S0-ANR-667

Inside AutoCAD 13 for DOS

Rick Llewellyn
David Byrnes
Larry Money
Jim Boyce
Michael Todd Peterson
Andrew Morris
William Valaski
B. Rustin Gesner
Kevin Coleman
Jim Fitzgerald

NEW RIDERS
PUBLISHING

New Riders Publishing, Indianapolis, Indiana

Inside AutoCAD 13 DOS

By Rick Llewellyn, David Byrnes, Larry Money, Jim Boyce, Michael Todd Peterson, Andrew Morris, William Valaski, B. Rustin Gesner, Kevin Coleman, and Jim Fitzgerald

Published by:
New Riders Publishing
201 West 103rd Street
Indianapolis, IN 46290 USA

All rights reserved. No part of this book may be reproduced or transmitted in any form or by any means, electronic or mechanical, including photocopying, recording, or by any information storage and retrieval system, without written permission from the publisher, except for the inclusion of brief quotations in a review.

Copyright © 1995 by New Riders Publishing

Printed in the United States of America 1 2 3 4 5 6 7 8 9 0

```
Inside AutoCAD 13 for DOS / Jim Boyce ... [et al.].
    p.      cm.
  Includes index.
  ISBN 1-56205-250-0
   1. Computer graphics.  2. AutoCAD (Computer file)  3. MS-DOS
(Computer file)  4. PC-DOS  (Computer file)  I. Boyce, Jim, 1958-
  .
T385.I4756   1995
620'.0042'02855369—dc20
```

Warning and Disclaimer

This book is designed to provide information about the AutoCAD computer program. Every effort has been made to make this book as complete and as accurate as possible, but no warranty or fitness is implied.

The information is provided on an "as is" basis. The author and New Riders Publishing shall have neither liability nor responsibility to any person or entity with respect to any loss or damages arising from the information contained in this book or from the use of the disks or programs that may accompany it.

Publisher	*Don Fowley*
Associate Publisher	*Tim Huddleston*
Product Development Manager	*Rob Tidrow*
Director of CAD Publishing	*Rusty Gesner*
Marketing Manager	*Ray Robinson*
Director of Special Projects	*Cheri Robinson*
Managing Editor	*Tad Ringo*

About the Authors

Rick Llewellyn is Director of Systems for HDR Engineering, Inc. in Omaha, Nebraska. Rick provides leadership in the planning, design, and implementation of information technology. He has worked for HDR since 1979, as drafter, designer, systems manager, and developer. He has designed, specified, purchased, and installed CAD networks, and written an extensive collection of software programs that include AutoCAD shareware, Microstation shareware, drawing management, and plot management. As a member of the Editorial Advisory Board for the A/E/C Systems Computer Solution magazine, Rick contributes articles and other services. He graduated from Florida A&M University with a BS in Architecture.

David Byrnes is a consultant in architectural conservation and historic preservation planning, based in North Vancouver, British Columbia. He is a part-time instructor at Emily Carr Institute of Art & Design in Vancouver, B.C., where he teaches AutoCAD in the Instructional Design department. He is also a private AutoCAD training consultant with clients in Canada, the United Kingdom, and Thailand.

David studied art history and earned a Diploma in Cultural Conservation from the University of Victoria (British Columbia).

David started learning AutoCAD on version 1.4 and has worked on all versions since 2.62. He is past vice-president of the Vancouver AutoCAD Users Society and an assistant sysop in Autodesk's AutoCAD Forum on the CompuServe Information Service. David is a contributing editor to *CADalyst* and *AutoCAD User* magazines and has also contributed to *CAD Systems* and *PC Magazine*.

David is a contributing author to several AutoCAD books from New Riders Publishing, including *Inside AutoCAD Release 11*, *Maximizing AutoCAD*, *The AutoCAD Professional Reference*, and *Hands-On AutoCAD 12*.

Larry Money received a Bachelor of Architecture degree from the College of Architecture and Design at the University of Michigan and has over 29 years experience in the architecture and construction business. He is an associate professor in the Technical Education Department at Del Mar College and serves as the program director for Architectural Technology. His teaching experience spans over 19 years, including more than 14 years of CAD instruction for college credit, as well as five years of professional development workshops in AutoCAD. Larry is a contributing author of *Hands-On AutoCAD 12.*

Jim Boyce is a Contributing Editor of *WINDOWS* magazine, a columnist for *CADENCE* magazine, and the author and co-author of 17 books on computers and software. Mr. Boyce has extensive experience in the CAD arena as a CAD user, system administrator, and programmer. He has worked with a variety of CAD applications and platforms, including AutoCAD, HP's ME-10 and ME-30, and others. Mr. Boyce also was a member of the faculty of Texas State Technical College, where he taught CAD use and programming, UNIX, DOS, and applications.

Michael Todd Peterson is currently a lecturer at the University of Tennessee School of Architecture, where he teaches an introductory computer course and sponsors independent study on advanced visualization with 3D Studio. He also owns a consulting firm, MTP Graphics, that specializes in AutoCAD and 3D Studio. He has used AutoCAD for 8 years and 3D Studio for 3 years. He graduated from the University of Tennessee College of Architecture in 1992 and is currently pursuing a Master's degree in Computer Science.

Andrew Morris is a freelance engineer in the broadcast, cable, and telecommunication industries. Employed for over 20 years by television and radio networks in New York City, he often has used AutoCAD for the design and documentation of audio, video, and RF systems. Mr. Morris writes on telecommunication technologies for *TV Technology, Computer Video,* and *Communications Technology* magazines. He holds a BFA degree from New York University's Tisch School of the Arts.

Bill Valaski graduated from the University of Cincinnati with a degree in Architectural Engineering. He works for CDS Associates, Inc., an A/E firm in Cincinnati, Ohio, where he practices architecture and manages computer operations for the firm. Bill is also a partner in Computer Projects Unlimited, a computer consulting firm, and a sysop for the Cincinnati Freenet, Tristate Online. Bill has been an author for Que and New Riders for over five years, working on projects such as *Using AutoCAD, 2nd Edition, The AutoCAD Quick Reference, AutoCAD: The Professional Reference, Killer AutoCAD Utilities,* and *Inside AutoCAD LT for Windows.*

Rusty Gesner is the CAD Publishing Director for New Riders Publishing. Rusty has been using and customizing AutoCAD since version 1.13, in 1983, and was one of the first six users of AutoCAD's first PC DOS release. Prior to joining New Riders, he was founder and president of CAD Northwest, Inc., in Portland, Oregon. He is a registered architect and formerly practiced the profession in Oregon and Washington after attending Antioch College and the College of Design, Art, and Architecture at the University of Cincinnati. Mr. Gesner has edited and co-authored several New Riders books, including *Maximizing AutoCAD, Maximizing AutoLISP, Customizing AutoCAD, Inside AutoLISP,* and nearly every edition of *Inside AutoCAD.*

Kevin Coleman is a Product Development Specialist at New Riders Publishing. He has been with New Riders since 1989. Kevin has been using AutoCAD and other computer graphics applications since 1985. He attended the University of Oregon, where he studied telecommunications and film.

Jim Fitzgerald is a CAD Product Development Specialist for New Riders Publishing in Gresham, Oregon. Prior to joining New Riders, he was the Director of Training for a CAD training and consulting organization in Philadelphia. He has been working with AutoCAD since 1988 and studied mathematics and education at Linfield College in McMinnville, Oregon.

Acknowledgments

Rick thanks Karan, Margaret, and Catherine for their support, patience, and cooperation. Also, I thank Mom and Dad. Thanks to my buddies at HDR (Rich, Perry, and Denis) for bearing the extra load. And thanks to the excellent staff at New Riders Publishing for their support and suggestions. I commend the team!

David thanks Delia for putting up with a dad who wasn't available as much as he should have been, and his best friend, Annie, for her support and patience while he worked on this book. He also thanks his friends and colleagues on the ACAD Forum who showed him the way many times. Finally, he thanks Rusty and Margaret in Gresham and Alicia and Rob in Indianapolis for all their support and help.

Larry thanks his wife Kasi for her patience and support during the 1994 holiday season. Working with the other authors, various editors, and staff at New Riders has again been a great experience for which I am grateful.

Jim thanks Rusty Gesner for his guidance over the years, and the rest of the New Riders Gresham team for their help and input. Thanks also go to the Indianapolis editing staff in general and to Stacia Mellinger in particular for an outstanding job in developing, editing, and review.

Todd thanks New Riders Publishing for their help and patience, especially Rob Lawson and Alicia Buckley. I would also like to thank all of my friends at the University of Tennessee for their support and encouragement.

Bill thanks Gretchen, his wife, for all her support and for putting up with the long hours during these projects. Thanks also to my parents for their encouragement over the years, and thanks to all the New Riders staff (Rob Lawson, Alicia Buckley, Rusty Gesner, Margaret Berson, Rob Tidrow, Cheri Robinson, and Tim Huddleston) for their continued interest in having me serve as an author on their projects.

Andy thanks his wife Linda for her love, support, and encouragement, and for turning down the TV throughout the creative process. He also thanks his parents, Mort and Elly, for their lifelong support and for banning daytime television during his formative years. And last of all he thanks CNBC for providing emotional ups and downs during the working day.

Rusty thanks Kathy, Alicia, Ricky, Damon, Dubs, Shatze, C.J., Buddy, Callie, and Kelsey. Also, I thank all the authors, editors, and technical editors, and lots of helpful folks at Autodesk. *Inside AutoCAD 13 for DOS* is based on the Inside AutoCAD 13 for Windows title that was authored by several of the preceding authors as well as Francis Soen, David Pitzer, Howard M. Fulmer, Kevin McWhirter, Jeff Beck, and Tom Boersma.

Trademark Acknowledgments

All terms mentioned in this book that are known to be trademarks or service marks have been appropriately capitalized. New Riders Publishing cannot attest to the accuracy of this information. Use of a term in this book should not be regarded as affecting the validity of any trademark or service mark. AutoCAD is a registered trademark of Autodesk, Inc.

Product Director
RUSTY GESNER

Acquisitions Editor
ALICIA BUCKLEY

Team Leader and Production Editor
ROB LAWSON

Copy Editors
MARGARET BERSON, LAURA FREY
JOHN KANE, SARAH KEARNS
STACIA MELLINGER, PHIL
WORTHINGTON, LILLIAN YATES

Technical Editors
WILLIAM BLACKMON
BILL SHANAHAN
PETER B. TOBEY

Marketing Copywriter
TAMARA APPLE

Acquisitions Coordinator
TRACEY TURGESON

Publisher's Assistant
KAREN OPAL

Cover Designer
DAN ARMSTRONG

Book Designer
KIM SCOTT

Production Team Supervisor
KATY BODENMILLER

Graphics Image Specialists
BRAD DIXON, JASON HAND
CLINT LAHNEN, DENNIS SHEEHAN
C. SMALL

Production Analysts
ANGELA BANNAN, DENNIS CLAY
HAGER, BOBBI SATTERFIELD
MARY BETH WAKEFIELD

Production Team
MONA BROWN, MICHAEL
BRUMITT, MIKE HENRY
LOUISA KLUCZNIK, DONNA
MARTIN, BRIAN-KENT PROFFITT
TINA TRETTIN, MICHELLE
WORTHINGTON, JEFF
WEISSENBERGER

Indexer
CHRIS CLEVELAND

New Riders Publishing
INSIDE
SERIES

Contents at a Glance

Table of Contents

Part Two: Basic 2D CAD Drafting

Part Five: Dimensioning

Introduction

AutoCAD is a software phenomenon; its users far outnumber those of any other CAD system. Since its introduction, AutoCAD has grown from a micro-curiosity to a full-fledged CAD system by any set of standards. AutoCAD also has grown from a relatively simple program to a large and complex one, but do not be intimidated by its size and complexity. More than a million designers and drafters have learned to use AutoCAD with the help of previous editions of *Inside AutoCAD*.

Inside AutoCAD 13 for DOS is your guide to a significant step in the evolution of AutoCAD: AutoCAD Release 13. *Inside AutoCAD 13 for DOS* helps you take advantage of the many new and improved user features that AutoCAD Release 13 offers over previous versions of AutoCAD, including an improved user interface with a comprehensive set of pull-down menus and improved dialog boxes, and many new and improved commands and features that make AutoCAD more powerful and efficient. These include true splines and ellipses; parallel multilines; complex linetypes with symbology; paragraph text; associative hatching; truly practical associative dimensioning with an improved interface, style families, and style overrides; GDT tolerance features; 3D solids and rendering; and numerous new and improved editing and construction features.

Who Should Read This Book—and How

Whether you are a new AutoCAD user or an experienced one, *Inside AutoCAD 13 for DOS* is your most complete and integrated introduction, tutorial, and reference manual for AutoCAD Release 13.

If You Are Upgrading from Earlier Releases of AutoCAD

This book is written specifically for the Release 13 version of AutoCAD. If you are upgrading from AutoCAD Releases 11 or 12, AutoCAD Release 13 offers you many new features, and provides comprehensive coverage of each.

The Benefits of This Book to Experienced AutoCAD Users

Even if you are experienced with previous releases of AutoCAD, Release 13 introduces enough new features to make this book valuable to you. Read Part One, "Getting Started," to learn about interface changes, the new menus, and the improved online help. Then skim through parts Two and Three—"Basic 2D CAD Drafting" and "Advanced 2D CAD Drafting," respectively—pausing as you encounter new features; don't skim too quickly, however, because many valuable tidbits—such as true ellipses and paragraph text—are included along the way.

In the more advanced sections, you learn to apply new sophistication and power to your AutoCAD work, such as copying AutoCAD data to other programs. In Part Four, "Automating Drafting," you learn AutoCAD's more advanced commands and methods to enhance your productivity, such as associative hatching and complex linetypes. In Part Five, "Dimensioning," you will find much has changed. Release 13 dimensioning is now fully associative, with dimension style families and overrides to prevent inadvertent changes during editing. Part Six, "Drawing and Data I/O," introduces new aspects of drawing and data exchange and output.

If you have only been using AutoCAD's 2D features, you might want to use Part Seven, "AutoCAD and 3D," to expand into 3D surface and solid modeling and rendering. Part Seven covers the new, integrated rendering and solids modeling features of Release 13. Further, the discussion and tips found in the appendixes are sure to help you optimize the performance of both AutoCAD and DOS.

The Benefits of This Book to New AutoCAD Users

If you are new to AutoCAD, skim through the book for an overview. Then, read all the chapters and work through the exercises; they will teach you how to use the AutoCAD interface and the program's commands, menus, and dialog boxes. Remember, this book requires no previous AutoCAD experience. It takes you from the beginning level and makes you an AutoCAD expert. This book covers AutoCAD more

completely than any other available source of information. Study it well and you will become an expert in the program's use. After you have completed parts One and Two, you will be able to take advantage of the book's benefits to experienced users.

The Benefits of This Book to All Readers

No matter how proficient you are with AutoCAD or your computer, and no matter how you read this book, you will revisit it again and again as a reference manual. You will find *Inside AutoCAD* indispensable as you use it to find explanations and examples of specific commands and techniques.

How This Book Is Organized

Inside AutoCAD is organized for both the beginner and the experienced user. It is designed both as a tutorial to help new users learn to master AutoCAD, and as a reference guide to be used over and over, long after you have mastered the basics of the program. To accomplish these goals, the book is organized into parts, each of which covers a specific group of concepts and operations.

Inside AutoCAD starts with the basics of 2D CAD drafting and ends with the construction and presentation of 3D models. The exercises and discussions do not assume that you have any prior knowledge of CAD in general or of AutoCAD in particular. If you study the entire volume, you will be able to use AutoCAD for 2D drafting, 3D modeling, and presentation. Further, you will be able to customize AutoCAD's interface so that the program works best for your unique needs, yet you do not need any knowledge of programming to do this.

Part One: Getting Started

The four chapters in Part One get you properly set up, teach you the basics of the AutoCAD Release 13 environment and interface, prepare you to begin drawing in AutoCAD, and cover the Help features. Part One familiarizes the AutoCAD system, preparing you to draw productively in Part Two.

Part Two: Basic 2D CAD Drafting

To produce good 2D drawings, you must know how to control the accuracy of AutoCAD's drawing tools. Part Two teaches you how to control the drawing display and how to create 2D drawings with AutoCAD's basic drawing and editing tools.

Upon finishing Part Two, you will be able to complete many 2D drawings; however, in Part Three you will learn to make your drafting much more efficient.

Part Three: Advanced 2D CAD Drafting

Part Three of *Inside AutoCAD* introduces many new and more advanced features of AutoCAD to improve your drawing versatility. These advanced drawing and editing commands and techniques include drawing polylines and splines, 2D regions, multiple-element lines, text (including paragraph editing, formatting, and spell checking), and the rest of AutoCAD's 2D editing and object modification tools. Upon completion of Part Three, you will have learned all but the most advanced 2D commands.

Part Four: Automating Drafting

Part Four automates drafting with blocks and text attributes for efficiency and control of repetitive drawing elements and data. It explains how to create, insert, and edit drawing symbols, called *blocks*. It also covers the rest of AutoCAD's most advanced editing commands—those that create objects through *constructive editing*. You learn how to access the same drawing data in multiple drawings, how to share drawings, and how to enable several people to work on one drawing through *xrefs* (external references) and overlays. Finally, Part Four discusses the enhancement of drawings through patterned linetypes and hatch patterns (*pochés*). When you complete the chapters in this section, you will have learned how to create finished complex 2D drawings, except for the dimensions.

Part Five: Dimensioning

Dimensioning is greatly improved in Release 13. Part Five covers the basics for placing various types of dimensions. You learn how to style and control the appearance of dimensions through dimension variable settings, dimension style families, and dimension style overrides; you also learn how to customize your dimensioning methods. This enables you to make AutoCAD's dimensioning meet your standards. You learn how to edit dimensions and dimensioned drawings; the style families and overrides protect the settings from inadvertent changes. The final two dimensioning chapters apply dimensioning features to architectural, civil (survey), and mechanical design applications, including Release 13's stacked fractions for architectural and GDT features for mechanical drawings.

By the time you complete Part Five, you will know all of AutoCAD's 2D drawing, editing, and dimensioning commands and techniques, and many tips and tricks for producing accurate, professional-looking 2D drawings.

Part Six: Drawing and Data I/O

Part Six covers drawing and data I/O (input/output), from how to compose drawings for plotting and how to plot or print them, to exchanging drawing images and data with other applications. This includes exporting and importing DXF files, using AutoCAD data and images with other applications, and using data and images from other applications in AutoCAD. When you finish Part Six, you will be able to plot your drawings, extract data from your drawings, and exchange graphic and nongraphic data with other users and programs.

Part Seven: AutoCAD and 3D

Part Seven covers 3D from isometrics to extruded 2D entities, to 3D surface entities, to solid models. You learn how to create, edit, and render presentations with 3D models. You use 3D models to create complex shapes or to find intersections and other design relationships that are difficult or impossible to draw manually; you then can generate 2D production drawing from those models. By the time you finish Part Seven, you will be an expert in AutoCAD, from 2D to 3D.

Part Eight: Appendixes

Inside AutoCAD 13 for DOS also has several useful appendixes:

◆ Appendix A covers installation and configuration.

◆ Appendix B covers problems and troubleshooting.

◆ Appendix C covers advanced configuration and settings.

◆ Appendix D provides tips and information for managing your AutoCAD work and drawings.

◆ Appendix E lists all AutoCAD commands, and the menu items, dialog boxes, and aliases that issue them.

◆ Appendix F provides a useful table of AutoCAD's system variables.

◆ Appendix G provides a useful table of AutoCAD's dimensioning variables.

◆ Appendix H lists and explains the contents of the IA Disk, including many free and useful utilities.

And, last but not least, inside the front and back of the book, you will find annotated illustrations of the AutoCAD Release 13 interface, including all pull-down menus.

How To Use the Tutorials

Each chapter provides a series of exercises, each of which teaches one or more AutoCAD commands. Explanatory text accompanies each exercise, puts commands and techniques into context, explains how commands behave, and shows you how to use different options. If you just read the text and exercises and look at the illustrations, you will learn a great deal about the program. But if you want to gain a greater mastery of AutoCAD Release 13, you need to sit down at a computer equipped with AutoCAD Release 13 and work through the exercises.

Using the IA Disk

To best utilize *Inside AutoCAD 13 for DOS,* work through every exercise in sequence. You can, however, select specific exercises to perform without backtracking by using files from the IA Disk. This disk contains starting drawings for many exercises.

Chapter 1, "Setting Up," explains how to prepare the IA Disk and AutoCAD Release 13 for use with *Inside AutoCAD.* The setup is designed to make sure the IA directory structure and exercises do not interfere with your normal AutoCAD settings or any other work you are doing. Chapter 1 also explains how to install the drawing and support files included with the IA Disk.

Stop The IA Disk and AutoCAD setup steps in Chapter 1 are an essential prerequisite for the rest of the book.

A Special Note to AutoCAD Instructors

Several editions of *Inside AutoCAD* have been used for classroom instruction, and *Inside AutoCAD 13 for DOS* is equally suitable for classroom use. Each chapter begins with a brief description of its contents and tells the student what he or she should be able to learn from it.

New Riders Publishing
INSIDE SERIES

Getting the Most from This Book

Regardless of how well you know AutoCAD, regardless of whether or not you have worked through all the exercises in this book, you can always use it as a reference, a constant resource. AutoCAD offers so many ways to accomplish the task of CAD design that you simply will not have the time to explore them all until specific needs arise for each. *Inside AutoCAD* will be an indispensable item on your bookshelf as you use it to find descriptions and examples of specific techniques. To ensure that you are getting the most from this book, read the following sections, which explain the notational conventions used throughout.

Notational Conventions

The conventions used for showing various types of text mirror—as closely as possible—those used in Autodesk's documentation. These conventions are shown in this section. Some conventions, such as the use of italic type to introduce a new term, are simple. Others, such as those used in the exercises, are worth a closer look.

How Exercises Are Shown

A sample exercise follows. You do not need to work through it or understand the content, but look over the format; note how the book's exercises are presented. Most exercises are accompanied by one or more illustrations, usually captured from the screen during an actual exercise. Exercises are arranged in two columns, with direct instructions on the left and explanatory notes on the right. Lengthy instructions or explanations sometimes extend across both columns.

Trying a Sample Exercise

Continue in the SAMPLE drawing from the preceding exercise.

Command: *Move the pointer to the top of the screen, and place it on* Assist	Displays the pull-down menu bar and highlights Assist
Click the left button (the pick button)	Chooses Assist and opens the Assist menu
Click on Snap mode, and closes the menu	Chooses the Snap menu item, turns on snap

<Snap on>

continues

continued

Command: *Move the pointer to the top of the screen and choose* Draw, Line	Displays the pull-down menu bar, then the Draw menu, and issues the LINE command
_line From point: **1,1** (Enter)	Starts a line at ① (see fig. I.1)
To point: *Pick* ②	Draws the line to point 1,2
To point: (Enter)	Ends the LINE command
Command: *Choose* Draw, Arc, *then* Start, Center, Angle	Issues the ARC command with Center and Angle options
_arc Center/<Start point>: @ (Enter)	Starts at last point, ②
Center/End/<Second point>: _c	The menu issues the Center option
Center: *Pick* ①	
Angle/Length of chord/<End point>: _a	The menu issues the Angle option
Included angle: **-90** (Enter)	Draws the door arc to ③
Command: *Choose* File, Save	Issues the QSAVE command and saves the drawing

Figure I.1

A sample exercise illustration.

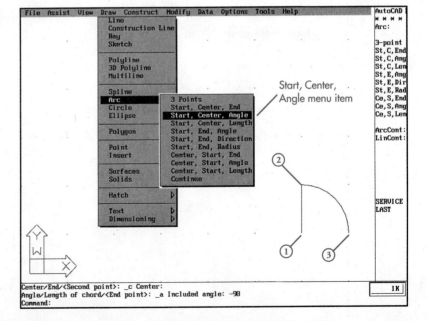

New Riders Publishing
INSIDE SERIES

As shown in the exercise, when you move the pointing device to the top of the AutoCAD screen, the pull-down menu bar is displayed. This pointing device (referred to throughout the book as a mouse) is used for much of your input in AutoCAD. Familiarize yourself with the following terms, which are used to describe mouse actions:

- ◆ **Click.** To press and release the pick button.

- ◆ **Click on, click in.** To position the cursor on the appropriate user interface object (icon, input box, menu item, and so on), or in the appropriate user interface area and click the pick button.

- ◆ **Double-click.** To press and release the pick button twice, in rapid succession.

- ◆ **Pick.** To position the cursor on the appropriate object or point and click the pick button.

- ◆ **Select.** To highlight an object in the AutoCAD drawing area by picking it or by using other object selection methods. Also, to highlight an item, word, or character in a drop-down or dialog box list or text input field by clicking on it.

- ◆ **Choose.** To select an item in a menu or dialog box by either clicking on it or typing its hot-key letter.

- ◆ **Drag.** To move the mouse and cursor, causing lines or objects on the screen to move with the cursor.

- ◆ **Press and drag.** To press and hold down a mouse button, drag something on screen, and then release the mouse button.

When you see an instruction such as "*Choose* Item" in an exercise, it means to move the pointer to Item and click the left mouse button. The instructions usually specify the location from which you are to initiate a command. Exercise steps that use the pull-down menus instruct you to choose the menu, then the item, as in "*Choose* File, Save." In a dialog box, you also can use a *hot key*—a key combination consisting of the Alt key and the letter underlined in the dialog box—to choose an item. To choose the File edit box in the Save Drawing As dialog box, for example, you would press Alt+F.

If a pull-down menu or dialog box is currently displayed, "*choose*" refers to an item on it. If no specific direction is given for the source of the command, feel free to use whatever serves you best. As you progress through the book, you will learn a variety of ways to issue a command. See Chapters 2 and 3—"Touring the AutoCAD Interface" and "Using the Drawing Editor," respectively—for more information on using the AutoCAD interface.

Your computer might have a key labeled Enter, or one labeled Return, or one with an arrow symbol. In any case, *Press Enter* or the symbol (Enter) means to press the key that enters a return.

You sometimes enter commands from the keyboard. Similarly, point coordinates, distances, and option keywords must be typed. The exercise text generally indicates when typed input is required by showing it in bold text following a prompt, such as Command: **UNITS** (Enter) or To point: **3,5** (Enter). You should type the input as it appears, and then press Enter.

Early in the book, you will notice that exercises contain numerous prompts and explanations of what is (or should be) happening as you enter commands. Later exercises often omit prompts that have become routine and explanations of familiar effects.

Note   Some menu items appear with three periods following the item name, and others have a right arrow at the right side of the menu. AutoCAD uses this notation to indicate items that activate dialog boxes and child menus. This book does not show this special punctuation in its text.

Do not be concerned about the leading underscore character that you see in many command prompts when commands and options are issued by the menus. This character is present to accommodate international versions of AutoCAD. You will see the underscore on the screen, but it is not actually part of the command name.

You should save your drawings when instructed, to help you build a habit of saving drawings at regular intervals. If you want to proceed at a leisurely pace, you can save and close your drawing whenever you see the save instruction and reload your drawing later.

Notes, Tips, and Stops

Inside AutoCAD features many special sidebars, which are set apart from the normal text by icons. The book includes three distinct types of sidebars: Notes, Tips, and Stops. These passages have been given special treatment so that you can instantly recognize their significance and easily find them for future reference.

Note   A *Note* includes extra information you might find useful. A Note might describe special situations that can arise when you use AutoCAD under certain circumstances, and might tell you what steps to take when such situations arise.

Tip A *Tip* provides quick instructions for getting the most from your AutoCAD system. A Tip might show you how to speed up a procedure, or how to perform one of many time-saving and system-enhancing techniques.

 Stop A *Stop* tells you when a procedure can be dangerous—that is, when you run the risk of serious problem or error, even losing data or crashing your system. Stops generally explain how to avoid such problems, or describe the steps you can take to remedy them.

Exercises and Your Graphics Display

The authors created this book's illustrations by capturing screen displays during the process of performing the exercises. Because AutoCAD supports many different video display controllers at many different resolutions, your screen displays might not agree exactly with the illustrations. Menus and screen elements might appear larger or smaller than they do in the illustrations, and you might want to zoom in or out further than the instructions indicate. You should learn from the outset, in fact, that you must adjust to the task at hand and the resources available. You might find that if you use colors different than instructed in the exercises, the entities are easier to see, depending on whether your system is configured for a white background or a black background.

What You Need To Use This Book

To use *Inside AutoCAD 13 for DOS,* you need the following software and hardware, at the least. This book assumes the following:

◆ You have a computer with MS-DOS 5.0 or later (we recommend 6.2 or later) and AutoCAD Release 13 for DOS installed and configured. Appendixes A and C—"Installation and Configuration" and "Advanced Configuration," respectively—provide more specific information and recommendations on system requirements, and on installing, configuring, and maximizing the performance of AutoCAD.

◆ You have at least 5 MB of free hard disk space left after you have installed and configured AutoCAD.

◆ You are familiar with MS-DOS/PC DOS and can use the basic DOS commands and utilities. (For help in learning DOS, refer to your DOS user's guide.)

Handling Problems

As you work through the exercises in *Inside AutoCAD,* you might experience some problems. These problems can occur for any number of reasons, from input errors to hardware failures. If you have trouble performing any step described in this book, take the following actions:

◆ Check the update text file on the IA Disk. You can use the MS DOS Editor (the DOS EDIT command) or any word processor or ASCII text editor to read or print the UPDATE.TXT file.

◆ Try again. Double-check the steps you performed in the previous exercise(s), as well as earlier steps in the current exercise.

◆ Check the settings of any AutoCAD system variables or dialog boxes modified in any previous exercise sequences. (See Appendix F, "System Variables Table," for a comprehensive listing.)

◆ Utilize Appendix B, "Troubleshooting."

◆ Check the AutoCAD Release 13 documentation or online help that came with your AutoCAD program.

If none of the above suggestions help, call New Riders Publishing (503-661-5745), *only* if the problem relates to a specific exercise, instruction, or error in the book. Otherwise, try the following for further help:

◆ Call your AutoCAD dealer.

◆ Log in to the ACAD forum on CompuServe, and ask or search for help.

Other AutoCAD Titles from New Riders Publishing

New Riders Publishing offers the widest selection of books on AutoCAD available anywhere. New Riders also offers an extensive selection of books on Windows, DOS, and other operating systems; on NetWare and other networking operating systems; and on communications, including the Internet and CompuServe. See the back of the book for information on selected New Riders titles, call New Riders at **1-800-581-5884** to request a catalog or information, or send in the *Want More Information* page in the back of the book. You can order any New Riders title by calling **1-800-858-7674** for customer service.

New Riders Publishing

The staff of New Riders Publishing is committed to bringing you the very best in computer reference material. Each New Riders book is the result of months of work by authors and staff who research and refine the information contained within its covers.

As part of this commitment to you, the NRP reader, New Riders invites your input. Please let us know if you enjoy this book, if you have trouble with the information and examples presented, or if you have a suggestion for the next edition.

Please note, however, that New Riders staff cannot serve as a technical resource for the AutoCAD program or for related questions about software- or hardware-related problems. Please refer to the documentation that accompanies Autodesk's AutoCAD or to AutoCAD's Help systems.

If you have a question or comment about any New Riders book, contact New Riders Publishing. We will respond to as many readers as we can. Your name, address, and phone number will never become part of a mailing list or be used for any purpose other than to help us continue to bring you the best books possible. You can write us at the following address:

New Riders Publishing
Attn: Associate Publisher
201 W. 103rd Street
Indianapolis, IN 46290

If you prefer, you can fax New Riders Publishing at (317) 581-4670.

You can send e-mail to New Riders from a variety of sources. New Riders maintains several mailboxes organized by topic area. Mail in these mailboxes will be forwarded to the staff member who is best able to address your concerns. Substitute the appropriate mailbox name from the following list when addressing your e-mail. The mailboxes are as follows:

ADMIN	Comments and complaints for NRP's Publisher
APPS	Word, Excel, WordPerfect, other office applications
ACQ	Book proposal inquiries by potential authors
CAD	AutoCAD, 3D Studio, AutoSketch and CAD products
DATABASE	Access, dBASE, Paradox, and other database products
GRAPHICS	CorelDRAW!, Photoshop, and other graphics products
INTERNET	Internet

NETWORK	NetWare, LANtastic, and other network-related topics
OS	MS-DOS, OS/2, all OS except Unix and Windows
UNIX	UNIX
WINDOWS	Microsoft Windows (all versions)
OTHER	Anything that doesn't fit the preceding categories

If you use an MHS e-mail system that routes through CompuServe, send your messages to:

mailbox @ NEWRIDER

To send NRP mail from CompuServe, use the following to address:

MHS: *mailbox* @ NEWRIDER

To send mail from the Internet, use the following address format:

mailbox@newrider.mhs.compuserve.com

New Riders Publishing is an imprint of Macmillan Computer Publishing. To obtain a catalog or information, or to purchase any Macmillan Computer Publishing book, call (800) 428-5331.

Thank you for selecting *Inside AutoCAD 13 for DOS*!

Part I

Getting Started

New Riders Publishing
INSIDE SERIES

CHAPTER 1

Setting Up

Inside AutoCAD 13 for DOS is a tutorial about AutoCAD. This chapter helps you set up the AutoCAD program on your computer, and then guides you as you explore the program's working relationship with the operating system. Appendix A, "Installation and Configuration," provides detailed instructions on loading and configuring the AutoCAD software. This chapter helps you start AutoCAD with the right parameters, and it shows you how to control AutoCAD's operating characteristics. After reading, you will be able to perform the following tasks:

- ◆ Install the IA Disk files

- ◆ Set up AutoCAD configuration, support, and working directories to prevent one working configuration from altering another

- ◆ Copy AutoCAD configuration and menu files

- ◆ Start AutoCAD with a special configuration

Even if you are an experienced DOS user and have some experience with AutoCAD, you need to make some preparations before moving on to any of the following chapters. You should start by performing several exercises in this chapter, beginning with the "Making the IA Directory" exercise, which appears in a later section.

Your understanding of the previously listed tasks also is necessary if you want to set up other AutoCAD configurations.

 Note   In addition to the setup covered in this chapter, you need to turn on the selection settings specified in Chapter 8, "Object Selection and Grip Editing," for exercises in subsequent chapters. If you jump around from chapter to chapter, turn on Use Shift To Add and Press And Drag in the Object Selection Settings dialog box for all chapters after Chapter 7. To open the Object Selection Settings dialog box, choose Selection from the Options pull-down menu.

A disk called the IA Disk is included with *Inside AutoCAD 13 for DOS*. The book and disk are designed for use on your existing AutoCAD system. The disk provides starting drawings for many of the exercises, saving you time by avoiding routine drawing setup. If you want to learn about dimensioning, for example, but do not want to first create a drawing to dimension, you can move right to the dimensioning section by using a preset drawing from the disk.

The disk also includes a freeware architectural AutoCAD text font, and other free or shareware AutoCAD utilities. Most of these are small files, so they are installed at the same time as the exercise and setup files. One utility, TEMPLATE!FREE, requires another 500 KB of disk space, so you might choose to install it now or later. See Appendix H, "The IA Disk," for more information.

Setting Up AutoCAD for This Book's Exercises

The setup for *Inside AutoCAD 13 for DOS* requires you to create a directory—named IA—on your hard disk. The book and disk are designed to ensure that the AutoCAD settings you use for the book's exercises do not interfere with any other AutoCAD settings or projects that you perhaps have under way. Also, you easily can remove all practice files after you are through with the book's exercises. The file names of the drawings you create during this book's exercises generally begin with "CHAP" to make their deletion easy.

Creating Directories

The following installation instructions assume that you are using the DOS operating system, that AutoCAD is installed in the C:\ACADR13\DOS directory, and that AutoCAD runs and is configured properly.

Note   If you do not yet have AutoCAD Release 13 installed, see Appendix A and install it now before continuing.

When this book shows a DOS prompt, the prompt includes the current path. When drive C's root directory is the current directory, for example, the DOS prompt looks like the following:

`C:\>`

When the IA subdirectory is the current directory, the prompt looks like the following:

`C:\IA>`

If your DOS prompt does not show the current path, you can enter the line **PROMPT=PG** at the DOS command line. You also can modify the prompt permanently by putting this line in your system's AUTOEXEC.BAT file.

Note   Your drive letter or subdirectory names may differ from those shown in this book. If they do, substitute your drive letter and directory names wherever you encounter drive letters (such as the C in C:) or the directory names (such as \ACADR13\DOS or \IA) in the book. If you are using an operating system other than DOS, your directory creation and setup will differ from those shown in the following pages. Even so, you should set up a directory structure that is similar to the one shown in this chapter. Also, if your disk drive is not drive A, substitute your drive letter for A when A: is shown.

Making the IA Directory

The book's setup also assumes that you work in the IA directory. You need to make an IA directory on your hard disk and then place a copy of your AutoCAD configuration file in this directory. By copying the configuration file into the working directory, you create a self-contained AutoCAD environment. To begin this task, make the hard disk's root directory the current directory. In the following exercise, you create the IA directory.

Making the IA Directory

Change to the root directory of drive C and perform the following steps:

`C:\> MD \IA` (Enter)   Creates the directory

`C:\> DIR *.` (Enter)   Displays a list of directory names, as shown in
                                                   the following listing:

continues

continued

```
Volume in drive C is DRIVE-C

Directory of  C:\

ACADR13   <DIR>   01-01-95   11:27a
DOS       <DIR>   12-22-93   10:53a
IA        <DIR>   01-01-95   11:27a
```

Your disk might show other directories, as in the following example:

```
123       <DIR>   12-01-88   11:27a
DBASE     <DIR>   12-01-88   11:27a

5 File(s) 48753472 bytes free
```

The ACADR13 subdirectory contains the AutoCAD program files, configuration files, and standard support files (in various subdirectories). The DOS subdirectory contains the DOS operating system files. The IA subdirectory contains the configuration files, prototype drawings, and other support files required for the *Inside AutoCAD 13 for DOS* exercises. Your directory listing almost certainly will be different from the one shown here.

Setting Up the AutoCAD Configuration Files

AutoCAD requires a *configuration file*—a file named ACAD.CFG—which specifies the hardware devices (such as video display cards and plotters) that you use with AutoCAD. This file is created the first time you run AutoCAD. The following exercise assumes that AutoCAD's configuration file resides in the \ACADR13\DOS directory. If your configuration file is not in the \ACADR13\DOS directory, substitute the correct directory name for \ACADR13\DOS in the exercise. By copying the ACAD.CFG file and the ACAD.INI file to the IA directory, you establish a separate AutoCAD configuration for this book. If AutoCAD has not yet been configured, see Appendix A of this book or your AutoCAD *Interface, Installation, and Performance Guide* for more information on configuring the program.

Configuring AutoCAD is a simple process of answering a series of prompts to tell AutoCAD what devices you are using, how they are connected, and what your preferences are for several optional settings that control AutoCAD's behavior.

New Riders Publishing
INSIDE SERIES

Copying the AutoCAD Configuration File to the IA Directory

Continue from the previous exercise, which created the IA directory.

`C:\> CD \ACADR13\DOS` (Enter)	Makes the AutoCAD program directory current
`C:\ACADR13\DOS> COPY ACAD.CFG \IA` (Enter)	Copies the AutoCAD configuration file from the AutoCAD directory to the IA directory
`1 File(s) copied`	
`C:\ACADR13\DOS> COPY ACAD.INI \IA` (Enter)	Copies the ACAD.INI file
`1 File(s) copied.`	

Installing the IA Disk

You are now ready to install the IA Disk files.

Installing the IA Disk

Put the IA Disk in drive A.

`C:\ACADR13\DOS>CD\IA` (Enter)	Makes the IA directory current
`C:\IA> A:IA-LOAD` (Enter)	Executes the IA Disk's installation program

Follow the prompts that appear next. If you have any problems, see the README.TXT file on the IA Disk. You can display the README.TXT file by changing to the IA Disk's drive and entering **MORE<README.TXT** at the DOS prompt.

Using a Batch File To Start AutoCAD

You now can create a simple batch file that starts AutoCAD so that it does not conflict with your current AutoCAD setup, and which keeps your drawing exercise files in one place. The batch file loads AutoCAD directly from your ACADR13 directory to avoid conflict with any startup batch file that you might already have. The batch file avoids conflicts by ensuring that the settings of two of AutoCAD's environment variables—named ACAD and ACADCFG—are correctly set when you run AutoCAD and then are cleared when you exit from AutoCAD. This section shows you how to make a batch file named IA.BAT to use with the directory you have created for the IA Disk. For more explanation of startup batch files and of the settings shown in this section, see Appendix A.

Note If you are using an operating system other than DOS, you can create a similar shell file rather than the batch file. See the AutoCAD *Interface, Installation and Performance Guide* for details.

After you create the IA.BAT batch file, you can start AutoCAD from any directory by entering **IA** at the DOS prompt. The backslash enables you to enter the IA batch command from any directory; if the IA.BAT file is placed in a directory on your path, you can omit the backslash.

The IA batch file sets the ACAD, ACADDRV, and ACADCFG settings; makes the IA directory current; and starts AutoCAD. When you exit from AutoCAD, the batch file clears ACAD, ACADDRV, and ACADCFG, and returns you to the root directory. Your configuration may require additional settings. The IA.BAT file requires (at the least) lines similar to the ten lines shown in table 1.1.

TABLE 1.1
Example IA.BAT Startup File

```
SET ACAD=C:\IA;C:\ACADR13\COMMON\SUPPORT;...DOS\SUPPORT;C:\ACADR13\COMMON\FONTS
SET ACADCFG=C:\IA
SET ACADDRV=C:\ACADR13\DOS\DRV
C:
CD\IA\DWGS
C:\ACADR13\DOS\ACAD %1 %2
SET ACAD=
SET ACADCFG=
SET ACADDRV=
CD\
```

Release 13 requires a startup batch file to set its environment variables. The standard Release 13 installation creates a startup batch file named ACADR13.BAT in the root directory of the drive where AutoCAD is installed. The differences between the standard ACADR13.BAT file and the standard IA.BAT file are shown in bold in table 1.1. (The first line in the table has been shortened to fit the page; additional path data exists where the ellipses is shown.)

In the sixth line of the file in table 1.1, the %1 and %2 are *replaceable parameters*. These parameters are used in batch files as placeholders for any command-line options that a program might take. Because AutoCAD can take two optional parameters (which can set a default drawing or script or enter AutoCAD's configuration when you start AutoCAD), this batch file includes two placeholders. See Appendix C, "Advanced Configuration," for more information on these settings.

 Note   The example IA.BAT file shows the default directories suggested by the AutoCAD installation program. If your AutoCAD support files are not installed in the AutoCAD program directory; or your font, support, sample, and ADS files (if installed) are not in the directories specified in the batch file, change the SET ACAD= line. If your device drivers are not in the \ACADR13\DOS\DRV directory, change the SET ACADDRV= line.

Your System's Requirements

Your system might require you to add other lines to the IA.BAT file. If you are using any AutoCAD ADI device drivers (for your video board, for example, or for your digitizer), you need to add commands to execute the device drivers just before the \ACADR13\DOS\ACAD %1 %2 line.

If your system is already configured and running AutoCAD and it needs such settings, you should find them in your AUTOEXEC.BAT file or in an AutoCAD startup batch file, such as the ACADR13.BAT file that the AutoCAD installation program creates. If so, include them in the IA.BAT file. Similarly, if you already have AutoCAD set up with a startup batch file that makes any memory or swap-disk configuration settings, you need to include them in your IA.BAT file. Do not, however, add any additional lines beginning with SET ACAD= or SET ACADCFG=. For more information, see Appendix C.

 Note   If your AutoCAD program files are not in a directory named \ACADR13\DOS, then substitute your directory name for \ACADR13\DOS where shown in the preceding listings and the following exercise.

Creating the IA.BAT File

The best way to create your batch file is to copy your existing startup batch file, such as ACADR13.BAT, to the name IA.BAT. Then use a word processor or text editor in ASCII-text mode to edit the IA.BAT file. As you edit the IA.BAT file, be sure to make any changes and add any extra lines you need.

The following setup exercise assumes that you have an ACADR13.BAT file in the root directory of drive C. If your startup file is named differently or located elsewhere, copy it rather than ACADR13.BAT to create IA.BAT in the exercise. If your startup settings are in your AUTOEXEC.BAT file, copy it to create IA.BAT, and delete all non-AutoCAD settings from the edited copy. The exercise assumes you use the DOS EDIT text editor to modify the IA.BAT file, but you can use any ASCII text editor you prefer. If you need help using EDIT, press F1 after you start EDIT. Remember to substitute your drive and directory names if they differ from the book's assumptions.

Creating the IA.BAT Batch File

C:\ACADR13\DOS> **CD** (Enter)   Returns to the root directory

C:\> **COPY ACADR13.BAT IA.BAT** (Enter)   Creates a file named IA.BAT

C:\> **EDIT IA.BAT** (Enter)   Opens the DOS EDIT editor, with the
                                                    IA.BAT file loaded

Make the changes and additions shown in bold in table 1.1.

Click on File, then Exit, then Yes   Closes EDIT and saves the changes

You now can start an *Inside AutoCAD 13 for DOS* session from any directory on your hard drive simply by entering **\IA**. For more information on the startup batch file's settings, see Appendix A.

 Note   If the root directory is on the path specified by your AUTOEXEC.BAT file, you can omit the backslash and just enter **IA**. If you want to keep your root directory uncluttered, you can move the IA.BAT file to any other directory on your path.

Using the IA Batch File

With these file-handling chores out of the way, you can now use the IA.BAT file to start up AutoCAD.

Starting AutoCAD

C:\> **\IA** (Enter)   Begins AutoCAD

A dialog box displays a message about the disk, including any last-minute information. Click on the up and down arrows at the right of the text listing to scroll up and down through the text. Click on the OK button when through to close the dialog box and display a new drawing.

Note If your system shows an `Error loading dialog` message, see Appendix B, "Troubleshooting." If your system displays a `Bad command or filename` error message when you try to start AutoCAD with the IA batch file, make sure that you have specified the correct path to the AutoCAD executable file. If AutoCAD is installed on a different drive than the IA subdirectory, you must also put the correct drive letter before the first backslash on the `\ACADR13\DOS\ACAD %1 %2` line of the IA batch file. If the ACAD.EXE file is located in the ACADR13 directory on drive E, for example, use the following command:

```
E:\ACADR13\ACAD %1 %2
```

As soon as you enter **\IA** from the operating system, the batch file takes control of your computer. The batch file makes IA\DWGS the current directory, and the AutoCAD program displays the opening screen.

Note To make absolutely sure that you are using the same default settings, the IA Disk includes a drawing named ACAD.DWG, which the book's exercises use as a prototype drawing. A *prototype drawing* is a drawing that AutoCAD uses as a template for creating a new drawing. All the AutoCAD settings that are stored in a drawing file, other drawing information, and any entities are transferred to the new drawing from the prototype. See Chapter 5, "Setting Up a CAD Drawing," for more information on prototype drawings.

Tip You can create additional AutoCAD configurations by creating directories like those created by the IA Disk installation, copying configuration and menu (optional) files to them as in the earlier exercise, and creating a new batch file to accommodate the new settings.

You are now set up and ready to move on to Chapter 2, "Touring the AutoCAD Interface."

Touring the AutoCAD Interface

Y ou probably are already familiar with manual drafting and design techniques or with CAD techniques used in programs other than AutoCAD. The drawing techniques and design methods used in AutoCAD are very similar to those used in manual drafting (and other CAD programs); only the tools are different. Learning to use those tools is as simple as learning to use AutoCAD's user interface. This chapter introduces and examines the components that make up AutoCAD's drawing editor.

This chapter covers the following topics:

- ◆ The AutoCAD drawing editor

- ◆ The AutoCAD graphics screen's components

- ◆ Using the pointing device

- ◆ AutoCAD's menus

- ◆ Communicating with AutoCAD

- ◆ The text screen and window

◆ Entering points and coordinates

◆ Correcting errors

◆ Using dialog boxes

The best way to learn about AutoCAD's interface is to both read about it and experience it. In this chapter, you start AutoCAD, use several commmands, draw an arc and some lines, and save the drawing file. By taking these steps, you learn to access commands from AutoCAD's menus and enter commands and other input from the keyboard. You also become familiar with AutoCAD's use of the pointing device (digitizer tablet or mouse), and you experiment with using dialog boxes.

The commands used in the following exercises are covered thoroughly in later chapters. This chapter focuses on understanding the AutoCAD for DOS user interface and on learning the different methods of choosing commands. When introducing new commands, this book emphasizes the use of pull-down menus, which seem to be the easiest interface for a new user. AutoCAD's pull-down menus are similar to those used in other software packages.

Along with pull-down menus, this chapter examines AutoCAD's various forms of command input, including command-line entry, the use of hot keys, aliases, dialog boxes, and the screen menu. These different types of command entry are covered to offer you a balanced overview of the many ways in which you can issue commands and choose options in AutoCAD.

Introducing the Drawing Editor

When you start AutoCAD, if it is correctly configured, the AutoCAD logo and software identification information appears, and then you enter the AutoCAD drawing editor.

Note   Starting AutoCAD by entering **IA** at the DOS prompt runs the IA.BAT batch file you created in Chapter 1. For all exercises in this book, start AutoCAD by entering **IA** at the DOS prompt.

In the following exercise, use the IA batch file to start AutoCAD so that you can examine the drawing editor.

Starting AutoCAD

Enter the following at the DOS command prompt.

C:\> **IA** (Enter)   Runs the IA.BAT file and starts AutoCAD

The AutoCAD logo and software identification information appears and then you enter the drawing editor (see fig. 2.1). AutoCAD creates a new, unnamed drawing.

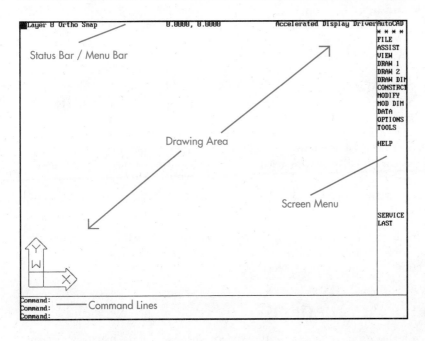

Figure 2.1

The AutoCAD for DOS screen menu.

2

The primary components of the drawing editor are contained in the AutoCAD graphics screen, which is discussed in the following section. The drawing editor also includes a text screen and window (see the illustration inside the front cover of this book). The text screen and window are discussed later in this chapter.

The AutoCAD Graphics Screen

Figure 2.1 shows the AutoCAD graphics screen and the various areas of that screen. The four primary areas of the AutoCAD screen are as follows:

◆ **Status bar/menu bar.** The status bar provides status on a variety of AutoCAD modes. When the pointer is placed on the status bar, the status bar becomes the pull-down menu bar. AutoCAD's pull-down menus are accessed through the menu bar.

◆ **Drawing area.** The center area, called the drawing area, is the area in which you draw.

◆ **Screen menu.** The screen menu was AutoCAD's original menu interface, but is now primarily used for option selection. When a command is issued by any method, the screen menu displays a set of relevant options for that command. Therefore, you can issue a command by any method you want, and then choose the options from the screen menu rather than typing them.

◆ **Command line.** The command line is the area where you enter commands and options from the keyboard. The command line prompts you for input and provides status on the results of AutoCAD commands, even when those commands are issued by the menus.

Move the pointer around the graphics screen. The center area is called the *drawing area*. Here, your pointer displays as a pair of crosshairs. The status bar, at the top, provides information on such items as the current active layer and the the coordinates of the current cursor position. See the illustration inside the front cover of this book for identification of the items on the status bar. When you move the pointer onto the status bar, the display changes and the status bar is replaced by the pull-down menu bar. The *screen menu* appears on the right side of the drawing area. Several command lines appear at the bottom of the screen. This is referred to as the Command: prompt.

Your pointing device is your primary means of communication with the drawing editor. The exercises often instruct you to use your pointing device to perform certain functions on the graphics screen.

Pointing Device Functions

Nearly everyone uses some type of pointing device with AutoCAD—usually a mouse or digitizer tablet puck (see fig. 2.2), or even the keyboard's cursor keys. This book assumes that you use a mouse or digitizer puck. AutoCAD reserves one button on the puck or mouse for picking points and choosing screen and tablet menu items. This *pick button* is the button that tells AutoCAD to pick a point or select an object or interface item at the cursor position. This usually is the mouse's left button or the lowest-numbered button (1 or 0) on the digitizer puck or stylus. You use this button to choose a menu item, click on a dialog box selection, or select an object on the graphics screen. Sometimes you must *double-click* the button if you want to choose a selection in a dialog box. This requires pressing the pick button twice in rapid succession.

The term *drag* is used in many applications to mean that you hold down the pick button while you move the cursor to another location. In AutoCAD, however, sometimes dragging may not require holding down the mouse button, and in fact, holding

down the mouse button would cause wrong input. Therefore, this book uses the term *press and drag* for instances in which you must hold down the mouse button while moving the cursor.

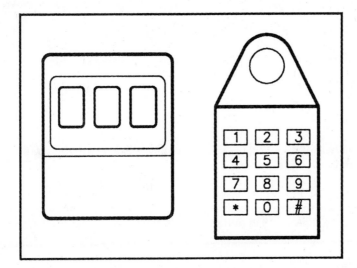

Figure 2.2

A typical mouse and puck.

A mouse usually has two or three buttons, and a puck can have up to 16 buttons. The position of the pick button varies with the device. The second button acts as an Enter key, and is called the Enter button in this book. The third button, if present, pops up a menu of object snap modes and point filters (see Chapter 6). You can also access this pop-up menu by holding down the Shift key and pressing the Enter button. The functions of the second and third buttons are defined by the AutoCAD buttons menu, described in the following section on menus. If your pointing device has additional buttons, their functions are also defined by the buttons menu.

One of the primary uses of the pick button is to choose menu items.

Understanding AutoCAD's Menus

AutoCAD has hundreds of commands, most of which feature numerous options. Almost all these commands relate to specific functions, such as drawing, editing, or dimensioning. Because it is difficult to remember the hundreds of AutoCAD commands with all their options and modifiers, the menu system offers an efficient alternative. AutoCAD's menus are organized for simple navigation through the software.

Menus provide a convenient way to organize and group commands so that they can be selected and executed with ease. AutoCAD has five primary types of menus; they include the following:

- ◆ Pull-down menu

- ◆ Screen menu

- ◆ Tablet menu

- ◆ Buttons menu

- ◆ Pop-up menu (also called cursor menu)

AutoCAD also has a type of menu called an *icon* or *image menu,* but it looks and acts like a dialog box, so it is discussed in the dialog box section of this chapter.

Menus are a powerful tool in AutoCAD, offering flexibility in command entry. AutoCAD's standard menus provide many different ways to execute the same commands. With a little practice, you will find the method of command entry that works best for you.

Most AutoCAD commands have options that you use to control the results of the command or the order or type of input the command requires. For example, you can specify an arc in numerous ways. You can use the ARC command's options to choose the method you prefer or the one that matches the available geometric information. Many menu items issue such options along with the command.

 Note   Most menu items are programmed to cancel any pending commands before issuing a new command.

Try all the types of menus available to see which menu method works best for you. The most commonly used type of menu is the pull-down menu.

Pull-Down Menus

When you move the pointer to the status bar/pull-down menu bar, the names of the 10 pull-down menus appear at the top of the screen. The names on the menu bar indicate the types of selections available in each pull-down menu. You make pull-down menu selections by highlighting the menu label or item with your pointing device and pressing the pick button.

Many pull-down menu selections open child menus (also called cascading menus or submenus), as shown in figure 2.3. Menu items followed by an arrowhead, such as the Arc or Text items in the Draw menu, display child menus. You can either click on the menu item or move the pointer to the arrowhead to open the child menu.

Tip   You can repeat the last menu item that you have selected from any pull-down menu by double-clicking on the pull-down menu's label on the menu bar.

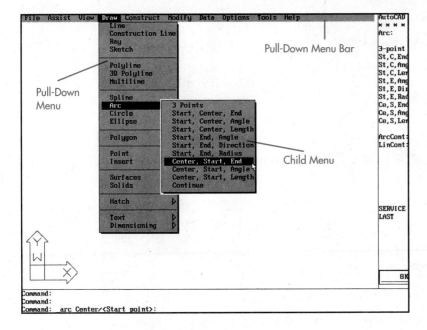

Figure 2.3

An AutoCAD pull-down menu and its child menu.

The menu map illustrations located at the back of this book show the complete AutoCAD Release 13 pull-down menu system.

In the following exercise, try choosing several items from the pull-down menus. Do not be concerned about the commands used; they will be fully explained later in the book.

Choosing Items from Pull-Down Menus

Continue from the previous exercise.

Command: *Move the pointer up to the status bar, then to the* Draw *label*

Displays pull-down menu bar and highlights the Draw menu label

Click the pick button

Selects and opens the Draw menu

Move the pointer down to the Arc *item, and click the pick button*

Highlights the Arc item, then opens the Arc child menu (see fig. 2.3)

continues

continued

Move the pointer over to the 3 Points *item and click the pick button*	Issues the ARC command
`_arc Center/<Start point>:` *Move the pointer to the status bar and choose* Draw *again*	Reopens the previous child menu, the Arc submenu
Move the pointer down to the Arc *item, then to the arrowhead at the right*	Closes the child menu, highlights the Arc item, then reopens the Arc child menu
Move the pointer down to the Center, Start, End *item and choose it*	Cancels the previous ARC command and reissues the ARC command with the Center option
`*Cancel*` `Command:`	
`Command:_arc Center/<Start point>: _c` `Center:` *Move the pointer into the drawing area and pick any point (click the pick button)*	The menu issues the *c* for the Center option, then the point you pick specifies the center of the arc
`Start point:` *Pick any other point*	Specifies the beginning of the arc
`Angle/Length of chord/<End point>:` *Pick any other point*	Draws the arc

 Note Unless a dialog box is open or unless otherwise specified, the instructions in exercises that begin *"Choose..."* refer to pull-down menus.

Some AutoCAD pull-down menu items open *dialog boxes*. If a pull-down menu item is followed by three dots (such as Preferences... or New...), that item opens a dialog box. Dialog boxes are provided for most operations that offer or require file specification or multiple settings (see fig. 2.4). Dialog boxes are covered later in this chapter.

Figure 2.4

The Create New Drawing dialog box.

New Riders Publishing
INSIDE
SERIES

Notice that when you used the Arc menu items in the previous exercise, the screen menu changed to display a set of arc menu items.

The Screen Menu

The screen menu appears on the right side of the screen in the drawing editor. You make screen menu selections by highlighting the item with your pointing device and pressing the pick button. The initial menu page displayed for the screen menu is the root menu, shown in figure 2.1 at the beginning of the chapter.

Most menu items, including those that issue commands, display (or branch to) other menu pages (also called submenus). The groupings of screen menu pages are for convenience only and have no effect on AutoCAD's command structure. If you become lost, just choose the AutoCAD item at the top of any screen menu. This choice returns you to the initial root page of the screen menu.

 Note   Exercise instructions referring to screen menus assume that their menu selections are currently visible on the screen menu. If they are not visible, choose the AutoCAD selection at the top of the screen menu.

When you choose a menu item, it changes menu pages and/or sends a command, option, or a series of commands to AutoCAD for execution. This command execution is the same as if you had typed the input. As you saw in the pull-down menu exercise, appropriate screen menus are usually displayed to offer command options when you enter commands or make pull-down selections. In this way, AutoCAD's screen menus are context-sensitive.

Choosing Items from the Screen Menu

Continue from the previous exercise, with the Arc page of the screen menu displayed. Notice the colon in the Arc: item near the top of the page.

Command: *Move the pointer to the* SERVICE *item and click the pick button*	Highlights and chooses the SERVICE item, then displays the Service menu, a page of commonly used options
Move the pointer to the Undo *item and choose it*	Issues the U command and removes the previously drawn arc
_u ARC GROUP	
Command: *Choose the* AutoCAD *item at the top of the menu*	Displays the root menu page

---

The U (undo) command, which reverses a previous command, is fully covered in Chapter 3, "Using the Drawing Editor."

Screen Menu Conventions

As you move through the screen menu, notice that the many selections, such as Arc, are followed by colons. These selections often branch to a new menu page and always start the indicated command. Items that automatically start commands generally have colons after their menu labels. The Undo item in the previous exercise, which was on a page of option items, did not have a colon. It does not have the colon because it issues only a U, which AutoCAD interprets as either the U command or the Undo option, depending on when it is used.

Many commands require options to complete their chores. These options are usually capitalized, like Undo.

At the bottom of most menu pages are shortcut branch items that enable you to return to your LAST menu page or to the SERVICE menu page.

As you flip through menu pages, remember that you can always return to the root menu by choosing the AutoCAD item at the top of the menu page. Every menu page also has an * * * * item below the AutoCAD selection. This selection displays a menu page containing choices for selecting object snaps. Object snaps are aids for drawing objects; Chapter 6 covers object snaps in detail.

Keyboard Access to the Screen Menu

You also can access the screen menu from the keyboard. The keyboard offers two methods of screen-menu selection. The first method is to press the menu cursor key (usually the Ins key) to highlight a menu selection. Use the up- and down-arrow keys to move the highlighted bar to the menu item you want and press Ins to choose the item.

The second method of accessing the screen menu from the keyboard is to start typing characters of the menu selection at the Command: prompt. As you type, the menu label beginning with the characters you type becomes highlighted. Most selections are highlighted by typing one or two characters; then you can press Enter or Ins to execute the selection.

Many users favor the tablet menu, which is described in the following section.

The Tablet Menu

AutoCAD comes with a standard tablet menu that performs many of the same functions as the screen and pull-down menus. Figure 2.5 shows the complete tablet menu. The tablet menu offers a few advantages over the other menu options. You can

easily remember where to find tablet menu selections, and you always can find them
without flipping through menu pages. The tablet menu also includes graphic images
to help you identify your selection. Many selections from the tablet menu activate the
appropriate screen menu pages to help you select option.

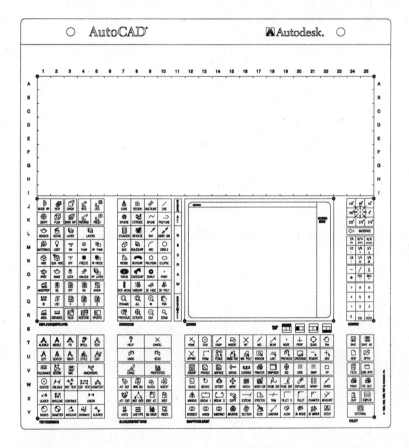

Figure 2.5

*The AutoCAD
tablet menu.*

 Note   To bring up AutoCAD's standard tablet menu, you need to configure your tablet.
See Appendix A for instruction in configuring the AutoCAD standard tablet menu.

Pop-Up Menu

As discussed earlier, in the pointing device discussion, the third mouse or digitizer
button (or the Shift key and Enter button) displays the pop-up (cursor) menu on the
screen at the pointer position. The pop-up menu gives you easy access to the object
snap modes and point filters. See Chapter 6 for more on the pop-up menu and object
snap modes and point filters.

Buttons Menu

Some digitizing pucks and other input devices have 16 or more buttons. AutoCAD's standard menu file, ACAD.MNU, also includes a buttons menu that assigns functions to the buttons. Remember, the first physical button (which may be labeled 0 or 1) is the pick button. AutoCAD assigns the other buttons as shown in table 2.1.

Table 2.1
Functions of the AutoCAD Buttons Menu

Physical Button Number	Button Menu Item Number	Button Function
1 or 2	1	Enter
2 or 3	2	Pop-up menu
3 or 4	3	Cancel
4 or 5	4	Snap On/Off
5 or 6	5	Ortho On/Off
6 or 7	6	Grid On/Off
7 or 8	7	Coordinate display On/Off
8 or 9	8	Isoplane On/Off
9 or 10	9	Tablet On/Off

You can assign the buttons to execute other menu selections by creating a custom button menu. For details on creating button menus, see the *AutoCAD Customization Guide.*

Communicating with AutoCAD

In addition to using the pointing device and menus, you can use the keyboard to communicate with AutoCAD. The drawing editor includes the command lines, status bar, and the text screen and window to communicate with you. When you choose a menu item, you can glance at the command lines at the bottom of the screen to see what information AutoCAD needs (such as a start point for drawing a line), or what action to take (such as selecting an object). Then watch the center of the graphics area for the action. You also can use the status bar to keep track of AutoCAD.

Reading the Status Bar

At the top of the drawing editor, in the area used by the pull-down menus, lies the status bar. This bar contains a combination of text and numbers. Here you find information about how AutoCAD is set up and how it reacts when you issue certain commands. Figure 2.6 shows the current color box; the layer name; mode names, such as snap and ortho; and the coordinate readout. The letter P also appears to the right of Snap if paper space is active.

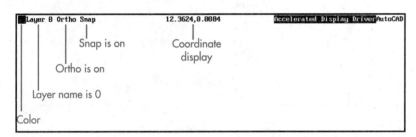

Figure 2.6

The AutoCAD status bar.

2

The settings of snap, ortho, and the coordinate display modes are most conveniently controlled by the buttons menu (if you have a multi-button digitizer) or by function keys.

Setting Modes with Function Keys

The function keys, usually at the top of the keyboard, can be used to turn a variety of AutoCAD modes—such as snap, grid, ortho, and the coordinate display—on and off. They can also be used to display the text screen window. Table 2.2 lists all the function keys.

Table 2.2
Function Keys for Mode Control

Mode	Function Key	Shown on Status Bar	Action
Text/Graphics	F1	No	Displays and hides text screen window
Isoplane	F5	No	Switches between top, left, and right
Coordinates	F6	Yes	Switches between coordinate display modes

continues

TABLE 2.2, CONTINUED
Function Keys for Mode Control

Mode	Function Key	Shown on Status Bar	Action
Grid	F7	No	Turns on/off grid dots in drawing area
Ortho	F8	Yes	Turns on/off ortho mode
Snap	F9	Yes	Turns on/off snap mode
Tablet	F10	Yes	Turns tablet mode on and off

The text screen and window are discussed in the following section. The coordinate display is briefly demonstrated in the exercise in the *Entering Points and Coordinates* section. The coordinate display, and the rest of the items in this table, are fully discussed in the following chapters.

Accessing the Text Screen and Window

AutoCAD has a text screen and window that display a full screen or window of command line text. The text screen window is shown in figure 2.7. You can press the F1 key to switch AutoCAD from the graphics screen to the text screen window. The button at the top left of the text screen window, labeled Send F1, closes the text screen window. Some commands (such as SHELL) cause the text screen window to appear. You can press F1 to switch back to the graphics screen. When the text screen window is displayed, you can choose a button labeled Go Text to display the text screen, a full screen of command-line text.

Switching between the Text Screen Window and Graphics Screen

Command: *Press F1*   Displays the text screen window

Move the cursor to the Go Text *button*   Flips to a full text screen
and click the pick button

Press F1   Displays the graphics screen

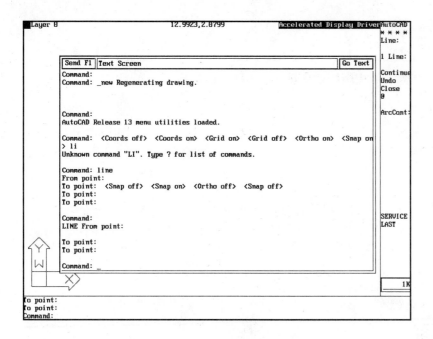

Figure 2.7

*The AutoCAD
text screen
window.*

2

On the text screen or window, you see the last sequence of commands that you have typed (or chosen from the menu). Use the text screen window to review a set of prompts. If you are interrupted or become confused, the text screen window can help you figure out what you and AutoCAD have been up to. You can display the text screen window at any time, except when a dialog box is open.

Using the Command Lines

At the bottom of the screen is the command-line area. This is where your typed input is displayed and where the Command: prompt and other prompts appear to guide you and provide information or command status.

AutoCAD enables you to issue any command by typing the command name at the keyboard in response to the Command: prompt. As you type, the letters appear after the Command: prompt. To execute any typed command, press Enter. If AutoCAD cannot interpret what you have typed, it will let you know after you press Enter, as shown in the following exercise.

Note   The Enter key is called the Return key by most AutoCAD prompts, and may be labeled Return or marked with only an (Enter) symbol on some systems. When you are entering commands and options, the spacebar and the Tab key are equivalent to using the Enter key. The exception to this is when you are entering text during one of the text drawing commands.

In the following exercise, try keyboard input.

Entering Commands at the Command Prompt

Command: **LI** (Enter)	Specifies an incorrect command name
Unknown command "LI". Type ? for list of commands.	Tells you that AutoCAD does not recognize the command as you have typed it
Command: **LINE** (Enter)	Starts the LINE command

AutoCAD displays a From point: prompt to tell you what input is expected.

From point: *Pick any point*	Starts a line at the point

AutoCAD displays a To point: prompt to tell you what input is expected. Move the cursor around and observe how the *rubber-band* line drags with the crosshairs.

To point: *Pick any point*	Draws a line to the point
To point: (Enter)	Ends the LINE command

Tip   Pressing Enter repeats the previous command. If the command was issued by a menu item that also issued options, the options are not repeated. Pressing Enter at the From point: prompt of the LINE command starts a new line at the end of the last one.

The exercise in the following section demonstrates repeating a command by pressing Enter, and the use of the Tab key and spacebar.

Entering Points and Coordinates

When you start AutoCAD, you can immediately go into the drawing editor and begin entering points. It does not matter whether you enter points by picking them with your pointing device or by entering them at the keyboard as coordinates. AutoCAD uses a relatively easy-to-use, standard Cartesian coordinate system that recognizes various types of drawing geometry.

When you enter the drawing editor, you enter a coordinate system called the *World Coordinate System* (WCS). When AutoCAD asks you to enter a point, you either pick the point with your pointing device or enter the point's coordinates from the keyboard. The simplest form of coordinate entry consists of a horizontal X displacement and a vertical Y displacement (and, in 3D, a Z displacement), separated only by a comma, such as 3,4. Both the X and Y are measured from a zero base point, called the origin, that is initially set at the lower left corner of your screen. This base point's coordinates are, of course, 0,0.

Try entering a few points in the following exercise.

Entering Points

Continue from the previous exercise, having just completed drawing a line.

Command: **Enter**	Repeats the LINE command
From point: *Press the Tab key*	Starts a line at the end of the last one

Move the cursor around and observe the coordinate display change with it. Move to where the coordinate display shows approximately 6.0000,5.0000.

To point: **6,5 Enter**	Draws a line to the point 6,5, which is near where you moved the cursor
To point: *Press the spacebar*	Ends the LINE command

In Chapter 6, you will learn to relocate and reorient the coordinate system. The icon that appears at the lower left corner of the screen near point 0,0 is called the UCS icon. It indicates the current state of the coordinate system.

Using Keyboard Commands and Aliases versus Menus

Many experienced users think keyboard command entry is just as fast if not faster than using menus. This is particularly true if you use AutoCAD's command alias feature. A command alias is an abbreviation of the command name. When you use an alias, AutoCAD replaces it with the full command name and executes the command. To execute the CIRCLE command from a menu, for example, you can use the pull-down menu to choose Draw, Circle; or you can choose the DRAW1 screen menu, then choose the Circle or CIRCLE items. Or, using the alias, you can merely type a **C** and press Enter. Some of AutoCAD's standard abbreviations are shown in table 2.3.

Table 2.3
Keyboard Command Abbreviations

Alias	Command	Alias	Command
A	ARC	LA	LAYER
C	CIRCLE	M	MOVE
CP	COPY	P	PAN
DV	DVIEW	PL	PLINE
E	ERASE	R	REDRAW
L	LINE	Z	ZOOM

These abbreviations cover only a few of AutoCAD's many commands, but you can easily create your own abbreviations by modifying the ACAD.PGP file. See Appendix H for more on aliases, and on using the more comprehensive NRP_ACAD.PGP file, which is included on the IA Disk.

AutoCAD offers similar keyboard shortcuts for command options. Instead of flipping through menus for command options, you can abbreviate virtually any command option to the one or two letters that are unique for that option at the current prompt. Recall, for example, the ARC prompt:

```
Center/<Start point>:
```

The Arc Center, Start, End menu item, which you used to issue the ARC command, responded to this prompt with merely a C for Center. You need only type the characters that are shown as uppercase in the AutoCAD command prompt to execute an option.

To learn AutoCAD thoroughly, it pays to become intimately familiar with the AutoCAD commands. Pull-down menu selection is emphasized in this book because that is probably the easiest interface for a new user. After you learn the commands, you can decide if keyboard entry, alias abbreviations, or other menus are better for you. Most users find that a combination of keyboard commands or abbreviations and menu selections works well.

AutoCAD's standard menus are general purpose, but custom menus are much more efficient for most applications. You can buy custom menus for many different applications—see your AutoCAD dealer. Or you can create your own custom menus—see the *AutoCAD Customization Guide.*

Correcting Errors

AutoCAD is forgiving. The program offers a variety of ways to correct mistakes. The worst that can happen when you type an incorrect command name is that AutoCAD warns you that it does not recognize the command as you typed it. Then AutoCAD gives you another chance or prompts you to get help.

If you notice a typing error before you press Enter, press the Backspace key on the keyboard to erase the characters. Then retype the entry. To start over, press Ctrl+X to display *Delete*, ignore all previous characters on the line, and get a blank new line to enter what you intended.

If you start the wrong command, and it is already showing on the Command: prompt, you can press Ctrl+C or Esc one or more times to cancel any command and return to the Command: prompt.

As you saw in an earlier exercise, you can use the U (undo) command to reverse a command. Choose Undo from the Assist menu to issue the U command. You can also remove an object using the ERASE command. The Erase item on the Modify menu issues the ERASE command. When you use ERASE, the crosshairs change to a *pick box*. You move the pick box until it touches the object you want to remove. Select each entity to erase by clicking on it with your pointing device's pick button. When you are finished selecting, press Enter to complete the command and erase them.

AutoCAD offers other ways to select objects and other ways to correct errors. Chapter 3 provides more information on error recovery. For now, the Escape key, and the U and ERASE commands are enough to get you out of a jam.

Most of AutoCAD's more complex commands use dialog boxes to make specifying settings and options easier.

Using Dialog Boxes

Dialog boxes are more convenient than AutoCAD's other data-entry methods because they present options for viewing or changing several items. In addition, dialog boxes provide the only means to view a list of files when you need to specify a file name within AutoCAD.

Although dialog boxes are usually accessed through menu selections that issue their commands, you can also access them by entering their command names at the Command: prompt. Many of these command names begin with DD, such as DDEMODES. Various commands that open dialog boxes are identified throughout the book.

The SAVEAS command opens the Save Drawing As dialog box (see fig. 2.8), which contains most typical dialog box features. The Save Drawing As dialog box is also displayed by the Save As menu item, and when you use the Save menu item or SAVE command if you have not yet named the current drawing. The Open Drawing dialog box and most other file dialog boxes in AutoCAD are almost identical to the Save Drawing As dialog box.

Figure 2.8

The Save Drawing As dialog box.

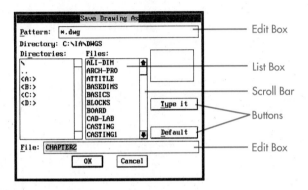

All dialog box features, including those that are not part of the Save Drawing As dialog box, are described in the following list:

Note Some commands, such as the INSERT command, do not display a dialog box unless you request it by entering a tilde symbol (~) at the prompt for a file name.

You can turn the file dialog box feature off by setting the FILEDIA system variable to 0. With the file dialog box turned off, all file menu selections and commands prompt for the file name at the Command: prompt. If you have the file dialog box feature turned off, you can still display file dialog boxes when you want to use them by entering a tilde symbol (~) when prompted for a file name.

All dialog box features, including those that are not part of the Save Drawing As dialog box, are described in the following list:

◆ **Button.** Buttons usually initiate an action. Typical examples are the OK and Cancel buttons found in practically all dialog boxes. The OK button accepts all changes made in the dialog box; the Cancel button closes the dialog box, ignoring any changes.

◆ **Check box.** Check boxes typically control on/off settings. Placing an X in the check box by clicking on it generally turns the setting on. Clicking on a box with an X removes it.

◆ **Edit box.** Edit boxes are used to enter text or numbers. Clicking in the box places an edit cursor in the box. You can then edit by using the Backspace and Delete keys or by dragging to highlight text. Typing over highlighted text replaces it. Edit boxes also are referred to as input or text boxes.

◆ **List box.** List boxes display lists of items, often file names. Clicking on a list item highlights or selects it. A list box with a large number of items usually has scroll bars. You can use the scroll bars (or the keyboard arrow keys) to advance through the list. Some list boxes normally are closed and have a down-pointing arrow at the right side. Clicking in the box or on the arrow displays the list. Such list boxes are called *drop-down list boxes.*

◆ **Radio button.** Like buttons on a car radio, radio buttons select among mutually exclusive choices. Selecting one option by clicking on it deselects the previous choice.

◆ **Slider bar.** Slider bars are used to adjust settings that are continuously variable. You can drag the slider, click in the slider bar area, or click on the arrows to make adjustments.

Edit boxes are used to enter text and values such as file, color, layer names, distances, or scale factors. In the Save Drawing As dialog box, the long rectangular box immediately above the OK button is the File edit box.

The Save Drawing As dialog box gives you the option of saving your current drawing session under the current name or under a file name of your choice. You can press Enter to accept the default name shown in the File edit box, or you can type a new name for the drawing. The following exercise shows you how to use this dialog box to save the current unnamed file with a new name.

Using the Save Drawing As Dialog Box

Command: *Choose* File, Save	Issues the SAVEAS command (not SAVE, because the drawing is unnamed) and opens the Save Drawing As dialog box (see fig. 2.8)

The File edit box, with no name, is highlighted.

Type **CHAPTER2**	Enters the name CHAPTER2
Press Enter	Accepts the name, closes the dialog box, and creates the CHAPTER2.DWG file

As you invest more time in your drawings, they become more valuable to you and should be saved frequently. Your work is not secure until it is saved to a file on hard disk, with periodic backups copied to another disk or tape.

The line above the Directories list and the File edit box shows the current defaults for the directory and file name. The Pattern edit box, at the top of the dialog box, enables you to specify file patterns to show in the list. You can filter the file names that are to be listed in the Files list box by entering DOS wild cards and text strings in the Pattern edit box. See Chapter 15 for more about wild card filters.

The following sections describe more about dialog box features, and then you will try some of them in an exercise.

Editing Text Boxes

When the text in an edit box is highlighted, the characters you type replace the current value. If you want to edit the current value rather than replace it, click on the edit box or press one of the cursor-control keys. A vertical-bar text cursor appears to mark the current character-entry position. The cursor-control keys are the four arrow keys, and the Home and End keys. The left- and up-arrow keys move the text cursor one character to the left; the right- and down-arrow keys move it to the right. The Home and End keys move the text cursor to the beginning and end of the line, respectively. The Backspace and Delete keys delete the character before and after the current text-cursor position, respectively. Any characters you type are inserted at the current text-cursor position. If the value is too long to fit into the edit box, it scrolls to the left or right. You can use the cursor keys to scroll the text in the box. When you have the desired text in the edit box, you can accept it by pressing Enter or by clicking on the OK button.

Selecting and Acting on Dialog Box Items

OK, Cancel, Type it and Default are examples of dialog box buttons. A button immediately executes an action when you click on it. Some buttons, such as the Set Color button in the Layer Control dialog box, open sub-dialog boxes, which are used to enter new values. You can select a button by clicking on it or by using its shortcut key (if it has one). In the file dialog boxes, the OK button accepts the current settings, exits, and performs the file action; the Cancel button exits without making changes. The Enter and Esc keys also are shortcut alternatives to the OK and Cancel buttons, respectively. If AutoCAD does not accept your new value, it is invalid and you must edit it or cancel the change. The Type it button closes the dialog box and returns you to the command line for you to type the file name, and the Default button restores all settings in the file dialog box to what they were when the dialog box first opened.

 Tip   Most dialog boxes contain a **H**elp button, which you can choose to call up the Help dialog box.

The File edit box is selected and highlighted when the Save Drawing As dialog box appears. To select an unselected dialog box item, you can click on it. Clicking on a button executes it, clicking on a radio button turns it on, and clicking on a check box

New Riders Publishing
INSIDE
SERIES

turns it on or off. If a dialog box item has a single underlined letter, that letter indicates a *hot key*, which can be typed from the keyboard to highlight that item. For example, the F in <u>F</u>ile is a hot key. The underlined T in the <u>T</u>ype it button is another hot key. If an edit box is in the text-entry mode, you must hold down Alt while typing the hot key. Selecting an item with a hot key also acts on it.

You can also select an item without acting on it. The Tab key moves between the edit boxes, buttons, and other dialog box items, selecting and highlighting each one as you move to them, but does not act on them. Shift+Tab moves through the items, in reverse order.

In dialog boxes, Enter, Tab, and the spacebar are not equivalent. When an item is selected, pressing Enter accepts it or acts upon it and often closes the dialog box. Pressing the spacebar acts on selected items, the same as clicking on them. In the case of a selected radio button, the spacebar turns it on. In the case of a selected check box, the spacebar turns it on or off. In the case of a selected button, pressing the spacebar acts on it, executing it or changing its value.

Note   If an item is gray in a dialog box, it usually means the item currently is not relevant and cannot be selected.

When you have finished entering or choosing items within a dialog box, you can close it in one of two ways. You can accept the changes made or you can cancel them. Choose OK to accept the current entries in the box; choose Cancel to ignore any changes to the current settings. You can also press Enter to accept the dialog box if the OK button is highlighted (shadowed). To cancel the dialog box, you can press either Esc, Ctrl+C, or you can click on the Cancel button with your pointing device.

Using Dialog Box Lists

You also can make selections in dialog boxes by selecting from lists. To select an item in a list, click on it or use the cursor keys to move up and down the list. In the file dialog boxes, the file name you select from the list appears in the file name edit box. Double-clicking on an item is the same as selecting the item and pressing Enter. When you double-click on a file name in the file list box, the file name is selected, accepted, the file action occurs on the chosen item, and the dialog box is closed.

The list of directory names below the Di<u>r</u>ectories label is also a list box. When you select a directory from it, its name appears on the line above the list box. You can, however, use the <u>F</u>ile edit box to change directories. If you enter a backslash in the text you enter in the <u>F</u>ile edit box, AutoCAD interprets it as a directory name rather than just a file name, changing the current directory and the contents of the file name and directory lists.

In the following exercise, try using the list boxes, buttons, Tab key, and spacebar in the Save Drawing As dialog box.

Using List Boxes, Buttons, and Keys

Continue from the previous exercise.

Command: *Choose* File, Save As	Issues the SAVEAS command and opens the Save Drawing As dialog box (see fig. 2.8)

The File edit box, with the default name CHAPTER2, is highlighted.

Press the Left arrow key	Places edit cursor between the R and the 2
Press Backspace	Deletes the R
Click on any name in the File *list box*	Selects a file name and puts it in the File edit box
Press the Page Down key	Scrolls down the Files list box, selecting another name
Click near the bottom of the scroll bar in the File *list, then click several times on the up arrow icon*	Scrolls down the Files list box, then single-steps up, but without selecting another name
Press on the scroll box in the scroll bar, drag it up and down, then release	Scrolls the Files list box up and down, without selecting another name
Double-click on the .. (parent directory symbol) in the Directories *list*	Changes the Files list to display the IA directory, which contains only the ACAD drawing that you made in Chapter 1
Press Tab three times	Highlights the Default button
Press the spacebar	Executes the Default button, restoring the CHAPTER2 name and \IA\DWGS directory
Click between the P *and the* T *in the* File *edit box*	Places edit cursor between the P and the T
Press Del three times and type 0	Deletes the TER and inserts 0, changing the name to CHAP02
Press Tab, then the spacebar	Highlights and executes the OK button, saving the drawing as CHAP02.DWG and closing the dialog box
Current drawing name set to C:\IA\DWGS\CHAP02.	Confirms the name change

New Riders Publishing
INSIDE SERIES

Using Buttons and Sliders

File-related dialog boxes contain all dialog features except check boxes, radio buttons, and horizontal slider bars. Figure 2.9 illustrates check boxes and radio buttons in the Drawing Aids dialog box. This dialog box appears when you choose Options, Drawing Aids.

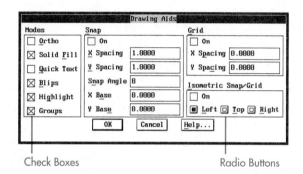

Check Boxes   Radio Buttons

Figure 2.9

Dialog box check boxes and radio buttons.

2

Check boxes are on/off switches that appear next to names of items that can only be on or off, such as the Grid On or Snap On items in the Drawing Aids dialog box. If an X mark appears in the box, the item the key word represents is on; if the box is blank, that item is off. Clicking on the box controls the setting. *Radio buttons* are groups of settings—only one radio button can be on at any one time. Radio buttons appear as a group of circles or squares enclosed in a box, with a black dot indicating which button is on, such as the Isometric Snap/Grid group in the Drawing Aids dialog box.

Slider bars are horizontal sliders that control values. They function the same as list box scroll bars. Figure 2.10 shows a slider bar in the Grips dialog box (choose Options, Grips). The slider controls the size of AutoCAD grip boxes. You can drag the slider bar by using your input device, or you can click on the arrows to adjust the grip size. A sample of the grip box size is shown beside the slider.

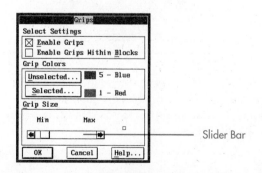

Slider Bar

Figure 2.10

Dialog box slider bar.

You can use the keyboard to select many items in a dialog box by typing the hot key (shown underlined in the dialog box, and bold and underlined in the text for this book) for that item. The hot key for the **T**op Isometric item in the Drawing Aids dialog box in the previous exercise, for example is the *T* key. You can use the Tab key to cycle through the dialog box items, highlighting them one at a time; Shift+Tab cycles in the reverse direction. Once displayed, dialog boxes can be moved with a drag-and-drop operation.

Pull-down menu items that display dialog boxes are followed by three dots. The New... and Open... items on the File pull-down menu are typical examples. Likewise, buttons in dialog boxes with labels followed by three dots display additional dialog boxes, as in the New Drawing **N**ame button in the Create New Drawing dialog box (refer back to figure 2.4).

Using Image Buttons

AutoCAD also displays menu selections as graphic images in certain dialog boxes. Selecting a graphic image—known as an *image button* or *tile* or an *icon*—is like selecting any other button. Several dialog boxes use image buttons, such as those used for linetypes (see fig. 2.11).

Figure 2.11

Dialog box image buttons.

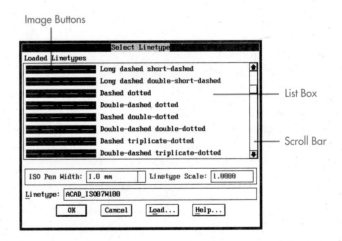

You should now be familiar with the major elements of AutoCAD's user interface and various ways to enter commands and options. In the next chapter, you gain a better understanding of the CAD drawing process and learn various coordinate entry methods. You also learn file handling, error recovery, and several basic drawing commands.

Using the Drawing Editor

Now that you are familiar with the elements of AutoCAD's user interface and how to enter commands, you need to understand the CAD drawing process. In this chapter, you learn many skills and concepts that you use repeatedly in AutoCAD. This chapter covers the following major topics:

◆ Starting and naming a new drawing

◆ Understanding AutoCAD's coordinate system

◆ Entering coordinates from the keyboard to set points

◆ Using relative coordinates

◆ Using several basic AutoCAD commands: OPEN, NEW, LINE, CIRCLE, ARC, QSAVE, SAVEAS, MOVE, ERASE, OOPS, U, PLOT, and QUIT

◆ Saving your work

Much of your work in AutoCAD depends on you identifying points within the drawing area. In AutoCAD, such points are located using *Cartesian (X,Y) coordinates,* and they define where objects as simple as a line begin and end. In this chapter, you learn about AutoCAD's coordinate system and how to enter coordinate points manually.

AutoCAD, by default, opens with a blank, generic, unnamed drawing, very similar to a blank drawing sheet fixed to a drawing board in manual drafting. As in manual drafting, you must name drawings so that you can refer to them and store them properly. This chapter covers opening, naming, and saving your drawing files.

This chapter introduces several AutoCAD commands. The LINE command, for example, is basic to almost all AutoCAD work. The chapter also discusses correcting errors. Knowing how to recover from any errors that you make is a vital learning tool; it gives you the confidence to explore AutoCAD's commands and features on your own and at your own pace. Finally, you carry out a quick plot of a practice drawing so that you can see your work off-screen. After you finish this chapter and its exercises, you will understand many of the basic operations you use to complete AutoCAD drawings.

Quick 5¢ Tour

Start AutoCAD by running the batch file you created in Chapter 1.

One of the most fundamental commands in AutoCAD is the LINE command, which enables you to draw line segments from one point to another on the drawing. You can simply pick points on-screen, but one of the ways to draw accurately is to use coordinates.

Command: *Choose* Draw, Line	Issues the LINE command
Command:_line From point: **5,5** (Enter)	Specifies first absolute Cartesian point
To point: **@2<30** (Enter)	Specifies second absolute Cartesian point
To point: **@2<90** (Enter)	Specifies third absolute Cartesian point
To point: **@2<150** (Enter)	Specifies fourth absolute Cartesian point
To point: **@2<210** (Enter)	Specifies fifth absolute Cartesian point
To point: **@2<270** (Enter)	Specifies sixth absolute Cartesian point

The LINE command has an Undo option. If you make a mistake, you can use it to "undraw" the last segment.

To point: **@2<340** (Enter)	Oops... a mistake
To point: **U** (Enter)	Undoes last segment

After you draw at least two line segments, you can create a closed shape by telling AutoCAD to draw a segment back to the first point.

To point: **C** (Enter)	Draws last segment to first point, then ends the LINE command

Your screen should look like figure 3.1. You devote additional time to coordinate entry later in this chapter. Another very basic AutoCAD object is the circle.

Command: *Choose* Draw, Circle, *then* Center, Radius	Issues the CIRCLE command
Command: _circle 3P/2P/TTR/ <Center point>: **4,6** `Enter`	Locates the center and displays a rubber-band line
Diameter/<Radius>: **3** `Enter`	Draws the circle

One of AutoCAD's most useful error-correcting tools is the ERASE command. The circle you just drew is too large, so you need to erase it and then draw another.

Command: *Choose* Modify, Erase	Issues the ERASE command
Command: _erase	
Select objects: *Select the circle*	
Select objects: 1 found	
Select objects: `Enter`	Erases the circle
Command: *Choose* Draw, Circle, *then* Center, Radius	Issues the CIRCLE command
Command: _circle 3P/2P/TTR/ <Center point>: **4,6** `Enter`	Locates the center and displays a rubber-band line
Diameter/<Radius>: **1.5** `Enter`	Draws the circle

Your screen should now look like figure 3.2. The circle is the right size now, but is in the wrong place. AutoCAD has a number of editing commands, and the one that will help you now is MOVE.

Command: *Choose* Modify, Move	Issues the MOVE command
Command: _move	
Select objects: *Select the circle*	
Select objects: 1 found	
Select objects: `Enter`	Selects the circle
Base point of displacement: **4,6** `Enter`	Sets base point for MOVE
Second point of displacement: **5,7** `Enter`	Sets new point

continues

continued

Command:

Your screen should now look like figure 3.3.

At this point, all your work exists only in your computer's memory. You must make a copy of your work on your computer's hard disk; otherwise, after you turn off your computer, you lose your work.

Command: *Choose* File, Save	Activates the Save Drawing As dialog box
Type **CH03**	Enters drawing name in the File edit box
Choose OK	Saves your work in a drawing file called CH03.DWG

Figure 3.1

Using the LINE command.

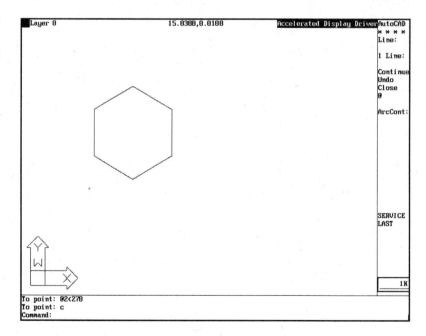

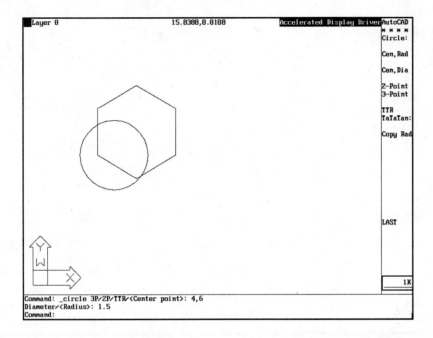

Figure 3.2

Using the CIRCLE command.

3

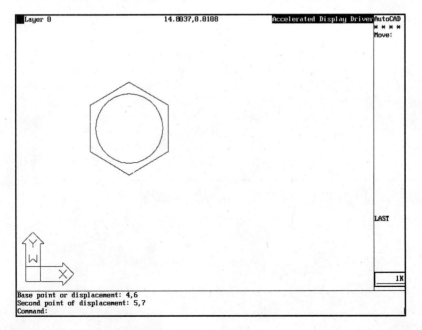

Figure 3.3

Using the MOVE command.

Opening and Creating Drawings

It might be stating the obvious, but in AutoCAD, you work with new and existing drawings. These drawings exist as files on your computer's hard disk. There are two commands you'll use as you work with your drawings: OPEN and NEW. The OPEN command enables you to select from a list of existing drawings and select one to load into the drawing editor for further work. The NEW command enables you to create a brand-new drawing file. This new file may be empty of objects and settings, or it may have settings that will let you create objects more easily, or it may already include objects that you want to use as starting points for your new drawing.

Previewing and Opening Existing Drawings

AutoCAD is a graphics application—the world's most popular desktop *computer-aided design* (CAD) software. Although AutoCAD is capable of linking large amounts of nongraphic data between the drawings it creates and external programs, AutoCAD's power and utility are based on visual data. File management interfaces, on the other hand, deal exclusively with textual/numerical data—file names, creation dates and sizes, hard drive directories, and subdirectories. Merging the two worlds—textual/numerical storage names versus visual data stored—often is difficult.

It was not until the relatively recent past that graphic elements derived directly from AutoCAD drawings began to appear as aids in selecting AutoCAD commands and command options. Icon menus, for example, first appeared in AutoCAD Release 9. Further refinements were made possible with the introduction of interactive dialog boxes that allowed AutoCAD's interface to become more graphic in nature. Now, for the first time, AutoCAD can display a preview of its graphics-based files before you perform such operations as opening a drawing, or choosing another drawing file to insert into the current drawing. The following exercise demonstrates this new capability of AutoCAD Release 13 for DOS to visually preview its own files.

Previewing AutoCAD Drawings

Start AutoCAD with the batch file you created in Chapter 1, "Setting Up." Perform the following steps.

Command: *Choose* File, Open   Displays the Open Drawing dialog box

The contents of the book's working directory, C:\IA\DWAS, appear in the file list box of the dialog box.

Click on any file name   Displays a preview of the drawing in the Preview box

You can preview drawing files one at a time by clicking once on the file name. If you find the drawing you want to open in the Open Drawing dialog box, you can open it by double-clicking on the file name or by choosing OK (see fig. 3.4). Drawing files—especially files stored in the same directory—often have similar file names, and if you have ever found it difficult to locate a particular drawing by its file name alone, you will appreciate the usefulness of this AutoCAD feature.

Click on the Cancel *button in the* Open Drawing *dialog box*	Closes the Open Drawing dialog box and cancels the OPEN command

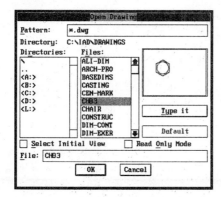

Figure 3.4

Previewing a drawing in the Open Drawing dialog box.

3

Creating and Naming a New Drawing

To ensure that you use the same default settings in AutoCAD as this book uses, follow the steps in the next exercise to set up AutoCAD. You first tell AutoCAD not to use a prototype drawing. A *prototype drawing* is a drawing AutoCAD uses as a template for creating a new drawing. The settings and other information, including previously drawn objects, that are stored in a prototype drawing are transferred to the new drawing. If you do not specify a prototype drawing, AutoCAD begins all drawings using the settings and other information stored in the initial default ACAD.DWG.

The prototype drawing is a very powerful tool and you learn to use it later in this book. The other settings you make in the exercise are necessary to ensure that your setup matches the book's or are appropriate for the work you carry out in this chapter. All these settings are covered in detail in later chapters of this book. In Chapter 5 "Setting Up a CAD Drawing," you will learn about other basic drawing settings. For now, you need only set them according to the exercises' directions.

You use the NEW command to start a new drawing. As with many of the commands in AutoCAD, you can issue the NEW command in several ways. You can type **NEW** from the command line, select the NEW command from the FILE item on the screen menu, or select the New item on the File pull-down menu. Whichever method you use, the Create New Drawing dialog box appears. In this exercise, you use the pull-down menu.

Note   In this and most of the remaining exercises in this book that involve choices from the pull-down menus, a shorthand method of designating menu choices is used. The pull-down menu's label is given first, followed by the menu item, separated by a comma. Choose File, New, for example, means to choose the File pull-down menu, then the New item. You can carry out these steps by clicking with the pointer.

In the following exercise, you create a new drawing named CHAP03, using AutoCAD's default settings.

Starting a New Drawing

Command: *Choose* File, New	Opens the Create New Drawing dialog box
Click inside the New **D**rawing Name *edit box and type* **CHAP03**	Assigns the name CHAP03 to the new drawing (see fig. 3.5)
Choose OK	Closes the dialog box, saves your settings, and opens a new drawing

Figure 3.5

The Create New Drawing dialog box.

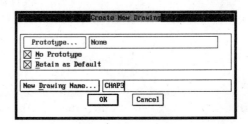

AutoCAD has created a new, named drawing, using the default ACAD.DWG as a prototype.

> **NEW.** The NEW command enables you to create a new drawing file.
> Pull-down: *Choose* File, New
> Screen: *Choose* FILE, New

Understanding the NEW Command Options

The NEW command provides the following options in the Create New Drawing dialog box:

New Riders Publishing
INSIDE
SERIES

- ◆ **Prototype.** This option enables you to specify the prototype drawing you want to use. Prototype drawings are covered in more detail in Chapter 5 "Setting Up a CAD Drawing."

- ◆ **No Prototype.** This option enables you to bypass a prototype drawing and use AutoCAD's default settings for all parameters.

- ◆ **Retain as Default.** This option enables you to set No Prototype as the default, or set the specified drawing as the default prototype drawing.

 Note   You can turn the file dialog box feature off by setting the FILEDIA system variable to 0. With the file dialog box turned off, all file menu selections and commands prompt for the file name at the Command: prompt. If you have the file dialog box feature turned off, you can still display file dialog boxes when you want to use them by entering a tilde symbol (~) when AutoCAD prompts you for a file name.

Exploring AutoCAD's Coordinate Systems

AutoCAD's default coordinate system is called the *World Coordinate System* (often referred to as the WCS throughout this book). One reason many new users find AutoCAD easy-to-use right away is that the WCS is based on a standard Cartesian (or X,Y) coordinate system. Anyone who has experience with standard manual drafting knows this system, and can easily understand and apply it to CAD drafting methods. Although AutoCAD supports other coordinate systems, such as spherical coordinates for 3D work, most of the points you need to specify are based on the standard Cartesian coordinate system.

The World Coordinate System

When you begin a new drawing, AutoCAD, by default, places you in the WCS. You can think of AutoCAD's opening graphics screen as a sheet of drafting paper with the WCS extending across the entire sheet. The WCS's coordinates consist of a horizontal or X axis, and a vertical or Y axis. (It also includes a Z axis above and below the plane of the paper for 3D work.) Displacements are from an *origin* that is initially located at the bottom-left corner of the sheet. The X,Y coordinates of the origin are 0,0. Displacements to the right along the X axis and upward along the Y axis are considered to be positive, and displacements to the left along the X axis and downward along the Y axis are considered to be negative.

You can describe any point on the sheet by specifying the distance, or displacement, from the origin. By convention, you describe points by specifying the X distance first, followed by the Y distance, separated by a comma. Figure 3.6 shows two points along with their coordinates. The point labeled 3,2 is located three units to the right and two units up from 0,0. The X and Y axes in figure 3.6 are represented by two lines that originate at 0,0. The tick marks along each axis represent 1 unit. As you pass through the 0,0 point or origin, the numbers become negative. The point –2,–1 in figure 3.6 is located two units to the left and one unit below point 0,0.

You can keep track of your location easily by following the coordinates display in the status bar. The following exercise shows you how coordinate display works.

Figure 3.6

Measuring coordinates in AutoCAD.

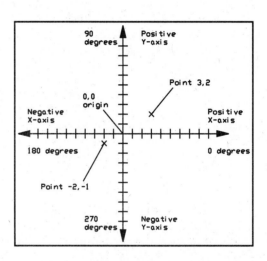

Understanding AutoCAD's Coordinate System

Command: *Choose* Draw, Line	Issues LINE command
Command: _line From point: **4,4** (Enter)	Sets start point
To point: *Move the cursor around the screen*	Coordinate display updates constantly as cursor moves
To point: *Press* Esc	Cancels the command

You can change the display mode of the coordinates readout. This is discussed later in this chapter.

To help you visualize this coordinate system, AutoCAD, by default, displays the WCS icon near the lower-left corner of the graphics screen or at the 0,0 point. Because the 0,0 point, by default, is in the extreme lower-left corner of AutoCAD's display, the WCS icon initially is offset from the origin (0,0) to make it more visible. The WCS icon is shown in figure 3.7, along with two points labeled with their respective coordinates. Using the UCSICON command to control the WCS icon is discussed in the following section.

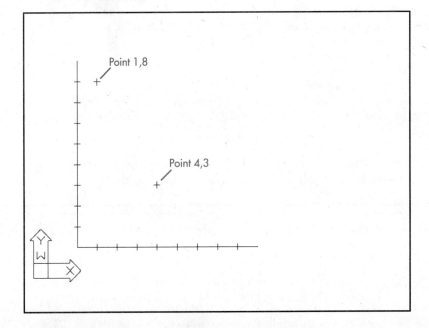

Figure 3.7

The World Coordinate System.

3

If you look at the WCS icon more closely, you see that the X arrow points to the right, or positive, direction on the X axis and the Y arrow points upward in the positive Y axis direction. The W on the Y arrow indicates that you are in the default World Coordinate System.

The User Coordinate System

Although the World Coordinate System is the default, you can create your own coordinate systems called *User Coordinate Systems (UCSs)*. As the name suggests, you, the user, can control a UCS. In a UCS, you can move and rotate the origin, and even make it align with particular objects in the drawing, and you can do the same with the directions of the X, Y, and Z axes. Even though the three axes of any UCS are mutually perpendicular to each other (as in the WCS), you can achieve a great degree of flexibility in UCS placement and orientation. The UCS icon is identical to the WCS icon, except the UCS icon lacks the *W*. User Coordinate Systems are indispensable in 3D design and drafting. Methods of creating and using the UCS are covered in Part Six, "AutoCAD and 3D." You also see how the UCS is of value in 2D applications in Chapter 6, "Drawing Accurately."

The WCS and UCS icons display other information about the current coordinate system's orientation in 3D space. A "+" in the corner of either icon, for example, indicates that the icon is placed at the exact origin of the current UCS. This, and other UCS icon symbology, is covered in Chapter 6.

 Note   If the screen display permits and the UCSICON command's Origin option is turned on, the WCS icon appears at point 0,0. In these instances, a cross appears in the corner box of the icon, marking the origin. This cross indicates that the WCS icon is at the origin.

As you work in 2D, you might find that the UCS icon obscures parts of your drawing. In the following exercise, you learn how to turn the UCS icon off and on.

Turning the UCS Icon Off and On

Choose Options, UCS   Displays the UCS submenu

Choose Icon   Turns the UCS icon off if it was on, and
                                                      on if it was off

The Icon item in the UCS submenu is a toggle; it appears with a check before it if the UCS icon is currently on and without a check if it is currently off (see fig. 3.8). In either case, clicking on it reverses the on/off condition of the icon.

You can also turn the UCS icon on and off by entering the UCSICON command at the Command: prompt and typing ON or OFF. The other options presented are for use mainly in 3D work and are covered in Part Six, "AutoCAD and 3D." For now, if the UCS icon is off, you should use the Options pull-down or the command-line method to turn it back on.

Command: **UCSICON** (Enter)   Turns the UCS icon back on

ON/OFF/All/Noorigin/ORigin <OFF>: **ON** (Enter)

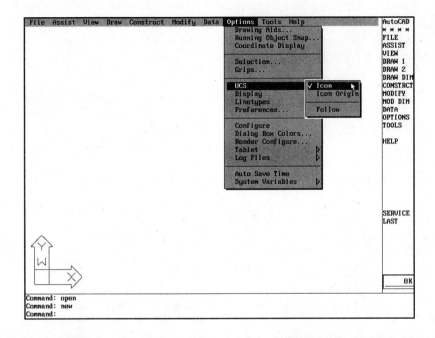

Figure 3.8
Toggling the visibility of the UCS Icon.

LINE. The LINE command enables you to draw a line with endpoints specified in 2D or 3D coordinates.
Screen: *Choose* DRAW1, Line:
Pull-down: *Choose* Draw, Line

The LINE command, used in the preceding exercise and later in this chapter, is one of AutoCAD's most frequently used commands. Although relatively straightforward, the LINE command has several options that increase and extend its usefulness. Those options are listed here and demonstrated in the exercises that appear throughout the rest of this chapter.

Line Command Options

The LINE command has two prompts displayed at the Command: prompt, and three options displayed on the screen menu when the LINE command is active, as follows:

◆ At the From point: prompt, you specify the point for the beginning of the first (and perhaps only) segment.

◆ At the To point: prompt, you specify the point to which AutoCAD draws a line from the previous point.

◆ Choosing the Continue option from the screen menu causes the line to begin from the end of the most recently drawn line or arc. If you drew an arc most recently, AutoCAD draws the line tangent to the endpoint of the arc.

Note Pressing Enter at the LINE command's From point: prompt has an effect similar to choosing the Continue option; that is, AutoCAD draws a new line segment from the end of the most recently drawn line or arc.

◆ At the To point: prompt, you can enter **U** or **UNDO**, or choose Undo from the screen menu, to erase the last line segment, stepping back to the previous point.

Entering Points

Now that you have been introduced to AutoCAD's standard coordinate system, you are ready to consider the various methods of entering or specifying points in AutoCAD. Many of the drawings you create in AutoCAD—from the very simple to the very complex—are composed of relatively few basic AutoCAD objects: lines, arcs, circles, and text elements. All these objects require that you enter points to specify their location, size, and direction. The center of a circle, the beginning of a line, and the end of an arc are all defined by points. Coordinate points are as basic to CAD as words are to word processing. You can enter coordinates in AutoCAD in several ways.

Using Absolute Coordinates

If you know the exact coordinates of your points, or their angle and distance from the drawing's origin, you can use the keyboard to enter coordinates in four formats: rectangular, spherical, cylindrical, or polar. These formats are known as *absolute coordinates*.

Note Absolute coordinates that involve points or angles in the Z axis, including absolute cylindrical and absolute spherical coordinates, apply only to 3D. A detailed discussion of 3D coordinate entry is given in Part Seven, "AutoCAD and 3D."

Absolute Cartesian or *X,Y coordinates* in 2D treat coordinate entry as X and Y displacements from the 0,0 origin of the current UCS. For example, the absolute Cartesian coordinates 6,5 define a point that is 6 units in the positive X direction and 5 units in the positive Y direction from the origin. This point is shown in figure 3.9. The UCS icon is also shown in figure 3.9.

New Riders Publishing
INSIDE
SERIES

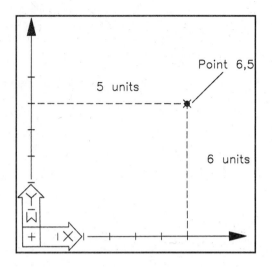

Figure 3.9

*Locating a point
with absolute
Cartesian
coordinates.*

If your displacement is positive, you do not need to use a plus (+) sign. Negative displacements are to the left of and down from point 0,0. You precede a negative displacement coordinate with a minus (–) sign; for example, –3.5,2.5 specifies a point 3.5 units below and 2.5 units to the right of the 0,0 point.

Absolute Polar coordinates also treat 2D coordinate entry as a displacement from 0,0 but you specify the displacement as distance and angle. The distance and angle values are separated by a left-angle bracket (<). Positive angles are measured clockwise relative to an assumed 0 degrees that, by default, lies along the positive X axis. In this system, then, 90 degrees lies along the positive Y axis, 180 degrees along the negative X axis and 270 degrees along the negative Y axis, all radiating from the drawing's 0,0 point. The default angle directions are shown in figure 3.10.

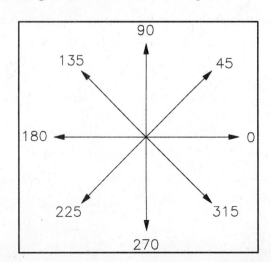

Figure 3.10

*Default angle
directions.*

In figure 3.11, the 2D point is defined using a distance of *D* and an angle of *a*. At the keyboard, you would enter: *D<a*. A specific polar coordinate, 2<60 for example, defines a point 2 units from 0,0 at an angle of 60 degrees from the X axis.

Figure 3.11

Locating a point using absolute polar coordinates.

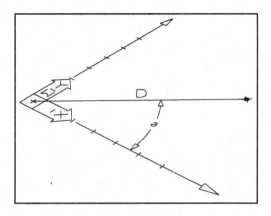

In the following exercise, you use both absolute Cartesian and absolute polar coordinates to draw some basic shapes.

Specifying Points with Absolute Coordinates

Continue to use the CHAP03 drawing.

Command: *Choose* View, Zoom, All	Zooms to display the entire drawing area
Command: *Choose* Draw, Line	Issues the LINE command
Command:_line From point: **7,2** (Enter)	Specifies first absolute Cartesian point
To point: **9,2** (Enter)	Specifies second absolute Cartesian point
To point: **9,4** (Enter)	Specifies third absolute Cartesian point
To point: **7,4** (Enter)	Specifies fourth absolute Cartesian point
To point: **7,2** (Enter)	Specifies fifth absolute Cartesian point
To point: (Enter)	Ends the LINE command
(Enter)	Reissues the LINE command
Command: _line From point: **1.25,5.25** (Enter)	Specifies an absolute Cartesian point
To point: **3,7.5** (Enter)	Specifies an absolute Cartesian point

To point: **7.08<47.86** (Enter)   Specifies an absolute polar point

To point: **C** (Enter)   Issues the Close option of LINE command
                                          and closes the triangle

Your drawing should now look like figure 3.12.

Command: *Choose* Assist, Inquiry,   Issues the ID command
Locate Point

Command: '_id Point: **ENDP** (Enter)   Issues the ENDpoint object snap and
                                          displays a box at the crosshairs

of *Pick the right end of the base
leg of the triangle and click*

of X = 4.7503   Y = 5.2499   Displays the exact coordinates of the
Z = 0.0000   endpoint of the right end of the base

Command: (Enter)   Repeats the ID command

'_ID Point: **ENDP** (Enter)   Issues the ENDpoint object snap

of *Pick the left end of the same line
and click*

of X = 1.2500   Y = 5.2500   Displays the exact coordinates of the
Z = 0.0000   endpoint of the left end of the base

Command: *Press F1*   Displays the text screen

In the text screen, note the Y coordinates that appear in the command history lines for the two
ID commands you issued.

Press F1   Displays the graphics screen

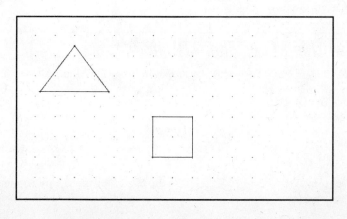

Figure 3.12

*Shapes drawn
with absolute
coordinates.*

The Y coordinates for the opposite ends of the triangle's base are not the same. Although the difference is small (0.001 units), it is unacceptable for most CAD work, in which this amount of inaccuracy can be significant, especially if magnified by a cumulative error effect. This inaccuracy is a major disadvantage of polar coordinate entry, by which angles specified with two places of precision, for example, are inadequate. Later in this book, you learn methods that you can use to increase the accuracy of your drawings.

Viewing the Coordinate Display

The preceding exercise used simple points. In a more realistic drawing, absolute points—especially absolute polar points—are usually more difficult to calculate. In addition to keyboard entry, you can use the AutoCAD crosshair cursor to pick polar coordinates by ensuring that the coordinate display on the mode status bar is set to display polar coordinates. The coordinate display has three modes of operation. You can switch through the three modes by pressing the F6 function key, or by pressing Ctrl+D.

The three modes of coordinate display are summarized here:

◆ Dynamic X,Y mode displays the absolute coordinates continuously and updates them as you move the cursor. This is the default mode.

◆ Dynamic polar mode displays distance<angle information during prompts that accept a distance and/or angle and otherwise displays dynamic X,Y coordinates.

◆ Static mode displays absolute coordinates that do not update as the cursor is moved. They always display the X,Y coordinates of the last point picked.

At the Command: prompt or a prompt that does not accept a distance and/or angle, you can only switch between static and dynamic X,Y modes—that is, absolute coordinates only. At a prompt that accepts a distance and/or angle, you can switch between all three modes. The following exercise demonstrates switching between coordinate display modes.

Switching Coordinate Display Modes

Continue to use the CHAP03 drawing. Pay particular attention to the coordinate display in the mode status line during the following steps.

Move the cursor around the screen	Updates the display of absolute coordinates continuously
Command: *Choose* Draw, Line	Issues the LINE command
Command: _line From point: *Pick a point somewhere below the triangle*	Displays the beginning of the line segments with a rubber band extending to the cursor

`To point:` *Pick a point inside the triangle, then press F6*	Draws the first line segment and changes coordinate display to static mode
`To point: <Coords off> U` [Enter]	Erases the last line segment

Responding to the `To point:` prompt with the LINE command's U option erases the most recent segment. The `<Coords off>` message indicates that the coordinate display mode has been switched during the LINE command.

`To point:` *Again pick a point inside the triangle, then press Ctrl+D*	Draws the first line segment and changes coordinate display to dynamic polar mode

This time you used Ctrl+D to switch the coordinate display to the dynamic polar mode.

`To point:  <Coords on> U` [Enter]	Erases the last line segment

The `<Coords on>` message indicates that the static mode coordinate display was switched to dynamic mode during the LINE command.

`To point:` *Press Esc*	Cancels the LINE command

3

In the preceding exercise, you used two methods of switching between the three modes of displaying coordinates on the mode status line. In the majority of your work with point entry, you will probably find it most useful to use dynamic polar coordinates. Although absolute coordinates have limited usefulness, they frequently are used to locate the first point of an object in a drawing or to establish a set of known points.

Using Relative Coordinates

If you had to enter all points in absolute coordinates, drawing in AutoCAD would be awkward. More often, you know the X,Y displacement or the distance and angle of points relative to previous points you have specified. Coordinates you enter in this manner are called *relative coordinates*. In 2D work, you can specify both Cartesian and polar coordinates as relative coordinates. When you use relative coordinates, AutoCAD treats the last point you entered as a temporary origin. The positive direction of the X and Y axes and the method of measuring angles is the same as for absolute coordinates.

You distinguish between absolute and relative point entry by placing an at symbol (@) before all relative coordinates. If you're using the LINE command, for example, and you want to add a line segment that is 2 units in the X direction and 1 unit in the Y direction from the last point you entered, type **@2,1** at the `To point:` prompt. You would enter a relative polar coordinate as @2<33, which defines a point 2 units at an angle of 33 degrees from the last point you specified. If you want to create a reference point by defining a new last point, you can use a zero distance in Cartesian or polar units, such as @0,0 or @0<*aa*, where *aa* is any angle, because the angle in this case makes no difference.

Tip   An even simpler way to enter a new point as the last point is to enter an @ without any distance or angle. AutoCAD interprets the @ symbol as specifying the last point.

Note   Defining and using last points is a valuable tool in AutoCAD editing operations, such as when you move or copy objects. These operations are covered in Part Two, "Basic 2D CAD Drafting."

In the following exercise, you use both relative Cartesian and relative polar coordinates to draw a parallelogram.

Drawing with Relative Coordinates

Continue with the CHAP03 drawing.

Choose Draw, Line	Issues LINE command
Command: _line From point: **2,3** (Enter)	Specifies an absolute Cartesian point
To point: **@2<0** (Enter)	Specifies a relative polar point
To point: **@1.5<260** (Enter)	

Remember that positive angles are measured counterclockwise from zero degrees. Refer again to fig. 3.10, if necessary.

To point: **@-2,0** (Enter)	Specifies a relative Cartesian point
To point: **@1.5<80** (Enter)	Completes the parallelogram (see fig. 3.13)

Recall that the close option of the LINE command could have been used in the last step to close this series of line segments.

To point: **U** (Enter)	Erases the last line using the Undo option of the LINE command
To point: **C** (Enter)	Closes the figure and ends the LINE command

---

Your CHAP03 drawing should now resemble figure 3.13. In some instances, it's easier to use relative polar coordinates to specify points than it is to use relative Cartesian coordinates; in other cases, the opposite is true. The angles involved or the distance information available often determines which method to use. Keep in mind that coordinate input (such as the input you use in this chapter) is useful when you already have the distance or angle information of drawing elements. In Part Two,

New Riders Publishing
INSIDE
SERIES

"Basic 2D CAD Drafting," you learn how to draw with the same accuracy when existing drawing objects and features determine point entry and not vice versa.

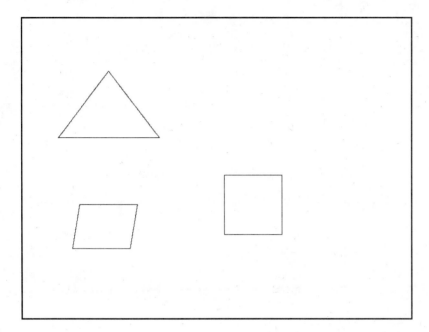

Figure 3.13

A parallelogram drawn with relative coordinates.

AutoCAD provides several commands that save the drawing by writing the drawing's database to a file on a permanent storage device, such as a hard drive. The drawing is saved with a DWG file-name extension. As a safeguard, AutoCAD further secures your work by assigning a BAK extension to the previous version of the drawing, if one exists. Three commands save drawings to a permanent file: SAVE, QSAVE, and SAVEAS. AutoCAD's terminology and menu structure are confusing here because the command labeled Save: on the screen menu and the Save item on the File pull-down menu actually issue the QSAVE command. The various commands you can use to save drawings to files are described in the following section.

QSAVE. The QSAVE (for Quick SAVE) command enables you to save the current, named drawing without any further input. If you issue QSAVE when a drawing has not been named, the Save Drawing As dialog box appears. See the following section for the SAVEAS command.

Pull-down:	*Choose* File, Save
Screen:	*Choose* FILE, Save:

In the following exercise, you practice using the File menu's Save item to save your CHAP03 drawing.

Saving Your Drawing File

To save your CHAP03 drawing, perform the following.

Command: *Choose* File, Save	Issues the QSAVE command and saves the drawing under its current name
Command: **QSAVE** (Enter)	Issues the QSAVE command and saves the drawing again

The QSAVE command saves the drawing under its current name with all changes since it was last saved.

The QSAVE command is a quick, easy way to ensure that the changes you make to the drawing are stored on your hard drive.

Saving Your Drawing Automatically

AutoCAD has a timed automatic save option. You set the time interval between automatic saves by using the SAVETIME system variable.

Note The SAVETIME system variable controls the automatic save option feature. SAVETIME is one of the many system variables that govern how AutoCAD works. You learn more about system variables in Part Two, "Basic 2D CAD Drafting." In the following exercise, you specify an interval (in minutes) for the SAVETIME system variable. You can set SAVETIME by choosing Options, Auto Save Time from the pull-down menu, or entering **SAVETIME** at the Command: prompt.

Using SAVETIME To Save Drawings Automatically

Continue to use the CHAP03 drawing from the preceding exercises.

Command: **SAVETIME** (Enter)	Accesses the SAVETIME system variable
New value for SAVETIME <120>: **15** (Enter)	Sets automatic save option to 15-minute intervals

---

New Riders Publishing
INSIDE SERIES

The default interval for SAVETIME is 120 minutes. Setting the interval to 0 minutes disables the SAVETIME feature. After you change the interval, the SAVETIME timer starts the next time you change the drawing and is reset and restarted any time you execute SAVE, SAVEAS, or QSAVE. AutoCAD's automatic saves do not affect your existing BAK files. Instead, AutoCAD uses a filename with the extension SV$. By default, the filename itself is AUTO.SV$ and is saved in the current directory. Each automatic save overwrites the existing AUTO.SV$. If you start working on another drawing, the filename is incremented to, for example, AUTO1.SV$.

Note   Automatic saving does not occur if there is no drawing activity. In other words, if you set SAVETIME to 10 minutes and then go for lunch, no automatic saves will take place.

AutoCAD's automatic save option provides a third copy of your drawing file. In the event that both your DWG and BAK files become unusable, you can rename AUTO1.SV$ to a name that has a DWG extension and open it as a drawing.

Tip   Even if the SAVETIME feature is active, you should develop the habit of manually saving the drawing at frequent intervals. Good habits are always operative—the automatic save option might not be!

Saving a Drawing under a Different Name

> **SAVEAS.** The SAVEAS command, like SAVE, enables you to save the drawing under any name. Issuing the SAVEAS command initiates the Save Drawing As dialog box. Using SAVEAS causes AutoCAD to change the current drawing name from its original name to the new name.
> Pull-down: *Choose File, Save As*
> Screen: *Choose FILE, Save As:*

AutoCAD Release 12 was the only version to date where its drawings could be loaded into the previous version of the program. Although some objects were not translatable, Release 11 had no difficulty opening a Release 12 drawing.

This does not hold for Release 13; you cannot load a Release 13 drawing into Release 12. To help users who need their drawings in Release 12 format, a special version of the SAVEAS command called SAVEASR12 is included in Release 13.

> **SAVEASR12.** The SAVEASR12 command enables you to provide backward compatibility with AutoCAD Release 12. When you issue the SAVEASR12 command, AutoCAD displays the Save Release 12 Drawing As dialog box, in which you enter a file name under which you want the Release 12 drawing to be saved. The original Release 13 drawing is stored with the same name but a BAK extension. Some of the Release 13 drawing information can end up lost or altered in this process. The SAVEASR12 command is available only at the command line.

As you saw in the definition of the SAVEAS command, you can save the current drawing to a different name. In the following exercise, you use the SAVEAS command to save the current CHAP03 drawing and rename it to CHAP03B.

Saving a Drawing to a Different Name

Continue to use the CHAP03 drawing from preceding exercise.

Choose File, Save As	Issues the SAVEAS command and displays the Save Drawing As dialog box (see fig 3.14)
Type **CHAP03B** *in the* File: *input box, then choose* OK	Saves the drawing to a new file and closes the dialog box

```
Current drawing name set to
C:\IA\DRAWINGS\CHAP03B.
```

`Command:` *Choose* File, Open	Displays the Open Drawing dialog box

Scroll down the list of drawing files. The drawing you saved with the SAVEAS command, CHAP03B, appears in the Files: list box.

Select the file name CHAP03B	Highlights the drawing name and displays a preview of the drawing in the Preview box (see fig. 3.15)
Choose OK	Loads the drawing into the drawing editor

If you want to exit AutoCAD at this point, you can choose File, Exit, which issues the QUIT command if you have made no changes to the drawing since you last saved it. You can return to this drawing later by using the OPEN command as described in the previous exercise.

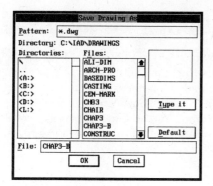

Figure 3.14

*The Save
Drawing As
dialog box.*

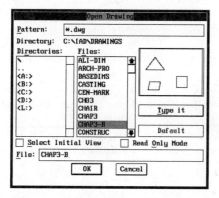

Figure 3.15

*The Open
Drawing dialog
box.*

3

QUIT. The QUIT command enables you to exit AutoCAD if you have made no
changes to the drawing since you last saved. If you have made changes to the
drawing, the Drawing Modification dialog box appears, prompting you to save
or discard the changes before you exit (see fig. 3.16).

Pull-down: *Choose* File, Exit
Screen: *Choose* FILE, Exit:

Figure 3.16

*The Drawing
Modification
dialog box.*

Learning More about Command Entry

In the exercises so far in this chapter and in Chapter 2, "Touring the AutoCAD Interface," you have issued numerous commands. After all, nothing gets done in AutoCAD until you issue a command. You have a basic understanding of the ways in which you can issue commands: from pull-down menus, from the screen menu, and of course, from the Command: prompt. You are now prepared to consider command entry more formally and to learn more about the mouse and keyboard entry.

Using the Mouse

The most common input device for AutoCAD—after the keyboard—is the mouse or digitizer puck; in AutoCAD, these are referred to as *pointing devices*. Most computer users are familiar with mice, and most computers come equipped with them.

Many CAD users have chosen digitizing tablets in preference to mice. A tablet is a very useful addition to an AutoCAD station. Not only does its puck act as a mouse, enabling you to input points and pick commands; you can also use it to copy paper drawings into AutoCAD by taping them to the tablet and tracing over them with the puck. AutoCAD even includes a digitizer template, with commands assigned to specific areas on it. AutoCAD's digitizer template has a screen pointing area and four command areas. Picking one of the boxes in the command areas initiates a command.

 Note   In this book, the term *mouse* means a digitizer puck, a trackball and a tablet stylus as well as a mouse.

You use the pointing device to control the AutoCAD cursor and the screen pointer. The AutoCAD cursor usually appears in the form of the drawing editor's crosshairs during drawing and editing functions. The cursor is of primary importance in a graphics-based application such as AutoCAD because you use it both to specify points and to select objects on which to perform editing operations. The cursor becomes a pointer when you position it over a menu selection or inside a dialog box. Whether it acts as a pointer or as crosshairs, you carry out commands or actions by clicking, or depressing, the device's buttons.

If you use a two-button mouse, the buttons are defined as follows:

◆ **Pick button.** The pick button is usually the left mouse button (unless a user has customized the menu). Use the pick button to select AutoCAD objects and menu items.

◆ **Enter button.** The Enter button is usually the right mouse button. Use the Enter button to issue a return; it is the functional equivalent of the Enter key.

Note If you have a three-button mouse, the middle button, by default, displays the floating cursor menu wherever the crosshairs sit on the screen. You can achieve the same thing with a two button mouse by holding down the Shift key and pressing the right button. The configuration of mouse buttons is sometimes not the same as described here; a user can change button configuration with relative ease. Experiment with your particular mouse. With tablet pucks, you might have additional buttons that you can use to turn on and off settings such as snap, ortho, and grid.

In the following exercise, you practice using the mouse and are introduced to the cursor menu and some AutoCAD commands you have not yet used. The CIRCLE command and the concept of object snap are covered in detail later in this book.

Practicing with the Mouse Buttons

Continue to use the CHAP03B drawing from the previous exercise.

Command: *Choose* Draw, Circle, *then* Center, Radius	Issues the CIRCLE command
Command: `_circle 3P/2P/TTR/ <Center point>: `Diameter/<Radius>:` *Pick a point near* ① *(see fig. 3.17)*	Locates the center and displays a rubber-band line
`Diameter/<Radius>:` *Move the cursor to* ② *and click the pick button on your mouse*	Draws a circle and ends the command

If you've already used the CIRCLE command in the current editing session, a default value for the radius will be shown inside angle brackets (<>) after the `Diameter/<Radius>:` prompt.

Command: *Press the Enter button on your mouse*	Repeats the CIRCLE command
`CIRCLE 3P/2P/TTR/<Center point>:` *Pick near* ③	Locates the center of a second circle
`Diameter/<Radius> <0.1555>:`	Defaults to last radius picked or entered
Command: *Hold down the Shift key and press the Enter button on your mouse (or just press the third button if you have one), then choose* Intersection	Pops up the cursor menu and activates INTersection object snap mode

continues

3

continued

`_int of` *Move the box appearing at the crosshairs over the upper right corner of the rectangle and click your Pick button*	Defines the radius of the circle at the intersection of the lines forming the upper right corner of the rectangle and completes the circle

You continue to use this drawing in the next section, but go ahead now and save your work.

`Command:` *Choose* File, Save	Issues the QSAVE command and saves the drawing

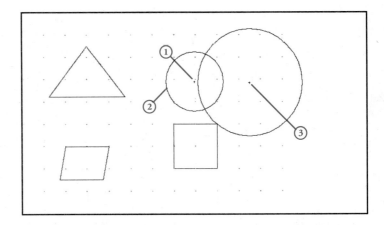

Figure 3.17

Using the CIRCLE command.

The mouse is very convenient for choosing commands and command options, and for selecting AutoCAD objects in the drawing editor. It provides the only means of accessing the pull-down and cursor menus.

Note   Many menu items issue commands along with specific options. The Circle item, for example, provides six different methods for drawing circles (plus the DONUT command). The first CIRCLE option, Center, Radius, is the default method for drawing a circle. The other five circle choices issue the command and specific options, sometimes prompting you for input before issuing the options. However, when you repeat a command by pressing Enter, it returns to the default—in the case of CIRCLE, to Center, Radius.

Using the Keyboard

The keyboard is essential to the operation of AutoCAD. It provides the primary means of entering text, including file names, and specific points. In addition, you can use the keyboard to perform many (but not all) mouse functions.

Note In the following exercise, and most of the exercises throughout the remainder of this book, when you are to enter commands at the Command: prompt, the input is shown in bold, monospaced type (for example **MOVE**), followed by (Enter), without additional instructions, such as a directive to type or enter said entry.

In the following exercise, you use the keyboard to issue commands and to access the items from the pull-down menus. It also introduces and demonstrates to you the concept of transparent commands.

Using the Keyboard To Enter Commands

Continue from the preceding exercise.

Command: **ARC** (Enter)	Issues the ARC command
Center/<Start point>: *Pick at* ① *in figure 3.18*	Locates the start of the arc

Notice the small Xs that appear on-screen whenever you pick a point. These are called *blips* and can be used as reference marks.

Center/End/<Second point>: *Pick* ②	Locates second point and displays rubber-band arc through the points
End point: **'REDRAW** (Enter)	Issues the REDRAW command transparently and performs a redraw

The REDRAW command clears the drawing blips and returns you to the ARC command.

Resuming ARC command.

End point: *Pick at* ③	Completes the ARC command
Choose Options, Drawing Aids	Displays the Drawing Aids dialog box
In the Modes *cluster, click inside the* **B**lips *toggle box*	Turns off BLIPMODE, disabling the creation of blips as points are picked
Choose OK	Closes the dialog box and accepts changes

Continue drawing with BLIPMODE turned off.

Command: **LINE** (Enter)	Issues the LINE command
From point: (Enter)	Begins a line from and tangent to the endpoint of the arc

continues

continued

Length of line: **1.0** (Enter)   Draws a line one unit long

To point: *Press Esc*   Cancels the LINE command

The blips no longer appear at screen pick points. You can also control blip creation by
entering the system variable BLIPMODE at the keyboard.

Command: **BLIPMODE** (Enter)   Prompts for blips setting

ON/OFF<off>: **ON** (Enter)   Turns blips back on

Figure 3.18

*Adding an arc to
your drawing.*

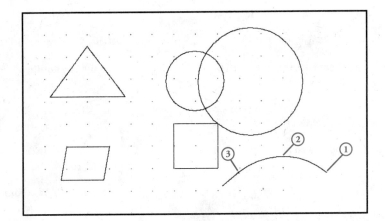

As you can see, you can use the keyboard to enter commands directly as well as to
input points. The keyboard also provides the primary way to enter text in your
drawings as well as into edit boxes. The domains of the mouse and the keyboard
overlap in many areas; in other areas, you must use each exclusively. When you have a
choice, the one you choose depends largely upon personal preference.

Transparent Commands

In the previous exercise, you issued the REDRAW command during the ARC command. AutoCAD redrew the graphics screen and the ARC command then resumed.
Commands that you can issue during another command are called *transparent
commands.*

Not all commands can be issued transparently, but most system variables and display commands can. You issue a transparent command from the keyboard by prefacing it with an apostrophe ('). If you are drawing a line, for example, and want to zoom your screen view, you can invoke the ZOOM command transparently by entering **'ZOOM**. When commands are used transparently, their prompts (if any) are preceded by two right angle brackets (>>), which calls attention to their transparent nature. Transparent commands are especially helpful when you work in large drawings. You encounter more examples and exercises using commands transparently in Part Two, "Basic 2D CAD Drafting." To identify commands that you can transparently, initial command definitions in this book precede the command name with an apostrophe.

Command Aliases

AutoCAD's command alias feature makes command entry from the keyboard easier and faster. A *command alias* is an abbreviation for a command that you can enter instead of the full command name. When you enter a command alias, AutoCAD enters the full name of the command and executes it. Table 3.1 lists some of AutoCAD's command aliases. The alias for the LINE command, for example, is L. If you type L at any Command: prompt, AutoCAD supplies the word *LINE* to the command input buffer, followed by an Enter, then issues the standard prompts for the LINE command normally. AutoCAD's standard command aliases cover only a few of AutoCAD's many commands, but you can easily create your own abbreviations by modifying the program parameter file, ACAD.PGP, that comes with AutoCAD. See Appendix H for more about the ACAD.PGP file. Command aliases are limited to top-level command names; you cannot assign aliases to subsequent command options and prompt responses.

TABLE 3.1
Keyboard Command Abbreviations

Alias	Command	Alias	Command
A	ARC	M	MOVE
C	CIRCLE	MS	MSPACE
CP	COPY	P	PAN
DV	DVIEW	PL	PLINE
E	ERASE	PS	PSPACE
L	LINE	R	REDRAW
LA	LAYER	T	MTEXT
LT	LINETYPE	Z	ZOOM

3

Note   You can find a listing of AutoCAD commands and their alternate forms of input in Appendix E, "Command Alias/Menu/Tool Equivalency Table." The IA Disk also includes the NRP.PGP file, which contains aliases for most drawing and editing commands. See Appendix H, "The IA Disk" for details.

Recovering from Errors

You inevitably make mistakes as you work in AutoCAD. More often than not, these mistakes result from erroneous input on your part, not from a defect in AutoCAD. AutoCAD provides a number of commands that help you recover from errors. Perhaps the most obvious, and one of the most frequently used "commands" in this category, is Cancel. Technically, Cancel is not an AutoCAD command at all, but a command-line "modifier" or function. Cancel interrupts any AutoCAD command in progress and returns you to an open Command: prompt. From the keyboard, you issue a Cancel function either by pressing Esc or using the Ctrl+C key combination. Although the Cancel function can cancel a command *in progress,* it usually does not undo the effect of any additions, deletions, or modifications to your drawing that have already taken place. For corrections of this nature, AutoCAD provides the ERASE command and the U command.

Note   You can also press Esc or Ctrl+C to cancel, or exit, most AutoCAD dialog boxes. When you cancel a dialog box, AutoCAD ignores any changes you have made to the settings in the dialog box.

Stop   Most menu items issue a Cancel before issuing their commands. Be sure to complete the current command before you use a menu item to choose a new command; otherwise, you can accidentally cancel the current command.

Using the ERASE Command

If you draw an object you do not want or if you place an object in the wrong place, you can use the ERASE command to remove it. When you use the ERASE command, AutoCAD's crosshairs change to a pick box. A *pick box* is a small square box that replaces the crosshairs when AutoCAD expects you to select an object. You move the pick box until it touches the object you want to erase, then select the object by clicking on it.

New Riders Publishing
INSIDE
SERIES

Note AutoCAD offers several other ways to select objects in addition to what is shown in the following exercise. These are covered in Chapter 8, "Object Selection and Grip Editing."

In the following exercise, you erase the circles in the CHAP03B drawing. You can find the ERASE command in the Modify pull-down menu.

Using ERASE To Remove an Object

Continue to use the CHAP03B drawing.

Command: *Choose* Modify, Erase	Issues the ERASE command and displays the pick box
_erase	
Select objects: *Select the larger circle*	Selects and highlights the circle

The object you selected should appear *highlighted* (as dashed or dotted), as in fig. 3.19.

Select objects: 1 found	Indicates that one object was selected
Select objects:	Prompts for other objects
Select objects: *Select the other circle*	Selects and highlights the other circle
Select objects: 1 found	Indicates that another object was selected
Select objects: (Enter)	Ends the selection process and erases the objects selected

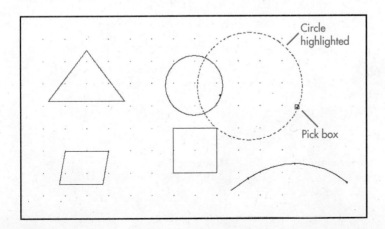

Figure 3.19

Selecting and highlighting AutoCAD objects.

Undoing Errors with the U and OOPS Commands

By default, AutoCAD keeps a record of every command you issue during a drawing session. The U command enables you to step back through these commands, one at a time, and undo their actions. This is a useful capability to have if you move, rotate, or otherwise edit some of your drawing objects and then want to return them relatively quickly to their original condition.

The OOPS command restores the object(s) deleted by the most recent ERASE command, regardless of whether or not other commands were executed since that erasure. The U command reverses any previous commands, including ERASE commands, except as noted in the Warning below. The REDO command reverses the most recent U or UNDO command.

Using the U and OOPS Commands

Continue from the previous exercise.

Command: **MOVE** (Enter)   Issues the MOVE command and displays a
                                                   pick box

Select objects: *Pick one of the*
three lines that form the triangle

Select objects: 1 found   Highlights the line and prompts for
                                                   another object

Select objects: *Pick another line*

Select objects: 1 found

Select objects: *Pick the third line*

Select objects: 1 found

Select objects: (Enter)   Ends the selection prompts

Base point or displacement: *Pick a*
point near the center of the triangle

As you move the cursor, the three highlighted lines move.

Second point of displacement: *Move*   Moves the triangle
the lines so that the triangle is
superimposed over the square, then click

New Riders Publishing
INSIDE
SERIES

Command: **OOPS** (Enter)   Issues the OOPS command and restores the circles erased in the previous exercise

Command: **U** (Enter)   Issues the U command and undoes the last command (OOPS), re-erasing the circles

Command: (Enter)   Repeats the U command and undoes the effect of the previous command (MOVE), returning the triangle to its previous position

Command: **REDO** (Enter)   Issues the REDO command

Command: (Enter)   Reissues the REDO command

Previous command did not undo things

AutoCAD takes no action, because you cannot redo a REDO command. Your CHAP03B drawing should now closely resemble figure 3.20.

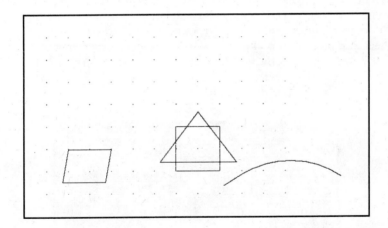

Figure 3.20
Using Undo and Redo.

3

The MOVE command is one of AutoCAD's many editing commands and is covered in Part Two, "Basic 2D CAD Drafting."

Stop You can only undo changes that affect the current drawing. You cannot reverse commands that write drawing information out to disk or create files outside of AutoCAD, such as the SAVE and WBLOCK commands. Sometimes, but not always, in these situations, if executing the command might destroy existing files, AutoCAD warns you before proceeding to carry out your bidding.

You now have a working knowledge of the primary commands that you can use to recover from most of the errors that you will inevitably make. Through the use of a combination of the Cancel function and the ERASE, U, REDO, and OOPS commands, you can easily correct most of the errors you normally commit in AutoCAD. As you progress through the remainder of this book, you need to have the freedom to experiment with AutoCAD's commands. In your regular AutoCAD work as well, being able to try out your ideas is an important facet of creative design and learning.

If you have a printer (or plotter) installed on your system and you have configured AutoCAD for that printer (see your *Installation and Performance Guide* or Appendix A "Installation and Configuration" of this book), take a moment now to make a quick plot. If you do not have a printer or plotter available, skip the following section.

Making a Quick Plot

Working through the following exercise will enable you to print a hard copy of the CHAP03B drawing. Do not be too concerned about the plotting sequence and the many settings in the Plot Configuration dialog box; they are fully explained in Chapter 25, "Sheet Composition and Plotting." The following exercise reflects settings for an HP LaserJet printer, but works for any 8 1/2-by-11-inch or larger printer or plotter. Figure 3.21 shows the Plot Configuration dialog box that you use in the following exercise to specify plot options.

Figure 3.21

The Plot Configuration dialog box.

Plot Configuration	
Device and Default Information	**Paper Size and Orientation**
HPLaserjet	■ Inches
[Device and Default Selection...]	□ MM [Size...] A
Pen Parameters	Plot Area 10.50 by 8.00.
[Pen Assignments...] [Optimization...]	**Scale, Rotation, and Origin**
Additional Parameters	[Rotation and Origin...]
□ Display □ Hide Lines	Plotted Inches = Drawing Units
■ Extents	8 = 7.75
□ Limits □ Adjust Area Fill	⊠ Scaled to Fit
□ View	**Plot Preview**
□ Window □ Plot To File	[Preview...] ■ Partial □ Full
[View...] [Window...] [File Name...]	
[OK] [Cancel]	[Help...]

New Riders Publishing
INSIDE
SERIES

Making a Quick Plot

Continue from the previous exercise.

Command: *Choose* File, Print   Displays the Plot Configuration dialog box
                                            (refer to figure 3.21)

In the Additional Parameters *cluster*   Tells AutoCAD to plot everything in the
click on the E<u>x</u>tents *radio button*   drawing

In the Scale, Rotation, and Origin   Tells AutoCAD to plot it as large as it
cluster, click on the Scaled <u>t</u>o Fit   will fit on the page
check box to place an X inside it

Choose OK   Starts plotting process

```
Command: _plot
Effective plotting area:
6.67 wide by 10.50 high
```

Your plotting area dimensions might differ from those shown.

`3150 raster data scan lines to be sent.`   Displays progress

Your scan line data might differ as well. After a few seconds, your plot should be completed.

`Scan lines complete.`

`Plot complete.`

Your plot should resemble what you see in figure 3.20. Yours might differ owing to the size of paper and your particular printer, but you should be able to see all the AutoCAD objects. In Chapter 25 "Sheet Composition and Plotting," you learn how to make adjustments that enable you to fully control your plots. For now, you have a hard copy of the CHAP03B drawing.

In this chapter, you have gained experience with several important AutoCAD concepts and skills that you use in virtually all AutoCAD drawings you make. If you want to review any of these concepts, go back to that section and use the ERASE command to delete any of the objects involved and perform the exercises again. For now, use the QSAVE command to save your drawing as you did earlier in this chapter and then exit AutoCAD by choosing File, Exit from the pull-down menu. In the next chapter, you learn about AutoCAD's extensive Help facility.

C H A P T E R

4

Getting Help

AutoCAD Release 13's Help facility is an online resource for getting assistance with AutoCAD. Help in Release 13 has been enhanced by the addition of a "What's New in Release 13" section. As well as context-sensitive online help, you can access a visual presentation that covers the new features of this release.

This chapter covers the following topics:

◆ Using AutoCAD's Help facility

◆ Accessing Help

◆ Using context-sensitive transparent help during a command

◆ Accessing the "What's New in Release 13" online learning tool

The AutoCAD Help facility is an online reference tool. You can use it to learn about AutoCAD's commands and features, or you can call it for complete context-sensitive help as you work within AutoCAD.

You access AutoCAD's Help facility by choosing the Help item from the pull-down menu, by choosing Help from the screen menu, or by entering HELP or a question mark (?) from the keyboard. Additionally, you can get context-sensitive help by entering a question mark after any command, or in response to any system prompt.

As you work through the exercises in this chapter, you become familiar with the kinds of information available in AutoCAD as you learn how to navigate through the various Help features.

As you learn about AutoCAD's Help facility, the concept of *jump text* becomes an important tool. In the following exercise, you read about hypertext *jumps* as you explore the How to Use Help feature.

Quick 5¢ Tour

If you are not already in AutoCAD, start AutoCAD by running the batch file you created in Chapter 1.

Command: *Choose* Help, How to Use Help	Displays the first page of the How to Use Help window (see fig. 4.1)

The Help on AutoCAD Help dialog box has a large, scrollable list box and a series of buttons. The contents of the list box explain the function of each button.

Notice that the word "topics" on this page is enclosed in double angle brackets (<<>>). Text so indicated is called *jump text.* Jump text uses hypertext links to move directly from topic to topic. To see how jump text works, perform the following steps:

Click on the OK button to close the Help on AutoCAD Help dialog box.

Command: *Choose* Help, Help	Displays the main AutoCAD Help dialog box

Notice the jump text entries enclosed in angle brackets in this dialog box.

Choose the phrase Definition of terms *at the bottom of the dialog box and click on the* <u>G</u>o To *button*	Displays an alphabetical list of items defined in the Glossary

Because of the size of the list, you have to use the scroll bar to move through it.

Click on the <u>C</u>ontents button *at the top of the window*	Displays the opening Contents page
Press Esc	Closes the AutoCAD Help dialog box

The preceding exercise introduced several of the features of AutoCAD's Help facility. The use of jump text, for example, is one of the basic tools for navigating the many topic and additional information pages that make AutoCAD Help a useful online tool for learning and using AutoCAD.

New Riders Publishing
INSIDE
SERIES

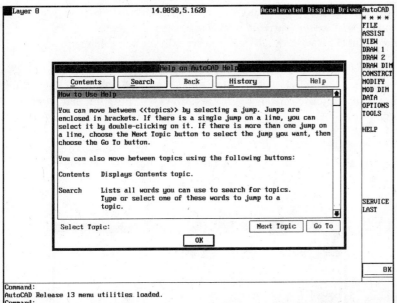

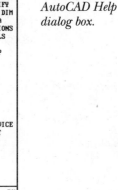

Figure 4.1

The How to Use Help window in the Help on AutoCAD Help dialog box.

Exploring AutoCAD's Help Facility

You can access the AutoCAD Help functions from the main AutoCAD Help dialog box, shown in figure 4.2. Like all AutoCAD dialog boxes, you can move it around the screen. Whether you browse through help topics at a leisurely pace, check the definition of a term in the glossary feature, or need immediate help to answer a command prompt, you enter AutoCAD Help through the AutoCAD Help dialog box.

Figure 4.2 shows the CONTENTS page of the Help dialog box. The CONTENTS page serves as the root page for AutoCAD Help. The CONTENTS page is broken down into three sections: Menu access, Command line access, and Glossary. Within these sections, you have access to the four primary help categories:

◆ **<<Pull-down Menus>>.** Clicking on Pull-down Menus takes you to the Pull-down Menus page, from which you can reach help on AutoCAD's pull-down menu items (see fig. 4.3).

◆ **<<Commands>>.** Clicking on Commands displays the Commands page, from which you can choose any of AutoCAD's commands, grouped alphabetically (see fig. 4.4). Clicking on a command takes you to the help page for that command.

◆ **<<System Variables>>.** Clicking on System Variables displays the System Variables page, with system variable names arranged alphabetically. You access Help for AutoCAD's system variables by clicking on the variable name.

◆ **<<Definition of terms>>.** Clicking on Definition of terms displays the beginning of the glossary section. Clicking on any item takes you to a definition of the item. You can move quickly to glossary topics by typing the first letter of the subject.

In any dialog box, you can highlight only one entire line. Sometimes, a line has more than one jump text item. When this is the case, the dialog box has a button labeled Next Topic. You press this button to cycle through all the jump text items in the line (see fig. 4.4).

Figure 4.2

The main AutoCAD Help dialog box.

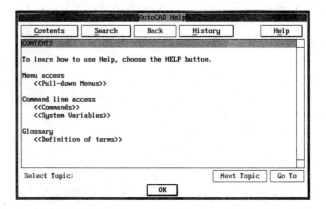

Figure 4.3

The Pull-down Menus Help page.

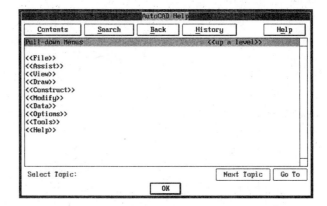

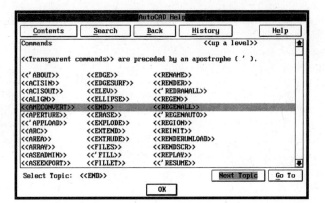

Figure 4.4
Choosing between multiple jump items.

Tip   Information that appears in "jumps" can offer still further jump text. No matter how many jumps you use, you can always return to your previous help page by using the **B**ack button, or to any previously read page by using the **H**istory button at the top of the AutoCAD Help dialog box. These functions are described later in this chapter.

Getting To the Help Dialog Box

Opening the AutoCAD Help dialog box is the key to accessing AutoCAD's Help facility. AutoCAD provides the following four ways to open this dialog box:

◆ Choose Help, Help from the AutoCAD pull-down menu

◆ Choose HELP, Help from the screen menu

◆ Enter **HELP** or **'HELP** at the Command: prompt, or **'HELP** during a command

◆ Enter **?** or **'?** at the Command: prompt, or **'?** during a command

Note   In the Windows version, F1 is for help and F2 is the text/graphics window toggle, whereas in the DOS version of AutoCAD, F1 is the toggle key for the text/graphics screens.

You can type **HELP** or **?** at the Command: prompt, or you can precede these commands with an apostrophe (') to make them transparent. Transparent commands are commands that you can issue during another command. Using the pull-down menu or screen menu automatically issues a transparent 'HELP command. Otherwise, no functional difference exists among the various methods; the **?** is merely an abbreviated keyboard convenience. Using a transparent HELP command to access the AutoCAD Help dialog box is discussed later in this chapter, when you learn about context-sensitive help.

In the following exercise, you practice methods of accessing the AutoCAD Help dialog box and using the jump text feature.

Becoming Familiar with Help

Start AutoCAD if it is not yet running.

Command: **?** (Enter)	Opens the AutoCAD Help dialog box (refer to figure 4.2)
Under Menu access, *double-click on* Pull-down Menus	Displays the Pull-down Menus topic page (refer to figure 4.3)
On the Pull-down Menus *page, double-click on* <<File>>	Displays the File Menu topic page
Double-click on <<Management>>	Displays the File>Management Menu topic page
Double-click on <<Utilities>>	Displays the File Utilities topic page
Double-click on the <<Unlock file>> *button*	Displays help information for Unlock file
Click on Close	Closes the More AutoCAD Help dialog box
Click on OK *or press Esc*	Closes the AutoCAD Help dialog box

---

In the preceding exercise, you saw how to advance through the pages of the AutoCAD Help dialog boxes in a logical, stepwise manner. The CONTENTS page serves as a home base for navigating the pages. You can always return to the CONTENTS page by choosing the <u>C</u>ontents button at the upper-left corner of the AutoCAD Help dialog box.

Using the Buttons in the Help Dialog Box

With jump text and the capability to move easily from topic to topic, also having the means to backtrack easily through help topics and return to previously displayed pages is essential. Several buttons in the Help dialog box provide this capability. Five buttons make moving between and within help categories easy and fast.

New Riders Publishing
INSIDE SERIES

The buttons in the Help dialog box perform the following functions.

◆ **Contents.** This button enables you to display the contents page of AutoCAD Help.

◆ **Search.** This button enables you to open the AutoCAD Help Search dialog box. You can select or enter key words and phrases to specify a search using a predefined index of topics.

◆ **Back.** This button enables you to return to pages you have viewed previously in the same help session. You can use this button to retrace pages one at a time.

◆ **History.** This button enables you to display a list of up to the last 40 help topics you have viewed in the current help session. If you choose a prior topic, you return directly to that topic or page.

◆ **Help.** This button enables you to activate the Help on AutoCAD Help dialog box.

Tip   The buttons in the Help dialog box have hot keys. With the AutoCAD Help dialog box open, for example, typing C and pressing Enter displays the Contents page.

Using the Contents, History, and Back Features

AutoCAD keeps track of your searches in HELP. You can investigate all the options of a command by moving efficiently through the History list, rather than starting a new search for each option.

The next exercise will give you some practice in using the buttons in the Help dialog box.

Navigating in the Help Dialog Box

Continue from the preceding exercise or start AutoCAD.

Choose Help, Help	Issues the 'HELP command and displays the AutoCAD Help Contents page
Double-click on <<Commands>>	Displays the top section of the Commands topic page (see fig. 4.5)
Scroll down the list and highlight the line with <<MTEXT>> *in the middle column*	

continues

continued

Click on the **N**ext Topic *button once,* *then click on the* **G**o To *button*	Displays the MTEXT command page
Click on the **B**ack *button or type* **B** *and press Enter*	Returns to the previous page of Command topics
Scroll down the list, highlight the line that contains <<DTEXT>> *and go to the DTEXT command page*	
Choose the **H**istory *button*	Activates the AutoCAD Help History dialog box (see fig. 4.6)

The History dialog box displays the help topics you have displayed so far in this exercise.

Double-click on MTEXT Command	Returns to the MTEXT command page

Scroll down the command description until you come to a section headed "See Also."

Figure 4.5

The main Commands topic page.

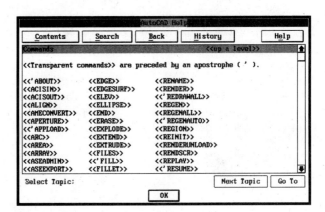

> **Note**   AutoCAD Help History dialog box displays all items you've looked at *in the current help session only*. As soon as you exit Help, the history clears.

Figure 4.6

The AutoCAD Help History dialog box.

The MTEXT topic page describes the MTEXT command. At the bottom of the initial screen are further jump text items that you can use to find out about the MTEXT command's options. The See Also feature, if present, displays references to related help topics. You can jump to these topics and then return to the base page with the back button.

After the first short paragraph in the See Also section, a new paragraph notes related commands.

Using the Help Buttons

Continue in the Help dialog box. You should be in the See Also section of the entry for the MTEXT command.

Choose the <<DDEDIT>> line	Specifies <<DDEDIT>> as the current Select Topic item (see fig. 4.7)
Click on the <u>G</u>o To *button*	Displays the DDEDIT command topic page

Help is available for main command entries as well as for individual command options.

Click on the <u>H</u>istory *button*	Opens the Help History dialog box
Double-click on DTEXT Command	Displays Help for the DTEXT command
Scroll down the box and highlight the line that has the jump text items <<Justify>> / <<Style>> / <<Start point>>: *(see fig. 4.8)*	
With Justify *as the current selected topic, choose* <u>G</u>o To	Displays Help for the text alignment options (see fig. 4.9)

System variable help topics appear much as command topics.

Choose <u>C</u>ontents	Returns to Contents page
On the Contents *page, double-click on* System Variables	Displays the System Variables index page
Scroll through the list of system variables and highlight the line containing SAVETIME *in the right-hand column*	Displays CIRCLERAD as the current SAVETIME item
Choose <u>N</u>ext Topic *twice*	Displays SAVETIME as current Select Topic item
Choose <u>G</u>o To	Displays help information on system variable

Press Esc to close the Help window

4

Figure 4.7

Using jump text with See Also topics.

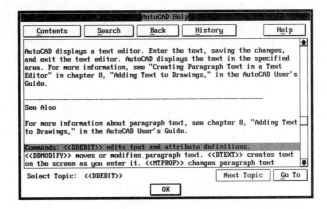

Figure 4.8

Using jump text for command options.

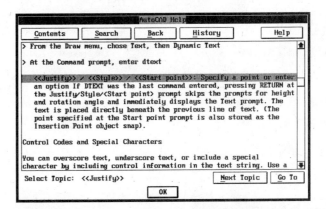

Figure 4.9

The AutoCAD Help on DTEXT's Justify option.

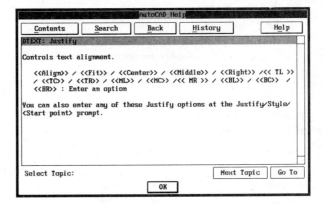

New Riders Publishing
INSIDE SERIES

Using the Glossary Feature

You access the AutoCAD Help Glossary feature by choosing the <<Definition of terms>> item from the AutoCAD Help dialog box's Contents page. The Glossary opens to an alphabetical index of help topics. Double-click on the topic to display a dialog box that has the definition. Related commands are indicated, but there is no jump text to the Commands help section. You can, however, use the <u>H</u>istory button to move between Glossary and help items. A typical Glossary page is shown in figure 4.10.

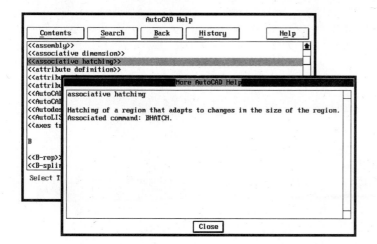

Figure 4.10

A typical Glossary entry.

Using the Search Feature

You can access the Help Search facility in two ways. If you choose Help from the Help pull-down, AutoCAD displays Help's Contents page. If you choose Search from the Contents page, AutoCAD displays the AutoCAD Help Search dialog box. You can go directly to the Help Search dialog box by picking Search for Help On from the Help pull-down.

Once the AutoCAD Help Search dialog box is displayed, you either enter the name of the command in which you are interested, or you scroll through the list box of commands, command options, and system variables, and highlight the one you want.

When the subject you're interested in is highlighted, you use the <u>S</u>how Topics button to place it in the topic list box, and then the <u>G</u>o To button to go to the Help entry.

4

Using the Search Feature

Continue from the preceding exercise or start AutoCAD.

Choose Help, Help

Issues the "? command and displays the Contents page

Choose Search

Displays the AutoCAD Help Search dialog box (see fig. 4.11)

Click in the subject text box to place the cursor there, and type **POLY**

Click on Show Topics

Displays polyface meshes, the first available help item that includes the text "POLY", and places PFACE Command in the topic list box (see fig. 4.12)

In the subject list box, click on POLYGON, *then click on* Show Topics

Places the POLYGON Command help topic in the topic list box

You also can scroll through the list of commands, options, and system variables until you find the item you want. Double-clicking on an item in the subject box has the same effect as clicking on it and then clicking on Show Topics.

Scroll up the list to the item ARC *and double-click on it*

Places the item "ARC Command" in the topic box

Click on Go To

Displays the ARC command help topic

Press Esc

Closes the Help Window

Figure 4.11

The AutoCAD Help Search dialog box.

Figure 4.12

Using a partial word in AutoCAD Help Search.

Tip

Because the **S**earch button is available at all times in the Help dialog box, using it is often the quickest way to go directly to the help topic of any command, command option, or system variable. The search facility does not search items in the glossary.

Understanding Context-Sensitive Help

One of the most helpful ways to use the HELP command is to issue it during another command—that is, to issue HELP transparently. Using help transparently is called *context-sensitive help* because you directly enter the Help feature for the command in progress, bypassing the opening Contents page.

Using Context-Sensitive Help

With AutoCAD open, perform the following steps to see how context-sensitive help works. In this exercise, you first draw a line and then issue the ROTATE command.

Command: *Choose* Draw, Line	Issues the LINE command
Command: _line From point: **2,2** (Enter)	Specifies the start point
To point: **@3<45** (Enter)	Specifies a relative point and draws a line
To point: (Enter)	Ends LINE command
Command: *Choose* Modify, Rotate	Issues the ROTATE command

continues

continued

```
Command: _rotate
```

```
Select objects: L Enter          Selects last object created
```

```
1 found
```

```
Select objects: Enter            Ends selection process
```

```
Base point: 2,2 Enter            Specifies endpoint of line
```

```
<Rotation angle>/Reference: '? Enter   Issues HELP command transparently and
                                       displays AutoCAD Help window
```

The ROTATE command topic page already is visible in the Help dialog box (see fig. 4.13).

In the Help dialog box,   Displays Reference option
select the jump text <<Reference>>, **N**ext Topic,   help information
and **G**o To *(see fig. 4.14)*

Click on the Close *button in the*   Closes the AutoCAD Help window
More AutoCAD Help *dialog box*
and press Esc

```
Resuming ROTATE command.
```

```
<Rotation angle>/Reference: 45 Enter     Rotates the line 45 degrees and completes the
                                         ROTATE command
```

Figure 4.13

*Context-sensitive
help for the
ROTATE
command.*

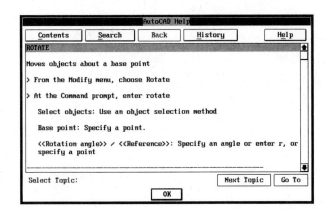

New Riders Publishing
INSIDE
SERIES

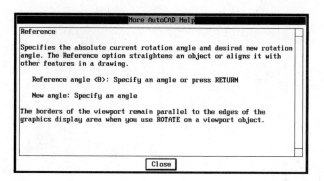

Figure 4.14

Context-sensitive help for the Reference option.

You can access context-sensitive help by choosing Help from the Help pull-down menu, or HELP, Help from the screen menu, or by entering '? or 'HELP. You can call upon context-sensitive help during any command. It provides a useful tool that you can use on the spot with minimal interruption of your work for help with commands and command options. In addition to context-sensitive help for commands, as shown in the preceding exercise, context-sensitive help is available in most of AutoCAD's dialog boxes. Choosing the **H**elp button in a dialog box activates the AutoCAD Help dialog box with help topics for the dialog box options and settings.

Learning about What's New in Release 13

Although not a part of the AutoCAD Help feature, an additional online learning tool is available from the **H**elp pull-down menu:

◆ **What's New in Release 13.** This online facility presents a concise, graphics-based review of many of the new features of AutoCAD Release 13. The format enables you to choose topics such as Usability, Design and Drafting, and Commands, and then advance through the material at your own pace. Figure 4.15 shows a typical page.

4

Figure 4.15

*A typical page
from What's New
in Release 13.*

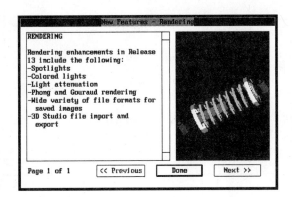

The AutoCAD Help facility provides an effective supplement to more extensive training sources such as the classroom or this book. Having a working knowledge of AutoCAD Help can make your work within AutoCAD faster and more efficient. This chapter has concentrated on those aspects of AutoCAD Help that you can use in your daily work with AutoCAD. Other features not covered can prove useful as well, and you might want to continue to explore the Help feature on your own.

Part II

Basic 2D CAD Drafting

New Riders Publishing
INSIDE SERIES

Setting Up a CAD Drawing

In many ways, setting up a CAD drawing is like preparing to draw on a drafting board. You determine the size of the paper sheet you need and the tools you need to use from the information you have about the drawing you want to make. In AutoCAD, you determine such things as the units you will use, the size of the drawing area, and the linetypes and layers you need. This chapter discusses these and other settings and drawing aids. Topics covered include the following:

◆ Understanding full-scale electronic drawing

◆ Determining scale factors for symbols and text

◆ Setting a drawing's working units and sizing its limits

◆ Organizing a drawing with layers

◆ Applying linetypes

Setting up your drawing is a key step. If you understand and use the electronic tools available in AutoCAD, you can draw more efficiently and accurately. If you plan ahead and anticipate your requirements, you can devote more time to the drawing and less time to the details of organizational concerns and how they affect the drawing outcome.

One of the most important and flexible tools you can use when you organize your drawings is AutoCAD's layers. You can plan and organize layers in many ways; the following Quick 5¢ Tour shows you one method. The Quick 5¢ Tour also examines some of the other settings that you learn to set up during this chapter. You use the Read Only feature of the OPEN command to avoid changing the HOSPROOM sample drawing.

Quick 5¢ Tour

If necessary, start AutoCAD.

Command: *Choose* File, Open   Issues the OPEN command and initiates the Open Drawing dialog box

Use the Directories *list boxes to display the* IA/DWGS *subdirectory, if required*

In the Files *list box, find and click on* HOSPROOM, *then choose* OK   Selects the HOSPROOM drawing (see fig. 5.1)

Figure 5.1

The HOSPROOM drawing.

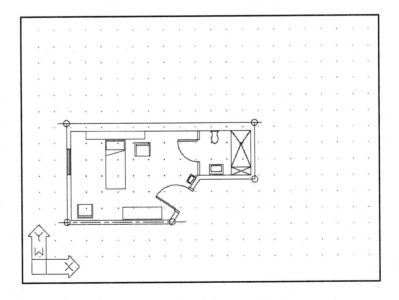

Command: *Choose* Data, Layers   Issues the DDLMODES command and opens the Layer Control dialog box (see fig. 5.2)

The HOSPROOM drawing shows the floor plan for a hospital room. You can see the layer names, their visibility status, their colors, and linetypes in the Layer Name list. Layer 0 is the current layer upon which you can draw.

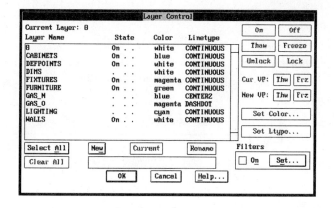

Figure 5.2

The Layer Control dialog box.

| Click on the GAS_N, GAS_O, *and* LIGHTING *layer names in the* Layer Name *list box* | Selects the layers for manipulation |
| Click on the On *button, then choose* OK | Turns on the selected layers (see fig. 5.3) |

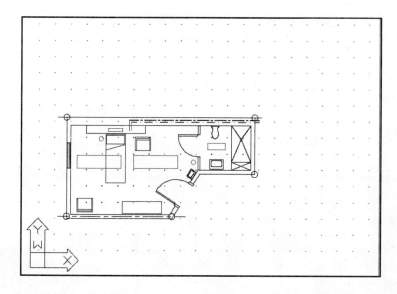

Figure 5.3

The HOSPROOM drawing with the LIGHTING, GAS_N, and GAS_O layers turned on.

Three additional layers are now on, or visible. These layers schematically represent overhead lighting fixtures and piping carrying medical gases into the room and appear with different colors and linetypes.

| Command: *Choose* Data, Units | Opens the Units Control dialog box and shows that the drawing is set up with Architectural units with 1/64" precision (see fig. 5.4) |

continues

continued

Choose Cancel	Closes the dialog box
`Command:` *Choose* Options, Drawing Aids	Opens the Drawing Aids dialog box showing various settings, including a snap of 6" and a grid of 2' (see fig. 5.5)
Choose Cancel	Closes dialog box

Figure 5.4

The Units Control dialog box.

Figure 5.5

The Drawing Aids dialog box.

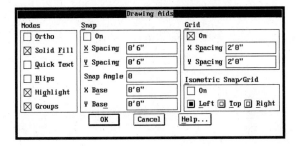

In the preceding exercise, you took a quick peek at a few of the settings you routinely make before you draw objects in a new drawing.

Understanding and applying an intelligent system of settings and layers is an important part of setting up a CAD drawing. You saw in the preceding exercise how layers can contain additional information about a drawing that you might not always want or need displayed. You also saw how you can selectively choose which layers you want visible. Layers serve several other useful functions and can have states other than only on and off. Most significantly, layers provide the primary mechanism for structuring the contents of a drawing. The last half of this chapter explores the uses of layers and the methods of creating and controlling them. But first you examine units and other settings.

New Riders Publishing
INSIDE
SERIES

Organizing Your Drawing

This chapter is about setting up and organizing your AutoCAD drawings. Before you begin to draw, you can take certain steps to save time and draw more efficiently. In this respect, drawing with AutoCAD is not that different from manual drafting, whereby you gather the tools you need and prepare the work area before you even put pencil to paper. When you draft manually, for example, one of the first questions you must answer is at what scale you will need to carry out the drawing. Unless the drawing fits comfortably on the drawing sheet at full scale, you must apply some reduction or enlargement. Although CAD drawings work somewhat differently in this respect, you still need to consider the form, scale, and size of the final output as you organize the electronic workspace. You should determine other important aspects as you set up and organize your drawing, as well, such as drawing units to use, settings that affect the way AutoCAD works, and naming and defining the properties of the layers you need.

Consider first what is perhaps the most important of all these considerations: understanding how working with AutoCAD differs from conventional manual drafting with respect to the concept of scale. Once you understand the concept of CAD scale, you can better understand the other steps you take to organize your drawings.

Drawing in Real-World Units

AutoCAD drawing elements are stored in real-world units. Therefore, when you use AutoCAD, you always draw in real-world units; that is, you always draw full scale. AutoCAD stores dimensional data—the length of a line, the radius of a circle—in real units of inches, feet, meters, millimeters, or just about any unit of measurement.

When you draw on a drafting board, you usually create the drawing to fit on a certain sheet size—the sheet taped to the board in front of you. If the objects your drawing represents are larger than the drawing sheet, you must scale them down as you draw. Conversely, if you represent relatively small objects on a large sheet, you scale up the dimensions by some factor, again, as you draw. In effect, you draw and plot simultaneously. As a consequence, the text, symbols, and line widths remain about the same size from drawing to drawing.

In AutoCAD, this process is reversed. You always draw objects at actual size (full scale) in real-world units. You do not need to worry about applying a scale as you actually draw. In fact, if your drawing is never plotted onto paper or some other physical medium, you need never worry about scale at all.

Most drawings, however, do get plotted onto some form of "hard" output. This stage, therefore, is the stage during which scale becomes a consideration. At plot time, AutoCAD enables you to scale the full-sized electronic drawing up or down to fit the plot sheet. In other words, you must apply some overall scale factor to the full-scale drawing as you plot it. A *scale factor* is a calculated number by which to multiply an object's real-world dimension to determine the object's plotted dimension. This scale factor affects everything in the drawing equally. You must, therefore, plan ahead for scaling a full-sized AutoCAD drawing and make the settings that adjust the scale of the text, symbols, and line widths as you add them to the drawing, so they appear at an appropriate size on the scaled plot. The first step is to determine the degree to which you must scale up or down your full-scale drawing to fit the actual plot sheet: the scale factor.

Determining a Scale Factor and Drawing Limits

Consider, first, an architectural drawing of a floor plan that has an overall dimension of 24 feet by 13 feet. Assume that you want to plot the drawing at a scale of 1/4" = 1' (12"). You need to know your scale factor and the size of electronic sheet you are going to use. You set the size of the electronic sheet by choosing the drawing's limits. You use AutoCAD's LIMITS command to set the X and Y values of the lower-right and upper-left corners of your electronic sheet. You still need to determine what values to use.

If you convert your intended drawing scale to a ratio of 1:*n*, then *n* is your scale factor. If you already have selected a drawing scale, determining the scale factor is easy. For your floor plan, you want a final plotted scale of 1/4" = 1'-0", so the scale factor is 48. You can think of the conversion in the following way:

> 1/4" = 1' (or 12") converts to 1" = 48" or a ratio of 1:48

Therefore, your scale factor is 48. If you select a scale of 3/8" = 1'-0", the scale factor is 32. The following is the conversion:

> 3/8" = 1' (or 12") converts to 3" = 96" or 1" = 32" or 1:32

Calculating Sheet Size for a Known Scale and Object Size

Now you can use the scale factor to determine the limits for your electronic drawing sheet by performing some test calculations for common plotting sheet sizes. The following is a sample set of calculations:

Size of floor plan: 24' × 13'

Scale: 1/4" = 12"

Scale factor: 48

Now test for a 17-by-11-inch B-sheet:

17" × 48 = 816" or 68'

11" × 48 = 528" or 44'

A 17-by-11-inch sheet equals 68' × 44' at a scale of 1/4" = 12".

The B-sheet is certainly large enough; the 24-by-13-foot floor plan would fit with ease. In fact, at this plotted scale, the floor plan would perhaps appear too small. Try the next smaller standard sheet, an 11-by-8.5-inch A-sheet:

11" × 48 = 528" or 44'

8.5" × 48 = 408" or 34'

An 11-by-8.5-inch sheet equals 44' × 34' at a scale of 1/4" = 12". This size offers a better fit with adequate room for dimensions, notes, and a border, and perhaps a title block.

In this example, you determined your limits by the number of units that fit across a standard A-sheet (44' across 11" at 1/4" = 12"). Sometimes you need to fit the full-scale drawing to a predetermined sheet size. In these instances, compare the sheet size to the size of your drawing, then calculate the scale. The following calculation applies to an 11-by-8.5-inch sheet and a 24-by-13-foot object:

24' = (24' × 12" per foot) = 288"

11": 288" (ratio of sheet size to object size)

11:288 equals a ratio of 1:26 (approximately)

The next highest scale is 1:32, or .375:12, or 3/8" = 1' scale.

Setting the Drawing Units and Limits

Now that you have determined the scale factor for a particular drawing and a final plotting scale, you are ready to set the units for the drawing and then set the limits. Figuring and setting the limits is easier if you first use the Units Control dialog box to set the units.

Setting Units

AutoCAD offers drawing units that are suitable for drawings in virtually any profession or discipline. If you normally use architectural units, for example, use AutoCAD's architectural units. Technical researchers might use decimal or scientific units; a mechanical designer would use metric units or inches; and a surveyor might choose decimal feet or miles. A wide range of precision settings also is available. Setting units accomplishes two things during the drawing setup process. First, it determines the input format you use for entering distances and angles from the keyboard. Second, it sets up the output format that AutoCAD uses when it displays the dimensioning distances and angles.

To get started with your drawing setup for the 24-by-13-foot architectural floor plan, perform the steps in the following exercise to create a new drawing and set the units and precision.

Using the UNITS Command

If necessary, start AutoCAD.

Command: *Choose* File, New	Opens the Create New Drawing dialog box (see fig. 5.6)
Type **ARCH** *in the* New **D**rawing Name *edit box, then choose* OK	Creates a new drawing named ARCH in the current directory
Command: *Choose* Data, Units	Issues the DDUNITS command and opens the Units Control dialog box (see fig. 5.7)
'_ddunits	
Choose the **A**rchitectural *radio button in the* Units *area*	Selects architectural units
Click in the **P**recision *list box in the* Units *area, then select* 0'-0 1/64"	Opens drop-down list and changes precision from 1/16" to 1/64"
Verify that the Dec**i**mal Degrees *radio button in the* Angles *area is selected*	Specifies the default, decimal degrees angles
Click in the Precisio**n** *drop-down list box in the* Angles *area, then select* 0.00	Changes the angular measurement precision from zero to two decimal places
Choose **D**irection	Opens the Direction Control dialog box (see fig. 5.8)

New Riders Publishing
INSIDE
SERIES

Verify that the **E***ast radio button in the* Angle 0 Direction *area is selected*	Specifies the default, East (right of screen), as the direction for angle 0
Verify that the **C***ounter-Clockwise radio button is selected*	Specifies angles to be measured counter-clockwise (the default) from 0
Choose OK, *then* OK *again*	Closes both dialog boxes and saves settings
Command: *Move the cursor in the drawing and note the coordinate display in the status bar*	

Save your drawing.

Figure 5.6

The Create New Drawing dialog box.

Figure 5.7

The Units Control dialog box.

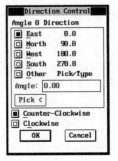

Figure 5.8

The Direction Control dialog box.

5

The coordinate display now shows Architectural units: feet, inches, and fractions. If the format of the current coordinate is too long to fit in the coordinate display area, it appears in scientific units, such as 1.704450E+03,95'-9 51/64".

Tip   If the status bar coordinate display is turned off (not tracking the coordinates as you move the pointing device), you can press F6 or Ctrl+D to turn it on.

'DDUNITS. The 'DDUNITS command enables you to open the Units Control dialog box, which enables you to set the current format for linear and angular units of measure. The Engineering and Architectural formats appear in feet and inches and assume a unit of one inch. The other formats can represent any real-world unit.
Pull-down: *Choose* Data, Units
Screen: *Choose* DATA, Units:

DDUNITS Command Options

The Units Control dialog box provides the following areas and options:

◆ **Units area.** Displays and sets the current format for units of linear measure. The Precision list box sets and displays the precision for the current units format.

◆ **Angles area.** Displays and sets the current angle format. The Precision list box sets and displays the precision for the current angle format.

You also can use the UNITS command to set linear and angular units and precision; however, the DDUNITS command and its Units Control and Direction Control dialog boxes are quicker and easier to use. The UNITS command simply steps you through the linear and angular settings as prompts on the command line, gathering the same information you supply when you use the DDUNITS dialog boxes.

'UNITS. The 'UNITS command enables you to set linear and angular units and precision with prompts from the command line. The functionality is the same as that offered by the DDUNITS command, but the UNITS command is slower and more difficult to use. You can issue this command only from the Command: prompt.

Note   Duplicate dialog box and command-line commands, such as DDUNITS and UNITS, might appear to be needless redundancy. Often the command-line version is a holdover from earlier versions of AutoCAD that did not support a dialog-box user

New Riders Publishing
INSIDE SERIES

interface. However, these command-line commands have been retained to provide a programming interface for AutoCAD scripts, menu macros, and user-defined AutoLISP functions. From a user's point of view, it almost always is preferable to use the dialog box version of these commands.

The precision defined for your drawing needs to be greater than you might think. As you draw an architectural section, you might think you never need to be more accurate with your measurements than 1/2". However, you might be surprised later when you need a more precise resolution of measurement, such as 1/64", to draw a joint detail. AutoCAD rounds the display, but maintains its internal accuracy. You can prove this by setting the precision for the units to 1/2" and drawing a line approximately 9" long. Then use the LIST command to display the actual length of the line. If you are accurate to 1/2", the LIST command reports the line to be 0'-9". Then change the precision for the units to 1/64" and use the LIST command on the same line. It displays the actual length as a fraction less than 9". The LIST command is fully explained in Chapter 15, "Object Modification, Inquiry, and Calculation." Therefore, you always set your precision at least one increment greater than you think you need.

Entering and Displaying Values in Various Units

No matter which units you use, you can enter values in integer, decimal, scientific, or fractional formats. When you use architectural or engineering units, you can enter values as feet, inches, or both. AutoCAD assumes that the value is in inches unless you use a foot mark (') to indicate feet. You can omit the inches mark ("), and if the inches value is zero, you do not need to type anything. The values 2'0", 2'0, 2', and 24" all are equivalent in engineering units. Thus, to signify one foot, three inches, you can enter 1'3" or 1'3.

AutoCAD's input and display formats differ. *Input format* refers to the form used to express a measurement in response to AutoCAD's prompts. *Display format* refers to the form AutoCAD uses to display measurements. An input of 1'3-1/2" appears as 1'-3 1/2". You can force feet and inches, angles, and fractions to appear in the same form as their entries by setting the UNITMODE system variable to 1. Enter **UNITMODE** at the Command: prompt, then enter the value **1**.

Stop   AutoCAD interprets pressing the spacebar the same as it interprets pressing Enter. Do not use the spacebar in an attempt to separate elements of a linear distance input. No space is allowed between feet and whole inches; use a hyphen between whole and fractional inches, as in 1'3-1/2" or, more simply, 1'3-1/2.

AutoCAD's scientific, decimal, and fractional units have no associated dimension, such as feet or inches. You can use them to represent any units. You can use AutoCAD's dimension text suffix feature to add an appropriate symbol. To represent millimeters, for example, use decimal units and then add mm as a suffix. See Chapters 21, "Introduction to Dimensioning," and 22, "Editing and Styling Dimensions," for details.

Setting Limits and Drawing Aids

After you establish your drawing's units, use the LIMITS command to set up your electronic drawing sheet. You also can set up various drawing aids, such as a cursor snap increment and a visual reference grid of dots. You set these to functions or multiples of the units you have specified.

> **'LIMITS.** The 'LIMITS command defines the drawing area by the coordinates of its lower-left and upper-right corners. The drawing limits are 2D points in the World Coordinate System. The drawing's limits also set the extents of the grid and determine the minimum area displayed when you use ZOOM All.
> Pull-down: *Choose* Data, Drawing Limits
> Screen: *Choose* DATA, Limits:

Earlier in this chapter, you calculated the scale factor and drawing limits for your electronic sheet. You must use the LIMITS command to input the lower-left and the upper-right coordinates of your electronic sheet. AutoCAD then defines the limits and warns you when you attempt to create an object existing outside of this area. The warning only appears if you choose the On option of the LIMITS command. You can type **LIMITS** at the Command: prompt or choose Data, Drawing Limits.

Note   You can define drawing limits separately for model and paper space. Chapter 10, "Working in Model and Paper Space Viewports," explains model and paper space. So far, you have been using model space.

LIMITS Command Options

The LIMITS command issues the following command-line options:

◆ **ON.** Turns on limits checking to prevent points from being specified outside the limits.

◆ **OFF.** Turns off limits checking (the default) to enable you to specify points outside the limits.

◆ **Lower left corner.** This prompt sets the coordinates for the lower left corner of the limits (the default is 0,0).

New Riders Publishing
INSIDE
SERIES

You previously determined that your 24-by-13-foot architectural floor plan would plot adequately on an 11-by-8-1/2-inch A-sheet at a scale of 1/4" = 1'-0", yielding a full-scale "sheet size" of 528 × 408 inches or 44 × 34 feet. Therefore, you now can apply this full-scale "sheet size" to the LIMITS command.

Setting the Limits for an Architectural Drawing

Continue to use the ARCH drawing.

Command: *Choose* Data, Drawing Limits	Issues the LIMITS command
Command: '_limits	
Reset Model space limits:	
ON/OFF/<Lower left corner> <0'-0",0'-0">: **Enter**	Retains the default 0,0 lower-left corner
Upper right corner <1'-0",0'-9">: **44',34' Enter**	Sets the value for the upper-right limit

The value in the preceding step is the sheet size value in drawing units that you calculated earlier. You could have entered the value in inches.

Command: *Choose* View, Zoom, All	Issues the ZOOM command with the All option
_zoom All/Center/Dynamic/Extents/ Left/Previous/Vmax/Window/ <Scale(X/XP)>: _a	Zooms to area bounded by current limits and regenerates the drawing
Regenerating drawing.	

Move the cursor around the drawing area and notice the coordinate display on the status bar. Near the upper-right corner of the drawing area, you can see that the display indicates approximately 44', 34'. You see the upper-left extent of the limits more clearly and precisely in the next section, when you turn on the grid and snap.

Command: *Choose* File, Save	Issues the QSAVE command and saves the drawing

Note The ZOOM command, used in the preceding exercise, is covered fully in Chapter 9, "Controlling the Display."

In the preceding exercise you set the limits of your ARCH drawing to the dimensions of an 11-by-8-1/2-inch physical sheet scaled up by an amount equal to the scale factor. This, in effect, defines an electronic drawing area within which you can create your 24-by-13-foot floor plan at full scale. When you actually plot the drawing, you scale the drawing down by the reciprocal of the scale factor (1/48 in this case) so that the objects in the drawing are physically plotted at a ratio of 48:1, or 48 real-world inches equals one plotted inch, or 12 real-world inches equals 1/4 plotted inches. Stated another way, 1/4" = 1'-0".

Setting the Snap and Grid

Now that you have set the limits of your electronic sheet, it would be useful to have some means of visualizing the limits. Unlike manual drafting, whereby the physical sheet on the drawing board clearly defines your boundary, AutoCAD's electronic screen has no physical bounds. You can use the Drawing Aids dialog box or the GRID command to establish a drawing grid that automatically extends to the current drawing limits. The grid also helps visualize and estimate coordinate values and distances. You also can set a snap increment in the Drawing Aids dialog box that causes the crosshairs to move in accurate increments. Appropriate snap and grid values, and the coordinates display, enable you to visually pick points accurately.

In the following exercise, you establish a drawing grid and snap increment and further investigate the function of the drawing limits.

Setting a Grid To Display the Drawing's Limits

Continue to use the ARCH drawing.

Command: *Choose* Options, Drawing Aids	Issues the DDRMODES command and invokes the Drawing Aids dialog box (see fig. 5.9)
'_ddrmodes	
Put a check in the G*rid* On *check box*	Turns on grid
In the G*rid area, double-click in the* X S*pacing edit box, then enter* **12**	Sets the X spacing to 12 and changes the Y spacing to 1'0" when you press Enter
Put a check in the S*nap* On *check box*	Turns on snap
In the Snap area, enter **3** *in the* X *Spacing box*	Sets X and Y spacing to 3"
Choose OK	Closes the dialog box and brings up the grid—an array of dots

```
Command: Z (Enter)                    Issues the ZOOM command

All/Center/Dynamic/Extents/          Zooms so that limits and grid cover 75
Left/Previous/Vmax/Window/           percent of the graphics window (see fig.
<Scale(X/XP)>: .75 (Enter)           5.10)
```

Move the cursor around the drawing area and notice the coordinate display on the status bar. Near the upper-right corner of the drawing area, the display indicates precisely 44'0", 34'0" at the upper-right grid dot.

Save your drawing.

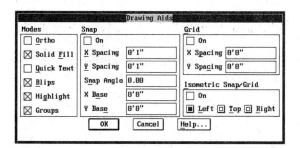

Figure 5.9

The Drawing Aids dialog box.

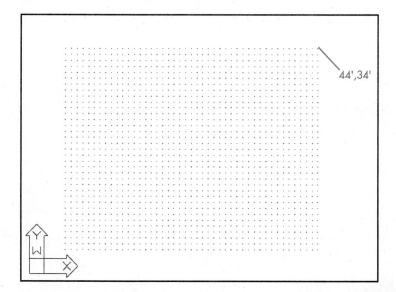

Figure 5.10

Drawing limits shown by a grid.

As shown in figure 5.10, the grid provides both a functional and visual boundary for your drawing. The area covered by the grid is the defined limits, representing an 11-by-8-1/2-inch sheet scaled up by a scale factor of 48, or 44' × 34' (528" × 408"). For clarity, the upper-right limits of the drawing are identified in figure 5.10.

This time, as you moved the cursor to the upper right, the coordinates display showed X,Y values in increments of three inches. This increment is the snap increment. The grid and snap modes help you pick points accurately. The grid and snap settings are discussed fully in Chapter 6, "Drawing Accurately," in which you develop methods to increase the accuracy of your drawings.

Turning On the Limits Checking

You can use AutoCAD's grid to visually identify the drawing's limits. The LIMITS command can be set to prevent you from drawing outside of these limits. This feature is called *limits checking* and is off by default. You use the LIMITS command's ON and OFF options to control limits checking. When limits checking is on, AutoCAD checks each point you specify to determine whether the point is within the drawing's current limits. If the point is outside the limits, AutoCAD prevents you from using the point.

The following exercise demonstrates limits checking and how to turn it on and off.

Turning Limits Checking On and Off

Continue from the previous exercise.

Command: **LIMITS** (Enter)   Issues the LIMITS command

Reset Model space limits:

ON/OFF/<Lower left corner>   Turns on limits checking
<0'-0",0'-0">: **ON** (Enter)

Next, you try to draw a line from within the drawing's limit to a point outside the limits. You can type the points shown in the following steps, or use the coordinates display to locate and pick them.

Command: *Choose* Draw, Line   Issues the LINE command

Command: _line From point: Begins a line from within the limits
24',13' (Enter)

To point: **-1',-1'** (Enter)

**Outside limits   Rejects the second point because it is
                                                 outside the limits, then reissues the prompt

To point: **1',1'** (Enter)   Draws the line and prompts for next point

To point: (Enter)   Ends the LINE command

New Riders Publishing
INSIDE
SERIES

The second line endpoint you specified was outside the limits, the first and third were not. Next, you turn limits checking off.

Command: *Choose* Data, Drawing Limits	Issues the LIMITS command
Command: '_limits	
Reset Model space limits:	
ON/OFF/<Lower left corner> <0'-0",0'-0">: **OFF** (Enter)	Turns limits checking off

Next, you try to draw outside the limits again.

Command: **L** (Enter)	Issues the LINE command
From point: **24',13'** (Enter)	Specifies a point within the drawing limits
To point: **-1',-1'** (Enter)	Specifies a point outside the drawing limits and draws the line
To point: (Enter)	Ends the LINE command

Do not save this exercise's changes to your ARCH drawing. You return to this drawing as it was saved in the previous exercise later in this chapter to set up a system of layers.

Setting Limits Automatically with MVSETUP

After you determine the size of plotted sheet or the final plotted scale for your drawing, you can determine the all-important scale factor that you use during plotting. Setting the drawing's limits is then largely a matter of simple arithmetic. You can use AutoCAD's MVSETUP command to perform most of these calculations. During MVSETUP, AutoCAD prompts you for the drawing units, the drawing scale factor, and the intended sheet dimensions, and then calculates the drawing's limits. MVSETUP also draws a rectangular border that represents the limits of the drawing. The border is a single object that becomes a part of your drawing. If you do not want the border, use the ERASE command to remove it.

> **MVSETUP.** The MVSETUP command (defined by an AutoLISP program) enables you to set the specifications for a drawing, including units, plotting sheet size, and plotting scale. Refer to the chapter on paper space for other MVSETUP functions. If you are in model space, you must enter **MVSETUP** at the Command: prompt.
> Pull-down: *Choose* View, Floating Viewports (for paper space only)

5

MVSETUP Prompts

For use in model space applications, MVSETUP has the following prompts:

◆ **Enable paper space? (No/,Yes>).** You must enter **N** or **n** to use the non-paper-space functions of this command.

◆ **Units type (Scientific/Decimal/Engineering/Architectural/Metric).** Entering one of these options (initial letter acceptable) displays a list of appropriate scales and associated scale factors.

◆ **Enter the scale factor.** Enter a value.

◆ **Enter the paper width.** Enter a value in actual sheet-size units.

In the following exercise, you use MVSETUP to determine the limits for a civil engineering drawing. For the purpose of this exercise, assume that you need to plot the drawing at a scale of 1" = 20' on a sheet that is 17" × 11".

Using the MVSETUP Command To Determine Limits

Begin a new drawing called ENG, using the default ACAD drawing as a prototype.

Command: *Choose* File, New	Issues the NEW command and opens the Create New Drawing dialog box
Type **ENG** *in the* New **D**rawing Name *box, then choose* OK	Begins a new drawing titled ENG, using the default ACAD prototype drawing
Command: **MVSETUP** (Enter)	Invokes the MVSETUP command
Initializing...	Indicates loading the command—it might take several seconds to initialize
Enable paper space? (No/<Yes>): **N** (Enter)	Forces the model space prompts
Units type (Scientific/Decimal/ Engineering/Architectural/Metric): **E** (Enter)	Specifies engineering units and prompts for engineering scale

AutoCAD switches to the text window and displays the following common engineering scales and their associated scale factors:

Engineering Scales
====================
```
(120)  1"=10'
(240)  1"=20'
```

New Riders Publishing
INSIDE SERIES

(360) 1"=30'
(480) 1"=40'
(600) 1"=50'
(720) 1"=60'
(960) 1"=80'
(1200) 1"=100'

Enter the scale factor: **240** (Enter)   Specifies 1" = 20' scale

Enter the paper width: **17"**   Specifies sheet width

Enter the paper height: **11"**   Specifies sheet height

The command MVSETUP calculates the drawings limits, sets units, and draws a border defined by the calculated limits, then zooms to the limits. Next, you zoom out a little farther.

Command: **Z** (Enter)   Issues the ZOOM command

ZOOM

All/Center/Dynamic/Extents/Left/   Zooms limits to cover 75 percent of
Previous/Vmax/Window/<Scale(X/XP)>:   drawing window
.75 (Enter)

Command: *Choose* Options, Drawing Aids   Activates the Drawing Aids dialog box
                                                 (refer to figure 5.9)

Put a check in the On *check box in*   Turns on snap
the Snap *area*

Double-click in the X Spacing *edit*   Sets both the X and Y snap interval to
box in the Snap *area, then enter* **10'**   10' after you press Enter

Put a check in the On *check box in*   Turns on the grid
the Grid *area*

Choose OK   Closes the dialog box and displays the
                                                 grid (see fig. 5.11)

Move the cursor around the drawing and note that it moves in 10-foot increments and coincides with the displayed grid. In the upper-right corner, note that the coordinate display reads 340' × 220'.

Save the drawing.

5

Figure 5.11

*The result of the
MVSETUP
command.*

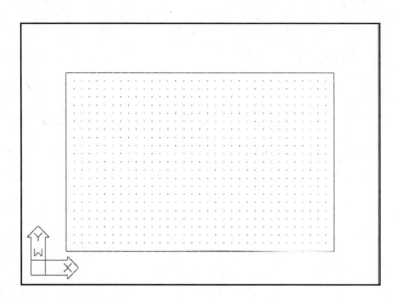

Note The MVSETUP command also enables you to set up multiple viewports in AutoCAD drawings in which you use paper space. When you use MVSETUP in paper space, it is available from the View menu. See Chapter 25, "Sheet Composition and Plotting," for details about using MVSETUP.

Figure 5.11 shows the ENG drawing after you have configured it for a 1" =20' scale. The border drawn by the MVSETUP command surrounds an area 340' × 220' within which you create your drawing at full scale. In the exercise, you turned on AutoCAD's snap feature and set the interval to a distance of 10'. Then you turned the grid feature on but left the grid spacing at the default of 0. The grid automatically displays at the snap interval when the grid spacing is set to 0. The snap feature restricts cursor movement to specified intervals. As you move the cursor around, it snaps to 10' intervals.

At plot time, you instruct AutoCAD to plot ENG drawing at a scale of 1 plotted inch equals 240 drawing units (20'). The border also will be scaled down to 17" × 11". This border forms the edge of the sheet—you need to draw or insert a standard title block and border.

Whether you use MVSETUP to set the limits for your drawing automatically or LIMITS to do so manually, defining limits is an important step of preparing drawings. First, you define the electronic drawing area, and if you define it visibly (by a grid or border) you can better conceptualize your position in electronic space. Secondly, unintentionally drawing objects outside of the limits is easy. You need only forget a negative sign or a digit and your door jamb can end up several thousand feet from

New Riders Publishing
INSIDE
SERIES

where you wanted it and you might not even notice. Enabling limits checking prevents this kind of mistake.

Note ACAD, the default prototype drawing file does not have limits set or limits checking enabled. The standard practice is to establish the drawing limits when the drawing size is determined. At that time, limits checking is usually set On unless you will intentionally draw outside the drawing limits.

Applying Scale Factors to Text and Symbols

When you use conventional manual drafting techniques, you add such features as text, standard symbols, linetypes, and line widths uniformly from drawing to drawing, in accordance with your own drawing standards and conventions. When you use AutoCAD and draw in real-world units, then plot at a scale, however, you need to apply a different technique. For example, if you want certain text elements in your plotted drawing to be 1/8" in height and you plot at a scale of 1/4 plotted inch equals 12 drawing inches, you need to figure out the height of the text in real-world units as you add it to your drawing. You need to know how wide to make a line in your full-scale drawing if you want it to be 1/16" wide when you reduce it to fit the plotted sheet at any given scale.

Answering these and similar questions is easy if you know the scale factor for your particular drawing size and plotted scale. Simply determine the size you want your symbols, text, and other elements to be in the final plot and then multiply that size by the scale factor. This is actually an extension of the principal involved in the scaling all CAD drawings discussed earlier in this chapter. You can use the following general formula:

Plotted Size × Scale Factor = Electronic Size

Applying this formula, 1/8" plotted text in a 1/4" = 1'-0" architectural drawing would be drawn at a height of 1/8" × 48, or 6". In a similar manner, you would draw a symbol you want plotted at a standard 3/4" height in an engineering drawing with a scale factor of 24 (1" = 2') at a real-world size of 3/4" × 24 = 18".

Use this formula with your ENG drawing (scale factor 240) and add some text as a title. Suppose, for example, that you want to add the title *I-24/SR-12 Interchange* in the lower left corner. Assume that you want the text to appear at a height of 1/4" on the plotted sheet. Use the following calculation:

1/4" × 240 = 60" or 5'-0"

5

Text drawn 60" or 5'-0" high at full scale will appear 1/4" in height on the plotted sheet. You apply this principle to text in the following exercise. Later in this chapter, you scale dashed linetypes.

Setting Text Height

Continue to use the ENG drawing.

Command: **DTEXT** (Enter)	Issues the DTEXT command
Justify/Style/<Start point>: **10',10'** (Enter)	Specifies the text insertion point coordinate
Height <0'-0.2000">: **60** (Enter)	Specifies a height of 60"
Rotation angle <0>: (Enter)	Accepts the default 0 degrees

In the following step, enter the text from the keyboard:

Text: **I-24/SR-12 Interchange** (Enter)	Draws the text (see fig. 5.12)
Text: (Enter)	Ends the DTEXT command

Save the drawing.

Figure 5.12

5'-0" tall, full scale text object.

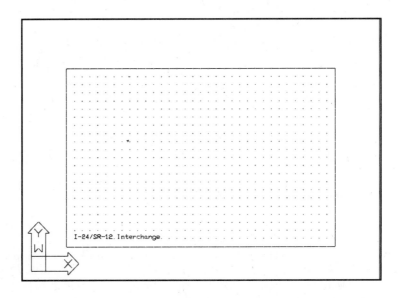

Applying a scale factor to a symbol is somewhat more complicated. You usually create a symbol, such as a sheet reference or note bubble, at its intended size. You can

address this type of symbol with the same logic you used for text scale factors. If you create the symbol with the same scale factor that you use on your drawing, they are at an equivalent scale and therefore the symbol scale factor is 1. Other occasions occur in which your symbol is already scaled, such as a roadway cross section that you must place on a drawing with other cross sections at a different scale. Scale factor is a difficult concept to grasp and apply, but it is a key factor in any CAD system.

 Note You specify the scale factor for symbols when you use the INSERT command, which is discussed in Chapter 16, "Basic Building Blocks for Repetetive Drawing."

Before you begin to explore other drawing setup features, such as creating layers and assigning colors and linetypes, a question may have occurred to you: "After I go to the trouble of setting up a drawing, can I save the setup to reuse it for other similar drawings?"

Using Prototype Drawings

After you set up units, limits, and scale factor and other settings, you probably will want to make many drawings with most, if not all, of the same settings. In an architectural setting, for example, you might need to make hundreds of drawings plotted at a scale of 1/8"=1'-0". If you use AutoCAD for a civil engineering application, you might need many drawings plotted at 1"=20'. The layers you use in one typical drawing might be the same layers you use in many others. Fortunately, AutoCAD provides a way that you can make a single drawing in which you can store the settings that you use regularly and use them again and again. Such drawings are called prototype drawings. *Prototype drawings* are drawings that you can use as the basis for new drawings. You can have many prototype drawings, each of which serve as the basis for new drawings of a specific type.

Actually, whenever you open a new drawing, AutoCAD refers to a prototype drawing to obtain the many settings needed to begin the drawing. If you do not specify a specific prototype drawing, AutoCAD uses it own prototype, named ACAD.DWG. AutoCAD reads the settings from ACAD drawing and uses them to get started. ACAD drawing contains only the bare necessities you need to start drawing any objects. It has one layer, layer 0, one linetype, CONTINUOUS, and a few other basic settings. Defining your own prototype drawings saves innumerable hours of drawing setup time and also imbues your work with an aura of consistency.

You use prototype drawings throughout this book as the basis for new drawings. In the next exercise, you use one of the book's prototype drawings, IAD-MECH, as the prototype for a new drawing named CHAP05 drawing.

5

The Create New Drawing dialog box enables you to specify a prototype drawing name to use as the starting point for a new drawing. Choosing the P̲rototype button opens the Prototype Drawing File dialog box, which contains the following elements:

◆ **F̲ile.** You enter a file name in the F̲ile edit box. If the cursor is not already in this box, you can click to place it there; you can double-click to highlight the text for replacement.

◆ **Di̲rectories.** The Di̲rectories list box enables you to select a different subdirectory or drive. Double-clicking selects a subdirectory or drive, then updates the Directory label and the contents of the F̲iles list box according to the current file pattern.

◆ **Fi̲les.** The F̲iles box lists the drawing files that match the file specification in the P̲attern edit box. You can click to select the file, which then updates the F̲ile edit box with the file name you select and updates the preview box. You can double-click to select the drawing file as the file name to use for the Create New Drawing dialog box.

The Create New Drawing dialog box is the parent dialog box for the Prototype Drawing File dialog box. It contains the following elements specifically related to prototype drawings:

◆ **P̲rototype.** The P̲rototype button opens the Prototype Drawing File dialog box.

◆ **N̲o Prototype.** Check the N̲o Prototype check box to begin a new drawing using AutoCAD's default settings.

 Note   You use the NEW command to open the Create New Drawing dialog box. The NEW command is covered in Chapter 3, "Using the Drawing Editor."

The following exercise explores using a prototype specification.

Using an Existing Drawing as a Prototype

Command: *Choose* File, New	Issues the NEW command and opens the Start New Drawing dialog box
Choose the P̲rototype *button*	Opens the Prototype Drawing File dialog box (see fig. 5.13)
Use the Di̲rectories *list box to access the* \IAD\DWGS *directory*	Selects the directory in which your IA Disk files are stored

New Riders Publishing
INSIDE
SERIES

In the F̲iles *list box, choose the* IAD-MECH *drawing file (scroll the list if required)*	Selects the IAD-MECH file as the prototype drawing file
Choose OK	Closes the Prototype Drawing File dialog box
In the New D̲rawing Name *edit box,* *type* **CHAP05** *and press Enter*	Closes the Create New Drawing dialog box and begins a new drawing named CHAP05

In the next step, take a look at the layer setup for the new CHAP05 drawing.

Command: *Choose* Data, Layers	Issues the DDLMODES command and opens the Layer Control dialog box

Note the 12 layers and their colors and linetypes. You do not need to save this drawing.

Figure 5.13

The Prototype Drawing File dialog box.

The CHAP05 drawing is an exact copy of the prototype IAD-MECH drawing, including all its settings, loaded linetypes, and layer configuration. After you expend the time and effort to set up the prototype, you can make an unlimited number of prototype clones. By their very nature, prototype drawings attempt to anticipate all layers, linetypes, and other named items and settings that you might need in the clone drawing. Therefore, they can contain layers and linetypes that you do not need in a specific drawing. You easily can use the AutoCAD commands to fine-tune the new drawing to your needs.

Tip

An alternative to using the Prototype Drawing File dialog box to specify a prototype drawing is to enter the file name (and path) directly in the input box next to the **P**rototype button.

Prototype drawings help avoid repetitious setup procedures, and using prototypes provides an excellent means for establishing standards. Any drawing can serve as a prototype. Because the prototype procedure essentially copies, renames, and opens a drawing in one step, existing drawings can serve as starting points for new drawings. After you open the new drawing, erase the unnecessary parts of the old drawing and keep the rest as the basis for your new drawing.

Prototype drawings are a powerful tool that you can use as you set up many of your drawings. Two prototype drawings are included on the IA Disk and are installed in the DWGS directory.

◆ **ARCH-PRO.** Provides settings and layers appropriate for many architectural drawings

◆ **IAD-MECH.** Provides settings suitable for many mechanical applications

In addition, AutoCAD ships with its own set of standard prototype drawings, including ACADISO, US_ARCH, and US_MECH, among others. You can find these drawing files in the Support directory of your AutoCAD installation.

Another important aspect of drawing setup—one you probably want to include in your prototype drawing—is establishing standard layer, color, and linetype setups.

Setting Up Layers, Colors, and Linetypes

Layers are one of the most effective tools you can use to help organize your drawing. You can conceive of almost everything you design or draw as separated into layers. You can layer buildings by floors; you can divide individual floors into electrical, plumbing, and structural elements. Even the simplest schematic drawing might have a layer devoted to annotation and another devoted to the schematic elements. AutoCAD offers a virtually unlimited number of electronic layers, which gives you a high degree of flexibility and control when you organize your drawing. You also use layers in CAD to separate different types of objects so that you can easily assign them different linetypes and plot them with different line weights.

In manual drafting, you often use physical layers made from clear plastic sheets to separate groups of related drawing elements. Think of AutoCAD's layers as similar transparent electronic sheets laid over one another. A typical AutoCAD 2D drawing looks like a stack of these transparent sheets (see fig. 5.14). You can see your entire drawing as it is being built from the superimposed sheets. You can "remove" sheets from the stack so that they do not interfere with the view of the other sheets, and you can add new sheets as the need arises. Each layer can have any of AutoCAD's colors and linetypes associated with it.

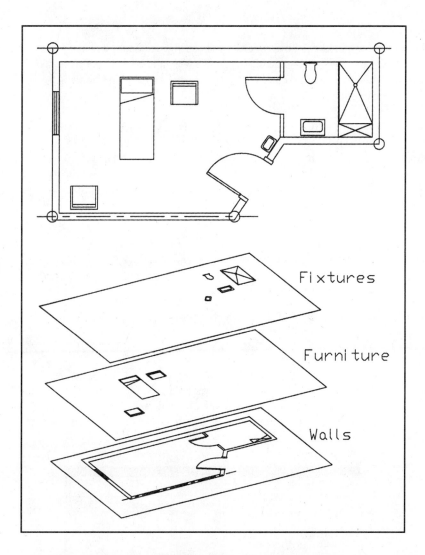

Figure 5.14

Using layers in AutoCAD.

Fixtures

Furniture

Walls

Understanding Objects and Properties

When you use any of AutoCAD's drawing tools to draw on one of the electronic layers, you create a *drawing object.* Lines, circles, and text are examples of AutoCAD objects. In addition to an object's geometric position, it has an associated layer, color, and linetype, called *object properties.* Normally, the color and linetype are inherited from the layer on which the object is drawn, although this you can override this association.

Note The color of an object can have special significance, because most plotting and printing devices used with AutoCAD assign line weight or other visual properties according to color. This and other plotting topics are discussed in Chapter 25, "Sheet Composition and Plotting."

When you have this degree of flexibility, one of the most important steps of organizing your drawing is to devise the layering scheme: which parts of the drawing you place on which layers, and the names, colors, and linetypes of each layer. You can make as many or as few layers as you need. There are many schemes for creating layers. Different professions have established standards and conventions that you can adopt, or you can devise your own.

Working with Layers

As a reflection of their importance, AutoCAD provides two ways to work with layers:

◆ Open the Layer Control dialog box by choosing Data, Layers from the pull-down menu or entering the DDLMODES command at the Command: prompt

◆ Enter the LAYER command, then enter options and layer names on the command line

In the preceding list, the first method affords complete layer control. Because of its advanced interface, you probably will use the Layer Control dialog box most often when you create layers and perform operations on groups of layers. The Layer Control dialog box is shown in figure 5.15.

Figure 5.15

The Layer Control dialog box.

Layer Name list box

Input box

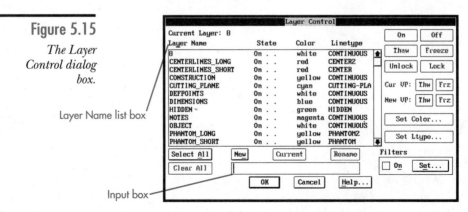

The Layer Control dialog box provides the easiest way to create layers, to change their colors and linetypes, and to manipulate groups of layers. The Layer Control drop-down list provides the easiest way to control layer visibility and set the current layer for drawing.

Using the Layer Control Dialog Box

The Layer Control dialog box is composed of a Layer Name list box, a user input box, and several buttons. The Layer Name list box displays a list of all the layers defined in the drawing, along with their assigned color, linetype, and current state. The Layer Name list box always contains a layer named 0. Layer 0 is AutoCAD's default layer and is assigned the default layer properties: color white and linetype continuous. The input box enables you to enter layer names. You use the DDLMODES command to open the Layer Control dialog box.

> **'DDLMODES.** The 'DDLMODES command enables you to open the Layer Control dialog box, which you can use to set a layer current, change a layer's assigned color and linetype, add new layers to your drawing, rename layers, turn layers on and off, freeze and thaw layers, and lock and unlock layers. You can use the Filters facility to control which layers appear in the Layer Name list box.
> Pull-down: *Choose* Data, Layers
> Screen: *Choose* DATA, DDlmode:

Creating New Layers

Although you always have layer 0 available, you need to begin setting up a layer system by making some new layers. In the following exercise, you begin a new drawing named LAYERS.

Creating New Layers

Use the NEW command to begin a new drawing named LAYERS, using the default ACAD.DWG as the prototype.

Command: *Choose* Data, Layers	Issues the DDLMODES command and opens theLayer Control dialog box
`'_ddlmodes`	
Type **OBJECT** *in the name input box* and *choose* New	Creates a new layer named OBJECT and adds it to the Layer Name list box (see fig. 5.16)

continues

5

continued

Select OBJECT *in the* Layer Name list box	Selects OBJECT layer for a subsequent operation
Choose Current	Makes OBJECT the current layer
Choose OK	Closes the Layer Control dialog box and saves the changes

Note that OBJECT now shows as the current layer in the status line.

Use the LINE command and enter the coordinates shown in figure 5.17 to draw the "Upper Shim" widget.

Save the drawing.

Figure 5.16

Creating the OBJECT layer in the Layer Control dialog box.

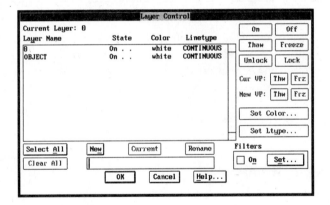

Figure 5.17

An Upper Shim widget drawn on the OBJECT layer.

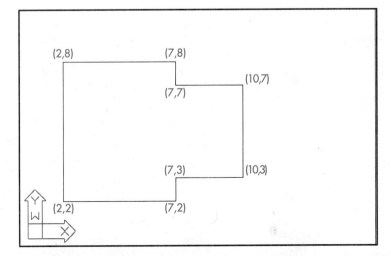

New Riders Publishing
INSIDE SERIES

After you created the new layer OBJECT, you made it the current layer, then drew the shim. Any objects you draw automatically are assigned to the current layer. The shim, therefore, appears on the OBJECT layer and has the associated properties of that layer. All new layers, by default, have a color of white and a linetype of continuous associated with them unless and until you change that association. You learn how to change the default color and linetype of layers in the section "Assigning Layer Properties," later in this chapter.

 Note If you use a white graphics background, AutoCAD's color 7 (white) appears black. Although it appears black, AutoCAD always calls it white. Certain light colors, such as yellow, can be difficult to see on a light background. You can reconfigure the AutoCAD display driver to change the background color. See the *AutoCAD Installation Guide For DOS* for more display driver configuration details.

Knowing which layer is the current layer is important because new objects are created on the current layer. AutoCAD displays the name of the current layer in the status line at the top of the graphics display. You frequently refer to this display since you often change the current layer.

 Note You can use the keyboard and the hot keys in the Layer Control dialog box to select layer names in the Layer Name list box. Press Alt+Y, use the up- and down-arrow keys to move the dotted box to the layer name, and then press the spacebar to select or deselect it.

Layer Control Dialog Box Options

The Layer Control dialog box contains numerous options and features that provide complete information about and control of AutoCAD layers (refer to figure 5.16).

♦ **Current Layer.** The Current Layer setting displays the name of the current layer.

♦ **Layer Name.** The Layer Name list displays the name, visibility state, color, and linetype of each layer in the drawing. To modify layer settings, select a layer name (or names) from the list and choose an option. You can use filters to control which layer names are listed. When you choose only one layer, its name appears in the input box.

♦ **Select All.** The Select All button selects and highlights all the layers currently displayed in the Layer Name list box.

♦ **Clear All.** The Clear All button deselects and dehighlights all selected and highlighted layers.

5

◆ **New.** The New button creates new layers with the name or names in the input box.

◆ **Current.** The Current button sets a selected layer current.

◆ **Rename.** The Rename button renames the selected layer to match the name in the input box.

◆ **Input box.** If you select only a single layer, the input box displays the name of that layer. If you select multiple layers, the input box is blank. Or, you can enter one or more layer names as input for the New or Rename buttons. A layer name can be as many as 31 characters long. The input box holds up to 255 characters for multiple entries.

◆ **On/Off.** The On/Off buttons enable you to control the on/off states of selected layers. Layers that are on are visible; layers that are off are invisible, but are still regenerated. If you turn off the current layer, any new objects you draw are not visible until you turn on the layer. The word ON in the State column of the Layer Name list box indicates which layers are on.

◆ **Thaw/Freeze.** The Thaw/Freeze buttons enable you to control whether the selected layers are frozen or thawed. AutoCAD neither displays nor regenerates a frozen layer. A thawed layer is simply one that is not frozen. An F in the State column of the Layer Name list box indicates a frozen layer. You cannot make a frozen layer current.

◆ **Unlock/Lock.** The Unlock/Lock buttons control the Unlock/Lock state of selected layers. *Locking* a layer prevents you from editing objects on that layer. AutoCAD displays locked layers and you can use their objects for object snaps. An L in the State column of the Layer Name list box indicates a locked layer.

◆ **Cur VP Thaw/Frz.** The Cur VP Thaw/Frz buttons enable you to control the Thaw/Freeze status of layers within individual viewports in model or paper space (see Chapter 10). This permits one viewport to have a layer thawed while the same layer is frozen in a different viewport.

◆ **New VP Thaw/Frz.** The New VP Thaw/Frz buttons enable you to control the default layer Thaw/Freeze status in subsequently created floating viewports (see Chapter 10).

◆ **Set Color.** You can use the Set Color button to open the Select Color dialog box, which enables you to assign a color to the selected layer(s).

◆ **Set Ltype.** You can use the Set Ltype to open the Select Linetype dialog box, which enables you to assign a linetype to the selected layer(s).

◆ **Filters On.** The Filters On check box enables you to limit the names that AutoCAD displays in the Layer Name list box. You use filters to group layers for

New Riders Publishing
INSIDE
SERIES

operations such as turning off, changing color, freezing, and so forth. When checked (on), AutoCAD displays only layer names that match the currently defined filter. You can filter layers based on state, name, color, or linetype. You also can filter layers based on whether they are frozen in the current viewport or in new viewports. Filters can use wild cards, which are explained in the section "Selecting Groups of Layers," later in this chapter.

◆ **Filters Set.** You can use the Filters Set button to open the Set Layer Filters dialog box, which enables you to choose the criteria by which AutoCAD displays layer names in the Layer Name list box.

◆ **OK.** The OK button closes the Layer Control dialog box and saves the current settings.

◆ **Cancel.** The Cancel button closes the Layer Control dialog box and discards any changes.

Naming Layers

Your layer names can be up to 31 characters long, so feel free to be as descriptive as you want. You must conform to a few restrictions, however: you are confined to the standard alphanumeric characters and the dash (-), dollar sign ($), and underscore (_) symbols. In addition, layer names cannot contain spaces. A name such as $CONTOUR 120 is not permitted, whereas $CONTOUR-120 is acceptable. Some planning of layer names enables you to effectively use layer name filters to manipulate groups of layers.

Creating Multiple Layers

Unlike mechanical drafting and design in which using a large number of overlays can become unwieldy and self-defeating, you can add as many layers to an AutoCAD drawing as necessary. Large drawings often contain hundreds of layers. On the other hand, you can eliminate needless or superfluous layers or combine them more meaningfully with other layers. Again, some thought to a layering scheme as you set up your drawing saves time and increases efficiency.

You can use the Layer Control dialog box to create multiple layers at one time. Simply enter several layer names, separated by commas (without spaces), into the input box and choose New.

In the next exercise you create three additional layers in your LAYERS drawing and place objects on two of them.

5

Creating Multiple Layers and Setting the Current Layer

Continue from the preceding exercise.

`Command:` *Choose* Data, Layers	Issues the DDLMODES command and opens theLayer Control dialog box
Type **CENTER,TEXT,DIMS** *in the input box and choose* Ne<u>w</u>	Creates three new layers—CENTER, TEXT, and DIMS—and lists them in the Layer Name list box
Select the CENTER *layer name in the* Layer Name *list box*	Selects and highlights the CENTER layer
Choose <u>C</u>urrent	Sets the selected layer—CENTER—current and displays its name as the current layer
Choose OK	Closes the Layer Control dialog box

Draw a line from point 1,5 to point 11,5 through the center of the shim.

`Command:` *Choose* Data, Layers	Issues the DDLMODES command and invokes the Layer Control dialog
Select the TEXT *layer name in the* Layer Name *list box*	Selects and highlights the TEXT layer
Choose <u>C</u>urrent	Sets the selected layer current
Choose OK	Closes the Layer Control dialog box
`Command:` **DTEXT** (Enter)	Issues the DTEXT command
`Justify/Style/<Start point>:` **2,8.25** (Enter)	Sets insertion point for text above shim
`Height <0.2000>:` **0.25** (Enter)	Sets a text height of 0.25"
`Rotation angle <0>:` (Enter)	Defaults to use a rotation angle of 0
`Text:` **Upper Shim** (Enter)	Draws text (see fig. 5.18)
`Text:` (Enter)	Ends DTEXT command

Save the drawing.

New Riders Publishing
INSIDE
SERIES

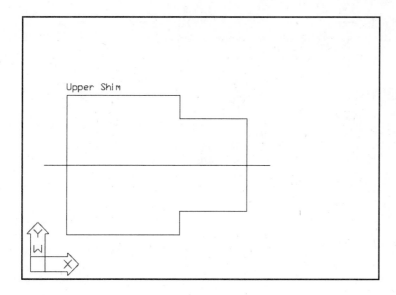

Upper Shim

Figure 5.18
*Creating objects
on various layers.*

Assigning Layer Properties

Currently all your layers have the same default properties: color white, linetype CONTINUOUS. Distinguishing between your layers will be difficult because everything looks the same. You need to take full advantage of the power of layers by assigning different colors and linetypes to some layers. AutoCAD supports 255 colors and 38 predefined linetypes. These colors and linetypes enable you to differentiate your layers.

Using Colors and Linetypes

Not only do various colors and linetypes make it easier to distinguish objects on-screen as you draw, they convey other important information. Some objects, for example, might require different line weights (widths) to make them stand out or to convey functional meanings. Colors are assigned to layers (or to objects—see Chapter 15) and then to different plotting pens.

Various design and drafting practices and standards require that certain linetypes be used to convey established meanings; examples of this include the use of the standard center linetype to denote the center of circles and other objects such as the shim in your LAYERS drawing. In mapping applications, certain standard linetypes denote various types of borders and other lines of demarcation. AutoCAD also offers a few complex linetypes that have embedded text and symbols, and you can create custom linetypes—see Chapter 12,"Drawing with Complex Objects," for complex linetype use and Chapter 20, "Linetypes and Hatching," for their creation.

5

Before you assign linetypes (other than CONTINUOUS) to any of your layers, you must first load the linetypes you need into your drawing, as shown in the next exercise.

Loading Linetypes

Linetype definitions are stored in specialized text files that AutoCAD uses to describe how a linetype appears. Standard linetypes are kept in a file called ACAD.LIN. Other special linetypes are stored in similar files. (See Chapter 20 for more about special linetypes.) Before you can assign linetypes to layers with the Layer Control dialog box, you must load them. AutoCAD provides several ways of loading linetypes. In this chapter, you use the linetype features of the Layer Control dialog box—see Chapter 19, "Using Xrefs and Overlays for Workgroups and Multiple Access Drawings," to use the DDLTYPE command and other methods. Before you can access the linetype features of the Layer Control dialog box, you must select one or more layers. The following exercise explains how to load all the linetypes available in the ACAD.LIN file.

Loading Linetypes

Continue to use the LAYERS drawing.

Command: *Choose* Data, Layers
Opens the Layer Control dialog box

Select CENTER *in the* Layer Name *list box*
Selects and highlights the layer

Choose Set Ltype
Opens the Select Linetype dialog box (see fig. 5.19)

Choose Load
Opens the Load or Reload Linetypes dialog box (see fig. 5.20)

Choose Select All
Selects and highlights all available linetypes from the ACAD.LIN file

Choose OK
Closes the Load or Reload Linetypes dialog box, loads all selected linetypes into the drawing, and displays them in the Loaded Linetypes list box

All the linetypes in the ACAD.LIN file are now loaded in the LAYERS drawing and are available to assign to layers. Leave the Layer Control dialog open for the next exercise.

New Riders Publishing
INSIDE
SERIES

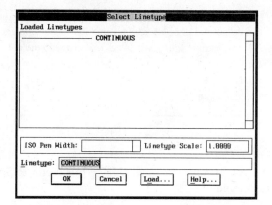

Figure 5.19

The Select Linetype dialog box.

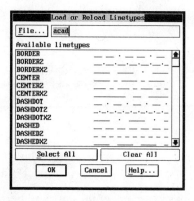

Figure 5.20

The Load or Reload Linetypes dialog box.

Rarely does a single drawing use all the available linetypes. The Load or Reload dialog box provides the capability to select individual linetypes so that you can load as few or as many as you require. Selectively loading linetypes reduces the overall storage size of your drawing; alternatively, you might find it more convenient to load all linetypes and use the PURGE command to remove ones you do not need.

You can select one or more linetypes in the Load or Reload linetypes dialog box by clicking on the linetype names of interest. Clicking on a selected linetype deselects it.

Tip   You can remove linetype definitions that are not used in your drawing with the PURGE command. The PURGE command is covered in the section "Deleting Named Items with the PURGE Command," later in this chapter.

'DDLTYPE. The 'DDLTYPE command enables you to open the Select Linetype dialog box, which you can use to view loaded linetypes, select a linetype to make it current, load linetypes, and set linetype scale.
Pull-down: *Choose* Data, Linetype
Screen: *Choose* DATA, DDltype:

DDLTYPE Command Options

The DDLTYPE command opens the Select Linetype dialog box (refer to figure 5.19), which contains the following elements:

- ◆ **Loaded Linetypes list box.** Displays the names and diagrams of available (loaded) linetypes. Clicking on the diagram selects the linetype and places its name in the Linetype text box.

- ◆ **ISO Pen Width list box.** Specifies pen width (in millimeters) for International Standards Organization (ISO) linetypes. This is available only for linetypes assigned directly to objects, not those assigned by layer, so it is grayed out when accessed through the Layer Control dialog box. See Chapter 20 for information about ISO linetypes.

- ◆ **Linetype Scale.** Displays the current linetype scale factor. You cannot modify this if you use the Layer Control dialog box to access it, but you can if you use the DDLTYPE command to access it.

- ◆ **Linetype text box.** Specifies the name of the current linetype.

Note The LINETYPE command, available only at the command line, offers many of the capabilities available with the Select Linetype dialog box and the additional capability to create linetypes on the fly. The LINETYPE command is covered in Chapter 20.

Assigning Colors and Linetypes

Now that you have loaded a series of linetypes to your LAYERS drawing, you can assign linetypes to individual layers. In the following exercise you assign nondefault colors and linetypes to some of your layers.

Assigning Properties to Layers

Continue from the preceding exercise, with layer CENTER selected, all linetypes loaded, and the Select Linetype dialog box open (see fig. 5.21).

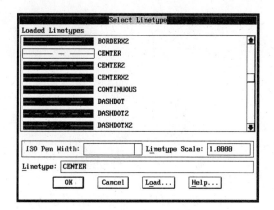

Figure 5.21

*The Select
Linetype dialog
box with linetypes
loaded from
ACAD.LIN.*

Click on the linetype pattern next to CENTER	Specifies and highlights the CENTER linetype; CENTER appears in the Linetype input box (see fig. 5.21)
Choose OK	Closes the Select Linetype dialog box

The linetype name *CENTER* appears in the Linetype column for the selected layer, CENTER, in the Layer Name list box.

Choose Set Color	Opens the Select Color dialog box (see fig. 5.22)
Click on the green box in the Standard Colors *area*	Specifies the color for the selected layer; green appears in the Color input box
Choose OK	Closes the Select Color dialog box and lists green in the color column of the CENTER linetype
Choose OK	Closes the Layer Control dialog box and saves the settings

The drawing regenerates and displays the center line with the CENTER linetype and color green properties. The green center line might be difficult to see if you have a white graphics background.

Use the Layer Control dialog box again to assign the color blue to the TEXT layer and red to the OBJECT layer. Leave the DIMS layer with the default color and linetype.

Command: *Choose* Data, Layers	Issues the DDLMODES command and opens the Layer Control dialog box

continues

continued

Click on the TEXT *layer in the* Layer Name *list box*	Selects and highlights the TEXT layer
Choose Set Color, *select* Blue, *then choose* OK	Sets the color for the TEXT layer to blue
Click on the TEXT *layer in the* Layer Name *list box*	Removes the highlight and deselects the TEXT layer
Click on the OBJECT *layer in the* Layer Name *list box*	Selects and highlights the OBJECT layer
Choose Set Color, Blue, *then choose* OK	Sets the color for the OBJECT layer to red
Choose OK	Closes the Layer Control dialog box and makes the changes to the layer colors

Save your drawing.

Your drawing should resemble fig. 5.23, with a **CENTER** linetype through the shim body.

Figure 5.22

Selecting a color in the Select Color dialog box.

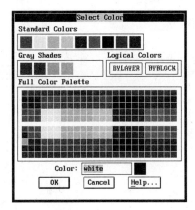

Understanding Linetype Scales

AutoCAD's standard linetypes are composed of repeating patterns of dashes, spaces, and, optionally, dots. The linetype itself and AutoCAD's system variable LTSCALE controls the number of defining patterns that AutoCAD draws per unit length. *System variables* are the settings and values AutoCAD uses to store its operating environment and many of its commands. The name of the current drawing, for example, is stored in a system variable. You learn more about system variables in Chapter 6. The

New Riders Publishing
INSIDE
SERIES

LTSCALE system variable acts as a multiplier, directly affecting the number of linetype repetitions per unit distance. LTSCALE acts globally on all noncontinuous linetypes in the drawing. The higher the value of LTSCALE, the fewer repetitions per unit distance, as shown in figure 5.24. With a default value of 1.0, for example, setting LTSCALE to 0.5 doubles the number of repetitions in a given distance. You can remember how LTSCALE affects linetypes by understanding that an LTSCALE of 2.0 takes twice the distance to display a pattern as an LTSCALE of 1.0. Likewise, an LTSCALE value of 0.5 takes half the distance to display the pattern.

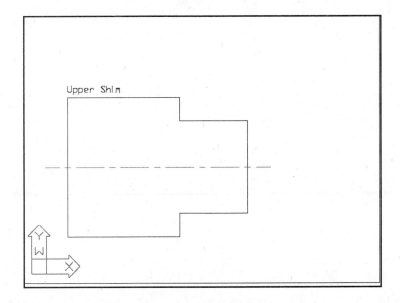

Figure 5.23

The center line displayed with the CENTER linetype on the CENTER layer.

```
LTSCALE = 2.0  ____  __  ____  __  ____

LTSCALE = 1.0  ____ _ ____ _ ____ _ __

LTSCALE = 0.5  __ _ __ _ __ _ __ _ __ _ __ _
```

Figure 5.24

The appearance of LTSCALE applied to a linetype.

5

In the LAYERS drawing, the CENTER linetype assigned to your CENTER layer has the default LTSCALE value of 1.0 applied to it. You might want linetypes to appear at a smaller scale to meet a specific drafting standard or convention. In the following exercise, you change the LTSCALE.

Changing the Appearance of Linetypes with LTSCALE

Continue from the preceding exercise.

Command: **LTSCALE** (Enter)   Accesses the LTSCALE system variable

New scale factor <1.0000>: **.5**   Sets the drawing's LTSCALE to 0.5 and
                                                regenerates the drawing to apply the new
                                                scale (see fig. 5.25)

Regenerating drawing

Save the drawing.

In this drawing, an LTSCALE factor of 0.5 yields an appropriate center line.

Figure 5.25

*The center line
with an
LTSCALE of 0.5.*

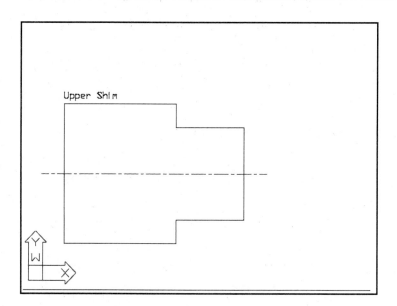

You scale linetypes for their plotted appearance, not their displayed appearance.
Setting the LTSCALE setting between one-half and one-fourth the drawing's scale
factor usually yields appropriate plotted linetypes. You also can set linetype scale per
object (see Chapter 20).

Stop   Assigning too small or too large a value to LTSCALE can cause all linetypes to
           appear continuous on-screen.

New Riders Publishing
INSIDE
SERIES

Understanding AutoCAD's Colors

A palette of 255 colors is available in AutoCAD, even if your graphics display supports fewer. The first 7 colors are standard and have both names and numbers: 1 = red, 2 = yellow, 3 = green, 4 = cyan, 5 = blue, 6 = magenta, and 7 = white. You can enter the color by name or number in the Color input box in the Select Color dialog box. Other colors are designated by numbers. You also can enter a color from the Select Color dialog box by clicking on the color patch. If your display supports fewer than 256 colors, the unsupported colors appear gray in the dialog box. You still can choose these unsupported colors; however, they appear in shades of gray. Assigning unsupported colors to layers in this manner still enables you to assign plotter pens to these colors. You also can use plotter pens to designate textures or other special effects when you export AutoCAD drawings to other graphics programs.

Renaming Layers

As you develop or adopt a structured layer naming scheme, you might want to rename layers on older drawings so that they comply compliance with your new scheme. You also might need to rename a layer due to a misspelling, or to make the name more descriptive, or because of layers in drawings received from others.

You can conveniently rename layers using the Rena<u>me</u> button in the Layer Control dialog box. You use this method in the following exercise as you rename the CENTER and DIMS layers in your LAYERS drawing.

Using the Layer Control Dialog Box To Rename Layers

Continue from the previous exercise.

`Command:` *Choose* Data, Layers	Opens the Layer Control dialog box
Select CENTER *in the* La<u>y</u>er Name *list box*	Selects the layer to rename and displays CENTER in the input box
Click to the right of the word CENTER *in the input box and type* **LINE**	Changes CENTER to CENTERLINE in the input box
Choose Rena<u>me</u>	Renames the layer in the La<u>y</u>er Name list box
Click on DIMS *in the* La<u>y</u>er Name *list box*	Selects DIMS, but grays out the Rena<u>me</u> button because two layers are selected
Click on CENTERLINE *in the* La<u>y</u>er Name *list box*	Deselects CENTERLINE and displays DIMS in the input box

continues

5

continued

Double-click on DIMS *in the input box and type* **DIMENSIONS**	Replaces DIMS with DIMENSIONS in the input box
Choose Rename	Renames the layer in the Layer Name list box
Choose OK	Closes the Layer Control dialog box and saves the new names

Save the drawing.

You also can rename layers by choosing Data, Rename, which issues the DDRENAME command and opens the Rename dialog box. You also can use the RENAME command at the Command: prompt to rename named items. Both of these commands are discussed in the section "Renaming Layers with the DDRENAME Command," later in this chapter.

Controlling Layer Status

Although assigning an adequate number of layers to your drawing is an effective way to help organize your work, a large number of layers visible at one time can lead to confusion and actually decrease efficiency, particularly if you have created a large number of layers and your drawing is complex. AutoCAD provides a number of ways to control the visibility and behavior of layers. A layer can be characterized by six states, or conditions, that affect layer visibility and behavior: on or off, frozen or thawed, and locked or unlocked. These states affect layers in the following combinations:

◆ **On, thawed, and unlocked.** Objects are visible, selectable, and require regeneration time.

◆ **Off and thawed.** Objects are invisible, not selectable, and require regeneration time.

◆ **Frozen.** Objects are invisible, not selectable, and do not require regeneration time.

AutoCAD regenerates a drawing in several circumstances, including certain viewing operations (see Chapters 9 and 10), text style and block redefinitions (see Chapters 13 and 16), and changing linetype scale. When you altered the LTSCALE for your LAYERS drawing earlier in this chapter, for example, AutoCAD automatically regenerated the drawing to display the change. AutoCAD automatically regenerates a drawing under many other circumstances.

New Riders Publishing
INSIDE SERIES

Regeneration can take a noticeable amount of time—especially with large drawings. Freezing layers can speed up regeneration because AutoCAD ignores the objects on a frozen layer during regeneration. Freezing a layer also renders the objects on that layer invisible.

Turn off a layer to suppress display of its objects in a crowded area of the drawing. Freeze layers when you want their objects to be invisible and do not want them to participate in regenerations. Lock layers when you want their objects to be visible for reference but do not want their objects to be selectable.

Even though the objects on a locked layer are not selectable for editing, you can use these objects as references and as object snap points. You learn about object snap points in Chapter 6.

Turning Layers Off and On

Turning a layer off or on controls the visibility of the objects on that layer. You might want to turn layers off that contain objects that are not relevant to your current work. You also might want to turn certain layers off for plotting purposes. You might not need or want a layer that contains annotations or material schedules, for example, on some plots.

In the following exercise, you use the Layer Control dialog box to turn layers on and off.

Turning Layers On and Off

Continue from the previous exercise.

Command: Data, Layer	Issues the DDLMODES command and opens theLayer Control dialog
Select the TEXT *layer*	Selects and highlights the TEXT layer
Choose the O__ff__ *button*	Changes the State of the TEXT layer to off and displays Warning: Current layer is off
Click on the TEXT *layer*	Deselects the TEXT layer
Click on the CENTERLINE *layer*	Selects and highlights the CENTERLINE layer
Choose the __C__urrent *button*	Sets the CENTERLINE layer current

continues

5

continued

Choose OK	Closes the Layer Control dialog and updates the display

The text "Upper Shim" is not visible. The TEXT layer has been turned off. CENTERLINE is now the current layer.

Command: (Enter)	Repeats the DDLMODES command

The TEXT layer shows a dot rather than On in the State column because you turned it off in the preceding steps.

Select CENTERLINE *in the* L<u>a</u>yer Name *list box*	Selects and highlights the layer name
Choose the O<u>f</u>f *button*	Removes On from the State column

Notice the Warning in the lower-left corner of the dialog box: Current layer is off. (see fig. 5.26).

Choose OK	Closes the dialog box and saves the change

AutoCAD displays another warning box. Choose OK. CENTERLINE still is the current layer but is set to off.

Command: **L**	Issues the LINE command
From point: **7,2**	Specifies the beginning point for the line
To point: **10,3**	Specifies the next point for the line
To point:	Ends the LINE command

The line you just drew is not visible. The current layer is turned off.

Command: *Choose* Data, Layer	Opens the Layer Control dialog box

Both the TEXT and CENTERLINE layers are turned off and CENTERLINE is current.

Select the CENTERLINE *and* TEXT *layers*	Selects and highlights both layers
Choose the O<u>n</u> *button*	Changes the state for the two selected layers to On
Deselect the CENTERLINE *and* TEXT *layers, then select the* OBJECT *layer*	Unhighlights the CENTERLINE and TEXT layers, then selects and highlights the OBJECT layer

Choose the Current *button*	Sets the current layer to be the OBJECT layer
Choose the OK *button*	Closes the Layer Control dialog box and updates the display

The line you drew is now visible because the CENTERLINE layer is now on (see fig. 5.27). OBJECT, the new current layer, appears on the status line.

`Command:` *Choose* Modify, Erase	Issues the ERASE command
`Command: _erase`	
`Select objects:` Pick the newest line	Highlights the line
Press Enter	Completes the object selection and erases the line

Save the drawing.

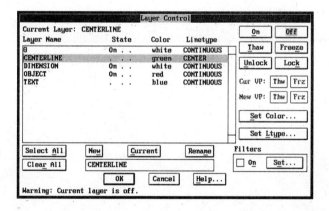

Figure 5.26

The Layer Control dialog box with a warning message.

The preceding exercise demonstrated how to turn multiple layers off and on. It also showed the effect of turning off the current layer, a practice that AutoCAD discourages with warnings. You can draw with the current layer turned off, but be careful, the objects you draw will not be visible.

Freezing and Thawing Layers

Freezing a layer makes objects on the layer invisible and exempt from screen regenerations. By freezing layers that you do not need to refer to, you can continue your work for an extended period of time.

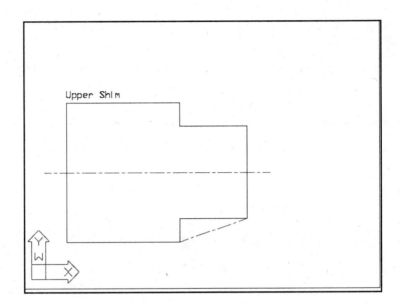

Figure 5.27

The LAYER drawing with a second CENTERLINE line.

When a frozen layer is thawed, AutoCAD performs a regeneration to update the objects on the formerly frozen layer. You cannot freeze the current layer.

In the following exercise, you demonstrate that you cannot freeze the current layer. You then freeze and thaw the TEXT layer.

Freezing and Thawing Layers

Continue from the preceding exercise with the OBJECT layer current.

`Command:` *Choose* Data, Layers	Opens the Layer Control dialog box
Notice `Current Layer: OBJECT` at the top of the dialog box.	
Select OBJECT *in the* Layer Name *list box*	Selects the layer to modify
Choose Freeze	Displays `Cannot freeze the current layer.` at the bottom of the dialog box
Click on OBJECT, *then* TEXT *in the* Layer Name *list box*	Deselects OBJECT and selects TEXT as the layer to modify
Choose Freeze	Sets the State to frozen and displays an *F* in the State column (see fig. 5.28)

New Riders Publishing

INSIDE SERIES

Choose OK	Closes the Layer Control dialog box and saves the setting

The text on the TEXT layer, *Upper Shim,* is not visible. Next, you thaw the TEXT layer.

Command: **(Enter)**	Repeats the DDLMODES command
Select the TEXT *layer in the* Layer Name *list box*	Selects and highlights the layer
Choose the Thaw *button*	Removes the F from the State column of the Layer Name list box
Choose OK	Closes the Layer Control dialog and updates the display

A regeneration has taken place, because you changed a layer's state from Frozen to Thawed.

Save the drawing.

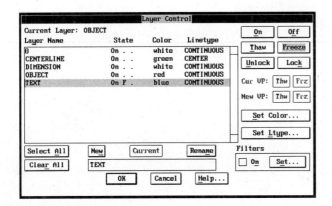

Figure 5.28

Freezing the TEXT layer.

Locking Layers

Locking a layer prevents you from editing any of the objects on the locked layer, but keeps the objects visible for reference. You also can make a locked layer current and add objects to it, and you can apply object snap modes to objects on a locked layer.

In the following exercise, you add objects to the Upper Shim in your LAYERS drawing while you investigate how locked layers work.

Locking and Unlocking Layers

Continue from the preceding exercise.

First, use any of the methods you have used so far in this chapter to make certain that all layers are on, thawed, and unlocked, and that the OBJECT layer is current.

Command: *Choose* Data, Layer	Opens the Layer Control dialog box
Select the OBJECT *layer in the* Layer Name *list box*	Selects and highlights the OBJECT layer
Choose the Lock button	Sets the state of layer OBJECT to locked, denoted by the L in the State column
Choose OK	Closes the Layer Control dialog box
Choose Modify, Erase	Issues the ERASE command
Command: _erase	
Select objects: **ALL** (Enter)	Specifies the ALL option to select all objects in the drawing
10 found	
8 were on a locked layer.	Reports objects on locked layer; these will be ignored by the ERASE command
Select objects: (Enter)	Erases the two objects not on a locked layer
Command: **OOPS** (Enter)	Restores the objects deleted by the ERASE command

The objects on the locked layer were ignored by the ERASE command.

Use the following steps to unlock the layer.

Command: *Choose* Data, Layers	Issues the DDLMODES command and opens the Layer Control dialog box

An *L* appears in the State column for the OBJECT layer in the Layer Name list box (see fig. 5.29).

Select OBJECT *in the* Layer Name *list box, then choose* Unlock	Unlocks the layer and removes the *L* from the State column

New Riders Publishing
INSIDE
SERIES

Choose OK	Closes the Layer Control dialog box and saves the changes

Save the drawing.

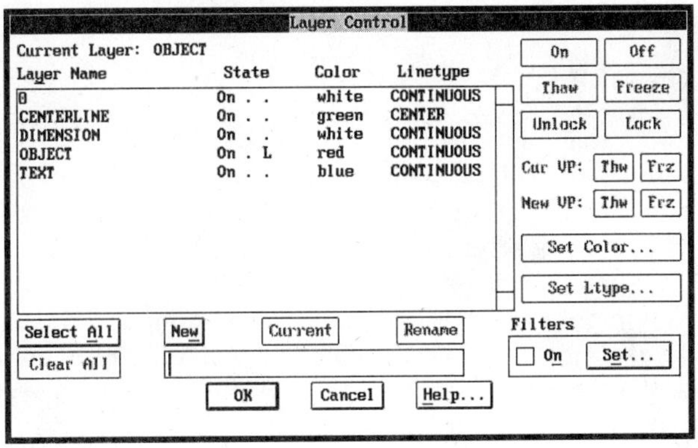

Figure 5.29

Unlocking a layer in the Layer Control dialog box.

Using the LAYER Command

Although the Layer Control dialog box provides complete control of AutoCAD's layers and usually is easier to use, you also can use the LAYER command available from the command line.

The LAYER command displays the following prompt:

```
?/Make/Set/New/ON/OFF/Color/Ltype/Freeze/Thaw/LOck/Unlock
```

The ? option displays a list of all current layers, their current state, and their color and linetype. You can filter this listing with the ? and * wild cards. The Make option creates a new layer and sets it current. The Set (current), New, ON, OFF, Color, Ltype, Freeze, Thaw, LOck, and Unlock options behave as they do in the Layer Control dialog box. These functions are described earlier in this chapter in the section "Layer Control Dialog Box Options."

'LAYER. The 'LAYER command provides layer control (except for paper space functions) from the Command: prompt, enabling you to create new layers, select the current layer, turn layers on and off, freeze and thaw layers, lock and unlock layers, list defined layers, and set the color and linetype for specified layers. The LAYER command is available only at the Command: prompt.

5

Tip   The Make option of the LAYER command is handy for quickly creating new layers. Minimally, you have to specify a name for the new layer you make. It then sets the new layer current and you can begin drawing on it. Later, you can go back and address the color, linetype, and visibility of your new layer.

Selecting Groups of Layers

When you work in a drawing that has a large number of layers, the Filters facility available in the Layer Control dialog box enables you to narrow the list of displayed layers by selectively filtering smaller groups of layers that share a common trait or property. You can filter layers using several criteria. You might, for example, want to have only layers sharing a common state, such as all locked layers, listed to globally change their state. Or, you might want to list all layers by a common characteristic of their name, such as all layers beginning with the characters "TXT-." By combining a well-planned layer naming scheme with AutoCAD's layer filter feature, you can perform operations on groups of layers easily and quickly.

Filtering Layers by State

When you work with layers, you often want to group layers by state. That is, you might want to thaw some or all frozen layers; you might want to list all of the layers currently turned off; or you might want to group all currently locked layers before you unlock any. Filtering layer names by state is an effective way to manage a large number of layers in a drawing in which you change layer states frequently.

In the following exercise you open the CHAP05A drawing, which represents a site plan for an imaginary office complex. Although the drawing is not complete, it does have 22 layers. By using your knowledge of the operation of the Layer Control dialog box and applying layer filters, you continue to learn how to make your work with layers more efficient. To open the drawing, use the prototype drawing option of the Create Drawing File dialog box that you learned earlier in the chapter.

Filtering Layers

Begin a new drawing named CHAP05A, using the SITE drawing from the IA Disk as a prototype drawing.

`Command:` *Choose* Data, Layers   Opens the Layer Control dialog box

Using the scroll bar, scroll through the Layer Name list box to familiarize yourself with the layer names and their states, colors, and linetypes. Some layers are frozen. In this exercise, you make a filter to list only these layers.

Choose S<u>e</u>t *in the* Filters *section*	Opens the Set Layer Filters dialog box (see fig. 5.30)

All of the visibility settings input boxes read "Both." In the case of <u>O</u>n/Off, this means that layers set to on or off are included. Therefore, you can include only layers that are on, only layers that are off, or layers that are both (on or off).

Click on Both *next to* <u>F</u>reeze/Thaw	Opens the Freeze/Thaw drop-down list
Select Frozen	Specifies that frozen layer names will be displayed
Choose OK	Closes the Set Layer Filters dialog box and checks the O<u>n</u> box in the Filters section

As shown in figure 5.31, only the layers that are frozen now appear in the La<u>y</u>er Name list box.

Click on the O<u>n</u> *check box in the* Filters *section to remove the X*	Removes the layer name filter and displays all layers in the La<u>y</u>er Name list box
Click on the O<u>n</u> *check box to restore the filter*	Reinstates the filter and displays the previously defined filtered list again

Stay in the Layer Control dialog box for the next exercise.

Set Layer Filters

On/Off:	Both
Freeze/Thaw:	Both
Lock/Unlock:	Both
Current Vport:	Both
New Vports:	Both
Layer Names:	*
Colors:	*
Ltypes:	*

Reset

OK	Cancel	Help...

Figure 5.30

The Set Layer Filters dialog box.

5

Tip You can use Alt keys to select the drop-down list boxes in the Set Layer Filters dialog box. When selected, you can set a filter by typing its first letter, such as F for frozen or B for both. Typing **O** alternates the filter on and off.

Figure 5.31

Filtering Layer names by state.

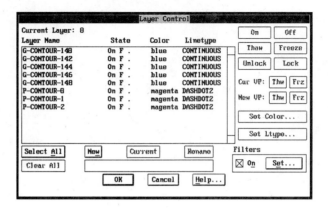

Filtering Layers by Layer Name

In addition to filtering layer names by state, you also can limit the number of layers that appear in the Layer Name list box by displaying only layers that have a common characteristic in their names. A structured layer naming scheme can be beneficial because it enables you to control logical groups of related layers. For example, you could freeze all of your existing construction layers and thaw all of your proposed construction layers.

In the following exercise, you continue from the preceding exercise, further filtering the layer list that you isolated by layer state by applying an additional filter based on layer name. In the filtered list you defined in the preceding exercise, all the layer names begin with the letter *P* or *G*. In the following exercise, you define a filter to thaw all the layers beginning with *G* and leave the *P* layers frozen.

Filtering Layers by Layer Name

Continue from the preceding exercise, with the Layer Control dialog box open and your filtered layer name list displayed (refer to figure 5.31).

Choose Set *in the* Filter *section*	Opens the Set Layer Filters dialog box (refer to figure 5.30)
Double-click in the Layer Names *input box and type* **G***	Defines a filter that matches all layer names that begin with G followed by any other characters
Choose OK	Closes the Set Layer Filters dialog box and displays a new filter layer name list (see fig. 5.32)

Your filter is further refined by filtering only frozen layers that begin with the letter G. Next, you select these layers and thaw them.

Choose Select **A**ll	Selects and highlights all displayed layers in the Layer Name list box
Choose **T**haw	Thaws selected layers and displays the message No layers match filter criteria. in the lower-left corner of the dialog box

When you thawed all the filtered layer names, no names met the filter criteria any longer, so the Layer Name list box is now empty.

Choose O**n** *in the Filters section to remove the X from the check box*	Deactivates the filter and displays all layers in the Layer Name list box

The F is removed from the State column of the G* layers.

Choose OK	Closes the Layer Control dialog box and regenerates the drawing with the filtered layers now thawed

Save the drawing.

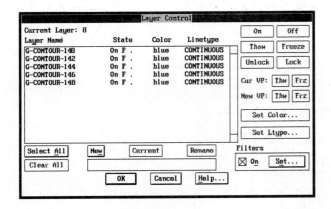

Figure 5.32

Filtering layers by name.

The thawed layers depict topographical contour lines that are now visible (see fig. 5.33).

Figure 5.33

The CHAP05A drawing with filtered layers thawed.

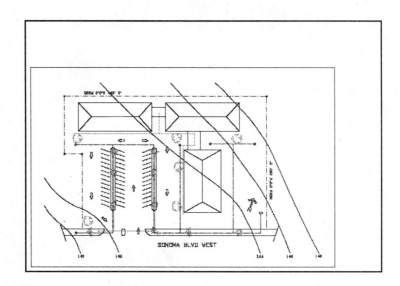

Filtering Layers by Color and Linetype

You can filter layer names based on their assigned color or linetype in a manner similar to that used in the preceding exercise. To display all layers assigned the color blue, for example, enter **blue** in the **C**olors input box of the Set Layer Filters dialog box. Entering **hidden** in the L**t**ypes input box filters all layers except those assigned the linetype HIDDEN.

Again, filter criteria are additive and you can filter for layer states, layer name characteristics, and color and linetype assignments simultaneously. For example, you can define a filter that would display only frozen layers that begin with the characters "1F-" and are assigned the color red and the linetype DASHED.

Tip   You can type multiple layer names, colors, and linetypes in the corresponding edit boxes of the Set Layer Filters dialog box by separating them with a comma. When input in this manner, the comma is interpreted as OR.

Note   Even though the Layer Control and the Set Layer Filters dialog boxes display layers names in uppercase letters, filter input data is not case-sensitive; you can enter filter criteria in uppercase or lowercase.

Filter Wild Cards

To increase the functionality of layer filters even further, you can use a number of wild-card characters in addition to the standard ? and *. You also can use these wild

New Riders Publishing
INSIDE
SERIES

cards in many other places in which AutoCAD accepts text string input, such as with the many commands that list items. The following wild cards are available:

TABLE 5.1
Available Wild Cards

Wild Card	Meaning
@	Matches any alphanumeric character.
#	Matches any number.
*	Matches any character or characters including an empty character string. You can use the asterisk anywhere in the string.
. (period)	Matches any nonalphanumeric character.
?	Matches any single character.
~ (tilde)	Matches any character except the one that follows the tilde.
[ ]	Matches any single instance of any characters enclosed between the brackets.
[~]	Matches anything except the enclosed characters.
- (hyphen)	Matches a range of characters when used within brackets, such as [5-9] to match 5, 6, 7, 8, or 9.
`	Matches the special character that follows; for example, `? matches a ? instead of using the ? as a wild card.
, (comma)	Separates wild cards, such as red,blue.

When you combine this flexibility in filtering layer names with a structured layer naming scheme, you can filter practically any set of layers using a wide variety of criteria. If you devise a standard layer naming format that you plan to utilize frequently, it might be worth the initial time and effort to consider groups of layers that you want to isolate using wild cards and establish your layer names accordingly. Do not be overwhelmed by the possibilities these wild cards afford. You probably can utilize a few of them to accomplish your filtering needs.

Renaming Layers with the DDRENAME Command

You can use wild cards effectively to edit named objects in other instances in AutoCAD. You use the DDRENAME command to rename objects in AutoCAD that are referred to by name, such as layers. You also use the DDRENAME command to rename blocks, dimension styles, linetypes, text styles, views, and user coordinate systems.

5

> **DDRENAME.** The **DDRENAME** command enables you to display the Rename dialog box, which you can use to rename blocks, layers, linetypes, text styles, dimension styles, named views, viewports, and user coordinates systems. You use this dialog box to select the object(s) by its current name and to assign the new name. You can use AutoCAD's wild cards to rename groups of objects (refer to table 5.1).
> Pull-down: *Choose* Data, Rename
> Screen: *Choose* DATA, Rename:

Rename Dialog Box Features

The DDRENAME command opens the Rename dialog box, which has the following features:

◆ **Named Objects list box.** Displays the types of objects you can rename.

◆ **Items list.** Displays the named objects, if any, that correspond to the category selected in the Named Objects list.

◆ **Old Name text box.** Specifies the object(s) to rename. Select a name from the Items list or enter a name in the Old Name text box. You can use wild cards in the Old Name text box.

In the following exercise, you use the DDRENAME command to rename some layers in the CHAP05A drawing. You use the * wild card to rename all layers that begin with the character *G* that you filtered in the preceding exercise. Assume that you want to rename these layers so that they conform to a different layering convention by replacing the *G* with *TOPO*. Using the DDRENAME command and a wild card enables you to rename these five layers in one fell swoop. You also rename another layer so that its name is more descriptive.

Using DDRENAME To Rename Layers

Continue from the preceding exercise.

Command: *Choose* Data, Rename

Issues the DDRENAME command, and opens the Rename dialog box (see fig. 5.34)

If not already highlighted, select
Layer *in the* Named Objects *list box*

Lists named objects, if any, of the selected category in the Items list box

Use the Items *list box scroll bars to display all five* G-CONTOUR-14X *layers*

Choose the <u>O</u>ld Name *input box, type* **G***, *and press Enter*	Highlights and selects all layers beginning with *G* followed by any other characters (see fig. 5.35)

Notice in the Items list box that only layers meeting the criteria of the G* filter are highlighted for renaming.

Click in the <u>R</u>ename To *input box and type* **TOPO***	Defines the new layer name prefix
Choose the <u>R</u>ename To *button*	Renames the selected layers in accordance with the wild-card specification

The renamed layers are moved to their alphabetical position at the bottom of the Items list.

Scroll to the bottom of the Items list to verify the name change. Next, you rename the layer PROP to the more descriptive name PROPLINE.

Find and choose the layer PROP *in the* Items *list*	Highlights the PROP layer name and copies it to the <u>O</u>ld Name input box
Double-click in the <u>R</u>ename To *input box and type* **PROPLINE**	Specifies the new layer name
Choose the <u>R</u>ename To *button*	Renames the layer
Choose OK	Closes the dialog box and saves changes

`Layers renamed.`

Save the drawing.

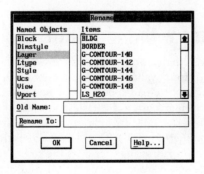

Figure 5.34

The Rename dialog box.

5

Figure 5.35

*Applying filters
with the
DDRENAME
command.*

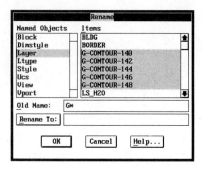

The RENAME Command

The RENAME command is available at the Command: prompt only. Unlike the
DDRENAME command and the Rename dialog box, the RENAME command does
not display a listing of current objects, nor does it enable you to rename groups of
objects with the use of wild cards. The RENAME command displays the following
prompt:

Block/Dimstyle/LAyer/LType/Style/Ucs/VIew/VPort:

You enter the option for the category of the named object you want to rename
(displayed uppercase letters for each option accepted), type the current name for the
object, press Enter, then enter the new name.

> **RENAME.** The RENAME command enables you to rename named AutoCAD items
> from the command line. AutoCAD prompts you for the old name then the new name.

Deleting Named Items with the PURGE Command

Earlier, when you set up the LAYERS drawing, you used the Select Linetype dialog
box to load all the linetype definitions available in the ACAD.LIN file at once.
Although you can use this dialog box to load specific linetypes, placing all the
linetype definitions into your drawing is often the easiest and fastest way to make a
wide variety of linetypes available, especially if you are first setting up a drawing and
do not know all the linetypes you might need. The disadvantage is that storing
unneeded linetype definitions in your drawing increases the size of the drawing,
which requires more disk storage space. You also might find your drawing populated
with unused layer definitions, especially if you create the drawing from a prototype
drawing that contains a large number of layers. In cases such as this, you can use the
PURGE command to delete named items like unused blocks, dimension and text
styles, layers, linetypes, and shapes.

> **PURGE.** The PURGE command enables you to delete unreferenced (unused) blocks, dimension styles, layers, linetypes, shapes, text styles, mline styles, and registered application IDs.
> Pull-down: *Choose* Data, Purge (Option)
> Screen: *Choose* DATA, Purge:

In the following exercise, you delete an unused layer. Although several loaded linetypes are not used in the drawing, the drawing is not yet completed. Therefore you should defer deleting linetypes until later.

Purging Unused Layers

Continue to use the drawing CHAP05A from the preceding exercise.

Command: *Choose* Data, Purge, Layers   Issues the PURGE command, Layers option
                                                                              (see fig. 5.36)

```
Command: _purge
Purge unused
Blocks/Dimstyles/LAyers/LTypes/
SHapes/STyles/APpids/
Mlinestyles/All: _la
```

In the above prompt, the menu issues the la (LAyers) option. Next, AutoCAD offers all unused layers (only one in this case) as candidates for purging from the drawing database.

Purge layer LY_CITY? <N> **Y**   Deletes the LY_CITY layer

Open the Layer Control dialog box so you can verify that the LT_CITY layer has been removed from the database.

You cannot purge an item that is referenced in any object or by any other item. If the LY_CITY layer contained a text object using the ROMANS text style, for example, neither the LY_CITY layer not the ROMANS text style could be purged. You can view items eligible for purging from several categories of named items by repeating the PURGE command and specifying different options each time. Alternatively, you can specify the All option to examine all categories in turn.

The PURGE command also is available from the command line. The prompts and mode of operation are the same as when issued from the pull-down menu; the pull-down menu adds the convenience of specifying an option as the command is issued.

5

Figure 5.36

*Issuing the
PURGE
command from
the Data pull-
down menu.*

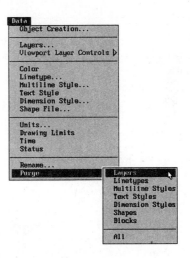

Note   Many of the categories of named items subject to the PURGE command have not been covered in this book yet. The PURGE command acts on all categories in the manner shown here.

The PURGE command is useful as a tool in setting up your AutoCAD drawing because you can use it to delete layers and other named items that might be included in prototype drawings. Prototype drawings are discussed in the section "Deleting Named Items with the PURGE Command," earlier in this chapter.

Developing a Layering Scheme

A layering scheme is easy to develop, a good layering scheme is not. You might be able to derive a suitable scheme from an existing one. The existing one might come from a partner, your professional society, a user group, or a client. Regardless, you need to understand key points.

◆ **No layering scheme is perfect.** Experience shows that few schemes exist without continuous improvements. If you believe your scheme will work for all situations, prepare for disappointment. Someone always finds a group of objects that do not seem to belong in this layer, that layer, or any other layer you provide. Too many variables that work against you are at play.

◆ **Schemes that have too many layers do not work.** Drawing is normally a situation in which a deadline is pressing. When you develop a scheme that has many layers, making sure that the object goes on the correct layer takes considerable time. Someone who works on a deadline takes shortcuts and inevitably fails to abide by the scheme, which defeats the purpose of having a scheme.

New Riders Publishing
INSIDE
SERIES

◆ **Naming schemes must be easy to remember.** A good scheme is one in which you do not have to constantly look at a list to determine upon which layer an object should be drawn. The scheme should be intuitive.

◆ **Schemes must befit the function.** A scheme should complement the drafter's needs. A scheme that works well for a plumbing contractor might not work at all for a piping contractor. If your business is a large piping contractor, your needs are different from a small piping contractor. You might find that as a part of a multi-office firm, a scheme that works for your office does not work for their office, although you all design schools.

In addition to the preceding points, keep in mind the elements of a layering scheme and the capabilities of AutoCAD. You have as many layers as you need. You can name the layers to facilitate grouping. The grouping at which you arrive should consider the relationship between color and plotted pen weights. See Chapter 25, "Sheet Composition and Plotting," for a broader discussion. You can override the default BYLAYER setting to achieve specific purposes (see the next section for a explanation of BYLAYER). For example, you might decide that setting linetypes by object reduces the number of layers you need—no need to have FLANGE-SOLID, FLANGE-CEN-TER, FLANGE-PHANTOM, and FLANGE-DASHED layers. You might decide to use layers to perform design analysis, such as arranging a first floor plan layer, a second floor plan layer, and a third floor plan layer to be sure utility chases are not passing through rooms. Your options are limitless.

Setting Color and Linetype by Object

Until now, you have created new objects that assume the color and linetype of the layer on which they were drawn. You can use the DDEMODES command to override this default method. The settings that you can use DDEMODES to make affect the subsequent creation of objects. You access the DDEMODES command from the Object Creation menu item of the Data pull-down menu, from the Ddemode: menu item of the Data screen menu, or from the Command: prompt. When you issue the command, the Object Creation Modes dialog box appears (see fig. 5.37).

5

Figure 5.37

The Object Creations Modes dialog box.

The Object Creation Modes dialog box consists of controls for the following settings:

◆ **Color button.** Activates the Select Color dialog box, which enables you to set the color for the subsequent creation of objects. You can specify the logical color assigments; BYLAYER or BYBLOCK. BYLAYER causes AutoCAD to assign the color of new objects according to the color value assigned to the current layer. BYBLOCK is explained in Chapter 16, "Basic Building Blocks for Repetitive Drawing."

◆ **Layer button.** Opens the Layer Control dialog box described earlier in this chapter. You can set the current layer and any other setting from the Layer Control dialog box. Changes you make here affect the creation of new objects.

◆ **Linetype button.** Opens the Select Linetype dialog box described earlier in this chapter. The setting you adjust here affect the creation of new objects. You also can specify the logical linetype assignments of BYLAYER or BYBLOCK.

◆ **Text Style button.** Opens the Text Style dialog box. Text styles are discussed in Chapter 13, "Annotation With Text." You can set the style that AutoCAD uses for the creation of new text objects.

◆ **Linetype Scale edit box.** You can set the value for the LTSCALE system variable here, which AutoCAD applies to new objects' linetype scales.

◆ **Elevation edit box.** Use this to set the Z value of the XY plane for new objects. Elevation is thoroughly discussed in Chapter 28, "3D Basics."

◆ **Thickness edit box.** The value you type is used to set the extrusion of new objects. This is used for 3D drawing and is discussed in Chapter 28.

The important concept introduced in the context of the DDEMODES command is that you can create objects that override the layer settings. Suppose you have a group of layers that contain the elements of a sprinkler system—the pipes and heads, the electrical system, the coverage of each head, and the text for the type of each head. As you draw on the layer that contains the text, you decide that you want a warning note to stand out from the other notes, but the layer's color plots a thin line. Do you make a new layer for the one note? In practice, you do not make a new layer for the one note, but rather, you set the color of the text note so that a heavier pen is used come plot time. The DDEMODES command provides you with this capability and more.

To demonstrate this capability, the exercise that follows adds more detail to the Upper Shim widget you drafted earlier in this chapter.

Setting Color and Linetype By Object

Open the LAYERS drawing used in the earlier exercises. Then open the Layer Control dialog box and reacquaint yourself with the layer names, colors, and linetypes. Make sure that OBJECT layer is current.

Command: *Choose* Data, Object Creation	Issues the DDEMODES command and opens the Object Creation Modes dialog box
Choose the Color *button*	Opens the Select Color dialog box

The BYLAYER is the setting in the Color edit box.

Select the dark blue color patch	Changes the color from BYLAYER to blue
Choose OK	Closes the Select Color dialog box
Choose the Linetype *button*	Opens the Select Linetype dialog box
Choose DASHED2 *from the* Loaded Linetypes *list box*	Changes the linetype from BYLAYER to DASHED2
Choose OK	Closes the Select Linetype dialog box
Choose OK	Closes the Object Creation Modes dialog box and adjusts the default settings

The current color patch on the status line is now set to blue.

Command: L (Enter)	Issues the LINE command
LINE From Point: 2,7 (Enter)	Specifies the start point
To point: 7,7 (Enter)(Enter)	Specifies the endpoint and draws the line
Command:(Enter)	Repeats the LINE command
LINE From Point: 2,3 (Enter)	Specifies the start point
To point: 7,3 (Enter)(Enter)	Specifies the endpoint and draws the line

continues

5

continued

You have drawn two blue dashed lines on layer OBJECT (see fig. 5.38). Open the Layer Control dialog box and inspect the color and linetype settings for the OBJECT layer. You can see that they remain unaffected by the settings you made in the Object Creation Modes dialog box. Continue the exercise to learn how to discontinue the override settings.

`Command:` *Choose* Data, Object Creation	Issues the DDEMODES command and displays the Object Creation Modes dialog box
Choose the Color *button*	Opens the Select Color dialog box
Choose the BYLAYER *button, then* OK	Sets the color back to BYLAYER (color patch is red, corresponding to the color of the current layer), then closes the Select Color dialog box
Choose the Linetype *button*	Opens the Select Linetype dialog box
Select the BYLAYER *picture from the list box, then choose* OK	Changes the linetype from DASHED2 to Loaded Linetypes BYLAYER and closes the dialog box
Choose OK	Closes the Object Creation Modes dialog box and restablishes the default color and linetype as BYLAYER

The current color patch on the status line is now the color (red) of the current OBJECT layer.

Save your drawing.

This exercise shows that you can draw the objects that you must draw on a specific layer without the layer's color or linetype settings affecting the object. Generally, using BYLAYER settings for color and linetype control is preferable. As you become more advanced, you may find occasion to not use BYLAYER, but only as special technique.

New Riders Publishing
INSIDE SERIES

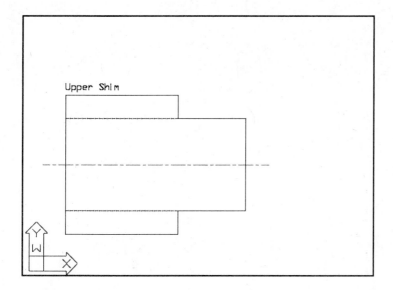

Figure 5.38

The lines drawn on the OBJECT layer.

Proper drawing setup is one of the keys to putting AutoCAD to work for you. Understanding and applying the concepts of drawing units, limits, and scale factors make working in real-world units intuitive and natural. Preparing a set of appropriate layers with their associated colors and linetypes makes your drawing both efficient and easy to work with. The next step is to learn how to take advantage of the precision AutoCAD places at your fingertips. In the following chapter you learn how to use object snap points, the grid, and the snap grid, as well as other commands and methods you need to construct a dimensionally accurate detail drawing.

5

Drawing Accurately

In Chapter 3, "Using the Drawing Editor," you learn about the way AutoCAD handles typed coordinate input and using absolute and relative coordinates to specify the position of objects in your drawings. In this chapter, you learn about the drawing aids that AutoCAD provides, which enable you to use the pointing device to input points in your drawing. This chapter covers the following topics:

◆ Using a reference grid to locate points

◆ Using snap to control points

◆ Using ortho mode to control angles

◆ Adjusting the UCS coordinate system in 2D

◆ Using object snap to snap points to existing objects

◆ Using point filters to align points

◆ Using construction lines to place objects

◆ Using the tablet to digitize points

Many of the tasks that arise in a CAD drawing are the same tasks you encounter in traditional manual drafting. The solutions in CAD, however, are often quite different and almost always consume less time. In this chapter's opening exercise, for example, you handle the construction of an arc tangent to two circles in a manner analogous to the method you might use in manual drafting. The difference lies not in the geometric principles, but rather, in the tools and methods. In the following exercise, you use some of AutoCAD's accuracy tools to solve a common geometric construction.

Quick 5¢ Tour

Using the prototype drawing method covered in Chapter 5, "Setting Up a CAD Drawing," use the NEW command to begin a new drawing named CHAP06, using the CIRCLES drawing from the IA\DWGS directory as a prototype. Use the Layer Control dialog box to set the layer OBJECT_LINES to on and current.

First, you draw a line that connects the centers of the circles.

Command: *Choose* Draw, Line	Issues the LINE command
_line From point: **CEN** (Enter)	Specifies the CENter object snap
_of *Pick the right circle*	Snaps to the center of the circle for the beginning of the line
To point: **CEN** (Enter)	Specifies the CENter object snap
_of *Pick the left circle*	Snaps and draws a line to the center of the second circle
To point: (Enter)	Ends the LINE command

In the next step, you realign AutoCAD's coordinate system by defining a User Coordinate System aligned with the line you just drew.

Command: **UCS** (Enter)	Issues the UCS command
Origin/ZAxis/3point/OBject/View /X/Y/Z/Prev/Restore/Save/ Del/?/<World>: **OB** (Enter)	Specifies the OBject option
Select object to align UCS: *Pick anywhere on the left side of the line*	Realigns the User Coordinate System with the line

The UCS icon's X axis is parallel to the line that connects the two circles (see fig. 6.1). Next, you construct a line that is perpendicular to the connecting line you just drew.

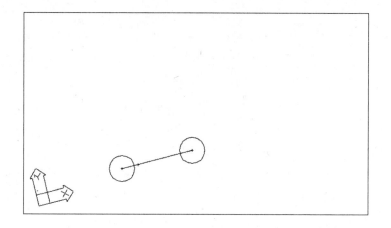

Figure 6.1

The UCS aligned with an object.

Command: **L** (Enter)	Invokes the LINE command
LINE From point: **MID** (Enter)	Specifies the MIDpoint object snap
of *Pick anywhere on the line*	Snaps to the midpoint of the line
To point: **@8<90** (Enter)	Specifies a line 8 units long at an angle of 90° to the current UCS
To point: **CEN** (Enter)	Specifies the CENter object snap
of *Pick the left circle*	
To point: (Enter)	Ends the LINE command

You now have the geometric construction lines required to draw an arc tangent to the two circles.

Command: *Choose* Draw, Arc *then* Center,Start,End	Issues the ARC command with the Center option and prompts for the center point
_arc Center/<Start point>: _c Center: **INT** (Enter)	Specifies the INTersection object snap

In the next step, make sure that the intersection falls within the box at the cursor.

of *Pick the intersection at* ① *(see fig. 6.2)*	Sets the center of the arc

6

Figure 6.2

Using geometry to construct and place an arc.

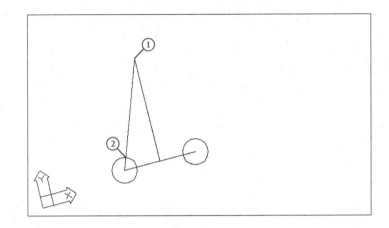

Start point: **INT** (Enter)	Specifies the INTersection object snap
of *Pick the point at the intersection of the line and the circle at* ②	Specifies the beginning of the arc
Angle/Length of chord/<End point>: **CEN** (Enter)	Specifies the CENter object snap
of *Pick the right circle*	Snaps the end of the arc to align with the angle from the arc's center to the circle's center

Now you can erase the three construction lines and return the UCS to the default World Coordinate System.

Command: *Pick each of the three lines you drew*	Highlights each line as it is selected
Command: *Choose* Modify, Erase	Issues the ERASE command and erases the highlighted lines
Command: **UCS** (Enter)	Issues the UCS command
Origin/ZAxis/3point/OBject/View /X/Y/Z/Prev/Restore/Save/ Del/?/<World>: (Enter)	Accepts the default option and returns the UCS to the World Coordinate System

Your drawing now should resemble figure 6.3.

Save the drawing.

New Riders Publishing
INSIDE
SERIES

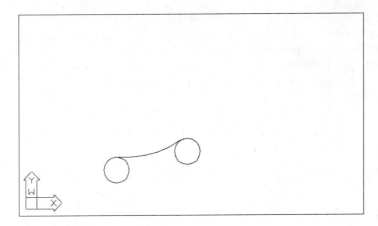

Figure 6.3

*An arc tangent to
two circles.*

In the preceding exercise you used two of AutoCAD's most powerful and flexible tools for making your drafting tasks easy to carry out and highly accurate. Object snaps enable you to precisely identify drawing geometry, such as midpoints and intersections. The capability to rotate and align the User Coordinate System (UCS) with drawing objects speeds tasks that are related to nonstandard X and Y axis orientations. Object snaps and the User Coordinate System are but two of the input accuracy control methods you learn about in this chapter.

Understanding Drawing Accuracy

The first step of creating an accurate drawing is to locate your drawing points. One way to do this is to enter coordinates from the keyboard. However, although you might know some of the coordinate values to start a drawing, you rarely know all of them as you continue a drawing. Besides, entering coordinates at the keyboard is grueling and tedious, and predisposes you to typing errors.

As you saw in Chapter 3, "The Basics of Drawing in AutoCAD," picking points accurately by simply moving the cursor and picking is difficult. AutoCAD provides several methods for controlling the movement of your cursor so that you can accurately select pick points. One method involves using the grid and snap functions; another involves using object snap. Still other methods involve using ortho mode, XYZ point filters, and two types of construction lines. All of these tools, used separately or in combination, enable you to take advantage of AutoCAD's capability to store data in a highly accurate drawing database.

AutoCAD's coordinate system is accurate to at least 14 significant digits. If you pick your drawing points without some form of control, however, AutoCAD must translate the cursor's pixel position into the current drawing units. That is, AutoCAD must approximate the coordinates you actually want. If you try to pick the point

6

2.375,4.625, for example, you might get such numbers as 2.3754132183649,4.6248359103856. If you set the coordinate display to show only three decimal places, these numbers appear to be rounded accurately, but AutoCAD stores them internally with their true precision—with several more decimal places of "inaccuracy." Even if you use the grid or other objects to visually align the crosshairs, you seldom can locate the point you want with complete accuracy.

Picking Accurate Points

Using your cursor to pick a point accurately is difficult. As you move the cursor, the digital readout of your coordinates should display the crosshair cursor's current X,Y position. If the coordinates are not active, you can turn on your coordinate display by pressing Ctrl+D or F6.

Try the following exercise to see how accurately you can pick your drawing points. To test your pick point, use the coordinate display and the ID command issued by the Assist, Inquiry, Locate Point pull-down menu item. Try to pick at coordinates 3.25,5. The ID command simply displays the picked point's coordinates.

Using ID Command To Test Pick Points

Continue from the preceding Quick 5¢ Tour and make sure that your coordinate display is turned on by pressing Ctrl+D, if necessary.

Command: *Choose* View, Zoom, All	Zooms drawing to its 11×17 limits
Command: **ZOOM** (Enter)	Initiates the ZOOM command
All/Center/Dynamic/Extents/Left/ Previous/Vmax/Window/<Scale(X/XP)>: .75 (Enter)	Zooms out to display a larger area
Command: *Choose* Assist, Inquiry, Locate Point	Issues the ID command
Command: '_id Point: *Try to pick the point* 3.2500,5.0000, *using the coordinate display to guide the crosshairs*	
X = 3.2456 Y = 4.9710 Z = 0.0000	Your point might differ, but you can't pick it exactly.

Save the drawing.

The ID command shows the X,Y,Z position of your pick point. Try the same thing with a few more points. Accurately picking the point you want is nearly impossible. AutoCAD's accuracy actually works against you here. If you don't use some form of control over the points you pick, a drawing can contain many inaccurate points.

ID. The ID command prompts for a point and returns the X,Y,Z coordinates of the point you specify. AutoCAD sets the system variable LASTPOINT to the point ID returns. You can reference the last point by entering @ when AutoCAD next prompts you for a point. Normally, the Z coordinate represents the current elevation. However, if you use object snap to snap to an object, the Z coordinate is the same as the selected feature of the object.
Pull-down: *Choose* Assist, Inquiry, Locate Point
Screen: *Choose* ASSIST, INQUIRY, ID:

Note   The ID command and the coordinates display might claim that the point is at exactly 3.2500,5.0000. When you change your units to six or eight decimal places, however, you see that AutoCAD really is rounding off an inaccurate point.

Although the coordinate display shows coordinates with the full precision set using the UNITS command, instructions to pick points at specific coordinates generally are abbreviated in exercises in this book. Leading and trailing zeros, and feet and inch marks that are not required for point entry might be omitted. For example, rather than "pick at 0'-3.25",0'-5.00"," you might be instructed to "pick at 3.25",5.00"" or to "pick or enter **3.25,5**."

Introducing AutoCAD's Drawing Accuracy Tools

As a first step to achieve some degree of drawing accuracy, you can use the grid or other objects to control your pick points. AutoCAD's *grid* serves as a visible template that shows the location of a set of points. The grid is a visual aid. Although it does help you see the location of points, it does not round the input points to accurate locations. *Snap,* on the other hand, is an invisible grid template that does control the points that you use your cursor to select. If you set snap to 0.5, you can select only points that fall exactly on 0.5-unit increments.

Grid and snap work well together and you easily can control many pick points by coordinating AutoCAD's grid and snap capabilities. If you set them equally, you can select only the visual grid points. If you set the snap increments to half the grid increments, you can select only the grid points or points that lie halfway between the grid points. Snap enables you to control the accuracy of your point selection; grid enables you to keep track visually of the points to which you snap.

6

A special form of snap, called *object snap,* enables you to accurately locate geometric points on objects or in relation to objects. Object snaps are among the most powerful tools available in AutoCAD for accurately defining relationships in your drawing. Object snaps are discussed in detail later in the section, "Examining Object Snaps."

Using Drawing Aids

You can control drawing accuracy by using the GRID, SNAP, and ORTHO commands and by using the Drawing Aids dialog box (see fig. 6.4). You access this dialog box by choosing the Drawing Aids item in the Options pull-down menu. You also can use function keys to turn grid, snap, and ortho on and off. Use the F7 key for grid, F8 for ortho, and F9 for snap. In addition, you can use the key combinations of Ctrl+B and Ctrl+G to turn snap and grid on and off, respectively. You can use Ctrl+O to turn ortho mode off and on.

Figure 6.4

The Drawing Aids dialog box.

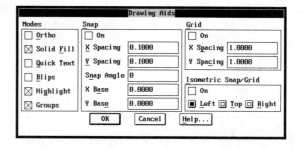

The Drawing Aids dialog box is organized into four groups, Modes, **S**nap, **G**rid, and **I**sometric Snap/Grid. The following list identifies the settings you can access in this dialog box.

In the Modes group:

◆ **O**rtho. When checked, turns on ortho mode.

◆ **Solid Fill.** When checked, turns on the solid filling of solids, wide polylines, and donuts.

◆ **Q**uick Text. When checked, text objects appear as rectangles.

◆ **B**lips. When checked, sets the BLIPMODE variable to 1 and marker blips appear on the display.

New Riders Publishing
INSIDE
SERIES

◆ **Highlight.** When checked, highlights selected objects.

◆ **Groups.** When checked, enables the selection of a group when you select only one group object within the group.

In the Snap group:

◆ **On.** When checked, snap mode is active.

◆ **X Spacing.** Sets the horizontal spacing increment of the snap mode.

◆ **Y Spacing.** Sets the vertical spacing increment of the snap mode.

◆ **Snap Angle.** Sets the angle used to rotate the snap mode grid.

◆ **X Base.** Sets the horizontal coordinate for the origin of the snap mode grid.

◆ **Y Base.** Sets the vertical coordinate for the origin of the snap mode grid.

In the Grid group:

◆ **On.** When checked, grid mode is on and the grid displayed.

◆ **X Spacing.** Sets the horizontal spacing increment for the grid.

◆ **Y Spacing.** Sets the vertical spacing increment for the grid.

In the Isometric Snap/Grid group:

◆ **On.** When checked, the snap mode and grid mode appears isometric format.

◆ **Left, Top, Right.** When one is selected, the isometric grid axis is switched to a left side, top, or right side view.

To investigate these drawing aids, you continue working in the CHAP06 drawing.

Using the Grid Display

To get accurate points, you first set up a grid template that helps you see points on-screen. A grid serves the same purpose as the lines or dots on a sheet of graph paper—it provides a frame of reference as you draw. AutoCAD's grid consists of an array of points that appear on-screen but are not part of the drawing file.

6

You use the GRID command or the Drawing Aids dialog box to set up a grid.

'DDRMODES. The 'DDRMODES command opens the Drawing Aids dialog box, which enables you to control the ortho, snap, and grid settings. It also enables you to control the FILLMODE, PICKSTYLE (for groups), BLIPMODE, and QTEXTMODE system variables.

Pull-down: *Choose* Options, Drawing Aids...
Screen: *Choose* OPTIONS, DDrmode:

In the next exercise, you set up a one-half-inch grid. When you try to pick a grid point, you see that grid points do not actually control input points.

Using GRID To Set Up a Grid

Continue using the CHAP06 drawing from the previous exercise.

Command: *Choose* Options, Drawing Aids	Displays the Drawing Aids dialog box (refer to figure 6.4)
In the **G**rid *group, put a check in the* On *box*	Turns on the grid
Double-click in the X S**p**acing *edit box, enter* **0.5**, *then choose* OK	Sets X to 0.5 units and, when you press Enter, defaults Y to equal X, then displays the 0.5 grid (see fig. 6.5)

Now use the ID command, as before, to try to pick a point that lies exactly on one of the grid marks.

Command: **ID** (Enter)	
Point: *Try to pick the point* 7.00,5.50	Displays the point you picked
X = 7.0170 Y = 5.5547 Z = 0.0000	Your point might differ, but you still can't pick it exactly.

Save the drawing.

This shows that the point is not precisely located on the grid. Using the grid, however, can give you a "target" and a better sense of the distances represented by the graphics window display. In addition, the grid gives you a visual indication of the drawing's limits because the extent of the grid is defined by the current limits when the UCS is set to the default.

New Riders Publishing
INSIDE
SERIES

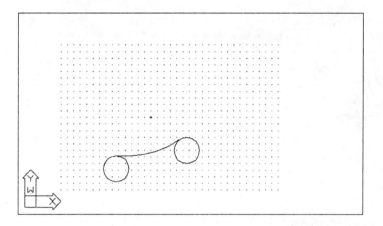

Figure 6.5

Adding a grid to the CHAP06 drawing.

Tip   When you set the grid spacing, avoid setting a grid that is too dense (one whose points are too close together). A too-dense grid obscures the drawing and causes slow screen redrawing.

You have several options when you set up a grid, and you are not limited to a square grid. Sometimes a grid that has an aspect ratio other than 1:1 might be useful. Figure 6.6, for example, shows a grid aspects ratio of 2X:1Y (the actual settings for the grid shown are X = 1.0, Y = 0.5).

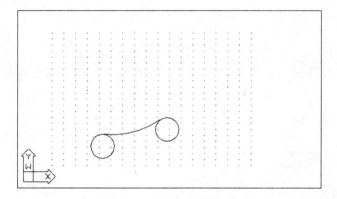

Figure 6.6

A grid that has a 2X:1Y aspect ratio.

6

> **'GRID.** The 'GRID command enables you to control the visibility and spacing of a visual reference grid of dots. You also can set the grid without using the GRID command, by using the Drawing Aids dialog box. You can turn the grid on and off by pressing Ctrl+G or F7.
> Pull-down: *Choose* Assist, Grid
> Screen: *Choose* ASSIST, Grid:

You can set the grid by using the Drawing Aids dialog box or the GRID command.

```
Grid spacing(X) or ON/OFF/Snap/Aspect <0.0000>:
```

Grid Command Options

The GRID command has the following options:

◆ **Grid spacing(X).** Sets the X,Y grid increment and activates it. If you enter **0**, AutoCAD makes the grid equal to the snap spacing, automatically adjusting when snap changes. If you enter a number followed by an X, AutoCAD sets the grid to the current snap increment multiplied by the specified number.

◆ **ON.** Makes the grid visible.

◆ **OFF.** Makes the grid invisible.

◆ **Snap.** Sets the grid increment to equal to the current snap increment (when you enter **0** or **1X** for the grid spacing, for example), except that it does not automatically change the grid as snap changes.

◆ **Aspect.** Enables you to set different increments for grid's horizontal and vertical dots.

Although the grid helps indicate how much you are zoomed into or out of the drawing and, along with the coordinate display, helps you find points, it provides no direct capability to pick points accurately. For that you need snap.

Setting Snap Points

The SNAP command enables you to set the smallest increment that AutoCAD can recognize when you move the cursor. If you turn snap on and set a spacing value, your cursor moves with an incremental motion; it jumps from snap point to snap point instead of tracking smoothly. Setting snap is equivalent to setting your smallest drawing increment. When you set snap spacing values, all drawing pick points are forced to multiples of your snap values.

A good practice is to set your snap to some fraction of your grid spacing. AutoCAD normally aligns snap points with the grid. As you draw, you can easily eyeball points that are one-quarter to one-fifth of the distance between grid points. In the following exercise, you set the snap increment to 0.25 units, or one-half of your grid spacing.

Using SNAP To Set Snap Points

Continue using the CHAP06 drawing from the preceding exercise with the grid on.

Command: *Choose* Options, Drawing Aids	Activates the Drawing Aids dialog box
In the S̲nap *group, choose the* On *check box*	Turns on snap
Double-click in the X̲ Spacing *box,* *enter* **.25**, *and choose* OK	Sets the X spacing and defaults the Y spacing to equal the X spacing
Try to move the cursor around	The crosshairs now jump to the snap increments

Save the drawing.

Notice that Snap now appears beside the layer name on the AutoCAD status line, indicating that snap mode is on, and that the coordinates display accurately in 0.25-unit increments. Think of snap as an invisible grid that constrains the points you can pick using the pointing device. Snap adds some real control to picking points. Combined with the grid and coordinate display, snap permits you to achieve a degree of accuracy comparable to that offered by manually typing coordinates.

 Note You can turn snap on and off by pressing Ctrl+B or F9. You must turn off snap before you can pick a point not on the snap grid.

Using Snap Points To Draw Objects

After you set a snap value, you can draw accurately in the CHAP06 drawing, as long as the points you need to pick are on snap points. The coordinate display shows the correct crosshairs position as it rounds the X,Y values to 0.25 units in your CHAP06 drawing.

Figure 6.7 shows a dimensioned drawing of a guide bar. At this stage of its design, all the points that you need to draw its outline fall upon convenient snap points. In the following exercise, you use the dimensions from figure 6.7 to duplicate the guide bar in your CHAP06 drawing aided by the current snap and grid settings.

6

Figure 6.7

Dimensioned guide bar drawing.

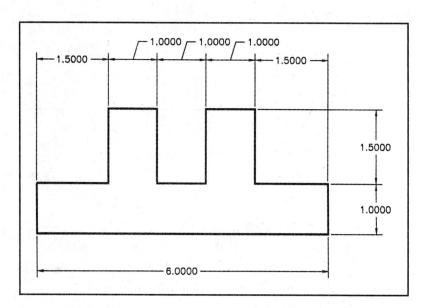

In the following exercise, you use the grid and coordinate display to help pick the points. As you pick the points, notice that the cursor snaps to the snap increments.

Using SNAP To Draw a Guide Bar

Continue to use the CHAP06 drawing. Use the Layer Control dialog box to set the layer OBJECT_LINES to off, then select the layer CONSTRUCT to make it current.

Command: *Choose* View, Zoom, All	Issues the ZOOM command and the All option and zooms drawing to limits
Command: *Choose* Draw, Line	Issues the LINE command
_line From point: *Using the grid and coordinate display, pick point 3.0000,3.0000*	Starts the outline at 3,3, which is the guide's lower-left corner

As you move the cursor, the coordinate's display now should display distance and angle from the last picked point. If necessary, press F6 one or more times in the coordinate display box to cycle the display to this mode.

To point: *Drag the line to 6.0000<0, as indicated by the coordinate display, and pick*	Draws the base line of the figure and prompts for the next point
To point: *Pick coordinates 1.0000<90*	Draws the right end line

New Riders Publishing

INSIDE
SERIES

Use the dimensions from figure 6.7 and the coordinate display, and proceed counterclockwise to each point, defining the outline of the guide. Enter **C** instead of picking the last point. C draws the closing line segment and ends the LINE command.

Save the drawing.

After you finish the exercise, your figure should look like the guide bar outline in figure 6.8.

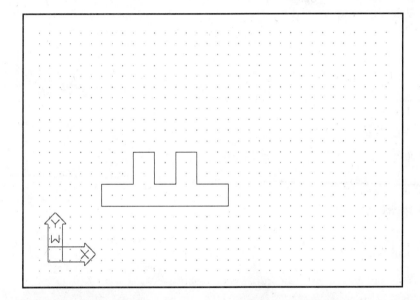

Figure 6.8

The completed guide bar drawing.

As you work with grid and snap, you might need to adjust the grid and snap settings as you zoom so that you can work in greater detail. If you start with a snap at 1 unit and a grid at 5 units on a whole drawing, you might want to reset your snap to quarter-units and your grid to 1 unit when you zoom in to work on a portion of the drawing. Before the grid can be a useful visual aid, you need to be able to see it in a context appropriate to the distances with which you work.

You can coordinate your snap and grid spacing to suit your needs. Make it a practice to set your grid and snap, and then leave them on most of the time. If you do not pick your drawing points with snap (or object snap) turned on, your drawings will not be accurate.

6

Tip In most real drawings, points often do not so conveniently coincide with small increments, so you usually must use the other accuracy methods covered in this chapter. However, keeping snap on for consistent placements, annotation, and dimensions is usually a good idea.

'SNAP. The 'SNAP command enables you to turn the snap grid on and off and set its spacing. It also provides options for setting the aspect ratio (different X and Y values) of the snap grid, rotating the snap grid about a base point, and switching to an isometric snap grid. You also use the Drawing Aids dialog box to set the snap grid.
Pull-down: *Choose* Assist, Snap (only ON or OFF option)
Screen: *Choose* ASSIST, Snap:

SNAP Command Options

The SNAP command offers the following options:

```
Snap spacing or ON/OFF/Aspect/Rotate/Style <current>:
```

◆ **Snap spacing.** Prompts you for a value to set the snap increment and to turn on snap.

◆ **ON.** Turns on snap.

◆ **OFF.** Turns off snap. This is the initial default setting.

◆ **Aspect.** Prompts for different horizontal (X) and vertical (Y) snap increments (except in isometric mode; see the description of the Style option).

◆ **Rotate.** Prompts you to specify an angle and a base point around which you can rotate the snap grid (and crosshairs).

◆ **Style.** Prompts for Standard or Isometric style. Standard sets the normal (default) snap style. See Chapter 27, "2D Isometric Drawings," for Isometric snap use.

Note The UCS command provides you with a better way to rotate snap, the grid, and the entire coordinate system. Rotating the snap grid does not affect the orientation of the drawing's X and Y axes. You use the User Coordinate System (UCS) to control axis orientation, discussed later in the section, "Creating Your Own Coordinate System."

New Riders Publishing
INSIDE
SERIES

Using Ortho Mode as a Special Snap

If you draw horizontal and vertical lines, you can constrain your cursor movements by turning on ortho mode. Ortho stands for *orthogonal* and limits cursor movement to right angles from the last point. When ortho is on, any lines you enter with the cursor are aligned with the snap axes. In effect, you can draw only at right angles. To turn on ortho mode, press Ctrl+O or F8. You also can use the ORTHO command or the Drawing Aids dialog box.

Ortho mode is easy to use and helpful any time you draw sets of horizontal and vertical lines. When you turn on ortho mode, `<Ortho on>` appears at the `Command:` prompt and Ortho displays beside the layer name on the AutoCAD status line. The rubber-band cursor that normally trails from the last point to the intersection of the crosshairs now goes from the last point to the nearest perpendicular point on the X or Y crosshairs.

In the following exercise, you make another copy of the guide bar shown in figure 6.7. As you pick points, notice that you do not actually need to place the cursor on the correct X and Y coordinates. The cursor need only align along one axis, X or Y, depending on the location of the next point.

Using ORTHO To Draw the Guide Bar

Continue from the previous exercise.

`Command:` *Choose* Draw, Line	Issues the LINE command
`_line From point:` *Using the coordinate display, pick the point* 3.0000,6.0000	Begins the line and rubber bands freely at any angle as you move the cursor
`To point:` *Press F8*	Turns on ortho mode and constrains the rubber-band line to 90° increments as you move the cursor
`To point:` `<Ortho on>` *Pick the point* 6.0000<0	Rubber-bands orthogonally and draws the line

Refer again to figure 6.7 for the guide bar dimensions and finish drawing the outline, picking points in a counterclockwise direction.

Your drawing now should resemble figure 6.9. Next, you use the U command to delete the second outline.

continues

6

continued

Command: *Choose* Assist, Undo	Issues the U command, deletes the lines of the second outline, and turns off ortho mode

Save the drawing.

Figure 6.9

A second guide bar drawn using snap and ortho modes.

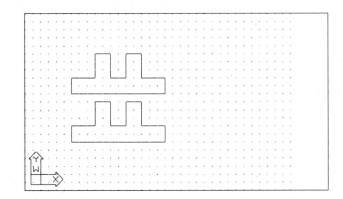

 Note   If you turn on ortho mode during the LINE command, undoing the line also undoes ortho.

You can quickly lay out many drawings—or portions of drawings—in the manner you used in the preceding exercise. If you use ortho in combination with snap, creating geometry that is parallel to the axes is simple, fast, and accurate.

 Note   In subsequent exercises, you should be aware of a few practices. The instructions usually simply say to turn ortho, snap, or grid on or off. You can use any of the various methods discussed in this chapter to accomplish these tasks. This arrangement avoids the confusion that you can experience if your current settings do not match the settings indicated in the exercise. Also, unless relative coordinates are specified or the @ sign is used in exercise instructions, coordinates in exercises refer to absolute coordinates.

Creating Your Own Coordinate System

Other than in the opening exercise, you have been using AutoCAD's default coordinate system, the *World Coordinate System (WCS)*, in this chapter. You can use the UCS command to create your own coordinate system. The UCS command enables you to position the 0,0 origin anywhere so that you can work relative to any point you want. You also can rotate the X, Y (and even Z) axes to any angle in 2D or 3D space (see fig. 6.10). Although the User Coordinate System (UCS) was developed to use in 3D drawings, it also can be useful for 2D drawings.

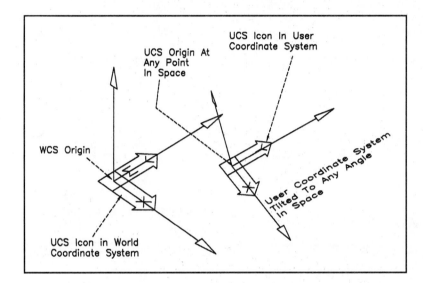

Figure 6.10

The World Coordinate System and a User Coordinate System.

One of the most useful applications of the UCS in 2D drafting is aligning a UCS with a feature or object in a drawing, analogous to rotating the drafting machine used in manual drafting. In this chapter's opening exercise, you defined a new UCS that aligned with a construction line in the drawing, which enabled you to easily draw a line perpendicular to the construction line that was not parallel to the X or Y axis of the WCS. Take another look at the Quick 5¢ Tour, then try another UCS method in the following exercise.

The following exercise demonstrates how to align the UCS with any two 2D points. To rotate the UCS in 2D, you rotate it about the Z axis.

Aligning the UCS with an Object

Continue from the preceding exercise in the CHAP06 drawing. Turn off the CONSTRUC-TION layer, then turn on the OBJECT_LINES layer and make it current. The CHAP06 drawing should again resemble the earlier figure 6.3. The *W* in the UCS icon indicates the default World Coordinate System is current.

continues

6

continued

Command: *Choose* View, Set UCS, Z Axis Rotate	Issues the UCS command and the Z option

`_ucs`

```
Origin/ZAxis/3point/OBject
/View/X/Y/Z/Prev/Restore/
Save/Del/?/<World>: _z
```

`Rotation angle about Z axis <0>:` **CEN** (Enter)	Specifies CENter object snap
of *Pick the left circle*	Snaps the angle's start point to the circle's center
`Second point:` **CEN** (Enter)	Specifies CENter object snap
of *Pick the right circle*	Snaps the angle to the circle's center and aligns the UCS icon with the circles

The *W* is not displayed in the UCS icon, because the UCS is no longer the World Coordinate System (see fig. 6.11).

Next, you make a copy of the two circles and the arc four units above the current objects and perpendicular to the X axis.

Command: *Pick each of the two circles and the arc*	Selects and highlights the three objects
Command: *Choose* Construct, Copy	Issues the COPY command and prompts for objects

`_copy 3 found`

`Select objects:`

`<Base point or displacement> /Multiple:` *Pick any point*	Sets a base point
`Second point of displacement:` *Pick point at* 4.0000<90 *on coordinate display*	Specifies a displacement of 4 units at 90° in the current UCS and copies the objects

Save the drawing.

The objects are copied 4 units above and perpendicular to the X axis of the UCS, as shown in figure 6.12.

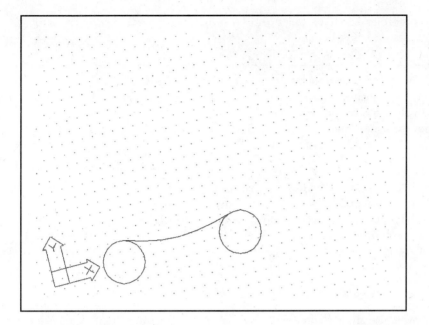

Figure 6.11

The User Coordinate System aligned to angle between circles.

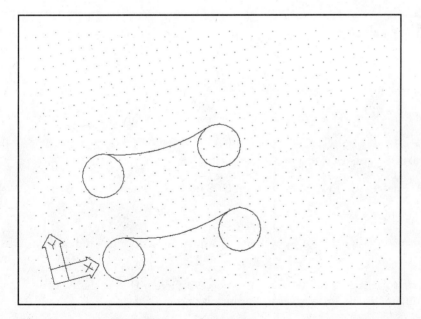

Figure 6.12

Objects in the new User Coordinate System.

In a short editing operation, like copying a few objects as you did in the previous exercise, you might not have to align newly defined UCSs with the graphics window.

However, for more extended editing operations, you probably will want to do so for visual orientation or convenience.

UCS. The UCS command enables you to set up and manage User Coordinate Systems. It provides a range of options, including setting the origin, specifying rotation about any axis, aligning with objects, saving, listing, and restoring.
Pull-down menu: *Choose* View, Set UCS
Screen menu: *Choose* VIEW, UCS:

In the preceding exercises, the UCS commands that you used are found as items on the Options and View pull-down menus. With the exception of the Follow item in the Options, UCS menu, these items actually issue the UCS or UCSICON commands with appropriate preset options. Both the UCS and UCSICON commands also are available at the Command: prompt. If you use the UCS command rather than the pull-down menu items, you see that the command has several options.

```
Origin/ZAxis/3point/OBject/View/X/Y/Z/Prev/Restore/Save/Del/?/<World>:
```

You learn how to use all these options in Part Seven, which covers 3D. You can use the following subset of options with most two-dimensional applications:

◆ **Origin.** Specifies a new X,Y,Z origin point relative to the current origin.

◆ **OBject.** Defines a new coordinate system based on a selected object.

◆ **Z.** Rotates the X,Y axes around the Z axis.

◆ **Prev.** Steps back to the previous UCS. You can back up through as many as 10 previously used UCSs.

◆ **Restore.** Sets the UCS to a previously saved UCS.

◆ **Save.** Enables you to store the current UCS under a name, which you specify.

◆ **Del.** Removes a saved UCS.

◆ **?.** Lists previously saved UCSs by name to display point of origin and orientation.

◆ **<World>.** This option is the default. It sets the current UCS to the World Coordinate System. Press Enter to accept this option.

In the following exercise, you use the PLAN and UCSICON commands to change your UCS view to a plan view and verify the origin of the UCS by moving the UCS icon to the current UCS origin. The PLAN command is covered in Chapter 28, "3D Basics."

Controlling the UCS, Original, Icon, and Plan View

Continue from the preceding exercise.

Command: *Choose* View, 3D Viewpoint Presets, Plan View, Current	Issues the PLAN command with the Current UCS option
Command: _plan \<Current UCS\>/Ucs/World: Regenerating drawing.	Changes to plan view and regenerates the drawing

Next, you use the UCSICON command to set the UCS icon at the origin of the current UCS.

Command: *Choose* Options, UCS, Icon Origin	Issues UCSICON command with ORigin option
_UCSicon ON/OFF/All/Noorigin/ORigin\<on\>: _OR	Sets the UCS icon at the current origin

You see no effect; the UCS is rotated, but still at the WCS 0,0 origin. If there isn't room for the entire UCS icon at the origin, AutoCAD ignores the UCSICON ON setting. Try relocating the UCS to the lower-left circle's center to see the UCS icon indicate the origin.

Command: *Choose* View, Set UCS, Origin	Issues UCS command with Origin option
_ucs Origin/ZAxis/3point/OBject/View/X/Y/Z/ Prev/Restore/Save/Del/?/\<World\>: _o	
Origin point \<0,0,0\>: **CEN** (Enter)	
of *Pick the lower left circle*	Sets the 0,0 origin and UCS Icon at the circle's center (see fig. 6.13)
Command: *Choose* View, 3D Viewpoint Presets, Plan View, World	Returns to plan view in the WCS orientation
Command: *Choose* View, Set UCS, World	Returns UCS to WCS origin and alignment

Save the drawing.

The UCS icon no longer fits at the origin.

6

Figure 6.13

The UCS icon placed at the current UCS origin.

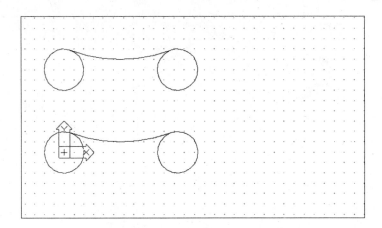

Stop Be careful using the PLAN command. It is easy to set the plan to the current UCS since <Current UCS> is the default option. Although the plan view of the current UCS might resemble the view using world coordinates, it is not. By the time you realize your mistake, it will be difficult to correct. Remember to use the UCS icon as your compass — the letter W indicates the world coordinate system.

You often might want to offset the origin of the UCS in 2D drawings to facilitate some aspect of editing or to carry out certain dimensioning tasks. Figure 6.14, for example, shows the guide bar that you drew earlier with the aid of the snap, grid, and ortho modes. Holes have been added to the guide bar in this figure and dimensioned from the lower-left corner of the bar. Adding these features is quick and accurate if you first define a UCS that has its origin at this corner.

Figure 6.14

The guide bar with holes added.

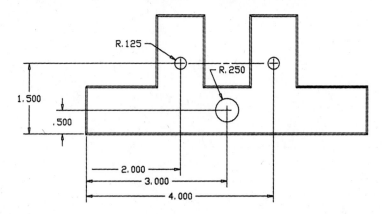

New Riders Publishing
INSIDE
SERIES

> **UCSICON.** The UCSICON command enables you to control the visibility and placement of the UCS Icon.
> Pull-down: *Choose* Options, UCS
> Screen: *Choose* OPTIONS, UCSicon:

UCSICON Command Options

The UCSICON command has the following options that control the display of the UCS icon:

```
ON/OFF/All/Noorigin/ORigin <ON>:
```

◆ **ON.** Turns on the UCS icon.

◆ **OFF.** Turns off the UCS icon.

◆ **All.** Displays the UCS icon in all multiple viewports.

◆ **Noorigin.** Displays the UCS icon at the lower-left corner of the viewports.

◆ **ORigin.** Displays the UCS icon at the 0,0 origin of the current UCS, unless the origin is out of the drawing area or too close to the edge for the icon to fit. The icon then appears at the lower-left corner.

Figure 6.15 shows the UCS icon. The X arrow points along the positive X axis, and the Y arrow points along the positive Y axis. The *W* on the Y arrow indicates that the current UCS is the default World Coordinate System (WCS). The + on the UCS icon indicates that the icon is placed at the origin of the current UCS.

The first two items shown in the Options, UCS menu in figure 6.16 correspond to options of the UCSICON command. Each of the items can be checked or unchecked as indicated by a check mark that precedes the menu item label. The Icon item corresponds to the ON/OFF options of the UCSICON command. A check mark preceding Icon corresponds to the ON option—the UCS icon is displayed. The absence of a check mark corresponds to the OFF option—the UCS icon is not displayed. The Icon Origin corresponds to the Noorigin/ORigin options of the UCSICON command. A check mark corresponds to the ORigin option; the absence of a check mark corresponds to the Noorigin option. The Follow item corresponds to the UCSFOLLOW system variable. If you set this variable to a value of 1, AutoCAD automatically generates a plan view when you change from one UCS to another. A check mark corresponds to a value of 1.

6

Figure 6.15

*The UCS icon at
the WCS origin.*

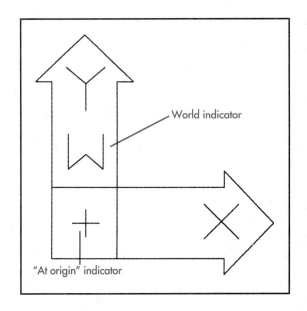

World indicator

"At origin" indicator

Figure 6.16

*The Options,
UCS menu.*

The power and flexibility that the User Coordinate System gives you is essential when you work in 3D drawings. The preceding few exercises in this chapter, however, show that being able to manipulate the orientation and origin of UCSs that you define enables you to work much more efficiently in many 2D drawings as well. To increase your ability to take advantage of the accuracy offered by electronic drafting, you next learn about object snaps.

Examining Object Snaps

Snap is useful if you want to draw an element that fits the snap increments exactly—such as the guide bar you drew earlier in this chapter. If you need to align new points, lines, and other objects with geometric points on entities you already have drawn, however, you need an easier, more accurate method.

Understanding Object Snap

As your drawing becomes more complex, points on circles, arcs, and intersections of angled lines no longer fall directly on snap points. AutoCAD offers a set of tools called *object snaps* to help you accurately pick such points. To understand object snaps, remember that objects such as lines have middle points and endpoints, and circles have center, quadrant, and tangent points. When you draw, you often need to attach lines to these points.

AutoCAD's *object snaps* are geometric filters that enable you to select your drawing-attachment points. If, for example, you want to draw to an intersection of two lines, you can set the object snap to filter for intersections, and then pick a point close to the intersection. The point snaps to the precise intersection of the lines. Although it takes a little time to get used to setting object snaps, it is the best way to maintain geometrically accurate drawings.

AutoCAD's OSNAP command and Running Object Snap dialog box (DDOSNAP command) enable you to set running object snap modes that calculate the attachment points you need to make accurate drawings. You also can enter object snap modes directly at any prompt that accepts point input. You tell AutoCAD which object snap attachment mode(s) to use—such as INT for INTersection or TAN for TANgent. After you pick a point or enter coordinates near the geometric point you want, AutoCAD snaps to the precise attachment point. Figure 6.17 shows all the filter modes you can use for picking attachment points on objects or for picking points in relation to objects. The OSNAP and DDOSNAP commands are discussed later in the section, "Using Running Object Snaps."

Using Overrides versus Running Modes

You can use object snaps as single-pick override filters at point-input prompts, or you can set a running object snap mode that is active until you turn it off. The OSNAP command sets running object snaps and is described in the "Using Running Object Snaps" section, later in this chapter.

6

Figure 6.17

*Object targets and
the points they
pick.*

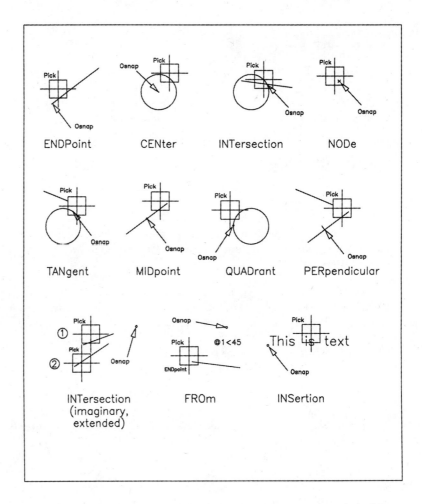

You can select object snaps as overrides (which interrupt any current running object snap) using several methods, as follows:

◆ **Screen menu.** The screen menu provides access to both the OSNAP command and object snap overrides. Click on the line of asterisks beneath the standard AutoCAD screen menu's title.

◆ **Pull-down menu.** The Assist, Object Snap menu provides access to both the OSNAP command and object snap overrides (see fig. 6.18).

New Riders Publishing
INSIDE
SERIES

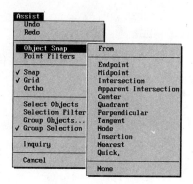

Figure 6.18

*The Object Snap
pull-down menu.*

◆ **Pop-up menu.** The cursor pop-up menu (see fig. 6.19) appears at the current
cursor position. It provides access to the object snap overrides. You can display
it by Shift-clicking the Enter button.

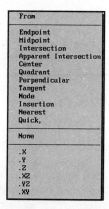

Figure 6.19

*The object snap
pop-up menu.*

◆ **Keyboard.** Each object snap mode has a unique abbreviation that you can
enter on the command line. This abbreviation is indicated by uppercase letters
in the following list.

Note When you choose object snap menu items from the pull-down menu while no
command is active, they issue the OSNAP command and the selected mode to set a
running object snap. When you choose object snap menu items during a command,
they issue only the selected mode as an object snap override. This feature, however,
is disabled during AutoLISP or ADS-define commands, such as those in third-party
application, or the AutoCAD RECTANG command. When you choose them during
AutoLISP or ADS-defined commands, they cause an error.

6

Whether invoked in the running or override mode, AutoCAD has 13 object snap modes. The following list gives a description of each.

Note In the following list, "line" includes polyline and spline segments, and floating viewports borders.

◆ **ENDPoint.** Snaps to the nearest endpoint of a line or arc.

◆ **MIDpoint.** When you use the MIDpoint option, AutoCAD snaps to the midpoint of a line or arc.

◆ **INTersection.** Snaps to the nearest intersection of any combination of two lines, arcs, or circles. If you select only one object with the first pick, AutoCAD prompts for a second object and the snap is to the real or projected intersection of the two objects.

◆ **APParent Intersection.** This option is identical to INTersection, except that it also snaps to the apparent intersection from the current viewpoint of two objects that might or might not actually intersect in 3D space. In 2D, the APParent Intersection and INTersection modes are equivalent. APParent Intersection is covered in Part Seven.

◆ **CENter.** Snaps to the center of an arc or circle.

◆ **QUAdrant.** Snaps to the closest 0-, 90-, 180-, or 270-degree point on an arc or circle.

◆ **PERpendicular.** Snaps to a point on a line, arc, or circle that, for the entity you pick, would form a perpendicular (normal) line from the last point to the entity you pick. The resulting point need not even be on the entity.

◆ **TANgent.** Snaps to a point on an arc, spline, or circle that forms a tangent to the picked arc, spline, or circle from the last point.

◆ **NODe.** Snaps to a point entity.

◆ **INSertion.** Snaps to the origin of text, attributes, and symbols (block or shape) that have been inserted into the drawing file. (You learn more about blocks, shapes, and attributes in Chapter 17, "Block Structure, Editing, Organization, and Management.")

◆ **NEArest.** Snaps to the nearest point on an entity; generally an endpoint, normal, or perpendicular point.

- **QUIck.** Forces all other object snap options to find the first potential target quickly. The point QUIck chooses is not necessarily the closest target. QUIck finds the potential point that is on the most recently qualified object in the target box.

- **NONe.** Removes or overrides any running object snap.

On the object snap menus, you will see a menu item called From. From does not appear as an option to the OSNAP command, nor does it appear in the Running Object Snap dialog box, because it technically is not an object snap mode. However, the FROm modifier is often used in conjunction with object snaps. The FROm modifier prompts for a base point to use when you specify for the next supplied point with relative coordinates. It establishes a temporary reference point similar to the last point used by the @ prefix for input. Dragging is disabled during FROm.

 Stop Although you can activate the ENDPoint object snap mode by entering **END**, use the four-letter abbreviation ENDP to help avoid accidentally issuing the END command and thereby ending your AutoCAD session.

You can use running object snaps or overrides. You use object snaps as overrides that apply to the next pick only. Running object snaps are described later in the section, "Using Running Object Snaps."

Using Object Snaps as Single-Pick Filters

To learn how overrides work, you draw the dimensioned transfer arm shown in figure 6.20. Refer to this illustration to obtain distances and other dimension data as you duplicate the part in the following exercise.

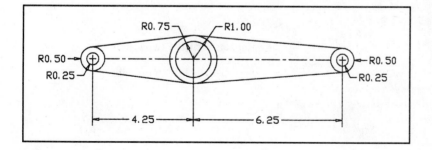

Figure 6.20

A dimensioned transfer arm.

6

As you might in conventional drafting, begin with the large circle in the center of the arm and work from there. Follow the steps of the exercise as you use object snaps and the FROm modifier to accurately create and place objects. In this exercise, you issue object snaps using the pull-down menu and the pop-up menu (refer to figures 6.18 and 6.19, respectively).

Using Object Snap Overrides

Begin a new drawing named CHAP06A, using the OBJECTS drawing from the IAD Disk as a prototype. The grid is set to .25, and snap is off. The X in the middle of the drawing is a point object.

Command: *Choose* Draw, Circle *then* Center, Radius	Issues the CIRCLE command
Command: _circle 3P/2P/TTR/ <Center point>: *Choose* Assist, Object Snap, Node	Specifies the NODe object snap override
_node of *Pick the point object at* ① *(see fig. 6.21)*	Snaps to the point object
Diameter/<Radius>: **1** (Enter)	Draws a circle with 1-inch radius
Command: (Enter)	Repeats the CIRCLE command
CIRCLE 3P/2P/TTR/<Center point>: *Press Shift and Right-Click and choose* Center	Displays the pop-up menu and specifies the CENter object snap override
_center of *Pick anywhere on the circle*	Snaps to the center of the circle
Diameter/<Radius> <1.00>: **.75** (Enter)	Draws a second circle concentric to the first
Command: (Enter)	Repeats the CIRCLE command
CIRCLE 3P/2P/TTR/<Center point>: *Press Shift and Right-Click to choose the pop-up menu and choose* From	Specifies the FROm modifier
_from Base point: *Press Shift and Right-Click* Center	Specifies the CENter object snap

New Riders Publishing
INSIDE
SERIES

`_center` of *Pick anywhere on either circle*   Establishes the FROm base reference point

Next, you supply the distance, as a relative coordinate, from the center concentric circles to the center of the left circles.

`<Offset>:` **@4.25<180** (Enter)

`Diameter/<Radius> <0.75>:` **.5** (Enter)   Draws the circle

`Command:` (Enter)   Repeats the CIRCLE command

`Command: _circle 3P/2P/TTR/`
`<Center point>:` *Press Shift and Right-click to display the pop-up menu and choose* Center   Specifies the CENter object snap

`_center` of *Pick on the left circle at* ②

`Diameter/<Radius> <0.50>:` **.25** (Enter)   Draws the smaller concentric circle

Repeat the steps used to draw the two left circles to draw the two right circles. Use a relative coordinate of 6.25<0 to draw the first circle. Your drawing now should resemble figure 6.22.

Save the drawing.

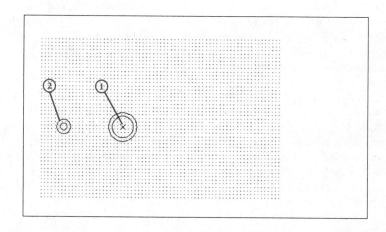

Figure 6.21

Placing the circles for the transfer arm.

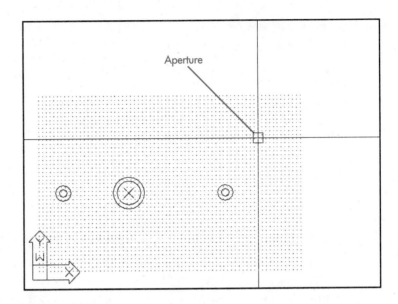

Figure 6.22

The Object Snap aperture.

Aperture

Note   If an object snap override pick fails to find an object to which to snap, AutoCAD warns you, reprompts for the point, and discards the object snap setting.

To begin this drawing, you used the NODe object snap to place the center of the first circle. Point objects are covered in the "Drawing Points" section, later in this chapter. The NODe object snap finds the location of point objects exclusively. You can take advantage of the unique nature of point objects and the NODe object snap by placing points in drawings that are, or will become, crowded with other objects. Later, you can use the NODe object snap to snap to the point when other objects present too many potential candidates for other snap modes.

You next used the FROm modifier to set a base point to place accurately two circles at either end of the arm. FROm is actually not an object snap but usually is used in combination with an object snap specification followed by a relative coordinate, as in the previous exercise. The relative coordinate specifies an offset distance and angle from the point set by the FROm modifier and its associated object snap mode. In the previous exercise, knowing that the circles were inline and knowing their relative distances from each other enabled you to place the end circles as relative distances from the center of the center circles.

Setting the Aperture To Control Object Finding

A dense drawing can have several attachment points close to your pick point. If you want to snap to an intersection, AutoCAD might find one, but it might not find the

intersection you want. Object snap uses a *aperture box* to identify the points it considers to be candidates for the snap attachment (refer to figure 6.22). The aperture serves as an electronic bull's-eye that homes in on object snap points. AutoCAD uses the object snap only for objects that fall in the aperture. You should size your aperture according to the entities you select, the drawing's zoom settings, the display resolution, and the drawing density.

In the following exercise, you set the aperture to control the size of the crosshairs' bull's-eye. You can adjust the aperture by using a slider bar in the Running Object Snap dialog box. The other features of this dialog box are discussed in the "Using Running Object Snaps" section of this chapter. To access this dialog box, use the DDOSNAP command or choose Running Object Snap from the Options pull-down menu. You also can use the APERTURE command to adjust the size of the aperture.

Adjusting the Aperture Size with DDOSNAP

Continue to use drawing CHAP06A from the preceding exercise.

Command: *Choose* Options, Running Object Snap	Issues the DDOSNAP command and initiates the Running Object Snap dialog box (see fig. 6.23)

`'_ddosnap`

In the Aperture Size section, adjust the size of the aperture box to match figure 6.23 by clicking on the left slider bar arrow (about 5 times).

Command: *Choose* OK	Closes the dialog box and saves the setting

---

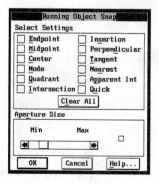

Figure 6.23

The Running Object Snap dialog box.

6

> **'APERTURE.** The 'APERTURE command sets the size of the object snap aperture box, or *target box*. This command is available at the command line. The command prompts for the height of the aperture box in pixels. Acceptable values range from 1 to 50.

Tip A smaller aperture size enables you to better pick specific objects to which to snap, but requires a slow, steady hand. A larger aperture makes it harder to select specific objects, but requires less coordination. You can issue the APERTURE and DDOSNAP commands transparently, so you can adjust the aperture size while being prompted for an object snap pick point. To avoid confusion with the pick box, you should usually make the aperture a couple of pixels larger than the pick box.

In the following exercise, you continue to use the transfer arm drawing as you learn about some other object snap modes.

Continuing with Object Snap Modes

Continue to use in CHAP06A drawing from the previous exercise. Turn off grid mode to provide a clearer working screen. In this exercise, you use the pop-up menu to issue object snaps.

Command: *Choose* Draw, Line	Issues the LINE command
_line From point: *Choose* Tangent *from the pop-up menu*	Specifies the TANgent object snap
_tan to *Pick near* ① *in figure 6.24*	Selects the circle but doesn't display rubber-band line yet
To point: *Choose* Tangent *from the pop-up menu*	Specifies TANgent object snap
_tan to *Pick near* ②	Draws a line tangent to the two circles
To point: *Press Enter twice*	Ends the LINE command, then reissues it
_line From point: *Choose* Tangent *from the pop-up menu*	Specifies the TANgent object snap
_tan to *Pick near* ②	Select the circle but doesn't display rubber-band line yet

New Riders Publishing
INSIDE SERIES

To point: *Choose* Tangent *from the pop-up menu*	Specifies TANgent object snap
_tan to *Pick near* ③	Draws a line tangent to the two circles
To point: *Press Enter twice*	Ends the LINE command, then repeats it

Continue to draw lines tangent to the bottom of the circles, picking near points ④, ⑤, and ⑥. Your drawing should resemble figure 6.24 after you finish.

Save the drawing.

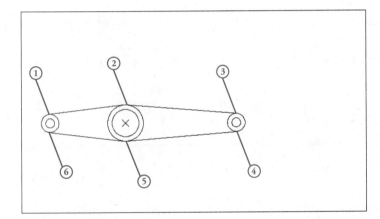

Figure 6.24

The completed transfer arm outline.

Tip If you accidentally specify the wrong object snap override mode, pick a point in a clear area. AutoCAD issues an error message and repeats its prompt for a point. You then can specify the correct mode.

When you use the TANgent object snap, the first end, the second end, or both ends of a line can snap to a tangent point. When you specify the TANgent object snap at the From point: prompt, no rubber-band line appears until you pick the next point, at the To point: prompt. The PERpendicular object snap exhibits the same behavior. Circles and arcs often have more than one point that qualifies for a TANgent or PERpendicular snap. In such cases, AutoCAD uses the point on the side closest to the pick point.

6

In the following exercise, you learn about the INSertion and NEArest object snap modes. In this exercise, you issue the object snap modes from the keyboard. You need enter only the uppercase letters (the first three) from the keyboard.

The INSertion and NEArest Object snap Modes

Continue from the preceding exercise and turn on layer TEXT.

Command: *Choose* Draw, Line	Issues the LINE command
`_line From point:` **INS** (Enter)	Specifies the INSertion object snap
`_ins of` *Pick on the text object* Centered	Snaps to insertion point of the center-justified text object
`To point:` **INS** (Enter)	Specifies the INSertion object snap
`_ins of` *Pick on the text object* Left	Snaps to the insertion point of the left-justified text object
`To point:` (Enter)	Ends the LINE command
`Command:` **U** (Enter)	Issues the U command and deletes the line
`LINE`	
`Command:` *Choose* Modify, Move	Issues the MOVE command
`_move`	
`Select objects:` *Pick anywhere on the arrow*	
`1 found`	
`Select objects:` (Enter)	End the Select objects prompts
`Base point or displacement:` **INS** (Enter)	Specifies the INSertion object snap
`_ins of` *Pick anywhere on the arrow*	Snaps to insertion point of block object
`Second point of displacement:` **NEA** (Enter)	Specifies the NEArest object snap
`_nea to` *Pick* ① *(see fig. 6.25)*	Snaps to nearest object

Your drawing should resemble figure 6.25.

Save your work.

New Riders Publishing
INSIDE
SERIES

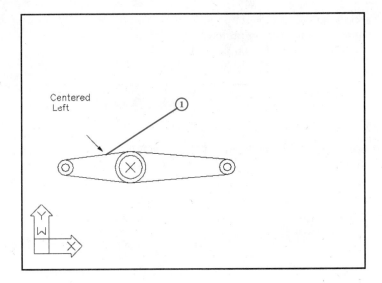

Figure 6.25

Working with the NEArest and INSertion object snaps.

The INSertion object snap snaps to the insertion point of block objects and text objects (blocks are discussed in Chapter 16 and text is discussed in Chapter 13). AutoCAD determines the insertion point for text objects according to the type of justification you specify when you create the text. Blocks also have their insertion points defined where they are created. Neither of these object types have natural geometric snap points other than their insertion points. You can, however, snap to the objects within blocks. Being able to use the INSertion object snap to snap to the insertion point of text objects is valuable if you must move the text or align it with other drawing geometry.

The NEArest object snap simply finds a point on an object closest to the point you specify—that is, closest to the center of the aperture box. NEArest object snap, although unable to snap to specific geometry, such as an endpoint or tangent point, has many uses. You frequently use it with measurements in conjunction with such commands as DIST. You use the NEArest object snap again in an exercise later in this chapter.

The next exercise looks at the ENDPoint, INTersection, MIDpoint, and PERpendicular object snaps. The ENDPoint and INTersection object snaps are two of the most frequently used object snaps in mechanical drafting and design, and the PERpendicular and MIDpoint object snaps are essential in most geometric construction. In the following exercise, you again specify object snaps by typing their abbreviations. Now that you have used all three methods of issuing object snap overrides in

6

the preceding exercises (pull-down menu, pop-up menu, and typed abbreviation), feel free to use whatever method(s) you prefer. The following exercise consists of completing a not-to-scale diagram of a simple roof truss.

Using MIDpoint, ENDPoint, INTersection, and PERpendicular Object Snaps

Continue from the previous exercise. Turn off layers TEXT and OBJECT, then turn on layer TRUSS and make it current.

Command: **L** (Enter)	Issues the LINE command
LINE from point: **MID** (Enter)	Specifies the MIDpoint object snap
of *Pick* ① *(see fig. 6.26)*	Snaps to midpoint of line
To point: **ENDP** (Enter)	Specifies the ENDPoint object snap
of *Pick* ②	Snaps to nearest ENDPoint
To point: *Press Enter twice*	Ends and repeats the LINE command
LINE from point: **INT** (Enter)	
of *Pick the intersection of the base and the line just drawn* ③	Snaps to intersection of lines
To point: **MID** (Enter)	Specifies the MIDpoint object snap
of *Pick* ④	Snaps to MIDpoint of line
To point: **PER** (Enter)	Specifies the PERpendicular object snap
to *Pick* ⑤	Snaps to PERpendicular point (see fig. 6.26)

Complete the right side of the truss by performing the following steps:

Command: *Press Enter twice*	Ends and reissues LINE command
LINE from point: **ENDP** (Enter)	Specifies the ENDPoint object snap
of *Pick* ① *(see fig. 6.27)*	Snaps to nearest ENDPoint
To point: **MID** (Enter)	Specifies the MIDpoint object snap

New Riders Publishing
INSIDE SERIES

of *Pick* ②	Snaps to MIDpoint
To point: **PER** (Enter)	Specifies the PERpendicular object snap
to *Pick anywhere on base line*	
To point: (Enter)	Ends LINE command

The truss diagram is complete and your drawing should look like figure 6.27.

Save your work.

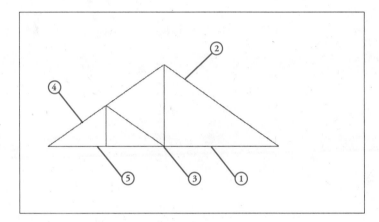

Figure 6.26

The truss figure, half completed.

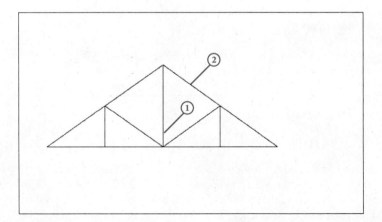

Figure 6.27

The completed truss outline.

You can be fairly indiscriminate when you pick ENDPoint, MIDpoint, and PERpendicular object snaps. Picking anywhere beyond the midpoint on a line with ENDpoint, for example, snaps to the nearest endpoint. Likewise, picking anywhere on a line or arc suffices when you snap to the MIDpoint. This can be beneficial in dense drawings when the geometric point to which you want to snap is crowded in with other objects or even out of view. INTersection object snaps must be precise or AutoCAD prompts you to pick the second object. Often, snapping to an ENDPoint rather than an INTersection is easier if you know that the ENDPoint of a line or arc coincides exactly with the INTersection. In dense drawings, changing the size of the aperture and zooming the view are beneficial. An added flexibility of the INTersection object snap is that if two objects do not actually intersect, AutoCAD calculates their projected intersection. Notice how INTersection is used in the following exercise.

Snapping to Imaginary INTersections

Continue from the preceding exercise. First, turn off layer TRUSS, then turn on layer VALVE and make it current.

Command: *Choose* Draw, Circle *then* Center, Radius	Issues the CIRCLE command and the Center, Radius option
_circle 3P/2P/TTR/<Center point>: **INT** (Enter)	Specifies the INTersection object snap
of *Pick* ① *(see fig. 6.28)*	Selects one object
and *Pick* ②	Selects another object and snaps to the imaginary extended INTersection of the two objects
Diameter/<Radius> <1.00>: **ENDP** (Enter)	
of *Pick* ②	Draws the circle (see fig. 6.28)

Save your work.

Using QUIck To Optimize Object Snap

When you use an object snap, AutoCAD must search every object in the drawing window to find all the objects that cross the aperture box. AutoCAD then calculates potential points for all qualified objects to find the best (closest) fit for the object snap you issue. This process can take some time if the drawing contains many objects.

You can shorten the object snap search process by reducing the size of the aperture to keep extraneous objects out of the target. You also can use the QUIck object snap option, which enables AutoCAD to take the most recently created object that meets

New Riders Publishing
INSIDE
SERIES

your object snap criteria, instead of doing an exhaustive search and comparison to find the closest object. You invoke QUIck by using it as a prefix for other object snap option(s), such as QUI,INT for a quick intersection.

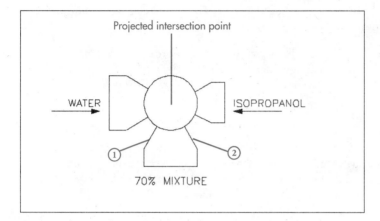

Figure 6.28

Snapping to a projected intersection.

Tip   When you invoke QUIck, AutoCAD occasionally finds a different fit from the one you want. If this happens, simply cancel the current command and initiate the object snap process again without the QUIck modifier.

When you use the keyboard, you can combine object snap modes to form multiple overrides, like MID,ENDP. The result is that the override finds a MIDpoint or an ENDPoint object snap. This is not usually necessary, because you normally need a specific object snap point. However, multiple overrides do make sense when you use running object snaps, discussed in the following section.

Using Running Object Snaps

An object snap condition that is set to be in effect until you change it is called a *running object snap mode.* You use the OSNAP command or Running Object Snap dialog box (DDOSNAP command) to set running object snap modes.

'DDOSNAP. The 'DDOSNAP command displays the Running Object Snap dialog box (see fig. 6.23). The DDOSNAP command enables you to set running object snaps and to set the size of the object snap aperture box.
Pull-down: *Choose* Options, Running Object Snap
Screen: *Choose* OPTIONS, DDosnap:

6

The Running Object Snap dialog box provides the following functions:

◆ **Select Settings area.** The Select Settings area provides check boxes for each of the object snap modes. You set a running object snap by placing a check in the box next to the associated object snap mode. The Clear All button enables you to turn off all object snap modes.

◆ **Aperture Size area.** The Aperture Size area provides a slider bar and an image box. You can change the size of the aperture by clicking on the slider bar arrows or dragging the slider. The image box shows the current size of the aperture.

'OSNAP. The 'OSNAP command enables you to set running object snap modes. If you enter it at the Command: prompt, the following prompt appears: Object snap modes:. Specify one or more object snap modes by entering the first three letters of the mode name. Separate multiple modes with a comma.
Pull-down: *Choose* Assist, Object Snap
Screen: *Choose* Object snap:

Tip   A quicker and easier way to set a single running object snap mode is to choose Assist, Object Snap from the pull-down menu for the mode you want while no command active. This issues the OSNAP command and sets the selected running mode. You cannot use the pull-down menu to set multiple (combined) object snap modes. The cursor pop-up menu does not support this mechanism.

Running object snap modes remain in effect until you replace them with another running mode setting or until you temporarily override them. If a pick fails to find an object to snap to when a running mode is set, AutoCAD finds the point that it would find if no object snap mode were set. You can use the NONe override or any other override to suppress a running mode temporarily.

In the following exercise, you set a running QUAdrant object snap and place a square inside a circle on the transfer arm drawing you completed in a previous exercise.

Using a Running Object Snap

Continue from the previous exercise. Turn off the layer VALVE, turn on the layer OBJECT, and set OBJECT current.

Command: *Choose* Options, Running Object Snap	Opens the Running Object Snap dialog box (refer to figure 6.23)

New Riders Publishing
INSIDE SERIES

`Command:` *Put a check in the* Q*uadrant check box, then choose* OK	Sets QUAdrant as the running object snap mode
`Command:` *Choose* Draw, Line	Issues the LINE command and displays the object snap aperture box
`_line From point:` *Pick a point near* ① *in fig. 6.29*	Snaps to the nearest quadrant of the circle
`To point:` *Pick a point near* ②	Snaps to the quadrant
`To point:` *Pick a point near* ③	Snaps to the quadrant
`To point:` *Pick a point near* ④	Snaps to the quadrant
`To point:` `C` `Enter`	Closes the square (see fig. 6.29)

Save the drawing.

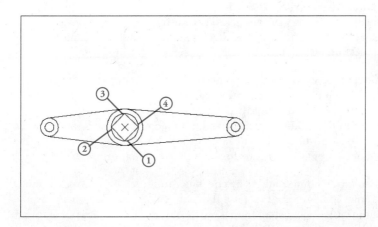

Figure 6.29

The completed transfer arm.

You can specify two or more running modes at once; AutoCAD finds the calculated point of the mode that is closest to the crosshairs. You could specify both CENter and ENDpoint in the Running Object Snap dialog box, then, as you pick a circle, AutoCAD snaps to the centerpoint, and, as you pick a line or an arc, AutoCAD snaps to the endpoint. AutoCAD considers the object type and their proximity within the object snap aperture, while comparing the modes you specify. Therefore, AutoCAD can determine that because the object you indicate is a circle, endpoint is not

6

appropriate but centerpoint is, and vice-versa. The combinations of object snap settings can quickly become complicated. Consider setting a combination of INTersection, ENDpoint, and CENter. If more than one object is within the aperture and they intersect, the INTersection setting prevails. If the object is an arc and the pick point is closer to the endpoint of the arc, the ENDpoint setting prevails. If the pick point is further away from an endpoint than the arc's radius, the CENter setting prevails. If the object is a circle, the CENter setting prevails. If the object is a line, the ENDpoint setting prevails.

Tip   CENter, INTersection, and ENDpoint is likely the most useful combination. It finds most of the points you intend on using and can be overridden if necessary.

Using combinations of object snap modes requires thoughtfulness when making object picks. When you use the MIDpoint and ENDpoint settings together, you have to pick nearer the end than the middle to indicate an endpoint. Likewise you need to pick nearer to the middle than the end to indicate a midpoint. The combination of PERpendicular and TANgent is another tricky combination. AutoCAD resolves it by inspecting the relative proximity of the pick. Try drawing a circle, then set the running object snap to PERpendicular and TANgent and draw a few lines to see how proximity of the pick affects the way AutoCAD applies the settings.

Some mode settings are useless when combined. The NEArest mode setting takes precedence over everything. If you combine NEArest and ENDpoint, then make a pick that suggests a line endpoint, AutoCAD just uses the suggested pick. If you combine CENter and QUADrant, and if the radius of a circle or arc is much larger than the aperture, you cannot snap to the centerpoint. Should you doubt the outcome of a particular combination, resort to a proven combination.

Specify object snap mode combinations by checking multiple check boxes in the Running Object Snap dialog box. If you use the OSNAP command at the Command: prompt, include multiple object snap modes at the Object snap modes: prompt and separate them with commas, as in END,MID,CEN.

Use the override modes whenever the need arises; they override running modes. Set up a running object snap whenever you repeatedly use the same object snap mode(s). The Running Object Snap dialog box provides a fast and efficient way to set running object snaps.

Note   When you use AutoCAD's grips autoediting feature, you can snap to various object-specific positions, such as an endpoint, without using object snaps. As you move the cursor over a grip, it snaps to the grip. Grips are discussed in Chapter 8, "Object Selection and Grip Editing."

New Riders Publishing
INSIDE
SERIES

Using Construction Methods

In manual drafting, you often draw light guidelines or temporary lines as construction to help you align or place objects accurately. The AutoCAD grid sometimes takes the place of guidelines, but you sometimes still need to use construction line methods in CAD drafting. AutoCAD offers two types of construction lines: infinitely long lines called *xlines*, and rays. AutoCAD also provides an alternative to drawing construction lines, called *point filters*. You also can use point objects as construction or marker points, and snap them with the NODE object snap mode.

The first construction tool you learn about is one of AutoCAD's basic drawing objects, the point, and the command that you use to draw points, the POINT command.

Drawing Points

The POINT command is the simplest of AutoCAD's drawing commands. It creates a point object.

> **POINT.** The POINT command enables you to draw a point object with X,Y,Z coordinates anywhere in 3D space. You often use points as reference marks and as nodes to which to snap with NODe object snap mode. You can use the PDMODE and PDSIZE system variables to control the display style and size of points.
> Pull-down: *Choose* Draw, Point, Point
> Screen: *Choose* DRAW2, Point:

The X in the center of the transfer arm (see fig. 6.29) is a point object. You can display point objects in twenty different styles, as shown in figure 6.30. If you use style 0, you must perform a display redraw after you create the point to see the actual point entity.

In the following exercise, you change point styles and draw a couple more points.

Using the POINT Command

Continue to use the CHAP06A drawing from the previous exercise, with OBJECT layer on. Notice the X, the point object in the center of the arm.

Command: *Choose* Options, Display, Point Style

Issues the DDPTYPE command and opens the Point Style dialog box (see fig. 6.31)

continues

6

continued

Click on the first point style in the first row, then choose OK	Sets the style to a dot (which is AutoCAD's default style)

The existing point is unchanged until you regenerate or zoom. Draw a new point.

Command: *Choose* Draw, Point, Point	Issues the POINT command
Command: _point Point: *Pick a point in any clear area*	Displays the usual blip mark at the specified coordinate—you must redraw to see the dot
Command: _point *Press Esc* Point: *Cancel*	Cancels the POINT command
Command: **R** (Enter)	Issues the REDRAW command
REDRAW	Leaves only a dot
Command: **REGEN** (Enter)	Starts the REGEN command
Regenerating drawing	Displays the old point as a dot

Save the drawing.

Figure 6.30

The 20 available point styles and their PDMODE numbers.

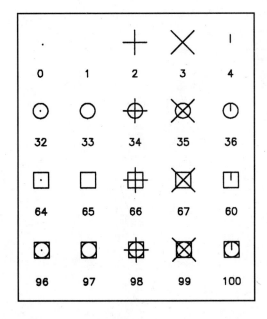

New Riders Publishing
INSIDE
SERIES

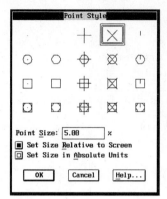

Figure 6.31
*The Point Style
dialog box.*

When you draw a point with the default dot (0) style, the usual mark appears at the specified coordinates. Issuing the REDRAW command clears the blip mark and leaves a small dot, or *point object.* (You might not easily see the point, but it is there.)

Note When you use the pull-down menu to issue the POINT command, it repeats until you cancel it. This is useful when you need to locate a number of points in sequence. You terminate the command by pressing Esc. If you issue the POINT command by typing it at the Command: prompt, AutoCAD requests only one point location, then the command terminates.

Twenty different "styles" of point objects are available (shown in figure 6.30 along with their corresponding number designation). You can set the display style of a point by changing the PDMODE system variable. The number you enter for the PDMODE variable corresponds to the numbers shown in figure 6.30. The system variable PDSIZE controls the display size of the point object. A positive PDSIZE value specifies an absolute size in drawing units for the point object; a negative value specifies a point object size that is a percentage of the viewport size. You can enable viewports within the graphics area to display multiple views of your drawing (see Chapter 10, "Working in Model and Paper Space Viewports," for more on viewports). Entering a size of 0 creates a point object that is 5 percent of the graphics area height.

Using the Point Style dialog box (refer to figure 6.31), which you issue by using the DDPTYPE command, is a much easier way to control point object style and size.

'DDPTYPE. The 'DDPTYPE command displays the Point Style dialog box, which enables you to set point object style and size.

Pull-down: *Choose* Options, Display, Point Style
Screen: *Choose* DRAW2, Point:, DDptype:

6

DDPTYPE Command Options

The Point Style dialog box enables you to change the point display by selecting an icon. Subsequent point objects you draw use the new style. The next regeneration updates all point objects to the current style.

The Point Style dialog box also provides the following controls:

◆ **Point Size.** Sets the size of the point display (in absolute drawing units or relative to the viewport).

◆ **Set Size Relative to Screen.** Sets the point object size as a percentage of the viewport size.

◆ **Set Size in Absolute Units.** Sets the point object size in actual units.

 Tip　Use an easily noticeable point style when you draw, but remember to set it to the default dot (PDMODE 0) before you plot. Or if you don't want points to plot, set them to the blank point style (PDMODE 1). You also can place construction points on their own layer and turn off or freeze the layer before you plot.

Using Point Filters

Point filters enable you to specify coordinates by choosing one value at a time, such as only the X value, and then combining values to form a complete 2D or 3D point. When you choose values, you can use object snaps to extract X, Y, or Z values from existing geometry to locate another point. You could use point filters, for example, to extract the X coordinate of the center point of an arc and combine that value with the Y coordinate of the midpoint of a line to yield an X,Y coordinate to serve as the center for a circle.

You can invoke point filters anytime AutoCAD requests a point. At the Point: prompt, you can respond with a point filter of the general form .*coordinate*, where *coordinate* is one or more of the letters X, Y, and Z. For instance, .X and .XY are valid filters. When you specify such a filter, AutoCAD responds with (of) and then extracts only those coordinates specified by the filter from the next point you designate. Point filters are used with object snaps to pick the filtered points. If a full point has not been formed, a prompt such as (need YZ) appears to tell you what is needed before a full point is complete. In 2D, the Z coordinate is the current elevation.

In addition to being able to enter point filters from the keyboard, you also can select them from the pop-up menu displayed by clicking the middle button (or

Shift+clicking the Enter button) of the pointing device. In the following exercise in which you use point filters, keyboard entry is indicated—but use the method you prefer.

The following exercise demonstrates a common application of point filters: finding the center of a rectangle. In this exercise, you begin a drawing of a simple flange.

Using Point Filters To Find the Center of a Rectangle

Continue to use the CHAP06A drawing. Turn off all layers, then turn layer FILTERS on and make it current. Make sure that grid is on and snap and ortho off.

Command: *Choose* View, Zoom, All	Issues the ZOOM command with the All option
``` _ZOOM All/Center/Dynamic/Extents/Left/ Previous/Vmax/Window/ <Scale(X/XP)>: _a ```	Zooms to the drawings limits and regenerates drawing

Next, you draw a 1-unit radius circle centered in the rectangle.

Command: *Choose* Draw, Circle then Center, Radius	Issues the CIRCLE command
Command: _circle 3P/2P/TTR/ <Center point>: **.X** (Enter)	Specifies X coordinate filter
of **MID** (Enter)	Specifies the MIDpoint object snap
of *Pick either the top or bottom line*	Filters the X coordinate of the midpoint of the line and prompts you for the Y and Z coordinates
(need YZ): **MID** (Enter)	Specifies the MIDpoint object snap
of *Pick either the left or right line*	Filters the Y and Z coordinates of the midpoint of the line and combines them with X coordinate; uses the result

After a valid X,Y,Z coordinate forms from the filters, the original prompt for a center point is answered.

Diameter/<Radius> <1.49>: **1** (Enter)	Draws the circle (see fig. 6.32)

Save your work.

6

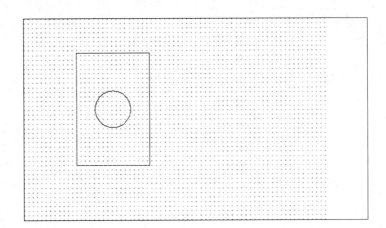

Figure 6.32

Using point filters to find the center of a rectangle.

In the preceding exercise, after you issued the prompt for the center of the circle, you isolated the X coordinate of the midpoint of either of the horizontal lines (the X coordinate of the midpoint of both lines are the same). Then, using the MIDpoint object snap, you ensured that the exact midpoint was chosen. Next, AutoCAD prompted for the Y,Z components, which you supplied by snapping to the midpoint of either vertical line, yielding a complete X,Y,Z coordinate for the circle's center.

In the following exercise, you begin a section view of the flange, using point filters to form points from existing drawing objects. Use the pop-up menu or type the object snap modes.

Using Point Filters To Make a New View

Continue from the preceding exercise. Turn on ortho mode.

Command: *Choose* Draw, Polygon, for Rectangle	Issues the RECTANG command and prompts first corner
Command: _rectang	
First corner: *Choose* .Y *from the pop-up menu*	Specifies a Y point filter
of **INT** (Enter)	Specifies the INTersection object snap
_int of *Pick the intersection at* ① *in figure 6.33*	Obtains Y coordinate of intersection
(need XZ): *Pick near* ②	Obtains X,Z coordinate; places first corner

New Riders Publishing
INSIDE
SERIES

Other corner: **.Y** (Enter)	Specifies a Y point filter
.Y of INT (Enter)	Specifies the INTersection object snap
of *Pick the intersection at* ③	Obtains Y coordinate of intersection
(need XZ): **@.25,0** (Enter)	Supplies X,Z coordinate and draws the rectangle

Next, you draw the cross section of the hole on a hidden-line layer. Set the layer HIDDEN on and make it current.

Command: *Choose* Draw, Line	Issues the LINE command
_line From point: **.Y** (Enter)	Specifies a Y point filter
.Y of QUA (Enter)	Specifies the QUAdrant object snap
of *Pick the top of the circle at* ④	Obtains the Y coordinate of the quadrant point
(need XZ): **NEA** (Enter)	Specifies the NEArest object snap
to *Pick anywhere on line at* ⑤	Obtains the X,Z coordinate of the line; establishes beginning of line
To point: **PER** (Enter)	Specifies the PERpendicular object snap
to *Pick anywhere on second line*	Draws the line
to point: (Enter)	Ends the LINE command

Use the same steps as for the top line to draw the bottom cross section line, but obtain the Y coordinate from the bottom quadrant of the circle.

Set layer CENTER on and current and draw the center line. Use a Y point filter and CEN object snap to locate its Y position, then pick with snap on to set its X position at ⑥ and second end at ⑦—ortho keeps it horizontal.

Next, you add some text centered below the front view of the flange. The DTEXT command is covered in Chapter 13, "Annotation with Text."

Set the layer FILTERS current.

Command: **DTEXT** (Enter)	Begins the DTEXT command
Justify/Style/<Start point>: **C** (Enter)	Specifies the Center justification option
Center point: **.X** (Enter)	Specifies an X point filter

continues

6

continued

of **MID** (Enter)	Specifies the MIDpoint object snap
of *Pick bottom line of flange, front view*	Obtains the X coordinate of the midpoint of the line
(need YZ): *Pick* (8)	Specifies a relative coordinate
Height <0.20>: **.25** (Enter)	Sets text height
Rotation angle <0>: (Enter)	Accepts the default angle of 0°
Text: **0.25 Flange** (Enter)	Draws the text and starts a new line
Text: (Enter)	Ends the DTEXT command

Save your work.

Figure 6.33

Two views of the flange.

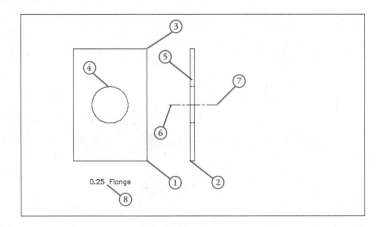

In effect, specifying a new point with the X value taken from one existing point and the Y value from another existing point finds the intersection of imaginary orthogonal construction lines projecting from each of the two points. Combining the accuracy of object snaps with point filters provides a powerful tool. Point filters help make working in three dimensions in the flat world of computer screens easy and intuitive.

 Tip If you make an error during point filtering, AutoCAD often prompts for the point again so you can respecify the filter and associated objects snaps. If not, most commands let you use U to undo, and then you can try again.

New Riders Publishing
INSIDE
SERIES

Using Xlines and Rays as Construction Lines

AutoCAD provides two methods of creating lines for construction that are visible, not imaginary. These special line objects extend to infinity in one or both directions, and are known as rays and construction lines, respectively. *Rays* have finite beginning points and extend from that point to infinity. *Construction lines* have no beginning point and extend to infinity in both directions. These characteristics and their methods of placement make them ideal for geometric locations and constructions.

 Note Although rays and construction lines extend to infinity in one or both directions, they do not change the total area of the drawing or have any affect on zooming or viewpoints.

XLINE. The XLINE command enables you to create construction lines, which possess infinite length.
Pull-down: *Choose* Draw, Construction Line
Screen: *Choose* DRAW1, Xline:

XLINE Command Options

The flexibility with which you use the XLINE command is greatly enhanced if you understand the command's six options:

◆ **From point.** The From point option is the default option. It specifies both the location of the infinite line and the point through which it passes. After you specify the first point, AutoCAD prompts you for the Through point. Specify the point through which you want the infinite line to pass. The first point you choose becomes the conceptual "midpoint" of the line. You can specify successive lines through this midpoint until you press Enter to end the command.

◆ **Hor.** The Hor (Horizontal) option creates an infinite line that passes through the point you specify. The line is parallel to the X axis of the current UCS.

◆ **Ver.** The Ver (Vertical) option creates an infinite line that passes through the point you specify. The line is parallel to the Y axis of the current UCS.

◆ **Ang.** The Ang (Angle) option creates an infinite line at a specified angle. After you specify an angle for the line, AutoCAD asks for the point through which the line, at the specified angle, is to pass. Enter **R** at the initial prompt if you want to specify a reference line, then an angle. The angle is measured counterclockwise from the reference line. You then specify the point through which the line at the specified angle is to pass.

6

◆ **Bisect.** The Bisect (Bisector) option creates an infinite line that passes through an angle vertex you select and bisects the angle formed between two points you specify. You can specify successive bisectors until you end the command by pressing Enter.

◆ **Offset.** The Offset option creates an infinite line parallel to another line object. You can specify the offset distance and direction or you can specify a point through which the line is to pass.

Xline objects behave like their cousin, the line, but have other properties of which you should be aware. Although the xline has no endpoints, you can use other object snaps modes with them. An xline object's midpoint is the first point used to define the xline and it acts as the object's primary grip. When you trim xline objects, AutoCAD converts them to ray or line objects. If you use the TRIM command to trim away one side of an xline, the remaining object becomes a ray because it still has one infinite end. If you use the TRIM command to trim away two sides of an xline, the remaining object becomes a line because it then has two endpoints.

The Construction Line menu item issues the XLINE command; however, the object it creates is called an *xline*. In discussing xlines and rays, the term construction line is used to mean both xline and ray objects.

RAY. The RAY command enables you to create a semi-infinite line. A ray has a finite starting point and extends to infinity.
Pull-down: *Choose* Draw, Ray
Screen: *Choose* DRAW1, Ray:

RAY Command Options

The RAY command displays the following prompts:

◆ **From point:.** At the From point: prompt, you specify the point from which you want the line to start.

◆ **Through point:.** At the Through point: prompt, you specify the point through which you want the ray to pass. AutoCAD prompts you for successive through points until you end the command by pressing Enter.

Other than their length and placement methods, AutoCAD's construction lines behave similarly to a conventional line object; for example, you can copy, rotate, move, break, and trim them. Certain editing operations, such as lengthening, do not

apply to infinite lines, although you can extend a ray object. You might want to create construction lines on a separate layer so that you can freeze or turn them off before you plot.

In the following exercise, you use the XLINE and RAY commands to create construction lines. For a point of departure, you use an identical rectangle to the one you used to begin the flange drawing in the previous exercise.

Working with Infinite Construction Lines

Continue to use the CHAP06A drawing or begin a new drawing named CHAP06B, using the OBJECTS drawing from the IAD Disk as a prototype.

Turn all layers off, then turn layer CONSTRUCTION on and set it current. Turn grid, snap, and ortho off. Use DDOSNAP to set a running INTersection object snap.

The following steps draw construction lines through the opposite corners of the rectangle.

Command: *Choose* Draw, Ray	Issues the RAY command
_ray From point: *Pick the intersection at* ① *(see fig. 6.34)*	Snaps to the intersection
Through point: *Pick the intersection at* ②	Snaps to the intersection and draws the ray
Through point: *Press Enter twice*	Ends and repeats the RAY command
RAY From point: *Pick the intersection at* ③	Snaps to the intersection
Through point: *Pick the intersection at* ④	Snaps to the intersection and draws the ray
Through point: (Enter)	Ends the command (see fig. 6.34)

Save the drawing.

After you draw the construction lines, you can change layers and use their intersection (with an INTersection object snap) to accurately place a circle as you did in the earlier exercise in which you used point filters to find the center of the rectangle.

In the following exercise, you use the XLINE command to place construction lines to use when you draw a side view of the flange.

6

Figure 6.34

Finding the center of a rectangle with rays.

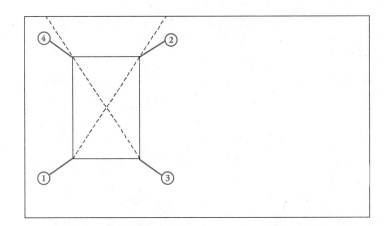

Using the XLINE Command To Draw Construction Lines

Continue from the previous exercise.

Command: *Choose* Draw, Construction Line	Issues the XLINE command
_xline Hor/Ver/Ang/Bisect/Offset/ <From point>: *Pick intersection at* ① *(see fig. 6.35)*	Snaps to the INTersection object snap
Through point: *Pick* ②	Snaps to the intersection and draws the construction line

Another Through point: prompt appears. As you move the cursor, a potential second line appears with the same "anchor" point.

Through point: *Press Enter twice*	Ends the XLINE command, then repeats it

To draw the next construction line, you use the horizontal option.

XLINE Hor/Ver/Ang/Bisect/Offset/ <From point>: **H** (Enter)	Specifies the horizontal option
Through point: **NEA** (Enter)	Specifies the NEArest object snap
_nea to *Pick anywhere along the top line of the rectangle*	Draws a horizontal construction line and prompts for another point

As you move the cursor, a potential second horizontal line appears at the cursor.

`Through point:` *Press Enter twice*	Ends and reissues the XLINE command

Next, you use the Offset option to create the vertical construction lines.

`xline Hor/Ver/Ang/Bisect/Offset/` `<From point>:` **0** (Enter)	Specifies the Offset option
`Offset distance or Through` `<Through>:` **4** (Enter)	Specifies the offset distance for the side view
`Select a line object:` *Pick the rectangle at* ③	Selects and highlights the rectangle
`Side to offset?` *Move the cursor any distance to the right and pick*	Specifies the offset direction and draws the line
`Select a line object:` *Press Enter twice*	Ends, then repeats the XLINE command
`XLINE Hor/Ver/Ang/Bisect/Offset/` `<From point>:` **0** (Enter)	Specifies the Offset option
`Offset distance or Through` `<4.00>:` **.25** (Enter)	Specifies the offset distance
`Select a line object:` *Pick the xline you just created*	Selects and highlights the xline
`Side to offset?` *Move the cursor any distance to the right and pick*	Specifies the offset direction and draws the line (see fig. 6.35)
`Select a line object:` (Enter)	Ends the command

In the preceding exercise, you used several of the options available to you for creating construction lines. All the constructions you drew were placed on layer CONSTRUC-TION; the layer has the color red and the linetype HIDDEN. Using a separate layer devoted to construction lines enables you to display these lines in a specific color and linetype to enhance their visibility. In the preceding exercise, you could use the geometry created by the construction lines (for example, intersections) to accurately place new objects (on another layer) by using point filters and object snaps. You could then freeze the layer that contains the construction lines, or erase the lines. Alternately, you could leave the construction lines in place, use the TRIM command to specify the two vertical xlines as trim boundaries, then trim the ends of the two horizontal xlines. This would leave line objects that represent the horizontal lines of the flange's side view. These two lines could then be used as trim boundaries and the ends of the vertical lines could be trimmed away. The result is a side view of the

6

flange with a HIDDEN line style on the layer CONSTRUCTION. You could then change the four line objects to the proper layer. You could also use the FILLET command on the xlines to achieve the same objective—AutoCAD offers you considerable flexibility and, in the future, your experience will help guide you through the alternatives.

Figure 6.35

Completed construction lines.

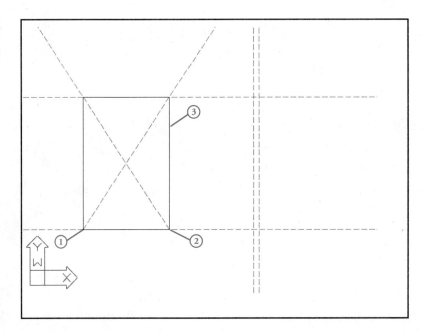

Tip   If you want automatically to have construction lines visible while drawing, but not have them plot, place them on the DEFpoints layer. The DEFpoints layer is never plotted—it is used by AutoCAD's associative dimensioning (see Chapter 21).

Transferring coordinate or geometric data from one location in the drawing to another is a basic technique for building and developing drawings. Using object snaps, point filters, and construction lines enables you to apply this technique to your CAD drawings with ease and accuracy.

Using the Tablet To Digitize Points

If you have a digitizer, you can use it to trace and digitize drawings into AutoCAD. AutoCAD has two modes for using digitizers: the screen pointing mode and a calibrated digitizing mode. You use the calibrated digitizing mode to establish a relation-

New Riders Publishing
INSIDE
SERIES

ship between points on a drawing taped to the tablet and points in your AutoCAD drawing. After the relationship is calibrated, you can pick points in the AutoCAD drawing fairly accurately by digitizing the corresponding points on the paper drawing. Although this is not as accurate as creating a new drawing entirely from accurate coordinate and measurement data, it often is the only efficient way to import existing drawing data.

Digitizing is well-suited to tracing contours, which do not demand absolute precision, with sketched lines. Digitizing, however, is not limited to sketching. You can use the full range of drawing commands and controls, even inserting blocks at datum points picked on the tablet.

To digitize, first use the CALibrate option of the TABLET command. It prompts you for two known points on the paper drawing and for the drawing coordinates to which to assign them. After calibration, the relationship between the drawing and tablet is maintained, even if you pan and zoom. The X and Y axes are calibrated with equal scales. If the tablet drawing is distorted (as are many paper drawings), you can compensate after you trace by blocking the results and inserting them with differing X and Y scales. If your paper drawing does not fit on the tablet menu's screen pointing area, you can reconfigure the tablet to use its full area for digitizing. To exit the calibrated tablet mode, use the TABLET command's OFF option; to reenter tablet mode, use ON. You also can switch between tablet mode and screen pointing mode by pressing Ctrl+T. For more information about tablet calibration and configuration, see Appendix A, "Installation and Configuration."

TABLET. The TABLET command enables you to calibrate the digitizing tablet to an independent coordinate system, as well as to turn tablet mode on and off and designate the tablet areas reserved for menu and screen pointing.
Pull-down: *Choose* Options, Tablet
Screen: *Choose* OPTIONS, Tablet:

TABLET Command Options

The TABLET command provides the following options:

- **ON.** Turns on tablet mode, as does setting the system variable TABMODE to 1.

- **OFF.** Turns off tablet mode, as does setting the system variable TABMODE to 0.

- **CAL.** Calibrates your digitizer to an outside coordinate system, such as a paper drawing or map, that is attached to the tablet, enabling you to digitize points on the drawing or map and transform them to coordinates in AutoCAD.

6

◆ **CFG.** Enables you to specify areas on the tablet for screen pointing and for menus to use.

The TABLET command offers extensive capabilities for transferring data from outside sources such as maps, drawings, and photographs. For details about tablet configuration, see Appendix A.

This chapter provided several methods for ensuring accuracy in your drawings. Use the GRID command for a frame of reference; use the SNAP command to limit crosshairs and picks to preset increments. If you need to draw at 90-degree increments, activate the ORTHO command. If you need to align your coordinate system with your drawing, you can change the UCS.

To construct geometrically accurate objects, use coordinate entry and object snap to snap to objects. You can invoke the object snap options temporarily to override any command that requests a point. A running object snap mode sets up a full-time mode and aperture that you still can override. Try to find a good aperture setting to control the reliability and speed of your object snap searches. The toolbars provide easy access to commands you use often.

Throughout the rest of this book, you often see coordinates given in response to prompts with the exercises. You can type them and press Enter, or you can use your pointing device to pick the coordinates if you are sure the pick is accurate. Remember that the crosshairs position is only accurate with snap on or with object snap. Use object snap whenever you can—your drawing productivity will improve, and you can be confident that your work is accurate. Now that you have had a chance to experiment with object snaps, point filters, and other accuracy tools, proceed to learn about some of AutoCAD's basic objects.

Drawing Basic Objects

No matter how complicated the drawing, no matter how many layers and linetypes, almost all AutoCAD drawings are comprised of relatively few basic shapes and forms. Circles and circular arcs, lines, rectangles, regular polygons, and ellipses are the elements from which both simple and complicated drawings are built. This chapter shows you the tools with which you need to be familiar before you can draw these simple objects. In this chapter you learn to draw the following objects:

- ◆ Circles

- ◆ Circular arcs

- ◆ Donuts—circles with wide, filled circumference lines

- ◆ Regular polygons

- ◆ Ellipses

You see circles in most drawings, representing various objects such as holes, wheels, trees, instruments, and numerous other real and symbolic entities. In mechanical drafting, as in AutoCAD, isolated circles are not particularly difficult to produce; you need only know the center point location and the radius or the diameter. Circles tangent to other objects—such as other circles, arcs, or lines—are somewhat more difficult when you use traditional means. AutoCAD, however, gives you the capability to draw tangent circles with an ease and precision that is impossible if you use only a compass, ruler, and straightedge.

In this chapter's first exercise, you use an option of AutoCAD's CIRCLE command (Tangent, Tangent, Radius) to provide the basic geometry for a drawing that depicts the design of a curved conveyor system (see fig. 7.1). In addition to the CIRCLE command, you use the LINE command, introduced in Chapter 3, "Using the Drawing Editor." Refer to that chapter for the use and options of the LINE command. The drawing has a 1-inch grid and .25-inch snap that you can use, along with the coordinates display, to pick the points in the exercise. If necessary, press Ctrl+D to change the coordinates display mode from a static display to a dynamic display. You can press Ctrl+D, once the LINE or CIRCLE command prompts for a second point, to change the coordinates display mode to relative distance and angle display mode.

Figure 7.1

Using tangent circles to design a conveyor.

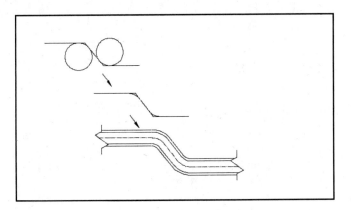

Quick 5¢ Tour

Begin a new drawing named CHAP07, using the BASICS drawing from the IA Disk as a prototype.

Command: *Choose* Draw, Line	Issues the LINE command

Draw lines from 1,9 to 3,9 to 6,7 to 9,7 (see fig. 7.2).

Turn off snap

Command: *Choose* Draw, Circle *then* Tan, Tan, Radius	Issues the CIRCLE command with TTR (Tangent, Tangent, Radius) option
`_circle 3P/2P/TTR/<Center point>: _ttr`	The crosshairs display the aperture box when the menu issues the TTR option

New Riders Publishing
INSIDE
SERIES

`Enter Tangent spec:` *Pick the line at* ① *(see fig. 7.2)*	Selects the first tangent object
`Enter second Tangent spec:` *Pick the line at* ②	Selects the second tangent object
`Radius:` **1.25** `(Enter)`	Draws a 2.50-unit diameter circle tangent to the two lines
`Command:` `(Enter)`	Repeats the CIRCLE command with the default `<Center point>` option
`CIRCLE 3P/2P/TTR/<Center point>:` **T** `(Enter)`	Specifies the TTR option
`Enter Tangent spec:` *Pick the line at* ②	Selects the first tangent object
`Enter second Tangent spec:` *Pick the line at* ③	Selects the second tangent object
`Radius <1.25>:` `(Enter)`	Accepts the default radius from previous circle and draws the circle tangent to the lines (see fig. 7.3)

Save the drawing.

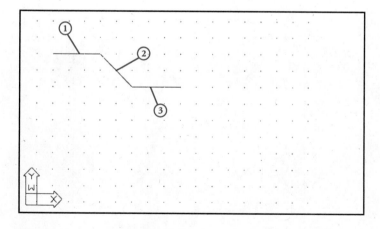

Figure 7.2

Conveyor center lines.

Drawing circles tangent to lines or other circles is quick and easy in AutoCAD. The lines and circles you drew in the preceding exercise form a precise template for the additional steps required to construct the curved conveyor depicted in figure 7.1. The intermediate steps outlined in figure 7.1 involve editing commands that are covered in later chapters of this book. You learn about other ways to draw precise, accurate circles in the following section.

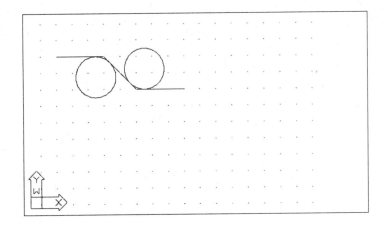

Figure 7.3

Circles tangent to two lines.

Creating Circles

AutoCAD offers five ways to construct a circle. The method you choose depends on the information you have about the geometry of the circle. Often, you know the center point and radius or diameter. At other times, you might know only where you want points on the circumference to lie. In the previous exercise, you knew the radius and tangent points. The CIRCLE command offers options to cover all these possibilities, as well as other situations. The various methods are illustrated in figure 7.4.

Figure 7.4

Methods of drawing circles.

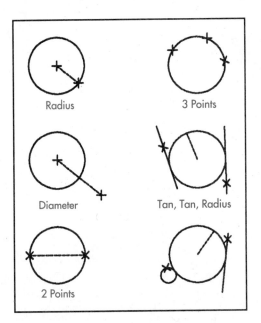

New Riders Publishing
INSIDE SERIES

Note Notice the difference between Center point/Diameter and 2P. Both options enable you to specify a diameter, but if you pick the second point with Center point/ Diameter, it merely indicates the diameter's distance, and the circle does not draw through the point. If you pick two points with 2P, you see a circle appear between those two points, and the distance is the diameter. The 2P option enables you to draw a diameter circle the way most people intuitively think about diameter.

CIRCLE. The CIRCLE command enables you to use a variety of geometric methods to draw circles. The most common (default) method requires you to specify the center point and the radius. You can drag and pick the size of the circle on-screen, or use the keyboard to specify the radius.
Pull-down: *Choose* Draw, Circle
Screen: *Choose* DRAW1, Circle:

CIRCLE Command Options

The CIRCLE command offers the following options:

```
3P/2P/TTR/<Center point>:
```

- ◆ **Center point.** Type or pick the center point and the CIRCLE command then prompts for a radius or diameter. This is the default option.

  - ◆ **Radius.** If you choose `Center point:`, you then use the Radius option to enter a distance or pick two points to show a distance for the radius.

  - ◆ **Diameter.** If you choose `Center point:`, use the Diameter option to specify a radius. You can either enter a distance or pick two points to show a radius.

- ◆ **3P (3 Point).** You use this option to specify the circumference by entering or picking three points.

- ◆ **2P (2 Points).** You use this option to specify two diameter points on the circumference.

Using the Circle Command

In the following exercise, you use the CIRCLE command as you begin to draw the components of a typical circuit board. Use the CIRCUIT-BOARD layer of the CHAP07A drawing. The outline of the circuit board and text already have been drawn on this layer. You now draw the outlines of two capacitors. You can use the coordinates display and the 0.25 snap to pick the points shown in figure 7.5.

Using the CIRCLE Command

Continue from the previous exercise or begin a new drawing named CHAP07A, using the BASICS drawing from the IA Disk as a prototype. Turn on the CIRCUIT-BOARD layer and set it to current, and turn all other layers off.

Command: *Choose* Draw, Circle *then* Center, Radius	Issues the default CIRCLE command
_circle 3P/2P/TTR/<Center point>: **3,8** (Enter)	Specifies the center at ① (see fig. 7.5)
Diameter/<Radius> <1.25>: **1** (Enter)	Draws the circle with a 1-unit radius

In the next step, you specify a circle with the Center point:, Diameter option.

Command: *Choose* Draw, Circle *then* Center, Diameter	Issues the CIRCLE command and the Diameter option
_circle 3P/2P/TTR/<Center point>: **6,8** (Enter)	Specifies the center at ②
Diameter/<Radius> <1.00>:_d	The menu issues the Diameter option
Diameter <2.00>: **2.2** (Enter)	Draws the circle with a 2.2-unit diameter

In the previous step, the default diameter value (2.00) is based on the most recent radius used (1.00).

Save the drawing.

Drawing circles with the Center point: option and then specifying a radius or a diameter is easy. You can drag the circle to the size you want or enter a value from the keyboard. You also can use object snap to place the circumference in relation to other geometry. If you issue the CIRCLE command from the Command: prompt, you can accept the default options by pressing Enter, or you can override the defaults by typing the command or option. Entering a **D**, for example, selects the diameter option at the Diameter/<Radius>: prompt.

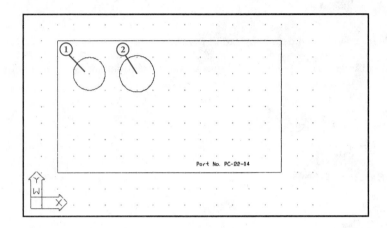

Figure 7.5

Drawing circles with a known radius or diameter.

7

In the following two exercises, you use the 2P, 3P, and TTR options to construct circles that are related to other drawing geometry. The 2P and 3P options, by definition, do not require radius or diameter input; AutoCAD calculates that information from the points you specify. You used the TTR option in the opening exercise; in this exercise you learn more about its capabilities. You also use the object snap and point filter features from Chapter 6; here, you can type them as shown or choose them from the pop-up menu.

Using the 2P Option

Continue from the preceding exercise. Turn off the CIRCUIT-BOARD layer, then turn on the CIRCLE layer and set it current. Your drawing should look like figure 7.6, except the circles are not yet drawn.

Command: **C** (Enter)	Issues the CIRCLE command
CIRCLE 3P/2P/TTR/<Center point>: **2P** (Enter)	Issues the 2 Point option
First point on diameter: **ENDP** (Enter)	Specifies the ENDPoint object snap
of *Pick* ① *(see fig. 7.6)*	Establishes the first point on diameter
As you move the cursor, the circle drags.	
Second point on diameter: **ENDP** (Enter)	Specifies the ENDPoint object snap
of *Pick* ②	Draws the circle

continues

continued

Next, you use an object snap to help define the radius of a TTR circle.

Command: *Choose* Draw, Circle *then* 2 Points	Issues the CIRCLE command with the 2 Point option
_circle 3P/2P/TTR/<Center point>: _2P First point on diameter: **ENDP** (Enter)	Specifies the ENDPoint object snap
of *Pick the line at* ③	Specifies first point
Second point on diameter: **ENDP** (Enter)	Specifies the ENDPoint object snap
of *Pick the line at* ④	Specifies second point and draws the circle

Save your drawing.

Figure 7.6

Drawing circles with the 2P, 3P, and TTR options.

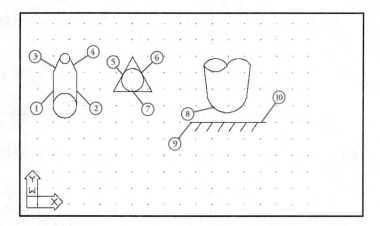

The 2P option of the CIRCLE command along with object snap is often useful. In the preceding exercise, it enables you to specify a diameter equal to the distance between the ends of the lines without having any information about that distance.

Tip You always can use the CAL command to specify a point halfway between two other points, regardless of whether adjacent geometry is available. The CAL command is covered in Chapter 15, "Object Modification, Inquiry, and Calculation."

New Riders Publishing
INSIDE SERIES

In the following exercise, you use the 3P option to draw a circle and you use the TTR option again.

Using the 3P Option and Learning More about the TTR Option

Continue from the preceding exercise.

7

Command: *Choose* Draw, Circle *then* 3 Points	Issues the CIRCLE command and the 3P option
`_circle 3P/2P/TTR/<Center point>:` `_3p First point:` **MID** (Enter)	Specifies the MIDpoint object snap
`_mid of` *Pick point* ⑤ *(refer to figure 7.6)*	Specifies first point on circumference
`Second point:` **MID** (Enter)	Specifies the MIDpoint object snap
`_mid of` *Pick point* ⑥	Specifies second point on circumference
`Third point:` **MID** (Enter)	
`_mid of` *Pick a point at* ⑦	Specifies third point on circumference and draws the circle
Command: *Choose* Draw, Circle *then* Tan, Tan, Radius	Issues the CIRCLE command and the TTR option
`_circle 3P/2P/TTR/<Center point>:` `_ttr`	
`Enter Tangent spec:` *Pick the arc at* ⑧	Selects the first tangent object
`Enter second Tangent spec:` *Pick the line at* ⑨	Selects the second tangent object
`Radius <0.70>:` **.4** (Enter)	Specifies the radius and draws the circle (see fig. 7.7)
`Command:` (Enter)	Reissues the CIRCLE command
`3P/2P/TTR/<Center point>:` **T** (Enter)	Specifies the TTR option
`Enter Tangent spec:` *Pick the arc at* ⑧	Selects the first tangent object
`Enter second Tangent spec:` *Pick the line at* ⑩	Selects the second tangent object

continues

continued

Radius <0.40>: (Enter)   Accepts the default radius and draws a
                                                second circle (see fig. 7.7)

Save your drawing.

Figure 7.7

*The completed
CIRCLE
command
exercise.*

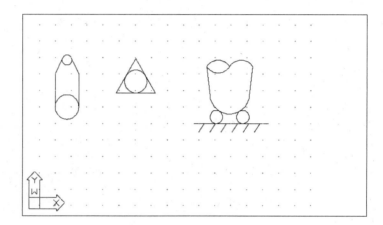

The 3P (3 Point) option of the CIRCLE command enables you to construct circles,
even when you have neither center point nor radius values. In the preceding exercise,
for example, drawing the circle inside the triangle without center point or radius
values would have been difficult. Both values would not be easy to obtain from the
information in the drawing. Because it was an equilateral triangle, the 3P option and
the MIDpoint object snap made the task easy.

Tip   To draw a circle tangent to any three lines (or arcs or curves), you use the 3 Point
option and then use the TAN object snap to pick each of the three lines.

When you use the TTR (Tangent, Tangent, Radius) option, you encounter situations
in which more than one circle matches the criteria specified by the command. In the
preceding exercise, for example, you could draw two possible circles that would satisfy
the radius and tangent specifications—one on either side of the arc's quadrant. In
such situations, AutoCAD draws the circle whose tangent points are closest to the
selected points. In the exercise, you forced both possible circles by picking near the
opposite ends of the line.

Depending on the information you have about the circle, the five options of
AutoCAD's CIRCLE command enable you to accurately draw and place virtually any
circle. Combined with object snaps and point filters, you need never calculate or
guess the information you need to draw circles correctly.

New Riders Publishing
INSIDE
SERIES

Creating Arcs

Unlike circles, which have only a center point and radius, arcs are difficult to define. In addition to center points and radii, arcs require that you begin and end angles to fully define them. Arcs, therefore, also have either a clockwise or counterclockwise nature to their creation, and are a little more difficult to draw than circles. AutoCAD offers 11 different methods for constructing arcs. Although this many choices might seem intimidating, you must understand only a few principles before you can use all the various methods. As with the five options of drawing circles, the information you have about the arc largely determines the method you choose. Often, more than one method can yield the arc you want with a given set of parameters. In the exercises in this section, you practice applying the most commonly used methods of constructing arcs in AutoCAD.

ARC. The ARC command enables you to create a circular arc. Three parameters enable you to choose the arc's dimensions and location. These parameters can be any combination of the start point, a point on the circumference, the endpoint, the center, the included angle, the chord length, or the tangent direction. The default method is a three-point arc that uses a starting point, a point on the circumference, and an endpoint.
Pull-down: *Choose* Draw, Arc
Screen: *Choose* DRAW1, Arc:

ARC Command Options

Figure 7.8 shows the various arc construction methods.

When you enter **ARC** at the Command: prompt, the following prompt appears:

Center/<Start point>:

If you pick a start point, your construction methods narrow to those that begin with Start (including 3 Points); if you begin with the C, AutoCAD restricts your options to those that accept the center point first. If, for example, you begin the arc with a center point, followed by a start point, the following prompt appears:

Angle/Length of chord/<End point>:

In this way, you are presented with remaining options as you supply each successive arc parameter. In most methods, when adequate information is supplied, AutoCAD drags the arc on-screen, and after you supply the third necessary parameter, draws the arc. Varying the order of the options enables you to choose the easiest order of input.

Figure 7.8

*Methods of
constructing arcs.*

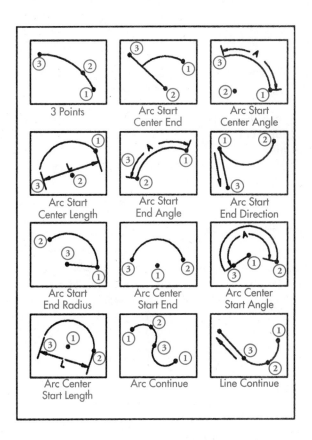

An example of input order is center-start-end versus start-center-end. The following list explains some combinations of the arc options.

◆ **3-Point.** This method creates an arc that passes through three specified points. The first point is the start point, the third point is the endpoint, and the second point is any other point on the arc. This is the default construction method.

◆ **Start,Center.** This method requires an arc starting point and the center point of the arc. This option group has a third parameter, which completes the arc by specifying an endpoint, an angle, or a length of chord. A counterclockwise arc is drawn if you give a positive included angle; a negative angle draws a counter-clockwise arc (from the start point). A positive chord length draws a minor arc (less than 180 degrees); a negative chord length draws a major arc (greater than 180 degrees).

◆ **Start,End.** This method enables you to define the starting and ending points of the arc first, and then to define how to draw the arc. You define the arc with

an angle, radius, direction, or center point. If you supply an angle, a positive angle draws the arc counterclockwise and a negative angle draws the arc clockwise (from the start point). If you choose the radius option, AutoCAD always draws the arc counterclockwise. A negative radius forces a major arc and a positive radius forces a minor arc.

◆ **Center, Start.** This method enables you first to identify the center of the arc, and then the start point. You complete the arc by supplying an angle, length of chord, or endpoint. If you choose a length of chord, a negative length forces a major arc. If you supply an angle, a negative angle draws a clockwise arc.

You can have additional control over the way AutoCAD draws the arc in several options by supplying negative values. A negative radius, for example, forces a major arc using the start, end, radius method; and if you specify negative included angles, AutoCAD constructs arcs in a clockwise direction.

Using ARC Command Options

You gain an understanding of several of the frequently used arc construction methods in the next two exercises. First, you use several options of the ARC command to draw the template shown in figure 7.9, beginning at the lower-left corner and proceeding counterclockwise. Then, in the second exercise, you use other arc options to draw the same part in a clockwise direction. As you proceed through these exercises, you can refer to the ARC command's options list and figure 7.8 to make sure that you understand why you use specific options.

 Note In many of the exercise's steps, you can type the coordinates shown, or you can use snap, ortho, and the coordinates display to pick the points. You might want to repeat the exercises on your own, using different methods.

Drawing the Template Counterclockwise

Continue to use the CHAP07A drawing from the preceding exercise, or begin a new drawing named CHAP07A, using the BASICS drawing as a prototype. First, turn on the layer TEMPLATE and set it current. Turn off all other layers. See figure 7.9 for dimensions. Turn on snap and ortho.

Command: *Choose* Draw, Line   Issues the LINE command

In the following six steps, you can type the relative coordinates or use ortho and snap along with the coordinate display to draw the lines from ① to ②.

continues

continued

`_line From point:` **1,2** (Enter)	Starts the lines at ① (see fig. 7.10)
`To point:` **@5<0** (Enter)	
`To point:` **@7<90** (Enter)	
`To point:` **@4<180** (Enter)	
`To point:` **@1<270** (Enter)	
`To point:` (Enter)	Ends the LINE command at ②

Next, you use the continue method to begin the first arc at ② where the last line segment ends. First turn off ortho.

`Command:` *Choose* Draw, Arc, Continue	Issues the ARC command and an Enter for the Continue option, and displays a rubber-band arc
`_arc Center/<Start point>:` `End point:` **@1,-1** (Enter)	Draws the arc from ② to ③

You must draw the next arc clockwise. Although you could use the continue method, use the start, center, angle method and specify a –90 degree angle.

`Command:` *Choose* Draw, Arc *then* Start, Center, Angle	Issues the ARC command and the Center option
`_arc Center/<Start point>:` **@** (Enter)	Specifies the last point—the end of the previous arc at ③
`Center/End/<Second point>:` `_c`	The menu issues the Center option
`Center:` **@1<270** (Enter)	Sets the center point; the arc rubber-bands as you move the cursor
`Angle/Length of chord/<End point>:` `_a Included angle:` **-90** (Enter)	Draws the 90° arc in a clockwise direction

Next, you use the Continue option of the LINE command to draw a 1-unit straight-line segment beginning from the end of the last arc.

`Command:` *Choose* Draw, Line	Issues the LINE command

`_line From point:` (Enter)	Specifies the Continue option; starts the line tangent to the end of the last arc
`Length of line: 1` (Enter)	Draws the line to ④
`To point:` (Enter)	Ends the LINE command

You must draw the next arc clockwise (beginning at ④). Use the start, end, angle method with a negative angle. The radius of the arc is 2 units.

Command: *Choose* Draw, Arc *then* Start, End, Angle	Issues the ARC command with the End and Angle options
`_arc Center/<Start point>: @` (Enter)	Starts the arc at the last point ④
`Center/End/<Second point>: _e`	The menu issues the End option
`End point: @-2,-2` (Enter)	Rubber-bands an arc in counterclockwise direction
`Angle/Direction/Radius/<Center point>: _a`	The menu issues the Angle option
`Included angle: -90` (Enter)	Draws the arc in clockwise direction

Next, you draw the last arc. Several methods work. Use start, center, end.

Command: *Choose* Draw, Arc *then* Start, Center, End	Issues the ARC command and the Center option
`_arc Center/<Start point>: ENDP` (Enter)	Specifies the ENDPoint object snap
`_endp of` *Pick the end of the arc at* ⑤	Specifies the arc start point
`Center/End/<Second point>: _c`	The menu issues the Center option
`Center: PER` (Enter)	Specifies the PERpendicular object snap
`to` *Pick the line at* ⑥	
`Angle/Length of chord/ <End point>: ENDP` (Enter)	Specifies the ENDPoint object snap
`_endp of` *Pick at* ①	Draws the arc and completes the template

Save your drawing.

Figure 7.9

The dimensioned template.

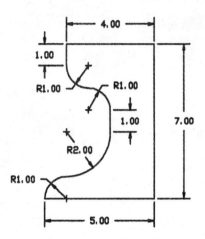

Figure 7.10

Drawing the template counterclockwise.

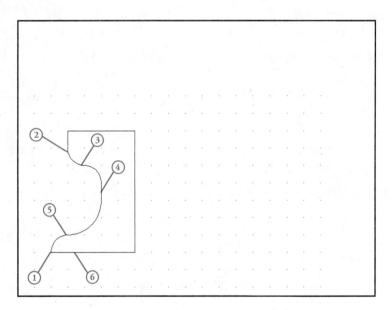

By using object snaps, relative coordinates, last point references, and four of the arc construction methods, you drew the template outline quickly and accurately. When you encounter a clockwise arc construction, you should, if possible, choose an option that forces arcs in that direction.

Now, you use some of the same and some other arc construction methods to draw the template in a clockwise direction. Now that you have experience with arcs from the preceding exercise, the steps in the following exercise are somewhat abbreviated. Again, refer to figure 7.9 for dimensions.

7

Drawing the Template Clockwise

Continue from the preceding exercise. Begin in the lower-left corner of the template and proceed clockwise; the first arc you draw is the last arc from the preceding exercise.

Command: **A** (Enter)	Issues the ARC command
ARC Center/<Start point>: **9,2** (Enter)	Specifies the arc start point (refer to ① in figure 7.11)
Center/End/<Second point>: **C** (Enter)	Specifies the Center option
Center: **@1<0** (Enter)	Sets the center; drags a rubber-band arc as you move the cursor
Angle/Length of chord/ <End point>: **A** (Enter)	Specifies the Angle option; arc drags in counterclockwise direction

The rubber-band angle drags from $0°$ (to the right of the center point), not from the start point.

Included angle: **-90** (Enter)	Forces and draws a clockwise arc

Now draw the next arc, using the start, end, direction method.

Command: (Enter)	Issues the ARC command
Center/<Start point>: **ENDP** (Enter)	

of *Pick the end of the arc at ②*

Center/End/<Second point>: **E** (Enter)	Specifies the End option
End point: **@2,2** (Enter)	Sets the endpoint
Angle/Direction/Radius/ <Center point>: **D** (Enter)	Specifies the Direction option; move the cursor and watch the arc drag with direction
Direction from start point: **0** (Enter)	Draws the arc

Note that in the last step, direction is reckoned in degrees from the start point. Next, you use the Continue option of the LINE command to draw the line segment.

Command: **L** (Enter)	Issues the LINE command
From point: (Enter)	Specifies the Continue option; drags a line

continues

continued

`Length of line: 1 (Enter)`	Draws the line
`To point: (Enter)`	Ends the LINE command

Use the center, start, angle method to draw the next arc.

`Command: A (Enter)`	Issues the ARC command
`Center/<Start point>: C (Enter)`	Specifies the Center option

Next, you use the @ (lastpoint) to specify the arc's center. Recall that the current lastpoint is the end of the line from the preceding step.

`Center: @1<180 (Enter)`	
`Start point: ENDP (Enter)`	Specifies the ENDPoint object snap
of *Pick at ③*	
`Angle/Length of chord/<End point>:` `A (Enter)`	Specifies the Angle option; drags a counterclockwise arc
`Included angle: 90 (Enter)`	Draws the arc

For the last arc, use the Continue option of the ARC command.

`Command: ` *Press Enter twice*	Repeats the ARC command and specifies the Continue option
`End point: @-1,1 (Enter)`	Draws the arc
`Command: L (Enter)`	Issues the LINE command
`From point: (Enter)`	Specifies the Continue option
`Length of line: 1 (Enter)`	Draws the line
`To point: (Enter)`	Ends the LINE command; you need not draw the remainder of the outline

The TEMPLATE layer of your CHAP07 drawing should now resemble figure 7.11.

Save your drawing.

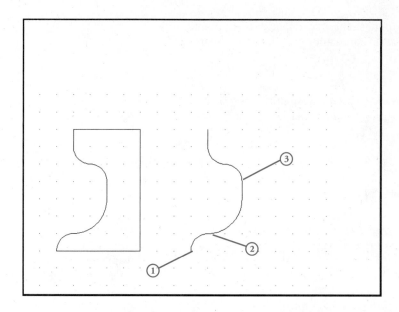

Figure 7.11
The completed templates.

In the two preceding exercises, you gain experience with seven of the arc construction methods. Again, more than one method often would work to construct the arc you need. In the template figure you use in those exercises, you have the opportunity to use the Continue options of both the ARC and LINE commands. In drawings that consist largely of orthogonal lines and arcs, these options often are available. Sometimes you draw objects that have unusual geometry. When you do, a knowledge of the ARC command's options provides you with a method to meet the challenge. You use few other AutoCAD commands in which thinking and planning ahead a step or two is as beneficial as when you use the ARC command.

While the TEMPLATE layer is still current, you might want to experiment with the remaining arc option combinations before you continue.

Creating Donuts, Polygons, and Rectangles

AutoCAD does not provide a specific object type for some of the basic geometric shapes like polygons, rectangles, or triangles. Instead, it borrows the capabilities of a special type of object called a polyline to construct the shapes. A *polyline* is a collection of connected line and/or arc segments that behave as a single object. This approach permits you to quickly create complex shapes that otherwise might take a great deal of time. Many of these shapes have their own command name: the DONUT, POLY-GON, and RECTANG commands enable you to create useful shapes that are discussed in the following sections.

Note Polylines are complex AutoCAD objects that can have the characteristics of width and curvature. Polylines are discussed in Chapter 11, "Drawing and Editing Polylines and Splines."

Creating Donuts

As you might imagine, the DONUT command enables you to create an object that looks like a doughnut. Donuts can have any inside and outside diameter. In fact, as figure 7.12 demonstrates, donuts that have an inside diameter of 0 appear as a filled-in circle. Donuts can serve many useful functions in a drawing, such as mounting holes, lugs, grounds, and so forth.

Figure 7.12

Some examples of donuts.

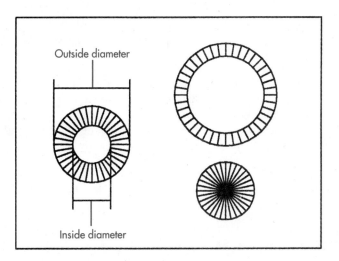

DONUT. The DONUT command enables you to create closed, filled polyline circles that can vary in width. Donuts have an inside diameter (which can be 0) and an outside diameter.
Pull-down: Choose Draw, Circle, Donut
Screen: *Choose* DRAW1, Donut:

New Riders Publishing
INSIDE
SERIES

DONUT Command Options

The DONUT command has the following options.

◆ **Inside diameter <current>.** At the `Inside diameter` prompt, you specify the inside diameter or press Enter to accept the default value. A diameter of 0 is acceptable; it causes DONUT to draw solid filled dots.

◆ **Outside diameter <current>.** At the `Outside diameter` prompt, you specify the outside diameter or press Enter to accept the default value.

You can use the PEDIT command to edit donuts; see Chapter 11, "Drawing and Editing Polylines and Splines."

In the following exercise, you return to the CIRCUIT-BOARD layer of the CHAP07A drawing and use the DONUT command to add mounting grommets and a grounding lug to the circuit board.

Adding Donuts to the Circuit Board

Continue to use the CHAP07A drawing from the earlier circuit board exercise. Turn on the CIRCUIT-BOARD layer and set it current. Turn off all other layers. Turn on snap mode.

Command: *Choose* Draw, Circle, Donut	Issues the DONUT command
_donut	
Inside diameter <0.50>: **.2** (Enter)	Specifies the inside diameter
Outside diameter <1.00>: **.4** (Enter)	Specifies the outside diameter

In the following steps, you can use snap and the coordinate display to locate the donut centers, or you can type the coordinates shown.

Center of doughnut: **1.5,9.5** (Enter)	Draws the donut
Center of doughnut: **14.25,9.5** (Enter)	Draws the donut
Center of doughnut: **14.25,2.5** (Enter)	Draws the donut
Center of doughnut: **1.5,2.5** (Enter)	Draws the donut
Center of doughnut: (Enter)	Ends the command

Next, you place a grounding lug on the board.

Command: (Enter)	Repeats the command

continues

continued

Inside diameter <0.20>: **0** (Enter)	Specifies the inside diameter
Outside diameter <0.40>: **.5** (Enter)	Specifies the outside diameter
Center of doughnut: **14,5** (Enter)	Draws the donut
Center of doughnut: (Enter)	Ends the DONUT command

Save your drawing.

Your circuit board drawing should now resemble figure 7.13. The DONUT command continues to prompt for donut center points until you end the command by pressing Enter.

Figure 7.13

Circuit board with donuts added.

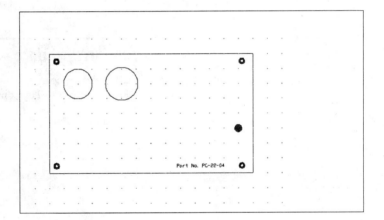

Port No. PC-22-04

 Tip   You can type **DONUT** or **DOUGHNUT**; AutoCAD recognizes both spellings.

Drawing Regular Polygons

Another composite polyline object is the polygon, which you create by using the POLYGON command. The POLYGON command enables you to draw regular (equilateral) polygons that can have from 3 to 1,024 sides. POLYGON gives you two ways to define the size of your figure (see fig. 7.14). You can show the length of one of the edges or you can define it relative to a circle. You then can inscribe the polygon in the circle or circumscribe it about the circle.

New Riders Publishing
INSIDE SERIES

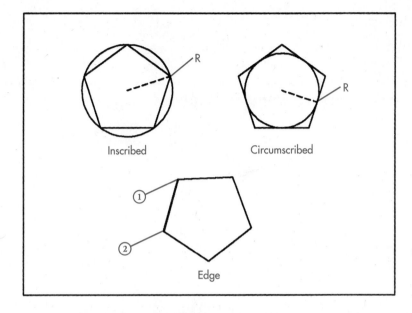

Figure 7.14

Three ways to draw regular polygons.

7

POLYGON. The POLYGON command enables you to draw regular (equilateral) polygons of from 3 to 1,024 sides. Polygon objects consist of polylines of zero width.

Pull-down: *Choose* Draw, Polygon
Screen: *Choose* DRAW1, Polygon:

Polygon Command Options

The POLYGON command offers the following options:

- ◆ **Number of sides <current>.** At the Number of sides prompt, you enter the number of sides between 3 and 1,024 or press Enter to accept the default.

- ◆ **Edge/<Center of polygon>.** At this prompt, you choose how you want to define the polygon. You can either specify its center point and then its radius, or the endpoints of an edge.

- ◆ **Inscribe in circle/Circumscribe about circle (I/C)<I>.** If you specify the center of the polygon, this prompt appears. If you choose inscribe in circle, all vertices of the polygon fall on the circle; if you choose circumscribe about circle, the radius equals the distance from the center of the polygon to the midpoints of the edges. If you use the pointing device to specify the radius, you dynamically determine the rotation and size of the polygon. If you specify the radius of the circle by typing a specific value, the angle at the bottom edge of the polygon equals the current snap rotation angle.

Regular polygons are easy to draw in AutoCAD. In the following exercise, you add two hexagonal inductance coils to the circuit board. You use the Edge option to place the first hexagon and the Center option to place the second hexagon.

Drawing Regular Polygons

Continue from the preceding exercise. Make sure that snap is on.

`Command:` *Choose* Draw, Polygon, Polygon	Issues the POLYGON command
`_polygon Number of sides <4>:` **6** `(Enter)`	Specifies a hexagon
`Edge/<Center of polygon>:` **E** `(Enter)`	Specifies the Edge option
`First endpoint of edge:` *Pick point* 9,7 (①) *(see fig. 7.15)*	Drags the polygon
`Second endpoint of edge:` *Pick point* 10,7 (②)	Draws the polygon
`Command:` `(Enter)`	Repeats the POLYGON command
`POLYGON Number of sides <6>:` `(Enter)`	Accepts the default hexagon
`Edge/<Center of polygon>:` *Pick point* 12,8 ③	Defaults to set the center point
`Inscribed in circle/` `Circumscribed about circle` `(I/C) <I>:` `(Enter)`	Accepts the default inscribed option

In the following step, you type the radius value to force the bottom edge of the hexagon to be parallel to the current snap angle (0 degrees).

`Radius of circle:` **1** `(Enter)`	Draws the polygon (see fig. 7.15)

Save your drawing.

After you draw a polygon object, you can use the PEDIT and EXPLODE commands to edit it. See Chapter 11, "Drawing and Editing Polylines and Splines," for information about editing polylines.

When you draw polygons, if you know the intended center point, the inscribed or circumscribed methods are the obvious choice. The edge method, on the other hand,

enables you to align the polygon with other objects. Using the edge method generates a polygon figure that continues counterclockwise from the two edge endpoints you specify.

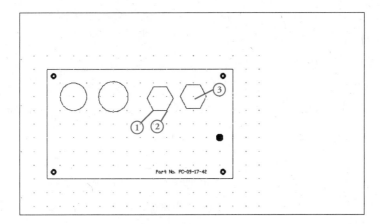

Figure 7.15

Adding a polygon to the circuit board.

7

Drawing Rectangles

Perhaps the simplest of the geometric shapes is the rectangle you draw when you use the RECTANG command. AutoCAD requests the opposite corners of the rectangle, then draws the rectangle.

RECTANG. The RECTANG command enables you to draw a rectangle by specifying the two opposite corners.
Pull-down: Choose Draw, Polygon, Rectangle
Screen: *Choose* DRAW1, Rectang:

RECTANG Command Prompts

Whether you issue the RECTANG command by using the pull-down menu or entering the command at the keyboard, RECTANG presents the following prompts:

◆ **First corner.** At this prompt, you specify a point to represent one corner of the rectangle. A rectangle drags on-screen as you move the cursor.

◆ **Other corner.** At this prompt, you specify a point to represent the opposite corner of the rectangle.

In the following two exercises, you draw several rectangles to represent additional elements on the circuit board: a transformer, three resistors, and a trimming capacitor. Use snap, the coordinate display, and figure 7.16 to help you find the points.

Adding a Rectangle to the Circuit Board

Continue from the previous exercise, with snap on.

`Command:` *Choose* Draw, Polygon, Rectangle	Issues the RECTANG command

`_rectang`

`First corner:` *Pick point* 2,6 (①) *(see fig. 7.16)*

As you move the cursor after you specify the first corner, a rectangle drags on-screen.

`Other corner:` *Pick point* 7.0,3.0	Draws the rectangle

Draw another rectangle inside the first one.

`Command:` **(Enter)**	Repeats the command

`First corner:` *Pick point* 2.5,5.5

`Other corner:` *Pick point* 6.5,3.5	Draws the second rectangle

Save your drawing.

Figure 7.16

Circuit board with rectangles added.

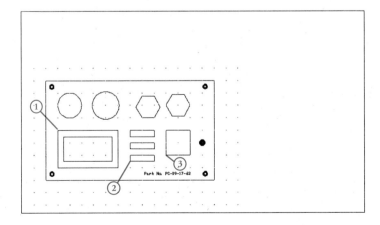

Using MULTIPLE To Repeat Commands

You can repeat commands automatically (without pressing Enter) by preceding the command with the MULTIPLE command.

> **MULTIPLE.** The MULTIPLE command enables you to repeat the next issued command. The command is repeated until you press Esc. Only the command name is repeated—you must specify any parameters to the command each time. MULTIPLE does not work with commands that you use from a dialog box. The MULTIPLE command is available only at the Command: prompt.

Use the MULTIPLE command in the next exercise to draw the remaining rectangles on the circuit board. Again, use snap and the coordinate display to help find the points quickly.

Adding Rectangles with the MULTIPLE Command

Continue from the preceding exercise.

Command: **MULTIPLE RECTANG (Enter)**   Issues and repeats the RECTANG command

No Command: prompt appears when you press the spacebar after you type **MULTIPLE**. Next, you draw the first resistor, beginning at ② in figure 7.16.

First corner: *Pick point* 8,3.5

Other corner: *Pick point* 10,4

First corner: *Pick point* 8,4.5

Other corner: *Pick point* 10,5

First corner: *Pick point* 8,5.5

Other corner: *Pick point* 10,6

Next, you draw the trimming capacitor, beginning at ③.

First corner: *Pick point* 11,4

Other corner: *Pick point* 13,6

First corner: *Press Esc*   Cancels the MULTIPLE RECTANG
command

continues

continued

Your circuit board should now resemble fig. 7.16.

Save your drawing.

Note Because pressing Enter (or the spacebar) at an empty Command: prompt repeats the last command, the MULTIPLE command is useful only if you need to repeat a command a substantial number of times.

Ellipses and Elliptical Arcs

AutoCAD is capable of constructing mathematically accurate ellipses and elliptical arcs. An AutoCAD ellipse can exist as a complete object or as a partial object. A partial object is called an *elliptical arc*. AutoCAD provides several methods you can use to accurately construct ellipses and elliptical arcs because you frequently need to depict views of the things you draft. A common drafting problem is the presentation of an ellipse or elliptical arc that has a rotation (into or out of the sheet) about one of its axes. You frequently use the rotated ellipse in piping to represent circular arcs that are turned toward or away from your view. Also, many machine made equipment parts require true ellipses and often require compound elliptical arcs—joined elliptical arcs that represent one surface. Fortunately, the ELLIPSE command and its options facilitate the brief process of creating what sometimes are rather complicated objects.

Note AutoCAD also provides the capability to draw an approximated ellipse using the polyline object, which you use the PELLIPSE system variable to control. A value of 1 forces AutoCAD to use the approximated method and draws a polyline object. The default value of 0 forces the mathematically correct method and draws an ellipse object.

An ellipse is defined by two axes, a short one called the *minor axis* and a long one called the *major axis*. The points you pick during the command define one or both axes, depending on the command options you use. You further define the elliptical arc by specifying a start angle and an end or included angle. In situations in which the mathematical method used to define the elliptical arc is of consequence to your application, you can use parameters to define the start and end angles, which causes AutoCAD to use a parametric vector equation. Refer to the *AutoCAD Command Reference* manual for more information.

> **ELLIPSE.** The ELLIPSE command enables you to create an ellipse object if the PELLIPSE system variable is set to 0; otherwise, it enables you to create a polyline approximation of an ellipse. You use centerpoints to define the ellipse and endpoints to define distances and radii. You can use an angle to define the ellipse with rotation about either axis. After you draw the ellipse, you also can use start and end angles or a parametric vector equation to draw an elliptical arc.
>
> Pull-down: *Choose* Draw, Ellipse
> Screen: *Choose* DRAW1, Ellipse:

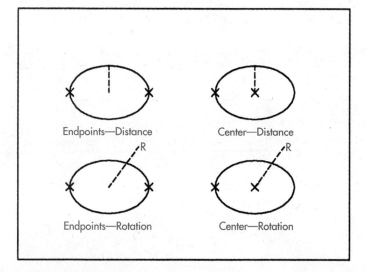

Figure 7.17

Methods of drawing an ellipse.

ELLIPSE Command Options

The ELLIPSE command has the following options:

♦ **<Axis endpoint 1>:.** Although this is a prompt, it begins the default procedure to define the first endpoint of the major or minor axis of the ellipse. Another prompt follows to define the last endpoint of the axis. To complete the definition, you can then choose to specify the distance for the remaining axis or choose the Rotation option.

♦ **Center.** Begins the definition of the ellipse by prompting you for a centerpoint. Another prompt follows and you define the endpoint of the first axis. To complete the definition, you can then choose to specify the distance for the remaining axis or choose the Rotation option.

◆ **Rotation.** Completes the definition of the endpoints/distance method or the center/distance method (refer to fig. 7.17). You can specify an angle measurement or pick a point. Specify an angle to ensure accurate input.

◆ **Arc.** Begins the definition of an elliptical arc. From this initial step, you can choose the endpoints/distance method or the center/distance method. The prompts that follow depend on which method you choose. After you define the ellipse, you must complete the command by indicating where the arc starts and ends, by specifying parameters or angles. The option requires one of six combinations—a start angle/included angle, a start angle/end angle, a start angle/parameter, a start parameter/end parameter, a start parameter/included angle, or a start parameter/end angle. The suboptions change according to the specification of parameter or angle to define the end of the arc.

The following exercise demonstrates how you can draw and rotate an ellipse, then how to construct an elliptical arc.

Constructing Ellipses and Elliptical Arcs

Continue from the preceding exercise. Turn off the CIRCUIT-BOARD layer, then turn on the ELLIPSE layer and set it current. Turn off snap mode and ortho mode.

Draw two lines, the first from 9,1 then vertically 10 units. Draw the second from 2,6 then horizontally 14 units.

Command: *Choose* Draw, Ellipse, Center	Issues the ELLIPSE command with the Center option
`_ellipse` `Arc/Center/<Axis endpoint 1>: _c`	
`Center of ellipse:` **INT** (Enter)	
of *Pick* ①	Selects the center of the ellipse (see fig. 7.18)
`Axis endpoint:` **ENDP** (Enter)	Defines the distance of the first axis
of *Pick* ②	

Drag your cursor to understand how you are interacting with the command.

`<Other axis distance>/Rotation:` **ENDP** (Enter)	Defines the remaining distance

New Riders Publishing
INSIDE
SERIES

of *Pick* ④	Completes the ellipse
Command: **U** `Enter`	Issues the UNDO command
Command: *Choose* Draw, Ellipse, then Axis, End	Issues the ELLIPSE command with the default distance option
`_ellipse` `Arc/Center/<Axis endpoint 1>:` **ENDP** `Enter`	Indicates the first axis endpoint
of *Pick* ③	
`Axis endpoint 2:` **ENDP** `Enter`	Indicates the second axis endpoint
of *Pick* ②	
`<other axis distance>/Rotation:` **R** `Enter`	Specifies the Rotation option
`Rotation around the major axis:` **60** `Enter`	Specifies a 60° angle and draws the ellipse

AutoCAD draws the ellipse with a flatness of 60°. Next, you draw an elliptical arc in the lower-left quadrant with a 60° flatness.

Command: **U** `Enter`	Issues the UNDO command
Command: **ELLIPSE** `Enter`	Issues the ELLIPSE command
`Arc/Center/<Axis endpoint 1>:` **A** `Enter`	Specifies the Arc option
`<Axis endpoint 1>/Center:` **ENDP** `Enter`	Specifies the first axis endpoint
of *Pick* ③	
`Axis endpoint 2:` **ENDP** `Enter`	Specifies the second endpoint of the first axis
of *Pick* ②	
`<other axis distance>/Rotation:` **R** `Enter`	Specifies the Rotation option to define the other axis
`Rotation around major axis:` **60** `Enter`	Specifies 60°
`Parameter/<start angle>:` **ENDP** `Enter`	Indicates the start angle of the arc
of *Pick* ③	

continues

continued

`Parameter/Included/<end angle>:`	Indicates the end angle of the arc
ENDP (Enter)	
of *Pick* ④ (see fig. 7.18)	Draws the elliptical arc (see fig. 7.19)

Erase the two lines, then use the Arc option of the ELLIPSE command to build three more arcs. Use the three arcs to build a full ellipse. Use object snaps on the elliptical arc to ensure accuracy.

The preceding exercise demonstrates the basics of building accurate ellipses. As an AutoCAD user, you will find that a good comprehension of the basics enables you to construct any ellipse.

Figure 7.18

Reference lines for building an ellipse.

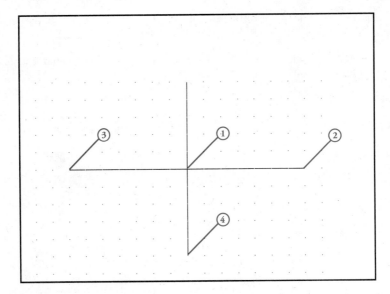

 Tip   You can construct elliptical arcs by making an ellipse and then using existing objects as trim boundaries for the TRIM command. This enables you to construct precise arcs without having to know odd angles and without having to use the added steps of the Arc option of the ELLIPSE command. For more on the TRIM command, refer to Chapter 14, "The Ins and Outs of Editing."

New Riders Publishing
INSIDE
SERIES

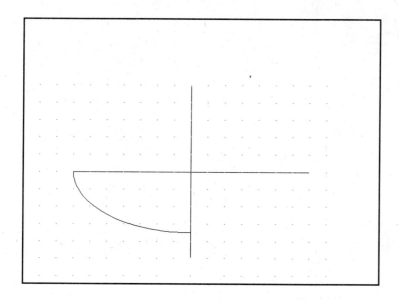

Figure 7.19

A completed elliptical arc.

In this chapter, you began earnest work on a real drawing. You used several concepts from preceding chapters as you used basic AutoCAD objects to begin to design. Throughout the circuit board drawing, for example, you used the convenience of snap, when possible, to speed the location and picking of points. The usefulness of object snap and point filters became evident in drawing arcs, for example. Even the value of having several layers that you turned on and off easily was evident.

When you draw circles and arcs, several methods are available. The method you select depends on what information you have. In the case of arcs, one or more methods often can accomplish the task.

The donuts, polygons, ellipses, and rectangles are common objects found in most drawings. Knowing how to draw them quickly and accurately increases your drawing efficiency.

Many of the exercises used methods that will be unnecessary after you learn about AutoCAD's editing commands. The next chapter introduces you to some of the basic operations of editing.

C H A P T E R

8

Object Selection and Grip Editing

A s your skills with AutoCAD develop, you use editing commands more often than drawing commands. You might, for example, use LINE and ARC (drawing commands) to represent a single chair in a room. You then would use COPY or ARRAY (editing commands) to generate the duplicates and fill up the room with chairs.

In addition to editing commands, such as MOVE, TRIM, and ARRAY, AutoCAD provides several quick, interactive, easy-to-use autoediting modes, such as stretch, move, and rotate. To use autoediting modes, you select objects and then use their geometric points, or *grip points*, to manipulate them. This chapter focuses on using autoediting modes with grips. Chapter 14, "The Ins and Outs of Editing," continues the discussion of editing techniques and selection options in more depth.

Before you can perform edit operations, AutoCAD must know which objects you select. This chapter covers the following activities:

◆ Selecting objects at the Command: prompt

◆ Using grips with the stretch, move, rotate, scale, and mirror autoediting methods and copy mode

◆ Using multiple hot grips to manipulate multiple points or objects

◆ Using the DDGRIPS and DDSELECT settings to control grip and selection behavior

Picking an object at the Command: prompt causes grips to appear. A *grip* is a convenient location on the object that helps you control and manipulate that object: think of it as a handle that you can grab and use to move the object. Each AutoCAD object has several grip points, which you can select accurately (without specifying object snap modes) by picking in the grip box. Figure 8.1 shows the grip locations of common objects.

Figure 8.1

Common object grip locations.

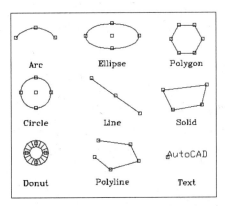

The grip points on a line, for example, are the endpoints and the midpoint. When grips are enabled (the default), the grips appear on an object when you select that object at the Command: prompt.

When you click on a visible grip, it becomes "hot" (selected) and appears highlighted. A hot grip becomes a base point for one of the autoediting modes to manipulate the object. The first exercise in this chapter demonstrates how you can select grips and use autoediting to construct a three-way valve.

Quick 5¢ Tour

Begin a new drawing named CHAP08 using the ACAD prototype drawing.

Command: *Choose* Options, Selection	Displays the Object Selection Settings dialog box
Choose the Default *button, choose* OK	Insures the proper settings for object selection and closes the dialog box
Command: *Choose* Draw, Polygon, Polygon	Issues the POLYGON command
_polygon	
Number of sides <4>: **3** (Enter)	Specifies a triangle

New Riders Publishing
INSIDE
SERIES

`Edge/<Center of polygon>: `**`6,6`** (Enter)	Specifies a centerpoint
`Inscribed in circle/Circumscribed` `about circle (I/C) <I>: `(Enter)	Specifies that the triangle is inscribed about a circle
`Radius of circle: `**`@3<0`** (Enter)	Specifies a 3 unit radius for the circle and draws the triangle
`Command: `*Choose* Draw, Line	Issues the LINE command
`_line`	
`From point: `*Pick* ① *using MIDpoint* *object snap (see fig. 8.2)*	Picks the midpoint of the triangle edge for the line's start point
`_mid of`	
`To point: `**`@3<180`** (Enter)	Specifies a line 3 units long to the left
`To point: `(Enter)	Completes the LINE command
`Command: `*Pick* ① *and* ②	Selects the triangle and the line, shows grips, and highlights each object
Pick the grip at the point of the *triangle*	Establishes the hot grip and starts autoedit mode
Press Enter 4 times	Switches from Stretch, to Move, to Rotate, to Scale, to Mirror mode

`** MIRROR **`
`<Second point>/Base point/Copy/`
`Undo/eXit: `**`C`** (Enter)
	Choose the Copy option

`** MIRROR (multiple) **`
`<Second point>/Base point/Copy/`
`Undo/eXit: `*Press F8 and pick a point*
above the triangle, then press Enter
	Turns on Ortho mode, then the new triangle
	is drawn, the Enter completes the autoedit

`Command: `*Select the new triangle and* *line*	Shows grips and highlights four objects
Select the grip at the valve center, *then press Enter 3 times*	Selects the hot grip for the selection set and switches to Scale mode

`** SCALE **`
`<Scale factor>/Base point/Copy/`
`Undo/Reference/eXit: `**`0.5`** (Enter)
	Scales the selection by half

continues

continued

`Command:` *Press Esc twice*	Unselects the object, then discontinues the grip edit mode
`Command:` *Select both lines and the right triangle*	Shows grips and highlights the objects
Select the grip at the valve center, then press Enter 2 times	Makes the selected grip hot and switches to Rotate mode

`** ROTATE **`
`<Rotation angle>/Base point/Copy/`
`Undo/Reference/eXit:` **C** (Enter)
	Chooses the Copy option

`** ROTATE (multiple) **`
`<Rotation angle>/Base point/Copy/`
`Undo/Reference/eXit:` **-90** (Enter) (Enter)
	Specifies a –90° angle, copies and rotates the selection, then exits autoedit mode

`Command:` *Pick the new line above the valve*	Selects the line
Select the new line's bottom grip, move the cursor to the grip at the valve center, then select that grip	Stretches and snaps the line's endpoint to the grip at the valve center
`Command:` *Press Esc twice*	Unselects the object, then discontinues the grip edit mode

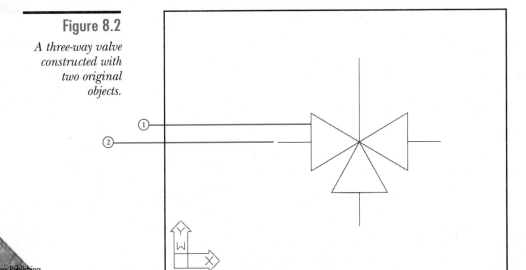

Figure 8.2

A three-way valve constructed with two original objects.

New Riders Publishing
INSIDE
SERIES

The next section explains the important features of grips and shows how using grips properly can make editing tasks less tedious. In this chapter, you further develop the TOOLPLAT drawing from the IA Disk. Figure 8.3 shows the initial view of the drawing.

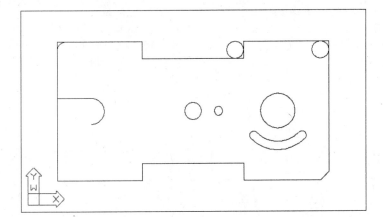

Figure 8.3

The TOOLPLAT drawing.

8

Introducing Autoediting Modes

Autoediting modes are a special group of common editing methods that are available when you choose a base grip. These modes are briefly explained in the following list:

◆ **Stretch.** Stretch mode modifies objects by moving one or more grips to another location while leaving the other part of the object intact. This can easily change the size or shape of an object or a group of objects. In some cases, the stretch mode moves an object.

◆ **Move.** Move mode relocates objects from a base point to another location you specify. The size and orientation do not change.

◆ **Rotate.** Rotate mode revolves objects around a base point. You can enter, drag, or use the Reference option to show the angle.

◆ **Scale.** Scale mode resizes objects up or down by a given scale factor about a specified base point. You can enter, drag, or use the Reference option to show scale factors.

◆ **Mirror.** Mirror mode reflects selected objects about a line described by the base point grip or a specified point, and another specified point.

All these autoediting modes have common properties. First, after you select objects and choose a base grip to issue the command, you can choose a mode by entering the first two letters of the mode (**SC** for scale, for example) or by pressing Enter, the spacebar, or the pointing device Enter button. Pressing Enter repeatedly cycles through the autoediting modes in the order they are presented in the preceding list. Each mode displays a set of options, such as the Copy option. If you want to make a copy while executing any autoediting mode, use the Copy option or hold down Shift while you make multiple second point picks. The Undo option enables you to undo the last edit, and the eXit option enables you to exit the autoediting modes. These modes and their options are similar to the corresponding commands, such as STRETCH and MOVE, which are discussed in Chapter 14.

The following exercises introduce you to using grips for selecting and editing objects to modify the TOOLPLAT drawing from the IA Disk. You use grips to stretch the top and side lines to the ends of the arc to form a fillet for the upper-left corner.

Stretching Lines with Grips

Begin a new drawing again named CHAP08, using the TOOLPLAT drawing as a prototype. Zoom to the drawing area shown in figure 8.4. Discard changes to the previous CHAP08 drawing.

Command: *Pick a point on the upper left arc*	Selects and highlights the arc and displays its grips
Command: *Pick line at* ① *(see fig. 8.4)*	Selects and highlights the top line and displays its grips
Command: *Pick grip at* ②	Enters stretch autoediting mode
** STRETCH ** `<Stretch to point>/Base point/Copy/` `Undo/eXit:` *Pick arc's grip at* ③	Stretches the line to the arc endpoint

Choose View, Zoom, Previous

Note   If you miss the object when you try to pick, a rubber-band box (a window) appears from the pick point. Pick again at the same point, or press Esc, and then try again. Window selection is covered later in this chapter in the section "Using DDSELECT To Control Selection."

New Riders Publishing
INSIDE
SERIES

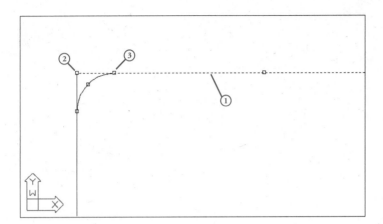

Figure 8.4

*Grip points and
pick points.*

8

Snapping with Grips

The preceding exercise could have used the endpoint object snap to lock the line
onto the arc's endpoint. Because the cursor automatically snaps to grips, however,
you generally do not need to use object snaps when you grip edit. (Some objects do
not provide grips for certain object snaps, so you need to use object snaps occasionally.) The trick to eliminating object snaps for editing is first to select the objects to
snap to as well as the objects to edit, which displays all their grips. Then, click on the
grips of the objects to edit, which makes their autoedit grips hot. You then can snap
to any of the displayed grips without using object snap modes. The hot grips remain
hot until the autoedit operation is completed or canceled by pressing Esc. All the
grips remain displayed until you enter a command or press Esc at the Command:
prompt. Depending on the autoediting mode being used, either all highlighted
objects or hot objects only are affected.

Grip Snapping

Continue in the CHAP08 drawing from the preceding exercise.

Command: *Pick* ① *and* ② *to*   Selects the objects shown in figure 8.5
indicate a crossing selection
(see fig. 8.5)

Slowly move your cursor near the grips   Makes the circle's centerpoint grip hot
of the selected circle, then select the circle's
center grip

Notice the snapping action, or gravity, of your cursor to a grip.

continues

continued

`** STRETCH **`
`<Stretch to point>/Base point/Copy/`
`Undo/eXit:` **(Enter)**
	Switches to the Move autoedit mode

`** MOVE **`
`<Move to point>/Base point/Copy/`
`Undo/eXit:` *Move the cursor to the*
grip at ③
	Moves the selection set toward the midpoint of the line

Click the grip at ③	Moves the selection set to the midpoint where the line was before the move
`Command:` **U** **(Enter)**	Undoes the edit, unselects the objects, and removes the grips

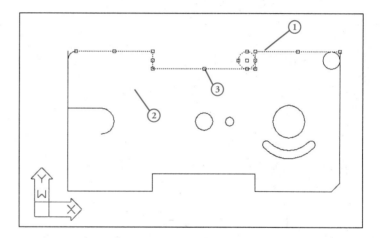

Figure 8.5

Snapping to objects using grips instead of object snaps.

To better control editing with grips, you must understand AutoCAD's grip settings and selection methods. The next section explains object selection methods.

New Riders Publishing
INSIDE
SERIES

Understanding Autoediting Object Selection

Object editing utilizes either verb/noun or noun/verb selection methods. One way to think of the verb/noun method is as the action/object method in which an action modifies the object you select. The noun/verb method is the reverse. You select the objects first, then apply the action. For example, when you use verb/noun object selection with the COPY command, you in effect tell AutoCAD to "copy these objects from point A to point B." When you use the verb/noun method, you tell AutoCAD, "These are the objects to copy from point A to point B." Autoediting objects uses a form of noun/verb object selection. Chapter 14 contains more information on object selection.

Controlling GRIPS and Selection Parameters

Grips must be on before autoediting modes can function. You can use the DDGRIPS command or choose Options, Grips to activate the Grips dialog box (see fig. 8.6).

Figure 8.6

The Grips dialog box.

'DDGRIPS. The 'DDGRIPS command enables you to open the GRIPS dialog box, in which you can enable grips, control their sizes, and manage their colors.
Pull-down: *Choose* Options, Grips
Screen: *Choose* OPTIONS, DDgrips

Putting a check mark in the <u>E</u>nable Grips check box turns on the GRIPS system variable; clearing the box turns it off. You can use the slider bar to easily adjust the grip size, which works similarly to object snap aperture size. You also can use the <u>U</u>nselected and <u>S</u>elected buttons to specify the color of both displayed and selected grips in this dialog box.

You have the useful option of displaying the grips of objects within blocks. In the Grips dialog box, the Enable Grips Within Blocks check box must be checked to provide this feature. Without enabling this setting, block objects have a single grip that corresponds to the block's insertion point. This allows limited grip editing— you can only snap, move, rotate, scale, or mirror about the insertion point. With the setting enabled, all of the block's objects have their grips displayed. Any of the displayed grips may be easily used as a move point, a rotation point, a scale point, or a snap point. It is much quicker to use grips within blocks than to specify object snaps, and you have much better visual feedback. Object snaps are usually more useful than grips when blocks are very complex and display too many grips. See Chapter 17, "Block Structure, Editing, Organization, and Management," for more about using blocks.

Tip You use the GRIPS system variable to store the grips on/off setting. On is 1 and off is 0. To check all the AutoCAD system variables related to grips, enter **SETVAR** at the Command: prompt, followed by **?**, then **GRIP***. See Appendix F, "System Variables Table," or use online help for the details on the corresponding values.

Using DDSELECT To Control Selection

Two selection settings in the Object Selection Settings dialog box—Use <u>S</u>hift to Add and <u>P</u>ress and Drag, enable you to improve the versatility and interaction of editing with grips (see fig. 8.7). You can access the Object Selection Settings dialog box by using the DDSELECT command or choosing <u>O</u>ptions, <u>S</u>election. The other settings in the Object Selection Settings dialog box are covered in Chapter 14.

'**DDSELECT**. The 'DDSELECT command enables you to open the Object Selection Settings dialog box, from which you can determine selection modes, pick box size, and object sort methods.
Pull-down: *Choose* Options, Selection
Screen: *Choose* OPTIONS, DDselec

New Riders Publishing
INSIDE
SERIES

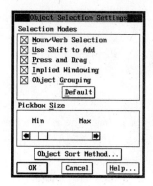

Figure 8.7

*The Object
Selection Settings
dialog box.*

AutoCAD editing modes and commands operate on a selection set of objects that
you select. The current selection generally is indicated by highlighting the objects.
You use the Use Shift to Add setting to control the way AutoCAD adds objects to
the selection set. When this setting is off (the default), AutoCAD adds objects to
the selection set as you select them. When it is on, AutoCAD replaces the existing
selection set with the new objects as you select them, unless you hold down Shift
as you do so. Holding down Shift and selecting (Shift+pick) currently highlighted
objects removes those objects from the selection set, independent of the Use Shift to
Add setting. To add objects when Use Shift to Add is on, hold down Shift as you select
objects. After you remove a selected object from the selection set, its grips still appear
until you clear them, as described later in this section. In the following exercise, you
experiment with Use Shift to Add.

Controlling Selection

Continue to use the CHAP08 drawing from the preceding exercise.

Choose Options, Selection	Activates the Object Selection Settings dialog box
Choose Default, *then* OK	Ensures default setting
Command: *Pick any object*	Highlights the object and starts a selection set
Command: *Pick two other objects*	Highlights the objects and adds them to the set
Command: *Shift+pick one of the highlighted objects*	Removes the object from the set, but leaves grips

continues

continued

Command: *Choose* Options, Selection	Displays the Object Selection Settings dialog box
Put a check mark in the <u>U</u>se Shift to Add *check box, then choose* OK	Turns Use Shift to Add on and exits
Command: *Pick any object*	Clears the selection set (leaving grips on) and starts a new set
Command: *Pick any other object*	Clears the selection set again and starts another new set
Command: *Shift+pick two other objects*	Adds the objects to the existing set
Command: *Shift+pick a highlighted object*	Removes the object from the set

The current <u>U</u>se Shift to Add setting (off or on) is obvious as you select objects. Whether you set it on is really a personal preference. Even if you are used to having it off, with practice you probably will find it more convenient to set it on. Just remember to use Shift to unselect objects or select additional objects. The exercises throughout the rest of this book assume that <u>U</u>se Shift to Add is checked on.

 Note The <u>U</u>se Shift to Add setting is stored in the PICKADD system variable. Confusingly, <u>U</u>se Shift to Add on means PICKADD=0 (off) and <u>U</u>se Shift to Add off (the default) means PICKADD=1 (on).

As an alternative to pressing Esc to clear a selection set or to clear grips (press Esc twice to clear both), you also can select in a clear area to accomplish the same result. When you do so, you actually select to clear the selection set. If <u>P</u>ress and Drag is off (the default), you must pick twice. (<u>P</u>ress and Drag is discussed in the next section.) If your first pick finds an object, you select the object. If, however, you miss with your first pick, you set the base corner of a rubber-banded window or crossing box. A second pick completes the window or crossing selection. A window selects all objects totally enclosed in its box; a crossing selects all objects in the box or that cross its box. If you pick window points left-to-right, the rubber-band box is shown solid; if you pick crossing points right-to-left, the rubber-band box is dashed. If the selection set is already empty, or if you just emptied it with a window or crossing selection of empty space, making another empty window or crossing selection removes all grips from the drawing window. The following exercise demonstrates this technique.

Clearing the Selection Set and Grips

Continue to use the CHAP08 drawing from the preceding exercise. You should have Use Shift to Add on and a few objects selected.

`Command:` *Pick points ① and ② (see fig. 8.8)*   Clears the selection set

`Command:` *Pick points ① and ② again*   Clears the grip markers

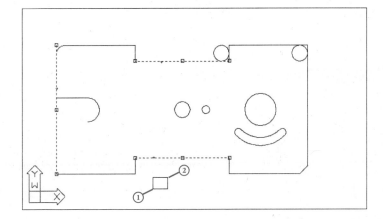

Figure 8.8

Selecting in empty space to clear grips.

8

The preceding exercise cleared the grip boxes and selection set from the drawing. You often need to clear grips to prevent the drawing area from becoming too cluttered. Alternatively, you can press Esc twice to clear the grips and selection set.

Window and crossing selections, including using the preceding method to clear a selection set and grips, are easier if you change the way AutoCAD makes window and crossing selections. The next section explains how and why.

Controlling Press and Drag

In earlier releases, AutoCAD always requires two picks to show a window. In most software that has a graphical interface, you can select a window by pressing and holding the button at the first point, dragging to the second point, and then releasing the button. The Object Selection Settings dialog box now offers a choice in the way you specify a window or crossing. When the Press and Drag box is checked (the PICKDRAG system variable is on, set to 1), you create a window by pressing the pick button, moving to the other corner of the window, and releasing. Even if you are used to the old two-pick method, after you get used to Press and Drag you will find it faster and more efficient. It also behaves in the same manner as other software you might use and enables you to clear selection sets or grips with a single pick. You try this technique in the next exercise.

Controlling Press and Drag

Continue in the CHAP08 drawing from the preceding exercise.

Command: **DDSELECT** (Enter)	Displays the Object Selection Settings dialog box
Put a check mark in the Press and Drag *checkbox, then choose* OK	Turns on Press and Drag and exits
Command: *Press and hold the pick button at* ① *(see fig. 8.9), drag to* ②*, and release the pick button*	Creates a crossing window selection
Command: *Press and hold the pick button at* ③*, then drag to* ④*, then release*	Creates a Window selection, clears the previous selection set, and starts a new set
Command: *Click once in empty space*	Clears the selection set
Command: *Click again in empty space*	Removes grip markers

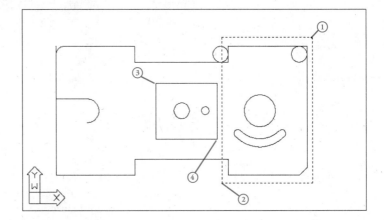

Figure 8.9

Selection points for press and drag windows.

Stop   Throughout the rest of the book, <u>P</u>ress and Drag (PICKDRAG on, 1) is the default window/crossing selection mode. When exercises direct you to use a crossing or window selection, remember to use the press-and-drag technique.

Controlling the Pick Box Sizes

The pick box is a small box that enables you to select objects. Unless both <u>N</u>oun/ Verb Selection (see Chapter 14) in the Object Selection Settings dialog box and grips are disabled, the pick box appears on the crosshairs at the `Command:` prompt. The pick box also appears without the crosshairs at the `Select objects:` prompt during editing commands such as ERASE, MOVE, and COPY. You use a system variable to control the size of the pick box. You can easily adjust the size by clicking and dragging a horizontal slider in the Object Selection Settings dialog box. The size usually ranges between 1 and 15 pixels, depending on your graphics resolution. Using a small pick box makes selecting an object from a group of tightly clustered objects easier. A large pick box enables you to be less precise with your selection and possibly select objects faster, depending on the drawing. But, a large pick box also can make object selection ambiguous. You might have several objects that pass through the pick box and miss the object you try to select. Use whatever is comfortable for your display and pointing device, but be sure to set it to a different size than the aperture (see Chapter 5, "Setting Up a CAD Drawing"). If you set the pick box and aperture to the same size, you may not be able to distinguish the two. This situation becomes very confusing when using a running object snap mode (see Chapter 6, "Drawing Accurately").

Tip   When multiple objects fall within the pick box, you can use the Cycle feature to select a specific object. You hold down Ctrl, then make your pick. Thereafter, each successive pick cycles to the next possible object. Stop picking when you have the correct selection, then press Enter and your object is selected.

Editing with the Autoediting Modes

Now that you understand <u>U</u>se Shift to Add and <u>P</u>ress and Drag, you can combine these techniques with the five autoediting modes to rapidly simplify editing tasks. The remainder of the sections in this chapter demonstrate how each of these modes work and how you can apply them.

Object Snapping and Stretching with Grips

In the following exercises, you continue to use the stretch autoediting mode and learn how to snap to specific points by using only grips. Grip editing usually involves fewer steps than regular object snap editing, and therefore is a great time-saver.

Object Snapping with Grips

Continue to use the CHAP08 drawing from the preceding exercise and zoom to the view shown in figure 8.10.

Command: *Pick the arc at* ① *(see fig. 8.10)*	Selects the arc and displays its grips
Command: *Pick line at* ②	Clears the previous set, selects the vertical line, and shows grips
Command: *Pick grip at* ③	Grips the line and enters stretch mode

`** STRETCH **`
`<Stretch to point>/Base point/Copy/`
`Undo/eXit:` *Pick the lower left grip on the arc at* ④ *in figure 8.11*
	Snaps the line to the arc endpoint

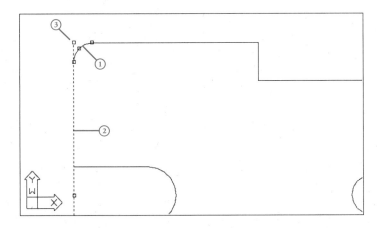

Figure 8.10

Grip and object selection points before stretching lines.

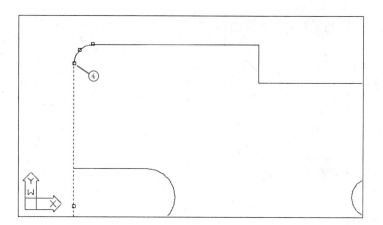

Figure 8.11

Tool plate after stretching lines.

With a few exceptions, depending on which grip you pick, the stretch autoediting mode changes the shape of objects. In the next exercise, you change one of the arcs in the radial slot.

Stretching Arcs with Autoedit

Continue to use the CHAP08 drawing from the preceding exercise and zoom to the previous view.

Command: *Pick any arc*	Selects arc and displays grips
Command: *Pick the arc's midpoint grip*	Grips the midpoint and enters stretch mode
** STRETCH ** `<Stretch to point>/Base point/Copy/` `Undo/eXit:` *Move and pick any other point*	Changes the arc's shape
Command: *Pick an endpoint grip on the arc*	Grips the endpoint and enters stretch mode
** STRETCH ** `<Stretch to point>/Base point` `/Copy/Undo/eXit:` *Pick any other point*	Changes the arc's shape
Command: **U** (Enter)	Undoes the last change
Command: **U** (Enter)	Returns the arc to its original shape

Copying and Moving with Stretch Autoediting Mode

In the stretch autoediting mode, you can move an object, change an endpoint, or resize an object, depending on the object type and grip you select. In the stretch editing mode, selecting a line's endpoint stretches the line, for example, whereas picking the middle grip moves it. Other objects behave similarly, like circles, while other objects, such as arcs, do not. You also can use the Copy option or hold the Shift key down as you pick the second point to create copies while stretching.

In this next exercise, you experiment with these methods and options, and use the Copy option of the stretch autoediting mode to complete the guide slot at the left of the tool plate.

Copying with Autoediting Modes

Continue to use the CHAP08 drawing from the preceding exercise.

Command: *Pick the line at* ① *(see fig. 8.12)*	Selects the line and displays grips
Command: *Pick the mid grip on the line*	Grips line and enters stretch mode, moving line

`** STRETCH **`
`<Stretch to point>/Base point/Copy/`
`Undo/eXit:` *Pick a point above the tool plate*
	Moves the line

Command: **U** (Enter)	Undoes the stretch move
Command: *Select the guide slot arc*	Selects and displays grips
Command: *Pick at* ①	Clears the arc from the set, selects the line, and displays its grips
Command: *Pick the line's midpoint grip*	Grips the line and enters stretch autoediting mode, moving the line

`** STRETCH **`
`<Stretch to point>/Base point/Copy/`
`Undo/eXit:` **B** (Enter)
	Specifies the Base point option

Base point: *Pick the right end grip of the line*	Changes the base (from) point for moving the line

`** STRETCH **`
`<Stretch to point>/Base point/Copy/`
`Undo/eXit:` **C** (Enter)
	Specifies the Copy (multiple stretch) option

New Riders Publishing
INSIDE
SERIES

`**STRETCH (multiple) **`
`<Stretch to point>/Base point/Copy/`
`Undo/eXit:` *Pick the bottom grip on*
the arc at ②
	Copies the line

`<Stretch to point>/Base point/Copy/` `Undo/eXit:` *Pick another point below* *the base plate*	Copies the line again
`<Stretch to point>/Base point/Copy/` `Undo/eXit:` **U** (Enter)	Undoes the last copy
`<Stretch to point>/Base point/Copy/` `Undo/eXit:` (Enter)	Exits from autoediting mode
`Command:` *Choose* File, Save	Clears the selection sets and grips, and saves the drawing

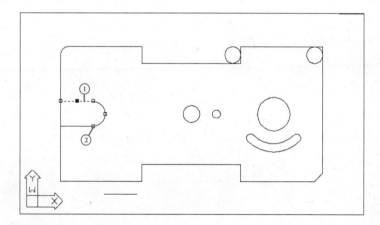

Figure 8.12

Copying with stretch autoediting mode.

 Note   You can exit from the multiple autoediting modes by pressing Enter, the spacebar, or Esc, or you can enter X. If you are not in multiple mode, you can exit from autoediting by pressing Esc or you can enter X.

Because it is so versatile—capable of stretching, moving, and copying objects—stretch is the default autoediting mode when grip editing. The move autoediting mode works similarly to stretch and is explained in the next section.

Using the Move Autoediting Mode

Instead of using the stretch autoediting mode to move an object, try using the move mode. To do so, enter **MO** at the autoedit prompt or press Enter or the spacebar once, and the move mode prompt appears. Specifying a point moves the selected object or objects the distance between the base point (selected grip) and the specified point. If you want a base point other than the selected hot grip, the Base point option enables you to specify it, as in the preceding exercise. You can specify points by any combination of grips, object snaps, or coordinate entry.

 Tip   When you try to move or stretch a grip point a small distance, the destination point might be within the grip box of the gripped point, frustrating your efforts. In such cases, just move or stretch the grip to an out-of-the-way point, repick the grip, and then repick the destination point, which is now clear of the grip.

In the next exercise, you use the move autoediting mode.

Using Move Autoediting Mode

Continue to use the CHAP08 drawing from the preceding exercise.

Command: *Pick, drag, and release to select from* ① *to* ② *(see fig. 8.13)*	Selects the radial slot and displays grips
Command: *Pick either large arc's mid grip*	Enters stretch mode

`** STRETCH **`
`<Stretch to point>/Base point/Copy/`
`Undo/eXit:` (Enter)
	Switches to move mode

`** MOVE **`
`<Move to point>/Base point/Copy/`
`Undo/eXit:`	

Move the cursor. The entire radial slot (the entire selection set) now moves with the cursor.

Pick any point below the tool plate	Relocates the slot
Command: **U** (Enter)	Undoes the move and removes the grips

New Riders Publishing
INSIDE
SERIES

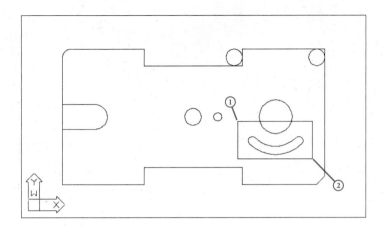

Figure 8.13

Window selection points for moving the slot.

As with stretch mode, you can make one or more copies from the original by using move mode. Use the Copy option or hold down the Shift key as you pick the first destination point. In the next exercise, you use the Copy option with the move mode.

Copying with the Move Autoediting Mode

Continue to use the CHAP08 drawing from the preceding exercise.

Command: *Select a window from ① to ② (refer to figure 8.13)*	Selects the radial slot and displays grips
Command: *Pick any of the large arc's grips*	Enters stretch mode
`** STRETCH **` `<Stretch to point>/Base point/Copy/` `Undo/eXit:` *Press the spacebar*	Switches to move mode
`** MOVE **` `<Move to point>/Base point/Copy/` `Undo/eXit:` **C** (Enter)	Specifies the Copy (multiple) option
`** MOVE (multiple) **` `<Move to point>/Base point/Copy/` `Undo/eXit:` *Pick two points below the tool plate (see fig. 8.14)*	Copies two new slots to below the tool plate
`<Move to point>/Base point/Copy/` `Undo/eXit:` (Enter)	Exits from autoediting mode

Save the drawing.

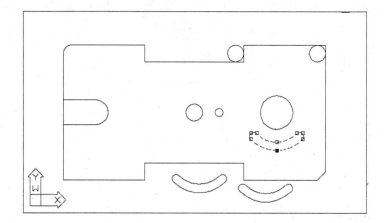

Figure 8.14

Two copies of the radial slot.

The preceding exercise illustrates the move autoedit mode and how you can make multiple copies. You should select all the objects to be included in the command, as well as make sure that any additional grips you might need for point selection are displayed. Using Shift to copy is shown next.

Using Shift To Copy

Using the Shift key as you autoedit initiates an incremental copy mode of operation. The distance from the hot grip to the first Shift+pick point establishes the increment. The grip you select affects the placement of incremental copies. Using a line's midpoint grip produces a different effect than using a line's endpoint grip. You can further control copy placement by using the ortho mode, in which the cursor snaps to points based on the increment distance.

In the following exercise, you use Shift+pick and stretch mode to copy the center hole.

Using Shift To Copy

Continue to use the CHAP08 drawing from the preceding exercise.

Command: *Press F8*   Turns on ortho mode

Command: *Pick the circle at* ①   Selects the center hole and displays its grips
(see fig. 8.15)

Command: *Click on the center grip*   Makes the center grip hot

New Riders Publishing
INSIDE
SERIES

```
** Stretch **
<Stretch to point>/Base point/Copy
Undo/eXit: Press and hold Shift and
pick a point above the center hole
```
Copies the center hole and specifies the copy increment

```
** Stretch **
<Stretch to point>/Base point/Copy
Undo/eXit: Continue to hold Shift and
pick a point below the center hole
```
Copies the center hole using the specified increment

```
** Stretch **
<Stretch to point>/Base point/Copy
Undo/eXit: Press F8
```
Turn off ortho mode

```
** Stretch **
<Stretch to point>/Base point/Copy
Undo/eXit: Press and hold Shift and
move the cursor around
```
Snaps cursor to points based on the copy increment

```
** Stretch **
<Stretch to point>/Base point/Copy
Undo/eXit: Press Esc
```
Cancels the autoedit operation

Command: **U** (Enter)   Undoes the copies

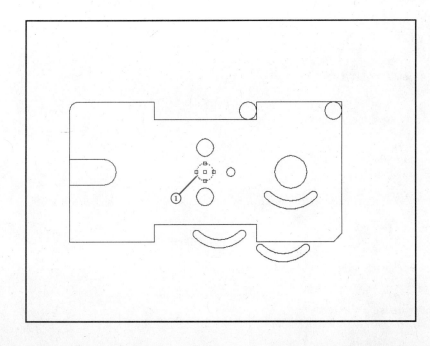

Figure 8.15

Center hole selection.

Rotating with Autoediting Mode

Often, drawing a shape in a normal orientation and then rotating it, or rotating and copying it into a different orientation is more convenient than drawing it at an odd angle. You can use the rotate autoediting mode to revolve selected objects about a base point. The default base point is the selected grip; you can use the Base point option to specify a new one. You enter rotate mode by pressing Enter or the spacebar twice, or entering **RO** at the stretch mode prompt, and then entering a rotation angle or picking a point to define a rotation angle. A positive value produces counterclockwise rotation; a negative value produces clockwise rotation.

In the following exercise, you use rotate mode.

Rotating and Moving Objects with Autoedit

Continue with the CHAP08 drawing from the preceding exercise. Make sure ortho mode is off.

Command: *Select a window from* ① *to* ② *(see fig. 8.16)*   Selects the radial slot and displays its grips

Command: *Pick either large arc's midpoint grip*   Highlights grip and enters stretch mode

```
** STRETCH **
<Stretch to point>/Base point/Copy/
Undo/eXit: Press the spacebar twice
```
Switches to rotate mode

```
** ROTATE **
<Rotation Angle>/Base point/Copy/
Undo/Reference/eXit:
```

Move the cursor, and note that the slot rotates dynamically as you do so.

```
<Rotation angle>/Base point/Copy/
Undo/Reference/eXit: Press F8, then
move the cursor up to rotate the slot 90° and pick
```
Turns on ortho mode and rotates the objects

Now, using figure 8.17 as a guide, move the slot into position near the guide slot at the left of the tool plate.

Command: *Press F8*   Turns off ortho mode

Command: *Pick either of the mid grips*   Enters stretch mode

```
** STRETCH **
<Stretch to point>/Base point/Copy/
Undo/eXit: Press the spacebar once
```
Switches to move mode

```
** MOVE **
<Move to point>/Base point/Copy/
Undo/eXit: B Enter
```
Make the grip hot

Base point: *Shift+right-click to*
pop-up the object snap menu and choose
CENTER, *then pick either of the large arcs*

Sets the base point at the arc's center

```
<Move to point>/Base point/Copy/
Undo/eXit: Use CENTER object snap
and pick the center of the guide slot arc
```
Moves the slot to a new location

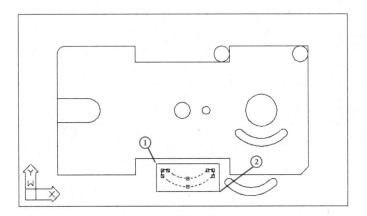

Figure 8.16

Slot selection window and grips.

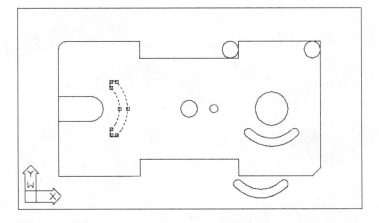

Figure 8.17

The rotated and relocated slot.

The autoedit rotate and move modes oriented the slot and moved it to the proper location. In the exercises, you used object snaps rather than grips because arc centers do not have grips. Remember that picking an empty window once clears the selection set; a second empty window removes the visible grips. You use that technique again in the following exercise.

Stop   Remember that picking an empty window clears the selection set; a second empty window removes the visible grips. If you accidentally clear the selection set, you have to reselect all of your objects.

In the next exercise, you use the Copy option of the rotate autoediting mode to complete the hole pattern at the center of the tool plate. You use the Shift+pick feature of Copy to snap copies to 45° increments.

Rotating and Copying with Autoedit

Continue with the CHAP08 drawing from the preceding exercise.

Command: *Double-click at* ① *(see fig. 8.18)*	Clears the selection set and grips
Command: *Pick the circle at* ②	Creates the set and displays grips
Command: *Pick the circle at* ③	Clears the previous set, selects the circle, and displays grips
Command: *Pick the larger circle's center grip*	Enters move mode, stretch mode is skipped because the base grip is not on a selected object
** MOVE ** <Move to point>/Base point/Copy/ Undo/eXit: *Press* (Enter)	Switches to rotate mode
** ROTATE ** <Rotation angle>/Base point/Copy/ Undo/Reference/eXit: **C** (Enter)	Enters multiple copy mode

`** ROTATE (multiple) **`
`<Rotation angle>/Base point/Copy/`
`Undo/Reference/eXit:` **45** (Enter)
	Makes the first copy at 45 degrees

`<Rotation angle>/Base point/Copy/` `Undo/Reference/eXit:` *Press and hold Shift, then snap to 90° and pick*	Makes the next copy at 90 degrees
`<Rotation angle>/Base point/Copy/` `Undo/Reference/eXit:` *Continue to press and hold Shift, then drag to 135° and pick*	Makes the next copy at 135 degrees
`<Rotation angle>/Base point/Copy/` `Undo/Reference/eXit:` *Continue to press and hold Shift, then drag to 180° and pick*	Makes the next copy at 180 degrees
`<Rotation angle>/Base point/Copy/` `Undo/Reference/eXit:` (Enter)	Exits from autoediting mode
`Command:` **QSAVE** (Enter)	Clears grips and the selection set, and saves the drawing

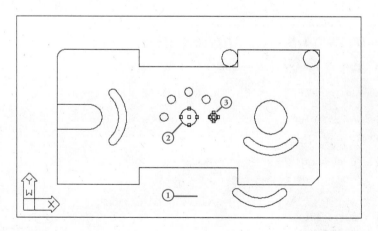

Figure 8.18

Circles copied with rotate autoediting mode.

The autoedit rotate mode conveniently changes the orientation of objects or creates circular patterns. Most of its options—Base point, Copy, Undo, and eXit—work the same as with the other autoediting modes. Use the Reference option to specify the current and new rotations. This latter method is handy when you must rotate a selection to align it with an object at an unknown angle. See Chapter 14, for details.

In this drawing, some of the work that you can accomplish by rotating you also can do by mirroring, which is discussed next.

Using Autoediting Mode To Mirror

In mirror mode, you can create a reflected image of the selected objects across an indicated mirror line. The mirror line is defined by the endpoints of the base point and a specified second point. AutoCAD assumes that the base point is the selected grip, unless you use the Base point option to override it. If ortho mode is on, you easily can pick a second point for a horizontal or vertical mirror line. The Copy option creates a mirrored copy of the original objects; otherwise, AutoCAD transforms the original objects. Enter **MI** at the autoedit prompt or cycle through the options by pressing Enter to access the mirror mode.

Try the mirror autoediting mode on the tool plate. Mirror the right radial slot to make a copy above the hole.

Mirroring Objects with Autoediting Mode

Continue to use the CHAP08 drawing from the preceding exercise.

Command: *Select the circle at* ① *(see fig. 8.19)*   Creates the set and shows grips

Command: *Select a window from* ②   Selects the radial slot and
to ③   displays grips

Command: *Pick one of the grips on the*   Enters stretch mode
slot

`** STRETCH **`   Switches to mirror mode
`<Stretch to point>/Base point/Copy/`
`Undo/eXit:` *Press Enter four times*

`** MIRROR **`   Prompts for a base point
`<Second point>/Base point/Copy/Undo/`
`eXit:` **B** (Enter)

`Base point:` *Pick center grip of the* *circle*	Specifies the new base point
`<Second point>/Base point/Copy/Undo/` `eXit:` *Pick the circle's right grip at* ①	Locates the second point directly to the right of the base point and mirrors the slot

Because you did not use the Copy option, the original slot was deleted.

`Command:` **U** (Enter)	Undoes the edit
`Command:` *Select the circle at* ① *and a window from* ② *to* ③ *(see fig. 8.19)*	Selects the circle and radial slot and displays grips
`Command:` *Pick one of the grips on* *the slot*	Enters stretch
`** STRETCH **` `<Stretch to point>/Base point/Copy/` `Undo/eXit:` *Press the spacebar four times*	Switches to mirror mode
`** MIRROR **` `<Second point>/Base point/Copy/Undo/` `eXit:` **B** (Enter)	
`Base point:` *Pick the center grip of* *circle*	
`<Second point>/Base point/Copy/Undo/` `eXit:` **C** (Enter)	Specifies the Copy option
`** MIRROR (multiple) **` `<Second point>/Base point/Copy/Undo/` `eXit:` *Pick the circle's right grip at* ①	Copies and mirrors in one operation
`** MIRROR **` `<Second point>/Base point/Copy/Undo` `/eXit:` (Enter)	Exits from autoedit

Save the drawing.

Figure 8.19

Upper slot created with mirror autoediting mode.

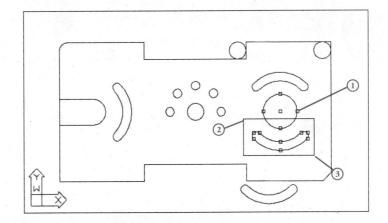

Next, you use the mirror mode to complete the hole pattern at the center of the tool plate. This time, instead of using the Copy option, press Shift as you pick the second point. Using Shift is an alternative way to copy with autoedit.

Finishing the Hole Pattern by Mirroring

Continue to use the CHAP08 drawing from the preceding exercise.

Command: *Pick the circle in the center of the hole pattern*   Creates the set and displays grips

Command: *Select a crossing window from points ① to ② (see fig. 8.20)*   Selects three circles and displays grips

Command: *Pick any one of the grip points on the small holes*   Enters stretch mode

```
** STRETCH **                          Enters mirror mode
<Stretch to point>/Base point/Copy/
Undo/eXit: MI Enter
```

```
** MIRROR **
<Second point>/Base point/Copy/Undo/
eXit: B Enter
```

Base point: *Pick the center hole's center grip*   Specifies a new base point

```
** MIRROR **
<Second point>/Base point/Copy/Undo/
eXit: Shift+pick the right grip of the
center hole
```

Enters copy (multiple) mode to make
copies while picking second point(s)

```
** MIRROR (multiple) **
<Second point>/Base point/Copy/
Undo/eXit: (Enter)
```

Exits autoedit mode

Your drawing should look like figure 8.21.

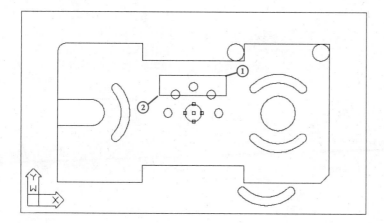

Figure 8.20

*Crossing selection
of holes to mirror.*

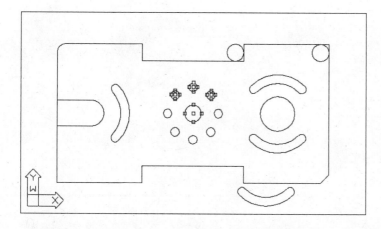

Figure 8.21

*The completed
hole pattern, with
grips.*

Look for opportunities to use mirror mode in your drawings to save time when you create objects. Remember to properly specify the two points that form the mirror line. Also, determine whether you need the Copy option.

Scaling with Autoedit

Scaling is another editing feature that is a great time-saver. You can use this autoedit mode to create blown-up views, resize standard shapes, or change from English to metric units. As the rotate mode, you scale from a base point. Unless you specify otherwise, the base point is the selected grip point.

Continuing with the project, assume that an engineering change requires a size reduction of the hole and radial slots at the right side of the tool plate. The pattern is proportional to its original size—just smaller. Use the scale autoediting mode in the following exercise to shrink the slots to three-fourths of their original size.

Using Scale Autoediting Mode

Continue to use the CHAP08 drawing from the preceding exercise.

Command: *Double-click in empty space*	Clears the selection set and grips
Command: *Pick a crossing window from* ① *to* ② *(see fig. 8.22)*	Selects slots and circle
Command: *Pick center grip of center circle*	Enters stretch mode
** STRETCH ** \<Stretch to point>/Base point/Copy/ Undo/eXit: *Press Enter three times*	Switches to scale mode
** SCALE ** \<Scale factor>/Base point/Copy/Undo/ Reference/eXit: *Move the cursor*	Dynamically scales objects in proportion
\<Scale factor>/Base point/Copy/Undo/ Reference/eXit: **.75** (Enter)	Scales objects to 3/4 original size

Save the drawing. Your drawing should now look like figure 8.23.

Because the proper scale—usually full—is so important in a CAD database, be sure to scale objects to their proper size. The scale mode is handy for adjusting items such as text, title blocks, and borders to complete a drawing. The autoediting modes have the same effect on text as on other graphics objects. You can scale, copy, move, and rotate text just like any other object.

New Riders Publishing
 INSIDE
 SERIES

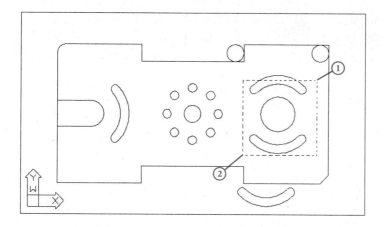

Figure 8.22

Crossing selection of slots.

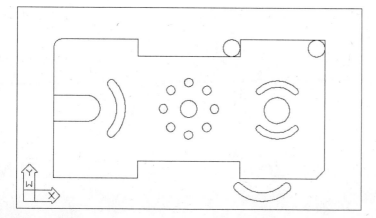

Figure 8.23

Scaled slots.

 Tip   The Reference feature of the scale autoediting mode can be a valuable technique when you need to accurately resize selected objects from one known size to another known size. It works by calculating the scale factor for you.

This chapter emphasized the procedures to create and modify objects from existing geometry, using the techniques of grip editing. As we have seen, one can generate fairly complex models from simple prototypes!

Many more drawing and editing techniques are explained in the following chapters. Your first challenge is to master the drawing and editing commands themselves, then start to develop a style of CAD drafting that best fits your needs. When you complete a drawing, think of ways to draw it more efficiently the next time. Eventually, you refine your skills and tap into those techniques that make your AutoCAD drafting and design work more productive.

As we progress on our AutoCAD journey, we'll discover in Chapter 9 ways to control the drawing display to get the job done even quicker.

Controlling the Display

Whether you use AutoCAD to draw a tiny machine screw or the side of a barn, you instruct the system to use "real-world" coordinates. Then, the AutoCAD drawing database maintains accurate sizes of objects. However, this can create a dilemma—for example, how do you represent the side of a barn at full scale on a screen that measures, say, 20 inches maximum?

To create drawings, you need to "move around" the drawing, locating and magnifying the work areas. This chapter includes the following 2D tools and techniques that you can use to control the view of the graphics screen:

◆ Using the ZOOM and PAN commands to view more or less of your drawing and to shift your view without changing the magnification

◆ Using the VIEW or DDVIEW commands to manage the use of saved views that you often use

◆ Controlling the display size and resolution

◆ Understanding the virtual screen and regenerations

Chapter 10, "Working in Model and Paper Space Viewports," discusses another way to control the display—using viewports.

What you see in the AutoCAD graphics window is actually a *viewport* into your drawing, enabling you to "zoom" in and out (like using a magnifying glass) and "pan" around (like using a pair of binoculars).

How far can you zoom in? In a moment, we'll look at the solar system, drawn at full scale (about seven million miles across—see fig. 9.1). If you include enough detail, you can position your view to the edge of the galaxy, and then zoom in to read the plaque attached to the leg of the lunar lander! AutoCAD is capable of such magnification levels because it is precise within at least 14 significant digits.

Figure 9.1

The solar system, at full scale.

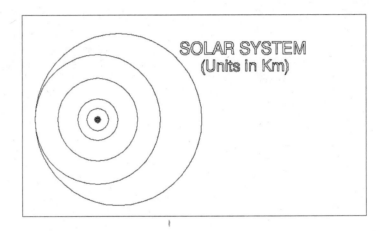

Let's see these zooming techniques in action in the following exercise.

Quick 5¢ Tour

Begin a new drawing named CHAP09, using the SOLAR drawing from the IAD Disk as the prototype (refer to figure 9.1).

Command: **VIEW** (Enter)	Accesses named views saved in drawing
?/Delete/Restore/Save/Window: **R** (Enter)	Specifies the Restore option
View name to restore: **SUN-AREA** (Enter)	Restores the named view (see fig. 9.2)
Command: (Enter)	Repeats the VIEW command
?/Delete/Restore/Save/Window: **R** (Enter)	
View name to restore: **MOON** (Enter)	Restores the view named MOON (see fig. 9.3)

New Riders Publishing
INSIDE
SERIES

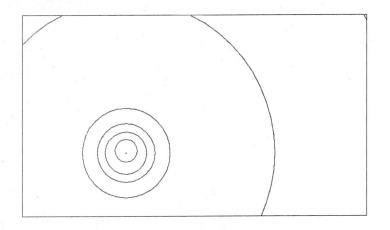

Figure 9.2

View of the sun area.

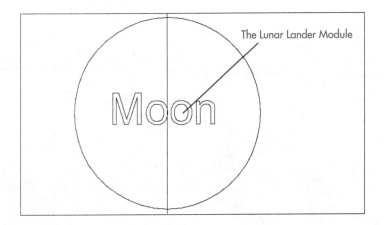

The Lunar Lander Module

Figure 9.3

View of the moon.

9

```
Command: Enter
```
Repeats the VIEW command

```
?/Delete/Restore/Save/Window:
R Enter
```

```
View name to restore: LEM Enter
```
Restores the view named LEM (see fig. 9.4)

```
Command: Z Enter
```
Starts the ZOOM command

```
ZOOM
All/Center/Dynamic/Extents/Left/
Previous/Vmax/Window/<Scale(X/XP)>:
Pick ① (refer to fig. 9.4)
```
Specifies first corner of a window to magnify

```
Other corner: Pick ②
```
Magnifies the lander leg (see fig. 9.5)

continues

continued

Figure 9.4
View of the lunar lander.

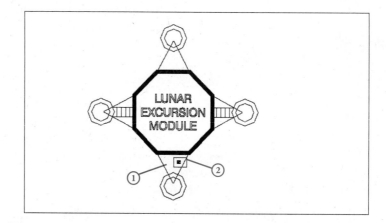

Figure 9.5
View of the lander leg.

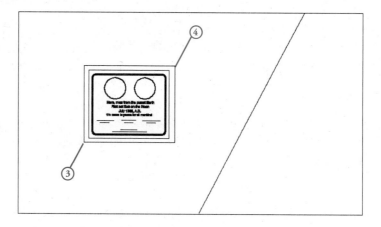

Command: **Enter**	Repeats the ZOOM command
All/Center/Dynamic/Extents/Left/ Previous/Vmax/Window/<Scale(X/XP)>: *Pick* ③ *(refer to fig. 9.5)*	Specifies first corner of a window
Other corner: *Pick* ④	Magnifies the lander plaque (see fig. 9.6)

New Riders Publishing
INSIDE
SERIES

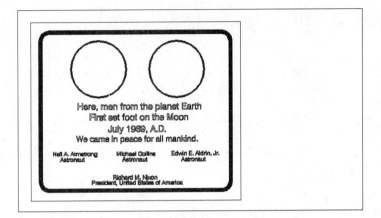

Figure 9.6

View of the lander plaque.

AutoCAD's display controls make drawing easier. Basic display-control commands, such as ZOOM and PAN, function in AutoCAD just like their photographic counterparts. Use the ZOOM command to magnify the drawing for detailed work. Use the PAN command to shift the drawing view at the current magnification. Panning enables you to work on large objects without having to return to a full-drawing view to determine your drawing location. Use the VIEW and DDVIEW commands to save and restore views by names you supply. Simple controls, such as REDRAW and REGEN, enable you to clean up your drawing or display its most current view.

AutoCAD's display controls are accessed through the View pull-down menu as shown in figure 9.7.

Figure 9.7

The View pull-down menu and VIEW screen menus.

Controlling the Drawing Display

Whenever you reopen a drawing, AutoCAD displays the last view that was on-screen at the time of the last save (not unlike an electronic bookmark). To look more closely at the current display, you might need to zoom in on the drawing. The most common way to tell AutoCAD what part of the current drawing you want to enlarge is to use the ZOOM command to pick diagonal corners of a box, or window, around the area of interest.

'ZOOM. The 'ZOOM command alters the current magnification level of the on-screen display. It is one of the most frequently used commands in AutoCAD.
Pull-down: *Choose* View, Zoom
Screen: *Choose* VIEW, Zoom

Using ZOOM Window

Do the following exercise to become more familiar with the ZOOM Window option. You do not need to pick exact coordinates; just indicate roughly the area you want to see in more detail.

Using the ZOOM Window

Begin a new drawing called CHAP09A, using the TOWER486 drawing from the IAD Disk as the prototype.

Command: *Choose* View, Zoom, Window	Issues the ZOOM command with the Window option
Command:_'zoom	
All/Center/Dynamic/Extents/Left/Previous/ Vmax/Window/<Scale(X/XP)>: w	
First corner: *Pick* ① *(see fig. 9.8)*	Sets the window's lower left corner
Other corner: *Pick* ②	Sets the window's upper right corner and zooms to the view in figure 9.9

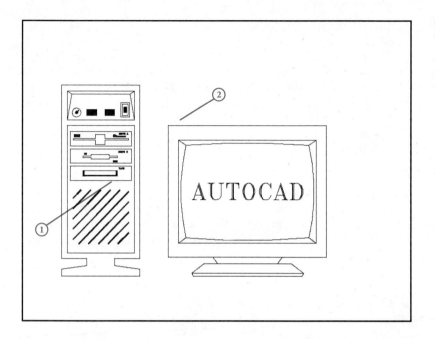

Figure 9.8

*Creating a
ZOOM Window.*

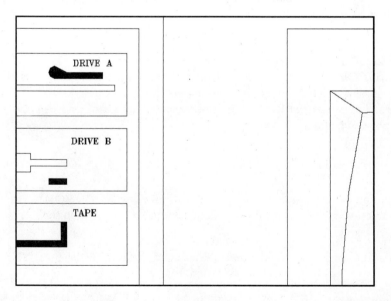

Figure 9.9

*The view of the
drawing after
ZOOM Window.*

9

Notice that after you pick the first corner, your cursor changes to a *rubber-band* box rather than the normal crosshairs. As soon as you pick the second corner, AutoCAD displays the area of the drawing that you enclosed in the window, as shown in figure 9.9. The corners that you pick determine the new area to display. Sometimes, the new area displayed shows more than you might expect. The reason is that your display area is rectangular and AutoCAD must maintain the aspect ratio of the window to the display area. Therefore, specifying a tall, narrow window causes AutoCAD to use the height of the window as the determining dimension and to fill the horizontal dimension as needed to maintain the aspect ratio.

 Tip You can use the PAN command to define your view with a tall, narrow window or a long, short window. A tall, narrow window at the right edge of the display pans right. A long, short window at the top edge of the display pans up. To keep the same magnification, make the tall or long side of the window as tall or as long as the display allows.

 Tip To use ZOOM Window to gain the best possible enlargement of the current view, drag the rectangle to describe roughly the same aspect ratio (proportions) as the current display. Describing a very tall, narrow window or a very long, thin window results in a negligible magnification.

 Tip You do not have to issue the Window option to perform a ZOOM Window. The default ZOOM command accepts two corner points and zooms to the window that they define. In fact, you do not even have to enter ZOOM, because AutoCAD defines Z as an alias that issues the ZOOM command. Just enter **Z** and then pick two points to perform a ZOOM Window.

Examining ZOOM's Other Options

The Window option enables you to move in closer to your drawing. The ZOOM command includes other options for display management, as described in the following list:

◆ **Extents.** This option displays the entire drawing in the current viewport. A regeneration occurs when this option is used.

◆ **All.** This option displays the drawing's limits or extents, whichever is larger. In a 3D view, All displays the drawing's extents. A regeneration occurs when this option is used.

 New Riders Publishing
INSIDE SERIES

◆ **Center.** This option prompts for a center point, then prompts for a magnification or height, and displays the view in the current viewport. The center point you pick becomes the viewport's center. If you press Enter instead of picking a center point, the display area's current center is maintained. For the second prompt, the magnification is specified by appending an X to the value you supply, otherwise the option uses the height of the display. Because the height is expressed in drawing units, you can specify a value relative to the size of your objects. For example, if your drawing is a floor plan of an office 170'0" long by 65'6" wide and you specify the center of the plan, you could specify a height of 65'6" to display the office so that the width fills the height of the display.

◆ **Dynamic.** This option graphically combines the PAN command with the ZOOM command's All and Window options. Dynamic displays an image of the entire generated portion of your drawing, and you use the cursor to tell AutoCAD where to zoom. Dynamic can zoom in or out, or it can pan the current viewport.

◆ **Left.** This option prompts for a point that becomes the lower left corner of the current viewport, then prompts for a magnification or height and displays the view in the current viewport. The Left option is the sister to the Center option, therefore the responses to the prompts are alike.

◆ **Previous.** This option restores the previous display for the current viewport, whether it was generated by the ZOOM, PAN, VIEW, DDVIEW, VPOINT, or DVIEW commands. AutoCAD stores up to ten previous views for each viewport; you can step back through them by using the Previous option repeatedly.

◆ **Vmax.** This option zooms to the currently generated virtual screen, to display the maximum possible drawing area without a regeneration.

◆ **Window.** This option zooms to the rectangular area you specify by picking two diagonally opposite corner points. When you issue the ZOOM command, you can automatically begin a zoom window by picking a point on the screen. This is the default zoom method; you need not enter W before picking points.

◆ **Scale(X/XP).** This option prompts for a scale factor relative to one of three things: the limits of the drawing, the current view, or paper space. When you specify a number alone, your number scales the limits of the drawing to the current viewport. When you specify a number followed by an X, your number scales the current view to the current viewport. When you specify a number followed by XP, your number scales the view relative to paper space.

Note   Zooms occasionally require a drawing regeneration. The ZOOM command's All and Extents options always cause at least one drawing regeneration. Such regens are not time-consuming in small or simple drawings, but large or complex drawings can take a long time to regenerate. If you use the ZOOM command's Previous or Vmax options, you can often avoid forcing AutoCAD to regenerate your drawing. There are more tips to avoiding regens in the section "Tips for Avoiding Regenerations" at the end of this chapter.

Keeping Track of Zoom Displays

Every time you zoom in or out, AutoCAD keeps track of the previous display, up to ten zooms. In the following exercise, you learn how to use the ZOOM command's Left, Center, Scale, Previous, and Extents options.

Using ZOOM Left, Center, Scale, Previous, and Extents

Continue in the CHAP09A drawing.

If snap is on, turn it off.

`Command:` *Choose* View, Zoom, All	Displays the drawing's limits (in this case)
`Command:` *Choose* View, Zoom, Left	Issues ZOOM with the Left option

`Command: _'_ZOOM`
`All/Center/Dynamic/Extents/Left/`
`Previous/Vmax/Window/<Scale(X/XP)>: '_l`
	Sets the lower left corner

`Lower left corner point:` *Pick the bottom of the tape drive (see fig. 9.10) at* ①	Sets the lower left corner
`Magnification or Height <26.190>:` *Pick* ② *(refer to fig. 9.10)*	Specifies the width of the tape drive as the height of the display and zooms (see fig. 9.11 for the resulting display)
`Command:` *Choose* View, Zoom, Center	Issues ZOOM with the Center option

`Command: '_zoom`
`All/Center/Dynamic/Extents/Left/`
`Previous/Vmax/Window/<Scale(X/XP)>: c`	

`Center point:` *Pick* ① *at the top of drive B (see fig. 9.11)*	Sets the window's center point

New Riders Publishing
INSIDE
SERIES

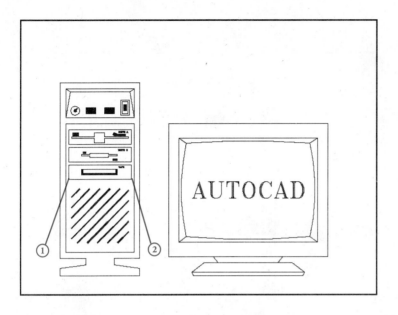

Figure 9.10

The drawing before using ZOOM Left.

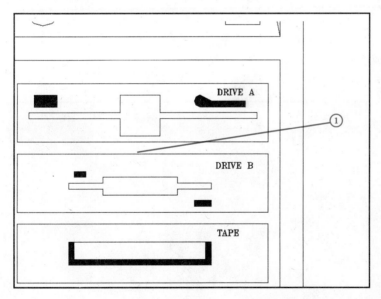

Figure 9.11

After ZOOM Left and before ZOOM Center.

9

`Magnification or Height <7.762>:` **0.5X** (Enter)	Reduces the view magnification by half (see fig. 9.12 for the resulting display)
`Command:` (Enter)	Repeats the ZOOM command

`'ZOOM`

continues

continued

Figure 9.12

After ZOOM Center and before ZOOM Scale.

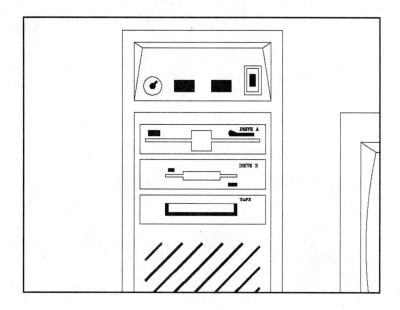

```
All/Center/Dynamic/Extents/Left/
Previous/Vmax/Window/<Scale(X/XP)>:
0.25X Enter
```

Reduces the view magnification to a quarter of its previous magnification (see fig. 9.13 for the resulting display)

Figure 9.13

After the ZOOM Scale 0.25X.

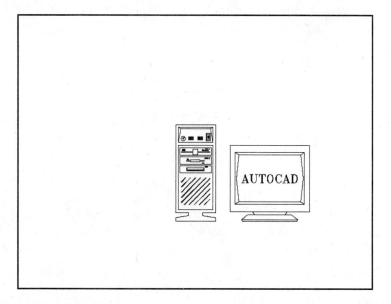

```
Command: (Enter)                          Repeats the ZOOM command

'ZOOM

All/Center/Dynamic/Extents/Left/          Zooms to the previous view
Previous/Vmax/Window/<Scale(X/XP)>:
P (Enter)

Command: (Enter)                          Repeats the ZOOM command

'ZOOM

All/Center/Dynamic/Extents/Left/          Zooms to the drawing extents (see fig.
Previous/Vmax/Window/<Scale(X/XP)>:       9.14 for the resulting display)
E (Enter)
```

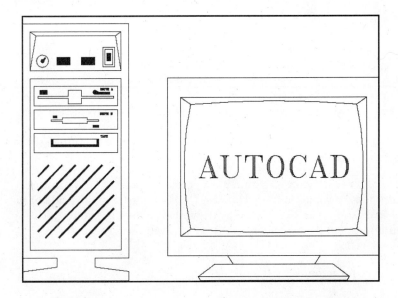

Figure 9.14

After ZOOM Extents.

9

```
Regenerating drawing.
```

If you followed the steps successfully, the window's height should be filled with a full view of your drawing.

Note   The Previous option does not necessarily zoom out. It simply returns to a previous view, whether larger or smaller than the current view, including views created by the PAN, VIEW, DVIEW, DDVIEW, and VPOINT commands.

Tip   Use the ZOOM Extents option just before you end your drawing session as a quick check to visually verify whether you drew outside your limits. Another advantage to issuing ZOOM Extents just before leaving a drawing is that the next person to open that drawing is immediately oriented within the file. You can terminate the zoom to save time while the screen is updating by pressing Esc.

You might have noticed a speed difference between zooms that regenerate the drawing and those that do not. In a complex drawing, this time difference can be considerable. To control drawing regenerations, you need to understand how ZOOM works. To understand the ZOOM command, you need to understand the relationship of REDRAW, REGEN, and the virtual screen. The following section explains AutoCAD's virtual screen.

AutoCAD's Virtual Screen

When you load a new drawing or use the REGEN command, AutoCAD recalculates the current view to its full 14 places of precision. The program treats the display as a 32,000×32,000-pixel screen area, referred to as the *virtual screen*. The virtual screen contains the last regeneration, or recalculation, of the graphic database. AutoCAD translates this calculated image to your actual display area and redraws the current viewport. AutoCAD performs a redraw much quicker than a regeneration. This translation is what occurs when you use the REDRAW command, turn on the grid, turn on layers, or change other settings that cause a redraw.

Many kinds of zooms require only a redraw, not a regeneration. The drawing does not regenerate as long as you do not use certain ZOOM options, zoom outside of the current virtual screen, or zoom so far into tiny detail that AutoCAD cannot translate accurately from the virtual screen. When a zoom occurs without a regeneration, it occurs at redraw speed.

Procedures available for minimizing the frequency of regens are listed at the end of this chapter.

Obtaining the "Big Picture" Using ZOOM Dynamic

You might have experienced situations in which you want to zoom to display an area, but first have to return to the extents or limits of your drawing before you can specify that area. In the CHAP09A drawing, for example, suppose your view was of the drive bays, but next you needed to view the monitor. Based on what you know now, you would use ZOOM Previous or ZOOM All to obtain the overall view of the drawing, then use ZOOM Window or ZOOM Center to display the monitor. As an avid AutoCAD user, you ask, "Why do I have to take this extra step?" The answer is that you might not have to if you learn to use ZOOM and its Dynamic option.

New Riders Publishing
INSIDE
SERIES

When you select ZOOM Dynamic, your display changes and now contains a reference display of your drawing, your current view, and your dynamic zoom window. The reference display contains the following four components:

◆ The current view, identifiable as a dashed rectangle

◆ The bounds of the drawing area—either the extents or the limits, whichever is the larger area

◆ The view window, which is connected to your pointing device

◆ The drawing

Also, you might see corners that define the virtual screen. If you move the view window outside the corners, the regeneration icon appears as an hourglass at the lower left corner of your display area. You might also see this icon if your view window is so small (50 times the current view) that it defines an area that requires regeneration.

In the following exercise, you learn how to use the ZOOM command's Dynamic option. You first must use the ZOOM command's All option.

Using ZOOM Dynamic

Continue using the CHAP09A drawing from the previous exercise.

Command: *Choose* View, Zoom, All	Displays the drawing to its limits
Command: *Choose* View, Zoom, Dynamic	Issues the ZOOM command with the dynamic option and builds the reference display

Your display should look like figure 9.15. By moving around your pointer, you can drag the view window as if it were held by the X handle in the middle of the window. Your pointer also controls the window's size. When you click your pointing device's button, an arrow appears within the view window and enables you to control the window's size. When you move the arrow to the right, you make the window larger; when you move it to the left, you make the window smaller.

When the window is the size you want, click again to lock in the size. You click the pointer button to move between the dynamic window size and its location.

After you capture the desired viewing area in the window, press Enter while holding the dynamic viewing window in place to select it. AutoCAD zooms to that new window.

continues

continued

Figure 9.15

The ZOOM Dynamic reference display.

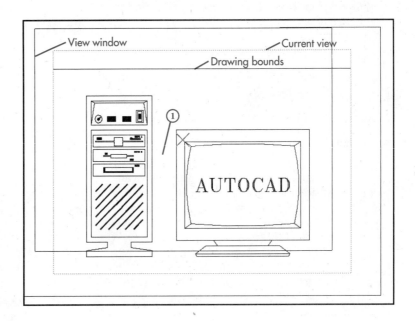

All/Center/Dynamic/Extents/Left/ Previous/Vmax/Window/<Scale(X/XP)>: _d *Move the pointer around*	Moves the view window around the display area
Click the pointer button	Switches pointer movement to control view window sizing
Click ① *(refer to fig. 9.15)*	Shrinks the view window

Notice that as you move the pointer, the view window now moves with it. The view window's size was locked at the previous click.

Move the view window to the center of the monitor in the drawing, then press Enter	Displays the new view of the drawing (see fig. 9.16)
Command: **Z** (Enter)	Starts the ZOOM command
All/Center/Dynamic/Extents/Left/ Previous/Vmax/Window/<Scale(X/XP)>: **D** (Enter)	Specifies the Dynamic option of the command and shows the reference display
Click the pointer and drag your view window to encompass the drive bays	
(Enter)	Displays the new view of the drive bays (see fig. 9.17)

New Riders Publishing
INSIDE
SERIES

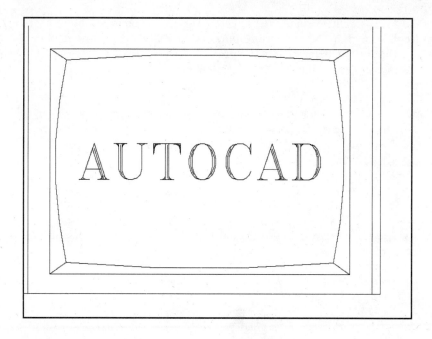

Figure 9.16

Display of the monitor in the drawing.

9

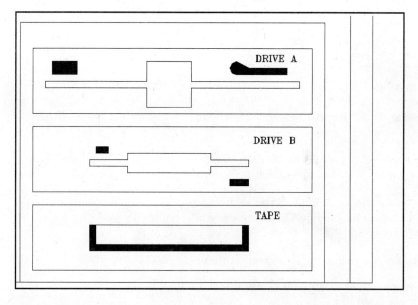

Figure 9.17

Display of the drive bays in the drawing.

Notice that you can press Enter while you are sizing the view window.

Save the drawing.

You can use ZOOM Dynamic to eliminate unneeded zooms and pans because it doesn't require the use of the All or Extents option of the ZOOM command to obtain an overall view as an intermediate step. In the preceding exercise you went from a tight view of the monitor to a tight view of the drive bays using one command.

Tip

If you are working with a large drawing, you might find that the reference display draws somewhat slowly. Do not wait on it! As soon as your view window becomes connected to your pointing device, you can define your new display area and complete the ZOOM command.

Using the Aerial View

The Aerial View is another feature that can help you get the "big picture." Aerial View is found on the Tools pull-down menu. The Aerial View is implemented as a resizeable window that contains five buttons, a resizeable view window, the drawing, and its own cursor crosshairs (see fig. 9.18).

Figure 9.18

Components of the Aerial View window.

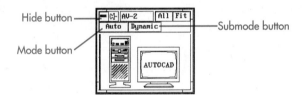

The five buttons in the Aerial View window are the mode button (labeled Auto), the submode button (labeled Dynamic), and the Hide, All, and Fit buttons. The labels of the mode and submode buttons change when they are selected. The mode button controls the following four modes of operation:

◆ **Auto.** Auto mode enables you to define an initial view window that can be moved within the Aerial View window.

◆ **Dzoom.** Dzoom mode enables you to define an initial view window that can be resized and repositioned just like the view window of the Dynamic option of the ZOOM command.

◆ **Zoom.** Zoom mode executes zooms within the Aerial View window.

◆ **Pan.** Pan mode executes pans within the Aerial View window.

The button labeled Dynamic controls two submodes of operation—Dynamic and Static. These submodes only apply to the Auto and Dzoom modes, however. They are defined as follows:

◆ **Dynamic.** The Dynamic submode causes the AutoCAD display to respond in real time to the cursor movements inside the Aerial View window.

◆ **Static.** The Static submode causes the AutoCAD display to respond to the cursor movements inside the Aerial View window after you use the pick button to locate the view window.

The other buttons are fixed—that is to say their labels do not change when they are selected. They are defined as follows:

◆ **Hide.** The Hide button, which is the box containing a thick black hyphen in the upper left corner, hides the Aerial View window.

◆ **All.** The All button displays in the Aerial View window either the area defined by the extents of the drawing or the area defined by the limits of the drawing.

◆ **Fit.** The Fit button displays in the Aerial View window the drawing area that will fit inside.

You might discover that one mode of operation works well in one situation but not in another. You should experiment with the different modes to determine if one works better for you than another. Try the Aerial View with a number of different drawings—large, small, 2D, and 3D, and try it with multiple viewports. See Chapter 10, "Working in Model and Paper Space Viewports," for an explanation of viewports.

Note The Aerial View is provided through the Accelerated Display Driver that comes with your AutoCAD software. If your software does not use this driver, you do not have this version of Aerial View available. Many third-party display drivers include more sophisticated viewers than this one. Check with the supplier of your graphics card about the features of your display driver.

The following exercise provides an introduction to the behavior of the Aerial View window using the Auto mode and Dynamic submode.

Understanding the Aerial View Window

Continue using the CHAP09A drawing from the previous exercise.

Command: *Choose* Tools, Aerial View	Displays the Aerial View window
Move the cursor into the Aerial View	Displays the Aerial View cursor as a crosshairs
Slowly move the cursor over the area of the drive bay	Changes the Aerial View cursor to a pointer

continues

Pick ① (see fig. 9.19)	Attaches the view window to the cursor
Move the cursor around inside the Aerial View window	Pans the AutoCAD display
Move the cursor to the center of the monitor and press the Alt key several times	Enlarges the view window and redisplays the AutoCAD screen with the enlarged view
Move the cursor to the center of the drive bay and press the Ctrl *key several times*	Shrinks the view window and redisplays the AutoCAD screen with the shrunken view
Select the All *button*	The Aerial View window redisplays the drawing to show this drawing's limits
Click the pointer in an open area	Starts dragging to define a new view window (the previous one is still there but probably is too small to see)
Click the pointer again	Defines the view window
Attach the view window to the cursor and drag it over the CPU and monitor, then click the pointer	Detaches the view window from the cursor
Select the Hide *button*	Closes the Aerial View window
Save the drawing.	

Figure 9.19

The view window.

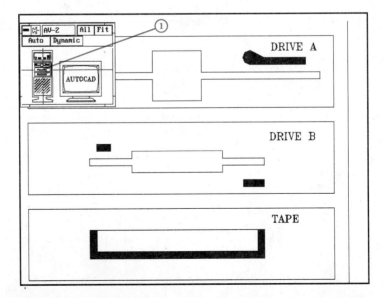

You can control the size and location of the Aerial View window to uncover a hidden part of the display or change the scope of the window's contents. However, the Aerial View window does not behave like other AutoCAD dialog boxes when you move or size it. The following exercise demonstrates how to move and size the Aerial View window.

Repositioning and Resizing the Aerial View Window

Continue using the CHAP09A drawing from the previous exercise.

Command: *Choose* Tools, Aerial View	Displays the Aerial View window
Move the cursor to the Aerial View window frame, then move it all the way around the frame	Displays four different cursors, one to drag the frame horizontally, one to drag it vertically, and two to drag the frame corners
Click the cursor while it is over the lower right corner frame	Attaches the outline of the window frame to the pointer
Drag the outline to cover one quarter of the AutoCAD display area, then click the cursor	Redefines the Aerial View window frame to the point you indicated with the click and the window is filled with the drawing
Move the cursor into the area between the Hide button and the All button, then click	Displays a cursor with four arrows and attaches the outline of the window to the cursor
Move the cursor as far right as you can and then click	Locates the Aerial View window to its new position

You now can close the Aerial View, or keep it open if you prefer. To close it, choose the Hide button.

As you can see, the Aerial View is simple, yet powerful. Aerial View enables you to zoom, magnify, and pan in near real time. Although the larger your drawings are, the more time required to update the display, Aerial View still offers significant advantages over time-consuming and imprecise zooms and pans. In spite of the time it takes to become comfortable and experienced with a tool like this, it is definitely worth mastering.

Using PAN To Slide a View

The PAN command enables you to position the view of your drawing to your specifications by relocating the drawing across the current viewport. If you are zoomed in and need to draw outside the current viewport, use the PAN command to shift the drawing to display the area of interest. Like a camera pan, the PAN command enables you to move around the drawing at your current magnification.

> **'PAN.** The 'PAN command shifts the drawing in the current viewport by a relative displacement.
> Pull-down: *Choose* View, Pan
> Screen: *Choose* VIEW, Pan

The Pan Point menu item issues the PAN command without specifying a displacement. The Pan submenu on the View pull-down menu includes eight versions of the PAN command with predefined displacements. These work opposite the way many people expect because they are named for the movement of the viewport (like an imaginary camera) as it pans across the drawing. For example, the Pan Left tool pans the viewport to the left, resulting in the drawing image being displaced to the right.

To use the PAN command, you supply AutoCAD with a displacement. A *displacement* is defined by two points, which determine the pan distance and direction. When you specify two points to identify a displacement, you specify a point at which AutoCAD picks up the drawing (the *first* displacement point) and then specify another point at which to place the drawing (the *second* displacement point). AutoCAD stretches a rubber-band line between the two displacement points.

In the following exercise, continue to use the CHAP09A drawing. Use the PAN command to shift the display to another area of the drawing.

Using PAN To Shift the Display

Continue in the CHAP09A drawing.

Command: *Choose* View, Zoom, All — Displays the drawing to its limits

Command: *Choose* View, Pan, Point — Issues the PAN command

Command:_'PAN displacement: *Pick the lower left corner of the main tower at* ① *(see fig. 9.20)* — Specifies the first displacement point

Second point: *Pick the lower left corner of the monitor at* ② — Specifies the second point and pans

Your screen should appear as shown in figure 9.21.

Save the drawing for a later exercise.

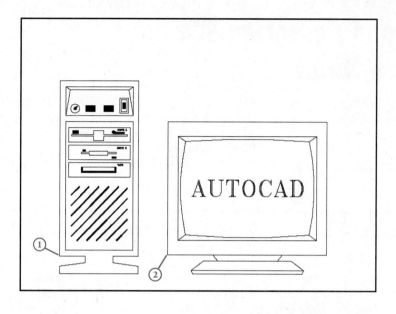

Figure 9.20

Using the PAN command to show displacement.

Figure 9.21

The view after using the PAN command.

9

By now you have sufficiently explored the ZOOM and PAN commands to be able to move around your drawing. Through the use of the ZOOM command and the Dynamic option your have even learned how to reduce the number of steps it takes to obtain the view you need. The next section can provide you with more ways to reduce steps by using named views.

Saving and Restoring Working Views by Name

As you develop a drawing, you might find that your zooms and pans frequently return to the same area. You can expedite the development process by storing a drawing "window" as a named view. You can use either the VIEW command or the View Control dialog box (accessed by the DDVIEW command).

> **'VIEW.** The 'VIEW command saves, restores, lists, and deletes views.

The VIEW command has the following five options:

◆ **?.** This option displays a list of all saved viewport configurations when you enter an asterisk (*). The ? option lists a specific set of views when you enter names using wild cards. The list includes an M or P with the view's name to indicate whether the view is defined in model space (M) or paper space (P). See Chapter 10 for a discussion of model space and paper space.

◆ **Delete.** This option prompts you to enter the name of a view to delete. You can use wild cards to delete a group of similarly named views.

◆ **Restore.** This option prompts you for the name of a saved view to display in the current viewport.

◆ **Save.** This option saves the current viewport's view.

◆ **Window.** This option enables you to define a window to save as a view by specifying its corners. You are prompted to enter a name for the view.

Note You can rename an existing view by using the RENAME command or the Rename dialog box (accessed by the DDRENAME command). The RENAME command is described in Chapter 5, "Setting Up a CAD Drawing."

The following exercise shows you how to use AutoCAD's VIEW command to save and restore named views.

Using VIEW To Save and Restore a View

Continue using CHAP09A, then zoom to the view shown in figure 9.22.

Command: **VIEW** (Enter)

?/Delete/Restore/Save/Window: Saves the current view under the name
S (Enter)   DRIVES

View name to save: **DRIVES** (Enter)

Command: *Choose* View, Zoom, Extents   Zooms to display the entire drawing as
                                                  large as possible (see fig. 9.23)

Command: **VIEW** (Enter)

?/Delete/Restore/Save/Window: Restores the saved view named DRIVES, as
R (Enter)   shown in figure 9.22

View name to restore: **DRIVES** (Enter)

Save the drawing.

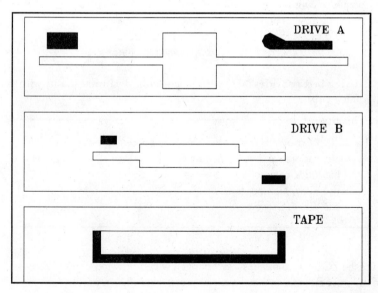

Figure 9.22

The saved and restored view named DRIVES.

9

Figure 9.23

The view after using ZOOM Extents.

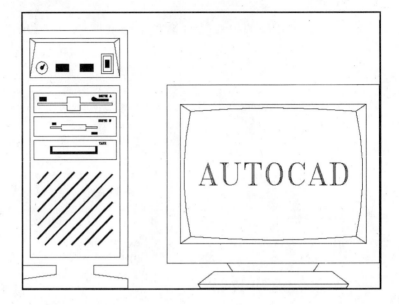

Tip   A useful named view is A for All. It is easy to type and can be used in place of the ZOOM command's All option to avoid regenerations. To easily restore the four "quadrants" of a drawing, use the view names LL, LR, UL, and UR. Similarly, use the standard named view called PLOT for consistency in plotting.

The View Control dialog box provides all the VIEW command's functionality with the convenience of a dialog box.

> **DDVIEW.** The DDVIEW command opens the View Control dialog box, which enables you to create, restore, and delete named views. The View Control options are similar to those of the VIEW command.
> Pull-down: *Choose* View, Named Views
> Screen: *Choose* VIEW, DDview

Tip   If you use the ZOOM command's Center option with a drawing already zoomed to its extents, press Enter to default the center point, enter **.8X**, and then save the view as **A** or **ALL**. This configuration provides a margin of safety in avoiding zoom and pan regenerations. Then use the VIEW command's Restore option to restore the All view, rather than the ZOOM command's All or Dynamic options.

New Riders Publishing
INSIDE
SERIES

When many view names are being saved and restored, the View Control dialog box is a useful tool (see fig. 9.24). Enter **DDVIEW** or choose Named View from the View pull-down menu to display this dialog box. The Views list box shows all defined view names. Use the buttons at the bottom of the dialog box to restore a named view, create a new view, delete an existing view, or see a description of a view's general parameters. The edit box enables you to type or change view names. As is the case with most dialog boxes, you can choose OK to accept the most recent changes in the dialog box; select Cancel to disregard the changes.

In the following exercise, you use the View Control dialog box to restore and save named views of the drawing.

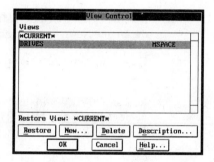

Figure 9.24

The View Control dialog box.

Using DDVIEW To Work with Views

Continue using drawing CHAP09A from the preceding exercise.

Command: *Choose* View, Zoom, All	Returns to the full view
Regenerating drawing.	Regenerates
Command: *Choose* View, Named Views	Issues the DDVIEW command and displays the View Control dialog box (see fig. 9.24)
Select DRIVES *in the* **V**iews *list box, then choose* **R**estore, *then* OK	Restores the view named DRIVES and closes the dialog box
Command: *Choose* View, Zoom, Previous	Issues ZOOM with Previous option and restores previous view
Command: *Choose* View, Named Views	Issues the DDVIEW command and displays the View Control dialog box
Choose **N**ew	Opens the Define New View dialog box

continues

continued

Choose the <u>D</u>efine Window *button*	Enables (darkens) the <u>W</u>indow button and corner coordinates
Choose <u>W</u>indow	Closes dialog boxes and prompts for window corner points
First Corner: *Pick the lower left corner of the monitor*	
Other Corner: *Pick the upper right corner of the monitor*	Specifies window to save and reopens dialog boxes
Type **MONITOR** *in the* <u>N</u>ew Name *text box, closes then choose* <u>S</u>ave View	Names the windowed view MONITOR and the Define New View dialog box
Choose OK	Closes the View Control dialog box and saves the view
Command: Enter	Repeats DDVIEW and displays the view names DRIVES and MONITOR in the View Control dialog box
Select MONITOR, *then choose* <u>R</u>estore, *then* OK	Closes the dialog box and restores the MONITOR view
Save the drawing.	

Stored with the view names are items such as clipping data, twist angle, and view size, which are useful for shading and rendering. (See Chapter 30 for a complete discussion.) To access this information, choose the Description button in the View Control dialog box. Delete any view names that you no longer need. (Remember, click on the <u>H</u>elp button if you forget how some of these options work.)

Controlling Display Size and Resolution

Adding more detail to a drawing increases its file size. AutoCAD uses the virtual screen to keep only a portion of the drawing generated at all times. With a small, uncomplicated drawing, the time difference between a redraw and a regen is negligible. But as your drawing file gets larger, the calculations necessary to regenerate the virtual screen take longer.

Usually, you use a PAN or ZOOM command at redraw (fast) speed to move between views in the generated portion of the drawing. There are times, however, AutoCAD

requires a regen (slow) to recalculate a different set of data that lies outside the virtual screen. The next section discusses a method of balancing display speed against drawing accuracy.

Using VIEWRES To Control Smooth Curve Regeneration

The AutoCAD VIEWRES (VIEW RESolution) command controls the speed of your zooms and regenerations in two ways. First, it turns fast zoom on and off. Fast zoom means that AutoCAD maintains a large virtual screen so that it can do most pans and zooms at redraw speed. The first prompt of the VIEWRES command is Do you want fast zooms?. If you answer with an **N**, fast zoom is off, then all pans and zooms cause a regeneration because AutoCAD disables the virtual screen. Second, VIEWRES determines how finely the curves should be displayed. When circles or arcs are tiny, AutoCAD need display only a few straight lines to fool your eye into seeing smooth curves. When arcs are larger, AutoCAD needs more segments (or vectors) to make an arc appear smoother. The VIEWRES circle zoom percent tells AutoCAD how smooth you want your curves, and AutoCAD then determines the number of segments necessary for the display contents.

> **VIEWRES.** The VIEWRES command sets the display resolution for objects in the current view.
> Screen: OPTIONS, Viewres

 Note   Views defined in model space (either tiled or floating model space viewports) are restored in model space, and views defined in paper space are restored in paper space. See Chapter 10 for details on paper space.

The following exercise shows you how AutoCAD alters the displayed smoothness of curved objects by generating fewer segments.

Using VIEWRES To Control Resolutions

Begin a new drawing named CHAP09C, and draw several random arcs and circles (see fig. 9.25).

Command: *Choose* View, Zoom, All	Displays the entire drawing
Regenerating drawing.	
Command: **VIEWRES** (Enter)	Issues the VIEWRES command

continues

continued

`Do you want fast zooms? <Y>` **Enter**	Accepts the fast zoom default
`Enter circle zoom percent (1-20000)` `<100>:` **5** **Enter**	
`Regenerating drawing.`	Displays curves as faceted segments See fig. 9.26
Draw several circles and arcs	
`Command:` **VIEWRES** **Enter**	Issues the VIEWRES command
`VIEWRES Do you want fast zooms? <Y>:` **Enter**	
`Enter circle zoom percent (1-20000)` `<5>:` **100** **Enter**	
`Regenerating drawing.`	Redisplays smoother curves

Save the drawing.

Figures 9.25 and 9.26 demonstrate the effect of **VIEWRES** on circles.

Figure 9.25

Smooth curves with a normal VIEWRES setting of 100.

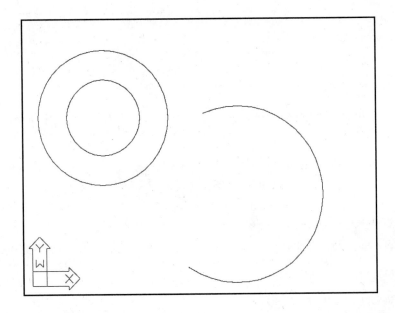

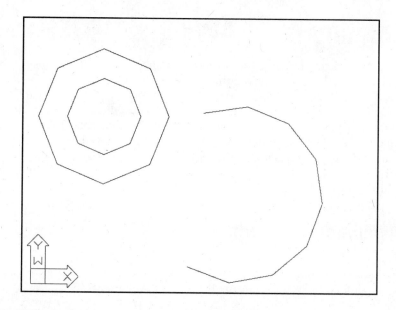

Figure 9.26

Curves after the VIEWRES command.

Fast zooms must be turned on to enable AutoCAD's large virtual screen, which effectively decreases the frequency of regens. When fast zoom is off, PAN and ZOOM operations always regenerate the drawing. So then, why not always keep fast zooms on? The minor disadvantage of fast zoom is that when a regeneration is required, AutoCAD takes longer than if fast zoom is off, because it must then recalculate a larger area.

Note When fast zoom is off, pans and zooms always cause a drawing regeneration. Although you probably never should turn off fast zoom, you might find that AutoCAD is more efficient when zooming large text-filled drawings or doing work that often causes regenerations, even if fast zoom is on. In addition, setting the VIEWRES circle zoom percent too large can cause slow regenerations.

Note VIEWRES has no effect on the plotted smoothness of circles and arcs—only the way circles and arcs appear on the screen.

Tip The default VIEWRES setting of 100 can yield some confusing results. For example, some unfortunate side effects are that door swings look like stop signs, lines trimmed against an arc appear too short, and so on. On today's more powerful PCs, try setting VIEWRES to a much higher value in the prototype drawing, such as 5000. This enables you to zoom in much further without curves becoming faceted.

Understanding REDRAWs and REGENs

There are two commands that the AutoCAD graphics window uses to refresh the screen to provide a cleaner look at your drawing: REDRAW and REGEN. The RE-DRAW command simply removes extraneous blips and pixels left over from prior editing operations. However, the REGEN command recalculates the drawing database and updates the virtual screen—a more CPU-intensive task. Therefore, for larger drawings, regenerations take time. Experienced AutoCAD users know that a desirable objective of drawing development is to avoid using the REGEN command. The next section lists some tips, tricks, and techniques to avoid, limit, or speed up the redraws and regens required.

Tips for Avoiding Regenerations

Although it is impossible to develop an entire drawing without a single redraw or regeneration, you can employ methods that greatly reduce the need to redraw or regenerate. As the situation arises, use any or all of the following suggestions:

◆ **Set BLIPMODE OFF.** Avoid placing blips in your drawing with each pick to minimize the frequency of redraws.

◆ **Set FILLMODE OFF.** Replace wide, filled-in object regions (polylines, solids, and traces) with their boundaries only. On some slower displays and plotters, this setting could enhance the regeneration speed or plotting time.

◆ **Set QTEXT ON.** Replace lines of text with approximate rectangular boundaries to speed the time required to regenerate more elaborate fonts. See Chapter 13, "Annotation with Text" for a discussion of QTEXT.

◆ **Use ZOOM Vmax.** Choose this option to zoom out as much as possible in the current viewport without forcing a regen.

◆ **Use ZOOM Dynamic.** Choose this option (with fast zoom on) to allow both panning and zooming without forcing a regen.

◆ **Avoid frequent ZOOM All or Extents.** These options always cause a regen.

◆ **Use LAYER Freeze.** Frozen layers are not subject to regeneration; therefore, any required regens are speeded up. Make sure you freeze any layers that are not involved in your current editing processes.

New Riders Publishing
INSIDE
SERIES

◆ **Use REGENAUTO OFF.** With this setting, whenever AutoCAD requires a regen, you are prompted to proceed. Then, you can "decline" the regen and try another strategy. For example, if you perform many linetype or text style changes, turn off REGENAUTO until all the changes are made. AutoCAD then queues the regen until appropriate.

◆ **Adjust VIEWRES.** Keep fast zooms on. Then, maintain a circle zoom percent large enough to discern true circles from polygons, but still within an acceptable regeneration time. This value depends on the CPU speed, so experiment!

◆ **Use VIEWs.** Define view names in prototype drawings to make them automatically available in generated drawings. Saving and restoring views minimizes the number of regens.

◆ **Limit active VIEWPORTs.** Turn off any viewports that you don't need, although viewports with zoomed drawing portions can save time. See Chapter 10 for a discussion on viewports.

◆ **Check your LIMITS.** Make sure that the LIMITS match the area within which you actually draw. For example, keeping the default LIMITS of 0,0 to 12,9 while drawing out to 50000,50000 usually increases the likelihood of regeneration when zooming in and out. If your drawing needs these new limits, zoom to this new size and set LIMITS to the sheet size or to a zoom factor slightly larger than the extents.

AutoCAD offers many ways to get around the graphics window. ZOOM gives you more (or less) detail. The most common, intuitive, and convenient zoom-in method is Window. The most common zoom-out methods are All and Previous, or named views. When zooming out, use ZOOM Dynamic or a view named ALL to get you there in a single step.

The next chapter discusses *viewports*—additional ways to work with your drawing as model geometry or plotted page composition.

Part III

Advanced 2D CAD Drafting

New Riders Publishing
INSIDE SERIES

Working in Model and Paper Space Viewports

In this chapter, you learn how to use multiple viewports to display and control several views on-screen simultaneously. So far, you have unknowingly been working in a viewport—a single viewport that fills the drawing window. You can subdivide the drawing window into two or more viewports and view different parts of your drawing in different viewports. You might want to do so to zoom in and add detail work while viewing a large area for reference. When you subdivide the drawing window, you create *tiled viewports*—so called because they must fill the drawing window like tiles, as shown in figure 10.1. That fact, the fact that you can make subdivisions only by halves or thirds of an existing viewport, and the fact that all tiled viewports share many of the same settings, such as layer visibility, might lead you to feel somewhat limited.

Figure 10.1

A drawing window with multiple viewports.

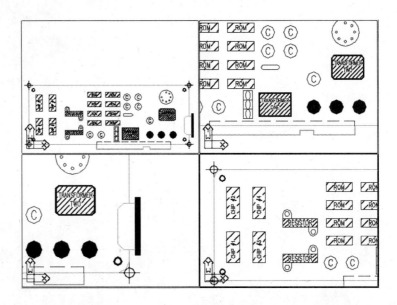

AutoCAD also has another type of viewport—*floating viewports*—which provides greater flexibility. Floating viewports can be any size, in any arrangement, and can differ in many current settings. Whereas tiled viewports exist in a drawing environment, called *tilemode* (the environment you've used so far), floating viewports exist in an environment called *paper space*. An AutoCAD drawing has two sides, just like a piece of paper. So far, you have been working on only one side—model space. In this chapter, you learn about the other side—paper space. Paper space is very versatile, and is covered in this chapter and in Chapter 25, "Sheet Composition and Plotting." In this chapter, you learn how to use paper space as an editing and drawing tool. In Chapter 25, you learn how to use paper space to compose your drawing layout for plotting.

In the following example, you create a new drawing for this chapter and explore the fundamental concepts of viewports.

Quick 5¢ Tour

Begin a new drawing named CHAP10, using the IAD Disk drawing BOARD as the prototype.

Command: *Choose* View, Tiled Viewports, 2 Viewports	Issues the VPORTS command with the 2 viewports option

New Riders Publishing
INSIDE
SERIES

```
Save/Restore/Delete/Join/
SIngle/?/2/<3>/4: 2
```

`Horizontal/<Vertical>: H` (Enter)	Splits the current viewport horizontally into two tiled viewports
Command: *Choose* View, Zoom, Extents	Zooms the (default) upper viewport to the drawing extents
Command: *Move the crosshairs into the lower window and click the pick button*	Makes the lower viewport the current viewport
Command: *Choose* Zoom, Window	Zooms to a window from 5,3.5 to 6.5,5
`First Corner: 5,3.5` (Enter)	
`Other Corner: 6.5,5` (Enter)	
Command: *Choose* View, Pan, Point	Pans the view from 6,4.5 to 7.5,4.5
`'_pan Displacement: 6,4.5` (Enter)	
`Second point: 7.5,4.5` (Enter)	
Command: *Choose* View, Paper Space	Switches you to paper space
Command: *Choose* View, Floating Viewports, 2 Viewports	Issues the MVIEW command with the 2 Viewport option
`ON/OFF/Hideplot/Fit/2/3/4/Restore/` `<First Point>: _2`	
`Horizontal/<Vertical>: H` (Enter)	Specifies a horizontal split
`Fit/<First Point>: 2,0.5` (Enter)	Specifies lower-left corner of the area to be split into two floating viewports
`Second point: 12,8` (Enter)	Specifies upper-right corner
`Regenerating drawing`	Displays previous current view in both viewports
Command: *Select the viewport at* ① *(see fig. 10.2) and choose* Modify, Move	Issues MOVE command with the viewport selected

continues

continued

`Base point or displacement:` `1<90` (Enter)	Specifies displacement
`Second point of displacement:` (Enter)	Moves viewport up one unit
Command: *Choose* View, Floating Model Space *and move the cursor into the* top viewport	Issues the MSPACE command, enters model space, and displays crosshairs in top viewport
Command: *Choose* View, Zoom, Extents	Zooms the (top) viewport to the drawing extents
Move the pointer into the lower viewport and click the pick button	Makes the lower viewport current
Command: *Choose* View, Zoom, Window	Zooms to a window from 5,3.5 to 6.5,5
`First Corner:` `5,3.5` (Enter)	
`Other Corner:` `6.5,5` (Enter)	
Command: *Choose* View, Pan, Point	Pans the view from 6,4.5 to 7.5,4.5
`'_pan Displacement:` `6,4.5` (Enter)	
`Second point:` `7.5,4.5` (Enter)	
Command: *Choose* Data, Layers	Opens the Layer Control dialog box
Select the layer HATCHING, *choose the* Cur VP Frz *button, then choose* OK	Freezes the layer HATCHING in the lower (current) viewport but not in the top viewport

You can use viewports to display different views of your objects. Also, you need not display layers that you display in one viewport in another viewport. Observe the difference between tiled viewports and floating viewports.

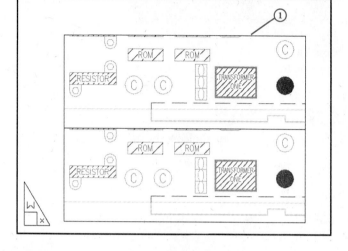

Figure 10.2
Moving the viewport.

Working with Tiled Viewports

AutoCAD has two distinct drawing environments: paper space and model space, either of which can have tiled or floating viewports. You use the MSPACE command to specify model space and the PSPACE command to specify paper space. You use the system variable TILEMODE to switch between tiled and floating viewports. TILEMODE is set to 1 to enable tiled viewports. When the TILEMODE variable is set to 0, floating viewports are enabled. You can use the menu item Paper Space in the View pull-down menu to set TILEMODE to 0 (off) and issue the PSPACE command to make sure you are in paper space. You can choose View, Tiled Model Space to set TILEMODE to 1 (on) and issue the PSPACE command. You can choose View, Floating Model Space to set TILEMODE to 0 (off) and issue the MSPACE command. More on paper space and floating viewports later; for this portion of the chapter on tiled viewports, you need to continue to work exclusively in model space only.

To display multiple views, you must use multiple viewports. A *viewport* is a rectangular area in which a single view of your model appears. In previous chapters, you have used only a single tiled viewport that AutoCAD automatically makes equal in size to your drawing window. In effect, your drawing window has been your single viewport.

The VPORTS command enables you to display and control multiple tiled viewports.

> **VPORTS.** The VPORTS command enables you to create, save, restore, delete, combine, and exit multiple tiled viewports in model space.
> Pull-down: *Choose* View, Tiled Viewports
> Screen: *Choose* VIEW, Vports

With VPORTS, you have the following options:

◆ **Save.** Enables you to save and name the current viewport configuration.

◆ **Restore.** Enables you to restore a saved viewport configuration.

◆ **Delete.** Enables you to delete a saved viewport configuration.

◆ **Join.** Enables you to merge the current viewport with another viewport. Both must have a common edge.

◆ **SIngle.** Enables you to restore the drawing window to a single viewport. The current viewport configuration is lost unless previously saved.

◆ **?.** Enables you to list any or all saved viewport configurations. You then can enter * for all viewports, or any combination of names or wild cards.

◆ **2.** Enables you to divide the current viewport into two viewports.

◆ **3.** Enables you to divide the current viewport into three viewports (the default).

◆ **4.** Enables you to divide the current viewport into four viewports.

Note   The word *tile* has recently appeared in two key phrases, TILEMODE and tiled viewports. *Tile* refers to the way the viewports appear in your drawing window, filling the area like floor or wall tiles.

In the sections that follow, you learn how to create and use tiled viewports.

Opening Tiled Viewports

Each tiled viewport displays a single view of the drawing. To display multiple views in your drawing window, you create additional viewports. You divide the current viewport into as many as four viewports. In the Tiled Viewports submenu, the following options create the additional viewports:

◆ **Layout ....** Opens the Tiled Viewport Layout dialog box. You can graphically select typical predefined viewport layouts (see fig. 10.3).

◆ **2 Viewports.** Divides the current viewport into two viewports. You can divide the current viewport vertically (the default) or horizontally (see fig. 10.4).

◆ **3 Viewports.** Divides the current viewport into three viewports. You can divide the current viewport vertically or horizontally, placing the major viewport above, below, left, or right, which is the default (see fig. 10.5).

◆ **4 Viewports.** Divides the current viewport into four equal viewports (see fig. 10.6).

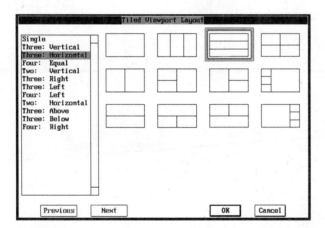

Figure 10.3

Tiled Viewport Layout dialog box.

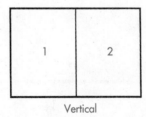

Horizontal

Vertical

Figure 10.4

Layout options for 4 viewports.

10

Figure 10.5

*Layout options
for 3 viewports.*

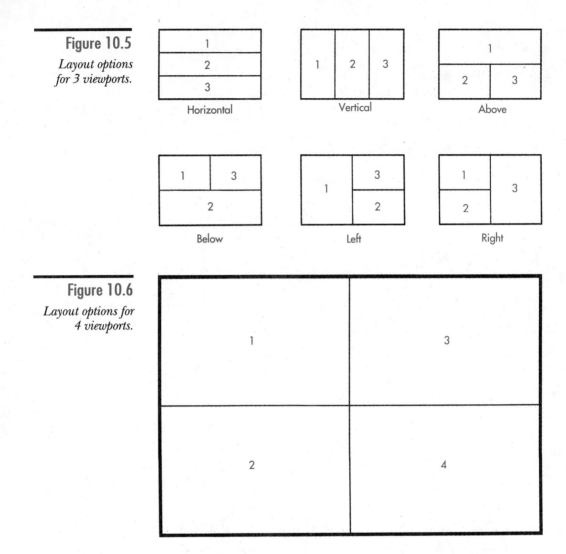

Figure 10.6

*Layout options for
4 viewports.*

The initial view in each of the new tiled viewports is the same as in the previous current viewport. You learn how to change the individual views in the next section.

 Tip   When you must choose whether to divide the current viewport vertically or horizontally, you should choose the option that gives you viewports that best fit the area(s) of your model that you need to see. If the area's extent is greater in the X than in the Y direction, divide horizontally. If the area's extent is greater in the Y than in the X direction, divide vertically.

New Riders Publishing
INSIDE
SERIES

In the following exercise, you display three views of a model simultaneously.

Creating Tiled Viewports

Begin a new drawing named CHAP10A using the IAD Disk drawing BOARD as the prototype.

`Command:` *Choose* View, Tiled Viewports, 3 Viewports	Issues the VPORTS command using the 3 Viewport option
`Save/Restore/Delete/Join/` `SIngle/?/2/<3>/4: 3`	
`Horizontal/Vertical/Above/` `Below/Left/<Right>:` `Enter`	Specifies the largest viewport to be on the right side

Save your drawing.

The board is now displayed in all three viewports, as shown in figure 10.7.

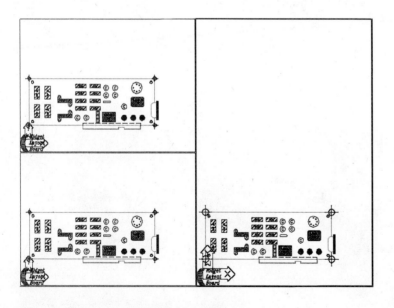

Figure 10.7

The CHAP10A drawing with three viewports.

10

Opening More Tiled Viewports

You can have more than four viewports open simultaneously by taking the current viewport and dividing it into multiple viewports. You can do this to each viewport, but the succeeding viewports are smaller and smaller. In practical terms, the maximum number of viewports with which you can work depends on the type of drawing and the size and resolution of your monitor. If you have a 14-inch monitor, two viewports probably is the maximum; if you have a 19-inch monitor, four viewports is quite possible. AutoCAD refuses to create more than 64 simultaneous viewports, and refuses to subdivide a viewport that it deems too small, but both of these limits are well beyond the number of viewports at which the size permits practical use.

Tip AutoCAD does have to do more work when you use multiple viewports. If you notice a performance degradation when you use multiple viewports with large drawings, reduce the number of viewports. Alternatively, you might want to freeze unneeded layers rather than reduce the number of viewports. Either action reduces the number of objects AutoCAD must calculate and display.

Choosing the Current Viewport

When you change the model, AutoCAD updates all viewports to reflect any change. There is, however, only one current or active viewport, the one in which you can draw and select points and objects, and the one that is affected by display commands (such as ZOOM, PAN, scroll bars, and so on). You can visually identify the current viewport in two ways (see fig. 10.8).

◆ The current viewport's border is heavier and darker than the other viewports' borders.

◆ The current viewport is the only viewport in which you can see the crosshairs. All other viewports display the pointer.

Figure 10.8

The current viewport has crosshairs and a heavier border.

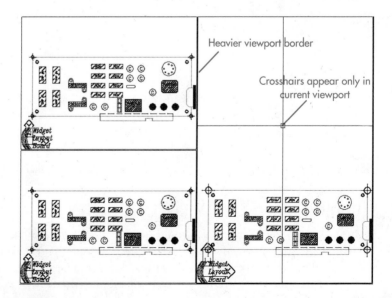

Heavier viewport border

Crosshairs appear only in current viewport

New Riders Publishing
INSIDE
SERIES

To set another viewport as the current viewport, just move the system pointer to that viewport and click the pick button. Immediately, the crosshairs appear in the selected viewport and the viewport's border becomes thicker and darker.

In the next exercise, you practice setting the current viewport.

Setting the Current Viewport

Continue to use the drawing CHAP10A.

The right viewport has a heavier border than the other two. The right viewport is the current viewport.

Move the cursor from one viewport to the next. The crosshairs appear in only the current viewport and the system pointer appears in the other viewports.

Click in the upper left viewport	Sets the upper left viewport current and displays a heavier border and crosshairs
Move the pointer to the lower left viewport	Displays the pointer
Click the pick button	Sets the lower left viewport current and displays a heavier border and crosshairs

---

Specifying the current viewports is quick and easy.

Changing the View

To change the view in a particular viewport, make that viewport the current viewport, then use the display commands (such as ZOOM and PAN) to adjust the view. To better grasp the concept of a viewport, imagine a viewport as an opening that exposes your model. If you have a large model, such as a state map, you might have a small opening that displays only a city in the state. You might have a larger opening that displays a county or you might have an even larger opening that displays the entire state. Using pan and zoom, the opening could display a different city or the state and all of its adjacent states. Using the display command within viewports is a powerful concept that you will find easy to learn and apply.

You can have different settings for the SNAP, GRID, and UCSICON commands in each viewport. You can have one spacing for the GRID command in one viewport, for example, and a different grid spacing in another viewport. You cannot, however, adjust the display of layers per individual viewport. If you turn off or freeze a layer in the current viewport, you turn off or freeze that layer in all the viewports. If you change the color of a layer in the current viewport, you change the color in all the viewports.

The REDRAW and REGEN commands affect only the current viewport. If you want to affect all viewports, you must use the equivalent commands REDRAWALL and REGENALL. You can activate REDRAWALL by choosing View, Redraw All. You must, however, type the REGENALL command, because it does not appear in a menu.

In the next exercise, you change the views in the viewports you created in the previous exercise.

Changing the Viewport Views

Continue to use the drawing CHAP10A; click in the upper left viewport, if necessary, to make it current.

Command: *Choose* View, Zoom, Extents

Zooms the view in the current viewport to the model's extents

Command: **SNAP** (Enter)

Issues the SNAP command

Snap spacing or ON/OFF/Aspect/Rotate/
Style <0'-0.10">: **ON** (Enter)

Turns snap on in the current viewport

Set the lower left viewport current.

Command: **GRID** (Enter)

Issues the SNAP command

Grid spacing(X) or ON/OFF/Snap/
Aspect <0'-0.00">: **ON** (Enter)

Turns the grid on in the current viewport

Command: *Choose* View, Zoom, Window

First corner: **6,3** (Enter)

Other corner: **7.5,4.5** (Enter)

Changes the view in the current viewport

Set the right side viewport current, then zoom its view with a window from 4.5,3 to 7,6.

Command: *Choose* Data, Layers, *select
the layer* HATCHING, *choose* OFF,
then choose OK

Reflects the change in all
viewports—the ROMs
are no longer hatched

Command: *Choose* Data, Layers,
select the layer HATCHING, *choose* ON,
then choose OK

New Riders Publishing
INSIDE
SERIES

| Command: *Choose* View, Redraw All | Issues the REDRAWALL command and redraws all viewports |

Save your drawing. See figure 10.9 for the results.

This exercise demonstrates how viewports can show different views and that some settings can be made on a per viewport basis whereas others affect all viewports.

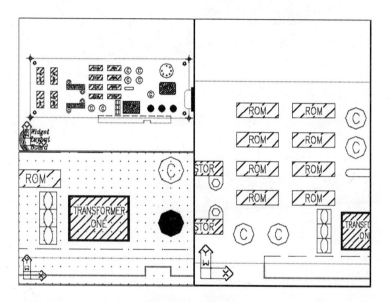

Figure 10.9

Tiled viewports with different views and settings.

10

Editing in Tiled Viewports

You always draw and edit in the current viewport, and you do all your object selection and point picking in the current viewport. Any changes you make to the model automatically appear in all viewports, assuming that the viewports show portions of the model that you edited.

You can change your current viewport while executing a command. You can start to draw a line in one viewport, for example, and change the current viewport before you pick the next point for the line. In general, the only commands during which you cannot change the current viewport are the display commands, such as ZOOM, PAN, and VIEW.

You can even change the current viewport during object selection. The objects you select are highlighted in each viewport in which the object is visible. This provides you with tremendous flexibility during object selection that is not available if you use a single viewport.

In the next exercise, you edit the drawing CHAP10A using multiple viewports.

Editing with Viewports

Continue to use the CHAP10A drawing.

Set the lower left viewport current.

Command: *Choose* Construct, Copy	Issues the COPY command
Select objects: *Pick* ① *and* ② *(see fig. 10.10)*	Selects the circle and letter *C*
Select objects: **Enter**	Completes object selection
<Base point or displacement>/ Multiple: *Using CEN object snap, pick the circle at* ①	Sets the center of the circle as the base point
Second point of displacement: *Click in the right viewport, then turn on* SNAP *and turn off* ORTHO	Changes the current viewport and settings during the COPY command
Second point of displacement: *Pick point* ③	Specifies the point in the right viewport to copy to
Command: *Choose* Assist, Undo	Undoes the copy

You can see that copying objects from one viewport to another is a simple matter. As in this exercise, you can use transparent commands to greatly enhance your editing capabilities by manipulating settings such as GRID, SNAP, and ORTHO as you work.

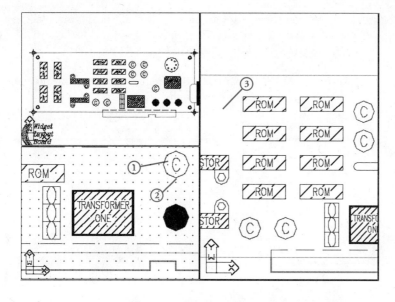

Figure 10.10

Copying objects across viewports.

Saving, Closing, and Restoring Tiled Viewports

In the View pull-down menu, the Tiled Viewports item has choices to Save, Delete, Join, and Restore viewports. These choices provide you with great flexibility when you work with tiled viewports. You might sometimes find that a viewport with which you work becomes unneeded, so you might close it or join it with another. Before you alter your viewport arrangement, referred to as a *viewport configuration*, you might want to save it for later use. For example, you might find that while creating a portion of a drawing, one viewport configuration makes it easier to work on details and notes while another viewport configuration makes it easier to work on the overall plan.

The four menu choices are options of the VPORTS command, as follows:

◆ **Save.** Choosing this option saves the current viewport configuration, allowing you to specify a name or display a listing of named viewport configurations.

◆ **Restore.** Choosing this option recalls a saved viewport configuration, allowing you to optionally display a listing of named viewport configurations.

◆ **Delete.** Choosing this option deletes a saved viewport configuration. As with Save and Restore, you can display a listing of named viewport configurations.

◆ **Join.** Choosing this option merges two adjacent viewports into a single viewport. You select two viewports. The view in the first viewport (the dominant viewport) is the view that appears in the new, combined viewports. Pressing

Enter selects the current viewport as dominant. The two viewports you select to join must combine to form a rectangle (new viewport). In figure 10.11, for example, you could join viewports 1 and 2, but not 1 and 3, nor 2 and 3.

When you use Save or Restore, AutoCAD maintains the tile arrangement and the view in each tile. The list options work just as they do with the other commands you have used—by specifying the list with a *?*.

Figure 10.11

You can join viewports 1 and 2, but not 1 and 3, nor 2 and 3.

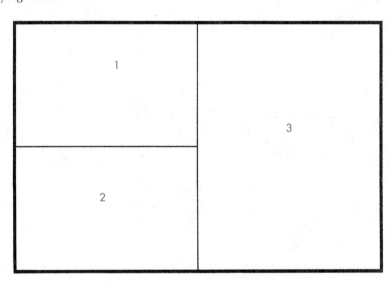

Saving, Closing, Joining, and Restoring Viewports

Continue to use the drawing CHAP10A.

Command: *Choose* View, Tiled Viewports, Save	Issues the VPORTS command with the Save option specified
Save/Restore/Delete/Join/SIngle/ ?/2/<3>/4: _s	
?/Name for new viewport configuration: **STD3** (Enter)	Specifies STD3 as the name used to save the viewport configuration
Command: *Choose* View, Tiled Viewports, Join	Issues the VPORTS command with the Join option
Select dominant viewport <current>: *Click in the upper left viewport*	Specifies the upper left viewport as the dominant viewport

`Select viewport to join:` *Click in the lower left viewport*	Specifies the lower left viewport and joins it with the dominant viewport

The resulting viewport has inherited the settings of the dominant viewport—SNAP is on but GRID is off.

`Command:` Choose View, Tiled Viewports, Save	Issues the VPORTS command with the Save option

`Save/Restore/Delete/Join/SIngle/`
`?/2/<3>/4: _s`

`?/Name for new viewport configuration:` save **SIDEBYSIDE** (Enter)	Specifies SIDEBYSIDE as the name used to the current viewport configuration

`Command:` *Choose* View, Tiled Viewports, 1 Viewport	Issues the VPORTS command with the SIngle option

The result is that the right viewport is closed and the current viewport is enlarged to the display area.

`Command:` *Choose* View, Tiled Viewports, Restore	Issues the VPORTS command with the option

`Save/Restore/Delete/Join/SIngle/?/2/`
`<3>/4: _r`

`?/Name of viewport configuration to` `restore:` **?** (Enter)	Displays a list of saved configurations

`Viewport configuration(s) to list <*>:` **S*** (Enter)	Displays all saved configurations that begin with the letter *S* (see fig. 10.12)

`?/Name of viewport configuration to` `restore:` **STD3** (Enter)	Restores configuration STD3 that we saved earlier

Save your drawing.

The preceding exercise demonstrates how viewport configurations are saved, modified and recalled for use at a later time. The viewport views are restored as they were when they were saved, including the settings you made in earlier exercises. You should now understand the dominant viewport and how you join viewports.

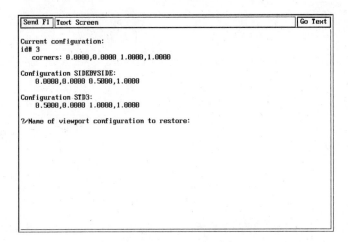

Figure 10.12

*Listing of
viewport
configurations.*

Tip   If you use the same viewport configurations repeatedly, you might consider defining
the viewport configurations in your prototype drawing so that every new drawing
has your viewport configuration ready to restore.

Working with Paper Space Viewports

Paper space originally was conceived as a tool to help you compose the layout of a
drawing before you plotted it, hence the term *paper space*. Paper space also can be a
useful environment from which to edit the model, and is discussed for the remainder
of this chapter.

In the sections that follow, you learn how to enter the paper space environment,
switch between paper and model space, and how to create and use floating viewports
for drawing and editing the model.

Entering the Paper Space Environment

You switch between the tiled viewport and paper space environments by changing the
setting of the system variable TILEMODE. When TILEMODE is set to 1 (on), you are
in the tiled viewport environment. When TILEMODE is set to 0 (off), you are in the
paper space environment. Within the paper space environment, you can be in model
space within a floating viewport or in paper space itself. Paper space is a special

New Riders Publishing
INSIDE
SERIES

drawing space intended for title blocks, borders, and similar features, and for the placement of floating viewports. You use the MVIEW command to place floating viewports in paper space, then you can enter model space and draw in the viewports. More on MVIEW and floating viewports later—first you need to know how to enable the paper space environment. You can type **TILEMODE** at the Command: prompt or you can use the View pull-down menu to set TILEMODE off. The Paper Space menu item not only turns off TILEMODE, it also issues the PSPACE command, which ensures you enter paper space itself and not model space within a floating viewport. When you are in paper space, a check mark appears beside this menu item.

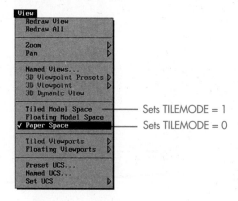

Figure 10.13

TILEMODE menu items.

Tip
If you use the sidebar menu, the Pspace: or Mspace: menu items in the View menu do not automatically switch TILEMODE to off. Therefore, if TILEMODE is on, you see the following message:

```
** Command not allowed unless TILEMODE is set to 0 **
```

You must first set TILEMODE to 0.

After you turn off TILEMODE, you are in the paper space environment. You know you are in paper space when you can see the paper space UCS icon (see fig. 10.14); otherwise you can see the model space icon.

The model space that exists in tiled viewports is the same model space that exists in floating viewports; however, paper space and model space are two separate areas of the same drawing file, and have a dividing wall between them. In the next exercise, you use various methods to move between tiled model and paper space.

Figure 10.14
The UCS icon in paper space.

Changing TILEMODE

Continue to use the CHAP10A drawing.

Command: *Choose* View, Paper Space   Changes to paper space

You can see the paper UCS icon and you cannot see your model yet.

Command: *Choose* View, Tiled Model   Changes back to tiled model space
Space

Now you can see the normal UCS icon.

When you are in tiled model space, the wall prevents you from seeing what is on the paper space side. When you are in paper space, you can see what is on the model space side only by opening some windows (viewports) in the wall. The viewports in model space are referred to as *tiled viewports,* but the viewports in paper space are referred to as *floating viewports.* In the following sections, you learn how to create and use floating viewports.

Opening Floating Viewports

When you opened tiled viewports in model space, you divided the current viewport into smaller multiple viewports. You had limited the control over the size and control over the positioning of the viewports. In contrast, when you create viewports in paper

space, you specify the size and location of the viewports. The viewports can float anywhere in paper space, hence the term *floating viewports*.

To work with the model in paper space, you use MVIEW to create floating viewports.

> **MVIEW.** The MVIEW command enables you to configure multiple floating viewports in paper space.
> Pull-down: *Choose* View, Floating Viewports
> Screen: *Choose* VIEW, Mview

With MVIEW, you have the following options:

◆ **ON.** Turns on a floating viewport.

◆ **OFF.** Turns off a floating viewport.

◆ **Hideplot.** Tags a floating viewport to have its hidden lines removed during plotting.

◆ **Fit.** Creates a single viewport to fit the drawing window.

◆ **2.** Divides a user-specified rectangular area into two viewports (refer to figure 10.4). It prompts you to specify the orientation (Horizontal or Vertical) and the location by specifying Fit or picking two points.

◆ **3.** Divides a user-specified rectangular area into three viewports (refer to figure 10.5). It prompts you to specify the orientation (Horizontal or Vertical) and the location by specifying Fit or picking two points.

◆ **4.** Divides a user-specified rectangular area into four viewports (refer to figure 10.6). It prompts you to specify the orientation (Horizontal or Vertical) and the location by specifying Fit or picking two points.

◆ **Restore.** Creates the equivalent of a tiled viewport configuration (saved using the VPORTS command) in paper space, using floating viewports.

◆ **First point.** The default option enables you to create a new floating viewport by picking two points that define its size and location.

To access the MVIEW command by using the pull-down menus, choose View, Floating Viewports (see fig. 10.15). Each menu item in the Floating Viewports submenu triggers the MVIEW command and then the appropriate option. The Floating Viewports submenu is active only in paper space.

10

Figure 10.15

The Floating Viewports submenu.

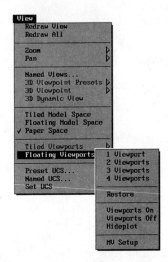

The default MVIEW command enables you to define the size and location of the floating viewport by defining a window or entering **F** to fill the paper space view. If you use the 2 or 3 options, AutoCAD prompts you for orientation. You can specify horizontal or vertical orientation, or if you use the 3 option, you can specify whether the major (larger) viewport is created above, below, left, or right of the others. After you specify orientation, or if you use the 4 option, you see the following prompt:

```
Fit/<First Point>:
```

At this prompt, you can define the window area (the default First Point option) or by specifying the area as the entire area visible in paper space (the Fit option).

The MVIEW options for creating floating viewports are very similar to the VPORTS options for creating tiled viewports, except that you choose the location and size of the floating viewports.

The menu items on the Floating Viewports submenu of the View menu (except MV Setup) all issue the MVIEW command. The 1 Viewport item issues MVIEW without options, and the rest of the menu items issue MVIEW with the options indicated in their menu labels.

In the following exercise, you use MVIEW to create floating viewports.

Creating Floating Viewports

Continue to use the CHAP10A drawing. If necessary, switch to paper space.

`Command:` *Choose* Data, Layers *then create
a new layer named FVPORTS, assign the
color green, set it current, and exit
the dialog box*

`Command:` *Choose* View, Floating Viewports, 3 Viewports	Issues the MVIEW command with the 3 option
`ON/OFF/Hideplot/Fit/2/3/4 /Restore/<First Point>: _3`	
`Horizontal/Vertical/Above/ Below/Left/<Right>:` (Enter)	Accepts the default arrangement, major viewport on the right
`Fit/<First Point>: 2,0.5` (Enter)	Specifies lower-left corner of the viewports
`Second point: 12,8` (Enter)	Specifies upper-right corner of the area and creates the three viewports (see fig. 10.16)

Save your drawing.

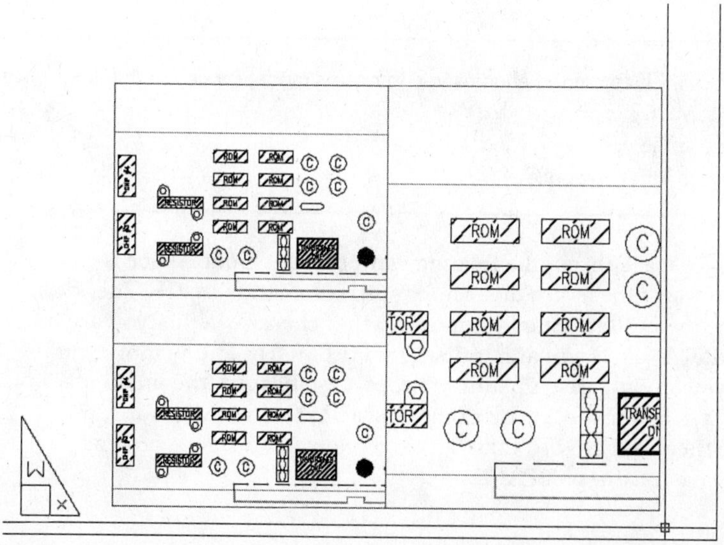

Figure 10.16

The CHAP10A drawing in paper space.

10

If you have several multiple floating viewports open, you might notice a degradation in your system's performance. Such a degradation is understandable when you consider that AutoCAD must do much more work to update multiple viewports. If the degradation becomes serious, you might want to turn off any unnecessary viewports temporarily. This allows AutoCAD to not update the display in the selected viewport. You can use the MVIEW command to turn viewports on and off.

 Note You can create as many viewports as you want. AutoCAD, however, by default updates the views in only 16 of them. The limit of 16 is set in the MAXACTVP (MAXimum ACTive ViewPorts) system variable. You can raise or lower it. If you create a new viewport that causes you to exceed the limit set in MAXACTVP, AutoCAD automatically turns off one of the older viewports. At no time does AutoCAD maintain (update) more floating viewports than is set in MAXACTVP.

After you create your floating viewports, you might need to make one of them the current viewport so that you can adjust the view in the viewport, and you must enter model space to work with your model. Initially, none of the viewports are current as long as you remain in paper space.

Choosing the Current Viewport and Entering Model Space

You use the MSPACE command to make the default floating viewport current and enter model space within that viewport.

> **MSPACE.** The MSPACE command enables you to access model space in a floating viewport while TILEMODE is off.
> Pull-down: *Choose* View, Floating Model Space
> Screen: *Choose* VIEW, Mspace

When you access model space through a floating viewport, the model space is called *floating model space*. However, be aware that there is only one model space. The View, Floating Model Space menu item actually is a macro that checks whether you are in model space (TILEMODE=1). If you are, it first sets TILEMODE to 0 to move you into paper space. If you already have floating viewports established, the menu macro then issues the MSPACE command. If you do not have any floating viewports, the MVIEW command is then triggered so that you can create one or more floating viewports before the macro issues MSPACE.

The views in the floating viewports are always current unless you have a particular viewport turned off or you have exceeded the maximum number of 64 active viewports. All viewports are normally active, so when you make changes to the model, AutoCAD updates all viewports to reflect the changes. There is, however, only one current viewport. The current viewport is the viewport in which you pick points and select objects, and that is affected by your display commands, such as ZOOM, PAN, and so on. When you are in floating model space, you can identify the current viewport based on the following indicators (see fig. 10.17).

◆ The model space UCS icon appears in each floating viewport.

◆ The (paper space indicator) is removed from the status bar.

◆ The current viewport has a heavier, darker border than the others.

◆ The crosshairs no longer cross the entire drawing window. The crosshairs appear only in the current viewport and only when the cursor is over that viewport. In the rest of the drawing window, the system pointer appears in place of the crosshairs.

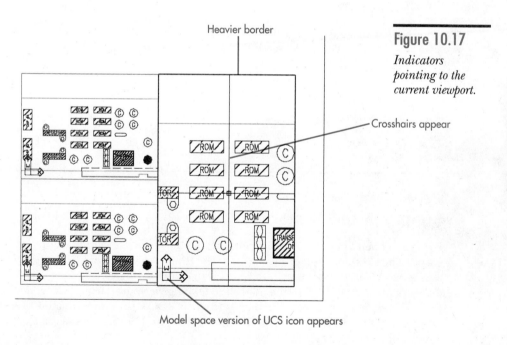

Figure 10.17

Indicators pointing to the current viewport.

Heavier border

Crosshairs appear

Model space version of UCS icon appears

10

Note If you are in model space when you issue the MVIEW command, it temporarily changes to paper space until the command is complete.

After you are in model space, to set another viewport current, move the pointer to the viewport you want to make current and click the pick button. That viewport immediately becomes the current viewport. After you make a viewport current, you can draw, edit, and adjust the view in that viewport.

In the following exercise, you set various floating viewports current.

Entering Model Space and Setting the Current Viewport

Continue to use the CHAP10A drawing, with three floating viewpoints visible.

Command: *Choose* View, Floating Model Space   Puts you into floating model space

Look at the viewports. The right viewport has a heavier border than the other two. The right viewport is the current viewport.

Move the cursor from one viewport to the next

The crosshairs appear only in the current viewport (see fig. 10.17). In all other viewports, you see the system pointer. The model space UCS icon now appears in each viewport.

Click in the upper left viewport   Sets the upper left viewport current, displaying heavier border and crosshairs

Click in the lower left viewport   Sets the lower left viewport current, displaying heavier border and crosshairs

Save your drawing.

Changing the View

When you open up a new floating viewport, the height of the view that appears corresponds to the height of the current view (the last view) in model space. Just as with tiled viewports, you can adjust the view in each floating viewport to show a different portion of the drawing. Make the floating viewport current that you want to work in, then use the display commands (such as ZOOM and PAN) to adjust the view. One viewport might show the overall drawing and another might display a close-up of a particular area.

Each viewport also can have individual settings for layer visibility and for the SNAP, GRID, and UCSICON states. You can, for example, have one spacing for the GRID command in one viewport and a different grid spacing in another viewport.

New Riders Publishing
INSIDE
SERIES

REDRAW and REGEN affect only the current viewport. If you want to affect all viewports, you must use the equivalent commands REDRAWALL and REGENALL. You can activate REDRAWALL by choosing View, Redraw All. You must enter REGENALL at the Command: prompt because it is not on a menu.

In the following exercise, you adjust the views and snap and grid settings in the floating viewports you created.

Adjusting the Viewport Views

Continue to use the CHAP10A drawing, in model space, with three floating viewports visible.

Set the upper left viewport current.

Command: *Choose* View, Zoom, Extents	Zooms the current viewport to the model's extents
Command: **SNAP** (Enter)	Issues the SNAP command
Snap spacing or ON/OFF/Aspect/Rotate/ Style <0'-0.10">: **OFF** (Enter)	Turns snap off

Set the lower left viewport current.

Command: **GRID** (Enter)	Issues the GRID command
Grid spacing(X) or ON/OFF/Snap Aspect <0'-0.00">: **ON** (Enter)	Turns the grid on
Command: *Choose* View, Zoom, Window *then zoom to a window from* 6,3 *to* 7.5,4.5	Changes the view in the current viewport

Set the right viewpoint current.

Command: *Choose* View, Redraw All	Issues the REDRAWALL command

Save your drawing.

10

The preceding exercise creates a viewport configuration similar to the one you created earlier in this chapter. The primary difference is that the three viewports do not occupy the entire display area. Unlike tiled model space, you cannot use the VPORTS command.

Editing the Viewports

Each floating viewport is an object—a VIEWPORT object. As an object, a floating viewport resides on the layer on which you draw it and has the current color and linetype. You even can edit it as an object.

To adjust the location of the viewport, you use the MOVE command. To change the size of the viewport, you use STRETCH or SCALE. You even can use GRIPS on a viewport object.

To edit the viewports, you need to be in paper space, not in floating model space. If you are in floating model space, you can use the PSPACE command to get back to paper space.

PSPACE. The PSPACE command puts you in paper space.
Pull-down: *Choose* View, Paper Space
Screen: *Choose* VIEW, Pspace

In the following exercise, you edit the viewport objects.

Adjusting Floating Viewports

Continue to use the CHAP10A drawing.

Command: *Choose* View, Paper Space	Changes to paper space
Command: *Choose* Modify, Move	Issues the MOVE command
Select objects: *Pick viewport border at ① (see fig. 10.18)*	Selects the upper left viewport object to be moved
Select objects: (Enter)	Completes object selection
Base point or displacement: **0,1** (Enter)	Specifies displacement
Second point of displacement: (Enter)	Moves viewport by specified displacements

Repeat the MOVE command and move the right viewport object one unit to the right. The three viewports should now be separated.

Command: *Choose* Modify, Stretch	Issues the STRETCH command

Select objects to stretch by crossing window or polygon.

Select objects: *Select a crossing window from* 14,9 *to* 7.5,6.5	Selects the right viewport as the object to be stretched
Select objects: (Enter)	Completes object selection
Base point or displacement: **0,1** (Enter)	Specifies displacement
Second point of displacement: (Enter)	Stretches viewport by specified displacement (see fig. 10.19)
Command: *Choose* View, Floating Viewports, Viewport Off	Issues MVIEW with the OFF option
Command: _mview ON/OFF/Hideplot/Fit/2/3/4/Restore/ <First Point>: _OFF	
Select objects: *Select the rightmost viewport and press Enter*	Turns off the rightmost viewport

The viewport display is blanked.

Command: *Choose* View, Floating Viewports, Viewport On	Issues MVIEW with the ON option
Command: _mview ON/OFF/Hideplot/Fit/2/3/4/Restore/ <First Point>: _ON	
Select objects: *Select the rightmost viewport and press Enter*	Turns on the rightmost viewport

Save the drawing.

You have by now realized that you can move and stretch the floating viewports you create as you like. Later, in Chapter 25, "Sheet Composition and Plotting," you see the benefits of floating viewports if you don't already.

Figure 10.18

Selecting viewports to modify.

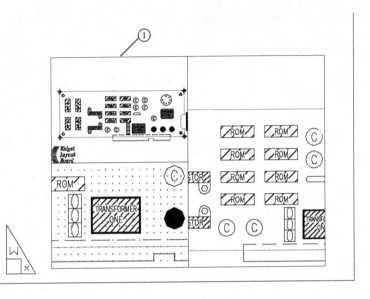

Figure 10.19

A stretched viewport.

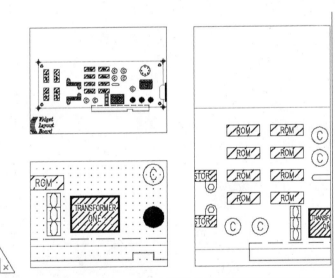

Editing in Model Space in Floating Viewports

After you make one of the floating viewports current, you also can edit the model in floating model space. (See Chapter 21, "Introduction to Dimensioning," for dimensioning in viewports.) Editing objects in model space using floating viewports (TILEMODE=0) is no different than editing the drawing in tiled model space

(TILEMODE=1). You draw and edit in the current viewport. You do all your object selection and point picking in the current viewport. Any changes you make to the model automatically appear in all viewports, assuming that they show portions of the model to which you made the changes and that the appropriate layers are thawed.

You even can change your current viewport while executing a command, just as you can with tiled viewports. You can start to draw a line in one viewport, for example, and then change the current viewport before you pick the next point for the line. In general, the only commands from which you cannot change the current viewport are the display commands, such as ZOOM, PAN, and VIEW.

Again, as with tiled viewports, you can even change the current viewport while selecting objects. The objects you select are highlighted in each viewport that the object is visible in. This provides you with tremendous flexibility during object selection not available if you use a single viewport.

Editing in Paper Space

So far, you have learned how to draw and edit in floating model space. You also know how to draw and edit in paper space itself. (See Chapter 21, "Introduction to Dimensioning," for dimensioning in paper space.) All the layers created in model space and in floating model space exist in paper space as well. AutoCAD, however, keeps objects you draw in paper space separate from the objects you draw on the same layers in model space. Basically, AutoCAD keeps two versions of the layers, one for model space and one for paper space.

You normally need only draw and edit in paper space (other than the viewport objects themselves) when you use paper space to compose your drawing. Paper space provides a way to put text into a final plot without the text becoming a part of the model. The most common use would be to have a 3D machine part that requires multiview projections to properly describe the object. You could define a viewport for each view of the part. View titles, such as "Left Side View," would be paper space text objects. You could draw two lines below the text in paper space, which would be more convenient because if the text were part of the model, subsequent scaling of the model would necessitate subsequent scaling of the text. Using paper space makes the text a nonissue. Laying out a drawing with paper space is covered in Chapter 25, "Sheet Composition and Plotting." For now, do not draw or edit in paper space. Always be sure to draw and edit in floating model space, with TILEMODE set to 0 (off).

Setting Layer Visibility in Viewports

You can control the display of layers globally (in all viewports) or per viewport. In contrast, you can affect layers in tiled viewports only globally. The only layer operations that you can set for an individual viewport are freezing and thawing. Setting a

10

layer's color and linetype or turning a layer on or off affects the views in all floating viewports. If you decide to freeze a layer, you can do it globally or for the current viewport only. In the Layer Control dialog box, if you choose the Free*z*e button, you freeze the layer globally. To freeze the layer for the current viewport only, choose the Fr button next to the label Cur VP. The letter *C* appears in the State column of the Layer Control dialog to indicate that the layer is frozen in the current viewport (see fig. 10.20).

Figure 10.20

The Layer Control dialog box.

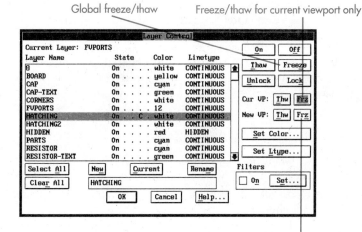

To thaw a layer that is frozen for the current viewport, choose the **T**hw button next to the Cur VP label. If you choose the regular **T**haw button, you do not thaw the frozen layer.

You also can use the VPLAYER command to set the freeze/thaw status. VPLAYER is discussed in greater detail in the next section.

In the following exercise, you control layer visibility in a single or all viewports.

Controlling Viewport Layer Visibility

Continue in the CHAP10A drawing from the previous exercise.

Command: *Choose View, Floating Model Space*   Changes to floating model space

Make the upper left viewpoint current.

Command: *Choose Data, Layers*   Opens the Layer Control dialog box

New Riders Publishing
INSIDE SERIES

Select layer HATCHING, *then choose* Free**ze** *(not the* Fr**z** *button), then* OK	Freezes the layer HATCHING in all viewports (the ROMs are no longer hatched)
Command: *Press* (Enter)	Reopens the Layer Control dialog box
Select layer HATCHING, *then choose* **T**haw *(not the* **T**hw *button), then* OK	Thaws the layer HATCHING in all viewports

Set the lower left viewport current.

Command: *Press Enter*	Reopens the Layer Control dialog box
Select layer HATCHING, *then choose* Fr**z** *(button next to* Cur VP, *not the* Free**ze** *button)*	Sets it frozen only in the current viewport and displays the letter *C* in the state column for HATCHING

The *C* indicates that the layer is frozen for the current viewport.

Choose OK	Freezes the layer HATCHING only in the current viewport; the hatching on the ROMs remains visible in the others
Click in the right viewport	Makes the right viewport current
Command: *Press Enter*	Reopens the Layer Control dialog box

The HATCHING does not have a letter *C* now. This is because for this viewport, HATCHING is not frozen.

Cancel the Layer Control dialog box.

Click in the lower left viewport	Makes the lower left viewport current

Save the drawing.

You can use the Layer Control dialog box to freeze unnecessary layers that slow AutoCAD. You can freeze layers in a viewport that might not be germane to the presentation of the drawing, but that is within the context of another viewport. For example, you might draw a complicated support detail once and display it at a reduced scale in an "elevation" viewport with the detail layers frozen. In the detail viewport, you could display the support detail at an enlarged scale with the detail layer thawed. In this manner, you draw it once and then let AutoCAD save you time.

Next to the label New VP is a pair of buttons labeled Fr**z** and **T**hw. If you choose the Fr**z** button, AutoCAD automatically freezes all selected layers in any new floating viewports you create. The letter *N* appears in the State column of the Layer Control dialog box to indicate that the layer will be frozen in new viewports. To remove the *N* state from a layer, choose the **T**hw button.

10

Another command you can use to manipulate layer visibility in lieu of the Layer Control dialog box is VPLAYER.

VPLAYER. The VPLAYER command enables you to control the visibility of existing and new layers, per viewport.
Pull-down: *Choose* Data, Viewport Layer Controls
Screen: *Choose* DATA, VPlayer

With VPLAYER, you have the following options:

◆ **?.** Lists all frozen layers in a selected viewport.

◆ **Freeze.** Enables you to freeze specified layers in a selected viewport.

◆ **Thaw.** Enables you to thaw specified layers in a selected viewport.

◆ **Reset.** Resets layers in a selected viewport to the default settings.

◆ **Newfrz.** Creates a new layer that is frozen in all current floating viewports and new viewports. The letters *C* and *N* appear in the State column of the Layer Control dialog box to indicate that the layer is frozen in the current viewport and will be frozen in new viewports.

◆ **Vpvisdflt.** Enables you to set the default visibility of existing layers to be used when you create new viewports. When you choose the Freeze option, the letter *N* appears in the State column of the Layer Control dialog box.

If you specify the Freeze, Thaw, or Reset options, you see the following prompt after you specify the layer name:

```
All/Select/<Current>:
```

This prompt enables you to choose whether you want to apply action to the current viewport (the default option), to all viewports, or to select viewports. If you choose the Select option, you are switched back to paper space (if necessary), where you can select the viewport objects you want to affect.

VPLAYER has the following two advantages over DDLMODES:

◆ You can choose to freeze or thaw selected layers for several viewports rather than just for the current viewport.

◆ You can use the Newfrz option to create a new layer that is frozen in all viewports and then thaw it for the current viewport, which is very handy when you want to create a layer to be visible in only a single viewport.

Stop   Unlike a frozen layer in normal model space (TILEMODE=1), a layer that is frozen for the current viewport can be the current layer. Freezing the current layer for the current viewport is allowed in floating model space. You receive a warning, but AutoCAD carries out the action. If a layer is frozen globally, you cannot make it the current layer, nor can you freeze the current layer globally (using the FREEZE button).

In the following exercise, you edit the model in floating model space, with the help of VPLAYER.

Editing in Floating Model Space

Continue to use the CHAP10A drawing.

Command: *Choose* Data, Viewport Layer Controls, Freeze	Issues VPLAYER with the Freeze option specified
Command: _vplayer ?/Freeze/Thaw/ Reset/Newfrz/Vpvisdflt: _f	
Layer(s) to Freeze: **HATCHING2** (Enter)	Specifies layer to be frozen
All/Select/<Current>: **S** (Enter)	Specifies the Select option
Switching to Paper space.	Indicates that the user is being switched back to paper space (PSPACE command)
Select objects: *Select the upper left viewport*	Selects the upper left viewport as one to be frozen
Select objects: *Select the lower left viewport*	Selects the lower left viewport as one to be frozen
Select objects: (Enter)	
Switching to Model space.	Indicates that the user is being switched back to model space (MSPACE command)
?/Freeze/Thaw/Reset/Newfrz/ Vpvisdflt: (Enter)	Ends the VPLAYER command

10

continues

continued

`Command:` *Choose* Data, Viewport Layer Controls, New Freeze	Issues VPLAYER with the New option specified
`?/Freeze/Thaw/Reset/Newfrz/` `Vpvisdflt:` `_n` (Enter)	
`New Viewport frozen layer names:` **TITLE** (Enter)	Creates a new layer named TITLE that is made frozen for all current viewports and new viewports
`?/Freeze/Thaw/Reset/Newfrz/` `Vpvisdflt:` **T** (Enter)	Specifies the Thaw option
`Layer(s) to Thaw:` **TITLE** (Enter)	Specifies the layer TITLE
`All/Select/<Current>:` **S** (Enter)	Specifies that the object be selected
`Switching to Paper space.`	
`Select objects:` *Select the upper left viewport*	Selects the upper left viewport
`Select objects:` (Enter)	Completes object selection
`Switching to Model space.`	
`?/Freeze/Thaw/Reset/Newfrz/` `Vpvisdflt:` (Enter)	Completes the VPLAYER command

Make the upper left viewport current. Make the layer TITLE the current layer.

`Command:` *Choose* Draw, Text, Dynamic Text	Issues the DTEXT command
`Justify/Style/<Start point>:` **4.5,6** (Enter)	Specifies the starting point of the text
`Rotation angle <0.00>:` (Enter)	Specifies no rotation of the text
`Text:` **Model 100X I/O Board** *Press Enter twice*	Makes the text object

Set the right viewport current. Issue ZOOM and choose the Extents option. The text you just drew does not appear, because the layer TITLE was created as a frozen layer in all viewports except the viewport in which you thawed it.

New Riders Publishing
INSIDE
SERIES

Controlling layer visibility in floating model space is very flexible and can save time. The exercise shows you how easily you can save several steps by specifying a new layer to be frozen, then thawing it in the viewport in which you will use it.

Closing Floating Viewports

Unlike tiled viewports, MVIEW does not have options you can use to merge or close multiple floating viewports. Instead, all you have to do to close a viewport is erase the viewport object. Deleting a viewport object does not delete the objects displayed in it.

In the next exercise, you close a floating viewport.

Closing Floating Viewports

Continue to use the CHAP10A drawing.

Command: *Choose* View, Paper Space	Switches from model to paper space
Command: *Choose* Modify, Erase	Issues the ERASE command
Select objects: *Select the upper left viewport*	Identifies the upper left viewport of the display
Select objects: (Enter)	Completes the object selection and closes the upper left viewport

---

Use this method of closing viewports to make room to stretch other viewports.

Opening More Floating Viewports

After you fill up your drawing window with floating viewports, you might find that you want to open up some more. You can make room for the additional viewports by shrinking (scaling down) some of the existing viewports, or you can use ZOOM to zoom out to see more paper space in the drawing window. If you choose to zoom out, make sure that you are in paper space; otherwise, you end up zooming the view in the current viewport.

 Tip If you want to blow up the view in a particular viewport before you work on the model, switch to paper space and zoom in on the viewport. If you issue ZOOM while in floating model space, only the view within the viewport confines is affected; before you can zoom in on or pan the viewports, you must be in paper space.

10

In the next exercise, you make more room for additional viewports.

Getting More Room

Continue to use the CHAP10A drawing.

Make sure that you are in paper space and not in floating model space.

Command: *Choose* View, Zoom, Out   Zooms halfway out making the viewports smaller and providing more paper space

You now have more room to place additional floating viewports. See figure 10.21 for the results of this exercise.

Figure 10.21

More room for paper space and viewports.

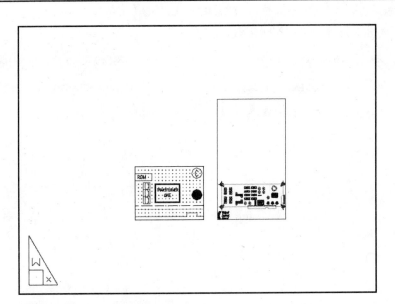

In this chapter, you have examined the behavior of paper space, model space and viewports. The viewports are just openings through which you view your model and you can zoom and pan around within the opening to display any portion of your model. The behavior of settings in the viewports is quite flexible and can be used to your advantage as you apply them to the real world in which you work.

In the next chapter, "Drawing and Editing Polylines and Splines," you discover how to create and edit the polyline object, control its appearance, and work with Splines and NURBS—the more advanced curves.

New Riders Publishing
INSIDE SERIES

C H A P T E R
11

Drawing and Editing Polylines and Splines

So far in this book you have used line and arc objects to draw straight lines and curves. Each line and arc segment has been a separate object, even when connected from end to end. If, for example, you used four lines to draw a box, you have had to select all the lines to move the box. Polylines are multisegmented objects; they can contain multiple straight and curved segments. If you want to move a box that was drawn using a polyline, you need only select any one segment to select the entire box.

In most CAD drawings, you use traditional drawing elements: lines, circles, ellipses, arcs, and so on. Sometimes, however, you need to draw smooth, irregular curves. You use splines to draw free-form, irregular curves. Splines are useful for drawing map contours, roads, walkways, and other smooth, flowing curves.

In this chapter, you learn how to do the following:

◆ Draw and edit multisegmented and multiwidth polylines

◆ Create a polyline from nonpolyline objects

◆ Fillet polylines and other objects

◆ Sketch freehand polylines

◆ Spline-fit a polyline

◆ Draw and edit splines

Although the PLINE, PEDIT, SPLINE, and SPLINEDIT commands consist of more options and suboptions than any other command in AutoCAD, you mostly use them with their defaults. As you become familiar with polylines in this chapter, you begin to understand when you can use polylines to your advantage.

In the following Quick 5¢ Tour exercise, you use polylines to draw a box that has a handle. First, you draw the outline of the box. You use snap and the coordinates display to pick the points shown. Then you use a wide polyline to draw the handle on the top of the box. Finally, you edit the box to change its linewidth and apply curves to it. When you select it to edit, you use only a single pick point to select the entire polyline object.

Quick 5¢ Tour

Begin a new drawing named CHAP11, using the default AutoCAD prototype, then set snap to .25 and grid to 1.

Command: *Choose* Draw, Polyline	Issues the PLINE command
_pline	
From point: *Pick point* 4,4	Specifies the starting point of the polyline
Current line-width is 0.0000	Tells you the current line width
Arc/Close/Halfwidth/Length/Undo/ Width/<Endpoint of line>: *Pick point* 12,4	Specifies vertex and draws line segment
Arc/Close/Halfwidth/Length/Undo/ Width/<Endpoint of line>: *Pick point* 12,1	Specifies vertex and draws line segment
Arc/Close/Halfwidth/Length/Undo/ Width/<Endpoint of line>: *Pick point* 4,1	Specifies vertex and draws line segment

New Riders Publishing
INSIDE SERIES

`Arc/Close/Halfwidth/Length/Undo/` `Width/<Endpoint of line>:` **C** (Enter)	Closes the polyline with another segment and ends the PLINE command
`Command:` (Enter)	Repeats the PLINE command
`PLINE` `From point:` *Pick point* 5,4	Specifies the starting point of the polyline
`Current line-width is 0.0000`	Tells you the current line width
`Arc/Close/Halfwidth/Length/Undo/Width/` `<Endpoint of line>:` **W** (Enter)	Specifies the Width option
`Starting width <0.0000>:` **.25** (Enter)	Specifies starting width
`Ending width <0.2500>:` (Enter)	Accepts starting width as ending width
`Arc/Close/Halfwidth/Length/Undo/Width/` `<Endpoint of line>:` **A** (Enter)	Changes to polyline arc mode

`Angle/CEnter/CLose/Direction/Halfwidth/`
`Line/Radius/Second pt/Undo/Width/`
`<Endpoint of arc>:` *Pick point* 6,5
	Specifies vertex of arc segment

`Angle/CEnter/CLose/Direction/Halfwidth/`
`Line/Radius/Second pt/Undo/Width/`
`<Endpoint of arc>:` **L** (Enter)
	Changes to polyline line mode

`Arc/Close/Halfwidth/Length/Undo/Width/` `<Endpoint of line>:` *Pick point* 10,5	Specifies vertex of line segment
`Arc/Close/Halfwidth/Length/Undo/Width/` `<Endpoint of line>:` **A** (Enter)	Changes to polyline arc mode

`Angle/CEnter/CLose/Direction/Halfwidth/`
`Line/Radius/Second pt/Undo/Width/`
`<Endpoint of arc>:` *Pick point* 11,4
	Specifies vertex of arc segment

`Arc/Close/Halfwidth/Length/Undo/Width/` `<Endpoint of line>:` (Enter)	Ends the PLINE command
`Command:` *Choose* Modify, Edit Polyline	Issues the PEDIT command
`Select polyline:` *Pick the box polyline*	Selects the entire polyline for object editing
`Open/Join/Width/Edit vertex/Fit/Spline/` `Decurve/Ltype gen/Undo/eXit <X>:` **W** (Enter)	Specifies the Width option

continues

continued

`Enter new width for all segments:` `.125` (Enter)	Changes the width of the entire polyline
`Open/Join/Width/Edit vertex/Fit/Spline/` `Decurve/Ltype gen/Undo/eXit <X>:` **F** (Enter)	Fits arc segments to all vertices, creating a circle
`Open/Join/Width/Edit vertex/Fit/Spline/` `Decurve/Ltype gen/Undo/eXit <X>:` **S** (Enter)	Spline-fits all vertices, creating an ellipse
`Open/Join/Width/Edit vertex/Fit/Spline/` `Decurve/Ltype gen/Undo/eXit <X>:` **D** (Enter)	Removes all curve information from polyline, restoring the box
`Open/Join/Width/Edit vertex/Fit/Spline/` `Decurve/Ltype gen/Undo/eXit <X>:` (Enter)	Exits the PEDIT command

Use REDRAW to clean up the image.

Figure 11.1

The created polyline rectangle and arcs.

The preceding quick exercise shows you that polylines are useful for drawing objects with multisegment outlines. This exercise also shows you that you can modify an entire polyline as one object. Finally, this exercise shows you that polylines are useful for drawing wide lines and arcs. Polylines have many more uses and features, which this chapter offers you the opportunity to explore.

Creating Polylines

You use the PLINE command to create polylines. Rather than use a wide plotter pen or create multiple lines to get a thick line, or create independent arcs and then connect them to lines, you can create a polyline. You can often draw an object of connected lines and arcs faster with the PLINE command than you can with separate ARC and LINE commands. Some samples of polylines are shown in figure 11.2.

New Riders Publishing
INSIDE SERIES

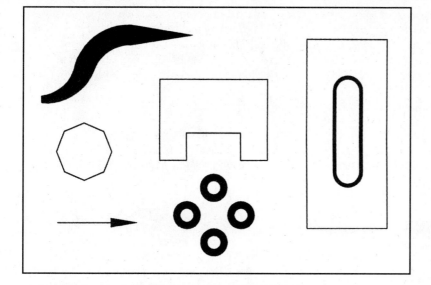

Figure 11.2

Several kinds of polylines.

> **PLINE.** The PLINE command enables you to draw polyline objects. Polylines consist of multiple straight and arc segments that you treat as a single object. Each segment also can possess width. The width of a segment can remain constant or can taper from one end to the other.
>
> Pull-down: *Choose* Draw, Polyline
> Screen: *Choose* Draw1, Pline:

Polylines versus Lines

Polylines are different from independent line objects that you use to LINE command to create, which only appear to be joined. AutoCAD treats a multisegment polyline as a single object. Polylines can include both line and arc segments connected at vertices (endpoints). AutoCAD stores information, such as tangent direction and line width, at each vertex.

Polylines offer two advantages over lines. First, versatility: they can be straight or curved, thin or wide, one width or tapered. You can, for example, draw a curved leader with an arrowhead as a single polyline.

Second, because a polyline is a single object, editing operations are easier and you make fewer errors when you use crosshatching or work in 3D. You can edit a polyline by selecting any segment, because all of a polyline's segments are connected. In

11

contrast, if you want to copy something that consists of individual line objects, you must select each individual line segment. If you crosshatch or create 3D objects from 2D lines, you must have edges that connect. Objects drawn with lines and arcs can have tiny gaps that cause hatch or 3D errors. Use polylines to draw any closed or connected object or polygon, particularly if you anticipate hatching it or working with your drawing in 3D.

 Tip If you plan to import your AutoCAD drawing into 3D Studio, polylines are indispensable. Use polylines to create all outlines, contours, and perimeters that you plan to loft in 3D Studio. Convert lines that make up walls in plan view drawings to polylines.

The PLINE Command

Because PLINE enables you to draw two basic kinds of segments, straight lines and curves, some PLINE prompts are similar to the LINE and ARC prompts. If you draw straight polyline segments, options such as Endpoint, Close, and Undo appear. Check out the possibilities on the PLINE prompt line. The default set of options applies to line mode, as described in the following list:

◆ **Arc.** Switches from drawing polylines to drawing polyarcs and issues the polyarc options prompt.

◆ **Close.** Closes the polyline by drawing a segment from the last endpoint to the initial start point, and then ends the PLINE command.

◆ **Halfwidth.** Prompts you for the distance from the center to the polyline's edges (half the actual width). See the Width option that follows for details.

◆ **Length.** Prompts you to enter the length of a new polyline segment. AutoCAD then draws the new segment at the same angle as the last line segment or tangent to the last arc segment. AutoCAD stores this angle in the LASTANGLE system variable. The last line or arc segment can be that of a previous polyline, line, or arc object.

◆ **Undo.** Undoes the last drawn segment. It also undoes any arc or line option that immediately preceded drawing the segment, but will not undo width options.

◆ **Width.** Prompts you to enter a width (default 0) for the next segment to create polylines. If you want to taper a segment, define different starting and ending widths. After you draw the tapered segment, AutoCAD draws the next segment with the ending width of the tapered segment. Unless you cancel the PLINE command before you draw a segment, AutoCAD stores the ending width as the new default width.

New Riders Publishing
INSIDE SERIES

◆ **Endpoint of line.** Prompts you to specify the endpoint of the current line segment. This option is the default.

The Arc option presents a set of arc mode options, including some familiar arc prompts, such as Angle/CEnter/Radius, Second pt, and Endpoint of arc.

The PLINE Arc options include the following:

◆ **Angle.** Prompts you to enter the included angle (a negative angle draws the arc clockwise).

◆ **CEnter.** Prompts you to specify the arc's center.

◆ **Close.** Closes the polyline by using an arc segment to connect the initial start point to the last endpoint, then ends the PLINE command.

◆ **Direction.** Prompts you to specify a tangent direction for the segment.

◆ **Halfwidth.** Prompts you to specify a halfwidth, the same as for the Line mode option of the PLINE command.

◆ **Line.** Switches back to line mode.

◆ **Radius.** Prompts you to specify the arc's radius.

◆ **Second pt.** Selects the second point of a three-point arc.

◆ **Undo.** Undoes the last drawn segment.

◆ **Width.** Prompts you to enter a width, the same way as in line mode.

◆ **Endpoint of arc.** Prompts you to specify the endpoint of the current arc segment. This option is the default.

◆**Note** When a polyline has width, you can control the line fill by turning FILL on or off.

Although using PLINE to draw lines and arcs is similar to using LINE and ARC to draw equivalent elements, you should be aware of several important differences, as follows:

◆ You get all the line or arc mode prompts every time you enter a new polyline vertex.

◆ Additional prompts, such as for Halfwidth and Width, enable you to control the width of the segment.

11

◆ You can switch back and forth from straight segments to curved segments and add additional segments to your growing polyline.

◆ You can apply linetypes continuously across vertices.

◆ You can apply the MEASURE and DIVIDE commands to complex polyline paths.

◆ You can use the AREA command to find lengths and areas of polylines.

◆ You can use the OFFSET command to great advantage to create new complex features, such as offsetting a foundation perimeter outline to create a footing.

 Note   Normal polylines are 2D objects. The command for drawing 3D polylines is 3DPOLY. 3D polylines only have straight, zero-width segments, so the 3DPOLY command prompt includes only the Close, Undo, and Endpoint of line options. See Chapter 28, "3D Basics," for more on 3D polylines.

Using PLINE To Draw Multisegment and Wide Lines

In the following exercises, you use polylines to draw a diagram of a street intersection as you use the PLINE command to create the most common types of objects: multisegmented lines and lines of varying widths.

You use normal zero-width polylines to draw the edge of the road where it meets the curb in the first exercise. You use the Arc, Line, and Length options. You also use the 5' grid and 6" snap to pick points.

Drawing Basic Polylines

Begin a new drawing named CHAP11A, using INTERSEC.DWG as a prototype.

Command: *Choose* Draw, Polyline	Issues the PLINE command
From point: *Pick point at* ① *(see fig. 11.3)*	Specifies the starting point of the polyline
`Current line-width is 0'-0.0000"`	Tells you the current line width
`Arc/Close/Halfwidth/Length/Undo/Width/` `<Endpoint of line>:` *Pick point at* ②	Specifies vertex of line segment
`Arc/Close/Halfwidth/Length/Undo/Width/` `<Endpoint of line>:` **A** (Enter)	Changes to polyline arc mode

`Angle/CEnter/CLose/Direction/Halfwidth/`
`Line/Radius/Second pt/Undo/Width/`
`<Endpoint of arc>:` *Pick point at* ③
	Specifies vertex of arc segment

`Angle/CEnter/CLose/Direction/Halfwidth/`
`Line/Radius/Second pt/Undo/Width/`
`<Endpoint of arc>:` **L** (Enter)
	Changes to polyline line mode

`Arc/Close/Halfwidth/Length/Undo/Width/` `<Endpoint of line>:` *Pick point at* ④	Specifies vertex of line segment
`Arc/Close/Halfwidth/Length/Undo/Width/` `<Endpoint of line>:` **A** (Enter)	Changes to polyline arc mode

`Angle/CEnter/CLose/Direction/Halfwidth/`
`Line/Radius/Second pt/Undo/Width/`
`<Endpoint of arc>:` *Pick point at* ⑤
	Specifies vertex of arc segment

`Angle/CEnter/CLose/Direction/Halfwidth/`
`Line/Radius/Second pt/Undo/Width/`
`<Endpoint of arc>:` **L** (Enter)
	Changes to polyline line mode

`Arc/Close/Halfwidth/Length/Undo/Width/` `<Endpoint of line>:` **L** (Enter)	Specifies Length option
`Length of line:` **21'6** (Enter)	
`Arc/Close/Halfwidth/Length/Undo/Width/` `<Endpoint of line>:` **A** (Enter)	Changes to polyline arc mode

`Angle/CEnter/CLose/Direction/Halfwidth/`
`Line/Radius/Second pt/Undo/Width/`
`<Endpoint of arc>:` *Pick point at* ⑦
	Specifies vertex of arc segment

`Angle/CEnter/CLose/Direction/Halfwidth/`
`Line/Radius/Second pt/Undo/Width/`
`<Endpoint of arc>:` **L** (Enter)
	Changes to polyline line mode

`Arc/Close/Halfwidth/Length/Undo/Width/` `<Endpoint of line>:` *Pick point at* ⑧	Specifies vertex of line segment
`Arc/Close/Halfwidth/Length/Undo/Width/` `<Endpoint of line>:` *Press Enter twice*	Ends and repeats the PLINE command
`PLINE` `From Point:` *Pick at* ⑨ *and use the* *Arc and Line options to draw segments* *to* ⑩, ⑪, *and* ⑫	Completes the curbs as shown in figure 11.3

continues

continued

Next, you move the right road edge to widen the lanes.

Command: *Select the right polyline and choose* Modify, Move	Issues the MOVE command with polyline selected
`Base point or displacement:` *Pick any point*	
`Second point of displacement:` `@9'6<0` *(see fig. 11.4)*	Moves the polyline

Next, you draw two polylines for the center lane stripes. You edit them into wide polylines in a later exercise.

Command: *Choose* Draw, Polyline
and draw a line from ① *to* ②

Command: *Choose* Draw, Polyline
and draw a line from ③ *to* ④

Save the drawing.

Figure 11.3

Polyline road boundaries using Line and Arc modes.

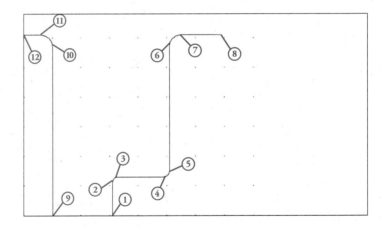

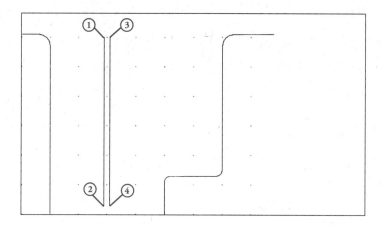

Figure 11.4

Added center lane stripes and moved right curb.

The drawing of the intersection looks anemic now, but you add some wide polylines in the next exercise to fill in the drawing. Later in this chapter, you edit the zero-width polylines into wide polylines.

A common use of wide and multiwidth polylines is as symbols and markings. Next, you add a stop line and some lane markers with wide polylines, and a fancy multiwidth polyline for the right-turn arrow. You use the Width and Halfwidth options.

Drawing Wide Polylines

Continue to use the CHAP11A drawing from the previous exercise.

Command: *Choose* Draw, Polyline	Issues the PLINE command
From point: *Pick point at* ① *(see fig. 11.5)*	Specifies the starting point of the polyline
Current line-width is 0'-0.0000"	Tells you the current line width
Arc/Close/Halfwidth/Length/Undo/Width/<Endpoint of line>: **W** (Enter)	Specifies the Width option
Starting width <0'-0.0000">: **10** (Enter)	Specifies a starting width of 10 inches
Ending width <0'-10.0000">: (Enter)	Accepts starting width as ending width
Arc/Close/Halfwidth/Length/Undo/Width/<Endpoint of line>: *Pick point at* ②	Specifies the endpoint of the polyline

continues

11

continued

`Arc/Close/Halfwidth/Length/Undo/Width/` `<Endpoint of line>:` *Press Enter twice*	Ends and repeats the PLINE command
`PLINE` `From point:` *Pick point at* ③	Specifies the starting point of the polyline
`Current line-width is 0'-10.0000"`	Tells you the current line width (AutoCAD remembers!)
`Arc/Close/Halfwidth/Length/Undo/Width/` `<Endpoint of line>:` *Pick point at* ④	Specifies the endpoint of the polyline
`Arc/Close/Halfwidth/Length/Undo/Width/` `<Endpoint of line>:` *Press Enter twice*	
`PLINE` `From point:` *Pick point 28'-6",22'*	
`Current line-width is 0'-10.0000"`	Tells you the current line width
`Arc/Close/Halfwidth/Length/Undo/Width/` `<Endpoint of line>:` *Pick point* *28'-6",23'*	
`Arc/Close/Halfwidth/Length/Undo/Width/` `<Endpoint of line>:` **H** (Enter)	Specifies the Halfwidth option and prompts with the current half-width
`Starting half-width <0'-5.0000">:` (Enter)	Accepts the default
`Ending half-width <0'-10.0000">:` **15** (Enter)	Specifies an ending width of 15 inches
`Arc/Close/Halfwidth/Length/Undo/Width/` `<Endpoint of line>:` **A** (Enter)	Changes to arc mode

Drag the cursor around and observe the tapered outline of the polyline arc.

`Angle/CEnter/CLose/Direction/Halfwidth/`
`Line/Radius/Second pt/Undo/Width/`
`<Endpoint of arc>:` *Pick point*
30'-6",25'
	Specifies the endpoint of the wide tapered polyline arc

`Angle/CEnter/CLose/Direction/Halfwidth/`
`Line/Radius/Second pt/Undo/Width/`
`<Endpoint of arc>:` **L** (Enter)
	Changes to line mode

`Arc/Close/Halfwidth/Length/Undo/Width/` `<Endpoint of line>:` **W** (Enter)	Specifies the Width option

New Riders Publishing
INSIDE SERIES

`Starting width <2'-6.0000">:` **60** (Enter)	Specifies a starting width of 60 inches
`Ending width <5'-0.0000">:` **0** (Enter)	Specifies an ending width of 0

`Arc/Close/Halfwidth/Length/Undo/Width/`
`<Endpoint of line>:` *Pick point*
`32'-6",25'`
	Specifies endpoint of tapered polyline segment

`Arc/Close/Halfwidth/Length/Undo/Width/` `<Endpoint of line>:` (Enter)	

Save the drawing.

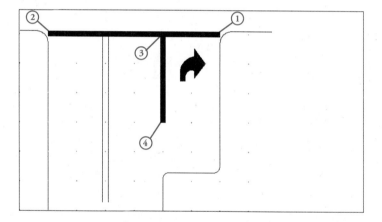

Figure 11.5

Enhanced drawing with wide polylines.

The preceding exercise emphasizes the versatility of polylines. Not only can polylines have varying width, but each segment can have different starting and ending widths. You might have also noticed that AutoCAD remembers the polyline width setting: it stores polyline width in the PLINEWID system variable.

Controlling Polyline Appearance with FILL

11

A drawing that consists of many wide polylines can dramatically increase the amount of time AutoCAD consumes to redraw the screen or plot a drawing. The FILL command enables you to control the visibility of the filled portion of wide polylines, multilines, traces, and solids. When you turn off FILL, AutoCAD displays or plots only the outline of the filled object. Before you can see the effect of the FILL command, you must regenerate the drawing.

'FILL. The FILL command enables you to change the state of the FILLMODE system variable, by which you can control the visibility of the filled portion of wide polylines, multilines, traces, and solids. When the fill mode is off, AutoCAD displays or plots only the outline of filled objects. Objects regenerate and plot faster when fill mode is off.

Screen: *Choose* OPTIONS, DISPLAY, Fill:

A certain pull-down menu item also enables you to control FILL, but it directly controls the FILLMODE variable and does not use the FILL command. If you choose Options, Display, you see the Solid Fill item on the Display menu. If a check appears beside this item, FILL is on (the default); if not, FILL is off. AutoCAD stores the setting with the drawing.

In the following exercise, you turn fill mode off and then back on.

Using the FILL Command

Continue to use the CHAP11A drawing from the previous exercise.

Choose Options, Display, Solid Fill	Turns off the FILLMODE system variable
Command: **REGEN** (Enter)	Regenerates the drawing to see changes (see fig. 11.6)
Command: **FILL** (Enter)	Invokes the FILL command
ON/OFF <Off>: **ON** (Enter)	Turns fill back on
Command: **REGEN** (Enter)	

Many commands other than the PLINE command enable you to create polylines. The DONUT, POLYGON, and RECTANG commands, for example, are covered in Chapter 7, "Drawing Basic Objects." The SKETCH command, which you learn about in the following section, is another such command.

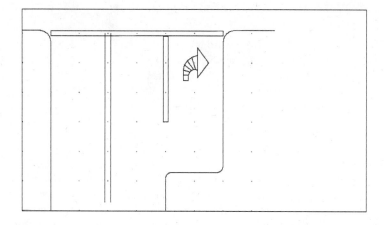

Figure 11.6

The drawing with FILL off.

Creating Polylines with SKETCH

You use the SKETCH command as a freehand drawing tool or use a drawing tablet as an input device to trace curves on a paper drawing. (See Appendix A, "Installation and Configuration," for information on tablet calibration.) During SKETCH, AutoCAD creates a contiguous series of lines or polyline segments as you move the cursor, drawing wherever you move your cursor. Because AutoCAD does not know where your sketching might lead, you and the program must take precautions to keep the amount of sketch information from getting out of hand. A few quick motions of the cursor while using the SKETCH command can create a huge number of short segments in the drawing file.

SKETCH. The SKETCH command enables you to create a contiguous series of lines or polyline segments as you move the cursor. The SKETCH command enables you to draw freehand or to trace curves from paper on a graphics tablet. The SKPOLY system variable enables you to control the type of object that you create when you use the SKETCH command. A value of 0 (the default) creates line objects; a value of 1 creates polylines.

Pull-down: *Choose Draw, Sketch*
Screen: *Choose DRAW1, Sketch:*

The Sketch screen menu also contains the SkpolOn: and SkpolOff: items, which you use to turn SKPOLY on and off.

Setting SKETCH Parameters

To help AutoCAD keep sketch information under control, you can specify the length of segment to use for storing your sketch data, known as the *record increment*. AutoCAD creates a new segment every time your pointer moves a distance greater than the record increment from the last segment endpoint. If you want to minimize the number of lines, try to keep the record increment as large as possible.

The record increment is in current drawing units, but the effect on your input coordination also depends on the area your mouse or digitizer cursor must move in your currently zoomed view. For example, if the width of your screen represents 300 feet (3,600 inches), and the screen pointing area on your digitizer is 6 inches wide, a 60-inch increment means your sketch segments are 5 feet and that AutoCAD records a new segment every time you move your pointing device about one-tenth of an inch (6 inches × 60 inches, divided by 3,600 inches). AutoCAD stores the record increment in the SKETCHINC system variable.

Tip   Some mouse drivers are speed sensitive; the faster you move the mouse, the faster the cursor moves across the screen. These drivers enable you to have fine positioning control when you move the mouse slowly for detail work, yet cover large distances on-screen for accessing menus when you move the mouse quickly. When you use the SKETCH command with speed-sensitive mouse drivers, move them at a slow, steady speed for best results.

You also must inform AutoCAD when it needs to consider the sketching pointer up (off the paper) or down (sketching). AutoCAD keeps all sketch input in a temporary buffer until you press R to record it into the drawing file database. SKETCH input appears in green until you record the input. You can press E to erase sketched lines before you record them. If you record sketched lines, AutoCAD turns them into regular line (or polyline) entities.

Note   Starting the SKETCH command begins an input mode that limits keyboard and mouse input. The sketch mode control keys P, X, Q, R, E, and C, need only be pressed, not entered. Pressing Enter ends the SKETCH command. You cannot choose from the pull-down menu during sketch mode and the screen menu is active only for the SKETCH command options. Object snap is not available, but you can use the mode toggle keys to turn off and on snap, grid, ortho, and the coordinates display.

To achieve smooth contour curves, you need to sketch with polylines rather than with lines (the default).

 Tip   You easily can sketch and edit polylines, but the foremost advantage of using polylines is that you can curve fit them and end up with a smooth curve. When you set SKPOLY to sketch polylines, you should set your record increment higher than when you sketch with lines. Use an increment one-half the smallest radius or turn that you might sketch. If this seems too large, just wait until you apply a curve fit to it.

To use the following options to control the SKETCH command, press the letter that corresponds to the uppercase letter of the option name without pressing Enter.

◆ **Pen.** This option tells AutoCAD to pick up or put down the tracing pen. Just type P, without pressing Enter, to change the mode. You also can click the pick button to raise or lower the pen.

◆ **eXit.** This option records the sketch segments you have been creating in the drawing file and returns you to the Command: prompt. You also can exit by pressing the spacebar or Enter.

◆ **Quit.** This option leaves SKETCH without storing the segments you have been creating. Pressing Esc does the same thing.

◆ **Record.** This option keeps you in SKETCH, but stores the segments you have been creating in the drawing file. This function is like a save, but after you record, the stored segments are not available for Erase.

◆ **Erase.** This option erases any unrecorded segment from a point you pick to the last segment drawn.

◆ **Connect.** This option connects the pen to the end of the last endpoint of an active sketch chain. You also can use normal AutoCAD editing techniques to connect finished sketch lines to other elements after you finish the sketch.

In the following exercise, you use the SKETCH command to make some contour lines, a common and extremely useful application of SKETCH. Getting the hang of sketching takes a little time, so don't hesitate to undo or erase and try again. First, you set up SKETCH to draw using polylines, then you sketch the contours.

11

Sketching Polylines

Continue to use the CHAP11A drawing from the previous exercise.

Command: **SKPOLY** (Enter)	Accesses the SKPOLY system variable
New value for SKPOLY <0>: **1** (Enter)	Causes SKETCH to draw polylines

Turn off snap

Command: *Choose* Draw, Sketch	Issues the SKETCH command
_sketch Record increment <0'-0.1000">: **1'** (Enter)	Specifies record increment

Sketch. Pen eXit Quit Record Erase Connect.

Move the cursor to the start of a contour and press P (see fig. 11.7)	Puts pen down and begins sketching

<Pen down>

Move the cursor along the contour	Draws sketch segments
Press P again	Raises the pen and stops sketching

<Pen up>

Draw the other three other contour lines.

After you finish drawing the contour lines, press R	Records the sketch data
4 polylines with 76 edges recorded.	Tells you how many polylines and how many segments were drawn by SKETCH (your number will vary)
Press X	Exits the SKETCH command

Nothing recorded

Save the drawing.

Do not worry if your sketched contours look too uneven; you use PEDIT to smooth them in the next section.

New Riders Publishing
INSIDE
SERIES

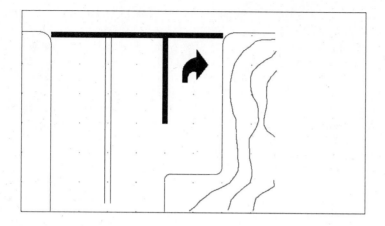

Figure 11.7

Contour lines created using the SKETCH command.

Tip Set the linetype to CONTINUOUS when you use the SKETCH command to create line objects. Noncontinuous linetypes do not work well for short line segments, such as those that SKETCH creates.

Next, you learn how to use the PEDIT command to change the characteristics of existing polylines.

Editing Polylines

Polylines can contain a complex, continuous series of line and arc segments, so AutoCAD provides the PEDIT command, which you use only to edit polylines. PEDIT also contains a large list of subcommands for polyline properties. To manage this list, AutoCAD divides PEDIT into two groups of editing functions. The primary group of functions works on the entire polyline that you edit, and the second group works on the vertices that connect segments within the polyline.

PEDIT. The PEDIT command enables you to modify 2D and 3D polyline objects and polygon meshes. You can use the PEDIT command to change the width of a polyline; add, delete, and move vertices; curve- or spline-fit the vertices; remove curve information from the vertices; adjust the tangent of a vertex; and close or open a polyline.

Pull-down: *Choose Modify, Edit Polyline*
Screen: *Choose Modify, Pedit:*

11

When you issue PEDIT, AutoCAD prompts `Select polyline:`, at which you can pick a polyline line, arc, or polyline object. The PEDIT command operates on only one polyline at a time. PEDIT does not support noun/verb object selection. Before you can select a wide polyline to edit, you must pick it at a vertex or an edge. This is true for any editing command. You can use a Window or Crossing selection, but before you can do so, you must enter W or C—PEDIT disables the implied windowing selection feature. You also can use the Last, Box, All, Fence, WPolygon, and CPolygon selection options. Selection ends as soon as PEDIT finds a line, arc, or polyline. If you select more than one, PEDIT finds only one, generally the most recently created one. If the first object you select is not a polyline, AutoCAD asks you if you want to turn it into one.

Although in this chapter you concentrate on editing two-dimensional polylines, you also can use PEDIT to modify three-dimensional polylines and meshes. The PEDIT command has fewer options and more restrictions when you edit three-dimensional polylines, as noted in the following list. See Chapter 29, "Editing and Drawing 3D Surfaces," for more details on 3D objects and editing.

The primary PEDIT options are as follows:

◆ **Close/Open.** Closes an open polyline or Opens a closed polyline. An open polyline is one that has not been closed using the PLINE command's Close option. If the startpoint of the first segment and the endpoint of the last segment do not coincide, AutoCAD adds another segment to the object. If the points do coincide (if, for example, you used ENDpoint object snap to join the last segment to the first), another segment is unnecessary and AutoCAD logically closes the polyline. You can identify whether a polyline is open or closed based on the PEDIT command prompt. When the polyline is open, the prompt shows Close; when closed, the prompt shows Open.

◆ **Join.** (2D only) Enables you to add selected arcs, lines, and other polylines to an existing polyline. Endpoints must coincide exactly before they can join.

◆ **Width.** (2D only) Prompts you to specify a single width for all segments of a polyline. The new width overrides any individual segment widths already stored. You also can use the Width suboption of the Edit vertex option to edit the width of individual segments.

◆ **Edit vertex.** Presents a prompt for a set of options that enable you to edit vertices and their adjoining segments. See the section "Editing Polyline Vertices with PEDIT" later in this chapter.

◆ **Fit.** (2D only) Creates a smooth curve through the polyline vertices.

◆ **Spline curve.** Enables you to create a curve controlled by, but not usually passing through, a framework of polyline vertices. System variables enable you to control the type of spline and its resolution.

◆ **Decurve.** Enables you to undo a Fit or Spline curve back to its original definition.

◆ **Ltype gen.** (2D only) Enables you to control whether AutoCAD generates linetypes between vertices (Ltype gen OFF) or between the polylines' endpoints (Ltype gen ON), spanning vertices. AutoCAD ignores this when polylines have tapered segments.

◆ **Undo.** Enables you to undo the most recent editing function.

◆ **eXit.** This option is the default <X> and enables you to end the PEDIT command and return to the `Command:` prompt.

Using PEDIT Width and Undo to Modify Polylines

In the following exercise, you use the Width option of the PEDIT command to modify the width of the center lane markings and the road boundaries. You also use the Undo option. These objects were created with zero-width polylines and need to have some width to fit into the diagram.

Changing the Width of Polylines

Continue to use the CHAP11A drawing from the previous exercise.

Command: *Choose* Modify, Edit Polyline	Issues the PEDIT command
`Select polyline:` *Pick left road edge at* ① *(see fig. 11.8)*	Selects the polyline for editing
`Close/Join/Width/Edit vertex/Fit/Spline/ Decurve/Ltype gen/Undo/eXit <X>:` `W` `(Enter)`	Specifies the PEDIT Width option
`Enter new width for all segments:` `6` `(Enter)`	Specifies new width and redraws entire polyline
`Close/Join/Width/Edit vertex/Fit/Spline/ Decurve/Ltype gen/Undo/eXit <X>:` `(Enter)`	Exits the PEDIT command

Press Enter to repeat the PEDIT command and use the above steps to change the right road edge at ② to 6" width.

Repeat the PEDIT command two more times, changing both center lane markers to 4" width.

Next, you try out the PEDIT Width option on a polyline that has multiple widths.

continues

continued

Command: **Enter**	Repeats the PEDIT command
PEDIT Select polyline: *Pick the right-turn arrow at* ③	Selects the arrow for editing
Close/Join/Width/Edit vertex/Fit/Spline/ Decurve/Ltype gen/Undo/eXit <X>: **W Enter**	Specifies the PEDIT Width option
Enter new width for all segments: **10 Enter**	Changes the width of all the segments in the polyline
Close/Join/Width/Edit vertex/Fit/Spline/ Decurve/Ltype gen/Undo/eXit <X>: **U Enter**	Restores the polyline to its original form
Command has been completely undone.	Tells you that all of the modifications to the polyline have been undone
Close/Join/Width/Edit vertex/Fit/ Spline/Decurve/Ltype gen/Undo/eXit <X>: **Enter**	Exits the PEDIT command

Save the drawing.

Figure 11.8

The INTERSEC drawing with modified polylines.

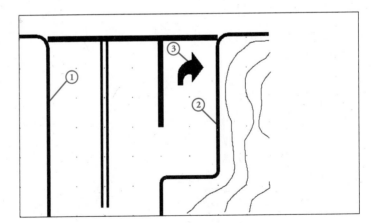

In the preceding exercise, you used the PEDIT Width option to change the width of all the polyline segments to the same value. The effect was particularly evident when you changed the width of the right-turn arrow. All the options at the main PEDIT prompt operate at the polyline level. You control the width of individual polyline segments at the vertex level. You use the PEDIT Edit vertex option and its suboptions

to change information at the vertex level. The Edit vertex option is explained in more detail in the "Editing Polyline Vertices with PEDIT" section, later in this chapter.

The ends of wide polylines are always square. When you trim or extend wide polylines, they still have square ends, regardless of the angle to which you trim or extend the object. If you trim a wide polyline to a nonperpendicular line, for example, AutoCAD does not miter the end of the wide polyline segment to the angle of the intersecting line. AutoCAD trims polylines so that the midpoint of the end segment exactly meets the trim boundary. This can cause half of the width to go beyond the trim boundary and the other half to fall short of the boundary. The more acute the angle of the two objects, the more pronounced the effect becomes.

 Tip   You can use a trick when you draw a polyline to create a wide polyline that seems to have a mitered end. After you specify the last vertex endpoint, set the width to taper from the full width to zero width. Then use typed relative polar input to draw another extremely short segment. The end of the polyline will appear to be mitered perpendicular to the angle you enter. Calculate the angle relative to the current UCS, not the angle of the polyline. For example, enter **@0.0000001<45** to miter the top of a vertically wide polyline to an angle of 135 degrees (145 plus 90). The end of the last segment is actually pointed, but the 0.0000001 segment is short enough to have the effect of ending the previous segment with a miter.

Exploding Polylines

In the following exercise, you use the EXPLODE command to change a polyline into individual line and arc objects. The EXPLODE command removes all width and tangent information from the polyline and breaks each segment into line or arc objects between each vertex. EXPLODE converts curve-fit and spline-fit polylines to many arc or line segments that approximate the shape of the spline. The EXPLODE command does not explode spline objects or ellipses.

> **EXPLODE.** The EXPLODE command enables you to reduce complex entities, such as 3D meshes, 3D solids, blocks, bodies, dimensions, groups, multilines, polyface meshes, polygon meshes, polylines, and regions, into their component parts.
> Pull-down: *Choose* Modify, Explode
> Screen: *Choose* MODIFY, Explode:

The EXPLODE command also reduces other complex objects, such as 3D meshes, 3D solids, blocks, bodies, dimensions, groups, multilines, polyface meshes, polygon meshes, polylines, and regions, into their component parts. See Chapter 16 for more information on blocks, Chapters 21 and 22 for information on dimensions, and

Chapter 29 for information on meshes. There also is a related XPLODE command, which is covered in Chapter 17.

In the following exercise, you use the EXPLODE command to reduce the right curb polyline to its component objects, arcs, and lines. The polyline's width property is lost.

Exploding Polylines

Continue to use the CHAP11A drawing from the previous exercise.

`Command:` *Choose* Modify, Explode	Issues the EXPLODE command
`Select objects:` *Pick the right road boundary*	Selects an object to explode
`1 found`	
`Select objects:` (Enter)	Explodes all selected objects
`Exploding this polyline has lost width information. The UNDO command will restore it.`	Warns you about explode and tells you how to fix an accidental explode
`Command:` *Pick line at* ① *(see fig. 11.9)*	Selects one of the exploded polyline line segments and shows its grips

AutoCAD explodes the polyline into its component parts; each polyline segment is now a separate object.

Save the drawing.

Figure 11.9

Wide polyline after EXPLODE.

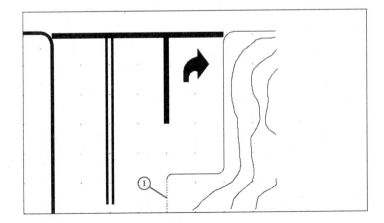

Joining Polylines with PEDIT

The PEDIT Join option enables you to add additional objects to a polyline to create a single larger polyline. You can add polylines, lines, or arcs—they must be contiguous and the endpoints must coincide exactly. The Join option reports the number of segments you add to the polyline.

You can use the PEDIT command to turn a line or arc object into a polyline. If you select a line or arc at the PEDIT `Select object:` prompt, AutoCAD asks you if you want to turn it into a polyline:

```
Object selected is not a polyline
Do you want to turn it into one? <Y>
```

Now that you have exploded the right road boundary into lines and arcs, you use the PEDIT command to turn a line into a polyline and then join the rest of the lines and arcs back together to again form a polyline in the following exercise.

Adding Segments to a Polyline

Continue to use the CHAP11A drawing from the previous exercise.

Command: *Choose* Modify, Edit Polyline	Issues the PEDIT command
Select polyline: *Pick line at* ① *(see fig. 11.10)*	Selects an object for editing
`Object selected is not a polyline` `Do you want to turn it into one? <Y>` (Enter)	Turns the line object into a polyline
`Close/Join/Width/Edit vertex/Fit/Spline/` `Decurve/Ltype gen/Undo/eXit <X>:` **J** (Enter)	Specifies the PEDIT Join option
Select objects: *Select objects with a crossing window from* ② *to* ③	Selects objects to add to polyline
`14 found`	
Select objects: (Enter)	Ends the selection process and adds segments to the polyline
`6 segments added to polyline`	Tells you the number of segments added
`Close/Join/Width/Edit vertex/Fit/Spline/` `Decurve/Ltype gen/Undo/eXit <X>:` (Enter)	Exits the PEDIT command

continues

continued

Command: *Pick line at* ①   Selects entire polyline and
                                                    shows its grips

The lines and arcs are now joined back into a single polyline object.

Save the drawing.

Figure 11.10

*Adding segments
to a polyline.*

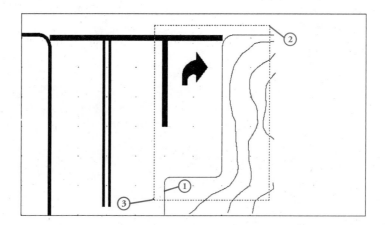

The PEDIT Join option starts with the initially selected (or converted) polyline and
sequentially joins each of the objects you select at the Join `Select objects:` prompt. It
ignores all but line, arc, and polyline objects, and joins an object only if its endpoint
coincides exactly with that of the previously joined segment. If more than one
joinable object coincides, the results can be unpredictable. You can use object snaps
and editing commands to fix the endpoints of objects that don't perfectly coincide
before you use PEDIT to join them.

Using the PEDIT Fit and Spline Options

The PEDIT command provides two options for making polyline curves that pass
through control points: a fit curve and a spline curve. A *fit curve* passes through vertex
control points and consists of two arc segments between each pair of vertices (see fig.
11.11). A *spline curve* interpolates between control points but does not usually pass
through the vertices (see fig. 11.12). The framework of vertices is called the *spline
frame*.

PEDIT spline curves create arcs or short-line segments that approximate the curve of
the arc. To help you visualize a spline curve, AutoCAD provides a system variable
called SPLFRAME. You can set SPLFRAME to 1 if you want AutoCAD to show you the
reference frame and vertex points for a spline curve. If you choose Options, Display,

you see a Spline Frame menu item that enables you to turn SPLFRAME on and off. If you see a check mark beside this item, SPLFRAME currently is on.

Note In early versions of AutoCAD Release 13 for DOS, the Spline Frame menu item in the Options, Display pull-down menu does not use a check mark to indicate the setting, however it does change the SPLFRAME system variable. You can use the screen menu OPTIONS, DISPLAY, SplFrame: to report the setting of this option. Unlike the pull-down menu item, you cannot use the screen menu item during the PEDIT command.

You use the SPLINESEGS system variable to control the fineness of the approximation and type of segment. The numeric value controls the number of segments. A positive value generates line segments; a negative value creates arc segments. Arcs are more precise, but slower.

You can generate two kinds of polyline spline curves: a quadratic B-spline (type 5) or a cubic B-spline (the default, type 6). You use the SPLINETYPE system variable to control both types of spline curves. The PolyVars item on the Pedit screen menu (choose MODIFY, Pedit:) opens the Set Spline Fit Variables dialog box. The Quadratic and Cubic selections control SPLINETYPE. AutoCAD stores all the Spline settings with the drawing.

Tip The easiest way to see where the vertices of a curve-fit or spline-fit polyline are is to select it at the Command: prompt, which displays grips at the vertices.

In the next exercise, you use the Fit and Spline options to smooth the sketched contour lines in your intersection drawing. Then, in a new drawing, you try both fit and spline curves to create an airfoil profile for a radio-controlled glider. The rough profile, already created, uses a closed polyline. After you generate the spline curve, turn on SPLFRAME to see the reference frame for the curve. The exercise shows you how to draw the polyline within the PEDIT command to make the frame visible. Figures 11.11 and 11.12 show a curve-fit and spline-fit polyline selected, so grips show at its vertices.

Using PEDIT To Make a Fit and a Spline Curve

Begin a new drawing named CHAP11B, using GLIDFUSE.DWG as a prototype, and zoom to the view that is similar to figure 11.11.

Command: *Choose* Modify, Edit Polyline   Issues the PEDIT command

continues

11

continued

```
_pedit Select polyline: Pick ①
(refer to fig. 11.11)
```

`Open/Join/Width/Edit vertex/Fit/`
`Spline/Decurve/Ltype gen/Undo/eXit`
`<X>: F ` **Enter**
	Specifies the Fit option and curve fits like that shown in figure 11.11

The PEDIT Fit option does not work well in this situation.

The PEDIT Spline option produces a better profile, but not a perfect one.

Choose Options, Display, Spline Frame	Turns on the spline frame (but you cannot see it yet)

`Open/Join/Width/Edit vertex/Fit/`
`Spline/Decurve/Ltype gen/Undo/eXit`
`<X>: S ` **Enter**
	Specifies the Spline option and spline fits the polyline, making the frame visible

`Open/Join/Width/Edit vertex/Fit/Spline/` `Decurve/Ltype gen/Undo/eXit <X>: ` **Enter**	Ends the PEDIT command
`Command: ` *Pick the polyline*	Highlights the polyline and displays grips at its vertices, as shown in figure 11.12.

Save the drawing.

Open the CHAP11A drawing from the previous exercise and use both PEDIT Fit, then Spline, to smooth the most jagged contour line. Fit smooths it, but Spline smooths it even more. Continue using PEDIT to smooth the rest of the contour lines, then save the drawing.

Figure 11.11

Airfoil using the Fit curve option.

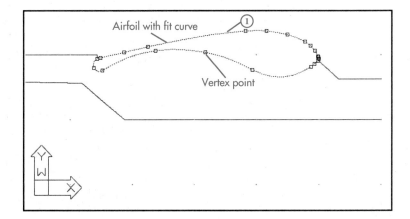

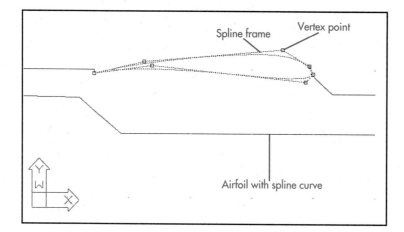

Figure 11.12
Airfoil using the Spline curve option.

Neither curve option creates a satisfactory airfoil profile with a closed polyline. The next section shows you how to open a polyline and insert a vertex.

Editing Polyline Vertices with PEDIT

Each polyline segment connects to, and is controlled by, the preceding vertex. The PEDIT Edit vertex option provides another prompt with a separate set of Edit vertex suboptions. When you use these options, the current vertex of the polyline is marked with an X, which shows you the vertex you are editing. Move the X until you mark the vertex you want to edit. Often the easiest way to edit the position of polyline vertices is to use grips rather than the PEDIT Edit vertex Move option, especially if you want to edit splined polylines. See Chapter 8, "Object Selection and Grip Editing," for information on editing with grips.

Options for the PEDIT Edit vertex command are as follows:

- ◆ **Next/Previous.** Moves the X marker to a new current vertex. Next is the initial default.

- ◆ **Break.** Splits the polyline into two, or removes segments of a polyline at existing vertices. The first break point is the vertex on which you invoke the Break option. Use Next/Previous to access another vertex for the second break point. The Go option performs the break.

  The BREAK command usually is more efficient than the PEDIT Break option, unless curve or spline fitting is involved. Chapter 18, "Constructive Editing," covers the BREAK command.

◆ **Insert.** Adds a vertex at a point you specify, following the vertex currently marked with an X. You can combine this option with the Break option to break between existing vertices.

◆ **Move.** Changes the location of the current (X-marked) vertex to a point you specify.

◆ **Regen.** Forces a regeneration of the polyline so that you can see the effects, such as width changes or the spline frame visibility, of your polyline editing.

◆ **Straighten.** Removes all intervening vertices from between the two you select and replaces them with one straight segment. It also uses the Next/Previous and Go options.

◆ **Tangent.** Sets a tangent to the direction you specify at the currently marked vertex to control curve fitting. You can see the angle of the tangent at the vertex with an arrow, and you can drag it with the cursor or enter it at the keyboard.

◆ **Width.** Sets the starting and ending width of an individual polyline segment to the values you specify.

◆ **eXit.** Exits vertex editing and returns to the main PEDIT command.

 top Choosing Undo at the main PEDIT prompt undoes an entire vertex editing session. Once the vertex editing session has been undone, your edits are lost. There is no way to undo the Undo option.

The airfoil profile needs a sharp trailing edge, but the closed polyline causes the splined polyline to use the common start/end vertex to influence the curve of the spline. If a splined polyline is open, the polyline starts and ends exactly on the first and last vertex. The PEDIT Edit vertex Break option cannot break a closed polyline at the first or last vertex. To get around this problem, you must first open the polyline, then add a new ending vertex.

The PEDIT Open option appears only when you edit closed polylines; otherwise, the Close option appears. The Open option deletes the closing segment of a polyline and, if the polyline is splined, updates the spline information. The deletion of the closing segment is true if the start and end points of the polylines do not coincide. If they do, the Open option simply changes the definition of the polyline and doesn't remove anything. In this case, the only visible effect is to polylines that have been spline-fit, as described.

In the following exercise, you use the PEDIT Edit vertex Insert option to open the splined polyline of the airfoil profile and insert a new ending vertex. The open polyline produces a nice, sharp edge for the airfoil trailing edge.

New Riders Publishing
INSIDE
SERIES

Opening a Polyline and Inserting a Vertex

Open the CHAP11B drawing from the previous exercise.

Command: *Choose Modify, Edit Polyline*	Issues the PEDIT command
Select polyline: *Pick the airfoil profile*	
Open/Join/Width/Edit vertex/Fit/Spline/ Decurve/Ltype gen/Undo/eXit <X>: **O** (Enter)	Specifies the Open option and opens the polyline by deleting the last segment (notice the difference in the spline format)

AutoCAD updates the polyline spline information when you open the polyline. The polyline now starts at the first vertex.

Close/Join/Width/Edit vertex/Fit/Spline/ Decurve/Ltype gen/Undo/eXit <X>: **E** (Enter)	Specifies the Edit vertex option and displays the Edit vertex prompt
Next/Previous/Break/Insert/Move/Regen/ Straighten/Tangent/Width/eXit <N>: *Press Enter six times*	Moves the X to the last vertex
Next/Previous/Break/Insert/Move/Regen/ Straighten/Tangent/Width/eXit <N>: **I** (Enter)	Specifies the Insert suboption and displays a rubber band from the last vertex to the cursor
Enter location of new vertex: *Use an ENDpoint object snap and pick* ① *(see fig. 11.13)*	Snaps the location for the new vertex to the line's endpoint
Command: *Choose* Options, Display, Spline Frame	Turns off SPLFRAME
Next/Previous/Break/Insert/Move/Regen/ Straighten/Tangent/Width/eXit <N>: **R** (Enter)	Regenerates the polyline and hides the frame
Next/Previous/Break/Insert/Move/Regen/ Straighten/Tangent/Width/eXit <N>: **X** (Enter)	Exits vertex editing
Close/Join/Width/Edit vertex/Fit/Spline/ Decurve/Ltype gen/Undo/eXit <X>: (Enter)	Exits PEDIT

Save the drawing.

Figure 11.13

*The completed
airfoil profile.*

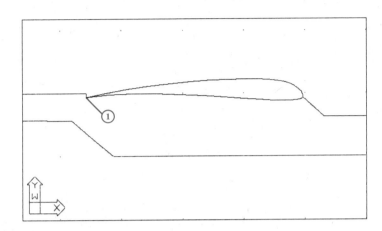

The airfoil looks much better. In the following section, you are introduced to the FILLET command and you fillet all vertices of the polyline fuselage at once.

Rounding Edges with the FILLET Command

A *fillet* is a tangent arc swung between any two lines, circles, or other arcs to create a round corner. In traditional drafting terms, a fillet is a rounded interior corner, and a *round* is a rounded exterior corner. AutoCAD uses the FILLET command to create both.

You can specify the radius of the arc to create the fillet corner. The default radius is 0. The fillet radius you set becomes the new default. The fillet radius must be less than the maximum distance between two line or polyline objects. You can use the Polyline option to fillet all of a polyline's segments at once. If the fillet radius is 0, the FILLET command enables you to trim or extend two lines or polylines so that the endpoints meet exactly.

FILLET works on any combination of two arcs, circles, or lines; or on a single polyline. The FILLET command is fully covered in Chapter 18, "Constructive Editing." This chapter focuses on applying FILLET to polylines. The Polyline option enables you to fillet an entire polyline at once. You can fillet only 2D polylines. AutoCAD ignores segments of a polyline that are shorter than the fillet radius. AutoCAD reports the number of lines filleted and the number ignored. If you fillet a polyline that has a radius of 0, AutoCAD removes all arcs and replaces them with a single vertex.

New Riders Publishing
INSIDE
SERIES

In the next exercise, you use the fillet command to fillet an entire polyline at once, rounding the edges of the glider fuselage to make it more aerodynamic. You work in a paper space viewport, which is already in the drawing.

Filleting Polylines

Continue to use the CHAP11B drawing from the previous exercise.

Command: *Choose* View, Zoom, Out	Reduce the zoom scale by one half to make more of the fuselage visible
Command: *Choose* Construct, Fillet	Issues the FILLET command

`_fillet`
`(TRIM mode) Current fillet radius =`
`0.1250`	

`Polyline/Radius/Trim/` `<Select first object>:` **R** (Enter)	Specifies the Radius option
`Enter fillet radius <0.1250>:` **1.25** (Enter)	Specifies a new fillet radius distance
Command: (Enter)	

`FILLET`
`(TRIM mode) Current fillet radius =`
`1.2500`
	Repeats FILLET command

`Polyline/Radius/Trim/` `<Select first object>:` **P** (Enter)	Specifies the Polyline option
`Select 2D polyline:` *Pick fuselage polyline at* ① *(see fig. 11.14)*	Fillets all corners that are equal to or greater than the fillet radius
`4 lines were filleted` `1 was parallel  1 was too short`	Tells you the number of lines filleted, the number not filleted, and why

Save the drawing.

You might wonder why the bottom corner of the fuselage nose was filleted rather than the top corner. The FILLET command progresses around the polyline from the start to the end when you make fillet arcs. When you filleted the bottom corner, no segment was left to fillet at the top corner of the nose. If you examine the tail, you can see that it was not filleted because the vertices were too close together. When you fillet polylines, you must consider the direction of the polyline and distances between vertices.

In the next section, you learn about the BOUNDARY command and use it to create a profile of the glider fuselage.

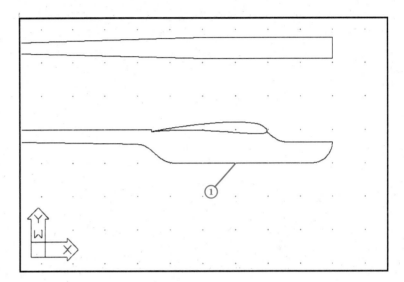

Figure 11.14

The filleted fuselage.

Creating Polyline Boundaries

The BOUNDARY command enables you to create a polyline boundary from contiguous or overlapping objects. The edges of the overlapping objects must form a completely enclosed area; otherwise, the command is doomed to fail. The BOUNDARY command also enables you to create a region object. BOUNDARY works like the BHATCH command, except it creates regions or polylines rather than hatches. See Chapter 12, "Drawing with Complex Objects," for more information on regions, and Chapter 20, "Hatching, Linetype Creation, Digitizing and Sketching," for more information on hatches.

> **BOUNDARY.** The BOUNDARY command enables you to create a polyline or region boundary from overlapping objects. The edges of the overlapping objects must form a completely enclosed area; if the perimeter contains a gap, the command fails.
> Pull-down: *Choose* Construct, Boundary
> Screen: *Choose* CONSTRCT, Boundar:

By default, issuing the BOUNDARY command opens the Boundary Creation dialog box (see fig. 11.15), which enables you to set its parameters. However, you can invoke a command-line version by preceding the command with a dash, as follows:

- BOUNDARY

New Riders Publishing
INSIDE
SERIES

Figure 11.15

The Boundary Creation dialog box.

You use the command-line version of the BOUNDARY command primarily to allow for script compatibility. *Scripts* are files that contain a list of AutoCAD commands that AutoCAD executes one at a time as the script file executes. See *Maximizing AutoCAD* from New Riders Publishing for more information on scripts.

> **-BOUNDARY.** -BOUNDARY is the command-line version of the BOUNDARY command. Its options are identical to the options available in the dialog box version.

The BOUNDARY command has the following options:

♦ **Object type.** You use the Object type option to specify whether to create a polyline boundary object or a region boundary object. The default setting is Polyline.

♦ **From Everything on Screen.** You use this option to use all objects to determine the boundary (On by default).

♦ **From Existing Boundary Set**. You use this option to use specific objects you select to create the boundary. Use this option if you want to avoid using certain objects for boundary determination or if you want to reduce the number of objects AutoCAD considers for the boundary perimeter. This option is available only after you use the Make New Boundary Set option and select objects.

♦ **Ray Casting.** The Ray Casting option controls the way AutoCAD looks for boundary objects. This option is enabled only if the Island Detection option is disabled. The default setting, Nearest, creates a correct boundary in most situations. If the boundary set contains objects that produce a narrow passage or slot, however, you might need to change the direction of the ray casting to parallel the slot. Chapter 20, "Linetypes and Hatching," discusses the BHATCH command and ray casting in more detail.

11

◆ **Island Detection**. When activated, this option causes AutoCAD to create polylines or regions for each object wholly contained within the boundary. BOUNDARY ignores islands when this option is off. (On by default.)

◆ **Boolean Subtract Islands**. In earlier versions of Release 13, this option does not function and is missing from the command-line version of the BOUNDARY command. This option should cause AutoCAD to subtract island regions from boundary regions that were created by using the BOUNDARY command. This option is not available for polyline boundaries.

◆ **Pick Points**. The Pick Points option prompts you to pick point(s) inside the perimeter of the boundary(ies). After you specify the point(s), AutoCAD creates the polyline or region boundary(ies). If you fail to define a valid perimeter, the Nothing was found to make a boundary out of error message appears and AutoCAD reprompts you to specify a point. If you pick more than one valid point, AutoCAD creates a boundary for each. (The Pick Points option is the default.)

See the BHATCH command in Chapter 20, "Linetypes and Hatching," for more information on methods for defining the boundary set.

In the following exercise, you use the BOUNDARY command, set to its defaults, to create a polyline boundary of the fuselage and airfoil profile.

Creating a Polyline Boundary

Continue to use the CHAP11B drawing from the previous exercise and restore the BOUND-ARY view shown in figure 11.16. The polyline boundary you create is the lowest of the three objects in the figure.

Command: *Choose* Construct, Boundary	Issues the BOUNDARY command and opens the Boundary Creation dialog box
Choose the Pick Points *button*	Prompts you to pick an internal point for the boundary calculation
Select internal point: *Pick point at* ①	Specifies what area to include inside the boundary
Selecting everything... Selecting everything visible... Analyzing the selected data... Analyzing internal islands...	Tells you the status of the boundary calculation and highlights the selected boundary elements
Select internal point: (Enter)	Ends the BOUNDARY command

New Riders Publishing
INSIDE
SERIES

`BOUNDARY created 1 polyline`	Draws the polyline
Command: *Choose* Modify, Move	Issues the MOVE command
`Select objects: L` (Enter)	Selects the last object, the boundary
`1 found`	
`Select objects:` (Enter)	Ends selection
`Base point or displacement:` `0,-5.25` (Enter)	Specifies displacement
`Second point of displacement:` (Enter)	Accepts displacement and moves boundary
Command: `R` (Enter)	Issues the REDRAW command
`REDRAW`	

Save the drawing. It should now look like figure 11.16.

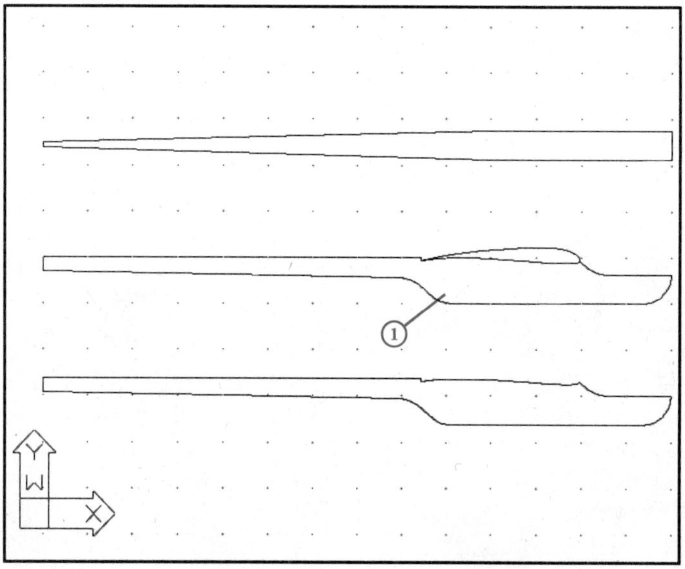

Figure 11.16

The polyline boundary created using the BOUNDARY command.

The boundary you created follows perfectly the curve of the fuselage and the airfoil profile. Although the airfoil and fuselage consisted of three objects, you created the boundary as a single polyline.

Tip

To create the boundary of the outside of a collection of objects, simply draw a polyline that encloses but does not touch all the objects, then use BOUNDARY and pick a point within the enclosing polyline, but outside the collection of objects. BOUNDARY creates two polylines, one that duplicates the enclosing polyline you drew, and one that forms the outside boundary of the collection of objects. If you enclose more than one collection of objects, you get an additional boundary polyline for each additional collection. This is useful when you need to find the area or perimeter of a building plan or any other object, because you can use the AREA and LIST commands to easily extract the area and perimeter of polyline objects (see Chapter 15, "Object Modification, Inquiry, and Calculation").

In the next section, you learn about spline objects and how to create them. Spline objects are not the same as a splined polyline; they are a separate object type.

Creating Splines

You use the SPLINE command to draw smooth, curved lines. Splines can be 2D or 3D objects. You draw the curve by specifying fit-data points (vertices) through which the curve passes. The fit-data points determine the location of the spline object's control points. The control points contain the curve information for the spline. Spline objects are true splines—unlike the spline approximation of spline-fit polylines. AutoCAD draws nonuniform rational B-splines (or NURBS) with the SPLINE command.

You use spline objects for the same purposes as you use spline-fit polylines. However, spline objects are far more accurate and can pass through their defining data points. Although more accurate, NURBS also consume less memory and disk resources than their polyline cousins; AutoCAD uses mathematical equations, rather than many short line or arc segments, to draw spline objects. You can use the SPLINE command to convert 2D and 3D spline-fit polylines to spline objects. If a portion of a boundary set is defined by a spline, the BOUNDARY command enables you to create only region boundaries. The SPLINETYPE system variable does not affect the type of spline you draw using the SPLINE command.

SPLINE. The SPLINE command enables you to draw 2D or 3D splines. *Splines* are smooth curved lines that fit to data points that you specify. You can control the tolerance of the curve to the fit-data points. SPLINE also enables you to convert spline-fit polylines into spline objects.
Pull-down: *Choose* Draw, Spline
Screen: *Choose* Draw1, Spline

The following list is of the SPLINE command options:

- ◆ **Object/<Enter first point>.** The default option of the main prompt specifies the starting point of the spline. After you specify a starting point, AutoCAD prompts you to specify a second point. Spline objects must consist of a minimum of two points.

- ◆ **Object.** The Object option enables you to convert existing spline-fit polylines to spline objects. After you specify this option, AutoCAD prompts you to select a splined polyline.

- ◆ **Close/Fit Tolerance/<Enter point>.** After you specify a second point for the spline, AutoCAD displays this prompt. The default option is to continue to specify additional data points for the spline you are drawing. If you press Enter here, AutoCAD prompts you to specify the tangent information for the start and endpoints of the spline, then ends the command. Entering U at this prompt undoes the last pick point.

- ◆ **Close.** The Close option operates identically to the PLINE command's close option. This option causes the start and end of the spline to coincide and share a common vertex and tangent information. When you close a spline, AutoCAD prompts you only once to specify the tangent information.

- ◆ **Fit Tolerance.** The Fit Tolerance option controls how closely the spline curve follows the data points. The distance of the Fit Tolerance is in current drawing units. The smaller the tolerance, the closer the spline fits the data points. A value of 0 causes the spline to follow the data points exactly.

- ◆ **Undo.** Although this option does not appear in the prompt, you can enter U after any point to undo the last segment.

In the following exercise, you use the SPLINE command. The fuselage of the glider is still a bit clunky, and a spline should give it a nice aerodynamic and sleek look. In the exercise, you explode the existing fuselage polyline and erase the bottom section, then use the SPLINE command to draw a new profile. It takes some practice to get a feel for drawing with the SPLINE command. If you don't like the profile you draw, feel free to use the Undo option to back up, or even cancel and start over.

Drawing a Spline

Continue to use the CHAP11B drawing from the previous exercise.

Command: *Choose Modify, Explode*   Issues the EXPLODE command

continues

continued

`Select objects:` *Pick the lower polyline of the middle fuselage profile and press Enter*	Explodes the polyline
`Command:` *Select all the lines and arcs of the bottom of the fuselage profile between ① and ③ (see fig. 11.17), then choose* Modify, Erase	Issues the ERASE command and erases the selected objects
`Command:` *Choose* Draw, Spline	Issues the SPLINE command
`Object/<Enter first point>:` *Use* ENDPoint *object snap to pick at* ①	Specifies the start of the spline
`Enter point:` *Pick another point*	
`Close/Fit Tolerance/<Enter point>:` *Pick point* ②	

Continue to pick points until you are ready to end the spline. You do not need many points to define the curve. Four points and a start and end vertex is enough. If you don't like the way the curve looks, don't worry—you edit it in the next exercise.

`Close/Fit Tolerance/<Enter point>:` *Use* ENDPoint *object snap to pick point at* ③	
`Close/Fit Tolerance/<Enter point>:` **Enter**	Ends the vertex input process
`Enter start tangent:` *Pick a point to the left of the first pick point* ①	Specifies the starting tangent
`Enter end tangent:` *Pick a point at 90 degrees to the spline endpoint at* ③	Specifies the ending tangent—this makes the nose bulbous, but you edit it in the next exercise

Save the drawing.

Spline objects are special objects that have their own editing command—similar to the relationship between PLINE and PEDIT. In the next section, you learn about the SPLINEDIT command and use it to change spline objects.

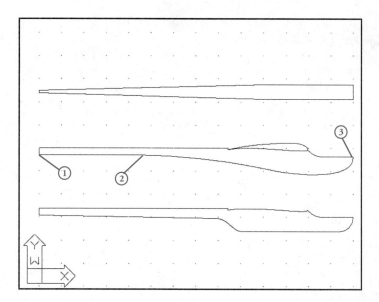

Figure 11.17
*The spline
fuselage bottom.*

Controlling Splines Using SPLINEDIT

The SPLINEDIT command enables you to edit the shape of all spline objects. Each spline object you draw initially has fit-data points and control points that are used to control the shape. The fit-data points are the points you pick as you use the SPLINE command. As you pick the fit-data point, AutoCAD calculates a corresponding control point. Also, AutoCAD adds a control point for each tangent point—one for a closed spline object, two for an open spline object. The control points are the defining points of the spline frame.

The SPLINEDIT command provides options for adding, deleting, and moving control points or fit-data points. If you add or delete a control point, the fit-data points are removed from the definition of the spline object and thereafter you must use control points to change the shape of the spline. You remove the fit-data points when you change the weight or add new control points. Also, you loose the fit-data when you elevate the order of the spline because an elevated order increases the number of control points and in turn refines the accuracy of the spline.

> **SPLINEDIT.** The SPLINEDIT command enables you to edit 2D or 3D spline objects. You can add additional control or fit-data points or move them. You can change the weight of control points and the tolerance of the spline. You also can close or open a spline and adjust the tangent information of the start and endpoints.
> Pull-down: *Choose* Modify, Edit Spline
> Screen: *Choose* MODIFY, SplinEd:

11

After you select a spline for editing, AutoCAD displays its control points as if you had selected the spline for grip editing (see fig. 11.18). However, you cannot perform grip editing on the spline during the SPLINEDIT command. The SPLINEDIT command permits you to work on only one spline object at a time. Also, you cannot use noun/verb selection during SPLINEDIT.

Figure 11.18

Control points of the fuselage spline.

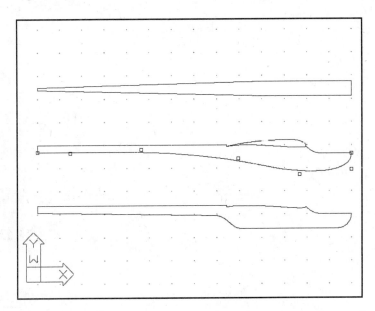

The SPLINEDIT command has the following options:

◆ **Fit Data.** Enables you to edit the fit-data points for spline objects that have them. AutoCAD displays another prompt of Fit Data options when you choose this option. AutoCAD does not present this as an option if the spline does not have any fit data information. A spline object cannot have fit data if it has been refined and elevated to a higher order (see the Refine option). The following list describes the Fit Data suboptions:

     ◆ **Add.** Adds additional fit-data points to the curve. Adding fit-data points changes the shape of the spline curve. Added fit-data points obey the current tolerance of the spline.

     ◆ **Close.** Performs the same function as the control point Close option, but uses fit-data points.

     ◆ **Open.** Performs the same function as the control point Open option, except that it uses fit-data points. The Open option replaces the Close option if the spline is already closed.

New Riders Publishing
INSIDE
SERIES

◆ **Delete.** Removes fit-data points and redraws the spline to fit the remaining fit-data points.

◆ **Move.** Enables you to move fit-data point vertices of a spline. You specify a vertex to edit by moving the current vertex to the next or previous vertex. You cannot use AutoCAD's grip editing feature to edit fit-data information.

◆ **Purge.** Removes all fit data from the spline.

◆ **Tangents.** Enables you to change the tangent information of the start and endpoints of a spline.

◆ **toLerance.** Changes the tolerance of the spline's fit-data points and redraws the spline. A spline loses its fit data if you both change the tolerance and move a control point or open/close the spline.

◆ **eXit.** Returns to the control point editing prompt.

◆ **Close.** Closes an open spline. This option adds a curve that is tangent between the start and end vertices for splines that do not have the same start and endpoints. If the spline does have the same start and endpoints, the Close option makes the tangent information for each point continuous. If the spline is already closed, the Close option is replaced by the Open option.

◆ **Open.** Opens a closed spline. If the spline did not have the same start and endpoints as before you closed it, this option removes the tangent curve and removes tangent information from the start and endpoints. If the spline shares the same start and endpoint before you close it, the option removes the tangent information from the points, but they continue to share the same point.

◆ **Move Vertex.** Enables you to move control point vertices of a spline. You specify a vertex to edit by moving the current vertex to the next or previous vertex. Often, using the grip editing features of AutoCAD to edit the control point vertices is easier. See Chapter 8, "Autoediting with Grips," for information on grip editing.

◆ **Refine.** Displays suboptions that enable you to add control points and adjust the weight of control points. You can add individual control points in areas where you want finer control of the curve. The following list describes the Refine suboptions:

◆ **Add control point.** This option enables you to add a single control point to a spline. AutoCAD locates the new control point as close as possible to a point you specify on the spline. Adding a control point does not change the shape of the spline.

◆ **Elevate Order.** The Elevate Order option elevates the order of the spline's polynomial, which adds control points evenly over the spline, giving you finer control of the spline. The Elevate Order option does not change the shape of the spline. You cannot decrease the order of the polynomial after you increase it.

◆ **Weight.** Controls the amount of tension that pulls a spline towards a control point.

◆ **eXit.** Returns to the main SPLINEDIT prompt.

◆ **rEverse.** Changes the direction of the spline; the start becomes the end and the end becomes the start.

◆ **Undo.** Undoes the most recently performed SPLINEDIT option.

◆ **eXit.** Ends the SPLINEDIT command.

The following are the suboptions of the Fit Data option, for editing spline object fit data.

Although this chapter concentrates on 2D spline curves, you also can use the SPLINEDIT command to edit 3D splines. In the following exercise, you edit the spline of the bottom of the fuselage. First, you reduce the number of fit-data points, then you add additional control points to the spline.

Editing Splines

Continue to use the CHAP11B drawing from the previous exercise.

Command: *Choose* Modify, Edit Spline	Issues the SPLINEDIT command
Select spline: *Pick the fuselage spline* at ① *(see fig. 11.19)*	Specifies the spline to edit and displays the control points
Fit Data/Close/Move Vertex/Refine/ rEverse/Undo/eXit <X>: **F**	Specifies the Fit Data option and displays the fit-data
Add/Close/Delete/Move/Purge/Tangents/ toLerance/eXit <X>: **D**	Specifies the Delete option
Select point: *Pick a few control points*	Deletes the points you pick
Select point:	Exits the delete points mode

`Add/Close/Delete/Move/Purge/Tangents/` `toLerance/eXit <X>: T`	Specifies the Tangents option
`System Default/` `<Enter start tangent>:`	Keeps current start tangent
`System Default/<Enter end tangent>:` *Pick a tangent point at about 60"* *from the endpoint*	Specifies new end tangent information to make a more aerodynamic profile
`Add/Close/Delete/Move/Purge/Tangents/` `toLerance/eXit <X>:`	Exits to the main control point prompt
`Fit Data/Close/Move Vertex/Refine/` `rEverse/Undo/eXit <X>: R`	Specifies the Refine option
`Add control point/Elevate Order/` `Weight/eXit <X>: E`	Specifies the Elevate Order option
`Enter new order <4>: 6`	Elevates order of spline polynomial and adds intermediate control points
`Add control point/Elevate Order/` `Weight/eXit <X>:`	Returns to the main prompt
`Close/Move Vertex/Refine/rEverse/` `Undo/eXit <X>:`	Exits the SPLINEDIT command

Save the drawing. See figure 11.20 for the completed fuselage with the new control points.

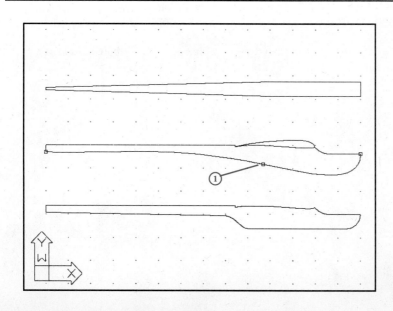

Figure 11.19

Fuselage spline with fit-data points deleted.

11

Figure 11.20

Fuselage with adjusted ending tangent

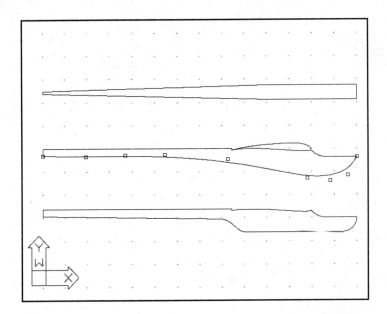

In this chapter, you explored the extremely versatile polyline. Using polylines can simplify editing by replacing separate line and arc segments with one continuous object. You created wide polylines to draw lines that are wider than the width of your plotter pen. You drew polylines that consist of multiwidth segments to use as symbols. Then you explored the PEDIT command to edit polylines.

You explored commands that are useful for working with polylines including EX-PLODE, FILLET, FILL, and SKETCH. You also learned how to draw smooth curves with the SPLINE command and edited them with the SPLINEDIT command.

In the next chapter, you learn how to draw complex AutoCAD objects, such as regions and multilines—objects that are even more complex than polylines.

Drawing with Complex Objects

I n Chapter 11, "Drawing and Editing Polylines and Splines," you
learn about two of AutoCAD's more complex objects, polylines,
and splines. In addition, AutoCAD offers a number of other
complex objects that you can use to increase your drawing productivity.

This chapter covers the following topics:

◆ Region modeling

◆ Boolean operations

◆ Creating multiple-line objects

◆ Creating custom multiline styles

◆ Creating TRACE and SOLID objects

The following exercise introduces you to some of the concepts presented in this chapter. In this exercise, you create a metric wrench by
drawing several objects and joining them as a region.

Quick 5¢ Tour

Begin a new drawing named CHAP12, using the ACADISO prototype drawing from the ACADR13\COMMON\SUPPORT directory. Create two layers named CONST and WRENCH. Make the CONST layer current. Set the grid spacing to 10 and snap spacing to 1 and turn on grid and snap.

Command: *Choose* Draw, Polygon, Rectangle *and draw a rectangle from* 100,100 *to* 300,132	Issues the RECTANG command and creates the rectangle (see fig. 12.1)
Command: *Choose* Draw, Circle *then* Center, Radius *and use* MIDpoint *object snap to draw a 16 mm radius circle at* ① *(see fig. 12.1)*	Issues the CIRCLE command and creates a 16 mm radius circle
Command: *Choose* Draw, Ellipse, Center	Issues the ELLIPSE command with the Center option
Center of ellipse: *Using the* MIDpoint *object snap, pick* ②	Places the center of the ellipse
Axis endpoint: **@35<0** (Enter)	Places the first axis endpoint
<Other axis distance>/Rotation: **@40<90** (Enter)	Places the second axis endpoint and creates the ellipse

Later, you use these three objects to create the main body of the wrench. First, you create the objects that you need for a 40 mm opening at the end of the wrench and a slot in the handle.

Figure 12.1

The wrench construction geometry.

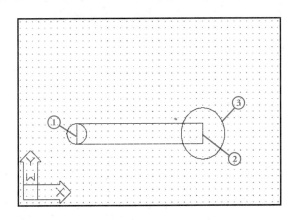

Command: *Choose* Draw, Line	Issues the LINE command
From point: *Using the* FROM *and* QUAdrant *object snaps, pick* ③	Places a reference point at the right quadrant of the ellipse

`<Offset>: @20<90` (Enter)	Places the first point of the line
`To point: @25<180` (Enter)	Draws the line from ① to ② (see fig. 12.2) and completes the LINE command
`To point:` (Enter)	
`Command:` (Enter)	Repeats the LINE command
`From point:` *Using the FROM and QUAdrant object snaps, pick* ③	Places a reference point at the right quadrant of the ellipse
`<Offset>: @20<270` (Enter)	Places the first point of the line
`To point: @25<180` (Enter)	Draws the line from ⑧ to ④
`To point:` (Enter)	

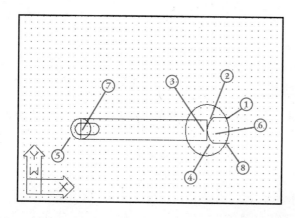

Figure 12.2

Subtracting the regions.

`Command:` *Choose* Draw, Arc, 3 Points *and use the* ENDpoint *and* MIDpoint *object snaps to draw an arc from* ② *to* ③ *to* ④ *(see fig. 12.2)*	Issues the ARC command and draws arc

Next, you create a new multiline style and use it to advance the slot.

`Command:` *Choose* Data, Multiline Style	Issues the MLSTYLE command
Choose the Multiline Properties *button* and turn *on the* Start *and* End Outer arc *options, then choose* OK	Turns on the multiline outer arcs
Double-click in the Name *edit box and type* **SLOT**, *then choose* Add, *then* OK	Creates a multiline style called SLOT
`Command:` *Choose* Draw, Multiline	Issues the MLINE command

continues

continued

`Justification/Scale/STyle` `/<From point>:` **S** (Enter)	Selects the Scale option
`Set Mline scale <1.00>:` **18** (Enter)	Sets an mline scale of 18
`Justification/Scale/STyle` `/<From point>:` **J** (Enter)	Specifies the Justification option
`Top/Zero/Bottom <top>:` **Z** (Enter)	Sets the mline justification to 0
`Justification/Scale/STyle` `/<From point>:` *Using the CENter object* *snap, pick* ⑤	Places the mline start point
`<To point>:` **@20<0** (Enter)	Places the end of the mline
`Undo/<To point>:` (Enter)	Ends the MLINE command

You now have the basic geometry for the wrench. First, make the WRENCH layer current, then in the following steps you use this geometry to create a region model of the wrench.

`Command:` *Choose* Construct, Boundary	Issues the BOUNDARY command
From the Object Type *list choose* Region, *then choose* Pick Points	Activates the Region option and begins the boundary selection
`Select internal point:` *Pick* ⑥ *and press Enter*	Creates the region
`Command:` *Choose* Construct, Region	Issues the REGION command
`Select objects:` *Select the circle,* *rectangle, and ellipse, and press* *Enter*	Creates three regions from the selected objects
`Command:` *Choose* Construct, Union	Issues the UNION command
`Select objects:` *Select the circle,* *rectangle, and ellipse, and press* *Enter*	Joins the selected objects into a single region
`Command:` *Choose* Construct, Boundary	Issues the BOUNDARY command
From the Object Type *list choose* Region, *then choose* Pick Points	Activates the Region option and begins the boundary selection
`Select internal point:` *Pick* ⑦ *and press Enter*	Creates the region

You now have created all the regions. Freeze layer CONST before you finish the model.

Command: *Choose* Construct, Subtract	Issues the SUBTRACT command
Select solids and regions to subtract from...	
Select objects: *Select the main body* *of the wrench and press Enter*	Selects the object to keep
Select solids and regions to subtract....	
Select objects: *Select the slot and* *end regions and press Enter*	Subtracts the two slots from the wrench

The wrench is now a single region. Finally, you take a look at the mass properties of the wrench.

Command: *Choose* Assist, Inquiry, Mass Properties	Issues the MASSPROP command
Select objects: *Select the wrench and* *press Enter*	Displays the mass properties of the wrench
Write to a file ? <N>: **(Enter)**	Ends the MASSPROP command

Save your drawing.

Your drawing should look like figure 12.3.

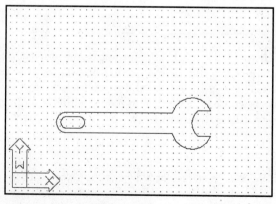

Figure 12.3

The finished wrench.

Creating Regions

A *region* is a 2D solid object formed from a closed area. You can think of a region as a flat surface. Although many commands in AutoCAD enable you to create closed shapes, regions are unique in the information they contain and in the way you can modify them.

Understanding Wire Models versus Solid Models

Circles are closed areas. Polylines, splines, and lines can be closed as well. Chapter 11, "Drawing and Editing Polylines and Splines," introduces you to the BOUNDARY command, which enables you to create closed polylines from any group of overlapping objects to form a closed area. The BOUNDARY command enables you to create what are known as wireframe models. A *wireframe model* consists only of the edges of an object. It is similar to taking a piece of wire and bending it into the shape of your model. The edges of the model are defined but the model has no surfaces.

Regions are solid 2D surfaces. A solid contains, not only the edge information, but also information about what is between the edges, such as holes, slots, and so on. AutoCAD can use this information to calculate engineering properties such as surface area, centroids, and moments of inertia.

The REGION command

You use the REGION command to create regions.

REGION. The REGION command enables you to create region objects from existing closed 2D objects, such as closed lines, polylines, circles, and splines.
Pull-down: *Choose* Construct, Region
Screen: *Choose* Construct, Region

When you issue the REGION command, AutoCAD prompts you to select objects that you want to convert to regions. Valid selections are closed lines, polylines, splines, circles, or any group of objects whose endpoints connect to form a closed loop. Self-intersecting objects or objects whose endpoints do not connect do not qualify. Figure 12.4 shows some examples of valid and invalid selections for the REGION command. The REGION command converts the valid selections to regions.

 Tip By default, the REGION command replaces the selected objects with regions and deletes the original objects. If you want to keep the original objects, set the AutoCAD system variable DELOBJ to 0 (off). AutoCAD then keeps the original objects.

In the following exercise, you use regions to create a front elevation of a small house.

New Riders Publishing
INSIDE SERIES

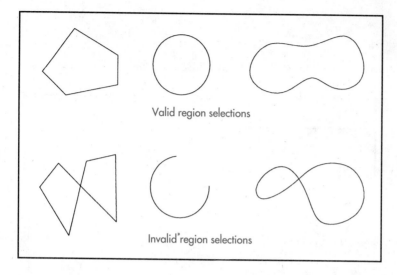

Figure 12.4

Examples of valid and invalid region selections.

Creating Regions

Create a new drawing named CHAP12A, using the IA Disk drawing PLANELEV.DWG as a prototype. The layer ELEV should be current.

`Command:` *Choose* Draw, Polygon, Rectangle *and draw a rectangle from* 60',30' *to* 82',38'	Issues the RECTANG command and draws the rectangle (see fig. 12.5)
`Command:` *Choose* Draw, Polyline	Issues the PLINE command
`From point:` *Using the ENDPoint object snap, pick* ①	Places the first point of the polyline
`Arc/Close/Halfwidth/Length/Undo/Width` `/<Endpoint of line>:` **@11',14'** (Enter)	Places the second point of the polyline
`Arc/Close/Halfwidth/Length/Undo/Width` `/<Endpoint of line>:` *Using the ENDPoint object snap, pick* ②	Places the third point of the polyline
`Arc/Close/Halfwidth/Length/Undo/Width` `/<Endpoint of line>:` **C** (Enter)	Closes the polyline
`Command:` *Choose* Construct, Region	Issues the REGION command
`Select objects:` **ALL** (Enter)	Selects the polylines
`Select objects:` (Enter)	Creates two regions from the polylines

continues

continued

Save your drawing.

The regions you created look the same as the polylines, but later in the chapter, you see how differently they act.

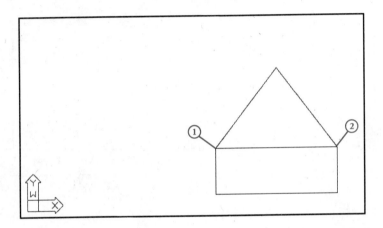

Figure 12.5

Creating regions from polylines.

Creating Regions with BOUNDARY

You can create regions in one other way. Chapter 11 introduces the BOUNDARY command, which enables you to create closed polylines by selecting a point within an enclosed area. You also can use the BOUNDARY command to create regions.

Figure 12.6

The Boundary Creation dialog box.

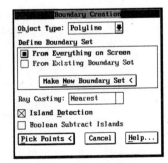

New Riders Publishing
INSIDE SERIES

Note Unlike the REGION command, BOUNDARY creates new regions but leaves the original objects in place regardless of the DELOBJ system variable's setting.

In the following exercise, you use the Region option of the BOUNDARY command to create some windows.

Creating Regions with BOUNDARY

Continue from the previous exercise. Thaw the layers CONST, ELEV_WINDOWS, and ELEV_DOORS. The layer ELEV should remain current.

Command: Choose Construct, Boundary	Issues the BOUNDARY command and opens the Boundary Creation dialog box
In the Object Type *drop-down list,* *select* Region	Selects the Region option
Choose Pick Points, *pick* ①, ②, ③, ④, ⑤, *and* ⑥ *(see fig. 12.7), and press Enter*	Determines the boundary areas and creates four regions

Freeze layers CONST, ELEV_WINDOWS, and ELEV_DOORS to see the six regions created by the BOUNDARY command (see fig. 12.8).

Save your drawing.

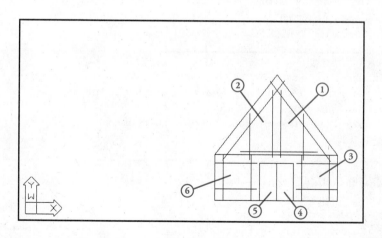

Figure 12.7

Creating boundary regions.

12

Figure 12.8

The resulting boundary regions.

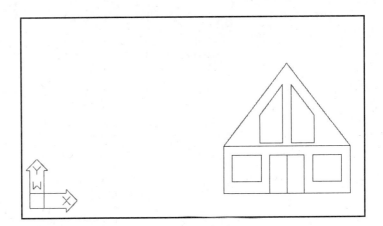

Understanding Boolean Operations

Because regions are solid objects, you act on them in the same manner as you would if you were to use real-world solid objects. If you had a flat piece of material, you might drill some holes in it, attach other pieces of material to it, or trim off excess material. Three commands (UNION, SUBTRACT, and INTERSECT), known collectively as *Boolean operations*, enable you to act similarly upon AutoCAD regions.

UNION. The UNION command enables you to combine multiple regions or 3D solids into a single region or 3D solid.
Pull-down: *Choose* Construct, Union
Screen: *Choose* DRAW 2, SOLIDS, Union

The UNION command enables you to join two or more regions into a single region of their combined areas. The regions do not have to touch before you can join them. The UNION command also combines 3D solids (see Chapter 31, "Solid Modeling," for more information along this vein). You can see an effect of using the UNION command in figure 12.9.

SUBTRACT. The SUBTRACT command enables you to subtract one set of regions or solids from another region or solid.
Pull-down: *Choose* Construct, Subtract
Screen: *Choose* DRAW 2, SOLIDS, Subtrac

The SUBTRACT command enables you to cut holes in regions. These holes and cutouts become a part of the region. If you move the region, the holes move as well.

New Riders Publishing
INSIDE
SERIES

You can see the effect of using the SUBTRACT command in figure 12.9. AutoCAD prompts you for the region you want to keep, then prompts you to select the regions you want to subtract.

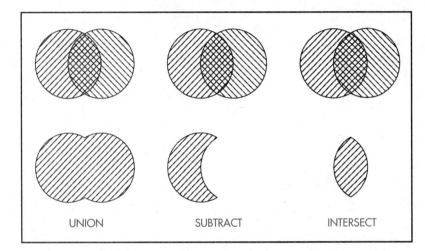

Figure 12.9

Examples of the effects of using the Boolean operations.

UNION   SUBTRACT   INTERSECT

Note The BOUNDARY command has an option to automatically Boolean subtract any islands AutoCAD detects within a region. However, in early releases of AutoCAD Release 13, this option is disabled.

INTERSECT. The INTERSECT command enables you to create a region from the overlapping area of two or more regions, or to create a single solid from the overlapping volumes of two or more solids.

Pull-down:　*Choose* Construct, Intersection
Screen:　　 *Choose* DRAW 2, SOLIDS, Intrsec

You can see the effect of the INTERSECT command in figure 12.9.

Stop Using INTERSECT on regions that do not overlap creates a region that has no area (a *null region*). AutoCAD deletes all the regions you selected. If this occurs, you can use an UNDO to restore the regions.

All the Boolean operations work on 3D solids as well as regions. Refer to Chapter 31 for more on using Boolean operations on 3D solids.

In the following exercise, you create some window and door openings in the elevation view.

12

Boolean Operations

Continue from the previous exercise and make the layer ELEV current.

Command: *Choose* Construct, Union	Issues the UNION command
Select objects: *Select the objects at* ① *and* ② *(see fig. 12.10) and press Enter*	Selects the two regions and joins them into a single region
Command: *Choose* Construct, Subtract	Issues the SUBTRACT command
`Select solids and regions to subtract from...`	
Select objects: *Pick* ① *(see fig. 12.10)and press Enter*	Selects the building elevation
`Select solids and regions to subtract...`	
Select objects: *Pick the point* ③ *and drag to* ④	Selects the door and window regions
`Select objects:` **Enter**	Ends UNION command and subtracts the door and window regions from the elevation

AutoCAD has subtracted the door sections from the shape.

Save your drawing.

Figure 12.10

Adding and subtracting regions.

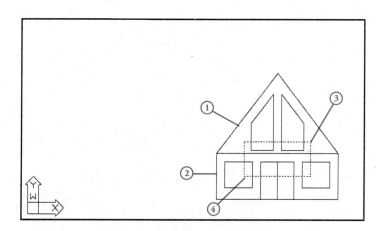

New Riders Publishing
INSIDE
SERIES

Note Because regions are solid models, you can change their shape only by using Boolean operations. If you want to convert regions back into lines and arcs, you must EXPLODE them. See Chapter 19, "Using Xrefs and Overlays for Efficiency and Sharing Data," for more information concerning the EXPLODE command.

Extracting Data from a Region Model

Because regions are solid objects, they contain a great deal more information than their wireframe counterparts. The MASSPROP command enables you to display engineering information about solid models.

> **MASSPROP.** The MASSPROP command enables you to display various engineering data about a region or 3D solid.
> Pull-down: *Choose* Assist, Inquiry, Mass Properties
> Screen: *Choose* ASSIST, INQUIRY, MassPro

When you issue the MASSPROP command, AutoCAD prompts you to select a region or regions. After you select the region(s), AutoCAD displays a list of engineering properties. The following is an example of the engineering data AutoCAD calculates.

```
---------------     REGIONS     ----------------

Area:                    12165.1412
Perimeter:               935.1617
Bounding box:         X: 34.0000  --  381.3532
                      Y: 21.0000  --  111.0000
Centroid:             X: 232.1490
                      Y: 66.0000
Moments of inertia:   X: 56095150.3085
                      Y: 774080785.1308
Product of inertia:  XY: 186392266.8312
Radii of gyration:    X: 67.9054
                      Y: 252.2520
Principal moments and X-Y directions about centroid:
                      I: 3103795.1893 along [1.0000 0.0000]
                      J: 118462957.3496 along [0.0000 1.0000]
```

After you display the information, you can save the information to an ASCII text file.

You also can use the MASSPROP command to obtain information about 3D solid models. See Chapter 31, "Solid Modeling," for information on 3D solid models. Chapter 15, "Object Modification, Inquiry and Calculation," offers more information on using AutoCAD's inquiry commands to obtain information from 2D wireframe objects.

12

Creating Multiple Lines

Multilines (referred to as mlines) are new in Release 13. *Multilines* are objects that contain multiple parallel lines called *elements*. Each element is defined by its distance or *offset* from the center. The center is *zero offset*. Figure 12.11 shows the parts of a typical mline object. You use the MLINE command to create mlines.

Figure 12.11

Multiline elements.

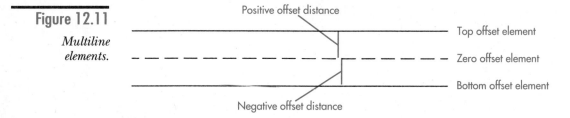

Drawing with the MLINE Command

You use the MLINE command to draw an mline object by indicating the mline's endpoints. The MLINE command is similar to the PLINE command in that you draw multiple segments until you press Enter or until you use the Close option. Unlike pline objects, the mline object has a justification that you set to determine how mline object endpoints are aligned to your specified points. You can set the justification at the center, or at an edge, of an mline object. You control the width of the mline object by setting the object's scale. You might use this scale setting to portray a 4" or a 6" brick wall using only one brick wall mline style. The MLINE command allows you to set the current mline style before you specify the first mline point. The styles from which you must choose depend on what styles are loaded.

MLINE. The MLINE command enables you to create multiple parallel line objects.
Pull-down: *Choose* Draw, Multiline
Screen: *Choose* DRAW 1, Mline

The MLINE command has the following prompts:

```
Justification/Scale/STyle/<From point>:
```

◆ **Justification.** The Justification option enables you to control whether AutoCAD draws the mline from the top offset, the zero offset, or the bottom offset.

◆ **Scale.** This option enables you to control the scale at which AutoCAD draws the mline. AutoCAD multiplies the offset distances by this scale factor.

◆ **STyle.** The STyle option enables you to set the current mline style. You use MLSTYLE command to define mline styles. Entering **?** at this prompt displays a list of currently defined mline styles.

◆ **From point.** This is the default option, which prompts you for the starting point of the mline. After you pick a starting point, AutoCAD prompts you for the To point. You also can use an Undo option to undo the last drawn segment. After you pick two points, you can use a Close option to close the mline and clean up the last corner.

 Note   The MLINE command creates only straight line objects. Curved multiline objects are not supported in R13.

By default, AutoCAD draws multilines with two elements, one having an offset of 0.5 and the other having an offset of –.5, which results in an mline that consists of two elements, 1 unit apart. You can control the distance between the elements by adjusting the mline scale. For example, setting the mline scale to 6 results in two parallel lines, 6 units apart.

In the following exercise, you begin to create a floor plan of the house, using the default multiline style.

Creating Multilines

Continue from the previous exercise. Make the layer PLAN current.

Command: *Choose* Draw, Multiline   Issues the MLINE command

Justification/Scale/STyle/   Specifies the Scale option
<From point>: **S** (Enter)

Set Mline scale <1.00>: **6** (Enter)   Sets the multiline scale factor

Justification/Scale/STyle/   Places the starting point
<From point>: **30',30'** (Enter)

<To point>: **@22'<0** (Enter)   Draws an mline segment

Undo/<To point>: **@26'<90** (Enter)   Draws another segment

Close/Undo/<To point>: **@22'<180** (Enter)

Close/Undo/<To point>: **C** (Enter)   Closes the multiline

Save your work.

12

Your drawing should now resemble figure 12.12.

Figure 12.12

Floor plan outline with mline object.

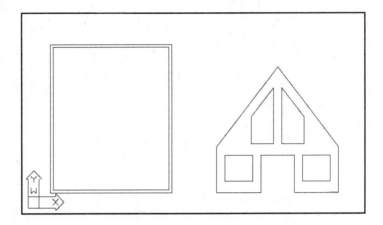

Defining Mline Styles with MLSTYLE

The default multiline style consists of two lines, each .5 units from the zero offset, and is known as the *Standard mline style.* By adjusting the scale and justification the STAN-DARD mline style can serve many purposes, but is limited to only two lines. The MLSTLYE command enables you to create much more complex multiline styles.

> **MLSTYLE**. The MLSTYLE command enables you to create, save, and load custom multiline styles.
> Pull-down: Choose Data, Multiline Style
> Screen: *Choose* Data, MLstyle

Issuing the MLSTYLE command initiates the Multiline Styles dialog box, shown in figure 12.13. The Multiline Style area of the dialog box gives you information about the multiline styles available in the drawing and gives you options for loading, saving, adding, and renaming multiline style definitions. Unless you save them to a file, multiline styles exist only in the current drawing. To share multiline styles between drawings, you must save the multiline style definitions to a file. Multiline styles are stored in MLN files. The STANDARD multiline style is stored in ACAD.MLN, in the \ACADR13\COMMON\SUPPORT directory.

Clicking on the Element Properties button brings up the Element Properties dialog box, shown in figure 12.14. The Element Properties dialog box enables you to define the elements of a multiline style. Each element is defined as a distance from the zero offset. AutoCAD draws elements that have a positive offset above the zero offset and draws elements that have a negative offset below the zero offset. The elements that have the greatest positive and negative offsets become the top and bottom justification elements.

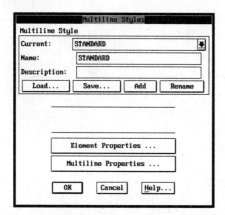

Figure 12.13

The Multiline Styles dialog box.

Figure 12.14

The Element Properties dialog box.

You can define as many as 16 elements in a multiline style. In addition to an offset distance, you assign each element a linetype and color, which enables you to create very complex multiline styles. For more on assigning linetypes and colors, see Chapter 5, "Setting Up a CAD Drawing." See Chapter 20, "Linetypes and Hatching," for more on creating custom linetypes.

Note Although you can assign a separate linetype and color to each multiline element, the multiline itself resides on a single layer. If you freeze a layer that contains a multiline, you freeze the entire multiline.

Clicking on the Multiline Properties button opens the Multiline Properties dialog box (see fig. 12.15). The Multiline Properties dialog box presents you with some options for the display and generation of the multilines. The Display joints check box provides you with the means to control the display of corner joints (see fig. 12.16).

12

Figure 12.15

*The Multiline
Properties dialog
box.*

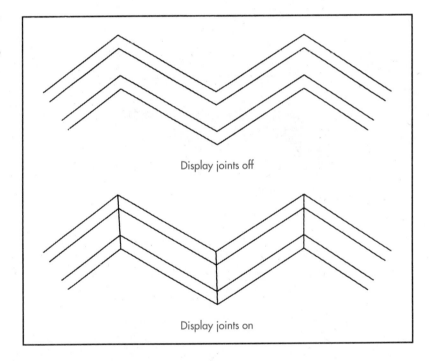

Figure 12.15

*The Multiline
Properties dialog
box.*

Figure 12.16

*Methods used to
display joints.*

The Caps area of the dialog box enables you to control the creation of the start and
end of the multilines. The Angle option enables you to control the miter angle of the
end cap. The various capping effects are shown in figure 12.17.

The options in the Fill area of the Multiline Properties dialog box enable you to fill in
the multiline with a solid color. If you set the Fill option to On (mark the On check
box), AutoCAD fills in the area between the outermost offset elements with the color
you define in the multiline style.

New Riders Publishing
INSIDE
SERIES

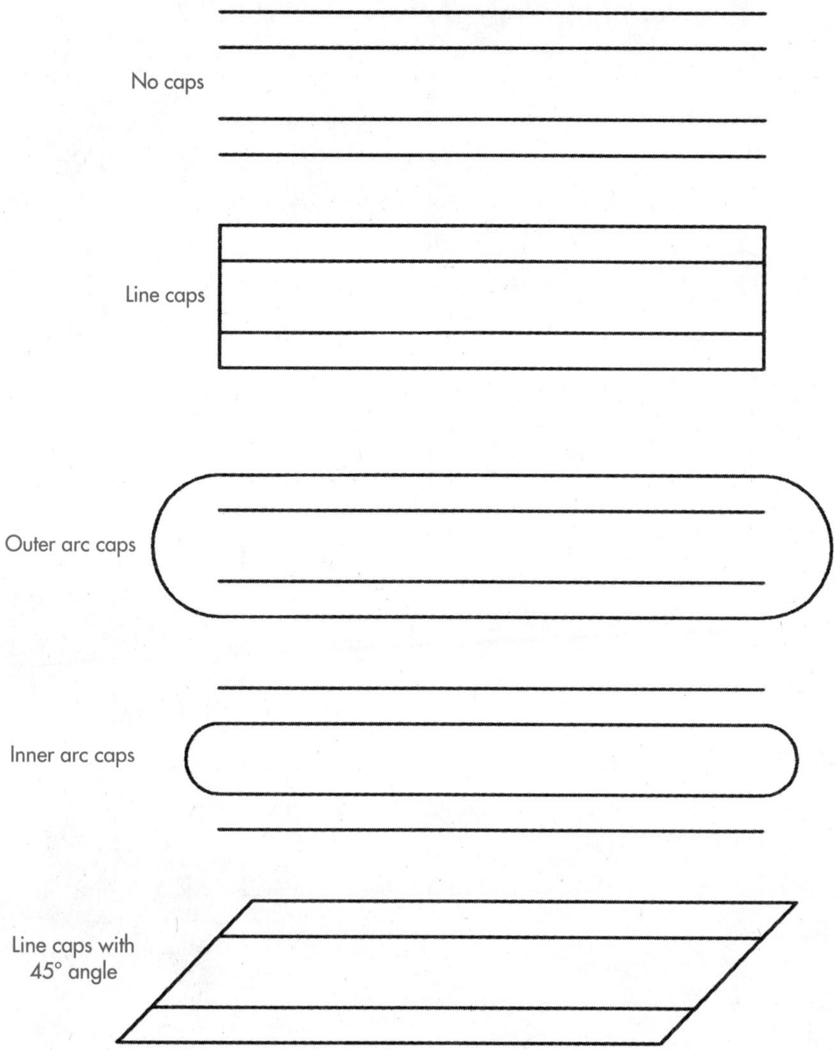

Figure 12.17

Multiline end cap options.

No caps

Line caps

Outer arc caps

Inner arc caps

Line caps with 45° angle

Note You use the 'FILL command to control the global display of solid fill. This sets the FILLMODE system variable to 1 for on or 0 for off. As an alternative, you can use the 'SETVAR command to set FILLMODE. See Chapter 11, "Drawing and Editing Polylines and Splines," for more information regarding the 'FILL command.

In the following exercise, you create two new multiline styles for the interior walls and closet shelves.

12

Creating Multiline Styles

Continue from the preceding exercise.

`Command:` *Choose* Data, Multiline Style	Issues the MLSTYLE command and opens the Multiline Style dialog box
Choose the Element Properties *button*	Activates the Element Properties dialog box
In the Elements *list, select the* 0.5 *element and enter a value of* **2** *in the* Offset *edit box*	Changes the top element to an offset of 2
Select the -0.5 *element and enter a value* **-2** *in the* Offset *edit box*	Changes the bottom element to an offset of –2
Choose OK	Exits the Element Properties dialog box
Choose the Multiline Properties *button, place an* X *in the* Start *and* End Line *boxes, then choose* OK	Opens the Multiline Properties dialog box and turns on the start and end caps
Enter `WALL_4` *in the* Name *box, enter* `4" WALL` *in the* Description *box, and choose* Add	Creates a new multiline style with the current setting

Next, you create a multiline style for a closet shelf.

Choose Element Properties	Activates the Element Properties dialog box
In the Elements *list, select the* 2.0 *element and enter a value of* **20** *in the* Offset *edit box*	Changes the top element to an offset of 20
Select the -2.0 *element and enter* **16** *in the* Offset *edit box*	Changes the bottom element to an offset of 16
Choose Linetype *and double-click on* Dashed *in the list of available linetypes*	Changes the element linetype to Dashed
Choose OK	Closes the Element Properties dialog box and returns to the Multiline Style dialog box
Choose Multiline Properties, *clear the* X's *from the* Start *and* End Line *check boxes, then choose* OK	Opens the Multiline Properties dialog box and turns off the start and end caps

Type **Shelf** *in the* Name *box, press Tab,* enter **20" Closet Shelf** *in the* Description *box, and choose* Add	Creates a new multiline style with the the current setting
Choose OK	Closes the Multiline Styles dialog box and creates the definitions in the drawing

Save your drawing.

In addition to the Standard multiline style, you now have two additional multiline styles. In the following exercise, you use these multiline styles to create the interior walls of your house.

Using Multiline Styles

Continue from the previous exercise. Before you begin, make sure ortho is on.

Command: *Choose* Draw, Multiline	Issues the MLINE command
Justification = Bottom, Scale = 6.00, Style = SHELF	
Justification/Scale/STyle/ <From point>: **S** (Enter)	Specifies the Scale option
Set Mline scale <6.00>: **1** (Enter)	Sets the multiline scale to 1
Justification = Bottom, Scale = 1.00, Style = SHELF	
Justification/Scale/STyle/ <From point>: **ST** (Enter)	Specifies the STyle option
Mstyle name (or ?): **WALL_4** (Enter)	Sets the multiline style to WALL_4
Justification = Bottom, Scale = 1.00, Style = WALL_4	
Justification/Scale/STyle/ <From point>: *Using FROM and the ENDPoint object snap, pick* ① *(see fig. 12.18)*	Picks a reference point at the end of the wall
<Offset>: **@13'<90** (Enter)	Places the first point of the mline

continues

12

continued

`<To point>:` `@9'6<0` **Enter**	Places the second point of the mline and draws a segment
`Undo/<To point>:` *Pick* ②	Draws another segment

This line is too short to meet the adjacent wall, but you can clean this up later.

`Close/Undo/<To point>:` **Enter**	Ends the MLINE command
`Command:` **Enter**	Repeats the previous command
`Justification = Bottom, Scale = 1.00,` `Style = WALL_4`	
`Justification/Scale/STyle/` `<From point>:` *Using the FROM and* *ENDPoint object snaps, pick* ③	Places a reference point at the end of the wall
`<Offset>:` `@13'<90` **Enter**	Places the first point of the mline
`<To point>:` `@7'6<180` **Enter**	Draws a segment
`Undo/<To point>:` **Enter**	Ends the MLINE command

Notice the end cap on the wall.

`Command:` **Enter**	Repeats the MLINE command
`Justification = Bottom, Scale = 1.00,` `Style = WALL_4`	
`Justification/Scale/STyle/` `<From point>:` *Using FROM the and* *ENDPoint object snap, pick* ④	Picks a reference point at the end of the interior wall
`<Offset>:` `@30<90` **Enter**	Places the first point of the mline
`<To point>:` `@6'<0` **Enter**	Places the second point of the mline
`Undo/<To point>:` *Using the* *PERPendicular object snap, pick* ⑤	Places the last point of the mline
`Close/Undo/<To point>:` **Enter**	Ends the MLINE command
`Command:` **Enter**	Repeats the MLINE command
`Justification = Bottom, Scale = 1.00,` `Style = WALL_4`	

`Justification/Scale/STyle/` `<From point>:` **ST** (Enter)	Specifies the STyle option
`Mstyle name (or ?):` **SHELF** (Enter)	Sets the multiline style to SHELF
`Justification = Bottom, Scale = 1.00,` `Style = SHELF`	
`Justification/Scale/STyle/` `<From point>:` **J** (Enter)	Specifies the Justify option
`Top/Zero/Bottom <top>:` **Z** (Enter)	Sets the justification to 0
`Justification = Zero, Scale = 1.00,` `Style = SHELF`	
`Justification/Scale/STyle/` `<From point>:` *Using the ENDPoint* *object snap, pick* ④	Places the first point of the mline
`Undo/<To point>:` *Using the ENDpoint* *object snap, pick* ⑥	Draws the closet shelf
`Undo/<To point>:` (Enter)	Ends the MLINE command

Save your drawing.

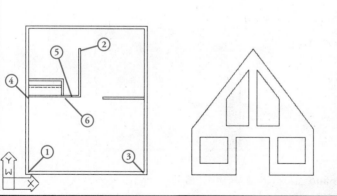

Figure 12.18
Floor plan with interior walls and a shelf.

Note AutoCAD does not provide a direct way to redefine an mline style or replace an mline object's style. You can overcome this first oversight by using the following procedure. Use the MLSTYLE command to change the style that you want to redefine, then add it as a new style using an interim name. Rename the old style to a useless name, then rename the interim style to the original name. If the original style is not already used by an mline object, you have effectively redefined the style. Unfortunately, if the style is used by an existing mline object, AutoCAD updates its style when you use the MLSTYLE command to rename it. Consequently, you cannot redefine the mline object's style after you draw it. Your only recourse is to use the EXPLODE command to reduce the mline object to line objects. For more information on the EXPLODE command, refer to Chapter 19, "Using Xrefs and Overlays for Workgroups and Multiple Access Drawings."

Editing Multilines with MLEDIT

Multilines are rather unique objects in AutoCAD R13. Insomuch as they are unique, they have a unique set of editing tools. The MLEDIT command gives you a set of tools for cleaning up and editing multilines.

> **MLEDIT.** The MLEDIT command enables you to control the way AutoCAD displays the intersections of mline objects. In essence, you can form tee and cross intersections, add or delete vertices, and cut or weld mline objects.
> Pull-down: *Choose* Modify, Edit Multiline
> Screen: *Choose* Modify, Mledit

When you issue the MLEDIT command, the Multiline Edit Tools dialog box appears (see fig. 12.19).

Figure 12.19

The Multiline Edit Tools dialog box.

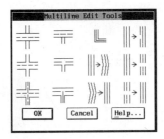

The MLEDIT command gives you a set of 12 tools for editing multilines. You can divide the MLEDIT tools into four categories: crosses, tees, corners, and cuts. AutoCAD does not break mline objects when you edit intersections, but rather, forms a gap on the mline object. Therefore, though a cross intersection might appear to have four mline objects, only two might exist. On the other hand, two mline objects perpendicularly extended to an mline object might appear to be four mline objects and in fact be three.

Note AutoCAD allows you to prefix the MLEDIT command with a –. The – commands AutoCAD to not display the Multiline Edit Tools dialog box. Instead, the 12 methods for controlling mline object intersections are available as options at the Command: prompt.

Crosses

The three cross tools (Closed Cross, Open Cross, and Merged Cross) enable you to clean up various crossing intersections. You can see the various effects of these tools in figure 12.20.

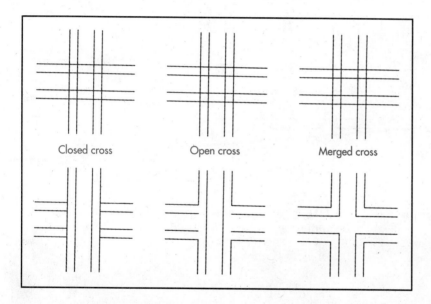

Figure 12.20

Closed, open, and merged crosses.

After you choose one of the cross tools, AutoCAD prompts you to select two mlines. AutoCAD always cuts the first mline you choose. AutoCAD cuts the second mline you choose according to the tool you use.

For merged crosses, AutoCAD creates a corner out of matching pairs of mline elements. In other words, the outermost elements of the first mline creates a corner with the outermost elements of the second mline, the second pair of elements in the first mline create a corner with the second pair of elements in the second mline, and so on. If AutoCAD encounters an unmatched element in one of the mlines, it is left uncut.

12

Tees

You use the next three multiline editing tools to clean up tee intersections. The tools behave much the same way the crossing tools behave. Figure 12.21 shows the effects of using the various tee tools on multilines.

Figure 12.21

Closed, open, and merged tees.

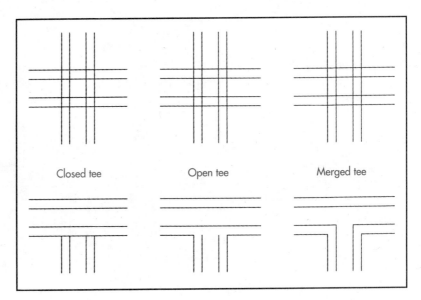

As with the cross tools, AutoCAD prompts you to select two mlines. AutoCAD cuts the first mline to make the base of the tee and cuts the second mline according to the tool you use.

Corners

The corner tools enable you to clean up corner intersections between two multilines, as well as give you the capability to add and remove vertices from multilines. The corner joint tool enables you to create a clean corner joint from two multilines. You can see the effect of the corner joint in figure 12.22.

After you select the corner joint tool, AutoCAD prompts you to select two mlines. Pick points on the portions of the mlines you want to keep. AutoCAD trims or extends the mlines to their respective intersection points.

Tip

When you make a corner joint, be sure that each mline has the same number of elements. This helps ensure that the corners miter properly. If you do not have the same number of elements, AutoCAD might trim or extend elements in a seemingly random manner.

New Riders Publishing
INSIDE
SERIES

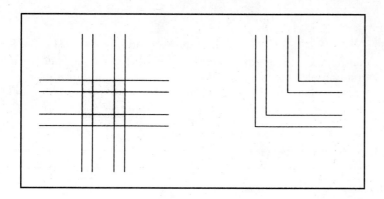

Figure 12.22
A corner joint.

When you create a multiline, AutoCAD places a vertex at each of the points you pick. The Add Vertex and Delete Vertex tools enable you to create and remove vertices from a multiline. Figure 12.23 shows the effect of adding a vertex. The top multiline is the original mline with a vertex at each endpoint. The middle multiline shows the effect of adding a new vertex, and the bottom shows the mline you use grips to stretch the mline.

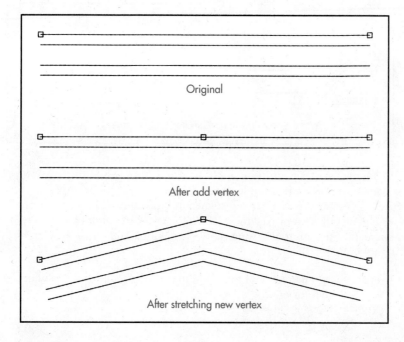

Original

After add vertex

After stretching new vertex

Figure 12.23
*Adding a vertex
to a multiline.*

You can use the Delete Vertex tool to remove a vertex from multilines that have three or more vertices. If you select an mline that has only two vertices, AutoCAD simply ignores the pick and allows you to try again.

Cuts

The cut tools enable you to break sections out of the individual elements of a multiline. You can use the Cut Single tool to break a section out of a single element of a multiline. You simply pick two points on the element and AutoCAD cuts the portion of the element between the two points. The Cut All tool works similarly, but cuts all of the elements. Figure 12.24 shows the effects of using the Cut Element and Cut All tools.

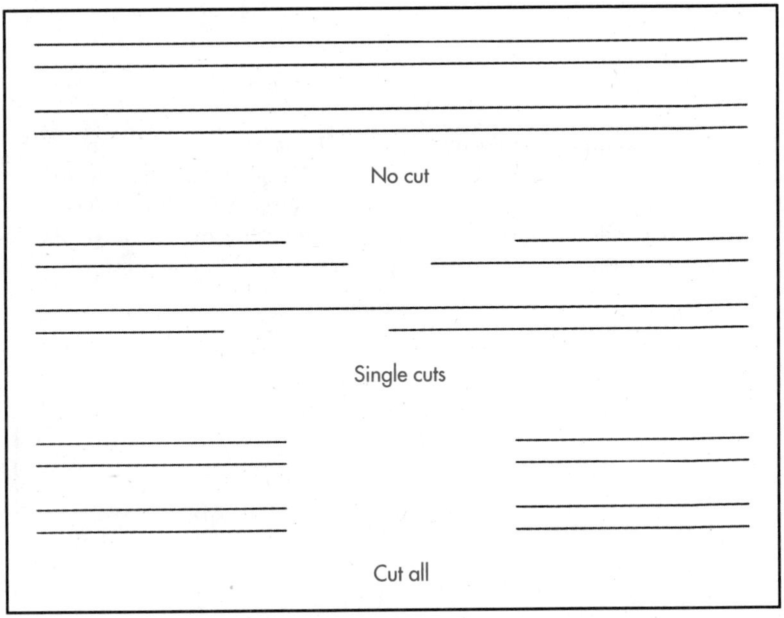

Figure 12.24

The multiline cut tools.

No cut

Single cuts

Cut all

AutoCAD doesn't actually cut the multiline itself—it simply suppresses display of those sections. The multiline is still a single object. The Weld All tool prompts you to pick two points on a multiline. AutoCAD redisplays any cut sections between the two points you pick. The fact that AutoCAD doesn't actually break the multiline enables you reverse the effects of the cut tools, using the Weld All tool. You can see the effect of the Weld All tool in figure 12.25.

In the following exercise, you use some of the multiline editing tools to create door openings in the walls of the floor plan.

New Riders Publishing
INSIDE
SERIES

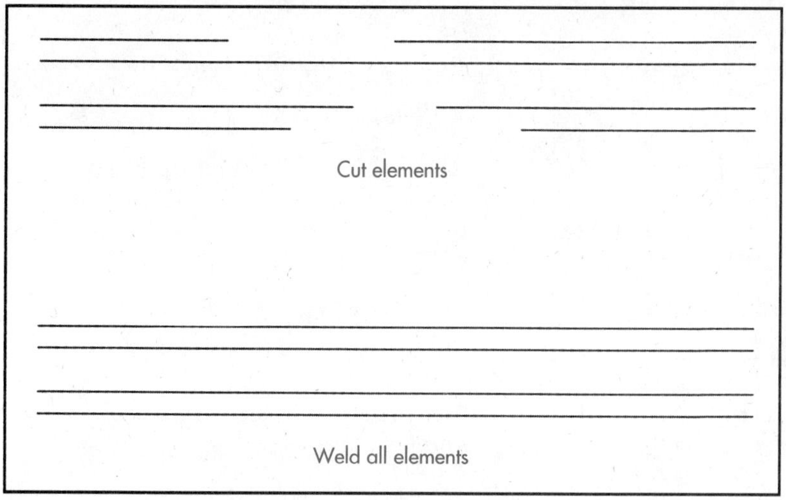

Figure 12.25
Welding a cut mline.

Cut elements

Weld all elements

Editing Multilines

Continue from the preceding exercise.

`Command:` *Choose* Modify, Edit Multiline	Issues the MLEDIT command
Double-click on the Closed Tee *icon*	Activates the Closed Tee tool
`Select first mline:` *Pick the mline at* ① *(see fig. 12.26)*	Selects the base of the tee intersection
`Select second mline:` *Pick the mline at* ②	Creates a closed tee intersection
`Select first mline(or Undo):` (Enter)	Ends the MLEDIT command
`Command:` (Enter)	Repeats the MLEDIT command
Double-click on the Merged Tee *icon*	Activates the Merged Tee tool
`Select first mline:` *Pick the mline at* ③	Selects the base of the tee intersection
`Select second mline:` *Pick the mline at* ④	Creates a merged tee intersection
`Select first mline(or Undo):` (Enter)	Ends the MLEDIT command

Next, you use the Cut All tool to create some door openings.

12

continued

Command: (Enter)	Repeats the MLEDIT command
Double-click on the Cut All *icon*	Activates the Cut All tool
Select mline: *Using the FROM and ENDPoint object snaps, pick* ⑤	Sets a reference point at the end of the closet wall
<Offset>: @6<0 (Enter)	Places the first point of the cut
Select second point: @4'8<0 (Enter)	Cuts a door opening in the wall

AutoCAD does not automatically cap the cut ends. Later, you cap these lines manually.

Select mline(or Undo): *Using the FROM and ENDPoint object snaps, pick* ⑥	Sets a reference point at the inside corner of the wall
<Offset>: @6<90 (Enter)	Places the first point of the cut
Select second point: @30<90 (Enter)	Creates a 30" door opening
Select mline(or Undo): *Using the FROM and MIDpoint object snaps, pick* ⑦	Sets a reference point at the midpoint of the wall
<Offset>: @3'<180 (Enter)	Places the first point of the cut
Select second point: @6'<0 (Enter)	Creates a 6' door opening
Select mline(or Undo): (Enter)	

Next, you use the LINE command and a running ENDPoint object snap to clean up the cut openings.

Command: *Choose* Assist, Object Snap, Endpoint	Sets a running ENDPoint object snap
Command: *Choose* Draw, Line	Issues the LINE command
From point: *Pick* ① *(see fig. 12.27)*	Places the start point of the line
To point: *Pick* ②	Draws the cap line
To point: (Enter)	Ends the LINE command

Use the LINE command to continue to connect the endpoints of the door openings. After you finish, your drawing should resemble figure 12.27. Leave the running ENDpoint object snap turned on—you use it in the next exercise.

Save your drawing.

New Riders Publishing
INSIDE
SERIES

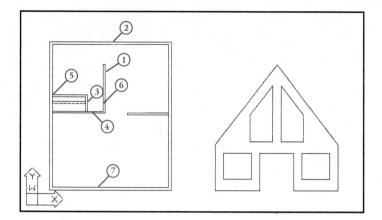

Figure 12.26

Editing with MLEDIT.

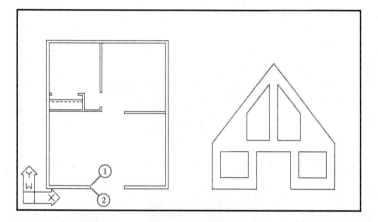

Figure 12.27

Capped door openings.

Drawing with TRACE and SOLID

Chapter 11,"Drawing and Editing Polylines and Splines," shows you how to use the PLINE command to create solid filled lines. Earlier in this chapter, you saw how to add solid fills to multilines. You can use two other commands to create solid filled objects: TRACE and SOLID.

Drawing Filled Lines with TRACE

A trace object is similar to the pline object, but much simpler. The TRACE command enables you to create a nonsegmented trace object—as when you use the LINE command, each successive endpoint creates another object. During the TRACE command, AutoCAD does not dynamically display the trace object; in fact, it does not display the trace object until you complete the command or until you specify the

12

subsequent object's endpoint. Uniquely, each trace object is mitered to the end of the previous one. Like the pline object, a trace object can have a width, but you cannot change it after you invoke the TRACE command. If the FILLMODE system variable is set to one, the trace object is filled according to the width you specified. The TRACE command is sometimes handy for quickly adding a width to an element of your drawing when your plotter pens cannot match the desired width. The only advantage the trace object has over a pline object is that it requires fewer bytes in your drawing file.

TRACE. The TRACE command enables you to create wide, solid-filled line segments.
Screen: *Choose* Draw 2, Trace

In the following exercise, you use the TRACE command to add some detail to the elevation.

Drawing with Trace

Continue from the preceding exercise. Thaw the layer ELEV_DOORS and set it current.

Command: **TRACE** (Enter)	Issues the TRACE command
Trace width <0'-2">: (Enter)	Accepts the default trace width
From point: *Pick points* ①, ②, ③, and ④ *(see fig. 12.28)*	Draws a trace around the door frame
To point: (Enter)	Ends the TRACE command
Command: *Choose* Assist, Object Snap, None	Turns off the running ENDpoint object snap

Save your drawing.

The TRACE command is not widely used because trace objects have some drawing and editing limitations that make working with them somewhat difficult. You cannot, for example, perform the following actions:

◆ Curve a trace

◆ Close a trace

◆ Continue a trace

◆ Undo a trace during the command

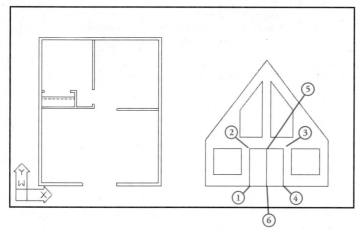

Figure 12.28
Tracing the door frame.

Polylines are more versatile, and thus used more widely, than TRACE. In general, you use polylines to create lines that have width, but you use traces if you need mitered corners.

Drawing Filled Areas with SOLID

Whereas the TRACE command enables you to create wide, solid-filled line segments, the SOLID command enables you to create solid-filled irregular polygons.

> **SOLID**. The SOLID command enables you to create solid-filled irregular polygons.
> Pull-down: *Choose* Draw, Polygon, 2d Solid
> Screen: *Choose* Draw 1, Solid

When you issue the SOLID command, AutoCAD prompts you to pick four points. The order in which you pick the points is important. Picking the points in the wrong order gives you bow ties rather than polygons. Figure 12.29 shows the proper order for picking points when you use the SOLID command.

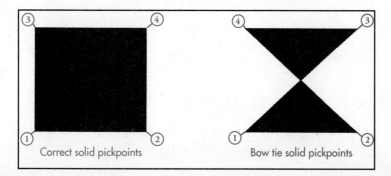

Correct solid pickpoints   Bow tie solid pickpoints

Figure 12.29
Solid pick points.

12

Note   Do not confuse the SOLID command with the REGION command or 3D solid modeling. The REGION command enables you to create 2D solid objects, whereas SOLID enables you to create filled 2D polygon areas. Solids contain no surface information. For information on 3D solid modeling, see Chapter 31, "Solid Modeling."

You can use object grips to edit solid or trace objects. You can use this method to edit the object's vertices, which allows you to quickly untie the aforementioned bow tie or collapse a four sided solid object to a triangle.

Note   You must select the SOLID object by indicating an edge of the object; otherwise AutoCAD responds 0 found when you pick from the Select objects: prompt.

In the following exercise, you use SOLID to add some additional details to the door elevations.

Drawing with the SOLID Command

Continue from the preceding exercise.

Command: **L** (Enter)	Invokes the LINE command
From point: *Use ENDP object snap to pick* ① *(see fig. 12.28)*	Specifies ENDpoint object snap and starts line
To point: *Use ENDP object snap to pick* ④	Specifies ENDpoint object snap and draws the door threshold
Command: (Enter)	Repeats the LINE command
From point: *Use MID object snap to pick* ⑤	Specifies MIDpoint object snap and starts line
To point: *Use PER object snap to pick* ⑥	Specifies PERpendicular object snap and makes two doors
To point: (Enter)	Ends the LINE command
Command: *Choose* Draw, Polygon, 2D Solid	Issues the SOLID command
First point: *Using the FROM and ENDPoint object snaps, pick* ① *(see fig. 12.30)*	Places a reference point at the corner of the door

`<Offset>: @6,6` (Enter)	Places the first point of the solid
`Second point: @24,0` (Enter)	Places the second point of the solid
`Third point: @-24,18` (Enter)	Places the third point of the solid
`Fourth point: @24,0` (Enter)	Creates the solid
`Third point:` (Enter)	Ends the SOLID command
Command: *Select the solid and pick one of the grips, then press Enter*	Displays the solid's grips, makes one of the grips hot, and cycles to the MOve grip edit mode
`<Move to point>/Base point /Copy/Undo/eXit: C` (Enter)	Specifies the Copy option
`<Move to point>/Base point /Copy/Undo/eXit: @24<90` (Enter)	Copies the solid 2' above the original
`<Move to point>/Base point /Copy/Undo/eXit: @48<90` (Enter)	Creates another copy of the solid 4' above the original
`<Move to point>/Base point/Copy/Undo /eXit:` (Enter)	
Command: *Select the three solids and pick one of the grips, then press Enter*	Displays the grips for the three solids, makes one of the grips hot, and cycles to the MOve grip edit mode
`<Move to point>/Base point /Copy/Undo/eXit: C` (Enter)	Specifies the Copy option
`<Move to point>/Base point /Copy/Undo/eXit: @3'<180` (Enter)	Copies the solids 3' to the right of the original
`<Move to point>/Base point /Copy/Undo/eXit:` (Enter)	Exits grip editing
Command: *Press Esc twice*	Clears the grips

Save your drawing.

Figure 12.31 shows the completed drawing.

12

Figure 12.30

Creating the solids.

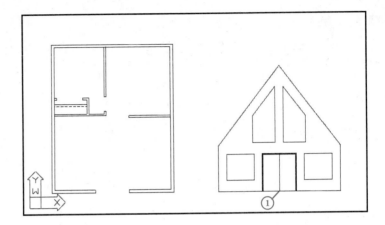

Figure 12.31

The completed plan and elevation views.

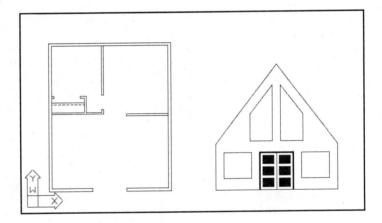

This chapter concludes 2D drawing commands in AutoCAD. You now should have a good feel for AutoCAD's drawing capabilities. In the next chapter, you learn how to add text and annotation to your drawing.

New Riders Publishing
INSIDE
SERIES

Annotation with Text

You often need to place lines of text in drawings to explain graphic objects. Although international logo symbols do support the philosophy that a picture is worth a thousand words (or at least several words), accompanying text can specify, clarify, and simplify drawing details. Textual data can refer to notes, specifications, schedules, leader callouts, or anything "character-string" based.

Historically, hand lettering a drawing was time-consuming and error-prone. Correcting a misspelled or omitted word was difficult. Today, using AutoCAD Release 13's powerful, yet easy-to-use text entry and editing methods, lettering generates faster, is more accurate, and follows a more uniform style than manual techniques.

This chapter covers the following procedures related to drawing annotation:

◆ Using TEXT, DTEXT, and MTEXT to place single, multiple, and paragraph text objects

◆ Using text styles and fonts

◆ Formatting basic line and paragraph text

◆ Formatting special characters and strings

◆ Formatting paragraph text using advanced methods

◆ Importing text

AutoCAD provides several methods to place text in your drawing. In the Quick 5¢
Tour, you see how to insert paragraph-style text, a new Release 13 feature.

 Stop The DOS version of AutoCAD Release 13 uses the default system editor, EDIT.EXE, for the MTEXT command. If EDIT.EXE is not your system editor, or not your preferred editor, you must first specify the editor with which you want to associate the MTEXT command; otherwise the MTEXT command will fail. Use the MTEXTED system variable to specify the system editor you use. For more information on the MTEXTED system variable, see "Using MTEXT To Place Text," later in this chapter.

Quick 5¢ Tour

Begin a new drawing called CHAP13, using the default ACAD prototype drawing.

Command: *Choose* Draw, Text, Text — Issues the MTEXT command

```
_mtext
Attach/Rotation/Style/
Height/Direction/<Insertion
point>: 2,7 (Enter)
```
Specifies the upper left corner of the paragraph

```
Attach/Rotation/Style/Height/Direction/
Width/2Points/<Other corner>: 10,2 (Enter)
```
Specifies width of paragraph and launches the system editor

Type the text shown in figure 13.1.

Your drawing screen should now look like figure 13.1.

Figure 13.1

*Typing
paragraph text
using the
MTEXT
command.*

```
This is an example of entering paragraph
text. Please note that you do not need
to use the <ENTER> key to format the
lines within a paragraph. Just keep typing
and allow AutoCAD to reformat the text
at the paragraph boundary. Start a new
paragraph. Press the <ENTER> key twice,
now.

In addition, you can add special codes to
format the paragraphs, assign fonts, and
assign color. Now save your file and exit
your editor.
```

New Riders Publishing
INSIDE
SERIES

Placing AutoCAD Text

AutoCAD provides the TEXT, DTEXT, and MTEXT commands so you can place text in your drawing. You use TEXT to create a single line of text. DTEXT enables you to generate multiple lines of text *dynamically,* by displaying the characters as you type. You use MTEXT to create paragraph-style text to fit within points you specify, which AutoCAD then treats as one object.

One common application of paragraph-style text is a leader callout, as shown in figure 13.2. Refer to Part Four, "Automating Drafting," for a complete discussion of leaders and dimension text, and Chapter 16, "Basic Building Blocks for Repetitive Drawing," for a discussion of attributes.

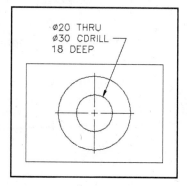

Figure 13.2

A leader text paragraph.

Plotted versus Drawn Text Height

Generally, AutoCAD draws all objects at full size. Therefore, you need to determine the corresponding text height so that AutoCAD can give geometry and text descriptions the proper proportions. What you really need to determine is the text height at which you should draw, so that the plotted height meets acceptable industry standards. See Chapter 25, "Sheet Composition and Plotting," for more information on plotted text heights at common plot scales.

Tip   Use snap for consistent, orderly text spacing and placement.

Using TEXT To Place Text

AutoCAD has always had a TEXT command. However, no one really needs to use it anymore, because the DTEXT and MTEXT commands are much more versatile. The TEXT command is retained for compatibility with older versions of the software.

> **TEXT.** The TEXT command enables you to place a single line of text in a drawing. AutoCAD prompts you for insertion point, style, justification, height, and rotation.
> Pull-down: *Choose* Draw, Text, Single-Line Text

In the following exercise, you place a single text label in the drawing at a specified location.

Placing a Single Text Label

Begin a new drawing again named CHAP13, using the HOSPROOM drawing from the IA Disk as the prototype. Zoom to the view shown in figure 13.3, then set snap to 3'' and grid to 6''. Set the FURN-TEXT layer current.

Command: *Choose* Draw, Text, Single-Line Text	Issues the TEXT command
_text Justify/Style/<Start point>: **12',11'6"** (Enter)	Specifies the start point 12',11'6''
Height <0'-0 1/4">: **6** (Enter)	Specifies 6'' text height
Rotation angle <0>: (Enter)	Accepts default baseline rotation
Text: **CHAIR** (Enter)	Draws text as shown in figure 13.3

Save your drawing.

Using DTEXT To Place Text

DTEXT provides more flexibility than TEXT. You can reposition the box cursor on the drawing area while you enter text by using the crosshairs to pick a new point. This feature enables you to use a single DTEXT command to place text throughout your drawing.

> **DTEXT.** The DTEXT command dynamically places multiple lines of text in a drawing, which enables you to preview and edit the characters as you type them. AutoCAD prompts you for insertion point, style, justification, height, and rotation.
> Pull-down: *Choose* Draw, Text, Dynamic Text
> Screen: *Choose* DRAW2, DText

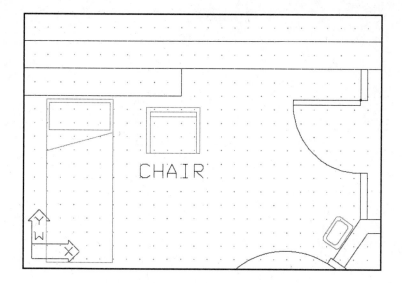

Figure 13.3

The chair annotated using TEXT.

13

Note AutoCAD does not create text objects until you press Enter, alone, at the Text: prompt. AutoCAD disables all menu access during the DTEXT command. You must use the keyboard to complete the command.

If you make a mistake as you type, you can backspace and correct your errors because the DTEXT command provides a screen preview.

In the next exercise, you label the remaining pieces of furniture in the room.

Placing Multiple Text Labels

Continue from the preceding exercise and zoom to view shown in figure 13.4. Label the remaining pieces of furniture in the hospital room.

Command: *Choose* Draw, Text, Dynamic Text	Issues the DTEXT command
Command: _dtext Justify/Style/ <Start point>: *Pick point* 5',7' at ① *(see fig. 13.4)*	Specifies start point for chair text
Height <0'-6">: (Enter)	Accepts default 6" text height, set by TEXT command in preceding exercise

continues

continued

`Rotation angle <0>:` **(Enter)**	Accepts default baseline rotation
`Text:` **CHAIR** **(Enter)**	Displays text as you type
`Text:` *Pick point* 9',7'6" *at* ②	Relocates next insertion point
`Text:` **BED**	Displays text (notice that you didn't press Enter this time)
`Text:` *Pick point* 12',6'6" *at* ③	Locates next insertion point
`Text:` **SOFA** **(Enter)**	Displays text
`Text:` **(Enter)**	Completes the DTEXT command

Save the drawing.

Figure 13.4

Hospital room furniture labeled with DTEXT.

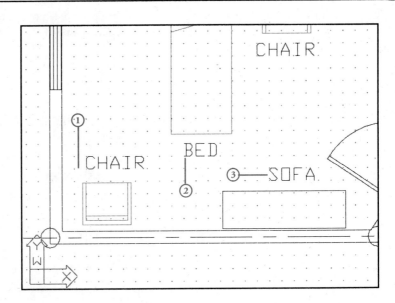

During the preceding exercise, you picked alternate text insertion points by reading the coordinate display in the status line. A single DTEXT command enables you to enter all three text labels.

If you do not use the default left justification, input for DTEXT still appears as left-justified during entry, but the alignment adjusts to the format you specify after you complete the command.

 Tip You also can use object snap modes to help place text. To add a line below existing text, use DTEXT with object snap mode INSert, pick the existing text, and enter only a space on the first line. Then press Enter to space down for the next line.

The DTEXT command enables you to place multiple lines of text at various locations in the drawing. Often, however, grouping several lines of text together so you can treat them as a single block becomes handy. Some examples are door schedules, design and build specifications, and mechanical tolerance notes. Rather than use the BLOCK command (see Chapter 16) to "glue" the text lines together, you can utilize a powerful, new Release 13 feature called MTEXT—paragraphs of text treated as objects.

Using MTEXT To Place Text

Because MTEXT enables you to create paragraph-style text that is treated as a single object, you can enter the text quickly and reposition its boundary frame to a new, uncluttered location in the drawing.

Before the MTEXT command will function, you must set the MTEXTED system variable correctly for your system. The default value is none, which directs AutoCAD to use EDIT.EXE as the system editor. You can specify the name of your preferred editor, prefixed with a path if not already in the DOS path.

> **MTEXT.** The MTEXT command enables you to create text paragraphs that fit within a boundary as a single object. The boundary specifies the width and alignment of the paragraph. You also can specify the text style, height, and direction.
> Pull-down: *Choose* Draw, Text, Text
> Screen: *Choose* DRAW2, MText

In the next exercise, you create a paragraph of text. You need not press Enter to format the text lines—MTEXT word-wraps like a word processor. Then, you see how to reposition the paragraph location.

Placing Paragraph Text with MTEXT

Continue to use CHAP13 drawing from the previous exercise, and zoom to the view shown in figure 13.5.

Command: *Choose* Draw, Text, Text	Issues the MTEXT command
Attach/Rotation/Style/Height/Direction/ <Insertion point>: *Pick point at* ① *(see fig. 13.5)*	Specifies upper left corner of paragraph
Attach/Rotation/Style/Height/Direction/ Width/2Points/<Other corner>: *Pick point at* ②	Specifies width of paragraph and launches the system editor

Enter the text shown in fig. 13.5, then save your file and exit the system editor.

Command: *Pick the text*	Selects the text and displays grips at its corner points
Pick either right grip, then move it 2' further right and click	Makes grip hot, enters autoediting stretch mode, changes the paragraph boundary and reformats the paragraph
Pick a grip, then press Enter	Makes grip hot, enters autoediting move mode, and drags text box with the cursor
Move the down text 2' and left 1' 6"	Dynamically relocates the paragraph

Save the drawing.

Figure 13.6 shows the results of this exercise.

AutoCAD word-wraps the text you enter. You have limited control over the appearance of the paragraph you type. If line breaks cause the paragraph to appear unsuitable, you can resize the paragraph boundary, which forces AutoCAD to recalculate the line breaks. You might want to use the DDEDIT command, which enables you to force line breaks by pressing Enter. See the section, "Using DDEDIT To Change Text," for more information.

 Note Entering **-MTEXT** at the Command: prompt causes AutoCAD to display all prompts at the command line rather than provide a dialog box.

New Riders Publishing
INSIDE SERIES

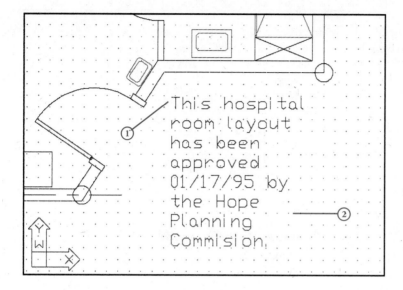

Figure 13.5

Completed approval note text.

13

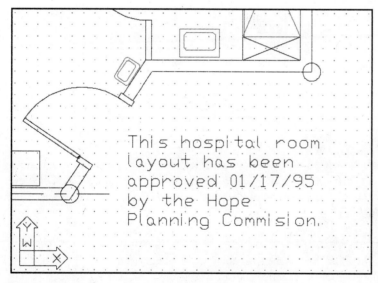

Figure 13.6

Reformatted and relocated approval note text.

Using Text Styles and Fonts

AutoCAD enables you to control the appearance of text in many ways, such as font, character width, character height, slant, and baseline format, all of which comprise a *text style*. AutoCAD provides a default text style called STANDARD, which uses a basic stick-lettering font called TXT. The STANDARD style does not meet the need of most users, therefore other styles need to be defined. You use the STYLE command to define the text characteristics, then name and save the definition.

STYLE. The STYLE command enables you to define, name, change, and list sets of text parameters, including the font, height, width factor, obliquing angle, as well as backwards, upside-down, and vertical orientation. This command also enables you to set the current style for the drawing.

Pull-down:	*Choose* Data, Text Style
Screen:	*Choose* DATA, Style

You can use the Select Text Style dialog box to select, but not modify, the current style. To access the dialog box from the pull-down menu, choose Data, Object Creation, then choose Text Style. Use this dialog box to set the text style or when you need visual confirmation of the appearance of a text style.

Figure 13.7

The Select Text Style dialog box.

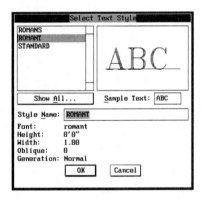

Note   AutoCAD Release 13 supports a variety of fonts from third-party vendors. Besides its native source (SHP) and compiled (SHX) shape file font formats, AutoCAD now handles Type 1 PostScript source (PFB) and compiled (PFA) fonts, as well as TrueType (TTF) fonts.

COMPILE. The COMPILE command enables you to compile shape (SHP) files and PostScript font files. You must compile shape files before you use them. Although AutoCAD Release 13 can use Type 1 PostScript source (PFB) files directly, compiling them improves loading speed. You enter the SHP or SHX file name in the Select Shape or Font File dialog box, then AutoCAD compiles it into a file that has the same name and gives it an SHX extension.

Pull-down:	*Choose* Tools, Compile
Screen:	*Choose* TOOLS, Compile

 New Riders Publishing
INSIDE SERIES

Figure 13.8 shows a selected sample of text fonts (in alphabetical order) included with AutoCAD.

FONT NAME	TYPE	SAMPLE
BGOTHL	TrueType	INSIDE AUTOCAD 13 FOR DOS
COBT	Postscript	Inside AutoCAD 13 for DOS
COMSC	TrueType	Inside AutoCAD 13 for DOS
DUTCH	TrueType	Inside AutoCAD 13 for DOS
GOTHICE	Shape	Inside AutoCAD 13 for DOS
MONOTXT	Shape	Inside AutoCAD 13 for DOS
PAR	Postscript	Inside AutoCAD 13 for DOS
ROMANS	Shape	Inside AutoCAD 13 for DOS
ROMB	Postscript	Inside AutoCAD 13 for DOS
SASB	Postscript	Inside AutoCAD 13 for DOS
SCRIPTC	Shape	Inside AutoCAD 13 for DOS
STYLU	TrueType	Inside AutoCAD 13 for DOS
SYMUSIC	Shape	♭♀♁♭oo ·♂⊕♒)·♪·o 13 ·♔:♔ o♒:---
TE	Postscript	INSIDE AUTOCAD 13 FOR DOS
VINET	TrueType	Inside AutoCAD 13 for DOS

Figure 13.8

AutoCAD font sampler.

13

Note The previous figure is by no means all-inclusive. AutoCAD ships with many more fonts, but does not provide a method to easily preview every possible one. As an interim solution, a sample drawing called TRUETYPE.DWG shows an example of each of the included TrueType (TTF) fonts.

In the following exercise, you assign another font to the default STANDARD style to enhance its appearance.

Revising a Text Style

Continue to use the CHAP13 drawing from the previous exercise.

Command: *Choose* Data, Text Style	Issues the STYLE command
`'_style`	
Text style name (or ?) <STANDARD>: (Enter)	Accepts the default style name and opens the Select Font File dialog box (see fig. 13.9)
Existing style.	

continues

continued

Choose <u>T</u>ype It	Closes dialog box and prompts for font name
Font file <txt>: **ROMANS** (Enter)	Specifies name without path—AutoCAD searches its support path and loads the font
Height <0'-0">: (Enter)	Defaults to zero height, which means variable-height text
Width factor <1.000000>: **0.8** (Enter)	Compresses the character width
Obliquing angle <0>: **10** (Enter)	Slants the text forward 10 degrees
Backwards? <N> (Enter)	
Upside-down? <N> (Enter)	
Vertical? <N> (Enter)	
STANDARD is now the current text style.	
Regenerating drawing.	Regenerates text with new style
Save your drawing.	

Figure 13.9

The Select Font File dialog box.

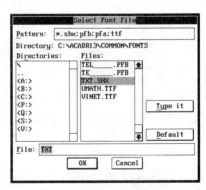

After you complete the exercise, your STANDARD style uses the smoother ROMANS font and is *slanted* (italicized) and slightly narrower than normal, as shown in figure 13.10.

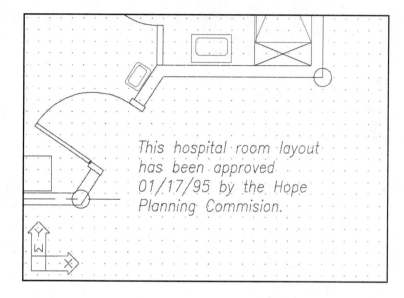

Figure 13.10

The modified STANDARD style.

13

Tip Use the RENAME command to change the name of an existing text style. By adopting a suitable naming convention for table entries (layers, blocks, and so on), you assist in the maintenance of company-wide standards. You can use the PURGE command to remove unused styles.

As the examples in figure 13.11 show, AutoCAD offers several text style effects. The following options are available:

◆ **Style name.** This option prompts you to name a new style to create or an existing style to edit. This style becomes the current default.

◆ **?.** This option lists named styles defined in the current drawing. You can enter an asterisk (the default) to list all named styles or use wild cards to list a specific set of styles.

◆ **Font file.** This option prompts you to specify a font file name for the style to reference. The default <TXT> references the TXT.SHX file.

◆ **Height.** This option prompts you to specify text height for a fixed height style, or enter **0** (the default) for a variable-height style. Text commands do not prompt for height unless you use a variable-height style.

◆ **Width factor.** This option prompts you for a width factor to expand or condense text (default 1 = normal).

◆ **Obliquing angle.** This option prompts you to specify a number to slant the text characters, italicizing them (default 0 = vertical). To slant toward the right, use a positive number; to slant toward the left, use a negative number.

◆ **Backwards.** This option mirrors text horizontally.

◆ **Upside-down.** This option mirrors text vertically.

Figure 13.11

*Examples of
text styles.*

PARAMETER	VALUE	RESULT
Width factor	0.50	ABC 123
Width factor	0.75	ABC 123
Width factor	1.00	ABC 123
Width factor	1.25	ABC 123
Obliquing angle	−20	ABC 123
Obliquing angle	0	ABC 123
Obliquing angle	20	ABC 123
Obliquing angle	45	ABC 123
Upside down	Y	ABC 123
Backwards	Y	ABC 123

Tip Limit the style's obliquing angle to within 20 degrees. A little slant goes a long way!

Operational Features of STYLE

The STYLE command has the following operational features:

◆ Many style names can exist in a single drawing. These style names refer to font files and affect only the current drawing. AutoCAD maintains style definition names in a tables section of the drawing database.

◆ If you give a new name at the prompt, AutoCAD creates a new style in the style table.

◆ If you supply an existing style name at the prompt, AutoCAD assumes that you want to change or edit the existing style. It prompts you for all the style parameters and offers the old settings as defaults.

◆ If you change a style currently defined in the drawing file, AutoCAD might regenerate the drawing. If the new style uses a different font, then AutoCAD will regenerate to display the text object's new font. If the new style changes characteristics other than the font, AutoCAD will not regenerate the display. Consequently, your update might not be apparent. If needed, you can use the **REGEN** command to update the display to reflect the text style changes.

Note Rather than define a standard set of styles each time you begin a new drawing, simply add your standard styles to your default prototype drawing (see Chapter 5 and Appendix D). Or, save them as part of another drawing file and insert them as a block (this does not override any existing definitions in an existing drawing). See Chapters 16 and 19 for more information.

13

Font Mapping and Substitution

AutoCAD accesses a variety of support files when you open a drawing for its initial screen display. In particular, AutoCAD checks to ensure that all the font files exist because text styles are linked to separate font files. If a font file does not exist or is linked to an invalid directory path, AutoCAD uses an alternate font or displays an error message and prompts for an alternate font file.

These situations can arise if you fail to load all the fonts when you install AutoCAD (see Appendix A for details). Another problematic scenario that involves missing fonts can occur if you send a drawing on disk to another user at another site. The drawing can contain styles linked to third-party, separately purchased font files. If the font files are not included on the disk (which could be a license infringement), the second user cannot access and match the corresponding styles.

 Stop Text styles are stored in the DWG file, but the fonts they reference are not. The font file must be available when you load the drawing. If not, AutoCAD might use the TXT font and display error messages. When you use the Select Font File dialog box to specify the font file, even if you just accept the default, the full path is stored with the font file name for the style, and if so, causes AutoCAD (at least in some versions of Release 13) to use the TXT font and/or display an error message if the font is available on AutoCAD's support path, but not in the same directory or on the same drive as it was when the font was originally specified for that style.

To prevent this error, do not use the Select Font File dialog box to load the font. Instead, make sure the font file is on AutoCAD's support path, choose Type It, and enter the font file name, without a path, at the Font file <default>: prompt that appears. This stores the font name without a path. To cure this error, redefine the style, using Type It to specify the font.

AutoCAD Release 13 provides a new mechanism you can use to address font issues such as compatibility, draft versus production output, missing fonts, and standards enforcement. The mechanism is available through two system variables, FONTALT and FONTMAP.

The FONTALT system variable specifies a single alternate font for AutoCAD to use if it cannot find the requested font file. If you use FONTALT to specify an alternate font, AutoCAD uses it during the drawing session, but does not redefine the style. The default for FONTALT is the TXT font. If you do not set FONTALT, AutoCAD displays an error message and a prompt or dialog box that requests a font selection. Selecting a font redefines the style, but if you close the drawing without making further changes, AutoCAD does not prompt you to save the change.

The FONTMAP system variable specifies a font mapping file (.FPM) that contains a line for each font to remap. Each line contains the name of the font to remap, a semicolon, and the font to substitute. The following line is typical:

```
scriptc;c:\acadr13\common\fonts\compi.ttf
```

Stop Font mapping files can be very useful. However, you must pay attention to character widths. Not all fonts take the same amount of width for a given character (see fig. 13.8). Substituting BGOTHL for STYLU, for example, causes the text objects with style STYLU to widen, which probably obscure other important objects.

When you specify the original font name, omit the directory name or path. After the semicolon, specify the substituted font name with the file-name extension. Unless the font can be found on AutoCAD's support path, specify the path. The preceding example replaces the SCRIPTC font with a cursive TrueType font. Font mappings specified by FONTMAP override the fonts for the drawing session, but do not redefine the style or cause any change in the drawing file—they only change the displayed and plotted appearance.

Note The SAVEASR12 command redefines any text style that uses an R13-specific font to use the TXT font.

You can use font mapping files for several purposes.

◆ **Compatibility.** Drawings are often shared: between systems such as DOS and Windows, between owners and consultants, and between users. By mapping the fonts, you can force AutoCAD to use a specific font that you know your counterpart will use and that you know you do not have.

◆ **Output.** Plots are often time-consuming to generate if they use complex fonts. Use different mapping files for check plots and final plots. The mapping file for a check plot uses a simple font. The mapping file for a final plot uses a complex, high-quality font.

◆ **Standards.** AutoCAD users often work as part of a team whose drawings must be consistent in appearance. Unfortunately, updates of third party fonts,

New Riders Publishing
INSIDE
SERIES

illegally licensed fonts, and shareware fonts can be unacceptable. Use a mapping file to substitute standardized fonts for bogus ones.

◆ **Conversion.** Sometimes you might want to convert your drawing's fonts to another font rather than redefine the drawing's text styles. Use a mapping file to substitute the old for the new.

Note The FONTMAP.PS and FONTMAP.BD files in the FONTS directory are not for the type of font mapping discussed here. They are used by AutoCAD's PostScript engine for PostScript font mapping.

Formatting Text

When you use the TEXT or DTEXT command to place text in a drawing, AutoCAD needs to know the format. The following options are available during text placement. The following four options apply to the initial `Justify/Style/<start point>:` prompt:

◆ **Justify.** This option issues the prompt for text justification. You also can enter justification directly at the `Justify/Style/<start point>:` prompt, or let it default to left justification.

◆ **Style.** This option specifies a new text style default. The style must have already been created using the STYLE command.

◆ **Start point.** This default option specifies the bottom left justification point.

After you specify the above information, AutoCAD prompts you for each of the following options:

◆ **Height.** This option specifies the text height (the default is 0.2). The height prompt is omitted if you use Align justification or any text style that has a predefined nonzero height.

◆ **Rotation angle.** This option specifies the baseline angle for text placement (the default is 0).

The default height shown in the TEXT command is rounded off to your units setting and might not accurately display its true value.

When you use AutoCAD text, you need to consider two angles. The *obliquing angle* is the slant of each character, and you use the STYLE command to control it. The *rotation angle* is the slope of the text baseline, and you use the TEXT, DTEXT, and MTEXT commands to control it.

You can specify the height or angle of the text object by picking a point, rather than entering a value at the height or rotation angle prompts. You can use several methods to ensure precise height or rotation angle. You can turn on ORTHO mode to force the rotation angle to be 0, 90, 180, or 270 degrees. You can turn on SNAP mode to ensure the text height is set to a multiple of an even snap increment. You can also use object snaps for either text height or rotation angle.

Text Justification

Justification (or alignment) specifies the positioning of the text, relative to the start and optional endpoint(s) you specify. The justification prompt shows all the options:

```
Align/Fit/Center/Middle/Right/TL/TC/TR/ML/MC/MR/BL/BC/BR:
```

The following list describes each option:

◆ **Align.** Specify the beginning and ending points of the text baseline. The text height is scaled so that the text between these points is not distorted.

◆ **Fit.** Specify the beginning and ending points of the text baseline. The text width is distorted to fit the text between these points without changing the height.

◆ **Center.** Specify a point for the horizontal center and the vertical baseline of the text string.

◆ **Middle.** Specify a point for the horizontal and vertical midpoint of the text string.

◆ **Right.** Specify a point for the right baseline of the text string.

◆ **TL.** Specify a point for the left of the text string, aligned with the top of an uppercase character.

◆ **TC.** Specify a point for the center of the text string, aligned with the top of an uppercase character.

◆ **TR.** Specify a point for the right side of the text string, aligned with the top of an uppercase character.

◆ **ML.** Specify a point for the left side of the text string, aligned halfway between the top of an uppercase character and the text baseline.

◆ **MC.** Specify a point for the center of the text string, aligned halfway between an uppercase character and the bottom of the text baseline.

◆ **MR.** Specify a point for the right side, between the top of an uppercase character and the text baseline.

◆ **BL.** Specify a point for the left side of the text string, aligned at the bottom of a
descender.

◆ **BC.** Specify a point for the center of the text string, aligned at the bottom of a
descender.

Figure 13.12 presents a graphical depiction of each option. After you have learned
these options, you can enter them directly at the `Justify/Style/<start point>:`
prompt, without first specifying the Justify option.

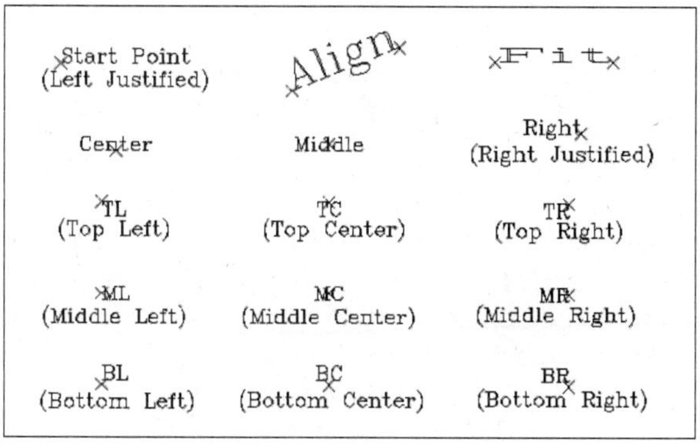

Figure 13.12

Text justification options.

The TL, TC, TR, ML, MC, MR, BL, BC, and BR justifications are the nine possible
combinations of the Top, Middle, and Bottom vertical alignments and the Left,
Center, and Right horizontal alignments. The default Left and the simple Center and
Right justifications all are baseline alignments, which could have fit into this same
matrix if B was not already taken by Bottom. You cannot use Fit, TL, TC, TR, ML, MC,
MR, BL, BC, and BR justified text with vertical text styles; the others work vertically or
horizontally.

Middle-justified text (unlike ML, MC, and MR) floats vertically, depending on
whether the particular text string includes uppercase characters or lowercase characters that extend below the line. The other options have three vertical positions
relative to a standard text cell height of a capital letter. The options TL, TC, TR, ML,
MC, MR, BL, BC, and BR each maintain vertical text positioning, regardless of the
string entered. Middle is designed to always be centered in both axes, for use in
bubbles, and similar applications. The other justifications are designed to give
consistent results for most other applications.

Tip If you respond to the DTEXT (or TEXT) start point prompt by pressing Enter, the new text starts one line below the last text you entered in the drawing. The new text assumes the height, style, and justification of the previous text, even if you have used intervening AutoCAD commands.

Formatting Paragraph-Style Text

When you use the MTEXT command to place paragraph-style text in a drawing, AutoCAD needs to know several of its properties. The initial prompt appears as follows:

```
Attach/Rotation/Style/Height/Direction/<Insertion point>:
```

Several options are available, as follows:

◆ **Attach.** This option controls the alignment of the text boundary to the insertion point. The Attach option issues the TL/TC/TR/ML/MC/MR/BL/BC/BR: attachment prompt, where T = top, M = middle, B = bottom, L = left, C = center, and R = right. TL (top left) is the default if you do not specify an attachment. You also can enter any of these attachment options directly at the <insertion point>: prompt without first using the Attach option. Attachment determines text justification and spill. Justification governs the text alignment to the left, center, or right of the text boundary, as in DTEXT. Spill manages the way excess text flows from the text boundary.

◆ **Rotation.** This option specifies the baseline angle of the text boundary.

◆ **Style.** This option specifies the default style used by the Mtext paragraph. The style must already have been created with the STYLE command.

◆ **Height.** This option specifies the default height of uppercase text for the Mtext paragraph.

◆ **Direction.** This option specifies the drawing direction (horizontal or vertical) of the paragraph text. In early versions of Release 13, vertical does not work correctly.

If you respond to the insertion point prompt, AutoCAD presents three additional options:

◆ **Width.** This option specifies the horizontal width of the text boundary. You can pick a point to indicate the width, or enter a width value.

New Riders Publishing
INSIDE
SERIES

◆ **2Points.** This option specifies the width of the text boundary, by specifying any two points.

The default style and height properties that the mtext paragraph uses are the current text settings stored in the TEXTSTYLE and TEXTSIZE system variables, which are set in the prototype drawing or by using the TEXT or DTEXT commands (you also can use the STYLE command to set the current style). You can use the MTEXT command's options to change the default style property which changes the value of the TEXTSTYLE system variable. The TEXTSIZE system variable is not affected by a change to the MTEXT command's Height option.

An important basic concept to grasp to understand how MTEXT works is that the mtext object has default *properties* (including style and height) but each character within the mtext object can have character *attributes* (including font and height) assigned to it, much like assigning italic or bold with a word processor.

In the following exercise, you use several options to place an MTEXT paragraph.

Using MTEXT Paragraph Insertion Options

Continue in the CHAP13 drawing from the preceding exercise. Zoom to the view shown in figure 13.13.

Command: *Choose* Draw, Text, Text	Issues the MTEXT command
`_mtext`	
`Attach/Rotation/Style/Height/Direction/` `<Insertion point>:` **A** (Enter)	Specifies the Attach option
`TL/TC/TR/ML/MC/MR/BL/BC/BR:` **BL** (Enter)	Specifies the bottom left attachment
`Attach/Rotation/Style/Height/Direction/` `<Insertion point>:` **H** (Enter)	Specifies the text Height option
`Height <0'-6">:` **4"** (Enter)	Changes text height to 4"
`Attach/Rotation/Style/Height/Direction/` `<Insertion point>:` *Pick* ① *(see* *fig. 13.13)*	Specifies the lower left corner
`Attach/Rotation/Style/Height/Direction/` `Width/2Points/<Other corner>:` *Pick* ②	Specifies width and launches the system editor

continues

continued

Type the following in the system editor
**Revise to meet handicapped accessibility
standards.** (Enter) **1) Lower lavatory** (Enter)
2) Specify C-type fixtures (Enter) **3)
Specify shower safety rails**,
*then save the file and exit
the system editor*

Save your drawing.

Figure 13.13

*Inserted
paragraph text.*

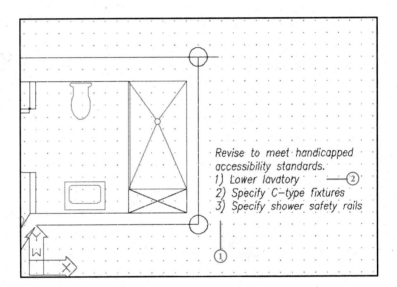

Using Special Characters with TEXT or DTEXT

Some symbols used in engineering drawings are not found on standard keyboards. These symbols include underscores, overscores, plus/minus, and so on. The coding methods that TEXT and DTEXT use differ from those used by MTEXT. To generate these symbols, you type special code entries that AutoCAD can translate, as shown in table 13.1.

TABLE 13.1
Special Characters with TEXT or DTEXT

Code Entry	Unicode Entry	Symbol Translation
%%O		Overscore
%%U		Underline
%%D	\U+00B0	Degree
%%C	\U+2205	Circle diameter
%%P	\U+00B1	Plus/minus

You can use the %%X codes only with TEXT or DTEXT. Now, you can use the Unicode codes with TEXT, DTEXT, or MTEXT. Unicode codes provide better international compatibility.

For example, to generate the character string

AutoCAD text entry has a <u>plethora</u> of options.

enter the following TEXT or DTEXT input:

Text: **AutoCAD text entry has a %%uplethora%%u of options.** (Enter)

You can enter the special character that follows the two percent signs in upper- or lowercase.

Note These special codes are not translated for PostScript fonts. International and special symbols, such as %%213, are properly translated by PostScript output; however, they do not appear on-screen translated.

In the following exercise, use DTEXT to dynamically enter multiple lines of text that include special symbols.

Using DTEXT Special Characters

Continue to use the CHAP13 drawing from the previous exercise, and zoom to the area shown in figure 13.14.

Command: *Choose* Draw, Text, Dynamic Text   Issues the DTEXT command

_dtext Justify/Style/   Specifies text insertion point

continues

continued

`<Start point>:` *Pick* ① *(see fig. 13.14)*

`Height <0'-6">: 4" `(Enter)	Specifies text height
`Rotation angle <0>: `(Enter)	Specifies baseline rotation
`Text: `**`Due to the nature of`** **`convalesince, `**(Enter)	Misspells first text line (see fig 13.14 and spaces down to next line
`Text: `**`do %%Unot%%U use 68%%D `**(Enter)	Specifies second text line, displaying %% codes
`Text: `**`thermostat setback. `**(Enter)	Specifies third text line,
`Text: `(Enter)	Completes DTEXT entry and redraws text with underline and degree symbol (see fig. 13.15)

Save the drawing.

Figure 13.14

DTEXT during text entry with special characters code.

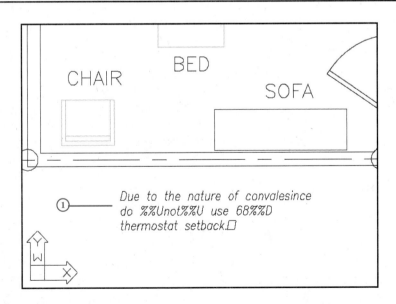

As you type DTEXT entries, AutoCAD displays the characters without modification or justification. When you press Enter for the final time on a separate line, AutoCAD translates any special character %% sequences and rejustifies the text as requested.

When you look at figures 13.14 and 13.15, you probably will notice a misspelled word. Don't worry—that was intentional. You use AutoCAD Release 13's new spelling checker to fix it later.

13

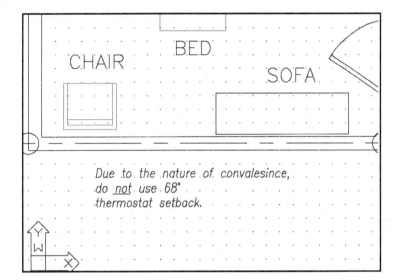

Figure 13.15

Completed DTEXT with formatted characters.

Controlling Text Display Quality and Speed

Adding many text objects to your drawing slows the performance of subsequent zooms, redraws, and regens. Filled PostScript or TrueType fonts and multistroke fonts, such as COMPLEX, are particularly slow to redraw and regenerate. To decrease regeneration time, AutoCAD offers two options for accelerating text display. The first alternative is to enter all text with styles that use a simple font, such as TXT, for initial drawing development or for test plotting. For the final plot, you can define the styles to a more elegant font, such as ROMANC. The second alternative is to use the QTEXT command. You use the QTEXT command to turn on the quick text display mode. This mode outlines the text object with a rectangle, but does not display the letters of the text string. The four lines used to display quick text is quicker to draw than each stroke of each letter of the text string. If your drawing is mostly composed of text, you should turn on the quick text mode to greatly reduce the time AutoCAD expends for zooms, pans, redraws, and regenerations. Be sure to turn off the quick text mode for plotting unless you intend to plot the text outlines.

QTEXT. The QTEXT (Quick TEXT) command enables you to control the screen and plotted appearance of text and attributes. When QTEXT is on, AutoCAD replaces text, dimensions, and attributes by approximating rectangles.

Pull-down: *Choose* Options, Display, Text Frame Only
Screen: *Choose* Options, DISPLAY, Qtext

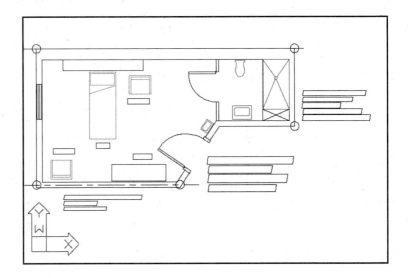

Figure 13.16

QTEXT turned on.

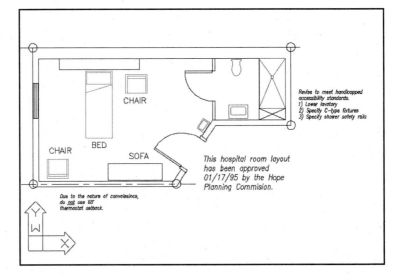

Figure 13.17

QTEXT turned off.

The Options, Display pull-down menu has four items that affect the display of text. The Filled Text, Outline Text, and Text Frame Only menu items are grouped to provide one of three possible settings to control the display of text. The fourth item, Text Quality, controls the resolution of the text. All of these settings apply to the graphics display and the plot. Use these settings to balance speed against quality.

Figure 13.18

The Options, Display pull-down menu and the text display menu items.

Text appears as filled text, outline text, or framed text. The QTEXT command was used to make framed text. Figure 13.19 shows filled text and figure 13.20 shows the same text as outline text. Most AutoCAD users work with outline text because filled text always takes more time to display and plot and because you cannot see the characters in framed text.

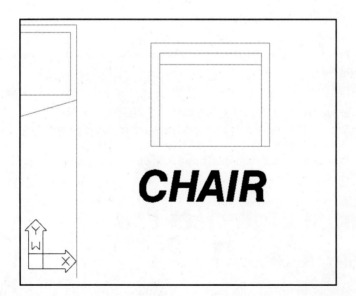

Figure 13.19

Text displayed as filled text.

Figure 13.20

Text displayed as outline text.

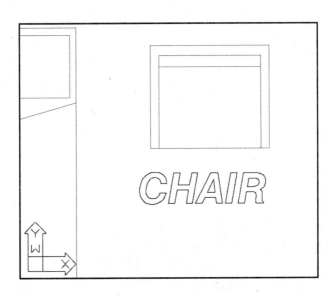

The Filled Text and Outline Text menu items enable you to control the TEXTFILL system variable. Only text, dtext, and mtext objects using styles with Adobe Type 1, Bitstream, or TrueType fonts are affected. You can set the TEXTFILL variable at the Command: prompt, use a value of 1 to display filled text, and use 0 to display outline text. Using the pull-down menu items also force framed text to be turned off by setting QTEXT. The Text Quality menu item sets the TEXTQLTY system variable. This variable sets the resolution of text objects that have styles derived from Adobe Type 1, Bitstream, or TrueType fonts. The values for this variable are whole numbers that range from 0 to 100. Use a lower value to increase display and plotting speed and decrease text resolution. A higher value increases text resolution but decreases display and plotting speed.

 Note   You do not see the effect of QTEXT, TEXTFILL, or TEXTQLTY until the next regeneration. You can use the REGEN command to force the regeneration.

The next section illustrates character formatting for MTEXT paragraphs.

Using Special Characters and Formats with MTEXT

MTEXT provides greater flexibility with formatting options than TEXT or DTEXT. You can apply several formatting properties and character attributes to MTEXT paragraphs. As you read the following, remember that an mtext object has global

New Riders Publishing
INSIDE SERIES

default *properties* (including style and height) but that you can assign overriding character *attributes* (including font and height) to each character within the mtext object.

AutoCAD accomplishes this by interpreting predefined format codes that it finds in the text file you create. There are many codes for various uses, such as underlines, colors, fonts, heights, and more. Unfortunately, this makes them cumbersome to use, although diligence and patience can yield great results. You can use your knowledge of format codes to create notes that have equations, construction notes, specifications, tables, and special effects.

The format codes control font selection, paragraph flow, and text characteristics. These codes are specific to mtext objects. You can use the following format codes in paragraph text:

◆ **\Ffontfilename;** Formats the text following this code with the font specified by *fontfilename* until another format code instructs otherwise

◆ **\~** Places a nonbreaking space in the text, which forces AutoCAD to keep the word immediately before and the word immediately after the code to remain on the same line

◆ **\P** Ends a paragraph

◆ **\Ooverlinetext\o** Draws *overlinetext* with an overline, where \O turns overline on and \o turns it off

◆ **\Ccolornumber;** Draws subsequent text using the color specified by *colornumber*

◆ **\Snumerator^denominator;** Creates stacked text in which the *numerator* appears immediately above the character box and the *denominator* appears along the text baseline

◆ **\Lunderlinetext\l** Draws *underlinetext* with an underline, where \L turns underline on and \l turns it off

◆ **\Htextheightvalue;** Uses *textheightvalue* as the text height for subsequent text

◆ **\Tcharacterspacevalue;** Adjusts the space between characters to *characterspacevalue*, where *characterspacevalue* is a factor, not an absolute distance, ranging from 0.75 to 4.0

◆ **\Qanglevalue;** Changes the obliquing angle of all subsequent text

◆ **\Wcharacterwidthvalue;** Widens each subsequent character by the factor specified by *characterwidthvalue*

Another powerful feature of format codes is that you can use braces ({}) to nest format codes. Use braces to limit the scope of the effect of format codes. For example,

```
{\C1;Not recommended} except when outside is not accessible.
```

draws the text, "Not recommended" using the color red (\C1), but subsequent text is not affected because it is not within the braces. Also, notice the semicolon, used to denote the end of the format code. Format codes that require a semicolon are shown above in the list.

Note The \, {, and } characters are characters that AutoCAD reserves for their special purpose in mtext objects. If you try to include them in your text, AutoCAD will discard them. To avoid this situation, prefix these characters with a \. Therefore, you would type \\ to have a single \ appear in your paragraph text.

In the following exercise, you use the MTEXT command to enter a paragraph that includes text stacking and character changes.

Using MTEXT Paragraph Formatting

Continue to use the CHAP13 drawing from the preceding exercise, turn off the grid, and zoom to a window from 7', 19' to 18' 6", 13'.

Command: *Choose* Options, Display, Filled Text	Turns off QTEXT and sets TEXTFILL to 1
Command: *Choose* Draw, Text, Text	Issues the MTEXT command
_mtext	
Attach/Rotation/Style/Height/Direction/ <Insertion point>: **7'6",18'0"** (Enter)	Specifies the upper left corner
Attach/Rotation/Style/Height/Direction/ Width/2Points/<Other corner>: **19'6", 16'9"** (Enter)	Specifies the paragraph width and starts the system editor
Type {\C5;\FSWISSBI.TTF;HOSPITAL ROOM LAYOUT}, \H3;by {\C12;{\SHIGH^LOW;} Associates} *then save and exit*	Enters text in the system editor and saves the text in a temporary file and draws the mtext object

The result is shown in figure 13.21. Carefully examine the text to determine how the format codes were applied.

Save the drawing.

New Riders Publishing
INSIDE SERIES

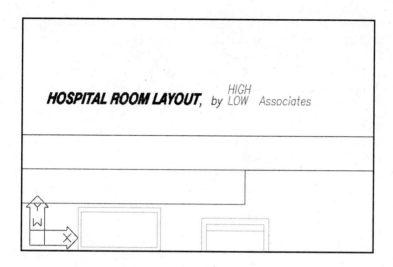

Figure 13.21

Completed MTEXT paragraph formatting.

13

Editing existing paragraph text works exactly the same as creating it. See the "Editing Paragraph Text" exercise later in this chapter for more examples of applying attributes and properties.

 Tip   Use the LIST command to examine the properties and font codes of an MTEXT object.

Editing Text

You must verify an AutoCAD drawing that contains both graphic objects and supporting text for technical accuracy. If the geometry is not consistent with the descriptive callouts, you lose the integrity of the design. Therefore, checking and rechecking the design must be thorough, yet cost-efficient. This section covers the various methods you can use to update existing textual information.

Using DDEDIT To Change Text

You can use the DDEDIT command to change the text contained in Text, Mtext, and Attribute Definition objects. Because the DDEDIT command does not honor the PICKFIRST system variable, you select the text after you enter the command. Once the text is selected, a dialog box is displayed. The type of object you select determines the type of dialog box. If you select an Mtext object, the system editor displays and you can edit your text using the features of your system editor.

If you select a text object, the Edit Text dialog box displays. The text displays in the Text: edit box, highlighted and with the cursor at the end of the text string. If you press a character, AutoCAD clears the text and begins a new text string. You can press the Home key to move the cursor to the beginning of the text string, then start making your corrections to prevent the loss of your text. Also, you can click in the box to precisely position the cursor at the character you must change. Choosing OK closes the dialog box and applies the change.

If you select an Attribute Definition object, the Edit Attribute Definition displays. In this dialog box, there are three edit boxes you use to correct tag, prompt, and values of the attribute. Refer to Chapter 16, "Basic Building Blocks for Repetitive Drawing," for more information concerning attributes.

The DDEDIT command continues to prompt for another text string to edit until you press Enter at the next selection prompt or cancel the command. You also can enter U to undo the previous change.

DDEDIT. The DDEDIT command prompts for a text, mtext, or attdef (attribute definition) object and then opens a dialog box or system editor appropriate to the text type you select. The DDEDIT command enables you to edit lines and paragraphs of text, and to modify block attribute definitions.

Pull-down: *Choose* Modify, Edit Text
Screen: *Choose* MODIFY, DDedit

Changing TEXT or DTEXT Objects

In the next exercise, you use DDEDIT to make a simple change to a line of text. You modify one of the furniture text labels.

Changing a Single Text Label

Continue to use the CHAP13 drawing from the preceding exercise. Pan the view so that one of the text objects labeled CHAIR appears.

Command: *Choose* Modify, Edit Text	Issues the DDEDIT command
_ddedit	
<Select a TEXT or ATTDEF object>/Undo: *Pick the text* CHAIR	Opens the Edit Text dialog box with the with the existing text highlighted (see fig. 13.22)
Type **RECLINER**, *then choose* OK	Closes dialog box, replaces text, and reprompts

New Riders Publishing
INSIDE
SERIES

```
<Select a TEXT or ATTDEF object>/        Exits the DDEDIT command
Undo: (Enter)
```

Save the drawing.

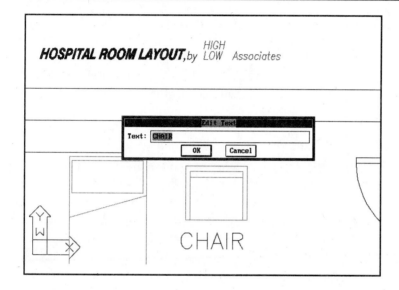

Figure 13.22

Replacing the CHAIR text object using the Edit Text dialog box.

Next, you use the DDEDIT command to edit an mtext object.

Changing MTEXT objects

In the next exercise, you use DDEDIT to change the content and format of a text paragraph. You change the phrase "hospital room" to "preliminary," underline the name "Hope Planning Commission," then change the width of the entire paragraph.

Editing Paragraph Text

Continue to use the CHAP13 drawing from the previous exercise. Restore the view named AAA.

Command: *Choose* Modify, Edit Text   Issues the DDEDIT command

`_ddedit`

```
<Select a TEXT or ATTDEF object>/Undo:    Opens the system editor with the
```
Pick the Hope Planning Commission   selected text displayed
paragraph

continues

continued

Replace the words hospital room *with the word* preliminary

Insert \L *before the* H *in* Hope, *then insert* \l *after the* n *in* commission	Specifies the underline format code for the words Hope Planning Commission
Save the file and exit the system editor	Displays the changed mtext object
`<Select a TEXT or ATTDEF object>/Undo:` (Enter)	Exits the DDEDIT command
`Command:` *Choose* Modify, Properties	
`Select objects:` *Select the* Hope Planning Commission *paragraph, then press Enter*	Selects the same mtext object, then issues the DDMODIFY command and opens the Modify MText dialog box
Choose the Edit <u>P</u>roperties *button*	Opens the MText Properties dialog box (see fig. 13.24)
Double-click in the Text Height *edit box, type* **4.0**, *then press Tab three times*	Changes the text height value to 4", then moves to the <u>W</u>idth: edit box
Type **80.0**, *then choose OK*	Closes the MText Properties dialog box
Choose OK	Closes the Modify MText dialog box and reformats the paragraph text

Save the drawing.

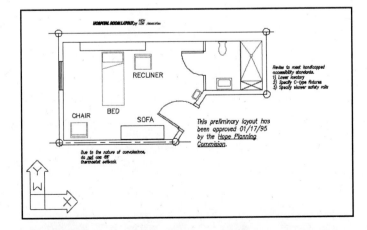

Figure 13.23

The corrected paragraph text.

New Riders Publishing
INSIDE
SERIES

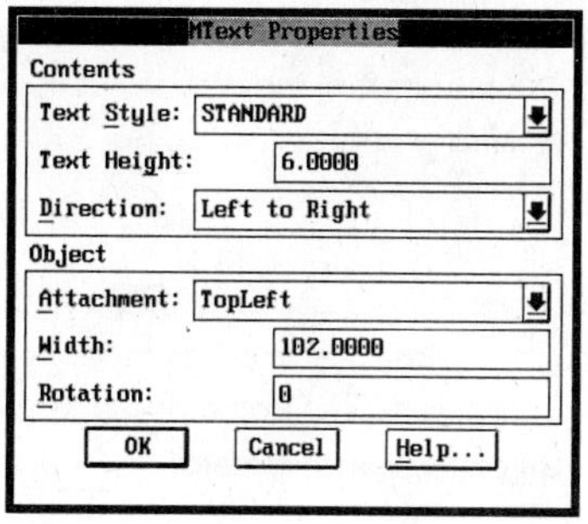

Figure 13.24

The MText Properties dialog box.

In the preceding exercise, you used the DDMODIFY command to modify the paragraph text. You can use this command when you need to change the text of the paragraph object (by choosing the <u>E</u>dit Contents button) and when you need to change the properties of the paragraph (by choosing the Edit <u>P</u>roperties button). The <u>E</u>dit Contents button links to the DDEDIT command and starts the system editor. The Edit <u>P</u>roperties button links to the MTPROP command and opens the Mtext Properties dialog box.

MTPROP. The MTPROP command enables you to change the properties of paragraph text. You can modify both the contents (text style, height, and direction) as well as the object boundary parameters (attachment, width, and rotation). MTPROP prompts you to select an mtext object, then opens the MText Properties dialog box.

Importing Text

So far, you have explored various methods for placing and editing text in a drawing. However, all the methods share a common text source —the keyboard. Occasionally, you need the capability to import text from an external file. For example, a secretary could type job specifications into a word processing document, save it as a plain ASCII file, then hand you the disk or, in a networked environment, load the file into a shared directory.

AutoCAD 13 for DOS provides no direct method to import text. You must use the MTEXT command and rely upon your skills with your system editor. Typically, once you were using your editor, you would open the file you need to import, copy it to a buffer, then paste it into the AutoCAD temporary file created by using the MTEXT command. This could be difficult, if not impossible, with some editors. If you need this capability, shop for a third party text editor to replace your system editor.

Stop In AutoCAD, you need to remember that the very versatile Import option in the File pull-down menu works only with graphic formats, not text.

 Stop If you exchange text files between Release 13 for DOS and Release 13 for Windows, you need two sets of files, one that has format codes and one that doesn't. Release 13 for Window's MTEXT command does not translate format codes. Therefore, the format codes become literal text.

After you place and edit your text, you are almost ready to print or plot your drawing. You should check your spelling first, though. For a long time, AutoCAD users bemoaned the lack of a built-in spelling checker. However, this latest release of AutoCAD makes this wish-list item a reality. The next section shows you how to use the AutoCAD Release 13 SPELL command.

Using the Spell Checker

The SPELL command enables you to verify the spelling of any selected text in your drawing. You can select a specific text object or you can select all of the objects displayed. AutoCAD reports the number of objects found and then displays the Check Spelling dialog box as shown in fig. 13.25. From this dialog box, you control the actions of the spell-checking process as AutoCAD finds words that are not contained in the current dictionary. You may cancel the process at any time.

Figure 13.25

The Check Spelling dialog box.

Check Spelling
Current dictionary: American English
Current word
xxUnotxxu
Suggestions:
Context
do xxUnotxxu use 68xxD

Cancel Help...

Ignore Ignore All
Change Change All
Add Lookup

Change Dictionaries...

New Riders Publishing
INSIDE SERIES

> **SPELL.** The SPELL command enables you to check the spelling of selected text, mtext, and attdef objects. The Check Spelling dialog box appears only if AutoCAD finds a questionable word. You can maintain custom dictionaries to minimize the unnecessary flagging of correctly spelled words.
>
> Pull-down: *Choose* Tools, Spelling
> Screen: *Choose* TOOLS, Spell

13

The spell-checking process is interactive—you must direct AutoCAD to accept a suggested change, ignore the suspicious word, look up related words, or add the word to a custom dictionary file. Also, you can refine how AutoCAD's spell checker checks recurring words. Recurring words can be changed or ignored. If your primary language is not English, you can select a different current dictionary. Words that are considered technical terms are stored in custom dictionaries. Custom dictionaries can also be used to store words that are not stored in the default American English dictionary.

The following dialog box items are available;

- ◆ **Current Word.** Displays the suspicious word.

- ◆ **Suggestions.** Displays the suggested word to use from the dictionary to replace the current word.

- ◆ **Context.** Displays the text string containing the current word.

- ◆ **Ignore.** Causes the check-spelling process to skip the current word and continue to the next suspicious word.

- ◆ **Change.** Replaces the current word with the suggested word.

- ◆ **Ignore All.** Causes the check-spelling process to skip all of the instances of the current word and continue to the next suspicious word.

- ◆ **Change All.** Replaces the current word and all of its instances with the suggested word.

- ◆ **Add.** Adds the current word to the custom dictionary.

- ◆ **Lookup.** Updates the **S**uggestions list box with words spelled similarly to the current word.

- ◆ **Change Dictionaries.** Displays the Change Dictionaries dialog box.

You use the Change Dictionaries button to display the Change Dictionaries dialog box (see fig. 13.26). This dialog box allows you to choose the main dictionary. AutoCAD provides three dictionaries: the American English, the British English (ise), and the British English (ize). Also, you can use this dialog box to create and/or modify your custom dictionaries. Words can be added to, or deleted from, any custom dictionary. It is your responsibility to create or obtain an appropriate custom dictionary file.

Figure 13.26

*The Change
Dictionaries
dialog box.*

 Note You must specify a custom dictionary filename before the **A**dd button in the Check Spelling dialog can be chosen. Use the Change **D**ictionaries button to open the Change Dictionaries dialog box. You must then type a file name in the **C**ustom dictionary edit box or use the **B**rowse button to select an existing custom dictionary file.

In the following exercise, you verify the spelling of the text in the hospital room layout drawing.

Using the Spell Checker

Continue to use the CHAP13 drawing.

Command: *Choose* Tools, Spelling	Issues the SPELL command
_spell	
Select objects: **ALL** ⟨Enter⟩	Selects all objects in drawing
81 found	Your count may slightly vary

New Riders Publishing
INSIDE
SERIES

`Select objects:` (Enter)	Ends selection and opens the Check Spelling dialog box (see fig. 13.25)

AutoCAD displays `%%Unot%%U` in the Current Word section—this code confuses the spell checker.

Choose Ignore	Skips to next word

AutoCAD displays the misspelled `convalesince` in the Current Word section, `convalesce` in the Suggestions box, and the correct `convalescence` in the Suggestions list box (see fig. 13.27).

Select convalescence, *then choose* Change	Corrects the spelling and continues to check each word

The spell checking continues until Change, Ignore, or Add each suspicious word. An AutoCAD Alert dialog box appears with a "Spelling check complete" message when all words have been checked.

Choose OK	Closes alert box and makes correction to drawing

Save the drawing

In the preceding exercise, you selected all objects in the drawing by simply typing **ALL** when prompted. Chapter 14, "The Ins and Outs of Editing," discusses the methods of selecting objects in more detail.

In this chapter, you learned that the TEXT, DTEXT, and MTEXT commands place lines or paragraphs of text into an AutoCAD drawing. Text also can be imported from external files. Using QTEXT optimizes the screen and plotted text display to roughly approximate the actual text characters.

The STYLE command customizes an existing font with parametric changes. The number and variety of styles are unlimited; truly to generate different strokes for different folks.

Formatting codes can be placed into text to generate special effects, either by character, line, or paragraph. The DDEDIT command is the primary method of editing text, whereas the MTPROP command alters the properties of paragraph-style text.

Finally, the new Release 13 SPELL feature is an extremely powerful tool to ensure that existing text is free of typographical errors.

The next chapter concentrates on the extensive set of tools available for selecting objects and editing graphic objects in drawings.

The Ins and Outs of Editing

Somebody said that the only thing constant in this world is change, and it is indeed true of engineering drawings—a change request invariably occurs before the drawing gets issued. Before you can use AutoCAD successfully and become a seasoned professional, therefore, you must become familiar with the program's editing functions. The benefits of electronic drawing editing are clear—as you master the commands and their options, you stay ahead of project changes without falling behind in your drawings.

In this chapter, you will learn about the following:

◆ The various methods of selecting objects for editing

◆ The MOVE and COPY commands

◆ Using UNDO to recover from mistakes

◆ Rotating objects using ROTATE and ALIGN

◆ Editing objects using the TRIM, EXTEND, and LENGTHEN commands

◆ How to change the size and shape of objects using STRETCH and SCALE

◆ How to group objects together

In the exercises up to this point, you spend most of the time creating new drawing objects. Chapter 8, "Object Selection and Grip Editing," explores several grip editing methods. AutoCAD, however, includes many more powerful and versatile modification commands and options. Figures 14.1 and 14.2 identify commands used to develop and refine the main exercise drawing for this chapter.

Figure 14.1

The CHAP14 drawing before editing.

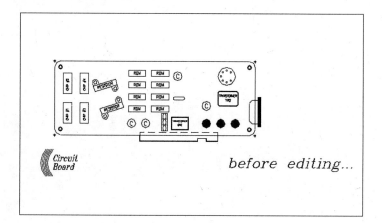

Figure 14.2

The CHAP14 drawing after editing.

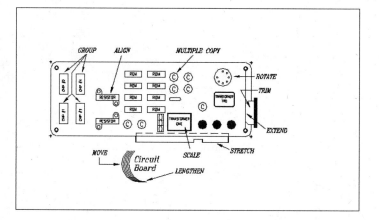

You perform three basic kinds of edits to drawings: changing, copying, and erasing objects. You can change an existing object's location, layer, and visual properties, such as color and linetype. You also can *break* objects by deleting portions of line and arc segments. Breaking an object reduces its length or divides it into multiple objects. You can copy objects singly or in a regular pattern. You also can erase objects to get rid of mistakes.

Most of AutoCAD's editing commands are gathered in the pull-down Modify menu. In addition, the Options pull-down menu includes the Selection item, which opens the Object Selection Settings dialog box. This latter dialog box was introduced in Chapter 8, and is covered in greater detail later in this chapter.

This chapter shows you how to change the spatial (location) properties of existing objects. Only a few basic editing commands are required to perform these simple functions. Chapter 15, "Object Modification, Inquiry, and Calculation," covers methods for changing the appearance (color and linetype) properties of existing objects.

Tip   If you want to practice individual editing commands as you work through the chapter, create a layer named SCRATCH. Create some objects on this layer, try out some editing variations, then freeze your SCRATCH layer and pick up again with the exercise sequences.

From a few simple geometric shapes, you generate a useful design with only edit commands. To appreciate the power and versatility of the various AutoCAD editing commands, try the Quick 5¢ Tour. Figure 14.3 shows the initial view of the drawing. During the exercise, refer to the figure for object snap locations.

Quick 5¢ Tour

Begin a new drawing named CHAP14, using EDIT1.DWG from the IA Disk as a prototype.

Command: *Choose* Modify, Align	Issues the ALIGN command
_align Initializing...	
Select objects: *Press and drag a window around the arrowhead and tail*	Selects objects with a window
5 found	
Select objects: (Enter)	Ends selection and proceeds
1st source point: *Use* INT *object snap to pick point* ① *(see fig. 14.3)*	Selects the first alignment source point
1st destination point: *Use* QUAdrant *object snap to pick point* ②	Selects the first alignment destination point

continues

continued

`2nd source point:` *Use* INT *object snap to pick point* ③	Selects the second alignment source point
`2nd destination point:` *Use* QUAdrant *object snap to pick point* ④	Selects the second alignment destination point
`3rd source point:` (Enter)	Ends point selection
`<2d> or 3d transformation:` (Enter)	Accepts default 2D alignment and performs edit

Figure 14.3

The TEST-ED1 drawing before editing.

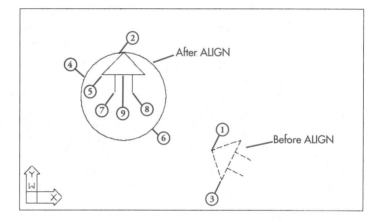

`Command:` *Choose* Modify, Scale	Issues the SCALE command
`_scale`	
`Select objects:` P (Enter)	Specifies the Previous selection
`5 found`	
`Select objects:` (Enter)	Ends selection and proceeds
`Base point:` @ (Enter)	Specifies the last picked point
`<Scale factor>/Reference:` R (Enter)	Specifies the Reference option
`Reference length <1>:` @ (Enter)	Sets first point of reference length

New Riders Publishing
INSIDE
SERIES

`Second point:` *Use* INT *object snap to pick point* ⑤ *on the relocated arrowhead*	Specifies the reference length
`New length:` *Use* QUAdrant *object snap to pick point* ④	Specifies length and selection by ratio of lengths
`Command:` *Choose* Modify, Extend	Issues the EXTEND command
`_extend`	
`Select boundary edges: (Projmode = UCS, Edgemode = No extend)`	
`Select objects:` *Pick the circle at* ⑥	Specifies the boundary for extensions
`1 found`	
`Select objects:` (Enter)	Ends selection and proceeds
`<Select object to extend>/Project/ Edge/Undo:` *Pick each of the lines at* ⑦ *and* ⑧	Extends each line to meet the circle
`<Select object to extend>/Project/ Edge/Undo:` (Enter)	Terminates the EXTEND command
`Command:` *Choose* Modify, Trim	Issues the TRIM command
`_trim`	
`Select cutting edges: (Projmode = UCS, Edgemode = No extend)`	
`Select objects:` *Press and drag a crossing window through the arrowhead tail*	Selects the two lines of the tail
`2 found`	
`Select objects:` (Enter)	Ends selection and proceeds
`<Select object to trim>/Project/ Edge/Undo:` *Pick the line between the tail lines at* ⑨	Trims the line

continues

continued

```
<Select object to trim>/Project/          Terminates the TRIM command
Edge/Undo: Enter
```

Your drawing should now resemble a "north arrow" symbol, as shown in figure 14.4.

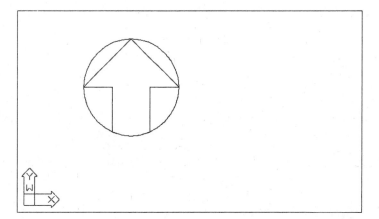

Figure 14.4

The CHAP14 drawing after editing.

How Editing Selection Works

Most editing commands involve deciding what kind of edit you want to do, which objects you want to edit, and how you want to edit them. The steps are as follows:

1. Issue the editing command

2. Select the objects

3. Enter the appropriate parameters and pick points

4. The edit occurs

With most editing commands, the order of the first two steps depends on whether you prefer noun/verb editing or verb/noun editing.

Noun/Verb versus Verb/Noun Selection

Noun/verb means that the objects (the nouns) are selected at the `Command:` prompt (as you did in Chapter 8 for grip editing) before the verb (the command or autoedit mode) is issued. *Verb/noun* means the command is issued, then the objects are selected at the `Select objects:` prompt.

Note Although most editing commands work well with noun/verb selection, some editing commands, such as FILLET and TRIM, ignore selections made prior to the command.

When you select objects at the Command: prompt and then issue most editing commands, such as MOVE, AutoCAD accepts the selected objects, skips the command's Select objects: prompt, and enters the command's editing mode. This is noun/verb editing.

When you issue most editing commands without objects selected, AutoCAD enters object selection, displaying the Select objects: prompt. At this prompt, you tell AutoCAD which objects you want to edit. When you complete object selection, AutoCAD enters the command's editing mode. This is verb/noun editing.

The following exercise demonstrates both the noun/verb and verb/noun selection methods with ERASE, AutoCAD's simplest editing command.

Noun/Verb and Verb/Noun Editing

Begin a new drawing named CHAP14A, using TOOLPLAT from the IA Disk as a prototype.

Command: *Choose* Modify, Erase	Issues the ERASE command and prompts for selection
_erase	
Select objects: *Pick the circle at* ① *(see fig. 14.5)*	Selects the circle
Select objects: *Hold down Shift while picking the cicle at* ②, *and while selecting a window from* ③ *to* ④	Adds the circle and the radial slot to the selections
Select objects: (Enter)	Erases the objects
Command: U (Enter)	Restores the objects
Command: *Select the circles and the slot again, then choose* Modify, Erase	Highlights selected objects and displays grips, then issues the ERASE command and erases the selections without additional input
erase 6 found	

Figure 14.5

*Selection points
for editing.*

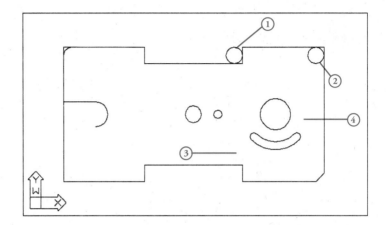

Verb/noun editing is always available. Noun/verb selection with editing commands is enabled by the **N**oun/Verb Selection setting in the Object Selection Settings dialog box, which is discussed in the next section. The default is on. The availability of noun/verb editing with grips and autoediting modes is controlled by the **E**nable Grips setting in the Grips dialog box (see Chapter 8), regardless of the **N**oun/Verb Selection setting. The default for **E**nable Grips is on.

There are several other aspects of object selection behavior that you can control.

Setting Object Selection Behavior

Object selection behavior, including the availability of noun/verb editing for editing commands, is controlled by the Object Selection Settings dialog box (see fig. 14.6).

Figure 14.6

*The Object
Selection Settings
and Object Sort
Method dialog
boxes.*

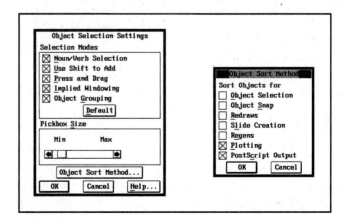

> **'DDSELECT.** The 'DDSELECT command displays the Object Selection Settings dialog box. You use this dialog box to set object selection behavior, the pickbox size, and to control the sorting of objects.
> Pull-down: *Choose* Options, Selection
> Screen: *Choose* OPTIONS, DDselec

Object Selection Settings Options

The controls in the Object Selection Settings dialog box are described in the following list:

- **Noun/Verb Selection.** For most editing commands, this setting enables selection of objects at the Command: prompt when turned on (the default). Its setting is stored in the PICKFIRST system variable (ON=1, OFF=0). Setting Noun/Verb Selection to on adds versatility to editing by allowing both noun/verb and verb/noun object selection methods. The crosshair cursor includes a pickbox at the Command: prompt when either grips (see Chapter 8) or Noun/Verb Selection is turned on, but if Noun/Verb Selection is turned off, the only method available to editing commands is verb/noun—selection at the Select objects: prompt.

- **Use Shift To Add.** When Use Shift to Add is on, additional objects selected by picking or implied windowing replace the previous selection set and start a new one. When on, objects selected while holding down Shift and picking or using implied windowing adds them to the existing selection. To remove previously selected objects from the selection set, hold down Shift as you pick or use implied windowing to select them. If you use Shift and an implied window to select both unselected and previously selected objects, the unselected ones are added and none are removed.

  When Use Shift to Add is off, objects are automatically added to the selection set as they are chosen. To remove previously selected objects from the selection set, hold down Shift as you select them. If you use Shift as you pick or use implied windowing to select both unselected and previously selected objects, the unselected ones are ignored and the previously selected ones removed.

  This setting is stored in the PICKADD system variable. When Use Shift to Add is off, PICKADD is on (1); when Use Shift to Add is on, PICKADD is off (0). See the Adding and Removing objects section of this chapter for more details and examples.

- **Press and Drag.** To make a a window or crossing selection, if Press and Drag is on, you press the pick button at the first corner point, move (drag) the cursor to the opposite corner point, then release. If it is off (the default), a separate pick is required for each corner point. Other window specifications, such as for ZOOM, always require two picks and are unaffected by this setting. This also affects clearing of a noun/verb selection and grips at the Command: prompt—if on, one pick clears grips and one pick clears a selection; but if off, two picks are required to clear grips and two more to clear a selection. The setting is stored in the PICKDRAG system variable (1=on, 0=off).

◆ **Implied Windowing.** If Implied Windowing is on (the default), a pick (or the press of a press-and-drag selection) at the Select objects: prompt selects an object, if any are in the pickbox. If no object is in the pickbox, the pick (or press) starts a selection window. If Implied Windowing is off, the pick (or press) either selects an object or returns a 0 found message. If off, you must use the Window or Crossing selection options to make window selections (see the "Building the Selection Set" section later in this chapter). This setting does not affect noun/verb selection at the Command: prompt, which always behaves as if Implied Windowing is on. This setting is stored in the PICKAUTO system variable (1=on, 0=off).

◆ **Object Grouping.** If Object Grouping is on, groups are selectable (selecting a member selects its group—see the "Grouping Objects" section at the end of this chapter). If off, groups are not selectable. This setting is stored in the PICKSTYLE system variable (on=1, off=0). This system variable also enables associative hatch selection (2 is hatch only, and 3 is both groups and hatches).

◆ **Default.** The Default button restores AutoCAD's initial default Selection Modes: all modes on except Use Shift to Add, and Press and Drag.

◆ **Pickbox Size.** Drag the slider box or click on the slider bar or arrows to set pickbox size from 1 to 20 pixels. The current size is indicated to the right of the slider. The size is stored in the PICKBOX system variable, which can directly set the size from 0 to 32,767 pixels. The size is the pixel distance from the crosshairs to the pickbox.

◆ **Object Sort Method.** The Object Sort Method button opens the Object Sort Method dialog box (see the following "Controlling Object Sorting" section in this chapter).

Press and Drag and Implied Windowing work well together. Without Press and Drag on, Implied Windowing can be a nuisance, because an accidental pick always either selects an object or starts a selection window.

 Note   From Chapter 8 on, the exercises in this book are written with the assumption that all Selection Modes are on (checked) in the Object Selection Settings dialog box.

New Riders Publishing
INSIDE SERIES

You can tailor object selection by varying the pickbox size. A large size makes selection quick and sloppy, and a small setting makes picking slower and more precise. You also can change the pickbox size transparently in the middle of a command by entering **'PICKBOX**, and then entering a new value. If you use the system variable to set it, you can set a 0 size pickbox for pinpoint accuracy.

Controlling Object Sorting

AutoCAD provides options for processing objects in their creation order. You can use these sort options if your drawing or application depends on the order in which objects were created. For example, the controller for a CNC milling machine critically depends on the vertex order of generated polylines to cut or route the proper tool paths.

AutoCAD Release 12 and later uses an oct-tree (octal tree) method of sorting the data base. This sometimes affects object selection. The newer oct-tree method sorts, selects, displays, and outputs objects in a grid arrangement of rectangular areas, whereas the older sort method favored the most recently created objects to process. These areas are visually evident during a complex redraw or regen because AutoCAD redraws or regenerates each area in sequence. By localizing the processing, AutoCAD optimizes tasks such as object selection and object snapping.

Tip To see the effect of an oct-tree sort, create a 50-row-by-60-column array of circles and perform a ZOOM All. (Refer to Chapter 18, "Constructive Editing," for details on the ARRAY command.)

Usually, the order of the objects is not important. You can use the Object Sort Method dialog box (refer to fig. 14.6), however, to override oct-tree sorting and consider the order of creation for specific operations.

To open the Object Sort Method dialog box, choose the Object Sort Method button from the Object Selection Settings dialog box (refer to fig. 14.6). A checked box indicates object creation sorting; an unchecked box (the default) indicates oct-tree sorting. The operations affected by the sorting method are as follows:

◆ **Object Selection.** If several objects fall within the pickbox and oct-tree sorting is in effect, it is difficult to predict which object will be selected. Under object creation sorting, the most recent object will be found. When you are editing recently created objects, as is often the case, setting oct-tree off will help select them. When making a window or crossing selection with oct-tree on, objects will be selected in an unpredictable order. With oct-tree off, they will be selected in the reverse of the creation order.

◆ **Object Snap.** As with Object Selection, oct-tree affects locating objects when using object snap. Turn it off when you use the QUIck object snap option if you want to reliably find the most recently drawn objects.

◆ **Redraws.** If the order in which objects appear during a redraw matters to you, turn oct-tree off to make them redisplay in creation sequence. Because many zooms merely redraw rather than regenerate, this might be an advantage. If, for example, you first draw a basic part outline, framework, or building grid in your drawings, you can use it to locate your zooms. With oct-tree off, any initial outline, framework, or grid appears first. You can do a rough zoom, cut the zoom short with Esc, and then zoom more precisely, using the outline, frame-work, or grid. With oct-tree on, the order of appearance is less predictable.

◆ **Slide Creation.** As with redraws, oct-tree controls the order of appearance of objects in slides created by using MSLIDE. This order is often important in a complex slide; a presentation might look odd if all the windows of a building appear before the wall outlines.

◆ **Regens.** As with redraws, oct-tree controls the order of appearance of objects during regens. See the preceding Redraw discussion.

◆ **Plotting.** Because AutoCAD's plot routine, and many plotters, perform their own vector sorting, oct-tree is generally not important here. If you plot to an image file format, however, you might want to control the order of appearance, as discussed in the preceding Slide Creation option.

◆ **PostScript Output.** As with slides and image file plotting, set oct-tree off if you need to control the order of appearance in the PostScript file.

Setting oct-tree off for any option causes only that option's operations to use old-style sorting; other operations still use oct-tree sorting. The SORTENTS system variable stores the current oct-tree sort setting; see Appendix F, "System Variables Table," for more information.

Building the Selection Set

AutoCAD offers more than a dozen ways to collect objects for editing. You can, for example, pick individual objects or enclose multiple objects within a window. As you select objects, AutoCAD sets up a temporary selection set and highlights the objects by temporarily changing their colors, making them blink, or giving them dotted lines. This highlighting confirms the objects that you have selected. You can enter any valid selection or selection option at the `Select objects:` prompt. If you enter invalid input, AutoCAD prompts you with all the available modes and reissues the `Select objects:` prompt, as follows:

```
Expects a point or
Window/Last/Crossing/BOX/ALL/Fence/WPolygon/CPolygon/Group/Add/
Remove/Multiple/Previous/Undo/AUto/SIngle
Select objects:
```

After you select all the objects you want, press Enter to end object selection and continue with the editing command.

Verb/noun editing is always available. Noun/verb selection with editing commands is enabled by the Noun/Verb Selection setting in the Object Selection Settings dialog box, which is discussed in the next section. The default is on. The availability of noun/verb editing with grips and autoediting modes is controlled by the Enable Grips setting in the Grips dialog box (see Chapter 8), regardless of the Noun/Verb Selection setting. The default for Enable Grips is on.

There are several other aspects of object selection behavior that you can control.

SELECT. The SELECT command enables you to select objects and build a selection set that you can later recall by using the Previous object selection option. SELECT lets you use all the selection options.
Pull-down: *Choose Assist, Select Objects*
Screen: *Choose ASSIST, Select*

The Select Objects Options and Methods

AutoCAD provides many ways to add objects to a selection set, as follows:

- ◆ **Object pick.** Enables you to pick individual objects. This method is the default. As you pick, AutoCAD finds the most recently created object that falls within or crosses the pick box. If you use snap and object snap together, AutoCAD snaps first, then performs the object snaps from that snapped point.

- ◆ **Window.** Selects objects within a window you specify. AutoCAD selects only those objects that are enclosed entirely within the window. AutoCAD considers lines that the window edge overlaps to be within this window. Technically, window selection selects an object which partially extends outside the current viewport if its entire visible portion is within or overlapped by the window; however, it is difficult to specify such a window. If Implied Windowing is on in the Object Selection Settings dialog box, you can select a window without first specifying the Window option.

- ◆ **Last.** Selects the last object created that is visible in the drawing window.

- ◆ **Crossing.** Works the same as Window, except that Crossing also selects any objects that are partially within, crossing, or touching the window. If Implied

Windowing is on, you can select a crossing window without specifying the Crossing option.

◆ **BOX.** Combines Window and Crossing into a single selection. Picking the points of your box from left to right produces a Window selection; picking from right to left produces a Crossing selection.

◆ **ALL.** Selects all objects in the drawing that are not on locked or frozen layer.

◆ **Fence.** Enables you to draw an open, multiple-point fence with which to select objects. All objects touched by the fence are selected.

◆ **Wpolygon.** This method is similar to Window selection but enables you to draw an irregular closed polygon to select objects. All objects completely within the polygon are selected.

◆ **Cpolygon.** This method is similar to the Crossing selection but enables you to draw an irregular closed polygon to select objects. All objects inside of or crossed by the polygon are selected.

◆ **Group.** Enables you to include a predefined group of objects by a specified name. (The GROUP command is covered later in this chapter.)

◆ **Remove.** Switches to Remove mode, so that you can remove selected objects from the selection set (not from the drawing). The Remove mode acts the same regardless of the setting of the Use Shift to Add setting in the Object Settings dialog box—picking a previously selected object removes it from the selection set. Picking unselected objects in the Remove mode has no effect. Previously selected objects, however, can be removed from the selection set without using the Remove option by simply holding the Shift key while picking them.

◆ **Add.** Switches from Remove mode back to normal, so that you again can add objects to the selection set, according to the setting of the PICKADD system variable.

◆ **Multiple.** Enables you to pick multiple objects in close proximity and speeds up selection by enabling you to make multiple selections without highlighting or prompting. Pressing Enter an extra time is required to complete the multiple selection and return to normal object selection.

◆ **Previous.** Selects the entire preceding selection set (from a previous command) as the current selection set. Previous does not recognize selections made at the Command: prompt for autoediting with grips.

◆ **Undo.** Undoes or reverses the last selection operation. Each **U** undoes one selection operation.

◆ **AUto.** Combines individual selection with the BOX selection. This selection performs the same as BOX, except that if the first pick point finds an object, that single object is selected and the BOX mode is aborted. This method is always available without entering **AU** if I̲mplied Windowing is on in the Object Selection Settings dialog box.

◆ **SIngle.** Works in conjunction with the other selection options. If you precede a selection with SIngle, object selection automatically ends as soon as an object is detected; pressing Enter to confirm is not required.

When do you use which mode? The default option, picking objects, is fast and simple, even for picking three or four objects, and it requires no mode setting. Selecting by window and crossing window are also always available without having to enter a **W** or **C** if I̲mplied Windowing is turned on in the Object Selection Settings dialog box. Last and Undo are obvious. Previous is great for repeated operations on the same set of objects, like a copy and rotate operation. The Wpolygon, Cpolygon, and Fence options are powerful tools for building complex selection sets, particularly when you must make the selections in a crowded area of the drawing. These selections take longer to specify than the Window and Crossing, but are more flexible and can save steps.

Note The selection set options BOX, AUto, and SIngle are primarily for use in menus. They offer no real advantages over the other options discussed in the preceding list when specifying modes by the keyboard.

Sometimes objects are so close to each other that you cannot pick the one you want; additional picks simply locate the same object over and over again.

In older versions of AutoCAD, you used Multiple and picked repeatedly to find multiple objects within the pickbox. Because each additional pick added objects to the selection set, however, you then had to remove any undesired objects—a tedious process.

AutoCAD Release 13 now supports object selection cycling. To obtain a single object in a crowded area, press Ctrl while picking repeatedly. Objects within the pickbox then highlight one at a time with each pick. When AutoCAD selects the desired object, simply release Ctrl, then press Enter—you now have the object you want.

Note Some editing commands, such as FILLET, TRIM, and EXTEND, require that you select a single object during the prompting sequence. In these cases, you must select by picking instead of using Crossing, Window, and so on.

You will use most of the preceding selection methods and options in the rest of this chapter and in subsequent chapters. First, you will take a better look at one of the most commonly used editing commands, MOVE, then use it as you further explore selection.

Exploring Selection and Editing with the MOVE Command

Because the MOVE command is a fairly typical editing command, it is used in the following sections to explore further object selection and editing. The MOVE command is one of the simplest editing commands to use. To move an object, you select it and issue the MOVE command, or vice versa, then specify the object's new location. Although the options for specifying the new location are unique to this command, the way you go about selecting objects for the MOVE command is typical of the way commands that prompt you to Select objects: work.

MOVE. The MOVE command relocates objects in 2D or 3D. You are prompted to specify two points, or a displacement. If you specify two points, the angle and distance from the first to the second point indicates the displacement for the move. Alternatively, if you specify a coordinate value (either X,Y or X,Y,Z, or polar or spherical) at the first prompt, Base point or displacement:, and then press Enter at the Second point of displacement: prompt, the specified coordinate value is interpreted as the displacement for the move. You move the logo using a window selection. The destination point (second point of displacement) is near the bottom center of the board. You will use verb/noun selection and two points to indicate displacement, then verb/noun selection and a displacement value.

Pull-down: *Choose Modify, Move*
Screen: *Choose MODIFY, Move*

Stop   To specify a displacement, type it as **2,3** for an X,Y displacement or **2<30** for a polar displacement. Do not enter it with an @ sign, (**@2,3** or **@2<30**) or you will get unexpected results, because you will have specified a point relative to the last point instead of a displacement value. You will probably get unexpected results if you pick a point at the Base point or displacement: prompt, then press Enter at the second prompt. In both cases, the displacement will be the distance and angle from 0,0 to the point you specified and the results often move the object out of the visible drawing area. If this happens, Undo and try again.

New Riders Publishing
INSIDE
SERIES

In the following exercise, you use the MOVE command to relocate the logo in the circuit board drawing. You move the logo using a window selection. The destination point (`second point_of displacement`) is near the bottom center of the board. You will use verb/noun selection, and two points to indicate displacement, then noun/verb selection and a displacement value.

Using MOVE To Reposition the Logo

Begin a new drawing named CHAP14B, using the BOARD2 drawing from the IA Disk as a prototype.

Command: *Choose* Modify, Move	Issues the MOVE command (verb)
Select objects: **?** (Enter)	Specifies invalid selection option
Invalid selection	
Expects a point or Window/Last/Crossing/BOX/ALL/Fence/ WPolygon/CPolygon/Group/Add/Remove/ Multiple/Previous/Undo/AUto/SIngle	Displays list of valid options
Select objects: **W** (Enter)	Specifies Window option
First corner: *Pick at* ① *(see fig. 14.7)*	Starts a window
Other corner: *Drag to* ② *and release*	Completes window and selects objects (noun)
8 found	
Select objects: (Enter)	Ends selection and enters edit mode
Base point or displacement: *Pick* ③ *point near the logo*	Specifies base point
Second point of displacement: *Drag and pick the crosshairs at* ④	Specifies second point of displacement and moves the object
Command: **U** (Enter)	Undoes the previous MOVE command
Command: *Select the logo with an implied window selection from* ① *to* ②	Selects the objects (noun)

continues

continued

`Command:` *Choose* Modify, Move	Issues the MOVE command (verb) with the objects selected
`move 8 found`	
`Base point or displacement:` **3.1<0** ⏎	Specifies a displacement
`Second point of displacement:` ⏎	Accepts displacement and moves the logo

Save the drawing.

Figure 14.7

Moving the circuit board logo.

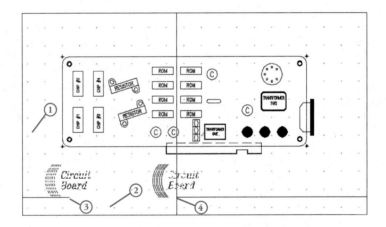

If you have set Implied Windowing on, you did not actually have to use the Window option to select a window. Sometimes, however, using the Window or Crossing option explicitly is essential. With Implied Windowing, picking selects an object (if any) within the pickbox. If such an object exists at the corner of the window selection area, it will be selected by the pickbox rather than the point starting a selection. To override this behavior, you must use the W or C options before you make your selection.

Object selection and moving is easy. After you select the logo with a window, the objects highlight. With verb/noun selection, you stop collecting objects by pressing Enter in response to the `Select objects:` prompt. With noun/verb selection, the command immediately enters editing mode. Then, pick your displacement points, and your logo moves.

You also can use move grip autoedit mode to move objects. See Chapter 8 for the use of grips autoedit modes.

New Riders Publishing

INSIDE SERIES

AutoCAD offers several alternative methods to perform the same task. In the case of a move operation, you can choose between many ways to define the distance, or *displacement*. The next section further explains the various techniques.

Displacement and Drag

The use of the MOVE command involves specifying a displacement. If you know the absolute X,Y, or polar displacement, you can enter it at the Base point or displacement: prompt. Entering **3.2,0** or **3.1<0** (do not preface the displacement with an @), for example, duplicates the second move made in the previous exercise. Press Enter, instead of entering a value, at the Second point: prompt to tell AutoCAD to use the first value as an absolute offset.

Often, you want to show a displacement by entering two points. Think of the first point (base point) as a handle on the selection set. The second point, then, specifies the new location for this handle and the selection set relative to it. The *displacement* is an imaginary line from the base point to the second point. AutoCAD calculates the differences between the base and second points. The new location of the object(s) is determined by adding this displacement to its current location. For visual confirmation, AutoCAD shows a rubberband line from the first point to the second, during the command.

Tip When you set a base point, try to pick one that is easy to visualize (and remember). Use a corner point for rectangular objects, a center point for circular objects, and appropriate object snap points for all other types of geometry. Otherwise, you appear to be carrying the selection set around without touching it.

Large selection sets may not drag well. You can turn dragging on or off by using the DRAGMODE command.

> **DRAGMODE.** The DRAGMODE command controls when AutoCAD drags an image of objects as you place them. The default DRAGMODE setting is Auto, which causes AutoCAD to drag everything, wherever possible. Setting DRAGMODE to on drags only when you enter **DRAG** during a command where dragging is possible. Turning DRAGMODE off disables dragging entirely. The DRAGMODE setting is stored in the DRAGMODE system variable (0=off, 1=on, and 2=Auto).
> Screen: *Choose* OPTIONS, Dragmod

Adding and Removing Objects from the Selection Set

AutoCAD's selection options include Add and Remove modes. Starting with Release 12, however, you rarely need to use Add or Remove. You can control adding and removing objects in the selection set using only the Shift key and picking, or the implied windowing methods.

If you turn on the Use Shift to Add setting in the Object Selection Settings dialog box, as is the book's assumed setting from Chapter 8, anything you select by picking, an implied window, or crossing box replaces the current selection set. To add objects to the selection set, press the Shift key while selecting them. To remove already selected objects from the selection set, just select them again by picking, an implied window, or crossing box while pressing the Shift key. If you press Shift and make a selection that includes both already selected and newly selected objects, the newly selected ones are added but the already selected ones are not removed.

If you have the Use Shift to Add setting off, as is the book's assumed setting up until Chapter 8, anything you select by any method without pressing Shift is added to the current selection set and anything you select by picking, an implied window, or crossing box while pressing Shift is removed from the current selection set.

Although adding and removing objects from the selection set might seem simpler with the Use Shift to Add setting off, you will probably find that, with practice, Use Shift to Add setting on is more efficient. The choice is yours.

To remove selections with options other than by picking, an implied window, or crossing box (such as CPolygon, Previous, Last, or Fence), you need to use the Remove option. To enter Remove mode, you enter an **R** (for Remove) at the `Select objects:` prompt. When the `Remove objects:` prompt appears, remove objects from the selection set by using any type of object selection. To exit Remove mode and again add to the selection set, you need to use the Add option. Add mode is the default, indicated by the `Select objects:` prompt. Enter an **A** to return to Add mode.

Adding and removing objects from the selection set is demonstrated in the next exercise, after you explore a few more options.

Using the Previous Selection Option

The Previous selection option is helpful when you cancel an editing command or use several commands on the same selection set. Previous object selection reselects the object(s) you selected in your most recent editing command.

Previous enables you to edit the preceding set without having to select its objects individually again. Note that Previous is different from Last, which selects the most recently created object visible in the drawing area.

Tip The Previous option is useful for removing specific objects from a difficult selection—if you plan ahead. You sometimes, for example, can turn off certain layers to simplify selection—use the SELECT command to create a selection set of objects you want to remove from a later selection set, then turn the layers back on, make the major selection, and finally use Remove mode and Previous to remove the previous selection from the current selection set.

Keeping Track of the Selection Set

Every time you select objects at the `Select objects:` prompt, AutoCAD shows the number you select and the number it actually finds. These numbers do not always match for two reasons. First, you can select objects that do not qualify for editing. When you are in model space, for example, ALL finds but then rejects paper space objects. In most cases, AutoCAD reports the number of objects rejected and the reason for their rejection. Second, you might already have selected an object. In the latter case, AutoCAD informs you that it found a duplicate. In all cases (except multiple mode selections), AutoCAD uses highlighting to show you what is currently in the selection set. Feel free to change the color of layers in the exercise drawing to better see the highlighting of selections.

Tip In a complex drawing, you might notice the time it takes AutoCAD to search through the drawing file for objects that qualify for the selection set. To expedite the selection of large selection sets, turn off the HIGHLIGHT system variable, enter **HIGHLIGHT**, and set it to 0 (off). If you operate in this mode, select carefully because you cannot tell which objects are selected. Highlight off is useful for selecting large, easily defined portions of the drawing. Also, consider using the DDSELECT dialog box to set Object Sort Method to fit your selection situation. (Object Sort is discussed later in this chapter.)

Using the COPY Command

The COPY command is similar to the MOVE command. The only differences between a copy and a move are that COPY leaves the original objects in place and provides a multiple option.

COPY. The COPY command copies objects in 2D or 3D. It works like the MOVE command, except the original objects remain unchanged. You are prompted to specify two points or a displacement. If you specify two points, the angle and distance from the first to the second point indicates the displacement for the copy. Alternatively, if you specify a coordinate value (either X,Y or X,Y,Z, or polar or spherical) at the first prompt, `Base point or displacement:`, and then press Enter at the `Second point of displacement:` prompt, the specified coordinate value is interpreted as the displacement for the copy. In addition, you can use the Multiple option to make several copies, specifying a single base point with repeated displacement points.

Pull-down: *Choose* Construct, Copy
Screen: *Choose* CONSTRCT, Copy

The Multiple option of the COPY command enables you to copy the contents of your selection set several times without having to respecify the selection set and base point. If you respond to the `Base point or displacement:` prompt by entering **M**, AutoCAD reprompts for base point, then repeatedly prompts you for multiple second point of displacement points. Press Enter or Esc to get out of the Multiple loop.

In the following exercise, you use a Fence selection with the COPY Multiple option to generate several copies of one of the circuit board's capacitors. The capacitors are the circles with Cs in them.

Using COPY To Duplicate the Capacitors

Continue in the CHAP14B drawing from either of the previous two exercises.

Command: *Choose* Construct, Copy	Issues the COPY command
_copy	
Select objects: **F** (Enter)	Specifies Fence option
First fence point: *Pick* ① *(see fig. 14.8)*	Specifies first fence point
Undo/<Endpoint of line>: *Pick* ②	Specifies next fence point
Undo/<Endpoint of line>: (Enter)	Ends fence specifications
2 found	Selects objects touching fence
Select objects: (Enter)	Terminates object selection

New Riders Publishing
INSIDE
SERIES

`<Base point or displacement>/` `Multiple:` **M** (Enter)	Specifies Multiple option
`Base point:` *Pick* ③	Specifies copy base point
`Second point of displacement:` `@0.5<0` (Enter)	Specifies offset to location of first copy
`Second point of displacement:` `@0.4<270` (Enter)	Specifies offset to location of third copy
`Second point of displacement:` `7.3,6.8` (Enter)	Specifies location for third copy
`Second point of displacement:` (Enter)	Ends COPY command

Save the drawing.

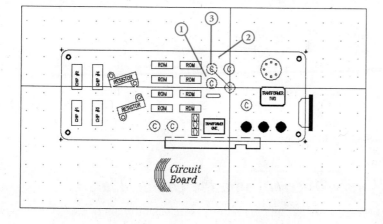

Figure 14.8

Copying multiple capacitors.

Remember, you can always use object snap and snap modes to help you get an exact displacement location.

Note Now that you have practiced using object selection, many exercises in the rest of the book omit the *nnn* found and Select objects: prompts (or both) and their responses, often simply telling you what to select and leaving you to complete the selection set on your own.

Using ROTATE To Turn Objects

The ROTATE command enables you to turn existing objects at precise angles. ROTATE, like MOVE, requires you to specify a rotation base point. After you specify the base point, you point to or enter a rotation angle. Negative angles produce clockwise rotation; positive angles produce counterclockwise rotation.

Another way to specify an angle is to use the reference method. You can specify a reference angle other than angle 0, then point to or enter a second angle relative to this reference angle. You need not know the actual angles—you can use pick points to instruct AutoCAD to calculate the angles. To align with existing objects, use object snaps when you pick the points of the angle(s).

ROTATE. The ROTATE command enables you to revolve your objects selected in the X,Y plane around a specified base point, using a rotation angle relative to the current angle 0 that you point to or enter, or relative to a reference angle that you can specify by either method.

Pull-down: *Choose Modify, Rotate*
Screen: *Choose MODIFY, Rotate*

In the following exercise, you use ROTATE to spin the contact plate so that the missing inner circle is in the upper left corner. The contact plate is the circular object that encloses a radial arrangement of smaller circles. You use two rotation methods in the exercise; figure 14.9 shows the final results.

Using ROTATE To Spin the Contact Plate

Continue in the CHAP14B drawing from the previous exercise, and zoom to the view shown in Figure 14.9.

Command: *Press and drag a window around the contact plate, then choose* Modify, Rotate	Issues the ROTATE command with the objects selected
8 found Base point: *Use* CENter *object snap to select the outer circle's center*	Specifies center of rotation
<Rotation angle>/Reference: *Drag the cursor around and the objects rotate, then pick point* ① *at 180 degrees*	Specifies the rotation angle relative to zero degrees and rotates the selected objects

Command: (Enter)	Repeats the ROTATE command
Select objects: **P** (Enter)	Specifies Previous selection set
Select objects: (Enter)	Ends object selection
Base point: *Use* CENter *object snap to select the outer circle's center*	Specifies center of rotation
<Rotation angle>/Reference: **R** (Enter)	Specifies the Reference option
Reference angle <0.00>: **@** (Enter)	Specifies last point (circle's center) as base point of reference angle
Second point: *Pick* ① *again*	Specifies 180 degree reference angle, from circle's center to ①

Drag the cursor around and see that it now drags relative to 180 degrees.

New angle: **135** (Enter)	Rotates the selected objects to position shown in figure 14.9

Save the drawing.

Figure 14.9 shows the rotated contact plate.

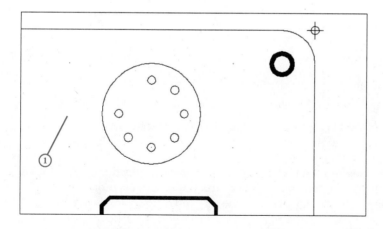

Figure 14.9

The contact plate after ROTATE.

This rotation base point does not need to be on the objects being rotated, although using an alternate point for rotation can be confusing if it is not logically placed relative to the objects being rotated.

Using the UNDO Command To Recover

As shown in Chapter 2, "Touring the AutoCAD Interface," you can use ERASE to delete objects from your drawing and OOPS to restore them. You also can use U to reverse the most recent procedure.

But what if you want to undo several steps, to a much earlier drawing state—can it be done? Sure, just use the UNDO command, the U command's big brother.

UNDO. The UNDO command enables you to reverse the effect(s) of one or more previous commands, to step back through the drawing to its state at the beginning of the drawing session. The UNDO command includes options that enable you to control the number of previous drawing steps stored, control how far back to undo previous steps, group operations as if single steps, and turn off the undo feature. The related U command (see Chapter 2) reverses a single operation at a time. The related REDO command (see Chapter 2) reverses a single UNDO (or U) if it was the last command.

Pull-down: *Choose* Assist, Undo
Screen: *Choose* ASSIST, Undo

The UNDO command provides the following options:

◆ **Number.** You can enter a number to tell AutoCAD to undo the last *number* of commands issued.

◆ **Auto.** Causes UNDO to interpret menu picks as one command. After you select this option, the following prompt appears:

```
ON/OFF <default>:
```

When on, UNDO reverses the effects of a menu selection, no matter how many steps it includes. If, for example, a menu selection changes layers, inserts a block, and rotates it as needed, one execution of UNDO treats all these steps as one. If the Auto option is off, each step is removed individually. The *default* displays the current setting. If the Control option has been turned off or has limited the UNDO command in some way, the Auto option is not available.

◆ **Control.** Enables the normal UNDO, disables it, or limits it to one step or command. If you select this option, the following options appear:

```
All/None/One <All>:
```

　　◆ **All.** Enables the UNDO command fully to operate.

New Riders Publishing
INSIDE
SERIES

◆ **None.** Disables completely the UNDO and U commands. If you select this option and then later enter the UNDO command, the `Control:` prompt immediately appears.

◆ **One.** Restricts U and UNDO to a single step. You cannot perform multiple UNDO commands if you select this option. When this mode is active, UNDO displays the prompt `Control /<1>` rather than the standard UNDO prompt. Press Enter to UNDO a single action, or enter **C** to modify the settings.

◆ **BEgin.** The BEgin and End options work together to group a sequence of commands together into one Undo operation. This option treats a sequence of commands as one command. Precede the commands with **UNDO BEgin**, finish the set with **UNDO End**, and then you can use a single U command to undo all the commands. Undo End is required to close a group. If a group is not properly Ended, the next BEgin option starts a new group, discarding the previous one. Also, issuing Undo will not back up past the Undo BEgin point. If an Undo Mark exists, it disappears inside the group.

◆ **Back.** Instructs AutoCAD to undo all commands until a mark is found. You can use the Mark option (explained later) to place multiple marks throughout the drawing. If no mark is in the drawing, AutoCAD displays the following prompt: `This will undo everything. OK? <Y>`.

◆ **End.** Closes a group of commands entered after the BEgin option was issued.

◆ **Mark.** Works in conjunction with the Back option. You can place marks periodically as you enter commands. Then you can use Undo Back to undo all the commands that have been executed since the last mark. Marks can be thought of as bookmarks—holding your place for a subsequent Undo operation.

In the next exercise, you use the UNDO command to mark your place in the drawing. Then you perform several operations, undo all the modifications back to the mark, and then undo again back to the beginning of the drawing session. Finally, use REDO to restore the drawing as it was before you started the exercise. If you make a mistake, reopen the drawing without saving changes—that will open it as saved in the previous exercise.

Using UNDO To Reverse Changes

Continue to use the CHAP14B drawing.

```
Command: UNDO (Enter)                          Starts the UNDO command
```

continues

continued

`Auto/Control/BEgin/End/Mark/` `Back/<Number>: M` **Enter**	Specifies a Mark for reference

Erase some objects, move some objects, and copy some more objects.

`Command: UNDO` **Enter**	Issues the UNDO command
`Auto/Control/BEgin/End/Mark/` `Back/<Number>: B` **Enter**	Reverts drawing back to the mark
`COPY MOVE ERASE`	Lists commands undone—see the following note
`Mark encountered`	The mark stops UNDO from undoing back to the beginning of the drawing session
`Command:` **Enter**	Repeats UNDO command
`UNDO Auto/Control/BEgin/End/Mark/` `Back/<Number>: B` **Enter**	Specifies Back option
`This will undo everything. OK? <Y>` **Enter**	Confirms undo

Undo lists all commands and groups undone.

`Everything has been undone`	Reports completion
`Command:` *Choose* Assist, Redo	Issues REDO command
`_redo`	Reverses the UNDO Back — the drawing should now be as it was at the start of the exercise

---

The list of commands reported as undone includes any commands issued and canceled, so take that into account when you use UNDO *<number>*. Also, some menu items cause their functions to be grouped as an UNDO Group, so they are undone as one operation and reported as GROUP. The operations of AutoLISP and ADS programs are also considered as single groups, even if they issue multiple commands.

Stop If you use transparent commands, such as 'ZOOM, or make settings, such as snap, ortho, or grid during another command, and then undo the command, the transparent commands and settings are also undone, without warning or notice.

Tip The UNDO Mark and Back options provide an excellent way to perform a "what if" scenario in your drawing. If you later determine the changes are not workable, simply undo back to the mark. UNDO resembles an electronic bookmark or even a time machine in your drawing.

So far, most of the editing commands with which you have worked are variations on a theme—moving or copying single objects, or making multiple copies of objects. The next group of editing commands involves deleting portions of objects, or—in the case of ERASE—deleting entire objects.

Advanced Editing

You can use advanced editing commands, such as EXTEND, STRETCH, and TRIM, for more than copying and moving objects. These commands build on AutoCAD's capability to recognize drawing geometry. By combining these commands with construction techniques, you can make a rough draft of a drawing quickly, and then finish it perfectly.

The key to using the TRIM, EXTEND, ALIGN, SCALE, STRETCH, and LENGTHEN editing commands in the next few sections is to plan ahead. The operational details of the commands can involve several objects, so think about the ways you will use them.

The TRIM and EXTEND commands shorten and lengthen existing lines, arcs, circles, ellipses, polylines, rays, and splines to meet existing polylines, arcs, circles, ellipses, lines, floating viewport edges, rays, regions, splines, text, and xlines.

Trimming Objects

The TRIM command either shortens the object or removes a section, depending on the objects and points you specify.

TRIM. The TRIM command enables you to remove portions of lines, arcs, circles, polylines, rays, and splines that cross a selected cutting edge. You can select polylines, arcs, circles, ellipses, lines, floating viewports, rays, regions, splines, text, and xlines as cutting edges. A selected object can be treated as both a cutting edge and an object to trim. The pick point on the object to trim determines what portion is trimmed.

Pull-down: *Choose Modify, Trim*
Screen: *Choose MODIFY, Trim*

Frequently, you need to trim existing lines in a drawing. If you work with a large number of objects, breaking individual objects is time-consuming. You can get the same results faster by using TRIM. The TRIM command uses boundary objects that include lines, arcs, circles, polylines, and, in paper space, viewports. The objects that you select as your boundary edge become your cutting edge(s). After you select your cutting edge, you pick the individual objects that you want to trim. You can trim lines, arcs, circles, and polylines. AutoCAD ignores other objects when you use the TRIM command; you can, therefore, select extra objects that are in the area.

Extending Objects

The EXTEND command is analogous to the TRIM command. EXTEND uses boundary edges, whereas TRIM uses cutting edges and projects objects back to the cutting edges.

EXTEND. The EXTEND command enables you to project selected lines, arcs, open polylines, and rays. Valid boundary objects include polylines, arcs, circles, ellipses, floating viewports, lines, rays, regions, splines, text, and xlines. A selected object can be treated as both a boundary edge and an object to extend. The pick point in the object to extend determines which end is extended.

Pull-down: *Choose Modify, Extend*
Screen: *Choose MODIFY, Extend*

TRIM and EXTEND Prompts and Options

Because the commands act in a similar fashion, the TRIM and EXTEND commands share the same prompts. The only difference between the prompts is that the TRIM command prompts for cutting edges, while the EXTEND command prompts for boundary edges. When you start either command, you see one of the following prompts:

```
Select cutting (or boundary) edges: (Projmode = UCS, Edgemode = No extend)
Select objects:
```

The first line in the preceding prompt displays the current projection mode and Edgemode for the TRIM and EXTEND commands. These can be changed at subsequent prompts. Select the objects that you want to use as the boundary or cutting edges for the command using any object selection method. If the view plan is not aligned with the current UCS, you see the warning, `View is not plan to UCS`. Command results may not be obvious. After you select the appropriate edges, you see the one of the following prompts:

New Riders Publishing
INSIDE
SERIES

```
<Select object to trim>/Project/Edge/Undo:
<Select object to extend>/Project/Edge/Undo:
```

- ◆ **<Select object to trim> or <Select object to extend>/.** Pick the object to trim or extend. Only one object can be picked at one time unless you use the Fence object selection method. The prompt repeats until you press Enter. If no intersection can be found between the object and the cutting edge, the message, Object does not intersect an edge, appears.

- ◆ **Project.** This option enables you to specify the mode of projection for subsequent options. The default mode is UCS. The Project option displays the following prompt:

```
None/Ucs/View <Ucs>:
```

- ◆ **None.** This option specifies that no projection will be used for trimming or extending. This means that the objects must intersect with the edges in order to be edited. Figure 14.10 shows objects before trimming. The circle in the drawing is two units in the positive Z direction above the other object. Figure 14.11 shows the objects trimmed using no projection.

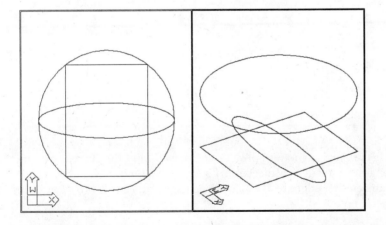

Figure 14.10

Objects shown in two views before trimming.

- ◆ **UCS.** This default projection method means that AutoCAD will project the objects and the edges onto the current UCS X,Y plane. The objects projected do not have to intersect the cutting edges in 3D space to be trimmed. Figure 14.12 illustrates this projection method.

Figure 14.11

Objects shown in two views after trimming using no projection.

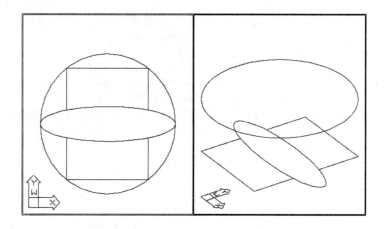

Figure 14.12

Objects shown in two views after trimming using UCS projection.

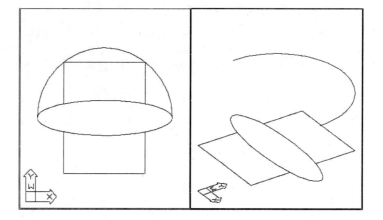

◆ **View.** This projection method projects the objects onto the current viewing plane along the current view direction. The objects do not necessarily have to intersect the cutting edges in 3D space to be trimmed. Figure 14.13 illustrates this projection method.

◆ **Edge.** The Edge option determines whether the objects are trimmed or extended to the implied edges, or only to the edge it actually intersects in 3D space.

◆ **Extend.** This option extends the edges through 3D space for objects that may intersect it.

◆ **No Extend.** This default option ensures that the objects are trimmed or extended only if they intersect the actual edges selected.

◆ **Undo.** Use the Undo option to reverse the most recent trim or extend operation. You can Undo to the start of selecting objects to trim or extend.

New Riders Publishing
INSIDE
SERIES

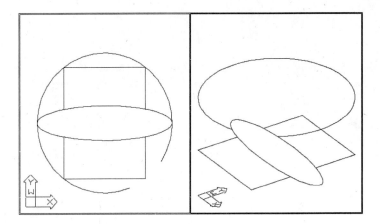

Figure 14.13

Objects shown in two views after trimming using View projection.

14

You can use lines, polylines, arcs, circles, and viewport objects (when in paper space) as the boundary edge(s). Use normal object selection to select the boundary edge(s) to which you want to extend, then pick the objects that you want to extend. You must individually pick each object to extend—you cannot use other modes to fill a selection set of objects to extend simultaneously. You cannot extend closed polylines or shorten objects (use the TRIM command to shorten lines).

 Tip   If an object to be trimmed or extended passes through or extends to multiple cutting or boundary edges, you can pick it multiple times until it meets the desired edge—each pick trims or extends it to the next edge.

In the next exercise, use TRIM and EXTEND to modify the geometry near the port connector. The port connector is located at the lower right corner of the circuit board.

Using TRIM and EXTEND To Adjust the Port Connector

Continue with the CHAP14B drawing from the previous exercise and zoom to the view shown in Figure 14.14.

Command: *Choose* Modify, Trim   Issues the TRIM command

```
_trim
Select cutting edges: (Projmode = UCS,
Edgemode = No extend)
```

Select objects: *Select a crossing*   Selects several lines and ends cutting
window from ① *(see fig. 14.14)*   edge selection
to ②, *then press Enter*

continues

continued

```
5 found.
```

```
<Select object to trim>/Project/
Edge/Undo:
```
Pick line through port connector at ③

Removes portion of the line between the nearest two selected cutting edges

```
<Select object to trim>/Project/
Edge/Undo:
```
Pick the same line again, near ①

Trims it back to the next vertex, near ④, because it is a polyline and was selected as both a cutting edge and object to trim

```
<Select object to trim>/Project/
Edge/Undo:
```
U (Enter)

Undoes the last trim

```
<Select object to trim>/Project/
Edge/Undo:
```
(Enter)

Exits TRIM

```
Command:
```
Choose Modify, Extend

Issues the EXTEND command

```
_extend
Select boundary edges: (Projmode = UCS,
Edgemode = No extend)
```

Notice that the prompt displays the current Projmode and Edgemode status

```
Undo/<Endpoint of line>:
```
Select a crossing window from ④ *to* ⑤, *then press Enter*

Selects the donuts near ④ and ⑤, and several other lines, and ends boundary edge selection

```
12 found 2 were not a valid edge.
```

```
<Select object to extend>/Project/
Edge/Undo:
```
Pick rear line of port at ⑥ *and again at* ⑦

Extends each picked line to nearest boundary object beyond the picked end—to the donuts

```
<Select object to extend>/Project/
Edge/Undo:
```
E (Enter)

Specifies Edgemode option

```
Extend/No extend <No extend>:
```
E (Enter)

Specifies Extend mode

```
<Select object to extend>/Project/
Edge/Undo:
```
Turn off snap, and pick the left end of each diagonal line at ⑧ *and* ⑨

Extends each line to meet the other

```
<Select object to trim>/Project/
Edge/Undo:
```
Enter **U** *twice*

Undoes the last two extends

```
<Select object to extend>/Project/        Exits EXTEND
Edge/Undo: (Enter)
```

Save the drawing.

Figure 14.14 shows the results of trimming and extending the port connector.

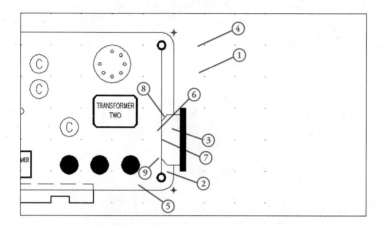

Figure 14.14

Detail of port connector after TRIM and EXTEND.

14

Note   Trimming a closed polyline creates two polylines unless the portion trimmed includes the starting or ending vertices.

You may have noticed in the previous exercise, the pick points used for selecting the edges were not very specific. In general, you usually don't have to be too careful in selecting cutting or boundary edges; a few extra objects in the selection set often do not interfere.

You may have noticed also that some of the objects used as edges were actually either trimmed or extended. The same object can act as both a cutting (or boundary) edge and an object to trim (or extend). After you trim (extend) it, it is no longer highlighted, but it still functions as an edge.

Tip   You can use the Fence selection option to select multiple objects to trim or extend. All eligible objects are simultaneously trimmed or extended when you end the fence specification. Ineligible objects are ignored.

Using ALIGN as a MOVE/ROTATE Alternative

Sometimes you need to be able to move objects to another location and then rotate them in place. In prior versions of AutoCAD, you have to issue separate MOVE and ROTATE commands to perform the task.

The ALIGN command combines the move and rotate operations into a single task. It is primarily intended for 3D transformations, but is also useful in 2D.

> **ALIGN.** The ALIGN command enables you to relocate and rotate objects to align with other objects, using at most three pairs of source and destination points. You can define a move, 2D or 3D transformation, a rotation, or any combination of these operations.
> Pull-down: *Choose Modify, Align*
> Screen: *Choose MODIFY, Align*

The ALIGN command provides the following options:

◆ **Select objects.** Select the objects to align in a new location by any object selection method. You then are prompted alternatively for a source point and its corresponding destination point.

◆ **1st source point.** Specify a point relative to the selected objects to align with its corresponding destination point. As each source point is specified, a rubber-band reference line is generated to assist in the specification of the associated destination point.

◆ **1st destination point.** Specify the location corresponding to the 1st source point.

◆ **2nd source point.** If you press Enter at this point, the ALIGN command moves the selected objects relative to the points specified. To perform 2D transformations, select a second source point.

◆ **2nd destination point.** Specify the location corresponding to the 2nd source point.

◆ **3rd destination point.** If you press Enter at this point, you receive an additional prompt prior to performing a 2D alignment. To perform a 3D transformation, specify a third point outside the plane of the first two pairs of points.

◆ **3rd destination point.** Specify the location corresponding to the 3rd source point. The 3D transformation is then performed and the Align command is complete.

◆ **<2d> or 3d transformation.** This prompt is issued only when you press Enter at the 3rd source point prompt. If you specify a 2D transformation, any Z axis differences in the pairs of source-destination points is ignored. If you enter **3** to specify a 3D transformation, the Z components of the source-destination points you specified are included in moving and rotating the selected objects.

In the following exercise, you use ALIGN to relocate and rotate the resistors on the circuit board. The resistors are clearly labeled.

Using ALIGN To Adjust the Resistors

Continue to use the CHAP14B drawing and zoom to the view shown in figure 14.15.

14

Command: *Choose* Modify, Align	Issues the ALIGN command
_align	
Select objects: *Press and drag a window around both resistors, then press Enter*	Selects objects to align, and ends object selection
1st source point: *Use* INT *object snap to pick* ①	Specifies base "move-from"
1st destination point: *Turn on snap and pick* ②	Specifies base "move-to"
2nd source point: *Use* INT *object snap to pick* ③	Specifies "rotate-from"
2nd destination point: *Pick* ④	Specifies "rotate-to"
3rd source point: (Enter)	Ends point specification
<2d> or 3d transformation: (Enter)	Accepts default 2D mode and completes alignment (see fig. 14.16)

Save the drawing.

Using LENGTHEN To Increase Sizes

Another editing task that you often are required to perform is to alter the length of a line or arc by a specific amount. In prior versions of AutoCAD, you must select a line, extend it to a boundary, offset that boundary, and finally, trim the line accordingly— quite a few steps. For arcs, the construction tasks were even more involved!

Figure 14.15

*Detail of resistors
before ALIGN.*

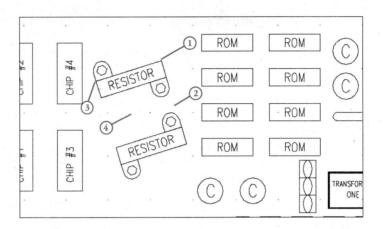

Figure 14.16

*Detail of resistors
after ALIGN.*

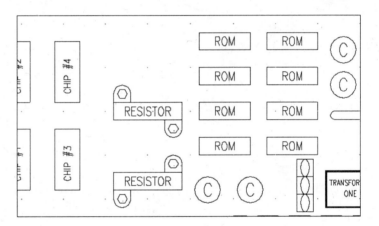

The Release 13 LENGTHEN command solves this problem with a minimum of fuss.

LENGTHEN. The LENGTHEN command enables you to change the length of objects and the included angle of arcs, but does not let you change closed objects. You can change lengths and angles by specifying an incremental amount, percentage of its total, new absolute total, or a dynamically dragged amount.

Pull-down: *Choose Modify, Lengthen*
Screen: *Choose MODIFY, Lengthn*

The LENGTHEN command presents the following options:

```
DElta/Percent/Total/DYnamic/<Select object>
```

◆ **Select object.** Use this default option to display the length and included angle of the object if applicable:

```
Current length: 3.5633, included angle: 205.6419
```

This is used for obtaining a reference length and angle only and does not necessarily define the selection set to be lengthened.

Note   The spline object typically can be shortened, but cannot be lengthened.

◆ **DElta.** Use the DElta option to lengthen or shorten an object by a specified increment. Specify a non-negative value to lengthen an object or a negative value to shorten the object. You can specify a length or an angle. The object is lengthened or shortened by the specified amount from the endpoint closest to the pick point used to select the object. The DElta option issues the prompt `Angle/<Enter delta length (0.0000)>`.

   ◆ **Angle.** Use the Angle option to incrementally change the included angle of an arc. Enter a positive or negative angle value at the prompt `Enter delta angle <0.0000>`; and select an object to modify at the prompt `<Select object to change>/Undo`. The Undo option reverses the change made to the last object.

   ◆ **Enter delta length.** This is the default option for the DElta method. Enter a positive or negative value at this prompt and select the object to modify at the prompt `<Select object to change>/Undo`. The Undo option reverses the change made to the last object.

◆ **Percent.** Use the Percent option to specify a percentage change for the object. A 50-percent change, for example, results in the object being shortened by half. A 200-percent change doubles the length of the object. This option changes the included angle of an arc by the specified percentage. The percentage must be a positive value greater than zero.

The Percent option issues the prompt `Enter percent length <0.0000>:`. Enter the percent change and select an object to modify at the prompt `<Select object to change>/Undo`. The Undo option reverses the change made to the last object.

◆ **Total.** Use the Total option to set an explicit length of an object from a fixed endpoint. For an arc, the Total option determines the total included angle of the arc. The Total option issues the prompt `Angle/<Enter total length (0.0000)>:`.

14

◆ **Angle.** The Angle option is used to specify the total included angle of an arc. Enter a value at the prompt `Enter total angle <0.0000>`; and select an object to modify at the prompt `<Select object to change>/Undo`. The Undo option reverses the change made to the last object.

◆ **Enter total length (0.0000).** At this prompt, enter the total length of the object and select an object to modify at the prompt `<Select object to change>/Undo`. The Undo option reverses the change made to the last object.

◆ **DYnamic.** Use this option to dynamically drag the length of the selected object. The endpoint closest to the pick point of the object is dragged to the desired length or included angle (for an arc), while the other endpoint remains fixed. The DYnamic option issues the prompt `<Select object to change>/Undo`. The Undo option reverses the change made to the last object. You cannot use the Dynamic option with Spline objects.

In the following exercise, you use LENGTHEN to increase all arc lengths within the circuit board logo to exactly 1.5".

Using LENGTHEN To Modify the Logo

Continue in the CHAP14B drawing and zoom the view shown in figure 14.17.

Command: *Choose* Modify, Lengthen	Issues the LENGTHEN command
_lengthen	
DElta/Percent/Total/ DYnamic/<Select object>: *Pick rightmost arc at* ①	Selects an arc to process
Current length: 1.01, included angle: 95.85	Reports arc data
DElta/Percent/Total/ DYnamic/<Select object>: **T** (Enter)	Specifies Total option
Angle/<Enter total length (1.00)>: **1.5** (Enter)	Specifies new total length but does not lengthen it yet
<Select object to change>/Undo: *Pick all arcs in sequence, right to left, and press Enter after the last pick*	Lengthens each arc in order

Save the drawing.

Figure 14.17
*Detail of logo
after using
LENGTHEN.*

14

Using STRETCH for Versatile Changes

The STRETCH command enables you to move and stretch objects. You can lengthen objects, shorten them, and alter their shapes. The results of stretching depend on the object types you select and how you select them.

In a stretch operation, you normally use a crossing window to select your objects and then indicate a displacement from a base point. Everything you select inside the crossing window moves, and objects crossing the window are stretched. The phrase *inside the window* means all endpoints and vertices of an object are within the window. The phrase *crossing the window* means that endpoints and other object elements can lie both inside and outside the window.

> **STRETCH.** The STRETCH command enables you to elongate objects selected with a crossing window. You can stretch lines, arcs, solids, traces, polylines (meshes), and 3D faces. For stretchable objects, endpoints that lie inside the crossing window are moved and endpoints that lie outside the crossing window remain fixed. All objects entirely within the window move. Text, blocks, shapes, and circles move only if their insert or center points are in the window.
> Pull-down: *Choose Modify, Stretch*
> Screen: *Choose MODIFY, Stretch*

The STRETCH command provides the following options:

◆ **Select objects to stretch by crossing-window or -polygon... Select objects.** At this prompt, you must use a crossing window or crossing polygon to select entities. AutoCAD accepts only one selection window. The STRETCH command ignores multiple selection sets, using the last one only. Use the BOX crossing option, Crossing window , or the Crossing Polygon (CP) object selection method to select the entities for stretching. You can use the Remove (R) option to remove objects from the selection set. You cannot use the Add (A) option, however, as AutoCAD ignores objects other than those originally selected using a crossing option. The prompt repeats until your selection set is complete. Press Enter to terminate object selection.

◆ **Base point or displacement.** Enter the base point of displacement or a coordinate amount of displacement.

◆ **Second point of displacement.** Enter the new point for the stretched entities.

In the following exercise, you use STRETCH to elongate the right side of the slot connector by 0.49". The slot connector runs along the bottom of the circuit board. This time, you use Noun/Verb selection.

Using STRETCH To Elongate the Slot Connector

Continue in the CHAP14B drawing from the previous exercise, and zoom to the view shown in figure 14.18.

Command: *Choose* Modify, Stretch	Issues the STRETCH command

```
_stretch
Select objects to stretch by crossing-window or -polygon...
```

Select objects: *Select a crossing window from* ① *to* ②	Selects objects and specifies window that determines what gets stretched

```
7 found
```

Notice which endpoints are within the window. The selection includes the polyline edge of the board, but no polyline endpoints are in the window. The selection also includes the objects at ③ and ④, which you next deselect.

Select objects: *Press Shift and pick the objects at* ③ *and at* ④	Removes both objects from selection set

```
1 found, 1 removed
1 found, 1 removed
```

Select objects: (Enter)	Ends selection
Base point or displacement: **.49<0** (Enter)	Specifies a polar displacement

New Riders Publishing
INSIDE SERIES

```
Second point of displacement: (Enter)
```
Accepts first point as displacement and stretches the objects

Notice that the endpoints within the window were moved, those outside the window were not, and the lines between those endpoints were stretched. The polyline edge of the board was unaffected.

Save the drawing.

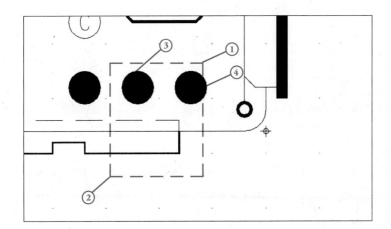

Figure 14.18

Detail of slot connector after STRETCH.

In the previous exercise, you also selected the bottom edge of the circuit board with the crossing window. Because neither endpoint of this line fell within the crossing window, it was not stretched.

 Note The following explanation of the effect of STRETCH is not well known, or even correctly documented in Autodesk's own documentation.

The results of STRETCH are controlled by the following three things:

◆ The selected objects. You can add or remove objects by any selection method.

◆ A window or polygon selection. Despite the command's prompt, it does not have to be a crossing selection. At least one window or polygon must be specified, although it does not have to select anything. You can use other methods to select the objects to be stretched or moved. It is only the relationship of each object's defining points to the last, and only the last, specified window or polygon that determines what gets stretched, moved, or ignored.

◆ The types of objects selected. Different types are affected differently.

Note In a crowded drawing, use the SELECT command before using STRETCH, to select the objects you do not want to be affected. Then start the STRETCH command, use a crossing window to select the objects to be stretched (and possibly many others) and determine the control points. Then switch to Remove mode and enter **P** to remove the objects selected by SELECT.

The effects of object stretching depend on the type of object. Some significant points to remember when you use STRETCH are as follows:

◆ The defining endpoints or vertices of lines, arcs, polyline segments, viewports, traces, and solids determine what stretches or moves. Those within the window or polygon get moved, those outside it remain fixed, and the geometry in between gets stretched.

◆ AutoCAD adjusts the center points of arcs or polyline arcs to keep the sagitta constant. The *sagitta* is the altitude or distance from the chord midpoint to the nearest point on the arc.

◆ Viewport contents remain constant in scale.

◆ A point, object, circle, block, shape, or text object never stretch. If the point object, the center of a circle, or the insertion point of a block, shape, or text object is in the stretch window or polygon, the object gets moved.

Tip Use the grip edit stretch mode for quicker stretching and as a copy option. You also can stretch a circle's radius with the grip edit stretch mode.

Using the SCALE Command

Occasionally, you use the wrong drawing symbol and text scale or need to change an object's size. The SCALE command enables you to shrink or enlarge existing objects. During a scaling operation, you use a scale factor or reference length to change the size of objects around a given base point. The base point remains constant; everything around it grows or shrinks by your scale factor. You can enter an explicit scale factor, pick two points to have AutoCAD compute the distance, or specify a reference length. To use the reference method, define a current length (generally on an object), then specify its new length.

New Riders Publishing
INSIDE SERIES

SCALE. The SCALE command enables you to change the size of existing objects relative to a specified base point, by a specified scale factor, by referencing one specified distance to another, or by using a combination of these two methods.
Pull-down: *Choose Modify, Scale*
Screen: *Choose MODIFY, Scale*

◆ **Select objects.** Choose all the objects you want to enlarge or reduce by means of any of the object selection methods.

◆ **Base point.** Enter a base point in the current coordinate system around which to scale objects. When the scaling occurs, all points on selected objects move closer to the base point or farther away from the base point as their scale is reduced and enlarged.

Tip   Choose a base point that relates to the object or objects being scaled and positions them correctly after scaling. You generally pick a corner or the center of the object being scaled.

After selecting a base point, you see the following prompt:

```
<Scale factor>/Reference.
```

◆ **Scale factor.** Specify a scale factor by which to scale objects. A number greater than one enlarges the objects; a number between zero and one reduces the objects. You can enter a number or pick a point to show a distance. If you pick a point, a rubber-band line appears between the base point and the crosshairs. The objects to be scaled are highlighted and dragged as you move the crosshairs.

◆ **Reference.** Enter **R** for the Reference option if you want to define the scale factor in reference to a length, such as the size of an existing object.

Note   You cannot scale the X, Y, or Z values independently.

◆ **Reference length <1>.** If you specify the Reference option, the scale factor is defined by the ratio of the two lengths that you specify. You also can pick two points, usually on an existing object, to show the reference length.

◆ **New length.** Enter the new length to scale the reference length to. The selected objects are then scaled by the ratio between the reference length and the new length. You also can pick one point to show the new length as a distance from the base point. As you move the cursor to pick the new length, AutoCAD shows a rubber-band line from the base point.

In the following exercise, you use the SCALE Reference option to make transformer number one exactly 0.8" long. The transformer is clearly labeled. To describe the original reference length to AutoCAD, you pick two points.

Using SCALE To Enlarge the Transformer

Continue to use the CHAP14B drawing and zoom to the view shown in figure 14.19.

Command: *Press and drag a crossing window around the transformer, from* ① *to* ②, *then choose* Modify, Scale
    Issues SCALE with preselected objects

_scale 3 found

Base point: *Use* INT *object snap to pick* ③ *(see fig. 14.19)*

Drag the cursor around and watch the selection scale relative to a one-unit length.

<Scale factor>/Reference: R (Enter)
    Specifies the Reference length method

Reference length <1>: @ (Enter)
    Issues @ to specify the last picked point at ③

Second point: *Use* INT *object snap to pick* ④
    Specifies existing transformer length as reference length

Drag the cursor around and watch the selection scale relative to the reference length.

New length: **0.8** (Enter)
    Specifies the new transformer length and scales the text proportionally

Save the drawing.

Tip
The scale base point is also the base point of the new length. You can pick points for the reference length on another object, but if you want to show the new length by picking points on another object, first use MOVE to move the selection to place the base point on the other object, then scale the selection. Then use the MOVE command to move the selection back to its original location. Use Previous to reselect the objects and object snaps to specify the moves.

New Riders Publishing
INSIDE
SERIES

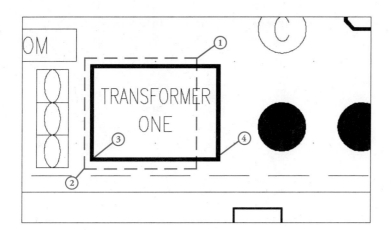

Figure 14.19

Detail of transformer number one after SCALE.

In the next section, you use selection filters to include and exclude specific objects, by object type and property, from your object selection sets.

Filtering the Selection Set

Despite the vast number of selection set options available, choosing the objects you want is still sometimes tricky in a complex drawing. Object-selection filters enable you to select only those objects that you specify in the filter description. Common filters can include object type, color, layer, or coordinate data. Although the concept of specifying filters is simple, the process can feel confusing because AutoCAD provides so many filter specifications and options for using them.

To explore the filter options, choose Selection Filters from the Assist pull-down menu. AutoCAD then presents the Object Selection Filters dialog box (see fig. 14.20). You can use this menu item or enter **'FILTER** to transparently open this dialog box at the Select objects: prompt.

'FILTER. The 'FILTER command enables you to activate the Object Selection Filters dialog box, in which you can create a list of conditions that an object must satisfy to be selected. You can use FILTER at the Command: prompt to create filter lists to use later at a Select objects: prompt. You also can use it transparently at a Select objects: prompt to select objects to use with the current command.

Pull-Down: *Choose Assist, Selection Filters*
Screen: *Choose ASSIST, Filter*

Figure 14.20

*The Object
Selection Filters
dialog box.*

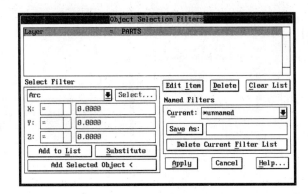

Note   FILTER finds objects by color or linetype only when they have been directly
assigned, rather than by layer.

The list box at the top of the Object Selection Filters dialog box is for displaying and
editing the filter criteria.

◆ **Select Filter.** This area of the dialog box contains features for specifying the
filter criteria for object selection.

◆ **Select Filter drop-down list box.** This list displays all the filter types
available. If you are editing an existing filter, this option shows the current
filter's type.

◆ **Select.** This button displays a dialog box with all the available items of the filter
type being edited. Valid types for the select are Xdata ID, Block Name, Color,
Dimension Style, Layer, Linetype, or Text Style Name.

◆ **X.** This drop-down list box displays the relational operators from which you can
choose. The relational operators are =, !=, <, <=, >, >=, *. X displays an X
coordinate value in the edit box when working with coordinates, such as the
starting point of a line. X displays the selected attribute when working with
properties such as the color of a layer.

◆ **Y.** Y displays the relational operators from which you can choose. The relational
operators are =, !=, <, <=, >, >=, *. This option displays a Y coordinate value in
the edit box when working with coordinates.

◆ **Z.** Z displays the relational operators from which you can choose. The relational operators are =, !=, <, <=, >, >=, *. This option displays a Z coordinate
value in the edit box when working with coordinates.

- ◆ **Add to List.** This button adds the current Select Filter settings to the Filters list box above the highlighted filter.

- ◆ **Substitute.** This button replaces the filter highlighted in the Filter list box with the current Select Filter settings.

- ◆ **Add Selected Object.** This button adds the properties of a selected object to the Filter list box. The dialog box is temporarily cleared from the screen while you select an object in your drawing.

- ◆ **Edit Item.** This option moves the filter highlighted in the Filters list box to the Select Filter group for editing.

- ◆ **Delete.** This option deletes the filter highlighted in the Filters list box.

- ◆ **Clear List.** This option deletes all the filters in the Filters list box.

The Named Filters group contains the following options:

- ◆ **Current.** This drop-down list box displays a list of the available named filters.

- ◆ **Save As.** This button saves the current set of filters in the Filter list box to the name entered in the Save As edit box. This creates a named filter list. You can have up to 18 named filters, each up to 25 characters in length, stored in the FILTER.NFL file.

Tip If you have a complicated selection filter that you want to use in other drawings, type a name in the Save As edit box and click on the Save As button. Your filter will be stored in the FILTER.NFL file in your AutoCAD directory. Use the Current drop-down list box to choose your saved filter and apply it.

- ◆ **Delete Current Filter List.** This button deletes the current filter from the list of available named filters in the FILTER.NFL file.

- ◆ **Apply.** This button exits the Object Selection Filters dialog box and applies the defined filter to all the objects you select. You are prompted to Select objects.

- ◆ **Select Objects.** You select the objects to which you want to apply the filter. This prompt appears after you click on Apply in the Object Selection Filters dialog box. You can use any valid object selection method. Use ALL to apply the filter to all objects in the drawing. AutoCAD reports how many objects were found and how many were filtered out.

You can specify object-selection filters by choosing an item from the drop-down list under Select Filter, then clicking on the Add to List button. That filter then appears in the current filter list at the top of the dialog box. You can repeat this process to add more condition to the filters. If you want to save the filter list to use at a later time, enter a name (up to 18 characters) in the edit box next to Sa<u>v</u>e As and then click on the Sa<u>v</u>e As button. You can find and retrieve all the defined filter names in the list box next to the C<u>u</u>rrent button. Choosing the <u>A</u>pply button closes the dialog box and prompts you for object selection, using the current filter. Choose Cancel to leave the dialog box without applying the filter.

The PARTS layer of the board drawing contains several objects in the default BYLAYER (red) color: the circular contact plate at the upper right, the switchbank at the bottom center, and the four chips at the left side. The PARTS layer also contains several other objects, which are magenta, with their color set explicitly. In the following exercise, you use filtering to select only the objects on the PARTS layer in the default BYLAYER (red) color.

Using FILTERS To Qualify Objects

Continue in the CHAP14B drawing from the previous exercise and zoom to the extents.

Command: *Choose* Assist, Selection Filters	Issues the FILTER command and opens the Object Selection Filters dialog box
Click in the Select Filter *drop-down list box and select* Layer	Puts Layer in Select Filter list box
Choose the S<u>e</u>lect button, *then select* PARTS, *then choose* OK	Opens Select Layer dialog box, enters PARTS in box below the S<u>e</u>lect button
Choose Add to <u>L</u>ist	Enters Layer = PARTS in the filter list at the top of the dialog box
Choose <u>A</u>pply	Closes the dialog box and prompts for objects
Applying filter to selection. Select objects: **ALL** (Enter)	Selects all, but filters out objects that do not meet the filter criteria
136 found, 97 were filtered out.	Highlights all objects on PARTS layer
Select objects: (Enter)	Exits selection
Exiting filtered selection	

The filtered selection included the unwanted magenta objects. You need to refine the filter specification, as follows.

Command: (Enter)	Repeats FILTER command and reopens Object Selection Filters dialog box with Layer = PARTS in the filter list

Click below the Layer = PARTS *line*	Highlights the next blank line
In the Select Filter *drop-down list,* *select* ** Begin NOT *from the end of* *the list, then Choose* Add to List	Puts ** Begin NOT in Select Filter list box and in the filter list
In Select Filter *drop-down list,* *select* Color, *choose* Select, *select* *the magenta color box, then choose* OK	Puts Color in Select Filter list box, opens Select Color dialog box, and returns to filters dialog box
Choose Add to List	Enters Color = 6-Magenta in filter list
In Select Filter *drop-down list,* *select* ** End NOT *from the end of* *the list, then Choose* Add to List	Puts ** End NOT in Select Filter list box and in the filter list
Choose Apply	Closes the dialog box and prompts for objects
Applying filter to selection. Select objects: **ALL** (Enter)	Selects all, but filters out all but the desired objects
136 found, 106 were filtered out.	Highlights all objects on PARTS layer except the magenta ones
Select objects: (Enter)	Exits selection
Exiting filtered selection	
Command: *Choose* Modify, Erase	Issues the ERASE command
Select objects: **P** (Enter)	Specifies Previous selection
30 found	Reselects the filter selection set
Select objects: (Enter)	Ends selection and erases objects
Command: *Choose* Assist, Undo	Restore objects

14

When a filter is active, AutoCAD selects only those objects that conform to that filter; it ignores all other objects. In the preceding exercise, the command prompt displays the number of objects selected and the number filtered out. You can use the Previous selection option to recall those objects during a subsequent editing command.

In the Object Selection Filters dialog box, you can create a list of filters to apply. After you add a filter to the list, you can highlight it by clicking on it. You might need to follow this procedure before you click on the Delete, Edit Item, or Substitute button. You can define and then save filters with a name that you specify, so that you can later recall and use them.

Do not get discouraged the first time you explore object filtering; with a little practice, filters can increase your productivity. If your drawings are not very complex, however, you might find the use of locked layers (see Chapter 5) to be more intuitive—just keep an open mind and see what works for you.

Note The 'FILTER command has many more uses beyond the scope of this book, such as Boolean filtering and conditional testing. For more information, consult the online help screens or the *AutoCAD Command Reference and User's Guide* or the *New Riders' Reference Guide to Release 13.*

Object Grouping

AutoCAD provides many ways to select objects. If you want to select several objects for subsequent reference, the Previous object selection option is somewhat limited, because it stores only the most recent set of edited objects.

One of the new Release 13 features is called *object grouping*, in which you can assign group names (saved with the drawing) to sets of selected objects. You can edit groups by referencing their names at any time during a drawing session; enter **G** at the Select objects: prompt to include a group of objects to process.

You use the Object Grouping dialog box (see fig. 14.21) to create groups.

GROUP. The GROUP command enables you to open the Object Grouping dialog box, in which you can create a named selection set of objects to facilitate subsequent edits. If you enter **-group** at the Command: prompt, GROUP displays prompts at the command line.
Pull-down: *Choose Assist, Group Objects*
Screen: *Choose ASSIST, Group*

The Object Grouping dialog box contains four basic areas: the Group Name list box, the Group Identification area, the Create Group area, and the Change Group area. The Group Name list box contains the names of all the groups defined within the drawing and whether they are selectable. *Selectable* means that if you select any one object within a group, the entire group is selected. Selectability is determined when you create a group and also can be changed at any time using the Selectable button.

The following sections discuss the other basic areas of the Object Grouping dialog box.

New Riders Publishing
INSIDE SERIES

Figure 14.21

*The Object
Grouping
dialog box.*

14

Group Identification

The <u>G</u>roup Name edit box is used for entering the name of a new group to create or showing the name of the highlighted group in the Group Name list box. Group names can be up to 31 characters in length, but cannot contain any spaces. AutoCAD converts the names to uppercase.

Use the <u>D</u>escription edit box to type an optional description of the group. Descriptions can be up to 64 characters in length and can contain spaces.

Choose the <u>F</u>ind Name button to list the groups that any one selected object belongs to. The <u>F</u>ind Name button prompts you to pick a member of a group. If the object you select is not a member of a group, AutoCAD prompts you as such. If you select an object that belongs to a group, the Group Member List dialog box appears, listing all the groups that include the selected object.

The <u>H</u>ighlight button is used to highlight all the objects in a drawing that belong to the selected group. First select the desired group in the Group Name list box, and then choose the <u>H</u>ighlight button.

Use the <u>I</u>nclude Unnamed check box to cause AutoCAD to display all group names, regardless of whether they are assigned an explicit name. All group names assigned by AutoCAD begin with *A*n* where *n* is a sequential number. (See the following Unnamed check box.)

Tip   When you copy a group, the copy is defined as an unnamed group. Use the <u>I</u>nclude Unnamed option to list such groups and then use the Change Group options to rename them, explode them, change their selection status, and so on.

Choose the **N**ew button to define a selection set for a new group. You must have a valid name entered in the **G**roup Name edit box unless the **U**nnamed check box is checked. Selecting the objects for the group is the last step in defining a group. Be sure you have entered the name and description for the group before choosing **N**ew.

The **S**electable check box affects only newly created groups and determines whether the new group will be selectable. Selectability means that the entire group is selected if any one object within a group is selected.

Use the **U**nnamed check box to specify whether you can create unnamed groups.

Change Group

Choose the **R**emove button to remove items from a group. You are prompted to `Select objects to remove`. If an object belongs to more than one group, it is removed only from the current group.

Choose the **A**dd button to add items to the current group. You are prompted to `Select objects to add`. If an object already belongs to other groups and any of those groups are selectable, the entire group is added to the current group.

Choose the Rena**m**e button to rename a group. Highlight the group you want to rename in the Group Name list box. Type over the name in the **G**roup Name edit box and choose the Rena**m**e button.

Objects are added to groups in the order you select them. If it is important to have them in a specific order, use the Re-**o**rder button. When you choose this button, an Order Group dialog box is displayed (see fig. 14.22). This dialog box provides functions for changing the position of objects within a group.

Figure 14.22

The Order Group dialog box.

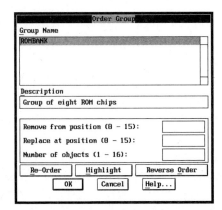

The Order Group dialog box contains the following options:

◆ **Group Name.** This list box displays the names of the groups defined in the drawing.

◆ **Description.** This text area lists the description, if any, of a selected group.

◆ **Remove from position (0 - nnn).** Object numbering with a group begins with 0. This edit box label shows the number of items within the selected group, starting at 0. In this edit box, enter the number of the item you want to move within the group.

◆ **Replace at position (0 - nnn).** Use this edit box to determine to what position within the group the item in the Remove from position edit box gets moved.

◆ **Number of objects (1 - xxx).** Use this edit box to enter a value or range of values to specify how many objects within the group will be moved to the new position.

The <u>R</u>e-order button performs the reordering of the objects within the group as specified earlier.

Choose the <u>H</u>ighlight button to selectively highlight individual objects within a group. When you select this button, the Object Grouping Highlight dialog box appears (see fig. 14.23). This dialog box contains a <u>N</u>ext and <u>P</u>revious button as well as a text label showing the current position of the highlighted object within the group. Use the buttons to work forward or backward through a group as AutoCAD highlights the object occupying that position within the group.

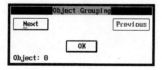

Figure 14.23

Dialog box for highlighting individual objects within a group.

Choose the Reverse <u>O</u>rder button to totally reverse the positions of objects within a group. In other words, the last becomes first and the first becomes last.

The <u>D</u>escription button in the Object Grouping dialog box is used to change a group description for an existing selected group. Type the new description in the <u>D</u>escription edit box and choose the <u>D</u>escription button to effect the change.

Choose the <u>E</u>xplode button to destroy a group, removing the objects from the group. The objects are not erased—they simply have their individual identity restored. The group name is deleted from the drawing.

The Se<u>l</u>ectable button turns the selectability of the highlighted group on or off.

In the following exercise you define two groups: one of all ROMs, and the other of all ROMs and chips, which includes the first group. You then experiment with group selectability.

Using GROUPs To Classify Objects

Continue in the CHAP14B drawing from either of the two previous exercises and zoom to the extents.

`Command:` *Choose* Assist, Group Objects	Issues the GROUP command and opens the Object Grouping dialog box
In the Group Identification *area,* *click in the* <u>G</u>roup Name *edit box and enter* `ROMBANK`	Names group
Press Tab (or choose <u>D</u>escription*) and enter* `Bank of eight ROM chips`	Describes group
Choose <u>N</u>ew	Closes dialog box and prompts for selection
`Select objects for grouping:` `Select objects:` *Select the eight ROMs with a window, then press Enter*	Selects ROMs (each is a polyline and text label), ends selection, reopens dialog box, and enters the name in Group Name list at the top of the dialog box
Enter another <u>G</u>roup Name `ALLCHIPS`, *and* <u>D</u>escription `Chips and ROMs`, *then choose* <u>N</u>ew	Names and describes group, closes dialog box, and prompts for selection
`Select objects for grouping:` `Select objects:` *Select the four CHIPs at the left with a window*	Selects CHIPs
`Select objects:` *Press Shift and pick one of the ROMs*	Selects all eight ROMs as a group
`16 found, 1 group`	
`Select objects:` (Enter)	Reopens dialog box, and enters the name in the Group Name list

Choose OK	Closes dialog box
Command: *Pick any ROM or CHIP*	Selects all objects in both groups
Command: *Choose* Assist, Group Objects	Opens Object Grouping dialog box
Select ALLCHIPS *in the* Group *Name list, and choose* Selectable, *then* OK	Changes the group's selectability from Yes to No, and closes dialog box
Command: *Pick any ROM*	Selects all ROMs
Command: *Pick any CHIP*	Selects only one object — the group's selectability is turned off

14

Tip   You can control group selectability globally with the Object **G**rouping check box in the Object Selection Settings dialog box.

After you finish the preceding exercise, the group name ROMBANK is now stored in the drawing. You can enter **G** and then the group name at any Select objects: prompt to edit a named group. Applications of group names are limited only by your imagination.

The advantages of groups over blocks includes the following:

◆ You can use the Selectable option to control access to the individual members of a group

◆ You can edit members of groups without affecting other members or removing them from the group

◆ Blocks are more efficient for multiple occurrences, but groups avoid increasing drawing size for single occurrences

◆ Any AutoCAD drawing object could be assigned membership in one or more groups, just as you can be a member of several groups.

Tip   When you use EXPLODE, AutoCAD replaces the selected block object with its component objects. When you use DIVIDE or MEASURE (see Chapter 16), AutoCAD creates points along the selected object. Use Previous to select the objects created (the points or component objects), and GROUP to name them. You then can later select the same objects by specifying the corresponding group name.

Final Editing Tips

From this chapter, you have seen the importance of editing during drawing development. Your job is to produce high-quality drawings in an efficient manner, so learning valuable techniques and adopting good work habits are key steps toward achieving your goal.

The following list outlines some procedures to help you edit your drawings in a professional style:

◆ Consider any repetitive or symmetric features. A good phrase to remember is "draw once, edit many."

◆ Familiarize yourself with all of the editing commands.

◆ Use snap, ortho, and object snaps to set up your MOVE and COPY displacements. If you find yourself in a tight space, try object selection cycling.

◆ Learn all of the object-selection options, including the Remove and Shift key usage. All selection-set options have their merits. Last and Previous are frequently used. The object-picking method is best for detail work, especially with object snap. If you want to edit most of the objects at once, use the All option, then remove the objects you did not want to include.

◆ Window is powerful, but it is not all inclusive. Remember, what you see in the window is what goes into the selection set. You can use Crossing as a knife to slice out a selection set. The WPolygon window is nice when a rectangular window can not enclose the objects. Previous saves time in repetitive editing. And lest you forget, a U undoes the last object selection operation.

◆ Explore the new Release 13 GROUP command, in combination with object filtering, to provide great flexibility with named selection sets.

When you work with all of the editing commands and investigate their capabilities, you expand your drawing knowledge and become a more valuable asset to your organization. In the next chapter, you will learn about direct modification of objects and their properties.

Object Modification, Inquiry, and Calculation

When you develop a drawing, you often find yourself making numerous inquiries about various aspects of the drawing.

◆ **How accurate is the drawing?** Did you place the center of the circle at coordinates 3,5 or 4,5? Is that line 6 inches or 6.5 inches long?

◆ **What are the coordinates at ...?** Now that you have laid out the floor plan, what is the square footage of the building? What are the coordinates of the point midway between the two reference points you laid out?

◆ **What layer and color was used?** You might want to move an object from one layer to another or change its color or linetype.

◆ **Is the object correctly placed?** You might need to change the radius of a circle, move the endpoint of a line, or move a text object.

◆ **What layers are created?** Which layers are on and which are off?

This chapter focuses on the tools that you can use to answer the preceding questions. Some of the tools enable you to edit the object and geometric properties of objects. *Geometric properties* define an object's size and location. Endpoints are a line's geometric properties, for example, and the center point coordinates and radius are a circle's geometric properties. *Object properties* are an object's color, linetype, layer, linetype, scale, and thickness.

Quite a number of commands are covered, so the new commands are presented in four groups, as follows:

◆ Commands that give you general information about the drawing, such as LAYER, STYLE, STATUS, TIME, SETVAR, and DDLMODES

◆ Commands that give you specific information about selected objects or points, such as LIST, ID, DIST, and AREA

◆ Commands that enable you to view and change specific properties of selected objects, such as DDMODIFY, DDCHPROP, and CHANGE

◆ The CAL command, which invokes the powerful, built-in calculator

The following exercise gives you a brief overview of the commands covered in this chapter. You see what information is available when you use the TIME and STATUS commands, then you see the information given by the ID and DIST command, and then you use the calculator and the DDMODIFY command.

Quick 5¢ Tour

Begin a new drawing named CHAP15, using the ACAD drawing as a prototype.

Command: *Choose* **D**ata, Tim**e**   Displays the current date and time and some other information

Press F1 or choose the Send F1 button on the text screen.

Command: *Choose* **D**ata, Stat**us**   Displays information about the overall state of your drawing (see fig. 15.1)

Press RETURN to continue: (Enter)   Terminates STATUS

New Riders Publishing
INSIDE
SERIES

Press F1 or choose the Send F1 button on the text screen.

`Command:` *Choose Assist, Inquiry, Locate Point*	Issues the ID command
`Point:` *Pick a point anywhere on the drawing*	Displays the coordinate of the point
`Command:` *Choose Assist, Inquiry, Distance*	Issues the DIST command
`First Point:` *Pick any point*	Establishes the starting point of the measurement
`Second Point:` *Pick any point*	Establishes the ending point of the measurement and displays coordinates, distances, and angles between the two points

Next, you use CAL to a perform calculation from within AutoCAD.

`Command:` *Choose* Tools, Calculator	
`Initializing...>>Expression:` **2+3** (Enter)	Adds 2 to 3 and displays the answer of 5

Next, you use the DDMODIFY command to get object data.

`Command:` *Draw a circle anywhere on your screen*	Places an object for the DDMODIFY command to examine
`Command:` *Choose* Modify, Properties	Prompts for selection
`Select objects:` *Select the circle and press Enter*	Selects circle, issues the DDMODIFY command, and opens the DDMODIFY dialog box (see fig. 15.2)

Explore the dialog box and cancel the DDMODIFY command after you finish. You do not use the CHAP15 drawing again, so you need not save it.

Figure 15.1

A typical report generated by STATUS.

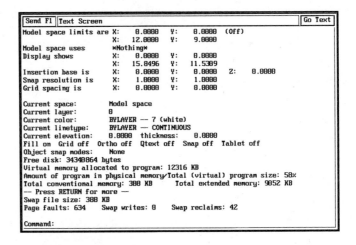

Figure 15.2

The DDMODIFY dialog box.

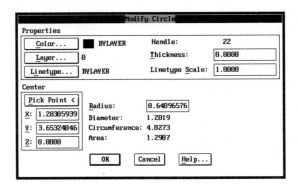

Note If one object is selected, the Modify, Properties menu item issues the DDMODIFY command. If two objects are selected, it issues the DDCHPROP command. Both commands are covered in this chapter, among others.

Getting General Drawing Data

STATUS and TIME are two commands that display information about the general state of your drawing. Additionally, several commands have a listing option you can use to get information about a specific aspect of your drawing, such as a listing of all layers and their states. STATUS, TIME, and these additional commands are covered in this section.

The STATUS Command

The STATUS command enables you to generate a report in the text window that describes the overall status of your drawing.

'STATUS. The STATUS command gives you some general information about the drawing file.
Pull-down: *Choose* Data, Status
Screen: *Choose* DATA, Status

In the "Quick 5¢ Tour" exercise, you issued the STATUS command; figure 15.1 shows a typical report that STATUS generates. You can see in the figure that the report contains much information. The following list describes what you see in each line of the report.

- The number of objects in the current drawing file and the drawing name.

- The coordinates of the lower-left corner of the drawing limits and the setting of limits checking.

- The coordinates of the upper-right corner of the drawing limits.

- The coordinates of the lower-left corner of the drawing space used by your drawing. This coordinate and the next are commonly referred to as the drawing extents.

- The coordinates of the upper-right corner of the drawing space used by your drawing. **Over might appear on this line, indicating that your drawing exceeds the limits you have set.

- The coordinates of the lower-left corner of the current viewport.

- The coordinates of the upper-right corner of the current viewport.

- The coordinates of the insertion base point.

- The X and Y distances used to define the snap resolution.

- The X and Y distances used to define the grid spacing.

- The setting of the current space, model space or paper space.

- The current layer setting.

- The current color setting.

◆ The current linetype setting.

◆ The current elevation and thickness setting.

◆ The settings of all of the modes.

◆ The running object snap modes that may be in effect.

◆ The amount of available disk space on the drive specified for AutoCAD temporary files.

◆ The amount of memory installed on your computer.

◆ The percent of memory installed on your machine that is occupied by the AutoCAD program.

◆ The amount of conventional DOS memory available to AutoCAD and the amount of extended DOS memory available to AutoCAD.

◆ The size of the swap file. The swap file is used to hold memory when AutoCAD exceeds conventional and extended DOS memory.

◆ The statistics concerning the DOS extender technology used to virtualize memory.

STATUS has no options. Using STATUS has no effect on the drawing.

The TIME Command

The TIME command enables you to keep track of time from within the drawing editor.

> **'TIME.** The TIME command enables you to display the current date and time, the date and time the drawing was created, the date and time the drawing was last updated, and the total cumulative time the drawing has been in the drawing editor.
> Pull-down: *Choose* Data, Time
> Screen: *Choose* DATA, Time

Figure 15.3 shows the typical output generated by TIME.

```
Send F1 | Text Screen                                          Go Text
Current color:        BYLAYER — 7 (white)
Current linetype:     BYLAYER — CONTINUOUS
Current elevation:    0.0000   thickness:     0.0000
Fill on  Grid off  Ortho off  Qtext off  Snap off  Tablet off
Object snap modes:    None
Free disk: 33374208 bytes
Virtual memory allocated to program: 12364 KB
Amount of program in physical memory/Total (virtual) program size: 58%
— Press RETURN for more —
Total conventional memory: 388 KB       Total extended memory: 9052 KB
Swap file size: 388 KB
Page faults: 639    Swap writes: 0    Swap reclaims: 42


Command:
Command:
Command: _time
Current time:           13 Dec 1994 at 14:06:56.070
Times for this drawing:
  Created:              13 Dec 1994 at 13:49:54.350
  Last updated:         13 Dec 1994 at 13:49:54.350
  Total editing time:   0 days 00:17:01.720
  Elapsed timer (on):   0 days 00:17:01.720
  Next automatic save in: 0 days 01:47:34.170

Display/ON/OFF/Reset:
```

Figure 15.3

The typical output generated by TIME.

The TIME prompt has the following options:

- ◆ **Display.** Choosing this option causes TIME to redisplay the time information.

- ◆ **ON.** Choosing this option starts the stopwatch function.

- ◆ **OFF.** Choosing this option stops the stopwatch function.

- ◆ **Reset.** Choosing this option resets the stopwatch function.

You can issue the TIME command transparently, and its usage does not affect the drawing.

Stop You might be tempted to use total editing time to track time for accounting purposes, but be careful. If an operator opens a drawing and then heads out for an hour lunch, AutoCAD includes that hour in the cumulative time if the operator subsequently updates the drawing file using the END command or the SAVE command. Also be aware that a copy of a drawing file contains the original file's total editing time. If you plan to track the total editing time, be sure to reset it.

In the following exercise, you use the TIME command to get some times relevant to the drawing file.

Checking on Some Times

Begin a new drawing, again named CHAP15, and use the CPLATE drawing from the IA Disk as the prototype.

continues

continued

Command: *Choose* Data, Time   Issues the TIME command

The current date and time, date and time of drawing creation, date and time of last update, elapsed time since opening the drawing, and time to next autosave are shown. The stopwatch function is automatically turned on when you open a drawing.

Display/ON/OFF/Reset: **OFF** (Enter)   Turns off the stopwatch function

Display/ON/OFF/Reset: **R** (Enter)   Resets the stopwatch function to zero

Display/ON/OFF/Reset: **D** (Enter)   Displays the current time information

The elapsed timer is now off and the time is 0.

Display/ON/OFF/Reset: **ON** (Enter)   Turns on the stopwatch function

So that you can accumulate some time in the timer, wait for several seconds before you proceed to the next step.

Display/ON/OFF/Reset: **D** (Enter)   Displays all time values

The elapsed timer is now on and the time has changed.

Display/ON/OFF/Reset: **OFF** (Enter)   Turns off the stopwatch function

Display/ON/OFF/Reset: (Enter)   Terminates TIME

Using the stopwatch options does not affect the drawing.

Other Listing Commands

A number of commands include a listing option, represented by the ? symbol in the command's options list. Here are some of the commands with the listing option:

Command	List Description
BLOCK ?	Displays a list of currently defined block definitions
DIMSTYLE ?	Displays a list of currently defined dimension styles
HATCH ?	Displays a list of all hatch patterns that reside in the ACAD.PAT file
INSERT ?	Displays a list of all currently defined block definitions (just like HATCH ?)
LAYER ?	Displays a list of all layers and their states

New Riders Publishing
INSIDE
SERIES

LINETYPE ?	Displays a list of all currently loaded linetypes
MLINE ST ?	Displays a list of all currently defined mline styles
SHAPE ?	Displays a list of currently loaded shapes
STYLE ?	Displays a list of all currently defined text styles and their settings
TEXT S ?	Displays a list of all currently defined text styles and their settings
UCS ?	Displays a list of all saved UCSs
VIEW ?	Displays a list of saved views
VPORTS ?	Displays a list of all saved viewport configurations
XREF ?	Displays a list of all currently attached XREFS

Out of the preceding commands, you can use only LAYER, SETVAR, and VIEW transparently.

After you specify the ? option of one of the preceding commands, another prompt usually asks you for the name of the item you want to list. The ? option of the LAYER command, for example, prompts you as follows:

```
Layer name(s) to list <*>:
```

The default value is the asterisk wild-card character, which specifies to list all layer names. If you want a specific layer or group of layers, type a layer name pattern. You can construct layer name patterns from wild-card characters.

Some of the patterns you might want to use can be formed by using individual or combined wild cards (refer to Chapter 5, "Setting Up a CAD Drawing"). Do not be overwhelmed by the possibilities; you usually use the question mark and asterisk. The other wild cards are available if you need them. Here are some common scenarios:

- Use S* to select all layer names that begin with the letter S.

- Use S???? to select all five character layer names that begin with the letter S.

- Use S## to select all three character layer names that begin with the letter S and end with two numbers.

- Use S-1# to select all four character layer names of the form S-nn that fall within the range of S-10 to S-19.

- Use ~# to select all layer names that end with a number.

- Use #* to select all layer names that begin with a number.

Some of the preceding commands with listing options have been superseded by dialog box-based successors. Consequently, you might be unable to find some of the aforementioned commands in any part of the menu system. You might find others only in the screen menu area. The commands, however, are still valid and you can always issue them by typing the command.

The newer dialog box versions of the commands usually have the information that was produced by the ? option incorporated directly into the dialog box format. The LAYER command, for example, has been superseded by the DDLMODES command, and the DDLMODES dialog box shows a list of all layers and their states.

Stop Unlike STATUS or TIME, the commands with listing options can affect your drawing. The ? option is harmless, but you can use the other options of these commands to save, delete, or change definitions and settings in your drawing.

In the following exercise, you get listings of various aspects of a drawing file.

Displaying Some Lists

Continue to use the drawing CHAP15.

Command: **LAYER** (Enter)	Issues the LAYER command
?/Make/Set/New/ON/OFF/Color/Ltype/ Freeze/Thaw/LOck/Unlock: **?** (Enter)	Specifies the listing option
Layer name(s) to list <*>: (Enter)	Instructs LAYER to list all layers

There should be four layers in the list.

?/Make/Set/New/ON/OFF/Color/Ltype Freeze/Thaw/LOck/Unlock: (Enter)	Ends the LAYER command

Next, you get a listing of all currently defined text styles and their settings.

Command: Choose Data, Text Style	Issues the STYLE command
Text style name (or ?) <STANDARD>: **?** (Enter)	Specifies the listing option
Text style(s) to list <*>: (Enter)	Instructs STYLE to list all text styles

There should be two styles in the list.

New Riders Publishing
INSIDE
SERIES

The SETVAR Command

Many drawing, editing, and dialog-box commands affect or are affected by settings. AutoCAD maintains these settings as system variables. SETVAR provides a means by which you can access these settings.

'SETVAR. The SETVAR command enables you to view and (usually) change the current value of a system variable.
Pull-down: *Choose* Options, System Variables
Screen: *Choose* OPTIONS, Sys Var

System variables perform several functions. Certain variables control various aspects of the drawing editor. FILEDIA, for example, controls whether a dialog box appears anytime you are prompted for a file name.

Other variables hold the results of various commands, such as AREA, which holds the last area recorded by the AREA command. Some variables even contain some environment settings. The variable DWGNAME, for example, contains the name of the current drawing file. DWGNAME also is an example of a read-only variable. *Read-only* means that AutoCAD maintains the variable and although you can view its value, you cannot change it directly.

Yet other variables hold the results of and control the actions of a number of AutoCAD commands. When you turn SNAP on or off, for example, the action is stored in the variable OSMODE as a 0 (for off) or 1 (for on). On the other hand, if you set the value of OSMODE directly, you can turn SNAP on or off.

SETVAR once was the primary means of accessing the system variables. AutoCAD now enables you to enter system variables the same as you enter commands, at the Command: prompt. As AutoCAD has developed, access to certain system variables (not all) has been integrated into the menu and command system. AutoCAD stores most dialog box settings as system variables. AutoCAD also stores dimension settings as system variables. You can access the system variable TILEMODE (which controls model space and paper space) through the View pull-down menu. On the other hand, FILEDIA (which controls the File dialog box) does not appear in the menu or any of the commands. To change FILEDIA, you must use SETVAR or enter it at the Command: prompt.

Tip   As a general rule, you can execute system variables transparently. If you are in the middle of the LINE command, for example, you can still execute the variable SNAPUNIT (which controls the snap spacing) and resume the LINE command.

15

When you save system variables, AutoCAD stores them either in the configuration file or with the drawing file. A few are not saved at all. As a general rule, any variables that are related to the drawing environment or editor (such as FILEDIA) are saved in the configuration file. All other variables are saved with the drawing file or not at all. If a particular variable is saved in the configuration file, then its setting carries over from one drawing session to another. If a variable is saved with the drawing, then its current value depends on the current drawing.

Quite a number of system variables exist in AutoCAD. This chapter does not focus on system variables; to learn more about specific system variables, see Appendix A, "Installation and Configuration," and Appendix F, "System Variables Table," of this book, or Appendix A of the *AutoCAD Command Reference*.

Although dated, SETVAR still has its uses. For one, the system variable AREA conflicts with the command AREA. If you enter the command AREA, you execute the command AREA; the only way to view the system variable AREA is to use SETVAR. More importantly, SETVAR is the only command you can use to list all or a group of system variables. You can use any of the wild cards listed earlier in this chapter to list specific sets of system variables.

In the following exercise, you use SETVAR to list and set some system variables.

Examining the System Variables

Continue to use the drawing CHAP15.

`Command:` *Choose* Options, System Variables, List	Issues the SETVAR command and specifies the ? option and * wild card automatically

At various points in the listing, you are prompted to press Enter to display more variables. Press Enter until the listing is completed and the `Command:` prompt reappears.

Some variables are accompanied by the notation (`read only`). This notation indicates that you can view, but not change, the system variable's value.

`Command:` *Choose* Options, System Variables, Set	Issues SETVAR and gives you the option of specifying a system variable name or the ? option

`Variable name or ?:` **?** (Enter)

`Variable(s) to list <*>:` **A*** (Enter)	Instructs SETVAR to list all system variables that begin with the letter A

`Command:` *Choose* Options, System Variables, Set

Variable name or ?: **SAVETIME** Enter	Specifies the system variable SAVETIME
New value for SAVETIME <15>: **20** Enter	Sets a new value for SAVETIME of 20 minutes

SAVETIME is the system variable that determines the time interval (in minutes) at which AutoCAD carries out the autosave function.

System variables are handy. They enable you to specify various settings directly and often are quicker to use than the commands you would normally use to set them. SETVAR is especially useful if you customize AutoCAD with custom menus and AutoLISP or ADS routines.

 Tip   The AutoCAD documentation still makes a distinction between a command and a system variable, even though system variables behave like commands. If you look up a command in Appendix E, "Command, Dialog Box, Alias, and Menu Equivalency Table," and cannot find it, check in Appendix F, "System Variables Table," because it might be listed as a system variable.

15

Getting Object-Specific Data

General information on the state of the drawing is handy, but you also need the capability to get object-specific information. In this section, you learn about commands that enable you to inquire about specific objects.

The DDMODIFY Command

You can use DDMODIFY to view geometric and property information on any drawing object.

> **DDMODIFY.** The DDMODIFY command enables you to display the object and geometric properties of any object you select. You can view or change the properties in the Modify object dialog box.
> Pull-down: *Choose* Modify, Properties
> Screen: *Choose* MODIFY, Modify

In figures 15.4 and 15.5, you can see the typical DDMODIFY dialog box for a line and a circle.

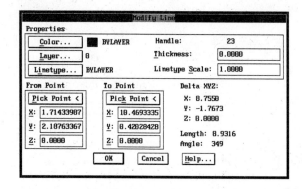

Figure 15.4

The Modify object dialog box for a line.

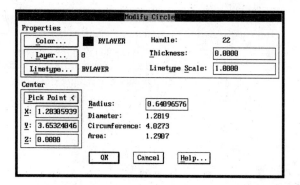

Figure 15.5

The Modify object dialog box for a circle.

Although both dialog boxes are produced by DDMODIFY, the dialog box title and format adjusts according to the type of selected object. The adjustments make it easier to read the object and geometric properties of the selected object.

The first time you invoke DDMODIFY during a drawing session, a message appears telling you that the command is being initialized. DDMODIFY is actually being loaded from a file, which can take several seconds. The next time you need DDMODIFY, it appears immediately because it has already been initialized.

Stop DDMODIFY actually enables you to modify some of the object's properties and geometry, so use it with care. The properties that you can change (such as the layer) appear next to buttons or in edit boxes. (Using DDMODIFY to change objects is covered later in this chapter.) To prevent accidental changes to an object's properties, press Esc or choose the Cancel button to exit the dialog box instead of choosing the OK button.

In the following exercise, you use DDMODIFY to view (not change) the object and geometric properties of selected objects.

Using DDMODIFY

Continue to use the drawing CHAP15.

Command: *Choose* Modify, Properties

Select objects: *Select a line* (Enter)　　　　　Issues the DDMODIFY command and opens
　　　　　　　　　　　　　　　　　　　　　　the Modify Line dialog box with line selected

Be careful not to change any of the settings, and explore the DDMODIFY dialog box. After you
finish exploring, click on the Cancel button.

Command: *Choose* Modify, Properties

Select objects: *Select a circle* (Enter)　　　　Opens the Modify Circle dialog box

Explore this version of the DDMODIFY dialog box. The appearance of the dialog box is
modified to suit the type of object. After you finish exploring, click on the Cancel button.

Tip　　When you choose Properties from the Modify pull-down menu, AutoCAD prompts
you to select objects. If you select more than one object, the command DDCHPROP
starts instead of DDMODIFY. This is because you are actually issuing a menu macro
that issues DDMODIFY if only one object is selected but issues DDCHPROP if
multiple objects are selected. If you want to issue DDMODIFY specifically, be sure to
select only one object. DDCHPROP is covered later in this chapter. If you type the
command DDMODIFY or select it from the screen menu, the actual command
DDMODIFY starts and AutoCAD prompts you to select an object. Invoking
DDMODIFY in this manner operates on only one object at a time.

The LIST Command

You can use the LIST command to list the object and geometric properties of several
objects simultaneously.

> **LIST.** The LIST command enables you to list the object and geometric properties of
> selected objects simultaneously.
> Screen:　　　　*Choose* ASSIST, INQUIRY, List

Unlike the DDMODIFY command, LIST displays the information in the text window.
You can see typical output of the LIST command in figure 15.6.

Figure 15.6

The typical output of LIST for an arc.

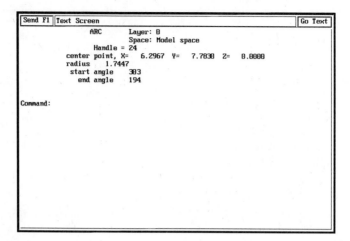

LIST and DDMODIFY display similar information; however, they differ on the following several points:

◆ DDMODIFY uses a dialog box to show the information, whereas LIST uses the text window.

◆ You cannot use LIST to change selected objects, unlike DDMODIFY.

◆ DDMODIFY and LIST sometimes display different calculated values for the same object. For example, LIST displays the area and perimeter of a polyline, whereas DDMODIFY does not. DDMODIFY displays the length of an arc, but LIST does not.

◆ If LIST displays an area, it updates the value of the AREA system variable with the area of the selected object. DDMODIFY does not affect AREA.

◆ LIST enables you to select more than one object. You can use this characteristic to display the information of several objects on one text window, for easier comparison.

◆ You do not have to wait for the LIST command to load—it is always loaded. If you have a slow machine, you might find that LIST responds significantly faster than does DDMODIFY.

In the following exercise, you use LIST to view the object and geometric properties of selected objects.

Listing Properties of Objects

Continue to use the CHAP15 drawing.

`Command:` *Choose* Assist, Inquiry, List	Issues the LIST command
`Select Objects:` *Select several objects*	
`Select Objects:` (Enter)	Displays the object and geometric properties of the selected objects in the text window

---

Note The DBLIST command is a cousin of the LIST command. DBLIST lists the same information for an object as does the LIST command, but does so for all objects in the drawing.

Distances, Areas, and Point Coordinates

The DIST, AREA, and ID commands are additional inquiry commands you can use to get information about selected objects or points. These commands are discussed to emphasize their role as inquiry tools.

The DIST Command

The DIST command enables you to measure the distance between any two selected points; the points do not have to be on the same object. Some distances are automatically measured and displayed by the LIST and DDMODIFY commands. For example, the length of a selected line is given by both LIST and DDMODIFY. You can use DIST transparently.

> **'DIST.** The DIST command enables you to measure the distance between any two selected points.
> Pull-down: *Choose* Assist, Inquiry, Distance
> Screen: *Choose* ASSIST, INQUIRY, Dist

In the following exercise, you use DIST to measure distances.

Measuring Distances

Continue using the CHAP15 drawing.

Command: *Choose* Assist, Inquiry, Distance	Issues the DIST command
First point: *Pick* ① *with* ENDPoint *object snap (see fig. 15.7)*	Picks the beginning point of the measurement
Second point: *Pick* ② *with* ENDPoint *object snap*	Picks the ending point of the measurement
Command: *Choose* Assist, Inquiry, Distance	Issues the DIST command
First point: *Pick* ② *with* ENDPoint *object snap*	Picks the beginning point of the measurement
Second point: *Pick* ① *with* ENDPoint *object snap*	Picks the ending point of the measurement

The distance also should be 6, but the Delta X is a now a negative number.

Figure 15.7

Starting and ending pick points.

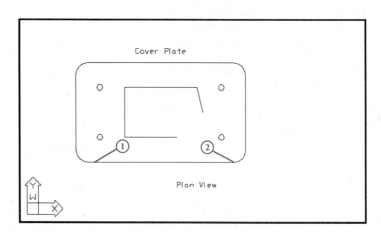

The information listed in both cases should be almost identical, except for the angle. The angle of the second distance is the reverse of the angle in the first, even though you picked the same two points. The angle depends on the order in which you pick the two points.

The AREA Command

You use AREA to measure areas and the perimeters of areas. You can define the area to be measured as the area enclosed by a single closed object (a circle or polyline) or by selected points that define the perimeter. You even can use the AREA command to get a net area of a complicated layout, by adding and subtracting subareas. You cannot execute AREA transparently.

The AREA command has four options—Object, Add, Subtract, and the default mode of identifying an area by picking points. The Object option permits you to select objects, only one at a time, for the calculation of an area. The Add option sums the areas you specify until you finish with the AREA command or until you change the mode's behavior by choosing the Subtract option. The Subtract option subtracts the areas you specify until you finish with the AREA command or until you change the mode to Add. You can mix the Add and Subtract options any time as you use the AREA command. You also can mix the Object option with Subtract or Add so that the object's calculated area is subtracted or added to the total area reported by the AREA command. You can easily indicate areas by using the default mode of picking points. Use the object snap as you pick points to make specific measurements.

AREA. The AREA command enables you to measure areas and perimeters of areas.
Pull-down: *Choose* Assist, Inquiry
Screen: *Choose* ASSIST, INQUIRY, Area

In the following exercise, you measure several areas.

Measuring Areas

Continue to use the drawing CHAP15.

Command: *Choose* Assist, Object Snap, Endpoint	Sets the endpoint object snap mode
Command: *Choose* Assist, Inquiry, Area	Issues the AREA command
<First point>/Object/Add/Subtract: *Pick* ① *(see fig. 15.8)*	Defines the first point of the area
Next point: *Pick* ②	Continue defining the area
Next point: *Pick* ③	Continue defining the area
Next point: *Pick* ④	Continue defining the area

continues

continued

Next point: *Pick* ⑤ **Enter** Area = 5.8181, Perimeter = 9.6618	Complete the definition of the area
Command: *Choose* Assist, Object Snap, None	Sets the object snap mode to none
Command: *Choose* Assist, Inquiry, Area	Repeats the last command
AREA <First point>/Object/Add /Subtract: **O** **Enter**	Tells AREA that you are going to select an object
Select Objects: *Pick* ⑥	Instructs AREA to measure the area and perimeter the polyline (edge of the plate)

Area = 27.7854, Perimeter = 21.1416

Even though the Select Objects: prompt implies you can select more than one object, you really can select only a single object unless you use the Add and Subtract options.

Command: **Enter**	Repeats the last command

Next, you use the Add and Subtract options to measure the net area of the cover plate by measuring the overall area of the plate and then subtracting the area of the circles (holes).

AREA <First point>/Object/Add/ Subtract: **A** **Enter**	Specifies the Add mode of AREA

AREA now adds the areas measured to the total area under its tracking. When you issue AREA, the total (net) area value is reset to zero.

<First point>/Object/Subtract: **O** **Enter**	Tells AREA that you will be selecting objects
(ADD mode) Select objects: *Pick* ⑥ Area = 27.7854, Perimeter = 21.1416 Total area = 27.7854	Area measures the area (27.7854) and perimeter (21.1416) of the polyline and adds the area to the value of the total
(ADD mode) Select objects: **Enter**	Ends the Add mode of AREA
<First point>/Object/Subtract: **S** **Enter**	Specifies the Subtract mode of AREA

AREA now subtracts the areas measured from the total area.

```
<First point>/Object/Add:
0 (Enter)
```

```
(SUBTRACT mode) Select objects:            Select the upper left hole
Pick upper left hole
```

```
Area = 0.0491, Circumference = 0.7854     AREA displays the area and circumference
Total area = 27.7363                       of the circle and then subtracts the circle's
                                           area from the total area
```

```
(SUBTRACT mode) Select objects:            Selects the lower left hole
Pick lower left hole
```

```
Area = 0.0491, Circumference = 0.7854     AREA displays the area and circumference
Total area = 27.6872                       of the circle and then subtracts the circle's
                                           area from the total area
```

```
(SUBTRACT mode) Select objects:            Select the upper right hole
Pick upper right hole
```

```
Area = 0.0491, Circumference = 0.7854     AREA displays the area (0.0491) and
Total area = 27.6381                       circumference (0.7854) of the circle
                                           and then subtracts the circle's area
                                           from the total area
```

```
(SUBTRACT mode) Select objects:            Select the lower right hole
Pick lower right hole
```

```
Area = 0.0491, Circumference = 0.7854     AREA displays the area (0.0491) and
Total area = 27.5890                       circumference (0.7854) of the circle
                                           and the
                                           from th
```

```
(SUBTRACT mode) Select objects: (Enter)    Ends th
```

```
<First point>/Object/Add: (Enter)          Ends th
```

Figure 15.8

Pick points for measuring areas.

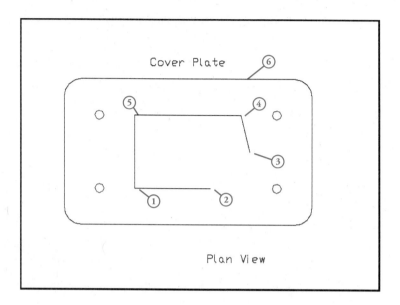

Tip   AutoCAD records the last area measured in the system variable AREA. Because the variable name is identical to the command name AREA, you must use the SETVAR command to retrieve the value of the AREA system variable. The AREA system variable is a handy way to retrieve the results of the last AREA command.

LIST also enables you to calculate and display the area and perimeter of circles and polylines. So, you could use BOUNDARY to outline the overall area with a polyline, then simply list the polyline for its area and perimeter. If you don't want to bother with the vertex data, just use AREA with the generated polyline. If islands are in the overall area, BOUNDARY can create polylines to delineate the islands, and you still can use AREA (using its Add and Subtract options) to get a net area.

The ID Command

The ID command enables you to identify the coordinates of a specified point and, if BLIPMODE is on, display the location. You can use ID transparently, which is handy for identifying coordinates while you accurately create objects. When you identify points on objects, you should pick the exact point, so use object snaps. If you need to see where particular coordinates are in the drawing, type the coordinates and look for the blip mark. You might want to use the REDRAW command first to clear existing blips.

> **'ID.** The ID command enables you to identify the coordinates of a specified point and display the location.
> Pull-down: *Choose* Assist, Inquiry, Locate Point
> Screen: *Choose* ASSIST, INQUIRY, ID

In the following exercise, you use the ID command to identify the coordinates of a point on an object, and to display a blip mark at known coordinates.

Identifying Points

Continue to use the drawing CHAP15.

`Command:` *Choose* Assist, Inquiry, Locate Point	Issues the ID command transparently
`_'id Point:` *Pick upper left hole using center object snap (refer to figure 15.9)* `X = 4.0000 Y = 6.0000 Z = 0.0000`	Displays the coordinates and a blip at the center of the hole

Next, use the ID command to visually locate known coordinates.

`Command:` (Enter)	Repeats the ID command
`_'ID Point:` **2,6** (Enter)	Displays the location of the point with a blip (see fig. 15.9)

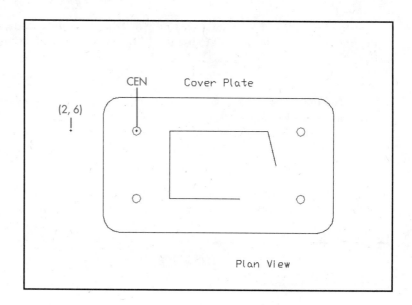

Figure 15.9

Pick points for identifying points.

Changing Object and Geometric Properties

At times, you need to change, not just examine, the object and geometric properties of selected objects. To modify objects, you use the DDMODIFY, DDCHPROP, CHPROP, and CHANGE commands, which are covered in this section.

The DDMODIFY Command

You can use DDMODIFY, not only to display information about a selected object, but also to change various object and geometric properties of the object. You can change any piece of information that appears next to a button or is in an edit field. You can use DDMODIFY to the following aspects of an object:

- ◆ Color or logical color—such as BYLAYER or BYBLOCK

- ◆ Layer

- ◆ Linetype and linetype scale

- ◆ Thickness

- ◆ Point coordinates—such as vertices, pick points, data points, and others

◆ Object geometry—such as radii, start angles, end angles, heights, widths, and other object specific geometries

Refer to figures 15.4 and 15.5 for examples of the DDMODIFY dialog box for a line and for a circle.

Regardless of the type of object you select, DDMODIFY always shows you the object's color, linetype, linetype scale, and thickness, and the layer on which the object resides. Furthermore, the geometric properties of the object (for example, a circle's center point and radius) are displayed. Some additional geometric information is calculated and displayed, such as a circle's circumference and area. The geometric properties that define the object appear in text edit boxes, which enables you to modify those values. You do not modify values that are calculated—DDMODIFY maintains and updates these automatically; for instance, you change a circle's radius and DDMODIFY automatically updates the area and circumference values.

A nice feature of DDMODIFY is that the dialog box adjusts according to the object you select. A shortcoming of the command is that it enables you to select only a single object at a time. When you need to affect several objects at once, use DDCHPROP, CHPROP, or CHANGE, all of which are covered in the following sections.

Tip DDMODIFY enables you to handle text, mtext, and dimension objects especially well. For example, using DDMODIFY, you can alter a text object's oblique angle and width factor, and you can determine whether you should generate the text upside-down or backward. No other editing command enables you to change all these aspects of a text or mtext object.

In the following exercise, you use DDMODIFY to edit selected objects.

Modifying Objects

Continue to use the drawing CHAP15, or create a new drawing named CHAP15, using the CPLATE drawing as a prototype.

Command: *Choose* Modify, Properties

Prompts for selection

Select objects: *Pick* ① *(see fig. 15.10) and press Enter*

Selects the circle, issues DDMODIFY, and opens the Modify Circle dialog box

Click in the **R**adius *text edit box and change the radius to* 0.25, *then choose* OK

Redraws circle with 0.25 radius

continues

continued

Command: *Select the circle at* ②,
then choose Modify, Properties

In the Radius text edit box, change the radius to 0.25.

Command: *Choose* Modify, Properties

Repeat DDMODIFY, choosing Modify, Properties, and change each of the circles at ③ and ④ to a 0.25 radius. Do not select both circles at once, or the DDCHPROP command (Change Properties dialog box) will open rather than DDMODIFY.

Command: **DDMODIFY** (Enter)   Issues the DDMODIFY command

The Properties menu item, from which you can issue DDMODIFY or DDCHPROP, prompts for multiple object selection, but when you enter DDMODIFY directly, it prompts for a single object.

Select object to modify: *Select the*
text string Cover Plate

From the Style drop-down list, select HEADING. In the Obliquing box, change the angle to 10. In the Height box, change the text height to 0.4. Choose OK after you make the changes.

Your drawing should look like figure 15.11.

Figure 15.10

Pick points for modifying objects.

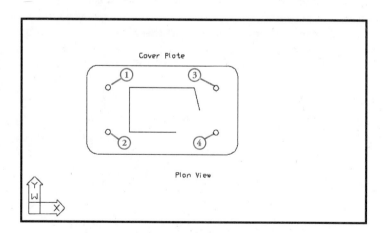

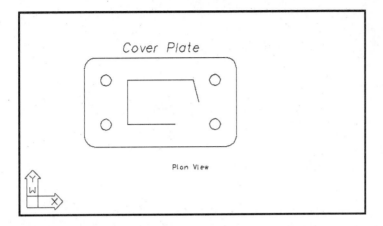

Figure 15.11

*The modified
cover plate.*

DDMODIFY gives you the most control over an object's properties, but unfortunately it works on only one object at a time.

The DDCHPROP Command

DDCHPROP does not enable you to change as many aspects of an object as does DDMODIFY, but it does enable you to edit multiple objects at one time. DDCHPROP enables you to set the following properties:

◆ Color or logical color—such as BYLAYER or BYBLOCK

◆ Layer

◆ Linetype

◆ Linetype scale

◆ Thickness

You can set the color of the selected objects to one color, even if each object has a different color. If the colors are not identical for each selected object, then the selected objects' color displays as "Varies". You can change all of the selected objects' color to one color by choosing the Color button, which activates the Select Color dialog box. In the Select Color dialog box, you can type the Color number or pick from the color palette. You can set BYLAYER or BYBLOCK here.

You can set the layer of the selected objects to one layer name, even if each object has a different layer name. The behavior is consistent with the Color property of DDCHPROP. You can choose the Layer button, which opens the Select Layer dialog box.

You can change the linetype of the selected objects, just as you can change Color and Layer. Choosing the Linetype button opens the Select Linetype dialog box, which contains BYBLOCK, BYLAYER, and the other linetypes you have loaded.

The linetype scale and thickness of the selected objects can be changed by entering the new value in the text input boxes labeled Linetype Scale and Thickness.

DDCHPROP. The DDCHPROP command enables you to change the object properties of selected objects.
Pull-down: *Choose* Modify, Properties
Screen: *Choose* MODIFY, Ddchprop

Issuing the DDCHPROP command invokes the Change Properties dialog box, as shown in figure 15.12.

Figure 15.12

The Change Properties dialog box.

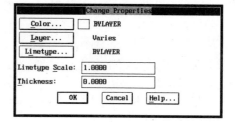

Tip If you work in 3D, you might have noticed that you can change the thickness assigned to objects, but not their elevations. If you do need to change the elevation of multiple objects, use the CHANGE command (described next).

In the following exercise, you use DDCHPROP to change the layer property of several objects simultaneously.

Using DDCHPROP To Change Properties

Continue to use the drawing CHAP15.

Choose Modify, Properties
Prompts for selection

`Select objects:` *Select the four circles and press Enter*
Opens Change Properties dialog box with the circles selected

Because you selected more than one object, the same menu item that you earlier used to issue DDMODIFY now issues DDCHPROP. The dialog box shows color BYLAYER (white) and layer 0.

Choose the **L**ayer button	Opens the Select Layer dialog box
Select layer SCREW_HOLES, *then choose* OK	Sets layer and returns to the Change Properties dialog box

The color shows BYLAYER (red) and the layer shows SCREW_HOLES.

Choose OK	Closes dialog box and redraws circles on layer SCREW_HOLES in red

You have just moved the four circles from layer 0 to layer SCREW_HOLES. The circles change color if you are successful.

Note CHPROP is the command-line version of DDCHPROP. CHPROP and DDCHPROP function identically. CHPROP grew out of the CHANGE command. In effect, CHPROP is the Properties option of the CHANGE command, minus the Elev option.

The CHANGE Command

CHANGE is the grandfather of all the commands covered in this section. CHPROP, DDCHPROP, and DDMODIFY evolved from CHANGE. Despite its age, CHANGE still has its uses.

> **CHANGE.** The CHANGE command enables you to change the object and geometric properties of selected objects.
> Screen: *Choose* MODIFY, Change

Unlike DDCHPROP, you also can use CHANGE to change an object's elevation (Z coordinate), and even an object's geometry, by using a "change point." A *change point* is a point you pick that redefines the object's geometry. The CHANGE command has the following two options:

◆ **Properties.** If you specify the Properties option, you are presented with six properties that you can modify: Color, Elev, LAyer, LType, ltScale, and Thickness.

◆ **Change point.** The default option is to specify a point to use to change the selected objects. You are prompted as follows:

```
Properties/<Change point>:
```

You can pick the change point, or press Enter (or the spacebar) to accept the default option.

You pick the change point, and AutoCAD uses it to modify the object. The effect of the change point depends on the type of object:

◆ **Attribute Definition.** The attribute definition moves to the change point. If you press Enter instead of picking a change point, AutoCAD prompts you for the new text insertion point. In either case, AutoCAD also prompts you for the attribute definition's style, height, rotation angle, tag, prompt, and default value.

◆ **Block.** The inserted block moves to the change point. If you press Enter instead of picking a change point, AutoCAD prompts you for a new insertion point. In either case, AutoCAD also prompts you for a new rotation angle.

◆ **Circle.** The circle's radius adjusts so that the circle passes through the change point. If you press Enter instead of picking a change point, AutoCAD prompts you for a new radius for the circle. Figure 15.13 shows how you can modify a circle's radius using a change point.

Figure 15.13

A change point with a circle.

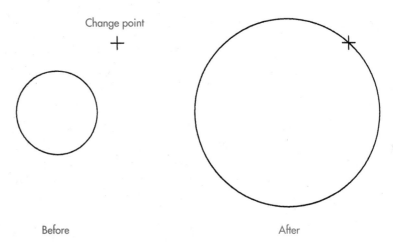

◆ **Line.** The nearest endpoint of the line moves to the change point. If you press Enter, AutoCAD does not prompt you again for a change point. Figure 15.14 shows how you can modify a line's endpoint using change point.

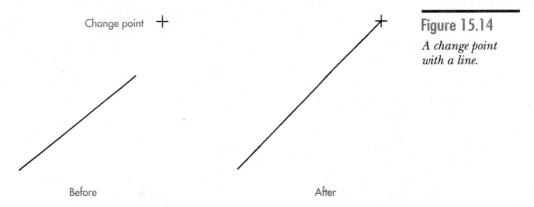

Change point

Before

After

Figure 15.14

A change point with a line.

◆ **Text.** The text moves to the change point. If you press Enter instead of picking a change point, AutoCAD prompts you for a new text insertion point. In either case, AutoCAD prompts you for the text's style, height, rotation angle, and value.

If you select multiple objects and pick a change point, CHANGE cycles through the selection set one object at a time, enabling you to pick a different change point for each object. One exception to this rule exists: If multiple lines are selected, all the lines are modified so that the nearest endpoint of each line moves to the change point. Figure 15.15 shows how a change point affects a multiple selection of lines.

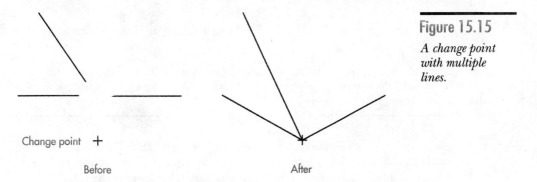

Change point

Before

After

Figure 15.15

A change point with multiple lines.

In the following exercise, you use CHANGE to alter the location and appearance of text and line objects.

Changing Some Objects

Continue to use the CHAP15 drawing.

Command: **CHANGE** (Enter)	Invokes the CHANGE command
Select objects: *Select the text* Plan View *and press Enter*	
Properties/<Change point>: **6.5,2** (Enter)	Moves the insertion point of the text object to the point 6.5,2
Text style: STANDARD	
New style or RETURN for no change: **HEADING** (Enter)	Changes the text style to HEADING
New height <0.2000>: **0.3** (Enter)	Changes the text size to 0.3 units
New rotation angle <0>: (Enter)	Accepts the current setting
New text <Plan View>: **Plan View** **(nts)** (Enter)	Changes the text string

Next, you modify the two lines shown in figure 15.16 so that they meet at the point 8,3.

Command: (Enter)	Repeats the last command
CHANGE	Selects the lines
Select objects: *Select the lines* ① *and* ② *and press Enter* *(see fig. 15.16)*	
Properties/<Change point>: **8,4** (Enter)	Stretches the lines to the change point 8,4

Because you selected only lines, AutoCAD changed the lines simultaneously so that the endpoint of each line nearest to the change point was moved to the change point. Your drawing should now look like figure 15.17.

One advantage of the CHANGE command over CHPROP, DCHPROP, and DDMODIFY is that you can use it to change the Z coordinate of multiple objects. Because Z coordinates are used only in 3D drawings, this aspect of the CHANGE command is not covered until Part Seven, "AutoCAD and 3D."

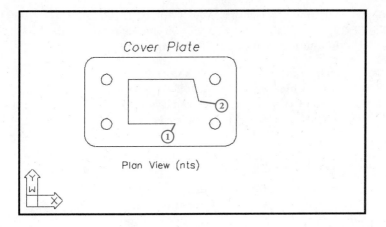

Figure 15.16

Changing text and change points for lines.

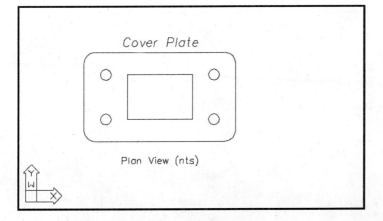

Figure 15.17

Changed lines.

15

Using the CAL Command

Issuing the CAL command invokes a powerful built-in calculator that you can use to perform numeric calculations, calculations involving point coordinates, and even calculations involving distances and angles. It is tightly integrated into the drawing editor, which gives you capabilities you do not have with an ordinary desktop calculator.

'CAL. The CAL command invokes the calculator included with AutoCAD.

Pull-down: *Choose* Tools, Calculator

Screen: *Choose* TOOLS, GeomCal

You can execute the CAL command transparently. If AutoCAD prompts you for the radius during the CIRCLE command, for example, you can enter CAL to help you calculate the radius without interrupting the CIRCLE command.

The CAL command is such a powerful tool and has so many capabilities that you should approach it in stages, which you do in the following sections. First, you learn how to use the CAL command as an ordinary desktop calculator. Then you learn how to use it to calculate points, distances, and angles of objects in your drawing.

CAL Command as a Desktop Calculator

You can use CAL to evaluate any mathematical expression that involves addition, subtraction, multiplication, and division. In the following exercise, you perform several such calculations.

Doing Math with the Calculator

Continue to use the drawing CHAP15.

Command: *Choose* Tools, Calculator	Issues the CAL command
Initializing...>> Expression: **5/16** (Enter)	Calculates the decimal equivalent of the fraction 5/16
0.3125	
Command: (Enter)	Repeats the CAL command
>>Expression: **7/32** (Enter)	Calculates the decimal equivalent of the fraction 7/32
0.21875	

If you execute CAL at the command prompt, the answer to your expression echoes to the screen. If you execute CAL transparently from within a command, AutoCAD interprets the calculated value as an input value by the command, as in the following exercise.

Using CAL Transparently

In the following sequence, you draw a circle and use CAL to specify the radius.

Command: *Choose* Draw, Circle, *then* Center, Radius	Issues the CIRCLE command

`3P/2P/TTR/<Center point>: ` **`3,5`** `(Enter)`	Places the center at 3,5
`Diameter/<Radius>: ` *Choose* Tools, Calculator	Issues CAL
`>> Expression: ` **`9/32`** `(Enter)` and draws the circle	Calculates the decimal equivalent of 9/32

In this case, you didn't really need to use CAL. CIRCLE would understand if you just type 9/32 as the radius. This was just an illustration of how the command captures the value CAL returns.

`Command: ` **`U`** `(Enter)`	Undoes the circle you just drew

The CAL command supports most of standard mathematical functions found on a scientific/engineering calculator, including the following:

sin(angle)	Returns the sine of the angle
cos(angle)	Returns the cosine of the angle
tang(angle)	Returns the tangent of the angle
asin(real)	Returns the arcsine of the number
acos(real)	Returns the arccosine of the number
atan(real)	Returns the arctangent of the number
ln(real)	Returns the natural log of the number
log(real)	Returns the base 10 log of the number
exp(real)	Returns the natural exponent of the number
exp10(real)	Returns the base 10 exponent of the number
round(real)	Returns the number rounded to the nearest integer
trunc(real)	Returns the integer portion of the number
sqr(real)	Returns the square of the number
sqrt(real)	Returns the square root of the number
abs(real)	Returns the absolute value of the number
r2d(angle)	Converts an angle from radians to degrees
d2r(angle)	Converts an angle from degrees to radians
pi	The constant pi

15

Unlike AutoLISP functions, the CAL command expects you to enter angles in decimal degrees and returns angular values in decimal degrees. You enter complicated expressions just as you would write them on a piece of paper, complete with necessary parentheses. The CAL command evaluates expressions using AOS (Algebraic Operating System) rules. In the next exercise, you enter longer expressions.

As part of your routine work, you might need to convert temperature readings from Fahrenheit to Celsius. The equation you use is Celsius = (5/9) × (Fahrenheit −32)). In the following exercise, you convert 76 degrees Fahrenheit to degrees Celsius.

Suppose you need to calculate the cost of moving dirt on your construction site. The calculation involves taking the volume in cubic feet, which you convert to cubic yards (27 cubic feet per cubic yard) and then multiply by a cost per cubic yard of $1.27. You then multiply the calculated dollar amount by a factor of 1.5 to get the amount you bill the client. Also in the following exercise, you convert the volume 15,000 cubic feet, price it, and round the final value to the nearest dollar.

Entering Longer Expressions

Continue to use the CHAP15 drawing.

First, convert 76° F to degrees Celsius.

Command: *Choose* Tools, Calculator

`>> Expression: (5/9)*(76-32)` (Enter)   Converts 76 degrees Fahrenheit to 24.4444
`24.444`   degrees Celsius

Next, you calculate the cost of excavation.

Command: *Choose* Tools, Calculator

`>>Expression:`   Returns an answer of 1058
round((15000/27)*1.27*1.5) (Enter)

You never enter commas as part of a number (such as 15,000), and integer values (whole numbers) that you enter or that are calculated must be between −32,768 and 32,767.

Variables

As when you use a desktop calculator, you can store the results in memory locations (variables) and then recall those values as the need arises. You can name the memory locations anything by using a combination of digits, letters, and other characters, except ( ) . ' " ; and spaces.

New Riders Publishing
INSIDE
SERIES

Tip Keep variable names short but meaningful. The variable name SUM, for example, communicates its purpose better than the name S.

You create the named memory location and store a value in it when you enter the expression at the CAL prompt. You type the variable name, followed by an equal sign, and then the expression you want AutoCAD to evaluate. When you need to use the variable outside of the CAL command, you access it by prefixing the variable name with an exclamation mark (!). The ! is a command prefix that you use to access AutoLISP variables. In the following exercise, you create and use a variable.

In the following exercise, you learn how to use CAL command variables and system variables to work through a simple problem.

Using Variables

Continue to use the CHAP15 drawing. Assume the rectangle of the cover plate is not a void, but a thickened portion that must have a large hole drilled at the center. The hole must not remove more then 50 percent of the thickened portion's area.

Command: *Choose* Assist, Inquiry, Area	Issues the AREA command
`<First Point>/Object/Add/Subtract:` `ENDP` (Enter)	Uses endpoint snap for accuracy
of *Pick* ① *(see fig. 15.18)*	Begins defining the thickened area
of Next point: `ENDP` (Enter)	
of *Pick* ②	Continues the definition
Next point: `ENDP` (Enter)	
of *Pick* ③	Continues the definition
Next point: `ENDP` (Enter)	
of *Pick* ④	Completes the definition
Next point: (Enter)	Completes the AREA command

`Area = 6.0000, Perimeter = 10.0000`

Now that you have determined the area of the thickened portion, you can calculate the center X coordinate of the area by subtracting the X coordinates of width, then dividing by two, and adding the result to the X coordinate at ①. Calculate the center Y coordinate of the area by subtracting the Y coordinates of the height, dividing by two, and adding the result to the Y coordinate at ②.

continues

continued

Command: *Choose* Tools, Calculator	Issues the 'CAL command
`'_cal >> Expression:` **`XCENTER=(8-5)/2+5`** (Enter)	Stores the result in variable XCENTER
`6.5`	
Command: (Enter) `'_CAL >> Expression:` **`YCENTER=(6-4)/2+4`** (Enter)	Repeats the 'CAL command Stores the result in variable YCENTER
`5.0`	

Next, you find the radius of the circle that will give a 50 percent area. Use the formula $A = pi\ r^2$.

Command: (Enter)	Repeats the 'CAL command
`'_CAL >> Expression:` **`MAXAREA=GETVAR(AREA)*0.5`** (Enter)	Retrieves the system variable AREA and stores half of it in variable MAXAREA
`3.0`	
Command: (Enter)	Repeats the 'CAL command
`'_CAL >> Expression:` **`MAXRAD=SQRT(MAXAREA/PI)`** (Enter)	Solves for r and stores the result in MAXRAD
`0.977205`	
Command: *Choose* Draw, Circle, *then* Center, Radius	Issues the CIRCLE command
`3P/2P/TTR/<Center point>:` **`'CAL`** (Enter)	Issues the CAL command
`>> Expression:` **`[XCENTER,YCENTER]`** (Enter)	Forms a point from our variables (see the next section for more on point specification)
`Diameter/<Radius>` **`!MAXRAD`** (Enter)	Uses the value stored in variable MAXRAD
Command: **`U`** (Enter)	Undoes the CIRCLE command

AutoCAD does not save variables and their contents with the drawing. When you QUIT or END the drawing, it discards the variables.

New Riders Publishing
INSIDE
SERIES

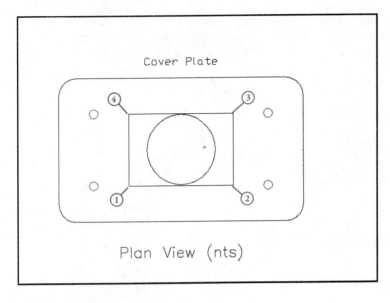

Figure 15.18
Pick points for defining the thickened area.

CAL as a Point Calculator

You also can use CAL to evaluate expressions that involve point coordinates. You can specify a point in any of the standard AutoCAD formats, but the most commonly used ones are Cartesian and polar coordinates.

Cartesian	[X,Y,Z]
Polar	[dist<angle]
Relative	[@dist<angle]

In CAL, you must enclose the coordinates in brackets ([]).

CAL can perform standard +1/* operations with points in the following manner:

multiplication	number * point or point*point
division	point/number or point/point
addition	point + point
subtraction	point – point

Expressions that involve point coordinates are also referred to as *vector expressions.* Suppose you want to find the coordinates of a point midway between the points 2,3 and 3,4. You can calculate the midpoint by averaging the X and Y values of the two points, as follows:

```
Command: CAL
>> Expression: ([2,3]+[3,4])/2
(2.5 3.5 0.0)
```

Performing operations with specific point coordinates in isolation probably does not excite you. But what if you could evaluate expressions using points that you select? The function CUR instructs CAL to let the user pick a point. The preceding example can be generalized as the following:

```
Command: CAL
>> Expression: (cur+cur)/2
```

Furthermore, you can incorporate object snap into your expressions by entering one of the following CAL functions rather than CUR:

> end (endpoint)
>
> ins (insert)
>
> int (intersection)
>
> mid (midpoint)
>
> cen (center)
>
> nea (nearest)
>
> nod (node)
>
> qua (quadrant)
>
> per (perpendicular)
>
> tan (tangent)

To take the preceding example a little further, you can calculate the point midway between an endpoint of a line and the center of a circle (see fig. 15.19). The command sequence might go as follows:

```
Command: CAL
>> Expression: (end+cen)/2
```

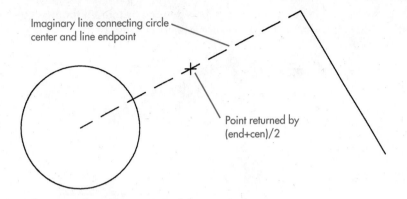

Figure 15.19

Finding a point midway between two other points.

Imaginary line connecting circle center and line endpoint

Point returned by (end+cen)/2

CAL also provides a set of functions to calculate points for certain scenarios:

◆ **ill(p1,p2,p3,p4).** Returns the intersection point of lines (P1,P2) and (P3,P4) (see fig. 15.20).

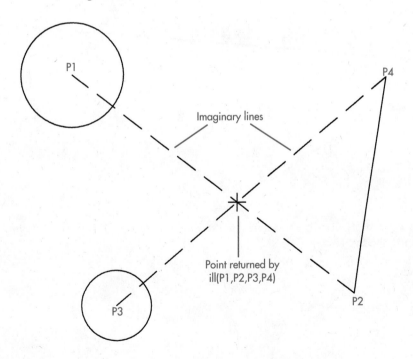

Figure 15.20

Finding an intersection of imaginary lines.

15

P1

P4

Imaginary lines

Point returned by ill(P1,P2,P3,P4)

P3

P2

◆ **ille.** Returns the intersection point of two lines defined by four endpoints. The shortcut for the expression is: `ill(end,end,end,end)` (see fig. 15.21).

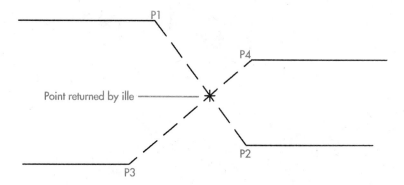

Figure 15.21

Finding an intersection of two imaginary lines.

◆ **mee.** Returns the midpoint between two endpoints (see fig. 15.22).

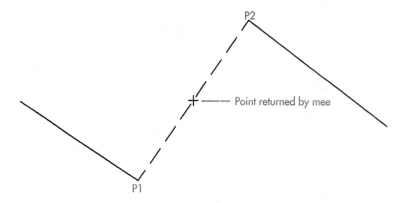

Figure 15.22

Finding a midpoint of an imaginary line.

◆ **pld(p1,p2,dist).** Returns the point on the line (p1,p2) which is *dist* units from point p1 (see fig. 15.23).

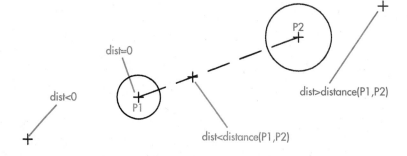

Figure 15.23

Finding a distance along an imaginary line.

New Riders Publishing
INSIDE SERIES

◆ **plt(p1,p2,t).** Returns the point on the line(p1,p2) at a distance from p1, where *t* is the ratio of the distance from p1 to the desired point, to the distance from p1 to p2 (see fig. 15.24).

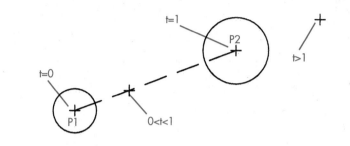

Figure 15.24

Finding a point at a parametric distance of an imaginary line.

Tip By invoking the CAL command from within AutoCAD commands, you can calculate point coordinates any time the need arises, which enables you to use CAL not only as an inquiry tool, but as a powerful construction aid.

In the following exercise, you use the CAL command to draw a new circle.

Calculating Points

Continue to use the CHAP15 drawing.

Command: *Choose* Draw, Circle, *then* Center, Radius	Issues the CIRCLE command
3P/2P/TTR/<Center point>: *Choose* Tools, Calculator	Issues the CAL command transparently
>>Expression: **(cen+cen)/2** (Enter)	Instructs CAL to return the point midway between the centers of two circles that you select next
>>Select entity for CEN snap: *Pick* ① *(see fig. 15.25)*	
>>Select entity for CEN snap: *Pick* ②	Sets center of circle
Diameter/<Radius>: **0.5** (Enter)	Finishes the CIRCLE command by specifying a radius of 0.5 units

Your drawing should look like figure 15.26.

Figure 15.25

Pick points on the cover plate.

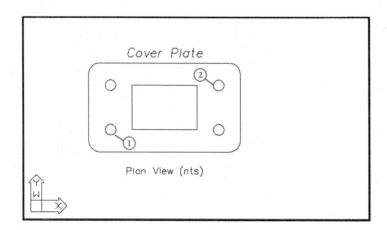

Figure 15.26

The circle is drawn at calculated midpoint.

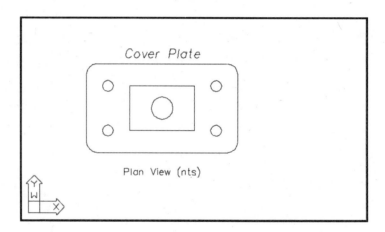

Using CAL can eliminate the need to draw intermediate construction lines.

CAL as a Distance Calculator

The CAL command also has functions for calculating distances, some of the more useful ones are discussed in the following list:

- ◆ **dee.** Distance between two endpoints; short for dist(end,end). See figure 15.27.

- ◆ **dist(p1,p2).** Distance between p1 and p2 (see fig. 15.28).

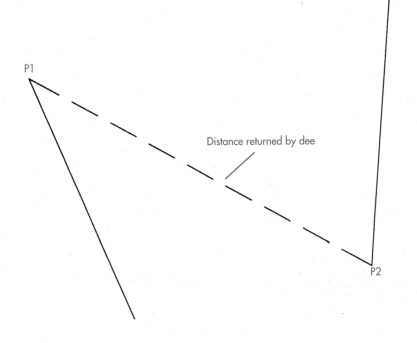

Figure 15.27

Finding a distance between two endpoints.

Distance returned by dee

P1

P2

15

Figure 15.28

Finding a distance between two points.

P1

P2

Distance returned by dist(P1,P2)

◆ **dpl(p,p1,p2).** Distance between point p and the line (p1,p2). See figure 15.29.

◆ **rad.** Radius of the selected object.

Figure 15.29

Finding the distance between a point and an imaginary line.

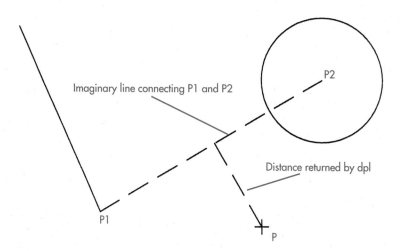

Imaginary line connecting P1 and P2

P2

Distance returned by dpl

P1

P

You can, of course, use DIST to measure distances, but you can integrate only these functions into more complicated CAL expressions.

In the following exercise, you measure some distances with CAL.

Calculating Distances

Continue to use the CHAP15 drawing.

Command: *Choose Tools, Calculator*

>> Expression: **rad** (Enter)	Instructs CAL to measure a curve's radius
Select circle, arc or polyline segment for RAD function: *Select the 0.5 radius circle*	Returns the radius
0.5	
Command: (Enter)	Repeats the CAL command
>>Expression: **rad*1.5** (Enter)	Instructs CAL to measure a curve's radius and multiply it by 1.5
Select circle, arc or polyline segment for RAD function: *Select the same circle*	Returns 1.5 times the radius
0.75	

New Riders Publishing
INSIDE
SERIES

Angle Measurement with CAL

Although you can use **DIST** to measure distances and **AREA** to measure areas, you do not have an equivalent command for measuring angles. Of course, you can use **DIMANGULAR** to dimension angles, but still, you have no command just for measuring an angle. Fortunately, the **CAL** command has several functions that enable you to make angular measurements:

◆ **ang(p1,p2).** Angle between the X axis and the line (p1,p2). See figure 15.30.

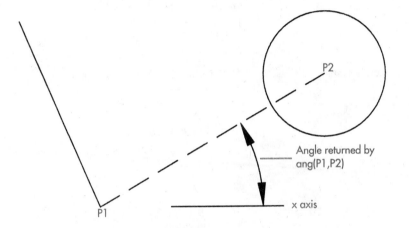

Figure 15.30

Finding the angle of an imaginary line.

◆ **ang(apex,p1,p2).** Angle between the lines (apex,p1) and (apex,p2) projected onto the XY plane (see fig. 15.31).

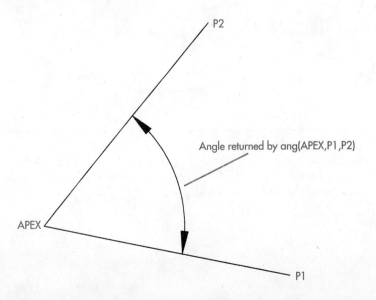

Figure 15.31

Finding the angle formed by three points.

In the following exercise, you measure the angle between two lines.

Measuring Angles

Continue to use the CHAP15 drawing.

Command: *Choose* Tools, Calculator

>> Expression: **ang(cen,cen,cen)** (Enter)	Instructs CAL to use the ang function with three center points you supply
>> Select entity for CEN snap: *Pick* ① *(see fig. 15.32)*	Selects the apex for the measurement
>> Select entity for CEN snap: *Pick* ②	Selects the end of the line from which the measurement begins
>> Select entity for CEN snap: *Pick* ③	Selects the end of the line at which the measurement ends

21.8014

Command: *Choose* Tools, Calculator

>> Expression: **ang(cen,cen,cen)** (Enter)	Instructs CAL to use the ang function with three center points you supply
>> Select entity for CEN snap: *Pick* ①	Selects the apex for the measurement
>> Select entity for CEN snap: *Pick* ③	Selects the end of the line from which the measurement begins
>> Select entity for CEN snap: *Pick* b	Select the end of the line at which the measurement ends

338.199

The angle measured the second time differed from the first angle because the angle is measured counterclockwise from the line (apex, p1) to the line (apex, p2). The order in which you select the points is very important.

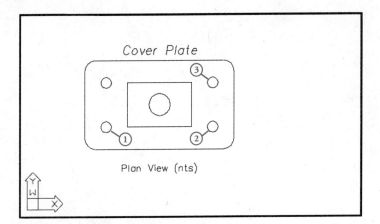

Figure 15.32

Pick points for angle measurements.

Other Uses for CAL

CAL has many other functions that enable you to calculate vectors, unit vectors, normal vectors, and filter point coordinates, and to convert points between the UCS and the WCS. To learn more about CAL, you can find a complete listing of CAL functions in the *AutoCAD Command Reference*, under CAL.

In this chapter, you have discovered many commands and functions that you can use to modify objects, report measurements of objects, and extend the function of other commands you previously learned. By now, you can set up a basic drawing and draw accurately.

Next, you venture into the part of this book that explains how you can automate drawings. You examine the use of symbols and drawing references, as well as other tools, that you can use to become truly productive.

15

Part IV

Automating Drafting

New Riders Publishing
INSIDE
SERIES

Basic Building Blocks for Repetitive Drawing

In this chapter you explore how to create and use blocks. *Blocks* are drawing elements grouped together so that you can place them easily throughout a drawing or use them in many different drawings. The use of blocks is similar to the use of templates in board drafting, but if you use blocks you control the scale and proportions of the symbols you draw. Just as when you use templates, using blocks eliminates repetitive drawing tasks and ensures standard symbols. You also are shown in this chapter how to attach text information to a block. Text information can be constant or can be defined each time you place the block.

In this chapter you learn how to do the following:

◆ Create a block of drawing objects

◆ Place blocks in your drawing

◆ Use blocks to increase drafting speed and technical accuracy and decrease file size

◆ Define block attributes that attach textual and numeric data to your block

◆ Insert attribute values with blocks

Using blocks enables you to increase the speed, uniformity, and efficiency of your work with AutoCAD. You increase drawing speed by eliminating the time you spend re-creating common elements, such as title blocks and drawing symbols. You increase uniformity, within a drawing or from one drawing to the next, through repetitious insertion of identical objects contained in a complex block reference. You also decrease drawing file size by using blocks for repetitive features because all block insertions make reference to a single complex of objects that reside in your drawing environment.

When to use blocks is as important to know as how to use them. Figure 16.1 shows some typical uses of blocks for common drawing symbols and parts. Blocks are most commonly used as the AutoCAD version of a drafting template. Other uses of blocks, however, go well beyond the capabilities of templates. For instance, if you create a standard title block with *attributes* (text attached to a block), you can automate the repetitive process of filling in the title block information for each drawing. Also, if you insert blocks that have variable X and Y scale factors, you can use the same block to generate several different sizes of the symbol, as shown in figure 16.2.

Figure 16.1

Blocks used as drawing symbols.

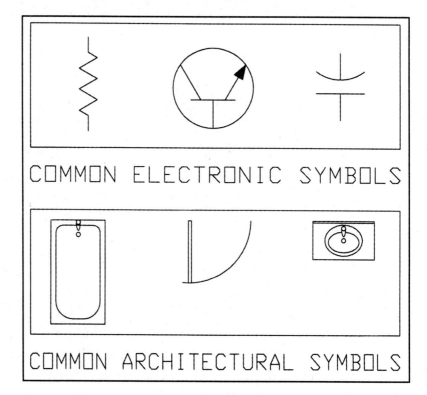

COMMON ELECTRONIC SYMBOLS

COMMON ARCHITECTURAL SYMBOLS

New Riders Publishing
INSIDE
SERIES

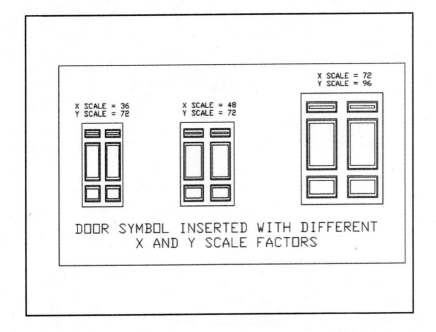

Figure 16.2
Scaling a block's proportions.

Blocks also can offer editing advantages. To move or copy symbol objects as individual drawing objects, you collect the individual objects into a selection set. As drawings become crowded, however, selecting the objects you want becomes more difficult. You can make selection much easier if you group the objects together as a block. AutoCAD blocks enable you to operate on the group as a whole. Objects in blocks stick together; if you move one part of the block, the whole block moves.

You save a block with a name and reuse it any number of times later in the same drawing or in other drawings. If you need to edit the individual elements of a block, you can explode the block.

The following exercise introduces you to some of the capabilities of blocks. In the exercise, you open a drawing of a simple office floor plan, insert a title block symbol, supply title information as attribute values, and insert a full-scale symbol of a workstation. Next, you insert the symbol of a chair twice—once at full scale, and again at a 3:1 scale to create a couch. All of these symbols are available to you as blocks of objects that have a fixed relationship to each other that enables their repetitive use.

You use the Insert dialog box to place blocks into your drawing. Figure 16.3 shows you where you can find this command in the pull-down menu.

Figure 16.3

Choosing the Insert dialog box.

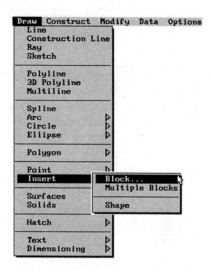

Quick 5¢ Tour

Begin a new drawing named CHAP16, using the file FLRPLN from the IA Disk as a prototype.

Command: *Choose* Draw, Insert, Block	Issues the DDINSERT command and opens the Insert dialog box
Type **TITLE** *in the box next to the* File *button*	Selects the file TITLE.DWG from the IA Disk
Clear the Specify Parameters on Screen *check box, then choose* OK	Sets insertion to use default location and scale, closes Insert dialog box, then opens Enter Attributes dialog box

You provide title block information for AutoCAD to automatically insert into the title block in the Enter Attribute dialog box. In the appropriate edit boxes, type your name, sheet number **1**, last sheet in package **10**, leave the scale at its default value, and type the current date. After you enter the information, choose OK. The title block is inserted with the information you entered as shown in figure 16.4.

Zoom in on the upper half of the floor plan, as shown in figure 16.5.

Set the FURNITURE layer current.

Command: *Choose* Draw, Insert, Block	Issues the DDINSERT command and opens the Insert dialog box
Choose the Block *button*	Opens the Defined Blocks dialog box

New Riders Publishing
INSIDE
SERIES

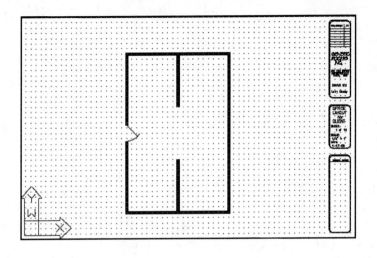

Figure 16.4

*Inserted title block
with attributes.*

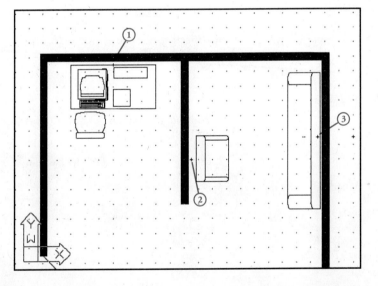

Figure 16.5

*The floor plan,
showing the
insertion points
for blocks.*

16

Select WORKSTATION *from the list, then choose* OK	Specifies the block to insert and returns to the Insert dialog box
Put a check in the <u>S</u>pecify Parameters on Screen *check box, then choose* OK	Closes the Insert dialog box and prompts for location
Insertion Point: *Pick* ① *(refer to figure 16.5)*	Specifies the insertion point of block origin

continues

continued

`X scale factor <1> / Corner / XYZ:` **Enter**	Accepts the default X scale factor of 1
`Y scale factor (default=X):` **Enter**	Accepts the default Y scale factor
`Rotation angle <0>:` **Enter**	Accepts the default block rotation angle
`Command:` **Enter**	Repeats the last command

`DDINSERT`

Type **CHAIR2** *in the box next to the* **B**lock *button, then choose* OK	Specifies block and closes the dialog boxes
`Insertion point:` *Pick* ②	Specifies insertion point of block
`X scale factor <1> / Corner / XYZ:` **Enter**	Accepts the default
`Y scale factor (default=X):` **Enter**	Accepts the default
`Rotation angle <0>:` **180** **Enter**	Specifies a rotation angle for the block
`Command:` **Enter**	Repeats the last command

`DDINSERT`

Choose OK	Defaults to insert the block CHAIR2 because it was the last used block
`Insertion point:` *Pick* ③	Specifies insertion point of block origin
`X scale factor <1> / Corner / XYZ:` **Enter**	Accepts the default
`Y scale factor (default=X):` **3** **Enter**	Specifies a Y scale factor of 3
`Rotation angle <0>:` *With ORTHO on, drag to a point toward angle 0 (to the right) and click*	Specifies a rotation angle for the block

See if you can insert the blocks in their proper positions to complete the drawing as shown in figure 16.6.

Save the drawing.

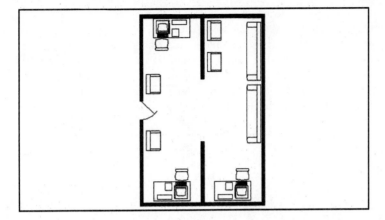

Figure 16.6

The completed office plan.

Blocks and Drawing File Size

Using blocks helps minimize a drawing's file size. If you draw 100 lines, for example, you add 100 objects to your drawing. If you make a block that contains 100 lines, AutoCAD creates a block definition that contains 100 objects, which then is stored as one object in the drawing file. When you insert a block in your drawing, you add only one new object—a reference to the block definition.

If you insert the block only once, you see nothing because the definition containing 100 lines is also stored in the drawing. However, if you insert a block that contains 100 lines into your drawing in 12 places, AutoCAD must store only 112 objects. These 112 objects include 100 lines in the block definition and 12 block references (properly called *insert objects*) for the visible references. If you draw and copy 12 groups of 100 lines, but do not use blocks, you add 1,200 objects to your drawing file. You can see, then, how using blocks can save huge amounts of disk and memory space. Using blocks to reduce the size of the drawing file also lowers the time required to load the file and leaves more memory free for other uses.

Understanding Types and Uses of Blocks

Drafting uses many symbols (such as thread symbols and surface finish symbols in mechanical drafting, window and door symbols in architectural drafting, fittings and equipment in pipe drafting, and so on) and common drawing elements (such as title blocks, standard details, and company logos). The varied use of symbols calls for various types of blocks.

You generally can divide types of drafting symbols into three categories. Certain common elements are not related to a specific type of drawing, such as the symbols illustrated in figure 16.7. Some common elements might pertain only to a specific drawing, such as the pump arrangements illustrated in figure 16.8. Also, you would use some symbols only on specific types of drawings, such as those illustrated in figure 16.9. Although these three categories don't cover every application of blocks for symbols, they do represent the largest use of blocks.

Figure 16.7

Common elements used in a variety of drawings.

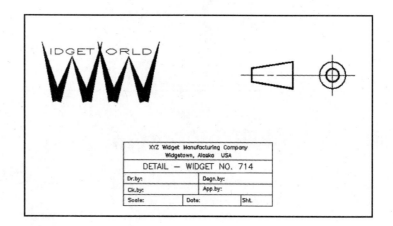

Figure 16.8

Common elements within a specific drawing.

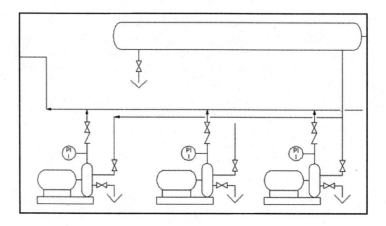

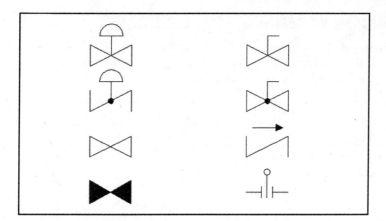

Figure 16.9

Symbols used within a specific type of drawing.

In addition to their use as symbolic objects in diagrammatic drawings, blocks often are used for real-world objects, such as toilets, light fixtures, fittings, or the furniture you inserted in the Quick 5¢ Tour exercise. Although you inserted one chair at a scale of 3:1 to create a couch, blocks used as real-world objects usually are defined at full scale and inserted at a 1:1 scale. Notice that the arms of the sofa became distorted when rescaled in one axis.

To accommodate these different applications, you use different methods of creating blocks. The WBLOCK command usually is suited best for common elements used in many drawings, such as a title block. The BLOCK command usually is suited best for common elements within a drawing. Finally, for symbols related only to specific types of drawings, the most efficient method of creating blocks is to use a symbol library of blocks. This chapter introduces you to the BLOCK and WBLOCK commands. Chapter 17, "Block Structure, Editing, Organization, and Management," deals with symbol libraries.

Creating and Using Blocks

AutoCAD provides several commands for grouping objects into blocks and inserting them. You use the BLOCK command to create a block definition, the DDINSERT command (which opens the Insert dialog box) or INSERT commands to place a block reference in a drawing, and the WBLOCK command to store a block's objects as a separate drawing file on disk. The BASE command enables you to reposition a block's insertion base point, and the MINSERT command enables you to insert blocks in a rectangular array.

Defining Blocks with the BLOCK Command

The BLOCK command defines a named reference in your drawing for the complex of drawing objects selected. The Block command can be issued from the Construct drop-down menu or entered on the command line.

> **BLOCK.** The BLOCK command has several prompts, and one option—the ? option—to list defined blocks.
> Pull-down: *Choose* Construct, Block

The prompts and the option for the BLOCK command are as follows:

- ◆ **Block name.** Supply a name for the block reference in your drawing.

- ◆ **Insertion base point.** Choose a reference point to use when placing the block in your drawing.

- ◆ **Select objects.** Select the objects to be included in the block reference.

Your response to the AutoCAD prompt for a block name can consist of any combination of letters and numbers up to a maximum length of 31 characters. In addition to letters and numbers, you can use the following characters: $, – (hyphen), and _ (underscore).

At the block name prompt, AutoCAD also gives you an opportunity to see a list of named blocks in the drawing if you type ?. AutoCAD lists the names of all blocks, and shows the number and types of blocks. The four types of blocks are described in the following list:

- ◆ **User blocks.** Blocks you use the BLOCK command to create.

- ◆ **External reference blocks.** Reference drawings attached to the drawing. (See Chapter 19, "Using Xrefs for Efficiency and Sharing Data," for more about reference drawings.)

- ◆ **Dependent blocks.** Blocks that belong to reference drawings.

- ◆ **Unnamed blocks.** Blocks that AutoCAD creates to perform hatching, associative dimensioning, PostScript importing, and solid modeling functions.

Next, AutoCAD prompts you for an insertion base point. You can enter the insertion base point as a coordinate or you can select it on-screen. The insertion base point becomes the point from which a block is justified when you place it in your drawing. Usually, you want to use an object snap mode to select the block insertion base point.

Before you pick a practical insertion base point while creating a block, you must consider how you plan to place the block in your drawing. Figure 16.10 shows some typical block insertion base points.

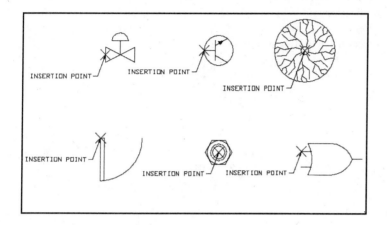

Figure 16.10

Typical block insertion base points.

Note Also consider the orientation of the objects in the block, and how the block is used. Symbols that point in a specific direction, such as North Arrows, should be defined pointing toward angle 0 so that they can be logically rotated to the desired angle when inserted.

Finally, AutoCAD prompts you to select the objects of which the block is to consist. You can use any of the object selection methods described in Chapter 14, "The Ins and Outs of Editing." After you select the objects, press Enter to create the block.

Tip You also can select the objects that make up a block from the Command: prompt before you issue the BLOCK command. If you do so, AutoCAD bypasses the Select objects: prompt and creates the block as soon as you specify a name and an insertion base point.

At this time, the objects that comprise the block are removed from the screen. The objects you used to create the block now exist as a block reference in the environment of your drawing.

Tip If you want to restore the objects used to define a block to the drawing, use the OOPS command. Using UNDO or U restores the objects, but also removes the block definition.

After you save a drawing in which you have created a block reference, AutoCAD stores the information that defines the block in the drawing file so that the next time you open this drawing file, you still have access to the named block reference.

In the following exercise, you create blocks of a tree and a group of shrubs. You create one by selecting the objects before you issue the BLOCK command and the other by selecting the objects after you issue the command.

Creating Blocks

Begin a new drawing named CHAP16A, using the file BLOCKS from the IA Disk as a prototype.

Command: *Choose* Construct, Block	Issues the BLOCK command
_block Block name (or ?): **TREE** (Enter)	Defines the block's name
Insertion base point: *Choose* Center *object snap*	
_center of *Pick circle at* ① *(see fig. 16.11)*	Specifies base point
Select objects: *Select a window from* ② *to* ③	Selects the objects for the block TREE.
4 found Select objects: (Enter)	Ends object selection

Now the objects that make up the TREE block are erased from the screen and are stored in the drawing's block definition table. To return the original objects to the screen, you can use the OOPS command.

Command: **OOPS** (Enter)	Starts the OOPS command

Next, use the noun-verb method of object selection.

Select a window from ④ *to* ⑤	Selects the objects that will make up the block named SHRUBS
Command: *Choose* Construct, Block	Issues the BLOCK command with the selected objects

Note that the `Select objects:` prompt is not issued when using the noun-verb method.

Command: _block Block name (or ?): **SHRUBS** (Enter)	Specifies the block's name
Insertion base point: *Pick* ⑥	Creates the block and deletes the selection
16 found	
Command: **OOPS** (Enter)	Returns the original objects

AutoCAD has defined the two blocks. Use the ? option of the BLOCK command to list all blocks in the drawing's block table.

Command: *Choose* Construct, Block	Issues the BLOCK command
Command: _block Block name (or ?): **?**	Specifies the List Blocks option
Block(s) to list <*>: (Enter)	Accepts the default to list all blocks

```
Defined blocks.
    SHRUBS
    TREE
  User          External         Dependent        Unnamed
  Blocks        References       Blocks           Blocks
    2              0                0                0
```

Use F1 to hide the AutoCAD text window, then save your drawing.

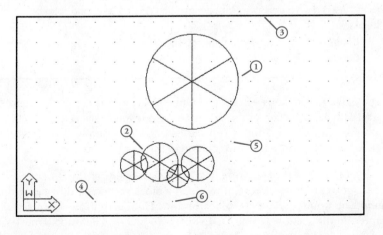

Figure 16.11

Landscape plants with pick points.

16

Placing Blocks into Drawings

Obviously, creating a block would be worthless if you lacked the means by which to place it in your drawing. But you don't lack the means—placing blocks is the purpose of the DDINSERT, INSERT, and MINSERT commands.

Remember that after you place a block in your drawing, AutoCAD considers the block to be one object, regardless of the level of complexity of the block. If you want to edit individual parts of a block, you must first explode the block, which you can do while using the INSERT or DDINSERT commands to place the block. An asterisk following the file name when using the INSERT command will explode the block as it is inserted. The Insert dialog box provides an Explode check box that causes the block to be exploded when inserted into your drawing. You also can use the EXPLODE or XPLODE command to explode a block; these commands are covered in the next chapter.

Using the DDINSERT Command

Issuing the DDINSERT command opens the Insert dialog box, which provides a convenient method of inserting block references from your drawing environment into your drawing while controlling the insertion point, the scale, and the rotated position. You are even able to explode the block into its original object components as it is inserted.

DDINSERT. The DDINSERT command opens the Insert dialog box, which enables you to specify a block name or a drawing file name to insert into your drawing. You also can use the Insert dialog box to specify an insertion point, scale, and rotation angle for the block.
Pull-down: *Choose* Draw, Insert, Block (see fig. 16.12)
Screen: *Choose* Draw2, DDinsert

The Insert dialog box has two sections—Block and Options—as well as the Explode check box (see fig. 16.13). The Block section of the dialog box allows you to select a block reference from your drawing or a disk file to be inserted into your drawing. The Options section allows you to control the location and rotation of the block being inserted.

In the Block section of the Insert dialog box, you must choose either the Block button or the File button. Because you want to insert a block you created by using the BLOCK command, you would choose the Block button. The File button is explained later in this chapter, in the section "Using DDINSERT To place a File into a Drawing." After you choose the Block button, AutoCAD displays a list of all user blocks in the drawing. Simply select the block you want to insert from this list.

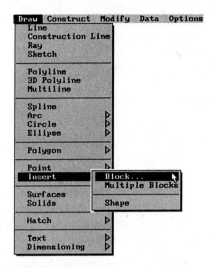

Figure 16.13

The Insert dialog box.

16

The Options section of the Insert dialog box is divided into three subsections. These subsections normally are grayed out because you usually specify a block's insertion point, scale, and rotation angle on-screen, which means that the Specify Parameters on Screen check box normally is selected. To access the options, you must deselect this check box. The first section, Insertion Point, enables you to supply an insertion point for the block using absolute coordinates. The second section, Scale, enables you to specify a scale for the X, Y, and Z axes of the block to create scaled blocks. The third section, Rotation, enables you to specify a rotation angle for the inserted block.

Also note the Explode check box at the bottom of the dialog box. If you mark this check box, AutoCAD inserts the block as individual objects rather than as one object. This is discussed in detail in Chapter 17, "Block Structure, Editing, Organization, and Management."

In the following exercise, you use the DDINSERT command to insert blocks identical to those you created in the previous exercise. You will insert them in a landscape drawing of a small park. The drawing contains the TREE and SHRUBS blocks, as well as several other blocks to be used in other exercises in this chapter.

Using DDINSERT To Insert Blocks into a Drawing

Create a new drawing named CHAP16B, using the drawing PARK from the IA Disk as a prototype. Restore the view named ENTRANCE to get a closer look at the park entrance (see fig. 16.14).

Next, place a few trees around the entrance.

Command: *Choose* Draw, Insert, Block	Issues the DDINSERT command and opens the Insert dialog box
Command: _ddinsert Initializing... DDINSERT loaded.	
Choose the **B**lock *button*	Opens the Defined Blocks dialog box with a list of block names
Select the block TREE *from the list,* *then choose* OK	Returns to the Insert dialog box
Check the **S**pecify Parameters on Screen *check box, then choose* OK	Closes the Insert dialog box
Insertion point: *Pick* ① *(see fig. 16.14)*	
X scale factor <1> / Corner / XYZ: **Enter**	Accepts the default X scale
Y scale factor (default=X): **Enter**	Accepts the default Y scale
Rotation angle <0>: **Enter**	Accepts the default rotation
Command: **Enter**	Repeats the DDINSERT command and opens the Insert dialog box
Choose OK	Defaults to the block TREE, the last block you selected
Insertion point: *Pick* ②	
X scale factor <1> / Corner / XYZ: **Enter**	Accepts the default X scale
Y scale factor (default=X): **Enter**	Accepts the default Y scale

New Riders Publishing
INSIDE
SERIES

`Rotation angle <0>:` (Enter)	Accepts the default rotation

The trees that you have been inserting have a foliage diameter of about 8'. Next, place a 16'-diameter tree where the walking path splits.

`Command:` (Enter)	Repeats the DDINSERT command
Choose OK	Defaults to place another tree
`Insertion point:` *Pick* ③	
`X scale factor <1> / Corner / XYZ:` **2** (Enter)	Specifies an X scale factor of 2
`Y scale factor (default=X):` (Enter)	Y scale defaults to 2 because X scale was entered as 2
`Rotation angle <0>:` (Enter)	Accepts the default rotation

Note that the scale factor of 2 doubles the size of the tree.

Next, you insert a tree by specifying its insertion point and scale factor in the Insert dialog box.

`Command:` (Enter)	Repeats the DDINSERT command and opens the Insert dialog box
Choose Block *button*	Opens the Defined Blocks dialog box
Select TREE *from the list of blocks,* *then* OK	Closes the Defined Blocks dialog box
Clear the Specify Parameters on Screen *check box*	Makes the edit boxes in the Options section available
Type **120'** *in the* X *edit box and* **190'** *in the* Y *edit box of the* Insertion Point *section.*	Locates the block insertion point
Type **2** *in the* X *edit box of the* Scale *section, then pick the* Y *edit box*	Set the scale in the X axis to 2 and makes the Y axis match it.

Figure 16.15 shows the dialog box with the proper settings.

Choose OK	Inserts the tree at ④ without further prompts (see fig. 16.14)

Save the drawing.

16

Figure 16.14

Closeup view of park entrance.

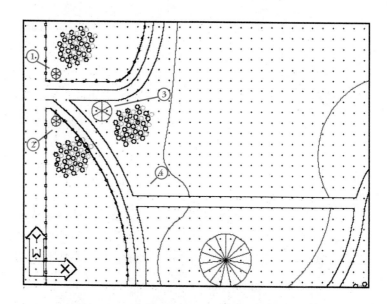

Figure 16.15

The Insert dialog box with insertion point and scale settings.

Insert

Block

Block...   TREE

File...

Options

☐ Specify Parameters on Screen

Insertion Point	Scale	Rotation
X: 120'	**X:** 2	**Angle:** 0
Y: 190'	**Y:** 2"	
Z: 0"	**Z:** 2"	

☐ Explode

OK   Cancel   Help...

Using the INSERT Command

The INSERT command provides another method for placing a block in your drawing. This command places the block without the use of a dialog box.

Tip   The INSERT command is useful for placing blocks from a custom menu macro or a LISP routine, because you do not need to select the block name from a list.

> **INSERT.** The INSERT command enables you to specify a block name or a drawing file name to insert into your drawing from the Command: prompt.
> Screen: *Choose Draw2, Insert*

When you insert a block without the dialog box, you must type the INSERT command from the Command: prompt or choose it from the screen menu. AutoCAD then asks you to supply a block name. You type the name of the block (or file) you want to insert, or type **?** if you want AutoCAD to list the names of all defined blocks in the current drawing. To insert a block as individual objects (exploded), you type the block's name with an asterisk (*) after it. (Exploded blocks are covered in Chapter 17, "Block Structure, Editing, Organization, and Management.") After you supply a block name, AutoCAD prompts for an insertion point, which you can supply by entering the coordinates or, more commonly, by picking it on-screen.

To insert a block reference, you can enter different values for the block's scale and rotation. To scale, you can enter X and Y scale factors. The default scale prompt for the Y factor uses the X factor you enter by default, which simplifies the process of scaling your drawing symbol at a 1:1 ratio. You can use different X and Y scales by entering different responses (the XYZ option is for 3D control). You also can supply an angle of rotation by entering an angle or by dragging the rotation and picking a point.

In the following exercise, you use the INSERT command to place the blocks you made previously. You also use the autoedit move copy mode to copy a block.

16

Using INSERT To Insert Blocks into a Drawing

Continue from the preceding exercise, or OPEN the drawing CHAP16B that you saved at the end of the preceding exercise. Restore the ENTRANCE view if it is not current (refer to fig. 16.14).

Use the Thaw option to unfreeze layer EXER_2 and set layer SHRUBS current.

Command: *From the screen menu choose* Draw2, Insert	Issues the INSERT command
Block name (or ?): **SHRUBS** (Enter)	Specifies the block to insert
Insertion point: **155',190'** (Enter)	Specifies insertion point by coordinates
X scale factor <1> / Corner / XYZ: (Enter)	Accepts the default X scale
Y scale factor (default=X): (Enter)	Accepts the default Y scale

continues

continued

`Rotation angle <0>:` (Enter)	Accepts the default rotation

It is easy to edit a block with grips. Because the block is considered one object, it has only one grip point.

Command: *Pick the* SHRUBS *block at* ① *(see fig. 16.16)*	Selects the block
Select its grip	Makes it a "hot" grip, and activates autoedit mode
`** STRETCH **` `<Stretch to point>/Base point/Copy/` `Undo/eXit:` (Enter)	Cycles to MOVE mode
`** MOVE **` `<Move to point>/Base point/Copy/` `Undo/eXit: C` (Enter)	Specifies the Copy option
`** MOVE (multiple) **` `<Move to point>/Base point/Copy/` `Undo/eXit:` *Pick at each of the shrub locations shown in figure 16.16*	Copies the inserted shrubs to several locations

Save the drawing.

Figure 16.16

Locations for copying shrubs.

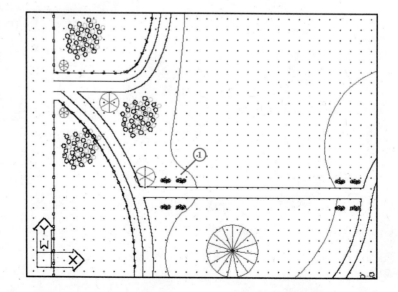

New Riders Publishing
INSIDE SERIES

Tip If you need to move a block by one of its component object's grips, choose Options, Grips, then turn on the Enable Grips Within **B**locks check box of the Select Settings section of the Grips dialog box.

When you accepted the default INSERT scale values in the preceding exercise, you might have noticed a second option, called Corner. When you use the Corner option to enter your scale values, you can scale the block by indicating the X and Y size of a rectangle. The insertion point is the first corner of the rectangle. Drag and pick the other corner to determine scale. AutoCAD uses the width as the X scale and the height as the Y scale, in current drawing units.

You do not need to enter C to use corner point scaling. If you move the pointer at the X scale prompt, you see the block being dynamically scaled. The Corner option is used in menus because it limits scale input to corner point picking and issues an Other corner: prompt.

 Tip Whether you use keyboard scale entry or the Corner option, you can specify negative scale factors to mirror the block's insertion, turn it upside-down, or both.

Be careful when you use corner point scaling. When you use a corner scale input, use snap or object snap to control accuracy. The dragged scale is relative to one drawing unit square, and it works well if your block definition is about one unit in size. (See the section "Using Versatile Unit Size Blocks" later in this chapter.) If your block definition is many drawing units in size, however, even a small rectangle yields a large size.

Using Preset Scales and Rotation Angle with INSERT

You have inserted blocks by specifying an insertion point, a scale, and an angle. You can preset the scale factor and rotation angle before you select the insertion point. When you preset the block's scale and angle, AutoCAD suspends insertion point dragging until you finish setting those options. You then see the block's scale and angle as you drag it to pick the insertion point.

Preset Scale and Rotation Options

Several options are available for presetting values, but they are not shown as prompts by the INSERT command. The following list shows every option:

- ◆ **Scale and PScale.** Sets the scale factor for the X, Y, and Z axes.

- ◆ **Xscale and PXscale.** These options preset only the X scale factor.

- ◆ **Yscale and PYscale.** These options preset only the Y scale factor.

- ◆ **Zscale and PZscale.** These options preset only the Z scale factor.

16

◆ **Rotate and PRotate.** These options preset the rotation angle. Enter this value from the keyboard or pick two points.

Type the first one or two characters of the preset option to tell AutoCAD what you want to preset.

The letter *P* stands for preliminary, not preset. Options prefixed with a *P* establish a preliminary scale and rotation value to visually aid in insertion. After you select the insertion point, you see the normal insert prompts and defaults.

Preset scale factors have limitations. You cannot mix fixed presets (such as Xscale) with preliminary presets (such as PYscale). If you try to mix them, the preliminary presets become fixed, and AutoCAD does not prompt you again for their values.

In the following exercise, you use preset values to insert a couple of blocks.

Using INSERT with Preset Scales

Continue from the previous exercise or open the CHAP16B drawing you saved at the end of the preceding exercise. Use the **R**estore option to retrieve the view named ENTRANCE as shown in figure 16.17.

Use the **T**haw option to unfreeze layers EXER_2 and EXER_3 and set layer BENCHES current.

Command: **INSERT** (Enter)	Issues the INSERT command
Block name (or ?): **BENCH** (Enter)	Specifies a block to insert
Insertion point: **X** (Enter)	Requests a preset X scale prompt
X scale factor: **2** (Enter)	Presets the X axis scale factor
Insertion point: **Y** (Enter)	Requests a preset Y scale prompt
Y scale factor: **1** (Enter)	Presets the Y axis scale factor
Insertion point: **R** (Enter)	Requests a preset rotation angle prompt
Rotation angle: **270** (Enter)	Presets the block rotation angle
Insertion point: **25',300'** (Enter)	Specifies the block insertion point at ① (see fig. 16.17)

Now repeat the procedure to place another bench with the same scale located at coordinate 25',250' on the other side of the entrance at ②.

Save the drawing.

The block you just inserted, BENCH, is a 3' by 10' park bench symbol. However, by inserting it with an X axis scale factor of 2 and a Y axis scale factor of 1, you have created 3' by 20' benches.

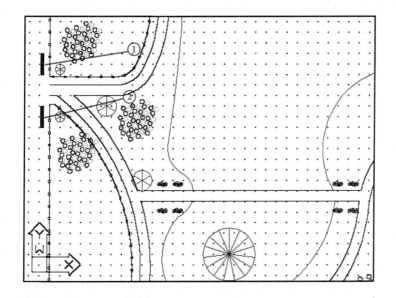

Figure 16.17

View of the park entrance with benches added.

Note   Preset options are most valuable when you use them in custom menu macros. Macros can apply preset options transparently, which simplifies the task of placing the block by enabling dragging with predetermined scale and rotations during an insertion.

Using the MINSERT Command

A block is more than a block if you use the MINSERT command to insert it. Suppose you want to put many blocks in your drawing in a rectangular pattern, such as placing columns or beams in a structural drawing or an array of tables and chairs in a school cafeteria. You could insert one copy of the block and then use the ARRAY command to make several columns and rows of copies, but each of these copies duplicates much of the insert object.

The MINSERT command provides another method. Think of MINSERT (Multiple INSERTion) as a single command that combines inserts and rectangular arrays. (You cannot use MINSERT to create a polar array.) Each object generated by using ARRAY is an individual object in the drawing file—you can edit, delete, copy, or even array the object individually. MINSERT differs from ARRAY in that each block component in the array that MINSERT generates is part of a single inserted object. You cannot edit the individual component blocks, but you save memory by not storing repetitive information.

MINSERT. The MINSERT command enables you to specify a block name or a drawing file name to insert into your drawing from the Command: prompt. AutoCAD then prompts you for the number of rows and columns to array the inserted block.

Pull-down: *Choose* Draw, Insert, Multiple Blocks *(see fig. 16.18)*
Screen: *Choose* Draw2, Minsert

Figure 16.18

Issuing the MINSERT command from the pull-down menu.

In the following exercise, you use MINSERT to place sprinklers in the park.

Using MINSERT To Insert an Array of Blocks

Continue from the preceding exercise or OPEN the CHAP16B drawing you saved at the end of the preceding exercise.

Thaw layers EXER_2, EXER_3, and EXER_4 and set layer IRRIGATION current.

Command: *Choose* View, Zoom, Window *and zoom a window from* 400',240' *to* 700',480'	Zooms to view shown in figure 16.19
Command: *Choose* Draw, Insert, Multiple Blocks	Issues the MINSERT command

```
minsert
Block name (or ?): SPRINKLER (Enter)          Specifies the block to insert

Insertion point: 450',260' (Enter)            Specifies insertion point

X scale factor <1> / Corner / XYZ: (Enter)    Accepts default X scale factor

Y scale factor (default=X): (Enter)           Accepts default Y scale factor

Rotation angle <0>: (Enter)                   Accepts default rotation

Number of rows (---) <1>: 7 (Enter)           Specifies 7 vertical rows of blocks

Number of columns (¦¦¦) <1>: 8 (Enter)        Specifies 8 horizontal columns of blocks

Unit cell or distance between rows            Specifies row spacing
(---): 30' (Enter)

Distance between columns (¦¦¦):               Specifies column spacing and draws the
30' (Enter)                                   sprinkler array (see fig. 16.19)
```

Save the drawing.

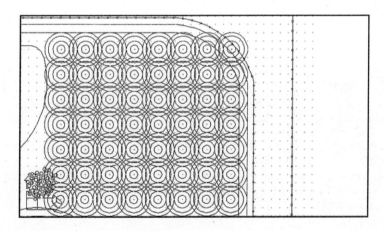

Figure 16.19

Sprinklers inserted with the MINSERT command.

16

Note When you specify a rotation in MINSERT, AutoCAD rotates the array, and the individual blocks maintain their position in the array.

MINSERT is an efficient way to place multiple copies of a block in a drawing file. In an array, every object occurrence takes up disk space. If you use MINSERT to insert, the block reference occurs once and includes information about the number of rows, columns, and spacing of elements.

Note Individual objects of a MINSERT cannot be edited with ERASE or otherwise edited, and objects inserted with MINSERT cannot be exploded.

You can use two additional commands, DIVIDE and MEASURE, to insert multiple copies of a block.

Using the DIVIDE Command

Sometimes you need to divide an object into an equal number of segments while laying out a drawing. For instance, a mechanical design might call for equally spaced holes along a part, or a landscape designer might want to plant shrubs at equal intervals along a pathway. The DIVIDE command provides a method by which you can do this automatically. You can accurately divide lines, circles, arcs, ellipses, polylines, donuts, polygons, and rectangles into equal intervals.

The DIVIDE command does not break these objects into separate segments. Instead, it places a point object at equal intervals along the divided object (see Chapter 6, "Drawing Accurately," for information about the point object). Or, you can specify a block rather than a point for AutoCAD to insert at these intervals.

> **DIVIDE.** The DIVIDE command enables you to divide an object into a user-specified number of equal divisions. You also can use it to place a block along the divided object at each division.
> Pull-down: *Choose* Draw, Point, Divide (see fig. 16.20)
> Screen: *Choose* Draw2, Divide

All you have to do after you issue the DIVIDE command is pick the object you want to divide, then specify the number of divisions you want AutoCAD to make. AutoCAD calculates the interval distance and places a point at each interval. If you want to place a block rather than a point, choose the Block option of DIVIDE before you specify the number of divisions.

 Tip Remember, you can use the NODE object snap to snap to a point object.

In the following exercise, you practice using the DIVIDE command to place the shrub block at equal intervals along the property line of the park. Then you place some benches along the park pathway, using the DIVIDE command to align the benches with the pathway.

New Riders Publishing
INSIDE
SERIES

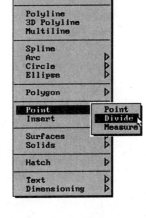

Figure 16.20
Using the pull-down menu to issue the DIVIDE command.

Using DIVIDE To Insert Blocks

Continue from the preceding exercise, or open the CHAP16B drawing that you saved at the end of the preceding exercise.

Thaw layers EXER_2, EXER_3, EXER_4, and EXER_5. Set layer SHRUBS current and restore the ENTRANCE view shown in figure 16.21.

`_divide` `Select object to divide:` *Pick* ① *(see fig. 16.21)*	Selects the perimeter fence
`<Number of segments>/Block:` **B** (Enter)	Specifies placing blocks rather than points
`Block name to insert:` **SHRUBS** (Enter)	Specifies the block to place
`Align block with object? <Y>` (Enter)	Accepts defaults to align blocks
`Number of segments:` **200** (Enter)	Inserts 199 shrub blocks along fence dividing the object 200 times (one at each division)
Change to Layer BENCHES.	
`Command:` *Choose* Draw, Point, Divide	Issues the DIVIDE command
`Select object to divide:` *Pick* ②	Selects edge of pathway

continues

16

continued

```
<Number of segments>/Block: B (Enter)

Block name to insert: BENCH (Enter)        Specifies the block to place

Align block with object? <Y> (Enter)

Number of segments: 20 (Enter)             Inserts blocks along pathway
```

Save the drawing.

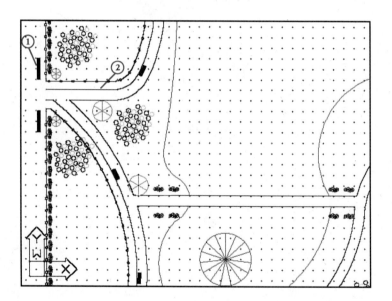

Figure 16.21

Park entrance with shrubs and benches inserted with DIVIDE command.

When you use DIVIDE to insert blocks (or points), AutoCAD saves the objects as a Previous selection set. To edit the group, you can use the Previous selection set option to select it again. If, for example, you want to change the layer of the benches in the preceding exercise, to select all of them, you would use the Previous option of the SELECT command or selection set options of various editing commands.

Tip

You can use a construction object for your block inserts, then use previous selections to erase it after you perform your DIVIDE (or MEASURE) insert. You can use groups (see Chapter 14, "The Ins and Outs of Editing") to save the selection for later access.

DIVIDE does not enable you to scale a block (nor does MEASURE). If you want to insert the original one-unit size trees at a different scale, for example, you need to create a larger block and insert it, or rescale each block after you insert it. You also

New Riders Publishing
INSIDE
SERIES

might need to adjust the insertion base point, the original rotation angle, or both for a block that you insert with DIVIDE and MEASURE.

Using the MEASURE Command

Placing objects at a set distance apart is another common necessity in drafting—placing a 2-by-6 stud every 24 inches along a wall in an architectural floor plan, for instance, or spacing 18 threads per inch in a mechanical drawing. AutoCAD enables you to do this automatically with the MEASURE command.

> **MEASURE.** The MEASURE command enables you to place a point or a block at a specified interval along the length or circumference of an object.
> Pull-down: *Choose* Draw, Point, Measure
> Screen: *Choose* Draw2, Measure

The MEASURE command works like DIVIDE, but, instead of dividing an object into equal parts, MEASURE enables you to specify the segment length. After you select the object to measure along, you can specify a block name to insert (rather than a point). Next, you specify a measured length (by entering a value or by picking two points), then AutoCAD inserts the specified block (rather than a point) at the segment-length intervals. Like DIVIDE, MEASURE works with points or blocks if specified, and it forms a Previous selection set that you can use for subsequent editing.

Tip As with DIVIDE, MEASURE creates a Previous selection set, which enables easy selection of inserted blocks for editing. You also can provide a group name for the selection set for future use.

In the following exercise, you use MEASURE to place some lightpoles along the pathway opposite the benches you placed earlier, using MEASURE to align the lights.

Using MEASURE To Insert Blocks

Continue from the preceding exercise and set layer LIGHTING current.

Command: *Choose* Draw, Point, Measure   Issues the MEASURE command

Command: _measure

Select object to measure: *Pick* ②   Selects edge of pathway
(refer to figure 16.21)

continues

continued

`<Segment length>/Block: `**`B`** Enter	Specifies placing blocks rather than points
`Block name to insert: `**`LIGHTPOLE`** Enter	Specifies block to insert
`Align block with object? <Y>` Enter	Accepts the default
`Segment length: `**`100'`** Enter	Places a lightpole every 100' around the pathway

Zoom out to see the shrubs, benches, and lightpoles along the complete fence and path (see fig. 16.22).

Save the drawing.

Figure 16.22

Full view of park with shrubs, benches, and lightpoles.

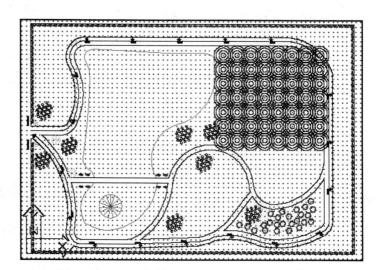

Using Blocks as Symbols

When drafting, you use many common symbols that never vary in shape or size. In board drafting, you have many templates to create these symbols. In AutoCAD, you can use blocks for the same purpose. Blocks are much more versatile because they enable you to scale the symbol, and because the amount of detail you can place in a block far exceeds what is possible when you use a template.

You might need to access these types of blocks from many different drawings. You can use two methods to make this possible—the WBLOCK command, discussed later in this chapter, and symbol libraries, discussed in Chapter 17.

Using Versatile Unit Size Blocks

A very important and versatile type of block is the *unit size block*, which you use for symbols that always have the same geometry, but vary in size and proportion. The unit size block is more versatile than the use of drafting templates. The template offers a limited number of available sizes of each geometric configuration, whereas the unit size block offers infinite sizes for your selection.

The applications of unit size blocks are not as obvious as the applications of blocks you use as symbols. Many situations occur in drafting in which symbols vary only in size and proportion. For instance, in structural drafting the basic geometry for most steel shapes is similar from one size to another; in mechanical drafting the geometry for fastener symbols is also consistent from one size to another. In building construction details, a 1×1 unit box with an X through it can be inserted at various scales to represent any piece of dimensioned lumber.

A unit size block is drawn to a 1 unit by 1 unit size, then inserted with appropriate X and Y scale factors to adjust its size and proportions. Figures 16.23 and 16.24 show the application of two unit size symbols for threaded holes. In figure 16.23, the symbols are drawn at a 1 unit by 1 unit scale—the circular view uses a major diameter of 1 unit, and the side view uses a major diameter of 1 unit and a depth of 1 unit. Figure 16.24 shows how you can insert this same block to create various threaded hole symbols simply by using the hole dimensions as X and Y scale factors when you insert the block.

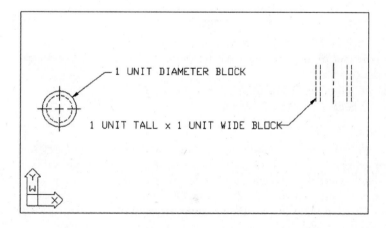

Figure 16.23

Threaded hole symbols drawn at a 1 × 1 scale.

16

Figure 16.24

Threaded hole symbols inserted with various X and Y scales.

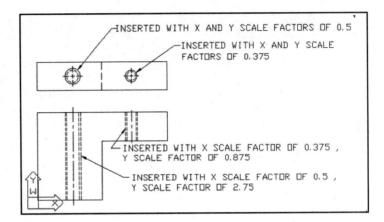

Storing Blocks with the WBLOCK Command

You have seen the way the BLOCK command enables you to make and use symbols repeatedly in a drawing. If this were the extent of its capabilities, the only advantage it would have over the COPY command would be a reduced file size. The main purpose of the WBLOCK command is to enable you to be able to reuse the same block from one drawing to another.

WBLOCK. The WBLOCK command enables you to create a drawing file from a block, a selection set, or an entire file, which makes the block or selections accessible from other drawing files.

Pull-down: *Choose* File, Export, Block
Screen: *Choose* FILE, EXPORT, Wblock

When you create a block, AutoCAD adds information that describes that block to a portion of the drawing file known as the *block table*. Because AutoCAD stores this information in the drawing file, you can access it only from within the drawing in which the information is stored. You use the WBLOCK command to write to disk a separate drawing file (a file that has the DWG extension) that contains the block information, which enables access of the block information from any drawing.

When using the Insert dialog box to place a file created with WBLOCK into a drawing, you use the File button instead of the Block button. This opens the Select Drawing File dialog box, in which you specify the directory and file name to insert. Or, if the file is on the search path, you simply can enter its name in the box next to the File button.

New Riders Publishing
INSIDE SERIES

The WBLOCK command has more uses than writing a block to disk. You also can create the disk file by using a selection set to define the objects that make up the WBLOCK, instead of supplying an existing block name to send to disk.

Writing a Block to Disk

To write an existing block to disk, you must first define a block as described earlier in this chapter, then issue the WBLOCK command. The Create Drawing File dialog box appears, and you supply the name with which you want to store the drawing. After you supply the name, choose OK in the Create Drawing File dialog box. The dialog box closes, and AutoCAD prompts you for a block name. You can specify the name of a block you have defined, or you can type = if the block name is the same as the drawing name you supplied. AutoCAD creates a drawing file that contains the block you specified, and you can insert this file as a block in any other drawing.

Note When you write a block to disk, the block's insertion point becomes the origin of the drawing file created.

Suppose you have decided to use the SHRUBS block and the EVERGREEN block in another drawing. In the following exercise, you write the blocks to disk files using the WBLOCK command and the EXPORT command. After writing the blocks, you start a new drawing and use the DDINSERT command to insert the files.

Writing a Block to Disk

Continue from the preceding exercise, or open the CHAP16B drawing that you saved at the end of the preceding exercise. Thaw layers EXER_2, EXER_3, EXER_4, EXER_5, EXER_6, and EXER_7.

Zoom to the view shown in figure 16.25, a window from 500',20' to 600',80'.

Command: **WBLOCK** (Enter)	Starts the WBLOCK command and opens the Create Drawing File dialog box
Select IA\DWGS *in the* Directories *list box*	Specifies the directory in which to store the SHRUBS file
In the File Name *edit box, type* **SHRUBS**, *then choose* OK	Specifies the file name to create
Block name: = (Enter)	Specifies that the block name is the same as the file name and writes the file

continues

continued

Next, to create a file of the EVERGREEN block, you use the File menu's Export sub-menu to select the Block command. Because a DOS file name can consist of no more than eight characters, you must give the file a shorter name than the block.

Command: *Choose* File, Export, Block	Issues the WBLOCK command and opens the Create Drawing File dialog box (see fig. 16.26)
Select \IA\DWGS *in the* Directories *list box, type* **EVERGRN** *in the* File Name *edit box, then choose* OK	Specifies the path, file type, and name,
File name: C:\IA\DWGS\EVERGRN.DWG Block name: **EVERGREEN** (Enter)	Specifies an existing block name and writes the EVERGRN.DWG file to disk

The files have been created. You do not need to save your changes; this will not delete the SHRUBS and EVERGRN files you just created.

Begin a new drawing named CHAP16C, using PROTOC as a prototype drawing from the IA Disk.

Command: *Choose* Draw, Insert, Block	Issues the DDINSERT command and opens the Insert dialog box
Choose the File *button*	Displays the Select Drawing File dialog box
Select the directory \IA\DWGS *and the* EVERGRN *file then choose* OK *twice*	Specifies the directory and file name and closes the dialog box
Insertion point: *Drag the block and pick at* 35',25'	Specifies location
X scale factor <1> / Corner / XYZ: (Enter)	Accepts the default X scale factor
Y scale factor (default=X): (Enter)	Accepts the default Y scale factor
Rotation angle <0>: (Enter)	Accepts the default rotation angle
Command: (Enter)	Repeats the DDINSERT command and opens the Insert dialog box
Choose the File *button*	Displays the Select Drawing File dialog box
Select the SHRUBS *file then choose* OK *twice*	Specifies file name and closes the dialog box
Insertion point: *Drag the block and pick at* 35',20'	Specifies location for block insertion
X scale factor <1> / Corner / XYZ:	Accepts the default X scale factor

Y scale factor (default=X): (Enter)   Accepts the default Y scale factor

Rotation angle <0>: (Enter)   Accepts the default rotation angle and inserts the block

Repeat the DDINSERT command and choose the **B**lock button in the Insert dialog box. You can see the block SHRUB and EVERGRN added to the current drawing, and you can now place it anywhere in the drawing without having to reload the files. Their block definitions now are a part of the drawing CHAP16C. Close the Insert dialog box. You do not need to save this drawing.

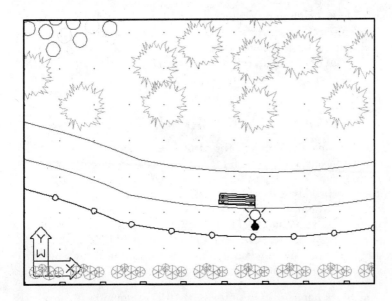

Figure 16.25

A zoomed view showing EVER-GREEN and SHRUBS blocks.

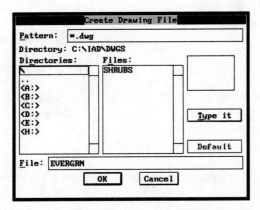

Figure 16.26

The Create Drawing File dialog box.

Writing a Selection Set to Disk

If you have drawn a symbol that you know you will need to write to disk using WBLOCK, you do not need to use the BLOCK command to define the block first. Instead, when the WBLOCK command prompts for a block name, press Enter. When no block name is supplied, AutoCAD enables you to define the block within the WBLOCK command. AutoCAD first prompts for an insertion point, then asks you to select the objects that comprise the block—exactly the same prompts AutoCAD issues when you use the BLOCK command.

As when you use the BLOCK command, when you use WBLOCK in this way, the objects you select are erased from the display. You can use OOPS or U (UNDO 1) to restore these objects to the screen. Using U deletes a block definition created using the BLOCK command, but does not affect a drawing file created using the WBLOCK command.

Writing an Entire File to Disk with WBLOCK*

Often as you create a drawing, you create many named items. Named items include blocks, dimension styles, layers, linetypes, and text styles. You can end up with many more named items than you need, depending on how you create the drawing. You might, for instance, use a prototype drawing with preset layers, linetypes, dimension styles, and text styles. If you complete the drawing and fail to use any one or more of these named items, they are saved along with the drawing file anyway. You can use the PURGE command to selectively delete the definitions of unused blocks and other named items. A simple way to remove *all* unused named items, thus decreasing the file size, is to issue the WBLOCK command and use the asterisk (*) as a block name.

If you respond to the block name prompt of the WBLOCK command with an asterisk, AutoCAD writes most of the entire current drawing to a disk file. AutoCAD does not write any unreferenced table definitions, such as unused blocks, text styles, layers, or linetypes. AutoCAD does write drawing-environment settings for UCSs, views, and viewport configurations, however.

 Tip Like the PURGE command, WBLOCK* often is used to remove unused blocks, layers, linetypes, and text styles. If you use WBLOCK* with the same file name as the current drawing, AutoCAD asks you if you want to replace it. If you answer Yes, AutoCAD saves the current drawing without any unused blocks, layers, and so on. Then you can simply quit the current drawing. This trick is commonly called a *"wblock star."* Use it with care—unlike PURGE, it does not prompt before deleting definitions.

Using the BASE Command To Set the Insertion Point

Every drawing file, whether created with the SAVE command or WBLOCK command, has a base location. The BASE command enables you to control the location of the insertion point for files that are to be inserted in other files.

> **BASE.** The BASE command enables you to control the insertion point for a drawing file when you want to set it for a coordinate other than the default 0,0,0. You must enter the command at the Command: prompt or issue the WBLOCK command using File, Export, Block from the pull-down or screen menu which will then display the BASE command on the screen menu. The coordinate of the base location is stored in a system variable named INSBASE.

Setting the Insertion Point When Writing a wblock star File

When using the WBLOCK command to create a disk file using the objects in your current drawing you should use the BASE command to set the insertion point for the file before issuing the WBLOCK command. You will not have the opportunity to do so when using WBLOCK command to create a "wblock star" file. By default the insertion point will be 0,0,0, which will not usually have a proper relationship to the objects in a file you intend to insert in other files as a block.

Setting the Insertion Point While Editing an Existing File

A convenient way to edit files created with the WBLOCK command is to open them as drawing files and perform the editing as you would for any other drawing file, then save the edited file by its original name or a new name. Frequently, relocation of the insertion point for the edited objects is as important as the editing itself. The BASE command is a convenient way to relocate the insertion point so that when you save the file and then insert it by name into a current drawing, the new block is inserted relative to an appropriate point.

Placing a Drawing File into a Drawing

Beyond placing blocks into a drawing, occasions arise in which you might want to place an entire drawing into another drawing. You might have a standard detail, such as a wall section, for example, that applies to many drawings. AutoCAD provides several ways in which you can perform such an action.

16

Note AutoCAD provides a command that enables you to visually attach one drawing file to another without merging their data. This is the XREF command, discussed in Chapter 19, "Using Xrefs and Overlays for Efficiency and Sharing Data." However, this command differs from the methods shown in this chapter, as the objects in the attached xref are not saved as part of the current drawing file.

Using DDINSERT To Place a File into a Drawing

In an earlier exercise, you used the Insert dialog box (accessed by the DDINSERT command) to place a file into a drawing. In that exercise, the file used had been created using the WBLOCK command. However, you can place any drawing file on disk into your drawing using the same method. Simply choose the File button in the Insert dialog box, then select the path and drawing file name. When inserting a drawing file into a drawing as a block, the origin point of the file (0,0) is used as the insertion base point of the block.

Tip If the file is on the AutoCAD support file search path, you need only enter the file name in the input box next to the File button in the Insert dialog box and AutoCAD will find the file. You also can enter a path and file name in the File input box if you want.

Using INSERT To Place a File into a Drawing

The INSERT command provides another way to insert a drawing file into the current drawing. You can specify the file name to insert at the command's block name prompt, or select the file from the Select Drawing File dialog box.

When you use the INSERT command, AutoCAD first prompts you for a block name to insert. When you supply a block name to the INSERT command, AutoCAD first searches the current drawing's block table for the name you specify. If AutoCAD does not find the block there, it then searches the current directory. If it still doesn't find a match, AutoCAD finally searches through the path defined by the Preferences dialog box and stored in your ACAD.INI file. You also can enter a drawing file name with its path, such as "\drawings\details\wallsect", in response to the block name prompt.

Tip An alternative to typing the name of the file to insert is to enter the tilde character (~) at the block name prompt, which causes AutoCAD to display the Select Drawing File dialog box, in which you can select the directory and drawing file name from lists.

In the following exercise, you use the DDINSERT command and the INSERT command to place a drawing file into a drawing.

Using DDINSERT and INSERT To Place a Drawing File into the Current Drawing

Begin a new drawing named CHAP16D using the PROTOD file from the IA Disk as a prototype drawing.

Command: *Choose* Draw, Insert, Block	Issues the DDINSERT command and opens the Insert dialog box
Command: _ddinsert Initializing... DDINSERT loaded.	
Choose the **F**ile *button*	Opens the Select Drawing File dialog box
Set the **D**irectories *list to* IA\DWGS, *select* KEYBOARD *from the* File **N**ame *list, then choose* OK	Specifies the file and closes the Select Drawing File dialog box
Choose OK	Closes the Insert dialog box and prompts for insertion
Insertion point: **1,1** (Enter)	Specifies insertion point ① in figure 16.27
X scale factor <1> / Corner / XYZ: (Enter)	Accepts the default X scale factor
Y scale factor (default=X): (Enter)	Accepts the default Y scale factor
Rotation angle <0>: (Enter)	Accepts the default rotation angle

Next, you use the INSERT command and the tilde (~) option to insert another file.

Command: **INSERT** (Enter)	Issues the INSERT command
Block name (or ?) <KEYBOARD>: **~** (Enter)	Opens the Select Drawing File dialog box
Select the **PHONE** *file in the* IA\DWGS *directory, then choose* OK	Specifies the file to insert, then closes the dialog box
Insertion point: **1,1** (Enter)	Specifies insertion point
X scale factor <1> / Corner / XYZ: (Enter)	Accepts the default X scale factor
Y scale factor (default=X): (Enter)	Accepts the default Y scale factor

continues

continued

Rotation angle <0>: (Enter)	Accepts the default rotation angle

To demonstrate that the drawing files are inserted as blocks, perform a simple edit operation on the phone.

Command: *Select the phone, then choose* Modify, Move	Issues the MOVE command with the phone selected
1 found Base point or displacement: **-5,-1** (Enter)	Specifies displacement
Second point of displacement: (Enter)	Accepts displacement and moves phone block to position shown in figure 16.27

Use ERASE to remove the keyboard from your drawing then set a new base location (for an insertion point) and create a "wblock star" file using the asterisk with the WBLOCK command. To prepare for this procedure erase the keyboard, explode the phone, and purge the blocks (keyboard and phone) from your current drawing.

Command: **BASE** (Enter)	Issues the BASE command
Base point <0.0000,0.0000,0.0000>: **1,1** (Enter)	Enters the new base location, which will match the base location of the KEYBOARD
Command: *Choose* File, Export, Block	Issues the WBLOCK command and displays the Create Drawing File dialog box
Set the directory to \IA\DWGS *and enter* **PHONE1** *in the F iles edit box*	Names the directory and new file name.
_wblock Block name: ***** (Enter) 100%	Entering the * causes AutoCAD to write the objects in the current drawing to the specified disk file

Quit your drawing and try the exercise again from the beginning but use your new PHONE1 block. This time you should not have to move the phone to a properly centered position relative to the keyboard. Because the two blocks have coordinated insertion points, the phone should be in the correct place.

The exercise above demonstrates simple techniques that are very useful when automating drafting with AutoCAD.

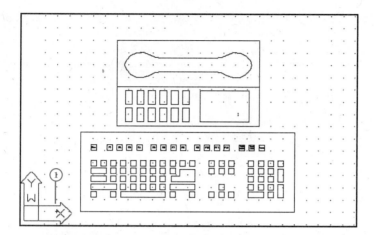

Figure 16.27

The completed drawing with keyboard and phone block files inserted.

The KEYBOARD and PHONE blocks were inserted with their insertion base points set by the 0,0 origin in their DWG files. As you saw in the exercise, these insertion base points were not well coordinated and required moving the PHONE after insertion. A good common practice is to define the insertion base point at the lower left corner of an object, or at a center line or center point. Another common practice for aligning multiple blocks is to coordinate their insertion base points so that the blocks properly align when all are inserted at the same point.

Automating Annotation with Attributes

16

Many types of information besides the graphical objects themselves are associated with a drawing. When you place symbols on a drawing, you often need to use textual information to provide specific information about that symbol. A window or door symbol on a floor plan contains a callout that refers it to a schedule in which more detailed information is provided. An electronic component on a schematic also would contain a reference designator to key it to a parts list. The Quick 5¢ Tour exercise at the beginning of this chapter used a title block to which attributes were attached. When you inserted the title block, you were prompted for title block text.

In AutoCAD, you can assign attributes to any block to provide extra information about that item. Attributes are like paper tags attached to merchandise with a string. They can contain all kinds of information about the item to which they are tied: the item's manufacturer, model number, materials, price, stock number, and so on. The information stored in the attribute is the attribute's *value*. Usually, you attach attributes to a symbol by selecting the attributes along with the objects that make up the symbol when you use the BLOCK command. You also can make a block that contains nothing but attributes.

Attributes originally were designed as a means of assigning information to blocks and exporting that information to generate reports. Attributes also are extremely useful as a means of automating and controlling text that appears in a drawing in the title blocks, schedules, and other items, even if you never need to export the text as data. Attributes can be used to predefine the text location, style, or even its content. They can be used to prompt the drafter for the text, and can offer defaults.

The remainder of this chapter deals with methods you can use to create and insert attribute information. Editing attributes is covered in Chapter 17, "Block Structure, Editing, Organization, and Management."

Creating Block Attributes

You can use the ATTDEF or DDATTDEF commands to create block attributes. In this chapter, you use the DDATTDEF command to create some simple attributes.

> **DDATTDEF.** The DDATTDEF command displays the Attribute dialog box, which enables you to create attributes as well as control constraints on values and appearance of the text.
>
> Pull-down: *Choose* Construct, Attribute

When you issue the DDATTDEF command, the Attribute Definition dialog box opens (see fig. 16.28). This dialog box has several sections, including Mode, Attribute, Insertion Point, and Text Options.

Figure 16.28

The Attribute Definition dialog box.

	Attribute Definition
Mode	**Attribute**
☐ Invisible	Tag: [ ]
☐ Constant	Prompt: [ ]
☐ Verify	Value: [ ]
☐ Preset	

Insertion Point	**Text Options**	
Pick Point <	Justification:	Left ▼
X: 0.0000	Text Style:	STANDARD ▼
Y: 0.0000	Height <	0.2000
Z: 0.0000	Rotation <	0

☐ Align below previous attribute

[OK]   [Cancel]   [Help...]

The Mode section of the dialog box enables you to create invisible attributes (the Invisible check box). Remember that attributes are text attached to a symbol—so why would you want invisible text? You can attach much information to a block that does not belong on the drawing, such as cost, catalog number, supplier, and so on. By attaching this information to the block, you can later extract the invisible (and visible) attributes to generate reports.

In the Attribute area, you define a name for the attribute (the Tag edit box), decide which prompt AutoCAD displays when inserting the attribute (the Prompt edit box), and optionally create default attribute text (the Value edit box). The following list describes each setting.

- ◆ **Tag.** Tag is a descriptive name for the attribute. It does not appear on the drawing after you insert the attribute, but it is needed for attribute data extraction. The tag name cannot have spaces; you need to use a hyphen or an underscore if you want to use a space, as in ITEM_COST. All attributes must have a tag.

- ◆ **Prompt.** When you insert a block that has an attribute attached, AutoCAD prompts you for the information. You define the prompt you receive, such as ENTER COST OF ITEM, here. You can have spaces in the attribute prompt. If you do not define a prompt, AutoCAD uses the attribute tag as a prompt. Prompts do not occur for attributes with a constant Mode setting because you cannot input or alter the attribute value for a constant attribute.

- ◆ **Value.** The attribute's value generally is supplied when you insert the block that contains the attribute. However, if the value is often the same, such as 1/4"=1' for a title block scale attribute, you can specify for AutoCAD to use this as a default to save the time it takes to type the attribute's value. Supplying a default value is optional.

When you define attributes, you should carefully consider prompts and values (default values) that you enter with each attribute tag. The clarity of the prompts and the convenience of the default values make a great difference in the efficiency with which the block is inserted. The prompt should read clearly and leave no doubt about the attribute value to be entered. The default value demonstrates the proper format for the attribute value. The attribute is only defined once but it is inserted many times.

Stop Although you can create an attribute tag and an attribute prompt of up to 256 characters each, the Enter Attributes dialog box (described later in this chapter in the section "Inserting Blocks with Attributes") can only display tags and prompts of 24 characters or less, so you should try to keep tags and prompts within this range.

The Insertion Point section of the Attribute Definition dialog box enables you to define an insertion point for the attribute text, just as you must define an insertion point when you use the TEXT or DTEXT command. You can supply absolute coordinate values, or, by clicking on the Pick Point button, you can select the insertion point on-screen.

When you create multiple attributes, you can use the Align below previous attribute check box to automatically line up one attribute under another. When you select this check box, the other Insertion Point options are grayed out. If you have not yet created any attributes, this check box is grayed out.

 Note   If you do not specify the insertion point for an attribute, it is placed at the drawing origin.

When you use the TEXT or DTEXT commands to place text on a drawing, you specify the text style, height, rotation angle, and justification. The Text Options section of the Attribute Definition dialog box enables you to make the same settings for the attributes you create. If you select a text style that has a predefined height or rotation angle, these buttons are grayed out.

In the following exercise, you use DDATTDEF to create some attributes for a title block. First you define an attribute for the drafter's name in the title block.

Using DDATTDEF To Create Attributes

Begin a new drawing named CHAP16E, using the drawing ATTITLE from the IA Disk as a default.

Command: *Choose* Construct, Attribute, _ddattdef Initializing... DDATTDEF loaded.	Issues the DDATTDEF command and displays the Attribute Definition dialog box
Type **DRAFTER** *in the* Tag *edit box,* *type* **Drawn By** *in the* Prompt *edit box,* *and type your name in the* Value *edit box*	Specifies the tag, prompt, and default (value) text
Choose the Height *button in the* Text Options *section of the dialog box*	Returns to the drawing for height specifications
Height: .125 (Enter)	Specifies the text height and returns to the dialog box
In the Insertion Point *section, choose the* Pick Point *button*	Returns to drawing for point selection

`Start point:` *Pick* ① *(see fig. 16.29)*	Specifies start point of text and returns to dialog box
Choose OK	Closes dialog box and inserts the attribute's tag at the start point

Next, create an attribute for the drawing scale. Note that no prompt or default value need be defined.

`Command:` (Enter) `_DDATTDEF`	Repeats the DDATTDEF command and opens the Attribute Definition dialog box
Type **Scale** *in the* Tag *box, then choose* Pick Point	Specifies tag and prompts for location
`Start point:` *Pick* ②	Specifies location and returns to dialog box
Choose OK	Closes dialog box and inserts tag at start point

Next, create an attribute for the drawing sheet number.

`Command:` (Enter) `_DDATTDEF`	Repeats the DDATTDEF command and opens the Attribute Definition dialog box
Type **SHEET** *in the* Tag *box and* **Sheet Number** *in the* Prompt *box, then choose* Pick Point	Specifies the tag and prompt, then prompts for location
`Start point:` *Pick* ③	Specifies location and returns to dialog box
Choose OK	Closes dialog box and inserts tag at start point

Next, create an attribute for the drawing title.

`Command:` (Enter) `_DDATTDEF`	Repeats the DDATTDEF command and opens the Attribute Definition dialog box
Type **TITLE** *in the* Tag *box,* **Drawing Name** *in the* Prompt *box, and enter* **.25** *for the* height, *then select* Fit *from the* Justification *list box and choose* Pick Point	Specifies tag, prompt, height, and text justification, then prompts for location
`Start point:` *Pick* ④	Specifies location and returns to dialog box
Choose OK	Closes dialog box and returns to drawing

continues

16

continued

First text line point: *Pick* ④	Closes dialog box and prompts for justification points
Second text line point: *Pick* ⑤	Specifies Fit width and inserts tag
Command: **BASE** (Enter)	Starts the BASE command
Base point <0.0000,0.0000,0.0000>: *Pick* ⑥	Specifies insertion base point

Save the drawing, which now looks like figure 16.30.

You do not need to use either the BLOCK or WBLOCK command to create a file that will insert into other drawings as a "title block" with attributes. You have set the insertion base point with the BASE command before you save the file with SAVE or SAVEAS, which produces the same result as using the WBLOCK command to produce a wblock star file as discussed in the previous section "Storing Blocks with the WBLOCK Command."

Figure 16.29

Title block with locations indicated for attributes.

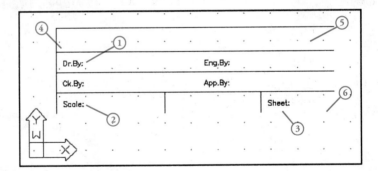

Figure 16.30

Title block with attribute tags in place.

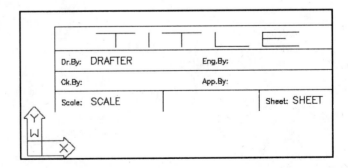

New Riders Publishing
INSIDE
SERIES

Inserting Blocks with Attributes

After you attach an attribute to a block or define one in a drawing, you simply insert the block or drawing in the manner described in section "Creating and Using Blocks" earlier in this chapter. When you insert a block or drawing that contains (or consists entirely of) attributes, AutoCAD prompts you for the information for the attribute. Then you define the attribute's value. You can supply the necessary information in a dialog box or at the Command: prompt.

You use the system variable ATTDIA to control whether AutoCAD displays the attribute prompts from the command line or in a dialog box. ATTDIA is set to 0 by default, which specifies for AutoCAD to prompt from the command line. Type **ATTDIA** and set its value to 1 to tell AutoCAD to issue the attribute prompts in a dialog box. Remember, you used DDATTDEF to assign the attribute prompt when you created the attribute.

In the following exercise, you use DDINSERT to insert the file you created in the previous exercise. You insert the file twice: once with ATTDIA at its default setting of 0, and once after you set ATTDIA to 1. Before you insert the title block, create a border on which to place it by drawing a 16-by-10-inch border with the RECTANG in which to place it.

Inserting a Block with Attributes

Begin a new drawing named CHAP16F, using the file IAD-MECH from the IA Disk as a prototype, and set the layer TITLE current. Set the drawing limits from 0,0 to 16,10.

Command: *Choose* Draw, Polygon, Rectangle *and draw a rectangle from* a 0,0 *to* 16,10	Issues the RECTANG command and draws rectangular border
Command: *Choose* View, Zoom, All	Zooms to new limits
Command: *Choose* Draw, Insert, Block	Issues the DDINSERT command and opens the Insert dialog box
Choose the File *button, then select the directory and file CHAP16E*	Specifies a file to insert as a block
Choose OK *twice*	Closes both dialog boxes and prompts for location
Insertion point: *Use* Endpoint *object snap to pick* ① *(see fig. 16.31)*	Specifies insertion point of block

continues

16

continued

```
X scale factor <1> / Corner / XYZ: Enter    Accepts the default X scale factor

Y scale factor (default=X): Enter           Accepts the default Y scale factor

Rotation angle <0>: Enter                    Accepts the default rotation angle

Enter attribute values
```

Drawn By <Your name here>: **YOUR NAME** Enter   Specifies value for the DRAFTER attribute

SCALE: **FULL** Enter   Specifies value for the SCALE attribute

Sheet number: **ONE** Enter   Specifies value for the SHEET attribute

Drawing name: **ATTRIBUTES INSERTED** Enter   Specifies value for the TITLE attribute

After you enter the last attribute value, the block is inserted with the attribute values in place of the attribute tags.

Next, erase the block you just inserted and place it again by using the Enter Attributes dialog box (ATTDIA set to 1).

Command: **ATTDIA** Enter   Accesses the ATTDIA system variable

New value for ATTDIA <0>: **1** Enter   Changes the system variable setting

Command: *Choose* Draw, Insert, Block   Issues the DDINSERT command and opens
the Insert dialog box

Choose OK   Closes dialog box and prompts for location
(it defaults to insert the last block, CHAP16E)

Insertion point: *Pick* ①   Specifies insertion point of block
(see fig. 16.31)

X scale factor <1> / Corner / XYZ: Enter   Accepts the default X scale factor

Y scale factor (default=X): Enter   Accepts the default Y scale factor

Rotation angle <0>: Enter   Accepts the default rotation angle and opens
                                                 the Enter Attributes dialog box

Fill in the attribute value edit boxes as   Specifies attribute values and inserts
shown in figure 16.32, then choose OK   title block

Save the drawing.

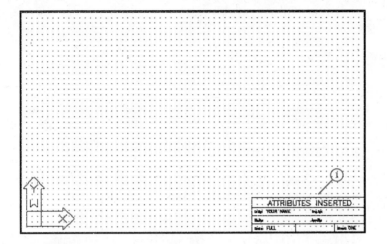

Figure 16.31

Title block with attribute values in place.

Figure 16.32

The attribute values shown in the Enter Attributes dialog box.

16

Note The order of attributes in the prompts or dialog box depends on the order of creation or selection. If you want the attributes in a specific order, select them in that particular order when creating the block definitions. Selection by window can make the order unpredictable. If you create them in a drawing that you later insert as a block, the order is the order of creation.

Using Attributes for Data Storage and Extraction

Attributes are great for automating and controlling text, and for minor data applications. They also can be used for applications that require significant data storage and extraction, but we recommend that you use AutoCAD's SQL (Structured Query Language) features (see the AutoCAD User's Guide) for those applications.

You can print extracted attribute data as lists or use the data in other programs, such as database, spreadsheet, and word processing programs. You also can put the data into a table and bring it back into your drawing as an mtext object.

Planning and Inserting Attribute Data

When you plan for attributes, lay out the data in a simple table. For example, the drawing shown in figure 16.33 lists employee names, type of phone, and extension number for each employee. Similar kinds of tables form the basis for bills of materials (BOM) lists, schedules, and specifications that regularly accompany professional drawings.

After planning the data, you define attributes and create a block or place the attributes in a drawing file for insertion in other drawings, using the techniques covered in the previous exercises. The IA Disk drawing named PHN-BLK contains attribute definitions for employee names, type of phone, and extension number. In the following exercise, you insert this block and enter attribute data.

Inserting Blocks with Attribute Data

Begin a new drawing named CHAP16G, using the OFFICE drawing from the IA Disk as a prototype. Zoom to the view shown in figure 16.33, then copy and mirror the furniture in the lower left cubicle to match the figure. Create a new layer named PHONES and set it current.

Command: *Choose* Draw, Insert, Block *enter* **PHN-BLK** in the File *edit box, then choose* OK	Opens the Insert dialog box, specifies the block, and closes the dialog box
Insertion point: *Pick* ① *(see fig. 16.33), then press Enter three times to accept default scale and rotation*	Inserts phone and opens Enter Attribute dialog box (because ATTDIA was on in the OFFICE prototype drawing)

Enter **Sam Smith** for the name, **Reception** for the type, and **586** for the extension, then choose OK to complete the INSERT command and attribute entry.

Repeat for name **Tonya White**, type **Desk**, and extension **486**.

Repeat for name **Susan Driscoll**, type **Desk**, and extension **386**.

Repeat for name **Harriet Sands**, type **Desk**, and extension **286**.

Save the drawing.

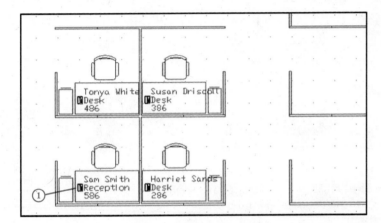

Figure 16.33

Office with attribute data phone blocks inserted.

Using the ATTEXT and DDATTEXT Commands To Extract Data

Although the ATTEXT command sounds like a text operation, it stands for ATTribute EXTraction. ATTEXT provides a way to extract attribute information from the drawing file and use that information in a text report.

> **ATTEXT.** Extracts the attribute data specified by a template file from the drawing. You can extract data from all or selected attributes, in CDF, SDF, or DXF format.

The ATTEXT command is provided for compatibility with previous versions of AutoCAD and for programming access to attribute extraction. It has no advantage over the DDATTEXT command, which is easier to use. DDATTEXT performs the same function with the Attribute Extraction dialog box. DDATTEXT is used in this chapter.

> **DDATTEXT.** Opens the Attribute Extraction dialog box, which extracts the attribute data specified by a template file from the drawing. You can extract data from all or selected attributes, in CDF, SDF, or DXF format.
> Pull-down: *Choose* File, Export, Attributes
> Screen: *Choose* FILE, EXPORT, DDattEx

16

ATTEXT and DDATTEXT (Attribute Extraction Dialog Box) Options

The functions and options of the DDATTEXT (Attribute Extraction dialog box) commands are described in the following list.

◆ **Comma Delimited File (CDF).** Specifies the CDF format for the extracted data file.

◆ **Space Delimited File (SDF).** Specifies the SDF format for the extracted data file.

◆ **Drawing Interchange File (DXF).** Specifies DXF the format for the extracted data file.

◆ **Select Objects.** This button closes the dialog box, prompts for object selection to extract data from specific blocks, and reopens the dialog box upon completion of object selection.

◆ **Template File.** This button and text box specifies the name and path of the template file. If you choose the button, it opens the Template File dialog box.

◆ **Output File.** This button and text box specifies the name and path of the data file to create. If you choose the button, it opens the Output File dialog box.

The prompts and options of the ATTEXT command are similar to the DDATTEXT functions and options described in the previous list.

 Stop   The output file overwrites existing files of the same name without warning you.

Examining ATTEXT Formats

AutoCAD provides three ways to extract attribute values from a drawing file and format them in a disk file. The following attribute extraction formats are templates that define the way the data is formatted in the extracted text file:

◆ **CDF (Comma Delimited Format).** CDF is easy to use with BASIC programs or with dBASE's "APPEND FROM . . . DELIMITED" operation.

◆ **SDF (Standard Data Format).** SDF is for FORTRAN and other programs that read a dBASE "COPY . . . SDF" file, or a dBASE "APPEND FROM . . . SDF" operation.

◆ **DXF (Drawing Interchange Format).** DXF is a subset of AutoCAD's full DXF file format that is used by many third-party programs.

New Riders Publishing
INSIDE
SERIES

You can extract data in any format suitable for your application. Many users (and vendors of third-party software) now have applications built around AutoCAD by using one or more of these data extraction interfaces.

Extracting Attribute Data Using CDF or SDF

CDF creates a file that has commas separating the data fields in the attribute extraction. The following is a simple example of a CDF format:

```
'Name1','Type1','Extension1'
'Name2','Type2','Extension2'
 ...
 ...
 ...
'Name9','Type9','Extension9'
'Name10','Type10','Extension10'
```

To format extract files, you need to place alphanumeric characters, commas, and spaces. In the CDF format, each data field is separated by a comma. The spacing of the data field is dependent on the data width in the field. Name10 in the preceding example takes up more room than Name9.

The SDF format creates a file similar to CDF, but without commas and with a standard field length and spacing, as shown in the following list:

```
Name1     Type1      Extension1
Name2     Type2      Extension2
...  ...  ...
...  ...  ...
Name9     Type9      Extension9
Name10    Type10     Extension10
```

In SDF format, the data field length is standardized and preformatted to a standard value, regardless of the data value length. If the data exceeds the length, the data is truncated.

Creating an Attribute Report Template File

Before you can extract attributes, AutoCAD needs a template file to create the SDF or CDF file. The *template file* is a format instruction list that tells AutoCAD what to put where in the extract data file. The IA Disk contains a template file called PHONE.TXT. This file provides an SDF template for the telephone data that you added to the office plan in the previous exercise. You use this file to create a report file.

16

The PHONE.TXT file was created as an ASCII text file. You can create similar files by using the DOS line editor (EDIT) utility. Use spaces, not tabs. Make sure you end the last line of your file with a return character (**Enter**). Also, make sure you do not have any extra spaces at the end of lines, or extra returns after the last line of text.

Table 16.3 shows the PHONE.TXT template file for your sample telephone data. The template outputs NAME first, TYPE second, and EXTENSION third.

TABLE 16.3
Viewing an SDF Template File

Data Code	Format Code
BL:NAME	C011000
BL:X	N006002
DUMMY1	C002000
BL:Y	N006002
DUMMY2	C002000
NAME	C015000
TYPE	C010000
EXTENSION	N005000

If you look at the right column, you can easily decipher the formatting information. The first C or N says this is a character or a number. The next three digits (011 in the BL:NAME line) tell the number of spaces to leave for the data. The final three digits specify the number of decimal places for floating point (decimal) numeric data. Integer data have 000 in the last three columns.

The BL:X and BL:Y are not blocks or attributes. They extract the X,Y coordinate values for the block.

DUMMY1 and DUMMY2 are not blocks or attributes; they are "dummy" codes used to provide space in the report. These dummy lines force a two-space blank between the X,Y coordinates (BL:X,BL:Y) and a two-space blank between the Y coordinate and the NAME, making the output easier to read.

Note If you get a ** Field overflow in record *nn* message from the ATTEXT or DDATTEXT commands, it means that the data for one of the fields in line *nn* of the output file contains too many characters.

Table 16.4 shows the complete list of the kinds of data that ATTEXT or DDATTEXT can extract.

TABLE 16.4
ATTEXT Template Fields

Field	Data Type	Description	Field	Data Type
BL:LEVEL level	integer	Block nesting	BL:XSCALE	decimal
BL:NAME	character	Block name	BL:YSCALE	decimal
BL:X	decimal	X insert coord	BL:ZSCALE	decimal
BL:Y	decimal	Y insert coord	BL:XEXTRUDE	decimal
BL:Z	decimal	Z insert coord	BL:YEXTRUDE	decimal
BL:NUMBER	integer	Block counter	BL:ZEXTRUDE	decimal
BL:HANDLE	character	Object handle	*attribute*	integer
BL:LAYER	character	Insertion layer	*attribute*	character
BL:ORIENT	decimal	Rotation angle		

Integer fields are formatted Nwww000, floating point (decimal) fields are Nwwwddd, and character fields are Cwww000, in which www is overall width (such as 012 for 12 characters wide and 000 is 0) and ddd is the width to the right of the decimal point.

Extracting the Data File

After you have the template file, you can extract data for all or some of the attributes. If you have the PHONE.TXT file, switch to AutoCAD. Extract the attribute data into a file called PHN-DATA.

Using DDATTEXT To Create an SDF Data File

Continue in the CHAP16G drawing from the previous exercise.

`Command:` *Choose* File, Export, Attributes	Opens the Attribute Extraction dialog box
`Initializing... DDATTEXT loaded.`	
Choose S̲pace Delimited File (SDF)	Specifies a space-delimited format
In the T̲emplate File *edit box, enter* **PHONE**	Specifies the template to use

Leave the default, the drawing name and TXT extension, in the Output F̲ile edit box.

continues

continued

Choose OK   Closes the dialog box and creates the file
                                                              on disk

```
4 records in extract file.
```

If you choose Select **O**bjects, AutoCAD closes the dialog box, prompts for object
selection to extract data from specific blocks, and reopens the dialog box upon
completion of object selection.

 Note   Do not use the same name for your template file as that of your extract file, or the
extract file overwrites the template.

The extracted SDF report file in the IA\DWGS directory, CHAP16F.TXT, is shown in
the following list. You can examine the file by using the DOS line editor (EDIT). Take
a look at your data text file.

SDF Report Example

```
PHN-BLK    646.00  384.00  Tonya White      Desk        486
PHN-BLK    646.00  288.00  Sam Smith        Reception   586
PHN-BLK    722.00  384.00  Susan Driscoll   Desk        386
PHN-BLK    722.00  288.00  Harriet Sands    Desk        286
```

Notice that the extracted data gives useful spatial information about this drawing as
well as the attribute data. The X and Y data fields give the X and Y insertion points of
each PHONE block. Your X,Y fields can vary from the ones shown here, depending
on where you insert the blocks. The PHONE column is set up to print the name of
the block that acts as the attribute data source. The PHONE column has character
data (see the C in the template) and an 11-character print width.

The next two columns give the X and Y locations of the block insertion point in numeric
form (see N in the template). (Your data can vary from the example.) The X and Y data
have two decimal places and the decimal point in a six-character print width. The X and Y
fields and the employee name would all run together if the two-character dummy fields
were not included. The other extracted attribute fields (a character field and a numeric
field) are in the last two columns. If an employee's name is unusually long, you can see
that the name would be truncated by the print width.

Block creating and inserting is one of the most powerful tools for automation of drafting
in AutoCAD. Your introduction to creating and inserting blocks in this chapter prepares
you for much more extensive information relative to block structure, editing of blocks
and attributes, organization of block data, and management of block making, and use of
blocks. The next chapter provides information in these areas.

New Riders Publishing
INSIDE
SERIES

C H A P T E R
17

Block Structure, Editing, Organization, and Management

C hapter 16, "Basic Building Blocks for Repetitive Drawing," illustrated several advantages of using blocks for recurring elements in your drawing, such as improved speed and uniformity of drawing symbols. Along with these advantages, blocks can represent a large reduction in drawing file size, which frees valuable disk space and leaves more memory free for AutoCAD to load its program modules. In this chapter, you explore specifically how AutoCAD stores this block information.

This chapter identifies the powerful methods AutoCAD provides for editing block references in your drawing, as well as the limitations imposed. This includes editing individual elements of a single block reference as well as simultaneously changing all occurrences of a block reference in your drawing.

A large number of standard symbols are used in any given drafting discipline, thus a large number of blocks should be created. You will learn some specific methods for storing and organizing your blocks, either as individual drawing files or in a special drawing file called a block library.

You will learn about some special considerations when creating and editing block references; for instance, how blocks and layers relate to each other, the uses of and difference between EXPLODE and XPLODE, and the use of nested blocks.

In the following exercise, experiment briefly with the EXPLODE command to learn how EXPLODE affects blocks and their layer and color settings.

Quick 5¢ Tour

Begin a new drawing named CHAP17 using EXPLODE.DWG from the IA Disk as a prototype.

First, attempt to erase the printer from the workstation on the left.

Command: *Choose* Modify, Erase	Issues the ERASE command
_erase	
Select objects: *Pick the printer in the upper corner of the left desk*	Selects the entire WORKSTATION block
Select objects: *Press Esc*	Cancels the ERASE command
Command: *Choose* Modify, Explode	Issues the EXPLODE command
_explode	
Select objects: *Pick any point on the left desk*	Selects the object to be exploded
Select objects: (Enter)	Ends objects selection and explodes the block

On your own, use the ERASE command to erase the printer from the left desk.

Command: **XPLODE** (Enter)	Issues the XPLODE command
Initializing...	
C:XPlode loaded.	
Select objects to XPlode.	
Select objects: *Pick the right desk*	Selects the object to be exploded
Select objects: (Enter)	Ends object selection
All/Color/LAyer/LType/Inherit from parent block/<Explode>: **I** (Enter)	Specifies the Inherit from parent block option
Object exploded.	

Notice that you were able to edit objects in the block only after exploding the block. Also, the colors of the objects in the first block changed when the block was exploded. This color change occurred because the EXPLODE command exploded the object onto the current layer, which was layer 0. Later in this chapter you will learn how to control a block's color, linetype, and layer properties. The next section will help you to understand how blocks are defined and stored.

Understanding Block Storage and Structure

You learn in Chapter 16 that the use of blocks can significantly reduce file size, which uses less disk space and less of your system's memory when loading the file. This section describes just how using blocks reduces file size. This section also describes a technique known as nesting blocks, which is very efficient if a block contains redundant features. Nested blocks also can be useful for certain editing operations.

One of the biggest problems AutoCAD users encounter when working with blocks is the way blocks and layers interact. A thorough understanding of the relationships between blocks and layers saves you quite a bit of frustration and expands the usefulness of your blocks. These relationships are explored in this section.

Block Storage

The AutoCAD drawing file contains a section known as the block table. In the block table, AutoCAD stores the information it needs to display the objects that are included in each unique block reference in your drawing, which is why the objects disappear when you create a block—the information needed to display the objects has been moved to the block table. When you insert a file into your drawing, the block table again is used to store all the object information for the file.

Because this information is stored in the block table, all AutoCAD needs to store in the object data area of the drawing file when you insert a block reference is the block's name, insertion point, scale factors, and rotation angle. This tells AutoCAD where and how to display that particular block reference.

Copying a Block and Multiple Insertions

Because the information describing a block's objects is stored in the block table, you can insert the block more than once in the drawing, and the information needed to display the objects doesn't need to be duplicated in the drawing file; this can represent a significant reduction in file size, especially if you have a complex block with

17

multiple occurrences in the drawing. The only thing you actually are adding to the drawing is the insertion information. Copying a block reference has the same effect as multiple insertions—all you actually are copying is the insertion information.

Do you remember the first exercise from Chapter 16? You inserted a block reference of a computer workstation in three places on an office floor plan. The size of the finished file was 14,003 bytes. The same drawing, if created without blocks, takes 41,857 bytes—almost triple the size! And that's only with three copies of the workstation.

Tip   If you are going to reuse a group of objects a number of times in a drawing, it might be more efficient to make a block of them instead.

You might remember from Chapter 16 the MINSERT command, which inserts a rectangular array of block references. If the block references of which you intend to copy or create multiple insertions follow a rectangular array pattern, MINSERT is an even more efficient method of placing them. When block references are placed this way, the only thing AutoCAD needs to store in the drawing file is one definition of the block in the block table and one insertion description containing information about the array.

Nested Blocks

A block can be made up of other blocks, a technique called *nesting*. You can place a block inside a block inside a block. AutoCAD does not place a limit on the number of block-nesting levels, although editing nested blocks can be confusing if you go more than a few levels deep. In the Quick 5¢ Tour exercise in Chapter 16, the WORKSTA-TION block that was inserted was made up of four nested blocks—a CHAIR, a KEYBOARD, a DESK, and a CPU block.

To nest one block in another block, first create blocks of the objects you want nested in the final block object. Next, reinsert the blocks in their original locations in the drawing. Then, use the BLOCK command and select the blocks, as well as all other objects that you want included in the final block object. You can use standard editing commands with nested blocks, such as ARRAY, COPY, and MOVE, just as you use them with normal block references.

Nested blocks further increase the efficiency and control of blocks. The WORK-STATION block contains only four objects (the four blocks mentioned) instead of all the lines, polylines, and arcs required to draw the individual blocks. In figure 17.1, the chair is a nested block, and the outer TABLE block needs to contain the table itself and six block references, rather than all the objects that make up each chair. Another advantage to nesting the TABLE block is that the CHAIR block can be redefined (changed) easily and independently of the TABLE block definition. Redefining blocks is covered later in this chapter in the section "Editing Blocks."

New Riders Publishing
INSIDE SERIES

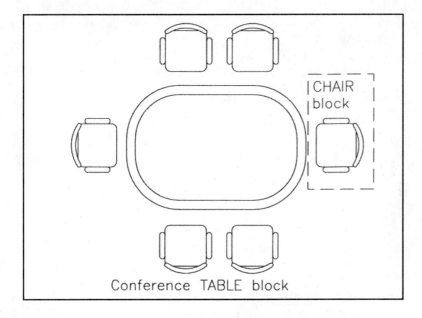

Figure 17.1
An example of a nested block.

Working with Nested Blocks

Begin a new drawing named CHAP17A, using the file NESTED from the IA Disk as a prototype.

Command: *Choose* Construct, Block	Issues the BLOCK command
Block name (or ?): **WORKSTATION** (Enter)	Names the block
Insertion base point: *Pick* ① *(see fig 17.2)*	Defines the block's insertion point
Select objects: **ALL** (Enter)	Selects all objects in the drawing
8 found	
Select objects: (Enter)	Ends object selection
Command: *Choose* Draw, Insert, Block	Issues the DDINSERT command
Choose **B**lock *and select* WORKSTATION *from the list of blocks, then choose* OK *twice*	Selects the block and starts the insertion process
Insertion point: *Pick some point near the middle of the drawing window*	Specifies insertion point

continues

17

continued

X scale factor <1> / Corner / XYZ: **Enter**	Accepts the default X scale factor
Y scale factor (default=X): **Enter**	Accepts the default Y scale factor
Rotation angle <0>: **Enter**	Accepts the default rotation angle

Now relocate the block reference to see how AutoCAD performs editing commands on block references.

Command: *Choose* Modify, Move	Issues the MOVE command
_move	
Select objects: **L** **Enter**	Selects the last object drawn
1 found	
Select objects: **Enter**	Ends object selection
Base point of displacement: **2'<30** **Enter**	Specifies displacement
Second point of displacement: **Enter**	Specifies distance to move with relative coordinates

Save this drawing for use in an exercise later in this chapter.

Figure 17.2

Pick point for nested block exercise.

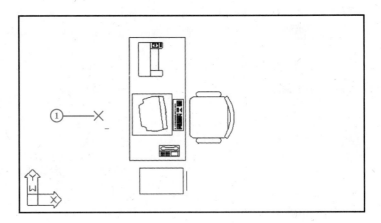

That's all there is to creating a nested block: simply select block references as the objects that make up a block. Any combination of objects and block references can be used for block creation. You also learned in the exercise that moving a block causes the entire object to be moved. This is because AutoCAD recognizes the contents of the block as a single object.

New Riders Publishing
INSIDE SERIES

Blocks, Layers, and Linetypes

AutoCAD keeps track of much more than the geometry of an object drawn on-screen. As you know, each object has certain properties, such as color, linetype, and layer, which provide very useful and even necessary features. If you don't consider these properties when creating blocks, however, you might experience some unexpected results.

When a block is created, the objects' properties of color, linetype, and layer are stored with the objects' data in the block definition. If the block is inserted in another drawing, these properties go along with it.

For example, consider a block created from objects drawn on layer PART and with color and linetype set to BYLAYER (the default setting for these properties). Assume that layer PART was defined as having blue phantom lines. The block table not only defines the objects, but also the properties of the blue phantom lines and of the layer PART. If you insert this block in a drawing that does not have this layer, AutoCAD automatically creates the layer PART to contain the block reference objects.

Taking the example one step further, what if you inserted the block in a drawing that *does* have a layer named PART, but the layer has different properties—such as yellow continuous lines? In this case, the block would not create a new layer, and the drawing's layer settings would override the block's settings. In other words, your block reference would end up with yellow continuous lines.

As you can see, the inner workings of blocks and their properties can become rather confusing. To understand these issues more clearly, consider the three methods of defining an object's linetype and color and see how these methods relate to block insertions. These three methods include setting the object's properties to BYLAYER, BYBLOCK, or specifying settings with the LINETYPE and COLOR commands. In addition, layer 0 has an effect on a block's properties, as you will read later in the section "Properties of Layer 0 Blocks."

Using BYLAYER with Blocks

The default setting for color and linetype properties is BYLAYER, which simply means the color and linetype of any object drawn is defined by the settings of the layer on which it resides. If you create a block of objects drawn on a specific layer, the color and linetype of that layer stay with the block, regardless of the layer on which it is inserted. This often is the desired effect. If you create a block of a tree using green continuous lines, you probably don't want to insert the tree and have it turn red with phantom lines.

Say you create a block of objects whose properties are set to BYLAYER, and the objects reside on layer RED, which is defined as having a linetype setting of CONTINUOUS lines and a color setting of RED. Regardless of the settings of the layer on which this block is inserted, it keeps red continuous lines. If it is inserted in a drawing that does not have a congruous layer named RED, AutoCAD creates one and assigns the CONTINUOUS linetype and red color to it.

17

Blocks created with BYLAYER can create some confusing results. For example, assume that you inserted the block from the previous discussion on a layer named BLUE with a color setting of BLUE and a linetype setting of HIDDEN. The block reference still appears red and has continuous lines, but if you select it with the DDCHPROP command, AutoCAD reports that the block reference is blue and has a hidden linetype! What's more, if you turn off the layer BLUE, the block reference is still displayed, even though it was inserted on layer BLUE.

The block reference is still displayed because AutoCAD placed the insertion point of the block reference on the layer BLUE, but the actual objects are still on whatever layer they were on when you created the block. The seemingly erroneous report from the DDCHPROP command is reporting the layer, color, and linetype of the block reference, not the block's objects. For the objects not to be displayed, you would have to turn off the layer RED. Freezing the layer BLUE also causes the objects not to be displayed.

Note   A block created from objects residing on layer 0 with the BYLAYER property settings does not behave as described in this section. The special case of layer 0 blocks is discussed later in this chapter.

See a later section of this chapter, "Using the EXPLODE Command," for special considerations when exploding blocks with BYLAYER properties. As you will learn in that section, exploding blocks converts the objects in the block back into individual, nonassociated objects.

If all this seems confusing, then you're on the right track. The following exercise helps clear things up by demonstrating the principles of blocks with BYLAYER properties. Figure 17.3 shows the drawing, which contains a symbol of an evergreen tree that was drawn with a polyline. The polyline was drawn on the layer EVERGREEN with its color and linetype properties set to BYLAYER. You will verify these settings in the next exercise using the DDCHPROP command.

Blocks with BYLAYER Properties

Begin a new drawing named CHAP17B, using the drawing BYLAYER from the IA Disk as a prototype.

Command: *Choose* Modify, Properties	Begins object selection
Select Objects: **L** ⏎	Selects the last object in the drawing
Select Objects: ⏎	Ends object selection and issues the DDMODIFY command

You can see in the Modify Polyline dialog box that the color and linetype for the evergreen symbol are set to BYLAYER. Choose OK to exit the dialog box.

New Riders Publishing
INSIDE
SERIES

Command: *Choose* Construct, Block	Issues the BLOCK command

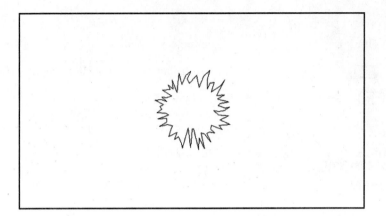

Figure 17.3

The symbol for an evergreen tree.

Block name (or ?): **EVERGREEN** (Enter)	Defines the block name
Insertion base point: *Pick a point near the middle of the evergreen symbol*	Sets the insertion point of the block
Select objects: **P** (Enter)	Selects the polyline
Select objects: (Enter)	Ends object selection
Command: *Choose* Data, Layers	Issues the 'DDLMODES command

Set layer EVERBLUE current. You can see in the Layer Control dialog box that the current layer (EVERBLUE) has its color property set to blue and its linetype property set to hidden. Now see what happens when you place the EVERGREEN block on this layer.

Choose OK	Ends DDLMODES
Command: *Choose* Draw, Insert, Block	Starts the DDINSERT command and opens the Insert dialog box
Choose **B**lock *and select* EVERGREEN *then choose* OK *twice*	Selects the block and starts the insertion process
Insertion point: *Pick a point near the middle of the drawing window*	Specifies the block insertion point
X scale factor <1> / Corner / XYZ: (Enter)	Accepts the default X scale factor
Y scale factor (default=X): (Enter)	Accepts the default Y scale factor
Rotation angle <0>: (Enter)	Accepts the default rotation angle

You can see that even though you inserted the block reference on a layer with blue hidden lines, it has retained its original green continuous lines. Now see what information AutoCAD gives you about this block reference with the DDMODIFY command.

continues

continued

Command: *Choose* Modify, Properties	Begins object selection
Select Objects: **L** (Enter)	Selects the last object in the drawing
Select Objects: (Enter)	Ends object selection, issues the DDMODIFY command, and opens the Modify Block Insertion dialog box

Note that AutoCAD says the block reference for EVERGREEN is blue and resides on the layer EVERBLUE. It sure looks green to me! Remember, AutoCAD is showing you the properties of the block reference, not the block's objects. The objects actually are on layer EVERGREEN, where they resided when you created them.

Choose OK	Ends DDMODIFY

Now, look at how layer settings will affect this block. Issue the DDLMODES command, set layer 0 current, and turn off layer EVERBLUE. Note that even though the layer on which the block reference resides is turned off, the objects that make up the block are still displayed.

Now use DDLMODES again to turn off the layer EVERGREEN. The objects that make up the block disappear. Turn back on all the layers to redisplay the block.

Next, freeze layer EVERBLUE. Again, the block disappears. Finally, thaw layer EVERBLUE and freeze layer EVERGREEN. The block is still frozen.

Turn on and thaw all layers, then save this drawing.

To summarize, if you want to suppress the display of a block reference with BYLAYER properties, you can either freeze or turn off the layer(s) on which the objects were created or freeze the layer on which they were inserted.

Using BYBLOCK with Blocks

You also can create blocks from objects with color and linetype properties defined as BYBLOCK. These blocks' properties behave quite differently from blocks with BYLAYER properties. You will be glad to know their behavior is much simpler.

 Stop   Remember that the default setting for object color and linetype properties is BYLAYER. If you want to create a block with BYBLOCK properties, you must define the objects' properties as BYBLOCK before creating the block. This can be done with the DDCHPROP, DDMODIFY, CHPROP, or CHANGE commands if the objects have already been drawn, or by setting the color and linetype to BYBLOCK with the COLOR and LINETYPE commands before drawing the objects.

If a block is created from objects whose color and linetype properties are set to BYBLOCK, the objects have no established color or linetype until they are inserted. They are displayed white with a continuous linetype until they are placed in a block. Upon insertion, they assume the color and linetype current in the drawing into which they are inserted. This makes these blocks act as sort of chameleon blocks, assuming whatever color and linetype is set for the environment they are placed in, whether these properties were set by layer settings or explicitly with the COLOR and LINETYPE commands. The layer on which the objects were drawn still stays with the block reference, just as it did for the BYLAYER blocks.

 Note See the section of this chapter titled "Using the EXPLODE Command" for special considerations when exploding block references with BYBLOCK properties.

In the following exercise, you will explore the methods of creating blocks with BYBLOCK properties. Figure 17.4 shows a hex head bolt symbol as it was drawn on the OBJECT layer with its linetype property set to BYLAYER.

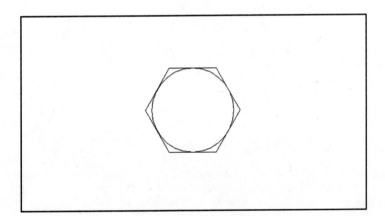

Figure 17.4
The symbol for a hexhead bolt.

17

Blocks with BYBLOCK Properties

Begin a new drawing named CHAP17C, using the drawing BYBLOCK from the IA Disk as a prototype.

Before making a block of the bolt head, change its color and linetype setting to BYBLOCK.

Command: *Choose* Modify, Properties   Begins object selection

Select objects: **ALL** (Enter)

Select objects: (Enter)   Ends object selection and issues 'DDCHPROP

continues

continued

In the Change Properties dialog box, choose the Color button. In the Select Color dialog box, choose BYBLOCK. Choose OK to exit the Select Color dialog box. Now from the Change Properties dialog box, choose the Linetype button and select BYBLOCK from the list box in the Select Linetype dialog box. Choose OK to exit the Select Linetype dialog box and choose OK again to exit the Change Properties dialog box.

Command: *Choose* Construct, Block	Issues the BLOCK command
Block name (or ?): **HEXBOLT** (Enter)	Names the block
Insertion base point: *Using the* CENter *object snap, select the circle*	Selects the insertion point of the block
Select objects: **P** (Enter)	Reselects the previous selection set
Select objects: (Enter)	Ends object selection and creates the block

Issue the LAYER or DDLMODES command and set current layer HIDDEN.

Command: *Choose* Draw, Insert, Block	Issues the DDINSERT command
Choose Block *and select* HEXBOLT *from the list of blocks, then choose* OK *twice*	Selects the block and starts the insertion process
Insertion point: *Pick a point near the center of the drawing window*	Sets the insertion point of the block
X scale factor <1> / Corner / XYZ: (Enter)	Accepts the default X scale factor
Y scale factor (default=X): (Enter)	Accepts the default Y scale factor
Rotation angle <0>: (Enter)	Accepts the default rotation angle

As you see, the block reference takes on the color and linetype of the layer on which it was inserted. Now see what properties AutoCAD reports for the block reference with the DDMODIFY command.

Command: *Choose* Modify, Properties	Begins object selection
Select Objects: **L** (Enter)	Selects the last object in the drawing
Select Objects: (Enter)	Ends object selection and issues the DDMODIFY command

The block reference's color and linetype properties have been changed to BYLAYER because that was the color and linetype setting when the block was inserted.

Choose OK	Ends DDMODIFY

Next you can see what happens when you insert a block with BYBLOCK properties when the color and linetype have been set explicitly.

`Command:` *Choose* Data, Color	Issues the DDCOLOR command
Choose the color red from the Standard Colors *area and choose* OK	Sets the current object color to red (1)
`Command:` *Choose* Data, Linetype, *choose* CENTER, *then choose* OK	Sets the current object linetype
`Command:` *Choose* Draw, Insert, Block	Issues the DDINSERT command
Choose OK	Accepts the default HEXBOLT block and starts the insertion process
`Insertion point:` *Pick a point to the right of the last block reference you placed*	Sets the insertion point of the block
`X scale factor <1> / Corner / XYZ:` (Enter)	Accepts the default X scale factor
`Y scale factor (default=X):` (Enter)	Accepts the default Y scale factor
`Rotation angle <0>:` (Enter)	Accepts the default rotation angle

This time the block reference was inserted to the current specifications of color red and linetype center, even though it is still on the layer HIDDEN. See what AutoCAD reports for this block reference's properties.

`Command:` *Choose* Modify, Properties	Begins object selection
`Select Objects:` L (Enter)	Selects the last object in the drawing
`Select Objects:` (Enter)	Ends object selection and issues the DDMODIFY command

The block reference's color and linetype properties have been changed to RED and CENTER because these were the color and linetype settings when the block was inserted. Figure 17.5 shows the two inserted block references of the block created with BYBLOCK properties.

Choose OK	Ends DDMODIFY

Save your drawing.

Figure 17.5

Inserts of block created with BYBLOCK properties.

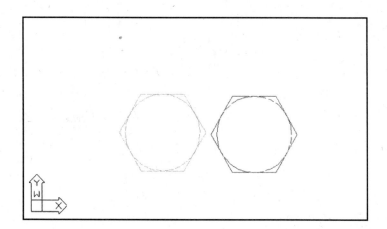

Using COLOR and LINETYPE with Blocks

You can create a block that always has the same color and linetype properties, regardless of the property settings in effect when the block is inserted. To do this, explicitly assign these properties to the objects before making a block of them.

Assignment is easily done by one of two methods. You can use the COLOR and LINETYPE commands to set explicit properties before drawing the objects, or you can use DDCHPROP, DDMODIFY, CHPROP, or CHANGE commands to reset these properties if the objects are already drawn.

Special Properties of Layer 0 Blocks

For general-purpose symbols, you might find that creating and blocking all objects on Layer 0 is the most efficient and least confusing method. Block objects created this way float to the layer current at the time of their insertion, meaning that the block reference's objects and its insertion point will always reside on the same layer. If you work with different layer schemes from one drawing to another, this can simplify block standardization.

Layer 0 blocks with properties set to either BYLAYER or BYBLOCK assume the color and linetype of the layer on which they are inserted. If the objects in a Layer 0 block were created with an explicit color or linetype setting, these settings are preserved.

 Note See a later section of this chapter, "Using the EXPLODE Command," for special considerations when exploding block references with Layer 0 objects.

Editing Blocks

In the first exercise of this chapter, you moved a workstation block reference and saw that it moves as a single object. Block references perform similarly when controlled by several editing commands, including COPY, MIRROR, ROTATE, and the various Autoedit modes. Block attributes also can be edited in many ways, using the DDEDIT, ATTEDIT, and DDATTE commands. There are, however, certain editing functions that cannot be performed on block references because of the nature of blocks. If you try to trim or extend a block reference, for example, AutoCAD has no way of describing this action in the block table, so it cannot enable you to use these commands on a block reference. Other editing functions that cannot be performed on block references include the OFFSET, STRETCH, BREAK, CHAMFER, FILLET, and LENGTHEN commands.

The EXPLODE and XPLODE commands enable you to turn a block reference back into the original objects used to create the block, which enables you to edit individual objects in the block. After a block reference has been exploded, it is stored as individual objects in the drawing file and no longer can be edited as a unit without first using the BLOCK command to redefine it as a block.

By far the most powerful aspects of block editing are the block substitution and block redefinition features. With these techniques, you automatically can change all occurrences of a block reference within a drawing simultaneously. These techniques have many applications that increase your productivity.

Editing a Block's Component Objects

When a block is placed in a drawing, AutoCAD treats it as a single object. If you try to select any part of the block reference for an edit command, such as ERASE or COPY, the entire block reference is selected. This can be very handy if you want to edit the entire block reference. If you want to edit any of the block reference's individual components, however, you must return the block reference to the original objects used to create it. This can be done with either the EXPLODE or the XPLODE commands.

If you know you will need to edit a block reference's individual components, you can insert the block as component objects, using either the Explode check box in the Insert dialog box, or you can issue the INSERT command and preface with an asterisk the name of the block to be inserted. Preceding the block name with an asterisk causes AutoCAD to insert the component objects from the block into the drawing as individual objects, not as a block, and has the same effect as choosing the Explode check box in the Insert dialog box. Both of these methods are explained in the section "Inserting Blocks as Component Objects."

17

Using the EXPLODE Command

The EXPLODE command is a simple command to use—it has no options; you are simply prompted to select the objects to explode. Exploding a block reference turns the block reference back into its original component objects.

> **EXPLODE.** The EXPLODE command has no command options. You are prompted to select the objects to be exploded. The EXPLODE command is used to break a compound object into its component objects. A *compound object* is an object that is made up of more than one object. Blocks, polylines, and dimensions are examples of compound objects.
>
> Pull-down: *Choose* Modify, then Explode
> Screen: *Choose* MODIFY, then Explode

As stated earlier, the EXPLODE command breaks apart a block reference, replacing it with its original objects. All of the objects used to create the block return to their original property setting upon being exploded.

Blocked objects created from BYLAYER objects return to their original layer and its property settings. Block objects created from BYBLOCK objects return to their original layer and retain their BYBLOCK color and linetype settings, but they are displayed as white objects of continuous linetype because they have no block to define these settings. Layer 0 blocks return to layer 0 with their original color and linetype settings.

When a block containing other blocks is exploded, it is broken down to the blocks used to create it, not to its original objects. These resulting component blocks then can be exploded to their original objects. In essence, therefore, the EXPLODE command explodes only one level at a time.

Stop   If you explode a block with attributes, any assigned attribute values are lost. The attribute definition is retained and the attribute tag is displayed.

When all block references are exploded, their component objects are stored as separate objects, but the block reference still is defined in the block table. The PURGE command, covered later in this chapter, should be used to remove these unneeded block definitions.

Using the XPLODE Command

When a block reference is exploded with the EXPLODE command, its component objects revert to their original settings. If this is not what you want them to do, you might want to use XPLODE instead. The XPLODE command enables you to explode the block and to specify what layer, color, and linetype you want the component objects to be given.

New Riders Publishing
INSIDE
SERIES

> **XPLODE.** The XPLODE command breaks a compound object into its component objects while enabling you to specify a new layer, color, and linetype for the component objects.

The XPLODE command provides more control over exploding block references than EXPLODE does, letting you specify in many ways how the component objects shall be displayed once exploded. To provide this kind of control, XPLODE has a number of options that overcome the limitations of EXPLODE but add a lot of complexity to the task of exploding a block reference.

If you select more than one block reference at the XPLODE command's Select objects: prompt, you will be asked if you want to XPLODE the objects individually or globally. If you explode them individually, you can define different properties for each block reference selected. AutoCAD highlights the block reference currently being exploded while it prompts you for the object properties of its components. If you choose to explode objects globally, the properties you specify are applied to all block references selected. If you only select one block reference to explode, this prompt does not appear.

After specifying whether to explode selected objects individually or globally, you are prompted for layer, color, and linetype information. The following list describes these prompts and their effects:

- ◆ **All.** Tells AutoCAD you want to change the layer, color, and linetype for the selected block reference. You will receive all the prompts described for the next three options in this list.

- ◆ **Color.** You can enter for this option the first letter of colors 1 through 7 or the number of any color. You can enter BYLayer or BYBlock.

- ◆ **LAyer.** You can type the name of any layer to which the component objects will be changed.

- ◆ **LType.** You can set the linetype of the component objects to BYLAYER, BYBLOCK, CONTINUOUS, or to any linetype that has already been loaded.

- ◆ **Inherit from parent block.** If you have blocks that were created on layer 0 and have their color and linetype set to BYBLOCK, this option will change the layer, color, and linetype of these objects to match the properties of their block reference. This enables you to explode blocks with BYBLOCK objects and have them retain their appearance after being exploded.

- ◆ **Explode.** This option causes AutoCAD to explode the block in the same manner as it would with the EXPLODE command.

Note   In early releases of R13, the Inherit from parent block option of XPLODE does not work properly. The blocks are simply exploded without changing the layer, color, and linetype properties.

Stop   The XPLODE command does not explode objects that are inserted with MINSERT.

In the following exercise, you try both the EXPLODE and XPLODE commands.

Using EXPLODE and XPLODE

Begin a new drawing named CHAP17D using the drawing EXPLODE, from the IA Disk, as a prototype. This drawing has two blocks, each containing a number of nested blocks created from objects on layer 0, having BYLAYER linetype and color. The blocks were inserted on layer WORKSTATION.

First, you will explode the left workstation using the EXPLODE command.

Command: *Choose* Modify, Explode	Issues the EXPLODE command
Select Objects: *Select the block at* ① *(figure 17.6) and press Enter*	Explodes the block

Notice that the objects that made up the block return to the layer, color, and linetype on which they were created. Verify this by looking at the object properties.

Command: *Choose* Modify, Properties	Begins object selection
Select Objects: *Select the blocks at* ② *and* ③ *and press Enter*	Selects the objects and issues the DDCHPROP command

You can see how the objects that made up the block return to their original state. This may not always be desirable. In the next steps, you will use XPLODE to change the layer and color of block components.

Choose OK	Ends the DDCHPROP command
Command: **XPLODE** (Enter)	Starts the XPLODE command
Select objects to XPlode. *Select the block at* ④ *and press Enter*	Selects the second block to explode
All/Color/LAyer/LType/Inherit from parent block/<Explode>: **A** (Enter)	Specifies the All option

`New color for exploded objects.`
`Red/Yellow/Green/Cyan/Blue/Magenta/`
`White/BYLayer/BYBlock <BYLAYER>:` (Enter)
	Accepts the default color for the component objects

`Enter new linetype name.` `<BYLAYER> :` (Enter)	Accepts the default linetype for the component objects
`XPlode onto what layer?` `<0>:` **WORKSTATION** (Enter)	Specifies the layer for the component objects

`Object exploded with color of Bylayer`
`linetype of BYLAYER, and layer`
`WORKSTATION.`

Notice that this block exploded onto the layer you specified instead of on the layer in which it was created. Also notice that you were able to separately set the color of the new objects. You can verify this by checking the properties of the new objects with DDCHPROP.

Save your drawing.

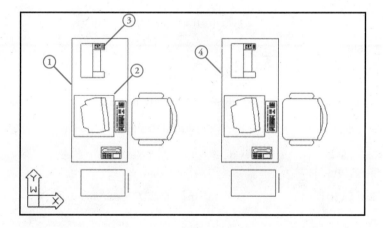

Figure 17.6

Workstation blocks to be exploded.

Inserting Blocks as Component Objects

If you have foreseen that a block reference will need editing after its insertion, you can insert it as an exploded block reference. If a block is inserted as an exploded block reference, AutoCAD disables dragging, which means the block is invisible to you as you place it. AutoCAD also does not enable the insertion of an exploded block reference with different X, Y, and Z scale factors. The property settings of a block reference inserted this way are the same as they would be if you inserted and then used the EXPLODE command on a block reference.

There are two methods of inserting blocks as component objects. You can use the DDINSERT command and choose the Explode check box of the Insert dialog box. Alternatively, you can use the INSERT command and simply type an asterisk (*) in front of the block name. The following exercise demonstrates both of these options.

Inserting Blocks as Component Objects

Begin a new drawing named CHAP17E using the drawing SLOTS from the IA Disk as a prototype.

Use DDLMODES to set layer OBJECT current.

Command: *Choose* Draw, Insert, Block	Issues the DDINSERT command

Select the block SLOT to be inserted. Place an X in the Explode check box and remove the X from the Specify Parameters on Screen check box. Set the X insertion point to 7.125 and the Y insertion point to 3.625. Set the X scale to .5. (Note the Y and Z scale are grayed out.) Set the Rotation Angle to 90. The Insert dialog box should appear like the one in figure 17.7. When you have made the settings, choose OK.

Command: **INSERT** (Enter)	Starts the INSERT command
Block name (or ?) <*SLOT>: ***SLOT** (Enter)	Specifies the block to insert
Insertion point: **2.875,3.625** (Enter)	Specifies insertion point by coordinates
Scale factor <1>: **.5** (Enter)	Scales the insertion to half scale
Rotation angle <0>: (Enter)	Accepts the default rotation angle

The slots should be inserted and appear as they do in figure 17.8. Next, you see why you inserted them as component objects.

Command: *Choose* Modify, Stretch	Issues the STRETCH command
Select objects: *Pick* ① *(see fig. 17.8)*	Selects right end of slot with a crossing box
Other corner: *Pick* ②	Selects the other corner of the crossing box
Select objects: (Enter)	
Base point or displacement: **.5<0** (Enter)	Sets the displacement for the stretch
Second point of displacement: (Enter)	Stretches the slot

Command: **Enter**	Repeats the last command
Select objects: *Pick* ③	Selects top of slot with a crossing box
Other corner: *Pick* ④	Selects the other corner of the crossing
Select objects: **Enter**	Ends object selection
Base point or displacement: **.5<90** **Enter**	Sets the displacement for the stretch
Second point of displacement: **Enter**	Completes the stretch

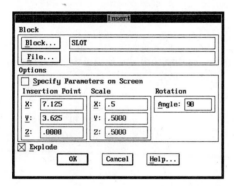

Figure 17.7

Settings for the Insert dialog box.

The slot you inserted was a 1-by-1 unit block—it was created with a 1-unit diameter and a center-to-center distance of 1 unit. By placing it as components with a .5 scale factor, you get a .5-wide slot that you can STRETCH to any desired length.

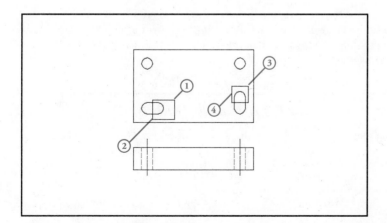

Figure 17.8

Pick points for STRETCH command.

17

Editing Attribute Information

Rather than editing the component objects of block references, you might need to edit their attributes. You might have entered information in the attribute incorrectly, or the information simply has changed since you inserted the block. In such a case, do not explode the block reference. Remember, exploding a block reference causes it to lose any attribute values you assigned when inserting the block.

There are only three commands with which to edit attributes, covered in the following section. The DDEDIT command can be used to edit text or attribute definitions. Note that it does not enable you to edit an attribute value, only its definition. It is useful only when creating attributes or after exploding a block reference with attributes.

The DDATTE command enables you to change an attribute value. After you select a block for attribute editing with this command, the Edit Attribute dialog box appears with the current values listed in the appropriate edit box. You simply make any changes needed in the edit box, then choose OK.

The ATTEDIT command gives you the most control over attributes, and has many options. Not only can you change an attribute's value, but you can change its position, text height, angle, text style, layer, and color.

Using DDEDIT To Change an Attribute Definition

If you make a mistake or change your mind about an attribute definition before you create a block of an attribute, it easily can be modified with the DDEDIT command, which also can be used to change the attribute definition of a block reference after it has been exploded.

All you need to do is select the attribute definition you want to change, and you are presented with a dialog box to make your changes. The following exercise demonstrates the use of DDEDIT.

Modifying an Attribute Definition

Begin a new drawing named CHAP17F using the drawing SCHEMATC from the IA Disk as a prototype.

First, you will create a couple of attributes with the DDATTDEF command.

Command: *Choose* Construct, Attribute	Issues the DDATTDEF command
Enter **Transistor_Number** *in the* Tag box *and* **Enter Transistor Number**	Specifies the tag, prompt, and default value, then prompts for the insertion

in the Prompt *box, in the* Value
box, enter **Q1***, then choose*
Pic<u>k</u> Point

point of the attribute

`Start point:` *Pick* ① *(see fig. 17.9)*

Selects insertion point for attribute text

Choose OK

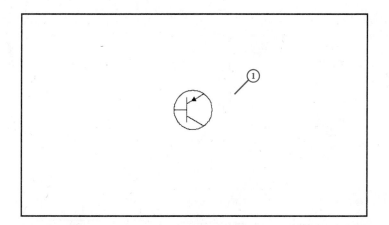

Figure 17.9

Pick points for DDEDIT exercise.

Figure 17.10

The transistor with attributes in place.

17

`Command:` `Enter`

Repeats the last command

Enter **Part_Number** *in the* <u>T</u>ag *box and*
Enter Transistor Part Number *in the*
<u>P</u>rompt *box, then place an X in the* <u>A</u>lign
below previous attribute *check box and
press* OK

Specifies the tag, prompt, and
placement of the attribute and
inserts the attribute

continues

continued

Your drawing now should look like the one in figure 17.10.

Suppose you decide on a better prompt for the TRANSISTOR_NUMBER attribute.

Command: *Choose* Modify, Edit Text	Issues the DDEDIT command
_ddedit <Select a TEXT or ATTDEF object>/Undo: *Select the TRANSISTOR_NUMBER attribute*	Specifies attribute definition to edit and displays the Edit Attribute Definition dialog box
Enter **Enter Reference Designation** *in the* Prompt *box and choose* OK	Changes the attribute prompt
<Select a TEXT or ATTDEF object>/ Undo: (Enter)	Ends editing selection

Save this drawing for use in the next exercise.

Using DDATTE To Change an Attribute Value

The DDATTE command is used to change the value of an attribute within an inserted block. It cannot be used to change attribute values defined as constant. Upon selecting a block with attributes, the Edit Attribute dialog box is displayed to make changes.

> **DDATTE.** The DDATTE command enables you to edit attribute values after a block reference with attributes has been inserted.
> Pull-down: *Choose* Modify, Attribute, Edit
> Screen: *Choose* MODIFY, AttEd

In the following exercise, you will create a block of the transistor and its attributes defined in the previous exercise. After inserting a block reference of this block, you will use DDATTE to change one of the values supplied on insertion.

Using DDATTE to Edit an Attribute Value after Insertion

Continue with the previous exercise.

To begin with, you must create a block containing the symbol and both of its attributes.

Command: *Choose* Construct, Block	Issues the BLOCK command
Block name (or ?): **TRANSISTOR** (Enter)	Names the block

```
Insertion base point: _int of Use
INTersection object snap to pick ①
(see fig. 17.11)
```

```
Select objects: ALL (Enter)          Selects all nonfrozen objects
```

```
Select objects: (Enter)              Ends object selection
```

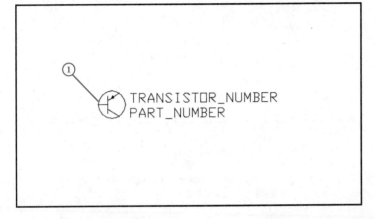

Figure 17.11

Pick point for the BLOCK command.

```
Command: Choose View, Zoom, All      Issues the ZOOM command with the All
                                     option
```

Use the DDLMODES or LAYER command to thaw layer SIGNAL_PATH.

```
Command: Choose Draw, Insert, Block  Issues the DDINSERT command
```

```
Choose Block and select              Selects the block and starts the
TRANSISTOR from the list             insertion process
of blocks, then choose OK twice
```

```
Insertion point: _endp of Use        Sets the insertion point for the block
ENDpoint object snap to pick ①
(see fig. 17.12)
```

```
X scale factor <1> / Corner / XYZ: (Enter)   Accepts default X scale factor
```

```
Y scale factor (default=X): (Enter)  Accepts default Y scale factor
```

```
Rotation angle <0>: (Enter)          Accepts default rotation angle
```

```
Enter attribute values
```

```
Enter Transistor Part Number:        Enters attribute value
2N6114 (Enter)
```

continues

continued

Figure 17.12

Pick points for the DDINSERT command.

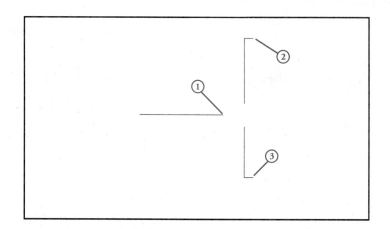

`Enter reference designation <Q1>:` **Enter**	Accepts default value

If you prefer entering values from a dialog box, remember that the ATTDIA system variable controls how AutoCAD will prompt for attribute values.

`Command:` **ATTDIA** **Enter**	Accesses the ATTDIA system variable
`New value for ATTDIA <0>:` **1** **Enter**	Turns on dialog box entry
`Command:` *Choose* Draw, Insert, Block	Issues the DDINSERT command
Choose OK	Inserts the TRANSISTOR block
`Insertion point: _endp of` *Use* ENDpoint *object snap to pick* ②	
`X scale factor <1> / Corner / XYZ:` **Enter**	Accepts default X scale factor
`Y scale factor (default=X):` **Enter**	Accepts default Y scale factor
`Rotation angle <0>:` **Enter**	Accepts default rotation angle
Enter **2N8601** *in the* Enter Transistor Part Number *box and* **Q2** *in the* Enter reference designation *box and choose* OK	Specifies the attribute information and inserts the block
`Command:` **Enter**	Repeats the last command
Choose OK	Inserts the TRANSISTOR block

New Riders Publishing
INSIDE
SERIES

```
Insertion point: _endp of Use
ENDpoint object snap to pick ③
```

`X scale factor <1> / Corner / XYZ:` (Enter)	Accepts default X scale factor
`Y scale factor (default=X):` (Enter)	Accepts default Y scale factor
`Rotation angle <0>:` (Enter)	Accepts default rotation angle
Enter **2B8088** *in the* Enter Transistor Part Number *box and* **Q3** *in the* Enter reference designation *box and choose* OK	Specifies the attribute information and inserts the block

Suppose you made a typo—you specified the third transistor's PART_NUMBER as 2B8088 when you meant to type 2N8088. This easily will be corrected using the DDATTE command.

`Command:` *Choose* Modify, Attribute, Edit	Issues the DDATE command
`Select block:` **L** (Enter)	Selects the last block and displays the Edit Attribute dialog box

Make the necessary change in the Edit Attribute dialog box, then choose OK. Figure 17.13 shows the final drawing. The attribute text is not very well placed; this can be fixed with the next command covered, the ATTEDIT command. Save this drawing for use in the next exercise.

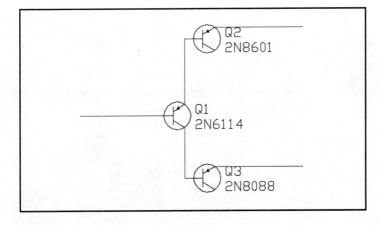

Figure 17.13

Three transistors with attributes.

17

Changing Attributes with ATTEDIT

The ATTEDIT command is used to change more than just attribute values; it is used to change the way the information is presented. With ATTEDIT, you can change the position, height, angle, style, layer, and color of attribute text.

> **ATTEDIT.** The ATTEDIT command enables you to edit attribute values globally and to change properties of the attribute text.
> Pull-down: *Choose* Modify, Attribute, Edit Globally

The first thing ATTEDIT asks is whether you want to edit attributes one at a time. If you want to change the way an attribute is displayed, you must answer yes (the default). If you answer no, you perform a global attribute edit. Global attribute editing enables you to change only attribute values, but it changes the value for all attributes selected at once. If you wanted to change the *Q* to a *V* in the transistor symbols in the previous exercise, for instance, you could change them all with one global edit.

If you answer yes to edit the attributes one at a time, you are allowed to select as many attributes as you want, then prompted to make changes to each attribute.

Tip When selecting attributes to edit, AutoCAD does not allow all normal object selection procedures. If you want to select more than one attribute, you must type **W** to select attributes with a window or **C** to use a crossing box. Any objects selected that are not attributes are ignored.

The following exercise takes you through the ATTEDIT options.

Using ATTEDIT for Global Editing Attributes

Continue with previous exercise.

To begin with, you will perform a global edit as described earlier—changing the Q designator for all transistors to a V.

Command: *Choose* Modify, Attribute, Edit Globally	Issues the ATTEDIT command
Edit attributes one at a time? <Y> **N** (Enter)	Specifies global editing of attribute values
Global edit of attribute values. Edit only attributes visible on screen? <Y> (Enter)	Accepts the default to edit only visible attributes
Block name specification <*>: **TRANSISTOR** (Enter)	Specifies which block's attributes to edit

You also could accept the default <*>, because TRANSISTOR is the only block reference in the drawing.

`Attribute tag specification <*>:` (Enter)   Accepts the default to edit all attributes

`Attribute value specification <*>:` (Enter)   Accepts the default to edit all attributes regardless of the present value

This option would be useful if you needed to change only a particular value. For instance, change all PART_NUMBER attributes set to 2N6017 to a new value of 2N8017.

`Select Attributes:` W (Enter)   Specifies window selection

`First corner:` *Pick* ① *(see fig. 17.14)*

`Other corner:` *Pick* ②

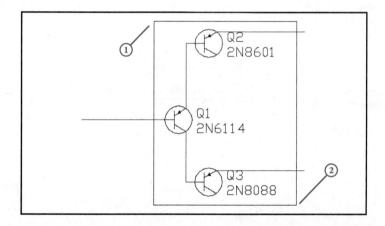

Figure 17.14

Pick points for Global Attribute Edit.

`String to change:` Q (Enter)   Specifies text to change

`New string:` V (Enter)   Specifies text to replace it with

A text string can be any number of letters to change. To change the text string BATTER to BOATER, for example, the string to change would be AT, and the new string would be OA.

You should now see all the transistors labeled Vn instead of Qn. Now you can edit attributes one at a time to clean up the drawing a bit.

`Command:` *Choose* Modify, Attribute, Edit Globally   Issues the ATTEDIT command

`Edit attributes one at a time?` <Y> (Enter)   Accepts the default

continues

continued

`Block name specification <*>:` (Enter)	Accepts default
`Attribute tag specification <*>:` (Enter)	Accepts default
`Attribute value specification <*>:` (Enter)	Accepts default
`Select Attributes:` **W** (Enter)	Specifies window selection
`First corner:` *Pick two points to select all three blocks with a window*	Specifies first corner
`6 attributes selected.`	Selects 6 attributes and highlights the first one for editing
`Value/Position/Height/Angle/Style /Layer/Color/Next <N>:` **P** (Enter)	Specifies Position option
`Enter text insertion point:` *Move attribute text to position shown in figure 17.15*	
`Value/Position/Height/Angle/ Style/Layer/Color/Next <N>:` (Enter)	Accepts default Next option and highlights attribute to edit
`Value/Position/Height/Angle/Style /Layer/Color/Next <N>:` **P** (Enter)	Specifies Position option
`Enter text insertion point:` *Move attribute text to position shown in figure 17.15*	
`Value/Position/Height/Angle/ Style/Layer/Color/Next <N>:`	

Continue to arrange the attributes so they appear as shown in figure 17.15.

 Tip   Grips are great for repositioning attributes, but not rotating them. Transistor symbols typically are inserted horizontally as in the previous exercises, but many symbols can be inserted at various angles. Therefore, you might need to change the angle of an attribute after it has been inserted. To do so, use the Angle option of the ATTEDIT command.

New Riders Publishing
INSIDE
SERIES

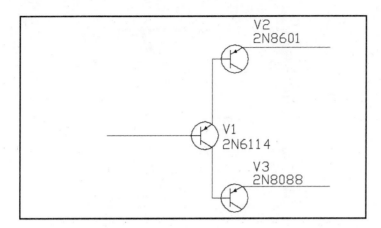

Figure 17.15

Final positions for all attributes.

Redefining a Block

You have seen how to edit individual block references, but what if you need to edit all occurrences of a block reference throughout a drawing? What if your client's standard for a symbol differs from your company's standard symbol? If you have placed quite a few copies of the symbol in your drawing, editing them individually would be very time-consuming.

AutoCAD enables you to change all occurrences of a symbol in your drawing simultaneously through a technique called *block redefinition,* with which you begin to see how the power to edit block references can be a real time-saver.

Block redefinition typically is accomplished with the BLOCK command, after inserting the block reference then exploding it to make the required changes. There are no new commands to learn, only a new application of these basic commands.

Figure 17.16 shows an office layout with 16 computer workstations. Each of these workstations is a nested block, as you might remember from a previous exercise—each workstation contains eight component blocks, one of which is a printer. Say you install a network so that these computers can share a printer, and at the same time add a mouse to each workstation. Without block redefinition, this would mean exploding each workstation block reference, erasing each printer block reference, and adding a mouse to each workstation. With block redefinition, the task is greatly simplified; simply explode one workstation, make the necessary changes, and redefine the workstation block. All workstation block references are automatically updated.

17

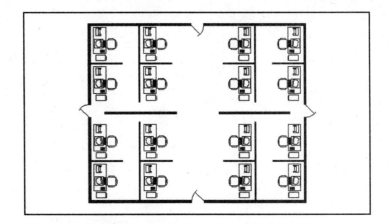

Figure 17.16

An office layout with 16 work-station block references.

The following exercise helps to illustrate the concept of block definition. You will make the changes previously described to the office layout.

Redefining Block References

Begin a new drawing named CHAP17G using the file REDEFINE, from the IA Disk, as a prototype. First, you will insert an exploded copy of the WORKSTATION block to edit.

Command: *Choose* Draw, Insert, Block	Issues the DDINSERT command
Choose the **B***lock button and double-click on* WORKSTATION*, then place an* X *in the* **E***xplode box and choose* OK	Specifies the block to be inserted and starts the insertion process
Insertion point: *Pick a point in the middle of the building*	Places the block insertion point
Scale factor <1>: (Enter)	Accepts the default scale factor
Rotation angle <0>: (Enter)	Accepts the default rotation angle

Next, you will edit the block by erasing the printer and replacing it with a mouse. First, zoom in on the workstation as shown in figure 17.17.

Command: *Choose* Modify, Erase	Issues the ERASE command
Select objects: *Pick* ① *(see fig. 17.17)*	Selects the PRINTER block reference
Select objects: (Enter)	Ends object selection and erases the printer

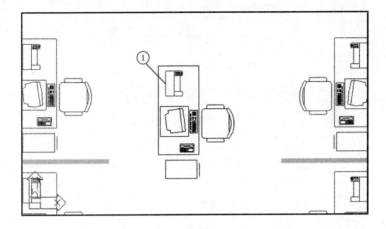

Figure 17.17

The exploded workstation.

A block for the mouse and mouse pad has already been created, so you can insert the mouse block at the workstation.

Command: *Choose* Draw, Insert, Block   Issues the DDINSERT command

Choose **B**lock *and select*   Selects the block and starts the
MOUSE *from the list of blocks,*   insertion process
then choose OK *twice*

Insertion point: *Pick a point on the*   Places the insertion point of the
desk to the right of the keyboard   block

X scale factor <1> / Corner / XYZ: (Enter)   Accepts default X scale factor

Y scale factor (default=X): (Enter)   Accepts default Y scale factor

Rotation angle <0>: (Enter)   Accepts default rotation angle

Now that the block reference has been exploded and modified, use the BLOCK command to redefine it.

Command: *Choose* Construct, Block   Issues the BLOCK command

Block name (or ?): **WORKSTATION** (Enter)   Gives the new block the same name as the
                                              original block

Block WORKSTATION already exists.   Redefines the block
Redefine it? <N> **Y** (Enter)

Insertion base point: *Using the*   Snaps to a POINT object
MID*point object snap, pick point*
① *(see fig. 17.18)*

continues

continued

Figure 17.18

Modified WORK-STATION with PRINTER erased and MOUSE added.

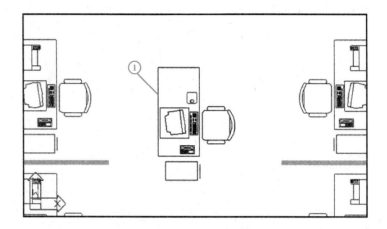

`Select objects:` *Select the 8 blocks that make up the workstation and press Enter*	Selects the objects and redefines the WORKSTATION block

To see that the redefinition changed all occurrences of the block reference WORKSTATION, zoom out to view the entire drawing.

`Command:` *Choose* View, Zoom, All	Issues the ZOOM command with the All option

Save this drawing for use in the next exercise.

Tip Before using EXPLODE on a block reference you want to redefine, note the location of the current block insertion point. Doing so enables you to choose the same insertion point when creating the new block, which keeps other references to the redefined block from shifting their position.

Block Substitution

As you have seen, block redefinition is a method of globally editing block references—changing all occurrences of a particular block reference in a drawing simultaneously. Another method of globally editing block references is the block substitution method.

Block substitution is simply the replacement of all occurrences of a block reference with a separate file, using the INSERT command. When supplying a block name for the INSERT command, you can set an existing block equal to a file, causing AutoCAD to substitute the specified file for the specified block.

New Riders Publishing INSIDE SERIES

Although the applications of block substitution are not so obvious, this method of global editing has two powerful uses. One common use is the replacement of complex blocks with simple blocks, which can tremendously reduce drawing regeneration time and time spent editing a drawing. When the drawing is completed, the simple blocks can be substituted with the complex blocks. This is a very efficient application of block substitution, as shall be seen in the following exercise.

Using Block Substitution for Efficient Drawing

Continue from the previous exercise. Zoom in on the upper left desk, as shown in figure 17.19, and turn on ortho mode.

First, you will draw an outline around the workstation to show its overall dimensions.

Command: *Choose* Draw, Polyline	Issues the PLINE command
From point: *Pick* ① *(see fig. 17.19)*	Specifies start point for polyline

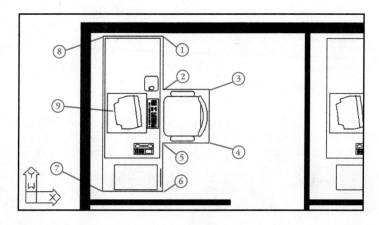

Figure 17.19
Envelope outline of the workstation.

Arc/Close/Halfwidth/Length/Undo/Width/ <Endpoint of line>: <Ortho on> *Pick* ②, ③, ④, ⑤, ⑥, ⑦, *and* ⑧	Specifies next point on polyline
Arc/Close/Halfwidth/Length/Undo/Width/ <Endpoint of line>: **C** (Enter)	Closes the polyline

Now you need to create a drawing file from the outline of the workstation.

Command: **WBLOCK** (Enter)	Starts the WBLOCK command

continues

continued

In the Create Drawing File *dialog box, specify the file name* OUTLINE, *then choose* OK	Specifies the name OUTLINE as the new drawing name
Block name: `Enter`	Specifies that no block is being used to create file
Insertion base point: *Using the object snap, pick* ⑨	Snaps to the insertion point of the INSertion workstation block
Select objects: **L** `Enter`	Selects the last object drawn to create the WBLOCK file
Select objects: `Enter`	Ends object selection and creates the new drawing file
Command: `Enter`	Repeats the last command
In the Create Drawing File *dialog box, specify the file name* WORKSTAT, *then choose* OK	Specifies the name WORKSTAT as the new drawing name
Block name: **WORKSTATION** `Enter`	Specifies the block to write to disk

To get an idea of how much time you will save substituting the simple outline for the workstation, note how long the drawing takes to regenerate when you select Zoom All. The time will vary depending on your hardware and configuration, but as an example, the author's 486DX66 machine took about 20 seconds to regenerate this drawing. Later in this exercise, you can compare this regeneration speed to the regeneration time using the simple outline block.

Command: *Choose* View, Zoom, All	Zooms to the drawing limits

Next you will substitute the OUTLINE block for the WORKSTATION block.

Command: **INSERT** `Enter`	Starts the INSERT command
Block name (or ?) <MOUSE>: **WORKSTATION=OUTLINE** `Enter`	Substitutes all block references to the block WORKSTATION with references to the block OUTLINE

At this time, the OUTLINE block should replace the WORKSTATION block, as shown in figure 17.20. Because you do not need to create any new references to the block, you should abort the command when you are prompted for an insertion point.

Insertion point: *Press Esc*	Cancels the INSERT command

Use the REGEN command to get an idea of regeneration time differences.

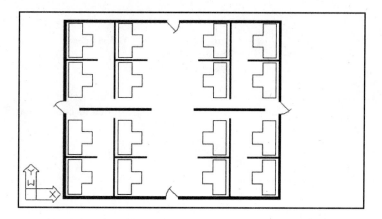

Figure 17.20
The WORK-STATION block replaced with the OUTLINE block.

Command: **REGEN** (Enter)   Issues the REGEN command

Regenerating drawing.

The author's computer, which took approximately 20 seconds to regenerate the drawing with the complex WORKSTATION blocks, regenerated the drawing with the substituted OUTLINE blocks in less than 1 second!

Save your drawing for the next exercise.

It was mentioned before the preceding exercise that block substitution has two powerful uses. The exercise demonstrated the timesaving capabilities of block substitution, but there is another powerful application of block substitution.

Suppose the office layout from the previous exercise is not the only option you want to show your client. Perhaps you want to provide the client with several other workstation design choices; for example, have one optional layout with smaller desks and another that eliminates the file cabinets. These changes do not require several layout drawings, only several files that can substitute the WORKSTATION block. These substitutions can be performed and the resulting layout plotted, or they can be incorporated into a presentation during which the client can watch as the layout transformations take place in seconds with the use of one command, INSERT. This use of block substitution is demonstrated in the following exercise.

Using Block Substitution for Multiple Designs

Continue from the previous exercise.

Command: **INSERT** (Enter)   Starts the INSERT command

continues

continued

`Block name (or ?) <MOUSE>:` **`WORKSTATION=WORKSTA2`** (Enter)	Substitutes all block references to the block WORKSTATION with references to the block WORKSTA2

As the block is substituted, you may see some messages about duplicate block definitions. That's OK, remember this is a nested block, and AutoCAD is telling you that its component blocks are already defined in this drawing.

`Insertion point:` *Press Esc*	Cancels the INSERT command

You should now see the new workstation layout as shown in figure 17.21.

Save your drawing for the next exercise.

Figure 17.21

Office Layout Alternative 2— desks shortened from 6' to 4.5'.

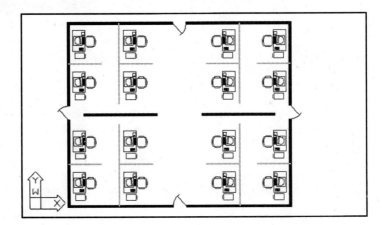

There is one more concept to illustrate involving block substitution. If you want to substitute a block reference with a file having the same name as the block, just type **BLOCKNAME=** when the INSERT command prompts for a block name, where *BLOCKNAME* is the name of the block being substituted.

For example, in the office layout of the previous exercises, suppose you also want to show your client a layout using tower PC cases rather than desktop cases. Because the case is the part of the nested block WORKSTATION defined by a block named CPU, you can substitute a file named CPU for the block named CPU. All occurrences of the block are automatically updated, even though it is nested in the WORKSTATION block. The following short exercise illustrates this point.

New Riders Publishing
INSIDE
SERIES

Using Block Substitution With BLOCKNAME=

Continue from the previous exercise.

Command: **INSERT** (Enter)	Starts the INSERT command
Block name (or ?): **CPU=** (Enter)	Substitutes all block references to the block CPU with references to the file named CPU
Insertion point: *Press Esc*	Cancels the INSERT command

You should now see the CPU block redefined in all of the WORKSTATION blocks as illustrated in figure 17.22.

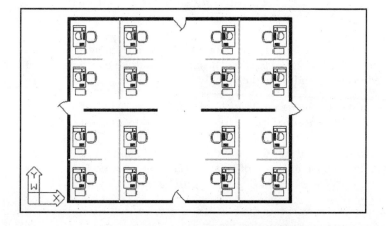

Figure 17.22

Office Layout Alternative 4— desktop CPUs replaced with tower CPUs.

Managing and Organizing Blocks

It should be obvious by now that an efficient CAD department makes extensive use of blocks. The amount and types of blocks you use depends on the types of drawings you produce, but any CAD discipline will find the use of blocks very advantageous.

When using large numbers of blocks, management and organization of your blocks greatly affects their efficiency. Block management encompasses the method used to organize your blocks, but also includes planning how your blocks should be created and used, as well as the setting of standards to ensure consistency in your block schemes.

17

Planning your block scheme involves deciding, before creating blocks, how they are to be used. Some of the questions you might ask at the planning stage are as follows:

◆ What is the most practical insertion point for each block?

◆ How will the block be placed (picked from a menu, inserted with an AutoLISP routine, with INSERT, with DDINSERT, as an XREF, and so forth)?

◆ Can several blocks be derived from one unit size block?

◆ Can several blocks be derived from one exploded block?

◆ Is the block complex enough to warrant the use of a simplified block and block substitution?

◆ How do the layer, linetype, and color properties of blocks relate to this block?

◆ At what scale should the block be drawn?

Although this list is far from complete, these questions are fairly generic and would apply to almost any extensive use of blocks. The answers to these questions will affect the methods used to create and store the blocks.

Consistency in your block scheme would include how your blocks will be named. If you are storing your blocks as separate files, you are limited to an eight-character name, which often isn't enough to be very descriptive. The use of mnemonic names or abbreviated names is a good solution, but don't get so elaborate with this that they become hard to interpret. An example of an abbreviated mnemonic file name would be 25SHCS20 for a 1/4" Socket Head Cap Screw with 20 threads per inch.

Keeping the standards used to create the blocks consistent with the standards used to create the drawings themselves is another aspect of block consistency. Layer names, linetypes, colors, and text style of attributes or blocked text are some of the things to consider in this area.

The organization of blocks pertains to deciding where and how the blocks shall be stored. There are two basic approaches to block organization: blocks can be stored as individual files in an intuitive directory structure, or they can be grouped into symbol libraries. A *symbol library* is a file made of a group of blocks, usually blocks that fall into some category, such as electronic control symbols, floor plan symbols, and so on. You often will find that a combination of these two approaches best suits your needs. The remainder of this chapter deals with the two approaches to block organization.

Again, the issues pointed out here concerning block management and organization are general in nature. Your specific application is bound to bring up other issues. Remember this: it is much more efficient to invest time before creating blocks to determine the best way to manage and organize your block scheme. Nobody wants to discover after creating several dozen blocks, or even several hundred blocks, that the blocks have an inconsistent text style or were drawn to an impractical scale.

Symbol Directories

The storage of symbols as individual files enables their easy editing and retrieval. The most common method of creating these files is to create a block of the symbol with the BLOCK command, then write the block to disk with the WBLOCK command. This method also enables symbols to be created on-the-fly; you simply draw the symbol the first time you need it, then use WBLOCK to store it as a file.

Another method of creating these files is to draw the symbol as a separate drawing and save it. Remember that any drawing file can be inserted—the WBLOCK command simply creates a drawing file. If the symbols are created in this manner, you must remember that the origin point (0,0,0) becomes the insertion point of the symbol. Alternatively, you can use the BASE command to specify the insertion point.

Storing symbols as individual drawings works best if you have a symbol that doesn't fall into a category of symbols. For instance, symbols for mechanical fasteners probably would be better stored in a symbol library, whereas symbols for your company's logo or a title block are good candidates for storage as individual drawing files.

As a rule of thumb, symbols that need to be accessed from a variety of drawings rather than from a particular type of drawing probably should be stored as individual drawing files. Also, symbols that are to be inserted from a menu selection or an AutoLISP routine usually should be stored as individual files.

If you decide to store symbols as individual files, you can save yourself a lot of time by creating a meaningful directory structure in which to store the files. A good directory structure makes selecting the files with the DDINSERT command much easier than if the files are all stored in one directory. The Select Drawing File dialog box only lists 10 files at a time. If there are more than 10 files in a directory, you must scroll to the file you need. The more files you have in the directory, the more you must scroll to get to the file you need. Figure 17.23 shows an example of a directory structure that would make symbols files easy to locate and would keep the directories from becoming too cluttered.

17

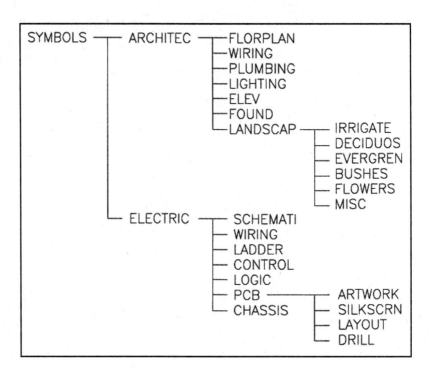

Figure 17.23

A sample directory structure.

There are disadvantages to storing symbols as separate files. Your computer's hard disk can quickly become cluttered with files stored this way, bogging down the hard disk and causing a decrease in your overall system performance.

Another less obvious disadvantage has to do with the way files are stored on a hard disk. File size limitations exist on your disk and operating system, and the end result is that a simple symbol can take more bytes of disk space than are needed to describe the symbol. Disk space for files is allocated in clusters, which are groups of sectors. Because of the method the operating system uses to allocate disk space, a typical file is slightly smaller than the amount of sectors the operating system allocates for the file. Therefore, virtually every symbol stored as a separate file is eating up more disk space than it requires. There also is a lot of information stored in a drawing file that might not be needed to describe the symbol, eating up even more bytes unnecessarily. These factors can account for several thousand bytes of disk space. Multiply that by several hundred symbol files and you can see this can be a real problem.

Symbol Libraries

Storing symbols in symbol libraries can overcome most of the disadvantages mentioned about storing symbols as separate files, but libraries have their own limitations. The next section explores the advantages and disadvantages of using symbol libraries.

New Riders Publishing
INSIDE
SERIES

As mentioned previously, creating a symbol library involves creating a drawing which contains nothing but the symbols and their block definitions. The block definitions are created with the BLOCK command, and the WBLOCK command is never used. Because the symbols are not saved as individual files, the hard disk clutter and hard disk space losses mentioned in the previous section are avoided.

Because the symbols are not stored as individual files, however, they cannot be directly inserted into a drawing. Remember, the BLOCK command creates only internal block definitions—these blocks are defined only in the symbol library file. If you insert the symbol library file into another drawing, however, all its block definitions are inserted along with it, and these blocks are then accessible from the new drawing. By canceling the INSERT command when it prompts for an insertion point, the symbol library file is not displayed in the current drawing, but its block definitions become part of the current drawing's block table.

 Tip   Another advantage to using symbol library files is the capability to give your symbols more descriptive names. Not limited to 8-character names, these symbols can have names up to 31 characters long.

The symbol names also can be placed in the drawing with the appropriate symbol, then plotted and used as a reference chart for the symbols.

Symbol libraries have two disadvantages. First, an extra step has been added to the process of inserting symbols. Before the symbol can be inserted into a drawing, the symbol library must be inserted, which causes a problem, especially when inserting the symbol from a menu selection or an AutoLISP program. Although you can work around this problem, it involves extra lines of code and slows down the symbol loading process.

Another disadvantage is the fact that all the block definitions from the symbol library are stored in the current drawing's block table—even if you needed to load only one block definition. This disadvantage can be overcome with the use of the PURGE command, which is described at the end of this chapter, or with the WBLOCK* technique, which is described in Chapter 16, "Basic Building Blocks for Repetitive Drawing."

Figure 17.24 shows a typical symbol library drawing. The symbols are generally associated in some way. In this example, they all are logic diagram symbols. The Xs represent the block insertion points. The labels and Xs have been added so that the drawing can be plotted and used as a reference chart. They are not part of the symbol.

Figure 17.24

A symbol library for logic symbols.

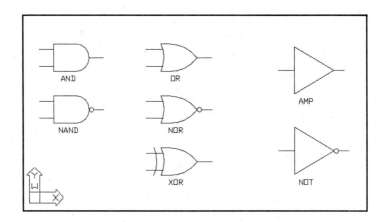

Inserting Symbols from a Library File

Using a symbol library file is a simple procedure. Before you can access the block definitions in the library file, you must insert the library file itself. It is helpful to think of the library file as a nested block. Upon inserting a nested block, AutoCAD stores a block definition for all nested blocks in the current drawings block table.

In the following exercise, you use the symbol library created in the preceding exercise to complete a logic diagram.

Using Blocks from a Symbol Library File

Begin a new drawing named CHAP17H using the default ACAD.DWG prototype drawing. Set the SNAP spacing to .25 and the GRID spacing to 1. Turn both GRID and SNAP on.

Command: *Choose* Draw, Insert, Block	Issues the DDINSERT command
Choose the **F**ile *button and select* LOGIC.DWG *from the file list, then choose OK twice*	Inserts the file LOGIC.DWG into the current drawing
Insertion point: *Press Esc*	Cancels the INSERT command
Command: **Enter**	Repeats the last command
Choose **B**lock *and select* AND *from the list of blocks and choose* OK, *remove the* X *from the* **S**pecify Parameters on Screen *box, enter* **2** *in the* **X** *Insertion Point box, enter* **8** *in the* **Y** *Insertion Point box, and choose* OK	Inserts the block AND at the coordinate 2,8
Command: **Enter**	Repeats the last command

New Riders Publishing

INSIDE SERIES

Command: *Enter* **2** *in the* X Insertion Point *box, enter* **6** *in the* Y Insertion Point *box, and choose* OK	Inserts the block AND at the coordinate 2,6
Command: (Enter)	Repeats the last command
Command: *Choose* **B**lock *and select* OR *from the list of blocks and choose* OK, *enter* **2** *in the* X Insertion Point *box, enter* **4** *in the* Y Insertion Point *box, and choose* OK	Inserts the block OR at the coordinate 2,4
Command: (Enter)	Repeats the last command
Command: *Choose* **B**lock *and select* XOR *from the list of blocks and choose* OK, *enter* **2** *in the* X Insertion Point *box, enter* **2** *sin the* Y Insertion Point *box, and choose* OK	Inserts the block XOR at the coordinate 2,2
Command: (Enter)	Repeats the last command
Command: *Choose* **B**lock *and select* OR *from the list of blocks and choose* OK, *enter* **6** *in the* X Insertion Point *box, enter* **7** *in the* Y Insertion Point *box, and choose* OK	Inserts the block OR at the coordinate 6,7
Command: (Enter)	Repeats the last command
Command: *Choose* **B**lock *and select* AND *from the list of blocks and choose* OK, *enter* **6** *in the* X Insertion Point *box, enter* **3** *in the* Y Insertion Point *box, and choose* OK	Inserts the block AND at the coordinate 6,3
Command: (Enter)	Repeats the last command
Command: *Choose* **B**lock *and select* NOR *from the list of blocks and choose* OK, *enter* **10** *in the* X Insertion Point *box, enter* **5** *in the* Y Insertion Point *box, and choose* OK	Inserts the block NOR at the coordinate 10,5

continues

continued

You should have all the symbols in place now, completing the diagram is just a matter of adding a few lines to connect the symbols. Figure 17.25 shows the completed logic diagram.

After adding the connecting lines, save your drawing for the next exercise.

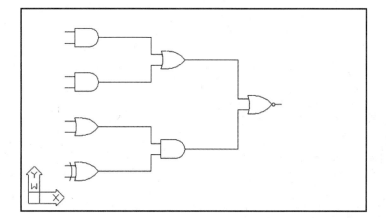

Figure 17.25

The completed logic diagram.

Purging an Unused Block from the Block Table

In the preceding exercise, you inserted into a drawing a symbol library file containing seven block definitions, which added eight block definitions to the block table of your drawing—seven definitions for the nested blocks in the symbol library file and one for the symbol library file itself. To create the drawing, however, you needed only four block definitions—you did not use the symbols for NAND, AMP, or NOT. Now that the drawing is complete, you should PURGE these three unused blocks from your drawing.

The PURGE command enables you to purge only unreferenced block definitions from your drawing. *Unreferenced block definitions* are block definitions that have no block references inserted in the drawing, or whose block reference(s) has been exploded. These block definitions are just taking up space; they increase the size of your drawing file and are not needed.

As the size of your symbols libraries and the complexity of your block definitions increase, the need to purge a drawing after inserting the symbol library becomes more and more important.

An alternative to using the PURGE command to remove unreferenced block definitions is the WBLOCK* procedure, which is discussed in Chapter 16, "Basic Building Blocks for Repetitive Drawing."

In the following exercise, you use the PURGE command to remove the unreferenced block definitions from the logic diagram completed in the previous exercise.

Mention should be made of one more aspect of purging blocks. When purging nested blocks, you are allowed to purge only the top level block, not the component blocks. After the top level block is purged, you can reissue the PURGE command to remove the component blocks. If any of the component blocks are also nested blocks, this procedure must be repeated as many times as is necessary to reach the lowest level of component blocks.

Purging Unreferenced Block Definitions

If you completed the last exercise, load that drawing and continue with this exercise. Otherwise, begin a new drawing named CHAP17I, using the file LOGIC2 from the IA Disk as a prototype.

Command: *Choose* Data, Purge, Blocks	Starts the PURGE command
`_purge`	

`Purge unused Blocks/Dimstyles/LAyers/`
`LTypes/SHapes/STyles/APpids/`
`Mlinestyles/All: _b`	

`Purge block LOGIC? <N>` **Y** (Enter)	Purges the definition from the block table
Command: (Enter)	Repeats the PURGE command

`Purge unused Blocks/Dimstyles/LAyers/`
`LTypes/SHapes/STyles/APpids/`
`Mlinestyles/All:` **B** (Enter)
	Specifies the Blocks option

`Purge block NAND? <N>` **Y** (Enter)	Purges the definition from the block table
`Purge block AMP? <N>` **Y** (Enter)	Purges the definition from the block table
`Purge block NOT? <N>` **Y** (Enter)	Purges the definition from the block table

17

This chapter has explored the intricacies of block storage and structure. The section of a drawing file AutoCAD uses to store block data and insertion information, known as the block table, was discussed. The relationships of blocks to the color, layer, and linetype object properties were outlined. Application of this information will insure you the most efficient use of blocks.

The methods of editing blocks were also shown, including exploding a block to edit its individual components, block substitution and redefinition, and commands used to edit block attributes. The techniques described for block editing make your use of blocks more flexible as well as more efficient.

Finally, the methods of organizing and managing your blocks were explained. Suggestions were given to help you decide the most beneficial way to organize and standardize your blocks.

After completing this and the previous chapter, you are ready to make extensive use of blocks to greatly increase your efficiency with AutoCAD. When doing so, bear in mind the advice given in this chapter concerning planning— time spent deciding how to create, use, and organize your blocks is time well spent.

Constructive Editing

Previous chapters introduce you to the concepts of drawing and editing. Many of AutoCAD's editing commands enable you to modify existing objects. This chapter merges the topics of drawing and editing to explain commands that you can use to edit existing geometry to create new geometry, a process known as *constructive editing*. This chapter covers the following constructive editing topics:

◆ Using the OFFSET command to create offset geometry

◆ Using the FILLET and CHAMFER commands to apply fillets and chamfers

◆ Using the MEASURE and DIVIDE commands to measure and divide objects

◆ Using the ARRAY command to create rectangular and polar arrays

◆ Using the BREAK command to break objects

◆ Using the MIRROR command to mirror objects

Chapter 14, "The Ins and Outs of Editing," introduces the concept of editing, which in AutoCAD generally means modifying existing objects. Typical editing includes erasing, copying, and moving objects. Many of AutoCAD's editing commands enable you to modify existing objects without changing the appearance of the original objects. When you copy or move a selection set, for example, the objects in their new location appear identical to the original objects.

Many of AutoCAD's editing commands, however, are *constructive editing commands*, tools that enable you to refine a sketchy design into a finished drawing. Like other editing commands, constructive editing commands modify existing objects, but they also create new objects, which enables you to construct a drawing quickly.

A good example of this type of command is the ARRAY command, which enables you to copy an existing object in a rectangular or circular (polar) array. Figure 18.1 shows a drawing before and after an array.

Figure 18.1

A drawing before and after an array.

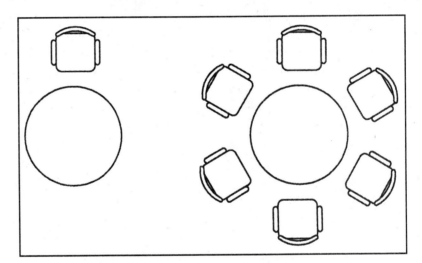

AutoCAD's constructive editing commands significantly speed up the drawing process because you can use existing geometry. You can use the ARRAY command, for example, to quickly create numerous copies of an object rather than individually draw or copy and rotate each new object.

AutoCAD's constructive editing commands enable you to modify existing objects quickly to add new features to the drawing, in turn enabling you to convert construction objects that need refinement into finished drawing geometry, modify existing parts and symbols to create new ones, and otherwise complete a drawing in as little time as possible. As you become proficient using AutoCAD, you will find that you use its constructive editing commands even more than its primary drawing commands to complete a drawing. For this reason, applying constructive editing is one of the most important skills you can learn.

The following sections explore several constructive editing commands, beginning with the FILLET command. First, however, you should take a few minutes to sample some constructive editing commands. Figure 18.2 shows a simple drawing to which you apply some constructive editing techniques in the following exercise.

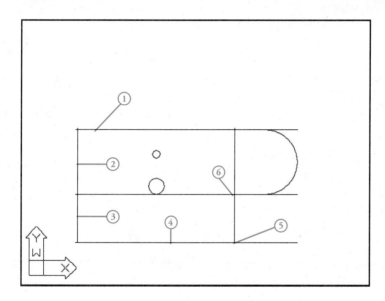

Figure 18.2

A sample drawing before constructive editing.

The drawing is a rough design of a mounting plate. Your task is to polish the rough geometry into a finished drawing. You use the FILLET command to fillet intersections of lines and the ARRAY command to create a mounting hole pattern.

After you complete the exercise, your drawing should resemble the one you see in figure 18.4.

Quick 5¢ Tour

Begin a new drawing named CHAP18 using CONSTRUC.DWG from the IA Disk as a prototype.

First, you apply a fillet to the intersection of two construction lines.

Command: *Choose* Construct, Fillet   Issues the FILLET command

```
_fillet
(TRIM mode) Current fillet
radius = 0.0000
```

continues

18

continued

`Polyline/Radius/Trim/<Select first` `object>:` **R** (Enter)	Specifies the Radius option
`Enter fillet radius <0.0000>:` `.25` (Enter)	Specifies the new default radius value
`Command:` (Enter)	Repeats the FILLET command

`FILLET`
`(TRIM mode) Current fillet`
`radius = 0.2500`	

`Polyline/Radius/Trim/<Select first` `object>:` *Pick line* ① *(refer to* *figure 18.2)*	Selects the first object to fillet
`Select second object:` *Pick line* ②	Selects the second object to fillet and creates the fillet
`Command:` (Enter)	Repeats the FILLET command

`FILLET`
`(TRIM mode) Current fillet`
`radius = 0.2500`	

`Polyline/Radius/Trim/<Select first` `object>:` *Pick line* ③	Selects the first object to fillet
`Select second object:` *Pick line* ④	Selects the second object to fillet and creates the fillet

Repeat the FILLET command two more times, and fillet the intersections at ⑤ and at ⑥.

Next, you array a circle to create a mounting hole pattern, using figure 18.3 as a reference.

`Command:` *Choose* Construct, Array, Polar	Prompts for selection
`Select objects:` *Pick circle at* ① *(see fig. 18.3) and* *press Enter*	Selects the object to be arrayed, ends selection, and issues the ARRAY command with the Polar option

`Command: _array`
`Select objects: _p`
`1 found`
`Select objects:`
`Rectangular or Polar array (R/P)`
`<R>: _p`	

New Riders Publishing
INSIDE
SERIES

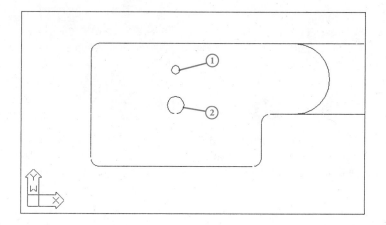

Figure 18.3

Selection points for the array.

Center point of array: *From the pop-up menu, choose* Center	Specifies the Center object snap mode
_center of *Pick circle* ②	Specifies the center point of the array
Number of items: **6** (Enter)	Specifies the total number of objects to be included in the array
Angle to fill (+=ccw, -=cw) <360>: (Enter)	Accepts default angle to fill with the arrayed objects
Rotate objects as they are copied? <Y> (Enter)	Causes objects to be rotated as they are arrayed

Save your drawing.

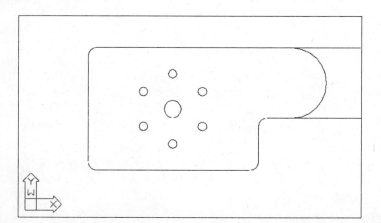

Figure 18.4

Sample drawing after constructive editing.

18

Using constructive editing commands enables you to modify the general shape and arrangement of objects. You learn more about the ARRAY command later in this chapter. The next section explains the FILLET and CHAMFER commands.

Applying Fillets and Chamfers

A *fillet* is an arc that you apply to the intersection of two objects—two lines, a line and an arc, two polyline segments, and so on. Figure 18.1 shows two lines before and after a fillet. A *chamfer* is a line segment that you apply to the intersection of two objects or two polyline segments. Figure 18.5 shows two lines before and after a chamfer.

Figure 18.5

Two lines before and after a chamfer.

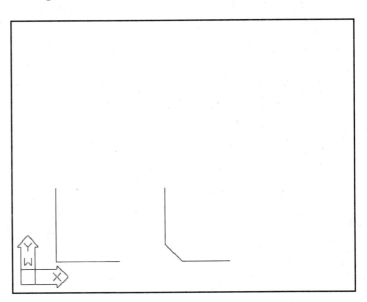

AutoCAD simplifies applying fillets and chamfers by completely automating the process. You simply specify a fillet radius or chamfer distance or angle and select the objects to which you want to apply the fillet or chamfer, rather than draw the fillet or chamfer manually. AutoCAD modifies the objects automatically.

Understanding the FILLET Command

The FILLET command enables you to apply a fillet to various types of objects, including the following:

New Riders Publishing
INSIDE
SERIES

- ◆ Lines

- ◆ Polyline vertices or entire polylines

- ◆ Arcs

- ◆ Circles

The most common use of the FILLET command is to apply an arc to the intersection of two objects, but other uses for the FILLET command exist. Because the two objects to which you apply the fillet do not have to meet at an intersection, for example, you can use the FILLET command to join two objects. You also can specify a radius of zero for the fillet, which enables you to "un-fillet" two objects and extend them to an intersection. Always, applying a fillet is as simple as specifying a radius and picking two objects.

FILLET. The FILLET command enables you to apply a fillet to two existing objects. You can apply a fillet to lines, arcs, circles, and polyline segments.
Screen menu: *Choose* CONSTRCT, Fillet:
Pull-down menu: *Choose* Construct, Fillet

The FILLET command provides three options that enable you to control the way in which AutoCAD applies the fillet:

- ◆ **Polyline.** Enables you to fillet all vertices of a polyline in a single operation.

- ◆ **Radius.** Enables you to specify the radius of the fillet arc.

- ◆ **Trim.** You can set this option to Trim (the default) or No Trim. Setting the option to Trim, causes AutoCAD to trim to the arc tangent points of the objects being filleted. If the option is set to No Trim, it causes AutoCAD to trim the fillet arc, but not the objects.

Applying Fillets

You used the FILLET command in the first exercise in this chapter to apply a fillet to the intersection of two lines that do not make a neat corner. You also can apply a fillet to two objects that do not intersect. If you set the Trim option to Trim, AutoCAD automatically trims or extends the objects as necessary to move their endpoints to the tangent points of the fillet arc. Although you probably usually want the objects to which you apply fillets to be trimmed to the tangent points of the fillet arcs, you occasionally might want the objects to remain as they are.

18

In the following exercise, you fillet two non intersecting lines on a scraper blade, extending the lines to the tangent points of the fillet arc. You use figure 18.6 as a guide, and use the Trim option to undo the previous fillet and experiment. You then set the Trim option set to No Trim and add a fillet to the upper-left and upper-right corners of the scraper blade. Figures 18.6 and 18.7 shows the selection points for the exercise.

Figure 18.6

A scraper blade before applying fillets.

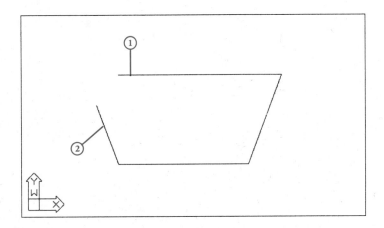

Using the Trim Option

Begin a new drawing named CHAP18A, using FEATURE.DWG as a prototype.

```
Command: Choose Construct, Fillet                Issues the FILLET command

_fillet
(TRIM mode) Current fillet
radius = 0.0000

Polyline/Radius/Trim/<Select first              Specifies the Radius option
object>: R Enter

Enter fillet radius <0.0000>: .5 Enter          Sets the radius

Command: Enter                                  Repeats the FILLET command
```

New Riders Publishing
INSIDE
SERIES

```
FILLET
(TRIM mode) Current fillet
radius = 0.5000

Polyline/Radius/Trim/<Select first          Specifies the first object to fillet
object>: Pick line ① (see fig.
18.6)

Select second object: Pick line ②          Specifies the second object to fillet and
                                            creates the fillet
```

Undo the previous fillet

Command: *Choose* Construct, Fillet   Issues the FILLET command

```
_fillet                                     Notice that the prompt indicates TRIM mode
(TRIM mode) Current fillet                  and the default radius
radius = 0.5000

Polyline/Radius/Trim/<Select first          Specifies the Trim option
object>: T (Enter)

Trim/No trim <Trim>: N (Enter)              Sets the Trim option to No Trim

Polyline/Radius/Trim/<Select first          Specifies first line to fillet
object>: Pick line ① (see fig.
18.7)

Select second object: Pick line ②          Specifies second line and creates fillet

Command: (Enter)                            Repeats the FILLET command

FILLET                                      Notice that the prompt indicates NOTRIM
(NOTRIM mode) Current fillet                mode
radius = 0.5000

Polyline/Radius/Trim/<Select first          Specifies first line to fillet
object>: Pick line ③

Select second object: Pick line ④          Specifies second line and creates fillet
```

Save your drawing, which should resemble figure 18.8

18

Figure 18.7

A scraper blade after adding a fillet.

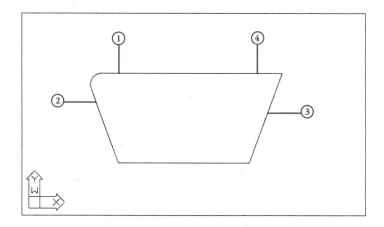

Figure 18.8

Fillets created with the Trim option set to No Trim.

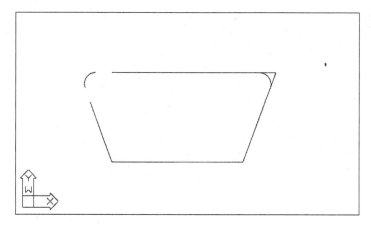

AutoCAD neatly trims the existing drawing objects when you apply a fillet in the default Trim setting, but does not alter the existing objects if you apply a fillet in the No Trim setting.

Trimming and Extending with a Zero-Radius Fillet

Although you can undo a fillet just like you can undo nearly any AutoCAD command, doing so is sometimes impractical. For example, you might apply a fillet, then realize an hour later—after a considerable amount of continuous editing—that you did not want the objects to be trimmed. Fortunately, you don't have to erase the objects and redraw them. Instead, you can use the FILLET command to re-extend the objects to an intersection.

If you specify a radius of zero for the fillet and set the Trim option to Trim, AutoCAD automatically extends the two objects to intersect. AutoCAD does not remove any fillet arcs, however.

New Riders Publishing
INSIDE
SERIES

Tip You can use the zero radius feature of the FILLET command to extend or trim lines and arcs, which enables you to make rough object drawings, then use FILLET later to clean up intersections and adjust endpoints, as shown in figure 18.9.

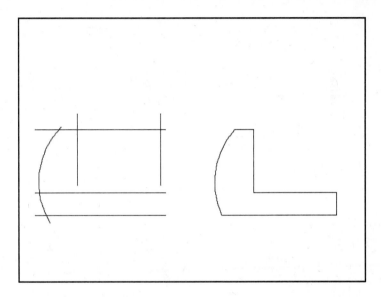

Figure 18.9

Editing using FILLET with a zero radius.

In the following exercise, you remove a fillet that you applied in the previous exercise. You use the FILLET command with a zero radius to extend the lines to their original intersection point.

Filleting with a Zero Radius

Continue to use the CHAP18A drawing from the preceding exercise.

Command: *Choose* Construct, Fillet   Issues the FILLET command

```
_fillet
(NOTRIM mode) Current fillet
radius = 0.5000
```

Polyline/Radius/Trim/<Select first   Specifies the Trim option
object>: **T** (Enter)

Trim/No trim <No trim>: **T** (Enter)   Turns on Trim

Polyline/Radius/Trim/<Select first   Specifies the Radius option

18

continues

continued

```
object>: R Enter
```

```
Enter fillet radius <0.5000>: 0 Enter
```
Sets the radius to zero

```
Command: Enter
```
Repeats the FILLET command

```
FILLET
(TRIM mode) Current fillet
radius = 0.0000
```

```
Polyline/Radius/Trim/<Select first
object>: Pick line ① (see fig.
18.10)
```
Specifies first line to fillet

```
Select second object: Pick line ②
```
Specifies second line and extends lines to their intersection

Save your drawing, which should now resemble figure 18.10.

Figure 18.10

A zero-radius fillet.

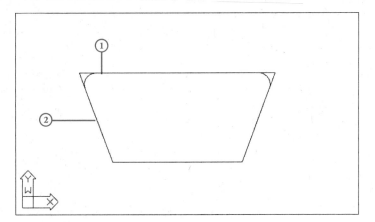

When you use FILLET with a zero radius, AutoCAD does not remove any previous fillet arcs. You must use the ERASE command to manually remove the fillet arc.

 Tip   You also can use the EXTEND command to extend the objects to an intersection after you apply a fillet. Set the EXTEND command's Edge option to Extend to cause AutoCAD to extend the lines to their projected intersection.

Filleting Arcs and Circles

In previous exercises, you filleted line segments. You also can fillet arcs, and even circles. Applying a fillet to a line and arc, or to two arcs, creates a tangent arc between the two objects. If you set the Trim option to Trim, AutoCAD trims the two objects to the tangent points of the fillet arc. If you set Trim to No Trim, AutoCAD draws only the tangent arc, but does not trim the objects.

Circles behave differently with fillets, however. AutoCAD does not trim a circle in any way when you apply a fillet to it, regardless of the Trim setting.

In the following exercise, you set the fillet radius to 20 and fillet lines, arcs, and circles, using figure 18.11 as a reference.

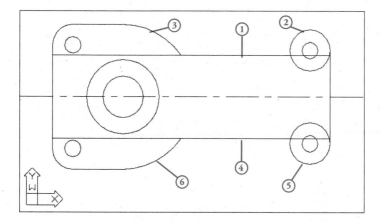

Figure 18.11

An incomplete top view of a casting ready for filleting.

Filleting Arcs and Circles

Begin a new drawing named CHAP18B, using CASTING as a prototype and zoom to the view shown in figure 18.11.

Command: *Choose* Construct, Fillet, *and set the fillet radius to 20*

Command: (Enter)   Repeats the FILLET command

FILLET
(TRIM mode) Current fillet
radius = 20.0000

Polyline/Radius/Trim/<Select first   Specifies the first object to fillet
object>: *Pick line* ① *(see fig.*
18.11)

continues

18

continued

`Select second object:` *Pick circle* ②	Creates fillet and trims the line but not the circle
`Command:` `Enter`	Repeats the FILLET command

`FILLET`
`(TRIM mode) Current fillet`
`radius = 20.0000`

`Polyline/Radius/Trim/<Select first object>:` *Pick line* ①	
`Select second object:` *Pick arc* ③	Specifies second object, trims line and arc, and creates fillet
`Command:` `Enter`	Repeats the FILLET command

`FILLET`
`(TRIM mode) Current fillet`
`radius = 20.0000`

`Polyline/Radius/Trim/<Select first object>:` `T` `Enter`	Specifies the Trim option
`Trim/No trim <Trim>:` `N` `Enter`	Sets Trim to No Trim
`Polyline/Radius/Trim/<Select first object>:` *Pick line* ④	Specifies first object
`Select second object:` *Pick circle* ⑤	Creates fillet without trimming the line or circle
`Command:` `Enter`	Repeats the FILLET command

`FILLET`
`(NOTRIM mode) Current fillet`
`radius = 20.0000`

`Polyline/Radius/Trim/<Select first object>:` *Pick line* ④	
`Select second object:` *Pick arc* ⑥	Creates fillet without trimming

Save your drawing, which should now resemble figure 18.12.

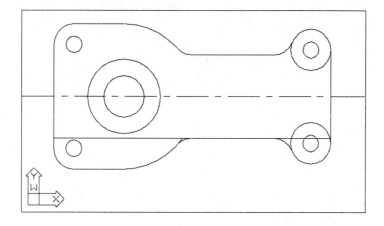

Figure 18.12

The casting after filleting arcs and circles.

AutoCAD does not trim circles when you fillet them, regardless of the Trim setting.

Filleting Polylines

You have applied fillets in the previous exercises primarily to noncomposite objects such as lines and arcs. The FILLET command also enables you to apply fillets to the vertices of polylines. You can apply a fillet to two polyline segments, just as you can to two line segments. The real advantage of using the FILLET command with a polyline is to apply fillets to all the vertices of a polyline. The Polyline option of the FILLET command enables you to apply fillets to all qualified vertices of the polyline in a single operation.

In the following exercise, you apply a common fillet radius to all the vertices of a polyline, then remove the arcs applied as fillets by setting the fillet radius to 0. Make sure that the Trim option is set to Trim.

Applying Fillets to All Vertices

Begin a new drawing named CHAP18C, using GASKET.DWG as a prototype.

Command: *Choose* Construct, Fillet
and set the fillet radius to .25

Command: (Enter)   Repeats the FILLET command

FILLET
(TRIM mode) Current fillet
radius = 0.2500

continues

continued

Polyline/Radius/Trim/<Select first object>: **P** (Enter)	Specifies the Polyline option
Select 2D polyline: *Pick any point on the polyline*	Selects the polyline to fillet and fillets the polyline
4 lines were filleted 10 were parallel	Creates 4 fillets between line pairs as shown in figure 18.13
Command: (Enter)	Repeats the FILLET command
FILLET (TRIM mode) Current fillet radius = 0.2500	
Polyline/Radius/Trim/<Select first object>: **R** (Enter)	Specifies the Radius option
Enter fillet radius <0.2500>: **0** (Enter)	Sets the radius to zero
Command: (Enter)	Repeats the FILLET command
FILLET (TRIM mode) Current fillet radius = 0.0000	
Polyline/Radius/Trim/<Select first object>: **P** (Enter)	Specifies the Polyline option
Select 2D polyline: *Pick any point on the polyline*	Selects the polyline to fillet and fillets the polyline
4 lines were filleted 10 were parallel	

AutoCAD did not apply a fillet to each vertex. AutoCAD does not fillet polyline arc segments. Instead, AutoCAD filleted only the four corners of the object. In addition, AutoCAD ignores all vertices that cause the loss of a polyline segment (the length of a segment is less than the radius of the fillet). The FILLET command behaves in this way with polylines only if you set the Trim option to Trim. If you set the Trim option to No Trim, AutoCAD creates the fillet arcs even when the polyline segments are too short to meet them with tangency. When you set the Trim option to Trim, FILLET modifies the original polyline with the fillet arcs. When you set the Trim option to No Trim, AutoCAD creates individual arc objects and does not change the polyline.

New Riders Publishing
INSIDE SERIES

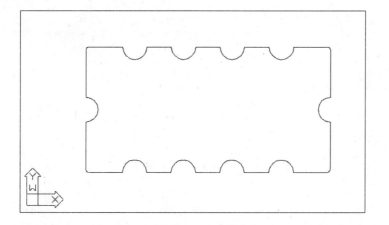

Figure 18.13

Fillets added to a polyline.

Understanding the CHAMFER Command

The CHAMFER command is similar to the FILLET command in the way it functions, but the results of the CHAMFER command are very different from those of the FILLET command. The CHAMFER command applies a chamfer to two objects; for example, you can quickly "trim" a corner where two line segments intersect and join them with a third line at a specific angle. You can base the chamfer on distances along each segment, or a distance and angle from one segment.

CHAMFER. The CHAMFER command enables you to chamfer two existing lines or polyline segments.
Screen menu:　　 *Choose* CONSTRCT, Chamfer:
Pull-down menu:　 *Choose* Construct, Chamfer

The CHAMFER command options in the following list enable you to control how you apply the chamfer.

◆ **Polyline.** This option enables you to apply a chamfer to all the vertices in a polyline.

◆ **Distance.** This option enables you to specify the chamfer distance along both objects.

◆ **Angle.** This option enables you to specify the angle of the chamfer from the first object.

◆ **Trim.** This option enables you to specify whether the CHAMFER command trims the objects (Trim mode—the default) or not (No Trim mode) when you apply the chamfer.

18

◆ **Method.** This option enables you to choose between chamfering using two distances (the distance along each object) or chamfering using a distance and an angle.

◆ **Select first line.** This option, which is the default, enables you to pick the first object of the two to be chamfered.

Applying Chamfers

You can use the CHAMFER command to apply chamfers in two ways. In the first method, you specify two distances, one along each of the objects to be chamfered. AutoCAD then draws the chamfer based on those two distances. In the second method, you specify the distance along the first line then specify the angle from the first line. AutoCAD then draws the chamfer relative to the first line and extends it to the second line.

In the following exercise, you use distances to apply a chamfer to one corner of a guide block. Use figure 18.14 as a reference.

Figure 18.14

Guide block prior to chamfering corners.

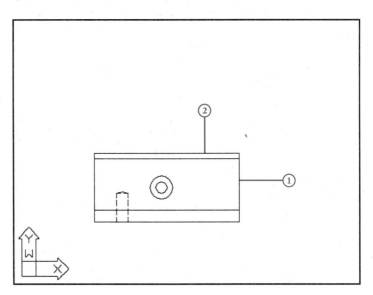

Applying a Chamfer to a Corner

Begin a new drawing named CHAP18D, using GUIDEBLK.DWG as a prototype.

Command: *Choose* Construct, Chamfer   Issues the CHAMFER command

`_chamfer`
`(TRIM mode) Current chamfer`
`Dist1 = 0.0000, Dist2 = 0.0000`
	Notice that the prompt indicates TRIM mode and the default distances

`Polyline/Distance/Angle/Trim/Method/` `<Select first line>:` **D** (Enter)	Specifies the Distance option
`Enter first chamfer distance` `<0.0000>:` **1.25** (Enter)	Sets the distance for the chamfer along the first object
`Enter second chamfer distance` `<1.2500>:` **2.5** (Enter)	Sets the distance for the chamfer along the second object
`Command:` (Enter)	Repeats the CHAMFER command

`CHAMFER`
`(TRIM mode) Current chamfer`
`Dist1 = 1.2500, Dist2 = 2.5000`
	Notice the new default distances

`Polyline/Distance/Angle/Trim/Method/` `<Select first line>:` *Pick line* ① *(see fig. 18.14)*	Specifies to which object to apply the 1.25 distance
`Select second line:` *Pick line* ②	Specifies the object for the 2.5 unit distance and creates the chamfer

Use the TRIM command (see Chapter 14) to trim the line at ① that represents the inner guide surface to the chamfered line at ② as shown in figure 18.15.

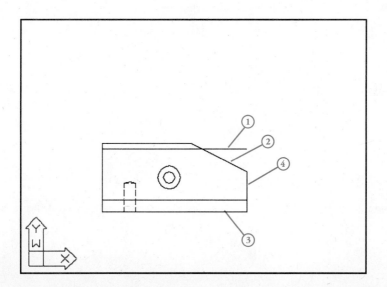

Figure 18.15

Guide block after chamfering.

18

The order in which you picked the objects to be chamfered in the above exercise was significant when using the Distance option. The first distance of 1.25 was applied to the first object you picked and the second distance of 2.5 was applied to the second object you picked.

Tip You create an equal-leg chamfer by specifying the same value for each of the two distances. To create an unequal-leg chamfer, you specify different values for the two chamfer distances.

When you apply a chamfer, the two objects do not have to intersect. If the Trim option is set to Trim, AutoCAD automatically extends the objects to intersect the newly created chamfer line segment. If Trim is set to No Trim, AutoCAD draws the chamfer line but does not modify the existing segments.

In addition to creating chamfers based on two distances, you can specify a distance and an angle to create the chamfer. The distance you specify is the distance from the theoretical point of intersection of the two objects to the starting point of the chamfer on the first segment. You then specify the angle between the first segment and the chamfer line. AutoCAD creates the chamfer accordingly.

In the following exercise, apply a 1'', 30° chamfer to the other corner of the guide block. Use figure 18.15 as a reference. Your drawing should look similar to figure 18.16 after you complete the exercise.

Creating a Chamfer at a Specific Angle

Continue to use the CHAP18D drawing from the preceding exercise.

Command: *Choose* Construct, Chamfer	Issues the CHAMFER command

`_chamfer`
`(TRIM mode) Current chamfer`
`Dist1 = 1.2500, Dist2 = 2.5000`	

`Polyline/Distance/Angle/Trim/Method/` `<Select first line>:` **A** (Enter)	Specifies the Angle option
`Enter chamfer length on the first` `line <0.0000>:` **1.25** (Enter)	Specifies the distance along the first object at which to start the chamfer
`Enter chamfer angle from the first` `line <0.0000>:` **30** (Enter)	Specifies the chamfer angle based from the first object

```
Command: (Enter)                          Repeats the CHAMFER command

CHAMFER
(TRIM mode) Current chamfer
Length = 1.2500, Angle = 30.0000

Polyline/Distance/Angle/Trim/Method/
<Select first line>: Pick line ③
(see fig. 18.15)

Select second line: Pick line ④
```

This time, try using FILLET with Trim mode on and a zero radius to trim the inside guide line to meet the newly created chamfer line at 1 (refer to figure 18.16). First, fillet at 1 by picking at 2 and 3. Then, fillet at 4 by picking at 2 and 5.

Save your drawing.

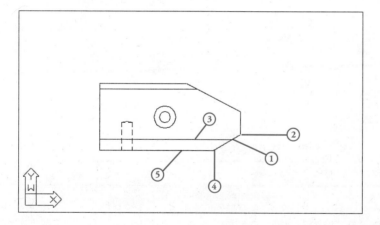

Figure 18.16

Guide block after angle chamfer.

Applying Chamfers to Polylines

Using the Polyline option of the CHAMFER command enables you to apply a chamfer to all of a polyline's vertices with a single operation. As when you use the FILLET command, the CHAMFER command ignores vertices of which the segments are shorter than the resulting chamfer distance, if the Trim option is set to Trim. If the Trim option is set to No Trim, CHAMFER creates the chamfer lines regardless of the length of the chamfer lines or their relationship to the original vertices.

18

Creating Offset Geometry

The OFFSET command enables you to offset certain types of objects through a point or at a specified distance from the original object. You can offset lines to represent the thickness of a wall, for example, or offset the outline of a gasket to create an interior cutout that is equidistant from the outer perimeter of the gasket. You can offset an object on one side of the entity or offset the entity on both sides. Figure 18.17 shows examples of offset geometry.

Figure 18.17

Examples of offset geometry.

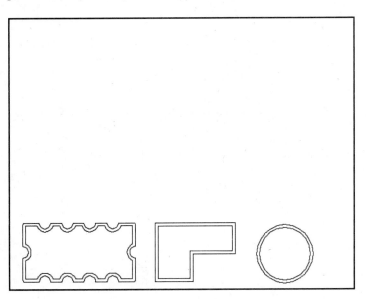

> **OFFSET.** The OFFSET command enables you to offset existing objects to create new objects. You can create the new offset object at a specific distance from the original, or you can create the offset object through a point.
> Screen menu: *Choose* CONSTRCT, Offset:
> Pull-down menu: *Choose* Construct, Offset

You can use the OFFSET command to offset only certain types of objects. Offsetting a single object such as a line or circle creates another singular object. Offsetting a polyline creates a new polyline with the same general shape as the original, but with a different size.

The OFFSET command offers two options:

- ◆ **Offset distance.** This option enables you to specify a distance from the original object to the new offset copy of the object.

- ◆ **Through.** This option enables you to specify a point through which the new offset object passes.

Creating Offsets at a Distance

The OFFSET command provides two methods for offsetting geometry. In the first method, you specify the offset distance between the original object and the new object. You can enter a value or pick two points to specify this distance. You would then pick a point on either side of the object to specify the general location of the new object. AutoCAD then constructs the offset geometry on the selected side of the original object, but spaces it away from the original object by the distance you specify.

Note   Offset distances cannot be negative values.

In the following exercise, you create the inner boundary of a complex gasket by offsetting the gasket's outer perimeter. Your drawing should resemble figure 18.18 after you complete the exercise.

Creating an Offset Boundary with OFFSET

Begin a new drawing named CHAP18E, using the GASKET1 drawing from the IA Disk as a prototype.

Command: *Choose* Construct, Offset	Issues the OFFSET command
_offset	
Offset distance or Through	Specifies the offset distance
<Through>: .5 Enter	
Select object to offset: *Pick the polyline at any point*	Specifies which object to offset
Side to offset? *Pick a point inside the polyline*	Creates the offset and prompts for another object
Select object to offset: Enter	Ends OFFSET command

18

Figure 18.18

*Inner perimeter of
a gasket created
using OFFSET.*

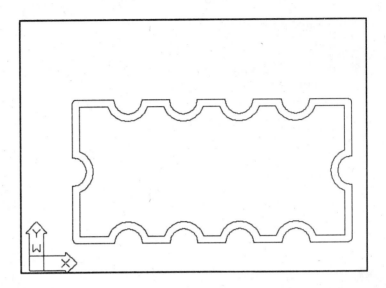

 Note If offsetting an arc will result in a radius of less than zero, AutoCAD doesn't create the arc. In figure 18.18, for example, the arcs at the four outer corners of the gasket were not duplicated in the interior perimeter of the gasket.

After you issue the OFFSET command, you can create more than a single offset. You can continue to specify offset distances and pick points to show the direction of other offset copies of the original object or (if you selected the Through option) show points for the offset object to pass through. You can, for example, create an inner and outer offset of an object without exiting and reissuing the OFFSET command. You can specify the offset distance only once, however, and AutoCAD makes all offsets at that distance. You can select any object for offsetting, in the same command (not just the original), including those just created by the command itself.

Creating Offsets through a Point

The second way to offset objects is to pick the object you want to offset and then pick a point through which the object is to be offset. You can enter a coordinate or pick the point, and you can use any point specification method—including object snap modes and filters—to pick the point. If this point falls beyond the end of the new object, AutoCAD calculates the offset as if the new object extended to the through point, but draws the object without that imaginary extension.

In the following exercise, you offset several of the existing lines and arcs, using the OFFSET command and a selected point on the existing objects to determine the size of the offset with the Through option.

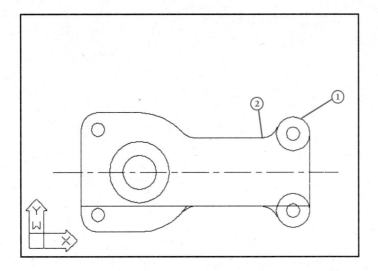

Figure 18.19

Casting before offsets.

Creating Offsets Through Points

Begin a new drawing named CHAP18F, using CASTING1.DWG as a prototype shown in figure 18.19.

Command: *Choose* Construct, Offset	Issues the OFFSET command
_offset Offset distance or Through <Through>: (Enter)	Selects the default Through option
Select object to offset: *Pick circle at* ① *(refer to figure 18.19)*	Specifies which object to offset
Through point: *From the pop-up menu, choose* Endpoint	
_endp of *Pick end of line at* ②	Creates the offset circle
Select object to offset: *Pick line at* ① *(see fig. 18.20)*	Specifies which object to offset
Through point: *From the pop-up menu, choose* Quadrant	
_qua of *Pick quadrant of circle at* ②	Creates the offset line
Select object to offset: *Pick circle at* ③	Specifies which object to offset

18

Figure 18.20

Casting after object offsets.

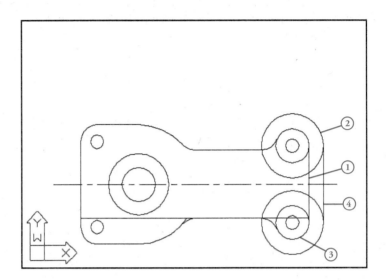

Through point: *From the pop-up menu, choose* Endpoint

_endp of *Pick end of line at* ④   Creates the offset circle

Select object to offset: (Enter)   Ends OFFSET command

You can see that considerable editing is necessary to trim circles to lines at intersections when you use the TRIM command.

Tip   Sometimes you need to offset a perimeter that consists of several objects. Use PEDIT to join objects and/or BOUNDARY to create a continuous object to offset.

In the following exercise, you continue to study offsets by joining objects to form a polyline that offsets much more conveniently. This exercise also demonstrates offsets that do not extend all the way to the point through which they are drawn.

Creating and Offsetting a Polyline Through a Point

Continue to use the CHAP18F drawing from the preceding exercise.

Command: *Choose* Modify, Edit Polyline   Issues the PEDIT command

New Riders Publishing
INSIDE
SERIES

Command: _pedit Select polyline: *Pick arc at* ① *(refer to figure 18.21)*	Specifies arc to change to a polyline
Object selected is not a polyline Do you want to turn it into one? <Y> ⏎**Enter**	Makes the selected arc a polyline segment
Close/Join/Width/Edit vertex/Fit/Spline/ Decurve/Ltype gen/Undo/eXit <X>: **J** ⏎**Enter**	Specifies the Join option
Select objects: *Select a crossing window from* ② *to* ③	
Select objects: ⏎**Enter**	Completes selection set.
6 segments added to polyline	Creates the polyline
Close/Join/Width/Edit vertex/Fit/Spline/ Decurve/Ltype gen/Undo/eXit <X>: ⏎**Enter**	Exits the PEDIT command
Command: *Choose* Construct, Offset	Issues the OFFSET command
_offset Offset distance or Through <Through>: ⏎**Enter**	Selects the default Through option
Select object to offset: *Pick polyline at* ④	Specifies which object to offset
Through point: *From the pop-up menu, choose* Endpoint	
_endp of *Pick end of line at* ⑤	Creates the offset polyline
Select object to offset: ⏎**Enter**	Ends the OFFSET command
Save your drawing.	

You might want to use the EXTEND command to fit the ends of the polyline neatly to the adjacent lines.

18

Figure 18.21

*The completed
casting after
polyline offsets.*

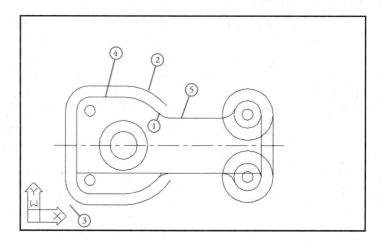

  Tip   You can use the OFFSET command to create concentric circles.

Objects that you can offset include lines, arcs, circles, splines, and 2D polylines. You also can offset objects that are created from polylines, which include donuts, ellipses, and polygons. Each offset creates a new object with the same linetype, color, and layer settings as the original object. Polylines also have the same width and curves as the original object, although the radius of curves and endpoints of objects change to allow a consistent offset distance between the original and the offset objects.

You cannot offset certain types of objects, such as blocks, text, dimensions, and view ports.

  Tip   OFFSET forms a new object by drawing the object parallel to the original object. OFFSET cannot form a new object inside an arc or circle if the offset distance exceeds the original radius. (You cannot create a negative radius.) Donuts, polygons, and arcs or short segments in other polylines are treated similarly. OFFSET attempts to duplicate small zigzag segments and loops with polylines, but you might get confused results. Use TRIM, BREAK, and/or PEDIT to clean up offset polylines if you do not like the results.

Creating Arrays of Objects

The ARRAY command is one of AutoCAD's most useful commands. ARRAY enables you to create a rectangular or circular array by copying one or more existing objects. Figure 18.22 shows a rectangular and polar arrays, respectively.

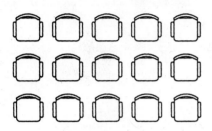

RECTANGULAR
ARRAY

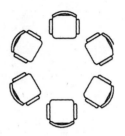

POLAR
ARRAY

Figure 18.22

A rectangular array and a polar array.

ARRAY. The ARRAY command enables you to create multiple copies of an object in a rectangular or circular (polar) pattern.

Pull-down: *Choose* Construct, Array, Rectangular
Screen: *Choose* CONSTRCT, Array, Rectangular

As with other commands that copy objects, new objects in an array have the same layer, color, and linetype settings as the original object. If necessary, however, you can change these object properties after you create the array.

Creating a Rectangular Array

A *rectangular array* is a group of objects arranged in rows and columns. To create a rectangular array, you first select the object(s) you want to copy. Then you specify the number of rows and columns in the finished array and the distance between rows and columns. AutoCAD automatically copies the object(s) into an array.

In the following exercise, you create an array of workstations in an office floor plan. You begin with a single four-cubicle group, then array more workstations to complete the layout. Use figure 18.23 as a reference. Your drawing should resemble figure 18.24 after you complete the exercise.

18

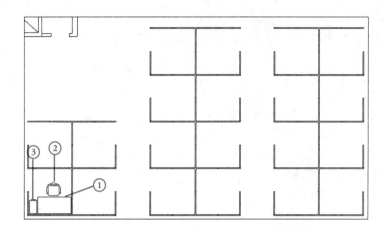

Figure 18.23

Workstation objects to array.

Creating a Rectangular Array

Begin a new drawing named CHAP18G, using OFFICE.DWG from the IA Disk as a prototype, then zoom to the view shown in figure 18.23.

Command: *Choose* Construct, Array, Rectangular	Issues the ARRAY command with the Rectangular option
`_select` `Select objects:` *Select objects* ①, ②, *and* ③ *and press Enter* (refer to figure 18.23)	Specifies the objects you want to array
`Command: _array` `Select objects: _p`	The tool issues the ARRAY command with the Rectangular option and selected objects

`3 found`
`Select objects:`
`Rectangular or Polar array (R/P)`
`<R>: _r`	

`Number of rows (---) <1>: 2` **Enter**	Specifies number of rows horizontally in the array
`Number of columns (¦¦¦) <1>: 2` **Enter**	Specifies number of columns vertically in the array
`Unit cell or distance between` `rows (---): 8'1` **Enter**	Specifies the distance vertically between objects in the array
`Distance between columns (¦¦¦):` `7'11` **Enter**	Specifies the distance horizontally between objects and draws the array

New Riders Publishing
INSIDE
SERIES

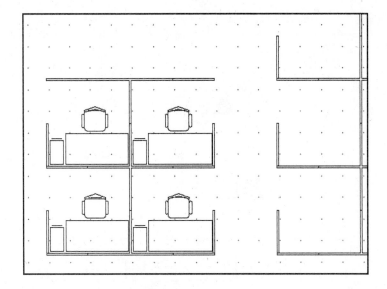

Figure 18.24

A two-by-two array of workstations.

Using the ARRAY command can be much faster than trying to copy or draw each workstation manually, particularly for large arrays.

Tip You can use the MINSERT command to create an array of blocks in a drawing. MINSERT offers one primary advantage over the ARRAY command in creating rectangular arrays. MINSERT inserts only one copy of the object in the drawing database, then represents that single block graphically in each of its locations in the drawing. The ARRAY command actually copies the objects for each instance in the array, which requires more memory to store the array of objects. Using ARRAY, however, is more flexible because you cannot edit multiple inserted blocks whereas you can edit arrayed objects.

Creating One-Column or One-Row Arrays

You frequently create one-column or one-row arrays. A *one-row array* is an equally spaced horizontal row of objects copied from the original object, and a *one-column array* is an equally spaced column of objects copied vertically from the original object. Using the ARRAY command makes it easy to create one-row and one-column arrays. To create a one-row array that consists of 12 objects, for example, you specify a value of 1 for the number of rows and a value of 12 for the number of columns in the array and specify a center to center distance between the columns. The result is a horizontal "line" of 12 objects equally spaced from each other.

18

In the following exercise, you create a one-row array to complete the first row of workstations in your office layout drawing. Use figure 18.25 as a guide. Your drawing should resemble figure 18.26 after you complete the exercise.

Figure 18.25

The office layout prior to the array.

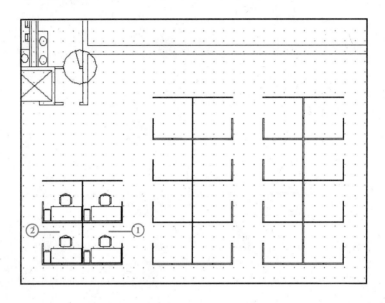

Creating a One-Row Array

Continue to use the CHAP18G (OFFICE) drawing from the preceding exercise, and zoom to the view shown in figure 18.25.

Command: *Choose* Construct, Array, Rectangular	Issues the ARRAY command with the Rectangular option
_select Select objects: *Pick the tables, chairs, and computer workstations in the two offices at* ① *and* ② *and press Enter* (refer to figure 18.25)	Specifies the objects to be arrayed
Command: _array Select objects: _p 6 found Select objects: Rectangular or Polar array (R/P) <R>: _r	The tool issues the ARRAY command with the Rectangular option and selected objects
Number of rows (- - -) <1>: (Enter)	Specifies a one-row array
Number of columns (¦¦¦) <1>: **3** (Enter)	Specifies number of rows in the array

New Riders Publishing
INSIDE
SERIES

```
Distance between columns (¦¦¦):          Specifies the distance between objects
22' Enter
```

Save your drawing.

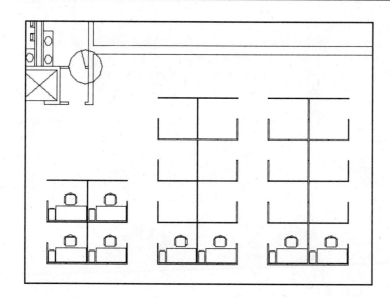

Figure 18.26

A one-row array.

Although you copied only two of the four offices in the array, you could have copied all four offices as a single-row array. Copying just one row of workstations, however, helps you understand the concept of one-row and one-column arrays.

Using a Negative Array Spacing

Row and column spacing of objects in an array is like using relative coordinate values in the Cartesian coordinate system. Positive row or column spacing causes AutoCAD to copy objects to the right or up from the original object. A negative row spacing value causes AutoCAD to array the object(s) to the left. Using a negative column spacing value causes AutoCAD to array the object(s) down, rather than up. You can use a combination of positive and negative row and column spacing values to control the directions in which AutoCAD arrays the objects.

Creating a Polar Array

A *polar array* is an array of objects created around a center point. You created a simple polar array in the first exercise in this chapter. To create a polar array, you pick the objects you want to array and choose a center point. AutoCAD then prompts you for

18

the angle to fill. Accepting the default angle of 360° arrays the objects in a complete circle. Specifying an angle less than 360° arrays the objects in a partial circle. For example, if you specify an angle of 180°, AutoCAD creates a semicircle of objects. If you specify a positive angle, AutoCAD copies the objects counterclockwise. If you specify a negative angle, AutoCAD copies the objects in a clockwise rotation.

 Tip You also can copy objects in an array by using the Copy (multiple) option with autoediting modes. If you press Shift while picking multiple copy displacements (to points), the cursor jumps to increments of the offset of the first displacement, in an array-like fashion. See Chapter 8, "Object Selection and Grip Editing," for details.

After you specify the angle for the array, AutoCAD prompts you to specify whether you want to rotate the objects as they are copied. Figure 18.27 shows two examples that illustrate object rotation. In the example on the left, the objects were not rotated during the array. In the example on the right, the objects were rotated.

Figure 18.27

The effects of object rotation on an array.

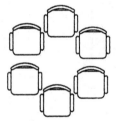
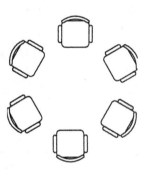

WITHOUT
ROTATION

WITH
ROTATION

 Note Sometimes it does not matter whether you rotate the objects during the array. Objects such as circles, for example, look the same regardless of whether you rotate them during the array.

In the following exercise, you use a polar array to copy the chairs around a table. Your drawing should look similar to figure 18.29 after you complete the exercise.

Creating a Polar Array

Continue to use the CHAP18G (OFFICE) drawing from the preceding exercise, and zoom to the view shown in figure 18.28.

Command: *Choose* Construct, Array, Polar	Issues the ARRAY command with the Polar option
_select Select objects: *Pick the chair at* ① *(see fig. 18.28) and press Enter*	Specifies an object to array
Command: _array Select objects: _p 1 found Select objects: Rectangular or Polar array (R/P) <R>: _p	Issues the ARRAY command with the Polar option and the selected object
Center point of array: *From the pop-up* *menu, choose Center*	Sets Center object snap
_center of *Pick circle* ②	Snaps the center of the array to the center of the circle
Number of items: **3** (Enter)	Specifies the total number of objects in the array
Angle to fill (+=ccw, -=cw) <360>: **180** (Enter)	Specifies the included angle of the array
Rotate objects as they are copied? <Y> (Enter)	Rotates the chairs as the array is created

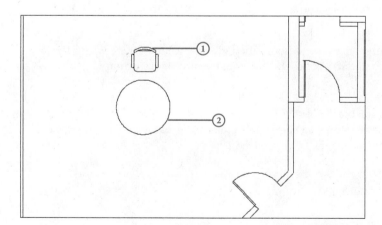

Figure 18.28

A table before a polar array.

18

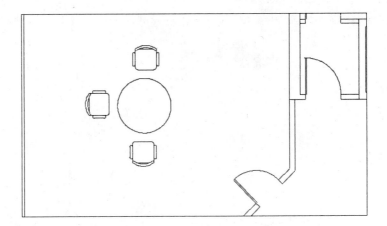

Figure 18.29

Chairs after completing the array.

The combination of the included angle and number of objects determines the angle between each object. To determine a combination of included angle and number of copies that will result in a specific angle between objects, multiply the angle between objects by the number of new objects (which is the same as "The number of items" specified for the array less one, the original). Dividing the included angle of the array by the angle between objects determines the number of new objects in the array, then add one for the original.

The following options are available for polar arrays during specification of "Angle of fill":

◆ Pressing Enter when AutoCAD prompts you for the number of objects simply proceeds to the `Angle to fill` prompt, then to an `Angle between items` prompt.

◆ Specifying a number of items, then giving a value of 0 (zero) for the `Angle to fill` prompt also issues the `Angle between objects` prompt.

 Note You can use the 3DARRAY command to create rectangular and polar 3D arrays. In addition to copying objects in the same plane as the original object, the 3DARRAY command copies the array in the Z axis.

Mirroring Objects

Many designs contain symmetrical objects, and AutoCAD's MIRROR command simplifies the task of drawing these symmetrical objects. The MIRROR command functions similarly to the Mirror Autoedit mode, which is introduced in Chapter 8, "Autoediting with Grips." MIRROR enables you to create a mirror image of an existing object and gives you the option of retaining (creating a mirrored copy) or deleting the original object.

MIRROR. The MIRROR command enables you to create a mirror-image copy of an object. The MIRROR command includes an option that enables you to specify whether the original object is deleted after the mirrored copy is created.
Screen: *Choose* CONSTRCT, Mirror:
Pull-down: *Choose* Construct, Mirror

After you issue the MIRROR command, AutoCAD prompts you to select the objects you want to mirror. Then, AutoCAD prompts you to define a mirror line about which to mirror the selected objects. You can pick two points to specify the mirror line. AutoCAD then uses this imaginary line as the axis around which it mirrors the selected objects.

The only command option that the MIRROR command offers is a choice of whether AutoCAD should retain the original objects or delete them. Directing AutoCAD to delete the original objects is conceptually similar to reversing (flipping) the selected objects. Directing AutoCAD to retain the original objects produces a mirror-image copy of the original.

Using the MIRROR Command

In the following exercise, you use the MIRROR command to copy a fixture and stall between two restrooms in the office layout you worked with in previous exercises. You specify a mirror line that falls midway between the original object and its mirrored copy. In this example, this means that the mirror line runs through the middle of the wall that separates the two rest rooms. Use figure 18.30 as a reference. Your drawing should resemble figure 18.31 after you complete the exercise.

18

Figure 18.30

The rest room layout prior to mirroring.

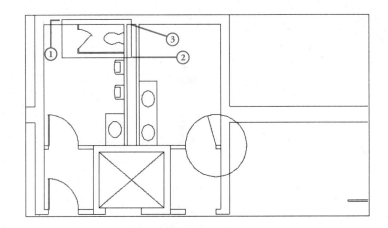

Mirroring an Object

Continue to use the CHAP18G (OFFICE) drawing from the previous exercise, and zoom to the view shown in figure 18.30.

Command: *Choose* Construct, Mirror	Issues the MIRROR command
_mirror Select objects: *Pick points* ① *and* ② *(see fig. 18.30) and* *press Enter*	Selects objects with a window
11 found	
First point of mirror line: *From the* *pop-up menu, choose* Midpoint	Sets Midpoint object snap
_mid of *Pick line* ③	Specifies first point on mirror line
Second point: *Turn on ortho mode and* *pick any point above or below the first* *point*	Defines the vertical mirror line
Delete old objects? <N> (Enter)	Creates a mirrored copy

Save your drawing.

New Riders Publishing
INSIDE SERIES

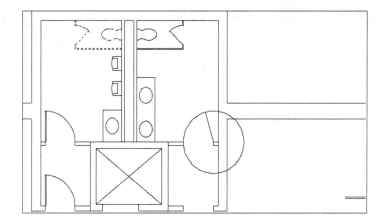

Figure 18.31

The stall after mirroring.

To examine the effect of using the MIRROR command to delete the original object, mirror one of the towel holders from the left restroom to the right rest room. Because the towel holders are mounted on the wall, you can use the same points to define the mirror line that you used in the previous exercise.

Deleting the Original Objects

Continue to use the CHAP18G (OFFICE) drawing from the preceding exercise, with ortho mode on.

Command: *Choose* Construct, Mirror	Issues the MIRROR command
_mirror Select objects: *Pick points* ① *and* ② *(see fig. 18.32) and press Enter*	Selects objects with a window
7 found	
First point of mirror line: *From the pop-up menu, choose* Midpoint	Sets Midpoint object snap
_mid of *Pick line* ③	Specifies first point of mirror line
Second point: *Pick any point above or below the first point*	Defines mirror line
Delete old objects? <N> Y (Enter)	Creates mirrored copy and deletes original objects

Save your drawing, which should look like figure 18.34.

18

Figure 18.32

*The fixture prior
to mirroring.*

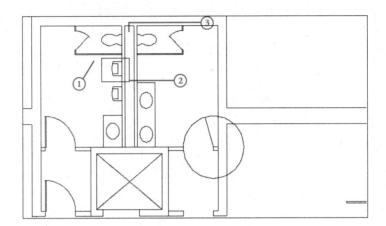

The MIRROR command is functionally similar to mirror autoedit mode. The MIRROR command is more useful than mirror autoedit mode when you need to work with a complex selection set because the MIRROR command supports all of AutoCAD's object selection methods.

Breaking Objects with BREAK

You often need to erase only a portion on an object. Although you can use the TRIM command in many situations, it is not useful unless your drawing contains an object that you can use as a cutting edge. If the drawing lacks a cutting edge with which you can properly trim an object, you can use the BREAK command to erase a part of the object.

BREAK. The BREAK command enables you to erase a portion of an object between two points, or to break an object into two separate objects that share a common endpoint.

Screen: *Choose* MODIFY, Break:

Pull-down: *Choose* Modify, Break, then one of four options available on the cascaded menu

---

The BREAK command requires that you select two points to define the points between which to break the object.

◆ **Select Object.** Selects the object and the first break point on the object.

◆ **First.** Use this option, after you select the object, to reselect the first point (different from the object selection point).

◆ **@.** Use this option, after you select the object, to make the second point the same coordinate as the first. Therefore, the object is broken into two parts without erasing any of the object.

The BREAK command options offer four predefined methods you can use to select the object you want to break and the points at which to break it. The following list defines these methods by their option names:

◆ **1 point.** You pick a point on the object and AutoCAD breaks the object at that point. If you pick a line, for example, AutoCAD breaks the line at the pick point and creates two separate lines that share an endpoint at the picked point.

◆ **1 point select.** AutoCAD prompts you to select the object you want to break, then prompts you for the first break point. AutoCAD automatically uses the same point for the second break point, breaking the object into two separate objects that share a common endpoint. This option is useful if you want to specify a break point other than the one by which you pick the object.

◆ **2 points.** AutoCAD prompts you to pick the object, then pick a point. AutoCAD uses the point at which you pick the object as the first break point and breaks the object between the two points, removing the portion of the object that falls between the two points.

◆ **2 points select.** AutoCAD prompts you to select the object, then pick two points. AutoCAD does not use the point at which you pick the object to determine the break points.

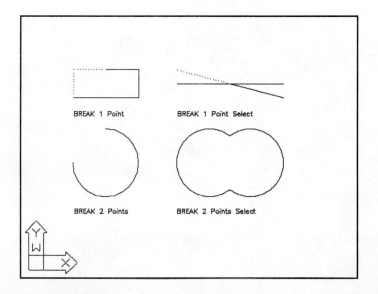

Figure 18.33

Four methods for breaking objects.

Tip   Circles are broken counterclockwise. Also, break points that you pick do not have to fall on an object. When a point does not fall on an object, AutoCAD calculates the apparent intersection between the point and the object, based on the geometry of the object. If the second point is beyond the end of the object, AutoCAD removes the end and does not create a new object.

Depending on the type of object and the points you specify, the BREAK command might both modify the existing object and create a new object, or simply modify the existing object.

In the following exercise, you use the BREAK command to create a simplified door symbol. You use the 2 points select method. Use figure 18.34 as a reference. Your drawing should resemble figure 18.35 after you complete the exercise.

Figure 18.34

The fixtures mirrored and door symbol ready to break.

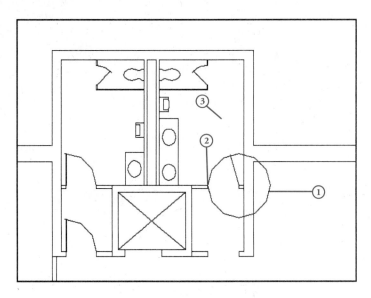

Using the BREAK Command

Continue to use your CHAP18G (OFFICE) drawing from the preceding exercise.

Command: *Choose* Modify, Break, 2 Points Select	Issues the BREAK command for the 2 points select method
_break Select object: *Pick circle* ① (*see fig. 18.34*)	Specifies object to break

New Riders Publishing
INSIDE
SERIES

```
Enter second point (or F for first
point): _f
```

Enter first point: *From the pop-up menu, choose* Endpoint

`_endp of` *Pick point* ②   Specifies first point at which to break the object

`Enter second point:` *Pick point* ③   Specifies second point and breaks the circle

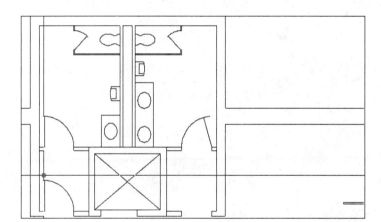

Figure 18.35

The door swing created using BREAK.

Sometimes using TRIM to erase a portion of an object is easier. If no trimming object exists, or drawing a trimming object is not feasible, the BREAK command is a good tool to use to erase part of an object.

Constructive editing is but one of many tools available for automating drafting by using efficient computer drafting methods. In the next chapter, "Using Xrefs for Efficiency and Sharing Data," you continue to investigate drafting automation.

18

CHAPTER

19

Using Xrefs for Efficiency and Sharing Data

This chapter explains the xref, or external reference, an AutoCAD object that in many ways is similar to a block. An *xref* is a reference in a drawing to another external drawing. All objects in an externally referenced drawing, including named items such as layers, linetypes, and blocks, are part of the xref in the active drawing.

This chapter covers the following topics:

◆ Explanation of xrefs

◆ When to use an xref

◆ How to use an xref

◆ New xref capabilities in Release 13

◆ Working in a multiple-user environment

Xrefs have two primary purposes. First, xrefs are an efficient way to import standard elements that you do not need to modify, such as title blocks, into a current drawing. Second, they provide a means by which you can use identical drawing data in multiple drawings. AutoCAD automatically updates any changes in an externally referenced drawing in all drawings that have xrefs to that drawing.

Through the use of xrefs, several people can work on a project and use the same data in a coordinated manner. For example, a building design team can simultaneously work on the building's structural plan, floor plan, electrical plan, and plumbing plan. All members of the team can use the same base plan by attaching or overlaying it as an xref. If anyone makes a change to the base plan, AutoCAD automatically updates it in the drawings to which it is attached or overlaid.

Understanding Xrefs

An xref is similar to a block in that it is a single object that can contain multiple objects. Like a block, an xref appears as an image of the referenced objects. The difference between an xref and a block is that AutoCAD stores a block's data in the current drawing, whereas it stores xref data in an external drawing. When you use an xref, AutoCAD places only an image of the data in the current drawing session—the xref data remains defined in the external drawing. You can create an xref as an attachment or as an overlay, and you can scale and rotate an xref when it is attached or overlaid.

Stop One potentially important part of a drawing that AutoCAD ignores when you attach it as an external reference is variable attributes in blocks. If, for example, you attach a title block as an xref, and that title block contains attributes for the drafter's name, project phase, and so forth, those parts of the xref do not appear in your current drawing. If you want to include variable data in your title blocks, do not use attributed blocks.

XREF. The XREF command enables you to attach, overlay, bind, or update external reference drawings. The xref's data resides entirely in the external drawing's database, and AutoCAD places only a reference to the external file in the current drawing's database.

Pull-down:　　*Choose* File, External Reference
Screen:　　　*Choose* FILE, Xref

New Riders Publishing
INSIDE
SERIES

When you issue the XREF command, AutoCAD prompts you as follows:

```
?/Bind/Detach/Path/Reload/Overlay/<Attach>:
```

The XREF command has the following options:

◆ **Attach.** This option creates a reference in the current drawing to the external drawing file, and displays the drawing as an object on-screen. Attach is the default option.

◆ **?.** This option lists the name, path, and type of each external reference in the drawing. The ? option does not indicate whether an external reference was loaded.

◆ **Bind.** The Bind option converts an xref to a block. In addition, it renames all dependent symbols, such as layers and linetypes, and places them into the current drawing.

◆ **Detach.** The Detach option removes xref objects from the current drawing. You can use AutoCAD's standard wild-card options when you specify xref objects to detach.

 Stop When you no longer need an xref in your drawing and want to remove it, be sure to use XREF Detach, rather than simply erase the xref. If you simply erase the xref, all of the xref's layers, linetypes, text and dimension styles, and blocks remain defined in the current drawing, and you must PURGE them one by one.

◆ **Path.** The Path option enables you to update the path of an xref object's associated drawing file.

◆ **Reload.** You use this option to force a reload of an attached drawing without having to reopen the current drawing. You use this option in a networked workgroup environment.

◆ **Overlay.** This option is similar to the Attach option; however, AutoCAD does not load nested, overlaid external references. It does load nested, attached external references as usual, however.

Advantages of Using Xrefs

Using xrefs rather than blocks or copied objects offers several advantages. First, an xref reduces the amount of disk space that a drawing consumes because the xref's data remains in an external drawing file—it's not re-created in the current drawing file as during a block insertion. Second, several other drawings can reference the external drawing. Third, each time the external drawing is referenced, AutoCAD saves the duplication of its contents in other drawings.

An xref also enables you to update drawing data easily. Each time you open a drawing that contains an xref, AutoCAD loads the referenced drawing, and any changes in the referenced drawing are automatically reflected in the drawing that contains the xref. You also can use the XREF command's Reload option to force a reload of the referenced drawing in the current drawing session.

Stop In a team situation, the person who changes a referenced drawing must notify the others; the XREF command does not provide automatic notification or identification of changes.

Planning for Xrefs

Using xrefs benefits from sound CAD management practices. Plan ahead when you develop a project that will involve a set of interrelated drawings that you want to use as xrefs. For example:

◆ Use a common origin point for each reference drawing to simplify the process of assembling and coordinating them.

◆ Decide which elements are truly common to your various drawings that reference base drawings. Sometimes labels and annotations are best stored in separate drawings that can be referenced as required, thus reducing the clutter in drawings that do not need them.

◆ Set up an appropriate directory structure in which to store the project's drawings if you foresee the use of many external reference drawings. Although the XREF command's Path option enables you to update the path to referenced drawings, if you change the location of a large number of xref files in the middle of a project, it can be very time consuming.

Working with Xrefs

You can attach or overlay any drawing file as an xref. Although xrefs take up less space in a drawing file than do blocks, you cannot edit them from within the drawing to which they are attached or overlaid. To edit the contents of an xref, you must edit the original external drawing file. You cannot use the EXPLODE command on xrefs to edit them in the current drawing as you can on blocks. Editing an external drawing affects all drawings that have a reference to that drawing.

New Riders Publishing
INSIDE
SERIES

Just as you cannot edit xrefs from the drawing to which they are attached, you cannot select objects in the xref either, should you need to list or otherwise query the object.

Note Although you cannot select individual objects in an xref, you can use object snap modes to snap to them. This means that you can, for example, place dimensions between objects in the attached drawing to objects in the current drawing.

After you attach or overlay an xref in a drawing, you can use the XREF command's Detach option to update the xref image, update the path to the external file, and remove them from the drawing. You also can list the xrefs in a drawing.

Attaching Xrefs

You use attached xrefs whenever you need to nest more than one level of xref. For example, attached xrefs are used when a master plan drawing references a new-construction drawing which, in turn, references an old-construction drawing. In this arrangement, the master drawing depends on information in the new-construction drawing, and the new-construction drawing depends on information in the old-construction drawing.

Attached xrefs cannot be circular. In other words, if drawing A references B, and drawing B references C, drawing C cannot reference drawing A.

The following exercise demonstrates how to attach nested xrefs. In the exercise, you place an xref to a plan drawing in a furniture layout drawing, and then place an xref to the furniture drawing in a master drawing. If the plan drawing changes, the changes show in the furniture layout drawing and the master drawing. Figure 19.1 shows the visual result of nesting attached xrefs.

Attaching Nested Xrefs

Start a new drawing named ATCHROOM.DWG, using DESKS.DWG as a prototype.

Command: *Choose* File, External Reference, *then* Attach	Opens the Select file to attach dialog box
Choose Type it	Switches from dialog-box to command-line input
?/Bind/Detach/Path/Reload/Overlay/ <Attach>: _a Select file to attach: **PLAN=ROOMPLAN** (Enter)	Specifies the drawing to attach (ROOMPLAN) and an alternate xref name (PLAN)

Insertion point: **0,0** (Enter)	Specifies insertion point
X scale factor <1> / Corner / XYZ: (Enter)	Accepts default X scale factor
Y scale factor (default=X): (Enter)	Accepts default Y scale factor
Rotation angle <0>: (Enter)	Accepts default rotation angle

Command: *Save the drawing*

Start a new drawing named CHAP19A, using XREFPROT as a prototype.

Command: *Choose* File, External Reference, *then* Attach	Opens the Select file to attach dialog box

Select the drawing ATCHROOM to attach to CHAP19A.

Insertion point: **0,0** (Enter)	Specifies insertion point
X scale factor <1> / Corner / XYZ: (Enter)	Accepts default X scale factor
Y scale factor(default=X): (Enter)	Accepts default Y scale factor
Rotation angle<0>: (Enter)	Accepts default rotation angle
Command: *Choose* File, External Reference, *then* List	Issues the XREF command with the List option
Xref(s) to list <*>: (Enter)	Lists all names and paths in the AutoCAD text screen

Xref name	Path	Xref type
ATCHROOM	ATCHROOM.dwg	Attach
PLAN	ROOMPLAN	Attach

Total Xref(s): 2

Save the drawing.

In the previous exercise, you placed an xref to ROOMPLAN.DWG in ATCHROOM.DWG, then placed an xref to ATCHROOM.DWG in CHAP19A.DWG. Now, whenever you open CHAP19A, AutoCAD loads ATCHROOM which, in turn, loads ROOMPLAN.

External references are named according to the referenced drawing file name by default. However, in the previous exercise, the xref to ROOMPLAN.DWG was named

PLAN. You can use this technique to name xrefs to specify longer or more meaningful xref names than eight-character file names allow. Also, this technique enables you to keep the names of dependent symbols the same if the xref file name changes.

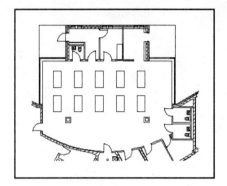

Figure 19.1

Xref ATCHROOM with nested xref ROOMPLAN in current drawing.

19

Overlaying Xrefs

The capability to overlay an xref is a new feature in Release 13. Overlaid xrefs are more flexible than attached xrefs. However, overlaid xrefs do not display nested, overlaid xrefs; an overlaid xref is not visible in a drawing if it is deeper than one attached or overlaid xref level. Overlaid xrefs can have circular references because AutoCAD ignores nested overlaid xrefs when you load them.

You use overlaid xrefs to see the way your current drawing relates to drawings of others in a concurrent-design workgroup. Overlaid xrefs enable each designer in the workgroup to see any other designer's drawings without worrying about creating circular xrefs or inflexible drawing interdependencies.

For example, what if the electrical designer attaches HVAC and plumbing information to his drawing at the same time as the HVAC designer needs electrical information? If the HVAC designer attaches the electrical drawing, a circular reference to the HVAC drawing occurs and the extra plumbing information is also loaded. With overlaid xrefs the electrical designer can see both HVAC and plumbing information in his drawing and the HVAC designer doesn't have to worry about getting plumbing information and referencing his own HVAC drawings.

Tip   If you use xrefs to share data in a concurrent design environment, use overlaid xrefs rather than attached xrefs to prevent circular xrefs and rigid, complex dependencies.

In the next exercise, you use the Overlay option of the XREF command to create a more flexible design drawing.

Overlaying Xrefs

Start a new drawing named OVLYROOM.DWG, using DESKS.DWG as a prototype.

Command: *Choose* File, External Reference, *then* Overlay	Opens the Select file to overlay dialog box
Choose Type it	Switches from dialog-box to command-line input
?/Bind/Detach/Path/Reload/Overlay/ <Attach>: _o Select file to overlay: **PLAN=ROOMPLAN** (Enter)	Specifies the drawing to overlay and an alternate xref name
Insertion point: **0,0** (Enter)	Specifies insertion point
X scale factor <1> / Corner / XYZ: (Enter)	Accepts default X scale factor
Y scale factor (default=X): (Enter)	Accepts default Y scale factor
Rotation angle <0>: (Enter)	Accepts default rotation angle
Command: *Save the drawing*	

Start a new drawing named CHAP19B, using XREFPROT as a prototype.

Command: *Choose* File, External Reference, *then* Overlay	Opens the Select file to overlay dialog box

Select the drawing OVLYROOM to overlay on CHAP19B.

Insertion point: **0,0** (Enter)	Specifies insertion point
X scale factor <1> / Corner / XYZ: (Enter)	Accepts default X scale factor
Y scale factor(default=X): (Enter)	Accepts default Y scale factor
Rotation angle<0>: (Enter)	Accepts default rotation angle
Command: *Choose* File, External Reference, *then* List	Issues the XREF command with the List option
Xref(s) to list <*>: (Enter)	Lists all names and paths in the AutoCAD text screen

New Riders Publishing
INSIDE
SERIES

```
     Xref name                    Path           Xref type
  .....................      ............      ..........
     OVLYROOM                   ovlyroom.dwg        Overlay
```

Total Xref(s): 1

ROOMPLAN isn't displayed because overlaid xrefs are displayed only one level deep (see fig. 19.2). If you want both the desks and the plan to show, you must overlay both xrefs (see fig. 19.3).

Command: *Choose* File, External Reference, *then* Overlay	Opens the Select file to overlay dialog box
Choose Type it	Switches from dialog-box to command-line input
?/Bind/Detach/Path/Reload/Overlay/ <Attach>: _o Select file to overlay: **PLAN=ROOMPLAN** (Enter)	Specifies the drawing to overlay and an alternate xref name
Insertion point: **0,0** (Enter)	Specifies insertion point
X scale factor <1> / Corner / XYZ: (Enter)	Accepts default X scale factor
Y scale factor (default=X): (Enter)	Accepts default Y scale factor
Rotation angle <0>: (Enter)	Accepts default rotation angle
Command: *Choose* File, External Reference, *then* List	Issues XREF command with the List option
Xref(s) to list <*>: (Enter)	Lists all names and paths in the AutoCAD text screen

```
     Xref name                    Path           Xref type
  .....................      ............      ..........
     OVLYROOM                   OVLYROOM.dwg        Overlay
     PLAN                       ROOMPLAN            Overlay
```

Total Xref(s): 2

Save the drawing.

Figure 19.2

Xref OVLYROOM overlaid in current drawing.

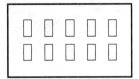

Figure 19.3

Xrefs OVLYROOM and ROOMPLAN overlaid separately in current drawing.

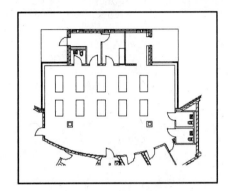

The next section discusses how changes to externally referenced drawings affect drawings that reference them.

Updating Xrefs

Now that you have created references to external drawing files, you are ready to see them in action. The primary advantage of using xrefs is that AutoCAD always loads the current version of the externally referenced drawing each time the referencing drawing is opened, which enables externally referenced design elements to change independently and ensures that the referenced drawing is up-to-date at the moment the referencing drawing is opened.

If an externally referenced drawing in your current open drawing changes, you can use the XREF command's Reload option to force a reload of the xref. The Reload option is covered later in this chapter in the section "Reloading Xrefs."

In the following exercise, you open and edit the ROOMPLAN drawing, the source of the PLAN xref. The demand for AutoCAD classes is so great that space for more desks is needed in the lecture room. Later you reopen CHAP19A to see the effects.

Modifying the Externally Referenced Drawing

Continue from the preceding exercise. Create a backup copy of ROOMPLAN.DWG named ROOMPLAN.SAV, using AutoCAD's file utilities. After you create the backup, open the ROOMPLAN drawing.

Command: *Choose* Modify, Stretch   Issues the STRETCH command

Select objects: *Specify a crossing window from* ① *to* ② *(see fig. 19.4)*

Select objects: **(Enter)**

Base point or displacement: **0,8'** **(Enter)**

Second point of displacement: **(Enter)**

Command: *Save the drawing*

You have now edited the xref object's source drawing, the externally referenced file, just as you might edit any drawing. Next, you open the CHAP19A drawing, which contains the xref to ATCHROOM, which contains the xref to ROOMPLAN, to see the effect of this modification.

Command: *Open the* CHAP19A *drawing*

Resolve Xref ATCHROOM: ATCHROOM.DWG   Loads each external reference drawing
ATCHROOM loaded.   and reports the status
Resolve Xref PLAN: ROOMPLAN
PLAN loaded. Regenerating drawing.

Your screen should look like figure 19.5.

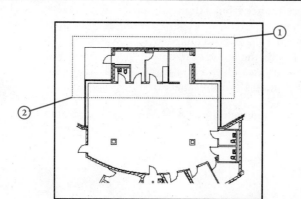

Figure 19.4

The drawing ROOMPLAN during STRETCH.

19

Figure 19.5

*The CHAP19A
drawing with the
ROOMPLAN xref
automatically
updated.*

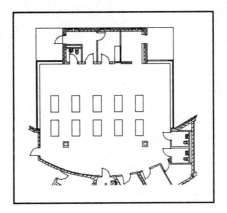

If you open the CHAP19B drawing with the overlaid xrefs, it will appear visually the same as CHAP19A. However, the drawing database contains two separate overlaid xrefs.

As AutoCAD loads a drawing, it finds and loads any external references. If an external drawing contains any attached xrefs, AutoCAD loads those drawings as well. If AutoCAD finds and loads drawings without any problem, it reports them as loaded.

If AutoCAD has difficulty when it tries to load any of the externally referenced drawings, a message dialog box appears. The dialog box reports where AutoCAD looked for the external reference files. Make sure that all the external reference files are in a directory in the AutoCAD search path. You can use XREF's Path option to respecify the drawing name and path for any unresolved xrefs.

Removing Xrefs

To remove an external reference from a drawing, you use the Detach option of the XREF command. Detaching an xref removes an xref object from the current drawing's database. You can detach both attached and overlaid xrefs. The Detach option prompts you to specify the name or names of the xrefs you want to detach. You can use any of AutoCAD's standard wild cards to specify xref names, or you can separate the names with commas (without spaces).

In the following exercise, you detach the ROOMPLAN drawing from the ATCHROOM drawing.

New Riders Publishing
INSIDE
SERIES

Detaching Xrefs

Continue from the preceding exercise and open the ATCHROOM drawing.

Command: *Choose* File, External Reference, *then* Detach	Specifies the XREF command's Detach option
Command: _xref ?/Bind/Detach/Path/Reload/Overlay/ <Attach>: -d	
Xref(s) to detach: **ROOMPLAN** (Enter)	Specifies the XREF name to detach
Scanning... No matching Xref names found.	

AutoCAD did not find the xref name because ROOMPLAN.DWG was attached with the PLAN xref name.

Command: *Choose* File, External Reference, *then* Detach	Specifies the XREF command's Detach option
Xref(s) to detach: **PLAN** (Enter)	Specifies the XREF name to detach
Scanning...	Scans the drawing database and removes the xref
Command: *Save the drawing*	
Command: *Open* CHAP19A	

When you reopened CHAP19A during the preceding exercise, AutoCAD loaded only the ATCHROOM xref because the PLAN xref was detached (see fig. 19.6).

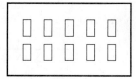

Figure 19.6

ATCHROOM drawing without PLAN xref.

Reloading Xrefs

Should another colleague in your workgroup update a drawing referenced by your current drawing, you can use the XREF command's Reload option to update your xref. The Reload option enables you to reload a specific xref or group of xrefs. Reloading specific xrefs saves time over reopening your current drawing; you don't have to save changes to your drawing, open the drawing, and then wait while every xref loads again.

The Reload option prompts you to specify the name or names of the xrefs to reload. You can use any of AutoCAD's standard wild cards to specify xref names, or you can separate the names with commas (without spaces).

The XREF command's Reload option usually is used in a networked, team design situation because AutoCAD Release 13 can edit only one drawing at a time. In a non-networked environment, you can use the Reload option to reload updated drawings copied from floppy disk or other storage devices.

In the next exercise, you open the CHAP19B drawing, which loads the OVLYROOM and PLAN xrefs. After you open the drawing, you copy the backup ROOMPLAN drawing over the ROOMPLAN drawing referenced by PLAN and then reload the PLAN xref. Figure 19.7 shows the reloaded xref.

Reloading an Xref

Continue from the preceding exercise and open the CHAP19B drawing. Use AutoCAD's file utilities to copy the ROOMPLAN.SAV backup file to ROOMPLAN.DWG.

Command: *Choose* File, External   Specifies the XREF command's Reload option
Reference, *then* Reload

Xref(s) to reload: **PLAN** (Enter)   Specifies XREF name to reload

   Scanning...   Scans the drawing database for the specified
Reload Xref PLAN: ROOMPLAN   XREF and reloads the external file
PLAN loaded. Regenerating drawing.

Your drawing should now use the original unstretched version of ROOMPLAN. Because AutoCAD does not update the image of an xref in the current drawing when changes are made to the source file, you must force a reload.

In the preceding exercise, you were aware that the ROOMPLAN drawing was updated. In a networked environment, you more than likely will be unaware of changes

as they occur. Take steps to make sure you're working with the latest drawing version as suggested in the following tip.

19

Tip AutoCAD does not notify you when it updates an externally referenced drawing. In a networked environment, therefore, you should reload xrefs periodically or adopt a departmental policy that requires all workgroup members to notify each other of significant changes as they occur. A network workgroup broadcast message is an easy way to handle notification.

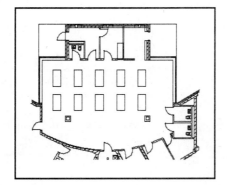

Figure 19.7

Updated ROOMPLAN reloaded.

Changing Xref Paths

AutoCAD stores the path to each external file as data in an xref object. If the structure of your project changes and referenced files are moved to another subdirectory, hard drive, or file server, you must also update the path information in the xref object. The XREF command Path option enables you to respecify a path to an external file.

The XREF command's Path option also enables you to specify a different file name for the xref. This is useful when you use simplified stand-in drawings in place of large complex drawings for positioning or rough-in purposes. When you need the detail of the complex drawing, you can substitute the file name of the alternate drawing in the xref.

In the following exercise, you move a referenced drawing to another subdirectory and use the XREF command's Path option to update the xref path.

Changing the Path of an External File

Use the SHELL command to exit AutoCAD to the DOS prompt. Then, create a \IA\TEMP subdirectory and move the ROOMPLAN drawing to the new subdirectory. After you move the file, return to AutoCAD and open the CHAP19B drawing.

When you open the drawing, a message box appears warning you that ROOMPLAN.DWG could not be found (see fig. 19.8). Choose OK.

Command: *Choose* File, External Reference, *then* Path	Specifies the XREF command's Path option
Edit path for which xref(s): **PLAN** (Enter)	Specifies the xref name to change
Scanning...	Searches the drawing database for the xref
Xref name: PLAN Old path: ROOMPLAN	Informs you of the old path
New path: **C:\IA\TEMP\ROOMPLAN** (Enter)	Specifies the new path and file name
Regenerating drawing	
Reload Xref PLAN: C:\IA\TEMP\ROOMPLAN.DWG PLAN loaded. Regenerating drawing.	Reloads the xref
Command: *Save the drawing*	

Use AutoCAD's file utilities to copy ROOMPLAN back to the original directory, because you use it in the remainder of the exercises in this chapter.

Figure 19.8

AutoCAD Alert indicating it cannot locate externally referenced files.

Archiving Xrefs

Archiving after finishing a project to make space for new projects is common practice. Archiving a single project drawing rather than a master drawing and its many individual external drawings is often easier. The XREF command's Bind option makes an

New Riders Publishing
INSIDE
SERIES

xref a permanent part of a drawing. Binding xrefs to the master drawing is safer than trying to remember to store a master drawing with its xrefs.

The Bind option prompts you to specify the name or names of the xrefs to bind to the current drawing. You can use any of AutoCAD's standard wild cards to specify xref names, or you can separate the names with commas (without spaces).

Stop   The All (External Reference, Bind) tool automatically binds every xref in the drawing! You can reverse the operation with the UNDO command.

Binding an xref to a drawing converts the xref to a block, making it a permanent part of the drawing and no longer an externally referenced file. You can use the XREF Bind option to bind the entire drawing's database, or you can use the XBIND command to individually bind the named items (referred to as *dependent symbols*) in the current drawing. The XBIND command is discussed later in this chapter, in the section "Using XBIND To Import Part of an Xref."

The following exercise uses the XREF command's Bind option to bind all the xrefs in CHAP19B into a single drawing.

Archiving an Xref

Continue to use the CHAP19B drawing from the previous exercise.

Command: *Choose* File, Bind, All   Issues the XREF command with Bind option

```
Xref(s) to bind: *
     Scanning...

Regenerating drawing
```

Command: *Choose* File, External   Issues the XREF command with the List
Reference, *then* List   option

```
?/Bind/Detach/Path/Reload/Overlay/
<Attach>: _?
Xref(s) to list <*>: (Enter)
```

Xref name	Path	Xref type
....	....	....

```
Total Xref(s): 0
```

Save the drawing.

The next time you open the CHAP19B drawing, AutoCAD will not load the xrefs; they no longer exist in the drawing. Visually, no changes occur when you bind an xref. However, when bound, the entire external file, including its dependent symbols, is incorporated into the referencing drawing. The dependent symbols are renamed so you can easily differentiate them from dependent symbols of xrefs.

Clipping Xrefs

The XREFCLIP command enables you create a specific view of an xref at a specific scale. XREFCLIP is useful for creating scaled detail views of a drawing in a plot drawing. XREFCLIP is also useful for importing standard details.

XREFCLIP. The XREFCLIP command enables you to attach an xref, then creates a floating viewport that displays a specified portion of the xref at a specified scale and location.
Pull-down: *Choose* File, External Reference, Clip

The XREFCLIP command attaches an xref on a layer you specify; displays the entire xref and prompts you to specify the area to display, the scale, and insertion point; and then creates a floating viewport based on your input. If TILEMODE is on, XREFCLIP prompts you to enable paper space. If you answer no to the prompt, the command fails; XREFCLIP requires paper space to be enabled. The layer you specify for the xref must not exist in the current drawing.

Stop The XREFCLIP command does not function properly if the xref you want to clip is already attached to the drawing. Use the XREF command's Detach option to remove the XREF before you use the XREFCLIP command.

In the following exercise, you use XREFCLIP to create a detailed view of a bathroom in ROOMPLAN and a full view of ROOMPLAN.

Using XREFCLIP

Start a new drawing named CHAP19C, using XREFPROT as a prototype.

Command: *Choose* File, External Reference, *then* Clip	Issues the XREFCLIP command
Initializing...	
Enable paper space? <Y>: (Enter)	Switches to paper space

New Riders Publishing
INSIDE
SERIES

Xref name: **ROOMPLAN** (Enter)	Specifies drawing name for xref
Clip onto what layer? **DET-BATH-1** (Enter)	Specifies the xref layer
First corner of clip box: *Pick* ① (*see fig. 19.9*)	Specifies first corner of clip box
Other corner: *Pick* ②	Specifies second corner of clip box
Enter the ratio of paper space units to model space units... Number of paper space units <1.0>: **12** (Enter)	Specifies the number of paper space units
Number of model space units <1.0>: **1** (Enter)	Specifies the number of model space units

AutoCAD switches back to a blank paper space screen, with the corner of the viewport at the crosshairs.

Insertion point for clip: *Pick* ① (*see fig. 19.10*)	Specifies point for lower-left corner of clip box

After the viewport is placed in the drawing, AutoCAD switches to model space, displays the entire xref in the viewport, and then scales it to the values you entered.

Repeat the process to place another scaled view.

Command: *Choose* File, External Reference, *then* Clip	Issues the XREFCLIP command
Xref name: **ROOMPLAN** (Enter)	Specifies drawing name for xref
Clip onto what layer? **PLAN-1** (Enter)	Specifies the xref layer
First corner of clip box: **'Z** (Enter)	Issues transparent zoom
>>Center/Dynamic/Left/Previous/Vmax/ Window/<Scale(X/XP)>: **.75X** (Enter)	Shrinks the view
First corner of clip box: *Enclose the entire xref with the clip window*	
Enter the ratio of paper space units to model space units... Number of paper space units <1.0>: **48** (Enter)	Specifies the number of paper space units

continues

`Number of model space units <1.0>:` `1` `Enter`	Specifies the number of model space units
`Insertion point for clip:` *Pick* ① *(see fig. 19.11)*	Specifies point for lower-left corner of clip box
`Command:` *Save the drawing*	

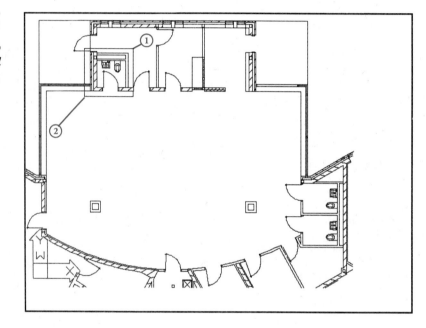

Figure 19.9

Specifying clip area for detail view of bathroom.

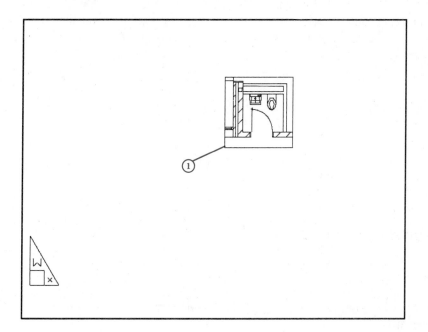

Figure 19.10

First clipped xref placed in paper space.

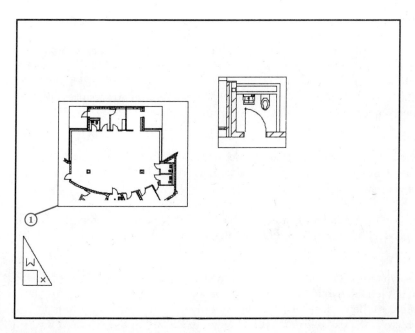

Figure 19.11

Two clipped xrefs created with XREFCLIP.

The next section explains what dependent symbols are and how they relate to xrefs. Up until now, dependent symbols have almost been ignored, but they are an important part of xrefs.

Understanding Xref Dependent Symbols

Layers, linetypes, text styles, blocks, and dimension styles are symbols; that is, they are arbitrary names that represent things such as layers or styles (not to be confused with graphic symbols). The symbols that are carried into a drawing by an xref are called *dependent symbols* because they depend on the external file, rather than on the current drawing for their characteristics.

To avoid conflicts, dependent symbols are prefixed with the name of the xref for which they are dependent. The only exceptions are unambiguous defaults like layer 0 and linetype CONTINUOUS. Because you can change text style STANDARD, it is prefixed. Prefixed dependent symbols also apply to nested xrefs. A vertical bar character (|) separates the prefix from the symbol name. For example, the layer named DESK-PLAN-1 in the ATCHROOM xref appears as the ATCHROOM|DESK-PLAN-1 dependent symbol.

To protect the integrity of an xref, AutoCAD limits the capability to change dependent symbols in your current drawing. You cannot make an xref's layer current and draw on it, for example, as you can with a standard drawing layer. You can modify an xref's appearance, however, by changing the color, linetype, and visibility of an xref's layers. Any changes you make are only temporary unless you set the VISRETAIN system variable to 1 (on). If you set VISRETAIN to 0 (off), AutoCAD restores all original dependencies when you reload the drawing or the xref.

 Note   If you change the linetype of an xref-dependent layer to any linetype defined in the current drawing, you cannot reset it back to its original linetype without reloading the drawing or xref.

The names of other dependent symbols, such as blocks, dimension or text styles, are similarly displayed but cannot be modified unless you use the XREF BIND or XBIND commands.

The XREF command's Bind option enables you to create a block from an xref. The Bind option also enables you to rename the dependent symbols that belong to xrefs. AutoCAD replaces the vertical bar (|) in the symbol name with $*n*$ (*n* is a number); for example, layer XSYMBOL|SYMLAYER changes to XSYMBOL0SYMLAYER. When AutoCAD renames bound symbols, it first uses 0 for the number. If a layer by that name already exists, AutoCAD increments the number by 1. AutoCAD continues

New Riders Publishing
INSIDE
SERIES

trying higher numbers until it reaches a unique layer name. You can use the RE-NAME command to change these strange layer names to whatever layer name you like.

Tip   If you want to insert a drawing as a block into your current drawing (and you have conflicting layer names), attach the drawing as an xref first, then bind it as a block. This step preserves the incoming block's unique layers.

You can use the XBIND command to selectively import these dependent symbols into your current drawing. You learn about the XBIND command in the next section of this chapter.

Tip   You can use the Filters feature of the Layer Control dialog box to display a specific group of dependent layers.

Using XBIND To Import Part of an Xref

In an earlier exercise in this chapter entitled "Archiving an Xref," you used the Bind option of XREF to convert an xref to a block. AutoCAD converted all the dependent symbols as well as all the geometry in the xref's file and made them part of the current drawing. The XBIND command binds only selected dependent symbols of an xref to the current drawing. Use XBIND if you only want to bring in a text style, dimension style, linetype, block, or layer defined in the xref without binding the entire xref.

XBIND. The XBIND command enables you to import dependent symbols (blocks, dimension styles, text styles, layers, and linetypes) that are defined in an externally referenced drawing into the current drawing. You specify what type of symbol to bind and XBIND prompts you for a specific symbol name of that type. You can enter a single name, several names separated by commas (without spaces), or AutoCAD standard wild cards.

Pull-down: *Choose* File, Bind, and one of the XBIND options
Screen: *Choose* FILE, Xbind

In addition to any symbols you explicitly bind by using XBIND, linetypes and other symbols that can be linked to one another are automatically bound to the current drawing. A linetype assigned to a layer is one such example. The entities (lines and so on) contained in the xref are not bound to the drawing. If you bind a block, however, you can then use INSERT to insert it in the current drawing.

In the following exercise, you bind the DOORR block and its layers from
ROOMPLAN. Then you set the bound layer current and insert a new door.

Binding Only Parts of an Xref by Using XBIND

Start a new drawing named CHAP19D, using XREFPROT as a prototype; attach ROOMPLAN at
0,0 with default scale and rotation; then zoom to the view in figure 19.12.

Command: **LAYER** (Enter)	Issues the LAYER command
?/Make/Set/New/ON/OFF/Color/Ltype/ Freeze/Thaw/LOck/Unlock: **?** (Enter)	Specifies the List option
Layer name(s) to list <*>: **ROOMPLAN*** (Enter)	Specifies layers to list

```
   Layer name        State         Color         Linetype
--------------------------------------------------------
ROOMPLAN¦A-DOOR      On          1 (red)        CONTINUOUS      Xdep: ROOMPLAN
ROOMPLAN¦A-FLOR-BATH On          1 (red)        CONTINUOUS      Xdep: ROOMPLAN
ROOMPLAN¦A-FLOR-WALL On          2 (yellow)     CONTINUOUS      Xdep: ROOMPLAN
ROOMPLAN¦A-IDEN-DIMS Frozen      1 (red)        CONTINUOUS      Xdep: ROOMPLAN

ROOMPLAN¦A-OVHD-FLOR On          1 (red)        ROOMPLAN¦SDASHED   Xdep: ROOMPLAN
ROOMPLAN¦A-WALL-FULL On          3 (green)      CONTINUOUS      Xdep: ROOMPLAN
ROOMPLAN¦A-WALL-FURR On          8              CONTINUOUS      Xdep: ROOMPLAN
ROOMPLAN¦A-WNDW-EXTR On          1 (red)        CONTINUOUS      Xdep: ROOMPLAN
ROOMPLAN¦A-WNDW-INTR On          1 (red)        CONTINUOUS      Xdep: ROOMPLAN

ROOMPLAN¦S-COLS      On          4 (cyan)       CONTINUOUS      Xdep: ROOMPLAN

Current layer: 0
```

?/Make/Set/New/ON/OFF/Color/Ltype/ Freeze/Thaw/LOck/Unlock: (Enter)	Cancels the LAYER command
Command: *Choose* File, Bind, *then* Layer	Issues the XBIND command with Layer option
Block/Dimstyle/LAyer/LType/Style: _la	
Dependent Layer name(s): **ROOMPLAN¦A-DOOR** (Enter)	Specifies layer to bind
Scanning... 1 Layer(s) bound.	Scans the drawing database and binds layer

New Riders Publishing
INSIDE
SERIES

```
Command: BLOCK (Enter)                          Invokes the BLOCK command

Block name (or ?): ? (Enter)                    Specifies the List option

Block(s) to list <*>: (Enter)                   Lists all blocks

Defined blocks.
  ROOMPLAN                     Xref: resolved
  ROOMPLAN¦COLCONC             Xdep: ROOMPLAN
  ROOMPLAN¦DOORR               Xdep: ROOMPLAN
  ROOMPLAN¦LAVFS               Xdep: ROOMPLAN
  ROOMPLAN¦TBL3672             Xdep: ROOMPLAN
  ROOMPLAN¦TEMP19              Xdep: ROOMPLAN
  ROOMPLAN¦WCWALL              Xdep: ROOMPLAN


User        External     Dependent   Unnamed
Blocks      References   Blocks      Blocks
  0            1           6           23
```

Command: *Choose* File, Bind, Block

Issues the XBIND command with the Block option

```
Block/Dimstyle/LAyer/LType/Style: _b
```

```
Dependent Block name(s):
```
ROOMPLAN¦DOORR (Enter)

Specifies block to bind

```
    Scanning...
1 Block(s) bound. Regenerating drawing.
```

Scans drawing database and binds block

Command: *Make the* ROOMPLAN0A-DOOR *layer current*

Command: *Choose* Data, Rename

Opens the Rename dialog box

In the Rename *dialog box,* Layer *is the default highlighted named object. Select* ROOMPLAN0A-DOOR *in the* Items *list, type* **A-DOOR** *in the* Rename *to: text box, and click on the* Rename *to: button*

Renames bound layer

Next, select Block *from the* Named Objects *list and* ROOMPLAN0DOORR *in the* Items *list, type* **DOORR** *in the* Rename to: *text box, click on the* Rename to: *button, then choose* OK

Renames bound block

continues

```
1 Block renamed.

1 Layer renamed.
```

Command: **INSERT** (Enter)	Invokes the INSERT command
Block name (or ?): **DOORR** (Enter)	Specifies block to insert
Insertion point: *Using endpoint object snap pick* ① *(see fig. 19.12)*	Specifies insertion point
X scale factor <1> / Corner / XYZ: **36** (Enter)	Specifies insertion scale
Y scale factor (default=X): (Enter)	Accepts default scale
Rotation angle <0>: (Enter)	Accepts default rotation angle
Command: *Save the drawing*	

Figure 19.12

Bound DOORR block inserted on bound A-DOOR layer.

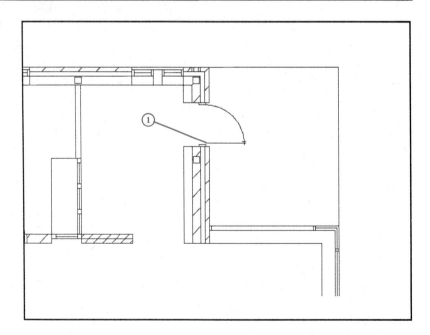

Use BIND if you want to bind the entire xref to make it a block. Use XBIND if you only want to bind layer, linetype, dimension styles, nested blocks, or text styles without binding any actual entities in the xref.

New Riders Publishing
INSIDE
SERIES

Tip
You can attach a library file that contains predefined named items, such as dimension styles or blocks. Use XBIND to import specific items, rename them to usable names, and then detach the xref.

Reading the XREF Log File

AutoCAD can be configured to maintain a log file of all xref activity in ASCII-text format. The log file is stored in the same directory as your drawing and has the same name as your drawing but with an XLG extension. The log file continues to grow as the drawing is edited over many sessions. Occasionally, you might want to delete all or part of the log file to save disk space. AutoCAD maintains this log file if the XREFCTL system variable is set to 1 (on). The default setting is 0 (off).

The log file indicates nested xrefs, dependent symbols, and any errors that occur. AutoCAD displays many of these messages in the command line, as well as writes them to the XREF log file. This log file can be a useful troubleshooting tool when you manage xrefs in your drawings. You also can use it to double-check when giving drawings that contain xrefs to others.

Managing Xref Layers, Colors, and Linetypes

When you insert a block into a drawing, any layers in the block's definition are added to the drawing. If a layer in a block already exists in the drawing, and the object properties in the block are set to BYLAYER, the block's objects take on the characteristics of the existing drawing's layer.

Xrefs work a little differently than blocks. When you attach an xref that contains layers other than layer 0, AutoCAD modifies the xref layer names to avoid duplication. A vertical bar (|) prefixes the xref layer names to separate the prefix from the layer name. Renaming layers prevents the xref's entities from taking on the characteristics of existing layers in the drawing.

As usual, the exception is layer 0. Any objects that exist on layer 0 in the xref come in on layer 0 in the destination drawing. They then assume the characteristics of the destination drawing's current layer, as would a block insert. The following list describes how xref objects created on layer 0 behave when you attach them to a drawing, based on their color and linetype settings:

◆ **BYLAYER.** The objects assume the color and linetype characteristics of the destination drawing's current layer.

◆ **BYBLOCK.** The objects assume the color and linetype characteristics that are current at the time the xref is attached.

◆ **EXPLICIT.** The objects retain their original explicit color and linetype settings.

Because an xref's layers do not merge with the destination drawing's layers (except layer 0), you can create the xref's objects on any layer other than 0 to make layers, colors, and linetypes remain as they are in the original drawing.

If you want an xref to temporarily assume different characteristics in the destination drawing, you can change the settings of the xref's layers in the destination drawing. Unless the VISRETAIN system variable is set to 1 (on), however, the changes do not survive from one drawing session to another, nor do they survive if the xref is re-loaded in the current drawing session.

Multiple Access Network Support Features

AutoCAD manages file locking in a networked workgroup environment. If simulta-neous reads and writes were allowed, files would become corrupt and AutoCAD could crash.

AutoCAD uses two type of locks: write locks and read locks. A write lock is placed on a file when you open the file for editing. Write locks prevent other users on the net-work from opening a drawing that you are editing. If you try to open a write-locked file, AutoCAD informs you that the file is write-locked and reports who is using the file and when it was opened. A file remains write-locked for the entire editing session.

You can open a write-locked file as read-only or as an external reference by another AutoCAD user. While the write-locked file is being loaded by another drawing session, AutoCAD places a read lock on the file. A *read lock* prevents the user who is editing the drawing from saving or writing a block to the opened drawing while another user is reading it. If the user editing a drawing attempts to write to a read-locked file, AutoCAD informs the user that the file is read-locked and reports who is reading the file and when the read lock was placed on the drawing. The read lock is removed after the file is finished being loaded.

If AutoCAD crashes during an editing session, or during a file read, read and write locks might not be removed. You can use AutoCAD's file utilities to remove a lock. Be sure to unlock only files that no other AutoCAD users are using.

In this chapter, you learned how to use references to external drawings to improve drawing efficiency and enable concurrent design practices. Xrefs give the same benefits as blocks, but they work with multiple drawings. Xrefs are most useful for keeping file size to a minimum and for ensuring that a drawing has the most up-to-date revision of the parts it contains. Xrefs act like blocks, and you can consider them special types of blocks. If you need to control the proliferation of common data, keep drawing size down, and decrease disk usage, use xrefs.

In the next chapter, you look at ways of enhancing the readability of your drawings by using hatching and special linetypes.

19

CHAPTER 20

Linetypes and Hatching

Although you can convey a great deal of information in a drawing using lines, arcs, circles and other AutoCAD primitive entities, you must show other kinds of information in different ways, such as areas sectioned by cutting planes and lines normally invisible in a particular view.

This chapter covers two major features of AutoCAD—linetypes and associative hatching. You can use special, noncontinuous linetypes in an AutoCAD drawing to show hidden objects, or to identify features such as center lines or property lines. You can apply hatch patterns to show areas in section, or to indicate different materials, to name just two uses. Linetypes and hatching enable you to highlight features in your drawings, which makes interpreting them easier.

In this chapter, you learn the following about linetypes:

◆ What linetypes are available

◆ How to assign linetypes to layers and objects

◆ How to edit linetypes of existing objects

◆ How to control the scale of linetypes

◆ How to define your own linetypes

Also, you learn the following about hatching:

◆ What hatch patterns are available

◆ How to define the areas to be hatched

◆ How to obtain additional hatch patterns

◆ What parameters control hatching, such as object proximity, pattern scale, and rotation

◆ How to edit existing hatched areas

The following exercise provides you with a brief overview of some of the commands covered in this chapter.

Quick 5¢ Tour

Begin a new drawing named CHAP20, using the ACAD drawing as the prototype drawing.

In the following steps, you create a couple of new layers, assign linetypes to them, and then draw on them.

Command: *Choose* Data, Layers   Opens the Layer Control dialog box

Next, you create two new layers, BORDER and CONTIN. Make CONTIN the current layer and choose OK.

Draw a circle that has a 3-unit radius and its center at 5,5 (see fig. 20.1).

Command: *Choose* Data, Layers, *and select the layer* BORDER	Make sure that BORDER is the only layer selected.
Choose Set **L**type	Opens the Select Linetype dialog box
Choose **L**oad; *select the linetype* BORDER *from the list of available linetypes and choose* OK	Loads linetype
Select BORDER *from the list of loaded linetypes and choose* OK	Sets linetype for selected layer

Make BORDER the current layer and choose OK.

Draw another circle that has a 3-unit radius and its center at 10,5 (see fig. 20.2).

The circle you drew on the BORDER layer automatically assumes the linetype assigned to that layer. Next, you hatch the two circles.

Command: *Choose* Draw, Hatch, Hatch	Activates the Boundary Hatch dialog box
Command: _bhatch	
Choose **P**ick Points	Highlights the circle
Select internal point: Pick any point inside the right circle	
Analyzing the selected data...	
Analyzing internal islands...	
Select internal point: **Enter**	Ends hatch selection mode and redisplays the Boundary Hatch dialog box
Command: *Click on* Apply	Applies hatch pattern, which also assumes layer's linetype setting (see fig. 20.3)

Change the current layer to CONTIN.

Command: *Choose* Draw, Hatch, Hatch	Initiates the Boundary Hatch dialog box
Click inside the Patte**r**n: *edit box and choose* ANSI32	Selects new hatch pattern
Double-click inside the Sca**l**e: *edit box and enter* **2**	Sets new hatch scale factor of 2
Press Tab to jump to the **A**ngle *edit box and enter* **90**	Sets new hatch rotation angle to 90
Choose **P**ick Points	Highlights the circle
Select internal point: *Pick any point inside the left circle*	
Analyzing the selected data...	
Analyzing internal islands...	
Select internal point: **Enter**	Ends hatch selection mode and redisplays the Boundary Hatch dialog box
Choose Preview Ha**t**ch *and then* Continue	Displays preview of applied hatch pattern
Click on Apply	Applies hatch pattern

Your drawing should now look like figure 20.4.

Figure 20.1

The first circle.

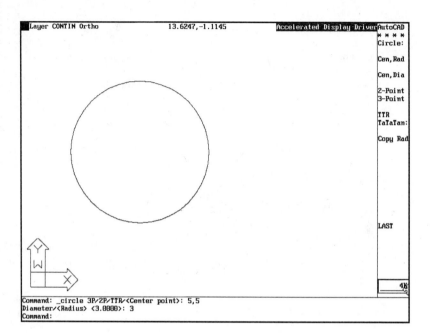

Figure 20.2

The second circle showing its layer's linetype.

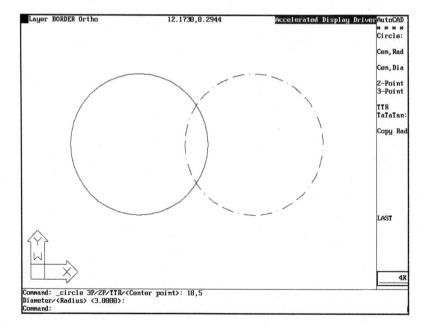

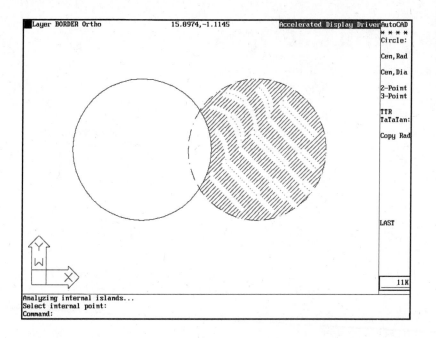

Figure 20.3

Hatching also takes on the layer's linetype.

20

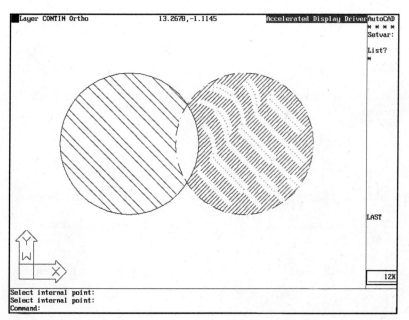

Figure 20.4

Options let you change hatch parameters.

Working with Linetypes

The majority of drawing work you do in AutoCAD involves using continuous lines. Sometimes, however, you need to show something in a different way, or indicate symbolically something that doesn't exist in the real world. To accommodate these needs, AutoCAD can draw with a series of noncontinuous linetypes. These noncontinuous linetypes follow long-established drafting conventions. For example, lines that consist of short dashes are used as *hidden* lines, to indicate objects or surfaces that are behind other objects. Or, lines that consist of alternating short and long dashes are used as *center* lines to indicate, for example, the mathematical center of a shaft.

You can apply a linetype to an object in the following three ways:

◆ Define a layer to have a default linetype—anything you draw on that layer takes on the assigned linetype

◆ Set a specific linetype as current—anything that you draw from that point on uses that linetype, regardless of the layer's linetype setting

◆ Use one of the entity modification commands to change the linetype of an existing object to a different linetype

Linetypes are defined in *linetype definition files.* The following two are supplied with AutoCAD:

◆ **ACAD.LIN.** Contains the standard linetypes

◆ **LTYPESHP.LIN.** Contains the definitions for complex linetypes that include shapes and text

Noncontinuous linetypes fall into the following three basic categories:

◆ Lines that have a repeating pattern of dashes, spaces and/or dots

◆ Lines that have a repeating pattern of text strings, dashes, spaces, and/or dots

◆ Lines that have a repeating pattern of shapes, dashes, spaces and/or dots (see fig. 20.5)

Despite the differences in appearance, you define, apply, and edit all linetypes in the same manner.

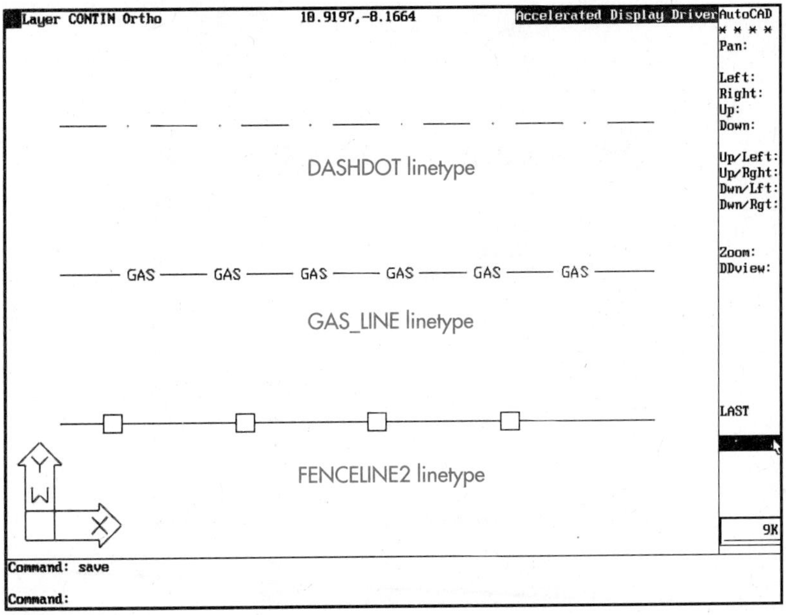

Figure 20.5
Sample linetypes.

20

The basic procedure for using additional linetypes in your drawing is as follows:

1. Load the linetypes into the drawing.

2. Set the current linetype, and if necessary, assign linetypes to layers.

3. Draw the objects.

Loading Additional Linetypes

By default, the only linetype you can use in a new drawing is the continuous linetype. If you want to use any other linetypes, you need to use the Select Linetype dialog box or the LINETYPE command to load them from the library file ACAD.LIN (stored by default in the directory \ACADR13\COMMON\SUPPORT).

'DDLTYPE. The DDLTYPE command enables you to open the Select Linetype dialog box, which enables you to load linetypes from a file and set the current linetype and global linetype scale.

Pull-down: *Choose* Data, Linetype
Screen: *Choose* DATA, DDltype:

To load additional linetypes, you use the Load button in the Select Linetype dialog box (see fig. 20.6). The Load button opens the Load or Reload Linetypes dialog box (see fig. 20.7).

Figure 20.6

The Select Linetype dialog box.

Figure 20.7

The Load or Reload Linetypes dialog box.

By default, the contents of the ACAD.LIN library are listed in the Load or Reload Linetypes dialog box. ACAD.LIN contains an extensive set of linetypes in two series: the standard linetype families and ISO linetypes (see figures 20.8 and 20.9).

◆ Note To provide greater flexibility when you scale linetypes, the standard linetype families each have three members. The BORDER family, for example, consists of BORDER, BORDER2, and BORDERX2. The element size and spacing in BORDER2 are half that of BORDER, and in BORDERX2, they are twice that of BORDER.

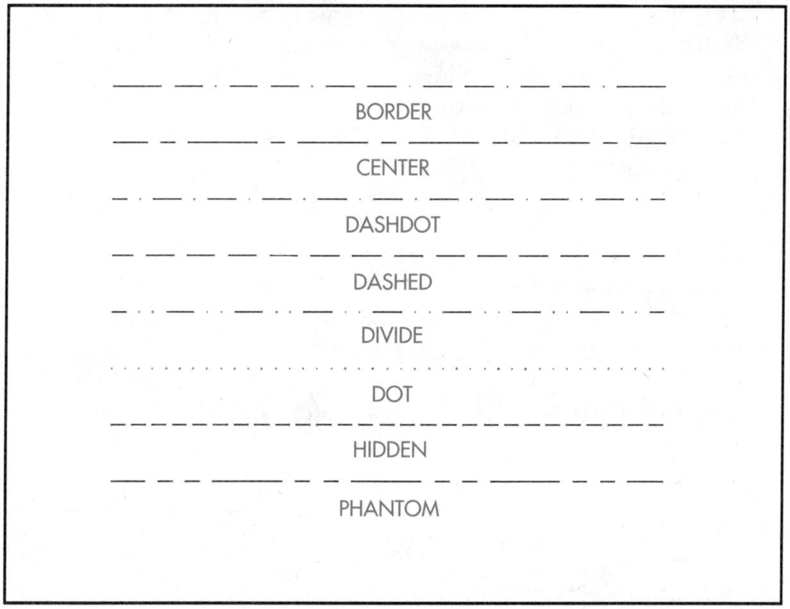

Figure 20.8

AutoCAD's Standard Linetype Families.

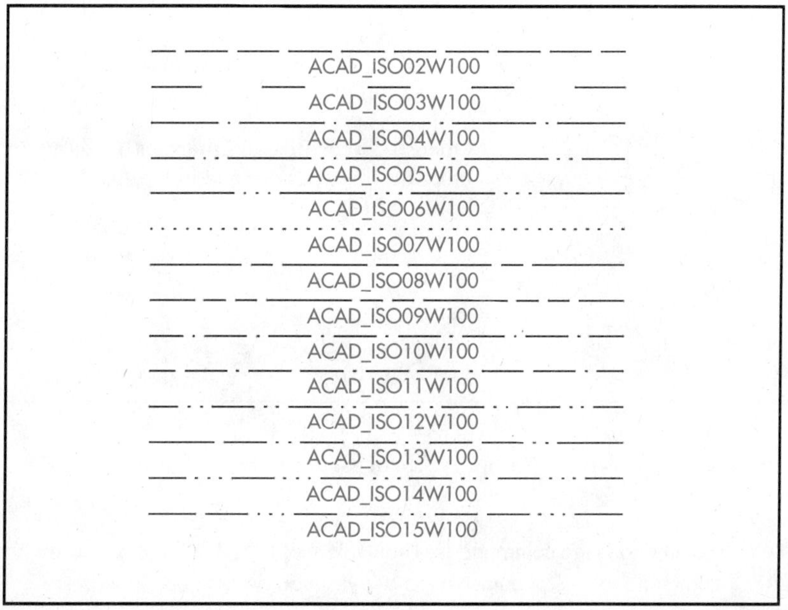

BORDER

CENTER

DASHDOT

DASHED

DIVIDE

DOT

HIDDEN

PHANTOM

Figure 20.9

AutoCAD's ISO linetypes.

ACAD_ISO02W100

ACAD_ISO03W100

ACAD_ISO04W100

ACAD_ISO05W100

ACAD_ISO06W100

ACAD_ISO07W100

ACAD_ISO08W100

ACAD_ISO09W100

ACAD_ISO10W100

ACAD_ISO11W100

ACAD_ISO12W100

ACAD_ISO13W100

ACAD_ISO14W100

ACAD_ISO15W100

20

To load or reload a linetype, you simply select the linetype from the list and choose OK. AutoCAD loads the linetype and returns you to the main Select Linetype dialog box. If you want to browse through another linetype file, use the File button to specify the file name and location. Creating your own linetype definitions and storing them in your own files is described later in this chapter in the section "Working with Linetype Files."

Tip If you know you are going to use several linetypes, you can save time by loading all the linetypes at one time and then purging the unused ones later. To load all the linetypes, choose the Select All button in the Load or Reload Linetypes dialog box to select all the linetypes and then choose OK to load them.

In the following exercise, you use the Select Linetype dialog box to load some linetypes from the file ACAD.LIN.

Loading Linetypes

Begin a new drawing again named CHAP20, using the TOPO drawing from the IA Disk as the prototype. You can discard the changes to the previous CHAP20.

You should see the drawing shown in figure 20.10.

Command: *Choose* Data, Linetype	Opens Select Linetype dialog box (see fig. 20.11)
Choose L**o**ad	Opens Load or Reload Linetypes dialog box with linetypes defined in the ACAD.LIN linetype definition file
From the list of linetypes, choose DASHED, HIDDEN, HIDDEN2, PHANTOM, *and* PHANTOM2	Selects linetypes to load (see fig. 20.12)
Choose OK *twice*	Loads linetypes

After you load the linetypes into your drawing, you can assign them to objects or layers.

Note The LAYER command is the command-line equivalent of DDLMODES. If you use the LAYER command to assign a linetype to a layer, you do not need to load the linetype before you assign it; AutoCAD automatically looks in the ACAD.LIN file for the linetype and loads it if it finds it.

New Riders Publishing
INSIDE SERIES

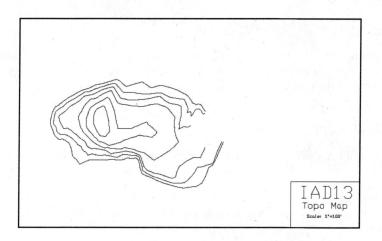

Figure 20.10

The topographical drawing with continuous linetypes.

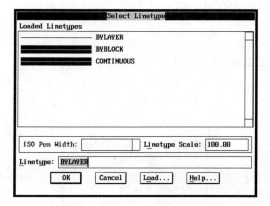

Figure 20.11

The Select Linetype dialog box.

Figure 20.12

The Load or Reload Linetypes dialog box.

20

Setting the Current Linetype

Chapter 5, "Setting Up a CAD Drawing," tells you that with a few exceptions, you draw objects using the current linetype. You can use the Select Linetype dialog box to set the current linetype. You simply choose the linetype you want from the Loaded Linetypes list box.

The current object linetype setting is set to one of the following three settings:

◆ **BYLAYER.** You draw objects set to BYLAYER using the linetype assigned to the layer on which you draw the object. BYLAYER is the default setting.

◆ **Specific linetype.** You draw all objects set to a specific linetype using that linetype, regardless of the linetype assigned to the layer on which you actually draw the object.

◆ **BYBLOCK.** You use this special setting to create block definitions. BYBLOCK is discussed in Chapter 17, "Block Structure, Editing, Organization, and Management."

You can use the Object Creation Modes dialog box (see fig. 20.13) to set the current linetype. When you do so, all entities added to the drawing from that point on will be created using the new linetype setting. See Chapter 5, "Setting Up a CAD Drawing," for details.

Figure 20.13

The Object Creation Modes dialog box.

Object Creation Modes	
Color... ◼	BYLAYER
Layer...	BORDER
Linetype...	BYLAYER
Text Style...	STANDARD
Linetype Scale:	1.00
Elevation:	0.00
Thickness:	0.00
OK Cancel Help...	

Choosing the Linetype button in the Object Creation Modes dialog box opens the Select Linetype dialog box.

Using BYLAYER versus Specific Linetypes

Forget about the BYBLOCK setting for now (it is covered in Chapter 17). A BYLAYER linetype setting is more appropriate to use than a specific linetype setting when you want to be able to modify the linetypes of objects on a layer-wide basis. You typically

New Riders Publishing
INSIDE
SERIES

want that flexibility with objects that describe a common feature (for example, property lines on a map). If objects have BYLAYER linetype assignments, all you have to do to change their linetypes is use DDLMODES to assign a new linetype to the layer on which the objects reside.

To draw using the current linetype setting of BYLAYER, you use DDLTYPE to load the linetypes you want, and then use DDLMODES to assign the linetypes to the appropriate layers. As you draw objects, you make current the layer to which you want to assign the appropriate linetype.

On the other hand, sometimes depicting a particular feature in your drawing might require several linetypes. In such a situation, you might wonder whether it would make sense to use several layers to draw that feature. A common example is the company border sheet that utilizes several linetypes. Should you draw the border and title block elements on one layer or on several layers? If you draw the border and title block drawn on one layer, you need to set the current linetype to the required linetypes as you draw your border sheet.

Tip   When you decide whether to use a BYLAYER setting, ask yourself whether you need the capability to isolate a particular group of subelements (for example, the phantom lines in a border sheet) by turning layers on and off. If you do, then you want to dedicate a layer for that group of objects, and if the objects have the same linetype, draw those objects with a BYLAYER linetype and assign the linetype to the layer.

No one answer fits all situations. You must make the decision based on the situation and your company's CAD standards.

In the following exercise, you draw with the current linetype set to both specific linetypes and to BYLAYER.

Setting the Current Linetype

Continue to use the CHAP20 drawing.

Command: *Choose* Data, Object Creation	Opens the Object Creation Modes dialog box
Choose Linetype	Opens the Select Linetype dialog box

Choose the linetype PHANTOM. Choose OK. Choose OK again to exit the dialog box.

Command: *Choose* Draw, Polygon, Rectangle *and draw a rectangle from* 200,200 *to* 1050,900	Draws a rectangle

continues

continued

Command: *Choose* Draw, Line *and draw*   Draws line segments
line segments from 1275,900 *to* 1200,900
to 1200,200 *to* 1275,200, *then press Enter*

Your drawing should look like figure 20.14. Because you set the current linetype to PHAN-
TOM, AutoCAD drew the rectangle and lines with a PHANTOM linetype rather than the
continuous linetype assigned to layer PROP_LINE.

Figure 20.14

*Property lines
drawn using the
PHANTOM
linetype.*

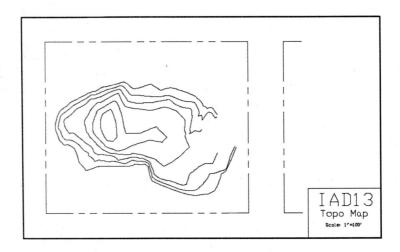

Command: *Choose* Data, Layers *and make*   Activates the Layer Control dialog box
SLUDGE_PIT *the current layer*

Command: *Choose* Data, Object Creation   Opens the Object Creation Modes dialog box

Choose Linetype   Activates the Select Linetype dialog box

Choose the linetype DASHED. Choose OK twice, the second time to exit the dialog box.

Command: *Choose* Draw, Polygon, Rectangle
and draw a rectangle with corners at 225,750
and 400,850. *Then draw two diagonal lines
from the opposite corners*

Your drawing should now look like figure 20.15.

Command: *Choose* Data, Object Creation   Opens the Object Creation Modes dialog box

New Riders Publishing
INSIDE SERIES

Choose L̲inetype

Choose BYLAYER, then OK *twice*   Resets the linetype to BYLAYER and closes
the dialog box

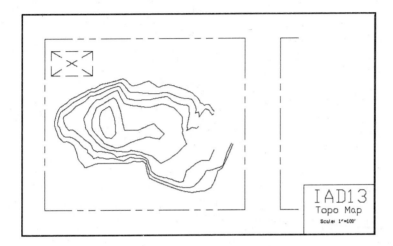

Figure 20.15

Additional site features using linetypes added.

20

In the preceding exercise, you drew several elements using different linetypes. At the end of the exercise, you reset the current linetype back to BYLAYER so that any new objects would be drawn with the linetype assigned to the current layer.

Modifying Existing Linetypes

If you want to change the linetype of entities on a layer-wide basis, you use the Layer Control dialog box (or the LAYER command) to assign a new linetype to the existing layer. At that point, all objects that reside on that layer and were drawn using a BYLAYER linetype setting take on the appearance of the newly assigned linetype. Objects on that layer that were drawn using a linetype other than BYLAYER remain unaffected.

AutoCAD has a series of commands for modifying entity properties: DDMODIFY, DDCHPROP, CHPROP, and CHANGE. You can use these commands to modify the linetype, layer, and color of entities.

If the entities were drawn with linetype set to BYLAYER, moving them to a different layer causes them to take on the linetype and color properties of the new layer.

In the following exercise, you edit the linetypes of existing objects.

Editing the Linetypes of Objects

Although you can have entities with explicitly set linetypes on layers that have the same default linetype assigned to them, it can be confusing when you (or someone else) must edit the drawings.

In the case of this drawing, none of the entities needs to have an explicitly set entity linetype. You can assign default linetypes to all the layers and let the layer itself determine the entity's linetype. You begin by resetting the linetype of all the entities in the drawing to BYLAYER.

Command: *Choose* Modify, Properties	Issues DDCHPROP command
Command: (ai_propchk)	
Select objects: **ALL** (Enter)	Selects all entities in drawing
19 found	
Select objects: (Enter)	
DDCHPROP loaded	Opens the Change Properties dialog box
Choose L̲inetype	Initiates the Select Linetype dialog box
Choose BYLAYER, *then choose* OK *twice*	Resets linetype to BYLAYER and closes the dialog box (see fig. 20.16)

Because all layers have CONTINUOUS as their default linetype setting, all the lines are now CONTINUOUS. Next, you apply default linetype settings to the layers in the drawing.

Command: *Choose* Data, Layers	Opens the Layer Control dialog box
Click on the layer SLUDGE_PIT *and choose* Set L̲type, *then choose* DASHED *from the* Select Linetype *dialog box and choose* OK	Highlights SLUDGE_PIT layer

Repeat and change the default linetype setting of the PROP_LINE layer to PHANTOM and the OLD_CONTOURS layer to HIDDEN2 (see fig. 20.17).

Choose OK	Closes the Layer Control dialog box

Figure 20.16

The Change Properties dialog box.

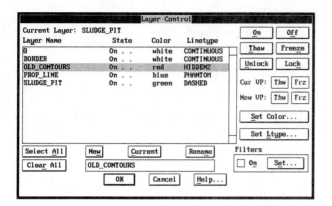

Figure 20.17

Setting default linetypes for layers.

Your drawing should now look like figure 20.18. The noncontinuous linetypes in the contour lines don't look right, but you fix them shortly.

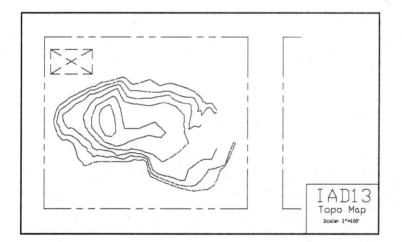

Figure 20.18

Noncontinuous linetypes applied to drawing elements.

Controlling Linetype Scales

Linetype definition files store the information AutoCAD needs to draw noncontinuous linetypes.

Every linetype has a linetype definition. A *linetype definition,* in its simplest form, consists of a series of numbers that instructs AutoCAD how long to make the dashes and spaces. The definition of the HIDDEN linetype, for example, instructs AutoCAD to draw dashes 0.25 units separated by spaces 0.125 units in length.

AutoCAD uses real world units to create noncontinuous linetypes. If you draw in architectural units (feet and fractional inches), AutoCAD tries to create the linetype patterns using the sizes specified in the linetype definition file. A hidden line, for example, would be drawn with 1/4" dashes and 1/8" spaces. In a drawing scaled to enable you to fit a building a hundred feet long onto a three-foot wide sheet, the hidden line is indistinguishable from a continuous line.

You need to be able to control the spacing of noncontinuous linetype elements, and AutoCAD provides a number of methods.

◆ You can set a global linetype scale factor called LTSCALE that's related to your intended plot scale factor.

◆ You can apply an additional scaling factor, CELTSCALE, and modify the linetype scaling of entities drawn from that point on.

◆ You can apply the same factor to existing lines with noncontinuous linetypes, and modify their appearance.

◆ Finally, you can use a system variable (PSLTSCALE) to allow linetype scaling if you're working with paper space viewports.

You compensate for the effects of the plot scale with the LTSCALE (LineType SCALE) command. This command sets the LTSCALE system variable, which AutoCAD uses as a global scaling factor for linetypes. By default, LTSCALE is set to 1, which means AutoCAD draws with a linetype that uses the exact lengths specified in the linetype's definition. If LTSCALE is set to 4, the lengths in the linetype definition are multiplied by 4 when the drawing is displayed or plotted. The HIDDEN linetype would be drawn as a series of 1-unit (0.25 * 4) dashes and 0.5-unit (0.125 * 4) spaces. Then, when a plot scale of 1=4 is applied, the linetype appears on the paper as a series of 0.25-unit dashes and 0.125-unit spaces. So, if you want the linetypes to appear on your plot with their defined lengths for the dashes and spaces, you need to set LTSCALE to the inverse of the plot scale. Here are some examples:

Plot scale	LTSCALE Setting
1/4"=1' (1=48)	48
1/8"=1' (1=96)	96
1/16"=1' (1=192)	192

Note   Regardless of how linetypes look on-screen, we need to remind ourselves that the final product of our work with AutoCAD is usually going to be a plotted drawing. Linetypes should be scaled so that they are easy to read on the drawing. Making LTSCALE the same as the inverse of the plot scale is not a hard-and-fast rule and many users prefer to set it to somewhere between 50% and 100% of the plot scale factor.

You should be aware that changing the value of LTSCALE not only affects new objects but existing objects as well. You might not have to issue a regeneration to see the changes made by a new LTSCALE value—it depends on whether the REGENAUTO system variable is set to on or off.

There are four ways of setting linetype scale:

◆ From the pull-down menus choose Options, Linetypes, then Global Linetype Scale

◆ From the pull-down menus choose Data, Linetype, Select Linetype to display the Select Linetype dialog box, and set a value in the Linetype Scale: edit box

◆ From the screen menu choose OPTIONS, DISPLAY, Ltscale

◆ Enter LTSCALE at the keyboard

Note If REGENAUTO is on (the default) when you set LTSCALE, AutoCAD automatically regenerates the drawing so you can see the results of the change in the Linetype scale. If REGENAUTO is off, you must issue the REGEN command before you can see the results of the change in linetype scaling.

You use LTSCALE to compensate for plot scale; however, you might also need to scale linetypes differently from object to object. Before you can do so, you must control the linetype scale of individual objects. In addition to the global linetype scaling factor LTSCALE, you also can set the system variable CELTSCALE (Current Entity LineType SCALE). By default, this system variable is set to 1. CELTSCALE is a scale factor applied to LTSCALE that enables you to apply linetype scaling factors to entities individually. You set CELTSCALE by using the Linetype Scale edit box in the Object Creation Modes dialog box (see fig. 20.13), or by using the Linetype Scale setting in the Select Linetype dialog box as accessed through the Object Creation Modes dialog box. The CELTSCALE setting that is current when an object is drawn determines the appearance of all subsequently drawn noncontinuous lines.

Note The naming that AutoCAD uses to control linetype scaling is potentially confusing. If you open the Object Creation Modes dialog box (see fig. 20.13), the value that you see in the Linetype Scale edit box is CELTSCALE. If you open the Select Linetype dialog box (see fig. 20.11), the value in the Linetype Scale edit box is LTSCALE.

An object's linetype scale and CELTSCALE interact to determine the final scale of an object's linetype. For example, if you draw an object with CELTSCALE set to 0.5, and LTSCALE is set to 2, then AutoCAD displays and plots the object with lengths in the linetype's definition multiplied by 0.5 (the Current Entity linetype scale) and 2 (the LTSCALE), which results in a net linetype scale factor of 1.

Sometimes all you really want is the linetype scaled up or down by a factor of 2. In such situations, you do not need to deal with CELTSCALE linetype scale factors because AutoCAD provides, not one, but three versions of each linetype. The three definitions are the original definition, the half-scale definition (the 2 version) and the double-scale definition (the X2 version). The 2 and X2 references derive from the suffixes used in the definition names. Figure 20.19 shows the three versions that AutoCAD provides of the hidden linetype.

Figure 20.19

The HIDDEN, HIDDEN2, and HIDDENX2 linetypes.

HIDDEN

HIDDEN2

HIDDENX2

Using Global and Entity Linetype Scaling

In the following exercise, you experiment with using the global linetype and entity linetype scale settings. The LTSCALE (global linetype scale) in your current drawing, CHAP20.DWG, scale) is set to 100 and CELTSCALE is set to 1.

Continue to use the drawing CHAP20.

Command: *Choose* Options, Linetypes, Global Linetype Scale	Issues the LTSCALE command
Command: _ltscale New scale factor <100.0000>: **50** (Enter)	Sets Global Linetype Scale factor to 50 and regenerates drawing to display change (see fig. 20.20)
Command: (Enter)	Repeats the LTSCALE command

Command: `_ltscale New scale factor` `<50.0000>:` **`100`** (Enter)	Sets global linetype factor to 100
Command: *Choose* Data, Object Creation	Opens the Object Creation Modes dialog box, showing CELTSCALE (still 1), not LTSCALE, in the Linetype Scale edit box
Click on the Cancel *button*	Exits the Select Linetype dialog box
Command: *Choose* Modify, Properties	
Command: `(ai_propchk)`	
`Select objects:` *Pick the rectangle with the diagonal lines you drew on the* SLUDGE_PIT *layer* `Select objects: 1 found` `Select objects: 1 found` `Select objects: 1 found`	
`Select objects:` (Enter)	Invokes the Change Properties dialog box
Change the Linetype S̲cale *value from* 1.0 *to* 0.5 *and choose* OK	

The linetype of the rectangle changes, but none of the other objects do (see fig. 20.21).

Note The Linetype Scale shown in the Object Creation Modes dialog box is the current entity linetype scale, or CELTSCALE. The value of CELTSCALE also appears in the Modify Objects and Change Properties dialog boxes.

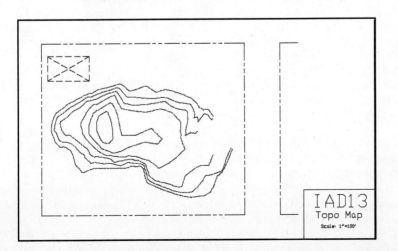

Figure 20.20
Changing the global linetype scale.

Figure 20.21

*Changing the
current entity
linetype scale.*

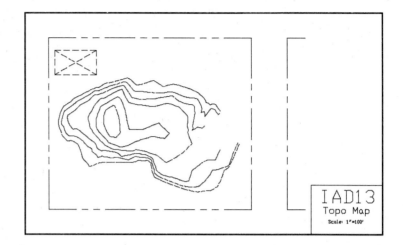

Using Paper Space Linetype Scaling

When paper space was introduced in AutoCAD Release 11, users discovered a problem when their drawings had several differently scaled viewports: linetype scaling observed the model space LTSCALE setting, and a larger-scale view would have a larger-scale linetype.

This is not acceptable in most drafting offices; regardless of view scale, non-continuous lines should have the same spacing throughout the drawing. Release 11 included half-size and double-size versions of all the standard non-continuous linetypes in the ACAD.LIN linetype definition file, but this was not really enough for most users.

Releases 12 and 13 provide a fix to this problem: paper space linetype scaling, controlled by the PSLTSCALE system variable. PSLTSCALE is a toggle. It's set to either 0 (Off) or 1 (on). If it's turned on, AutoCAD will read the scale of the viewport and set the linetype scale to an appropriate value.

The key to using paper space linetype scaling successfully is to understand how to set the LTSCALE system variable. As you've already seen, in model space you set LTSCALE to a value more or less equivalent to the scale at which the drawing will ultimately be plotted. In the case of a 1/4"=1'-0– drawing, you would set LTSCALE to 48.

When you use paper space linetype scaling, you set LTSCALE *as if you were going to draw the non-continuous linetypes in paper space*. In a 1/4"=1'-0– drawing using paper space, your viewport would be scaled to 1/48xp, but you would set the PLOT command to plot at 1:1. You should therefore set LTSCALE to a value of 1. With PSLTSCALE turned on, AutoCAD will check the scale of each viewport and scale the non-continuous linetypes to the same, consistent appearance.

Applying Linetypes to Polylines

When you apply a linetype pattern to an object, AutoCAD begins the pattern generation from the object's start point and continues to the object's next vertex or endpoint—differently than simple objects.

If you look closely at the polylines in your drawing that represent the contour lines, you see that their layer's noncontinuous linetype has not been applied very well. In some parts of the contour lines, where the polylines are smoother, you can see the pattern of the hidden lines; in other parts, the lines appear continuous. Polylines are a special case where noncontinuous linetypes are involved.

A polyline has a start point and an endpoint and, usually, numerous intermediate points (vertices) that help define it. A good example of such a polyline is a contour line on a topographic drawing. Unlike other objects that have a start and endpoint (such as lines and arcs), AutoCAD does not consider the distance between the start and endpoints of a polyline when it determines whether enough space exists for the linetype pattern, but rather, checks the space between each pair of vertices to see whether it can apply the linetype pattern along that portion of the polyline.

So no matter how long a polyline might be, it still might not have enough space for the linetype pattern because of closely spaced vertices. Another polyline might have enough space between adjacent vertices along only one certain portion of its length to accommodate the linetype pattern.

AutoCAD draws linetype patterns from vertex to vertex for all polylines, whether they've been curve-fit or spline-fit or left intact. Figure 20.22 shows the same polyline in its original form at the left, spline fit at the lower right, and curve fit at the upper right. In all three cases, there is not enough space between some of the vertices to draw the linetype properly.

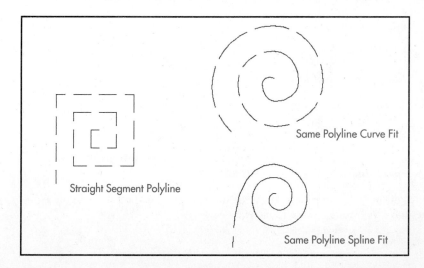

Straight Segment Polyline

Same Polyline Curve Fit

Same Polyline Spline Fit

Figure 20.22

A polyline that is incapable of displaying a noncontinuous linetype.

If the distance between the vertices is not enough for AutoCAD to complete the pattern at least once, AutoCAD draws a continuous line. If conditions ever change so that AutoCAD can draw the linetype, AutoCAD automatically regenerates the object with the assigned linetype.

So, what conditions might change that would allow that? If you set the linetype scale factor to a smaller value, the pattern might be reduced enough to fit between the existing endpoints of the object. Alternatively, increasing the distance between the object's endpoints (lengthen the line) might allow the linetype pattern to fit.

You can force AutoCAD to apply noncontinuous linetypes to polylines in the same way it applies them to lines and other simple entities—that is, from start point to endpoint. You can do this in two ways:

◆ To create new polylines with smoothly-applied noncontinuous linetypes, choose Options, Linetypes, Linetype Generation.

◆ To modify existing polylines that currently do not show smoothly applied noncontinuous linetypes, choose Modify, Properties and switch on LT Gen in the Modify Polyline dialog box.

In the following exercise, you use Modify, Properties to apply a smooth HIDDEN linetype to the contour lines.

Applying Linetype Generation to Existing Polylines

Continue to use the CHAP20 drawing.

Before the noncontinuous linetypes can display properly in the contours lines, you must edit them. You begin by zooming into the drawing so that the contour lines fill most of the screen.

Command: *Choose* Modify, Properties

Command: (ai_propchk)

Select Objects: *Select one of the contour lines*

Select Objects: 1 found

Select Objects: (Enter)   Displays Modify Polyline dialog box

Click the LT Gen *check box to turn it on*   Regenerates polyline with smooth pattern
(see fig. 20.23), then choose OK   (see fig 20.24)

Recall the Modify Polyline dialog box and repeat the steps for the next polyline. Continue until all polylines show their noncontinuous linetypes correctly.

New Riders Publishing
INSIDE
SERIES

One of the contour lines is at a major contour interval, so its linetype should look different to make it stand out. Finish the exercise by recalling the Modify Polyline dialog box and selecting the polyline at ① (see fig. 20.25). In the Linetype Scale edit box, change the value of the Current Entity Linetype Scale to 2.5, then choose OK.

Your drawing should look like figure 20.25.

Save your drawing.

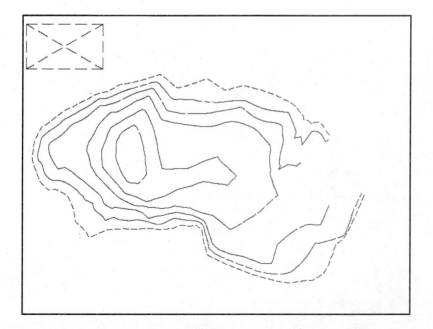

Figure 20.23

The Modify Polyline dialog box.

20

Figure 20.24

The outer polyline using linetype generation.

Figure 20.25

The finished contour lines.

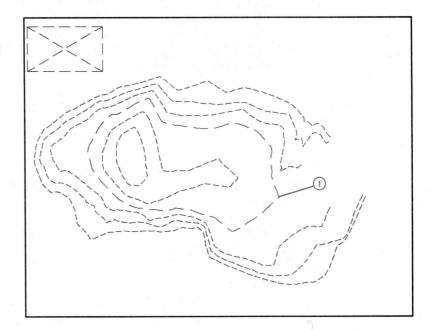

Using ISO Linetypes

ACAD.LIN contains linetype definitions for linetypes that meet ISO standards. The linetypes names all begin with the ISO prefix.

ISO linetypes are used in the same way as the rest of the linetypes defined in the ACAD.LIN file, with one important exception. The standard linetype patterns—B ORDER, DASHED, HIDDEN, and so on, are designed to be used when AutoCAD's base unit represents one inch. The ISO linetypes are designed for use in metric drafting, where the base unit represents one millimeter. For this reason, where an LTSCALE of 1 is suitable for full-size drawing in inches, you must set LTSCALE to 25 (1 inch equals 25.4 millimeters) before you can see the ISO linetype patterns in the same drawing.

This means that using linetypes from both the standard and ISO families in the same drawing is impractical, although you can do so if you use CELTSCALE. In fact, they are not intended to be used side-by-side; rather the ISO set is purpose-designed for metric drafting.

Defining Linetypes

AutoCAD's linetype definitions are supplied in simple ASCII text files. You can use a text editor or the LINETYPE command to modify or create new linetypes.

> **'LINETYPE.** The LINETYPE command has options for loading linetypes, listing the contents of linesetting the current linetype, and creating new linetype definitions. The LINETYPE command is not included in AutoCAD's menus, so you must enter it at the Command: prompt.

The LINETYPE command is the command-line version of the Select Linetype dialog box. LINETYPE, however, has a Create option that the dialog box does not. LINETYPE's Create option enables you to modify an existing linetype definition or create a new definition without using a text editor.

Working with Linetype Files

Because linetype files are just text files, you can use any ASCII text editor to work with them. Every version of MS-DOS comes with an editor called EDIT.COM. (If you use PC-DOS, your version comes with an editor called ED.EXE.) A host of other text editors work equally well.

Stop If you are more comfortable with your word processor than with DOS Edit or any other text editor, it is perfectly all right to use it. Just be careful how you save the files. Word processors insert formatting codes that a DOS editor—or AutoCAD—cannot understand. If you use your favorite word processor, be sure to save the file as an ASCII text file.

The two linetype files supplied with AutoCAD are ACAD.LIN and LTYPESHP.LIN, and are located in the \ACADR13\COMMON\SUPPORT directory. You can modify the linetype definitions in these files or create or add new linetype definitions. If you decide to create your own linetype files, be sure to use the file-name extension of LIN.

In the following sections, you learn how to put together the linetype definitions that go into the linetype files.

Tip A good guide for assembling linetype definitions is the structure of the ACAD.LIN and LTYPESHP.LIN files. Print out the contents of the files and use them as examples. Also, before you make any changes to these files, you should make copies of the originals, in case you need to restore them later.

Defining Simple Linetypes

The simplest linetypes consist of a repeating pattern of dashes, spaces, and/or dots. The basic pattern is recorded in a linetype definition. A linetype definition always consists of two lines of text. The first line begins with an asterisk and is immediately followed by the linetype name and some optional description text:

```
*linetype_name[,linetype description]
```

You can use as many as 31 characters for the linetype name. You can use alphanumeric characters and the $, -, and _ characters for a linetype name. A linetype name cannot have any spaces. You can use as many as 47 characters for the optional description text. The optional description of the linetype appears in the Load area of the Select Linetypes dialog box. The dash, underline, period, space, and other keyboard characters are commonly used to create a pictorial representation of the linetype. As an example, the actual definition of the hidden linetype stored in ACAD.LIN is as follows:

```
*HIDDEN,__ __ __ __ __ __ __ __ __ __ __ __ __ __ __
A,.25,-.125
```

The second line of the definition consists of the character A, immediately followed by a series of numbers that tells AutoCAD how long to make the dashes and spaces. The A is the alignment type, which controls how the linetype pattern begins and ends. Currently, AutoCAD supports only one alignment type, so the second line must always begin with the letter A.

The numbers that follow the alignment type are the default lengths of the dashes and spaces in drawing units. A positive number represents a dash and a negative number represents a space. A zero represents a dot. The preceding hidden linetype definition specifies a linetype that consists of a 0.25 drawing unit-long dash, followed by a 0.125 drawing unit space.

You need only define one instance of the pattern; AutoCAD automatically repeats the pattern. A hidden line is drawn by repeating the basic pattern of a dash and a space, so the definition has only two numbers, one for the dash and one for the space. A linetype definition must always begin with a dash or dot, never a space.

Tip Set the lengths of the dashes and spaces in the linetype definition to be equal to what you want to see on a 1:1 scale plot.

You don't have to use a text editor at all to create a new linetype definition; you can create it "on the fly" with the LINETYPE command's Create option.

Note The LAYER command automatically loads linetypes from the ACAD.LIN file types to layers. If you want to assign linetypes, but do not have them stored in ACAD.LIN, LAYER cannot load them automatically. You must use DDLTYPE to load them first.

In the following exercise, you create your own linetype definition and apply it.

You should place your new linetype file in a support directory where AutoCAD can find it, so that your new linetype file is available whenever you work on the exercises in this book. To keep your AutoCAD installation tidy, be sure to save this IAD.LIN file in your C:\IA directory.

Creating Your First Linetype

Continue to use the drawing CHAP20. Zoom back out to a full view of the drawing.

Command: **LINETYPE** (Enter)	Issues the LINETYPE command
?/Create/Load/Set: **C** (Enter)	Specifies the Create option
Name of linetype to create: **DITCH** (Enter)	Names linetype you want to create
When the Create or Append Linetype File *dialog box appears, change to the* C:\IA *directory, then enter the file name* **IAD** *(see fig. 20.26)*	Creates new linetype file

Descriptive text:

Type three underscore characters, then a space, a period, a space, a period, a space, a third period, and another space. Repeat this pattern one more time, then press Enter. You should end up with something like "___ . . . ___ . . ."

This descriptive text is optional. It does not actually affect the definition.

Enter pattern (on next line):
A,0.25,-0.125,0,-0.125,0,-0.125,0,-0.125 (Enter)

The pattern specified is a 0.25 unit-long dash, followed by a 0.125 unit-long space, a dot, a 0.125 unit-long space, a dot, a 0.125 unit-long space, a dot, and one more 0.125 unit-long space.

New definition written to file.

?/Create/Load/Set: **L** (Enter)	Specifies the Load option
Linetype(s) to load: **DITCH** (Enter)	Invokes the Select Linetype File dialog box

Select the file you just created, C:\IA\IAD.LIN

Linetype DITCH *loaded.*

continues

continued

?/Create/Load/Set: (Enter)

Command: *Choose* Data, Layers	Opens the Layer Control dialog box

Create a new layer DITCH, *apply the*
DITCH *linetype to it and make it current,*
then choose OK

Command: *Draw lines from* 400,840 *to*	Your drawing should look like figure 20.27
1075,840 *and from* 400,830	
to 1075,830	

Save your work.

Figure 20.26

The Create or
Append Linetype
File dialog box.

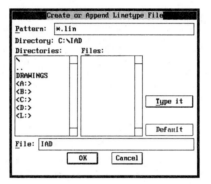

Figure 20.27

A newly created
linetype applied to
drawing objects.

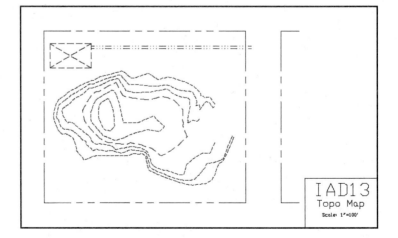

New Riders Publishing
INSIDE
SERIES

Modifying Existing Linetype Definitions

You can modify an existing linetype definition in exactly the same manner as you create new ones. When you enter the name of an existing linetype definition at the LINETYPE command's `Name of linetype to create:` prompt, AutoCAD returns the following:

```
Wait, checking if linetype already defined...

DASHED already exists in this file.  Current definition is:
   *DASHED,__ __ __ __ __ __ __ __ __ __ __ __ __ __ __
   A,0.5,-0.25
Overwrite? <N>
```

If you respond with a Y (for Yes), the LINETYPE command continues to use the same prompts that it uses when you create a new linetype and replaces the existing definition.

You also can modify an existing linetype definition by directly editing it in a linetype file, such as ACAD.LIN, using any ASCII text editor.

In the preceding exercise, you used LINETYPE to create the new linetype pattern and store it in the file IAD.LIN. You can examine or edit the resulting file with a text editor. Remember, you can use any ASCII text editor you are comfortable with to do the work.

Stop Do not attempt to edit a linetype file that is currently open (currently accessed by the Select Linetype File dialog box or LINETYPE Load option). Most text editors do not allow you to do so; however some editors do not protect you from doing so, which can bring about errors or a loss of work.

Defining Linetypes with Shapes

A linetype also can consist of symbols, dashes, spaces, and/or dots (see fig. 20.28).

The symbols you use in linetype definitions must be shape definitions. A shape definition is a little like a block definition, but unlike blocks, you must load shapes into the drawing before you can insert them. You insert a shape similarly to a block, but you use the SHAPE command rather than INSERT. You have to define an insertion point, a height (scale factor), and a rotation angle. Defining a shape, however, is considerably more cumbersome than defining a block. Defining a shape is like defining a text font character, and is beyond the scope of this book. (See New Riders Publishing's *Maximizing AutoCAD* for more on defining shapes.)

Figure 20.28

A linetype with symbols.

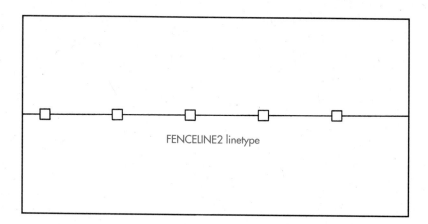

The basic format of the linetype definition you use to include shapes is the same as for simple linetypes, except that is has additional information. For each shape in the pattern, you supply the following:

```
[Shape_name,shape_file_name,S=scale_factor,R=rotation_angle,X=xoffset,Y=yoffset]
```

To define a linetype that has a symbol in it, you use the same basic linetype definition format; for example, the linetype definition for the line shown in figure 20.28 is as follows:

```
*FENCELINE2,----[]-----[]----
A,.25,[BOX,ltypeshp.shx,s=.1],-.2,1
```

You can store multiple shape definitions in one file, much as you can store multiple linetype definitions in one file. You must begin the shape definition with a shape name and the file in which the shape definition is stored. The file name can include a path name.

You also can supply an optional insertion scale factor (S=0.1). If you do not specify one, a scale factor of 1 is the default. The scale factor must have a prefix of *S=*. The shape BOX is a 2 × 2 unit rectangle, so a scale of 0.1 results in a 0.2 × 0.2 unit rectangle.

You also can specify a rotation angle (in decimal degrees). If you do not specify one, a rotation angle of 0 is the default. You can use R= or A= as the prefix for the rotation angle to specify whether the rotation angle is relative or absolute, respectively. *Relative rotation* means that the shape always has the same angular orientation to the line segment. *Absolute rotation* means that the shape is always oriented the same way no matter what the orientation of the line segment. The default rotation is R=0; in other words, the shape is always aligned with the line segment. Figure 20.29 shows the results of changing the rotation angle in the FENCELINE2 linetype.

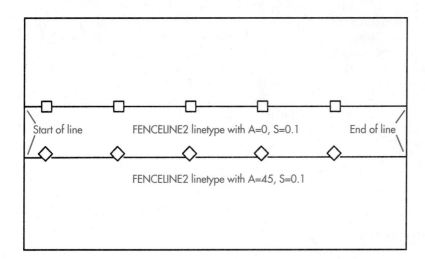

Figure 20.29

The effect of a rotation angle.

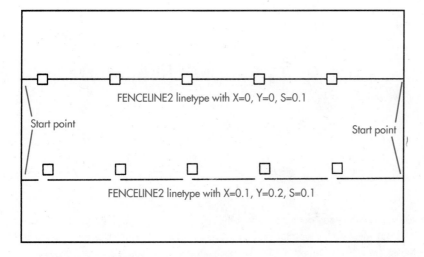

Figure 20.30

The effect of an X and Y offset.

As with blocks, shapes have an insertion point. You normally insert a shape so that the insertion point is on the line itself. You can specify an X and/or Y offset if you want AutoCAD to shift the shape insertion relative to its normal position. The X offset is the offset along the line and the Y offset is the offset perpendicular to the line. See figure 20.30 to see the effect of an X and Y offset.

In the following example linetype, the shape definition is followed by a space (–2 value). This space is very important since, if you omit it, the line portion of your linetype will superimpose itself on the symbol.

```
*FENCELINE2,----[]-----[]----
A,.25,[BOX,ltypeshp.shx,s=.1],-.2,1
```

Imagine yourself holding the pen and drawing the linetype. You first drop the pen onto the paper and draw the 0.25 dash. Then you draw the BOX shape (0.2×0.2 rectangle), after which you return the pen to the insertion point (end of the dash). Now, unless you want to draw the next dash through the BOX shape, you need to lift the pen and move it 0.2 units away from the shape's insertion point. The space specification moves the pen to the other side of the box to begin the next dash. The construction of the shape definition determines where the pen ends up after drawing the shape, but if a shape is designed for linetypes, the pen should return to the insertion point.

AutoCAD includes some sample shape definitions in the file LTYPESHP.SHP and linetype definitions that use them the file LTYPESHP.LIN, both in the directory \ACADR13\COMMON\SUPPORT\ Figure 20.31 shows you how lines created with these sample linetypes appear.

Figure 20.31

Linetypes incorporating shapes in LTYPESHP.LIN.

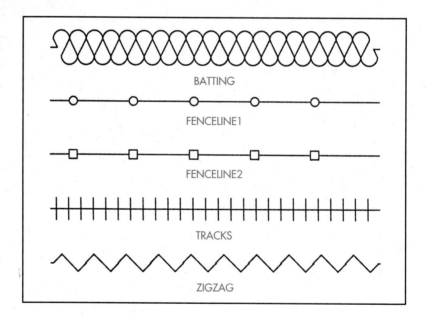

If you work with shape definitions that other people have defined, the simplest way to find out what each shape looks like at a scale factor of 1 and rotation angle of 0 is to use the SHAPE command to insert each shape. By inserting each shape, you also see the position of the insertion point relative to the shape. Before you can use

Tip

New Riders Publishing
INSIDE
SERIES

the SHAPE command, you must use the LOAD command to load the shape file into your drawing. You also can use an ASCII text editor to view the contents of a shape file, because the shape file is just another text file.

In the following exercise, you apply one of the sample linetypes from the file LTYPESHP.LIN.

Using Linetypes with Shapes

Continue to use the drawing CHAP20.

Command: *Choose* Data, Layers   Opens the Layer Control dialog box

Make a new layer named FENCE. Set its linetype to FENCELINE2 from the LTYPESHP.LIN linetype definition file, and make it the current layer.

Draw a polyline from 225,650 to 530,775 to 730,775 to 950,650. Your drawing should look like figure 20.32.

Finish the fence by using Modify, Properties, select the polyline you just drew, then set Linetype Scale to 0.5 and turn on LT Gen (see fig. 20.33) by clicking in its toggle box.

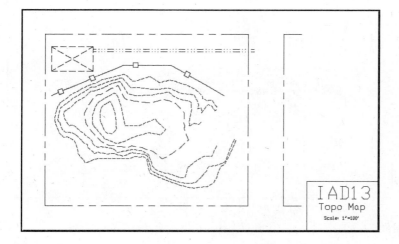

Figure 20.32

Using shapes in linetypes.

20

Figure 20.33

The finished fence line.

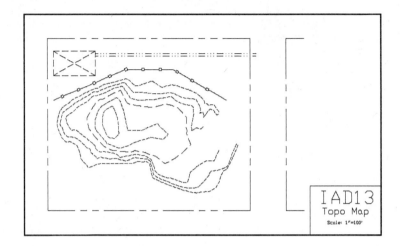

Defining Linetypes with Text

You can incorporate text strings into a linetype definition, as in figure 20.34

Figure 20.34

A linetype with text.

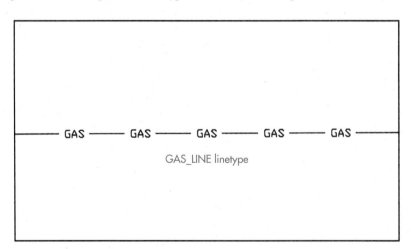

The specification for a text string in a linetype is similar to that for a shape:

```
["string",text style,S=scale_factor, R=rotation_angle, X=x_offset, Y=y_offset]
```

For example, one of the linetypes supplied in the file LTYPESHP.LIN is shown in figure 20.35. Figure 20.35 also shows the difference between relative and absolute rotation. The box at the left has no setting for text rotation, so it defaults to R=0, or the text always relative to and aligned with the line segments. The box at the right has

New Riders Publishing
INSIDE
SERIES

text rotation set to A=45, so no matter what the orientation of the line, the text always is at an absolute angle of 45 degrees.

The definition of the GAS_LINE linetype is as follows:

```
*GAS_LINE,____GAS____GAS____GAS____GAS
A,.5,-.2,["GAS",STANDARD,S=.1,A=0.0,X=-0.1,Y=-.05],-.25
```

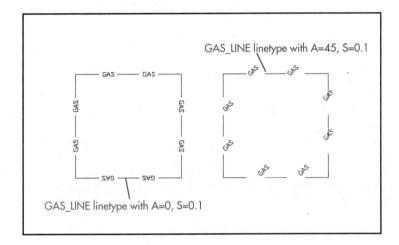

GAS_LINE linetype with A=45, S=0.1

GAS_LINE linetype with A=0, S=0.1

Figure 20.35

The effect of a rotation angle.

You must enclose the text in quotes ("GAS") and you must specify a text style (standard) that exists before you load the linetype.

The scale factor (S=0.1) is really the height of the text and is optional. If you do not specify a text height, the default height is 1 drawing unit. This text height is independent of the text height set in a fixed height text style. You must use the prefix *S=*.

The X and Y offsets (X=–0.1 and Y=–0.05) are optional parameters as well. The X offset is parallel to the direction of the line and the Y offset is perpendicular to the direction of the line. If you do not supply offsets, AutoCAD draws the text such that the text baseline is in line with the rest of the line. Normally, you want the text to be offset in the negative Y direction so that the text is centered within the gap in the line. Figure 20.36 shows you the effects of changing X and Y offsets.

Imagine yourself holding the pen and drawing the linetype. You first put pen to paper and draw the 0.5 dash. You lift the pen and move it 0.2 units. Now you draw the text *GAS* with a height of 0.1 units and offset from the line –0.1 units along the line and –0.05 below the line.

After you draw the word *GAS*, you move the pen back to the beginning of the text string. To avoid drawing a line through the text, you must pick the pen up and move it 0.25 units to the other side of the word *GAS* before you repeat the pattern.

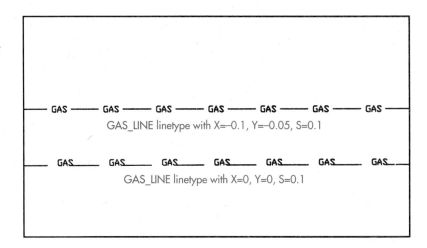

Figure 20.36

The effect of an X and Y offset.

AutoCAD comes with two linetypes that have text defined, in the file **LTYPESHP.LIN** in the directory **\ACADR13\COMMON\SUPPORT** (see fig. 20.37).

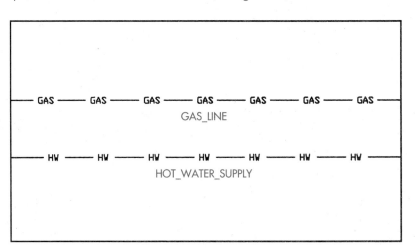

Figure 20.37

Linetypes with text in LTYPESHP.LIN.

In the following exercise, you use one of the linetypes in **LTYPESHP.LIN** that incorporates text.

Using Linetypes with Text

Continue to use the drawing CHAP20. You use a linetype that has text to indicate gas lines on your drawings.

Make a new layer named GAS. Set its linetype to GAS_LINE from the LTYPESHP.LIN linetype definition file, and make it the current layer.

Command: *Choose* Draw, Line *and*   Draws line segments
draw two lines, from 1150,900 *to*
1150,200 *and from* 1150,500 *to* 800,500

The text in the horizontal line reads upside-down, because this linetype is defined so that the text is always aligned with the line, and this line runs from right to left. The easiest way to deal with this is to simply erase the line and redraw it from left to right.

Command: *Erase the last line and draw*   Your drawing should look like figure 20.38
a new line from 800,500 *to* 1150,500

Save your work.

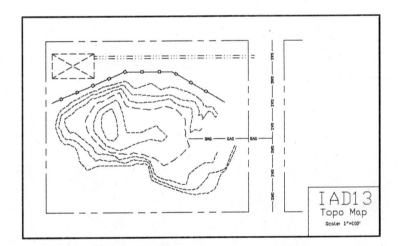

Figure 20.38

Using linetypes that have text.

Looking at Other Forms of Linetypes

You can define linetypes with dashes, spaces, and/or dots; with symbols; and with text. You even can define a linetype that consists of dashes, spaces, dots, text, and shapes in one definition. Designing such a linetype is just a matter of combining the elements of each of the three basic linetype forms into one definition.

You also can design linetypes that do not look like lines. A good example is the BATTING linetype (see fig. 20.39), which is used in architectural drawings to represent insulation in a wall section.

Figure 20.39

The BATTING linetype, which represents insulation section of wall.

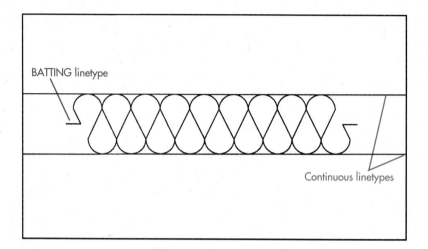

The BATTING linetype definition consists of a very short dash (0.0001 units), the shape itself, and a space. In effect, the linetype is a repetition of a single shape, end to end. Be careful when you use linetypes such as BATTING when it comes to corners and intersections (see fig. 20.40). Linetypes are not "smart" enough to clean up correctly at corners and intersections. You must clean them up. For corners, stop one line at the corner and then continue a new line around the corner. For intersections, break one of the lines at the intersection. Refer to figure 20.41.

Figure 20.40

Examples of a linetype such as BATTING in a corner or an intersection.

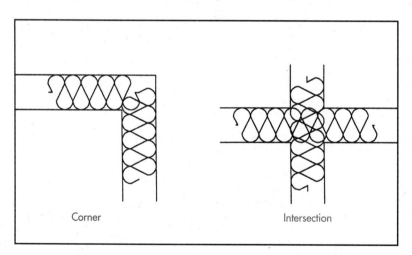

If you ever have to work with drawings created in earlier versions of AutoCAD, you might encounter objects that look like linetypes with shapes and text, but which are, in fact, not linetypes at all. Before Release 13, if you wanted to draw a linetype that

New Riders Publishing
INSIDE
SERIES

incorporated text and/or symbols, you had to draw lines, then place the text or symbols along the lines. These remained separate entities and were difficult to edit, unlike Release 13's single-entity complex linetypes.

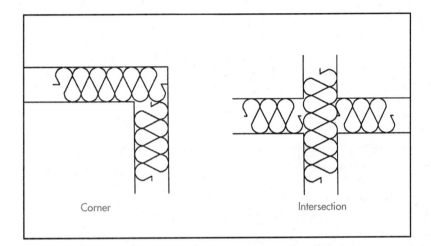

Figure 20.41

BATTING linetype corner and intersection after hands-on cleanup.

Corner

Intersection

20

Working with Hatch Patterns

Hatching enables you to fill a selected area with a pattern. AutoCAD comes with a library that contains over 50 hatch patterns, some of which are shown in figure 20.42.

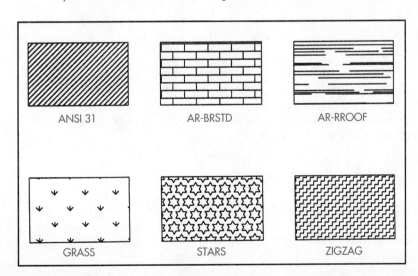

Figure 20.42

Some sample hatch patterns.

ANSI 31

AR-BRSTD

AR-RROOF

GRASS

STARS

ZIGZAG

In AutoCAD Release 13, hatching is associative. Associativity offers the following advantages over hatching in previous releases of AutoCAD:

◆ Hatching changes to accommodate changes in the hatch boundaries

◆ You can set hatch parameters by picking an existing hatch object to copy

◆ You can edit hatch objects and can change their pattern, scale and rotation

You can find illustrations of all available hatch patterns in Appendix C of the *AutoCAD User's Guide.*

The command you use to apply hatch patterns is the BHATCH command.

BHATCH. The BHATCH command enables you to draw a hatch pattern in a selected area.
Pull-down: *Choose* Draw, Hatch, Hatch
Screen: *Choose* CONSTRCT, Bhatch:

In this section, you learn how to use BHATCH to apply a hatch pattern to an area.

You typically follow these steps when you draw a hatch pattern:

1. Define the area you want to hatch.

2. Choose the pattern you want to apply.

3. Apply the pattern.

Note   The command-line version of BHATCH is –BHATCH. –BHATCH is useful for programmers who want to incorporate hatching into their routines. An obsolete and less-capable hatching command named HATCH is included in Release 13 for compatibility, but it lacks many of the features of BHATCH, primarily, associativity. HATCH is covered later in this chapter.

Setting the Current Properties

You draw a hatch, as you do most objects, on the current layer with the current color and linetype. If the current color is set to BYLAYER, the hatch pattern takes on the color of the layer on which it is drawn. If the current color is set to a specific color, the hatch pattern takes on that color, regardless of the layer on which it is drawn. The same is true regarding the current linetype.

New Riders Publishing
INSIDE
SERIES

Tip Hatching can clutter up a drawing very quickly, so you generally want the capability to turn hatching off and on. To control hatch visibility by layer, dedicate one or more layers on which to draw your hatches.

Defining Simple Areas To Be Hatched

You always apply a hatch pattern to an area delineated by one or more objects. In the simplest case, the area is delineated by a single closed object, such as a circle or closed polyline. An area also can be delineated by a series of objects that intersect, such as a series of lines and arcs, as long as the area is closed.

The objects that form the boundary are referred to as *boundary objects*. You can select boundary objects in two ways. You can select the objects themselves, or you can simply pick a point inside the area you want to hatch, and AutoCAD finds the boundaries for you. The following brief exercise shows you how these options work.

Selecting Hatch Boundaries

Continue to use drawing CHAP20.

Make a new layer named GATEHOUSE. Leave its linetype as CONTINUOUS and make it the current layer.

`Command:` *Choose* Draw, Polygon, Rectangle *and draw a rectangle from* 970,670 *to* 1035,715	Draws a rectangle

Make a new layer named HATCH. Leave its linetype as CONTINUOUS and make it current.

`Command:` *Choose* Draw, Hatch, Hatch	Opens the Boundary Hatch dialog box

`Command: _bhatch`

Leave the Pattern Type *as is, but change the* Scale *value to* 50 *(see fig. 20.43)*

Choose Pick Points	Clears the Boundary Hatch dialog from screen

`Select objects:`

`Select internal point:` *Pick a point inside the rectangle you just drew*

continues

continued

```
Selecting everything visible...
Analyzing the selected data...
Analyzing internal islands...

Select internal point: Enter
```

Click on Apply   Fills the shape with hatching and terminates command

Your screen should look like figure 20.44.

Figure 20.43

Setting Pattern Scale in the Boundary Hatch dialog box.

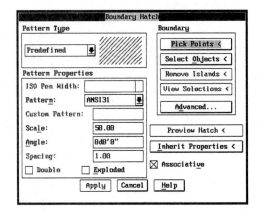

Figure 20.44

Boundary hatching a simple area.

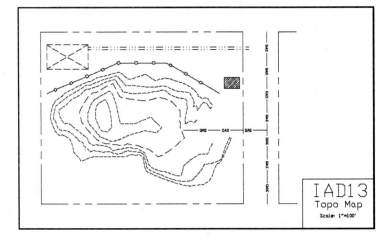

Note   When you use the <u>P</u>ick Points button, you must pick a point within the area you want to hatch. BHATCH then applies the BOUNDARY command (see Chapter 11, "Drawing and Editing Polylines and Splines") to define a closed boundary that surrounds the point you select.

Selecting and Applying the Hatch Pattern

After you define the area you want to hatch, you must define the pattern you want to apply. Defining a pattern involves choosing the pattern and then the parameters that control its generation.

You can choose from three types of patterns, described in the following list:

◆ **Predefined.** This category refers to the patterns defined in the file ACAD.PAT (the hatch pattern file supplied with AutoCAD). See figure 20.42 for some samples.

◆ **User defined.** This category refers to patterns you can define using the BHATCH command. These patterns consist of one or two sets of parallel lines. You can choose the angle and spacing of the lines in the first set, and you also can choose to have a second set of lines generated perpendicular to the first set. The second set of lines have the same spacing as the first set of lines.

◆ **Custom.** This category refers to hatch patterns that are defined in a file other than ACAD.PAT (the default hatch pattern file). This option is discussed in greater detail in the section "Defining New Hatch Patterns."

After you select the hatch pattern, you need to set the parameters that control the pattern generation. For a predefined pattern, the parameters are scale and angle.

When you set the scale to 1 (default), AutoCAD generates the pattern with the exact distances you specify in the definition. If the scale factor is greater than 1, AutoCAD enlarges the lengths proportionately. If the scale factor is less than 1, AutoCAD reduces the lengths proportionately. The effect is similar to that of LTSCALE on linetypes.

The angle affects the rotation of the pattern. The default value of 0 results in no rotation of the pattern; any other angle value results in a corresponding rotation of the pattern.

Tip   The hatch patterns that AutoCAD supplies are designed to use with the continuous linetype. You can generate variations of the basic patterns, however, by using other linetypes and varying linetype scales.

The parameters that define a user-defined pattern are angle, spacing, and whether to use double-hatching.

A user-defined pattern consists of one or two sets of parallel lines. The following parameters determine the appearance of a user-defined pattern:

◆ The <u>A</u>ngle value (default 0) defines the angle of the lines or, when <u>D</u>ouble is set, the angle of the first set of lines.

◆ The <u>S</u>pacing value (default 1 unit) defines the distance between the parallel lines.

◆ The <u>D</u>ouble option tells AutoCAD to generate a second set of parallel lines perpendicular to the first set (see fig. 20.45).

Figure 20.45

Two user-defined hatch patterns.

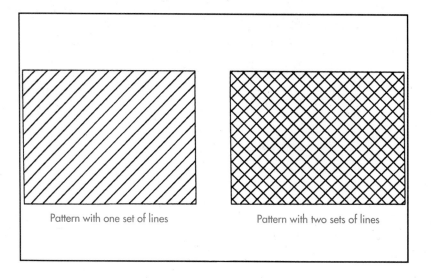

Pattern with one set of lines   Pattern with two sets of lines

Tip You can use a user-defined pattern that has a tight line spacing to hatch an area to make it appear to be a solid filled area. Although this is a valid use of hatching, be careful. Such a tight hatch pattern usually takes up a substantial amount of storage space in the drawing file. Using solids or wide polylines to fill an area is much more efficient than using a tight hatch pattern.

When you set the parameters for a pattern type, you can choose the Preview Hatch button to view the resulting pattern without actually drawing the pattern. If you like the pattern, draw it by choosing the Apply button. If you do not like it, go back and change the parameters, or the pattern type itself, and preview it again. Continue to fine-tune the pattern until you like it, then apply it.

New Riders Publishing
INSIDE
SERIES

Sometimes you might want to match a pattern that already exists in the drawing. A quick way to set your BHATCH pattern parameters to match an existing hatch is to choose the Inherit Properties button. You select the hatch you want to duplicate, and the pattern parameters in BHATCH are set to reproduce that hatch.

If you run into trouble or decide to abandon the hatching operation, click on the Cancel button or press Esc to exit BHATCH.

 Note Sometimes you inadvertently use a scale factor that results in a very dense hatch pattern. When you do, the Preview (and Apply) operation can take quite a while to complete. Wait several seconds, even minutes, before you decide your system has locked up. If you can see any flicker of motion in the area being hatched, BHATCH is still at work. Similarly, if you use too large a scale, you might think BHATCH is failing to hatch the objects, because the hatched area fails to intersect any lines in the pattern.

To avoid such situations, set the initial value of the pattern scale equal to the inverse of the plot scale (just as with LTSCALE). Then you can adjust the scale to get pattern you want.

Understanding ISO Hatch Patterns

Included in ACAD.PAT are a set of patterns that conform to the ISO standards. The names of these patterns have an ISO prefix. Should you select any of these patterns, you enable the ISO Pen Width option in the Boundary Hatch dialog box. When you choose a particular pen width for the pattern, the Scale option automatically is set equal to the pen width. You can change the scale after you set the pen width.

Defining Complicated Areas To Be Hatched

Now that you know how to hatch a simple area, you are ready to learn to deal with more complicated areas. Quite often, you want to hatch an area but leave subareas within the overall area unhatched, or hatch them with a different pattern (see fig. 20.46).

The subareas within the overall area are called *islands*. As with the overall hatch area, an island must be a closed area. The BHATCH command treats text and mtext objects as islands, which ensures that text within a hatch area is not hatched over.

Defining islands is easy. If you use the Select Objects button to define the area to be hatched, all you have to do is to select the objects that define the boundaries of the islands. For text or mtext objects, just selecting them is sufficient.

Figure 20.46

*Complex area
with islands.*

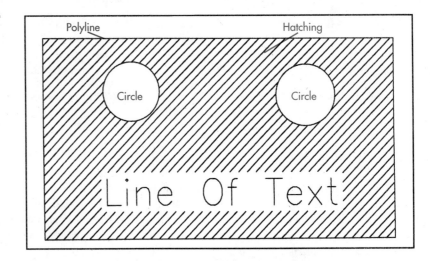

If you use the **P**ick Points button to define your areas, the islands automatically are
defined as found. Sometimes this method finds islands that you don't want BHATCH
to consider. In such cases, use the **R**emove Islands button to remove them from
consideration. Be careful when you pick the point(s) used to define the boundary
area and islands. The point(s) should be external to the islands you want BHATCH to
consider, but internal to the overall hatch area. For example, a pick point outside of
the circles but within the overall polyline would result in a hatch like that shown in
figure 20.46.

In the following exercise, you hatch an area that contains islands. You begin by
drawing a new feature—a tank pen—on the site plan.

Hatching with Islands

Continue to use the CHAP20 drawing.

Make a new layer named TANK_PEN. Leave its linetype as CONTINUOUS and make it the
current layer.

Zoom in on the lower-left area of the site (see fig. 20.47)

Command: *Choose* Draw, Polygon Rectangle *and draw a rectangle from* 230,230 *to* 520,350	Draws a rectangle
Command: *Draw three circles of radius* 30 *and centers at* 450,270; 370,270 *and* 290,270	Draws circles for tanks

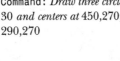

New Riders Publishing
INSIDE
SERIES

Place a text label inside the tank pen area.

Command: *Choose* Draw, Text, Dynamic Text	Issues DTEXT command
Command: _dtext Justify/Style/<Start point>: **315,315** (Enter)	Sets start point for text
Height <12.50>: **15** (Enter)	Your default text may be different
Rotation angle <0d0'0">: (Enter)	
Text: **TANK PEN** (Enter)	
Text: (Enter)	Places text in drawing

Your drawing should look like figure 20.47. After all that drawing, the hatching is the easy part!

Command: *Make the* HATCH *layer current*	
Command: *Choose* Draw, Hatch, Hatch	Opens the Boundary Hatch dialog box
Click in the Pattern: *edit box. Scroll down the list and choose* NET. *Leave* Scale *at* 50 *but change* Angle *to* 45	Opens Pattern pop-up list
Command: *Choose* Pick Points	Clears the Boundary Hatch dialog box from screen
Select internal point: *Pick a point at* ① *in fig. 20.47*	
Selecting everything visible... Analyzing the selected data... Analyzing internal islands...	
Select internal point: (Enter)	Ends boundary object selection; Boundary Hatch dialog box reappears
Choose Preview Hatch	Previews hatch pattern
Choose Continue, Apply	Applies hatch pattern to area

Your drawing should look like figure 20.48.

Figure 20.47

Tank pen before hatching.

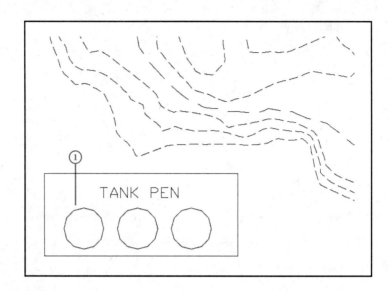

Figure 20.48

Tank pen after boundary hatching.

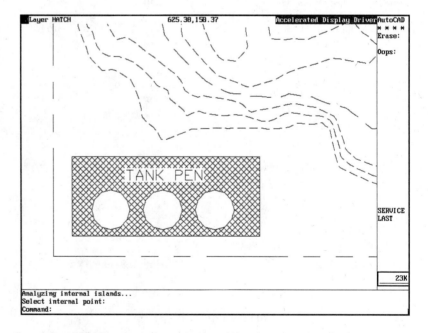

Editing Hatches

Using the HATCH Command

The HATCH command is a less sophisticated version of the BHATCH command.

> **HATCH.** The HATCH command enables you to draw a hatch pattern in a selected area. HATCH is not available from any of the menus, so you must enter it at the `Command:` prompt.

The HATCH command was the command-line predecessor of the BHATCH command. For Release 13, it has a new option that enables you to define the area to be hatched by picking points that outline the boundary. This option (not available with BHATCH) enables you to hatch an area without first having to draw objects to delineate the area.

You are first prompted for the name of the pattern to apply, and its scale and rotation angle. After you supply these answers, the following prompt appears:

```
Select hatch boundaries or RETURN for direct hatch option,
```

Here you can select the objects that make up the hatch boundary or press Enter for the direct hatch option. If you select the direct hatch option, you see the following prompt:

```
Retain polyline? <N>
```

If you answer Yes, the polyline generated to delineate the areas to be hatched is not erased after the hatch is generated. The default answer of No results in the polyline being removed at the end of the command.

Finally, the next prompt appears:

```
From point:
```

Now you pick the beginning point of the hatch boundary, after which you see the following options:

◆ **Arc.** The Arc option enables you to define an arc as part of the boundary. After you specify this option, you have several options to define the arc. The arc options are similar to the options for the ARC command. To exit the arc option, you need to select Close or Line.

◆ **Close.** This option closes the boundary and returns you to the previous prompt. You want to always end your boundary definition with the Close option to ensure a closed boundary.

◆ **Length.** This option draws a line of a length that is tangent to the previous line or arc segment.

◆ **Undo.** This option undoes the last segment.

◆ **Next point.** The default option is to pick the next point that defines the boundary.

After AutoCAD generates the boundary, you see the following prompt:

```
From point or RETURN to apply hatch:
```

You can define another boundary (an island perhaps) or press Enter to generate the hatch and end the command.

 Stop One major drawback of the HATCH command is that it always generates nonassociative hatches, meaning that hatches generated using HATCH do not work with HATCHEDIT, nor do they update automatically when you edit the boundary objects.

In the next exercise, you use the HATCH command's Direct option to create a little grassy area just above the tank pen.

Using HATCH To Create a Grassy Area

Continue to use the CHAP20 drawing. Make sure that the HATCH layer is current.

Command: **HATCH** (Enter)	Issues the HATCH command
Pattern (? or name/U,style) <NET>: **GRASS**	Specifies pattern name of GRASS
Scale for pattern <50.0000>: **25**	Specifies new pattern scale
Angle for pattern <45d0'0">: **0** (Enter)	
Select hatch boundaries or RETURN *for direct hatch option,*	
Select objects:	Specifies Direct option
Retain polyline? <n>	

From point: **220,380**	Pick first point for hatch area
Arc/Close/Length/Undo/<Next point>: **220,470**	Specifies second point for hatch area
Continue drawing the hatch area to 240,490 to 270,440 to 300,440 to 330,380 and then enter C to finish drawing the boundary	Finishes drawing area for hatch
From point or RETURN to apply hatch:	Applies hatch and erases boundary

Your drawing should look like figure 20.49.

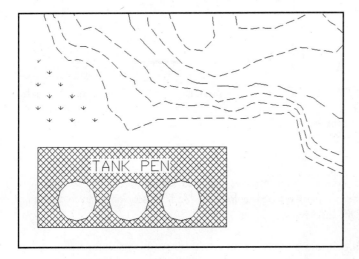

Figure 20.49

Using the HATCH command's Direct option.

Editing Associative Hatches

By default, the patterns that you generate using the BHATCH command are associative patterns. The major advantage of associative hatches over nonassociative hatches is the ease with which you can edit them.

HATCHEDIT. The HATCHEDIT command enables you to edit an existing associative hatch.
Pull-down: *Choose* Modify, Edit Hatch
Screen: *Choose* MODIFY, HatchEd:

The Hatchedit dialog box is the same as the Boundary Hatch dialog box, except for the Advanced button, all of the boundary options are disabled. Of Hatchedit's advanced options, the only item you can change is the hatch style (that is, Normal, Outer, or Ignore). The main Hatchedit dialog box is shown in figure 20.50.

Figure 20.50

The Hatchedit dialog box.

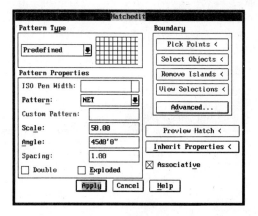

After you select the hatch you want to edit, you can change the pattern type, the parameters that control the pattern, the hatch style (Advanced button), and you can even explode the hatch or make it nonassociative. If you make a hatch nonassociative, you cannot use HATCHEDIT to edit it.

Tip You also can edit other properties of a hatch object with DDMODIFY, and you can access the Hatchedit dialog box from the Modify Associative Hatch dialog box that DDMODIFY displays.

If you use any edit command to change the boundary objects of an associative hatch, the hatch automatically regenerates to fit the modified boundary. If the boundary modification results in an open boundary, then you cannot update the hatch, nor make it nonassociative. An example of such a boundary change would be to make a break in a circle that was hatched. The associativity of a hatch also is removed if you remove any boundary objects or islands that were used to generate the original hatch. An associative hatch is updated if it is on a layer that is turned off or frozen; however, if it is on a layer that is locked, it will be updated. If the hatch is not associative, the hatch is not adjusted to fit the changed boundary objects.

When you select hatches for editing commands, the system variable PICKSTYLE plays a very important role. PICKSTYLE has four potential settings, as follows:

| 0 | No group or associative hatch selections |
| 1 | Group selection enabled |

2	Associative hatch selection enabled
3	Group and associative hatch selections enabled

The default for PICKSTYLE is 3, which means that when you select a hatch, you also select the boundary objects associated with that hatch—sometimes leading to unwanted results. For example, if you select a hatch you want to erase, but you left PICKSTYLE set at 3, not only do you erase the hatch, but you erase all associated boundary objects. To avoid this sort of calamity, set PICKSTYLE to 0 or 1. PICKSTYLE is not on the menu, so to set it, you need to enter it at the Command: prompt.

Selecting boundary objects without also selecting the hatch pattern can be tricky. Window selections work well. Grips are a very good way to edit the boundary objects of a hatch. A hatch is a special type of block and therefore has a single grip point (unless you have grips in blocks enabled). This point is the insertion point of the hatch, which is always 0,0, no matter where the hatch actually resides on the drawing. If the view of the drawing in your window does not show the point 0,0, you will never see the grip point. If you have PICKSTYLE set to 2 or 3, selecting a hatch results in the grip points of the boundary objects appearing as well. If you edit the boundary objects that have grips, AutoCAD updates the associated hatch to reflect the changed boundaries.

In the following exercise, you use the HATCHEDIT commands options to modify the hatching in the tank pen.

Editing Hatches and Their Boundaries

The size of the tank pen can be reduced and the hatching in the tank pen area is too dense. Begin by modifying the area of the pen.

Command: **PICKSTYLE**   Accesses the PICKSTYLE system variable

New value for PICKSTYLE <1>:   Sets the PICKTYLE variable to 1

Stretch the top edge of the tank pen 10 units toward the bottom of the pen. The hatch automatically updates.

Command: *Choose* Modify, Properties,
select the text, and change its height to 12

Again, the hatch automatically updates (see fig. 20.51).

The hatch pattern looks too dense for this area. Use HATCHEDIT to modify the pattern, scale, and rotation.

continues

continued

Command: *Choose* Modify, Edit Hatch *and pick the tank pen hatch*	Invokes the Hatchedit dialog box
Click the down arrow in the Patter**n** *edit box, scroll up the list and choose* DOTS. *Change the* Sca**l**e *to* 100, *the* **A**ngle *to* 0, *and click on* Apply	Resets pattern, scale, and angle of existing hatch (see fig. 20.52)

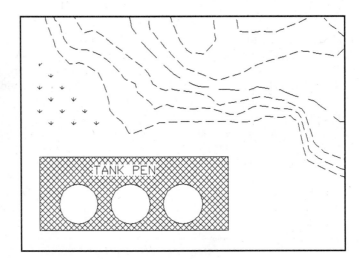

Figure 20.51

Associative hatching automatically updates.

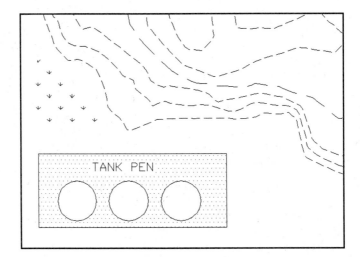

Figure 20.52

Associative hatching after HATCHEDIT.

Exploding Hatches

A hatch is a special type of block known as an anonymous block. Because a hatch is a block, no matter how complicated the hatching, each generated hatch is a single object. A single object is much easier to select to edit. You can, however, have the hatch generated in an exploded form (as individual lines) by enabling the xploded option in the Boundary Hatch dialog box.

In an exploded form, a hatch is not a single object but a collection of lines or dots that form the pattern. When you edit using an exploded hatch, you gain some editing flexibility within the hatched area. You can, for example, clear a portion of a hatched area by erasing the entities in the area.

However, this increase in flexibility is offset by what you lose. An exploded hatch is not an associative hatch. Should you edit the boundary objects of the hatch, AutoCAD cannot automatically adjust the hatch to fit the new boundaries. You must erase the old hatch and use the BHATCH command to regenerate the hatch.

You also can use the EXPLODE command to explode an associative hatch after it has been drawn. The EXPLODE command is covered in more detail in Chapter 16, "Basic Building Blocks for Repetitive Drawing."

Tip   The bottom line is that you lose more than you gain by generating an exploded hatch or by exploding an existing hatch. After you explode a hatch, you can undo the action only by using the UNDO command. You are much better off working with associative hatches.

Controlling Hatch Boundaries and Style

If you choose the Advanced Options button in the Boundary Hatch dialog box, the Advanced Options dialog box appears (see fig. 20.53).

Normally, you do not need to change any of the settings in the Advanced Options dialog box to draw hatches. Understanding the options, however, gives you more control over the hatching process. The first option is Object Type, which is active only if the option Retain Boundaries is enabled (near the bottom of the dialog box). When you create a hatch, BHATCH creates temporary polylines that delineate the area to hatch and any islands within the area. These temporary polylines are erased by default after the hatch is drawn. You can retain them, however, by enabling the Retain Boundaries option. Furthermore, you can retain them as polylines or as regions (see Chapter 12, "Drawing with Complex Objects," for more information on regions).

Figure 20.53

The Advanced Options dialog box.

You also can define the boundary set that BHATCH uses. The *boundary set* is the set of all objects that BHATCH examines when you use the Pick Points option to define the area to be hatched. Initially, the boundary set is every object in the current viewport. If you have a very crowded drawing, that boundary set might be so large that it significantly slows down the BHATCH command. If so, choose the Make New Boundary Set button to explicitly select the objects to consider as you define the area to be hatched. If you choose to select another area to be hatched after already selecting one area to be hatched, the default boundary set is the Existing Boundary Set, the most recently used boundary set. You can use the Make New Boundary Set button to select a new boundary set.

Tip Normally you do not need to define your own boundary set. The default, every object visible in the current viewport, usually is satisfactory.

The Style option controls how BHATCH treats islands within islands, within the overall hatch area. The default style is Normal. The Normal style results in alternating areas being hatched, as shown in figure 20.54.

Figure 20.54

Hatching a complex area with normal style.

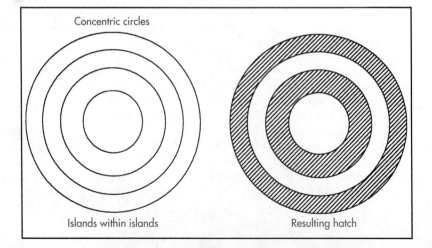

You also can choose the Outermost style. The Outermost style results in the outermost area, the area between the two outermost boundaries, being hatched (see fig. 20.55).

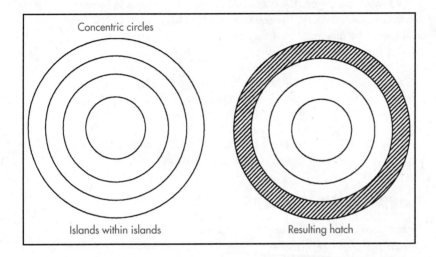

Figure 20.55

Hatching a complex area using outermost style.

The last style is the Ignore style, which results in the islands being ignored and the overall area being completely hatched, as shown in figure 20.56.

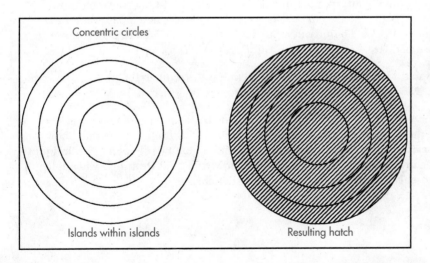

Figure 20.56

Hatching a complex area with the Ignore style.

Tip Instead of changing the style, use the Remove Islands option to remove any islands you don't want considered. The equivalent of the Ignore style is to remove all islands within the overall boundary. The equivalent of the Outermost style is to remove all islands except the outermost boundary and the next boundary in.

The Ray Casting option is enabled only if the Island Detection option is disabled. *Ray casting* refers to the method used for finding a boundary when the Pick Points option is used to define the overall hatch area. A line is projected from the pick point until a boundary object is encountered, then the algorithm follows the boundary object in a counterclockwise direction until it finds another boundary object or ends up at the starting point. If the algorithm can trace a boundary to the starting point, it has successfully defined a hatch area. If not, you get an error message.

Defining New Hatch Patterns

Even with a library of over 50 predefined hatch patterns, you might find yourself needing additional patterns. AutoCAD does enable you to define your own hatch patterns. You can add to the ACAD.PAT file or define a new hatch pattern in its own PAT file (the Custom pattern type). In theory, hatch patterns are easy to create because each pattern is only a collection of sets of parallel lines or dots. In practice, defining a new hatch pattern often proves complicated and time-consuming. You would be much better advised to purchase one of the many hatch pattern libraries commercially available. To find out more about available products, check with your dealer, *The AutoCAD Resource Guide*, or Autodesk's ACAD forum on CompuServe.

If you want to find out more about how to define your own hatch patterns, *Maximizing AutoCAD* by New Riders Publishing, is a good source of information.

This chapter covered much ground. You learned about simple and complex linetypes: how to use them, how to create them, and how to modify them. You learned how to create associative and nonassociative hatches. In the next two chapters, "Techniques for Architectural Drafting" and "Techniques for Mechanical Drafting," you apply some of those techniques and others from earlier chapters.

Part V

Dimensioning

New Riders Publishing
INSIDE SERIES

C H A P T E R

21

Introduction to Dimensioning

To communicate a design, a drawing must convey more than mere graphic entities and text. Many drawings require additional annotations in the form of dimensions to show what lengths, angles, diameters, and sizes are required to construct the design. The necessary dimensions often are more important than the graphic entities themselves. For example, an object not drawn to scale might not affect the project if the dimensions are correct, but if a dimension is incorrect, you can end up with delays and additional costs to the production of the design.

You must, therefore, have accurate dimensions in your drawings. AutoCAD's dimensioning environment is dynamic. As you place dimensions, AutoCAD reads the size of the object or the distance between points and automatically places that size or distance as the text component of the dimension. This feature forces you to construct accurate drawings before you place your dimensions.

In this chapter, you learn the following about dimensions and dimensioning in your AutoCAD drawings:

◆ How associative dimensions work

◆ The components of associative dimensions

◆ How to control the size of dimension components

◆ The different types of AutoCAD dimensions

◆ How to place leaders and notes in your drawings

◆ How to dimension in paper space

Understanding Associative Dimensions

The key to working successfully with AutoCAD's dimensioning abilities is an understanding of *associative dimensions*. Associative dimensions have three important attributes that give you a great deal of control and flexibility over the appearance of your dimensions. These attributes are as follows:

◆ **Associative dimensions are single entities.** If you have to erase a dimension, or select it for some other purpose, you only have to pick once, anywhere on the dimension to select it.

◆ **Associative dimensions are linked to the geometry they describe.** If you modify an object with an associative dimension, AutoCAD sees the change and puts the new value in the dimension text.

◆ **Associative dimensions are governed by dimension variables.** Groups of dimension variable settings can be stored as dimension styles. If you notice your dimension text is too small, or you want to change its color so it will plot with a different pen, you simply adjust the variable or modify the dimension style. Then all dimensions created with that style are automatically updated.

You create dimensions that are non-associative by turning off the system variable DIMASO; you change associative dimensions to non-associative ones by using AutoCAD's EXPLODE command—although you cannot do the reverse.

Non-associative dimensions differ from associative dimensions in the following ways:

◆ **Non-associative entities are made up of separate entities.** A non-associative linear dimension, for example, is made up of eight or nine components: two definition points, two extension lines, one or two dimension lines, two arrowheads, and a text string. If you want to erase them, you have to carefully find each component individually and select it.

◆ **Non-associative dimensions are not linked in any way to the geometry from which they were created.** If you modify an object with non-associative dimensions, the dimension does not show the new value. Figure 21.1 shows the effect of stretching associative and non-associative dimensions.

New Riders Publishing
INSIDE SERIES

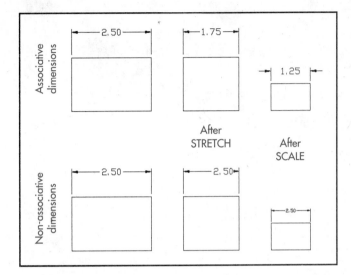

Figure 21.1

The effects of stretching and scaling dimensions.

◆ **Non-associative dimensions are not governed by dimension variables or dimension styles after they've been placed in the drawing.** If you need to change the size of your arrowheads, you have to go around your drawing, dimension by dimension, and replace each arrowhead individually. Figure 21.1 shows the effect of scaling non-associative dimensions. Each dimension component—including the text that is now incorrect—has been scaled just like the object it dimensions.

In spite of the seeming superiority of associative over non-associative dimensions, some users prefer to use non-associative dimensions, as they perceive them to be easier to edit than associative dimensions. Using associative dimensions in AutoCAD can be complex. You are liable to find the dimensioning environment very frustrating if you don't understand the factors that control the way dimensions work. After you work through this chapter, you should feel much more in control of the dynamic dimensioning features available in AutoCAD.

Given that the majority of dimensions in most drafting disciplines are linear, the command you will probably use the most to place dimensions is DIMLINEAR. The next most common type of dimension is a radius dimension; the DIMRADIUS command lets you place radius dimensions on arcs or circles. The following exercise helps you get started with dimensioning. In the exercise, you will place horizontal, vertical, and radius dimensions on a drawing.

Quick 5¢ Tour

Begin a new drawing called CHAP21 using the DIM1 drawing from the IA Disk as your prototype.

First, use DIMLINEAR to place a vertical dimension.

Command: *Choose* Draw, Dimensioning, Linear	Issues the DIMLINEAR command
Command: _dimlinear First extension line origin or RETURN to select: Enter	
Select object to dimension: *Pick* *arc at* ① *(see fig. 21.2)*	Specifies object to dimension
Dimension line location (Text/Angle/ Horizontal/Vertical/Rotated): *Pick* ②	Locates dimension line and text

Now place a horizontal dimension for the overall length of the part.

Command: Enter	Reissues DIMLINEAR command
DIMLINEAR	
First extension line origin or RETURN to select: *Use QUAdrant* *object snap to pick arc at* ③	Sets extension line origin
Second extension line origin: *Use* *QUAdrant object snap to pick arc* *at* ④	Specifies second extension line origin
Dimension line location (Text/Angle/ Horizontal/Vertical/Rotated): *Pick* ⑤	Sets dimension line location

Next place a radius dimension.

Command: *Choose* Draw, Dimensioning, Radial, Radius	Issues the DIMRADIUS command
_dimradius Select arc or circle: *Pick the arc* *at* ① *(see fig. 21.3)*	Selects object to dimension

New Riders Publishing
INSIDE
SERIES

```
Dimension line location          Locates arrowhead for radius dimension
(Text/Angle): Pick ②
```

Save your drawing.

As you can see, placing linear and radius dimensions is very easy.

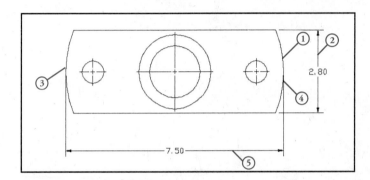

Figure 21.2

Placing linear dimensions.

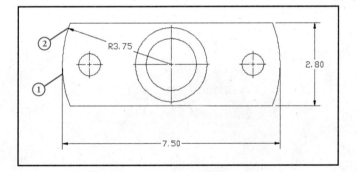

Figure 21.3

Placing a radius dimension.

 Note When you use the DIMLINEAR command to place linear dimensions, you do not have to specify whether you want a vertical or horizontal dimension, owing to the new inference dimensioning feature in Release 13. AutoCAD automatically infers the appropriate dimension command according to the direction you drag your cursor from the object you are dimensioning. This new technique makes dimensioning in AutoCAD faster and more efficient.

The DIM Mode and Equivalent Commands

When you enter **DIM** at the Command: prompt, AutoCAD enters the old (Release 12 and prior) dimensioning mode, which enables you to use the dimension subcommands from earlier releases of AutoCAD. In Release 13, the dimensioning commands are mainstreamed with all other commands and can be entered at the Command: prompt. Now you don't have to enter a "dim mode" before you can issue dimension commands.

The DIM command is still available in Release 13, but only to maintain compatibility with Release 12. The following is a list of dimension commands used in the DIM mode and their Release 13 equivalents:

DIM Mode Command	Release 13 Command
ALIGNED	DIMALIGNED
ANGULAR	DIMANGULAR
BASELINE	DIMBASELINE
CENTER	DIMCENTER
CONTINUE	DIMCONTINUE
DIAMETER	DIMDIAMETER
HORIZONTAL	DIMLINEAR Horizontal
LEADER	LEADER
ORDINATE	DIMORDINATE
RADIUS	DIMRADIUS
ROTATED	DIMROTATE
VARIABLES	DIMSTYLE Variables
VERTICAL	DIMLINEAR Vertical

Exploring the Release 13 Dimensioning Environment

The Release 13 dimensioning commands are accessed through the pull-down menus, as shown in figure 21.4. Most of these commands are covered in this chapter. The rest are covered in the next three chapters.

Placing dimensions in AutoCAD can be quick and easy. AutoCAD takes as much work as it can out of dimensioning by automatically calculating distances based on the size of the objects you select. Style settings control the sizing of the various parts of the dimensions, such as arrowheads, extension lines, and dimension text, by keeping all

New Riders Publishing INSIDE SERIES

the dimensions in a drawing consistent. After you select where you want to place a dimension, AutoCAD automatically creates all the dimension parts. If you compare this process to board drafting, whereby you must draw every part of every dimension, you begin to see the real power of using AutoCAD to create your drawings.

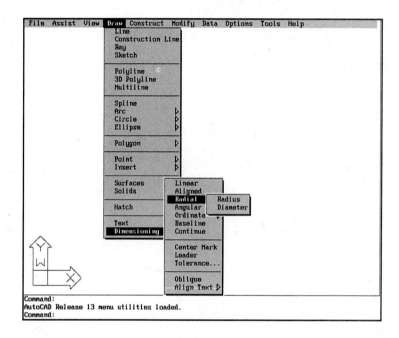

Figure 21.4

Selecting a dimensioning command from the pull-down menu.

21

Tip

Quick and accurate dimensioning relies more on drawing technique than on dimensioning. The accuracy of the objects in your drawing controls the accuracy of the drawing's dimensions because AutoCAD calculates dimensions based on the points you specify. When you draw an object out of scale or at an incorrect size, the drawing's dimensions reflect the incorrect size unless you override the dimension text. If you have to override the dimension text by typing the correct size every time, you defeat the speed advantage that AutoCAD provides when it calculates dimensions and places the correct text for you.

Creating drawings accurately from the beginning greatly increases the speed at which you can place your dimensions.

When you start a drawing from scratch, AutoCAD has a basic dimensioning environment already set up for you. This basic setup works fine for some drawings, but you might have different dimensioning needs. The problem with the basic setup is that it is so basic that it works with only one type of drawing environment and with only one scale factor. Most of the drawings you create require you to adjust this basic dimensioning setup.

Preparing Your Drawing for Dimensions

Every drawing you create requires that you prepare a few settings before AutoCAD can place your dimensions. You should adhere to the following basic procedure before you place dimensions in any drawing.

Here are the five basic steps for setting up a drawing for dimensioning:

◆ Create a separate layer for all your dimensions. Keep your dimensions separate from all other information in your drawing.

◆ Create a text style to use only when you create dimensions.

◆ Set your dimension units to the type of measurement that you want your dimensions to reflect (decimal, architectural, engineering, and so forth), and set the precision to the smallest unit you want your dimensions to show.

◆ Set the Overall Scale Factor to the plot scale factor of your drawing.

◆ Set the running object snap to ENDPoint, INTersection, CENter to speed up picking points on objects that you want to dimension.

Tip   When you create prototype drawings from which to start your new drawings, be sure to do the basic steps for setting up dimensioning in each prototype. Then whenever you start a new file, you automatically are set up for dimensioning. Otherwise, you have to go through the dimensioning setup steps every time you start a new drawing.

In the exercises in the following sections, you create a layer for dimensions, create a text style to use only for dimensions, set the units for dimensions, set the appropriate dimension scale factor, and turn on the running object snaps for quicker placement of dimension origin points. Snap is already set on in the prototype DIM-EXER drawings, to aid in dimension placement.

Creating a Dimension Layer

The first step is to create a layer for your dimensions, as shown in the following exercise.

Starting Your Basic Dimensioning Setup

Create a new exercise drawing called CHAP21A. Use the DIM-EXER drawing from the IA Disk as a prototype. Your drawing should look like figure 21.5.

Choose Data, Layers   Opens Layer Control dialog box

New Riders Publishing
INSIDE
SERIES

Type **DIMS** *in the text box, then choose* Ne<u>w</u>	Creates new layer DIMS
Select DIMS *in the* La<u>y</u>er Name *list box*	Selects layer for subsequent actions
Choose <u>S</u>et Color	Opens Select Color dialog box
Choose the green color box in the Standard Colors *cluster*	Sets color green for DIMS layer
Choose OK	Exits the Set Color dialog box
Choose <u>C</u>urrent	Makes DIMS current layer
Choose OK	Closes Layer Control dialog box and saves changes

The current layer is now DIMS.
Save the Drawing.

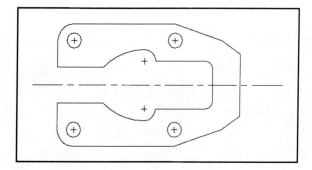

Figure 21.5

The CHAP21A drawing ready for dimensioning.

21

Controlling Dimension Text

When you place a dimension in a drawing, AutoCAD creates the dimension text using the current text style. The STYLE command for text is covered in Chapter 13, "Annotation with Text." You need to create a text style called DIMS to use specifically for your dimensions so that you can control the font and the size of the dimension text without affecting the other text in your drawing. Be sure to set the DIMS text style to current before you place your dimensions.

Tip Creating a DIMS text style enables you to set a width factor for your dimension text. If the dimension text does not fit within the extension lines of a dimension, AutoCAD places the text outside of the extension lines. Dimension text that is a little bit thinner than normal (for example, with a width factor of .75) stays inside the dimension lines better if the extension lines are close together.

Figure 21.6 illustrates the difference between a dimension style that has a width of 1.0 and a style that has a width of .75.

Figure 21.6

Using text styles with different width factors.

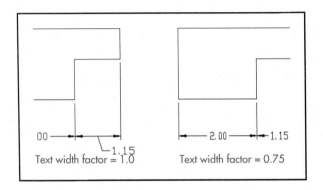

In the following exercise, you create a dimension text style called DIMS.

Creating a Text Style for Dimension

Continue working in drawing CHAP21A.

Command: *Choose* Data, Text Style	Issues STYLE command
`_'style Text style name (or ?)` `<STANDARD>:` **DIMS** (Enter)	Creates new text style called DIMS and opens Select Font File dialog box
Scroll to and double-click on the ROMANS.SHX *font file in the* File Name *list box*	Specifies Roman Simplex font
`Height <0.0000>:` (Enter)	Accepts current default text height
`Width factor <1.000>:` **.75** (Enter)	Specifies narrower text width than normal
`Oblique angle <0>:` (Enter)	Accepts default obliquing angle
`Backwards? <N>:` (Enter)	Defaults to forward-reading text
`Upside-down? <N>:` (Enter)	Defaults to right-side-up text
`Vertical? <N>:` (Enter)	Accepts default

DIMS is now the current text style.

Save the Drawing.

Note You should always set the height of the text style you use for dimensions to zero so that the setting for text height in the Annotation dialog box can control the dimension's text height.

If you set the text height in the current text style to anything other than zero, that height setting overrides the dialog box setting, which prevents the DIMTXT variable from controlling the dimension text height. For more information, refer to Chapter 22, "Editing and Styling Dimensions."

Preset Dimension Style Families

All characteristics of dimensions are controlled by values stored in dimension variables. Rather than setting and resetting these values over and over again whenever you want to change the appearance of a dimension, AutoCAD lets you save groups of settings in *dimension styles*. You give your dimension styles names as you save them, and you can restore any of them to the status of *current* style at any time. All dimensions made when a particular dimension style is current take on the settings of the dimension variables saved in that dimension style.

Each named dimension style is a *family style*; within each style are family members representing the different types of dimensions that you can use (linear, radial, angular, diameter, ordinate, and leader). You can apply different settings to each of the different family members. You can apply one group of settings to your linear dimensions and another to your diameter dimensions, for example, but still use only one named dimension style, eliminating the need for a new dimension style for each type of dimension you place in the drawing.

When you start a new drawing using AutoCAD's ACAD.DWG as your prototype, you have one ready-made default dimension style called STANDARD. Other prototype drawings have additional dimension styles created in them, as discussed in the following chapter. STANDARD gives you a quick foundation on which to set up the dimension variables necessary to get your dimensions to look the way you want. You use the STANDARD dimension style (with a few minor adjustments) for your dimensions in this chapter. In Chapter 24, you design your own dimension style according to your specific needs.

In a single drawing you might need several different types of variable settings for the different objects you dimension. Working with these variables by modifying dimension styles is covered in more detail in Chapter 24.

DDIM. DDIM enables you to create dimension styles and to set the dimension variables.
Pull-down: Choose Data, Dimension Style
Screen: Choose DRAW DIM, Ddim

21

Dimension Styles Dialog Box Options

The Dimension Styles dialog box (see fig. 21.7) includes the following options:

- ◆ **Current.** Sets a dimension style current.

- ◆ **Save.** Saves the current settings to the style.

- ◆ **Name.** Creates a new dimension style name.

- ◆ **Rename.** Renames a style.

- ◆ **Parent.** Creates a style family parent.

- ◆ **Geometry.** Sets all variables for dimension components.

- ◆ **Format.** Controls text formatting and location.

- ◆ **Annotation.** Sets variables for controlling text.

Figure 21.7

The Dimension Styles dialog box.

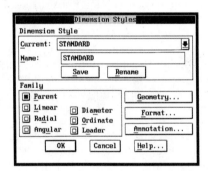

See Chapter 22, "Editing and Styling Dimensions," for additional options and sub-dialog boxes.

 Note Appendix G contains a complete list of dimension settings that make up a dimension style along with a brief definition of each variable.

In the following exercise, you will use the Dimension Styles dialog box to set the units and precision for the dimension text.

Setting Your Units and Feature Scaling

Continue in the CHAP21A drawing.

Choose Data, Dimension Style   Displays Dimension Styles dialog box

New Riders Publishing
INSIDE
SERIES

Choose **A**nnotation	Displays Annotation dialog box (see fig. 21.8)
In the Primary Units *cluster,* *choose* **U**nits	Displays Primary Units dialog box

You want Decimal units (the default), and you will set the precision to two places.

In the Dimension *cluster, click in the* **P**recision text box	Opens the Precision drop-down list
Select 0.00	Sets precision to two places
Choose OK, *then* OK *again*	Closes Primary Units and Annotation dialog boxes and accepts changes to precision setting

Remain in the Dimension Styles dialog box for the next exercise.

Figure 21.8

The Annotation dialog box.

21

Annotation

Primary Units

Units...
Prefix:
Suffix:
1.00

Alternate Units

☐ Enable Units   Units...
Prefix:
Suffix:
[25.4]

Tolerance

Method: None
Upper Value: 0.0000
Lower Value: 0.0000
Justification: Middle
Height: 1.0000

Text

Style: STANDARD
Height: 0.1800
Gap: 0.0900
Color...   BYBLOCK
Round Off: 0.0000

OK   Cancel   Help...

Note In Release 13, you no longer control the precision of dimension values with the UNITS commands. Precision for dimensions is set using the Dimension Styles dialog box; precision for units in the coordinates readout and for drawing queries is set using the Units Control dialog box. In Release 13 your coordinates display can show four decimal places of precision, and your dimensions can be placed with two decimal places of precision.

Drawing Scale Factor and Dimensions

When you're preparing your drawing for dimensioning, the most important setting to make is the overall scale factor. This setting governs the plotted size of the dimension components—that is, the arrowhead size, the text size, the size of center marks, and so on. In a drawing plotted at 1=2 (for a drawing scale factor of 2), for example, you want to set your overall scale factor (the scale factor for the drawing) to 2. If your arrowhead size is then set to 0.25 units, AutoCAD automatically scales up your arrowhead and draws it 0.5 units long. When plotted at 1=2, however, the arrowhead actually measures 0.25 units long.

Drawing and plotting scale factors are covered in Chapters 5, "Setting Up a CAD Drawing," and 27, "Isometric Drawing."

To set the overall dimension scale factor for your drawing, you use the Geometry dialog box in the following exercise.

Setting the Dimension Scale Factor

Continue in the CHAP21A drawing, in the Dimension Styles dialog box.

Choose **G**eometry	Opens Geometry dialog box (see fig. 21.9)

In the Scale section, the default setting in the O**v**erall Scale text box is 1.00000. The scale factor for the exercise drawing is 1=1, so accept the default setting.

Choose OK	Accepts settings and closes Geometry dialog box
Choose **S**ave	Saves changes to STANDARD dimension style
Choose OK	Exits Dimension Styles dialog box

Save the drawing.

Figure 21.9

The Geometry dialog box.

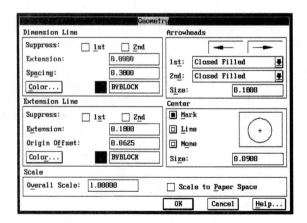

Tip   You can find all the settings you need for your dimension sizes and distances in the Dimension Styles dialog box. Some people make adjusting dimension settings much more difficult than necessary by failing to use the overall scale setting. This forces them to calculate all the correct sizes for each of the individual components of a dimension.

The best way to set up dimensioning is to set all your individual dimension component sizes and distances to the size you want them to be when you plot them and let the Overall Scale setting in the Geometry dialog box globally scale your dimensions to the correct size in the plotted AutoCAD drawing.

Fast Dimensions with Automatic Object Snaps

If you create a perfectly accurate drawing, you will not want to turn around and place inaccurate dimensions by simply putting your cursor on top of on-screen points and picking them. To place dimensions accurately on objects in a drawing, you must select the objects or use AutoCAD's object snap options. Object snaps are covered in Chapter 6, "Drawing Accurately."

When you place your dimensions, you use object snaps quite often. To avoid having to set object snaps every time you place a dimension, use one or more running object snaps.

Tip   One of the most important speed tips for placing dimensions is to set your running object snap mode. You use object snaps to place many of your dimensions, and if you have to set an object snap mode every time you place an extension line, you are wasting time.

If you set the running object snap to endpoint, intersection, and center, you can enter each dimension command and just select the features you want to dimension. AutoCAD automatically places your dimensions exactly where you want them.

In the following exercise, you set the running object snap modes to speed up the dimensioning process.

Setting Running Object Snap Modes

Continue in the CHAP21A drawing.

Command: *Choose* Options, *then* Running Object Snap	Opens Running Object Snap dialog box (see fig. 21.10)

continues

continued

Initializing...   DDOSNAP loaded.

Put a check in the **E**ndpoint, **C**enter   Sets running object snap modes
and **I**ntersection *boxes*

Choose OK   Closes Running Object Snap dialog box and
                                                        accepts changes

Save the drawing.

Figure 21.10

*Optimum
dimensioning
settings in the
Running Object
Snap dialog box.*

Your basic dimensioning setup is now complete. Saving changed settings to new
dimension styles is covered in more detail in the next chapter. But, for now, you are
ready to begin dimensioning.

Understanding the Components of a Dimension

Every dimension in AutoCAD is composed of standard components. All these component parts are grouped together like a block and edited as a single object. The
component parts of a basic dimension, identified in figure 21.11, are as follows:

◆ **Defpoints or definition points.** Defpoints are points placed at the exact
   locations the dimension is referencing (① in figure 21.11). The defpoints are
   the elements that make AutoCAD dimensions associative.

◆ **Extension lines.** Extension lines project away from the objects being dimensioned toward the dimension line, indicating exactly what is being dimensioned
   (see ②).

◆ **Dimension lines.** The dimension lines carry the value of the dimension, usually parallel to the objects being dimensioned and stretching between the extension lines (see ③). If the text breaks the dimension line as in figure 21.11, two dimension lines result. If the text is placed above the dimension line, one continuous dimension line exists.

◆ **Dimension text.** The dimension text is the part of the dimension entity that carries the value for the dimension as calculated by AutoCAD or entered by the user (see ④).

◆ **Terminators.** The terminators are the dimension objects located at the end of the dimension lines where they meet the extension lines (see ⑤). By default these are arrowheads, although a number of options are available.

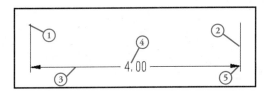

Figure 21.11

The components of an AutoCAD associative dimension.

21

Associativity

You place each dimension in a drawing with all the individual parts grouped together. *Definition points* (or *defpoints*) mark where the extension lines originate on the selected objects and the second arrowhead tip. If you select these points along with the objects to be edited—for example, if you select the definition points along with an object, and then stretch the object to a new length—you stretch the definition points as well, and AutoCAD automatically updates the text, dimension, and extension lines to reflect the new distance. AutoCAD's dynamic capability of updating dimensions when you edit them is called *associativity*.

Note In the drawing file, each dimension is considered to be a block. Dimensions are called *unnamed blocks,* because they are treated as blocks but have no name assigned to them. If you list all the blocks in a file and see that you have a number of unnamed blocks in your drawing, don't be alarmed—the dimensions in your drawing make up some of those unnamed blocks. Other unnamed blocks are hatch patterns, pfaces, and meshes.

Any time you use associative dimensions, AutoCAD automatically creates a layer called DEFPOINTS, which holds the definition points at the origin of the extension lines and the second arrowhead. You can see the entities on this layer, but they do not plot. Don't try to remove this layer—it is a natural part of any AutoCAD drawing that has dimensions.

Using Dimensioning Commands

Now that you understand the basic setup for preparing to place dimensions, you're ready to being using the dimensioning commands. Placing dimensions in a drawing can be frustrating because dimensions don't always come in the way you want them on your first try, and controlling them seems to be a mystery. When you drew dimensions using manual board drafting techniques, you could fudge the tight areas, but when you are beginning to learn AutoCAD, this isn't as easy.

If all the features of a dimension do not fit between the extension lines, AutoCAD places the dimension as it deems appropriate. You might not like the way AutoCAD positions the dimension, and you will probably feel powerless to correct its position. Starting out by using a correct dimensioning setup, however, eliminates some of the early frustration when you begin to dimension. In Chapter 22, "Editing and Styling Dimensions," you will learn how to edit dimensions to solve other problems.

Earlier in the chapter, we looked at one technique to give you more control over dimension placement: creating a text style for dimensions that has a narrower text width. As you work through the following dimension commands, you will be introduced to additional tips and techniques to further give you better control of the dimensioning environment. Chapter 22, "Editing and Styling Dimensions," introduces all the tools that enable you to have complete control of the way you create dimensions. After you work through the rest of this and the next chapter, dimensioning will be a mystery to you no longer and you will have control of AutoCAD's dynamic dimensioning features.

Linear Dimensions

Dimensions that measure the straight-line distance between two points are called *linear dimensions*. The two points can be endpoints of lines, intersections, arc chord endpoints, or any other points you can identify (usually by selecting an entity or using object snap). AutoCAD can create the following types of linear dimensions:

◆ **HORIZONTAL.** This linear dimension shows the horizontal distance relative to the screen and the plotted drawing between two points (see fig. 21.12). Horizontal dimensions are drawn with the DIMLINEAR command, which is accessed from the Draw, Dimensioning, Linear pull-down menu.

◆ **VERTICAL.** This linear dimension shows the vertical distance relative to the screen and the plotted drawing between two points (see fig. 21.12). Vertical dimensions are drawn with the DIMLINEAR command.

◆ **ALIGNED.** This linear dimension shows the straight-line distance between any two points that are not horizontal or vertical in relation to the screen or the plotted drawing (see fig. 21.12). Aligned dimensions are drawn with the DIMALIGNED command, which is accessed from the Draw, Dimensioning, Aligned pull-down menu.

◆ **ROTATED.** This linear dimension shows the distance at a specified angle between two points (see fig. 21.12). The dimension might not necessarily be aligned with the points that define the dimension. Rotated dimensions are drawn with the Rotated option of the DIMLINEAR command.

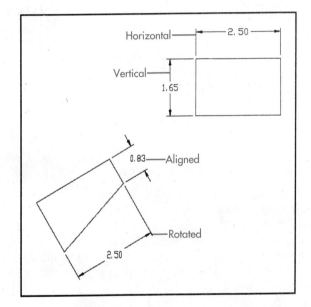

Figure 21.12

Horizontal, vertical, aligned, and rotated linear dimensions.

21

In addition to these types of linear dimensions, the following two other linear dimension commands help you create multiple dimensions:

◆ **CONTINUE.** This command creates a series of linear dimensions, with each dimension using the previous dimension's second extension line as the new dimension's first extension, and each dimension line meeting the previous dimension line in end-to-end fashion (see fig. 21.13). To create continuous dimensions, choose Draw, Dimensioning, Continue to issue the DIMCONTINUE command.

◆ **BASELINE.** This command creates a series of linear dimensions whereby each dimension line is offset from the previous one, and all dimensions share a common first extension line (see. fig. 21.13). To create baseline dimensions, choose Draw, Dimensioning, Baseline to issue DIMBASELINE command.

Figure 21.13

Continuous and baseline dimensions.

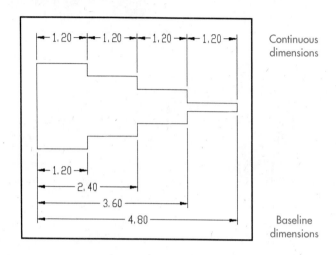

Continuous dimensions

Baseline dimensions

You will become more familiar with these dimension types and commands in the next few exercises in this chapter.

Automated Horizontal and Vertical Dimensions

New in Release 13 is a linear dimensioning feature called *inferential dimensioning*. AutoCAD executes this feature whenever you use the DIMLINEAR dimension command. After you pick an entity or two points, you can place a horizontal or vertical dimension by simply picking the location for the dimension line on-screen. You can place a rotated dimension by using DIMLINEAR's Rotated option. This feature enables you to use one linear dimension command to place all your horizontal, vertical, and rotated dimensions.

> **DIMLINEAR.** The DIMLINEAR command is a new enhancement to AutoCAD's dimensioning features. It enables you to place horizontal, vertical, and rotated dimensions.
> Pull-down: Choose Draw, Dimensioning, Linear
> Screen: Choose DRAW DIM, Linear

DIMLINEAR Command Options

The DIMLINEAR command is three dimensioning commands and two dimension text customizing commands built into one dimension command. The command options for DIMLINEAR are as follows:

◆ **TEXT.** Before you place a dimension, the text option enables you to specify or add to the dimension text.

◆ **ANGLE.** This option changes the default angle of the dimension text. The Dimension Styles dialog box controls whether the default angle is aligned with the dimension line or is horizontal—see Chapter 22.

◆ **HORIZONTAL.** This option places a horizontal dimension.

◆ **VERTICAL.** This option specifies a vertical dimension.

◆ **ROTATED.** This option rotates the dimension line to the angle you specify.

The Horizontal and Vertical options of DIMLINEAR function identically, except that one places the dimension line horizontally and the other places the dimension line vertically. After issuing the DIMLINEAR command, you pick one point for the first extension line and then a second point for the second extension line, or else press Enter and select a single object (such as a line, arc, or circle) in order to place the extension origins on that object. Then, when you specify the point, or as you move the cursor to the point where you want the dimension line, AutoCAD makes its best guess whether you want a horizontal or vertical dimension. If it guesses wrong, or if you want a rotated dimension, you can enter an H, V, or R to force AutoCAD to draw the type of dimension you want.

Placing Horizontal Dimensions

In the following exercise, you place horizontal dimensions on the CHAP21A drawing. Remember that you have running object snaps set so you don't need to select an object snap mode each time you pick a point.

Using DIMLINEAR for Horizontal Dimensions

Continue in the CHAP21A drawing, with the setup from the previous exercises.

Choose Draw, Dimensioning, Linear	Issues DIMLINEAR command
`First extension line origin`	Sets first extension line origin

continues

continued

`or RETURN to select:` *Carefully pick*
the lower endpoint of the vertical
center mark at ① *(see fig. 21.14)*

`Second extension line origin:` *Carefully*   Sets second extension line origin

Figure 21.14

Placing
horizontal
dimensions.

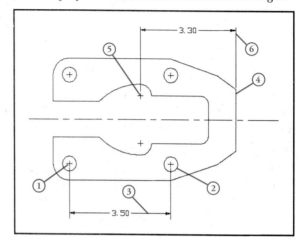

pick the lower endpoint of the vertical
center mark at ②

`Dimension line location (Text/Angle/`   Sets dimension line location and draws
`Horizontal/Vertical/Rotated):`   dimension
Pick ③

Next, place the second horizontal dimension.

`Command:` (Enter)   Repeats DIMLINEAR command

`DIMLINEAR`

`First extension line origin or`   Sets first extension line origin
`RETURN to select:` *Pick the vertical*
line at ④

`Second extension line origin:`   Sets second extension line origin
Carefully pick the top endpoint of
the center mark at ⑤

`Dimension line location (Text/Angle/`
`Horizontal/Vertical/Rotated):`
Pick ⑥
	Sets dimension line location and draws dimension

Save the drawing.

Placing Vertical Dimensions

You have now placed your first horizontal dimensions. In the next exercise you will use exactly the same technique to place some vertical dimensions.

Adding Vertical Dimensions

Continue in the CHAP21A drawing.

Choose Draw, Dimensioning, Linear	Issues DIMLINEAR command

`_dimlinear`
`First extension line origin or`
`RETURN to select:` *Carefully pick the left endpoint of the horizontal center mark at* ① *(see fig. 21.15)*
	Sets first extension line origin

`Second extension line origin:` *Carefully pick the left endpoint of the horizontal center mark at* ②	Sets second extension line origin

`Dimension line location (Text/Angle/`
`Horizontal/Vertical/Rotated):`
Pick ③
	Sets dimension line location and draws vertical dimension

The second vertical dimension defines the hole placement off the center line.

`Command:` `Enter`	Repeats DIMLINEAR command
`First extension line origin or` `RETURN to select:` *Carefully pick again at* ①	Sets first extension line origin
`Second extension line origin:` *Pick the horizontal line at* ④	Sets second extension line origin

As you move your cursor, watch it drag the dimension.

Move the cursor so it's to the left and vertically between the two points you picked	Drags a vertical dimension

continues

continued

Move the cursor so it's above and horizontally between the points	Drags a horizontal dimension

`Dimension line location (Text/Angle/`
`Horizontal/Vertical/Rotated):`
Pick ⑤
	Sets dimension line location and draws vertical dimension

`Command:` *Save your work.*	

Figure 21.15

Applying vertical dimensions.

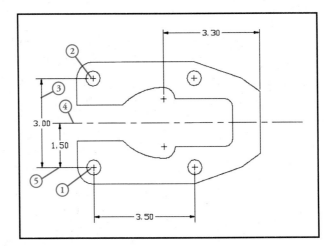

The DIMLINEAR command enables you to place horizontal, vertical, and rotated dimensions without having to enter a different command each time, thus greatly reducing the amount of time it takes to place dimensions. In addition, DIMLINEAR has two options for rotating the text independent of the dimension, and for modifying or replacing the text itself.

In the next exercise, you'll use DIMLINEAR's Text option to add an annotation to a dimension.

Using DIMLINEAR's Text Option

Continue in drawing CHAP21A.

`Command:` **⟮Enter⟯**	Reissues DIMLINEAR command
`Command: _dimlinear`	

New Riders Publishing
INSIDE SERIES

```
First extension line origin or
RETURN to select: Pick line at ①
(see fig. 21.16)

Second extension line origin: Pick line
at ②
```

Before you locate the dimension, specify DIMLINEAR's Text option.

`Dimension line location (Text/Angle` `Horizontal/Vertical/Rotated): T (Enter)`	Specifies Text option
`Dimension text <6.30>: <> OVERALL (Enter)`	Appends text string to dimension value

`Dimension line location (Text/Angle`
`Horizontal/Vertical/Rotated):`
Pick at ③
	Locates dimension

Save your work.

The text you appended appears on the dimension line as part of the associative dimension. The pair of angle brackets (<>) act as a placeholder for the dimension value.

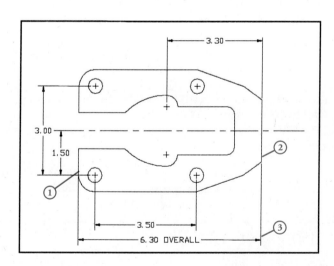

Figure 21.16

Using DIMLINEAR's Text option.

21

Tip   It is important to use the paired angle brackets (<>) as placeholders for your dimension value when you use DIMLINEAR's Text option. Doing so maintains the associative dimension's capability to update its value as the dimension is stretched or moved. In the preceding exercise, had you entered "6.30 OVERALL" rather than "<> OVERALL," the dimension value would have been set to 6.30 and would no longer have updated as the dimension was stretched.

Fast Chain Dimensions with the DIMCONTINUE Command

The DIMCONTINUE command enables you to place dimensions in single row with ease and speed. You begin a series of continuous dimensions with any LINEAR dimension. Next, you use the DIMCONTINUE command to string together subsequent dimensions in a series. The DIMCONTINUE command automatically begins each new dimension line at exactly the point at which the last dimension line leaves off. You do not have to specify where to place each dimension line in the series because the DIMCONTINUE command automatically uses the specified dimension's placement and lines up additional dimensions perfectly. DIMCONTINUE defaults to continue from the last linear dimension, or you can press Enter at the prompt and then select a dimension from which to continue.

DIMCONTINUE. The DIMCONTINUE command enables you to continue a string of dimensions in a row.

Pull-down: Choose Draw, Dimensioning, Continue

Screen: Choose DRAW DIM, Continu

 Tip   Before you begin to use the DIMCONTINUE command, make sure that the running object snap is set to ENDPoint, CENter, INTersection, or all of them. This enables you to pick the second extension line location very quickly. After you specify the second extension location, AutoCAD automatically asks for the next second extension line origin, and repeats itself until you press Enter to stop.

The following three exercises introduce the DIMCONTINUE command. In the first, you set up for DIMCONTINUE by creating a linear dimension. Then, continue it as a string of dimensions. The option to select an existing dimension from which to start a string of continuous dimensions is covered in the third exercise.

First, you place a horizontal dimension at the lower left corner of the gasket in the following exercise. The running object snap is already set to ENDPoint.

Placing the First Dimension

Begin a new drawing named CHAP21B, using the DIM-CONT drawing from the IA Disk as a prototype.

Choose Draw, Dimensioning, Linear   Issues DIMLINEAR command

`First extension line origin or`   Sets the first extension line origin
`RETURN to select:` *Pick the line at*
① *(see fig. 21.17)*

`Second extension line origin:` *Pick the line at* ② — Sets the second extension line origin

`Dimension line location (Text/Angle/ Horizontal/Vertical/Rotated):` *Pick* ③ — Sets the dimension line placement and draws dimension

Save your work.

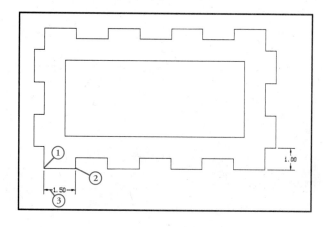

Figure 21.17

The first dimension for a chain.

 Note The order in which you select the extension line origins is important. The DIMCONTINUE command continues from the second extension line, so make sure that you pick the first and second extension line origins according to the direction in which you want to proceed.

After you place the first linear dimension, you can place continuous dimensions very quickly. In the following exercise, you create a continuous chain of dimensions from the first dimension, which you placed in the preceding exercise. You begin by issuing the DIMCONTINUE command.

Starting the Continuous Chain

Continue in drawing CHAP21B.

Choose Draw, Dimensioning, Continue — Issues DIMCONTINUE command

`Second extension line origin or RETURN to select:` *Pick the line at* ① *(see fig. 21.18)* — Sets second extension line origin, draws dimension, and prompts for another

continues

continued

`Second extension line origin or` `RETURN to select:` *Pick the line at* ②	Sets next second extension line origin
`Second extension line origin or` `RETURN to select:` *Pick* ③, ④, ⑤, *and* ⑥	Sets four more second extension line origins and draws dimensions
`Second extension line origin or` `RETURN to select:` *Pick the line at* ⑦	Sets second extension line origin and draws dimension, placing text with a leader

Keep the DIMCONTINUE command active for the next exercise.

If running object snap is set to endpoint, placing a string of dimensions as you did in the preceding exercise is quick and efficient. The dimension text for ⑦ wouldn't fit between the extension lines, so it was automatically placed with a leader.

Figure 21.18

Placing continuous dimensions.

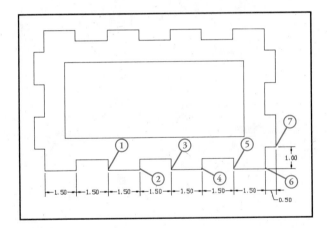

Note If you are using the DIMCONTINUE command and the text does not fit between two extension lines, AutoCAD offsets the text from the dimension line and draws a leader from the text to the dimension line. In some cases in which there is a series of tight dimensions, the leaders and dimension text overlap the previous dimension, and you must edit the text location. Refer to Chapter 24 "Techniques for Mechanical Dimensioning" for details.

DIMCONTINUE is useful in creating strings of continuous dimensions. You've just seen how to create a string from the most recently created dimension, but you're not limited to using the command from the last dimension.

New Riders Publishing
INSIDE
SERIES

Tip By default, the DIMCONTINUE command strings dimensions from the most recently drawn linear dimension in the current drawing session. By pressing Enter, you can then select any existing linear dimension from which to continue a string of dimensions. When you do so, the point you use to select the dimension determines which extension line DIMCONTINUE continues from.

In the following exercise, you begin a string of continuous dimensions from an existing dimension in the drawing. There is a vertical dimension on the lower right side of the gasket. You will select it as the starting dimension in a string of continuous dimensions.

Starting Continuous Dimensions from an Existing Dimension

Continue from the previous exercise, with the DIMCONTINUE command running.

`Second extension line origin or` `RETURN to select:` **Enter**	Stops sequence and prompts you to select dimension from which to continue
`Select continued dimension:` *Pick the dimension at* ① *(see fig 21.19)*	Selects dimension from which to continue

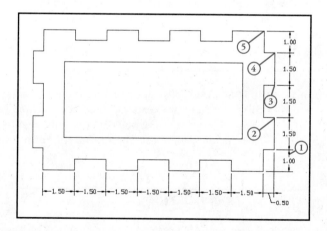

Figure 21.19

Continuing dimensions from an existing dimension.

`Second extension line origin or` `RETURN to select:` *Pick* ②	Sets second extension line origin
`Second extension line origin or` `RETURN to select:` *Pick* ③, ④, *and* ⑤	Sets three more second extension line origins

continues

---

continued

`Second extension line origin or` `RETURN to select:` [Enter]	Stops sequence
`Select continued dimension:` [Enter]	Ends DIMCONTINUE command

Save your drawing.

You also can use DIMCONTINUE to place continued angular dimensions. Angular dimensioning is covered later in this chapter.

Stacking Dimensions with BASELINE

Continuous dimensions give you the distance between each feature in a linear direction. You can use baseline dimensions to dimension each feature of a part, giving baseline measurements from one reference point, or *datum line*. This datum line is always the first extension line of the specified dimension, regardless of pick point or the first extension line of the default, last-created dimension. You create baseline dimensions with the DIMBASELINE command.

> **DIMBASELINE.** The DIMBASELINE command enables you to stack dimensions on top of each other, using a common first extension line.
> Pull-down: Choose Draw, Dimensioning, Baseline
> Screen: Choose DRAW DIM, Baseline

The sequence and options for the DIMBASELINE command are the same as for the DIMCONTINUE command. In the following two exercises, you place baseline dimensions from an existing dimension, after you first place a linear dimension. You will start by placing a horizontal dimension. Again, remember that the running object snap is set to endpoint.

Applying BASELINE Dimensions

Start a new drawing named CHAP21C. Use the BASEDIMS drawing from the IA Disk as a prototype. You will be dimensioning to the centers of the circles in this drawing and you will find a center running object snap as well as an endpoint object snap very handy.

`Command:` *Choose* Options, Running Object Snap, *turn on* Endpoint *and* Center *object snap modes, and* *choose* OK	Displays Running Object Snap dialog box

New Riders Publishing
INSIDE SERIES

`Command:` *Choose* Draw, Dimensioning, Linear	Issues DIMLINEAR command
`First extension line origin or` `RETURN to select:` *Pick the line at* ① *(see fig. 21.20)*	Sets first extension line origin
`Second extension line origin:` *Pick the circle at* ②	Sets second extension line origin
`Dimension line location (Text/Angle/` `Horizontal/Vertical/Rotated):` *Pick* ③	Places dimension

Next, issue the **DIMBASELINE** command and select the second extension line origins.

`Command:` *Choose* Draw, Dimensioning Baseline	Issues DIMBASELINE command
`Second extension line origin or` `RETURN to select:` *Pick the circle at* ④	Sets second extension line origin
`Second extension line origin or` `RETURN to select:` *Pick the circles at* ⑤ *and* ⑥	Sets two more second extension line origins
`Second extension line origin or` `RETURN to select:`	

Keep the **DIMBASELINE** command active for the next exercise.

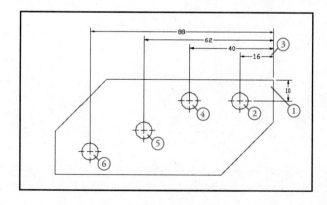

21

Figure 21.20

BASELINE dimensions.

In the following exercise, starting from the vertical dimension on the right of the plate drawing, you create vertical baseline dimensions using a selection to specify the initial dimension.

Baseline Dimensions from an Existing Dimension

Continue from the previous exercise using the DIMBASELINE command.

Second extension line origin or RETURN to select: **Enter**	Prompts you to select dimension from which to start baseline dimensions
Select base dimension: *Pick the dimension at* ① *(see fig. 21.21)*	Selects dimension from which to start baseline dimensions
Second extension line origin or RETURN to select: *Pick the circle at* ②	Specifies second extension line origin
Second extension line origin or RETURN to select: *Pick the circle at* ③	Specifies second extension line origin
Second extension line origin or RETURN to select: **Enter**	Stops baseline sequence
Select base dimension: **Enter**	Exits DIMBASELINE command

Save your drawing.

Figure 21.21

Baseline dimensions from an existing dimension.

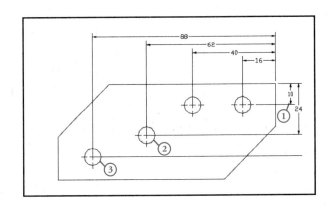

Note You can use the DIMCONTINUE and DIMBASELINE dimension commands not only on horizontal and vertical dimensions, but on any linear or angular dimension at any angle.

Using ALIGNED Dimensions

Some dimensions require the dimension line be aligned with an object, usually at an angle parallel to the extension line origins. In the following exercise, you must align the dimension for an hexagon object by using the DIMALIGNED command to follow the angle of the flat sides. Using horizontal and vertical dimensions would result in an inaccurate dimension length.

DIMALIGNED. The DIMALIGNED command places a dimension line parallel to the origin points of the two extension lines. If you press Enter to select an object to dimension, the dimension line is placed parallel to the object.
Pull-down: Choose Draw, Dimensioning, Aligned
Screen: Choose DRAW DIM, Aligned

As usual, a running object snap mode will prove helpful in quickly finding points for dimensions. Running object snap is already set to endpoint in the drawing used for the following exercise.

Placing Aligned Dimensions

Begin a new drawing named CHAP21D using the ALI-DIM drawing from the IA Disk as a prototype.

Command: *Choose* Draw, Dimensioning Aligned	Starts DIMALIGNED command
First extension line origin or RETURN to select: *Pick the line at* ① *(see fig. 21.22)*	Sets first extension line origin
Second extension line origin: *Pick* ②	Sets second extension line origin
Dimension line location (Text/Angle): *Pick* ③	Places dimension line in alignment with extension line origins

Save your drawing.

Although DIMALIGNED always aligns dimensions with the extension line origins, you sometimes need a dimension at another angle that is not parallel to an object or to the extension line origins. AutoCAD calls this a *rotated dimension*.

Figure 21.22

Placing an aligned dimension.

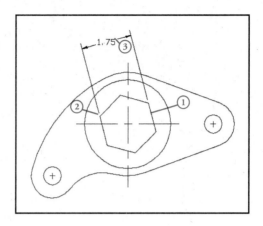

Applying Rotated Dimensions

You do not use the Rotated dimension as often as the other linear dimensions, but when it is needed, the Rotate option of the DIMLINEAR dimension command is the only way to get the correct measurement. In the drawing used in the following exercise, you need to dimension the slot to show its length, and neither the aligned, horizontal, nor vertical dimensions can give you the correct distance measurement.

The Rotate option of the DIMLINEAR command works perfectly here. You define the two extension line origins (which are not parallel to the line being dimensioned) and specify an angle at which to place the dimension line. The dimension line angle must be parallel to the line being dimensioned.

You can access the DIMLINEAR Rotate option by choosing Dimensioning, Linear from the Draw pull-down menu, specifying the extension line origins, then entering R for Rotated.

In the following exercise, the bracket needs a dimension placed on the slot to measure its length, so use the Rotate option in the DIMLINEAR command to place the correct dimension.

Creating a Rotated Dimension

Begin a new drawing named CHAP21E using the DIM-ROT drawing from the IA Disk as a prototype.

Choose Draw, Dimensioning, Linear	Issues DIMLINEAR command
`Select first extension line origin or RETURN to select:` *Pick the angled line at* ① *(see fig. 21.23)*	Selects first extension line origin

`Second extension line origin:` *Pick the line at* ②	Specifies second extension line origin

Move the cursor around and see the dimension drag as horizontal or vertical.

`Dimension line location (Text/Angle /Horizontal/Vertical/Rotated):` `R` Enter	Enables Rotate dimension option

`Dimension line angle <0>: 45` Enter	Sets angle for dimension line

Move the cursor around and see the dimension drag.

`Dimension line location (Text/Angle /Horizontal/Vertical/Rotated):` *Pick* ③	Sets dimension line location and draws dimension at 45°

Save your drawing.

Notice that the dimension line is not parallel to the angle of the extension line origins, as in an Aligned dimension, but rather the dimension line follows the angle you specified.

21

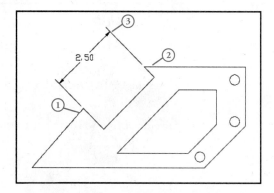

Figure 21.23

Placing a rotated linear dimension.

Dimensioning Curved Objects

You can use the LINEAR dimension commands to dimension circles and arcs, depending on the type of dimension information you need.

AutoCAD has the following three specific dimension commands for putting information on circles and arcs:

◆ **DIMRADIUS.** The DIMRADIUS command is used to place radius dimensions on circles and arcs. It is accessed from the Draw, Dimensioning, Radial, Radius pull-down menu.

◆ **DIMDIAMETER.** The DIMDIAMETER command is used to place diameter dimensions on circles. It is accessed from the Draw, Dimensioning, Radial, Diameter pull-down menu.

◆ **DIMCENTER.** The DIMCENTER command places center marks with or without center lines on arcs and circles. It is accessed from the Draw, Dimensioning, Center Mark pull-down menu.

Placing Radius Dimensions

The DIMRADIUS command calculates an arc's radius and places the information with a leader.

DIMRADIUS. The DIMRADIUS command enables you to place a dimension leader and text for the size information on circles and arcs.
Pull-down: Choose Draw, Dimensioning, Radial, Radius
Screen: Choose DRAW DIM, Radius

The drawing in the following exercise needs several RADIUS dimensions placed.

Placing Radius Dimensions

Begin a new drawing named CHAP21F using the HOLE-DIM drawing from the IA Disk as a prototype.

Command: *Choose* Draw, Dimensioning Radial, Radius	Issues the DIMRADIUS command
_dimradius Select arc or circle: *Pick the arc* at ① *(see fig. 21.24)*	Specifies arc on which to place radius dimension

Move the cursor and watch the leader drag.

Dimension line location (Text/Angle): *Pick* ②	Sets leader and text placement, and draws dimension
Command: (Enter)	Repeats DIMRADIUS command
Select arc or circle: *Pick the arc* at ③	Specifies arc on which to place radius dimension
Dimension line location (Text/Angle): *Pick* ④	Draws dimension

Save your drawing.

New Riders Publishing
INSIDE
SERIES

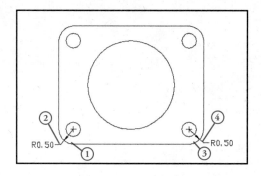

Figure 21.24

Placing radius dimensions.

The radial dimension commands give you the same flexible options of modifying text value and text angle as the DIMLINEAR command.

Dimensioning Circle Diameters

The DIMDIAMETER command works similarly to the DIMRADIUS command. You select the circle to dimension and then place the leader.

DIMDIAMETER. The DIMDIAMETER command enables you to place diameter dimensions on circles.

Pull-down: Choose Draw, Dimensioning, Radial, Diameter

Screen: Choose DRAW DIM, Diametr

In the following exercise, you place some diameter dimensions in the drawing.

Applying Diameter Dimensions

Continue from the previous exercise.

Command: *Choose* Draw, Dimensioning Radial, Diameter	Issues DIMDIAMETER command
_dimdiameter Select arc or circle: *Pick the circle at* ① *(see fig. 21.25)*	Selects circle on which to place diameter dimension
Dimension line location (Text/Angle): *Pick* ②	Sets leader and text locations, and draws dimension
Command: **Enter**	Repeats DIMDIAMETER command

continues

continued

`DIMDIAMETER`

`Select arc or circle:` *Pick the circle at* ③	Selects circle on which to place diameter dimension
`Dimension line location (Text/Angle):` *Pick* ④	Draws dimension

The previous two dimensions call out the dimension with a leader and no internal dimension line because one will not fit in the circle. The next dimension adds a dimension line and puts the text in the circle because the circle is larger.

`Command:` **Enter**	Repeats DIMDIAMETER command

`DIMDIAMETER`

`Select arc or circle:` *Pick the circle at* ⑤	Selects circle
`Dimension line location (Text/Angle):` *Pick* ⑥	Draws dimension

Save your drawing.

Figure 21.25

Placing diameter dimensions.

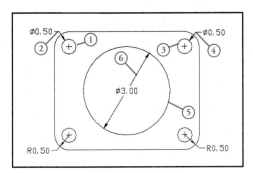

Note All the dimensions you've placed so far have been created according to the default settings of AutoCAD's dimension variables. In the next chapter, you'll learn how to work with these dimension variables, saving different groups of settings in named dimension styles. You could modify the dimension style with which you created the last diameter dimension, for instance, so there was no internal dimension line, but rather the dimension appeared as a leader.

Adding Center Marks to Arcs and Circles

You use the DIMCENTER command to designate the center origin point of a circle or arc.

The size of the center mark placed by the DIMCENTER command on a circle or arc is set in the Geometry sub-dialog box of the Dimension Styles dialog box. This value is multiplied by the overall scale factor, also set in the Geometry dialog box, to ensure it is drawn at the correct size at plot time. You can set center marking so it draws a cross at the center of the circle, a cross plus center lines that extend to just beyond the circumference, or no marks at all.

Note   All dimension settings you make in the Dimension Styles dialog box are stored in dimension variables. The dimension variable that controls the size and configuration of center marks is DIMCEN.

A positive DIMCEN value draws only center marks. A negative value draws center marks with extensions to just beyond the circle's quadrant points. In the Geometry dialog box, you set the size in the Size box and set the type of mark with the radio buttons. Mark (DIMCEN +) draws only center marks, Line (DIMCEN -) draws both marks and extension lines, and None (DIMCEN 0) draws neither.

DIMCENTER. The DIMCENTER command enables you to place center crosshair marks at the origins of arcs and circles.
Pull-down: Choose Draw, Dimensioning, Center Mark
Screen: Choose DRAW DIM, Center

In the following exercise, you use the DIMCENTER dimension command to place center marks in all the circles and at all the fillet origins.

Putting Center Marks in Fillets and Holes

Begin a new drawing named CHAP21G using the CEN-MARK drawing from the IA Disk as a prototype.

Command: *Choose* Draw, Dimensioning   Issues DIMCENTER command
Center Mark

Command: _dimcenter

Select arc or circle: *Pick the*   Places center mark at center of circle
hole at ① *(see fig. 21.26)*

continues

continued

Command: **Enter**	Repeats DIMCENTER command

```
DIMCENTER
Select arc or circle: Pick the hole
at ②
```

Small crosses are suitable when the circles they annotate are small too, but they can get lost in larger circles. Place center marks with lines on the other four circles. You'll have to turn on this option by using the Dimension Styles dialog box.

Command: *Choose* Data, Dimension Style	Opens Dimension Styles dialog box
Choose **G**eometry	Opens Geometry dialog box
In the Center cluster, turn on the **L**ine *option*	Sets center marks to include lines
Choose OK, *then* OK *again*	Closes Geometry dialog box, then Dimension Styles dialog box without saving change to dimension style
Command: *Double-click on the* Draw *label of the pull-down menu bar to recall the last command*	Issues DIMCENTER command
Select arc or circle: *Pick the hole* at ③	Selects circle and places center mark

For each of the holes at ④, ⑤, and ⑥ and each of two fillets at ⑦ and ⑧, press Enter to repeat the DIMCENTER command and place a center mark.

The **L**ine option affects not only center marks, but radial dimensions as well. Use the DIMRADIUS command to place two radius dimensions where you placed the first two lineless center marks.

Erase the first two center marks you drew (① and ② in figure 21.26).

Command: *Choose* Draw, Dimensioning, Radial, Radius	Issues DIMRADIUS command
Select the hole at ① *(fig. 21.27), then place the dimension at* ②	Places first radius dimension
Repeat for hole at ③, *placing dimension at* ④	Places second radius dimension

After you finish, the CHAP21G drawing should look like figure 21.27. Save your drawing.

New Riders Publishing

INSIDE
SERIES

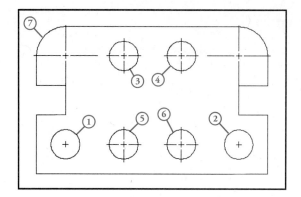

Figure 21.26

Placing center marks on circles and arcs.

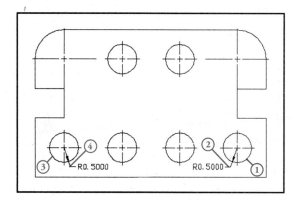

Figure 21.27

Placing radius dimensions with center lines.

21

If you look closely at your CHAP21G drawing, you can see that the center lines on the fillets are longer than the ones on the circles. How did AutoCAD do that?

When you used the Geometry dialog box to turn on the Line option for center marks, you might have noticed a Size box with a default value of 0.09 in it. This value controls several settings for center marks. When Mark is turned on, four lines 0.09 units long are drawn from the center of the circle toward the quadrant points. If Line is turned on, those same four lines are drawn at the center of the circle, then there is a gap of 0.09 units, then four longer lines are drawn through the quadrant points 0.09 units beyond the circumference of the circle.

 Note   Center marks placed by DIMCENTER are placed as individual lines, but those placed by DIMRADIUS and DIMDIAMETER are part of the associative dimension object.

Dimensioning Angles

In the design process, the relationship of two objects and the angle between them can be critical to the final product. If the angle is not correct, you can end up with a flawed design. AutoCAD has the capability to create and measure the angle between objects very accurately.

Placing ANGULAR Dimensions

You use the DIMANGULAR command to measure the angle between two objects.

> **DIMANGULAR.** The DIMANGULAR command measures the angular distance between two objects. You can select two objects, or specify three points to calculate the angle.
> Pull-down: Choose Draw, Dimensioning, Angular
> Screen: Choose DRAW DIM, Angular

If you pick an arc, DIMANGULAR dimensions it. If you pick a circle, its center sets the vertex, the pick point sets one endpoint, and DIMANGULAR prompts for the second endpoint. If you pick a line, DIMANGULAR prompts for another line and uses the two lines' intersection as the vertex and their ends as the endpoints.

Note   DIMANGULAR works in an opposite fashion from DIMLINEAR. Whereas with DIMLINEAR you are prompted to pick extension line origin points and have the option of selecting an object, with DIMANGULAR, the *default* is to select an object, and you must press Enter if you want to pick points for the angle vertex and endpoints.

In the following two exercises, you place an angular dimension, then use the DIMCONTINUE command to create a string of angular dimensions.

Placing Dimensions between Angled Objects

Start a new drawing named CHAP21H using the DIMANG drawing from the IA Disk as a prototype.

Command: *Choose* Draw, Dimensioning Angular	Issues DIMANGULAR command
`_dimangular`	Selects first line
`Select arc, circle, line, or RETURN:` *Pick the line at* ① *(see fig. 21.28)*	

New Riders Publishing
INSIDE
SERIES

`Second line:` *Pick the line at* ②   Selects second line

Move the cursor around and watch the dimension drag to dimension the various inside and outside angles formed by the two lines.

`Dimension arc line location`   Places arc dimension line and text
`(Text/Angle):` *Pick* ③

Save your work.

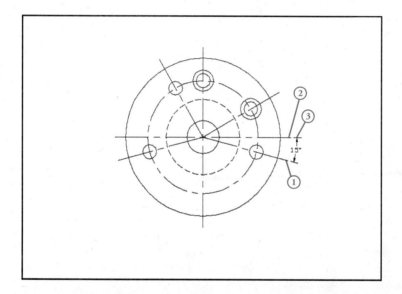

Figure 21.28

Placing an angular dimension.

Just like DIMLINEAR, DIMRADIUS, and DIMDIAMETER, DIMANGULAR has options for text value and text angle.

Tip   You can use DIMANGULAR to find the angle between two objects but not place the dimension. Just issue the DIMANGULAR command and select two objects to dimension. When the dimension begins to drag and you can see the text, read the angle and then press Esc to cancel the command without placing the dimension.

Creating Continuous or Baseline Angular Dimensions

A new feature in Release 13 is the capability to create continuous or baseline angular dimensions. After you place the first angular dimension, you can start the DIMCONTINUE or DIMBASELINE dimension commands (as you did earlier with the linear dimensions) and pick the next features or points that you want to dimension.

The next exercise illustrates how this new feature works for continuous angular dimensions.

Creating Continuous Angular Dimensions

Continue from the previous exercise.

You have placed one angular dimension in the previous exercise; now continue the angular dimensioning around the drawing.

Command: *Choose* Draw, Dimensioning Continue	Issues DIMCONTINUE command and snaps drag line to default vertex

If you are continuing from the previous exercise, skip the following prompt—you will not see it.

`_dimcontinue` `Select continued dimension:` *Pick dimension at* ① *(fig. 21.29)*	
`Select next feature on RETURN to select:` *Pick end of line at* ②	Specifies second extension line and draws dimension

> **Note** In early versions of Release 13, attempting to place a continuous angular dimension would dimension the external angle rather than the internal angle. If your drawing looks like figure 21.29, continue with the exercise. If AutoCAD drew an external dimension, erase it and use the DIMANGULAR command to dimension each angle separately until your drawing looks like figure 21.30.

`Select next feature or RETURN to select:` *Pick the line at* ①	Specifies second extension line
`Select next feature or RETURN to select:` *Pick the line at* ②	Specifies the second extension line
`Select next feature or RETURN to select:` *Pick the lines at* ③, ④, *and* ⑤	Specifies three more second extension lines
`Select next feature or RETURN to select:` (Enter)	Stops the sequence and asks for another dimension from which to continue
`Select continued dimension:` (Enter)	Exits the DIMCONTINUE command

Save the drawing.

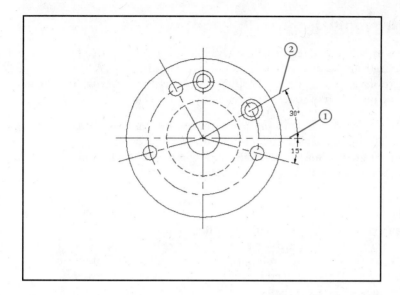

Figure 21.29

Placing the first continuous angular dimension.

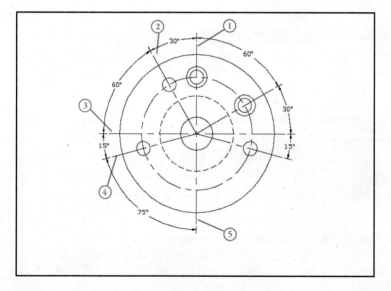

Figure 21.30

Placing the remaining continuous angular dimension.

21

Adding continuous angular dimensions is an easy task. The vertex point is automatically set, and you simply use an object snap to pick the next object feature to dimension.

 Stop   Don't let the `Select next feature...` prompt fool you into thinking that AutoCAD somehow finds a geometric point on an object if you pick at this prompt. You must use object snaps to accurately pick a point.

Placing Drawing Notes with Leaders

You use leaders to point out a feature, then give information about that feature. Unlike dimension commands, a leader does not measure distances. A leader is composed of an arrowhead, a straight line or splined shaft, and a horizontal line called a *flat* or *hook line.* Annotation of some form generally is placed at the end of the leader.

The standard dimension commands put measurement information on your drawings. Sometimes you need to use text to call out information on a drawing to some feature, or to point out design information. The LEADER command enables you to use a pointer to identify features or add text information.

The LEADER command has some new enhancements in Release 13. You now have many options to place information at the end of the leader. The default for annotation is single-line text. You can enter an option for multiple-line text; you can copy an existing single or multiline text, attribute definition, block, or tolerance object and attach it; or you can attach a block tolerance control frame in lieu of text. You also can specify a straight or spline-curved leader line, and whether the leader has an arrowhead. These new features greatly enhance the flexibility of the LEADER command.

LEADER. The LEADER command draws an arrowhead and leader and places text or other annotation objects. This enables you to point to a feature and place text information about that feature.

Pull-down: Choose Draw, Dimensioning, Leader
Screen: Choose DRAW DIM, Leader

Leader Command Options

The LEADER command has been enhanced to give you more capabilities with the following prompts and options:

◆ **Annotation.** When you press Enter to accept the default Annotation option, LEADER prompts you to enter text (Annotation) or to press Enter for other options. If you type a line of text and then press Enter, LEADER prompts `Mtext:`. If you press Enter, LEADER creates a single line of mtext. If you enter additional lines and press Enter, LEADER creates multiple lines of mtext. If you press Enter instead of entering *any* text annotation, LEADER prompts with the following:

`Tolerance/Copy/Block/None<Mtext>:`

◆ **Tolerance.** Prompts you to create a Tolerance Control Frame to add to the end of the leader.

◆ **Copy.** Prompts you to select any existing text, mtext, block, attribute definition, or tolerance object to copy and attach to the leader. If you select an attribute definition, its default value is inserted as an mtext object. If you select a text object, it is inserted as mtext.

◆ **Block.** Prompts you to specify a block to insert, and continues with the normal block insertion prompts.

◆ **None.** Draws the leader without annotation.

◆ **Mtext.** Pressing Enter to accept the default Mtext option shells out of AutoCAD and loads your configured text editor (by default, MS-DOS Editor).

◆ **Format.** Prompts for options for formatting the leader to be splined, straight, arrowhead, or none (no arrowhead):

```
Spline/STraight/Arrow/None/<Exit>:
```

◆ **Spline.** Formats leader as a spline curve.

◆ **STraight.** Formats leader as a series of straight lines.

◆ **Arrow.** Places the default arrowhead style on the leader.

◆ **None.** Places no arrowhead on the leader.

◆ **Exit.** Exits format options.

◆ **Undo.** Undoes the last leader vertex point.

Straight leaders with arrowheads are the default each time you use leaders, so you need not use the Arrow or STraight options unless you use the None or Spline options and then change your mind.

In the drawing in the following exercise, the holes need to be called out with size information. The LEADER command is perfect for this. In the following exercise, you use the default method for text entry.

Using Leaders To Place Information

Continue in the CHAP21H drawing.

Command: *Choose* Draw, Dimensioning   Issues LEADER command
Leader

continues

continued

From point: *Pick the circle at* ① *(see fig. 21.31)*	Sets arrowhead point
To point: *Pick* ②	Specifies end of first leader
To point (Format/Annotation /Undo)<Annotation>: (Enter)	Accepts default and prompts for annotation
Annotation (or RETURN for options): **14 DIA - 3 HOLES THROUGH**	Enters text for leader information
Mtext:	Places text on drawing

In the preceding exercise, LEADER automatically supplied a short hook line from the second point you picked to the text. Your drawing should look like figure 21.31.

Figure 21.31

Placing a leader with text.

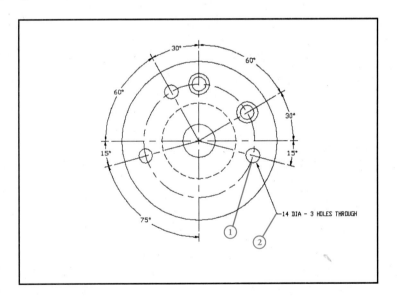

The new feature of adding multiline text to leaders enables you to add as many lines of text to your leaders as you need, which you could not do in previous releases.

In the following exercise, you work through the multiline text option.

New Riders Publishing
INSIDE SERIES

Multiline Text with Leaders

Continue from the previous exercise.

Command: *Choose* Draw, Dimensioning, Leader	Issues LEADER command
From point: *Pick* ① *(see fig. 21.32)*	Sets start point for arrow
To point: *Pick* ②	Sets end of leader shaft
To point (Format/Annotation/ Undo)<Annotation>:	Accepts default for Annotation
Annotation (or RETURN for options):	Gives you further options
Tolerance/Copy/Block/ None/<Mtext>:	Shells from AutoCAD and loads MS-DOS Editor
Type: **12 DIA - 18 CBORE** **12 DEEP**	Specifies text
Save this text in your editor , and exit	Closes MS-DOS Editor and returns to AutoCAD and draws leader and text as shown in figure 21.31

Save the drawing.

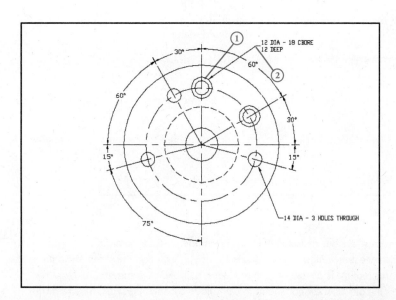

Figure 21.32

Adding multiline text to a leader.

Further flexibility in Release 13's leader object lies in its ability to use curved—or splined—leader lines, and to copy text from another leader and have it inserted in exactly the right place.

In the next exercise, you'll use the LEADER command's Copy option, and spline-fit a leader line.

Creating Splined Leaders and Copying Leader Text

Continue in drawing CHAP21H.

Command: *Choose* Draw, Dimensioning, Leader	Starts LEADER command
Command: _leader From point: *Pick at* ① *(see fig. 21.33)*	Sets start point for leader arrowhead
To point: *Pick at* ②	Sets end point for leader line
To point: (Format/Annotation/Undo) <Annotation>: **F** (Enter)	Initiates Format option
Spline/STraight/Arrow/None/<Exit>: **S**	Sets Spline option
To point: (Format/Annotation/Undo) <Annotation>: *Pick at* ③	Initiates Format option and draws a splined leader line
To point: (Format/Annotation/Undo) <Annotation>: (Enter)	Initiates Format option and ends splined leader
Annotation (or RETURN for options): (Enter)	Displays annotation options
Tolerance/Copy/Block/None/<Mtext>: **C** (Enter)	Sets Copy option
Select an object: *Pick the text at* ④	Copies selected text to end of new leader line

Your drawing should look like figure 21.33. Save your work.

Note   In previous versions of AutoCAD, the DIM mode LEADER command incorporated the last measured dimension in leader text if you included the string <> in the leader text. This feature is absent from the Release 13 LEADER command, but you can access the old LEADER command in DIM mode by entering **DIM**, then **LEADER**. Press Esc to exit DIM mode when finished.

New Riders Publishing
INSIDE
SERIES

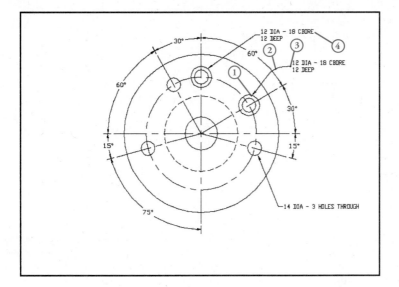

Figure 21.33
*Creating splined
leader lines and
copying Mtext.*

Dimensioning with Alternate Units

In the majority of cases, you place standard dimensions with a single unit type for the dimensional text information. In certain industries, however, you need to represent two types of units on each dimension line. For instance, manufacturers might need feet and inches measurements as well as total inches on each dimension. You might also need metric measurements.

If you are only using a single system of measure for your dimensions, but you are drawing in a different system, AutoCAD is very capable of performing the conversion for you. You can also tell AutoCAD to create dimensions displaying two systems of measure.

You see an example of using two systems of measurement in one dimension in figure 21.34. For more detailed information on setting up for alternate units of measurements in dimensions, see Chapter 24, "Techniques for Mechanical Dimensioning."

Ordinate Dimensions

Ordinate dimensions (sometimes called *datum dimensions*) are a series of dimensions that are offset from a common base point without dimension lines. Ordinate dimensions measure the X datum or Y datum of the point you specify from the current 0,0 origin. They have only one extension line, a leader on which the dimension text is placed. The dimension text is always aligned with the leader.

Figure 21.34

Figure 21.34

A dimension with multiple units of measurement.

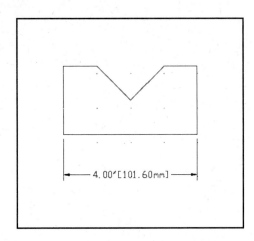

You must use the UCS command to place the current drawing origin at the base point you want, then use object snaps to ensure accurate datum points. Using ortho mode helps keep straight leader lines. Otherwise, when you pick a point for the end of the leader that is not in line with the dimension point (at an angle), AutoCAD draws an offset line or "dogleg" as the leader. Doglegs are useful, however, if you want to avoid overlapping dimension text in closely spaced dimensions. For more detailed information on ordinate dimensions, see Chapter 24.

Creating Tolerance Dimensions

A new addition to AutoCAD's dimensioning features is geometric tolerancing. *Geometric tolerancing* enables you to place more information about certain characteristics of the object on the drawing. Tolerance information includes information such as maximum allowable variations in form or profile, orientation, location, and runout. This information is placed in the drawing in feature control frames. See Chapter 24 for more information on geometric tolerancing.

Dimensioning in Paper Space

There are two methods for placing dimensions when you use paper space to plot your drawings:

◆ Place your dimensions in model space in a floating viewport and use automatic paper space scaling to control your dimension sizes.

◆ Place your dimensions in paper space.

New Riders Publishing
INSIDE
SERIES

These methods require different setups to work properly. You will begin by placing dimensions in model space in floating viewports, as explained in the following section.

Placing Dimensions in Model Space

In the following exercise you'll work on a drawing that has been set up to use paper space and model space (see fig. 21.35).

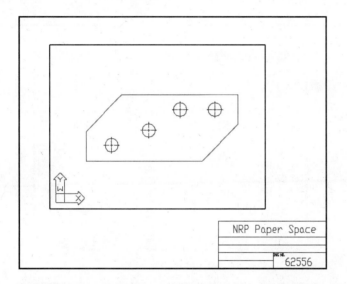

Figure 21.35

The CHAP21I drawing ready to be dimensioned.

NRP Paper Space

DWG NO.
62556

The paper space sheet is set up to plot an A-size (8.5-by-11) paper at 1=1 (full scale). The scale factor for the model space viewport is 1=25. First, set the Scale to Paper Space setting to on; you will find this setting in the Geometry dialog box accessed through the Dimension Styles dialog box.

Setting Dimension Scale Factor for Paper Space

Begin a new drawing named CHAP21I using the PS-DWG drawing from the IA Disk as a prototype.

Command: *Choose* Data, Dimension Style	Opens Dimension Styles dialog box
Choose Geometry	Opens Geometry dialog box
Put a check in the Scale to Paper Space *box (see fig. 21.36)*	Turns on paper space scaling

continues

Choose OK	Exits the Geometry dialog box
Choose <u>S</u>ave	Saves the changes to the current dimension style
Choose OK	Exits the Dimension Style dialog box

Now, make sure that model space is the current space. Set Endpoint and Center object snaps and place linear baseline dimensions so that your drawing looks like figure 21.37.

Save the Drawing.

Figure 21.36

Setting paper space scaling in the Geometry dialog box.

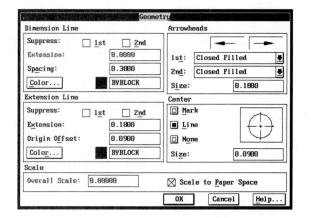

Figure 21.37

Dimensions placed in model space.

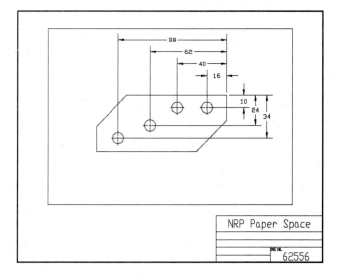

New Riders Publishing
INSIDE
SERIES

Turning on the Scale to Paper Space feature instructs AutoCAD to multiply the dimension variables settings by the zoom magnification factor for each model space viewport. This feature keeps your dimension component sizes the same size in all the viewports, regardless of the zoom scale factor in a model space viewport. For example, in the preceding exercise, your viewport was scaled at 1:25. AutoCAD applied the *plot* scale factor of 25 to all the distances that were dimensioned, but left the dimension components themselves at their original *paper space* scale factor of 1.

◆ Tip   As you learned in the beginning of this chapter, it's important to take control of your dimensions. Set all your dimension variables to the size you want on the piece of paper, then let the Overall Scale setting control your dimension component sizes. If you follow this setup, when you use the Scale to Paper Space feature, the sizes of your dimensions when you plot are equal to the sizes you actually set for your variables. For more information on scaling and floating viewports to paper space, see Chapter 25, "Sheet Composition and Plotting."

Placing Dimensions in Paper Space

In the previous exercise, you placed the dimensions in model space. The other option for dimensioning in the paper space environment is to place your dimensions in paper space itself, which requires a different technique to get the correct size for dimension components.

Using the DIMLFAC Variable

When you want to place your dimensions in paper space you need to set the variable DIMLFAC to match the zoom scale factor of the viewport in which you want to place dimensions.

◆ Note   DIMLFAC stands for DIMension Linear FACtor. The DIMLFAC dimension variable sets the linear factor by which AutoCAD scales distances when you dimension. The DIMLFAC variable scales the view of the geometry to equal its actual size, so the dimension text you place in paper space matches the geometry's actual size.

It's important to understand the difference between DIMLFAC and DIMSCALE. Both dimension variables control scaling of dimensions, but there the similarities end. DIMLFAC controls the scaling of real distances in your drawing. DIMSCALE controls the scaling of dimension objects; that is, the arrowheads, text size, extension line offsets, center mark sizes, and so forth.

The DIMLFAC variable works in two ways. In a strictly model space environment, it's used to scale distances and apply those scale factors to the dimension value. In model space, you may have a sheet of details that you want to have plotted on the same sheet at different scales. You would set DIMLFAC to "fool" AutoCAD into thinking distances were less or greater than they seemed.

For example, you might have a 1/2"=1'-0" (or 1:24) view of a column layout, and want to show a 1"=1'-0" (or 1:12) detail of the anchor bolts. You would probably make a copy of one of the columns, then scale it up by a factor of 2 (the difference in the scale factors). AutoCAD, of course, doesn't know what you're doing. It sees the distance between the bolts in the 1:12 detail as twice the distance between the same bolts in the 1:24 detail, and wants to dimension them accordingly.

This is where DIMLFAC comes in. If you set DIMLFAC to 0.5 before you dimension the enlarged detail, AutoCAD sees the distance between the bolts, multiplies it by the value of DIMLFAC, and places the "correct" dimension on the drawing.

DIMLFAC also has a purpose if you want to place your dimensions in paper space. Floating viewports must be scaled in order for the drawing to plot to scale. If the value of DIMLFAC is set to the inverse of the viewport scale, AutoCAD applies the absolute value of DIMLFAC to the distance you indicate in the drawing.

For example, you might have a wall that's 20 feet long in model space. You've set up a viewport and you want to display the view of this wall at 1/4"=1'-0" (or 1:48). If you dimension this distance in paper space, AutoCAD returns the true distance—in paper space, that's five inches. Now if you set your DIMLFAC to –48, the inverse of the plotscale, AutoCAD recognizes that you are dimensioning in paper space, and it multiplies whatever distance it calculates by the absolute value of DIMLFAC, or 48. Now your dimension reads 20'-0".

 Tip   You don't have to know the scale of your floating viewport to give AutoCAD a negative DIMSCALE value. If you are in paper space, use the DIM command to switch to the Dim: prompt. Now enter **DIMLFAC**. You will be prompted with the current value of DIMLFAC and asked to set a new value. The default new value is Viewport; enter a **V**, and AutoCAD prompts you to select a viewport and calculate the scale factor from it. Note that if you are using the Dimension Styles dialog box, you must know the scale factor so you can enter it in the edit box. The only place that you can perform a DIMLFAC V is from the Dim: prompt, in paper space.

Setting DIMLFAC for Paper Space Dimensioning

Continue from the previous exercise. Erase all the dimensions and set paper space to current.

You must use the dim mode command to set DIMLFAC for paper space.

Command: **DIM**	Enters dim mode
Dim: **DIMLFAC**	Shows DIMLFAC options

 New Riders Publishing
INSIDE SERIES

`Current value <1.0000>` `New value (Viewport): V` ⏎**Enter**	Sets Viewport option
`Select viewport to set scale:` *Pick the viewport border at* ① *(see fig. 21.38)*	
`DIMLFAC set to -25.0000` `viewport`	Sets DIMLFAC to zoom scale factor of
`Dim: E` ⏎**Enter**	Exits dim mode to command prompt

Now use DIMLINEAR to place dimensions in paper space. As you work your way around the part, placing dimensions, notice the way AutoCAD uses the correct dimension sizes. Pick points still use object snap, snapping to objects in the floating viewport.

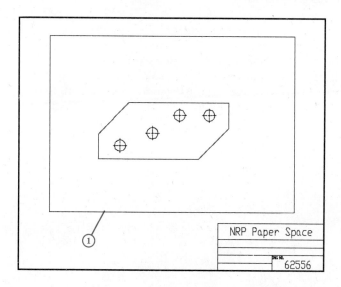

Figure 21.38

Setting DIMLFAC to the viewport.

21

Tip   If you have two floating viewports in your drawing, and both viewports are zoomed to the same scale factor, you can begin a dimension in one and end it in another.

Now that you know how to dimension in paper space, you should have an understanding of the drawbacks of doing so. Although model space is supposed to be the space for the model, and paper space the space for everything that documents it, most users stop short of putting dimensions in paper space.

Stop   Consider the following three strong reasons not to place your dimensions in paper space:

◆ You cannot pan or zoom in paper space without causing the drawing to regenerate is not possible. Placing dimensions often involves a great deal of zooming and panning to be able to select points accurately. Paper space dimensioning is extremely inefficient for this reason alone.

◆ You cannot select model space objects to dimension from paper space. You *can* use object snaps, but you can't select objects directly. This means you can't dimension arcs or circles without laborious workarounds.

◆ Paper space dimensions are not associative with the model space objects they reference. If you stretch geometry in model space, the paper space dimensions will not move.

This chapter has given you a basic understanding of the dimensioning environment and its commands. You have used all the core dimensioning commands and many advanced options. As you work more with dimensions, you'll discover the need for more control over the way your dimensions are created in the drawing. In the next chapter you will learn how to use dimension styles and editing options to manipulate and control the appearance of your dimensions.

C H A P T E R

22

Editing and Styling Dimensions

Chapter 21, "Introduction to Dimensioning," shows you how to set up for a basic dimensioning environment and how to use the basic dimension commands. This chapter takes you through the commands and tools available for creating and manipulating dimensions to make your drawings look the way you want them to. AutoCAD provides several options for controlling your drawing's dimensions.

After reading this chapter, you will be able to perform the following tasks:

◆ Manipulate dimension style families

◆ Control each component of the dimension

◆ Place dimension text where you want it

◆ Place multiline text in dimensions

◆ Control the appearance of groups of dimensions

◆ Use your standard dimension styles in all your projects

When you first start to use AutoCAD, you probably will find that one of the most frustrating and mysterious tasks is controlling your dimensions. After this chapter guides you through the new dimensioning features in Release 13, you will no longer be in the dark.

When you set your drawings up properly (as outlined in Chapter 21) and see the power of dimension styles, you start to understand how easy it can be to control and edit the dimensions and associated geometry in your drawings.

All dimensions you place in a drawing are controlled by dimension styles. The default AutoCAD prototype drawing has one dimension style already created called STANDARD. You can make changes to this default style or create your own dimension style, as illustrated in the following quick exercise. To create a new dimension style, use the Dimension Styles dialog box. After you have created a new dimension style, dimensions that you place in the drawing will observe that style's settings. Making changes to the style in the Dimension Styles dialog box will cause all dimensions created using that style to take on the new settings.

The following exercise offers a brief overview of some of the commands covered in this chapter.

Quick 5¢ Tour

Begin a new drawing called CHAP22 using the STYLE-EX drawing from the IA Disk as a prototype.

Command: *Choose* Data, Dimension Style	Displays Dimension Styles dialog box (see fig. 22.1)
Double-click inside the **N**ame *edit box to highlight* STANDARD *and type* **MECHANICAL**	Sets name for new dimension style
Choose **S**ave, *then* OK	Creates new dimension style, sets it current, and closes Dimension Styles dialog box

Subsequent dimensions will be created using the settings in the current dimension style until the style is changed. Now that you have created a dimension style, add some dimensions.

Command: *Choose* Draw, Dimensioning, Linear	Issues DIMLINEAR command
_dimlinear First extension line origin or RETURN to select: **Enter**	Enables you to select object to dimension

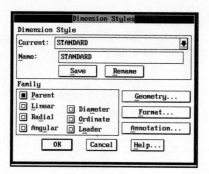

Figure 22.1

The Dimension Styles dialog box.

`Select object to dimension:` *Pick the line at* ① *(see fig. 22.2)*	Selects line object to dimension
`Dimension line location (Text/Angle/ Horizontal/Vertical/Rotated):` *Pick* ②	Specifies dimension line location
`Command:` (Enter)	Repeats DIMLINEAR command
`DIMLINEAR` `First extension line origin or RETURN to select:` *Use ENDPoint object snap and pick* ③	Sets first extension line origin at endpoint of line at ③
`Second extension line origin:` *Use ENDPoint object snap and pick* ④	Sets second extension line origin at endpoint of line at ④
`Dimension line location (Text/Angle/ Horizontal/Vertical/Rotated):` *Pick* ⑤	Specifies dimension line location

With two dimensions placed (see fig. 22.2), edit the new dimension style to change the number of decimal places displayed from two to three. This can be done easily using the Dimension Styles dialog box.

`Command:` *Choose* Data, Dimension Style	Displays Dimension Styles dialog box
Choose **A**nnotation	Displays Annotation dialog box
In the Primary Units *cluster, choose* **U**nits	Displays Primary Units dialog box

continues

continued

In the Dimension *cluster, choose the* Precisio**n** *text drop-down list and then select* 0.000	Sets units precision for dimensions to 3 places
Choose OK, *then* OK *again*	Closes Primary Units and Annotation dialog boxes, returns to Dimension Styles dialog box

In most drawing offices, the convention for all linear dimension text is that it aligns with the dimension line. You'll need to revise the dimension style to make this change. You'll also change the distance that extension lines extend beyond dimension lines.

Choose **F**ormat	Displays Format dialog box
Click on the **I**nside Horizontal *and* **O**utside Horizontal *toggle boxes*	Removes Xs, turning options off
Choose OK	Closes Format dialog box, returns to Dimension Styles dialog box
Choose **G**eometry	Displays Geometry dialog box
In the Extension Line *cluster, double-click inside the* E**x**tension *edit box and type* **0.125**	Changes value of extension line extension
Choose OK	Closes Geometry dialog box, returns to Dimension Style dialog box
Choose **S**ave	Saves changes to MECHANICAL dimension style
Choose OK	Exits Dimension Styles dialog box and updates all dimensions created with MECHANICAL style (see fig. 22.3)

Notice that the dimensions made with the MECHANICAL dimension style automatically updated to the new settings, as shown in figure 22.3. Later in this chapter you are shown how to update selected dimensions without globally updating their styles.

New Riders Publishing
INSIDE SERIES

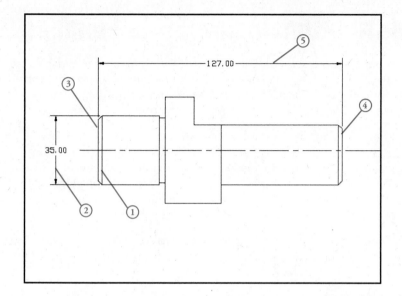

Figure 22.2

Using DIMLINEAR to dimension a mechanical part.

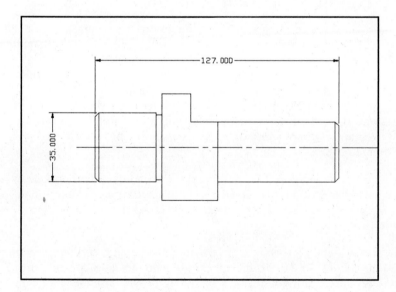

Figure 22.3

Dimensions with new settings.

22

Manipulating Dimension Style Families

The individual components of a dimension are controlled by dimension variables, as shown in Chapter 21. There is a complete list of each dimension variable with a brief description in Appendix G of this book. You can adjust and set any dimension variable by typing the variable name at the Command: prompt.

It's easier, however, to control dimension variables through the Dimension Styles dialog box. The Dimension Styles dialog box also controls and creates dimension styles. A *dimension style* is a group of dimension variable settings that control how your dimensions look when placed in a drawing. All dimensions are controlled by the dimension style that is current at the time you place the dimension. If you do not create your own styles, you are using the default dimension style.

It is best to use your own styles in a drawing. Your own styles enable you to dimension according to your own standards or preferences, or to industry standards.

Creating a Parent Dimension Style

Because dimensions are created using whichever dimension style is current, you need to verify the current dimension style *before* you place your first dimension. By default, the STANDARD style is current in the prototype drawing ACAD.DWG. Other prototype drawings supplied with AutoCAD Release 13 have additional dimension styles. US_ARCH.DWG has an ARCH dimension style, US_MECH.DWG has an ANSI dimension style, and ACADISO.DWG has several ISO dimension styles. The settings in these dimension styles are generic; although they might work well for basic drawings, you need to create your own styles for your dimensions to be created exactly the way you need them to be.

When making your own dimension style, you first set up a parent dimension style by naming and saving a style. Within this named parent style are family members that control the different types of dimensions: Linear, Radial, Angular, Diameter, Ordinate, and Leader.

For each of the family members there are three dialog boxes that control how each type of dimension will look. The three dialog boxes—Geometry, Format, and Annotation—are accessed by the buttons of the same names in the Dimension Styles dialog box (refer to fig. 22.1). The Geometry dialog box controls the layout of the dimension's individual parts, the Format dialog box controls the placement of the dimension text, and the Annotation dialog box controls the appearance of the dimension text.

New Riders Publishing
INSIDE
SERIES

You will now open the DIM-STYL.DWG file and create a dimension style and adjust the components within that dimension style.

DDIM. Dimensions are controlled by dimension variables, and there are 58 of them in AutoCAD Release 13. The DDIM command displays the Dimension Style dialog box, in which you can make adjustments to these variables and create new dimension styles.

Pull-down: *Choose* Data, Dimension Style
Screen: *Choose* DRAW DIM, DDim

Using Dimension Style Options

The Dimension Style dialog box provides you with the following options:

- ◆ **Current.** Selects an existing style to set current.

- ◆ **Name.** Enters a new name for a dimension style.

- ◆ **Save.** Saves the style specified in the Name text box, including any changes made to the style settings.

- ◆ **Rename.** Renames the current dimension style to the name in the Name text box.

- ◆ **Family.** Parent, Linear, Radial, Angular, Diameter, Ordinate, and Leader create family members within the parent dimension style. Family members can have different settings from the parent style.

- ◆ **Geometry.** Displays the Geometry dialog box to set variables for the dimension geometry.

- ◆ **Format.** Displays the Format dialog box for text formatting.

- ◆ **Annotation.** Displays the Annotation dialog box to control how the dimension text looks.

The first step when working with dimension styles is to create a new dimension style parent. AutoCAD starts all drawings with its default STANDARD style. This style contains very basic settings, and you will want to refine the dimensioning environment to meet your specific needs.

Creating a New Dimension Style

Begin a new drawing called CHAP22A using the DIM-STYL drawing from the IA Disk as a prototype. Your screen should look like figure 22.4. Begin by making the DIMs layer current, then create a new named dimension style.

Command: *Choose* Data, Dimension Style	Displays Dimension Styles dialog box
Double-click in the N*ame text box,* *type* **PROJECT**, *and then choose* S*ave*	Creates new parent dimension style and sets it current
Choose OK	Closes dialog box and saves changes

Next, before placing some dimensions, set the running object snap to ENDPoint.

Command: *Choose* Options, Running Object Snap	Displays Running Object Snap dialog box
Choose E*ndpoint, then* OK	Sets running object snap to Endpoint (see fig. 22.5) and closes dialog box

With both the PROJECT dimension style and the running object snap set, place a couple of dimensions as shown in figure 22.6.

Command: *Choose* Draw, Dimensioning Linear	Issues DIMLINEAR command
First extension line origin or RETURN to select: *Press Enter, then pick line at* ① *and place dimension at* ②	Places overall horizontal dimension
Command: **Enter**	Issues DIMLINEAR command
DIMLINEAR First extension line origin or RETURN to select: *Press Enter, then pick line at* ③ *and place dimension at* ④	Places overall vertical dimension

Save your drawing.

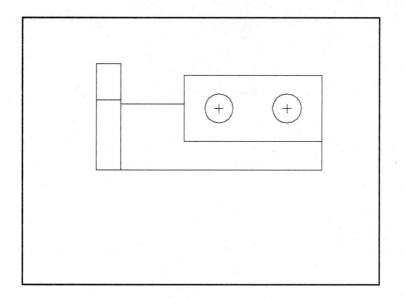

Figure 22.4

*The CHAP22A
drawing ready for
dimensioning.*

Figure 22.5

*The Running
Object Snap
dialog box.*

22

Figure 22.6

Dimensions created using PROJECT dimension style.

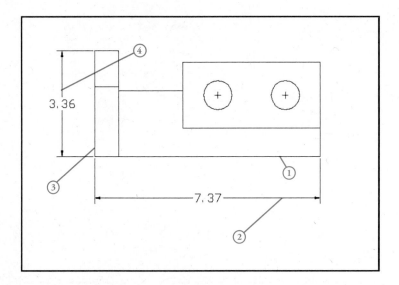

Now that you have created your own dimension style and placed some dimensions, take a look at the characteristics of dimensions that you need to control.

Making Adjustments to Dimension Geometry

Chapter 21 covers AutoCAD's associative dimensions, and how they update as the geometry they describe changes. As you make changes in a dimension style, note the dynamic power of associativity when *all* the dimensions created with that style automatically update to the new settings.

The Geometry dialog box (see fig. 22.7) has settings for all the individual parts that make up a dimension. Those parts consist of the dimension line, the extension lines, and the arrowheads. Center marks for circles and arcs are also controlled here, and you set the overall dimension scale factor in this dialog box.

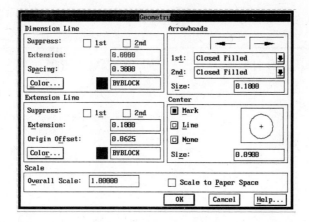

Figure 22.7

The Geometry dialog box.

22

Changing Dimension Lines

The Dimension Line cluster in the Geometry dialog box controls the variables that affect the dimension lines. The dimension line options are discussed in the following list:

◆ **Suppress.** The Suppress 1st and 2nd settings control the visibility of the first and second dimension line. When the text divides the dimension line in two, you can turn off the visibility of the first or second dimension line. The first dimension line is determined by the first extension line origin you select when placing the dimension.

◆ **Extension.** Extends the dimension line out past the extension lines. This is often used in architectural dimensioning when using oblique terminators (ticks) to give the dimension more of a hand-drawn look.

◆ **Spacing.** Controls the distance between the dimension lines when they are stacked, such as when using baseline dimensions.

◆ **Color.** By default, your dimension's color is BYBLOCK, so dimensions adopt the current entity color or layer color setting. The Color option enables you to override the color setting, using any color you want for the dimension lines. The color of arrowheads matches the setting for dimension lines.

Tip Adding color to parts of your dimensions does two things for you. First, having differently colored dimension parts helps make the dimensions easier to read on the monitor. Second, by making certain parts of the dimension a different color, you can assign different pen widths to those colors at plotting time. This can help make your dimensions easier to read on the plotted drawing.

In the next exercise, you make a change in the color of your dimension lines.

Controlling the Color of Dimension Lines

Continue in the CHAP22A drawing.

Command: *Choose* Data, Dimension Style	Displays Dimension Styles dialog box with PROJECT displayed as current style
Choose <u>G</u>eometry	Displays Geometry dialog box
In the Dimension Line *cluster, choose* <u>C</u>olor	Displays Select Color dialog box
Choose the red *color box, then* OK	
Choose OK	Closes Select Color dialog box

The dimension line and arrowhead color are now set to red.

Choose OK	Closes Geometry dialog box
Choose Save, *then* OK	Updates dimension style and closes Dimension Styles dialog box

Save your drawing.

Notice that the dimensions you created with the PROJECT dimension style are now updated automatically to the new dimension line color setting.

Controlling Extension Lines

How you adjust your extension lines can help make your drawing easier to read. When dimensioning certain objects, set your extension lines so they don't interfere with any of the lines defining the object to be dimensioned. The following list discusses the controls in the Extension Line cluster of the Geometry dialog box. These controls aid in making your dimensions easier to read.

◆ **Suppress.** The Suppress 1<u>s</u>t and 2<u>n</u>d settings control the visibility of the first and second extension line. If one or both of the extension lines are going to overlap an object line, it is best to suppress the visibility of the extension line to make the dimension easier to read. The first extension line is determined by the first dimension origin you select when placing the dimension. The definition points themselves are unaffected.

New Riders Publishing
INSIDE
SERIES

◆ **Extension.** Controls the distance the extension lines extend past the dimension line.

◆ **Origin Offset.** Controls the distance that the extension lines start from the object. The defpoints are unaffected, and are still placed on the selected object or at the points you pick.

◆ **Color.** By default, your dimension's color is BYBLOCK, so dimensions adopt the current entity color or layer color setting. The Color option enables you to override the color setting, using any color you want for the extension lines.

Setting Extension Line Offset

You will often need to increase the distance for the extension line offset from the object. The next exercise shows you how to do just that.

Defining Extension Line Offset

Continue in the CHAP22A drawing.

Command: *Choose* Data, Dimension Style	Displays Dimension Styles dialog box
Choose Geometry	Displays Geometry dialog box

The origin offset is set to 0.0625 by default; set it to 0.125.

Double-click in the Origin Offset *text box*	Highlights 0.0625 for deletion
Type .125	Sets extension line offset to 0.125
Choose OK	Returns to Dimension Styles dialog box
Choose Save, *then* OK	Saves changes to PROJECT style and exits Dimension Styles dialog box

Save your drawing.

Notice that all the dimensions created with the PROJECT dimension style are automatically updated to the new extension line offset setting (see fig. 22.8).

Figure 22.8

Extension line offset changes.

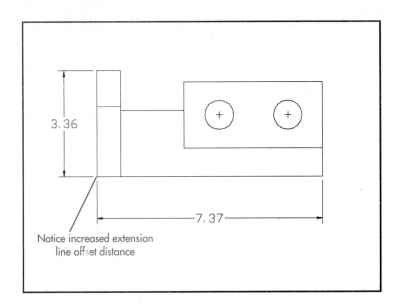

Suppressing Extension Lines

Good dimensioning standards require that the extension lines never overlap the object lines of the part to be dimensioned. You can suppress either or both extension lines if they overlap object lines. In the following exercise, you apply dimensions under both of these situations.

Suppressing Visibility of Extension Lines

Continue in the CHAP22A drawing. You will place dimensions that require one dimension line to be suppressed, and a dimension with both extension lines requiring suppression. Start by suppressing one extension line.

Command: *Choose* Data, Dimension Style	Displays Dimension Styles dialog box, confirming PROJECT as current style
Choose **G**eometry	Displays Geometry dialog box
In the Extension Line *cluster, choose* Suppress 2**n**d	Suppresses visibility of second extension line (see fig. 22.9)
Choose OK, *then* OK *(don't save it this time)*	Closes Geometry dialog box, then closes Dimension Styles dialog box

Do not save the changes to the PROJECT style, or all the existing dimensions will have suppressed extension lines.

New Riders Publishing
INSIDE
SERIES

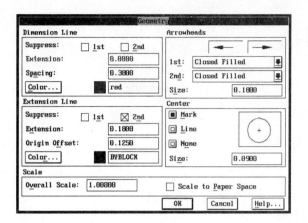

Figure 22.9

Suppressing 2nd extension line visibility in Geometry dialog box.

Note By not choosing the **S**ave option before exiting the Dimension Styles dialog box, you initiated a dimension override. This override is indicated by a plus sign before the style name in the **C**urrent style box (see fig. 22.10). This means that you have not made changes to the current dimension style, and only the following dimensions will show the changes just made to the dimension variables. Previously created dimensions are unaffected. You will learn more about overrides later in this chapter.

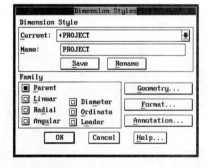

Figure 22.10

The Current style name indicating a dimension override.

22

Dimensioning with Suppressed Extension Lines

Continue in the CHAP22A drawing.

Command: *Choose* Draw, Dimensioning, Linear	Issues the DIMLINEAR command
First extension line origin or RETURN to select: *Pick the line at* ① *(see fig. 22.11)*	Specifies the first extension line origin

continues

continued

`Second extension line origin:` *Pick the line at* ②	Specifies the second extension line origin
`Dimension line location (Text/Angle /Horizontal/Vertical/Rotated):` *Pick* ③	Sets the dimension line location

Because the second dimension line would have overlapped an object line, you suppressed it (see fig. 22.11).

When both extension lines overlap object lines, you need to suppress both extension lines. In the PROJECT dimension style, you will now suppress both extension lines and place a dimension.

`Command:` *Choose* Data, Dimension Style, Geometry	Displays Dimension Styles dialog box, then Geometry dialog box
In the Dimension Line *cluster, choose* Suppress 1st (2nd *should already be suppressed*)	Suppresses the visibility of both extension lines
Choose OK, *then* OK *(don't save it)*	Closes Geometry and Dimension Style dialog boxes
`Command:` *Choose* Draw, Dimensioning Linear	Issues DIMLINEAR command
`First extension line origin or RETURN to select:` *Pick the line at* ① *(see fig 22.12)*	Specifies the first extension line origin
`Second extension line origin:` *Pick the line at* ②	Specifies the second extension line origin
`Dimension line location (Text/Angle /Horizontal/Vertical/Rotated):` *Pick* ③	Sets the dimension line location

Save your drawing.

Notice that both extension lines are not showing on the dimension just placed (see fig. 22.12).

New Riders Publishing
INSIDE
SERIES

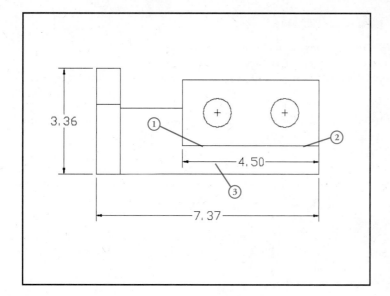

Figure 22.11

The second dimension line suppressed.

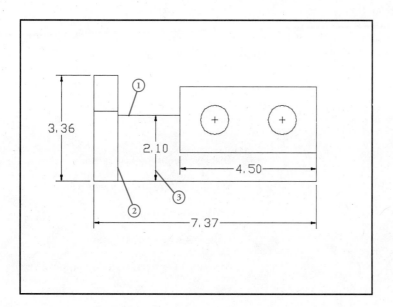

Figure 22.12

Dimension with both extension lines suppressed.

22

Modifying Arrowheads

At the end of dimension lines are terminators. A *terminator* is a symbol that indicates the extents of the dimension. The default terminator symbol in AutoCAD is an arrowhead, which designates the point at which the dimension line is stopped by the extension line.

You can specify the type of terminator and its size in the Geometry dialog box. The default setting is Closed Filled arrowheads. The next exercise shows you how to change the size of the current arrowhead.

Changing the Arrowhead Size

Continue in the CHAP22A drawing.

In the Dimension Styles, Geometry dialog box, you have access to seven arrowhead variations. The default setting for arrowhead size is 0.1800. Change that to 0.25 to enlarge the arrowhead size for all the arrowheads in the drawing.

Command: *Choose* Data, Dimension Style   Displays Dimension Styles dialog box

Notice that the current dimension style is +PROJECT; the plus indicates that a variable was set and not saved to the parent style. This is called an override. You need to reset the PROJECT dimension defaults.

Press Alt+C	Highlights Current style text box
Open the drop-down list and *choose* PROJECT	Sets PROJECT style current
Choose Geometry	Displays Geometry dialog box
Press Alt+I	Highlights Arrowhead Size box
Type .25	Changes arrowhead size
Choose OK	Closes Geometry dialog box
Choose Save	Saves changes to current dimension style
Choose OK	Closes Dimension Styles dialog box and updates arrowhead size

Save your drawing.

New Riders Publishing
INSIDE SERIES

Notice that all the dimensions created with the **PROJECT** dimension style have been automatically updated to the larger arrowhead size. The dimensions created with overrides, however, retain their special settings (see fig. 22.13).

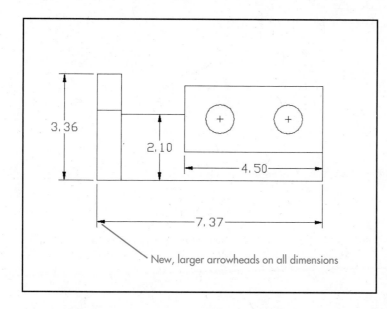

Figure 22.13

All dimensions now have larger arrowheads.

Many drafting standards require different types of terminators, and certain types of dimensioning situations—such as isometric dimensions—require custom arrowheads. AutoCAD provides eight predefined selections for dimension line terminators, plus the capability to define custom terminators. The following list explains the arrowhead controls in the Geometry dialog box for manipulating arrowhead appearance:

◆ **1st.** Controls the type of arrowhead placed at the first extension line.

◆ **2nd.** Controls the arrowhead placed at the second extension line.

◆ **Size.** Controls the size of the arrowheads.

The dimensions that have been placed so far with the **PROJECT** dimension style have used the default Closed Filled arrowhead type. In the following exercise, you modify the arrowheads by changing them to the Open arrowhead type.

22

Defining Arrowhead Type

Continue in the CHAP22A drawing.

Command: *Choose* Data, Dimension Style	Displays Dimension Styles dialog box
Choose Geometry	Displays the Geometry dialog box
Click on the 1st *arrowhead drop-down list box*	Displays a list of all the arrowhead options
Select Open	Sets the Open arrowhead current (see fig. 22.14)

Notice that the image tile for arrowheads updates automatically to show you the type of arrowhead you select.

Choose OK	Closes the Geometry dialog box
Choose Save	Saves the changes to the current dimension style
Choose OK	Closes the Dimension Styles dialog box

Again, watch the dynamic capability of associative dimensions as all the dimensions automatically update to the new arrowhead type (see fig. 22.15).

Save your drawing.

Figure 22.14

The Arrowhead type drop-down list.

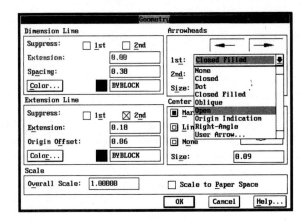

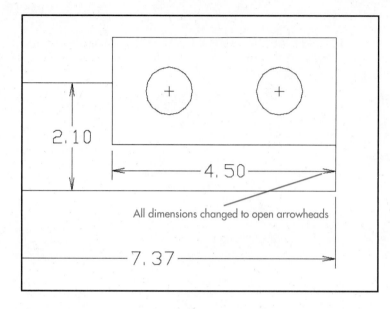

Figure 22.15

*Detail of
dimensions with
different
arrowheads.*

 Note When you set the 1s<u>t</u> arrowhead, the 2n<u>d</u> arrowhead automatically changes to match. If you want different arrowheads, set the 2n<u>d</u> arrowhead; the 1s<u>t</u> will not automatically change to match it.

Controlling Center Marks in Circles and Arcs

Indicating the center point of circles and arcs is a standard part of placing dimension information on a drawing. AutoCAD makes this very easy with the DIMCENTER command. Center marks are nonassociative and consist of two or more individual lines.

Center marks in circles can be placed with or without center lines extending out past the perimeter. You can set center lines on or off in the Center section of the Geometry dialog box.

Placing Center Lines for Circle Diameters

Continue in the CHAP22A drawing.

Begin by restoring the size and type of arrowhead and the dimension line color to their original settings. Dimension line color should be BYBLOCK, arrowhead type should be Closed Filled, and arrowhead size should be 0.18. Save the changes to the PROJECT dimension style.

continues

continued

In this exercise, you will place center marks with center lines. The drawing includes existing center marks without center lines. You will erase the existing center marks and place new center marks with center lines.

`Command:` *Choose* Modify, Erase	Issues ERASE command
`Select objects:` *Select the four center mark lines at* ①, ②, ③, *and* ④ *(see fig. 22.16)*	
`Select objects:` (Enter)	Erases center marks

Next, use the Dimension Styles dialog box to reset center line type.

`Command:` *Choose* Data, Dimension Style, *then* Geometry	Displays Dimension Styles dialog box, then Geometry dialog box
In the Center *cluster, choose the* Line *radio button*	Turns center lines on
Choose OK, *then* OK *(don't save it)*	Closes Geometry and Dimension Styles dialog boxes without updating style

Next, use this override to place a center mark with center lines on the circles.

`Command:` *Choose* Draw, Dimensioning	Issues DIMCENTER command
`Command: _dimcenter`	
`Select arc or circle:` *Pick the circle at* ① *(see fig. 22.17)*	Places center mark with center lines at center of circle
`Command:` (Enter)	Repeats DIMCENTER command
Pick the circle at ②	Places center mark with center lines at center of circle (see fig. 22.17)

Save your drawing.

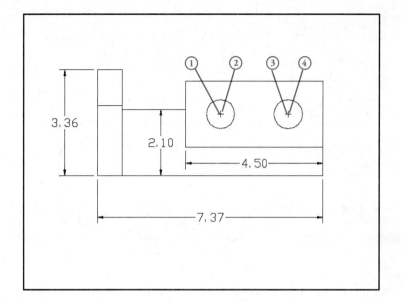

Figure 22.16

Erasing center marks.

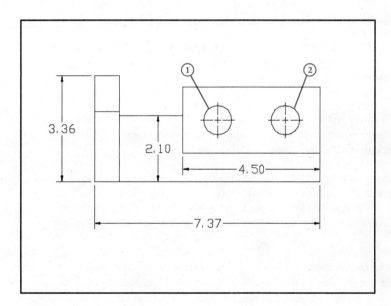

Figure 22.17

Center marks with center lines.

22

The DIMCENTER command has no options, but the Geometry dialog box provides the following settings that control the different ways to place your center marks:

◆ **Mark.** Turns on the center mark when using the DIMCENTER, diameter, and radial dimension commands.

◆ **Line.** Extends center lines from the center mark to beyond the circumference of the circle.

◆ **None.** Turns off the center mark. Placing radial dimensions on very small holes where the center mark would be too large is an example of when not to place a center mark.

◆ **Size.** Controls the size of the center mark. The size you specify is one-half the total length of the center mark. When using center lines with center marks, this setting also determines the distance the center line extends past the circumference of the circle.

Defining Dimension Text Format

You can adjust the position of text, arrowheads, and leader lines in relation to the dimension and extension lines to meet your drafting standards. AutoCAD enables you to justify the dimension text both horizontally and vertically in relation to the dimension and extension lines.

Managing how the dimension text is placed in relation to the extension lines is one of the most important aspects of controlling how well your dimensioning works. Chapter 21 explains how the current text style is used for dimension text.

When placing dimension text, AutoCAD has to calculate the distance between the two extension lines and then place two arrowheads, two dimension lines, two text gaps, and the text (see fig. 22.18). If there isn't enough room for all the dimension information, AutoCAD places some of the information outside the extension lines.

Tip You can create a special text style for dimensions, to squeeze the text width thinner so that text fits better between the extension lines. In addition to using a narrow text style, you can reduce the arrowhead size and the text gap size to help AutoCAD keep the information inside the extension lines.

New Riders Publishing
INSIDE
SERIES

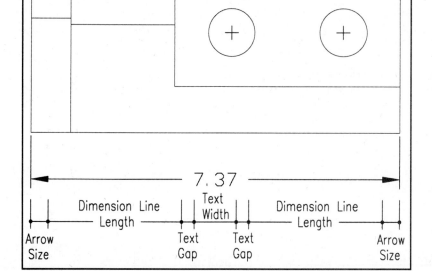

Figure 22.18

AutoCAD automatically places the dimension text and arrowheads according to its internal calculations.

You tell AutoCAD how to locate dimension text by setting the Fit option in Dimension Styles' Format dialog box (see fig. 22.19). Best Fit is the default. When Best Fit is set, AutoCAD checks the distance between the dimension's extension lines. If you do not have room for both the text and arrowheads, you can use the other options in the Fit drop-down list to specify either the text or the arrowheads (or both) be placed outside the extension lines. The Leader option tells AutoCAD to use a leader to place the text away from the dimension line when there isn't enough room between the extension lines. This option is useful for continuous dimensions in tight areas.

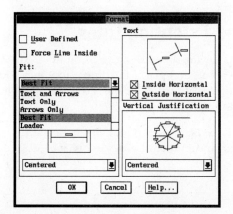

Figure 22.19

The Format dialog box.

Format Dialog Box Options

You have the following options within the Format dialog box:

- ◆ **User Defined.** When you check this option, the point you specify during dimensioning for the dimension line location also specifies where to place the dimension text.

- ◆ **Force Line Inside.** Places a dimension line between the extension lines even when the dimension text and arrowheads are placed outside of the extension lines.

- ◆ **Fit.** Controls dimension text and arrowhead placement in relation to the extension lines. A drop-down list gives you a variety of ways to place dimension text in tight spots.

- ◆ **Horizontal Justification.** Provides options for controlling the text placement along the dimension line. Text can be placed at the center of the dimension line, at the right end or the left end, or perpendicular to the dimension line over either extension line.

- ◆ **Inside Horizontal.** When checked (turned on), this option sets all the dimension text inside the extension lines to read horizontally. When off, the text aligns with the dimension line.

- ◆ **Outside Horizontal.** When checked (turned on), this option sets all the dimension text outside the extension lines to read horizontally. When off, the text aligns with the dimension line.

- ◆ **Vertical Justification.** Controls the position of the text in relation to the dimension line. The text can be placed above, centered, or below the dimension line, or in accordance with the Japanese (JIS) drafting standard.

Controlling Text and Extension Lines

After you select the two points for the dimension extension lines, AutoCAD calculates the distance between the two points and places the dimension lines and the dimension text accordingly. When there isn't room for the arrowheads and text, AutoCAD uses the Best Fit setting to place the information.

If you want more control over the placement of dimension text and arrowheads so that you can better follow your drafting standards, you can set a different option for the Fit setting.

New Riders Publishing
INSIDE
SERIES

In the CHAP22A drawing, you're going to place some dimensions that are too tight for all of the dimension to fit inside the extension lines. In the following exercise, you switch those dimension lines so that both the arrowheads and the text are outside.

Controlling Arrowhead Placement

Continue in the CHAP22A drawing.

Place a horizontal dimension as shown in figure 22.20. When text is placed outside the extension lines, AutoCAD places the text outside the second extension line.

Command: *Choose* Draw, Dimensions, Linear	Draws horizontal dimension
Pick ①*, then* ② *and locate* ③	

AutoCAD places the arrowheads inside the extension lines if they will fit. You will now force the arrowheads outside to go with the text.

Command: *Choose* Data, Dimension Style*, then choose* Format	Displays Dimension Styles dialog box, then Format dialog box
Click on the Fit *drop-down list*	Displays options list
Select Text and Arrows	Sets Text and Arrows to be outside extension lines
Choose OK	Closes Format dialog box
Choose Save	Saves setting to PROJECT style
Choose OK	Closes Dimension Styles dialog box

Save your drawing.

The dimension with inside text has been updated so that the text and the arrows are outside the extension lines (see fig. 22.21).

Figure 22.20

*Placing a
horizontal
dimension over a
small distance.*

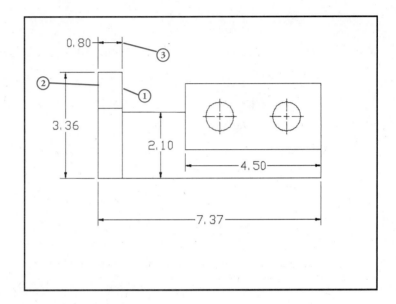

Figure 22.21

*Arrowheads are
forced outside
extension lines.*

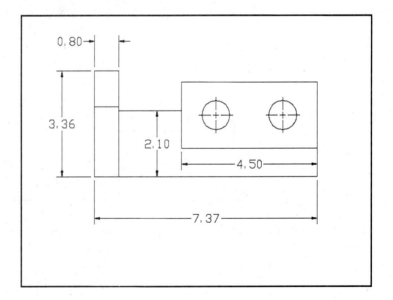

Forcing an Internal Line

When the arrowheads are placed outside the extension lines, you have an option to place a dimension line between the extension lines. This is called *forcing an internal line,* and you can set it in the Format dialog box.

The upper left dimension (0.80) has outside arrowheads and text. In the following exercise, you force a dimension line inside the extension lines.

Forcing Internal Dimension Lines

Continue in the CHAP22A drawing.

Choose Data, Dimension Style	Displays Dimension Styles dialog box
Choose **F**ormat	Displays Format dialog box
Place an X inside the Force **L**ine Inside *box*	Turns on Force Line Inside option
Choose OK	Closes Format dialog box
Choose **S**ave	Saves new setting to PROJECT style
Choose OK	Closes Dimension Styles dialog box and updates dimensions

Save your drawing.

Notice how the dimension is updated automatically to have an interior dimension line (see fig. 22.22).

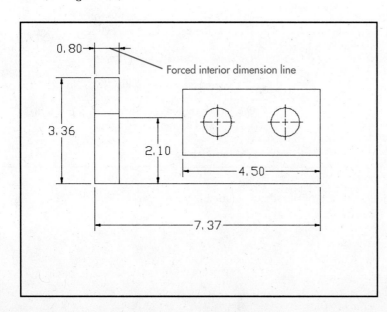

Figure 22.22

Forcing an interior dimension line.

22

Setting Text Orientation

Dimension text orientation observes either unilateral or bilateral placement. With the unilateral format, all the text is placed so that it reads horizontally and is read from the bottom of the drawing. In the bilateral format, the text follows the angle of the dimension line, and all vertical dimensions are read from the right side.

Text orientation is controlled in the Format dialog box. The Text section illustrates an image tile of dimension text inside and outside the extensions lines. The settings for inside and outside text are controlled by separate variables. The default settings for both are horizontal.

In the CHAP22A drawing, all the vertical dimensions have horizontal text. Use the Format dialog box to reset the text to follow the dimension lines. In the following exercise, you will reset all your dimensions to follow the bilateral format.

Applying Bilateral Text Placement

Continue in the CHAP22A drawing.

Choose Data, Dimension Style, *then* **F**ormat	Displays Dimension Styles dialog box, then Format dialog box
Clear the Force **L**ine Inside *check box*	Turns off forced interior lines
Clear the **I**nside Horizontal *and* **O**utside Horizontal *check boxes*	Sets all dimension text to follow orientation of dimension lines
Choose OK	Closes Format dialog box
Choose **S**ave	Saves new setting to PROJECT style
Choose OK	Closes Dimension Styles dialog box and updates dimensions

Save your drawing.

The vertical dimensions are updated automatically to realign the text with the dimension line (see fig. 22.23).

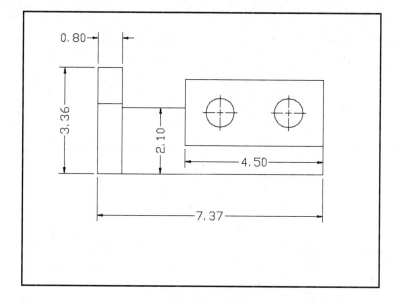

Figure 22.23

*Vertical
dimensions with
new text
alignment.*

Adjusting Vertical Text Justification

You control how your text is placed vertically in relation to the dimension line with the Vertical Justification section in the DDIM Format dialog box. Dimension text can be positioned above, below, or centered within the dimension line.

Using ANSI standards, the text is vertically centered on the dimension line, splitting the dimension line in two. According to ISO standards, the text is usually centered above the dimension line. With most architectural standards, the text is above the dimension line, and preferably centered. Depending on the drafting standards that you follow, you will want to have your dimension text either centered between or centered above the dimension lines.

In the CHAP22A drawing, all the dimension text is vertically centered on the dimension line. The following exercise shows you how to change it to be above the dimension line.

Forcing Text above the Dimension Line

Continue in the CHAP22A drawing.

Choose Data, Dimension Style,   Displays Dimension Styles dialog box, then
then **F**ormat   **F**ormat dialog box

continues

continued

Click on the Vertical Justification *drop-down list box*	Opens Vertical Justification options list
Select Above	Sets text justification to above dimension line
Choose OK	Closes Format dialog box
Choose <u>S</u>ave	Saves new setting to PROJECT style
Choose OK	Closes Dimension Styles dialog box and updates dimensions

Save your drawing.

The dimension text is changed to be above the dimension line (see fig. 22.24).

Figure 22.24

The new position of the vertical dimension text.

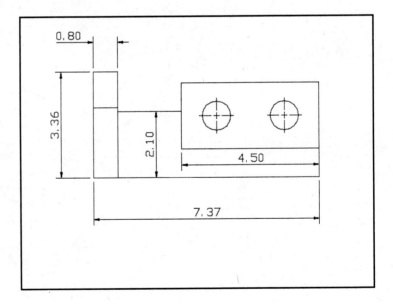

Managing Text Appearance in Dimensions

You have several options for controlling text appearance in dimensions. You can add prefixes and suffixes to the default text, such as RAD for radius dimensions, or TYP for typical dimensions. Before you start to adjust the variables in a dimension style, it is a good idea to create a text style for dimensions only.

Setting Dimension Text Style

The text style AutoCAD uses when placing a dimension is the current drawing text style. Among other features, the text style controls the font and the width of the dimension text. In Chapter 21, you create a text style called "DIMS" for dimensions, which squeezes the width of the text by 75 percent to help arrowheads and dimension text stay inside the extension lines more often.

Stop When creating a text style, one of the options you can set is the height of the text. Setting a text height as you define the text style will predetermine the height of your dimension text, no matter what you set it to in the Dimension Styles, Annotation dialog box. For dimension text to conform to your office practices, regardless of the scale of the drawing, it is essential to set the height in the text style definition to 0 and use the Dimension Styles, Annotation dialog box to set your dimension text height.

The Dimension Styles, Annotation dialog box (see fig. 22.25) enables you to control the appearance of your dimension text by providing the following options:

- ◆ Text style to be used

- ◆ Text height

- ◆ Prefixes and suffixes for dimension text

- ◆ Tolerances

- ◆ Alternate units

- ◆ Units precision

22

Figure 22.25

*The Annotation
dialog box.*

Controlling Dimension Text Height

With the height of your current text style set to 0, you can control the dimension text height in the Annotation dialog box. You then set the Overall Scale value in the Geometry dialog box to be the reciprocal of the plot scale.

The dimension text height in the CHAP22A drawing is set to the default height of 0.25. You want the dimension text to be 0.185, so set the height in the Annotation dialog box in the following exercise.

Controlling Text Height

Continue in the CHAP22A drawing.

Choose Data, Dimension Style, *then* **A**nnotation	Displays Dimension Styles dialog box, then Annotation dialog box
Press Alt+T	Highlights text Heigh**t** box
Type **.185**	Sets text height to .185
Choose OK	Closes the Annotation dialog box
Choose **S**ave	Saves the new setting to PROJECT style
Choose OK	Closes the dialog box and updates dimensions

Save your drawing.

All the dimension text automatically updates to the new .185 unit text height (see fig. 22.26).

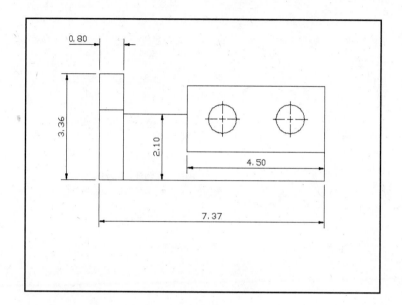

Figure 22.26

*The new
dimension text
height.*

Setting Primary Units for Dimensions

Chapter 5, "Setting Up a CAD Drawing," shows you how to set the units for a drawing using the Units Control dialog box. The drawing units setting controls the type and precision of units you use for coordinate display and input. With Release 13, AutoCAD has separate settings for dimension text precision, which you can set in the Dimension Styles, Annotation dialog box.

The Primary Units dialog box—accessed by choosing Units in the Primary Units cluster of the Annotation dialog box—provides the option to set the type of units you want for linear and angular dimension text.

The dimension units are currently set to two decimal places. The following exercise shows you how to set the primary units to a three-place decimal for dimension text using the Units option in the Primary Units cluster:

22

Adjusting Dimension Units Precision

Continue in the CHAP22A drawing.

Choose Data, Dimension Style, *then choose* **A**nnotation	Displays Dimension Styles dialog box, then Annotation dialog box
In the Primary Units *cluster, choose* **U**nits	Displays the Primary Units dialog box
In the Dimension *cluster, click on the* **P**recision *drop-down list (see fig. 22.27)*	Drops down the list of dimension text precision options
Choose the three-decimal place (`0.000`) *option*	Sets precision to three places
Choose OK	Closes the Primary Units dialog box
Choose OK	Closes the Annotation dialog box
Choose **S**ave	Saves the new setting to **PROJECT** style
Choose OK	Closes the dialog box and initiates the changes

Save your drawing.

All the dimension text automatically updates to the new three-decimal place precision (see fig. 22.28).

Figure 22.27

Setting dimension precision in the Primary Units dialog box.

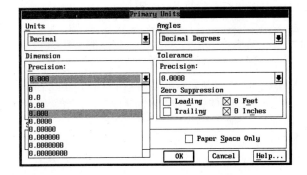

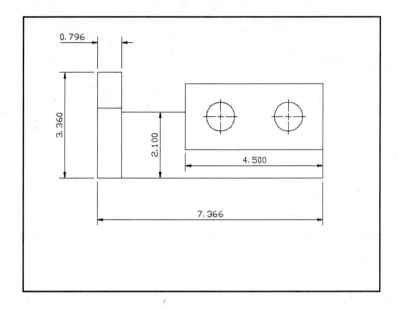

Figure 22.28

The dimensions with three-place decimal precision.

Controlling Zeros in Dimension Text

Depending on your drafting standards or just how you want your dimensions to look, you might need to control how AutoCAD uses zeros in the dimension text.

Drafting conventions established over many years of manual drafting have determined that, for example, for machining operations, you usually show the leading zero in your dimensions; in architectural drawings, however, you would not want leading zeros for feet measurements when dimensions show inches only. Convention also dictates that when using decimal units, you include leading zeros, but in imperial units, you do not include a leading zero feet indication.

Note   With decimal dimensions, you can turn off either the leading zeros in front of the decimal point or the trailing zeros after the last number. More is covered in Chapter 24, "Techniques for Mechanical Dimensioning." When using architectural units, you can control when zeros are used for feet or inches. Chapter 23, "Techniques for Architectural and Civil Dimensioning," goes more in depth on this topic.

Using Alternate Units

You can place dimensions that show two types of units for a single measurement. An example is when the primary dimension value shows inches, and a secondary value—in brackets—shows the metric equivalent within the same dimension. In this case, the metric measurement is called the *alternate* unit (see fig. 22.29).

Figure 22.29

A dimension showing alternate units.

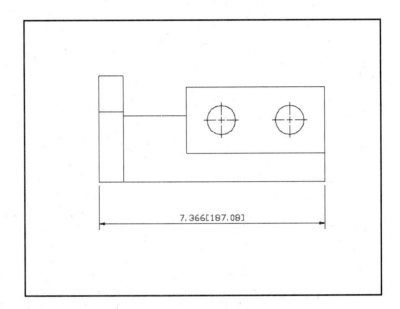

You set alternate units in the Alternate Units cluster of the Annotation dialog box. Within the Alternate Units cluster are several settings that control how alternate units are formatted. Options exist for the type of unit used for alternate dimensions, prefixes, and suffixes. An image tile illustrates graphically how your alternate units are set to look. Put a check in the Enable Units box to turn on alternate units.

The Units button displays the Alternate Units dialog box, which enables you to set the type of units and precision, to control zero suppression, tolerance precision, zero suppression for tolerances, and the linear scale factor (see fig. 22.30). The only difference between the Alternate Units dialog box and the Primary Units dialog box is that in the former, a Linear Scale Factor for the alternate unit—by default, 25.4— can be set.

For more information about managing alternate dimensions, see Chapter 24.

Figure 22.30

The Alternate Units dialog box.

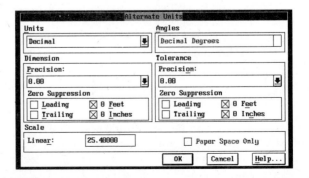

Dimensioning with Lateral Tolerances

In machining parts for manufacturing, part sizes and shapes can vary depending on the lateral tolerance that is acceptable for that part. When a cylinder needs to fit inside a hole, the acceptable tolerance determines whether the cylinder fits tightly or moves freely inside the hole. For more information on adding tolerances to dimensions, and creating geometric tolerances, see Chapter 24.

Applying Dimension Styles

After you create a dimension style family, you can apply variations to each of the family members. These family members represent the different types of dimensions found in the Family cluster of the Dimension Styles dialog box: Linear, Radial, Angular, Diameter, Ordinate, and Leader dimensions (refer to fig. 22.1). Having these members at your fingertips enables you to have different settings for each type of dimension, while still only using one dimension style.

 Note In a slightly confusing manner, AutoCAD groups diameter and radius dimensions as *radial* dimensions on the pull-down menu, but defines family members as *diameter* and *radial*, not *radius*. When working with dimension style family members, remember that "radial" means radius.

You might want your diameter dimensions to have the text forced inside, for example, and your radius dimensions to have the text outside the arc or circle. Within a parent style, you would set radius dimensions to force the text outside and the diameter dimensions to force the text inside. When you apply either a radius or a diameter dimension, AutoCAD understands the type of dimension placed and uses the appropriate setting for that dimension. This prevents the need for a different dimension style when you need only a minor change in dimension settings for each type of dimension.

In the following exercise, you create "child" dimension styles within the parent "PROJECT" style. Until now, the Parent radio button in the Family cluster has been selected, so changes made to dimension geometry, format, and annotation have applied to all members of the "PROJECT" family. Selecting one of the other radio buttons in the Family cluster will cause any changes in settings to apply only to the selected "child" style.

22

Creating "Child" Dimension Styles

Continue in the CHAP22A drawing.

Command: *Choose* Draw, Dimensioning, *then* Radial, Radius	Issues DIMRADIUS command

```
Command: _dimradius
Select arc or circle: Pick
```
① *(see fig. 22.31)*

```
Dimension line location (Text/Angle):
```
Pick ②   Places radius dimension (see fig. 22.31)

The radius dimension is accurate but not well formatted; erase it, and place a better-formatted one. First, you create a special style for radius dimensions.

Command: *Choose* Data, Dimension Style	Displays Dimension Styles dialog box
In the Family *cluster, choose* Radial	Sets Radius member of PROJECT family as current
Choose Format	Displays Format dialog box

The User Defined option in the Format dialog box gives you additional control over text placement. Normally, you would want this option turned off so the Horizontal Justification settings control text placement. In the case of radius and diameter dimensions, however, you do not have enough control with Horizontal Justification settings enabled. Turning on User Defined overrides the Horizontal Justification settings.

Choose the User Defined *option*	Disables Horizontal Justification settings for Radial member of PROJECT family

You also need to allow dimension text for radial dimensions to be horizontal, so the dimension can have the appearance of a leader notation. Finally, the dimension text needs to have a Centered vertical justification.

Choose Outside Horizontal *in the* Text *cluster*	Allows dimension text to be placed horizontally
Choose Above *in the* Vertical Justification *cluster and change the setting to* Centered	Places dimension text vertically centered on the dimension line

The Format dialog box should look like figure 22.32 when you are finished.

Choose OK, *then* <u>S</u>ave, *then* OK	Confirms settings in Format dialog box, saves settings to Radial member of PROJECT dimension style, and closes Dimension Styles dialog box
Command: *Choose* Draw, Dimensioning, Radial, Radius	Issues DIMRADIUS command
`Command: _dimradius` `Select arc or circle:` *Pick* ① *(see fig. 22.33)*	
`Dimension line location (Text/Angle):` *Pick* ②	Places radius dimension

The new radius dimension automatically conforms to the settings made to the Radial member of the PROJECT parent dimension style (see fig. 22.33).

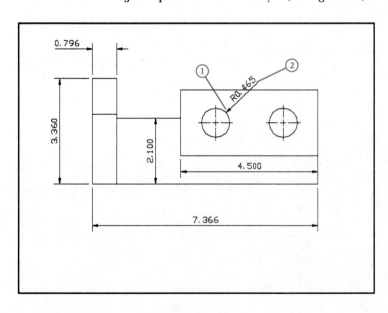

Figure 22.31

A radial dimension observing the parent PROJECT style settings.

22

Figure 22.32

The Format dialog box with settings for radial dimensions.

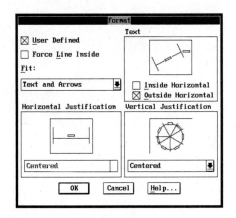

Figure 22.33

Radial "child" dimensions of the PROJECT family.

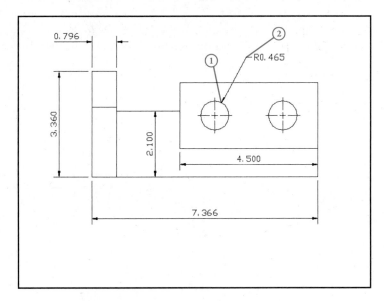

Overriding Style Settings

For most of the dimensions you place in your drawings, you make an existing dimension style current and use the settings in that style to control the way your dimensions are created. At times you might want to adjust a single dimension variable to place a dimension that looks different. You already did this when you suppressed the extension lines of two dimensions in an earlier exercise.

As you saw then, rather than create a completely new style, you can override your current style's settings by changing a variable to place a single dimension. Overrides

New Riders Publishing
INSIDE
SERIES

enable you to create and keep current one base dimension style, yet maintain the ability to make small adjustments for individual dimensions that must be different. This eliminates the need to create a new dimension style for every dimension that needs a different setting.

In the CHAP22A drawing, a new vertical dimension will indicate the distance from the top of the block to the centers of the two holes. This dimension should show two decimal places of accuracy. Set the dimension unit's precision to two places in the following exercise. You will not save the changes to the current style; the change in settings will be used only for the next dimension. Then place a dimension as shown in figure 22.34.

Stop When you set an override for one or more dimensions that you are ready to place, do not save the changes in the Dimension Styles dialog box. This would save the change to the current dimension style and would update *all* the existing dimensions created with that style. When the current style name is prefaced with a plus sign, it has not been saved.

Setting Dimension Style Overrides

Continue in the CHAP22A drawing.

Choose Data, Dimension Style, *then choose* **A**nnotation	Displays Dimension Styles dialog box, then the Annotation dialog box
In the Primary Units *cluster, choose* **U**nits	Displays Primary Units dialog box
In the Dimension *cluster, click on the* **P**recision *box*	Drops down options list for dimension text precision
Select the two-decimal place (`0.00`) *option*	
Choose OK *three times*	Closes Primary Units, Annotation, and Dimension Styles dialog boxes without saving change
Command: *Choose* Draw, Dimensioning Linear	Issues DIMLINEAR command

`_dimlinear`
`First extension line origin or`
`RETURN to select:` *Pick the line at* ① *(see fig. 22.34)*
	Specifies the first extension line

continues

continued

`Second extension line origin:` *Pick the line at* ②	Specifies the second extension line origin
`Dimension line location (Text/ Angle/Horizontal/Vertical/Rotated):` *Pick* ③	Places the dimension line

Save your drawing.

Using this technique of changing a variable without saving it to the current style enables you to add dimensions with small variations without having to create a new dimension style (see fig. 22.34).

Figure 22.34

Using a dimension override to adjust decimal precision.

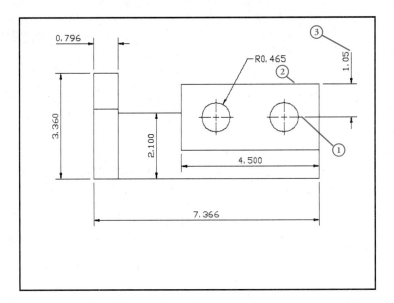

Applying Overrides to Existing Dimensions

Existing dimensions can be changed by adding an override to them. The DIMOVERRIDE command enables you to change any variable settings and select the dimension to which you want to apply the changes. The dimension then updates to the new settings.

New Riders Publishing
INSIDE SERIES

> **DIMOVERRIDE.** The DIMOVERRIDE command provides the capability to change individual dimension variables without having to create a whole new dimension style. DIMOVERRIDE is not in any menu and must be entered from the Command: prompt.
> `Command: DIMOVERRIDE`

Note The Dimension Styles dialog box shields users from the often arcane names of dimension variables. It's easy to modify existing dimensions by using the Dimension Styles dialog box to set overrides, and then using the Apply option of the DIMSTYLE command to select the dimensions to modify. Using DIMOVERRIDE from the Command prompt requires that you enter the name of the dimension variable you want to change; you, therefore, need to know the actual variable names.

In the following exercise, the upper left dimension (0.796) needs its text forced inside the extension lines and the leading zero suppressed.

Overriding Settings in Existing Dimensions

Continue in the CHAP22A drawing.

`Command: DIMOVERRIDE` (Enter)	Starts DIMOVERRIDE command
`Dimension variable to override: (or Clear to remove overrides): DIMTIX` (Enter)	Forces text inside extension lines
`Current value <Off> New value: ON` (Enter)	
`Dimension variable to override: DIMZIN` (Enter)	Suppresses leading zeros
`Current value <0> New value: 4` (Enter)	
`Dimension variable to override:` (Enter)	Exits variable prompts
`Select objects:` *Pick the upper left dimension* (0.796)	Selects dimension to override
`1 found`	
`Select objects:` (Enter)	Exits command and applies overrides

continues

continued

The text is moved inside the extension lines, and the leading zero is suppressed (see fig. 22.35).

Save your drawing.

Figure 22.35

Realigning text with overrides.

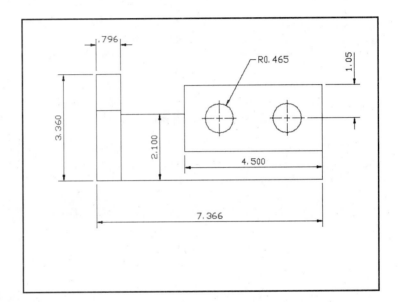

Changing an Existing Dimension's Style

At times you will need to change existing dimensions to a new dimension style. A new dimension style can be applied to any existing dimension.

> **DIMSTYLE.** The DIMSTYLE command provides the capability to restore dimension styles, save the current settings to a style name, list the current variable settings, current overrides, or the settings in another dimension style, update dimensions to the current settings, and list the dimension styles that are available in a drawing. DIMSTYLE is not available in any menu and must be entered from the Command prompt.

Using the Dimension Styles dialog box, you will set a different dimension style current and then use the DIMSTYLE command to select the dimensions that you want changed to that style. The existing vertical dimensions were created with the

New Riders Publishing
INSIDE
SERIES

PROJECT dimension style. You now will change their dimension style to the VERT-DIMS style. The text will be switched to horizontal.

Applying a Dimension Style to an Existing Dimension

Continue in the CHAP22A drawing.

`Command:` *Choose* Data, Dimension Style	Displays Dimension Styles dialog box
Click on the <u>C</u>urrent *text box*	Displays drop-down list of styles
Choose VERT-DIMS	Selects VERT-DIMS dimension style
Choose <u>A</u>nnotation	Displays Annotation dialog box
Choose <u>U</u>nits	Displays Primary Units dialog box
Open the <u>P</u>recision *drop-down list and choose* 0.0000	Sets decimal precision to four places
Choose OK *twice, then* Save	Closes Primary Units and Annotation dialog boxes, and saves changes to VERT-DIMS dimension style
Choose OK	Exits dialog box
`Command:` **DIMSTYLE** (Enter)	Issues DIMSTYLE command

`Dimension style: VERT-DIMS`
`dimension Style Edit (Save/Restore`
`/STatus/Variables/Apply/?)`
`<Restore>:` **A** (Enter)
	Selects Apply option

`Select objects:` *Pick the three vertical dimensions (see fig. 22.36)*	Selects all vertical dimensions to change to VERT-DIMS style
`Select objects:` (Enter)	Ends command and changes all selected dimensions to VERT-DIMS style

Save your drawing.

Notice that all the vertical dimensions have text that is now horizontal and are set with four-place decimal precision (see fig. 22.36). Notice also that the overrides you set earlier, to suppress both extension lines on the 2.10 dimension, are not honored, as they were applied to a different dimension style.

Figure 22.36

The new dimension style applied to the vertical dimensions.

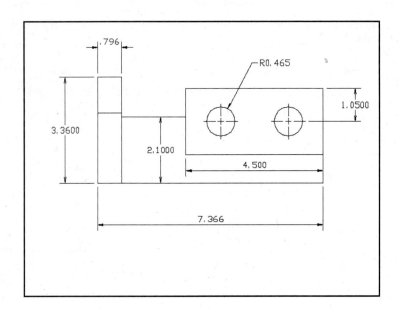

The following list describes the command options for DIMSTYLE:

◆ **Save.** Saves the current dimension variable settings to a new style name.

◆ **Restore.** Restores another dimension style's variables to make them current.

◆ **STatus.** Displays the current setting for all the current style's variables.

◆ **Variables.** Displays a list of variable settings for any dimension style without affecting the current style settings.

◆ **Apply.** Applies the current dimension style settings and any current dimension overrides to any dimension objects you select.

◆ **?.** Provides a list of the dimension styles created in the current drawing.

Getting a List of Dimension Variable Settings

To determine the dimension variable settings for the current dimension style, you can use the DIMSTYLE command. The following exercise shows you how to list the current settings of all dimension variables.

Listing Current Dimension Variable Settings

Continue in the CHAP22A drawing.

Command: **DIMSTYLE** (Enter)	Issues the DIMSTYLE command
dimension style: VERT-DIMS Dimension Style Edit (Save/Restore /STatus/Variables/Apply/?) <Restore>: **ST** (Enter)	Selects the STatus option and displays the current settings in the text window

Press Enter several times, until the command: *prompt reappears*

DIMSTYLE's STatus option also shows you if any overrides are currently set. Set some temporary dimension overrides.

Command: **DDIM** (Enter)	Displays Dimension Styles dialog box
Choose Geometry, *then* Suppress 2nd Extension Line, *then* OK	Suppresses second extension line
Choose Format, *then* Force Line Inside, *then* OK	Forces dimension line between extension lines
Choose Annotation, *then* Enable Units, *then* OK	Turns on alternate units display
Choose OK *(do not save)*	Does not save changes to dimension style
Command: **DIMSTYLE** (Enter)	Issues DIMSTYLE command

dimension style: VERT-DIMS
dimension style overrides:
    DIMALT   On
    DIMSE2   On
    DIMTOFL On
	Lists current dimension style
	Lists current dimension overrides
	Alternate units dimension variable
	Suppress second extension line variable
	Force interior dimension line variable

Dimension Style Edit (Save/Restore/
STatus/Variables/Apply/?) <Restore>:
Press Esc to break out of command

The text screen lists one page of dimension variables; press Enter to see the next pages. The dimension variables are listed in Appendix G.

Open the Dimension Styles dialog box, restore the VERT-DIMS style and save your drawing.

22

Editing Existing Dimensions

Where new dimensions are concerned, you can cover practically every eventuality by using the style families and the Dimension Styles dialog box. At times, however, you have to make a change to a dimension that has already been placed in a drawing, and styles will not handle what you want to do. For those cases, there are dimension editing commands.

Exploding Dimensions

The real power of editing dimensions comes from the associativity of each dimension. In the early versions of AutoCAD, it was sometimes quicker to use the EXPLODE command on a dimension and then to edit its parts to get the dimension to look the way you wanted it. In the last few releases of AutoCAD, there have been great improvements made to dimension editing.

Exploding dimensions for editing is no longer necessary because of the new variables that control every part of a dimension. Before you start to explode dimensions, make sure you have examined all the dimension editing commands and dimension style options. Exploding dimensions converts intelligent dimension entities to an unrelated group of primitive entities. When you explode dimensions, you defeat the dynamic capabilities of controlling associative dimensions with dimension styles.

 Stop Associative dimensions are *unnamed blocks*. After you explode a dimension, it is changed into individual objects, and all the objects float down to layer 0. If you need to explode a dimension, make sure you change all the resulting objects back to your dimension layer, and change the color and linetype properties of the objects back to BYLAYER. Alternatively, you can use the XPLODE command, which gives you the option of placing the exploded entities on any layer.

Changing Dimension Position with Grips

The best way to edit a dimension's basic geometry is with grips. Once dimensions have been placed on the drawing, they can be difficult to modify. Without using grips, for example, it's impossible to move the dimension line or defining points of an individual dimension.

The grips autoediting modes are introduced in Chapter 8, "Object Selection and Grip Editing." Grips enable you to edit the definition points of a dimension, the dimension line location, and the text location.

New Riders Publishing
INSIDE SERIES

In the CHAP22A drawing in the following exercise, the left vertical dimension needs to be moved out farther away from the object, and the right vertical dimension modified to show the overall height of that side of the part.

Changing Dimension Line Position

Continue in the CHAP22A drawing.

Before you start this exercise, make sure you have a clear Command: prompt.

Command: *Pick the left vertical dimension*	Selects dimension and displays grips
Pick the grip at ① *(see fig. 22.37)*	Enters Stretch autoediting mode
STRETCH <Stretch to point>/Base point/ Copy/Undo/eXit: *Drag the dimension line and pick at* ② *(see fig. 22.38)*	Moves the dimension line position

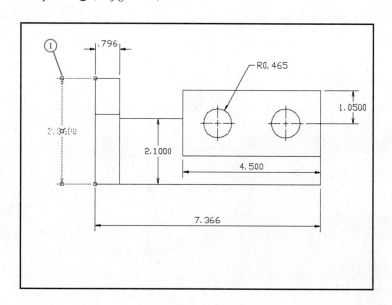

Figure 22.37

Using Autoedit Stretch to move a dimension line.

22

continues

continued

Figure 22.38

Simple relocation of a dimension line using grips.

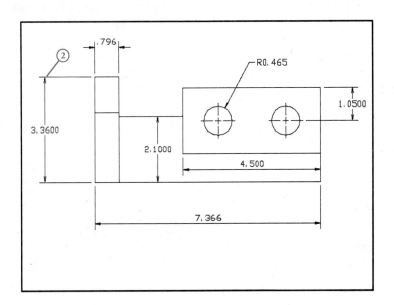

After placing the dimension line in its new position, press Esc twice to cancel the autoediting mode.

Next, use grips stretch mode to modify the vertical dimension at the right of the drawing.

Command: *Pick the right vertical dimension*	Selects dimension and displays grips
Pick the grip at ① *(see fig. 22.39)*	Enters Stretch autoediting mode
STRETCH <Stretch to point>/Base point/ Copy/Undo/eXit: *Drag the dimension line and pick at* ② *(use ENDPoint object snap)*	Moves the extension line and defpoint

After placing the dimension line in its new position (see fig. 22.40), press Esc twice to cancel the autoediting mode.

Finally, use grips to relocate the text on the uppermost horizontal dimension. Note that, unlike in Release 12, it is not possible to move the text without also moving the dimension line.

Command: *Pick the horizontal dimension at the upper left* Selects dimension and displays grips

Pick the grip at ① *(see fig. 24.41)* Enters Stretch autoediting mode

STRETCH
<Stretch to point>/Base point/
Copy/Undo/eXit: *Drag the dimension text and pick at* ② Moves the dimension line and text

After placing the dimension line and text in their new position, press Esc twice to cancel the autoediting mode.

Save your drawing.

With your final autoediting completed, your drawing should look like figure 22.42.

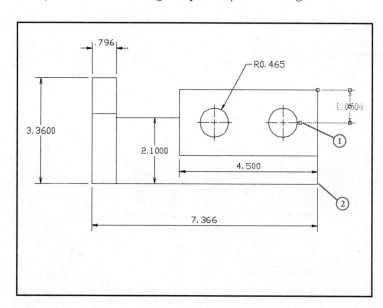

Figure 22.39

Turning on grips in the second dimension to adjust.

22

Figure 22.40

*Dimension
adjusted using
Autoedit's stretch
mode.*

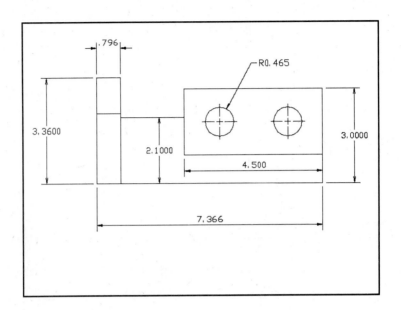

Figure 22.41

*Selecting
dimension text for
grip editing.*

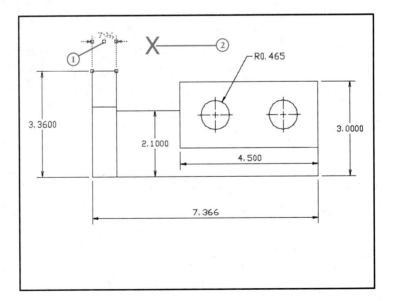

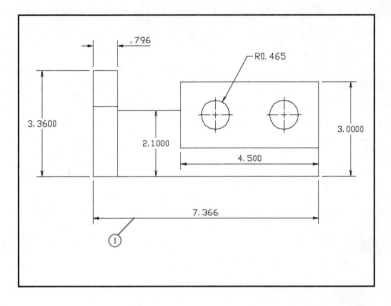

Figure 22.42

Dimension text after move using grips.

Editing Dimension Text

After you place your dimensions, you might need to adjust certain aspects of the text to have the dimension look the way you want it. The DIMEDIT command enables you to manipulate your dimension in several ways.

DIMEDIT. The DIMEDIT command provides the capability to assign new text to a dimension, adjust the text position, rotate the text, and oblique the extension lines. The DIMEDIT command can be used to edit one or more dimensions at a time. Specific options can be issued from the pull-down menus, but the full range of options is only available from the Command prompt.

Pull-down: Draw, Dimensioning, Oblique
Pull-down: Draw, Dimensioning, Align Text, <options>
Command: DIMEDIT

In the following exercise, the New option in DIMEDIT is used to replace the overall dimension's text (7.366) with 7.500.

Editing Dimension Text

Continue in the CHAP22A drawing.

Command: **DIMEDIT** (Enter)   Starts DIMEDIT command

Dimension Edit (Home/New/   Selects New option
Rotate/Oblique) <Home>: **N**

Dimension text <0.000>: **7.500** (Enter)   New value entered

Select objects: *Pick dimension at*
① *(see fig. 22.42)*

Select objects: 1 found   Selects dimension to modify

Select objects: (Enter)   Updates dimension

Save your drawing.

The dimension text changes from 7.366 to 7.500 without editing the geometry (see fig. 22.43).

Figure 22.43

Using DIMEDIT to reposition dimension text.

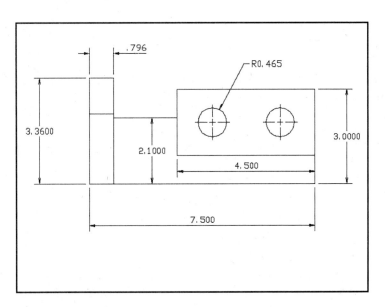

DIMEDIT Command Options

The DIMEDIT command provides the following options to help manage your dimension text:

◆ **Home.** Repositions the text to its original position.

◆ **New.** Enables you to edit dimension text without having to edit the geometry to which the dimension is attached.

◆ **Rotate.** Rotates the dimension text without affecting the dimension geometry itself. The dimension lines will adjust to the new text width according to the DIMGAP setting.

◆ **Oblique.** Rotates the extension lines of a dimension to an angle you specify.

The next exercise illustrates how DIMEDIT's other options work.

Using DIMEDIT's Options

Continue in drawing CHAP22A. Use DIMEDIT's Home option to return the text of the dimension you just used grips to move to its default location.

Command: **DIMEDIT** (Enter)	Starts DIMEDIT command
Dimension Edit (Home/New/ Rotate/Oblique) <Home>: (Enter)	Selects Home option
Select objects: *Select text at* ① *(see fig. 22.44)*	Selects dimension to modify
Select objects: 1 found	
Select objects: (Enter)	Returns dimension text to home position

Next, use DIMEDIT's Rotate and Oblique options to modify the vertical dimension at the right side of the part.

Command: **DIMEDIT**	Starts DIMEDIT command
Dimension Edit (Home/New/ Rotate/Oblique) <Home>: **R** (Enter)	Selects Rotate option
Enter text angle: **15**	Enters angle for text rotation
Select objects: *Pick dimension at* ②	Selects dimension to modify

continues

continued

```
Select objects: 1 found
```

```
Select objects: (Enter)              Rotates dimension text
```

```
Command: (Enter)                     Reissues DIMEDIT command
```

```
DIMEDIT Dimension Edit (Home/New/    Selects Oblique option
Rotate/Oblique) <Home>: 0 (Enter)
```

```
Select objects: Pick dimension       Selects dimension to modify
at ② again
```

```
Select objects: 1 found
```

```
Select objects: (Enter)              Ends object selection
```

```
Enter obliquing angle (RETURN for    Sets extension lines to oblique angle
none): 15 (Enter)
```

```
Command:
```

Save your drawing. It should look like figure 22.45.

Figure 22.44

Selecting the dimensions to modify with DIMEDIT.

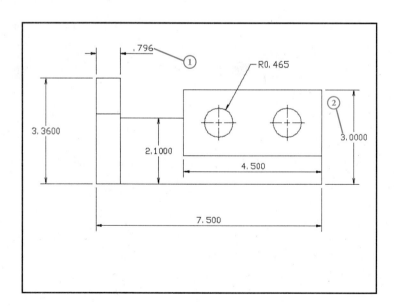

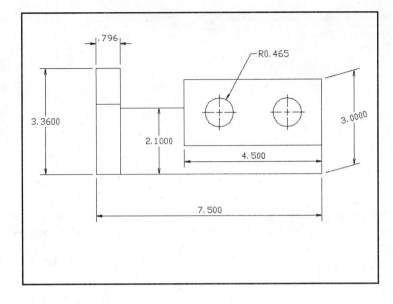

Figure 22.45

Using DIMEDIT to modify dimension text and extension lines.

Editing MTEXT in Dimensions

In addition to DIMEDIT New, you can also use a full-screen editor to revise your dimension text. Selecting Modify, Edit Text from the pull-down menus causes dimension text to be treated like MTEXT objects (see Chapter 13 "Annotation with Text," for a discussion of MTEXT).

In the following exercise, MTEXT editing is used to add a notation to the overall dimension.

Editing MTEXT in Dimensions

Continue in drawing CHAP22A.

`Command:` *Choose* Modify, Edit Text	Issues DDEDIT command
`<Select a TEXT or ATTDEF object>/` `Undo:` *Select the overall horizontal dimension text (7.500)*	AutoCAD shells to MS-DOS Editor with dimension text loaded

Add the text **FACE TO FACE** after the dimension value (see fig. 22.46) and exit MS-DOS Editor, saving your changes by pressing Alt+F, then X. You are notified that the loaded file is not saved. Press Enter to save it now.

You are returned to the drawing editor with the dimension text revised (see fig. 22.47)

Figure 22.46

Using Modify Text switches to MS-DOS Editor.

Figure 22.47

Dimension text modified as MTEXT.

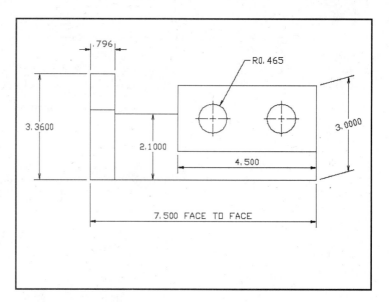

Using DIMTEDIT To Edit Dimension Text

When placing dimensions, there are times when the dimensions must be placed closely together because of the limited space available. When this happens, you need to reposition the dimension's text to be read easily. The DIMTEDIT command offers four options for changing the text position.

New Riders Publishing
INSIDE
SERIES

> **DIMTEDIT.** The DIMTEDIT command is used to reposition text within associative dimensions.
> Pull-down: *Choose* Draw, Dimensioning, Align Text

DIMTEDIT Command Options

When using DIMTEDIT to change text placement, the following options are available:

◆ **Left.** Places the dimension text as far to the left as possible while still showing a minimum dimension line length.

◆ **Right.** Repositions the dimension text to the right with a minimum dimension line length.

◆ **Home.** Moves the text back to its original position and orientation.

◆ **Angle.** Rotates the dimension text to an angle you specify.

Calling the command from the pull-down menu presents you with a fifth option, Center. This option, while not part of the DIMTEDIT command, will relocate dimension text to the center of the dimension line; note that this may be different than DIMTEDIT's Home option.

The DIM Mode and Basic Edit Commands

When you enter **DIM** or **DIM1** at the Command: prompt, you turn on AutoCAD's dimensioning mode. Dim mode enables you to use the dimension subcommands from earlier releases of AutoCAD. In Release 13, the dimensioning commands have been mainstreamed so you can enter them at the Command: prompt like the other commands. Now you don't have to enter a "dim mode" to start dimension commands.

The DIM command is still available in this release only for compatibility with the last release. Table 22.1 shows dimension editing commands used in the Dim mode and their equivalent Release 13 commands.

22

TABLE 22.1
DIM Mode Editing Commands and Their Release 13 Equivalents

DIM Mode Command	Release 13 Command
HOMETEXT	DIMEDIT Home
NEWTEXT	DIMEDIT Text
OBLIQUE	DIMEDIT Oblique
OVERRIDE	DIMOVERRIDE
RESTORE	DIMSTYLE Restore
ROTATED	DIMLINEAR <angle>
SAVE	DIMSTYLE Save
STATUS	DIMSTYLE Status
TEDIT	DIMTEDIT
TROTATE	DIMEDIT Rotate
UPDATE	DIMSTYLE Apply

Managing Dimensions in Projects

An important consideration in managing projects is the consistent dimensioning of all the drawings throughout all the departments. Dimension styles can be a great management tool in accomplishing this goal.

Place all your dimension styles in the prototype drawings; then, when new drawings are started from these prototypes, the dimension styles will already be available to all CAD operators, eliminating the need for each operator to define his or her own dimension styles. After everyone learns the dimension style to use for each dimensioning situation, all the drawings will have consistent-looking dimensions.

 Tip You can import dimension styles by inserting as a block a drawing that contains the needed styles. When you do so, cancel the insertion at the Insertion point: prompt and the block won't actually be inserted. Definitions of the styles as well as blocks, text styles, and other named definitions from the inserted drawing will, however, be imported. You later can purge any unwanted definitions, but it is best to insert a drawing that includes only the dimension styles, and no objects or other definitions. It need not even include any dimension objects.

New Riders Publishing
INSIDE
SERIES

In this chapter, you have learned some of the advanced techniques of working with dimensions in AutoCAD. You have learned how to create and modify dimension styles so you can have total control over their appearance in the drawing. The next chapter explains how to apply what we've learned to specific drawing disciplines: architecture and civil drafting.

22

Techniques for Architectural and Civil Dimensioning

AutoCAD is the CAD software of choice for the majority of CAD software users. The prime reason for its popularity is its flexibility. AutoCAD has been called a "graphics engine," which means that it contains a great set of generic tools. You can modify the basic engine by creating your own specific environment, by changing AutoCAD's default environment, by doing your own customization, or by buying a third-party software add-on. Being able to change the way AutoCAD works to suit your own standards and specifications is why so many different drafting and design disciplines use AutoCAD. AutoCAD lends itself easily to whatever type of drawings you need to create, be they architectural, civil, mechanical, electrical, piping, or clothing design.

AutoCAD's flexibility extends to most aspects of the package. One area where users take advantage of this flexibility is in controlling the appearance of dimensions.

Both architectural and civil drawings require different dimension settings to get dimensions that look correct for that discipline. This chapter shows you how to set up the basic AutoCAD dimensioning environment for architectural and civil drawings, and then works through exercises for each. You will learn about the following:

- ◆ Defining architectural dimension standards

- ◆ Creating dimension style families for architectural drawings

◆ Using hand-lettering fonts included with this book to add architectural flavor to dimensions

◆ Placing architectural dimensions

◆ Defining civil dimension standards

◆ Creating a dimension style family for civil drawings

◆ Using fonts that mimic Leroy template lettering in dimensions for civil drawings

AutoCAD's default dimension settings enable you to create a very basic type of dimension. You can change some of those settings so that the dimensions you place follow the standards for architectural dimensions. The architectural industry has its own dimension standards; most firms use oblique ticks as terminators, place the dimension text above the dimension line, and allow the dimension line to extend past the extension line. Figure 23.1 shows a typical floor plan dimensioned according to the dimension settings for architectural standards.

Figure 23.1

Example of architectural dimensions.

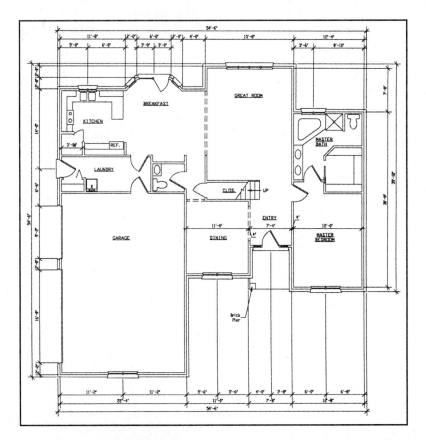

Creating Dimension Style Families for Architectural Drawings

In Chapter 22, "Editing and Styling Dimensions," you learn that creating a dimension style gives you control of all the components that comprise a dimension. Dimension style family members give even more control over how each of the different dimension commands work within a certain dimension style family.

Dimension style families is one of the major enhancements to dimensioning in Release 13. Frequently, architectural dimensions use oblique tick marks as terminators for dimension lines. In past releases of AutoCAD, you had to create two separate dimension styles to have leaders with arrowheads and linear dimensions with ticks. In Release 13, you no longer need to create a new dimension style for minor changes with the different types of dimension commands. Dimension style families give you the capability to create leaders with arrowheads and linear dimensions with ticks, all in the same dimension style.

For a complete architectural dimension style, you create a dimension style family member under the ARCH family name for each of the different dimensioning commands.

Tip

Remember that if you create and save your dimension styles in your prototype drawings, all your dimension styles will be immediately available when you begin a new drawing. Doing so lends consistency to your dimensioning in all your drawings.

A variation of the prototype drawing setup is to have a completely empty drawing file that has only the dimension styles added. You can insert this type of drawing into any existing drawing, so all you really add are the defined dimension styles. This enables you to have consistent dimension styles in drawings not started from your standard prototype.

A prototype drawing called US_ARCH.DWG comes with your AutoCAD software, and you should be able to find it in the C:\ACADR13\COMMON\SUPPORT directory on your hard drive. Autodesk also provides a mechanical prototype called US_MECH.DWG in the same directory. The US_ARCH drawing provided with AutoCAD is a good beginning of an architectural prototype, but it is not complete. The dimensioning setup lacks a few features

23

that need to be set to make it a complete architectural dimension style. The following list indicates the limitations of the AutoCAD prototype in the dimensioning setup:

- ◆ Does not have a text style that uses an architectural font

- ◆ Does not force a dimension line inside the extension lines when the text is outside the extension lines

- ◆ Does not extend the dimension lines past the extension lines

- ◆ Does not center fractions vertically relative to the main text

- ◆ Leaves the angular dimensions reading to four decimal places instead of changing angular dimension precision to the usual whole number values

- ◆ Sets the DIMRADIUS, DIMDIAMETER, and LEADER commands to use oblique ticks when they should use arrowheads

- ◆ Leaves the format for text alignment at horizontal when it should align with the dimension line

- ◆ Suppresses zero inches on even foot dimensions

In the following exercise, you develop a better overall architectural dimension style that has complete settings. You create a dimension style called ARCH that you can use when you place dimensions on a floor plan.

Creating an Architectural Dimension Style

Begin the exercise by creating a new drawing called CHAP23, using the FLORPLAN drawing from the IA Disk as a prototype.

Choose Data, Dimension Style	Displays Dimension Styles dialog box
Double-click in the Name *edit box, and type* **ARCH**	
Choose Save	Creates new dimension style ARCH from existing style STANDARD and sets ARCH current (see fig. 23.2)

Remain in the Dimension Styles dialog box for the next exercise.

Now that you have created a new dimension style called ARCH, you need to adjust the dimension features to follow architectural standards. You created the new style from the STANDARD dimension style, which has very basic settings.

New Riders Publishing
INSIDE
SERIES

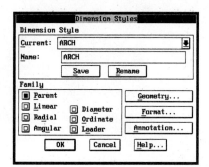

Figure 23.2

Creating a new dimension style called ARCH.

Note When you create a new dimension style, the new style is always created from the dimension style that is current at the time. If you have existing dimension styles, and you want to create a new one, be sure to set a dimension style current that has the most settings similar to your new style.

If you create a new dimension style for the first time in a drawing, AutoCAD copies the STANDARD style to create your first new dimension style.

Setting the Overall Dimension Scale Factor for Architectural Drawings

The most important dimension variable to set correctly is the Overall Scale factor for your dimensions. Chapter 22 emphasizes the importance of setting your dimension feature sizes to the size you want on the paper. You set the Overall Scale factor to match your drawing scale factor. The Overall Scale factor multiplies the size of each dimension component and enlarges or reduces the dimension components to match the scale of the drawing.

In the following exercise, you set the overall dimension scale factor to the correct value for the FLORPLAN drawing. The CHAP23 drawing is going to be plotted at 1/4''=1'-0''. You should set the Overall Dimension Scale factor to this scale, but first you must find out the correct scale factor. The easiest way to figure out the correct scale factor is to determine the number of quarter-inches in a foot, which is 48. Therefore, in the following exercise you set the Overall Scale factor to 48.

Setting the Overall Dimension Scale Factor

Continue working in the Dimension Styles dialog box.

Choose **G**eometry   Displays Geometry dialog box (see fig. 23.3)

continues

continued

Double-click inside the O<u>v</u>erall Scale *edit box and type* **48** *to reset the value*	Sets Overall Scale factor to 48
Choose OK	Exits Geometry dialog box
Choose <u>S</u>ave	Saves new settings to ARCH parent style

Remain in the Dimension Styles dialog box for the next exercise.

Figure 23.3

Setting the Overall Scale factor in the ARCH dimension style.

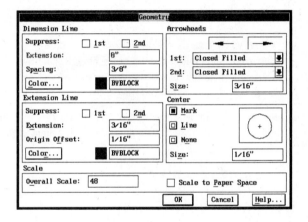

Table 23.1 lists the most common drawing scale factors in architectural drawings and the associated Overall Scale settings.

TABLE 23.1
Dimension Scale Factors in Architectural Drawings

Drawing Scale Factor	Overall Scale Settings
1-1/2''=1'-0''	8
1''=1'-0''	12
3/4''=1'-0''	16
1/2''=1'-0''	24
3/8''=1'-0''	32
1/4''=1'-0''	48
1/8''=1'-0''	96
1/16''=1'-0''	192
1/32''=1'-0''	384

Creating Architectural Dimension Style Family Members

You have created a new dimension style called ARCH, and set one of the elements common to all its family members—the Overall Scale factor. You are now ready to adjust settings for individual family members—Linear, Radial, and so on—of the ARCH dimension style family.

Fine-Tuning the Linear Dimensions

Most architectural firms use oblique tick marks rather than arrowheads as dimension line terminators. The default setting for terminators is set to filled arrowheads. In the following exercise, you create a LINEAR family member that has settings specific to linear dimensions.

Setting Oblique Terminators

Continue in the Dimension Styles dialog box, and use the Geometry dialog box to set the linear terminators to oblique ticks.

In this exercise, you set most of the variables for the Linear member of the ARCH family.

Choose **L**inear	Sets Linear member of ARCH dimension style current
Choose **G**eometry	Displays Geometry dialog box
Click on the left arrowhead image until you get the Oblique *option (see fig. 23.4)*	Sets terminator to Oblique ticks for linear dimensions

Remain in the Geometry dialog box for the next exercise.

Extending Your Dimension Line

Architectural dimensions have another setting that is specific to an architectural style of dimension standards. The dimension line itself extends past the extension lines (see fig. 23.5). The setting for the dimension line extension is in the Geometry dialog box.

23

Figure 23.4

Selecting oblique terminators.

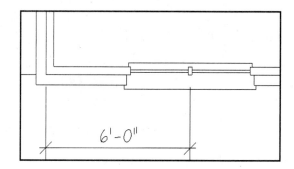

Figure 23.5

Dimension lines extended past the extension lines.

Note If you select any arrowhead option other than Oblique, the **E**xtension option in the Dimension Line section of the Geometry dialog box is grayed out, which means you cannot extend your dimension lines unless you first set your arrowheads to Oblique.

In the next exercise, you continue in the Geometry dialog box and set a dimension line extension, so your dimension lines will extend beyond your extension lines.

Making the Dimension Lines Extend Past the Extension Lines

Continue working in the Geometry dialog box.

Double-click in the **E**xtension *edit box in the* Dimension Line *cluster and type* **1/8"** *(see fig. 23.6)*	Sets dimension line extension to 1/8"
Choose OK	Exits Geometry dialog box

New Riders Publishing
INSIDE
SERIES

Choose **S**ave	Saves all changes made to the Linear dimension family member

Remain in the Dimension Styles dialog box for the next exercise.

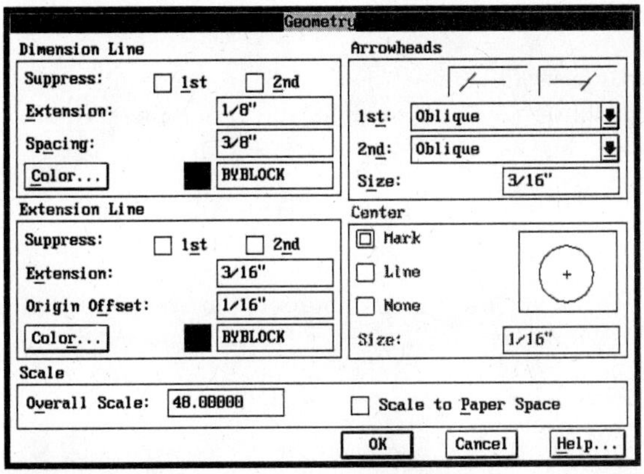

Figure 23.6

Setting a dimension line extension.

Managing the Dimension Text for Architectural Drawings

Most architectural dimension standards require that the dimension text aligns with and sits above a continuous dimension line. In the next exercise, you set the dimension text format so that the text aligns with the angle of the dimension line for all linear dimensions.

Aligning the Text with the Dimension Line

Continue in the Dimension Styles dialog box. You now use the Format dialog box to set your dimension text to the correct format for linear dimensions.

Choose **F**ormat	Displays Format dialog box
In the Text *cluster, clear the* X *from the* **I**nside Horizontal *box*	Turns off Inside Horizontal
Clear the X *from the* **O**utside Horizontal *box*	Turns off Outside Horizontal

continues

These two settings enable the dimension text to align with the dimension line for all linear dimensions. The next setting forces a dimension line between the extension lines no matter how small the distance being dimensioned. This helps clarify the dimension that the text is calling out.

Place an X *in the* Force **L**ine Inside   Sets Force Line Inside on
check box

The next setting determines what part of the dimension will be placed inside the extension lines when the distance being dimensioned is too small for the entire dimension to fit between them.

Choose the **F**it *list box and select*   Turns on Text Only fit option
Text Only

If space allows for only the text or the arrowheads but not both, the Text Only setting places the text inside the extension lines and places the arrowheads outside the extension lines.

Next, set the vertical justification so that dimension text for all linear dimensions is placed above a continuous dimension line.

Click on the Vertical Justification   Sets vertical placement of dimension text
icon until it is set to Above   to above dimension line

Your Format dialog box should now look like figure 23.7.

Choose OK   Closes Format dialog box

Choose **S**ave   Saves changes to ARCH style

Leave the Dimension Styles dialog box open for the next exercise.

Figure 23.7

Format settings
for the Linear
family member.

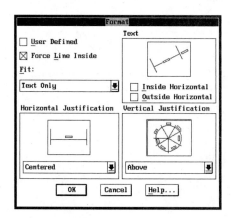

New Riders Publishing
INSIDE SERIES

Using Architectural Units for Dimensions

By default, units for dimensions are set to a four-place decimal. Architectural drawings are usually done in feet-and-fractional-inches—AutoCAD's "architectural" units. In the next exercise, you use the Annotation dialog box to set architectural units for linear dimensions.

 Note Unlike previous versions of AutoCAD, Release 13 enables you to set dimension units differently than drawing units. You can set your drawing units to decimal, for example, but show your dimensions in architectural units. Also, within a dimension family, each family member can have a different units setting. Later in this chapter, you set angular dimensions to use different units than the linear dimensions.

Setting Architectural Units for Linear Dimensions

With the Dimension Styles dialog box still open, and Linear still the current family member, you open the Annotation dialog box and set the units for dimensions to architectural.

Choose Annotation	Displays Annotation dialog box
Choose Units	Displays Primary Units dialog box
Click on the arrow in the Units box	Opens drop-down list for dimension units
Select Architectural	Sets dimension units to architectural

In architectural dimensions, you want AutoCAD to display zero inches in even-foot dimensions (for example, 4'-0").

In the Dimension Zero Suppression *cluster, clear the* X *in the* 0 Inches *box*	Turns off zero suppression for inches

Figure 23.8 shows the Primary Units dialog box as it should now appear.

Choose OK	Closes Primary Units dialog box
Choose OK	Closes Annotation dialog box
Choose Save	Saves changes to ARCH Linear dimension family member
Choose OK	Exits Dimension Styles dialog box

23

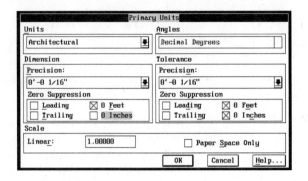

Figure 23.8

Primary Units settings for linear dimensions.

You have now established settings for a basic architectural dimensioning style. In the next exercise you place some dimensions on the floor plan as shown in figure 23.9. Make sure that you set the DIMS layer current. Just place a couple of dimensions, because before you place all your dimensions you need to do more setup in the following exercises.

Tip You can speed up the placement of linear dimensions by using running object snaps. Look at the type of drawing in which you're working and decide which object snap modes would be most appropriate. For example, in the current drawing, Endpoint and Midpoint would be useful ones.

Placing the First Linear Dimensions

Use the ZOOM command to zoom in on the part of the floor plan shown in figure 23.9. Check the Status line to make sure DIMS is the current layer.

Command: *Choose* Options, Running Object Snap	Displays Running Object Snap dialog box
Turn on **E**ndpoint *and* **M**idpoint *running object snap modes, then choose* OK	
Command: *Choose* Draw, Dimensioning, Linear	Issues DIMLINEAR command
First extension line origin or RETURN to select: *Pick endpoint of line at* ① *(see fig. 23.9)*	Sets first extension line origin
Second extension line origin: *Pick at center of windowsill at* ②	Sets second extension line origin

New Riders Publishing
INSIDE SERIES

Dimension line location (Text /Angle/Horizontal/Vertical/Rotated): *Pick at* ③	Sets dimension line location
Command: *Choose* Draw, Dimensioning Baseline	Invokes Baseline dimension mode
Second extension line origin or RETURN to select: *Pick at* ④	
Second extension line origin or RETURN to select: **⏎Enter**	Cancels current Baseline sequence
Select base dimension: **⏎Enter**	Cancels Baseline command

Save your drawing.

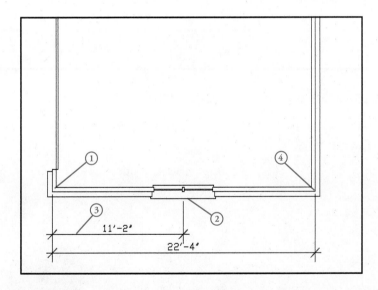

Figure 23.9

Placing the first dimensions on the CHAP23 drawing.

Adding Architectural Hand Lettering to Your Dimensions

One of the myths about using CAD for architectural drafting is the loss of the artistic hand-drawn look that makes architectural drawings so unique. If you use AutoCAD in its basic, out-of-the-box form, then this myth is quite true. But that is why you custom-ize the dimension setup to follow architectural standards. Many architectural

23

"hand-lettering" fonts are available from third-party developers. The ARCHS architectural font comes on the IA Disk that accompanies this book. See Appendix H for more information about ARCHS.

Note Unlike all previous versions of AutoCAD, Release 13 lets you create dimensions with a different text style than the one you have current. For example, if your current text style is STANDARD, you can set your dimension style's text style to ARCH. Then dimensions created with that style will use the ARCH, not the STANDARD, text style. This change in the way you use Release 13 dimension text also prevents changes in the appearance of dimension text when a dimension is stretched.

In the following exercise, you create a new text style for your dimension text. You will define it with an architectural font, ARCHS.SHX, so that you can use an artistic hand-lettering style of text in your dimensions. After you create this text style, you can use it in your ARCH dimension style.

Creating a Text Style Using an Architectural Font

Continue in drawing CHAP23.

Command: *Choose* Data, Text Style	Issues STYLE command
Command: '_style Text style name (or ?) <TEXT>: **DIMS** (Enter)	Creates new named text style
New Style.	Displays Select Font File dialog box
Set the C:\IA *directory current,* *highlight* ARCHS.SHX, *and choose* OK	
Height <0'-0">: (Enter)	Confirms default setting
Width factor <1.0000>: **.75** (Enter)	Sets width factor to .75

Accept the remaining defaults. DIMS will be set as the current text style.

Save your drawing.

Note Remember from Chapter 21 that the text height in a text style to be used for dimensions must be set to 0. You control the plotted dimension text height through settings in the Dimension Styles dialog box. You use the Annotation dialog box to set the dimension text height you want on your plotted drawing—that is, 1/8″. In addition, you set your Overall Scale factor in the Geometry dialog box to 48. Using a zero-height text style and setting dimension text height and overall scale factor in this manner gives the current dimension style all the control for your dimension text height settings.

In the next exercise, you assign the newly created architectural text style to the ARCH dimension style. Because all members of the ARCH family should use this font so that all dimensions in the drawing have a consistent appearance, the logical thing to do would be to change to this text style with Parent as the current family member.

AutoCAD, however, doesn't work in quite that way. You can make the change to the parent style, and it will be honored in all the family members—except for Linear. Because you already made modifications to the Linear member and saved them, AutoCAD assumes you want the text style that was current when you saved those changes. In other words, you must change the text style for linear dimension text explicitly.

Assigning a Hand-Lettering Font to Dimensions

Continue in the CHAP23 drawing.

Choose Data, Dimension Style	Displays Dimension Styles dialog box
With the Parent family member current, choose **A**nnotation	Displays Annotation dialog box
In the Text *cluster, click on the arrow in the* Sty**l**e *box*	Opens text styles drop-down list
Select DIMS	Sets DIMS text style current for all dimensions except Linear
Choose OK	Closes Annotation dialog box
Choose **S**ave	Saves change to Parent family member

continues

23

continued

The preceding steps set DIMS as the text style to use for all dimensions except linear ones. You must repeat the same process with the Linear family member current to reset the text style for linear dimensions.

Choose **L**inear	Sets Linear family member current
Choose **A**nnotation	Displays Annotation dialog box
In the Text *cluster, click on the arrow in the* Sty**l**e *box*	Opens text styles drop-down list
Select DIMS	Sets DIMS text style for linear dimensions
Choose OK	Closes Annotation dialog box
Choose **S**ave, *then* OK	Saves changes to ARCH dimension style and closes Dimension Styles dialog box

The dimensions that you placed now update to an artistic hand-lettering style of text (see fig. 23.10).

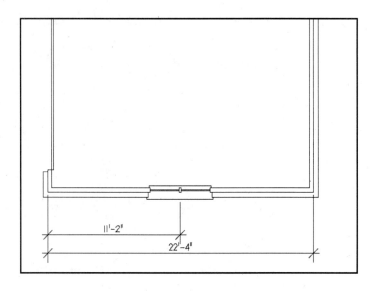

Figure 23.10

Dimensions using the hand-lettering font of the DIMS text style.

Controlling Dimension Layer Visibility in Architectural Drawings

In an architectural drawing, different sets of dimensions might refer to different aspects of the structure. You need a way to separate the different dimension types so dimensions for one part of a structure don't appear on another part, such as the dimensions for a reflected ceiling plan appearing on your foundation drawing. You can control architectural dimensioning by setting up separate layers for the different types of dimensions.

You might need three or four layers for dimensions in an architectural drawing. These layers enable you to control the visibility of each set of dimensions, associating them with the appropriate drawing data when you plot. For example, you might need to show a few dimensions on a reflected ceiling plan, but you do not want to show all the dimensions that might be in the architectural base plan. To control the dimensions you want to show for the reflected ceiling plan, you must have two different layers for the base plan dimensions and the reflected ceiling plan dimensions.

Placing Continuous Dimensions Quickly

Continuous dimensions make up a large portion of the dimensioning you do in architectural drawings. Chapter 21, "Introduction to Dimensioning," introduces the DIMCONTINUE command. You must start all continuous dimensions with one of the linear or angular dimension commands, then use the DIMCONTINUE command to continue a string of dimensions from that first dimension.

Tip   The first dimension you use to start a continuous dimension string must have its first and second extension lines selected in the right order. After you select the first extension line origin, the second extension line origin must be in the direction in which you want the continuous dimension string to follow. If you switch the order, your continuous dimensions cannot start correctly.

In the following exercise, you finish dimensioning the CHAP23 drawing with linear, baseline, and continuous dimensions. In general, you'll find it easier to place the inner dimensions first, and the outer, overall dimensions last. The detailed instructions for the first set of dimensions should make this clear.

23

Completing the Dimensions on the Architectural Plan

Continue in drawing CHAP23. Begin by setting the display so the bottom left half of the plan almost fills the screen (see fig. 23.11). Start off by using continuous dimensions to fill in the first-level dimensions.

Command: *Choose* Draw, Dimensioning, Continue

Issues DIMCONTINUE command

Command: _dimcontinue
Second extension line origin or RETURN to select: Enter

Enables you to start from existing dimension

Select continued dimension: *Pick the 11'-2' dimension at* ① *(see fig. 23.11)*

Sets dimension to continue from

Second extension line origin or RETURN to select: *Pick end of inner wall line at* ②

Places continuous dimension

Second extension line origin or RETURN to select: *Pick center of sill at* ③

Places continuous dimension

Second extension line origin or RETURN to select: *Pick corner of porch at* ④

Places continuous dimension

Second extension line origin or RETURN to select: *Pick center of door sill at* ⑤

Places continuous dimension

Second extension line origin or RETURN to select: *Pick end of inner wall line at* ⑥

Places continuous dimension

At this point, use a transparent pan to move over to the right just far enough so you can see the right corner of the plan (see fig. 23.12).

Second extension line origin or RETURN to select: *Pick center of sill at* ① *(fig. 23.12)*

Places continuous dimension

Second extension line origin or RETURN to select: *Pick end of inner wall line at* ②

Places last continuous dimension in first-level dimension string

New Riders Publishing
INSIDE
SERIES

You can start a second continuous dimension string without exiting the command. Stay in the DIMCONTINUE command and place the continuous second-level dimension string.

`Second extension line origin or` `RETURN to select:` **(Enter)**	Enables you to start from existing dimension
`Select continued dimension:` *Pick the 22'-4' dimension at* ③	Sets dimension to continue from
`Second extension line origin or` `RETURN to select:` *Pick extension line at* ④	Places continuous dimension
`Second extension line origin or` `RETURN to select:` *Pick extension line at* ⑤	Places continuous dimension
`Second extension line origin or` `RETURN to select:` *Pick extension line at* ⑥	Places continuous dimension
`Second extension line origin or` `RETURN to select:` **(Enter)**	Breaks out of continued dimension sequence
`Select continued dimension:` **(Enter)**	Ends DIMCONTINUE command sequence

End this set of horizontal dimensions by placing an overall dimension across the outer corners of the exterior wall.

`Command:` *Choose* Draw, Dimensioning Linear	Issues DIMLINEAR command
`First extension line origin or` `RETURN to select:` *Pick the corner at* ⑦	

Finish this overall dimension by transparently issuing the ZOOM Previous command, and pick the corner at ①, in figure 23.13, for the second extension line origin. Place the dimension line at ②.

Finish dimensioning the floor plan using the same techniques of continuous dimensioning. You also can try baseline dimensioning where appropriate. Refer to figures 23.14, 23.15, and 15.23 for dimension locations.

Save your work.

Figure 23.11

Continuing the first-level horizontal dimensions.

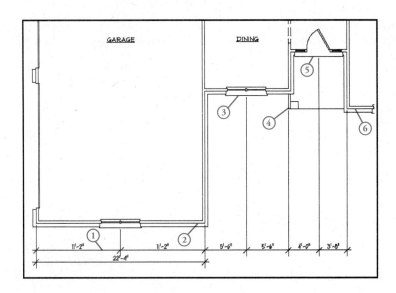

Figure 23.12

Adding first- and second-level dimensions.

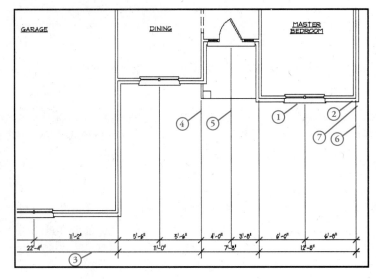

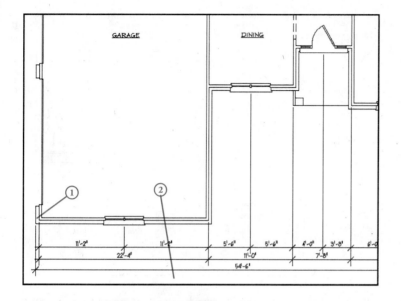

Figure 23.13

Finishing the lower dimensions with an overall dimension.

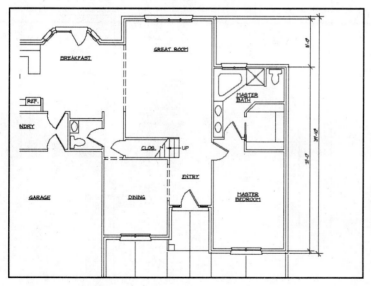

Figure 23.14

Placing continuous vertical dimensions.

23

Figure 23.15

Placing continuous and baseline horizontal dimensions.

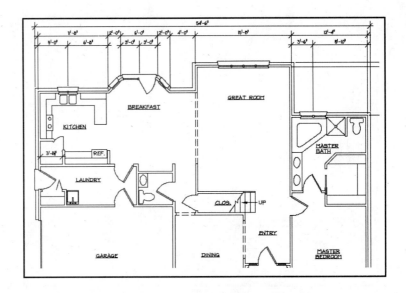

Figure 23.16

Placing additional continuous vertical dimensions.

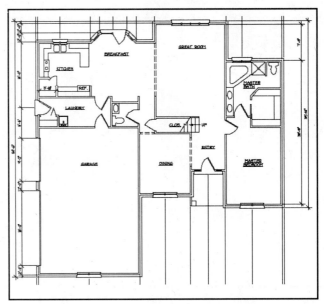

Using Stacked Fractions in Dimensions

Dimensions created using architectural units now use stacked fractions, whereas previously the fraction took the form of a continuous line with numerals of uniform height. Stacked fractions take up less space between the extension lines, reducing the total width of the dimension text and helping the dimension text fit between the extension lines more easily.

New Riders Publishing
INSIDE
SERIES

In the following exercise, you place a dimension to see how the new stacked fractions feature works.

Placing a Dimension with a Stacked Fraction

Continue in drawing CHAP23. Zoom in to the pantry area of the kitchen as shown in figure 23.17.

Command: *Choose* Draw, Dimensioning Linear	Issues DIMLINEAR command
Command: `_dimlinear` `First extension line origin or` `RETURN to select:` *Pick wall line at* ①	Sets first extension line origin
`Second extension line origin:` *Pick wall line at* ②	Sets second extension line origin
`Dimension line location (Text/Angle/` `Horizontal/Vertical/Rotated):` *Pick at* ③	Locates dimension line

Save your work.

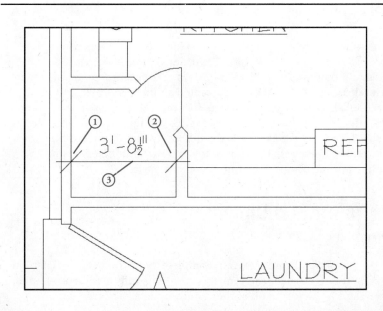

Figure 23.17

A dimension showing a stacked fraction.

23

Automatic Leaders in Continuous Dimensions

Another new feature in Release 13 is automatic leaders in continuous dimensions. AutoCAD automatically draws leaders when the text does not fit inside the extension lines. This new feature greatly reduces the amount of time you spend editing dimension text placement. See figure 23.18 for an example of stacked fractions and the automatic leader with continuous dimensions.

Figure 23.18

Automatic leaders and stacked fractions.

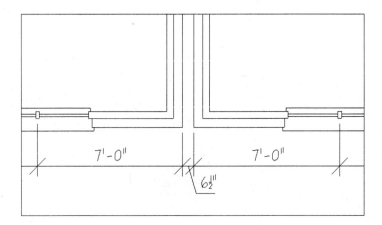

Using Dimension Style Family Members

Dimension style families is a major enhancement to dimensioning in Release 13. (Chapter 22, "Editing and Styling Dimensions," introduced dimension styles and families.) Architectural dimensions use oblique tick marks as terminators for dimension lines. In past releases of AutoCAD, if you created a dimension style that used oblique tick marks, you had to create a new style for your leaders so that they could have arrowheads rather than tick marks. In Release 13, you no longer need to create a new dimension style for minor changes with the different types of dimension commands. Dimension style families enable you to use arrowheads for leaders and oblique ticks for linear dimensions, all in one dimension style.

Completing Your ARCH Dimension Style Family Members

The settings for the Linear family member are complete. Now you need to finish the family by completing the settings for the remainder of the family members—Radial, Angular, Diameter, and Leader. The one other family member is Ordinate, but you do not use ordinate dimensions in architectural drawings.

In the following exercise, you complete the settings for all the remaining family members.

Adding the Settings for All the Family Members

Continue in drawing CHAP23. Use the Dimension Styles dialog box to change the dimension settings for the Radial family member.

Choose Data, Dimension Style	Displays Dimension Styles dialog box
Choose Radial	Sets following variable changes to Radial family member
Choose Format	Displays Format dialog box
Place a check mark in the User Defined *check box*	Enables you to select text position
Place a check mark in the Force Line Inside *check box*	Forces leader line inside radius or circle
In the Fit *edit box choose* LEADER	Places text outside if text and arrowhead cannot both fit
Choose OK	Exits Format dialog box
Choose Save	Saves new settings
Choose Annotation	Displays Annotation dialog box
Choose Units	Displays Primary Units dialog box
Click on the arrow in the Units *box*	Opens drop-down list for dimension units
Select Architectural	Sets dimension units to architectural
In the Zero Suppression *cluster, clear the* X *in the* 0 Inches *box*	Turns off 0 Inches suppression
Choose OK	Exits Primary Units dialog box
Choose OK	Exits Annotation dialog box
Choose Save	Saves new changes

continues

23

continued

You have completed the Radial family member. Next, you create the Angular family member.

Choose Ang<u>u</u>lar	Sets following changes to Angular family member
Choose <u>F</u>ormat	Opens Format dialog box
Place a check mark in the <u>U</u>ser Defined *check box*	Enables you to select text placement
Choose OK	Closes Format dialog box
Choose <u>A</u>nnotation	Displays Annotation dialog box
Choose <u>U</u>nits	Displays Primary Units dialog box
Open the <u>P</u>recision *drop-down list in the* Dimension *cluster area and choose* 0	Sets angular units to no precision past decimal point
Choose OK	Closes Primary Units dialog box
Choose OK	Closes Annotation dialog box
Choose <u>S</u>ave	Saves new changes

The Angular family member is now complete; you are ready to start the Diameter family member.

Choose Dia<u>m</u>eter	Sets following changes to Diameter family member
Choose <u>F</u>ormat	Displays Format dialog box
Place a check mark in the <u>U</u>ser Defined *check box*	Sets user to select text position
Place a check mark in the Force <u>L</u>ine Inside *check box*	Forces line when text is outside
In the <u>F</u>it *edit box, choose LEADER*	Sets leader inside
Choose OK	Closes Format dialog box
Choose <u>A</u>nnotation	Displays Annotation dialog box
Choose <u>U</u>nits	Displays Primary Units dialog box
Click on the arrow in the <u>U</u>nits *box*	Opens drop-down list for dimension units

Select Architectural	Sets dimension units to architectural
In the Zero Suppression *cluster, clear the* X *in the* 0 Inches *box*	Turns off 0 Inches suppression
Choose OK	Exits Primary Units dialog box
Choose OK	Exits Annotation dialog box
Choose Save	Saves new settings

You now have finished the Diameter family. It's not necessary to modify the remaining family member, Leader, because all the parent style settings apply to this style without any changes.

Choose OK	Closes Dimension Styles dialog box

Save your drawing.

Now place a leader in the CHAP23 drawing. The leaders use arrowheads and the leader text is centered off of the leader shaft (see fig. 23.19). If you also place a linear dimension, the linear dimensions will use the tick marks. Using dimension style family members makes placing dimensions correctly and quickly in your drawings much easier.

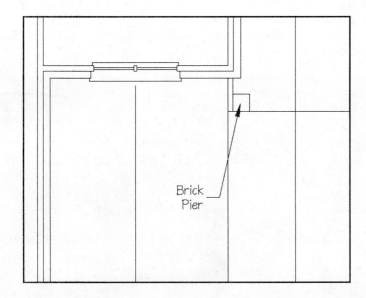

Brick
Pier

Figure 23.19

Placing a leader in the CHAP23 drawing.

23

The ARCH dimension style family is now complete. All the dimension commands should now be set to follow a basic architectural standard. You can use these settings to create an architectural dimensioning setup in any drawing.

Tip Creating dimension style families and family members enables you to control the way all the dimension commands work in your drawings. Take the time to set up your dimension families in your prototype drawings so they are available whenever you start a new drawing.

Suppressing Extension Lines

The dimensions that you place inside the floor plan designate the distance between walls. You do not need extension lines for these dimensions, as the dimension lines run directly between the wall lines. Figure 23.17 shows this type of internal dimension, although it does not have suppressed extension lines.

As you saw in Chapter 22, you can easily override dimension style settings by making changes in the Dimension Styles dialog box but not saving the changes to the style. Any dimensions you place before electing not to save the changes will honor the changed settings; when you're finished with the overrides, restoring the unaltered dimension style restores the original settings.

In architectural dimensioning, however, you will have to place a great many dimensions with no extension lines. It's therefore far more efficient to set up a special dimension style for interior dimensions. Simply set that dimension style current when you have to create this type of dimension. You use the Geometry dialog box to control the settings for extension lines.

In the following exercise, you create a new dimension style called INTERIOR and then adjust the dimension variables to suppress both extension lines. After you create the dimension style, you place a few dimensions in the CHAP23 drawing.

Creating a Dimension Style with Suppressed Extension Line

Continue in the CHAP23 drawing.

Choose Data, Dimension Style	Displays Dimension Styles dialog box
In the Name *edit box, type* **INTERIOR**	Creates new dimension style family based on ARCH dimension style
Choose Save	Saves new style and sets it current
Choose Linear	Sets INTERIOR family member for changes
Choose Geometry	Opens Geometry dialog box

New Riders Publishing
INSIDE SERIES

Click on the left arrowhead icon in the Arrowheads *cluster and change both arrowheads to* Oblique	Changes arrowhead setting
Double-click in the Extension *edit box of the* Dimension Line *cluster and type* **1/8"**	Sets dimension line extension to 1/8''
Choose 1st *and* 2nd Suppress *in the* Extension Line *cluster*	Turns on suppression of both 1st and 2nd extension lines
Choose OK	Exits the Geometry dialog box
Choose Format	Opens Format dialog box
Check the Force Line Inside *check box*	Forces dimension line in all dimensions
Open the Fit *drop-down list and choose* Text Only	Forces text inside dimension lines for short dimensions
In the Text *cluster, clear the* Xs *in the* Inside Horizontal *and* Outside Horizontal *check boxes*	Forces dimension text to align with dimension line
Click on the Vertical Justification *icon until the setting reads* Above	Forces dimension text above a continuous dimension line
Choose OK	Closes Format dialog box
Choose Save	Saves the changes to the INTERIOR dimension style
Choose Annotation	Displays Annotation dialog box
Choose Units	Displays Primary Units dialog box
Pick the down arrow in the Units *box and choose* Architectural	Sets dimension units to architectural
In the Zero Suppression *cluster, clear the* X *from the* 0 Inches box	Allows 0'' display in dimensions
Choose OK	Closes Primary Units dialog box
In the Text *cluster, pick the down arrow in the* Style *box and choose* DIMS	Sets the text style for dimensions

continues

23

continued

Choose OK	Closes Annotation dialog box
Choose <u>S</u>ave	Saves changes to INTERIOR dimension style
Choose OK	Closes Dimension Styles dialog box

INTERIOR is now the current dimension style.

Save your work.

In the next exercise, you place a string of interior dimensions through the dining room, entry, and master bedroom (see fig. 23.20). Notice that both extension lines are suppressed. When you need to revert to standard dimensions, set the ARCH dimension style current, and when you need suppressed extension lines, set the INTERIOR dimension style current.

Dimensioning Using Suppressed Extension Lines

Continue in drawing CHAP23. Use the ZOOM command to make your display appear like figure 23.20. The running objects snaps Endpoint and Midpoint are still set.

Command: *Choose* Draw, Dimensioning, Linear	Issues DIMLINEAR command
Command: _dimlinear First extension line origin or RETURN to select: *Pick wall at* ①	Sets first extension line origin
Second extension line origin: *Pick wall at* ②	Sets second extension line origin
Dimension line location (Text/Angle/ Horizontal/Vertical/Rotated): *Pick* ③	Places dimension text
Command: *Choose* Draw, Dimensioning, Continue	Issues DIMCONTINUE command
Command: _dimcontinue	
Second extension line origin or RETURN to select: *Pick wall at* ④	Sets next continuous dimension extension line origin

`Second extension line origin or` `RETURN to select:` *Pick wall at* ⑤	Sets next continuous dimension extension line origin
`Second extension line origin or` `RETURN to select:` *Pick wall at* ⑥	Sets next continuous dimension extension line origin
`Second extension line origin or` `RETURN to select:` *Pick wall at* ⑦	Sets next continuous dimension extension line origin
`Second extension line origin or` `RETURN to select:` (Enter)	Ends continuous dimension string
`Select continued dimension:` (Enter)	Exits DIMCONTINUE command

Save your work.

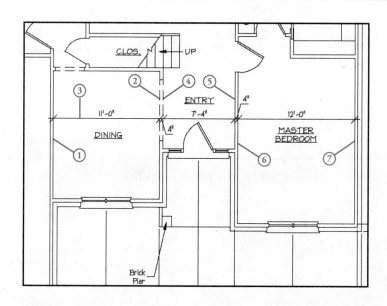

Figure 23.20

Using dimensions with suppressed extension lines.

You have finished dimensioning an architectural floor plan using two dimension styles you created especially for architectural dimensioning. You can re-create these dimension styles in your own prototype drawing so they'll be available the next time you have to draw a building plan.

You'll finish the chapter by looking at another discipline with specific dimensioning requirements: civil engineering.

Exploring the Civil Dimensioning Environment

Proper dimensioning in civil projects can require different setups, depending on the types of drawings with which you work. Site plans have different dimension information from road or bridge construction details. Plan and profile drawings also must contain specific information. Construction details use architectural units, depending on your company's standards, whereas site plans use decimal units. In the following exercises, you set up a dimension style and family members for a site plan drawing.

Creating a Civil Dimension Style Family

The architectural dimensioning setup in the first part of this chapter required that you create a dimension style family and then create all its family members. Similarly, civil applications, from construction details to site plans, also require a complete dimension style family so that all the dimension commands work properly.

When you place information on property lines for a legal description, you use both decimal units and surveyor's units to give the length and the angle for the property line.

In the following series of exercises, you begin a new drawing using a prototype drawing from the IA Disk, create a civil site plan dimension style, then dimension a property line and add text for the angular information.

Creating a Property Line Dimension Style

Begin a new drawing called CHAP23A, using the SITE-DIM drawing from the IA Disk as a prototype.

Command: *Choose* Data, Dimension Style	Displays Dimension Styles dialog box
Double-click in the Name *edit box, then enter* **PROPLINE**	Names the new dimension style family
Choose Save	Saves the new dimension style

Stay in the Dimension Styles dialog box for the next exercise.

New Riders Publishing
INSIDE
SERIES

Setting Up Units, Scale, and Text Style

Before you make settings to specific family members, you need to globally set units, scale, and the text style for the entire dimension style.

Setting Dimension Units and Scale

With the Dimension Styles dialog box still open and Parent selected, you use the Annotation dialog box to set the dimension commands to use decimal units with two-place decimal precision.

Choose Annotation	Opens Annotation dialog box
Choose Units	Opens Primary Units dialog box
Click in the Precision *edit box in the* Dimension *cluster*	Opens drop-down list for precision
Select 0.00	Sets decimal precision to two places
Choose OK	Closes Primary Units dialog box
Enter ' *in the* Suffix *edit box*	Sets suffix to single quote (foot mark)
Choose OK	Closes Annotation dialog box
Choose Geometry	Opens Geometry dialog box
In the Overall Scale *edit box, enter* **20**	Sets overall dimension scale factor to 20
Choose OK	Closes Geometry dialog box
Choose Save	Saves changes
Choose OK	Closes Dimension Styles dialog box

23

Using a Civil Lettering Style in Dimensions

In manually prepared civil engineering drawings, lettering was usually not done by hand at all, but by a machine called a *Leroy lettering template*. For civil drawings in AutoCAD, you will find that the ROMANS font that comes as a standard font with AutoCAD is similar to Leroy lettering style. If you need an exact match to the Leroy standard, several third-party fonts are available. You need to create a text style that uses the ROMANS font before you can apply it to your PROPLINE dimension style. In the following exercise, you create and set this new text style to be used by your dimension style.

Applying the DIMS Text Style to Your Dimension Style

Continue from the preceding exercise.

Use the STYLE command to create a new text style called DIMS. When the Select Font File dialog box displays, choose Type It and enter **ROMANS** to select the font file (this avoids path problems—see Chapter 13, "Annotation with Text"). Accept the defaults for the rest of the style options.

Choose Data, Dimension Style	Displays Dimension Styles dialog box
Choose Annotation	Opens Annotation dialog box
Click in the Text Style *edit box*	Opens drop-down list of text styles
Select DIMS	Sets DIMS text style for dimension text
Choose OK	Exits Annotation dialog box
Choose Save	Saves your changes
Choose OK	Exits Dimension Styles dialog box

Save the drawing.

Setting Up the Linear Family Member

With the parent PROPLINE dimension style created, you will now set up the Linear family member to dimension property lines.

Creating a Linear Dimension Style Family Member

Choose Data, Dimension Style	Displays Dimension Styles dialog box
Choose Linear	Selects Linear family member for changes
Choose Geometry	Displays Geometry dialog box
In the Dimension Line *cluster,* *place a check mark in the* Suppress 1st *and* 2nd *check boxes*	Suppresses both ends of dimension lines
In the Extension Line *cluster,* *place a check mark in the* Suppress 1st *and* 2nd *check boxes*	Suppresses both extension lines
Choose OK	Closes Geometry dialog box

New Riders Publishing
INSIDE
SERIES

Choose **F**ormat	Opens Format dialog box
Put a check in the **U**ser Defined *box*	Enables user to specify text location
Clear the **I**nside Horizontal *and* **O**utside Horizontal *check boxes*	Sets all text to align with dimension line
Click on the Vertical Justification *image tile until the* Above *option appears*	Sets dimension text above dimension line

The Format dialog box should match the one shown in figure 23.21.

Choose OK	Closes Format dialog box
Choose **S**ave	Saves changes to Linear family member
Choose OK	Closes Dimension Style dialog box and saves style changes

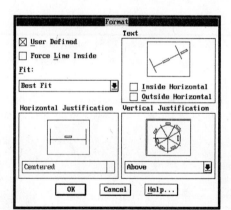

Figure 23.21

Establishing format settings for civil linear dimensions.

Creating Property Line Dimension Text

You need to place dimensional information for the angle direction and the length of each property line on site plans. AutoCAD cannot place both the angle direction and the distance without editing the text. You can use the Linear dimension family member settings you made and the DIMALIGNED command to align distance text with the property lines to place dimensions that have no extension lines and no dimension lines. In Release 13, dimension text is a special form of mtext, so you can use the Mtext editor—by default, MS-DOS Edit—to add the angle direction to the dimension line text.

23

To open the Mtext editor for editing dimension text, you press Enter at the `Dimension line location (Text/Angle):` prompt. AutoCAD shells to DOS and opens the Mtext editor which displays <> to indicate the measured dimension text. You can add any other text before or after the <>, or replace the <> with whatever text you want in the editor. When you save the file and exit the editor, you are returned to AutoCAD and the dimension shows the changes you made in the editor.

In the following exercise, for the property line dimension, you add the bearing angle to the default dimension value <>. To obtain the bearing angle, you use the LIST command to select the property line. AutoCAD will display this information in its text screen, and you must write it down or remember it. In order to obtain this angle in the correct format, Surveyor angular units with `N 0d00'00" E` precision must be set, as they are in this drawing. Then you place the dimension using the DIMALIGNED command and the new PROPLINE dimension style, adding and editing the angle text in the Mtext editor.

Placing a Property Line Dimension

Zoom to the area shown in figure 23.22.

Command: *Pick the property line at* ①, *then choose* Assist, Inquiry List	Issues LIST command and displays selected lines in text window (see fig. 23.23)

The LIST command returns entity properties on the selected line, including its angle, which is returned in surveyor's units. Make a note of the angle before you clear the text window.

Command: *Return to the graphics screen and choose* Draw, Dimensioning, Aligned	Issues DIMALIGNED command
`First extension line origin or RETURN to select:` (Enter)	Prompts for line to be dimensioned
`Select object to dimension:` *Pick the property line at* ① *again*	
`Dimension line location (Text/Angle):` `T` (Enter)	Enables modification of default dimension text
`Dimension text <420.03>:` *Type* `S89\U+00B019'05"`, *followed by five spaces to separate the two parts of the dimension. Then type a left and right angle bracket* <> *and press* (Enter)	Returns default dimension text string Formats angle value using Unicode setting for degree symbol (U+00B0) Places marker for dimension value

New Riders Publishing
INSIDE SERIES

```
Dimension line location (Text/Angle):        Draws the dimension as
Pick point ① (see fig. 23.22)                S89°19'05"E      420.03'
```

If you want to dimension the other property lines, you can use the same technique.

Save the drawing.

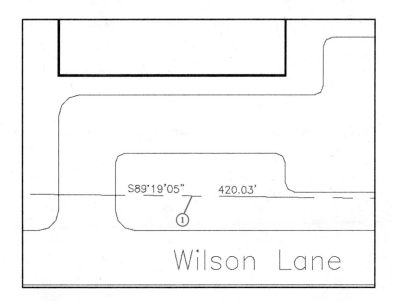

Figure 23.22

Placing a property line dimension.

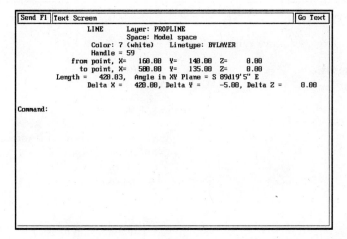

Figure 23.23

Properties of the selected line including its angle.

23

Note The IA Disk includes the PROPLINE.LSP file, which defines the NRP_DIMPL command. This command places a complete bearing and distance dimension (like the preceding exercise) automatically when you pick a line or polyline object. It requires Surveyor's units with N00d00'00"E precision and a dimension style like the one you created in the previous exercises.

You now have completed the settings for your Linear family member, under the PROPLINE dimension style family. For a complete site dimensioning style, you can complete the rest of the dimension style family members, setting the options for dimension geometry, text format, and annotation to follow your standards.

Placing Dimensions with No Extension Lines

When you use site plans, you need to indicate distances between two lines, such as the distance between property lines and utility easement lines. When you want to place dimensions in this manner, the dimension lines should not overlap the property and easement lines, because the extension lines can sometimes cover linetypes and cause confusion. To avoid this problem, you want to suppress the extension lines. In the next exercise, you create a new dimension style and suppress the Linear family member's extension lines. The new dimension style will be called NOEXTN. You will create it from a copy of the PROPLINE dimension style, so the global settings of the Parent will be inherited—all you need to do is suppress the extension lines for the Linear family member.

Creating a Dimension Style with No Extension Lines

Continue from the preceding exercise, with the PROPLINE dimension style set up.

Choose Data, Dimension Style	Displays Dimension Styles dialog box with PROPLINE current
Enter **NOEXTN** *in the* **N**ame *edit box*	Names new dimension style
Choose **S**ave	Creates a new dimension style, identical to PROPLINE Parent's settings
Choose **L**inear	Specifies Linear family member
Choose **G**eometry	Opens Geometry dialog box
In the Extension Line *cluster,* *choose* Suppress 1**s**t *and* 2**n**d	Suppresses both extension lines
Choose OK	Closes Geometry dialog box
Choose **F**ormat	Displays Format dialog box

Turn off **I**nside Horizontal *and* **O**utside Horizontal, *set* Vertical Justification *to* Above, *then choose* OK	Sets format and closes Format dialog box
Choose **S**ave	Saves changes to new NOEXTN dimension style
Choose OK	Closes Dimension Styles dialog box

Use **DIMLINEAR** to place some dimensions similar to the dimensions in figure 23.24 in the SITEPLAN drawing.

Save the drawing.

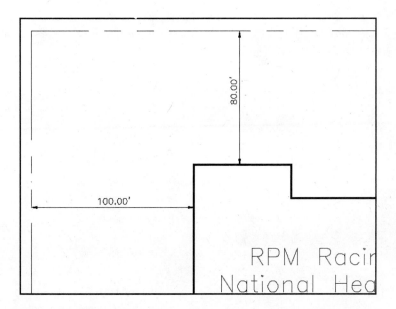

Figure 23.24

Placing dimensions with suppressed extension lines.

 Tip When you use a dimension style that has suppressed extension lines, you should use the NEArest object snap mode to place extension lines. If you need to place several dimensions, set the running object snap mode to NEArest to speed up the process.

Dimension styles give you a great amount of flexibility to create your dimensions to fit your specific application. In Release 13, with the addition of dimension style families, you can create dynamic dimension families for any application, not just architectural and civil. In Chapter 24, "Techniques for Mechanical Dimensioning," you work through a detailed setup for mechanical applications.

Techniques for Mechanical Dimensioning

Completing a drawing that has dimensions both pleasing to the eye and technically correct remains a challenge. Two particular skills are required to dimension using CAD. First, you need a good understanding of the way the dimensioning commands function. Second, you must understand the technical requirements of the type of drawing with which you work.

Chapters 21 and 22 cover many of the fundamentals of dimensioning with AutoCAD. However, learning individual commands is not enough; you must develop techniques that are effective for dimensioning on the type of drawings with which you work. This chapter helps you apply AutoCAD's dimensioning commands to mechanical drawings, providing the following information:

◆ A brief review of general mechanical dimensioning practices and techniques

◆ A review of the specific standards as defined by the *American National Standards Institute* (ANSI) and the *International Standards Organization* (ISO)

◆ Techniques for styling and applying AutoCAD dimensions and dimension style families to mechanical drawings

◆ Coverage of AutoCAD's new ANSI-based Geometric Dimensioning and Tolerancing feature

◆ Emphasis on the need for using these standards in your dimension styles; several useful drawing exercises give you hands-on practice with mechanical dimensioning techniques

Now, you probably are curious about the new dimensioning features in AutoCAD, so try the following introductory exercise, which briefly introduces you to some of the concepts covered in this chapter. To make placing dimension origins easy, the drawing you use already has running object snap set to ENDPoint and CENter.

Quick 5¢ Tour

Begin a new drawing called CHAP24, using the GDT-DIM drawing from the IA Disk as a prototype.

Command: *Choose* Draw, Dimensioning Linear	Issues the DIMLINEAR command

Create the two linear dimensions shown in figure 24.1.

Command: *Choose* Draw, Dimensioning, *then* Radial, Diameter	Issues the DIMDIAMETER command

Create the diameter dimension shown in figure 24.1.

Figure 24.1

Creating the first three dimensions.

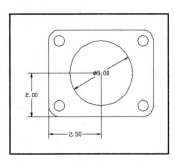

Command: *Choose* Data, Dimension Style	Opens the Dimension Styles dialog box
From the Current *drop-down list,* *select* GDT, *then choose* OK	Sets GDT as current dimension style and closes the dialog box

New Riders Publishing
INSIDE SERIES

Now erase the three dimensions and use the GDT dimension style to re-create them. Your dimensions should now resemble figure 24.2.

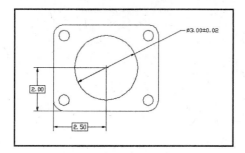

Figure 24.2

Using the GDT dimension style.

`Command:` *Choose* Draw, Dimensioning, *then* Tolerance	Opens the Symbol dialog box
Choose the Position *symbol (see fig. 24.3), then choose* OK	Opens the Geometric Tolerance dialog box with the Position symbol in first box

Enter the values shown in the **dialog box in figure 24.4**

Click in the edit box at ① *and type* **.01**	Enters Tolerance 1 value
Click in the edit box at ② *and type* **-D-**	Enters Datum Identifier symbol
Click in the edit boxes at ③, ④, *and* ⑤ *and type* **A**, **B**, *and* **C**, *respectively*	Enters Datum reference letters
Click on the image button at ⑥	Toggles on display of diameter symbol
Click on the image button at ⑦	Opens the Material Condition dialog box
Choose the first symbol, a circled **M** *and choose* OK *then* OK *again*	Adds Maximum Material Condition symbol and closes the Geometric Tolerance dialog box
`Command: TOLERANCE` `Enter tolerance location:`	
`Enter tolerance location:` *Pick at* ① *(see fig. 24.5)*	Places feature control frame

24

Figure 24.3

The GDT position symbol in the Symbol dialog box.

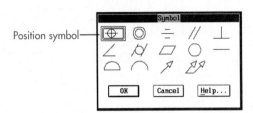

Figure 24.4

The Geometric Tolerance dialog box.

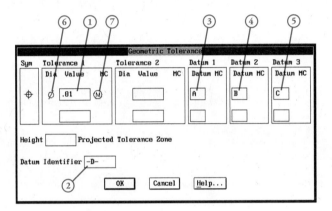

Figure 24.5

The completed feature control frame.

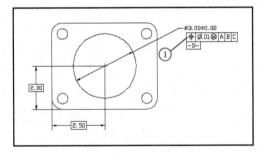

Imagine creating feature control frames as individual objects. You can see the amount of time you can save by using the new TOLERANCE command, covered fully in this chapter. Several of the other dimensioning techniques, such as putting a box around the basic dimensions and a tolerance on the diameter, are controlled by the GDT dimension style settings. You also explore using the GDT dimension style settings in this chapter.

New Riders Publishing
INSIDE SERIES

Understanding Dimensioning Standards

If you work in a large engineering or manufacturing company, you might be aware of existing internal design standards for mechanical drawings. The major topics of discussion usually include the following:

◆ Standard sheet sizes to be used for various projects

◆ Conventional view layout and placement

◆ Title blocks and notes appropriate to the drawing

◆ Dimension features and locations

◆ Tolerance specifications

◆ Physical size and characteristics of notes, dimension text, and arrows

◆ Datums and references for dimensioned objects

Even if you do not have your own standards, you probably possess a good working knowledge of mechanical drawings based on your education or experience. You might wonder about the origin of engineering specifications. Most drafting and detailing standards used in industry have their origins in one or more of the following sources:

◆ Senior designers who know how to implement good design practices

◆ Industry groups, such as automotive, aerospace, or military suppliers, who have agreed on certain standards

◆ Large companies, such as General Motors, who have defined their own standards

◆ Governmental bodies who develop their own specifications, such as Mil-Spec standards written by the Department of Defense

◆ National and international standards committees, such as ANSI and ISO, that have both the authority and expertise to write and administer standards that apply to all design and manufacturing activities

The current trend is away from the first three types of standards and toward universal engineering and design standards that are much more conducive to a global economy.

24

Note   Many companies develop a CAD Operations Manual. This ties in the engineering standards of the company with the way the CAD draftspersons specifically implement those standards.

Some flexibility is needed regarding how closely CAD dimensioning and tolerancing matches previous manual drafting techniques. Most CAD software, however, is written to closely emulate the current ANSI and ISO dimensioning standards, which are examined more closely later in this chapter.

Placing Dimensions Correctly

Many general rules are applied to the location and placement of dimensions in a mechanical drawing. *Placement* refers to the general part of the drawing in which the dimension is placed, and *location* refers to the distance between the view and the dimension, as well as the distance between dimensions.

 Note   Absolute sizes and locations are derived from the values that will appear on the final plot. You control the sizes and locations by setting dimension variable values in the Dimension Styles dialog box. The size of dimension elements, for example, is controlled by the DIMSCALE variable, which you set as the Overall Scale factor in the Geometry dialog box.

When you create several orthogonal views of a part, you try to anticipate the amount of room that the dimensions will require. When you place dimensions in CAD, you can find comfort in the fact that you can always reposition the views to allow for more dimensioning area. The dimensions in figure 24.6 illustrate some of the rules for dimension placement.

Figure 24.6

Proper location and placement of dimensions.

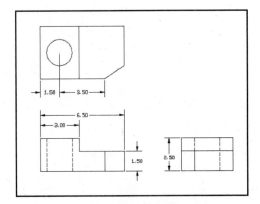

New Riders Publishing
INSIDE
SERIES

The specific locations of dimensions are generally related to the text size used on the drawing. For standard dimension text size of 3/16", you should place dimensions at least 7/16" from the view, and subsequent dimensions 3/8" from each other.

Note When you use the baseline dimensioning feature, you can specify the distance between dimensions. The distance between dimension lines is controlled by the DIMDLI variable which you set in the Dimension Line pacing box of the Geometry dialog box. The default setting is 0.3800".

Tip Use proper snap and grid settings for uniform placement of dimensions.

The rules of dimension placement obviously are flexible to a certain extent in special situations. The following list emphasizes good general dimension placement guidelines. Note that these are rules based on practice, and your knowledge of mechanical drafting must be your guide. There are no particular settings in AutoCAD that will help you observe these standard practices.

◆ Place dimensions between the orthographic views as shown in figure 24.6

◆ Try to keep the dimensions off objects in the view

◆ Do not dimension to hidden lines or features

◆ Place dimensions in the view that best shows the outline of a feature

◆ Position the dimensions so that extension lines do not cross other extension lines or object lines

AutoCAD's dimensioning tools can help you follow some of these rules. For example, you can use the From object snap mode to move the origin point of a dimension, where the extension line would otherwise lie on top of an object.

One of the most important rules of dimensioning applies to the number of dimensions used: Do not leave out dimensions required to define a part, but at the same time, do not use more dimensions than necessary. Keep the number of dimensions minimal, and ask yourself if you could make the part from the dimensions you supplied.

Establishing Tolerances

Although tolerances are almost nonexistent on most architectural drawings, they are very important on mechanical drawings. Often, improper tolerancing of mating parts is one of the most costly errors that occurs in the design and manufacturing process. If you fail to

24

sufficiently control the tolerances, mating parts might not properly fit. On the other hand, excessively close tolerances are wasteful because of the extra manufacturing costs.

Five types of tolerance specification are used in mechanical drawings, as follows:

◆ **Assumed Tolerance.** If you do not give a tolerance, the default tolerance is one-half of the distance between the nominal dimension value and the next logical counting number. For instance, a dimension that reads 2.83 is assumed to be between 2.825 and 2.835.

◆ **General Tolerance.** You usually specify general tolerances in a tolerance block near the title block. The number of decimal places of the dimension indicates the tolerance to be used from the tolerance block.

◆ **Deviation Tolerance.** A deviation is shown at the dimension as the amount the dimension can vary from the nominal size. A *bilateral* tolerance, sometimes called a *symmetrical tolerance,* is an equal distance above and below the nominal value. A *unilateral* tolerance specifies a separate value for deviation above and below the nominal value. You can set your dimensions to display deviation tolerances by choosing Symmetrical or Deviation as the Tolerance **M**ethod in the Annotation dialog box, then setting appropriate values in the edit boxes.

◆ **Limits Tolerance.** Limits dimensions often are easier to interpret because they consist of only two numbers: the maximum value and the minimum value of the dimension. You set up for Limits dimensioning by choosing Limits as the Tolerance **M**ethod in the Annotation dialog box, and then setting appropriate upper and lower values.

◆ **Geometric Tolerance.** Geometric dimensions and tolerances are certainly the most complicated method of tolerancing. However, they also are far superior in their capability to clearly define the intended use of a part. Geometric tolerances use many different symbols and labels that are not easy to interpret if you do not have prior knowledge of the GDT system. AutoCAD provides a special command, TOLERANCE, for creating GDT dimensions.

Note Not specifying a tolerance is unacceptable on most mechanical drawings. Achieving an "exact" dimension in a manufacturing process is impossible.

Figure 24.7 shows a typical deviation, limits, and geometric tolerance generated in AutoCAD.

AutoCAD Release 13 provides the proper tools to apply all these tolerancing systems. You always need to control the number of decimal places for a dimension value, and you do so best by specifying the number of decimal places for the dimension and

New Riders Publishing
INSIDE
SERIES

tolerance in the <u>A</u>nnotation group of settings found in the Dimension Styles dialog box.

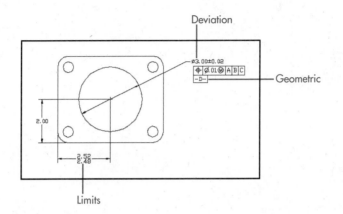

Figure 24.7

Using geometric, limits, and devia-tion tolerances.

General tolerances are certainly the easiest to specify. Limits and deviation tolerances require additional dimension style settings, and if you use them often you should define them as separate dimension styles. Chapter 22, "Editing and Styling Dimensions," introduces you to these dimension settings and you learn more about them in the next exercise. Geometric tolerances are covered later in the chapter.

The following exercise reviews the dimension style settings required to generate the appropriate tolerances. Remember that in the parent/child family member relationship of dimension settings, you can have different tolerance specifications for different child categories of dimensions.

Controlling Dimension Tolerances

Begin a new drawing called CHAP24T, using the GDT-DIM drawing from the IA Disk as a prototype.

Place the horizontal 2.50 dimension as shown in figure 24.8.

`Command:` *Choose* Data, Dimension Style	Opens the Dimension Style dialog box
Choose the <u>L</u>inear *radio button, then* <u>A</u>nnotation	Opens the Annotation dialog box for linear family member (see fig. 24.9)
Select Limits *from the* Tolerance <u>M</u>ethod *drop-down list*	Specifies limits tolerance

Set both Upper <u>V</u>alue and Lo<u>w</u>er Value to .02.

continues

continued

Choose the **U**nits *button and set the* Tolerance Precisi**o**n *to 2 places* (0.00)	Opens the Primary Units dialog box and sets tolerance precision

Place the 2.00 vertical dimension, as shown in figure 24.8.

Reopen the Dimension Styles dialog box.

Choose the **D**iameter *radio button, then* **F**ormat	Opens the Format dialog box for diameter family member
Place an X in the **U**ser Defined *toggle box, then choose* OK	Allows user-positioned text
Choose **A**nnotation	Opens the Annotation dialog box for diameter family member
Select Deviation *from the* Tolerance **M**ethod *drop-down list*	Specifies deviation tolerance

Set both Upper **V**alue and Lo**w**er Value to .02, as shown in figure 24.9.

Choose the **U**nits *button and set the* Tolerance Precisi**o**n *to 2 places* (0.00)	Opens the Primary Units dialog box and sets tolerance precision
Choose OK, OK, **S**ave, *and* OK	Saves settings and exits dialog boxes

Finish the exercise by placing the diameter dimension, as shown in figure 24.8.

The use of dimension style family members enables you to set different settings for various types of dimensions, yet have the settings defined in a single dimension style.

Figure 24.8
Three dimensions with different tolerance specifications.

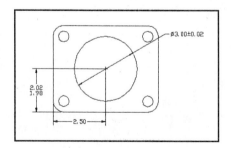

Note   The Deviation and Symmetrical tolerance options are very similar. Symmetrical tolerances have the same upper and lower tolerance value, whereas the upper and lower values of deviation tolerances can vary.

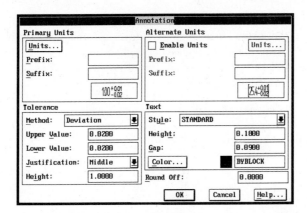

Figure 24.9

Specifying tolerance type and value in the Annotation dialog box.

Again, creating dimensions that have all the proper tolerances is not always easy or convenient, but doing so in mechanical drawings is very important.

 Tip In mechanical drafting, you frequently need to use all three types or tolerance dimensioning. Create different dimension styles that are similar in their overall features but are set up for different types of tolerances.

Controlling Special Dimension Types

Several special types of dimensions are used in mechanical drawings. You must properly identify these dimensions to avoid confusing them with regular dimensions. Figure 24.10 shows three special types of dimensions.

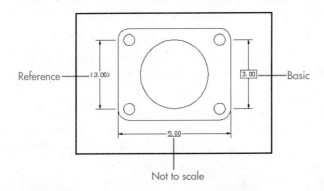

Figure 24.10

A reference, basic, and unscaled dimension.

24

The dimensions shown in figure 24.10 are explained in the following list:

◆ **Reference.** A reference dimension is identified by placing the text in parentheses or by adding the text string REF to the dimension. A reference dimension does not need a tolerance and is not required to produce the part. It often is for information only. To create a reference dimension style in AutoCAD, open the Annotation dialog box and place an open parenthesis in the Prefix box and a closed parenthesis in the suffix box, or "REF" (note the leading space) in the suffix box.

◆ **Not to Scale.** Although you should always properly scale your CAD drawings, it might be necessary at times to show some objects out of the proper scale. A not-to-scale dimension is underlined to identify it as such. To create underlined dimension text, you have to use special Unicode settings at the `Dimension text <default>:` prompt; you place `\L` before the dimension place holder (<>), and `\l` after it.

◆ **Basic.** Basic dimensions do not have tolerances because the tolerance is specified in the GDT feature control frame. The text in a basic dimension is placed in a box for easy identification. To create a basic dimension style in AutoCAD, open the Annotation dialog box and pick Basic as the Tolerance Method.

Applying ANSI and ISO Standards

Many companies now recognize that if they want to remain competitive, they must orient themselves to a more global economy. Although the United States has the advantage of the universal English language, it needs to cover much ground in terms of engineering standards. Several terms need to be defined at this point.

◆ **ANSI.** The American National Standards Institute is a body that has the resources and the recognition to define a set of engineering standards that is recognized nationally and is compatible with international standards.

◆ **ASME.** The American Society of Mechanical Engineers is a national organization that publishes ANSI standards and assists in the implementation of them, among other activities.

◆ **ANSI Y14.5M.** This is the specific set of standards that defines proper dimensioning and tolerancing procedures. Copies of this standard are available directly from ASME. The Release 13 US_MECH.DWG prototype drawing contains an ANSI dimension style.

New Riders Publishing
INSIDE SERIES

◆ **ISO.** The International Standards Organization is a European-based group that tries to coordinate and define standards that are recognized by all of the major industrial countries. The Release 13 ACADISO.DWG prototype drawing contains a set of 8 ISO-compatible dimension styles.

◆ **SI Units.** The International System of Units (Systeme Internationale) is based on metric units. Most international standards, therefore, are defined in metric terms.

◆ **JIS.** The Japanese Industrial Standard is a set of engineering standards similar to ANSI. The Release 13 JIS_MECH.DWG prototype drawing has a set of JIS dimension styles.

◆ **DIN.** The DIN specification is an older European standard now being merged with ISO standards.

Note One of the greatest sources of conflict and confusion in many engineering departments is the process of converting between SI and English units. As we pass through this transitional period of switching from the old imperial system of measure ("English" units) to SI Metric units, many firms are hedging their bets with dual dimensioning. AutoCAD makes dual dimensioning easy, as you will see in the last section of the chapter.

Interpreting the Standards

Although the latest version of a standard is written in black and white, many gray areas begin to appear. Textbooks often contain various translations of these standards. Trainers and consultants often are swayed by the way some large companies apply these standards. Even the programmers at Autodesk who write the code for AutoCAD must decide how to implement these standards in the automatic dimensioning capabilities of AutoCAD.

Perhaps you have heard of the ISO 9000 series of manufacturing-related guidelines that many companies are trying to adopt. Unfortunately, it often takes a high-priced consultant to help a company determine the best way to conform to the standards.

The ANSI Y14.5M document *Dimensioning and Tolerancing* probably is the best place to start for good design standards. The document is written well and contains many useful illustrations of how to properly dimension and tolerance a mechanical drawing.

24

Choosing the Best Standard

Some CAD software packages come complete with several standards built-in as dimension styles or prototype drawings. You probably need to modify these settings slightly to meet your specific needs. Before Release 13, many AutoCAD users bought third-party dimensioning and tolerancing software or customized AutoCAD themselves using the capability to insert dimensioning symbols and create GDT feature control frames.

Your customer base and the type of industry with which you work probably will influence your choice of standards. AutoCAD has several different prototype drawings available for which dimensioning styles are already defined for specific standards. Figure 24.11 shows a metric prototype drawing (ACADISO.DWG) set in the Preferences dialog box. Note also the English and Metric **M**easurement choices in that dialog box.

Figure 24.11

Prototype drawing options in AutoCAD.

Preferences

Measurement:	Metric	⬇
	English	
Environment	Metric	
Prototype drawing:	Metric/ISO Size A3	⬇
File name:	acadiso.dwg	

[OK] [Cancel] [Help...]

Note Although only two prototype drawings (ACAD.DWG and ACADISO.DWG) are listed in the Preferences dialog box, a total of six are supplied with AutoCAD. As well as these two, there are also US Architectural (US_ARCH.DWG), US Mechanical (US_MECH.DWG), Japanese Architectural (JIS_ARCH.DWG), and Japanese Mechanical (JIS_MECH.DWG). To use any of these other four drawings, you must specify them with the Prototype button in the Create New Drawing dialog box.

Many standards are moving toward icons rather than notes. (Think of the No Left Turn icon you see in traffic signs.) Many standard callouts on mechanical drawings, such as the diameter or counterbore symbol, appear as icons. To help you see how closely ANSI and ISO symbols appear, compare them in figure 24.12.

New Riders Publishing
INSIDE
SERIES

Symbol Name	ANSI	ISO
POSITION	⊕	⊕
CONCENTRICITY/COAXIALITY	◎	◎
SYMMETRY	NONE	⌯
PARALLELISM	//	//
PERPENDICULARITY	⊥	⊥
ANGULARITY	∠	∠
CYLINDRICITY	⌭	⌭
FLATNESS	▱	▱
CIRCULARITY	○	○
STRAIGHTNESS	—	—
PROFILE OF A SURFACE	⌓	⌓
PROFILE OF A LINE	⌒	⌒
CIRCULAR RUNOUT	↗	↗
TOTAL RUNOUT	⌰	⌰
AT MAXIMUM MATERIAL CONDITION	Ⓜ	Ⓜ
AT LEAST MATERIAL CONDITION	Ⓛ	NONE
REGARDLESS OF FEATURE SIZE	Ⓢ	NONE
DIAMETER	∅	∅
DATUM	–A–	–A–
BASIC DIMENSION	50	50
REFERENCE DIMENSION	(50)	(50)
DIMENSION NOT TO SCALE	50	50
COUNTERBORE/SPOT FACE	⌴	NONE
COUNTERSINK	⌵	NONE
DEPTH	⌉	NONE

Figure 24.12
ANSI and ISO symbols.

24

Exploring GDT Dimensioning Features

Full support of Geometric dimensioning and tolerancing is a long-awaited feature in AutoCAD. As you might well imagine when you look at a GDT-based mechanical drawing, it can take far longer to dimension the part than to draw it. For many AutoCAD users, the hardest part of using the new GDT features will be understanding how to apply them. Of course, if you merely are trying to duplicate a drawing using CAD, the thought process behind the GDT feature control frames is already complete. You need only duplicate the GDT symbols.

Understanding the Need for GDT

In an ideal environment, the toolmakers and manufacturing personnel would understand the exact intent of the designer who applied the dimensions and tolerances. Quality control departments would position and inspect the part in the same fashion. Finally the customer would verify the dimensional integrity of the part, and everyone would agree on how well the part met the design specifications. If you have any experience in manufacturing, you know an ideal environment does not often describe the situation.

For reasons too lengthy to explore here, conventional dimensioning and tolerancing present many shortfalls. In the following sections of this chapter, you are introduced to many of the improvements that GDT adds to a mechanical drawing, including datums, tolerance zones, material condition, and geometric characteristics.

One of the historical problems with GDT is that it has been very difficult to verify part features using traditional measuring tools such as a caliper, micrometer, or a height gage and surface plate. Now that many companies have access to coordinate measuring machines, GDT features are now easy to verify.

Using the TOLERANCE Command

The new TOLERANCE command in Release 13 enables you to automatically generate most types of feature control frames.

TOLERANCE. The TOLERANCE command opens a series of dialog boxes that enable you to define all the necessary components of a feature control frame. The command finally places the feature control frame at the specified point in your drawing.

Pull-down: *Choose* Draw, Dimensioning, Tolerance
Screen: *Choose* DRAW DIM, Toleran

Before you explore this command, review the parts of a typical feature control frame (see fig. 24.13).

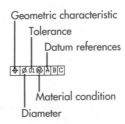

Figure 24.13

A typical feature control frame.

A brief list of explanations of the components follows.

◆ **Geometric characteristic.** You can choose from 1 of 14 geometric characteristics (refer to figure 24.13 for a illustration). If you do not require a symbol, simply choose OK.

◆ **Diameter symbol.** This diameter symbol is required on only a few of the geometric characteristics. You use it to specify a round tolerance zone, and you place it before the tolerance value.

◆ **Tolerance value.** You specify the total tolerance of the feature as a numeric value.

◆ **Material condition.** You use the material condition with some of the features to modify the tolerance value based on the true size of the feature.

◆ **Datum reference.** Again, you use datums with only some of the features. Depending on the application, between one and three datums are required.

Issuing the TOLERANCE command opens the Symbol dialog box, in which you can choose one of these tolerance symbols, or choose OK if you do not require any of them (see fig. 24.14).

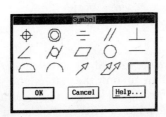

Figure 24.14

The Symbol dialog box.

Next, after you choose OK to close the Symbol dialog box, the main Geometric Tolerance dialog box appears (see fig. 24.15).

Figure 24.15

The Geometric Tolerance dialog box.

```
┌─────────────────────────────────────────────────────────────┐
│                    Geometric Tolerance                        │
│  Sym   Tolerance 1      Tolerance 2     Datum 1  Datum 2  Datum 3 │
│        Dia  Value   MC  Dia  Value   MC Datum MC Datum MC Datum MC │
│  ┌──┐  ┌──────────┐    ┌──────────┐    ┌─────┐  ┌─────┐  ┌─────┐ │
│  │  │  │          │    │          │    │     │  │     │  │     │ │
│  │  │  └──────────┘    └──────────┘    └─────┘  └─────┘  └─────┘ │
│  │  │  ┌──────────┐    ┌──────────┐    ┌─────┐  ┌─────┐  ┌─────┐ │
│  └──┘  │          │    │          │    │     │  │     │  │     │ │
│        └──────────┘    └──────────┘    └─────┘  └─────┘  └─────┘ │
│                                                               │
│  Height ┌──────┐ Projected Tolerance Zone                     │
│         └──────┘                                              │
│  Datum Identifier ┌──────┐                                    │
│                   └──────┘                                    │
│              ┌──────┐  ┌────────┐  ┌──────┐                   │
│              │  OK  │  │ Cancel │  │ Help...│                 │
│              └──────┘  └────────┘  └──────┘                   │
└─────────────────────────────────────────────────────────────┘
```

You seldom have to address all the values in the Geometric Tolerance dialog box. If you did address all the values, your complex feature control frame would appear similar to the one shown in figure 24.16.

Figure 24.16

A complex feature control frame.

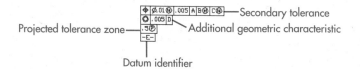

Projected tolerance zone —

Secondary tolerance —

Additional geometric characteristic —

Datum identifier

Identifying Datums

The simplest way to use the TOLERANCE command is to create a datum label. Datums are very important to GDT because they specify exactly how to set up a part in manufacturing or inspection. *Datums* typically are flat surfaces or the centerlines of cylinders. A datum should be a capital letter in a box, connected to the feature or the dimension of the feature. The datum identifier label is shown in figure 24.16.

Although you are free to name datums as you please, you really do need to call out datums in the proper order in the feature control frame. In a typical rectangular part, the *primary datum* establishes the reference plane. The *secondary datum* establishes the alignment of the part. Finally, the *tertiary datum* locates the part in the third axis of movement. Figure 24.17 shows the points that you can use to establish the respective datums.

You can use the TOLERANCE command to easily create a separate datum label by choosing none of the symbols and filling in only the datum letter in the Datum 1 box of the Geometric Tolerance dialog box. If you want to add a datum identifier along with a feature control frame, fill in the datum letter in the Datum Identifier edit box.

After you identify the datums, you can reference these datums in the Datum 1, Datum 2, and Datum 3 areas of the Geometric Tolerance dialog box—the primary, secondary, and tertiary datums, respectively.

New Riders Publishing
INSIDE
SERIES

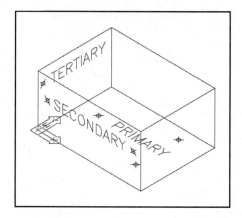

Figure 24.17

A primary, secondary, and tertiary datum.

Building the Feature Control Frame

The symbol you choose from the Symbol dialog box appears in the first box in the Sym area of the Geometric Tolerance dialog box, as you saw in the Quick 5¢ Tour exercise. If you click on this box, the Symbol dialog box reappears so that you can make another selection. You use any part of the second line of the Geometric Tolerance dialog box only if you want to create an additional geometric characteristic, such as that shown in figure 24.16.

 Tip   You also can stack additional feature control frames by adding additional ones at a later time.

You also can activate a Projected Tolerance Zone symbol by choosing that box, as well as specify the height for that tolerance zone.

Specifying Tolerance and Material Conditions

The Tolerance 1 area of the Geometric Tolerance dialog box enables you to specify the tolerance by typing the correct value. Optionally, you can use the DIA box if you need to specify a round tolerance zone. The Tolerance 2 area enables you to specify a secondary tolerance, normally not required.

Finally, if you want to include a material condition in the tolerance or datum areas of the Geometric Tolerance dialog box, choose any of the MC boxes to open a secondary Material Condition dialog box. You have the three choices (see fig. 24.18).

24

Figure 24.18

The Material Condition dialog box.

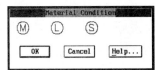

Material conditions are important to GDT. The three options are briefly explained in the following list, based on an example that deals with the locational tolerance of a hole.

◆ **Maximum Material Condition.** When the hole is on the small side of the tolerance, the maximum amount of material is left on the workpiece, often meaning that the location must be the most precise at this point before it can accept a mating part. When the M is present with the tolerance, as the hole is opened up towards the largest acceptable size, the locational tolerance relaxes by the difference between the maximum and minimum diameter.

◆ **Least Material Condition.** This defines the condition in which the hole diameter is on the large side of the tolerance, meaning that the least amount of material is present. This symbol is not used nearly as often as the Maximum Material Condition symbol.

◆ **Regardless of Feature Size.** You use the S symbol to specify that material condition does not affect the tolerance. Some argue whether the absence of this symbol altogether would not imply the same concept.

You can use a tolerance or a datum reference to specify material conditions.

 Note Further study of GDT applications might be necessary to determine which symbols are required and which symbols are optional for a given tolerance.

Now that you know about the TOLERANCE command and its options, you will apply it in the following exercise. The part that you dimension has five holes that are critical to the function of the part. Instead of being located from the edge of the part, the holes are located from the theoretical center of the part. Imagine that this part needs to fit into a pocket and have all five holes align with a mating part. This is how you try to define these locations using GDT. Notice that the size tolerances are regular deviation tolerances.

You begin by drawing the side view, then you place the appropriate dimensions of size and location. Remember to identify the locational dimensions as basic. Then, you use the TOLERANCE command to label the necessary datums. Finally, you use the TOLERANCE command to create the feature control frames.

New Riders Publishing

INSIDE SERIES

Applying GDT to a Mechanical Drawing

Begin a new drawing called CHAP24GD, using the GDT-DIM drawing from the IA Disk as a prototype.

Use snap mode and draw the side view on layer OL, as shown in figure 24.19, then reset layer DIMS current.

Set the Dimension Style to GDT and create the 3.00 and 4.00 basic dimensions shown.

Reopen the Dimension Styles dialog box and choose <u>L</u>inear. Choose <u>A</u>nnotation and change the tolerance <u>M</u>ethod to Symmetrical, the tolerance value to .01, and the Primary Units tolerance precision to 2 places (0.00). Choose OK, then OK again to get back to the Dimension Styles dialog box.

Choose <u>S</u>ave, then <u>D</u>iameter, then <u>A</u>nnotation, and make the same settings as you made for the <u>L</u>inear family member. Save the settings and exit the dialog box.

Create the length, width, and height dimensions as shown in figure 24.19.

Dimension both circle diameters as shown in figure 24.19.

Command: *Choose* Draw, Dimensioning Tolerance	Opens the Symbol dialog box
Choose OK	Selects no symbol and opens the Geometric Tolerance dialog box
Type A *in the* Datum 1 *box, then choose* OK	Names datum and closes the dialog box
Enter tolerance location: *Pick at* ① *(see fig. 24.20)*	Locates datum label

Draw the line at ②.

Repeat this procedure to place datum labels B and C.

Command: *Choose* Draw, Dimensioning Tolerance	Opens the Symbol dialog box
Choose the Position *symbol, then choose* OK	Selects the Position symbol and opens the Geometric Tolerance dialog box

Refer to figure 24.21 to complete the feature control frame by the following steps.

In the Tolerance 1 *cluster, click on the* Dia *image button*	Turns on display of diameter symbol

continues

24

continued

Click in the Tolerance 1 Value *edit box and type* **.01**	Enters tolerance value
In the Tolerance *1 cluster, click on the* MC *image button*	Opens the Material Condition dialog box
Choose the M *symbol, then choose* OK	Places Maximum Material Condition symbol in frame
Click in the Datum 1 Datum *edit box and type* **A**	Labels Datum 1
Click in the Datum 2 Datum *edit box and type* **B**	Labels Datum 2
In the Datum 2 cluster, click on the MC *image button*	Opens the Material Condition dialog box
Choose the M *symbol, then choose* OK	Places Maximum Material Condition symbol in frame
Click in the Datum 3 Datum *edit box and type* **C**	Labels Datum 3
In the Datum 3 cluster, click on the MC *image button*	Opens the Material Condition dialog box
Choose the M *symbol, then choose* OK	Places Maximum Material Condition symbol in frame

The Geometric Tolerance dialog box should now look like fig. 24.21

Choose OK	Closes Geometric Tolerance dialog box
Command: _tolerance Enter tolerance location: *Locate the frame at* ③	Places feature control frame on drawing

Now create a second feature control frame to be placed beside the diameter dimension for the larger hole.

Command: (Enter)	Reissues TOLERANCE command
Choose the Position *symbol, then choose* OK	Selects the Position symbol and opens the Geometric Tolerance dialog box
In the Tolerance 1 *cluster, click on the* Dia *image button*	Turns on display of diameter symbol
Click in the Tolerance 1 Value *edit box and type* **.015**	Enters tolerance value

In the Tolerance *1 cluster, click on the* MC *image button*	Opens the Material Condition dialog box
Choose the M *symbol, then choose* OK	Places Maximum Material Condition symbol in frame
Click in the Datum 1 Datum *edit box and type* **A**	Labels Datum 1
Click in the Datum 2 Datum *edit box and type* **B**	Labels Datum 2
In the Datum 2 cluster, click on the MC *image button*	Opens the Material Condition dialog box
Choose the M *symbol, then choose* OK *in frame*	Places Maximum Material Condition symbol
Click in the Datum 3 Datum *edit box and type* **C**	Labels Datum 3
In the Datum 3 cluster, click on the MC *image button*	Opens the Material Condition dialog box
Choose the M *symbol, then choose* OK *in frame*	Places Maximum Material Condition symbol
Choose OK	Closes Geometric Tolerance dialog box
`Command: _tolerance` `Enter tolerance location:` *Locate the frame at* ④ *(fig 24.20)*	Places feature control frame on drawing

Save your work.

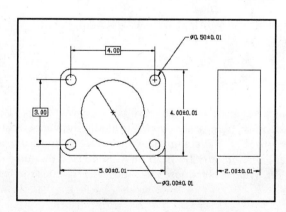

Figure 24.19

Creating the side view and linear and diameter dimensions.

24

Figure 24.20

Placing the datum labels and feature control frames.

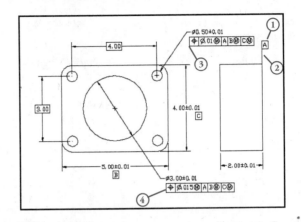

Figure 24.21

Creating a feature control frame in the Geometric Tolerance dialog box.

> **Note** In some early versions of Release 13, placing only a datum label may draw an extra small box above the datum frame. As a workaround, you can use the Tolerance 1 box to specify the datum, without selecting any symbols.

Now you have used the TOLERANCE command to create datum identifier labels and complete feature control frames.

Editing the Feature Control Frame

A *feature control frame* is a single object that you can move, copy, or erase. Grips also are useful for modifying feature control frames. The best way to modify the characteristics of the feature control frame is to use the DDEDIT command. When you select the feature control frame, all the current characteristics are shown in the Geometric Tolerance dialog box for you to view and edit. When you choose OK, AutoCAD updates the feature control frame.

New Riders Publishing
INSIDE
SERIES

Note Some AutoCAD users have been known to explode dimensions so they can edit them. Although TOLERANCE is a dimensioning command, the feature control frames you create with it are *not* a dimension, but rather, a *tolerance*. You cannot explode feature control frames that you use the TOLERANCE command to create.

Using Dimension Style Families

As you can see from the exercises so far in this chapter, you can spend a considerable amount of time changing the Dimension Style settings for various types of dimensions, especially if tolerances are involved. Learning to utilize a number of dimension styles can help you reduce the time you spend changing the dimension style settings. Just as using several text styles is desirable, you should organize your dimensions according to dimension style.

This section focuses on how to use the Dimension Style dialog box to effectively control your dimensions, which is the easiest way to keep track of numerous variables. Of course, many shortcuts are available if you are familiar enough with AutoCAD's dimension styles and variables to control them at the Command: prompt.

Determining How Many Styles To Define

In Chapter 22, "Editing and Styling Dimensions," you learned about dimension style overrides and dimension style families. When you modify the settings in a dimension style, and save the changes, all dimensions created using that style are affected. If you want to change only the settings to create one special dimension, do not save the changes. This is called an *override,* and a + sign appears in front of the dimension style name in the Dimensions Styles dialog box to indicate that unsaved changes exist in that style.

Some common cases in which overrides are useful in a mechanical drawing include the following:

♦ A special tolerance not often used. You would change the Tolerance **M**ethod setting in the Annotation dialog box, then exit the Dimension Styles dialog box without choosing **S**ave.

♦ One or both extension lines suppressed. To achieve this, use Extension Line Supress 1**s**t and 2**n**d in the Geometry dialog box. For an override, do not choose **S**ave before you exit the Dimension Styles dialog box.

♦ Unique text or dimension line placement. Here you might use one of the Horizontal Justification options, again without saving the style.

24

◆ Alternate units or places of precision not commonly used. You set alternate units in the Annotation dialog box, and set places of precision in the Primary Units dialog box.

In other words, use overrides for special situations that occur in mechanical dimensioning.

You can anticipate certain types of dimensions when you work on mechanical drawings. Because you might need to alter several settings before you can create a certain type of dimension, always using overrides is not practical, such as in the following cases:

◆ Basic dimensions required on GDT-type drawings. Basic dimensions are common enough that it's worth creating a dimension style for them. Create a new style based on the GDT style, then, with the Parent family member current, open the Annotation dialog box and set the Tolerance Method to Basic.

◆ Common text strings appended to certain dimensions. You may frequently work with reference dimensions. As you learned earlier in the chapter, reference dimensions are enclosed in parentheses. Create a reference dimension style based on your GDT style. Open the Annotation dialog box and in the Primary Units cluster place an opening parenthesis in the Prefix edit box and a closing parenthesis in the Suffix edit box.

◆ Dual dimensioning. Create an alternate units dimension style by turning on Enable Units in the Alternate Units cluster of the Annotation dialog box. When Alternate Units are enabled, you can set units, or add a prefix or suffix.

◆ Other types of tolerancing, such as limits or deviation. In any kind of dimension that occurs more than a few times in a drawing, it is very much worth the extra time to create a special dimension style.

Often, you should save separate dimension styles so that you can quickly choose another style rather than have to check all the settings.

Note In a CAD drafting department in which many different designers try to conform to a standard, a standard set of dimension styles is very important. This helps ensure a uniform drawing appearance throughout your office, and it makes it easier for checkers to spot errors.

New Riders Publishing
INSIDE
SERIES

Understanding Parent and Child Relationships

Although the concept of dimension styles is not new to AutoCAD, the parent and child relationship *is* new in Release 13. Using different settings for different types of dimensions is common practice; for example, the type of tolerance or the places of accuracy of a linear dimension can differ from an angular or diameter dimension.

When you define a new dimension style, you choose the Parent radio button in the Dimension Styles dialog box (see fig. 24.22). First, make all the necessary settings in the Geometry, Format, and Annotation pages of the dialog box. Try to choose settings such as units, text style, and arrows that are appropriate for most of your dimensions of that style. AutoCAD stores all these settings as parent settings.

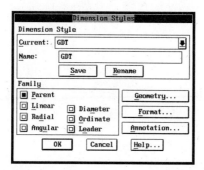

Figure 24.22

Preparing to create a parent dimension style in the Dimension Styles dialog box.

Next, choose one of the six child categories and alter any settings that affect only those types of dimensions. Continue to modify the various child categories until you create your best combinations of settings.

Finally, you save this dimension style and continue to define as many other different styles as you will need for your drawings. A sample of mechanical dimension styles is shown in the following list:

- ◆ **MECH-NT.** A dimension style that has no tolerance.

- ◆ **MECH-BA.** A dimension style to create basic dimensions.

- ◆ **MECH-DT.** A dimension style for creating oversize datum labels with a special font.

- ◆ **MECH-DD.** A dimension style for creating dual dimensions.

After you have included some familiar dimension styles in your prototype drawings, mechanical dimensioning should become less of a chore.

24

Experimenting with Other Mechanical Dimensioning Techniques

Along with Geometric dimensioning and tolerancing, you encounter many other special situations on mechanical drawings. Sometimes labeling holes or keyways according to the mating part is appropriate, assuming that the production department understands the sizes and tolerances involved. Some examples of this would be tapped holes, counterbored screw holes, or woodruff keyways. Figure 24.23 shows some examples of these notes, which are a lot less work than specifying all the exact sizes and tolerances. You can use the AutoCAD LEADER command for these notes.

Figure 24.23

Common mechanical dimensioning techniques.

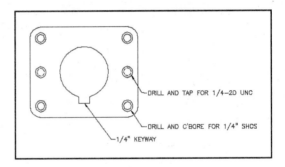

When you create a family of similar parts from a common drawing, letters or symbols can take the place of dimension values. A table is then constructed that lists several sets of values for different-sized parts, which leads to some very advanced CAD applications for which a parametric drawing is created. The actual feature size and locations are then driven by external data imported through a variety of methods that AutoCAD supports.

Controlling the Appearance of Dimensions and Tolerances

Many of the components of a dimension are controlled by the dimension style settings. In mechanical dimensioning applications, you might want to optimize the appearance of the dimensions. One item that you might want to control is the leading 0 in front of a decimal fraction. While some mechanical drafters feel this extra 0 is unnecessary, others want to see it because it helps the decimal point stand out if the drawing is faded and hard to read. The Units portion of the Annotation settings has a leading 0 switch for both the primary value and the tolerance. Figure 24.24 shows a dimension created with and without the leading 0.

Also, in the interest of saving space, you might want to modify the text height of deviation tolerances, for which you would use the tolerance portion of the A̲nnotation settings. Figure 24.24 also shows an example of the tolerance text at full scale and at half scale of the dimension text.

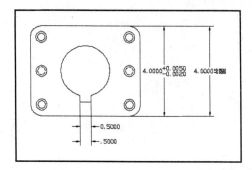

Figure 24.24

Dimensions with modified leading 0 and tolerance text height.

One final dimensional feature you might want to control is the color of the various dimension components. This is especially useful if you want to assign different plotting pens or plotting line widths to these components.

Creating Ordinate Dimensions

On mechanical designs that contain many features requiring locational dimensions, ordinate dimensions are very useful. Because ordinate dimensions do not use dimension lines and use only one extension line, far less clutter occurs on the drawing.

> **DIMORDINATE.** The DIMORDINATE command enables you to place ordinate (also known as datum-line) dimensions on a drawing. Ordinate dimensions measure the perpendicular distance from an origin point on the part being dimensioned to any other point on the part. You can indicate whether you want to dimension along the X-datum or the Y-datum, or let AutoCAD decide the direction according to the points you pick.
>
> Pull-down: *Choose* Draw, Dimensioning, Ordinate
> Screen: *Choose* DRAW DIM, Ordinat

The first step in using ordinate dimensions is to set the current UCS to the dimensioning datum point. In the next exercise, you practice placing some ordinate dimensions.

Applying Ordinate Dimensions

Begin a new drawing called CHAP24O, using the BASEDIMS drawing from the IA Disk as a prototype. To make finding points and placing ordinate dimensions easier, turn on ortho mode, and set an ENDPoint running object snap.

Command: *Choose* View, Set UCS, *then* Origin	Issues the UCS command with Origin option

`Origin/ZAxis/3point/OBject/View`
`/X/Y/Z/Prev/Restore/Save/Del/?`
`/<World>: _o`	

`Origin point <0,0,0>:` *Pick* ① *(see fig. 24.25)*	Sets 0,0 to the corner of the plate

Because the UCS is no longer the same as the WCS, the W indicator from the UCS icon has disappeared.

Command: *Choose* Draw, Dimensioning *then* Ordinate, Automatic	Issues the DIMORDINATE command in automatic mode
`_dimordinate` `Select feature:` *Pick* ②	Selects endpoint of centerline
`Leader endpoint (Xdatum/Ydatum/Text):` *Pick point at* ③	Specifies leader length and draws dimension

Continue to add ordinate dimensions until your drawing resembles figure 24.25.

To create the 21 dimension with a staggered leader line, turn off ortho before picking ④. Otherwise, keep ortho on to ensure straight lines.

Figure 24.25

Ordinate dimensions applied to the drawing

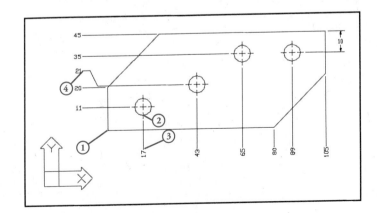

Tip There are no dimension variables to control the distance away from the object that the leader line ends and the dimension is placed. To work around this problem and give your ordinate dimensions a neat appearance, set your snap so that you can easily end the leader lines at a uniform distance.

You can see how quickly you can dimension a detail drawing when you use ordinate dimensions. You end up with very little clutter and the extension lines do not interfere with each other.

Tip When dimensions are very close to each other you can use a staggered leader to bring the dimension text to a better position, as shown in the 21mm dimension in figure 24.25.

Using Alternate Units

You really want to avoid creating a design that uses both SI and English units. Because of standard stock sizes, as well as standard component compatibility with items such as threads and keyways, the design must originate in either metric or English standards. Owing to customer requirements, however, or the insistence of shop workers, you sometimes must show both units in a dimension.

If you activate the Enable Units function in the Alternate Units cluster of the Annotation dialog box, AutoCAD automatically generates dimensions with alternate units. After you activate the alternate units, you have complete control over the units and tolerance settings of the alternate units. The most common conversion factors are 25.4 when inch units are standard and millimeters are the alternate unit, and 0.03937 when millimeters are standard and inches are the alternate unit.

As you can see in figure 24.26, dual dimensioning text strings can become very long and hard to place. Local tolerances are almost out of the question.

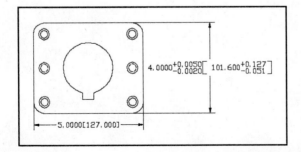

Figure 24.26

Alternate units for dual dimensioning.

24

Stop You might find that in some engineering standards, dual dimensions must be placed so that the alternate units are under, rather than behind, the normal dimension text. It is currently not possible to create associative dual dimensions in AutoCAD where the alternate dimension is below the dimension line.

Reviewing Dimensioning Techniques

Perhaps you already had a pretty good idea of how your detailed and dimensioned drawings should appear before you started this series of chapters on dimensioning. Possibly some of the mechanical dimensioning concepts discussed in this chapter helped you connect AutoCAD capabilities with your technical drawing requirements.

The first step of dimensioning with AutoCAD involves learning the basic dimensioning tools. Chapter 21, "Introduction to Dimensioning," introduces the dimensioning commands and demonstrates how you can apply them. After you learn how to use these tools, in Chapter 22, you learn how to control your dimensions by changing settings and using dimension styles.

Finally, Chapters 23 and 24 give you some useful information for applying AutoCAD dimensioning to your specific needs. Those who read Chapter 23 were probably not interested in the TOLERANCE command, and Chapter 24 did not cover many of the dimension settings primarily used by surveyors, architects, or civil engineers.

Continue to explore better ways to utilize AutoCAD dimensioning on your projects. This is the end of Part 5. Now that you can dimension your drawing, turn to Part 6, where you learn how to compose your final drawing layout and generate the plot.

Part VI

Drawing and Data I/O

New Riders Publishing
INSIDE SERIES

CHAPTER 25

Sheet Composition and Plotting

In previous chapters, you saw how to construct a model. In this chapter, you learn how to use the PLOT command to put that model on a piece of paper, vellum, or other media (also referred to as your *hard copy* or *plot*).

This chapter also shows you how to compose the layout of your plot in both model and paper space. The phrase "compose the layout of your plot" refers to when you sit at a drafting board and decide what views to draw and where to place them on the sheet of paper. You learn the equivalent process for an AutoCAD drawing.

In this chapter you learn how to do the following:

◆ Configure plotters for plot output

◆ Configure the output format, size and orientation

◆ Preview plot output

◆ Compose drawings in tiled model space for plotter output

◆ Compose drawings in the floating viewports of paper space

◆ Annotate drawings for consistency in both environments

In this exercise, you compose a 2D drawing on a typical drawing sheet as it will appear when plotted.

Quick 5¢ Tour

Begin a new drawing named CHAP25, using the IA Disk drawing BOARD as the prototype.

Command: *Choose* View, Paper Space	Turns off TILEMODE and enters paper space
Command: *Choose* View, Floating Viewports, MV Setup	Issues the MVSETUP command
Initializing... _mvsetup	
Align/Create/Scale viewports /Options/Title block/Undo: **T** (Enter)	Specifies the Title block option
Delete objects/Origin/Undo/ <Insert title block>: (Enter)	Accepts Insert title block option to list title block choices

```
Available title block options:
0:  None
1:  ISO A4 Size(mm)
2:  ISO A3 Size(mm)
3:  ISO A2 Size(mm)
4:  ISO A1 Size(mm)
5:  ISO A0 Size(mm)
6:  ANSI-V Size(in)
7:  ANSI-A Size(in)
8:  ANSI-B Size(in)
9:  ANSI-C Size(in)
10: ANSI-D Size(in)
11: ANSI-E Size(in)
12: Arch/Engineering (24 x 36in)
13: Generic D size Sheet (24 x 36in)
```

25

| Add/Delete/Redisplay/ | Specifies an ANSI-B size title block |
| `<Number of entry to load>:` **8** (Enter) | |

| Create a drawing named | Specifies to not save the title block in |
| `ansi-b.dwg? <Y>:` **N** (Enter) | another drawing file and inserts the title block (see fig. 25.1) |

| Align/Create/Scale viewports | Specifies the Create option |
| /Options/Title block/Undo: **C** (Enter) | |

| Delete objects/Undo/ | Accepts the default option of creating |
| `<Create viewports>:` (Enter) | viewports and lists choices |

```
Available Mview viewport layout options:
 0:  None
 1:  Single
 2:  Std. Engineering
 3:  Array of Viewports
```

| Redisplay/`<Number of entry to` | Specifies the single viewport option |

Bounding area for viewports.	Specifies corner of the area in which the
Default/`<First point >` *Pick* ①	viewports are to be located
(see fig. 25.1)	

| Other points: *Pick* ② | Inserts a single viewpoint and restores the current view to the viewport |

| Align/Create/Scale viewports/ | Quits the MVSETUP command |
| Options/Title block/Undo: (Enter) | |

Save the drawing.

The composition of technical drawing, sheet border line and title block that results from the previous exercise will plot on a B size sheet for a finished drawing.

MVSETUP enables you to automate composing views for plotting in paper space. You explore this in more detail later in this chapter and in Chapter 28, "3D Basics," but first you learn about plotting.

Figure 25.1

*ANSI-B drawing
with title block.*

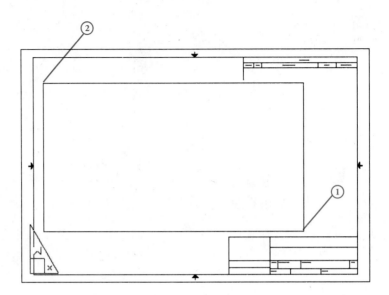

Plotting

Despite the incessant talk of a "paperless" office, the reality is that producing plots is still a major factor in CAD work. You create plots for checking (sometimes called *check plots*), and of course, you create plots of the finished product. The PLOT command is the primary command you use to produce hard copies.

PLOT. The PLOT command opens the Plot Configuration dialog box and enables you to generate plots on a printer or plotter.

Screen: *Choose* FILE, Print

Pull-down: *Choose* File, Print

PLOT has quite a number of options, described in detail in the following section.

The basic procedure for producing a plot is as follows:

1. Make sure that your plotter is ready to plot.

2. Issue the PLOT command.

New Riders Publishing

INSIDE SERIES

3. Select the plotter you want to use.

4. Set the pen table.

5. Specify the area of the drawing to plot.

6. Select a sheet size.

7. Set a plot scale.

8. Preview your settings, and if satisfied, start the plot.

Checking Your Plotter Configuration

You can use CONFIG to configure AutoCAD to use a particular output device, when you install AutoCAD or any time thereafter. The exact options available in the Plot Configuration dialog box vary from one plotter model to another. To ensure that you can carry out the exercises, you configure an HP DesignJet 600 plotter as one of your output devices.

 Note Even if you do not have an HP DesignJet 600 plotter, you can configure for it and follow the exercise. You then can use the Preview Full feature in the Plot Configuration dialog box to simulate the plot, then use Cancel rather than OK to exit the dialog box without actual plotter output.

To find out whether you even have a plotter currently configured, simply issue the PLOT command. If AutoCAD has not yet been configured to use an output device, an error message box appears (see fig. 25.2).

Figure 25.2

The AutoCAD Alert box appears with a message that no plotter is configured.

If AutoCAD is configured for an output device, the Plot Configuration dialog box appears, as shown in figure 25.3.

Figure 25.3

*The Plot
Configuration
dialog box.*

```
                        Plot Configuration
Device and Default Information      Paper Size and Orientation
 Laser Printer                       ■ Inches
   Device and Default Selection...   □ MM        Size...  MAX
 Pen Parameters                      Plot Area 8.00 by 10.50.
   Pen Assignments...  Optimization... Scale, Rotation, and Origin
 Additional Parameters                  Rotation and Origin...
   ■ Display    □ Hide Lines        Plotted Inches = Drawing Units
   □ Extents
   □ Limits     □ Adjust Area Fill        8      = 1'5.00"
   □ View                           ⊠ Scaled to Fit
   □ Window     □ Plot To File      Plot Preview
   View...  Window...  File Name...   Preview...  ■ Partial □ Full
              OK    Cancel    Help...
```

This chapter does not intend to teach you how to configure AutoCAD for your specific plotter. If this is what you need, consult the *AutoCAD Installation Guide* and the plotter manufacturer's installation guide.

In the following exercise, you configure for an HP DesignJet 600 plotter. Do not be alarmed if you do not have the plotter that is specified in the following instructions. You do not actually plot to the specified plotter.

Configuring a Plotter

Begin a new drawing named CHAP25A, using the IA Disk drawing BOARD as the prototype.

Command: *Choose* Options, Configure   Issues the CONFIG command and the main
                                              configuration menu appears, after some
                                              configuration information

```
Configuration menu
 0. Exit to drawing editor
 1. Show current configuration
 2. Allow detailed configuration
 3. Configure video display
 4. Configure digitizer
 5. Configure plotter
 6. Configure system console
 7. Configure operating parameters
```

Enter selection <0>: **5** **(Enter)**   Specifies the plotter configuration option

Next, you see the plotter configuration menu, which has options that you can use to add, delete, or modify plotter configurations.

```
Plotter Configuration Menu
 0. Exit to configuration menu
 1. Add a plotter configuration
 2. Delete a plotter configuration
 3. Change a plotter configuration
 4. Rename a plotter configuration

Enter selection, 0 to 4 <0>: 1 (Enter)        Specifies the Add plotter option

Available plotter:

   1.  None
   2.  ADI plotter or printer (installed - pre v4.1) - by Autodesk, Inc
   3.  AutoCAD file output formats (pre 4.1) - by Autodesk, Inc
   4.  CalComp ColorMaster Plotters ADI 4.2 V2.8 - by Autodesk
   5.  CalComp DrawingMaster Plotters ADI 4.2 V2.8 - by Autodesk
   6.  CalComp Electrostatic Plotters ADI 4.2 V2.8 - by Autodesk
   7.  CalComp Pen Plotters ADI 4.2 V2.8 - by Autodesk
   8.  Canon Bubble Jet Printers, ADI 4.2 - for Autodesk by Canon
   9.  Canon Laser Printer ADI 4.2 - by Autodesk, Inc
  10.  Epson printers ADI 4.2 - by Autodesk, Inc
  11.  Hewlett-Packard (HP-GL) ADI 4.2 - by Autodesk, Inc
  12.  Hewlett-Packard (PCL) LaserJet ADI 4.2 - by Autodesk, Inc
  13.  Hewlett-Packard (PCL) PaintJet/DeskJet ADI 4.2 - by Autodesk, Inc
  14.  Hewlett-Packard HP-GL/2 devices, ADI 4.2 - for Autodesk by HP
  15.  Houston Instrument ADI 4.2 - by Autodesk, Inc
  16.  IBM Proprinter ADI 4.2 - by Autodesk, Inc
  17.  PostScript device ADI 4.2 - by Autodesk, Inc
  18.  Raster file export ADI 4.2 - by Autodesk, Inc

Select device number or ? to repeat        Specifies the HP-GL/2 driver
list <1>: 14 (Enter)
```

The list of plotters might vary from version to version, so make sure that the number 14 still corresponds to HP-GL/2 devices before you enter 14.

```
Supported models:
   1. HP DesignJet 650C
   2. HP DesignJet 600
   3. HP DesignJet 200
   4. HP DraftMaster with Roll Feed
   5. HP DraftMaster Plus Sheet Feed
   6. HP DraftMaster SX/RX/MX Sheet Fd
   7. HP PaintJet XL300
   8. HP DraftPro Plus
   9. HP 7600 Color (obsolete)
```

continues

continued

```
10. HP 7600 Monochrome (obsolete)
11. HP LaserJet III
12. HP LaserJet 4
```

Enter selection, 1 to 12 <1>: **2** (Enter)   Specifies the HP DesignJet 600 plotter

The list of HP models might vary from version to version, so make sure that the number 2 still corresponds to the HP DesignJet 600 before you enter 2.

You then get some device-specific instructions, after which you see the following prompt.

Press a key to continue (Enter)   Continues the configuration process

Is your plotter connected to a <S>erial,   Selects a parallel rather than a serial
or <P>arallel port? <P> (Enter)   port

You then get some port-specific instructions, after which you see the following prompt.

Enter parallel port name for plotter   Selects the parallel port 1 (LPT1:) for
or . for none <LPT1>: (Enter)   output to the plotter

```
Plot will NOT be written to a selected file
Sizes are in Inches and the style is landscape
Plot origin is at (0.00,0.00)
Plotting area is 43.00 wide by 33.00 high (E size)
Plot is NOT rotated
Hidden lines will NOT be removed
Plot will be scaled to fit available area
```

Do you want to change anything?   Accepts the listed defaults
(No/Yes/File) <N>: (Enter)

Enter a description for this plotter: Assigns the name IAD PLOTTER to the new
IAD PLOTTER (Enter)   plotter configuration and returns you to
          the plotter configuration menu

```
Plotter Configuration Menu
 0. Exit to configuration menu
 1. Add a plotter configuration
 2. Delete a plotter configuration
 3. Change a plotter configuration
 4. Rename a plotter configuration
```

New Riders Publishing
INSIDE
SERIES

```
Enter selection, 0 to 4 <0>: (Enter)     Exits plotter configuration menu and
                                          returns you to the configuration menu


Configuration menu
  0. Exit to drawing editor
  1. Show current configuration
  2. Allow detailed configuration
  3. Configure video display
  4. Configure digitizer
  5. Configure plotter
  6. Configure system console
  7. Configure operating parameters


Enter selection <0>: (Enter)              Exits configuration menu

If you answer N to the following question, all configuration
changes you have just made will be discarded.


Keep configuration changes? <Y> (Enter)   Saves configuration and returns you to the
                                          drawing editor
```

You use the IAD PLOTTER configuration in the following exercises.

Previewing Your Plot

As you decide on the exact settings for the plot, you can use the Preview options to preview the expected results at any time (see fig. 25.4).

Plot Preview

Preview... ☐ Par**ti**al ☐ F**u**ll

Figure 25.4

The Plot Preview options in the Plot Configuration dialog box.

You can perform a Partial (default setting) or a Full preview. If you select a Partial preview, you see a dialog box similar to the one figure 25.5.

Figure 25.5

A partial preview in the Preview Effective Plotting Area box.

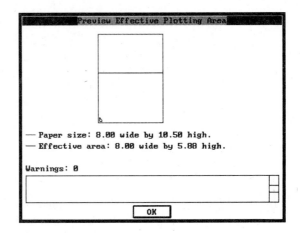

The larger rectangle (usually red in color) represents the specified plot area (paper size) and the smaller rectangle (usually blue in color) represents the area that the plot actually uses. You are given the actual dimensions below the rectangles. The preview function warns you if it detects any possible errors, such as specifying a scale that requires more plot area than you indicate is available.

If you opt for a full preview, you see an image of the actual plot, similar to figure 25.6.

Figure 25.6

A full preview.

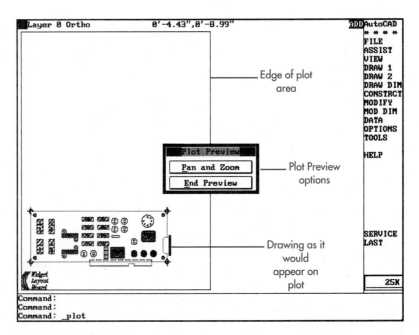

You can use the <u>P</u>an and Zoom button to zoom into an area. If you choose <u>P</u>an and Zoom, a rectangle replaces your normal cursor. You position the rectangle in the area into which you want to zoom. If you click the pick button, you can size the rectangle. If you click the pick button again, you can position the resized rectangle. Clicking the pick button switches you between resizing and positioning the rectangle. Zoom, Dynamic works in a similar manner. After you are satisfied with the size and location of the rectangle, press Enter or the spacebar, and the specified area appears. You then see the following options, as shown in figure 25.7.

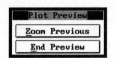

Figure 25.7
Full preview options.

If you want to zoom into another area, choose the Zoom Previous button. The previous view appears and you can zoom and pan to another area. After you are satisfied, you can end the preview by clicking on the <u>E</u>nd Preview button. Naturally, it takes longer to generate a full preview than a partial preview.

If you do not like what you see in the preview, go back and change your settings. After you decide that everything looks satisfactory, choose OK from the Plot Configuration dialog box to proceed with the actual plot.

Note Zooming and panning in preview mode does not actually change the view that is plotted. It simply enables you to see the details of the plot that might be too small to read.

In the exercises that follow, you use the preview function to view the effects of changing the various plot configuration settings.

Selecting the Plotter

You can configure AutoCAD to work with multiple output devices. If you have only one plotter configured, PLOT automatically uses that one. If, however, you have several plotters configured, you need to select the plotter you want to use by choosing the <u>D</u>evice and Default Selection button in the Device and Default Information group of the Plot Configuration dialog box (refer to figure 25.3). Choosing the <u>D</u>evice and Default Selection button opens the Device and Default Selection dialog box (see fig. 25.8).

Figure 25.8

*The Device and
Default Selection
dialog box.*

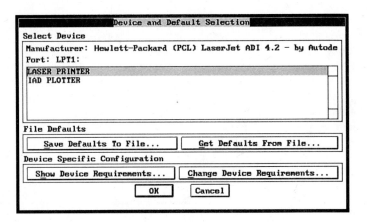

To select a particular plotter configuration, simply select it from the Port list at the top of the dialog box. At times, you can set some device-specific options. To see if the selected plotter has any options, choose the Show Device Requirements button. If you want to set device-specific options, choose the Change Device Requirements button. The device-specific options, of course, vary from device to device, and simply do not exist for some devices.

Tip

The plotter configuration names that appear in the list are the names you specify during the configuration process. Use descriptive names that will be meaningful even to a novice user.

In the following exercise, you issue the PLOT command and select the plotter you configured in the previous exercise.

Selecting a Plotter Configuration

Continue to use the drawing CHAP25A.

Command: *Choose* File, Print	Issues the PLOT command and opens the Plot Configuration dialog box
Choose the **D**evice and Default Selection *button*	Opens the Device and Default Selection dialog box

If you have multiple plotter configurations, you select the plotter configuration you want to use in the Device and Default Selection dialog box.

Select IAD PLOTTER *from the list
of plotters*

New Riders Publishing
INSIDE
SERIES

Choose the Change Device Requirements *button*	Opens the Device Requirements dialog box

You set device-specific options in the Device Requirements dialog box. The HP DesignJet displays settings, but you must use the HPCONFIG command (supplied with the plotter driver) to change them.

Choose OK	Exits the Device Requirements dialog box
Choose OK	Exits the Device and Default Selection dialog box and returns to Plot Configuration dialog box
Choose the Full *button,* *then* Preview	Displays a detailed preview of the image that will be output to the plotter
Choose End Preview	

Remain in the Plot Configuration dialog box for the next exercise. If you cancel, your settings are lost.

The preview simulates actual plotting, scaled to fit the display, but you need to consider several other options before you actually create a finished plot.

Setting Pen Parameters

After you select the device to use, you want to set up the pen table for the plot to allow control of line weights (line thickness) for each object plotted. You access the pen table by using the Pen Assignments dialog box (see fig. 25.9), which you bring up by choosing the Pen Assignments button in the Pen Parameters group of the Plot Configuration dialog box (refer to figure 25.3).

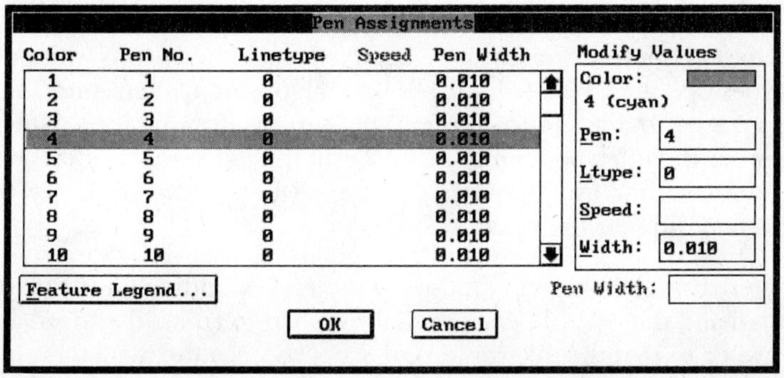

Figure 25.9

The Pen Assignments dialog box.

The Pen Assignments dialog box enables you to assign a pen, speed, linetype, and line weight to a particular drawing color. You might ask "Why pens?" especially if your output device does not even use pens (for example, if you have a laser jet or ink jet printer).

In the early days of CAD, the basic output device was a pen plotter. The simplest ones were *single pen plotters* (could load with only one pen at a time). The more sophisticated ones were *multi-pen plotters*, which employed pen carousels. The *carousel* was a storage unit for the pens. Each pen was stored in a numbered position in the carousel. The pen in position #1 was referred to as pen #1, the pen in position #2 was referred to as pen #2, and so on. Multi-pen plotters facilitated the generation of plots that used varying colors and/or line weights. For example, if you stored a pen with red ink in position #3 and wanted to draw red lines on the plot, you would instruct the CAD software to pick up pen #3 to draw certain objects.

In AutoCAD, you assign pens by color. You can instruct PLOT to use pen #2 for all objects drawn in red or pen #1 for all objects drawn in green by setting the pen table. Then, if you actually insert pens that have color ink into the carousel, you end up with a color plot. On the other hand, if you put pens that have different line weights into the carousel, you end up with a plot that has different line weights.

So in AutoCAD, you use the Pen Assignments table to assign line weights to objects by drawing the objects in specific colors and then assigning specific numbered pens to those colors. If you do not use a pen plotter, such as a laser or ink jet plotter, plotting technology has moved away from using physical pens but still employs logical pens. *Logical pens* basically are imaginary pens to which you can assign properties such as line weight or color. You can use logical pens to program a laser plotter to draw a line of a certain width and/or color whenever it receives instructions to use a certain logical pen.

The linetype parameter is another holdover from the old plotting technology. The earliest CAD software could draw only continuous lines. To draw noncontinuous linetypes, the software had to rely on linetypes defined in the plotter itself. These linetypes were referred to by number. Linetype 1, for example, might have been a hidden linetype, whereas linetype 2 might have been a dotted linetype. As with pens, you assigned linetypes by colors. Plotter linetypes became obsolete when AutoCAD evolved to enable the user to draw noncontinuous lines in the drawing itself. Nowadays, you no longer use the linetype setting. Instead, you leave it set at the default value of 0 (for continuous) and use AutoCAD's linetypes when you want to draw objects that have noncontinuous linetypes.

The speed parameter also is a holdover from pen plotters. Depending on the media on which you plotted and the type of pen specified, you had to adjust the speed at which the pens traveled so that the ink would flow properly onto the media. Even today, if you use a pen plotter, you sometimes have to adjust the pen speeds. With technology that does not employ pens, such as lasers or ink jets, the pen speed setting

is not relevant and you can leave it at the default setting. For some devices, you use the pen speed setting to control some other parameters, such as the darkness of lines for a laser jet.

The pen width setting enables you to set the pen width of a particular pen. AutoCAD uses this information when it draws solid filled areas and for the Adjust Area Fill option of the Plot Configuration dialog box. To fill in a solid area, AutoCAD draws one stroke and then moves the pen over one pen width to draw the next stroke. If the pen width setting is smaller then the actual pen width, you get many redundant overlapping of strokes. If the pen width setting is larger than the actual pen width, you get gaps (blank space) between the strokes. For some plotters, you can set a pen width for each pen, whereas for others you can only set a global pen width for all pens. When you elect to define your paper size in inches (which is the default setting), remember that the pen width is set in inches, not millimeters. So, if you use a 0.35 mm pen, enter a pen width of 0.014 inches. Usually leaving this setting at its default value of 0.01 (equivalent to 0.254 mm) is satisfactory. ISO pen widths from the Select Linetype dialog box and ISO hatch patterns, with ISO linetypes, from the Boundry Hatch dialog box are defined in mm even if the drawing units are inches.

Tip If you are accustomed to working with line weights defined in millimeters, set the paper size units to mm, then assign the pen widths. After you assign the pen widths, you can change the paper size units back to inches.

To set the values for a particular pen, just select the pen you want to set. AutoCAD then places the pen's current values into the Modify Values edit boxes on the right side of the Pen Assignments dialog box (see fig. 25.9), which enables you to change them. To set several pens simultaneously, select several pens and then change the values in the edit boxes.

In the following exercise, you change the default pen table.

Changing the Pen Assignments

Continue to use the drawing CHAP25A. If you canceled the PLOT command in the previous exercise, reissue it and make sure that the IAD PLOTTER is still the selected configuration.

In the following steps, you use the **P**en Assignment button located in the upper left portion of the Plot Configuration dialog box.

Command: *Choose the* **P**en Assignments   Opens the Pen Assignments dialog box
button

Select colors 1, 2, 3, *and* 4

continues

continued

Replace the value in the **P**en *edit box with the value 1 and press Enter*	Changes the Pen No. column to 1 for the selected pens
Deselect colors 1, 2, 3, *and* 4	
Select colors 5, 6, *and* 7	
Replace the value in the **P**en *edit box with the value* **2** *and press Enter*	Changes the Pen No. column to 2 for the selected pens
Choose OK	Exits the Pen Assignments dialog box

Remain in the Plot Configuration dialog box for the next exercise.

 Note If you need to exit, choose OK to save your settings, then quickly use Ctrl+C to cancel the plot. If you choose Cancel in the Plot Configuration dialog box, your settings are not saved.

Defining the Area To Be Plotted

You specify the portion of the drawing you want to plot in the Additional Parameters section of the Plot Configuration dialog box (see fig. 25.10).

Figure 25.10

The Additional Parameters section from the Plot Configuration dialog box.

Additional Parameters

☑ Display   ☐ Hide Lines
☑ Extents
☑ Limits   ☐ Adjust Area Fill
☐ View
☐ Window   ☐ Plot To File
[View...] [Window...] [File Name...]

You have the following choices in the Additional Parameters section:

◆ **Display.** Choose this radio button to plot the portion of the drawing in the current viewport. If you are in paper space or in the default single tiled viewport, Display plots the portion of the drawing displayed in the drawing window. If you are in a model space tiled or floating viewport, then the portion of the drawing visible in that viewport is plotted.

New Riders Publishing
INSIDE SERIES

◆ **Extents.** Choose this radio button to process the rectangular portion of your drawing that actually has objects drawn in it. Extents plots the extents of model space or paper space, whichever is current.

◆ **Limits.** Choose this radio button to process the area defined by the drawing limits (as set by using the LIMITS command). The limits of model space or paper space according to which environment is current (limits usually are different for the two environments.

◆ **View.** This radio button initially is grayed and disabled. Choose this button to plot views previously saved with DDVIEW or VIEW. If you opt to plot a view, choosing the View button at the bottom of the Additional Parameters area opens the View Name dialog box, in which you can select from a list of defined views. Then the View radio button becomes enabled and ungrayed so that you can choose it.

◆ **Window.** This radio button initially is disabled. To window a rectangular area to be processed, first you define the area by choosing the Window button at the bottom of the Additional Parameters area. A Window Selection dialog box appears (see fig. 25.11) that displays the points defining the current window. If you want to define another window area, enter the coordinates of two opposite corners in the edit boxes, or choose the Pick button, to specify the corners on-screen. When you choose OK to close the Window Selection dialog box, the Window radio button is ungrayed and enabled.

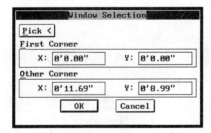

Figure 25.11

The Window Selection dialog box.

Stop If you recently changed the extents you might need to perform a ZOOM All or ZOOM Extents before you plot. You can change extents accidentally, for example, if you mistakenly move or copy an object to somewhere "out in space." Even if you use Undo to reverse the mistake, the extents will be oversized. If you find your plot is scaled small and placed in a corner of the plotted area, this probably is the cause. Use ZOOM Extents to discover whether you have this problem.

In the following exercise, you use the various options to define the area to plot. You also use the preview buttons located in the lower-right corner of the Plot Configuration dialog box to simulate the plot.

Defining the Area To Plot

Continue to use the drawing CHAP25A. If you canceled the PLOT command in the previous exercise, reissue it and make sure that the IAD PLOTTER is still the selected configuration and that the previous pen assignments are intact.

Choose P**r**eview	Displays a partial preview (default setting) of the plot using the current settings
Choose OK	Ends the partial preview
Choose F**u**ll	Enables a full preview for next preview operation
Choose P**r**eview	Displays a full preview of the plot using the current settings and displays the Plot Preview dialog box (see fig. 25.12)

Figure 25.12

Full preview of plotter output with Plot Preview dialog box.

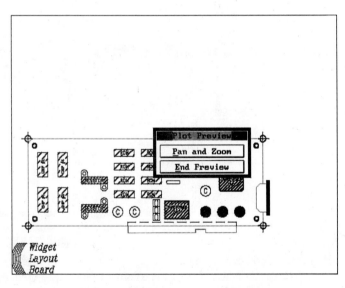

Choose **P**an and Zoom	Enters the pan and zoom mode

Your cursor is replaced with a box that represents the area you are panning or zooming. Position the box anywhere on-screen. Click the pick button once and you can size the box. If

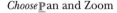

you want, click the pick button once again and you can reposition the box. After you are satisfied with the size and location of the box, press Enter to redisplay the Plot Preview dialog box.

Choose E̲nd Preview	Ends the preview function and redisplays the Plot Configuration dialog box

In the following steps, you work with the options for defining the area to plot. These options are in the left side of the Plot Configuration dialog box in the Additional Parameters section.

Choose the E̲x̲tents *radio button*	Sets the drawing extents as the area to be plotted
Choose P̲r̲eview	Displays a full preview (see fig. 25.13)

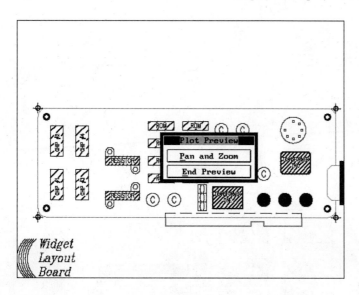

Figure 25.13
Full preview of Extents to be plotted.

Choose E̲n̲d Preview

Choose the Wi̲n̲dow *button at the bottom*	Displays the Window Selection dialog box with the coordinates of the current window
Choose p̲ick	Closes dialog boxes and prompts for a new windowed area
First corner: *Pick* ① *(see fig. 25.14)*	
Other corner: *Pick* ②	Defines new windowed area and returns dialog boxes, automatically selecting the W̲indow radio button

continues

continued

Choose OK   Accepts the new windowed area

Figure 25.14

*The window
selected for plotter
output.*

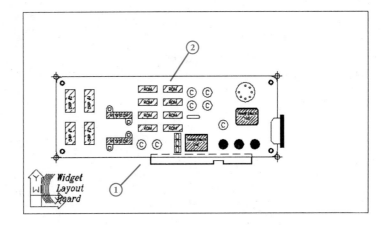

Choose P<u>r</u>eview

You should see the area you windowed as the area on the plot preview (see fig. 25.15).

Figure 25.15

*Full preview of
Window to be
plotted.*

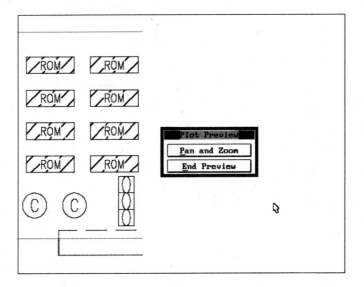

Choose <u>E</u>nd Preview

Remain in the Plot Configuration dialog box for the next exercise.

New Riders Publishing
INSIDE
SERIES

Tip Consistently using the name PLOT for the view you are plotting can help you avoid confusion about what you output to the plotter.

Setting the Paper Size

You also must decide the size of media on which to plot and the units—inches or millimeters—to define that media size. You set these options in the Paper Size and Orientation section of the Plot Configuration dialog box, as shown in figure 25.16.

```
Paper Size and Orientation
■ Inches
                 Size... E       [    ]
□ MM
Plot Area 43.00 by 33.00.
```

Figure 25.16

The Paper Size and Orientation section from the Plot Configuration dialog box.

Unless you work with metric standards, the default units of inches is appropriate. To set the actual paper size, click on the Size button to open the Paper Size dialog box (see fig. 25.17).

```
                    Paper Size
Size   Width   Height      Size    Width    Height
A      10.50    8.00    ▲  USER:   [      ]  [      ]
B      16.00   10.00
C      21.00   16.00       USER1:  [      ]  [      ]
D      33.00   21.00
E      43.00   33.00       USER2:  [      ]  [      ]
F      40.00   28.00
G      90.00   11.00       USER3:  [      ]  [      ]
H     143.00   28.00
J     176.00   34.00       USER4:  [      ]  [      ]
K     143.00   40.00
A4     11.20    7.80       Orientation is landscape  [  ]
A3     15.60   10.70
A2     22.40   15.60    ▼
            [  OK  ]      [  Cancel  ]
```

Figure 25.17

The Paper Size dialog box.

The term *paper size* is misleading because what you really define is the area on which you plot (also referred to as the *plot area*). The difference is that a plotter cannot plot right up to the edges of a sheet of paper. There always is a margin around the edges that the plotter cannot access, as shown in figure 25.18.

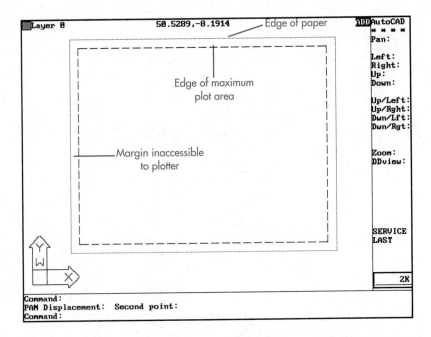

Figure 25.18

Physical area versus maximum available plot area.

The actual margin varies from plotter to plotter, so you need to look up that information in the plotter manuals. When you subtract the margins from the sheet size, you obtain the maximum available plot area, which is what you usually want to enter in the Paper Size dialog box. Suppose the instruction manual of your plotter states that the plotter leaves a half-inch margin all the way around the edge of the paper. Then on a 24-by-36-inch piece of paper, the maximum usable area (or plot area) is going to be 23 inches by 35 inches.

On the left of the Paper Size dialog box is a list of standard sheet sizes and their associated plot areas. You can select a plot area from the list or you can enter custom dimensions by using the edit boxes on the right, labeled U̲SER, USER1, and so on. A sheet size defined using these edit boxes is referred to as a *user defined sheet*. After you define a sheet size, the associated label (USER, USER1, and so on) appears in the list of available sheet sizes.

The list of predefined plot areas usually is not optimized for the specific plotter you use. You usually can get more plot area for a specific sheet size than what is stated on the list. If this is true for your plotter, use the edit boxes to define your own user-defined sheet size.

Tip
You can test the maximum available plot area by selecting the MAX size and separately plotting two xline objects (one horizontal and one vertical), then measuring the results of each plot. Use a tall, skinny window for the vertical xline plot and a short, wide window for the horizontal one.

You might wonder how critical it is to enter the correct plot area. If you are going to plot using a specific scale (like 1/8"=1'), the sheet size usually is not critical. If you choose a sheet size larger than what you actually have (such as the MAX sheet size), however, the plotter still only plots according to the limits of the plotter. If you choose a sheet size less than the maximum plot area, you lose use of some of the sheet.

In the lower-right corner of the Paper Size dialog box is a message that indicates the orientation of the paper. This is the default orientation of the loaded media. It is just a message, not a choice. The message varies for different plotters. For some, it indicates landscape; for others, it indicates portrait.

After you select a sheet size, choose the OK button to return to the Plot Configuration dialog box.

Setting the Rotation and Origin

Choosing the Rotation and Origin button in the Scale, Rotation and Origin section of the Plot Configuration dialog box opens the Plot Rotation and Origin dialog box (see fig. 25.19

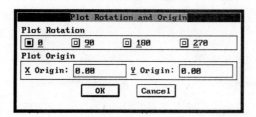

Figure 25.19

The Plot Rotation and Origin dialog box.

A plotter has its own X,Y axes and origin point. A rotation angle setting of 0 and an origin setting of 0,0 ensures that the area to be plotted (limits, extents, or whatever) is oriented on the paper so that the model's X axis is parallel to the plotter's X axis and that the lower-left corner of the area to be plotted coincides with the plotter's origin point.

You might want to change the orientation so that the area to be plotted can be better accommodated on the paper. Typically, the paper is loaded in a plotter so that the plotter's X axis runs along the longer length of the sheet. If your model's extents is greater in the Y direction than in the X direction, you might need to rotate the plot to get the largest possible plot onto the paper.

 Stop Be careful when you change the rotation angle. The settings rotate the plot in a clockwise direction and you can rotate the plot off the physical paper area. If this occurs, no plot is produced, and you have to adjust the origin point to accommodate the rotation angle.

Some plotters have a smaller margin on one side of the paper than the other. In such cases, your plot might appear off balance with more blank space on one side than the other. To even the margins out, you can adjust the origin to center the plot.

You also can use the origin option to fit several small plots onto a single large sheet of paper. After you generate the first plot, you would set the origin so that the next plot does not overlap the area occupied by the first plot. Not all plotters enable you to use this technique because it requires that you can reuse the same sheet of paper for several plots. This technique is most commonly used with pen plotters. Composing your plot in paper space, as discussed later in this chapter, is probably easier than offsetting multiple plots.

In the following exercise, you change the paper size and set the rotation and origin of the plot.

Setting the Rotation and Origin

Continue to use the drawing CHAP25A. If you canceled the PLOT command in the previous exercise, reissue it and make sure that the IAD PLOTTER is still the selected configuration.

First you work with the paper size options located in the upper-right portion of the Plot Configuration dialog box.

Choose the E**x**tents *radio button*	Sets the drawing extents as the area to be plotted
Choose **S**ize	Opens the Paper Size dialog box
Select the A size sheet *from the list*	Sets the current plot area to that of an A size sheet
Choose OK	Closes the Paper Size dialog box
Choose P**r**eview	Displays a full preview (see fig. 25.20)

New Riders Publishing
INSIDE
SERIES

Choose **E**nd Preview

Compare the results of the Full Preview with figure 25.13, keeping in mind that the sheet size in figure 25.13 is 43" by 33" (your current sheet size is 10.5" by 8").

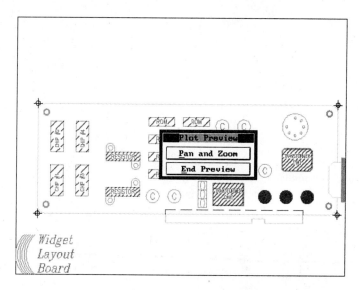

Figure 25.20

Full Preview with Extents of A-size sheet.

25

Then, you set the origin and rotation of the plot (using the Rotation and Origin command button in the Scale, Rotation, and Origin section of the Plot Configuration dialog box).

Choose Rotation and Origin	Opens the Plot Rotation and Origin dialog box
Type **2.0** *in the* **Y** Origin *edit box*	Offsets the origin of the plot 2 inches along the plotter's Y axis
Choose OK	Returns you to the Plot Configuration dialog box
Choose F**u**ll, *then* **P**review	Offsets the plot in the vertical (Y axis) direction (see fig. 25.21)
Choose **E**nd Preview	
Choose Rotation and Origin	
Choose the **9**0 Plot Rotation *radio button*	Rotates the plot 90 degrees clockwise

continues

continued

Type **0.0** *in the* Y Origin *edit box*	Resets the plot origin back to 0,0
Choose OK	
Choose Full, *then* Preview	Previews the plot, rotated clockwise 90 degrees (see fig. 25.22)
Choose End Preview	
Choose Rotation and Origin	
Choose the 0 Plot Rotation *radio button*	Rotates the plot back to 0 degrees

Remain in the Plot Configuration dialog box for the next exercise.

Figure 25.21

Full Preview with plot origin offset of 2 inches.

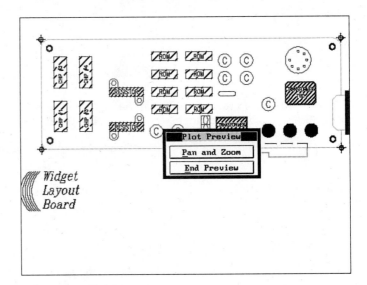

Setting the Plot Scale

The *plot scale* is the relationship you set between a distance on your final plot (inches or millimeters) to the equivalent distance in your drawing (drawing units). One inch on your drawing to 10 feet (drawing units) on your drawing would produce a drawing at 1"=10' (or 1=120). You set the plot scale in the Scale, Rotation, and Origin section of the Plot Configuration dialog box (see fig. 25.23).

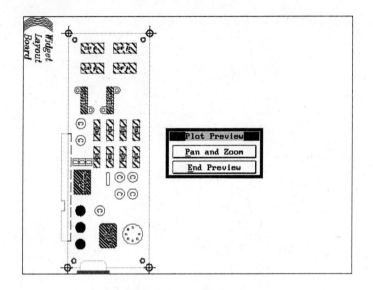

Figure 25.22

Full Preview with plot rotated 90°.

25

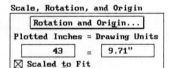

Figure 25.23

The Scale, Rotation, and Origin section of the Plot Configuration dialog box.

If you set your units for architectural or engineering units, you can include the foot and inch marks in your scale specification. Regardless of the units you set, you always can set the scale in decimal units. For example, if you work on a drawing that you have set up in architectural units and intend to plot at a 1/8"=1' scale, you can enter any of the following values for the scale:

  1" = 8'

  1/8" = 1'

  1=96"

  1=96

Sometimes, you might want to generate a plot that has no particular scale. In such situations, use the Scaled to Fit option. Turning on Scaled to Fit instructs AutoCAD to calculate and use the largest scale possible to fit the area you want to plot onto the specified plot area (Paper Size section). The drawback of using Scaled to Fit is that you cannot scale anything off the drawing because a nonstandard scale was used for the plot.

In the following exercise, you set the plot scale for the plot in the Scale, Rotation, and Origin section of the Plot Configuration dialog box.

Setting the Plot Scale

Continue to use the drawing CHAP25A. If you canceled the PLOT command in the previous exercise, reissue it and make sure the IAD PLOTTER is still the selected configuration.

Choose Size	Displays the Paper Size dialog box
Select B *size from the list*	Sets the paper size to the B size
Choose OK	
Clear the Scaled to Fit *check box*	Enables you to set a specific scale, the default is 1=1.00" scale

Make sure that the values in the scale edit boxes read 1 = 1.00", meaning that 1 inch on the plot is equal to 1 inch in the model.

Choose Preview

The plot no longer fills the sheet (see fig. 25.24).

Choose End Preview

Type 2.00" *in the Drawing Units edit box*

Choose Preview	Decreases the plot size with 1 inch on the plot equal to 2 inches in the model

Choose End Preview

Type 0.25" *in the Drawing Units edit box*

Choose Preview	Enlarges the plot but it is not complete with only part fitting on the specified paper size (see fig. 25.25)

Choose End Preview

Remain in the Plot Configuration dialog box for the next exercise.

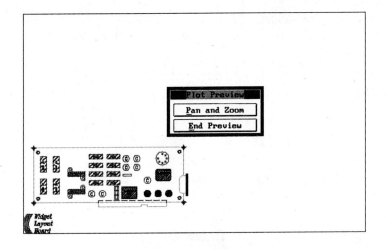

Figure 25.24

Full Preview of a plot scaled at 1"=1.00".

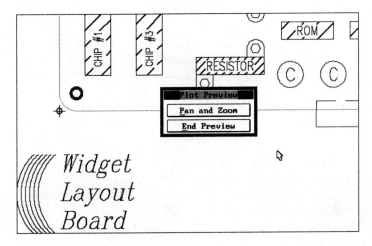

Figure 25.25

Full Preview of a plot scaled at 1"=0.25".

Where Does the Plot Information Go?

You might wonder where the plot information goes after you choose the OK button in the Plot Configuration dialog box. By default, the data is sent to the parallel or serial port that you specify in your plotter configuration. You can, however, send the plot data to a file by enabling the Plot To File option. You then can specify a file name by choosing the File Name button. If you do not specify a file name, a default file name is used that is the same as the drawing file name but with a PLT extension. The plot file is written in the current working directory (IAD\DWGS). Plotting to a file is common when you do batch plotting of many files at a central location for many users. The use of a network plotter, shared by many users, also requires plot files. Plot files are used to send information ready to be plotted to a remote location either electronically or by mail.

If you specify the file name as LPT1, LPT2, LPT3, COM1, COM2, COM3, or COM4, the file is sent directly to the associated parallel or serial port.

To enable AutoCAD's plot spooler, you use the file name AUTOSPOOL. For details on how to configure a spooling program to work with AutoCAD, see the *AutoCAD Installation Guide*.

If your plotter is connected to a network, you should consult your network administrator concerning how you should send the plot information.

Setting the Pen Motion Optimization

When you process the drawing data for plotting, you can use the <u>O</u>ptimization button of the Plot Configuration dialog box to access the Optimizing Pen Motion dialog box (see figure 25.26), in which you can instruct AutoCAD to try to optimize the order in which the information is sent to the plotter. The goal is to minimize wasted motion (such as moving pens or changing pens) that the plotter physically must undertake to plot. Efficient use of a pen plotter is for it to draw all the lines that require a particular pen in one area, then move to a different area or use a different pen, rather than to jump around the sheet and switch pens throughout the plot. If you turn on *pen sorting,* AutoCAD processes the entire drawing and sends out all plotting instructions for pen one first, then repeats the process for the next pen, and so on.

The Optimization button in the Pen Parameters section of the Plot Configuration dialog box enables you to open the Optimizing Pen Motion dialog box, in which you can set the level of pen motion optimization.

 Note Some plotters have a built-in plot and pen optimization that might be more efficient than that offered by AutoCAD.

You can use the Optimizing Pen Motion dialog box to set specific levels of optimization of pen plotters. The levels are arranged in order of complexity and are cumulative. If you select the 3rd level of optimization, the 1st and 2nd levels are selected automatically. The greater the optimization, the more time AutoCAD requires to generate plot data, but usually enables pen plotters to plot more quickly. Normally, the configuration process includes the automatic setting of the optimization level. For raster image devices (laser jets, inkjets, and so on), optimizing the data is a waste of time because physical pen movements are not involved. If you use such a device, you want to choose the <u>N</u>o optimization level.

```
┌──────────────────Optimizing Pen Motion──────────────────┐
│ ☐ No optimization                                        │
│ ☒ Adds endpoint swap                                     │
│ ☐ Adds pen sorting                                       │
│ ☐ Adds limited motion optimization                       │
│ ☐ Adds full motion optimization                          │
│ ☐ Adds elimination of overlapping horizontal or vertical vectors │
│ ☐ Adds elimination of overlapping diagonal vectors       │
│          ┌──────────┐    ┌──────────┐                    │
│          │    OK    │    │  Cancel  │                    │
│          └──────────┘    └──────────┘                    │
└──────────────────────────────────────────────────────────┘
```

Figure 25.26

The Optimizing Pen Motion dialog box.

Tip   Plot optimization can improve the consistency of plotted lines, particularly by eliminating overlapping vectors.

In the following exercise, you set the level of pen optimization.

Setting the Pen Optimization Level

Continue to use the drawing CHAP25A. If you canceled the Plot Configuration dialog box in the previous exercise, reissue it and make sure that the IAD PLOTTER is still the selected configuration.

Choose <u>O</u>ptimization	Opens the Optimizing Pen Motion dialog box
Put a check in the <u>N</u>o Optimization *box*	Disables all optimization

For raster devices such as the HP DesignJet 600, this setting is optimal.

Choose OK

Remain in the Plot Configuration dialog box for the next exercise.

Hiding Lines for 3D Drawings

The Hide <u>L</u>ines check box (in the Additional Parameters section of the Plot Configuration dialog box) results in *hidden lines*—lines that lie behind an opaque surface—being removed from the plot of a 3D surfaced model. This option is discussed in more detail in Part 7, "AutoCAD and 3D," which deals with working in 3D. This option is unnecessary for plotting 2D models, to which your work has been limited thus far.

Enabling the Adjust Area Fill Option

If you turn on the Adjust Area Fill check box, plotting adjusts for the pen width when you draw solid filled areas. This adjusts the location of the plotter pen inward by half its pen width when you draw the edges of a filled area.

If Adjust Area Fill is enabled, the edges of filled areas better match the coordinates of the filled area boundaries as measured in the drawing. Objects that this setting affects include traces, solids, and polylines that have width.

Unless you require an extreme degree of accuracy in the placement of lines on your plots (such as for printed circuit board artwork), you do not want to enable the Adjust Area Fill option.

Saving Your Plot Parameters

AutoCAD stores the current plot parameters in the ACAD.CFG file when you exit the Plot Configuration dialog box. Sometimes, however, you need multiple sets of plot parameters.

In the Device and Default Selection dialog box (refer to figure 25.8), you can choose the **S**ave Defaults To File button to save the current plot parameters to a file. You supply the file name and AutoCAD creates a file that has a file-name extension of PCP (Plot Configuration Parameters). Choose the **G**et Defaults From File button from the same dialog box to restore a saved set of plot settings. The **G**et Defaults From File option is especially handy for saving and restoring pen settings when you switch from one set of pen settings to another.

 Tip You can store the name of the PCP file to use with a drawing as an invisible attribute attached to an inserted block, such as the title block. Then, in a couple of years when you replot the drawing, you can check the name and quickly access the PCP file.

In the next exercise, you save the current plot settings to a file.

Saving the Plot Settings

Continue to use the drawing CHAP25A. If you canceled the Plot Configuration dialog box in the previous exercise, reissue it and make sure the IAD PLOTTER is still the selected configuration.

Choose **D**evice and Default Selection	Opens Device and Default Selection dialog box

Choose Save Defaults to File	Activates the Save to File dialog box
Enter **PLTSET1** *in the* File edit *box*	Specifies saving the plot parameters as PLTSET1.PCP
Choose OK	Initiates the save operation
Choose Get Defaults From File	Opens the Obtain from File dialog box, listing PLTSET1.PLT in the file list
Select PLTSET1.PLT *from the list, then* OK	Closes the Obtain from File dialog box and displays the message "Plot configuration updated without error" in the lower left corner of the Device and Default Selection dialog box.
Choose OK	Closes the Device and Default Selection dialog box

You now can cancel the PLOT command. If you choose OK, AutoCAD attempts to generate a plot.

Plotting Hints and Tips

Inevitably, you run into problems plotting at one time or another. To minimize the chances of problems, check on the following items before you even trigger the PLOT command:

- ◆ Make sure that the plotter is turned on and is online.

- ◆ Make sure that the necessary paper and pens are loaded. If you use a penless device, make sure that the ink cartridges have sufficient ink, especially if you plan multiple plots.

- ◆ Make sure that you know the scale you should use.

- ◆ Decide what area (extents, window, and so on) of the drawing you want to plot.

- ◆ Make sure that the appropriate layers are turned on or off.

Some other steps you can take to ensure fewer problems when you plot are as follows:

- ◆ **Read the instructions that came with the plotter and the driver you use.** Different models of plotters have different capabilities. You must read the instructions to get the most out of your plotter. In some cases, AutoCAD might come with a driver for your device, but a more up-to-date driver might be supplied by the plotter manufacturer. The instructions would indicate whether such a device driver is supplied.

◆ **Create standards for your pen settings.** If you have standard pen settings for your plots, you can save them in PCP files and restore them when necessary.

◆ **Create standards for your drawing creation.** Everybody in your organization should set up the drawing the same way. A standard setup makes it easier to standardize the settings used for plotting.

◆ **Always check out drawings from other sources.** If you get drawings from a client or a subcontractor, do not assume that the drawings are set up the same way as your drawings. Check the units and colors. Ask whoever supplied the drawings how the drawings were set up.

Some of the more common problems encountered when you plot are as follows:

◆ **Part of the plot gets chopped off.** Be sure to specify the right scale and sheet size. You might accidentally specify a scale that requires more paper than you have. Alternatively, you might specify a plot area smaller than the drawing sheet that is available. PLOT does not plot beyond the plot area you specify, even if the drawing sheet is large enough.

◆ **Solid filled areas are not getting filled.** Do you have your FILL turned off? Also, check on the pen widths. If the pen width is too large, PLOT might move the pen over too far to overlap the previous pen stroke. A common mistake is to specify the pen widths in millimeters when the units are still set for inches.

◆ **Text characters are being connected together or are missing parts.** Again, check your pen widths. When the width is too large, text characters are chopped off or connected together.

◆ **The plot comes out the size of a postage stamp.** Check the scale. If you specify a Fit scale with the plot area set to Extents, check the drawing extents. Sometimes the drawing extents are not reset correctly prior to plotting, so PLOT thinks the drawing occupies more room than it actually does. The drawing might contain objects that were generated by mistake while copying or moving and extents takes those into account as well as the objects intended to be in the drawing. The easiest way to check the extents is to issue the ZOOM command and use the Extents option.

◆ **The PLOT command completes, but the plotter does not respond.** This problem is most commonly encountered on networks. Usually, the problem is that the plot data gets sent to the wrong device. Make sure that the correct LPT ports are being captured correctly by the network.

♦ **PLOT command says plotter is not responding.** Check to see whether the plotter is online. Make sure that the cable is connected correctly and that the plotter configuration is set to the right parallel or serial port.

♦ **Pen seems to be skipping on the plot.** The pen is moving too fast. Lower the pen speeds. Also, check the type of pens you are using. The types of pens that work best with different types of media vary.

Composing Plots in Tiled Model Space and Paper Space

In this section, you learn how to compose the layout of your plot. You can compose the layout in tiled model space or paper space. You first learn how to compose a layout in tiled model space. Then, you learn how to compose a layout with floating viewports in paper space and why paper space is preferable to model space for complicated layouts. See Chapter 10, "Working in Model and Paper Space Viewports," for more information about model space, viewports, and paper space. To help compose, you use the MVSETUP command.

MVSETUP. The MVSETUP command facilitates setting up a layout in model or paper space.
Pull-down: *Choose* View, Floating Viewports, MVSetup

MVSETUP actually is two routines in one: one routine is for model space and the other routine is for paper space. The details of MVSETUP are covered in the following sections.

Sheet Composition in Tiled Model Space

The drawings you produce can have one of two types of layouts: layouts with scale and layouts without scale. Although layouts without scale are not recommended, you learn in the following sections how to compose both types of layouts in model space.

Layouts with Scale

In the previous chapters, you have been encouraged to draw your model full size— that is, as the model would appear in the real world. This approach eliminates scaling errors and enables you to use your model as a design tool for making accurate measurements. Of course, you must consider the scale you eventually use to plot the model, in drawing elements such as text and symbols (border, bubbles, north arrows, and so on). This approach works well if you produce a drawing that has a single view or multiple views at the same scale. But what if you want to create a plot with multiple views at varying scales? Suppose, for example, you want to produce the drawing in figure 25.27.

Figure 25.27

A plan drawing layout with multiple scales.

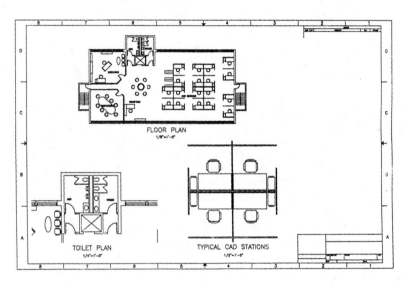

The best approach, when you mix drawing scales on one drawing, is to use paper space. If for some reason you choose not to use paper space, you can use the following approach to compose the layout in model space. If you use the preceding figure as an example, you could do the following:

1. Choose one of the views and use its scale for a new drawing and draw the border. The new drawing will be referred to as the parent drawing.

   In the preceding example (refer to figure 25.27), suppose you chose to use the 1/8"=1' scale (FLOOR PLAN View) and a 23" × 35" border for the parent drawing. You begin a new drawing and draw a 184' (23" × 8'/inch) × 280' (35" × 8'/inch) border.

2. Draw any views that share the parent drawing's scale in the parent drawing itself.

   The border line, title block, and the FLOOR PLAN view are in the parent drawing, because it too is to be at a 1/8"=1' scale.

3. Draw the other views in their own individual drawing files.

   The TOILET PLAN detail and TYPICAL CAD STATIONS plan detail views have scales that differ from the parent drawing. Draw the TOILET PLAN detail view in

New Riders Publishing
INSIDE
SERIES

the TOILT-PL drawing, and the TYPICAL CAD STATIONS plan detail view in the T-CAD-ST drawing. Set up each drawing for the appropriate scale and draw each view at full size. Set up the TOILT-PL drawing for a scale of 1/4"=1'. Set up the T-CAD-ST drawing for a scale of 1/2"=1'.

4. Use the INSERT or XREF commands to insert the other drawings into the parent drawing and scale them by the ratio of the drawing's scale to the parent drawing's scale.

   Insert drawings TOILT-PL and T-CAD-ST into the parent drawing as blocks or xrefs. For the TOILT-PL drawing, use an insertion scale of 2 (1/4" divided by 1/8"). Use an insertion scale of 4 (1/2" divided by 1/8") for the T-CAD-ST drawing.

   Not convinced about the scale factors? Suppose all text in the plot is to be 1/8" in height. In the parent drawing itself, draw text with a height of 1' (1/8"=1' plot scale). In the TOILT-PL drawing, use a text height of 0.5'. After you insert the TOILT-PL drawing with a scale factor of 2, the text in the TOILET PLAN detail view appears to be 1/8" high, which is, of course, what you want. In the T-CAD-ST drawing, use a text height of 0.25'. After you insert the T-CAD-ST drawing with a scale factor of 4, the text in the TYPICAL CAD STATION detail view appears to be 1/8" high.

5. If you dimension the views in the parent drawing, compensate for the insertion scale factors by setting the DIMLFAC dimension variable to the inverse of the insertion scale.

   For the TOILET PLAN detail view, set DIMLFAC to 0.5 (1/2). For the TYPICAL CAD STATION detail view, set DIMLFAC to 0.25 (1/4).

6. Plot the parent drawing at the appropriate scale.

   Plot the parent drawing using a scale of 1/8"=1' (1=8' or 1=96" in the Plot Configuration dialog box).

A variation of the preceding approach would be to generate a parent drawing that is set up for a 1=1 plot scale. Then you would draw the three plan views at full size in their individual drawing files. Then, you would insert the three drawing files into the parent drawing at their respective plot scales. You would insert the FLR-PLAN drawing with a 1/96 scale factor, the TOILT-PL drawing with a 1/48 scale factor, and the T-CAD-ST drawing with a 1/24 sale factor.

The drawback to both approaches is that instead of having to deal with only a single drawing, you must contend with multiple drawings. To update the views, you must change the drawings individually and update their insertions in the parent drawing. All in all, the solution, though workable, is cumbersome and less than efficient.

If all this seems complicated, that's because it is. Using paper space to compose a plot is a much more efficient method and takes full advantage of your computer drafting system.

Layouts without Scale

Some types of drawings are not scaled, such as schematics and sketches. The best way to deal with these types of drawings is to treat the model space like the final plot sheet. Treat each drawing unit as equal to one inch on the final plot. Then, size everything you draw just as you would on a piece of paper. If you want a 23"-by-35" border, you draw a 23-by-35-unit border. If you want 1/8" high text, draw 1/8" high text. You then use a 1=1 scale to plot the drawing. In effect, you can use model space to simulate paper space while drawing without a scale.

Using MVSETUP in Tiled Model Space

You can find the MVSETUP command in the Floating Viewports submenu of the View pull-down menu. The Floating Viewports submenu is inactive when you are in tiled model space, so you have to enter **MVSETUP** at the Command: prompt.

In the following exercise, you use MVSETUP to set up a drawing in Tiled Model Space.

Drawing Setup in Tiled Model Space

Begin a new drawing named CHAP25B, using the ACAD.DWG drawing file as the prototype. Create a new layer named border-line with the red pen and continuous line type, then make it the current layer.

Command: **MVSETUP** (Enter)   Issues the MVSETUP command

mvsetup

Enable paper space? (No/<Yes>): **N** (Enter)   Retains Tiled Model Space as the current
                                                     environment

Units type (Scientific/Decimal/   Selects Architectural units (feet, inches
Engineering/Architectural/Metric):   and fractions)
A (Enter)

Architectural Scales
======================
 (480) 1/40"=1'
 (240) 1/20"=1'
 (192) 1/16"=1'

New Riders Publishing
INSIDE
SERIES

```
(96)   1/8"=1'
(48)   1/4"=1'
(24)   1/2"=1'
(16)   3/4"=1'
(12)   1"=1'
(4)    3"=1'
(2)    6"=1'
(1)    FULL
```

Enter the scale factor: **48** (Enter)   Selects 1/4"=1' as the scale at which the drawing will be plotted

Enter the paper width: **23** (Enter)   Sets the width of the border line

Enter the paper height: **17** (Enter)   Sets the height of the border line

Save your drawing setup for use in the next exercise or keep this drawing current and proceed to the next exercise.

In the preceding exercise, you used MVSETUP to set the drawing units to Architectural, set the limits at 0',0' to 92',68', and draw a rectangle to represent the border. The limits and rectangle size are at the edges of the drawing output to the plotter. Your drawing setup should look like figure 25.28.

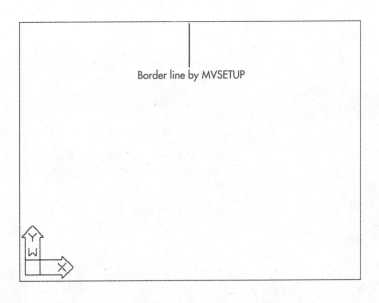

Border line by MVSETUP

Figure 25.28

Border line using MVSETUP in tiled model space.

In the following exercise, you insert a foundation plan at the same scale as your drawing setup (1/4"=1'), then insert two details at twice the size to represent a scale of 1/2"=1'. In the exercise, you use the XREF command to insert the plan and details, however, you also can use the INSERT block command for similar results.

Inserting Objects in Tiled Model Space at More Than One Scale

Continue to use the CHAP25B drawing.

Command: *Choose* File, External Reference, Attach	Issues the XREF command with the Attach option and opens the Select File to Attach dialog box
`_xref` `?/Bind/Detach/Path/Reload/Overlay/<Attach>:` (Enter)	
Choose the FOUNDTN *drawing from the* IA Disk directory, *then* OK	Selects the drawing file to be attached
`Attach Xref FOUNDTN: C:\IAD\DWGS\FOUNDTN.DWG` `FOUNDTN loaded.`	
`Insertion point:` **0,0** (Enter)	Sets the absolute coordinate 0,0 as the insertion point
`X scale factor <1> / Corner / XYZ:` (Enter)	Accepts the default scale factor of 1 for 1/4'=1" plotter output
`Y scale factor (default=X):` (Enter)	Accepts the default scale factor to match the X scale factor
`Rotation angle <0>:` (Enter)	Accepts 0 rotation angle
`Command:` (Enter)	Repeats the XREF command

`_xref`
`?/Bind/Detach/Path/Reload/Overlay/`
`<Attach>:` (Enter)
	Accepts the default Attach option and opens the Select File to Attach dialog box

Choose the FND-D1 *drawing from the* IA Disk directory, *then* OK	Selects the drawing file to be attached

New Riders Publishing
INSIDE
SERIES

```
Attach Xref FND-D1: C:\IAD\DWGS\FND-D1.DWG
FND-D1 loaded.
```

Insertion point: *Pick point at* ①   Locates the insertion point on your
(see fig. 25.29)   drawing

X scale factor <1> / Corner / XYZ: **2** (Enter)   Sets an X scale factor of 2 that will double the size of the objects inserted

Y scale factor (default=X): (Enter)   Sets the Y scale factor equal to the X
scale factor

Rotation angle <0>: (Enter)   Accepts 0 rotation angle

Command: (Enter)   Repeats the XREF command

```
_xref
?/Bind/Detach/Path/Reload/Overlay/
<Attach>: (Enter)
```
Accepts the default Attach option
and opens the Select File to Attach
dialog box

Choose the FND-D2 *drawing from the*   Selects the drawing file to be attached
IA Disk directory, then OK

```
Attach Xref FND-D2: C:\IAD\DWGS\FND-D2.DWG
FND-D2 loaded.
```

Insertion point: *Pick point at* ②   Locates the insertion point on your drawing

X scale factor <1> / Corner / XYZ: **2** (Enter)   Sets an X scale factor of 2 that will double the size of the objects inserted

Y scale factor (default=X): (Enter)   Sets the Y scale factor equal to the X
scale factor

Rotation angle <0>: (Enter)   Accepts 0 rotation angle

Save your drawing setup for use in the next exercise or keep this drawing current and proceed to the next exercise.

Your drawing now has a plan that plots at 1/4"=1' scale and two details that insert at double size so they will plot at 1/2"=1' scale (refer to figure 25.30).

Figure 25.29

Plan inserted into tiled model space.

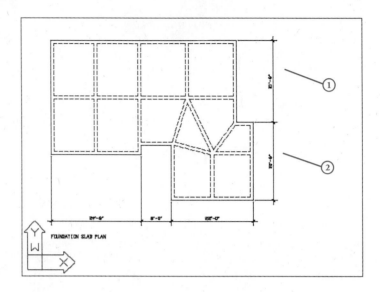

Figure 25.30

Objects inserted into tiled model space at different scales.

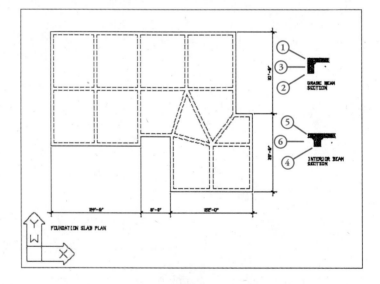

The text in drawing FOUNDTN.DWG is 9" in height (plots at 3/16") whereas the text in FND-D1.DWG and FND-D2.DWG is 4.5" in height. Therefore, when you insert the two details at double scale, the text doubles to match that in the plan drawing. This kind of planning is necessary if you work in more than one scale on a single drawing.

In the next exercise, you insert dimensions for the detail drawings and adjust the size to be consistent with the DIMSTYLE of the FOUNDTN.DWG plan drawing.

Dimensioning Objects in Tiled Model Space at Different Scales

Continue to use the CHAP25B drawing.

Command: *Choose* File, Bind, Dimension Style	Issues the XBIND command with the Dimstyle option
`_xbind` `Block/Dimstyle/LAyer/LType/Style: _d`	
`Dependent Dimstyle name(s):` **`FOUNDTN¦FNDTN`** (Enter)	Names the FNDTN dimension style from the FOUNDTN reference drawing for binding
`    Scanning...` `1 Dimstyle(s) bound.`	Locates and binds FNDTN to your current drawing
Command: *Choose* Data, Dimension Style	Issues DDIM command and opens the Dimension Styles dialog box
Command: *Select* FOUNDTN0 FNDTN *from* Current *list, then* OK	Makes FNDTN the current dimension style
Command: **`DIMLFAC`** (Enter)	Accesses the DIMLFAC variable
`New value for DIMLFAC <1.0000>:` **`1/2`** (Enter)	Sets the dimension length factor variable value
Command: *Choose* Options, Running Object Snap	Issues DDOSNAP and opens the Running Object Snap dialog box
`_ddosnap` *Pick* Endpoint, OK	Starts Endpoint running object snap
Command: *Choose* Draw, Dimensioning, Linear	Issues the DIMLINEAR command

`_dimlinear`
`First extension line origin or`
`RETURN to select:` *Pick* ①
(see fig. 25.30)
	Specifies point for first extension line of the dimension

`Second extension line origin:` *Pick* ②	Specifies point for second extension line of the dimension

continues

continued

Dimension line location (Text/Angle/ Horizontal/Vertical/Rotated): *Pick* ③	Locates the dimension line
Command: **Enter**	Repeats the DIMLINEAR command
DIMLINEAR First extension line origin or RETURN to select: *Pick* ④	Specifies point for first extension line of the dimension
Second extension line origin: *Pick* ⑤	Specifies point for second extension line of the dimension
Dimension line location (Text/Angle/ Horizontal/Vertical/Rotated): *Pick* ⑥	Locates the dimension line

Set running object snap back to NONE. Save your drawing, which should look similar to figure 25.31.

It is apparent in the preceding drawing that mixing scales in a tiled model space drawing requires considerable planning and manipulation, even when only using 2 scales. The use of a paper space environment for this purpose offers much more flexibility and allows further refinement through additional control of layers, and simpler editing.

Figure 25.31

Dimensioned drawing with different scales in tiled model space.

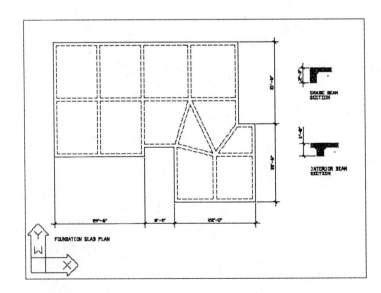

New Riders Publishing
INSIDE
SERIES

Using MVSETUP for Sheet Composition in Paper Space

Composition of a drawing that has multiple views at varying scales is simpler and more flexible when you use paper space. In paper space, you compose the arrangement of viewports, scale each viewport individually, then plot the whole composition at 1':1[in], while in paper space with the contents of each viewport plotted at its preset scale. The views might be completely different from each other (for example, a plan view versus an elevation view) or they might be different views of a common model. Either way, the general approach is the same. In Chapter 10, "Working in Model and Paper Space Viewports," you learn how to use TILEMODE to switch to paper space, create the needed floating viewports, and use the viewports to edit the model. Now, you learn how to use paper space to compose a layout for your plot. The procedure is quite simple and broken down in the sections that follow.

Using MVSETUP in Paper Space

You can use AutoCAD commands such as TILEMODE, PSPACE, and MVIEW to compose floating viewports in a paper space environment, however, using MVSETUP is faster and offers several title block and border line layouts not otherwise available. After you issue MVSETUP in paper space, AutoCAD prompts you as follows:

```
Align/Create/Scale viewports/Options/Title block/Undo:
```

The following sections explain these options.

Align

The Align option enables you to align and rotate views. Your alignment options are as follows:

```
Angled/Horizontal/Vertical alignment/Rotate view/Undo:
```

◆ **Angled.** You pick a base point in the first viewport (point 1) and then a point in the second viewport (point 2). Then you specify a second point in the first viewport (point 3) by specifying a distance and angle from point 1. MVSETUP then pans the view in the second viewport so that point 2 coincides with point 3. The angled alignment is primarily intended for viewports that overlap, as shown in figure 25.32.

◆ **Horizontal.** You pick a base point in the first viewport (point 1) and then a point in the second viewport (point 2). MVSETUP then pans the view in the second viewport so that point 2 lines up with point 1 horizontally (see fig. 25.33).

Figure 25.32

Angled alignment.

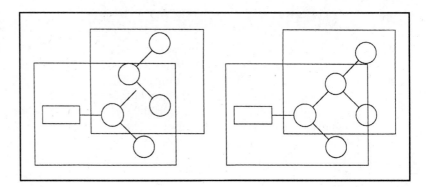

Figure 25.33

Horizontal alignment.

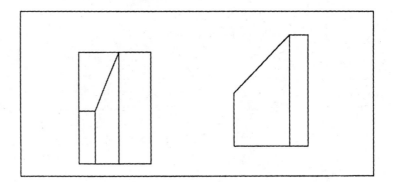

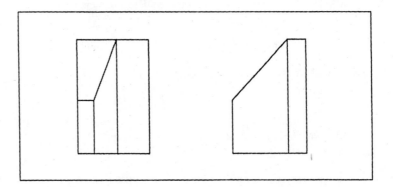

◆ **Vertical alignment.** You pick a base point in the first viewport (point 1) and then a point in a second viewport (point 2). MVSETUP then pans the view in the second viewport so that point 2 lines up with point 1 vertically (refer to figure 25.34).

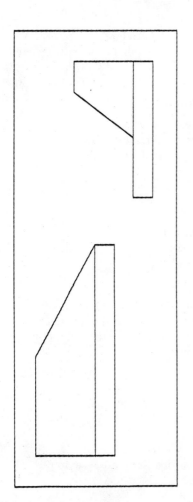
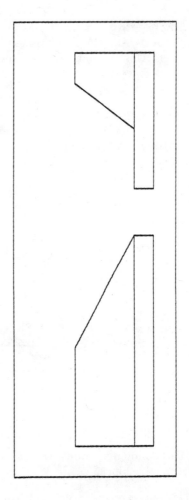

Figure 25.34
Vertical alignment.

25

◆ **Rotate view.** You also can rotate the view in a viewport. Bear in mind that you are not rotating the model itself, only its view.

Create

The Create option enables you to create viewports. You have the following choices:

◆ **0: None.** Skips viewport creation.

◆ **1: Single.** If you choose to create a single viewport, AutoCAD prompts you to locate and size the viewport by using a Window to select an area. This option is identical to the MVIEW command's default option of creating a single viewport.

◆ **2: Std. Engineering.** If you choose to create a standard engineering arrangement of viewports, AutoCAD asks you to window an area that it then divides into four viewports. This option is similar to the MVIEW command's 4 viewport option, except that you can specify a vertical (X) and horizontal (Y) separation distance between the viewports.

◆ **3: Array of Viewports.** If you choose to create an array of viewports, AutoCAD asks you to window an area that it then divides into m rows and n columns of viewports. You get to specify the m and n values and the vertical (X) and horizontal (Y) separation distance between the viewports.

Scale Viewports

Scale Viewports enables you to scale the view in a viewport. This option issues the ZOOM command and supplies it with an XP scale factor.

Options

Options enables you to create a new layer, select units, set the limits to match the title block, and determine how AutoCAD will insert the title block. You should select this option before you use any of the other MVSETUP options, because the other options are affected by these settings. You can control settings as follows:

```
Set Layer/LImits/Units/Xref
```

◆ **Set Layer.** This option enables you to specify the layer on which to draw the title block. The specified layer can be an existing or new layer. If it is new, MVSETUP creates it for you.

◆ **LImits.** This option determines whether the drawing limits are reset to the extents of the title block.

◆ **Units.** This option enables you to determine whether to interpret paper space units as inches, feet, meters, or millimeters.

◆ **Xref.** This option enables you to determine whether the title block is inserted as a block or attached as an xref.

Title Block

Selecting this option brings up another list of options, as follows:

```
Delete objects/Origin/Undo/<Insert title block>:
```

◆ **Delete objects.** This option enables you to delete selected objects.

New Riders Publishing
INSIDE
SERIES

25

◆ **Origin.** This option enables you to determine a new insertion point for the title block. The default origin point is 0,0.

Note The title block normally is inserted at 0,0, unless you use the Options option to specify a different origin.

◆ **Undo.** This option undoes the last option.

◆ **Insert title block.** This option is the default, and if you select it, a list of available title blocks appears, as follows:

```
0:      None
1:      ISO A4 Size(mm)
2:      ISO A3 Size(mm)
3:      ISO A2 Size(mm)
4:      ISO A1 Size(mm)
5:      ISO A0 Size(mm)
6:      ANSI-V Size(in)
7:      ANSI-A Size(in)
8:      ANSI-B Size(in)
9:      ANSI-C Size(in)
10:     ANSI-D Size(in)
11:     ANSI-E Size(in)
12:     Arch/Engineering (24 x 36in)
13:     Generic D size Sheet (24 x 36in)
```

If AutoCAD finds a drawing of which the name matches the selected size in the directory specified by the ACADPREFIX system variable, it inserts that drawing as the title block, which enables you to use your own title block drawings with MVSETUP. If you want MVSETUP to recognize and use it as a title block drawing, the name of the drawing should follow the following form (where *??* is A0, A1, A2, A3, or A4):

```
ANSI-? (where ? is V, A, B, C, D, or E) or ISO_??
```

If AutoCAD does not find a drawing that has the name of the selected size, MVSETUP creates one and you then can write out (WBLOCK) to a drawing file.

Note The directories listed in the ACADPREFIX system variable are determined by the ACAD system variable or the support field in the environment section of the PREFERENCES command. The search for the title block files will be controlled by these settings.

The Initial Steps

You have used paper space and floating viewports using various AutoCAD commands and options in Chapter 10. Applying the methods you have used in Chapter 10, you can compose a drawing in the following sequence with AutoCAD commands and options:

1. Draw all the views in the model space of a single drawing file. If the views are different views of a single model, just draw the one model. Name the various views so they can be restored into the floating viewports of paper space. Draw the model at full size.

2. Change to paper space by turning off TILEMODE.

3. Draw the border in paper space on a layer named to associate with paper space objects. Treat paper space like your sheet of drafting paper. To end up with a 23-inch-by-35-inch border on the plot, draw a 23-inch-by-35-inch border in paper space. Eventually, you plot the entire paper space layout at a 1=1 scale.

4. Use MVIEW to create the required views of the model as floating viewports of the desired shape and size. If you do not want viewport borders on the final plot, be sure to draw the viewports on a separate layer. Before you plot, you can turn off the layer that contains the viewport objects, which makes the viewport borders invisible but still leaves the views in them visible.

Tip Draw the viewports on the DEFPOINTS layer. If you do so, the viewports do not plot, even if the DEFPOINTS layer is on.

You now use MVSETUP with its options and suboptions to compose a paper space environment with floating viewports. Your work with MVSETUP will parallel the sequence of steps used when composing a drawing using the individual AutoCAD commands and their options; however, notice that you can do the work more efficiently with fewer steps and achieve the same result.

In the following exercise, you use the MVSETUP command and its options to compose an initial layout in paper space.

Setting up a Paper Space Drawing Environment

Begin a new drawing named CHAP25C, using the IA Disk drawing OFFICE1 as the prototype.

Command: *Choose* View, Paper Space   Switches to paper space

New Riders Publishing
INSIDE SERIES

Command: *Choose* View, Floating Viewports, MV Setup	Issues the MSVSETUP command
Initializing... Align/Create/Scaleviewports/ Options/Title block/Undo: **O** (Enter)	Specifies the Options option
Set Layer/LImits/Units/Xref: **L** (Enter)	Specifies the Layer option
Layer name for title block or . for current layer: **TITLE_BLOCK** (Enter)	Sets the layer TITLE_BLOCK as the layer on which the title block is to be drawn
Set Layer/LImits/Units/Xref: (Enter)	Returns you to the main MVSETUP options list
Align/Create/Scale viewports/ Options/Title block/Undo: **T** (Enter)	Specifies the Title block option
Delete objects/Origin/Undo/<Insert title block>: (Enter)	Accepts the default of inserting a new title block

```
Available title block options:
 0:  None
 1:  ISO A4 Size(mm)
 2:  ISO A3 Size(mm)
 3:  ISO A2 Size(mm)
 4:  ISO A1 Size(mm)
 5:  ISO A0 Size(mm)
 6:  ANSI-V Size(in)
 7:  ANSI-A Size(in)
 8:  ANSI-B Size(in)
 9:  ANSI-C Size(in)
10:  ANSI-D Size(in)
11:  ANSI-E Size(in)
12:  Arch/Engineering (24 x 36in)
13:  Generic D size Sheet (24 x 36in)
```

Add/Delete/Redisplay/<Number of entry to load>: **10** (Enter)	Specifies #10, ANSI-D, as the title block to be inserted
Create a drawing named ansi-d.dwg? <Y>: **N** (Enter)	Declines the option of writing the newly created title block out to a file (WBLOCK)
Align/Create/Scale viewports/ Options/Title block/Undo: (Enter)	Ends the MVSETUP command

Make a new layer named FLOAT-VPORT and set it current.

continues

continued

Command: *Choose* View, Floating Viewports, MV Setup	Issues the MVSETUP command
Align/Create/Scale viewports/ Options/Title block/Undo: **C** (Enter)	Specifies the Create option
Delete objects/Undo/ <Create viewports>: (Enter)	Accepts the default option of creating viewports

```
Available Mview viewport layout options:
  0:  None
  1:  Single
  2:  Std. Engineering
  3:  Array of Viewports
```

Redisplay/<Number of entry to load>: **3** (Enter)	Specifies the Array layout
Bounding area for viewports. Default/<First point >: *Pick* ① *(see fig. 25.35)*	Sets the right corner
Other point: *Pick* ②	Finishes specifying the area that will be divided into viewports
Number of viewports in X. <1>: **2** (Enter)	Defines two columns of viewports are to be created
Number of viewports in Y. <1>: **2** (Enter)	Defines two rows of viewports are to be created
Distance between viewports in X. <0.0>: **1** (Enter)	Specifies a separation of 1 inch in the X direction
Distance between viewports in Y. <1.0>: (Enter)	Accepts the default separation of 1.0 inches in the Y direction
Align/Create/Scale viewports/ Options/Title block/Undo: (Enter)	Ends the MVSETUP command

Save your work.

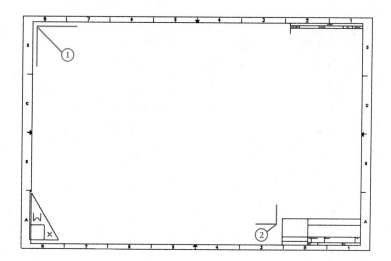

Figure 25.35

Specifying the area for viewports.

25

Adjusting the Views

To select and adjust the view displayed in the viewports, you must enter model space (MSPACE) and, in turn, make each viewport current. You can restore named views to each viewport or use the ZOOM and PAN commands to select the appropriate view for each viewport. To scale each view correctly, use the XP option of the ZOOM command. XP stands for "relative to paper." You should enter a number that represents the scale of the view. For example, after you issue the ZOOM command, use the zoom factor of 1/96XP (1 plotted inch equals 96 drawing units). This is the same scale factor you would use to plot each viewport separately; instead, you scale the viewports floating in paper space and plot at 1 plotted inch = 1 paper space unit.

 Tip   You can use the LIST command on a viewport to obtain the zoom scale.

After you scale a view correctly, you use PAN to center the view in the floating viewport while in model space. You can enlarge or shrink the viewport to better accommodate the view using the SCALE or STRETCH commands in paper space. You can use the PAN command or change the viewport size without affecting the scale of the view. But do not use the ZOOM command unless you intend to alter the scale of the view.

Tip Because "locking" in a view is impossible, you might want to draw some reference points or lines after you set your views. These objects would act as registration points to help you realign the views, should it ever be necessary. For example, you might draw several points in paper space that coincide with the ends of several lines that appear in a view. You can then use PAN to reposition a view in a floating viewport after editing of the model.

When you deal with noncontinuous linetypes and multiple viewports at varying scales, you want the various linetypes to have the same appearance in all viewports. It is not desirable to have the dashed linetype in one viewport appear different from the dashed linetype in another viewport or from that drawn in paper space. To prevent this from occurring, you need to turn on the PSLTSCALE system variable. When PSLTSCALE is on and CELTSCALE is 1, all linetypes in all viewports are drawn at a 1 to 1 scale factor, as if they were drawn in paper space. If CELTSCALE is set to a value other than 1, the linetypes are proportionately affected. To see the effect on existing linetypes, you must issue a REGENALL.

Tip If you use a limited number of layouts, consider creating the layouts in your prototype drawings. That way, every new drawing has the paper space already prepared for usage.

In the following exercise, adjust the views in the viewports for scale and the size and location of the viewports.

Restore and Adjust the Views

Continue to use the drawing CHAP25C.

Command: *Choose* Modify, Stretch	Issues the STRETCH command
_stretch Select objects to stretch by crossing-window or -polygon... Pick ① *(see fig. 25.36)*	Locates the first corner of crossing window
Select objects: Other corner: Pick ②	Completes the crossing window
1 found	

New Riders Publishing
INSIDE
SERIES

`Select objects:` (Enter)	Completes selection set
`Base point or displacement: END` `of` *Pick* ③	Uses Endpoint to pick base for stretch
`Second point of displacement: END` `of` *Pick* ④	Uses Endpoint to pick point to stretch to
`Command:` **E** (Enter)	Issues the ERASE command
`ERASE` `Select objects:` *Pick* ⑤	
`1 found`	
`Select objects:`	Completes the ERASE command
`Command:` *Choose* View, Floating Model Space	Issues the MSPACE command and makes one of the viewports current
`Command:` *Click in the top viewport*	Makes top viewport current
Choose View, Named Views	Opens the View Control dialog box
`_ddview`	
Choose FULL *from* Views *list, choose* *the* Restore *button, choose* OK	Restores the Full view to the current viewport
`Command:` **Z** (Enter)	Issues the ZOOM command

`All/Center/Dynamic/Extents/Left/`
`Previous/Vmax/Window/<Scale(X/XP)>:`
1/96XP (Enter)
	Zooms view in current viewport to a scale
	relative to paper space of 1=96 (1 paper
	space inch = 96 model space drawing unit)

`Command:` *Click in the bottom left viewport*	Makes the lower-left viewport current
Choose View, Named Views	Opens the View Control dialog box
`_ddview`	
Choose TOILETS *from* Views *list, choose* *the* Restore *button, choose* OK	Restores the TOILETS view to the current viewport
`Command:` **Z** (Enter)	

continues

continued

`All/Center/Dynamic/Extents/Left/`
`Previous/Vmax/Window/<Scale(X/XP>:`
1/48XP (Enter)
	Zooms view in current viewport to a scale relative to paper space of 1=48 (1 paper space inch = 48 model space drawing unit)

`Command:` *Click in the bottom right viewport*	Makes the lower-right viewport current
Choose View, Named Views	Opens the View Control dialog box.
`_ddview`	
Choose CAD-STNS *from* Views *list, choose the* Restore *button, choose* OK	Restores the CAD-STNS view to the current viewport
`Command:` **Z** (Enter)	

`All/Center/Dynamic/Extents/Left/`
`Previous/Vmax/Window/<Scale(X/XP>:`
1/24XP (Enter)
	Zooms view in current viewport to a scale relative to paper space of 1=24 (1 paper space inch = 24 model space drawing unit)

Save your work.

Figure 25.36

Stretch the top viewport.

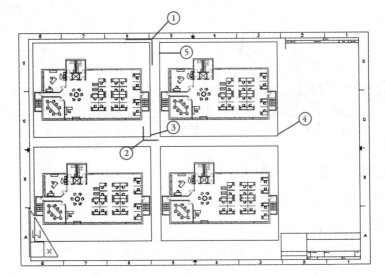

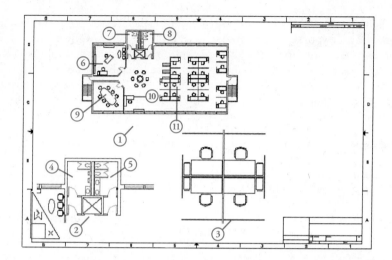

Figure 25.37

Scaled views in paper space viewports.

25

Annotating the Paper Space Layout

You also must annotate the drawing with necessary symbols or text. You should draw text or symbols that are not directly related to the views in paper space. These should be objects that are not normally affected when you edit (stretch, move, and so on) the views. Examples include general notes, scale bars, labels for the views, information in the title block, dimensions that span across viewports, and so forth.

You should draw text or symbols that are directly related to a particular view in the floating model space of that view. These should be objects that should be affected when you edit the views. Examples include normal dimensions, section lines, labels for parts of the views, callout symbols, revision symbols, and so forth.

When you draw in paper space, you can use all the layers created in model space. AutoCAD keeps track of and keeps separate the objects you draw in paper space from the objects you draw in model space. If need be, you can create and use additional layers while in paper space. Remember, all objects drawn in paper space are not visible when you switch back to tiled model space (TILEMODE=1).

Remember that although you can pick points and use object snap to snap to objects while in floating model space, you cannot select those objects when you are in paper space. While you are in paper space, you can select and edit only objects that reside in paper space. When you are in floating model space, you can select and edit only objects that reside in model space. You are able to verify whether you're in paper space or floating model space by the presence of a "P" on the left end of the upper prompt area. The "P" indicates that the current drawing environment is paper space.

When you use floating viewports, you can freeze a layer in specific viewports and leave it on in the remaining viewports. When you deal with multiple views of the same model, you can use this feature to draw text and other objects so that they appear only in specific viewports. You begin by drawing the objects specific to the current view, on a separate layer. Then, you use DDLMODES or VPLAYER to freeze that layer in the other viewports so that the layer is visible only in selected viewports. See Chapter 10 for more information on using floating viewports.

In the following exercise, you add some annotation in paper space.

Adding Annotation in Paper Space

Continue to use the drawing CHAP25C. Make sure that you are in paper space before you proceed with the exercise. Turn off layer FLOAT-VPORT.

Make a new layer named TXT-PS and set it current, then make new layers named TXT-FPLAN and TXT-TOILT to use in the floating model space viewports.

Command: *Choose* Draw, Text, Single-line Text	Issues the TEXT command
_text Justify/Style/<Start point>: **C** (Enter)	Specifies the text centering option
Center point: *Pick* ① *(see fig. 25.37)*	Locates the center of the title
Height <0'-0 1/4">: **3/8** (Enter)	Specifies a new text height
Rotation angle <0>: (Enter)	Accepts the default rotation
Text: **FLOOR PLAN** (Enter)	Specifies the title
Command: (Enter)	Repeats the TEXT command

Locate a title for TOILET PLAN centered on ② and a title for TYPICAL CAD STATION centered on ③.

Command: (Enter)	Repeats the TEXT command
TEXT Justify/Style/<Start point>: **C** (Enter)	Specifies the text centering option
Center point: *Pick point centered under FLOOR PLAN title*	Locates the center of the title

New Riders Publishing
INSIDE
SERIES

Height <0'-0 3/8">: **3/16** (Enter)	Specifies a new text height
Rotation angle <0>: (Enter)	Accepts the default rotation
Text: **1/8"=1'-0"** (Enter)	Specifies the scale notation
Command: (Enter)	Repeats the TEXT command

Locate scale notations of 1/4"=1'-0" centered under the TOILET PLAN title and 1/2"=1'-0" centered under the TYPICAL CAD STATION title.

Command: *Choose* View, Floating Model Space	Changes to floating model space environment

Make the lower-left viewport current and make the TXT-TOILT layer current.

Command: *Choose* Draw, Text, Single-line Text	Issues TEXT command
_text Justify/Style/<Start point>: *Pick* ④	Locates the text
Height <0'-0 3/16">: **6** (Enter)	Specifies a new text height in model space units for a 1/4"=1'-0" scale plot
Rotation angle <0>: (Enter)	Accepts the default rotation
Text: **MEN** (Enter)	Specifies the room name notation
Command: (Enter)	Repeats the TEXT command

Locate a room title for WOMEN at ⑤.

Make the top viewport current and make the TXT-FPLAN layer current.

Command: *Choose* Draw, Text, Single-line Text	Issues the TEXT command
_text Justify/Style/<Start point>: *Pick* ⑥	Locates room title text
Height <0'-6">: **1'** (Enter)	Enters a new text height in model space units for a 1/8"=1'-0" scale plot
Rotation angle <0>: (Enter)	Accepts the default rotation

continues

continued

`Text: EXECUTIVE` ⌨Enter	Specifies the room name notation
`Command:` ⌨Enter	Repeats the TEXT command

Locate room titles for MEN at ⑦, for WOMEN at ⑧, for CONFERENCE at ⑨, for RECEP-TION at ⑩, and for CAD STATIONS at ⑪.

Choose Data, Layers *and select* TXT-TOILT, *then* Cur VP: Frz *button*	Freezes the specified layer in the current viewport (FLOOR PLAN)

Make the lower-left viewport current and freeze the TXT-FPLAN layer for the current viewport. Make the lower-right viewport current and freeze the TXT-PLAN layer for the current viewport.

Choose View, Paper Space	Changes to the paper space environment
Choose File, Print	Issues the PLOT command and opens the Plot Configuration dialog box

Make sure the IAD PLOTTER is current plotter, the plot area is 35 by 23 (to match your drawing), and do a Full Preview to display your drawing as you would plot it in paper space (see fig. 25.38).

The text height entered in paper space as paper space objects will be plotted the height given when inserted. The text in the floating viewports must be adjusted in height in the same fashion using the same rationale as discussed in the "Sheet Composition in Tiled Model Space" section earlier in this chapter. When properly planned and executed, the 3 different text heights inserted in the 3 separate floating viewports will plot at the same height in the resulting paper space drawing.

Dimensioning the Views

If a view requires dimensions, draw them in floating model space so that the measured distances are the correct real-world dimensions. Drawing the dimensions in model space also enables you to edit (move, stretch, and so on) them while you edit the model.

New Riders Publishing
INSIDE
SERIES

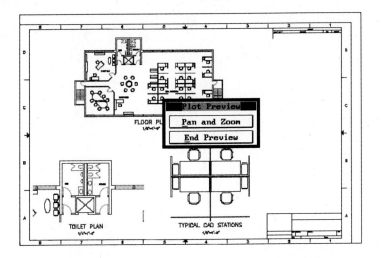

Figure 25.38

Completed drawing with paper space text.

Setting the dimension variable DIMSCALE to 0 forces AutoCAD to automatically use the inverse of the XP scale factor of the current viewport as you draw dimensions. In the example problem, setting DIMSCALE to 0 results in dimension objects being drawn with a scale of 96 while the full floor plan viewport is current; a scale of 48 while the toilet plan viewport is current; and a scale of 24 while the typical CAD station plan viewport is current (refer to figure 25.38), thus ensuring that the dimensions are scaled correctly for the current viewport.

If the views show common portions of the model, you might see a dimension in more than one viewport. If a dimension drawn in one viewport is visible in another viewport, the dimension appears to be twice as big as a dimension drawn in the first viewport. To avoid this, you must dedicate a layer for the dimensions in each viewport and then freeze that layer for all other viewports. See Chapter 23, "Techniques for Architectural and Civil Dimensioning," for more information on dimensioning in model and paper space.

Your experience with the complexities of plotter configuration and composition of drawings for controlled plotter output, both in tiled model space and floating viewports in paper space, prepares you for the study of drawing and graphic data exchange.

C H A P T E R
26

Exchanging Drawing and Graphic Data

Data exchange is the process of importing and exporting textual and graphic data between applications. AutoCAD drawings contain a great deal of data and are the product of a great deal of work. You can increase the value of your drawings and lower the cost of preparing them by exporting data from them to other applications, and by bringing data from other applications into your drawings.

This chapter discusses the advantages of using data exchange and explains how you can exchange data between AutoCAD and other applications. The following topics are covered:

◆ The advantages of data exchange

◆ Importing graphics and text from other applications into AutoCAD

◆ Exporting graphics and text from AutoCAD drawings to other applications

◆ Exporting AutoCAD drawings to other file formats

In the Windows environment, applications have had to conform to a uniform operating environment imposed by Microsoft. In the world of DOS, on the other hand, applications have developed independently of each other, making it difficult to move data from one of those applications to another.

Several "neutral" formats have been developed to make data exchange for DOS easier. In text applications, the ASCII file format is used. Most word processors, spreadsheet programs and database programs can save data in ASCII format. ASCII files can be readily imported into any application; text files saved in ASCII format can be imported into AutoCAD drawings and placed as normal AutoCAD text objects.

Another common exchange format is DXF (for Drawing Interchange Format). The DXF format was developed by Autodesk to be as complete as possible a representation of the drawing data, only saved in a format readable by other applications.

Graphics formats have proven more difficult to work with than ASCII files, but AutoCAD is capable of importing and exporting graphic data in a number of formats. AutoCAD now can even convert raster image files to vectors, which can be imported into a drawing.

 Note   There are two types of computer graphics: raster images and vector drawings. *Raster images*, also known as bitmaps, consist of a pattern of adjacent dots that make up a picture. Raster files are typically created by paint programs, by fax software, and by scanners. *Vector drawings* are actually database files, with drawing entities mathematically defined using coordinates. Vector files are created by CAD programs such as AutoCAD, and by the more sophisticated illustration programs such as CorelDRAW! and Micrografx Designer. The two types of graphic data are mutually incompatible; raster files must be converted to vector format before they can be used in a vector drawing program.

The following exercise shows you how to import a raster image—a *Graphic Interchange File* (GIF) to be precise—into AutoCAD's drawing editor.

Quick 5¢ Tour

Begin a new drawing named CHAP26 using the default prototype drawing ACAD. Create a new layer named GIF and set it current.

Command: *Choose* File, Import, Raster GIF	Issues GIFIN command
Command: _gifin GIF file name: **NRP** (Enter)	
Insertion point<0,0,0>: **4,4** (Enter)	Specifies insertion point for image

New Riders Publishing
INSIDE SERIES

Scale factor: **5** (Enter)   Specifies insertion scale for image

The image is placed in the drawing (see fig. 26.1).

Figure 26.1

A raster image imported into AutoCAD.

Understanding Data Exchange

Computers excel at automating processes that would otherwise make many jobs difficult or impractical. Design and drafting are often repetitive processes—you probably use parts of one drawing or design in others. Computers have given us the ability to transfer information from drawing to drawing or between applications. Without this, you would spend a lot of time recreating drawing data each time you needed to use it.

Chapter 17, "Block Structure, Editing, Organization, and Management," discusses the most common way to transfer data from drawing to drawing—using the WBLOCK and INSERT commands. Transferring graphic data from AutoCAD to another application is also possible. Figure 26.2, for example, shows an AutoCAD drawing inserted into a Lotus Ami Pro document.

Figure 26.2

*Drawing data
copied from
AutoCAD to Ami
Pro.*

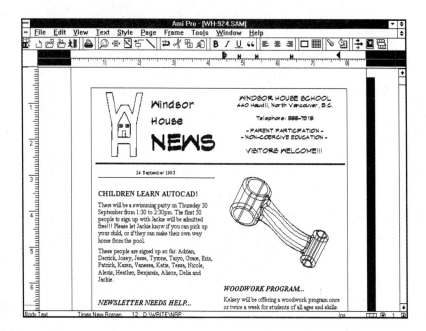

There are many advantages to transferring data to and from AutoCAD, but the two most important are efficiency and accuracy. Reusing data saves time—you don't have to recreate an object each time you need to use it. Reusing data also improves accuracy because you eliminate the possibility of errors being introduced when the data is recreated from scratch.

AutoCAD can *export* data to several different graphics and data file formats, enabling you to use AutoCAD drawings in many other applications. AutoCAD enables you to *import* data in various graphics and data file formats, making it possible to use drawings in AutoCAD that were created using other applications.

The following list summarizes the options available for exchanging data between AutoCAD and other applications:

◆ **DXF and DXB exchange.** A DXF file is an ASCII (text-only) or binary file that contains AutoCAD drawing data in a format understandable by other programs. Many graphics applications, in addition to AutoCAD, can export and import DXF files, making DXF a common means of moving data between AutoCAD and other graphics applications. DXB files are binary only; all entities in a DXB file are brought into AutoCAD as line entities.

◆ **Common data file formats.** AutoCAD can import and export data in common file formats, including 3D Studio and other 3D modeling formats.

◆ **Graphics file exchange.** AutoCAD can import and export drawing data in a variety of different graphics file formats, including bitmapped formats such as GIF, PCX, and TIF. This capability makes it possible for you to exchange drawing data between AutoCAD and a wide variety of non-CAD graphics applications.

Importing and Exporting Data

AutoCAD has the capability to export AutoCAD drawings to other applications in a format readable by those other applications. It can also convert graphic models from other applications into its native drawing format. AutoCAD can directly import, for example, a 3D model created using 3D Studio—you don't have to export from 3D Studio in a special format.

AutoCAD can export data from a drawing using a variety of formats. You can export data by choosing Export from AutoCAD's File menu, or you can use specific commands for each exported file type.

The following list describes the options available in the Export pull-down menu. Each option item includes the extension of the file created and the AutoCAD commands that you can use to create the export file:

◆ **Block.** Displays the Create Drawing File dialog box. Using the Block option is the simplest way to export graphic data for subsequent importing into another AutoCAD drawing. File extension: DWG. AutoCAD command: WBLOCK.

◆ **Release 12 DWG.** Displays the Save Release 12 Drawing As dialog box. Using this option creates a Release 12-compatible drawing file. File extension: DWG. AutoCAD command: SAVEASR12.

Note A drawing created and saved in Release 13 cannot be loaded into Release 12. Use the SAVEASR12 command when you have to save your drawing in a format that can be loaded into Release 12.

◆ **DXF.** An ASCII or binary file format that stores as much as possible of the AutoCAD drawing data. You can use this format to exchange data between AutoCAD and other graphics applications that support DXF input. File extension: DXF. AutoCAD command: DXFOUT.

◆ **3D Studio.** The native data file format for Autodesk's 3D Studio animation and rendering program. You can export an AutoCAD 3D model to 3D Studio using this format. File extension: 3DS. AutoCAD command: 3DSOUT.

26

◆ **SAT.** An ASCII file format that contains a description of a 3D model, which can include trimmed non-uniform rational B-spline (NURB) surfaces, regions, and solids. Use this format to export a 3D AutoCAD model to other 3D modeling applications that support the ACIS format. File extension: SAT. AutoCAD command: ACISOUT.

◆ **Stereolithography.** An ASCII or binary file format containing a description of an AutoCAD solid object that can be understood by a *Stereolithograph Apparatus*, or SLA. Solids are stored as meshes. File extension: STL. AutoCAD command: STLOUT.

◆ **PostScript.** *PostScript* files can be imported by many applications; these include most wordprocessing, desktop publishing, and illustration programs. You also can print a PostScript file by using the PLOT command and a PostScript printer. Choosing PostScript from the File, Export pull-down menu presents two further options: Export and Prolog. Export issues the PSOUT command and displays the Create PostScript File dialog box. Prolog enables you to enter a value for the PSPROLOG system variable. File extension: EPS. AutoCAD commands: PSOUT, PSPROLOG.

Note PSPROLOG enables you to modify the prolog, or header, of the PostScript output file, providing you with a great deal of control over the appearance of your final image. You can, for example, modify PSPROLOG to produce different lineweights depending on the color of the AutoCAD entities. A full discussion on PSPROLOG is beyond the scope of this book.

◆ **Attributes.** Issues the DDATTEXT command and displays the Attribute Extraction dialog box. Refer to Chapter 16 for information on this option.

In addition to exporting data from AutoCAD to various file types, you also can import data into AutoCAD from specific types of data files. Choose Import from the File pull-down menu to access the various options for importing external data files.

You can import graphic files in eight different formats. The following list describes these eight file types, their extensions, and the AutoCAD commands you can use to import them. Some of the file types are explained in the previous section on exporting files; their descriptions are abbreviated in the following list.

◆ **DXF.** The standard AutoCAD DXF format. File extension: DXF. AutoCAD command: DXFIN.

◆ **DXB.** A binary version of DXF. DXB files consist entirely of line segments. File extension: DXB. AutoCAD command: DXBIN.

New Riders Publishing
INSIDE
SERIES

◆ **3D Studio.** The standard 3D Studio file format. You can import a 3D Studio data file directly into AutoCAD. File extension: 3DS. AutoCAD command: 3DSIN.

◆ **SAT.** 3D model in ASCII format. File extension: SAT. AutoCAD commands: IMPORT, ACISIN.

◆ **PostScript.** Imports Encapsulated PostScript files. File extension: EPS. AutoCAD command: PSIN.

◆ **PCX.** The bitmap format used by Windows Paintbrush and other graphics applications. This format was developed by Z-Soft and has become a standard graphics format. AutoCAD converts the bitmap to a block that contains a series of solids. File extension: PCX. AutoCAD command: PCXIN.

◆ **GIF.** Common bitmapped graphics file format developed by the CompuServe Information Service as an efficient compressed format for electronic file transfer. As with the PCX format, AutoCAD converts the image to a block that contains a series of solids. File extension: GIF. AutoCAD command: GIFIN.

◆ **TIFF (Tagged Image File Format).** A standard bitmapped graphics file format recognized by many graphics and desktop publishing applications. As with PCX and TIFF formats, AutoCAD converts the image to a block that contains a series of solids. File extension: TIF. AutoCAD command: TIFFIN.

 Tip Importing a PCX, TIF, or GIF file is practical only for relatively small files. The amount of data in these types of files, and the fact that AutoCAD converts the pixels to solids (the 2D solid object, not 3D ACIS solids), can cause the drawing size to grow tremendously.

Using DXF

Autodesk developed the *Drawing Interchange Format* (DXF) to accurately describe an AutoCAD drawing file in an ASCII text-file format. Although AutoCAD's proprietary binary (or compiled) DWG drawing file is efficient for a computer to use, it is difficult to manipulate outside of AutoCAD. An ASCII text file, on the other hand, is more cumbersome, but most software applications can read and write to it.

Because of AutoCAD's market dominance, the DXF format has become an industry standard. One frequent use of the DXF format is as the end product of the automatic conversion of scanned raster images to vector drawing files ready for import to AutoCAD (see fig. 26.3).

Figure 26.3

A scanned raster image converted to DXF and imported to AutoCAD.

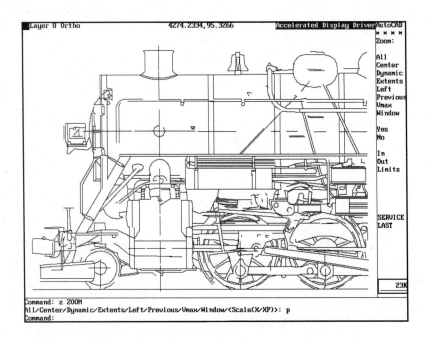

To create a DXF file from your current drawing, either choose File, Export, DXF from the pull-down menu, or enter **DXFOUT** at the keyboard. With either method, the Create DXF File dialog box appears. After you've entered a file name, you are prompted to enter the number of decimal places of accuracy AutoCAD will use to create the DXF file. Six is the default and works well in most cases, although some applications might require even more precision. The DXFOUT command outputs to an ASCII file, unless you specify the Binary option. The Binary option outputs to a more efficient but less readable binary DXF file.

Try creating a DXF file in the next exercise, using the EXCHANGE drawing from the IA DOS Disk as a prototype.

Using DXFOUT To Export Data

Begin a new drawing named CHAP26A using EXCHANGE.DWG as a prototype.

Command: *Choose* File, Export, DXF	Displays Create DXF File dialog box
Select the \IA\DRAWINGS *directory, then type* **DXFTEST** *in the* File *text box, then choose* OK	Specifies directory and file name for exported DXF file

New Riders Publishing
INSIDE
SERIES

```
Command: _dxfout
Enter decimal places of accuracy
(0 to 16)/Objects/Binary <6>: (Enter)
```
Confirms default setting of six decimal
places of accuracy

The previous exercise creates a text file that accurately describes the drawing database. If you open the resulting DXF file in a text editor or word processor in text mode, the text might look a little confusing; but you can learn to read this type of file. Because there were so few objects in this drawing, most of the file is filled with the first two sections, called the header and tables, which define all the drawing's variables, settings, and feature definitions. The last part of the file lists the objects and their coordinates.

In addition to exporting an entire drawing, you can export only a selection of objects by using the DXFOUT command.

> **DXFOUT.** The DXFOUT command enables you to create a drawing interchange (DXF) file from the current AutoCAD drawing. By default, the resulting DXF file is accurate to six decimal places and is in ASCII text format. Command options enable you to change the precision within a range of 0 to 16 decimal places, select specific drawing objects to include in the file, or create a binary DXF file.
> Pull-down: *Choose* File, Export, DXF
> Screen: *Choose* FILE, EXPORT, DXFout:

The following exercise exports a selection set to a new DXF file.

Exporting Selected Objects with DXFOUT

Continue in the CHAP26A drawing from the previous exercise.

```
Command: DXFOUT (Enter)
```
Displays Create DXF File dialog box

Type **LINES** *in the* File *text box,*
then choose OK
Specifies file name LINES.DXF

```
Enter decimal places of accuracy
(0 to 16)/Objects/Binary <6>: O
```
(the letter O, not the number 0) (Enter)
Specifies Objects option

```
Select objects: Select the two lines (Enter)
```
Specifies objects to be exported

```
Enter decimal places of accuracy
(0 to 16)/Binary <6>: 3 (Enter)
```
Specifies three decimal places of accuracy
and creates DXF file

Note The DXFOUT command also features the Binary option, which creates a binary DXF file. A binary DXF file is about 25 percent smaller than a text file and can be read much faster by AutoCAD. A binary DXF file can be read and written by sophisticated third-party programs, but you cannot read or edit the file with a text editor.

Next, import into a new drawing the DXF file you just created. Use the Import option in the File pull-down menu to initiate the import process. Your drawing should look similar to figure 26.4 when you complete the following exercise.

Importing a DXF File

Command: *Choose* File, New, Discard Changes, *then choose* OK *in the* Create New Drawing *dialog box*	Begins new unnamed drawing using default ACAD.DWG prototype
Command: *Choose* File, Import, DXF	Displays Select DXF File dialog box
From the Files *list box, select* LINES, *then choose* OK	Issues the DXFIN command and imports file LINES.DXF

Figure 26.4

Lines imported from a DXF file.

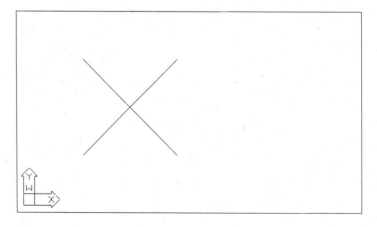

It is not necessary to specify a file extension because the DXFIN command applies it automatically. You also can enter the DXFIN command directly at the Command: prompt.

> **DXFIN.** The DXFIN command enables you to import an existing drawing interchange (DXF) file into the current AutoCAD drawing. There are no command options.
> Pull-down: *Choose* File, Export, DXF
> Screen: *Choose* FILE, EXPORT, DXFout

To import block definitions into a drawing, you must import a full (not objects-only) DXF file into a new drawing. The LINES.DXF file in your text editor appears much shorter than the DXF file created from the entire drawing because only those objects that you chose (the two lines) were included. Selecting objects to create a DXF file is often preferred to creating a complete DXF file because the header and tables in a complete DXF might conflict with settings in your current drawing. You should use this option if you want to import data into an existing drawing file, rather than into a new one.

Note A full DXF file can only be imported into a new, empty drawing file. Three options exist for creating a new drawing. Using the Create New Drawing dialog box, you must either use the default *original* ACAD.DWG prototype file, or specify **N**o Prototype, or set the new drawing name equal to nothing (blank), such as CHAP26A= in the New **D**rawing Name edit box.

Note Another file format, even more compact than a binary DXF file, is the Binary Drawing Interchange (DXB) format. DXB format is not as complete as DXF, but it can handle large amounts of object data very efficiently, and it maintains greater accuracy. A special command, DXBIN, is used to read a DXB file. Although AutoCAD has no direct command for creating one of these files, it can be done indirectly by configuring an ADI plotter driver to plot in a DXB format. DXB files are not the same as binary DXF files that are created with the DXFOUT command or export option. The disadvantage to binary DXB output is that it converts everything, including text and curves, to straight line segments.

Exchanging Data through PostScript

PostScript is a type of graphics file that is popular in many desktop publishing and illustration applications. The advantage PostScript has over regular raster images is that it contains special shapes and fonts that are stored more efficiently and generated with better resolution. You can use PostScript fonts in AutoCAD drawings, as well as TrueType and the old SHX fonts. PostScript files are more compatible with other devices or applications that recognize PostScript entities. The standard file extension for PostScript is EPS, for Encapsulated PostScript. EPS files are text files that can be read by many different graphics software packages, as well as by hard-copy output devices.

You can access AutoCAD's PostScript commands, PSIN and PSOUT, from the Import and Export options of the File pull-down menu, or you can issue the commands from the Command: prompt.

PSIN. The PSIN command enables you to import an Encapsulated PostScript file into the current AutoCAD drawing. There are no command options, but you can control whether the image displays accurately or as an outline *bounding box* as you drag it into place; you can also control whether or not solid areas are filled or left as outlines.

Pull-down: *Choose* File, Import, PostScript, Import
Screen: *Choose* FILE, IMPORT, PSin:

PSOUT. The PSOUT command enables you to export all or part of the current AutoCAD drawing as an Encapsulated PostScript file. Command options enable you to select the area of the drawing you want included; control whether or not a screen preview image is included in the file header, plotting units and scale; and control the physical size of the image.

Pull-down: *Choose* File, Import, PostScript, Export
Screen: *Choose* FILE, EXPORT, PSout:

The process of creating an EPS file is very similar to plotting. If you have used a PostScript text font (by using a style defined with a font file that has a PFB extension) or a PostScript fill pattern (by using the PSFILL command), these fonts and fills will be exported along with the rest of the image. If the system variable FILEDIA is set to 1, a File dialog box appears to name the file. The next prompt offers the same five choices as plotting for the area to output: Display, Extents, Limits, View, or Window. A screen preview can be added to the EPS file in either an EPSI or TIFF format, and several choices are offered for the resolution of that image. Then the scale and output size is specified. The next exercise shows how to export a drawing to a PostScript file.

 Stop You can only use files generated by the PSOUT command with a PostScript printer or a software PostScript emulator.

New Riders Publishing
INSIDE SERIES

Exporting to a PostScript File

Begin a new drawing named CHAP26B using EXCHANGE.DWG as a prototype.

Command: *Choose* File, Export, PostScript, Export	Displays Create PostScript File dialog box with CHAP26B in File edit box
Choose OK	Accepts default name (CHAP26B) and begins file export

Confirm the default values for all the command options.

```
Command: _psout
What to plot—Display, Extents, Limits, View, or Window <D>: (Enter)
Include a screen preview image in the file? (None/EPSI/TIFF) <None>: (Enter)
Size units (Inches or Millimeters) <Inches>: (Enter)
Specify scale by entering:
Output Inches=Drawing Units or Fit or ? <Fit>: (Enter)

Standard values for output size
Size      Width       Height
A          8.00        10.50
B         10.00        16.00
C         16.00        21.00
D         21.00        33.00
E         33.00        43.00
F         28.00        40.00
G         11.00        90.00
H         28.00       143.00
J         34.00       176.00
K         40.00       143.00
A4         7.80        11.20
A3        10.70        15.60
A2        15.60        22.40
A1        22.40        32.20
A0        32.20        45.90
USER       7.50        10.50

Enter the Size or Width,Height (in Inches) <USER>: (Enter)
Effective plotting area: 7.50 wide by 5.46 high
```

 Note The PSOUT command lacks control for lineweight, color, and grayscale. The IA Disk includes the PSLWAS.EXE file, which adds these controls. See Appendix H, "The IA Disk," for details.

26

AutoCAD created a PostScript file named CHAP26B.EPS that contains the contents of the drawing in PostScript format.

Using PostScript To Import Data

The PSIN command inserts an EPS file similar to the way the INSERT command inserts a block. If the system variable FILEDIA is set to 1, the Select PostScript File dialog box assists in selecting the EPS file. The PSQUALITY system variable is used to define the resolution of the image. A higher number provides higher resolution. A negative number outlines the polygons rather than filling them.

You might need to experiment with the PSQUALITY variable to see what resolutions work the best for graphics display and hard copy output. Try to maintain a balance between a good image and a reasonable file size.

PostScript capability enables you to use AutoCAD to exchange information with other software packages without converting the image to a raster image. PostScript also gives AutoCAD a better interface with output devices that directly support this type of file.

This chapter covers importing and exporting graphic data to and from AutoCAD. You can also work with text data, both by importing and exporting, and by linking with external files. The next chapter outlines how to work with textual data and AutoCAD.

Part VII

AutoCAD and 3D

New Riders Publishing
INSIDE
SERIES

Isometric Drawings

AutoCAD is capable of very sophisticated three-dimensional drawing; in fact, 3D drawings in AutoCAD are usually referred to as models rather than drawings. The following four chapters introduce you to the basics of creating and viewing 3D models.

This chapter stays within the realm of 2D drawings, but uses an old technique from the days of manual drafting. Before computers, drafters still had to convey three-dimensional impressions of their designs. Several techniques for creating 3D drawings evolved under the general label of *parallel projection drawings.*

You use parallel projection drawings to simulate a 3D view in such a way that you can take accurate measurements—in some directions—from the view. The various types of parallel projection drawings each require you to use a distinct construction technique. The most common types of parallel projections are as follows (see fig. 27.1):

◆ **Axonometric projection.** Presents an accurate plan view of an object, oriented at 45° to normal. You can take accurate measurements anywhere on plan view and along lines at multiples of 45°.

◆ **Oblique projection.** Presents an accurate elevation of an object, with projection lines at 30° to normal. You can take accurate measurements anywhere on the elevation plane and along lines at 0, 30, 90, or 150°.

◆ **Isometric projection.** All planes are distorted, but the overall view is more realistic than the other two. You can take accurate measurements along lines at multiples of 30° regardless of the plane they are in.

Figure 27.1

Types of parallel line projection.

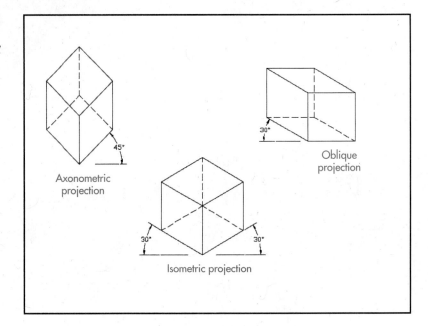

 Note This chapter does not intend to teach you isometric drawing techniques, but rather how to use AutoCAD's isometric capabilities. If you want to explore isometric drawings in detail, refer to a drafting techniques book.

The most common type of parallel line projection is isometric, particularly in the process piping industry, in which it serves as the standard format for preparing piping and instrumentation diagrams (P&IDs). AutoCAD has a built-in feature that enables you to create isometric drawings with relative ease.

The material in this chapter is divided into the following parts:

◆ How to invoke isometric mode and control the isometric environment

◆ How to maneuver in isometric mode

◆ How to draw in isometric mode

◆ How to plot an isometric drawing

New Riders Publishing
INSIDE SERIES

You might wonder why you would draw an isometric view when you can generate 3D models in Release 13. Using AutoCAD's isometric mode presents a couple of advantages over generating a 3D model. Under certain circumstances, drawing an isometric view of a model is faster than creating a full-fledged 3D model. The other major advantage is simplicity; you need learn only one new command: ISOPLANE.

2D isometric views present disadvantages, as well. An isometric drawing is not a 3D model, so you cannot rotate the model to get other 3D views. You cannot generate a rendered image from an isometric drawing. You can make measurements only along an isometric view's X, Y, or Z axes; any measurement along any other axis is distorted. Depending on the model, drawing it in isometric mode can take longer than creating a true 3D model. Drawing some features in isometric mode can be cumbersome and can require you to use intermediate construction lines.

In the following exercise, you draw an isometric view of a 2-by-2-by-2 cube, and you are asked to snap to some points. Use the coordinates display. Be sure that the point you pick snaps to the coordinates given.

Quick 5¢ Tour

Begin a new drawing named CHAP27, using the default prototype drawing ACAD. Create a new layer named PART and set it current.

Command: *Choose* Options, Drawing Aids	Opens Drawing Aids dialog box
Put a check in the Grid On *box and leave the X and Y spacing set to 0*	Turns on grid
Put a check in the Snap On *box and leave the X and Y spacing set to 1*	Turns on snap
Put a check in the Ortho *box*	Turns on ortho
Put a check in the On *box in the* Isometric Snap/Grid *cluster*	Turns on isometric mode
Choose the Right *radio button*	Sets right isoplane current

Your Drawing Aids dialog box should now look like the one in figure 27.2.

Choose OK	Closes Drawing Aids dialog box and saves settings

Next, you draw the right isoplane of the cube.

continues

continued

Figure 27.2

Isometric settings in the Drawing Aids dialog box.

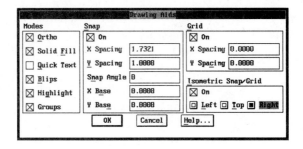

As you work, notice how the crosshairs indicate the current isometric plane.

Command: *Choose* Draw, Line	Issues the LINE command
_line From point: *Pick point* ① *(see fig. 27.3) at coordinates* 6.9282,1.0000	Starts line at snap point
To point: *Pick point* ② *at coordinates* 8.6603,2.0000	Places point 2 snap points to right of previous point in right isoplane
To point: *Pick point* ③ *at coordinates* 8.6603,4.0000	Places point 2 snap points directly above previous point
To point: *Pick point* ④ *at coordinates* 6.9282,3.0000	Places point 2 snap points to left of previous point
To point: C (Enter)	Closes isometric box and ends LINE command (see fig. 27.3)

Figure 27.3

Drawing in the right isoplane.

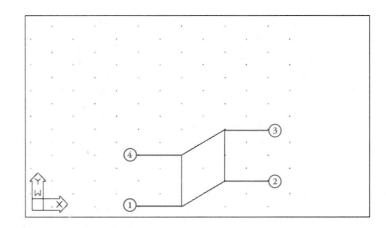

`Command:` *Choose* Options, Drawing Aids	Opens the Drawing Aids dialog box
Choose the T*op radio button, then* OK	Switches to top isoplane
`Command:` *Choose* Draw, Line	Issues the LINE command
`From point:` *Pick* ① *(see fig. 27.4)*	Starts line at snap point
`To point:` *Pick point* ② *at coordinates* 6.9282,5.0000	Places point 2 snap points to left of previous point in top isoplane
`To point:` *Pick point* ③ *at coordinates* 5.1962,4.0000	Places point 2 snap points to left of previous point
`To point:` *Pick* ④	Places point 2 snap points to right of previous point
`To point:` (Enter)	Ends the LINE command

Your drawing now should look like figure 27.4.

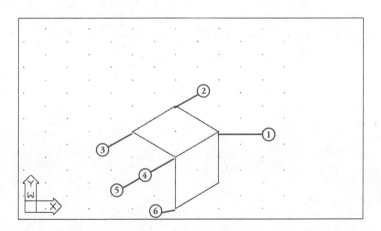

Figure 27.4
Drawing in the top isoplane.

27

Using the radio buttons in the Drawing Aids dialog box to switch isoplanes is easy enough, but using the Ctrl+E key combination to alternate between the three isometric planes is easier still.

`Command:` *Press Ctrl+E twice*	Switches to left isoplane
`Command:` *Choose* Draw, Line	
`From point:` *Pick* ③	Places start point of line
`To point:` *Pick point* ⑤ *at coordinates* 5.1962,2.0000	Places point 2 snap points directly below previous point

continues

continued

To point: *Pick* ⑥	Places point 2 snap points to right of previous point
To point: (Enter)	Ends the LINE command

Save the drawing.

You have just created your first isometric drawing of a cube. Your drawing should look like figure 27.5.

Figure 27.5

Isometric view of a 2"-by-2"-by-2" cube.

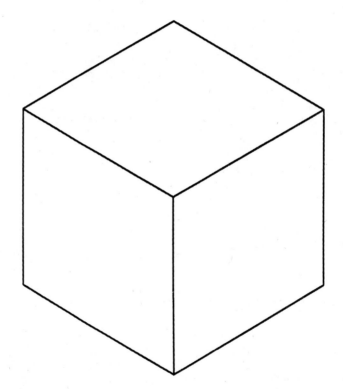

Invoking Isometric Mode

Using AutoCAD's isometric mode is the easiest way to draw an isometric view. When you invoke isometric mode, AutoCAD adjusts the snap and grid to the orientation of the X, Y, and Z axes of an isometric view.

Using the Drawing Aids Dialog Box

If you want to switch to isometric mode, choose Options, Drawing Aids, which opens the Drawing Aids dialog box (see fig. 27.6).

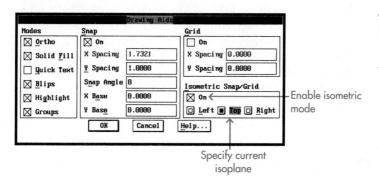

Figure 27.6

The Drawing Aids dialog box.

— Enable isometric mode

Specify current isoplane

Note In isometric mode, the snap and grid's Y spacing values control their spacing, and their X spacing values are grayed out.

You can open the Drawing Aids dialog box transparently by entering **'DDRMODES**.

Using the SNAP Command

You can use the Style option of the SNAP command to switch between isometric and standard (nonisometric) mode. When you issue the SNAP command, AutoCAD prompts you as follows:

```
Snap spacing or ON/OFF/Aspect/Rotate/Style <1.0000>:
```

Enter **S** to specify the Style option. AutoCAD then prompts you with two styles from which to choose:

```
Standard/Isometric <S>:
```

Enter **I** to specify isometric mode. AutoCAD then prompts you for the spacing of the snap grid:

```
Vertical spacing <1.0000>:
```

After you enter a vertical spacing value, AutoCAD returns you to the Command: prompt and turns on the snap grid in isometric mode. To use SNAP to turn off isometric mode, use the Style option and specify the Standard style.

You can also invoke SNAP transparently.

Understanding Isoplanes

In an isometric view, only three faces of a cubic object are visible. In isometric drafting, place points and create entities using these three faces. To help you, AutoCAD creates the illusion of working on one of these three distinct surfaces, or planes. These three planes are referred to as *isometric planes,* or *isoplanes,* for short. The three planes are called the left, right, and top isoplanes (see fig. 27.7). As you switch isoplanes, AutoCAD automatically changes the appearance of the crosshairs and grid to make it look as though they lie in the current isoplane. This is all an illusion—you draw the isometric in 2D just as you would on a sheet of paper.

Figure 27.7

Isometric view of a cube.

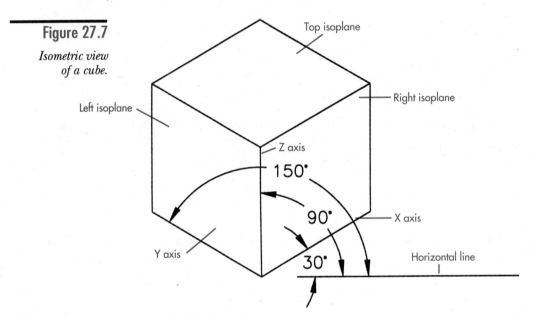

You can use several methods to switch between isoplanes. The Drawing Aids dialog box has radio buttons that enable you to set the current isoplane to the left, top, or right isoplane (refer to fig. 27.6). You also can use the ISOPLANE command to set the current isoplane.

'ISOPLANE. The ISOPLANE command enables you to set the current isoplane. ISOPLANE does not appear anywhere in AutoCAD's menu, and the only way you can invoke it is to enter ISOPLANE at the Command: prompt.

When you issue the ISOPLANE command, AutoCAD prompts you as follows:

```
Left/Top/Right/<Toggle>:
```

You specify an isoplane explicitly by entering L, T, or R, or by pressing Enter to accept the default option Toggle, which changes in a clockwise direction to the next isoplane.

You also can change isoplanes by pressing Ctrl+E. Repeatedly pressing the Ctrl+E combination cycles clockwise through the three isoplanes. Pressing F5 also cycles through the three isoplanes. Finally, the isoplane toggle is assigned to puck button #8, if your puck has that many buttons. You can issue the ISOPLANE command and press Ctrl+E transparently.

In the Quick 5¢ Tour, you used the Drawing Aids dialog box to turn on isometric mode. In the following exercise, you turn isometric mode on and off with the SNAP command and the Drawing Aids dialog box to switch between isoplanes.

Initiating Isometric Mode

Continue to use the CHAP27 drawing from the Quick 5¢ Tour. The crosshairs are in the left isoplane.

Command: *Press Ctrl+E several times*	Changes current isoplane to next isoplane in clockwise direction
Command: *Press F5 several times*	Changes current isoplane to next isoplane in clockwise direction
Command: *Choose* Options, Drawing Aids	Opens the Drawing Aids dialog box

Isometric snap is turned on. Clear the check mark in the On box in the Isometric Snap/Grid cluster to turn it off, then close the dialog box. You are now out of isometric mode.

Command: (Enter)	Redisplays Drawing Aids dialog box
Put a check in the On *box in the* Isometric Snap/Grid *cluster*	Turns isometric mode back on
If it's not already turned on, choose the Top *radio button*	Changes current isoplane to top

Save your work.

27

Maneuvering in Isometric Mode

Isometric mode is a 2D simulation of 3D space. In reality, you are still working in a flat environment with an X,Y coordinate system that has not changed. This requires a little adjustment on your part when you specify points and angles.

Specifying Points

In an isometric view of a cube, the cube's visible edges are aligned at 30, 90, and 150° relative to a horizontal line (refer to figure 27.7). The visible edges are referred to as *isometric lines,* and any lines parallel to the visible edges are also isometric lines. The Z axis is the 90° line. Using the right-hand rule, the X axis is the 30° line and the Y axis is the 150° line.

Note The *right-hand rule* was invented by Autodesk to help clarify 3D coordinates. Hold your right hand in front of you and make a letter *L* with your thumb and forefinger. The right-hand rule says your thumb is pointing along the X axis and your forefinger along the Y axis. Now, if you point your index finger at yourself, according to the rule it's pointing along the Z axis.

In an isometric view, you can measure distances accurately only along an isometric line. Any measurement along a nonisometric line will not be correct. If you measure the length of one of the diagonals of an isoplane, for example, the measurement is incorrect. If, however, you measure the length of one of the isometric lines, the measurement is correct.

To further the illusion of working in 3D, when you turn on isometric snap/grid, AutoCAD adjusts the crosshairs and the snap and grid points so that they appear to lie in the current isoplane (see fig. 27.8), by realigning the crosshairs and the snap and grid dots along isometric lines. The result, however, is that the coordinates of a snap point in normal space end up being rotated 30° or 150° about the origin, because the coordinate system remains unchanged. This explains why the snap points end up with strange X coordinate values, like 0.8660. Using absolute coordinates is rather difficult; using snap points, object snap modes, grip points, and relative coordinates to pick specific points is much easier.

Note When you specify angles for relative coordinates, remember that lines that are supposed to run parallel to the X or Y axes actually are aligned along 30° and 150°, respectively.

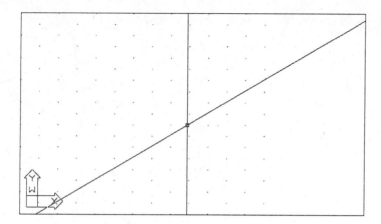

Figure 27.8

The isometric drawing environment.

Using Ortho Mode

AutoCAD also adjusts ortho mode to create the illusion of working in the current isoplane. If you need to use ortho to help you draw orthogonal lines in one of the isoplanes, you should make that isoplane current, and then ortho appears to lie in that plane.

Drawing in Isometric Mode

Drawing lines, circles, arcs, text, and dimensions is easy in isometric mode. You must enlist the aid of construction lines when you draw other geometry, such as spiral curves or ellipses.

Drawing Lines

The easiest way to draw lines in isometric mode is to use your snap points, object snap modes, and relative coordinates whenever possible. If you are going to use relative coordinates to draw a line parallel to the X axis, use an angle of 30° or 210°. If you want the line to be parallel to the Y axis, use an angle of 150° or 330°. If you want the line to be parallel to the Z axis, use an angle of 90° or 270°. If you need to draw a line that is not parallel to any of the three axes, you must fall back on using object snap modes, snap points, or standard drafting construction techniques.

27

In the following exercises, you create the first lines of the drawing shown in figure 27.9.

Figure 27.9

The finished isometric part drawing.

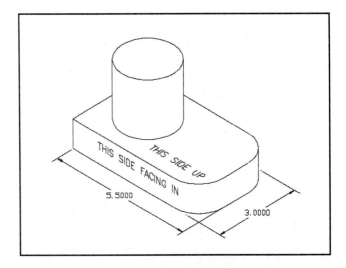

Drawing Isometric Lines

Continue to use the drawing CHAP27 and erase the cube you drew. The top isoplane should be current.

In the following steps, you draw the lines that form the right face of the part.

Command: *Choose* Draw, Line	Issues LINE command
_Line From point: *Press Ctrl+E*	Sets right isoplane current
From point: *Pick point at* coordinates 6.9282,1.0000	Starts line at snap point
To point: **@3<30** (Enter)	Draws isometric line to right
To point: **@1<90** (Enter)	Draws isometric line going "upwards"
To point: **@3<210** (Enter)	Draws isometric line to left
To point: **C** (Enter)	Closes isometric box and ends LINE command

Your drawing should look like figure 27.10. Next, you draw the top face of the part.

Command: *Press Ctrl+E twice*	Sets top isoplane current
Command: (Enter)	Repeats the LINE command

New Riders Publishing

INSIDE
SERIES

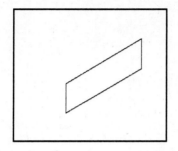

Figure 27.10

*Drawing a face in
the right isoplane.*

`_Line From point:` *Pick* ① *(see fig. 33.11)*	Starts line at snap point
`To point:` *Pick the snap point at the coordinates* 5.1962,6.0000	Draws isometric line to left
`To point:` *Pick the snap point at the coordinates* 2.5981,4.5	Draws isometric line to left
`To point:` *Pick* ②	Draws isometric line to right
`To point:` **Enter**	Ends the LINE command

Your drawing now should look like figure 27.11.

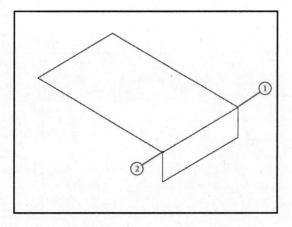

Figure 27.11

*Drawing a face in
the top isoplane.*

Next, you draw the left face of the part.

`Command:` *Press Ctrl+E twice*	Sets left isoplane current
`Command:` **Enter**	Repeats the LINE command

continues

continued

_Line From point: *Pick* ① (see fig 27.12)	Starts line at a snap point
To point: **@1<-90** (**Enter**)	Draws an isometric line going directly down
To point: *Pick* ②	Draws an isometric line going to the right
To point: (**Enter**)	Ends the LINE command

Save your work. Your drawing should look like figure 27.12.

Figure 27.12

Drawing a face in the left isoplane.

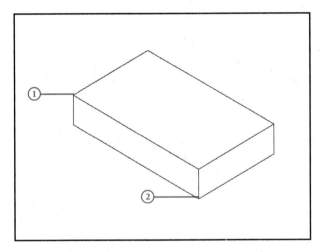

You have finished drawing the base of the part. Next, you need to add a circular feature.

Drawing Circles and Arcs

Circles in orthogonal views, such as plan and elevation views appear as ellipses in isometric views. To draw a circle in an isoplane, you must draw an ellipse, and you must align its axes in such a way as to make it appear that the ellipse lies in that isoplane. To help draw such ellipses, you can use the Isocircle option of the ELLIPSE command. The Isocircle option appears in the ELLIPSE prompt only if you are in isometric mode. AutoCAD prompts you as follows:

```
Arc/Center/Isocircle/<Axis endpoint 1>:
```

After you specify the Isocircle option, AutoCAD prompts you for the location of the "circle's" center point and its radius or diameter. AutoCAD automatically adjusts the appearance of the ellipse for the current isoplane.

New Riders Publishing
INSIDE
SERIES

Just as circles appear as ellipses, arcs appear as portions of ellipses in isometric views. You can approach drawing these elliptical arcs in two ways. You can draw a full isocircle and then trim or break the unneeded portion, or, you can select the Arc option of the ELLIPSE command, which gives you the following options:

```
<Axis endpoint 1>/Center/Isocircle:
```

After you specify Arc, Isocircle in the ELLIPSE command, AutoCAD prompts you for the center of the isocircle:

```
Center of circle:
```

AutoCAD also prompts you to supply the circle's radius (default) or its diameter:

```
<Circle radius>/Diameter:
```

Then, you must supply a starting angle or parameter for the elliptical arc:

```
Parameter/<start angle>:
```

After you enter P, for parameter, AutoCAD returns the following prompt:

```
Angle/<start parameter>:
```

You use the parameter option when you need to project an arc onto a plane that is not parallel to one of the isoplanes. You input the same values as when you use the standard option, but AutoCAD uses a different formula to create the arc, so that it appears correct in the nonisometric plane.

Finally, you must specify an ending angle (default option), the included angle, or a parameter, for which AutoCAD prompts you as follows:

```
Parameter/Included/<end angle>:
```

As when you use the standard arc option, AutoCAD temporarily changes the orientation of 0° to align 0° with the first axis endpoint, while prompting you for a start and end angle. Unfortunately, in isometric mode, this behavior makes specifying the angles with typed values difficult. To overcome this difficulty, use the distance and angle display on the status bar, snap points, or object snap modes to specify the start and end angles. To draw any other type of curve, you must use standard isometric drafting construction techniques, as you would on paper.

In the following exercise, you draw several isometric curves for the model.

27

Drawing Isometric Curves

Continue to use the CHAP27 drawing and use Ctrl+E to set the current isoplane to the top isoplane. Make sure that the SNAP button is on.

In the following steps, you round off the corners on the right side of the part. You must enter ELLIPSE at the Command: prompt because the Isocircle option is not available from menu selections.

Command: **ELLIPSE** (Enter)	Issues the ELLIPSE command
Arc/Center/Isocircle/ <Axis endpoint 1>: **I** (Enter)	Specifies the Isocircle option
Center of circle: *Pick* ① *at* *coordinates* 6.9282,3.0000 *(see fig.* *27.13)*	Locates center of circle

---

Figure 27.13

*Drawing ellipses
and elliptical
arcs.*

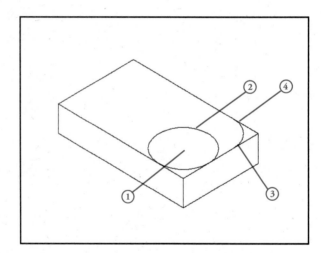

<Circle radius>/Diameter: **1** (Enter)	Sets isocircle radius to 1 and draws ellipse
Command: (Enter)	Repeats the ELLIPSE command
ELLIPSE Arc/Center/Isocircle/ <Axis endpoint 1>: **A** (Enter)	Specifies the Arc option
<Axis endpoint 1>/Center/ Isocircle: **I** (Enter)	Specifies the Isocircle option

`Center of circle:` *Pick* ② *at* *coordinates* 7.7942,3.5000	Locates center of isocircle
`<Circle radius>/Diameter: 1` (Enter)	Sets radius to 1
`Parameter/<start angle>:` *Pick* ③ *at coordinates* 8.6603,3.0000	Sets start angle of elliptical arc
`Parameter/Included/<end angle>:` *Pick* [bub4] *at coordinates* 8.6603,4.0000	Sets end angle of elliptical arc

Next, you use the TRIM command to create the rounded corners at the right side of the part. You need to temporarily turn snap off before you complete this command.

`Command:` *Choose* Modify, Trim	Issues the TRIM command
`Select cutting edges: (Projmode = UCS,` `Edgemode = No extend)`	
`Select objects:` *Select the ellipse at* ① *(see fig. 27.14), the arc at* ②, *and* *the lines at* ③ *and* ④, *then press Enter*	Specifies cutting edges
`<Select object to trim>/Project/` `Edge/Undo:` *Pick the ellipse at* ①	Trims ellipse to lines to form elliptical arc
`<Select object to trim>/Project/` `Edge/Undo:` *Pick the line at* ⑤	Trims line to arc
`<Select object to trim>/Project/` `Edge/Undo:` *Pick the lines at* ⑥, ⑦, *and* ⑧	Trims lines to arcs
`<Select object to trim>/Project/` `Edge/Undo:` (Enter)	Terminates the TRIM command

Your drawing should now look like figure 27.15. Next, you use the COPY and TRIM commands to shape the bottom right edge of the part.

`Command:` *Choose* Construct, Copy	Issues COPY command
`Select objects:` *Select the two* *elliptical arcs and press Enter*	Select objects to copy
`<Base point or displacement>/` `Multiple: 1<270` (Enter)	Specifies displacement
`Second point of displacement:` (Enter)	Copies arcs with specified displacement

continues

continued

Figure 27.14

Selecting cutting edges for TRIM.

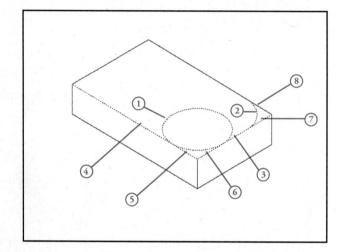

Figure 27.15

Finishing the face in the top isoplane

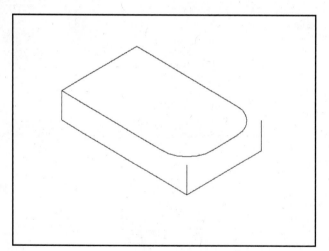

Your drawing should appear as figure 27.16.

Command: *Choose* Modify, Trim	Issues the TRIM command
Select cutting edges: (Projmode = UCS, Edgemode = No extend)	
Select objects: *Select the arcs at* ① *and* ② *(see fig. 27.16) and press Enter*	Selects the arcs as cutting edges

New Riders Publishing
INSIDE
SERIES

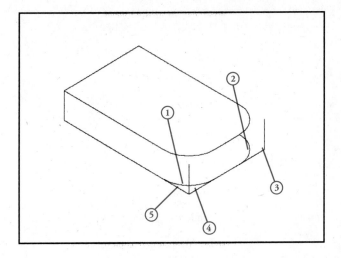

Figure 27.16

*Copying and
trimming the
bottom arcs.*

```
<Select object to trim>/
Project/Edge/Undo: Pick the lines at
③, ④, and ⑤ and
press Enter
```
                                    Trims the lines to the arcs

Save your work.

Your drawing now should look like figure 27.17.

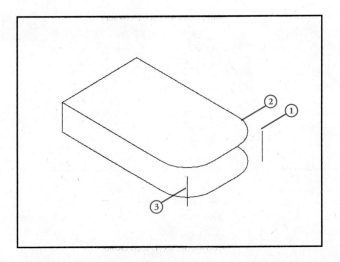

Figure 27.17

*The partly
completed part.*

In the following exercise, you use the MOVE and TRIM commands to draw the silhouette edge of the rightmost corner.

Using Snaps on Isometric Arcs

Continue from the previous exercise.

Command: *Choose* Modify, Move	Issues the MOVE command
Select objects: *Pick the line at* ① *(refer to fig. 27.17) and press Enter*	Selects line to move
Base point or displacement: *Using ENDP object snap, pick the line at* ①	
Second point of displacement: *Using* QUAdrant *object snap, pick arc at* ②	Moves line to create visual edge to filleted corner
Command: *Choose* Modify, Erase	Issues the ERASE command
Select objects: *Pick the line at* ③	Selects line to erase
Select objects: **Enter**	

Your drawing should look like figure 27.18. Trim one more line to finish off the corners.

Command: *Choose* Modify, Trim	Issues TRIM command
Select cutting edges: (Projmode = UCS, Edgemode = No extend)	
Select objects: *Pick line at* ① *(see fig. 27.18) and press Enter*	Selects the line as cutting edge
<Select object to trim>/ Project/Edge/Undo: *Pick* arc at ②	Trims the isometric arc
<Select object to trim>/ Project/Edge/Undo: **Enter**	Exits the TRIM command

Save the drawing.

In the next exercise, you use the same commands you used to draw the base to draw a cylinder on the top surface of the part. You begin by resetting the snap increment to make picking points easier.

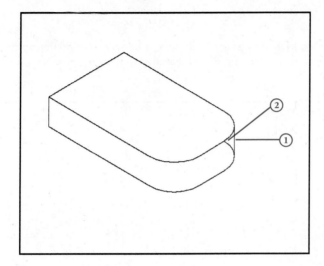

Figure 27.18

*Trimming
the arc.*

Drawing an Isometric Cylinder

Continue from the previous exercise.

Command: *Choose* Options, Drawing Aids, *set the* Y Spacing *in the* Snap *section to 0.5, turn Snap mode on, and choose* OK	Sets snap to 0.5 in the Drawing Aids dialog box
Command: **ELLIPSE** (Enter)	Issues the ELLIPSE command
Arc/Center/Isocircle/ <Axis endpoint 1>: **I** (Enter)	Specifies isocircle option
Center of circle: *Pick point* ① *(see fig. 27.19) at coordinates* 5.1962,4.5	
<Circle radius>/Diameter: **1** (Enter)	Draws ellipse for base of cylinder
Command: *Choose* Construct, Copy	Issues the COPY command
Select objects: *Select the ellipse you just drew and press Enter*	
<Base point or displacement>/ Multiple: **2<90** (Enter)	Specifies displacement
Second point of displacement: (Enter)	Copies ellipse for top of cylinder

continues

continued

Your drawing now should look like figure 27.19. Next, you draw the silhouette edges of the cylinder. Set a QUAdrant temporary running object snap to draw the next two lines. You might need to turn snap off again.

Figure 27.19

Drawing the base and top of the cylinder.

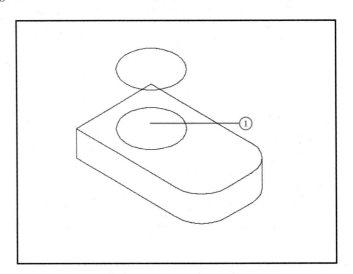

Command: *Choose* Options, Running
Object Snap   Displays Running Object Snap dialog box

Place an X beside **Q**uadrant, *then* OK   Sets QUAdrant running object snap

Command: *Choose* Draw, Line   Issues LINE command

From point: *Pick the lower ellipse
at* ① *(see fig. 27.20)*   Starts line at ellipse's quadrant

To point: *Pick the upper ellipse at*
②   Draws first silhouette edge

To point: **Enter**   Ends the LINE command

Repeat the preceding LINE command and draw the other edge from ③ to ④, then turn off the running object snap. Your drawing now should look like figure 27.20.

In the next step, you do some final trimming.

Command: *Choose* Modify, Trim   Issues TRIM command

Select cutting edges:
(Projmode = UCS, Edgemode = No extend)

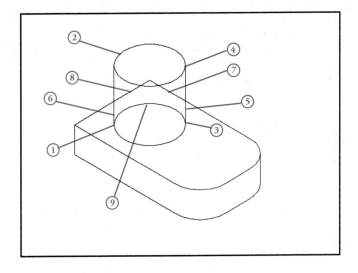

Figure 27.20

Drawing edge lines and trimming the base ellipse and corners.

`Select objects:` *Pick the lines at* ⑤ *(see fig. 27.20) and* ⑥ *and press Enter*	Selects cutting edges
`<Select object to trim>/ Project/Edge/Undo:` *Pick the lines at* ⑦ *and* ⑧	Trims corner lines
`<Select object to trim>/ Project/Edge/Undo:` *Pick* ⑨	Trims ellipse to form ellipse arc
`<Select object to trim>/ Project/Edge/Undo:` (Enter)	Exits the TRIM command

Save your work. Your drawing should now look like figure 27.21.

Drawing Text

To draw text that appears to lie in the current isoplane, you must use multiples of 30° for the obliquing and rotation angles (see fig. 27.22 for examples of text aligned with isoplanes). You need to make the baseline of the text and the verticals of the letters appear to be parallel to the appropriate isometric lines. To make text appear to lie upright in the right isoplane, for example, use an obliquing angle of 30° and a rotation angle of 30°.

Figure 27.21
Isometric view of the cylinder and base.

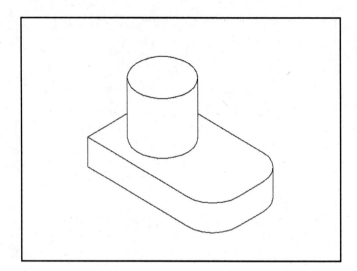

Figure 27.22
Text in isoplanes.

To make text appear to lie upright in the left isoplane, use an obliquing angle of –30° and a rotation angle of –30°. To make text appear to lie in the top isoplane and run parallel to the Y axis, use a 30° obliquing angle and a –30° rotation angle. To make text appear as though it is running parallel to the X axis, use the same 30° obliquing angle but a rotation angle of 30°, the same as for the right isoplane.

Tip
You need two distinct text styles for creating isometric drawings, one with an obliqing angle of 30° and one with an obliquing angle of –30°. Make text styles for the left and right isoplanes with the appropriate obliquing angles. Then, just set the style appropriately before drawing text in an isoplane. Use the left style for the top isoplane along the Y axis, and the right style for the top isoplane along the X axis, reversing the text rotation angles from those used in the left and right isoplanes.

In the following exercise, you create two text styles and use them to draw isometric text.

Drawing Isometric Text

Continue to use the drawing CHAP27. Create a new layer named TEXT, and make it the current layer. First, you create the needed text styles.

27

`Command:` *Choose* Data, Text Style	Issues the STYLE command
`Text style name (or ?)` `<STANDARD>:` **ISOLEFT** `Enter`	Opens the Select Text Font dialog box
`New style.`	
Select the ROMANS *font file and* *choose* OK	Specifies font file
`Height <0.0000>:` `Enter`	
`Width factor <1.0000>:` `Enter`	
`Obliquing angle <0>:` **-30** `Enter`	Sets obliquing angle to –30, which makes letters appear to lean backwards
`Backwards? <N>` `Enter`	
`Upside-down? <N>` `Enter`	
`Vertical? <N>` `Enter`	

continues

continued

`ISOLEFT is now the current text style.`	Sets the ISOLEFT text style current

Next, you repeat the STYLE command and define **ISORIGHT** with a 30° obliquing angle, which makes the letters appear to lean forward.

Command: (Enter)	Repeats the STYLE command
`ISORIGHT is now the current text style.`	Sets the ISORIGHT text style current

Now, you draw some text on the top isoplane. Change your current isoplane to the top isoplane by pressing Ctrl+E and turning on **SNAP**, if necessary.

Command: *Choose* Draw, Text, Dynamic Text	Issues the DTEXT command
Justify/Style/<Start point>: *Pick point* ① *at coordinates* 5.1962,3.5000 *(see fig. 27.23)*	Sets the left justification point
Height <0.2000>: (Enter)	
Rotation angle <0>: **-30** (Enter)	Rotates text along Y axis
Text: **THIS SIDE UP** (Enter)	Draws text
Text: (Enter)	Ends the DTEXT command

Next, you draw text on the left isoplane. Change your current isoplane to the left isoplane by pressing Ctrl+E twice.

Command: (Enter)	Repeats the DTEXT command
Justify/Style/<Start point>: **S** (Enter)	Specifies the style option
Style name (or ?) <ISORIGHT>: **ISOLEFT** (Enter)	Sets ISOLEFT style current
Justify/Style/<Start point>: *Pick point* ② *at coordinates* 3.4641,3.500	
Height <0.2000>: (Enter)	
Rotation angle <330>: **-30** (Enter)	Rotates text for left isoplane

New Riders Publishing
INSIDE
SERIES

Text: **THIS SIDE FACING IN** (Enter)

Text: (Enter)

Save your drawing.

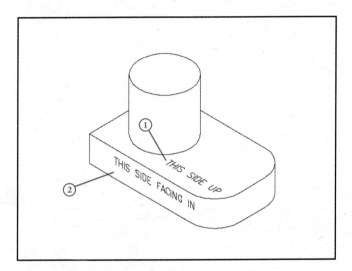

Figure 27.23
*Adding isometric
text for isoplanes.*

27

Dimensioning in Isometric Drawings

When you dimension in isometric drawings, you want the dimensions to appear to lie in a particular isoplane just like the text with which you have been working. You want AutoCAD to draw the extension lines and dimension lines parallel to the appropriate isometric lines (see fig. 27.24). Just as with text, you use increments of 30° to create the illusion.

The general procedure for placing dimensions in isometric drawings is as follows:

1. Make two text styles with the appropriate obliquing angles necessary to orient the text with the desired isoplane (see the preceding discussion on isometric text).

2. Use the DIMALIGNED or DIMLINEAR Rotated command to draw the initial dimension.

3. Use the DIMEDIT Oblique command to change the angle of the extension lines to be parallel to the appropriate isometric lines.

4. Use the DIMEDIT Rotate command to rotate the text's baseline parallel to the appropriate isometric line.

Figure 27.24

Isometric dimensions.

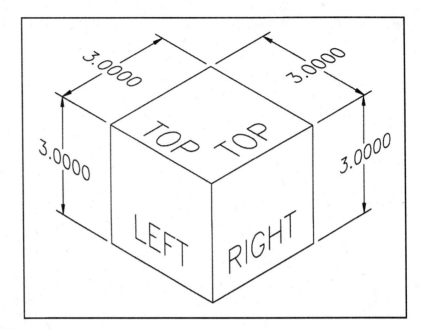

For dimensions that lie in the left isoplane, use the DIMEDIT Oblique option to change the angle of the extension lines to 150° or –30°. For dimensions that lie in the right isoplane, change the angle of the extension lines to 30° or 210°. For dimensions that lie in the top isoplane, change the angle of the extension lines to 30, –30, 150 or 210°. You must define text styles with the appropriate oblique angles, because you cannot modify the oblique angle of the dimension text style after the dimension is drawn, unless you redefine its style.

Tip   Although the obliqued text styles you defined in the previous section work in dimensions, you might want to define styles with narrower width, as discussed in Chapter 21, "Introduction to Dimensioning."

If you use the wrong text style to draw a dimension, you can use the DDMODIFY command to change the text style of the dimensions object.

In the following exercise, you dimension the part you drew in the previous exercise.

Dimensioning in Isometric Drawings

You finish off the CHAP27 drawing by dimensioning the part. You begin by adding an overall length dimension along the bottom plane of the base. Because some of the points you dimension are not on an isoline, but all the dimensions are parallel to isolines, you must use the DIMLINEAR Rotated command to place some of these dimensions.

`Command:` *Choose* Draw, Dimensioning, Linear	Issues the DIMLINEAR command
`First extension line origin or RETURN to select:` *Use ENDP object snap and pick at* ① *(see fig. 27.25)*	Sets first extension line origin
`Second extension line origin:` *Use ENDP object snap and pick at* ②	Sets second extension line origin
`Dimension line location (Text/Angle/ Horizontal/Vertical/Rotated:` `R` `Enter`	Sets rotated option
`Dimension Line angle <0>:` `-30` `Enter`	Sets dimension line angle to –30°
`Dimension line location (Text/Angle/ Horizontal/Vertical/Rotated:` *Pick at* ③	Places linear dimension

Next, you use the DIMEDIT Oblique command to align the extension line with the isoplane.

`Command:` *Choose* Draw, Dimensioning Oblique	Issues the DIMEDIT command, Oblique option
`Command: _dimedit Dimension Edit (Home/New/Rotate/Oblique) <Home>: _o Select objects:` *Pick the dimension you just created, and press enter*	
`Enter obliquing angle (RETURN for none:` `30` `Enter`	Sets angle of extension lines to 30°

Repeat the process and place a dimension across the width of the part at the right end. You will encounter a problem, however. You trimmed away the hidden lines as you drew the part. You need to cheat a little to place this dimension.

`Command:` *Choose* Draw, Dimensioning, Aligned	Issues the DIMALIGNED command
`First extension line origin or RETURN to select:` *Use an ENDP object snap and choose the end of the line at* ④	Places first dimension point
`Second extension line origin:` *Use an ENDP object snap and pick at* ⑤	Places second dimension point
`Dimension line location (Text/Angle):` *Pick at* ⑥	Locates dimension line

continues

continued

Command: *Choose* Draw, Dimensioning Oblique	Issues the DIMEDIT command, Oblique option
```Command: _dimedit Dimension Edit (Home/New/Rotate/Oblique) <Home>: _o Select objects:``` *Pick the dimension you just created, and press Enter*	
```Enter obliquing angle (RETURN for none: -30``` (Enter)	Sets angle of extension lines to –30°

Next, you use the MOVE command to move the dimension from the upper plane of the base to the lower plane.

Command: *Choose* Modify, Move *and pick the last dimension*	Issues the MOVE command
```Base point or displacement: 1<270``` (Enter)	Moves dimension to align with bottom of base
```Second point of displacement:``` (Enter)	
Command: (Enter)	Reissues MOVE command
```Select objects: P``` (Enter)	Selects Previous selection set
```Base point or displacement: .5<330``` (Enter)	Moves dimension away from drawing entities
```Second point of displacement:``` (Enter)	

Figure 27.25

Isometric dimensions.

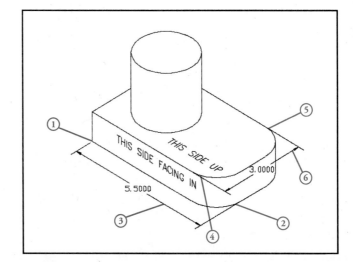

Drawing Other Types of Features

If you need to draw types of features (such as an inclined plane or an ellipse) other than those already discussed, you need to apply the appropriate drafting construction techniques. If you draw a certain type of feature repeatedly, consider having an AutoLISP routine written to automate it. Alternatively, you might be able to create a block out of the feature and just insert it whenever you need it.

Note An isometric drawing is just another 2D drawing. Everything you learned about plotting 2D drawings applies to isometric drawings. If the plot is to be just a pictorial (which is true more often than not), use the Scaled to Fit plot scale section.

In this chapter, you learned how to make a crude but serviceable imitation of a 3D drawing. Although isometrics like this are easy to create, they are limited compared to true 3D models. In the next three chapters, you learn how to create true three-dimensional objects.

27

CHAPTER

28

3D Basics

Generally speaking, you deal with three basic forms of 3D modeling: wireframe, surface, and solid modeling. You can use AutoCAD to generate all three types.

A *wireframe model* consists of a framework of 3D lines and curves and has no surfaces whatsoever. In effect, a wireframe model is a skeletal model. You can see right through a wireframe model because no surfaces block your view. For example, suppose you create a wireframe model of two cubes lined up one behind the other (see fig. 28.1).

Figure 28.1

Wireframe models versus surface models.

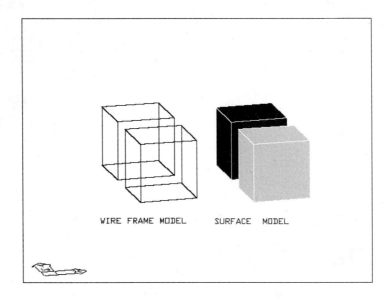

WIRE FRAME MODEL   SURFACE MODEL

You can see right through the first cube to the second cube because no surfaces block your view.

A *surface model*, on the other hand, consists of surfaces only. The surfaces are opaque and can block your view. The second cube is partially obscured in the second illustration of figure 28.1, blocked from your view by the first cube.

A *solid model* also has surfaces that are opaque but more importantly, by definition, the surfaces of a solid model enclose a portion of space. Software capable of handling solid models can distinguish the interior of a solid from the exterior, which in turn, enables you to manipulate solid models in ways unavailable when you use other types of models.

You can use AutoCAD to generate all three types of models. AutoCAD, however, normally displays all forms as wireframe models. This means that if you were to create a wireframe, surface, and solid model of the preceding example of two cubes, all of them would appear identical and as a wireframe model most of the time. Only when you use certain commands does the true nature of a model become obvious. In the strictest definition of the term wireframe, you can only call a model a wireframe model if it consists exclusively of lines and curves and no surfaces. In the AutoCAD world, however, the term wireframe model applies to all three forms of models if you are displaying them as wireframes.

In this chapter, you learn how to do the following:

◆ Generate simple surface models by extruding 2D objects

- ◆ View 3D models from various viewing angles

- ◆ Plot a 3D model directly from model space

- ◆ Compose a layout for a 3D model using paper space

- ◆ Pick points in 3D space using XYZ point format, object snap modes, point filters, cylindrical coordinates and spherical coordinates

- ◆ Carry out basic editing and construction commands on 3D models

- ◆ Apply UCSs in a 3D environment

This chapter serves as an introduction to 3D modeling. You learn how to create more sophisticated surface and solid models in the remaining chapters of this book. The first step, however, is to try some of the 3D modeling methods. In the following exercise, you create a three-dimensional wireframe of a workbench (see fig. 28.2) and view it in 3D space.

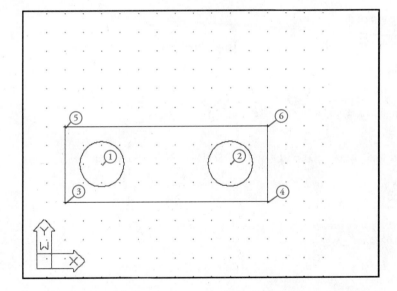

Figure 28.2

Plan view of bench.

28

Quick 5¢ Tour

Begin a new drawing named CHAP28, using the ACAD.DWG drawing as the prototype drawing.

Create a new layer named BENCH and make it current. Set the limits from 0,0 to 80,70. Set snap spacing to 5 and turn it on. Turn on the grid. Turn off solid fill. Set object thickness to 15, and then zoom all.

continues

continued

In the following steps, you create cylinders that serve as the legs of the bench.

Command: *Choose* Draw, Circle, *then* Center, Radius	Issues the CIRCLE command
_circle 3P/2P/TTR/<Center point>: *Pick* ① at 20,30 *(see fig. 28.2.)*	Sets the center of the circle
Diameter/<Radius>: **6** (Enter)	Sets the radius
Command: (Enter)	Repeats the last command
CIRCLE 3P/2P/TTR/<Center point>: *Pick* ② at 55,30	Sets the center of the circle
Diameter/<Radius> <6.0000>: (Enter)	Accepts default radius

Next, you draw the top of the bench.

Command: *Choose* Data, Object Creation	Issues the DDEMODES command and opens the Object Creation Modes dialog box
'_ddemodes *Type* **15** *in the* Elevation *edit box, type* **3** *in the* Thickness *edit box,* choose OK	Changes the current elevation and thickness settings
Command: *Choose* Draw, Polygon, 2D Solid	Issues the SOLID command
First point: *Pick the snap point with the coordinates 10,20 at* ③	Sets first point of solid
Second point: *Pick the snap point with the coordinates 65,20 at* ④	Sets second point of solid
Third point: *Pick the snap point with the coordinates 10,40 at* ⑤	Sets third point of solid
Fourth point: *Pick the snap point with the coordinates 65,40 at* ⑥	Sets fourth point of solid
Third point: (Enter)	Ends the SOLID command

Next, you view the 3D model.

New Riders Publishing
INSIDE SERIES

Command: *Choose* View, 3D Viewpoint Presets, SE Isometric	Displays nonplanar view of 3D model
Command: **HIDE** (Enter)	Generates a view with all hidden lines removed

Save your drawing.

The bench is viewed in wireframe as shown in figure 28.3 even though it has surfaces. The surfaces become apparent only after you issue the HIDE command.

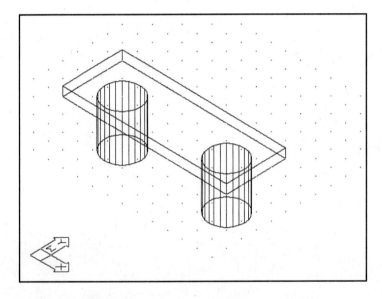

Figure 28.3

3D wireframe of bench.

Adding Elevation and Thickness

Before you learn how to make your first 3D model, you should understand the following terms:

♦ **XY plane.** An XY plane is a flat, 2D surface that contains the X and Y axis. There are an infinite number of parallel XY planes but every 2D drawing you have created up to this point has utilized the XY plane with a Z coordinate of 0.

♦ **Z axis.** The Z axis is the third axis of a 3D coordinate system. The other two are the X and Y axes. The Z axis is always perpendicular to the XY plane (see fig. 28.4).

28

Figure 28.4

Z coordinate or elevation.

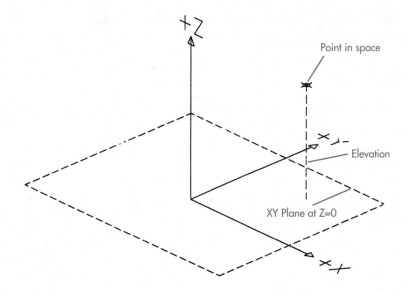

◆ **Plan view.** A plan view is a view of the XY plane in which the Z axis is parallel to your line of sight.

◆ **Elevation.** An object's elevation is its position as measured along the Z axis from the XY plane that has a Z value of 0. An object elevation also is referred to as its Z coordinate.

◆ **Thickness.** An object's thickness is its length as measured along the Z axis. Thickness describes an object's height when the object is an extruded 2D object.

You can create a basic 3D surface model by taking an ordinary 2D object and giving it a third dimension: thickness. You might be wondering where you can find this third dimension in an AutoCAD drawing. If you visualize your monitor screen as the XY plane (refer to fig. 28.4) on which you draw, then the Z axis is perpendicular to the monitor screen. You cannot see the Z axis because until now you have been working in a plan view of 3D space.

In the next two sections, you learn how to set an object's elevation and thickness.

Setting the Current Elevation

So far, you have not had to supply Z coordinates when you specify points. When you type in coordinates, you supply only a pair of numbers, X and Y. In fact, point coordinates are a triplex of numbers —X, Y, and Z, and are recorded as such in the

drawing database. When you do not supply a Z coordinate, AutoCAD automatically assigns the default Z coordinate (which is normally 0) to your points. Did you ever notice that the coordinates displayed by ID, LIST, or DDMODIFY always have a Z component that always seems to be zero? Now you know where the zero came from and why.

You can use the DDEMODES command to change the default Z coordinate (also known as the *current elevation*) at any time. You access DDEMODES, if you recall, by choosing Data, Object Creation.

You also can use the ELEV command to change the default elevation.

'ELEV. The ELEV command enables you to change the current elevation and thickness.

ELEV does not appear anywhere on the menus, so you must type it before you can use it. After you issue ELEV, AutoCAD prompts you to enter a new current elevation and thickness. The next section covers thickness. The current elevation is stored in the system variable ELEVATION, so another way to change the value is to type the system variable ELEVATION.

The current elevation can be positive or negative. All objects are at the current elevation plane unless you override it by specifying an absolute Z coordinate value. AutoCAD displays the grid on the elevation plane.

In a 3D model, you can draw an object above or below another object by using different Z coordinates. In addition to being able to set the elevation of 2D objects, you also need to know how to give a 2D object thickness.

Setting the Current Thickness

Before you can call an object a 3D object, you must give it three dimensions. Everything you have drawn up to this point has had only two dimensions: length and width as measured along the X and Y axes. You can create a 3D object from a 2D object simply by giving the 2D object a thickness.

AutoCAD automatically assigns the current thickness to every object you draw. By default, the current thickness is normally zero and that is why all the objects you have drawn thus far have been 2D. Just as you can use the DDEMODES command to set the current elevation, so too can you use it to set the current thickness. You also can use the ELEV command to change the current thickness. The system variable THICKNESS holds the current thickness and you can use it to change the value directly, as well.

When you assign a 2D object a nonzero thickness, AutoCAD extrudes that object along the Z axis, which transforms it into a 3D object. If the thickness is positive, AutoCAD extrudes the 2D object in the positive Z direction, which converts the original 2D object to the base of the new 3D object. If the thickness is negative, AutoCAD extrudes the 2D object is extruded in the negative Z direction, which changes the original 2D object to the top of the new 3D object. Figure 28.5 provides examples of a cylinder on the left projected up with positive thickness value and a cylinder on the right projected down with a negative thickness value.

Figure 28.5

Extruding 2D objects.

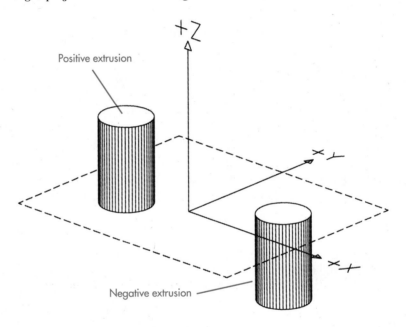

If you do an inquiry on a 3D object formed by extrusion, the Z value of the object's defining points is always the Z value of the original 2D object. For example, if you list a 3D cylinder that was formed by extruding a circle in the positive Z direction, the coordinates that appear are those of the original 2D circle, which is the base of the cylinder.

All the objects you have learned to draw, other than text and dimensions, are affected by the current thickness. Text and dimension objects are always drawn with zero thickness, regardless of the current thickness setting.

In the following exercise, you take an incomplete 3D model of a city's downtown area and add a new building.

Extruding 2D Objects

Begin a new drawing named CHAP28A, using the IA Disk prototype drawing CITY.DWG with the named view BLOCK_F restored and current. The restored view is a plan view of the area for this drawing exercise.

Command: *Choose* Data, Object Creation	Issues DDEMODES command and opens the Object Creation Modes dialog box
'_ddemodes *Type* **50** *in the* Thickness *edit box and choose* OK	Changes the current thickness settings
Command: *Choose* Draw, Polygon, 2D Solid	Issues the SOLID command
_solid	
First point: *Pick the snap point with the coordinates 420,820* ① *(see fig. 28.6)*	Sets the first point to 420,820
Second point: *Pick the snap point with the coordinates 680,820* ②	Sets the second point to 680,820
Third point: *Pick the snap point with the coordinates 420,1080* ③	Sets the third point to 420,1080
Fourth point: *Pick the snap point with the coordinates 680,1080* ④	Sets the fourth point to 680,1080
Third point: **Enter**	Ends the SOLID command

Because you do not specify a Z coordinate, AutoCAD uses the current elevation (which is currently 0) as the Z coordinate when it records the points in the drawing database.

Command: *Choose* Data, Object Creation	Issues DDEMODES command and opens the Object Creation Modes dialog box
'_ddemodes *Type* **50** *in the* Elevation *edit box*, **300** *in the* Thickness *edit box and choose* OK	Changes the current elevation and thickness settings
Command: *Choose* Draw, Circle, *then* Center, Radius	Issues the CIRCLE command
3P/2P/TTR/<Center point>: **550,950** **Enter**	Sets the center point at ⑤

continues

28

continued

Because you did not supply a Z coordinate, AutoCAD uses the current elevation and records the point as 550,950,50.

```
Diameter/<Radius>: 100 (Enter)          Sets the radius
```

Save your work.

Your drawing should now resemble figure 28.6 and although it might not look like it, your two extruded 2D objects, a solid and a circle, occupy 3D space. In the next exercise, you issue some commands so that you can actually view the 3D building you just drew.

Figure 28.6

The new building you just drew.

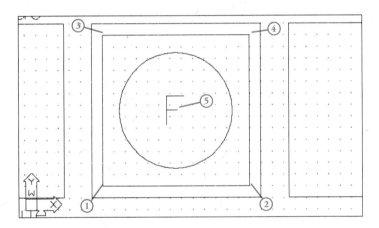

Coplanar... What's That?

Coplanar, in the context of AutoCAD, means "on the same XY plane." All the objects you have learned to draw thus far are considered to be 2D objects, even after you extrude them into 3D objects. Unlike true 3D objects, all points within 2D objects must be coplanar. In practical terms, this means that the points that define the object must all have the same Z coordinate. For example, the vertex points of a polyline must all have the same Z coordinate. A true 3D object, on the other hand, can be defined by points that have differing Z coordinates. In the next chapter, you learn to draw true 3D objects. For now, you work with extruded 3D objects only.

As a rule of thumb, for a 2D drawing command that requires that you select several points, only the Z coordinate of the first point is significant because it defines the elevation of the entire object. If you try to specify points of varying elevations for a particular drawing command, the exact results vary from command to command but, in general, the command refuses to use the points. For example, the SOLID and

PLINE commands refuse to accept XYZ coordinates for all points except the first point.

An additional general rule is to not try to supply XYZ coordinates after the first point prompt of a 2D drawing. The exception is the LINE command. LINE accepts XYZ coordinates at all times and interprets them correctly, because a line is actually a true 3D object. Until now, you simply have not been using the LINE command to its full potential.

Viewing Your 3D Model

Your current viewpoint is directly above the XY plan. Your line of sight is parallel to the Z axis, perpendicular to the XY plane. The resulting view is a 2D plan view of the model, whether it is a 2D or 3D model. Because of this viewpoint, you cannot see an object's height or its elevation relative to other 3D objects.

To see the third dimension, you need to learn a couple new display commands. Before you proceed with the new commands, now is a good time to learn a few terms, as defined in the following list.

◆ **Camera position.** If you use the analogy of a camera, you, the observer, are the camera through which the 3D model is being viewed. This is also known as the viewpoint.

◆ **Target point.** When you point a camera at a particular subject or concentrate on something in your field of vision, you are focusing on a distinct point known as the target point.

◆ **Line of sight.** This is the imaginary line that connects the camera's position with the target point.

The following sections introduce you to several new display commands that enable you to generate both planar and nonplanar views of a 3D model.

The DDVPOINT Command

The DDVPOINT command is the first new display command you learn. DDVPOINT uses the Viewpoint Presets dialog box (see fig. 28.7).

DDVPOINT. The DDVPOINT command enables you to use the Viewpoint Presets dialog box to set the current viewpoint for the current viewport.
Pull-down: *Choose* View, 3D Viewpoint, Rotate

28

Figure 28.7

*The Viewpoint
Presets dialog
box.*

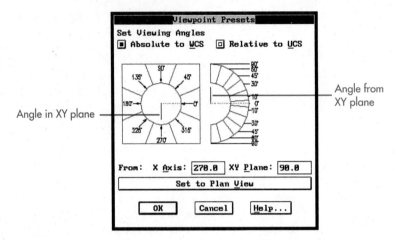

You define the viewpoint with the two angles: an angle in the XY plane and an angle from the XY plane (see fig. 28.8).

Figure 28.8

*The defining
angles for
viewpoint.*

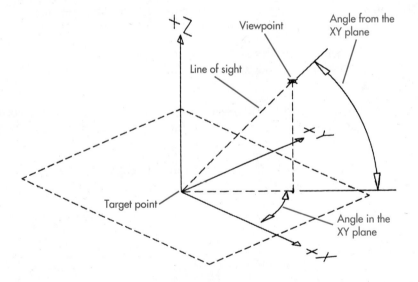

These two angles combine to determine the observer's position relative to the target point. The target point itself is unchangeable and is always positioned in the middle of the drawing extents.

The graphics on the left side of the Viewpoint Presets dialog box represent the angle to the viewpoint in the XY plane as measured from zero degrees (X axis). The red line indicates the current angle, which also appears in the From X axis edit box. The target point is in the middle of the circle and the observer's point is outside of the

circle. You also can think of the red line as the current line of sight connecting the two points. You set this angle by picking points in the graphics or by typing a value in the edit box. If you pick a point beyond the circle, AutoCAD rounds the angle to the nearest displayed angle. If you pick a point within the circle, the angle is set to the point you select.

The graphics on the right side represent the angle from the XY plane, to the observer's position. The red line indicates the current value, which also appears in the From XY plane edit box. The target point is in the center of the arc and the observer's point is outside of the arc. You also can think of the red line as the current line of sight that connects the two points. You can set this angle by picking points in the graphics or by typing a value in the edit box. If you pick a point beyond the arc, AutoCAD rounds the angle to the nearest displayed angle. If you pick a point within the arc, AutoCAD sets the angle to the point you select.

As you pick points, AutoCAD draws a white or black line to represent the new angle (or line of sight).

By default, the two angles are defined relative to the world coordinate system (WCS). To define the angles relative to the current user coordinate system (UCS), select the Relative to UCS option at the top of the Viewpoint Presets dialog box.

Tip Do not set the option to define the angles relative to the current UCS until you are completely comfortable with working with UCSs in a 3D environment. You easily can get disoriented doing so. Working with UCSs in a 3D environment is discussed in the section "Using UCS in 3D" later in this chapter.

When you use the DDVPOINT command, the target point is always located in the middle of the drawing extents and the observer point is always located beyond the drawing extents. Consequently, the view you get is always that of an observer standing beyond the periphery. The actual distance between the target and observer points does not effect the generation of the view. AutoCAD uses the two points only to define the line of sight.

After you define the line of sight, AutoCAD generates the corresponding view in the current viewport. The initial view always is one of the entire model. After AutoCAD displays the initial view, you can zoom or pan the view.

If you want to generate a plan view, you set the angle from the XY plane to 90 degrees. DDVPOINT automatically resets the angle in the XY plane to 270 degrees after you choose the OK button. Choosing the Set to Plan View button is a quick way to set the angle from the XY plane to 90 and the angle in the XY plane to 270.

In the following exercise, you use DDVPOINT to get a 3D view of the CHAPT28A drawing of the city.

28

Getting a Nonplanar View

Continue to use the drawing CHAP28A. In the following steps, you generate a nonplanar view and zoom in on the building you just drew.

Command: *Choose* View, 3D Viewpoint, Rotate	Issues the DDVPOINT command and opens the Viewpoint Presets dialog box
Command: *Pick* ① *(see fig. 28.9)*	Sets the angle in the XY plane
Command: *Pick* ②	Sets the angle from the XY plane
Command: *Choose* OK	Ends the DDVPOINT commands
Command: *Choose* Zoom, Window	Issues ZOOM with the Window option
First corner: *Pick* ① *(see fig. 28.10)*	
Other corner: *Pick* ②	Zooms in along the current line of sight

Save your work.

Figure 28.9

Set angles in the Viewpoint Presets dialog box.

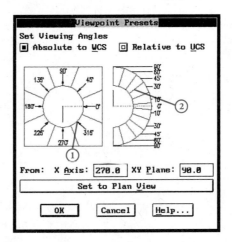

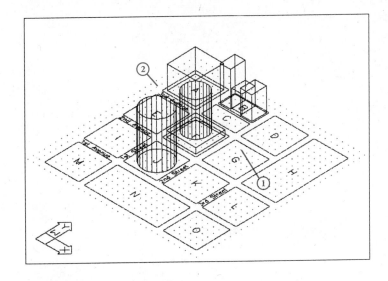

Figure 28.10

3D view of city.

28

The VPOINT Command

The VPOINT command is the ancestor of the DDVPOINT command. DDVPOINT's Viewpoint Presets dialog box provides you with the functionality of the VPOINT command (selection of angles in the XY plane and from the XY plane), but in a more graphic manner.

> **VPOINT.** The VPOINT command enables you to set the current viewing point for the current viewport.
> Pull-down: *Choose* View, 3D Viewpoint
> Screen: *Choose* VIEW, Vpoint

The prompt of the VPOINT command is as follows:

```
Rotate/<View point> <0.0000,0.0000,1.0000>:
```

Although VPOINT does not have the nice graphics that DDVPOINT has, it still is a useful command that offers three options. The 3D Viewpoint submenu has two menu items that trigger options of the VPOINT command, Tripod and Vector. The third option, Rotate, does not appear on the submenu.

◆ **Tripod.** Selecting this menu item brings up VPOINT's compass and axes tripod display (see fig. 28.11). The compass and tripod display enables you to set your viewing position dynamically. The icon in the upper-right corner of the screen is the compass. A pair of shorter crosshairs appears in place of the usual crosshairs. The XYZ icon in the center of the display is the tripod. The tripod represents the positive direction of the X, Y, and Z axes. As you move your crosshair about the compass, the tripod display adjusts to show the corresponding orientation of the XYZ axes.

◆ **Vector.** This menu item issues the VPOINT command with its default option of setting the viewing position by vector. The vector is simply a set of XYZ coordinates to the viewing point from the target point.

◆ **Rotate.** The third option of VPOINT, Rotate, enables you to set the viewing point by defining an angle in the XY plane and an angle from the XY plane, to the new viewing point. The Rotate option is the command-option equivalent of the Viewpoint Presets dialog box (DDVPOINT command). The Rotate menu item in the 3D Viewpoint submenu triggers the DDVPOINT command, not the Rotate option of the VPOINT command, therefore, you must use the screen menu VPOINT command to access the rotate option.

Figure 28.11

VPOINTS's compass and axes tripod.

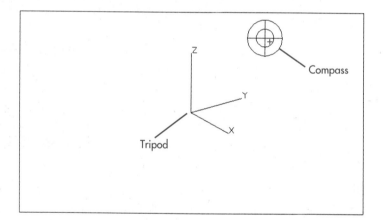

The Compass and Tripod

The compass is a 2D representation of 3D space. You set the viewing point by picking a point within the compass, which sets the angle in the XY plane and the angle from the XY plane simultaneously (see fig. 28.12).

New Riders Publishing
INSIDE SERIES

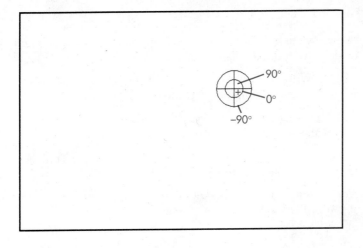

Figure 28.12

The angle from the XY plane.

The center point of the compass and the two circles define the angle from the XY plane. If you pick the exact middle of the compass, you place the observer directly above the XY plane (90 degrees) and the resulting view is a plan view. If you pick a point within the inner circle, the angle from the XY plane is between 0 and 90 degrees. If you pick a point on the inner circle, the angle from the XY plane is 0 and the resulting view is an elevation view of the model.

If you pick a point between the inner and outer circles, the angle from the XY plane is between 0 and –90 degrees and you see your model from a point below it. If you pick a point on the outer circle, then the angle from the XY plane is –90 degrees. You should not pick a point beyond the outer circle—it is ineffective and the results are unpredictable (although harmless).

The vertical and horizontal lines in the compass represent 0, 90, 180, and 270 degrees in the XY plane. The pick point's position relative to the vertical and horizontal compass lines determines the new angle in the XY plane.

If you type the VPOINT command and want to access the Tripod option, simply press Enter at the first VPOINT prompt.

The Vector as a Line of Sight

The following is a series of commonly used vectors and the orthographic views that correspond to them:

Vector	Resulting View
0,0,1	Plan view. The equivalent of an angle in the XY plane of 270 and an angle from the XY plane of 90.
1,0,0	Right Elevation view. The equivalent of an angle in the XY plane of 0 and an angle from the XY plane of 0.
0,1,0	Back Elevation view. The equivalent of an angle in the XY plane of 90 and an angle from the XY plane of 0.
–1,0,0	Left Elevation view. The equivalent of an angle in the XY plane of 180 and an angle from the XY plane of 0.
0,–1,0	Front Elevation view. The equivalent of an angle in the XY plane of 270 and an angle from the XY plane of 0.

Tip Use DDVPOINT when you want to set the viewpoint precisely and use VPOINT's Tripod option when you want some visual feedback as you choose angles. Use VPOINT's Vector or Rotate options when you want to change the viewpoint from within a LISP or ADS program, or script file.

Unlike DDVPOINT, VPOINT does not have an option that allows you to choose the WCS or UCS as the basis of the angle settings. If you set the system variable WORLDVIEW to 1, VPOINT uses the WCS. If you set WORLDVIEW to 0, VPOINT uses the UCS. Using the system variable WORLDVIEW, you can change the variable setting to affect VPOINT in the desired manner.

WORLDVIEW also affects DDVPOINT. As a matter of fact, the option in DDVPOINT that enables you to choose the WCS or UCS is a direct link to the WORLDVIEW variable. When you choose Absolute to WCS in the Viewpoint Presets dialog box (DDVPOINT command), AutoCAD sets the WORLDVIEW variable value to 1. When you choose Relative to UCS, AutoCAD sets the WORLDVIEW variable value to 0.

In the following exercise, you use the VPOINT command to get another 3D view of the city.

Getting Another View

Continue to use the drawing CHAP28A.

Command: *Choose* View, 3D Viewpoint, Tripod	Issues VPOINT with the Tripod option
Command: *Pick* ① *(see fig. 28.13)*	Sets the angle in the XY plane and angle from the XY plane

New Riders Publishing
INSIDE SERIES

The resulting viewpoint is on the left side and above the model.

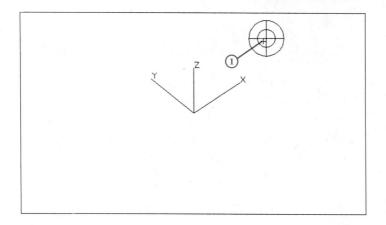

Figure 28.13

Viewpoint selection with the Tripod option.

The PLAN Command

You can use the PLAN command to generate plan views.

> **PLAN.** The PLAN command enables you to generate a plan view of your model in the current viewport.
> Pull-down: *Choose* View, 3D Viewpoint Presets, Plan View
> Screen: *Choose* VIEW, Plan

The options of PLAN are as follows:

```
<Current UCS>/Ucs/World:
```

The default option is to generate a plan view of the current UCS. The Ucs option enables you to generate a plan view of a named UCS. The World option enables you to generate a plan view of the world UCS, regardless of the current UCS.

In the following exercise, you use the PLAN command to generate a plan view of the city.

Returning to a Plan View

Continue to use the drawing CHAP28A.

Command: *Choose* View, 3D Viewpoint Presets, Plan View, Current	Issues the PLAN command with the Current UCS option

---

Another way to generate a plan view is to use the Viewport Presets dialog box (DDVPOINT command) and choose the Set to Plan View button to reset the angles to correspond to a plan view.

3D Viewpoint Presets

Choosing 3D Viewpoint Presets from the View pull-down menu brings up the submenu shown in figure 28.14.

Figure 28.14

The 3D Viewpoint Presets submenu.

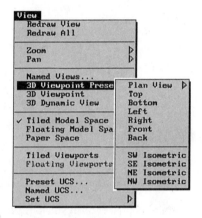

You can use this submenu to change your viewing point to one of several preset positions. The top menu item, Plan View, brings up another submenu that lists the options for the PLAN command (see the section "The Viewpoint Command"). The other menu items issue the VPOINT command with preset vectors. The following table lists the vectors used for each menu item and the equivalent angles you would use with VPOINT's Rotate option or DDVPOINT to get the same view.

TABLE 28.1

The 3D Viewpoint Presets Menu with Corresponding Vectors and Angles

Menu Item Label	Equivalent Vector	Equivalent Angles (in degrees)	
Top	0,0,1	In XY: 270	From XY: 90
Bottom	0,0,−1	In XY: 270	From XY: −90
Left	−1,0,0	In XY: 180	From XY: 0

New Riders Publishing
INSIDE SERIES

Menu Item Label	Equivalent Vector	Equivalent Angles (in degrees)	
Right	1,0,0	In XY: 0	From XY: 0
Front	0,–1,0	In XY: 270	From XY: 0
Back	0,1,0	In XY: 90	From XY: 0
SW Isometric	-1,-1,1	In XY: 225	From XY: 45
SE Isometric	1,–1,1	In XY: 315	From XY: 45
NE Isometric	1,1,1	In XY: 45	From XY: 45
NW Isometric	–1,1,1	In XY: 135	From XY: 45

Four possible isometric views of the object from the bottom (in addition to the four preset isometrics) are available using vectors (– Z vector) or angles (– angle).

Note   The orientations defined in the Presets submenu are always relative to the WCS, regardless of the WORLDVIEW setting.

In the following exercise, you use the 3D Viewpoint Presets pull-down menu to generate a 3D view, then save it by name for future reference.

Yet Another View

Continue to use the drawing CHAP28A.

Command: *Choose* View, 3D Viewpoint Presets, NE Isometric	Issues the VPOINT command with a vector of 1,1,1

The resulting view is an isometric of the front, right side, and top of the city.

Command: *Choose* View, Named Views	Issues the DDVIEW command and opens the View Control dialog box
Choose the New *button*	Opens the Define New Name dialog box
Type **NE-ISO** *in the* **N**ew Name *edit box and choose the* **S**ave View *button, then* OK	Saves the new view name

Save your drawing for future use.

28

3D Model Views in Multiple Viewports

At times, you might discover that you need to switch back and forth between certain views of your model as you draw and edit. Although naming the views certainly eases switching them, a yet easier alternative exists. Remember viewports, discussed in Chapter 10, "Working in Model and Paper Space Viewports"? If you configure your drawing window for multiple viewports, each viewport can have a different view (with its own viewpoint) of the model. For example, if you have three viewports configured, one viewport can have a plan view, another can have an elevation view, and the third can have an isometric view. You then can select the view that is convenient for editing and drawing and make it the current viewport. You even can pick a different current viewport as you edit when that particular view becomes more convenient, freely moving from one viewport to another as you work.

In the following exercise, you set up multiple viewports and restore a different view of your 3D model in each of the viewports.

Working with Multiple Viewports

Begin a new drawing named CHAP28B, using the CITY1 drawing from the IA Disk as a prototype.

Command: *Choose* View, Tiled Viewports, 3 Viewports	Issues VPORTS with the 3 Viewports option
`Save/Restore/Delete/Join /SIngle/?/2/<3>/4:` **3**	
`Horizontal/Vertical/Above/Below/ Left/<Right>:` (Enter)	Accepts the default 3 Viewport division with the larger vertical viewport on the right
Pick the top left viewport to make it current	
Command: *Choose* View, Named Views	Issues the DDVIEW command and opens the View Control dialog box
Pick BLOCK_F *from the* Views *list and choose the* Restore *button*	Restores the selected view to the current viewport
Pick the bottom left viewport to make it current	
Command: *Choose* View, 3D viewpoint Presets, Right	Issues the VPOINT command with a vector of 1,0,0

Save the drawing.

You now have three viewports with three individual views (each with its own view-point) of the same 3D model. Your drawing should look like figure 28.15.

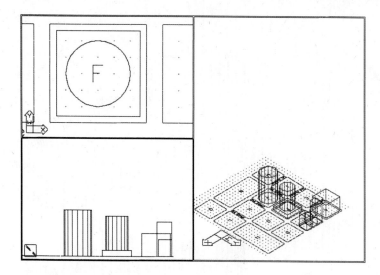

Figure 28.15

Multiple views of the city model.

Removing Hidden Lines

AutoCAD usually displays extruded 3D objects as wireframe models, even though they actually are surface models. The surfaces, however, do not become apparent in the model display until you issue one of several display control commands. One such display control command is the HIDE command.

HIDE. The HIDE command enables you to remove hidden lines from the current view.
Screen: *Choose* Tools, Hide
Pull-down: *Choose* Tools, Hide

The HIDE command enables you to generate a version of the current view in which objects or portions of objects are being obscured by surfaces. Edges that are obscured are referred to as *hidden lines*. Figure 28.16 shows two cylinders with their hidden lines removed.

You can work in a view in which the hidden lines are removed, just as you can with a normal wireframe view. You must keep in mind that you simply cannot see portions or all of certain objects. Because parts of the model are missing, you should avoid using this view to edit your model. To restore the wireframe view, issue the REGEN command.

28

Figure 28.16

Hidden lines removed from back cylinder.

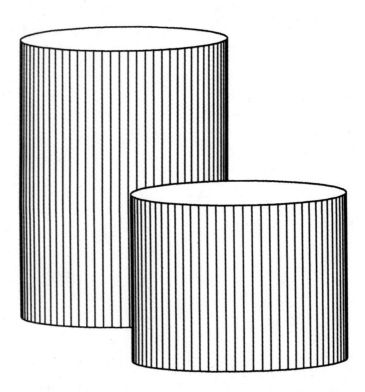

If you have multiple viewports configured, HIDE affects only the view in the current viewport. If you issue the HIDE command in several viewports and want to restore all viewports to a wireframe display, just issue the REGENALL command.

The DDVIEW and VIEW commands do not save the actual display information, just the locations of the observer and target points. You cannot use these commands to save the views you generate when you use the HIDE command. In Chapter 30, "3D Views, Renderings, and Presentations," you learn how to use slides to save views generated by HIDE so that you can recall them quickly and easily at a later date.

HIDE enables you to see the surfaces generated by giving objects thickness. Some 2D objects, such as circles, solids, and polylines, that have a width, have top and bottom surfaces. For example, a circle that has a thickness is a cylinder that has a top and bottom (see fig. 28.17).

Tip

The SOLID command is a quick and easy way to generate triangular and quadrilateral 3D shapes that have top and bottom surfaces. A solid is filled in plan view, but not in a nonplanar view. If you prefer not to have the solids filled in plan view, use the FILL command or the FILLMODE variable to turn off FILLMODE. To affect existing solids, issue the REGEN command.

New Riders Publishing

INSIDE
SERIES

Other 2D objects, such as lines, arcs, and polylines that have a width of 0, do not have top and bottom surfaces. If you use the RECTANG command with a polyline width set for 0 and extrude it through some given thickness to draw a rectangle, you get a box that has four sides but no top or bottom (see figure 28.17).

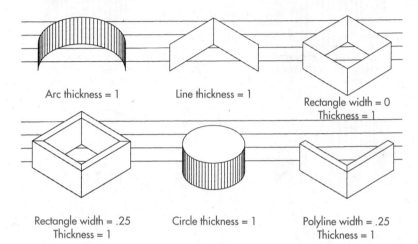

Arc thickness = 1   Line thickness = 1

Rectangle width = 0
Thickness = 1

Rectangle width = .25   Circle thickness = 1   Polyline width = .25
Thickness = 1   Thickness = 1

Figure 28.17

Examples of 2D objects extruded into a 3D model.

 Tip   Circles extruded into cylinders of a given thickness always have a top and bottom, therefore you cannot have an open ended cylinder as an extrusion of a circle. You can extrude a pair of semicircles (closed on each other) to generate an open ended cylinder.

Text objects (created using TEXT, DTEXT and MTEXT), as you may recall, are always drawn with zero thickness. Unfortunately, HIDE does not properly recognize text objects that have zero thickness. Consequently, text objects are not hidden correctly until you assign the objects at least some nominal thickness (such as 0.01 units). You can use DDMODIFY, DDCHPROP, or CHANGE to change an object's thickness or, preferably, set the correct thickness before you insert the text objects into your drawing.

The other object that is never given a thickness is a dimension. Unlike text objects, HIDE does recognize dimension objects correctly.

 Tip   A wireframe model can play tricks with your vision. You might think you are viewing the model one way, but in fact, you are viewing the model from a completely different viewing point. You might think you are seeing the top-front-right isometric view and actually you are seeing the bottom-front-right view. You can issue the HIDE command to clarify the situation (see fig. 28.18). After you finish using the view, issue the REGEN command to restore the wireframe display of the model.

28

Figure 28.18

Using the HIDE command to understand 3D models.

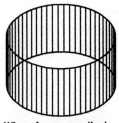

Wire frame cylinder
(BOTTOM—FRONT—RIGHT)
VPOINT <1,1,-1>

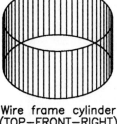

Wire frame cylinder
(TOP—FRONT—RIGHT)
VPOINT <1,1,1>

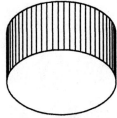

Cylinder after hide
(BOTTOM—FRONT—RIGHT)
VPOINT <1,1,-1>

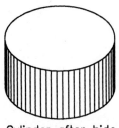

Cylinder after hide
(TOP—FRONT—RIGHT)
VPOINT <1,1,1>

In the following exercise, you use the hide command to more clearly understand your 3D model of the city.

The Effect of HIDE on Text

Continue to use the drawing CHAP28B. You should have three viewports open with the right viewport as the current viewport.

Command: *Choose* Tools, Hide	Issues the HIDE command, which performs hidden line removal in current viewport
Command: *Pick the lower-left viewport to make it current*	
Command: (Enter)	Repeats the HIDE command, which performs hidden line removal in current viewport

In the right viewport, you can see the text through the surfaces, because the text objects have zero thickness. Before HIDE can recognize the text properly, you must change the thickness of the text.

Command: *Pick the right viewport to make it current*

New Riders Publishing
INSIDE
SERIES

Command: *Choose* Modify, Properties	Starts selection set

```
(ai_propchk)
Select objects: Select all the
text objects
```

Select objects: (Enter)	Issues DDCHPROP command and opens the Change Properties dialog box

Change the value in the Thickness *edit box to* **0.1** *and choose* OK

Command: **HIDE** (Enter)	Issues the HIDE command, which performs hidden line removal in current viewport

This time, HIDE recognizes the text and that some of the text objects should now be hidden.

Command: **REGENALL** (Enter)	Regenerates the views in all viewports

The model reappears as a wireframe model in all viewports.
Save the drawing.

Plotting Your 3D Model

Now you know how to create and view simple 3D models. How about plotting the model? You still use the PLOT command (Chapter 25, "Sheet Composition and Plotting"), but with a couple of twists. If you plot from model space or floating model space, you must enable the Hide option in the PLOT command to have hidden lines removed from the plot. The HIDE command affects only the display, not the plotted output.

As far as scale is concerned, more often than not, you plot 3D views for pictorial purposes. Consequently, you find that you use the Scaled to Fit option more with plots of 3D views.

Paper space (covered in Chapters 10 "Working in Model and Paper Space Viewports," and 25 "Sheet Composition and Plotting") is a powerful tool for composing a layout that consists of multiple views of the same model. You can set each floating viewport to display a different view of the model. One floating viewport can display a plan view while another displays an elevation view. Composing a layout of a 3D model is similar to composing a layout of a 2D model. The main difference is the use of the DDVPOINT, VPOINT, or PLAN commands when you set the views in the individual floating viewports. Paper space also allows you to scale each viewport separately, control layers differently in each viewport, freeze edges of viewports, and turn the view within each viewport on or off as needed.

MVSETUP is the command that enables you to automate laying out a title block and floating viewports. If you use MVSETUP with a 3D model and choose the Standard Engineering viewport layout (under the Create option), MVSETUP creates four viewports and automatically sets the views as follows:

Viewport Location	View
Upper-left viewport	Plan View
Upper-right viewport	SE Isometric
Lower-left viewport	Front Elevation
Lower-right viewport	Right Elevation

If you want to remove the hidden lines from the viewports when you plot, you must use the Hideplot option of the MVIEW command to tag the viewport objects from which you want to remove the hidden lines. Then, when you go to plot in paper space, the hidden lines are removed. The Hide option of the PLOT command does not work when you plot from paper space but does work when you plot from a floating model space viewport.

 Tip Unfortunately, the extra lines AutoCAD draws to show curved surfaces (tessellation lines) do plot. You cannot suppress display or plotting of tessellation lines. If you absolutely cannot live with the tessellation lines, you must generate a solid model rather than a surface model. Solid models are covered in Chapter 31, "Solid Modeling."

In the following exercise, you compose a layout for the 3D model of the city.

Composing a Layout for CITY

Continue to use the drawing CHAP28B. Create a new layer named TITLE and make it the current layer.

In the following steps, you switch to paper space, create a title block, and create four viewports.

Command: *Choose* View, Paper Space	Sets TILEMODE to 0 and issues PSPACE command
Command: *Choose* View, Floating Viewports, MV Setup	Issues the MVSETUP command
Initializing...	

 New Riders Publishing
INSIDE
SERIES

`Align/Create/Scale`
`viewports/Options/Title`
`block/Undo:` **T** (Enter)
	Specifies the Title block option

`Delete objects/Origin/Undo` `/<Insert title block>:` (Enter)	Accepts the default option
`Available title block options:`	Lists available title block/sheet borderline combinations 1 through 13
`Add/Delete/Redisplay/` `<Number of entry to load>:` **11** (Enter)	Specifies an ANSI-E title block
`Create a drawing named` `ansi-e.dwg? <Y>:` **N** (Enter)	Declines the option to write the title block out to a drawing file (WBLOCK)

`Align/Create/Scale`
`viewports/Options/Title`
`block/Undo:` **C** (Enter)
	Specifies the Create option

`Delete objects/Undo/` `<Create viewports>:` (Enter)	Accepts the default option to create floating viewports

`Available Mview viewport layout options:`

```
0:  None
1:  Single
2:  Std. Engineering
3:  Array of Viewports
```

`Redisplay/<Number of entry to` `load>:` **2** (Enter)	Specifies a Standard Engineering layout that consists of four viewports

`Bounding area for viewports.`

`Default/<First point >:` *Pick* ①
(see fig. 28.19)

`Other point:` *Pick* ②	Defines the area in which to locate the viewports
`Distance between viewports in X.` `<0.0>:` **.5** (Enter)	Sets the horizontal spacing between viewports to 0.5 units
`Distance between viewports in Y.` `<0.5>:` (Enter)	Sets the vertical spacing between viewports to 0.5 units

`Align/Create/Scale viewports/Options/`
`Title block/Undo:` (Enter)

continues

continued

In the following steps, you turn on the hideplot setting for the viewports to ensure that the views have their hidden lines removed during PLOT.

Command: *Choose* View, Floating Viewports, Hideplot	Issues the MVIEW command with the Hideplot option
ON/OFF: **ON** (Enter)	Specifies the ON option
Select objects: *Select the four viewports*	Turns on hiding for the selected viewports
Select objects: (Enter)	Terminates selection
Command: *Choose* File, Print	Issues the PLOT command

Choose F̲u̲ll *preview and choose the* P̲review *button*

You should see that the views do get the hidden lines removed in the plot preview.

Choose OK *(if plotter set up and ready)*

Save your drawing.

Figure 28.19

Place viewports on ANSI-E drawing.

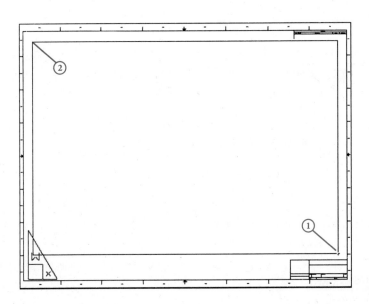

Picking Points in 3D

In the first portion of this chapter, you learned to assign elevations to points by setting the current elevation before you pick new points. This technique is not always convenient, so this section provides you with several methods that enable you to override the default elevation setting and explicitly assign the Z coordinate for the pick point.

Typing in Z Values

All points are recorded in the AutoCAD database in an XYZ format. When you specify a point by entering just an XY coordinate pair, AutoCAD automatically uses the current elevation as the missing Z coordinate. An easy way to override the current elevation is to specify a point by supplying the point's Z coordinate, in addition to just the X and Y coordinates.

In the following exercise, you add another building to the CITY model.

Adding Another Building

Continue to use the drawing CHAP28B, and set layer BUILDINGS current.

Command: *Choose* View, Tiled Model Space   Switches you back to model space

Command: *Pick the right viewport*
to make it current

Command: *Choose* View, Named Views   Issues DDVIEW command and opens the
View Control dialog box

Select BLOCK_L *from the* Views *list,*   Restores the view to the current viewport
choose Restore *button, then* OK

Next, you add a building in the area you just set up.

Command: *Choose* Data, Object   Issues the DDEMODES command and opens
Creation   the Object Creation Modes dialog box

Change the value in the Thickness   Changes Thickness, keep Elevation set
edit box to 100   at 50

Choose OK   Closes dialog box with current settings

continues

28

continued

Choose Draw, Polygon, 2D Solid	Issues the SOLID command
_solid First point: **1120,470,0** (Enter)	Sets first point at elevation 0
Second point: **1380,470** (Enter)	Sets second point
Third point: **1120,730** (Enter)	Sets third point
Fourth point: **1380,730** (Enter)	Sets fourth point
Third point: (Enter)	Terminates SOLID
Command: *Choose* Data, Object Creation	Issues the DDEMODES command and opens the Object Creation Modes dialog box
Change the value in the Thickness *edit box to* **200**	Changes Thickness, keep Elevation set at 50
Choose OK	Closes dialog box with current settings

Next, you draw the remainder of the building.

Choose Draw, Polygon, 2D Solid	Issues the SOLID command
First point: **1160,510,100** (Enter)	Sets first point at elevation 100
Second point: **1340,510** (Enter)	Sets second point
Third point: **1160,690** (Enter)	Sets third point
Fourth point: **1340,690** (Enter)	Sets fourth point
Third point: (Enter)	Terminates SOLID

Save your drawing, which should look like figure 28.20.

AutoCAD ignored the current elevation setting for both objects because the Z coordinate was supplied for the first point. The rule of thumb when you specify a Z coordinate for a draw command is to supply it only for the first point. All other points for a draw command assume the Z coordinate of the first point. As a matter of fact, if you try to specify a Z coordinate for any other points of the SOLID command, you receive an error message.

New Riders Publishing
INSIDE SERIES

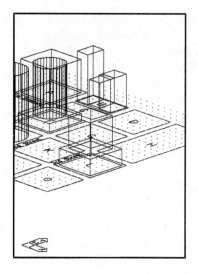

Figure 28.20

*Building with
elevations
specified in Z
coordinates.*

Using Object Snap

If you use object snap to pick a point, AutoCAD uses the XYZ coordinate of the
selected point, regardless of the current elevation setting. You might wonder what
object snap modes work with extruded 2D objects.

Any object snap mode that works with the original 2D object works with the extruded
version. Furthermore, the object snap modes work with both the top and bottom
surfaces of the 3D object. For example, an extruded circle becomes a cylinder. Using
center object snap mode, you can pick the center point of the top circular face or the
bottom circular face.

You might wonder whether you can use object snap on the vertical lines of the
cylinder. The purpose of the vertical lines, also referred to as *tessellation lines*, is to
help you better visualize the curved surface. You cannot select them in any way,
except for the tessellation lines that appear at the endpoints of a line or line segment
of a polyline—you can select these tessellation lines with object snap modes, just like
an ordinary line.

 Tip   As a rule, never try to select an object snap point on the plan view of an extruded
3D object. The problem is that in plan view, every point you can select on the top
surface has a corresponding point immediately below it on the bottom surface. Your
pick is ambiguous—AutoCAD doesn't know whether you mean to select the point
on the top or bottom surface. To avoid ambiguity when you select points, use a view
that clearly isolates the point you want to select.

28

One object snap mode designed specifically for 3D work is the APPINT, or apparent intersection, mode. This mode enables you to select the apparent intersection point of two objects that have different elevations but that overlap each other in the current view. AutoCAD uses the smallest Z coordinate of the objects involved for the apparent intersection point. For example, if you use object snap to attach to the apparent intersection point of two circles, the first with an elevation of 1 and the other with an elevation of 2, AutoCAD assigns the apparent intersection point the Z coordinate of 1. Be careful when you use this mode, because the apparent intersection of two objects changes according to the selected viewing point.

Using Object Snap

Continue to use the drawing CHAP28A. Restore the view BLOCK_M to the right viewport.

Command: *Choose* Data, Object Creation	Issues the DDEMODES command and opens the Object Creation Modes dialog box
Change the value in the **T**hickness *edit box to* **50**	Changes Thickness, keep Elevation set at 50
Choose OK	Closes the dialog box with current settings

Next, you draw the bottom portion of the building with a cylinder.

Command: *Choose* Draw, Circle, *then* Center, Radius	Issues the CIRCLE command
3P/2P/TTR/<Center point>: **200,250,0** (Enter)	Sets center at elevation 0
Diameter/<Radius>: **125** (Enter)	Sets radius

Next, you draw the top portion of the building with an elliptical cylinder.

Command: *Choose* Ellipse, Center	Issues the ELLIPSE command with the Center option
Center of ellipse: *Use* CEN *object snap mode and pick* ① *(see fig. 28.21)*	Sets center of ellipse at the center of the top circular surface
Axis endpoint: **@100<0** (Enter)	Sets first axis endpoint
<Other axis distance>/Rotation: **@75<90** (Enter)	Sets second axis endpoint

Save your drawing.

New Riders Publishing
INSIDE
SERIES

The preceding exercise demonstrates that you can use object snap to pick points on solids (the center of the extruded top of the cylinder) and that the ellipse cannot have thickness greater than 0. The ellipse and SPLINE commands always generate objects that have 0 thickness, regardless of the setting for THICKNESS.

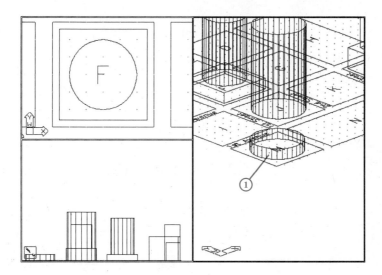

Figure 28.21

Cylindrical solid extruded from a circle.

Using Grips

If you use grip points to edit your objects, AutoCAD always uses the elevation of the grip points rather than the current elevation setting. What grip points are on an extruded 3D object? The same grip points that were on the original 2D object are on the top and bottom surfaces of the extruded 3D object. Tessellation lines do not have grip points.

Never try to select a grip point on an extruded 3D object using the plan view of the object, because in plan view, every point you can select on the top surface has a corresponding point immediately below it on the bottom surface. Use a view that clearly shows the separation between the top and bottom objects such as an isometric view.

In the following exercise, you use grip points to edit the building you drew in the previous exercise.

Editing Solids with Grip Points

Continue to use the drawing CHAP28B. You still should have a 3D view of the building you just drew in the right viewport. Use the PAN command to adjust the view to match figure 28.22.

Command: *Pick the cylinder at* ① *(see fig. 28.22)*	Preselects object and displays available grip points

You can see all grip points clearly in this view.

Command: *Press Esc*	Deselects object but leaves grip points available
Command: *Pick the ellipse at* ②	Preselects object and displays available grip points
Command: *Pick* ③	Makes the grip point hot and initiates grip editing commands

```
** STRETCH **
<Stretch to point>/ Base point/Copy/
Undo/eXit: Enter
```
Skips to the next grip command

```
** MOVE **
<Move to point>/Base point/Copy/
Undo/eXit: C Enter
```
Selects the Copy option

```
** MOVE **
<Move to point>/Base point/Copy/
Undo/eXit: Pick grip at ④
```
Copies selected object to the selected grip point

```
** MOVE **
<Move to point>/Base point/Copy/
Undo/eXit: X Enter
```
Terminates grips editing

Press Esc twice   Turns off grip points

Save your work for future use.

This exercise demonstrates that you can use grip points on solids to copy from one Z coordinate elevation to another without needing to worry about current settings of thickness and elevation.

New Riders Publishing
INSIDE SERIES

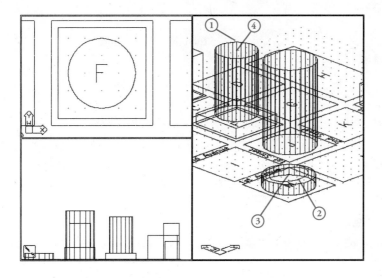

Figure 28.22

Solids and grip points.

Using Filters

Usually, if you pick points without using object snap or grips, AutoCAD uses the current elevation setting for the elevation of those points. If you want to override the current elevation without using object snap or grips, invoke the .XY filter before you pick the point. The .XY filter tells AutoCAD that the new point will be a combination of the X and Y coordinates of the point you are about to pick and a Z coordinate that you will supply separately (by typing or picking another point). You even can use filters in combination with object snap, but remember to invoke the filter before the object snap mode.

In the remaining exercises, you develop a series of models for a library of 3D furniture. In the following exercise, you use filters to create a table.

Using Filters

Begin a new drawing named CHAP28C, using the default prototype drawing ACAD.DWG.

Set limits from 0,0 to 60,60. Set snap spacing for 2 and turn it on. Turn on the grid. Turn off solid fill, then zoom all.

The table you are about to draw will be part of a library of symbols, so draw it on layer 0.

Command: **THICKNESS** (Enter)   Starts system variable THICKNESS

continues

continued

New value for THICKNESS <0.0000>: **24** (Enter)	Sets the current thickness
Command: *Choose* Draw, Circle, *then* Center, Radius	Issues the CIRCLE command
_circle 3P/2P/TTR/<Center point>: **30,30** (Enter)	Sets the center of the circle
Diameter/<Radius>: **6** (Enter)	Sets the radius

In the following steps, you draw the table top.

Command: **THICKNESS** (Enter)	Starts THICKNESS system variable
New value for THICKNESS <24.0000>: **2** (Enter)	Sets the current thickness
Command: *Choose* Draw, Circle, *then* Center, Radius	Issues the CIRCLE command
CIRCLE 3P/2P/TTR/<Center point>: *Type* **.XY** (Enter)	Specifies .XY point filter
of *Pick the snap point with coordinates* 30,30	Specifies point for center
(need Z): **24** (Enter)	Sets Z coordinate of center point
Diameter/<Radius> <6.0000>: **24** (Enter)	Creates a circle with radius of 24
Command: *Choose* View, 3D Viewpoint Presets, SW Isometric	Generates a 3D view
Command: **HIDE** (Enter)	Issues the HIDE command
Command: **BASE** (Enter)	Issues the BASE command
Base point <0.0000,0.0000,0.0000>: *Using Center object snap, pick the base of the table*	Sets new drawing insertion point

Use the SAVEAS command to save your drawing as TABLE-24, which should appear as shown in figure 28.23.

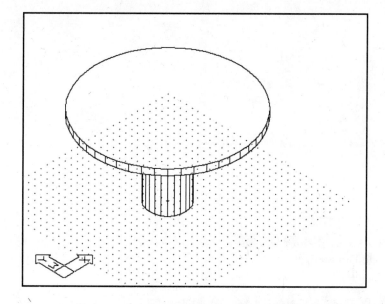

Figure 28.23
Solids and point filters.

Cylindrical and Spherical Coordinates

Besides being able to specify points in the Cartesian format of X, Y, Z, you also can use cylindrical or spherical coordinates. Cylindrical coordinates are defined as an angle in the XY plane and a distance along the Z axis as shown in figure 28.24. The format for cylindrical coordinates is as follows:

```
XY distance<angle,Z distance (for absolute coordinates)
```

or

```
@XY distance<angle,Z distance (for relative coordinates)
```

To define the point, you specify the point's projected distance and angle in the XY plane from the origin, and the Z distance from the XY plane. The term *cylindrical* derives from the fact that if you vary the angle and Z distance values for a given XY distance, the resulting points form a cylinder.

Tip Another way to think of cylindrical coordinates is that they consist of a polar coordinate, distance<angle, with a Z component. Cylindrical coordinates can be especially useful when you specify 3D relative coordinates because it allows input of polar distance and angle, and elevation in the Z coordinate as a single input step.

28

Figure 28.24

Cylindrical coordinates.

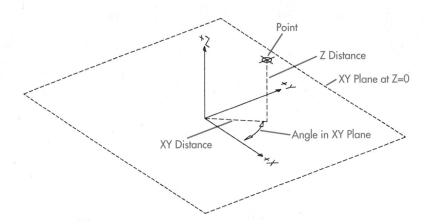

Spherical coordinates are defined as a distance from the origin to the point, an angle in the XY plane, and an angle from the XY plane, as shown in figure 28.25. Spherical coordinates use a different format, as follows:

```
XYZ distance<Angle in XY plane<Angle from XY plane (for absolute coordinates)
```

or

```
@XYZ distance<Angle in XY plane<Angle from XY plane (for relative coordinates)
```

Figure 28.25

Spherical coordinates.

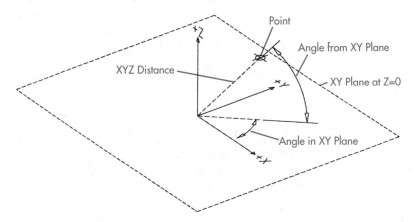

Spherical coordinates require the XY distance from the origin to the point, an angle in the XY plane, and an angle from the XY plane.

This format is called *spherical* because all the possible combinations of angle values for a given distance produce a group of points that form a sphere. Describing a point in spherical coordinate format is very similar to what you do to set a viewing point. In

New Riders Publishing
INSIDE
SERIES

both cases, you give two angles, an angle in the XY plane, and an angle from the XY plane. You just have the additional information of the actual distance to the point for spherical coordinates.

Editing in 3D

So far, you have learned to assign an elevation and thickness to new objects. Now, you learn how to change an existing object's elevation and thickness and to perform other common editing functions in 3D.

Modifying Thickness and Elevation

You can take several approaches to edit the elevation and/or thickness of existing objects. If you just want to change the elevation or thickness of one or a few select objects, you can use DDMODIFY.

In the DDMODIFY dialog box (the Modify Circle dialog box in figure 28.26 is an example), an edit box exists for the object's thickness, but not a field for the object's elevation. You must remember that an object's elevation is synonymous with the Z coordinate of the points that define the object. So, for this example (see fig. 28.26), the circle is defined by a center point and radius. Therefore, to change the elevation of the circle, you change the Z coordinate of the center point.

 Note The name and arrangement of the dialog box that appears when you issue the DDMODIFY command varies according to the object type.

28

```
                    Modify Circle
  Properties
    Color...      ■ BYLAYER    Handle:            24
    Layer...      0            Thickness:       2.0000
    Linetype...   BYLAYER      Linetype Scale:  1.0000
  Center
    Pick Point <
    X: 30.0000     Radius:         24.0000
    Y: 30.0000     Diameter:       48.0000
    Z: 30.0000     Circumference:  150.7964
                   Area:           1809.5574

            OK       Cancel     Help...
```

Figure 28.26

The Modify Circle dialog box.

If you want to change the thickness of a number of objects, you should use the DDCHPROP command. DDMODIFY and DDCHPROP are triggered by choosing Edit, Properties from the pull-down menu. If you select a single object, AutoCAD issues DDMODIFY, but if you select several objects, AutoCAD issues DDCHROP. Unfortunately, you cannot use DDCHPROP to change the elevation of objects.

To change the elevation of a group of objects, you can resort to using the CHANGE command, which does have an option for changing the elevation of selected objects. You also can use the MOVE command (or the move mode of grips) to move the objects to the new Z coordinate.

Tip
A good way to change an object's elevation is to use the MOVE command with relative coordinates. For example, to move an object 2 units in only the positive Z direction, you would type **@0,0,2** for the point to which to move after you select an appropriate base point. If you want to move an object a certain distance and direction in the XY plane and also change its elevation, use cylindrical coordinates. For example, if you want to move an object 2 units in a 45 degree direction in the XY plane and 3 units in the Z direction, you would type **@2<45,3** for the point to which to move after you select an appropriate base point.

When you change the thickness of an extruded 3D object, the surface that was the original 2D object remains stationary. The other surface—the extruded surface—moves.

In the following exercise, you change the thickness and elevation of several objects.

Changing Elevation and Thickness

Continue to use the drawing you saved as TABLE-24. First, you change the thickness of the base of the table.

`Command:` *Choose* Modify, Properties	Starts menu macro
`(ai_propchk)` `Select objects:` *Select the base of the table (12-unit cylinder)*	
`Select objects:` **Enter**	Menu macro initiates DDMODIFY because only one object is selected
Change the value in the Thickness *edit box to* **30**	
Choose OK	The table top is 6 units below the top of the base
`(ai_propchk)`	
`Command:` *Choose* Modify, Properties	Starts menu macro
`Select objects:` *Select the table top*	

New Riders Publishing
INSIDE
SERIES

Select objects: (Enter)   Initiates DDMODIFY because only one object
                                           is selected

Change the value in the Z *edit box*
for the center point to **30**

Choose OK   The table top now moves up 6 units

Use the SAVEAS command to save your drawing as TABLE-30 as a part of a library of symbols.

Using Z in the Commands You Know

For the most part, all the editing commands with which you are already familiar
accept XYZ points. Remember, not only can you specify Z by typing XYZ coordinates,
but also by using filters, grips points, and object snap modes. What the commands do
with the Z, however, varies with the individual command.

◆ **MOVE.** This command enables you to move an object from one elevation to
  another while at the same time moving the object in the XY plane.

◆ **STRETCH.** In general, this command does not enable you to stretch a portion
  of an object from one elevation to another with one exception, LINE. If you try
  to stretch an extruded 3D object in the Z direction, the object just ends up
  moving in the Z direction. You can use STRETCH to move the endpoint of a
  line from one elevation to another, which stretches the entire line, because a
  line is not coplanar. You can stretch a line because it is the only object that you
  know how to draw that does not have to be coplanar. You cannot use STRETCH
  to change the thickness of any object.

◆ **COPY.** This command enables you to create copies at elevations different from
  the original object's elevation.

◆ **SCALE.** This command enables you scale up or down a 3D object, in a uniform
  manner about the specified base point. If the base point you pick has a Z
  coordinate different from the object's, the scaling operation also changes the
  object's Z coordinate.

◆ **ROTATE.** This command accepts XYZ points but treats the angle of rotation as
  the rotation angle in the XY plane. The net effect is that you can use ROTATE
  only to rotate objects in the XY plane.

◆ **MIRROR.** This command accepts only a 2D mirror line. If you try to use
  coordinates with Z values to specify the mirror line, you get an error message.
  The end result is that you can use MIRROR only to mirror objects in the XY
  plane.

◆ **ARRAY.** This command accepts only 2D points. If you try to specify any XYZ points, you get an error message. The net effect is that you can use ARRAY only to create new objects in the XY plane.

In the following exercise, you use some editing commands to create a new table.

A Square Table

Begin a new drawing named CHAP28D, using the default prototype drawing ACAD. First, you set up the drawing environment.

Set limits from 0,0 to 60,60. Set snap spacing for 2 but turn it off. Turn on the grid. Turn off solid fill, then zoom all.

The table you are about to draw will be part of a library of symbols, so draw it on layer 0.

Now you draw the table leg.

Command: **ELEV** (Enter)	Issues the ELEV command
New current elevation <0.0000>: (Enter)	Accepts current elevation
New current thickness <0.0000>: **15** (Enter)	Sets current thickness
Command: *Choose* Draw, Line	Issues the LINE command
From point: **4,6** (Enter)	Starts line
To point: **@1<0** (Enter)	
To point: **@1<90** (Enter)	
To point: **@1<180** (Enter)	
To point: **C** (Enter)	Closes and ends LINE

Next, you create the three remaining table legs.

Command: *Choose* Construct, Array, Rectangular	Issues Array with Rectangular option
_select Select objects: *Select the four lines you just drew*	

New Riders Publishing
INSIDE SERIES

```
4 found
Select objects: (Enter)

_array
Select objects: P
4 found
Select objects
Rectangular or Polar array(R/P) <R>:_r
```

`Number of rows ( --- ) <1>: 2 `(Enter)	Specifies number of rows
`Number of columns ( ¦¦¦ ) <1>: 2 `(Enter)	Specifies number of columns
`Unit cell or distance between rows` `( --- ): 17 `(Enter)	Sets row separation
`Distance between columns ( ¦¦¦ ): 17 `(Enter)	Sets column separation
Command: *Choose* View, 3D Viewpoint Presets, SE Isometric	Issues the VPOINT command

```
_vpoint
Rotate/<View point> <0.0000,0.0000,1.0000>:
_non *1,-1,1 Regenerating drawing.
```

Next, you draw the table top.

Command: **THICKNESS** (Enter)	Issues the THICKNESS system variable
`New value for THICKNESS` `<15.0000>: `**1.5** (Enter)	Sets current thickness
Command: **SOLID** (Enter)	Issues the SOLID command
`First point: `**8,32** (Enter)	
`Second point: `**@20<0** (Enter)	
`Third point: `**@-20,20** (Enter)	
`Fourth point: `**@20<0** (Enter)	
`Third point: `(Enter)	Ends SOLID
Command: **Z** (Enter)	Issues the ZOOM command

`ZOOM`
`All/Center/Dynamic/Extents/Left/Previous/`
`Vmax/Window/<Scale(X/XP)>: `**a** (Enter)
	Issues Zoom with All option

```
Regenerating drawing.
```

continues

28

continued

Command: **Z**   Issues the ZOOM command, using alias

ZOOM   Zooms with image reduced to 90% of
All/Center/Dynamic/Extents/Left/Previous/   previous to provide working space
Vmax/Window/<Scale(X/XP)>: **.9X** (Enter)

Regenerating drawing.

Command: **HIDE** (Enter)   Issues the HIDE command and removes
                                                             hidden lines showing 3D position of objects

Regenerating drawing.

Next, you move the table top onto the legs.

Command: *Choose* Modify, Move   Issues the MOVE command

_move
Select objects: *Select the solid you
just drew*

1 found

Select objects: (Enter)   Completes selection of objects to move

Base point or displacement: *Choose* From   Specifies the From object snap
from pop-up menu

_from
Base point: *Using* ENDPoint object snap,   Specifies the point to offset from
pick ① *(see fig. 28.27)*

_endp of <Offset>: **@1,1** (Enter)   Specifies the offset

Second point of displacement: *Using*
ENDPoint object snap, *pick* ②

Command: **BASE** (Enter)   Issues the BASE command

Base point <0.0000,0.0000,0.0000>:
Select From *option from pop-up menu*   Select From option

_from Base point: *Select* Endpoint *option
from pop-up menu*

_endp of *Pick* ③   Specifies the point to offset from

<offset> @-1,-1 (Enter)   Specifies the offset

Use the SAVEAS command to save your drawing as TABLE-S, a square table in your new symbol library.

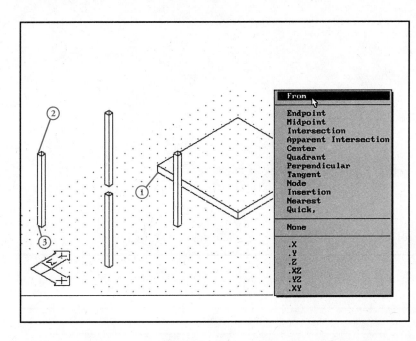

Figure 28.27
MOVE table top.

The next exercise is a continuation of the previous square table drawing exercise and you use your previous work, modified using the STRETCH command, to produce a second similar rectangular table. The resulting table will be another symbol (the fourth) in your growing library of symbols.

A Rectangular Table

Continue to use the drawing you saved as TABLE-S in the previous exercise.

Command: PLAN (Enter)   Generates a plan view

<Current UCS>/Ucs/World: (Enter)   Accepts the Current UCS default

Command: Z (Enter)   Issues the ZOOM command, using alias

ZOOM   Zooms with image reduced to 75% of
All/Center/Dynamic/Extents/Left/Previous/   previous to provide working space
Vmax/Window/<Scale(X/XP)>: **.75X** (Enter)

continues

continued

Regenerating drawing.

Command: *Choose* Modify, Stretch	Issues the STRETCH command

```
_stretch
Select objects to stretch by crossing
-window or -polygon
```

Select Objects: *Pick first corner at* ① *(see fig. 28.28)*	Sets a crossing window
Other corner: *Pick* ②	
9 found	
Select objects: **(Enter)**	Completes selection set
Base point or displacement: *Pick* ③	
Second point of displacement: @6,0 **(Enter)**	Stretches table 2 units in the 0 degree direction

Use the SAVEAS command to save your drawing as TABLE-R, a rectangular table in your new symbol library.

Figure 28.28

Stretch table to rectangular shape.

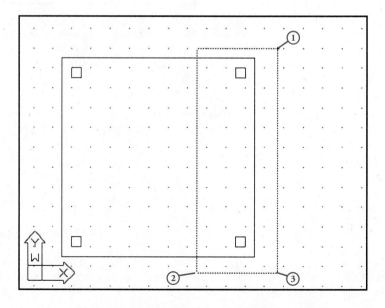

The ROTATE3D Command

The ROTATE3D command is the 3D version of the ROTATE command.

ROTATE3D. The ROTATE3D command enables you to rotate objects about any axis you want to define in 3D space.
Screen: *Choose* CONSTRCT, Rotat3D
Pull-down: *Choose* Construct, 3D Rotate

Unlike the ROTATE command, ROTATE3D does not restrict you to rotating objects in the XY plane. In other words, ROTATE3D enables you to rotate objects about the Z axis. 3DROTATE enables you to rotate objects about the X, Y, or Z axis, or even an arbitrary axis that you define.

ROTATE3D has the following options:

◆ **Entity.** The Entity option enables you to set the axis of rotation based on a selected object. The only objects you can select are a line, circle, arc, or 2D polyline. If you select a line or a line segment of a polyline, AutoCAD determines the axis of rotation according to the endpoints of the line. If you select a circle, arc, or an arc segment of a polyline, AutoCAD defines the axis as a line that passes through the center of the arc or circle, perpendicular to the plane of the arc or circle.

◆ **Line.** ROTATE3D uses the endpoint of the line as its rotation point and uses the two endpoints of the line to define the axis.

◆ **Circle.** The line that is perpendicular to the plane in which the circle lies and also passes through the center of the circle becomes the axis of rotation.

◆ **Arc.** Same as for a circle.

◆ **Pline.** If you pick a line segment, AutoCAD defines the axis as when you select a line. If you pick an arc segment, AutoCAD defines the axis as when you select an arc.

◆ **Last.** The Last option uses the axis of rotation defined the last time ROTATE3D was used during the current AutoCAD session. This option works only after ROTATE3D has been used at least once during the current AutoCAD session.

◆ **View.** Sets the axis of rotation to be perpendicular to the plane of the current viewport, passing through a point you select.

28

◆ **Xaxis.** Sets the axis of rotation parallel to the X axis and passing through the point selected.

◆ **Yaxis.** Sets the axis of rotation parallel to the Y axis and passing through the point selected.

◆ **Zaxis.** Sets the axis of rotation parallel to the Z axis and passing through the point selected.

◆ **2points.** This is the default option and enables you to set the axis of rotation by picking two points through which the axis goes.

The hardest part of using 3DROTATE is figuring out the direction of positive rotation, which is where the right hand rule comes to the rescue. The right hand rule states that if you stick your right thumb out in the positive direction of the axis about which you are rotating, the curl of your fingers is the direction of positive rotation. Figure 28.29 shows the results of applying the right hand rule to the X, Y, and Z axes.

Figure 28.29

Direction of Positive Rotation about the X, Y and Z axes.

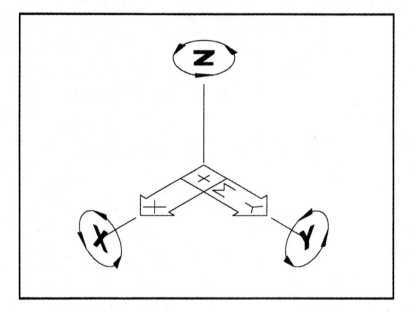

If you use the 2point option to define a rotation axis, the positive direction of the axis runs from the first point to the second point.

New Riders Publishing
INSIDE SERIES

Tip Using the Entity option to set the axis can be confusing, because the results vary according to the type of object. Avoid using this option unless you intend to use it often enough to get familiar with the object-dependent results. The other options are much easier to use and understand.

In the following exercise, you use ROTATE3D to construct a bookcase.

Construct Bookcase with ROTATE3D

Begin a new drawing named CHAP28E, using the default prototype drawing ACAD. First, you set up the drawing environment.

Set limits from 0,0 to 40,30. Set snap spacing for 2, but turn it off. Turn on the grid. Turn off solid fill, and then zoom all.

The bookcase you are about to draw will be part of a library of symbols, so draw it on layer 0.

Command: *Choose* Data, Object Creation	Issues the DDEMODES command and opens the Object Creation Modes dialog box
Change the value in the **T**hickness *edit box to* **72**	
Elevation is set to 0, *choose* OK	Closes dialog box with current settings
Command: *Choose* View, 3D Viewpoint Presets, SE Isometric	Issues the VPOINT command

```
_vpoint
Rotate/<View point> <1.0000,1.0000,1.0000>:
_non *1,-1,1 Regenerating drawing.
```

Next, you draw one side of the bookcase.

Command: *Choose* Draw, Polygon, 2D Solid	Issues the SOLID command

```
_solid
First point:6,18 (Enter)

Second point: @1<0 (Enter)

Third point: @-1,9 (Enter)
```

continues

continued

```
Fourth point: @1<0 (Enter)
```

```
Third point: (Enter)
```
Ends the SOLID command

Next, you copy the side you have drawn to use as the other side of the bookcase.

Command: *Select the solid*
you drew

Selects the solid and displays its
grips points

Command: *Make one of the grip*
points hot

Initiates grip command mode

```
** STRETCH **
<Stretch to point>/Base point/Copy/
Undo/eXit: (Enter)
```
Cycles to the MOVE grip edit mode

```
** MOVE **
<Move to point>/Base point
/Copy/Undo/eXit: C (Enter)
```
Specifies Copy option

```
** MOVE (multiple) **
<Move to point>/Base point
/Copy/Undo/eXit: @31<0 (Enter)
```
Specifies point to copy to

```
** MOVE (multiple) **
<Move to point>/Base point
/Copy/Undo/eXit: X(Enter)
```
Ends grip command mode

Next, you draw the two boards to use as the shelf.

Command: *Choose* Data, Object Creation

Issues the DDEMODES command and opens
the Object Creation Modes dialog box

Change the value in the Thickness
edit box to 1

Change Thickness, keep elevation set
at 0

Choose OK

Closes dialog box with current settings

Command: *Choose* Draw, Polygon, 2D Solid

Issues the SOLID command

```
_solid
First point: 7,19 (Enter)
```

```
Second point: @30<0 (Enter)
```

```
Third point: @-30,6 (Enter)
```

New Riders Publishing
INSIDE
SERIES

Fourth point: @30,0 `Enter`

Third point: `Enter`   Ends SOLID command

Command: *Choose* Data, Object Creation   Issues the DDEMODES command and opens
                                                 the Object Creation Modes dialog box

Change the value in the T̲hickness   Change Thickness, keep elevation set
edit box to **6**   at 0

Choose OK   Closes dialog box with current settings

Command: *Choose* Draw, Polygon,   Issues the SOLID command
2D Solid

_solid
First point: **7,25** `Enter`

Second point: **@30<0** `Enter`

Third point: **@-30,1** `Enter`

Fourth point: **@30<0** `Enter`

Third point: `Enter`   Ends SOLID command

Next, you rotate the shelf 10 degrees.

Command: *Choose* Construct, 3D Rotate   Issues the ROTATE3D command

_rotate3d

Select objects: *Pick* ① *and*   Selects objects to be rotated
② *(refer to figure 28.30)*

1 found
1 found

Select objects: `Enter`   Completes selection set

Entity/Last/View/Xaxis/Yaxis   Sets first point on axis of rotation,
/Zaxis/<2points>: *Using* Endpoint   you may need to zoom into view for control
object snap, pick ③   of endpoint selection

2nd point on axis: *Using* Endpoint   Sets second point on axis of rotation
object snap, pick ④

<Rotation angle>/Reference: **-10** `Enter`   Specifies rotation angle

continues

continued

Now, you move the shelf up three units.

Command: *Choose* Modify, Move	Issues the MOVE command
Select objects: **P** (Enter)	Selects previous selection set for MOVE
Select objects: (Enter)	Completes the selection set
Base point or displacement: *Pick* ① (*refer to figure 28.31*)	Sets base point for MOVE
Second point of displacement: @0,0,3 (Enter)	Sets point to move to

Save your work, so you can finish the shelves in the next exercise.

Figure 28.30

Construct and rotate 3D shelf.

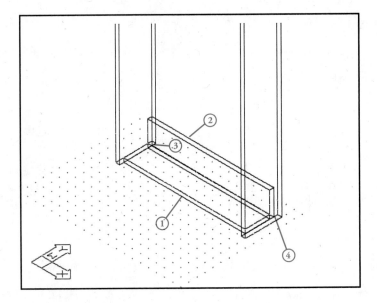

New Riders Publishing
INSIDE SERIES

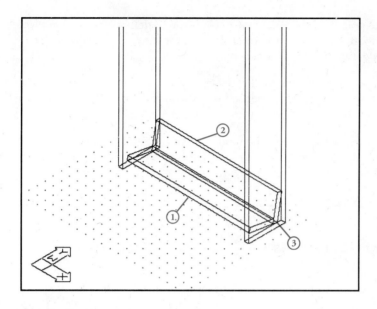

Figure 28.31
MOVE 3D shelf.

The 3DARRAY Command

The 3DARRAY command is the 3D version of the ARRAY command.

> **3DARRAY.** The 3DARRAY command enables you to construct rectangular and polar arrays in 3D space.
> Screen: *Choose* CONSTRCT, 3Darray
> Pull-down: *Choose* Construct, 3D Array, Rectangular

After you select the objects you want to array, you see the following prompt:

```
Rectangular or Polar array (R/P):
```

The options are very similar to the options you have with the ARRAY command. If you choose to construct a rectangular array, then in addition to asking you for the number of rows and columns, AutoCAD also asks you for the number of levels. The number of levels dictates the number of copies made in the Z direction. AutoCAD also asks you for the distance that separates adjacent rows, columns, and levels. If you use a negative row distance, AutoCAD builds the array in the negative Y direction; otherwise, it builds the array in the positive Y direction. If you use a negative column distance, AutoCAD builds the array in the negative X direction; otherwise, it builds the array in the positive Y direction. If you use a negative level distance, AutoCAD builds the array in a negative Z direction; otherwise, it builds the array in the positive Z direction.

28

If you choose the polar option (P), AutoCAD asks you to define an axis about which to make the rotation, in addition to prompting you for the number of items and angle to fill. You define the axis by selecting two points.

If you are not going to array through 360 degrees, you must take into account the direction of positive rotation. The direction of positive rotation is derived by using the right hand rule.

In the following exercise, you finish the model of the shelf unit that you started in the previous exercise. You use the ARRAY3D command to copy a column of shelves vertically up the side panels of the bookcase.

The 3DARRAY Command

Continue to use the drawing CHAP28E.

Command: `Z` **(Enter)**	Issues ZOOM command

`ZOOM`
`All/Center/Dynamic/Extents/Left`
`/Previous/Vmax/Window/<Scale`
`(X/XP)>:` `.7X` **(Enter)**
	Zooms out

Command: *Choose* Construct, 3D Array, Rectangular	Issues 3DARRAY menu macro
`_select` `Select objects:` *Pick* ① *and* ② *(refer to figure 28.31)*	Selects objects to be arrayed
`Select objects:` **(Enter)**	Completes selection set

`_3darray`
`Select objects: _p`
`2 found.`
`Select objects:`
`Rectangular or Polar array (R/P): _r`	

`Number of rows (---) <1>:` **(Enter)**	Accepts default number of rows
`Number of columns ( ¦¦¦ ) <1>:` **(Enter)**	Accepts default number of columns
`Number of levels (...) <1>:` `6` **(Enter)**	Sets number of levels
`Distance between levels` `(...):` `12` **(Enter)**	Sets distance between copies in the Z direction

New Riders Publishing
INSIDE
SERIES

Command: **BASE** (Enter)   Sets a base location

Base point <0.0000 0.0000 0.0000>:
Using ENDpoint objectsnap, pick ① (see fig. 28.32)

Command: **HIDE** (Enter)   Issues the HIDE command and displays the
                                                       bookcase (see fig. 28.32)

Use the SAVEAS command to save your drawing as BK-CASE in your library of symbols.

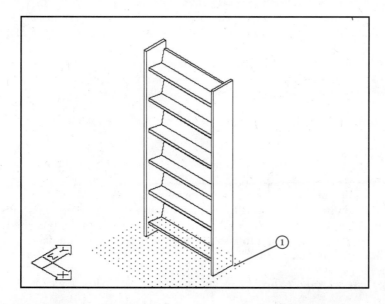

Figure 28.32
*Completed 3D
bookcase.*

28

The ALIGN Command

The ALIGN command is a combination of the MOVE and ROTATE commands
designed specifically for 3D space.

ALIGN. The ALIGN command enables you to align one surface with another surface
in 3D space.
Screen: *Choose* MODIFY, Align
Pull-down: *Choose* Modify, Align

After you select the objects you want to align, the ALIGN command prompts you to
supply up to three pairs of points. Each pair of points consists of a source point and a
destination point. A *source point* is a point on the selected objects. The *destination point*
is the point to which you want to move the source point. Every time you define a pair

of points, ALIGN draws a temporary line that connects the two to help you visualize the results. The temporary lines disappear when you issue a REDRAW or REGEN.

You do not have to supply all three pairs of points. If you supply one pair of points, the ALIGN command simply moves the selected objects in the direction and distance defined by the source (s1) and destination (d1) points. The net effect is the same as when you use the MOVE command.

When you supply two pairs of points, the ALIGN command moves the selected objects to the destination points so that the first source point (s1) coincides with the first destination point (d1) while the edge defined by the two source points (s1 and s2) is rotated to be in line with the edge defined by the two destination points (d1 and d2). You choose whether this rotation is to be a 2D or 3D transformation. If you opt for a 2D transformation, the move does not involve any change in elevation and the edge is rotated only enough to make them overlap in plan view but not necessarily to coincide.

With a 3D transformation, the first source and destination points coincide and the edges are rotated so that the edges coincide.

If you supply all three pairs of points, the plane (or face) defined by those three source points aligns with the plane (or face) defined by the three destination points. This alignment is carried out so that the first source point is moved to the first destination point. Then the edge defined by the first two source points coincides with the edge defined by the first two destination points. Then another rotation is carried out to make the plane defined by the three source points coincide with the plane defined by the three destination points.

In the following exercise, you use the ALIGN command to fit two parts of a table together.

The ALIGN Command

Begin a new drawing named CHAP28F, using the default prototype drawing ACAD. First, you set up the drawing environment.

Set limits from 0,0 to 30,30. Set snap spacing for 2 but turn it off. Turn on the grid. Turn off solid fill, and then zoom all.

The furniture you are about to draw will be part of a library of symbols, so draw it on layer 0.

Command: *Choose* Data, Object Creation	Issues the DDEMODES command and opens the Object Creation Modes dialog box
Change the value in the Thickness *edit box to* **15**	Change Thickness, Elevation is set to 0

New Riders Publishing
INSIDE
SERIES

Choose OK	Closes dialog box with current settings

Command: *Choose* View, 3D
Viewpoint Presets, SE Isometric

Issues the VPOINT command

```
_vpoint
Rotate/<View point> <1.0000,1.0000,1.0000>:
_non *1,-1,1 Regenerating drawing.
```

Next, you draw one side of the table.

Command: *Choose* Draw, Polygon, 2D Solid   Issues the SOLID command

```
_solid
First point: 5,8 (Enter)
```

Second point: **@.5<0** (Enter)

Third point: **@-.5,15** (Enter)

Fourth point: **@.5<0** (Enter)

Third point: (Enter)   Ends the SOLID command

Next, you use grips while you make a copy of the table leg.

Command: *Select the solid*
you just drew

Preselects object and displays grip
points

Command: *Make one of the*
grip points hot

Starts grip commands

```
** STRETCH **
<Stretch to point>/
Base point/Copy/Undo/eXit: (Enter)
```

Moves to the next grip command

```
** MOVE **
<Move to point>/Base point/
Copy/Undo/eXit: C (Enter)
```

Specifies the Copy option

```
** MOVE (multiple) **
<Move to point>/Base point/
Copy/Undo/eXit: @15.5<0 (Enter)
```

Sets destination of copy

```
** MOVE (multiple) **
<Move to point>/Base point/
Copy/Undo/eXit: X (Enter)
```

Ends GRIP command

Command: *Press Esc twice*   Deselects object and grip points

continues

28

continued

Command: *Choose* Draw, Circle, *then* Center, Radius	Issues the CIRCLE command
3P/2P/TTR/<Center point>: **13,5** (Enter)	Sets center point of circle
Diameter/<Radius>: **3** (Enter)	Sets radius of circle
Command: *Choose* Modify, Align	Issues the ALIGN command
Select objects: **L** (Enter)	Selects the last object drawn
Select objects: (Enter)	Ends selection
1st source point: *Using* Center *object snap pick* ① *(refer to figure 28.33)*	Sets first source point
1st destination point: **.XY** (Enter)	Specifies .XY point filter
of *Using* Midpoint *object snap,* pick ②	Specifies object you want the midpoint of
(need Z): **7.5** (Enter)	Supplies the missing Z coordinate
2nd source point: *Using* Center *object snap,* pick ③	Sets second source point
2nd destination point: **.XY** (Enter)	Specifies .XY point filter
of *Using* Midpoint *object snap,* pick ④	Specifies object you want the midpoint of
(need Z): **7.5** (Enter)	Supplies the missing Z coordinate
3rd source point: (Enter)	Skips third point
<2d> or 3d transformation: **3D** (Enter)	Completes the transformation, cylinder positioned as shown in figure 28.34
Command: *Choose* Data, Object Creation	Issues DDEMODES command and displays the Object Creation Modes dialog box
Change the value in the **T**hickness *edit box to* **1**	Change Thickness, keep Elevation set to 0
Choose OK	Closes the dialog box with current settings

Command: *Choose* Draw, Polygon,　　　　Issues the SOLID command
2D Solid

_solid
First point: *Using Endpoint object*
snap, pick ① *(see fig. 28.34)*

Second point: *Using Endpoint object*
snap, pick ②

Third point: *Using Endpoint object*
snap, pick ③

Fourth point: *Using* ENDpoint *object*
snap, pick ④

Third point: (Enter)　　　　　　　Ends the SOLID command

Command: **BASE** (Enter)　　　　　Sets a base location

Base point <0.0000 0.0000 0.0000>:
_endp of *Pick* ①(see fig. 28.35)

Command: **HIDE** (Enter)　　　　　Issues the HIDE command and displays the
　　　　　　　　　　　　　　　　bookcase (see fig. 28.35)

Use the SAVEAS command to save your drawing as TABLE-F in your library of symbols.

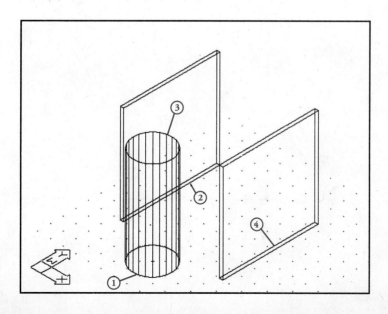

Figure 28.33

*Cube table
components.*

28

Figure 28.34

Cube table components assembled without top.

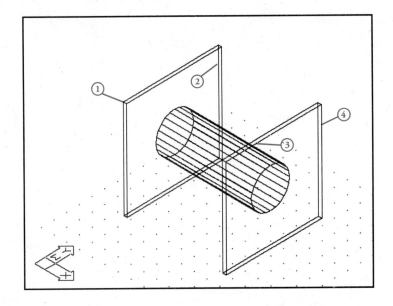

Figure 28.35

Cube table assembled with top (hidden lines removed).

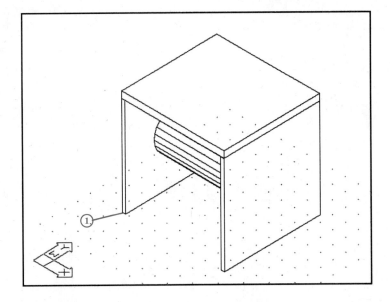

New Riders Publishing
INSIDE
SERIES

The MIRROR3D Command

MIRROR3D is the 3D version of the MIRROR command.

> **MIRROR3D.** The MIRROR3D command enables you to mirror selected objects about a user-defined plane.
> Screen: *Choose* CONSTRCT, Mirro3D
> Pull-down: *Choose* Construct, 3D Mirror

The MIRROR3D command has the following options for defining the mirror plane:

```
Plane by Entity/Last/Zaxis/View/XY/YZ/ZX/<3points>:
```

- ◆ **Entity.** Sets the plane in which the selected object resides as the mirror plane. The selected object can be a circle, arc, or 2D polyline.

- ◆ **Last.** Sets the mirror plane to the mirror plane used in the last MIRROR3D command.

- ◆ **Zaxis.** Sets the mirror plane by defining a line that has two points. The line you specify is assumed to be the Z axis and the mirror plane is set perpendicular to the Z axis, passing through the first point.

- ◆ **View.** Sets the mirror plane parallel to the viewing plane of the current view but passing through a user selected point.

- ◆ **XY/ZY/ZX.** Sets the mirror plane parallel to the XY, ZY, or ZX plane but passing through a user-defined point.

- ◆ **3points.** The default option enables you to define the mirror plane by picking three points that lie in that plane.

After you define the mirroring plane, you see the following prompt:

```
Delete old objects? <N>
```

The default option is No, which results in AutoCAD leaving the original objects in place and creating the new, mirrored objects. If you answer Yes, AutoCAD deletes the original objects.

28

Using UCS in 3D

With the exception of the LINE command, every drawing command you know so far creates an object that must lie in the current XY plane. Situations will arise in which you need to draw objects in other planes. For example, suppose you were required to draw a circle (to represent a hole) on each face of a cube (see fig. 28.36).

Figure 28.36

A cube with a circle on each face.

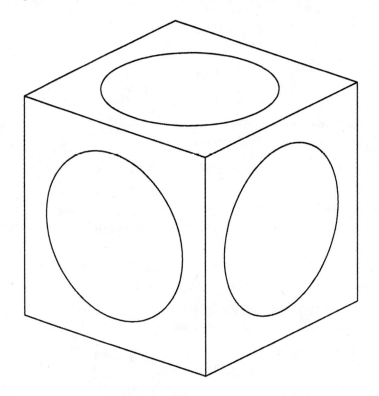

You might wonder how you would approach drawing circles. If the draw commands are restricted to creating objects in the XY plane, you need to be able to temporarily define each face as the XY plane in which you want to draw.

In Chapter 6, "Drawing Accurately," you learn how to define UCSs in a 2D environment. Changing the current UCS enables you to change the origin point and even to rotate the XY axes. In this chapter, you take UCSs one step further and learn how to define the current XY plane anywhere you want in 3D space, which enables you to draw 2D objects in various vertical planes (frontal and profile), inclined planes, and skewed planes. In the preceding example, to draw on a particular face of the cube you would make that face the current UCS and draw the circle in the new XY plane.

In the sections that follow, you learn how to use the UCS and control the UCS icon in a 3D environment.

Controlling the UCS Icon

In Chapter 6, you learned to use the UCSICON command to control the display of the UCS icon. The UCSICON command gave you the option of turning the icon off or on, or displaying it at the origin point. When you work with 3D models, you should leave the icon on and even turn on the Origin option. The icon is on by default but is set for NOORIGIN so that it always appears in the lower left corner on-screen. Without the icon, you can become disoriented relative to the plane of the UCS in 3D space.

Stop When you enable the Origin option, AutoCAD displays the UCS icon at the origin point only if enough area exists on your current viewport to see the entire icon. If not, the icon appears in the lower-left corner of the viewport. If this glitch occurs, simply shrink the display by performing a ZOOM, using roughly a 0.9X magnification factor, which should provide the necessary area to display the icon at the origin point.

In a 3D environment, it is quite possible to generate a view in which you can view the current UCS edge on. For example, in an elevation view, the world UCS would be viewed edge on, making the XY plane appear as a line. In this orientation, you cannot pick points in the XY plane and your 2D objects appear as dots or lines. To warn you that the current UCS is not properly visible, AutoCAD substitutes a broken pencil icon for the standard UCS icon (see fig. 28.37).

Figure 28.37

The broken pencil icon.

Tip If a view displays the broken pencil icon, avoid picking points. The only time it is safe to pick points is when you use object snap modes to select existing points.

Changing the Origin

In 3D, the Origin option of the UCS command is a very good way to relocate the current XY plane to any Z coordinate, thereby establishing the current UCS as parallel to the old UCS as shown in figure 28.38. The orientation of the XYZ axes remain unchanged. You can use this technique to work at any elevation without having to change the current elevation setting.

Figure 28.38

Setting the origin of the current UCS.

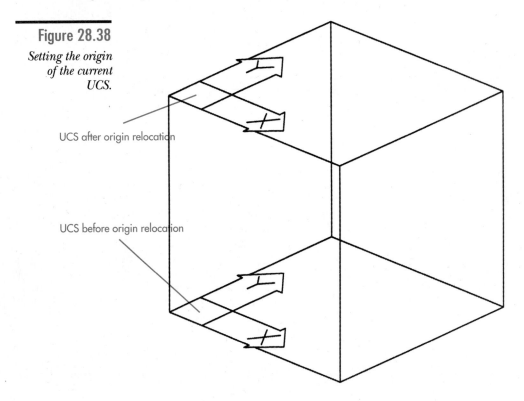

UCS after origin relocation

UCS before origin relocation

Tip Using a nonzero value for the current elevation setting while setting a new UCS can be confusing. You might end up with AutoCAD drawing objects at some distance away from the current XY plane rather than in the current XY plane. Consider keeping the current elevation set to zero, and then just setting the UCS at the elevation you want.

Establishing the Z

The ZAxis option of the UCS command enables you to set the current XY plane by defining the positive direction of the Z axis. You select two points (refer to figure 28.39). The first point you pick (①) is the new location of the 0,0,0 point and the second point (②) determines the positive direction of the Z axis. The XY plane is then established as perpendicular to the new Z axis.

New Riders Publishing
INSIDE SERIES

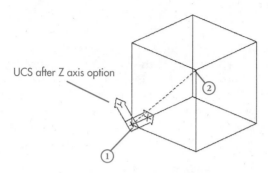

Figure 28.39

The ZAxis option.

The advantage of the ZAxis option is that you can use it as a quick way to establish the current UCS when you can visualize the Z axis clearly. The downside is that AutoCAD uses an algorithm that establishes the actual orientation of the X and Y axes rather arbitrarily. Use this option if all you care about is establishing which way positive Z is pointing.

The 3Point Option

The 3Point option is an accurate and easy method for establishing your current XY plane at any orientation in 3D space. The 3Point option of the UCS command enables you to establish the new UCS by selecting three points (refer to figure 28.40). The first point (①) establishes the new location of the 0,0,0 point. The second point (②) establishes the positive direction of the X axis and the third point (③) establishes the direction of the Y axis.

This option is very nice because you get to explicitly set the location of the origin and the orientation of the X and Y axes.

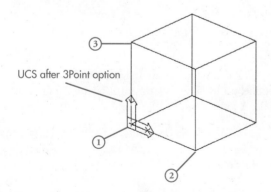

Figure 28.40

The 3Point option.

Using Objects

The Object option of the UCS command is a quick and easy way to establish the current UCS so that the selected object ends up lying in the new XY plane. All you have to do with this option is select the object. AutoCAD then establishes the orientation of the X and Y axes. The downside is that the rule used to establish the orientation of the XY axes depends on the type of object you select. The following is a list of object types and the way the origin and orientation of the UCS is determined for each type of object:

◆ **Arc.** The arc's center point becomes the new origin. The X axis is aligned to pass through the endpoint nearest the pick point.

◆ **Circle.** The circle's center point becomes the new origin. The X axis is aligned to pass through the pick point.

◆ **Dimension.** The middle point of the dimension text becomes the new origin. The X axis is aligned to be parallel to the X axis in effect at the time the dimension was drawn.

◆ **Line.** The endpoint nearest the pick point becomes the origin. The line becomes the X axis.

◆ **Point.** The point becomes the origin. AutoCAD determines the orientation of the X axis arbitrarily, using an algorithm.

◆ **2D Polyline.** The start point of the polyline becomes the new origin. The X axis is aligned to go through the next vertex point.

◆ **Solid.** The first point of the solid becomes the origin. The X axis is aligned to go through the second point.

◆ **Trace.** The first point of the trace becomes the origin. The trace itself becomes the X axis.

◆ **3DFace.** The first point of the 3D Face becomes the origin. The X axis is aligned to pass through the second point. The fourth point of the 3D face determines the orientation of the Y axis.

◆ **Complex Objects (Shape, Text, Block Reference, Attribute, and Definition).** The insertion point becomes the origin. The X axis is defined by the rotation of the object around its extrusion direction.

You cannot select all objects using the Object option; you can select only the objects listed in the preceding table. Objects not available for selection with this option are 3D Solid, 3D Polyline, 3D Mesh, Viewport, Mline, Region, Spline, Ellipse, Ray, Xline, Leader, and Mtext.

Tip   Because the results vary with the object you select, this option is most useful if your primary goal is to establish the UCS so that the selected object lies in the current XY plane. Before some editing commands can function properly (or at all), the current UCS must be parallel to the object's UCS. For example, to use DDMODIFY on a text object, the current UCS must be parallel to the UCS with which the object was drawn. A quick way to make the current UCS parallel to an object's UCS is to use the Object option and select the object in question.

Using the Current View

The View option of the UCS command enables you to set the current UCS parallel to your current view. In effect, it makes the new UCS parallel to your monitor screen (see fig. 28.41). The origin is set arbitrarily. The View option is most useful when you want to annotate the current view but want the text to appear flat.

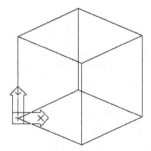

Figure 28.41

The View option.

Rotating about the Axes

The X, Y, and Z options of the UCS command are very handy when you can establish the new UCS by rotating about one of the axes of the existing UCS.

The hardest part is to figure out which direction corresponds to a positive rotation angle. You can easily establish this direction by using the old right hand rule—if you stick the thumb of your right hand in the positive direction of the axis about which you are rotating, the curl of your fingers is in the direction of a positive rotation.

Going Home Again

Working in 3D space can be very disorienting; if you get dizzy, go back to home base—the World Coordinate System (WCS), by using the World option of the UCS command, which is the default option.

The UCS Presets

You also can use the DDUCSP command to select a UCS orientation from a set of preset orientations.

> **DDUCSP.** The DDUCSP command enables you to select from a set of several preset UCS orientations (see fig. 28.42).
> Screen: *Choose* VIEW, DDucsp
> Pull-down: *Choose* View, Preset UCS

Figure 28.42

The UCS Orientation dialog box (DDUCSP command).

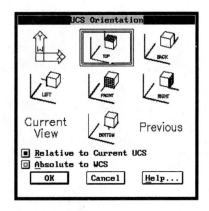

In effect, DDUCSP issues the UCS command with the X, Y, or Z axis options specified. Keep in mind that you do not get a chance to set an origin point for the new UCS.

Making a Viewport Follow

When you configure multiple viewports, you can specify that a viewport always display the plan view of the current UCS, by making the desired viewport the current viewport and then turning on the UCSFOLLOW system variable. You can set UCSFOLLOW independently for each viewport.

Stop   If you use multiple viewports, be sure to turn off the UCSFOLLOW system variable in the viewport you want to use when you set the current UCS. If you don't turn off UCSFOLLOW in the viewport you use to set the UCS, as soon as you finish using the UCS command, a plan view of the current UCS replaces the view in the current viewport.

In the following exercise, you implement many of the topics discussed in this section on UCSs to draw a 3D model of a cardboard box.

Working with UCSs

Begin a new drawing named CHAP28G, using the default prototype drawing ACAD. Make a new layer named BOX and make it the current layer. Set the drawing limits of 0,0 to 40,40, and the current thickness to 12. Turn on grid and snap and use Zoom All to zoom to the drawing limits.

Command: *Choose* View, Tiled Viewports, 2 Viewports	Issues the VPORTS command with the 2 Tiled viewport option
Save/Restore/Delete/Join/ SIngle/?/2/<3>/4: **2**	
Horizontal/<Vertical>: (Enter)	Accepts the default option
Command: **UCSICON** (Enter)	Issues the UCSICON command
ON/OFF/All/Noorigin/ ORigin <ON>: **A** (Enter)	Specifies the All option
ON/OFF/Noorigin/ORigin <ON>: **OR** (Enter)	Specifies the Origin option
Command: *Make the left viewport current*	
Command: *Choose* View, 3D Viewpoint Presets, SE Isometric	Issues the VPOINT command
_vpoint Rotate/<View point> <1.0000,1.0000,1.0000>: _non *1,-1,1 Regenerating drawing.	
Command: *Make the right viewport current*	
Command: *Choose* Options, UCS, Follow	Sets UCSFOLLOW on for the current viewport

Next, you draw the four sides for the box.

Command: *Choose* Draw, Line	Issues the LINE command
From point: **10,10** (Enter)	

continues

continued

To point: **@30<0** (Enter)

To point: **@15<90** (Enter)

To point: **@30<180** (Enter)

To point: **C** (Enter)   Closes the line and ends the LINE
                                           command

Next, you change the UCS to draw the bottom surface and a couple of the flaps for the top of
the box.

Command: *Choose* View, Set UCS,   Issues UCS with X axis option
X Axis Rotate

Rotation angle about X axis   Specifies 90 degree rotation
<0>: **90** (Enter)

The view in the right viewport has automatically changed to display a plan view of the current
UCS. Make the left viewpoint current.

Next, you change the origin of the UCS.

Command: *Choose* View, Set UCS,   Issues UCS with Origin option
Origin

Origin point <0,0,0>:   Moves UCS to new origin
Using ENDPoint object snap,
pick ① *(see figure 28.43)*

Figure 28.43

Box with
ORigin option
set for UCS.

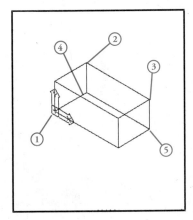

Make the right viewport current

Choose View, Zoom, Out | Moves the icon to the lower-left corner of the box

Make the left viewport current

Command: **THICKNESS** (Enter) | Initiates THICKNESS system variable

New value for THICKNESS <12.0000>: **15** (Enter) | Sets current thickness

Next, you draw two of the flaps for the top.

Command: *Choose* Draw, Line | Issues the LINE command

From point: *Using ENDPoint object snap, pick* ② | Starts line

To point: **@6<150** (Enter)

To point: (Enter) | Ends line

Command: (Enter) | Repeats the LINE command

From point: *Using* Endpoint *object snap, pick* ③ | Starts the LINE command

To point: **@6<-30** (Enter)

To point: (Enter) | Ends LINE

Next, you draw the bottom surface of the box.

Command: (Enter) | Repeats the LINE command

From point: *Using* Endpoint *object snap, pick* ④ | Starts LINE

To point: *Using* Endpoint *object snap, pick* ⑤

To point: (Enter) | Ends LINE

Next, you name the current UCS in case you need to restore it in the future.

Command: *Choose* View, Named UCS | Issues the DDUCS command and opens the UCS Control dialog box

Select *NO NAME* *from the* UCS Names *list box*

continues

28

continued

Enter BACKFACE *in the edit box*

Choose the **R**ename To *button,*
then the OK *button*

Now change the UCS to draw the remaining flaps for the box.

Command: *Choose* View, Set UCS, 3 Point	Issues UCS with 3Point option
Origin point <0,0,0>: *Using ENDPoint object snap, pick* ① *(refer to figure 28.44)*	Sets origin of new UCS

Figure 28.44

Completed box with hidden lines removed.

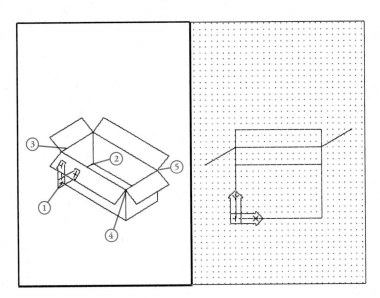

Point on positive portion of the X-axis <1.0000,0.0000,0.0000>: *Using ENDPoint object snap, pick* ②	Sets direction of X axis
Point on positive-Y portion of the UCS XY plane <0.0000,1.0000,0.0000>: *Using ENDPoint object snap, pick* ③	Sets direction of Y axis

The view in the right viewport now displays the plan of the current UCS. You need to zoom out to fix the icon again.

Make the right viewport current

Choose View, Zoom, Out   Moves the icon to the lower-left corner of
                                                 the box

Make the left viewport current

Command: **THICKNESS** (Enter)   Initiates THICKNESS system variable

New value for THICKNESS   Sets current thickness
<15.0000>: **30** (Enter)

Command: *Choose* Draw, Line   Issues the LINE command

From point: *Using ENDPoint object snap,*   Starts line
pick ③

To point: **@6<210** (Enter)

To point: (Enter)   Ends LINE

Command: (Enter)   Repeats LINE command

From point: *Using ENDPoint object snap,*
pick ④

To point: **@6<30** (Enter)

To point: (Enter)   Ends LINE

Save your drawing.

The preceding exercise is an introduction to handling of the UCS in a 3D drawing
environment. Your continued use of the 3D environment will require that you master
the use of the UCS.

This chapter introduced you to many new commands and options, enabling you to
work in and control AutoCAD's 3D environment. In the next chapter, you expand
your knowledge and ability to design and edit 3D models using even more powerful
AutoCAD tools for the 3D environment.

Drawing and Editing 3D Surfaces

Previously, you learned how to create pseudo 3D objects by extruding 2D objects. AutoCAD, however, is capable of creating true 3D objects, and you learn how to generate them in this chapter. The 3D surface models you created in the previous chapter have two major restrictions. The first restriction is that the original object has to be 2D—that is, lying in a single XY plane. The second restriction is that the 2D object can be extruded only in a direction perpendicular to the object's XY plane. These restrictions combine to limit the variety of 3D shapes you can create and require you to constantly change your UCS when creating a model of any complexity. For example, given the restrictions, how would you create a model of a sphere?

This chapter covers the following topics:

◆ How to create 3D curves using line, spline, and 3D polyline entities

◆ How to modify 3D entities using the DDMODIFY command

◆ How to create simple three-dimensional objects such as boxes, cones, hemi-spheres, and spheres

◆ How to create 3D mesh surfaces with a variety of tools such as 3DMESH, TABSURF, RULESURF, and REVSURF

In the following sections you learn to draw 3D curves. A *3D curve* is an object that has no thickness. A 3D object's points have varying Z coordinates, which enables the curve to meander through 3D space, allowing for fewer UCS changes. Three objects qualify as 3D curves, two of which you already know how to draw—lines and splines. You can draw a line starting from one elevation and ending at another elevation without changing your UCS. The third type of 3D curve is a 3D polyline, a cousin of the polyline you already know how to create. Using 3D curves you can create complex wireframe models. You then can use these 3D curves to generate complex surface and solid models.

You also learn to create 3D surfaces and generate 3D surfaces from 3D curves in this chapter. A *3D surface* is an object that has no thickness and can be defined with points with varying Z coordinates. The latter characteristic enables you to create a curved surface, such as the surface of a sphere. Generating the points for a 3D surface is tedious work, but AutoCAD supplies a number of commands that do the work for you.

Note When you use the Surfaces, 3D Objects menu item, AutoCAD displays a dialog box of icons that issue commands such as AI_BOX or AI_CONE. These commands access AutoLISP-defined functions that provide much of AutoCAD's 3D surfacing capabilities. If you enter the 3D command at the Command: prompt, you can access the same functions with options such as Box or Cone. Whether accessed by specific commands or equivalent 3D options, the functions issue the same prompts and draw the same objects.

This chapter completes the discussion on creating surface models. To learn more about surface modeling, please see *AutoCAD in 3D*, by New Riders Publishing.

In the following exercise, you will create a table with some items on the tabletop. Here you begin to work with some of the basic three-dimensional entities available in AutoCAD.

Quick 5¢ Tour

Begin a new drawing named CHAP33 using the default prototype drawing ACAD.

Change the drawing limits so that the lower left corner is at 0,0 and the upper right corner is at 80,40. Issue a ZOOM All to see the entire drawing area.

First, you draw the top of the table.

Command: *Choose* Draw, Surfaces, 3D Objects	Displays the 3D Objects dialog box
Choose 3D Box, *then* OK	Issues the AI_BOX command
Corner of box: **0,0** (Enter)	Sets corner of box at 0,0
Length: **80** (Enter)	Sets length of box at 80
Cube/<Width>: **30** (Enter)	Sets width of box at 30
Height: **1.5** (Enter)	Sets height of box at 1.5
Rotation angle about Z axis: **0** (Enter)	Sets rotation angle of box at 0 degrees

Now, you draw the leg of the table.

Command: (Enter)	Repeats the AI_BOX command
Corner of box: **12,5,-30** (Enter)	Sets corner of box at 12,5
Length: **2** (Enter)	Sets length of box at 2
Cube/<Width>: **20** (Enter)	Sets width of box at 20
Height: **30** (Enter)	Sets height of box at 30
Rotation angle about Z axis: **0** (Enter)	Sets rotation angle at 0 degrees

Next, you modify the shape of the table leg to make it appear flared.

Command: *Choose* View, 3D Viewpoint Presets, SE Isometric	Sets isometric viewpoint
Zoom in on the table leg.	
Command: *Select the table leg*	Selects the object and displays its grip points
Command: *Hold down the Shift key while you pick* (1) *and* (2) *(see fig. 29.1)*	Makes the grip points hot

continued

29

continued

`Command:` *Release the Shift key and pick* ①	Initiates grip editing modes
`** STRETCH **<Stretch to point>/` `Base point/Copy/Undo/eXit:` `@0,-5` (Enter)	Stretches the selected grip points
`Command:` *Hold down the Shift key while you select* ③ *and* ④	Selects the grip points
`Command:` *Release the Shift key and select* ③	Initiates grip editing modes
`** STRETCH **<Stretch to point>/` `Base point/Copy/Undo/eXit:` `@0,5` (Enter)	Stretches the selected points

Next, you make a copy of the table leg to be used as the other table leg.

`Command:` *Pick* ① *(see fig. 29.2)*	Initiates grip editing

`** STRETCH **`
`<Stretch to point>/Base point/`
`Copy/Undo/eXit:` (Enter)
	Switches to the next grip command

`** MOVE **`
`<Move to point>/`
`Base point/Copy/Undo/eXit:` `C` (Enter)	

`** MOVE (multiple) **`
`<Move to point>/Base point/`
`Copy/Undo/eXit:` `@54<0` (Enter)
	Sets position of copy

`** MOVE (multiple) **`
`<Move to point>/Base point/`
`Copy/Undo/eXit:` (Enter)
	Exits grip editing

Next, reset the UCS to the tabletop and draw some items on the table surface.

`Command:` *Choose View, Zoom, All option*	Issues the ZOOM command with the All
`Command:` *Choose View, Set UCS, Origin*	Issues the UCS command with Origin option

`Origin point <0,0,0>:` *Using END object snap, pick* ① *(see fig. 29.3)*	Sets origin of UCS at the top corner of the tabletop

Next, you draw a set of bookends holding up some books.

`Command:` *Choose* Draw, Surfaces, 3D Objects	Displays the 3D Objects dialog box
Choose Wedge	Issues the AI_WEDGE command
`Corner of wedge:` **25,20** (Enter)	Sets corner of wedge at 25,20
`Length:` **2** (Enter)	Sets length of wedge at 2
`Width:` **5** (Enter)	Sets width of wedge at 5
`Height:` **5** (Enter)	Sets height of wedge at 5
`Rotation angle about Z axis:` **180** (Enter)	Sets rotation of wedge at 180 degrees
`Command:` *Choose* Draw, Surfaces, 3D Objects	Displays the 3D Objects dialog box
Choose 3D Box, *then* OK	Issues the AI_BOX command
`Corner of box:` *Using END object snap, pick* ②	Sets corner of box at corner of wedge
`Length:` **1.5** (Enter)	Sets length of box at 1.5
`Cube/<Width>:` **10** (Enter)	Sets width of box at 10
`Height:` **10** (Enter)	Sets height of box at 10
`Rotation angle about Z axis:` **0** (Enter)	Sets rotation angle at 0 degrees
`Command:` (Enter)	Repeats AI_BOX command
`Corner of box:` *Using END object snap, pick* ③	Sets corner of box at corner of previous box
`Length:` **2** (Enter)	Sets length of box at 2
`Cube/<Width>:` **8** (Enter)	Sets width of box at 8

continues

29

continued

Height: **12** (Enter)	Sets height of box at 12
Rotation angle about Z axis: **0** (Enter)	Sets rotation angle of box
Command: *Choose* Construct, Mirror	Issues the MIRROR command
Select objects: *Select the wedge and two boxes you just drew*	
Select objects: (Enter)	
First point of mirror line: *Using END object snap, pick* ④	Sets base of mirror line at corner of last box drawn
Second point: *Using END object snap, pick* ⑤	Sets mirror line at other end of previous box
Delete old objects? <N> (Enter)	Completes MIRROR

You complete the model by drawing a ball lying on the tabletop.

Command: *Choose* Draw, Surfaces, 3D Objects	Displays the 3D Objects dialog box
Choose Sphere	Issues the AI_SPHERE command
Center of sphere: **47,12,3** (Enter)	Sets center of sphere three units above the tabletop
Diameter/<radius>: **3** (Enter)	Sets radius at 3
Number of longitudinal segments <16>: (Enter)	Sets number of segments for sphere
Number of latitudinal segments <16>: (Enter)	Sets number of segments for sphere
Command: *Choose* Tools, Hide	Issues the HIDE command

New Riders Publishing
INSIDE
SERIES

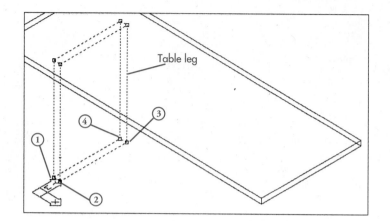

Figure 29.1

Stretching the table leg.

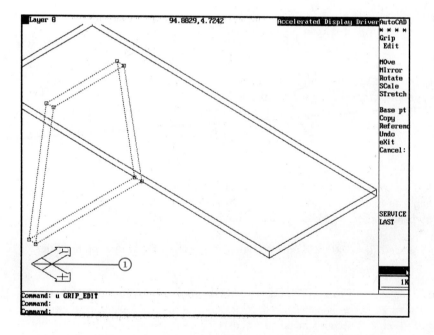

Figure 29.2

Creating a second table leg.

29

Figure 29.3

Drawing items on the tabletop.

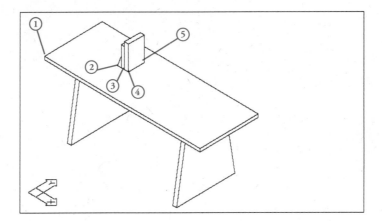

Drawing 3D Lines

In the previous chapter, you learned to create a 3D surface from a line by assigning a thickness to the line. You also can draw a line from one elevation to another elevation. The capability to pick endpoints with varying Z coordinates means that you do not have to change your UCS just to draw a line that is nonplanar relative to the current UCS. Not having to change the current UCS as often can be a significant time-saver when constructing 3D models.

Tip If you draw a line from one elevation to another, with non-zero thickness, the result might be confusing to look at. The lines thickness extrudes in the Z direction perpendicular to the current XY plane, not perpendicular to the line.

In the exercises to follow, you will have a chance to draw several non-coplanar lines.

Note In Chapter 11, "Drawing and Editing Polylines and Splines," you learned to draw complex 2D curves with the SPLINE command. Just like lines, splines actually are true 3D objects because the points that define a spline do not have to be coplanar. Because a spline is basically one continuous curve, SPLINE enables you to generate complex curves through 3D space. In conjunction with some of the new commands covered in this chapter, you will be able to use splines to generate surfaces with complex, curved boundaries.

New Riders Publishing
INSIDE
SERIES

Drawing 3D Polylines

The PLINE command you learned about in Chapter 11 generates 2D polylines. There is, however, a 3D version of the PLINE command called 3DPOLY.

> **3DPOLY.** The 3DPOLY command enables you to draw a polyline consisting of multiple 3D points.
> Pull-down: *Choose* Draw, 3D Polyline
> Screen: *Choose* DRAW 1, 3Dpoly

When you enter the 3DPOLY command you are prompted for a start point. After you pick a start point, the following options appear:

```
Close/Undo/<Endpoint of line>:
```

- ◆ **Close.** Draws a closing segment to the start point and ends 3DPOLY.

- ◆ **Undo.** Undoes the last segment drawn.

- ◆ **Endpoint of line.** Picks the next point to draw a segment to. (The default option.)

Even though the object generated by 3DPOLY is referred to as a polyline, it is quite different from the polyline generated by PLINE. These differences are described as follows:

- ◆ The vertices of a 3D polyline can have differing Z coordinates.

- ◆ A 3D polyline cannot have arc segments, only straight line segments.

- ◆ You cannot assign a width to a 3D polyline.

- ◆ You cannot assign a thickness to (extrude) a 3D polyline.

- ◆ A 3D polyline cannot be displayed with any linetype other than a continuous linetype.

Along with these differences, polylines and 3D polylines share the following characteristics:

- ◆ A 3D polyline consisting of multiple segments is considered a single object.

- ◆ You can explode a 3D polyline into multiple line segments.

29

◆ You can edit a 3D polyline with the PEDIT command. You do not have as many options using PEDIT on a 3D polyline as you do when editing a polyline, however. The missing options include Width, Join, Ltype gen, and Fit. The options you do have include Close, Edit Vertex, Spline curve, and Decurve.

So, when do you use 3D polylines? If you have to model an outline that does not lie in an XY plane (is not coplanar) and consists of multiple segments that you want to be treated as a single object, then the model is a candidate for the 3DPOLY command. You also can export 3D polylines to 3D Studio where you can use them for lofting, the process of creating a 3D shape from a 2D object, or camera paths used for walk-throughs of a 3D model.

Examining 3DMESH

3DMESH is the first of several commands covered in this chapter that generate a surface. Particularly, 3DMESH creates a polygon mesh surface (see fig. 29.4). The points that define the polygon mesh are arranged into an M × N matrix of points.

Figure 29.4

Two views of a polygon mesh.

N direction

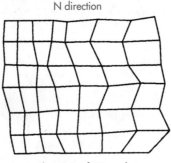

Plan view of 3D mesh

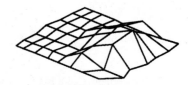

Isometric view of 3D mesh

3DMESH. The 3DMESH command generates a polygon mesh surface defined by an M × N matrix of 3D points.
Pull-down: *Choose* Draw, Surfaces, 3D Mesh
Screen: *Choose* DRAW2, SURFACES, 3Dmesh

The minimum values of M and N are 2, which means you need a minimum of 4 points to define a polygon mesh. The maximum values of M and N are 256, which means the maximum number of points you can use to define a 3D mesh is 65,536. The points are referred to as *vertex points* or *vertices,* just as with a polyline. As a matter

New Riders Publishing
INSIDE
SERIES

of fact, a 3D mesh is considered a polyline and is identified as such by LIST and DDMODIFY. Although the points of a 3D mesh typically are arranged in a loose matrix of rows and columns, the vertices themselves do not have to have uniform spacing. The vertices also can have varying Z values, making this an excellent tool for modeling irregular and curved surfaces.

When generating a polygon mesh surface with varying Z elevations along the vertices, the surface tends to be jagged unless the variation in Z is gradual. Because a polygon mesh is a polyline, you can use PEDIT to smooth over a jagged 3D mesh (see fig. 29.5).

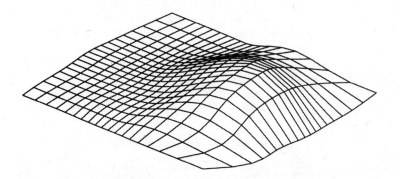

Figure 29.5

The polygon mesh in figure 29.4 smoothed by using PEDIT.

PEDIT's Smooth option can generate the following three types of surfaces, depending on the value of the system variable SURFTYPE:

SURFTYPE Value	Type of Surface Generated
5	Quadratic B-spline
6	Cubic B-spline (default)
7	Bézier surface

The higher the value of SURFTYPE, the smoother the resulting surface becomes. When you smooth a 3D mesh, you are in effect replacing the original 3D polygon mesh with another mesh made up of vertices calculated with the set of equations specified by SURFTYPE. The density of the replacement mesh is controlled by the system variables SURFU and SURFV (equivalent of M and N in the 3DMESH command).

Tip If you are smoothing a polygon mesh, be sure to set the values of SURFU and SURFV greater than or equal to the M and N values of the original unsplined 3D polygon mesh; otherwise, you will end up with a surface showing fewer vertices than you started with.

29

To edit the vertices of a polygon mesh, you can use either grips or the Edit vertex option of the PEDIT command. If the polygon mesh has been smoothed, then you have to edit the vertices of the original 3D mesh—the spline frame—to affect the smoothed surface. The spline frame is automatically displayed if you use grips. If you want to see the spline frame of a smoothed 3D mesh without using grips, set SPLFRAME to 1 and issue the REGEN command.

DDMODIFY is an excellent tool to change the type of surface or the density in a smoothed mesh. DDMODIFY, which is covered in Chapter 15, "Object Modification, Inquiry, and Calculation," is different for each type of object created in AutoCAD. When editing a 3D mesh object, for example, DDMODIFY displays the Modify Polyline dialog box (see fig. 29.6). This dialog box enables you to change all of the mesh's properties. In addition to basic object properties such as color, layer, and linetype, you also can list the location of individual mesh vertices and the number of mesh elements in the M and N directions. The Modify Polyline dialog box also enables you to change the type of mesh smoothing applied (the SPLFRAME value) and the smoothing density (the SURFU and SURFV values). To access DDMODIFY from the pull-down menu, choose Modify, then Properties.

Figure 29.6

The Modify Polyline dialog box.

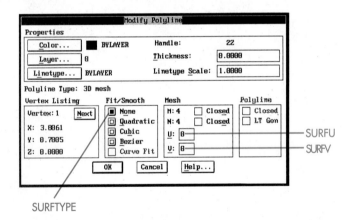

A polygon mesh also can be closed or open in the M or N direction or both directions. When you close a mesh, you force the starting and ending edges to meet. You see good examples of closed polygon meshes in the following sections.

The internal lines in a polygon mesh are called *tabulation lines*. The generation of tabulation lines cannot be suppressed.

Generating a mesh requires a lot of work. To generate a 4 × 4 mesh requires that you pick 16 points. Because of the work involved, the 3DMESH command rarely is used directly. Instead, routines are written to generate the needed points to define a mesh

to simulate a specific shape. AutoCAD includes several such routines, which are covered in the sections to follow.

Examining Basic 3D Shapes

AutoCAD provides several commands for generating polygon mesh objects that look like several basic 3D shapes. These commands are issued by the 3D Objects dialog box (see fig. 29.7). The 3D Box selection issues the AI_BOX command. Each of the other selections issues a command whose name matches that option, plus an "AI_" prefix.

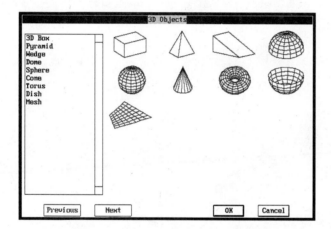

Figure 29.7

The 3D Objects dialog box.

In lieu of the dialog box, you also can use the 3D command.

3D. The 3D command enables you to generate 3D polygon meshes in the form of several basic shapes. The 3D command is not listed in a menu and therefore must be typed at the Command: prompt.

The 3D command issues the following options:

Box/Cone/DIsh/DOme/Mesh/Pyramid/Sphere/Torus/Wedge:

These options are the shapes that can be generated with the 3D command, and are the same as those shown in the 3D Objects dialog box. These shapes are described in the following sections. You generated several of them when you created the table in the exercise at the beginning of the chapter. Except for the Mesh item, the shapes created by these 3D commands or options are created with their base planes parallel to the X,Y plane of the current UCS.

29

Tip Because the shapes are 3D polygon meshes, you can edit the vertices to stretch the initial shape. You used this capability in the first exercise to stretch a box into the shape of the table leg. You do not have as much flexibility in stretching extruded 2D objects. Each of these shapes can be accessed directly from the command line by entering **AI_** followed by the option name. For example, to issue the Box option of the 3D command, you enter **AI_BOX**.

Box

The Box option enables you to generate a 3D polygon mesh in the shape of a box (see fig. 29.8).

Figure 29.8

A shape generated by the Box option.

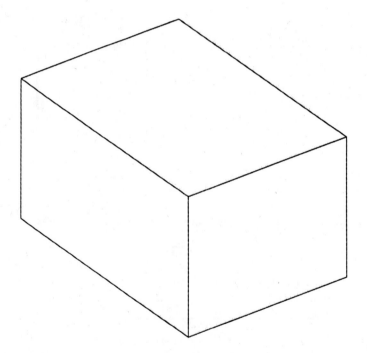

You must answer the following prompts to generate a box:

◆ **Corner of box.** Initially, the box is generated so that its edges are parallel to the X, Y, and Z axes. The point you pick at this prompt will be the lower left corner point of the base of the box.

◆ **Length.** This option specifies the length of the box along the X axis.

- ◆ **Cube/<Width>.** If you choose the Cube option, a cube with the length specified for the preceding prompt is generated. The default option is to specify the width of the cube as measured along the Y axis.

- ◆ **Height.** You see this prompt only if you are not generating a cube. This is the height of the box as measured along the Z axis.

- ◆ **Rotation angle about Z axis.** After the box is generated, you can rotate it about the point you picked to be the corner of the box. This is a rotation angle in the XY plane.

Cone

Using the Cone option, you can generate a right circular cone or a frustum (see fig. 29.9). A *frustum* is the bottom portion of a cone.

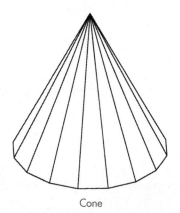

Cone   Frustum

Figure 29.9

Shapes generated by the Cone option.

You must answer the following prompts to generate a cone:

- ◆ **Base center point.** You must pick the center of the circular base of the cone or frustum as the base center point of the cone.

- ◆ **Diameter/<radius> of base.** You must specify the diameter or radius (default option) of the circular base.

- ◆ **Diameter/<radius> of top <0>.** Your answer to this prompt determines whether a cone or a frustum is generated. A cone is generated if the radius of the top circular surface is 0, which is the default radius. If you specify a nonzero value for the radius or diameter of the top circular surface, a frustum is generated.

29

◆ **Height.** Use this prompt to specify the height of the cone or frustum.

◆ **Number of segments <16>.** This prompt determines the number of mesh segments that are generated. The higher the value, the more the base and top appear like circles.

Dish

A *dish* is the bottom half of a sphere, as shown in figure 29.10.

Figure 29.10

A hemispherical shape generated by the Dish option.

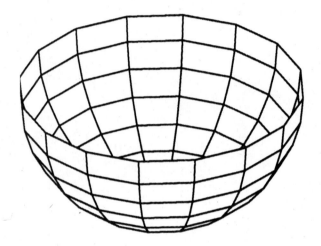

You must answer the following prompts to generate a dish:

◆ **Center of dish.** The point you pick will be the center of the dish's top circular edge.

◆ **Diameter/<radius>.** You must specify the diameter or radius (default option) of the dish. Remember that a dish is the bottom half of a sphere.

◆ **Number of longitudinal segments <16>.** Use this prompt to specify the number of mesh segments generated along the dish's circumference.

◆ **Number of latitudinal segments <8>.** Use this prompt to specify the number of mesh segments generated along the dish's vertical axis (Z axis).

New Riders Publishing
INSIDE
SERIES

Dome

A *dome* is the top half of a sphere. Figure 29.11 shows a dome created by using the Dome option of the 3D command.

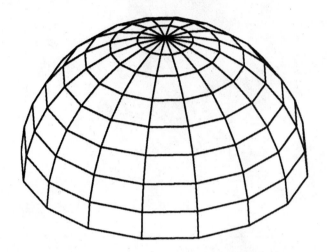

Figure 29.11

A hemispherical shape generated by the Dome option.

The prompts are identical to the prompts for a dish. The center point you specify becomes the center of the circular base of the dome.

Mesh

The Mesh option creates an M × N 3D mesh. The number of vertices you specify for the M and N directions defines how smooth the resulting mesh will look after it is created. You first are prompted to pick four corners as shown in figure 13.12. These corners define the border of the mesh. After picking the four corners you are prompted as follows:

- ◆ **Mesh M size.** Valid sizes are 2–256. AutoCAD creates M number of vertices between corners 2 and 3, and corners 1 and 4.

- ◆ **Mesh N size.** Valid sizes are 2–256. AutoCAD creates N number of vertices between corners 1 and 2, and corners 3 and 4.

29

Figure 29.12

A 3D mesh.

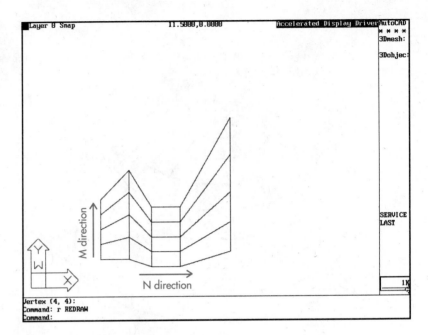

Pyramid

This option can be used to generate several prismoidal shapes. You must answer the following prompts to generate a pyramid:

◆ **First base point.** This point is the first point that defines the shape of the base.

◆ **Second base point.** This point is the second point that defines the shape of the base.

◆ **Third base point.** This point is the third point that defines the shape of the base.

◆ **Tetrahedron/<Fourth base point>.** If you want to define a triangular base, specify the Tetrahedron option. If you want to define a quadrangle for the base, pick a fourth base point.

◆ **Ridge/Top/<Apex point>.** The default option is to specify a single additional point, the *apex* point. The resulting shape is a three-sided pyramid (a tetrahedron) or a four-sided pyramid, depending on your response to the preceding prompt (see fig. 29.13).

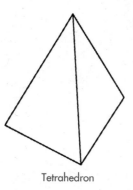 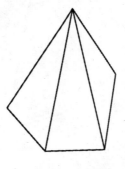

Tetrahedron   Four-sided pyramid

Figure 29.13

Two pyramid shapes generated with an apex point.

You also can specify the Top option, which enables you to specify a top surface. If you defined a tetrahedron for the base surface, you are asked to pick three points for the top surface; otherwise, you are asked to pick four points for the top surface (see fig. 29.14).

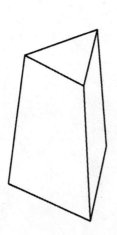 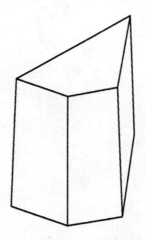

Figure 29.14

Two pyramid shapes generated with the Top option.

29

The Ridge option is available only when you define a base with four points. The ridge is defined by two additional points (see fig. 29.15).

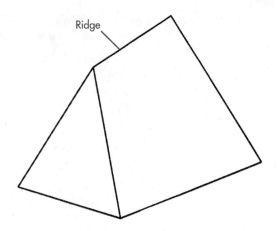

Figure 29.15

A pyramid shape generated with the Ridge option.

Ridge

Spheres

The Sphere option generates a polygon mesh in the shape of a sphere, as shown in figure 29.16.

Figure 29.16

A sphere generated by the Sphere option.

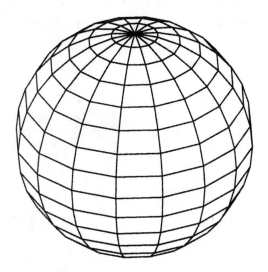

You must answer the following prompts to generate a sphere:

◆ **Center of sphere.** You pick the center of the sphere.

◆ **Diameter/<radius>.** You specify the diameter or radius (default option) of the sphere.

New Riders Publishing

INSIDE SERIES

◆ **Number of longitudinal segments <16>.** If you think of a sphere as a globe of the world, then this number is the number of segments that run north to south.

◆ **Number of latitudinal segments <16>.** This number is the number of segments that run east to west if you think of a sphere as a globe.

Torus

The Torus option generates a ringlike shape, as shown in figure 29.17.

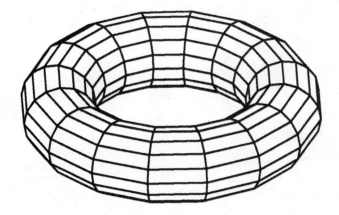

Figure 29.17

A ring-like shape generated by the Torus option.

You must answer the following prompts to generate a torus:

◆ **Center of torus.** This point will be the center of the ring.

◆ **Diameter/<radius> of torus.** You must specify the diameter or radius (default option) of the shape. The diameter or radius is measured to the centerline of the ring itself.

◆ **Diameter/<radius> of tube.** You also must specify the diameter or radius (default option) of the ring itself.

◆ **Segments around tube circumference <16>.** Use this prompt to specify the number of mesh segments generated along the circumference of the ring.

◆ **Segments around torus circumference <16>.** Use this prompt to specify the number of mesh segments generated along the cross section of the ring.

29

Wedge

The Wedge option generates a rectangular wedge, as shown in figure 29.18.

Figure 29.18

A shape generated by the Wedge option.

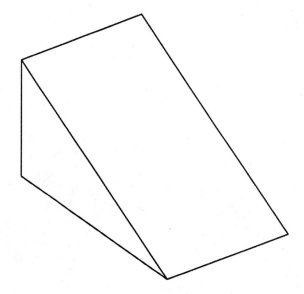

You must answer the following prompts to generate a wedge:

◆ **Corner of wedge.** This point will be the lower left corner point of the base of the wedge.

◆ **Length.** This option specifies the length of the rectangular base of the wedge as measured along the X axis.

◆ **Width.** This option specifies the width of the rectangular base of the wedge as measured along the Y axis.

◆ **Height.** This option specifies the height of the wedge. The high side of the wedge initially is generated parallel to the Y axis, on the side of the corner point.

◆ **Rotation angle about Z axis.** After the initial generation of the wedge, you can specify a rotation angle about the point you picked as the corner of the wedge.

Examining 3DFACE

The 3DFACE command, like the 3DMESH command, generates a 3D surface, an AutoCAD 3Dface object, as shown in figure 29.19.

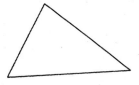

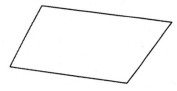

Figure 29.19

3DFACE objects.

Three-sided 3D face   Four-sided 3D face

3DFACE. The 3DFACE command generates a three- or four-sided surface.
Pull-down: *Choose* Draw, Surfaces, 3D Face
Screen: *Choose* DRAW 2, SURFACES, 3Dface

The following list explains the 3DFACE prompt sequence:

◆ **First point.** Pick the first point of the 3D face.

◆ **Second point.** Pick the second point of the 3D face.

◆ **Third point.** Pick the third point of the 3D face.

◆ **Fourth point.** You can either press Enter or pick a fourth point. If you press Enter, a 3D face with three edges is created. If you pick a fourth point, a 3D face with four edges is created.

After pressing Enter or picking a fourth point, the prompt for a third point is repeated. If you press Enter, the 3DFACE command sequence ends. If you select a new third point, then the previous third and fourth points are recycled as the first and second points of the next 3D face, which is created adjacent to the first 3D face (see fig. 29.20).

The prompts for the third and fourth points repeat until you press Enter at the prompt for a third point.

29

Figure 29.20

Continuing a 3D face.

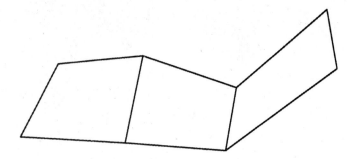

Making 3D Face Edges Invisible

You have the option of making one or more of the edges of the 3D face invisible. This feature is especially useful when you have several 3D face objects adjacent to each other, sharing common edges. When you make the common edges invisible, the 3D faces appear to be a single, seamless surface (see fig. 29.21).

Figure 29.21

3D faces of figure 29.20 with shared invisible edges.

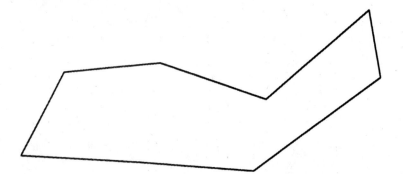

To make a particular edge invisible, you type the letter *I* followed by the Enter key at the prompt for that point, before picking the point. If you want to make the third edge invisible, for example, type **I** followed by the Enter key at the prompt for the third point before picking the third point. If you make the third edge invisible and then continue the 3DFACE command by picking new third or fourth points, 3DFACE automatically makes the first edge (the common edge) of the new continuing 3D face invisible.

If you want to control the visibility of the edges of existing 3Dfaces, use the DDMODIFY command. When you issue the DDMODIFY command, the Modify 3D Face dialog box opens (see fig. 29.22). In the Modify 3D Face dialog box you can set the visibility controls for the edges of a 3D face.

New Riders Publishing
INSIDE
SERIES

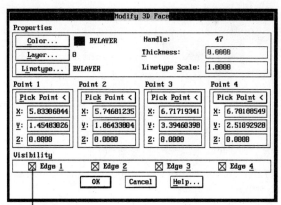

Figure 29.22

The Modify 3D Face dialog box.

Visibility controls for edges

Stop If you make all the edges of a 3D face invisible, you easily can lose track of the 3D face.

You also can use the EDGE command to control the visibility of the edges of a 3D face object.

EDGE. The EDGE command enables you to control the visibility of the edges of a 3D face object.
Pull-down: *Choose* Draw, Surfaces, Edge
Screen: *Choose* DRAW2, SURFACES, 3Dface, Edge

After issuing the EDGE command, you see the following prompt:

`Display/<Select edge>:`

The default option is to select an edge. If the edge is visible, then selecting it makes it invisible. If the edge is invisible, then selecting it makes it visible. To select an invisible edge to make it visible, you first use the Display option.

The Display option shows all invisible edges as dashed lines. After selecting the Display option, you see the following prompt:

`Select/<All>:`

You then can select the 3D face objects of which you want to see the invisible edges, or accept the default option of viewing the invisible edges of all 3D face objects. After the invisible edges are displayed as dashed lines, you can select the edges you want to make visible. When you are done selecting edges, press Enter to end the command.

29

If you want to see all invisible edges, you can make them visible by setting the SPLFRAME system variable to 1 (on) and then issuing the REGEN command.

In the following exercise, you create a trash can to add to the furniture symbols you created in the previous chapter.

Surfacing with 3DFACE

Begin a new drawing named TRASH1 using the default prototype drawing ACAD.

Create a new layer named OUTLINE and make it the current layer. Now you draw the outline of the top and bottom of the rectangular trash can.

Command: *Choose* Draw, Polygon, Rectangle	Issues the RECTANG command
First corner: **3,2** (Enter)	Anchors rectangle at coordinates 3,2
Other corner: **@8,5** (Enter)	Specifies size of rectangle
Command: *Choose* Construct, Offset	Issues the OFFSET command
Offset distance or Through <Through>: **1** (Enter)	Specifies distance of offset at 1
Select object to offset: *Select the rectangle*	Selects the rectangle to be offset
Side to offset? *Select a point outside the rectangle*	Specifies direction of offset
Select object to offset: (Enter)	Ends OFFSET
Command: *Choose* View, 3D Viewpoint Presets, SE Isometric	Sets isometric viewpoint
Command: *Choose* Modify, Move	Issues the MOVE command
Select objects: **L** (Enter)	Selects the last rectangle
Select objects: (Enter)	
Base point or displacement: **0,0,10** (Enter)	Specifies displacement of rectangle 10 units in the Z direction

New Riders Publishing
INSIDE
SERIES

`Second point of displacement:` (Enter)	Accepts displacement and moves the rect angle 10 units in the Z direction

Zoom to see the entire drawing.

Create a new layer named SURFACES and make it current. In the following steps, you create the surfaces of the trash can.

`Command:` *Choose* Options, Running Object Snap	Issues the DDOSNAP command
Choose Endpoint *then* OK	Sets endpoint running object snap and exits the Running Object Snap dialog box
`Command:` *Choose* Draw, Surfaces, 3D Face	Issues the 3DFACE command
`First point:` *Pick* ① *(see fig 29.23)*	Sets first point
`Second point:` *Pick* ②	Sets second point
`Third point:` *Pick* ③	Sets third point
`Fourth point:` *Pick* ④	Sets fourth point
`Third point:` (Enter)	Ends 3D face
`Command:` (Enter)	Repeats 3D face
`First point:` *Pick* ① *(see fig. 29.23)*	
`Second point:` *Pick* ⑤	
`Third point:` *Pick* ⑥	
`Fourth point:` *Pick* ②	
`Third point:` *Pick* ③	
`Fourth point:` *Pick* ⑦	
`Third point:` *Pick* ⑧	
`Fourth point:` *Pick* ④	
`Third point:` *Pick* ①	

29

continued

Fourth point: *Pick* ⑤

Third point: **⟨Enter⟩**   Ends 3D face

Command: **HIDE** **⟨Enter⟩**   Displays hidden line views

Notice that the top of the model is open and you can look inside the trash can (see fig. 3.24).

To finish this model, you should use the BASE command to pick an appropriate insertion base point and freeze the layer OUTLINE.

Figure 29.23

Surfacing the trash can.

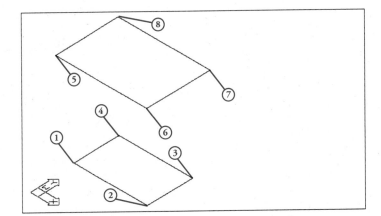

Figure 29.24

The trash can with hidden lines removed.

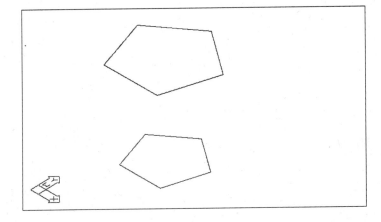

New Riders Publishing
INSIDE
SERIES

Creating Polyface Meshes

The PFACE command generates another surface object that is a variation of a polyline object known as a *polyface mesh*.

> **'PFACE.** The PFACE command creates a multisided 3D surface or collection of surfaces.
> Screen: *Choose* DRAW 2, SURFACES, Pface

Whereas the 3DFACE command is restricted to generating surfaces with three or four edges, PFACE can generate surfaces with multiple edges and even multiple surfaces that behave as a single unit.

After PFACE is started, you see prompts similar to the following:

```
Vertex 1:
Vertex 2:
...
...
Vertex n: (where n is some number)
```

At each prompt for a vertex, you are expected to pick a point. These points are later used to define the corners on the perimeter of the generated surface(s). The ellipses in the preceding and following command prompts indicate that there is no preset number of vertices for you to locate. When you finish picking points, press Enter. Then you see prompts similar to the following:

```
Face 1, vertex 1:
Face 1, vertex 2:
...
...
Face m, vertex n: (where m and n are numbers)
```

In response to the preceding prompts, you type the vertex number corresponding to the point you want to use to define the face (or surface). The vertex number of a point is the number in the prompt `Vertex n:`, to which you responded by picking the point.

PFACE is ideally suited for two basic scenarios. The first scenario is one in which you generate a surface with more than four edges (the maximum number of edges for a 3D face). Suppose you want to generate a surface for a six-sided object (see fig. 29.25). The following command sequence enables you to create such an object:

29

```
Vertex 1: Pick ①
Vertex 2: Pick ②
Vertex 3: Pick ③
Vertex 4: Pick ④
Vertex 5: Pick ⑤
Vertex 6: Pick ⑥
Vertex 7: (Enter)
Face 1, Vertex 1: 1 (Enter)
Face 1, Vertex 2: 2 (Enter)
Face 1, Vertex 3: 3 (Enter)
Face 1, Vertex 4: 4 (Enter)
Face 1, Vertex 5: 5 (Enter)
Face 1, Vertex 6: 6 (Enter)
Face 1, Vertex 7: (Enter)
Face 2, Vertex 1: (Enter)
```

Figure 29.25

Generating a six-sided surface with PFACE.

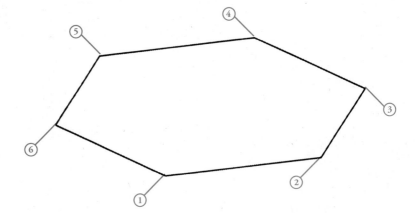

Tip

The polyface mesh generated by the PFACE command resembles a whole series of 3D face objects with the common edges made invisible. The invisible edges in the interior of the surface all meet at the first vertex point you specified.

To generate the surface correctly, you must make sure that these invisible interior lines do not cross each other or the perimeter of the surface. Imagine that you are standing at the point you want to specify as the first vertex point of the face. Can you see each of the other corners without another corner point intervening? If your answer is Yes, then the surface will be generated correctly. If the answer is No, then

New Riders Publishing
INSIDE
SERIES

the surface will not be generated correctly. If the surface is not generated correctly, choose another point to be the first vertex point or define multiple surfaces rather than a single surface. You can see the internal lines if you set the SPLFRAME system variable on before drawing the P face. To see the mesh lines of existing polymeshes, set SPLFRAME on and issue the REGEN command.

The prompt sequence for this type of scenario seems redundant. Why do you have to pick the points first and then type the point numbers? Why not just pick the needed points and skip the Face m, Vertex n prompts? The reason is that PFACE also was designed to handle the next scenario, in which you create multiple surfaces that behave as a single unit. You can create, for example, a wireframe model of a box using lines with zero thickness (see fig. 29.26). To cover two of the faces, you can execute PFACE in the following manner:

Vertex 1: Pick ①
Vertex 2: Pick ②
Vertex 3: Pick ③
Vertex 4: Pick ④
Vertex 5: Pick ⑤
Vertex 6: Pick ⑥
Vertex 7: (Enter)
Face 1, Vertex 1: 1
Face 1, Vertex 2: 2
Face 1, Vertex 3: 5
Face 1, Vertex 4: 4
Face 1, Vertex 5: (Enter)
Face 2, Vertex 1: 2
Face 2, Vertex 2: 3
Face 2, Vertex 3: 6
Face 2, Vertex 4: 5
Face 2, Vertex 5: (Enter)
Face 3, Vertex 1: (Enter)

The result appears to be two separate surfaces, but in reality is a single polyface mesh that is treated as a single object. This multiple-surfaces scenario is what PFACE was ultimately designed to handle and explains why you are asked to pick the points first and then specify the points to be used for a particular face.

As when using the 3DFACE command, you can specify certain edges on the perimeter of the surface to be invisible. You enter the point number as a negative number at the prompt for the nth vertex point to make the nth edge invisible. Unlike a 3D face object, you cannot use DDMODIFY or EDGE or any other command to control the visibility of existing polymeshes.

29

Figure 29.26
*Wireframe model
of a box to be
surfaced.*

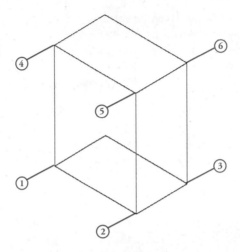

As with the 3DMESH command, using PFACE requires a lot of work and therefore is rarely used directly by the user. The number of points and the difficulties of keeping track of the proper face and vertex numbers usually keeps this command from being used by all but the most dedicated of 3D element creators. The PFACE command is mostly used by programs that create meshes from a number of input points—for example, creating a digital terrain map from a collection of survey points.

Revolving a Surface with REVSURF

REVSURF generates a 3D mesh object in the form of a surface of revolution. REVSURF generates a surface of revolution by taking an outline—the path curve—and revolving it about a user-defined axis. As shown in figure 29.27, the path curve is revolved around the axis of revolution to create the surface.

REVSURF. The REVSURF command enables you to generate a surface of revolution.
Pull-down: *Choose* Draw, Surfaces, Revolved Surface
Screen: *Choose* DRAW 2, SURFACES, Revsurf

When REVSURF is invoked, the following prompts appear:

◆ **Select path curve.** The path curve is the outline that will be revolved. The outline is a single object that can be a line, arc, circle, 2D or 3D polyline (splined or unsplined), ellipse, or elliptical arc.

◆ **Select Axis of revolution.** The axis of revolution is the axis about which the path curve will be revolved. The axis can be a line or an open 2D or 3D polyline. If a polyline is selected, the axis is assumed to be an imaginary line running through the first and last vertices.

◆ **Start angle <0>.** The start angle is the angular offset from the path curve, at which the surface of revolution is to begin. The default value 0 indicates that the surface of revolution will begin at the location of the path curve.

◆ **Included angle (+=ccw,-=cw)<Full circle>.** The included angle is the angular distance over which the path curve will generate a surface. The default is a full circle, 360 degrees, which results in the generation of a closed surface of revolution. If you specify a positive angle less than 360 degrees, then the surface is generated in a counterclockwise direction. If you specify a negative angle less than 360 degrees, then the surface is generated in a clockwise direction.

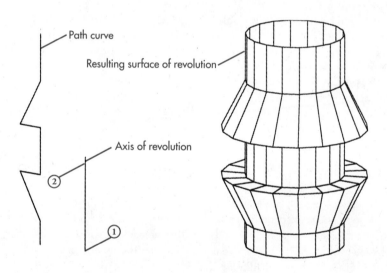

Figure 29.27

Creating a surface of revolution.

Determining Rotation Direction

To have a start angle other than 0 or an included angle other than a full circle (360 degrees), you must be able to determine the positive direction of rotation; a negative value dictates an angular distance in the clockwise direction, whereas a positive value dictates an angular distance in the counterclockwise direction. You determine the direction of rotation by applying the right-hand rule.

29

According to the right-hand rule, if you point your right thumb in the positive direction of the axis about which you are rotating and then wrap the other fingers of your right hand around the axis, the curl of the fingers indicates the direction of positive rotation about the axis. Now the question becomes How do you determine the positive direction of the axis of rotation?

The positive direction along the axis of rotation runs from the endpoint of the object nearest the pick point used to select the object to the other endpoint. For example, in figure 29.25, if you select the line with the point ①, then the positive direction of the axis runs from ① to ②. If you select the line with the point ②, then the positive direction of the axis runs from ② to ①.

Generating a Smooth Mesh

The surface generated by REVSURF is a 3D polyline mesh. The density, M × N, of the 3D mesh is determined by the system variables SURFTAB1 and SURFTAB2. The default value for both variables is 6. SURFTAB1 determines the number of segments generated along the direction of revolution, the M direction of the mesh. SURFTAB2 determines the number of segments generated along the path curve, the N direction of the mesh. If the profile is an unsplined polyline, then one mesh segment is generated per line segment and SURFTAB2 segments are generated for each arc segment. SURFTAB2 segments are generated for any other type of object selected as the path curve.

Tip   The original objects that define the profile and axis are left untouched by the REVSURF command and are not integrated into the final surface of revolution. They might be difficult to spot, however, because the surface of revolution can envelope them. A good habit is to generate the surface of revolution on a layer separate from the layer containing the path curve and axis. This method gives you some flexibility should you need to use the path curve and axis again. This tip also applies to TABSURF, EDGESURF, and RULESURF.

REVSURF is a superior tool for creating any sort of 3D object that is symmetrical about some axis. In the following exercise, you use REVSURF to create a model of a vase.

Creating a Surface of Revolution

Begin a new drawing named VASE1 using the default prototype drawing ACAD. Create two layers named OUTLINE and SURFACE and set the layer OUTLINE current. You start by creating the profile of the vase.

New Riders Publishing
INSIDE
SERIES

Command: *Choose* View, 3D Viewpoint   Sets isometric viewpoint
Presets, SE Isometric

Command: *Choose* View, Preset UCS	Displays the UCS Orientation dialog box
Select the Front *icon and choose* OK	Creates a UCS rotated about the X axis
Command: *Choose* Draw, Polyline	Issues the PLINE command
From point: **10,1** (Enter)	Places the start point of the polyline
Current line-width is 0.0000 Arc/Close/Halfwidth/Length/Undo /Width/<Endpoint of line>: **@2<180** (Enter)	Places the second vertex
Arc/Close/Halfwidth/Length/Undo /Width/<Endpoint of line>: **@4<90** (Enter)	Places the third vertex
Arc/Close/Halfwidth/Length/Undo /Width/<Endpoint of line>: **A** (Enter)	Selects the Arc option
Angle/CEnter/CLose/Direction Halfwidth/Line/Radius/Second pt /Undo/Width/<Endpoint of arc>: **@1,2** (Enter)	Creates a polyline arc segment
Angle/CEnter/CLose/Direction Halfwidth/Line/Radius/Second pt /Undo/Width/<Endpoint of arc>: **L** (Enter)	Selects the Line option
Arc/Close/Halfwidth/Length/Undo /Width/<Endpoint of line>: **@2<90** (Enter)	Places the next segment
Arc/Close/Halfwidth/Length/Undo /Width/<Endpoint of line>: **@.5<120** (Enter)	Places the last segment
Arc/Close/Halfwidth/Length/Undo /Width/<Endpoint of line>: (Enter)	Ends the PLINE command
Command: *Choose* Construct, Fillet	Issues the FILLET command
Polyline/Radius/Trim /<Select first object>: **R** (Enter)	Selects the Radius option
Enter fillet radius <0.0000>: **.25** (Enter)	Sets the fillet radius to .25
Command: (Enter)	Repeats the FILLET command

continues

29

continued

`Polyline/Radius/Trim` `/<Select first object>:` **P** (Enter)	Specifies the Polyline option
`Select 2D polyline:` **L** (Enter)	Fillets the polyline with a .25 radius

This polyline will be the path curve for the surface of revolution. Next you draw the axis of revolution.

`Command:` *Choose* Draw, Line	Issues the LINE command
`From point:` *Using the ENDpoint object snap, pick* ① *(see fig. 29.28)*	Places the starting point of the line
`To point:` **@10<90** (Enter)	Creates the axis of revolution
`To point:` (Enter)	Ends the LINE command

Next you create the surface of revolution. Set the SURFACE layer current.

`Command:` **SURFTAB1** (Enter)	Issues the SURFTAB1 system variable
`New value for SURFTAB1 <6>:` **16** (Enter)	Sets SURFTAB1 to 16
`Command:` *Choose* Draw, Surfaces, Revolved Surface	Issues the REVSURF command
`Select path curve:` *Select the* *polyline at* ②	Selects the profile as the path curve
`Select axis of revolution:` *Select the* *line at* ③	Selects the line as the axis
`Start angle <0>:` (Enter)	Accepts the default starting angle of 0
`Included angle (+=ccw, -=cw)` `<Full circle>:` (Enter)	Accepts the default included angle and creates the surface

The surface of revolution is created. Before hiding it, freeze the OUTLINE layer.

`Command:` **HIDE** (Enter)	Displays a hidden line view of the surface

To create a smoother surface, set SURFTAB1 to a higher value. For a more angular surface, set SURFTAB1 to a lower value. Before saving this model, use the BASE command to set an appropriate base point. Your drawing should look like figure 29.29.

New Riders Publishing
INSIDE
SERIES

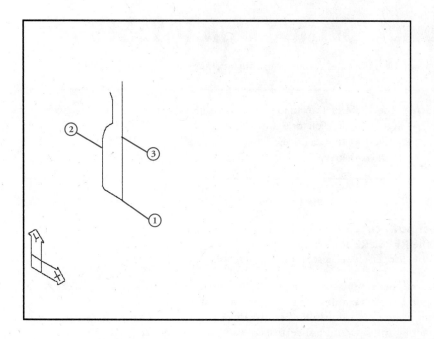

Figure 29.28

*The path curve
and axis of
revolution.*

Figure 29.29

*The finished
surface of
revolution.*

29

Extruding a Surface with TABSURF

TABSURF is another command for generating surfaces.

> **TABSURF.** The TABSURF command generates a surface by extruding a path curve—a profile—in a given direction for a given distance.
> Pull-down: *Choose* Draw, Surfaces, Extruded Surface
> Screen: *Choose* DRAW 2,SURFACES, Tabsurf

After you start TABSURF, you are prompted to select two objects:

◆ **Select path curve.** The path curve is the outline that is to be extruded. As with the REVSURF command, the path curve can be any single object consisting of a line, arc, circle, ellipse, elliptical arc, spline, or 2D or 3D polyline.

◆ **Select direction vector.** The direction vector is a line, or a 2D or 3D polyline, that determines the direction and distance of the extrusion. If the direction vector is a polyline, then the direction vector is an imaginary line connecting the first and last vertices of the polyline.

The direction of extrusion is along the direction vector, starting from the endpoint nearest the point used to select the direction vector to the furthest endpoint. For example, in figure 29.30, if you select the line to be the direction vector by picking ①, then the extrusion direction is from ① to ②. If the pick point is ②, then the extrusion direction is from ② to ①.

Figure 29.30

The TABSURF elements.

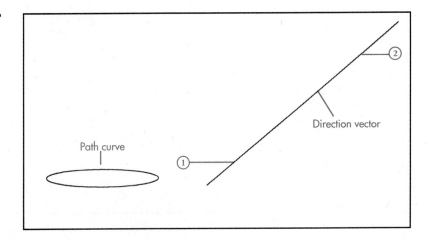

New Riders Publishing
INSIDE
SERIES

The distance of the extrusion is equal to the length of the direction vector. This extrusion is similar to the extrusion you performed on 2D objects. The difference is that when you were extruding 2D objects, the extrusion always was in a direction perpendicular to the XY plane, or, in other words, along the Z axis. With TABSURF, the direction vector can be oriented any way you choose relative to the XY plane; the extrusion need not be perpendicular to the XY plane.

TABSURF actually creates a 3D polyline mesh object. You control the number of mesh segments through the SURFTAB1 system variable. If the path curve is an unsplined polyline, one mesh segment is generated per line segment and then each arc segment is divided into SURFTAB1 number of segments. For all other types of objects, SURFTAB1 number of equal length segments are generated along the path curve.

Extruding Surfaces

Begin a new drawing named STOOL using the default prototype drawing ACAD. Enlarge the drawing limits so that the upper right corner is at 20,20. Zoom to view the enlarged area.

Make a new layer named OUTLINE and make it the current layer. First draw a circle to use as a reference.

`Command:` *Choose* Draw, Circle, *then* Center, Radius	Issues the CIRCLE command
`3P/2P/TTR/<Center point>:` **10,10** (Enter)	Sets center point at 10,10
`Diameter/<Radius>:` **6** (Enter)	Sets radius at 6

Next, draw the path curve to be extruded.

`Command:` (Enter)	Repeats last command
`3P/2P/TTR/<Center point>:` *Choose* Assist, Object Snap, From	Invokes From object snap
`Base point:` *Using CEN object snap, select the circle*	Sets base point for From object snap
`<Offset>:` **@4<-30** (Enter)	Sets offset
`Diameter/<Radius> <6.0000>:` **.75** (Enter)	Sets radius at .75

Next, draw the direction vector for the extrusion.

`Command:` *Choose* Draw, Line	Issues the LINE command

continues

continued

From point: *Using CEN object snap,*
select the smaller circle you just drew

To point: **@2<-30,-12** (Enter)　　　　　　Sets the endpoint of the line using cylindrical
　　　　　　　　　　　　　　　　　　　　　coordinates

To point: (Enter)　　　　　　　　　　　　Ends the LINE command

Command: *Choose* View, 3D Viewpoint　　　Sets isometric viewpoint
Presets, SE Isometric

Make a new layer named SURFACES and make it current. Next, carry out the extrusion to
create a leg for the table.

Command: **SURFTAB1** (Enter)　　　　　　　Accesses SURFTAB1 system variable

New value for SURFTAB1 <6>: **18** (Enter)　　Sets SURFTAB1

Command: *Choose* Draw, Surfaces,　　　　　Issues the TABSURF command
Extruded Surface

Select path curve: *Pick* ① *(see*　　　　　Selects object to be extruded
fig. 30.31)

Select direction vector: *Pick* ②　　　　　Selects direction vector

Next, copy the extruded circle two times in a polar array because this stool has three legs.

Command: *Choose* Construct, Array,　　　　Issues the ARRAY command with the Polar
Polar　　　　　　　　　　　　　　　　　option

Select objects: *Pick* ① *(see fig.*　　　　　Selects object to be arrayed
30.32)

Select objects: (Enter)

Center point of array: *Using CEN*　　　　　Sets center of array
object snap, pick ②

Number of items: **3** (Enter)　　　　　　　Sets number of copies at 3

Angle to fill (+=ccw, -=cw)　　　　　　　Accepts default angle to fill of 360
<360>: (Enter)　　　　　　　　　　　　　degrees

Rotate objects as they are copied?
<Y> (Enter)

Create the seat for the stool by using DDMODIFY to change the thickness of the large circle,
②, to 1.5 and its layer to SURFACES.

Command: *Choose* Tools, Hide   Issues the HIDE command

To finish this model, you use the BASE command to pick an appropriate insertion base point and freeze the OUTLINE layer.

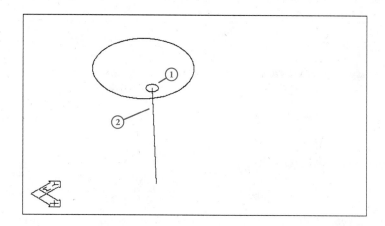

Figure 29.31

Creating a leg for the stool.

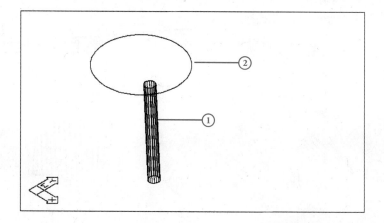

Figure 29.32

Creating the remaining legs and seat.

Creating a Surface with RULESURF

Another command for creating a surface is RULESURF. A ruled surface is a 3D mesh that is generated between two objects. You can use any valid AutoCAD objects except dimensions, text, mlines, blocks, or xrefs. Each border is divided evenly based on the value of the SURFTAB1 variable, and mesh elements extend between each division point, creating a smooth, continuous mesh.

RULESURF. The RULESURF command enables you to create a surface between two objects.
Pull-down: *Choose* Draw, Surfaces, Ruled Surface
Screen: *Choose* DRAW 2, SURFACES, Rulsurf

After you start RULESURF, you see the following prompts:

◆ **Select first defining curve.** Select an object. You can select a line, circle, arc, ellipse, elliptical arc, spline, point, polyline, or 3D polyline.

◆ **Select second defining curve.** Select a second object from those mentioned above.

The two selected objects act as the "edges" of the generated 3D mesh. The two objects can be any combination of lines, circles, ellipses, elliptical arcs, splines, points, or 2D or 3D polylines, subject to the following conditions (see fig. 29.33):

◆ The two objects can both be open or closed curves, but cannot be a combination of the two. A closed curve is a circle, closed spline, closed polyline, or ellipse. All other objects are open curves.

◆ The two objects can consist of a point and either a closed or an open curve, but not two points.

Figure 29.33

Three types of ruled surfaces.

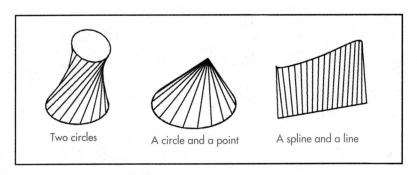

Two circles   A circle and a point   A spline and a line

The number of segments in the resulting 3D polyline mesh is controlled by the SURFTAB1 system variable.

If you choose to generate a surface between two open boundaries, you have to be careful about the point you use to select the boundaries. RULESURF starts generating the mesh at each boundary by dividing each boundary curve into SURFTAB1 segments, starting from the endpoint nearest the pick point. If you use pick points on opposite sides of the two boundary curves, you end up with a surface that intersects itself.

In the following exercise, you use the RULESURF command to draw a tapered cylindrical base for another table to add to your library of furniture symbols.

Creating a Ruled Surface

Begin a new drawing named TABLE3 using the default prototype drawing ACAD. Create a new layer named OUTLINE and make it current.

Set your drawing limits to a lower left corner point of 0,0 and an upper right corner point of 40,40. Issue a ZOOM All. Next, you draw the outline of the cylindrical base of the table.

*Draw a circle with its center point
at* 20,20 *and a radius of* 10

Command: *Choose* Construct, Offset	Issues the OFFSET command
Offset distance or Through <Through>: **1** (Enter)	Sets the offset distance at 1
Select object to offset: *Select the circle*	Selects object to be offset
Side to offset? *Select a point inside the circle*	Sets the direction of offset
Select object to offset: (Enter)	Ends the OFFSET command
Command: *Choose* Modify, Move	Issues the MOVE command
Select objects: **L** (Enter)	Selects last object
Select objects: (Enter)	
Base point or displacement: **0,0,30** (Enter)	Sets displacement at 0,0,30
Second point of displacement: (Enter)	Moves the circle 30 units in the Z direction

Create a new layer named SURFACES and make it the current layer. Next, you draw a surface using the two circles as the boundaries.

Command: *Choose* View, 3D Viewpoint Presets, SE Isometric	Sets nonplanar viewpoint

Next, you connect the two circles with a surface using RULESURF.

Command: **SURFTAB1** (Enter)

continues

29

continued

`New value for SURFTAB1 <6>:` **18** (Enter)	Sets the number of segments in the 3D mesh
Command: *Choose* Draw, Surfaces, Ruled Surface	Issues the RULESURF command
`Select first defining curve:` *Pick the lower circle*	Selects first boundary object
`Select second defining curve:` *Pick the upper circle*	Selects second boundary object

Next, draw the square tabletop.

Command: *Choose* Draw, Surfaces, 3D Objects	Displays the 3D Objects dialog box
Choose 3D *Box*	Issues the AI_BOX command
`Corner of box:` *Using CEN object snap, pick the top circle*	Sets corner of box
`Length:` **40** (Enter)	Sets length
`Cube/<Width>:` **40** (Enter)	Sets width
`Height:` **1** (Enter)	Sets height
`Rotation angle about Z axis:` **0**	Sets rotation angle
Command: *Choose* Modify, Move	Issues the MOVE command
`Select objects:` **L** (Enter)	Selects last object drawn
`Select objects:` (Enter)	
`Base point or displacement:` **-20,-20** (Enter)	Sets displacement
`Second point of displacement:` (Enter)	Centers the tabletop
Command: *Choose* View, Zoom, All	Issues ZOOM command with the All option
Command: *Choose* Tools, Hide	Issues the HIDE command

To finish this model, you should use the BASE command to pick an appropriate insertion base point and freeze the layer OUTLINE.

Creating **EDGESURF** Elements

EDGESURF is a surfacing command that creates a 3D mesh that resembles a Coons surface path. A *Coons surface path* is a mesh bounded on four sides, which smoothly transitions between each of the edges.

EDGESURF. The EDGESURF command creates a 3D mesh that approximates a Coons surface path.
Pull-down: *Choose* Draw, Surfaces, Edge Surface
Screen: *Choose* DRAW 2, SURFACES, Edgsurf

After you start EDGESURF, you see the following prompts:

```
Select edge 1:

Select edge 2:

Select edge 3:

Select edge 4:
```

The constructed surface requires that you select four boundary edges. These boundary edges can be any combination of lines, arcs, elliptical arcs, or 2D or 3D polylines, and they need not be coplanar. However, the four objects must meet end to end to form a closed boundary. Figure 29.34 shows the border of an Edgesurf mesh created from arcs and lines.

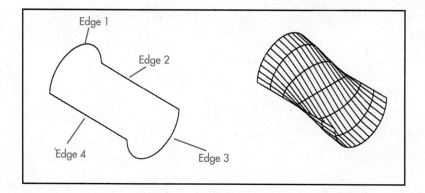

Figure 29.34

The borders of an EDGESURF mesh, and the resulting mesh.

29

SURFTAB1 controls the number of segments generated along the first edge, the M direction. SURFTAB2 controls the number of segments generated in the other direction, the N direction.

Using Regions for Surfaces

In Chapter 12, "Drawing with Complex Objects," you learned about regions—how to create and use them. Regions also are very useful in 3D. When you issue the HIDE command, a region is automatically converted into a surface; when you issue a REGEN, the region reverts to its normal wireframe display. A region is not a 3D object, which means that all the objects you use to define a region must be coplanar. By using the SUBTRACT command, however, you easily can create surfaces with holes in them.

When converting a region to a surface, AutoCAD is replacing the wireframe display of the surface with a polygon mesh with invisible tabulation lines. Because the edges of a polygon mesh are straight lines, any curved edges in the region are approximated with a series of straight edges. To control the number of straight edges used to approximate curves, use the system variable FACETRES. The higher the value, the more straight edges are used.

Removing Tabulation Lines

You have probably been wondering about those unsightly tabulation lines that are part of 3D mesh objects. You cannot prevent them from being created, but you can choose whether or not they are displayed when you hide or plot your drawing.

The trick is to realize that HIDE and PLOT recognize surfaces on layers that are turned off when removing hidden lines. Therefore, the solution is to turn off (not freeze) the layer containing 3D mesh objects. This technique works only if the edges of the surface also are delineated by other objects.

To learn more about this technique and other techniques for 3D surface modeling, see *AutoCAD in 3D* by New Riders Publishing.

In this chapter you learned how to create complex 3D curves and surface models. You also learned how to adjust the smoothing settings for 3D mesh objects with the DDMODIFY command, and you created basic 3D objects such as boxes, cones, and spheres from the 3D Objects dialog box. In the next chapter you learn how to add a touch of realism to the model with rendering and perspective views.

New Riders Publishing
INSIDE
SERIES

C H A P T E R

30

3D Views, Renderings, and Presentations

Knowing how to present the model as a finished product is almost as important as knowing how to create a 3D model. AutoCAD provides you with several presentation tools. You already know about some of them, such as HIDE, VPOINT, and DDVPOINT. VPOINT and DDVPOINT enable you to generate nonplanar views of your model and HIDE enables you to generate views in which the hidden lines are removed. In this chapter, you learn additional presentation commands and techniques, such as how to perform the following actions:

◆ Generate perspective views

◆ Generate "clipped" views

◆ Generate rendered views

◆ Put together slide shows

◆ Transfer your AutoCAD 3D model to other media

In the following exercise, you use the SHADE and RENDER commands to render a drawing, and you use DVIEW to establish a new view.

Quick 5¢ Tour

Begin a new drawing named CHAP30, using the IA Disk prototype drawing CITY.

First, you use SHADE and RENDER to render the current view.

Command: *Choose* Tools, Shade 256 Color	Issues the SHADE command
Command: *Choose* Tools, Render, Render	Issues the RENDER command

If you have not configured for rendering, you are prompted to do so—see the note following this exercise.

Choose the Render Scene *button*	Renders the view
Command: **R** (Enter)	Redraws the screen and returns to the drawing

Next, you use DVIEW to change the view.

Command: *Choose* View, 3D Dynamic View	Issues the DVIEW command
Select objects: **ALL** (Enter)	Selects all objects
Select objects: (Enter)	
Camera/TArget/Distance/POints /Pan/Zoom/TWist/CLip/Hide/ Off/Undo/<eXit>: **PO** (Enter)	Specifies the Points option
Enter target point <768.9048, 778.0894, 176.1489>: *Using END object snap,* pick ① *(see fig. 30.1)*	Sets target point at the top corner of the building
Enter camera point <770.5113, 775.5968, 178.7834>: *Using CEN object snap,* pick ②	Sets camera point at the center of the top of the round building and establishes a new line of sight to the corner of the square building
Camera/TArget/Distance/POints /Pan/Zoom/TWist/CLip/Hide /Off/Undo/<eXit>: **H** (Enter)	Removes the hidden lines from the view

`Camera/TArget/Distance/POints`
`/Pan/Zoom/TWist/CLip/Hide/`
`Off/Undo/<eXit>:` **CA** (Enter)
	Specifies the Camera option

`Toggle angle in/Enter angle` `from XY plane <17.9477>:` **45** (Enter)	Sets the angle from the XY plane
`Toggle angle from/Enter angle in XY` `plane from X axis <-68.62938>:` *Move* *crosshairs left to right until the angle in the* *status bar displays approximately 60 degrees,* *then pick*	Dynamically sets the angle in the XY plane

`Camera/TArget/Distance/POints`
`/Pan/Zoom/TWist/CLip/Hide/`
`Off/Undo/<eXit>:` **Z** (Enter)
	Specifies the Zoom option

`Adjust zoom scale factor <1>:` *Move the* *slider bar until the scale factor in* *the status bar reads approximately 2,* *then pick*	Magnifies the view

`Camera/TArget/Distance/POints`
`/Pan/Zoom/TWist/CLip/Hide/Off`
`/Undo/<eXit>:` (Enter)
	Exits DVIEW

`Command:` *Choose* Tools, Hide	Issues the HIDE command
`Command:` **REGEN** (Enter)	Regenerates the image

Save your drawing.

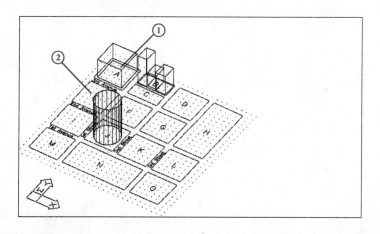

Figure 30.1

Establishing a line of sight.

30

The previous example assumed that you have already configured the rendering devices you will use with AutoCAD. If, instead of displaying the Render dialog box, AutoCAD switches to a text screen, you will need to define which video and printer devices you will be using for rendering. Please refer to the AutoCAD Installation Guide for DOS for instructions on configuring your rendering devices.

Examining the DVIEW Command

You already know how to use DDVPOINT to achieve nonplanar views of your model. As useful as DDVPOINT is, it the following major shortcomings:

◆ You can use DDVPOINT to generate only views in which the viewing point is positioned beyond the model extents. In the model of the city, for example, you cannot generate the view you would get if you were standing on top of one of the buildings, looking out toward the city limits.

◆ You cannot set a specific distance between the viewing point and target point.

◆ The views generated by DDVPOINT are parallel projection views. DDVPOINT does not provide the capacity to generate perspective views.

DVIEW is a more powerful command for generating views of 3D models and addresses the shortcomings of DDVPOINT and more. You can use DVIEW to generate perspective views of your 3D model, establish target and camera placements, and create clipping planes to limit which parts of the 3D model you need to see.

> **DVIEW.** The DVIEW command enables you to generate nonplanar parallel and perspective views of your model.
> Pull-down: *Choose* View, 3D Dynamic View
> Screen: *Choose* VIEW, Dview

When you first invoke DVIEW, AutoCAD prompts you to select objects, then the following options list appears:

CAmera/TArget/Distance/POints/PAn/Zoom/TWist/CLip/Hide/Off/Undo/<eXit>:

The DVIEW options are explained in detail in the following sections.

The Initial Selection of Objects

After you issue the DVIEW command, AutoCAD asks you to select objects. The selected objects then appear and remain listed in the current viewport for the duration of DVIEW. Several DVIEW options enable you to dynamically set settings. *Dynamically* means that the display changes as you decide on a value for a setting. The result is similar to the dragging that occurs during the MOVE or COPY commands. You can imagine that a dynamic display can be very slow for complicated models. Because you can select the objects to display in DVIEW, you should restrict your selection to just the salient parts of a model to use as a frame of reference for setting the options, thereby speeding up dynamic display of DVIEW.

If you choose not to select any objects, DVIEW automatically uses a block named DVIEWBLOCK as the view to display within DVIEW. DVIEWBLOCK's just a simple wireframe 3D model of a house (see fig. 30.2).

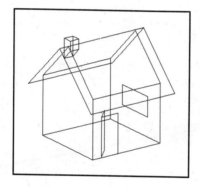

Figure 30.2

A block named DVIEWBLOCK.

The idea behind DVIEWBLOCK is that you need something to display and use as a frame of reference when you are in DVIEW, even if you choose not to select any portion of your model. DVIEWBLOCK provides that frame of reference. You can even define your own block named DVIEWBLOCK (draw it as a 1-by-1-by-1 block) and use it in DVIEW.

Tip

For large models, the trick is to select just enough of the model to provide an accurate frame of reference while you set the various parameters. If the model is very complicated and is a single object, you can use the DVIEWBLOCK (by not selecting anything) as a reference picture within DVIEW.

30

Positioning the Camera and Target

DVIEW was programmed with the analogy of a camera in mind. You are the camera and the view on-screen is the view through the lens of the camera. The first chore you want to accomplish is to establish the location of the camera (yourself) and the target (the point at which the camera is pointed).

The initial view you see in DVIEW is that of the current view in your current viewport. DVIEW has three options that you can use to set the positions of the camera and target:

◆ **Points.** This option enables you to set the position of the target and camera by picking points. The target point initially is at the center of the current view and a rubber band extends from it. If you want to leave the target point at its current position, press Enter; otherwise, pick another location.

After you select a new target point, a rubber band extends from the new target point. The rubber band helps you visualize your line of sight as you pick a new camera point.

◆ **Camera.** This option enables you to set a new camera position by rotating the camera about the target point. You can rotate the camera in the XY plane and/ or the camera's angle relative to the XY plane (similar to DDVPOINT).

You choose the angles dynamically by moving your crosshairs. When you move your crosshairs horizontally (left to right), you rotate the camera in the XY plane. If you move the crosshairs vertically (up and down), you affect the camera's angle relative to the XY plane.

Controlling both angles can be confusing or unwanted, so you can lock in one of the angles as you dynamically set the other angle. In the command window, you see the following prompt:

```
Toggle angle in/Enter angle from XY plane <-8.8035>:
```

To lock the angle from the XY plane, type an angle or accept the default (the current angle), after which your crosshairs affect only the angle in the XY plane. Locking the angle from the XY plane limits the motion of the camera to circling the target point.

Choosing the Toggle option enables you to unlock the angle, and at the same time lets you lock the other angle, the angle in the XY plane:

```
Toggle angle from/Enter angle in XY plane from X axis <-3.96373>:
```

To lock the angle in the XY plane, type an angle or accept the default (the current angle), after which your crosshairs affect only the angle from the XY plane. The effect of locking the angle in the XY plane is to limit the motion of the camera to going up and down relative to the target point. If you find that after you lock the angle, you want to unlock it, choose the Toggle option and the preceding prompt appears. Toggle enables you to switch back and forth between the two angles.

You can type both angles and forego using the crosshairs.

♦ **Target.** This option is similar to the Camera option except that it controls the angle of the target point in the XY plane and from the XY plane. AutoCAD measures the angles relative to the camera position. The net effect is similar to the effect of swiveling a camera about its tripod, pointing the camera in different directions.

Of the three options, only Points enables you to set a distance between the target and camera points while defining their positions. The other two options, Camera and Target, only enable you to set angles, not distances. Distance is crucial for generating perspective views.

Even when you use the Points option to set the actual locations of the target and camera points, the generated view is not the view you would get if you actually stood at the camera point. The points only establish the line of sight. To generate the view you get when you stand at the camera point, you must enable DVIEW's perspective viewing mode.

Tip Before you begin DVIEW, think about the possible positions at which you would like to place the camera and target points. If these positions are not already on objects (which then enables you to use object snap to select), you can draw some points at those locations so that you easily can use object snap to select them while you are in DVIEW.

Zooming, Panning, and Twisting

The ZOOM and PAN commands do not work in DVIEW. DVIEW has its own Zoom and Pan options. The Zoom option enables you to zoom in and out. You set the zoom scale factor by positioning the slider bar (see fig. 30.3), ranging from 0x to 16x.

You also can type a scale factor. AutoCAD always applies the scale factor to the current view (similar to the X option of Zoom).

30

Figure 30.3

Defining the twist angle.

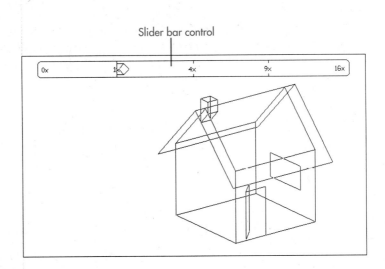

The Pan option enables you to pan your view, and is similar to the PAN command. You define the distance to pan by picking a base point and a point to which to pan; there is no displacement option.

The Twist option enables you to twist the view around the line of sight. A rubber band extends from the center of your view to your crosshairs. You determine the twist angle by setting the angle of the rubber band. The standard 2D angle orientation applies where 0 degrees is horizontal and pointing to the right. The effect is similar to the effect of rotating the camera in your hands.

Clipping the View

A *clipping plane* is an opaque plane positioned somewhere along, and perpendicular to, the line of sight. Two clipping planes are available: the front and back clipping planes. A clipping plane's function is to block from the camera's view whatever is behind the back clipping plane and whatever is in front of the front clipping plane, relative to your line of sight. Figure 30.4 shows an example of front and back clipping planes.

When you specify the Clip option, the following prompt appears:

```
Back/Front/<Off>:
```

◆ **Off.** The default option is to turn off all clipping planes.

◆ **Back.** This option enables you to position the back clipping plane and turn it off or on.

◆ **Front.** This option enables you to position the front clipping plane and turn it off or on.

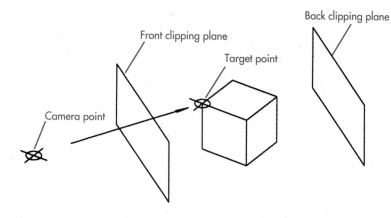

Figure 30.4
Clipping planes.

When you select the Front option, the following prompt appears:

```
Eye/ON/OFF/<Distance from target> <11.1394>:
```

Specifying the Eye option positions the front clipping plane at the camera point. ON turns on the clipping plane at its present location. OFF turns off the clipping plane.

You can use the slider bar at the top of the screen to set the distance of the front clipping plane from the target point. The distance corresponding to the position of the slider bar appears in the status bar. Or, you can type a specific distance. After you position the clipping plane, AutoCAD automatically turns on clipping. A positive distance places the clipping plane in front of the target and a negative clipping plane places the plane behind the target.

If you select the Back option, you have the same options as when you select the Front clipping plane, except that you have no Eye option (placing the back clipping plane at the camera point would hide the entire model from sight).

Tip You need not bother to place the front clipping plane behind the camera. Keep the plane in front of the camera. Also, be careful not to place the back clipping plane so close to the camera that you obscure too much of the model.

After you turn on the clipping planes, they stay on even after you exit DVIEW. To turn off clipping planes, issue the DVIEW command, select the Clip option, and specify the OFF option.

30

Stop Other views as well are clipped until you turn off the Clip option.

Tip Although you can edit the drawing with clipping planes on, you should avoid doing extensive editing in this mode. For example, you might move a model so that one of the clipping planes obscures it entirely.

In the next exercise, you use DVIEW to generate a clipped view of your model.

Clipping Your Model

Continue to use the drawing CHAP30. Restore the view OVERALL.

Command: *Choose* View, 3D Dynamic View	Issues the DVIEW command
Select objects: **ALL** (Enter)	Selects all objects
Select objects: (Enter)	
Camera/TArget/Distance/Points/ PAn/Zoom/TWist/Clip/Hide/Off/ Undo/<eXit>: **CL** (Enter)	Specifies the Clip option
Back/Front/<Off>: **F** (Enter)	Specifies Front clipping plane
Eye/ON/OFF/<Distance from target> <3.9667>: *Move the slider until the* *distance displayed in the status bar* *is approximately 32, then pick*	Sets clipping plane between the camera point and the target and produces the clipped view
Camera/TArget/Distance/POints /Pan/Zoom/TWist/CLip/Hide/ Off/Undo/<eXit>: **CL** (Enter)	Specifies the Clip option
Back/Front/<Off>: (Enter)	Accepts default of turning off clipping planes
Camera/TArget/Distance/POints /Pan/Zoom/TWist/CLip/Hide/ Off/Undo/<eXit>: **Z** (Enter)	Specifies the Zoom option

```
Adjust zoom scale factor <1>: 2 (Enter)      Sets zoom factor at 2

Camera/TArget/Distance/POints              Exits DVIEW
/Pan/Zoom/TWist/CLip/Hide/
Off/Undo/<eXit>: (Enter)
```

Save the drawing.

Hiding the View

The Hide option shows you a temporary hidden line removal of the objects within the DVIEW command. AutoCAD restores the full wireframe view when you leave DVIEW or select another option. The Hide option enables you to preview the results of the regular HIDE command only on the objects you select for the DVIEW command.

Generating Perspective Views

By default, DVIEW generates parallel projection views, just like DDVPOINT or VPOINT. To generate a perspective view, you must specify the Distance option. The Distance option enables you to set the camera a specific distance away from the target. The default distance is the current 3D distance between the camera and target points.

When you use the Distance option, AutoCAD automatically generates a perspective view and, if clipping is not turned on, turns on the front clipping plane and positions it at the camera. The resulting view is what you would actually see through the camera lens at the specified distance from the target along the line of sight established between the target and camera points.

When perspective mode is on, the icon you see in figure 30.5 appears in the lower left corner of your screen.

Figure 30.5

The perspective mode icon.

This icon (which resembles a box in a perspective view) is to remind you that the view on-screen is a perspective view. You cannot pick points when you are in perspective view, which makes it very difficult to perform general drawing and editing work. To turn off perspective viewing, use the Off option of DVIEW.

30

Tip Use multiple viewports to draw or edit while displaying a perspective view in one viewport.

When perspective mode is on, you can use the Zoom option to adjust the field of vision. Zoom's prompt is different when you are in perspective mode. AutoCAD asks you for a lens length rather than a zoom factor. The default is a 50mm lens. If you want a wider angle shot, specify a shorter lens length, like 35mm. If you want a tighter shot, use a larger longer lens length, like 75mm. You can use the slider bar to set the lens or you can type a value. Zoom does not affect the distance between the camera and target points.

To plot perspective views, just use the PLOT command as you normally would. You can save a named view in perspective view, and later specify it as a view to plot.

In the next exercise, you generate a perspective view of your model.

Generating Perspective Views

Continue to use the drawing CHAP30. Restore the view OVERALL.

Command: *Choose* View, 3D Dynamic View	Issues the DVIEW command
Select objects: **ALL** (Enter)	Selects everything
Select objects: (Enter)	
Camera/TArget/Distance/POints /Pan/Zoom/TWist/CLip/Hide/ Off/Undo/<eXit>: **PO** (Enter)	Specifies the Point option
Enter target point <1044.2557, 1039.4883,255.5651>: *Using END object snap*, pick ① *(see fig. 30.6)*	Sets the target point
Enter camera point <1045.8622, 1036.9956,258.1996>: **.XY** (Enter)	Specifies the .XY point filter
of *Using END object snap*, pick ②	Sets camera point's XY coordinates
(need Z): **5** (Enter)	Sets camera's height

New Riders Publishing
INSIDE SERIES

```
Camera/TArget/Distance/POints/            Specifies the Distance option
Pan/Zoom/TWist/CLip/Hide/
Off/Undo/<eXit>: D (Enter)

New camera/target distance                Accepts the default distance, which is the
<882.7655>: (Enter)                       current 3D distance between the target and
                                          camera points
```

Using the Distance option generates a perspective view.

```
Camera/TArget/Distance/POints            Specifies the Zoom option
/Pan/Zoom/TWist/CLip/Hide/
Off/Undo/<eXit>: Z (Enter)

Adjust lenslength <50.000mm>: 35 (Enter)  Sets the camera lens at 35mm
```

While in perspective mode, the Zoom option prompts for a lens length rather than a zoom factor.

```
Camera/TArget/Distance/POints            Exits DVIEW with perspective mode on
/Pan/Zoom/TWist/CLip/Hide/Off
/Undo/<eXit>: (Enter)
```

Use the DDVIEW command to name the current perspective view as PERS1.

```
Command: Choose View, 3D Dynamic View   Issues the DVIEW command

Select objects: P (Enter)               Selects the previous selection set

Select objects: (Enter)

Camera/TArget/Distance/POints            Turns off perspective mode
/Pan/Zoom/TWist/CLip/Hide/Off
/Undo/<eXit>: O (Enter)

Camera/TArget/Distance/POints            Ends DVIEW
/Pan/Zoom/TWist/CLip/Hide/Off
/Undo/<eXit>: (Enter)
```

Use the DDVIEW command to restore the PERS1 view.

```
Regenerating drawing.
```

Save the drawing.

30

Figure 30.6

Setting the camera and target points.

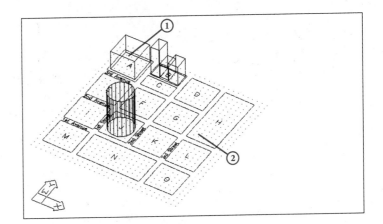

You can save and restore perspective views. To turn perspective mode off again, you must use the Off option of DVIEW or restore another saved view with DDVIEW.

Tip   Saving and restoring perspective views is a timesaving technique. Using the DVIEW command to generate the same perspective twice can be difficult.

Shading Your Views

Besides having AutoCAD remove the hidden lines from the current view, you also can render the view. Two levels of rendering are available in R13, SHADE and RENDER. SHADE level rendering is simple to use and quick. RENDER level rendering is more realistic, but requires more knowledge to use and takes longer. RENDER level rendering also requires a graphics card capable of at least 256 colors, preferably more.

The SHADE Command

SHADE creates a flat shaded rendering in the current viewport.

SHADE. The SHADE command enables you to render the current view as a flat shaded model.
Pull-down: *Choose* Tools, Shade, 256 Color
Screen menu: *Choose* TOOLS, SHADE, Shade

New Riders Publishing
INSIDE
SERIES

SHADE does not enable you to produce shadows, but you can set the SHADEDGE system variable so that it shades a surface to simulate the effect of differing amounts of light reflecting from different portions of the surface (referred to as *shading*). By default, SHADE simply colors the surfaces of your model with their assigned colors.

SHADE affects only objects that are on visible layers. The image that SHADE produces remains in the viewport until you issue a REGEN or use a command that causes a regeneration, in which case, AutoCAD redisplays the wireframe model. You cannot select objects during the display of a shaded image, so you must regenerate the display before you can perform further work on the model. You cannot, moreover, directly plot a shaded image. The shaded image must first be saved to a file with a command such as SAVEIMAGE, discussed later in this chapter. Once the shaded image has been saved to a file, it can then be plotted from a graphics program such as Windows Paintbrush.

SHADE has no options, but its actions are affected by two system variables, SHADEDGE and SHADEDIF.

SHADEDGE

SHADEDGE is one of two system variables that you can use to control the effects of the SHADE command. You can set SHADEDGE to one of four values, as follows:

- ◆ **0.** Causes surfaces to be shaded but with none of the edges highlighted. The color used to shade the edge varies according to the viewing angle.

- ◆ **1.** Causes surfaces to be shaded with the edges highlighted in the background color. The color used to shade the edge varies according to the viewing angle.

- ◆ **2.** Causes surfaces to be shaded in the background color with the edges drawn in the object's color. The effect is similar to the HIDE command.

- ◆ **3.** Causes the surfaces to be shaded in the object's color with the edges drawn in the background color. This is the default option.

Options 0 and 1 cause SHADE to account for various portions of the surface reflecting varying amounts of light. The amount of light a surface reflects depends on its angle to the light source. A surface reflects the most light if it is at a right angle to the light rays. A surface at another angle to the light reflects less light and appears darker. You can see this effect most easily with curved surfaces, such as a cylinder's side.

SHADE utilizes a single light source for the shading calculations. This light source is located behind the observer and shines directly on the model. You cannot do anything to affect the location of this light source.

30

The curious effect of setting SHADEDGE to a value of 0 or 1 is that you can actually end up with AutoCAD drawing an object's surface using colors other than the assigned color. For example, you might draw a cylinder in red but after you issue a SHADE command, see portions of the cylinder in magenta, purple, or some other color, especially if your graphics card is capable of only 16 colors. SHADE is not capable of more realistic renderings because it is designed for cards that can display only 256 or fewer colors; more realistic renderings require many more colors.

Tip If the results of the HIDE command are not satisfactory, (HIDE is not hiding lines that should be hidden), try using the SHADE command with SHADEDGE set to 2. This setting might not always correct defects in the shaded image.

SHADEDIF

The SHADEDIF system variable enables you to control the amount of reflection from the model's surface due to diffuse reflection of light versus ambient light. *Ambient light* is light that appears to come from all around the model with the same intensity. *Diffuse reflection* is reflection that bounces off a surface in various directions—that is, uneven reflection off a surface. The value of SHADEDIF is 70, by default, which indicates that 70 percent of the light from the model is diffuse reflective light from SHADE's single light source. The remaining 30 percent is from ambient light. The more light that comes from ambient light, the less contrast you get with the rendered model (the effect is similar to a white out that you sometimes can see during snow storms).

SHADEDIF only affects SHADE if SHADEDGE is set to 0 or 1.

Making and Viewing Slides

AutoCAD can save and display images in a *slide* file format (SLD). These images can be views of ordinary 2D drawings, or 3D views with shading or hidden line removal applied. Slide files are used for presentations and for the images in image tiles in dialog boxes and icon menus. Creating a slide show of slide file images is covered in the section "Putting Together a Slide Show" later in this chapter.

You cannot save shaded and hidden line views within the drawing. You must have AutoCAD regenerate them each time you want to see one. AutoCAD does, however, give you several ways to take snapshots of your screen, which you can save and restore at any time. Using the MSLIDE command is one way you can take a snapshot of your screen.

New Riders Publishing
INSIDE
SERIES

> **MSLIDE.** The MSLIDE command enables you to take a snapshot of the view in your current viewport.
> Pull-down: *Choose* Tools, Slide, Save
> Screen: *Choose* TOOLS, Mslide

Making a slide is easy. Just display the view you want to save on your screen, then issue the MSLIDE command and supply a file name. AutoCAD tags slide files with an SLD file-name extension. You can use MSLIDE to save any wireframe, shaded views, or views with hidden lines removed.

To view a slide created using MSLIDE, you use the VSLIDE command.

> **VSLIDE.** The VSLIDE command enables you to display in the current viewport snapshots you took with the MSLIDE command.
> Pull-down: *Choose* Tools, Slide, View
> Screen: *Choose* TOOLS, Vslide

All you do is issue the VSLIDE command and supply the name of the slide file you want to view, and the slide appears in the current viewport. It temporarily replaces the current view, but issuing the REDRAW command immediately restores the current view.

Tip If you want to show someone views of a drawing without sending the actual drawing file, you can just send slide files. Because slide files are separate and independent from the drawing from which they were created, you can view slides without the drawing from which they were created.

In the next exercise, you create and view a slide file.

Creating and Viewing Slides

Continue to use the drawing CHAP30. Restore the view PERS1.

Command: *Choose* Tools, Shade 256 Color	Issues the SHADE command
Command: *Choose* Tools, Slide, Save	Issues the MSLIDE command and opens the Create Slide File dialog box

continues

30

continued

Enter **CITY1** *in the* File *box, then* *choose* OK	Creates a new slide file with the name CITY1
Restore the view OVERALL	
Command: *Choose* Tools, Slide, View	Issues the VSLIDE command and opens the Select Slide File dialog box
Select CITY1.SLD, *and choose* OK	Displays the slide image
Command: *Choose* View, Redraw View	Issues the REDRAW command

The slide only temporarily displaces the current view. REDRAW restores the current view.

Save your work.

Rendering Your Views

SHADE is the lowest level of rendering available in AutoCAD. The next level of rendering uses the RENDER command. With RENDER, you can work the following wonders:

◆ Specify multiple light sources

◆ Specify different types of light sources

◆ Specify different combinations of views and lights

◆ Assign materials to the model

The end result of the RENDER command is a much higher quality rendering than you can achieve using the SHADE command. Actually, several commands are involved in the rendering process; RENDER simply is the command that actually generates the rendered view.

The RENDER Command

The RENDER command initiates the rendering process.

New Riders Publishing
INSIDE SERIES

> **RENDER.** The RENDER command enables you to generate a rendered image of the view in the current viewport.
> Pull-down: *Choose* Tools, Render, Render
> Screen: *Choose* TOOLS, RENDER, Render

Issuing the RENDER command opens the Render dialog box (see fig. 30.7).

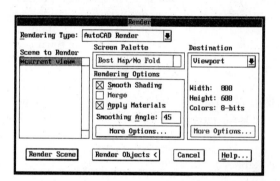

Figure 30.7

The Render dialog box.

The various components of the dialog box are as follows.

♦ **Rendering Type list box.** You use this list box to choose the type of rendering program you want to use with RENDER. Unless you purchase additional add-on programs, such as AutoVision, you have only one choice: AutoCAD Render.

♦ **Scene to Render list box.** You use this list box to specify the scene you want to render. Scenes are discussed later in the section "Creating Your Scenes." For now, you should use the default scene, *current view*.

♦ **Screen Palette list box.** You use this list box to select a color map to use when AutoCAD is configured for a 256-color rendering driver. If you use a driver that supplies more than 256 colors (a continuous color rendering driver), this option is not available.

♦ **Rendering Options section.** Smooth Shading, on by default, creates a smoother blend of colors between adjacent faces in a curved polygon mesh surface, such as one you might use the REVSURF command to generate. This setting works in tandem with the Smoothing Angle value, which is set to 45 degrees by default. The 45 degrees dictates that if the outside angle between two adjacent faces on a polygon mesh is greater than 45 degrees, RENDER

30

should render the two faces with a distinct edge separating the two faces; otherwise, RENDER tries to blend one face into the next face.

The Merge option is off by default. When it is on, RENDER does not clear the previous render image in the *frame buffer* (the area of memory that holds the most recent rendering) before creating the new image. The result is a merged image of the new image and the image that previously was in the frame buffer.

The Apply Materials option, which is on by default, instructs RENDER to take into account any materials that have been applied to the model, when rendering. By default, AutoCAD assigns the material *global* to all objects to which you have not explicitly assigned a material, for rendering purposes. See the section "Adding Materials to the Rendering," later in this chapter for more details.

◆ **Destination section.** You use this section to specify where to display the rendering. The default is the current viewport. Other options include rendering to a file and rendering to a separate render window. The options of rendering to a file and rendering to the Render screen are discussed in greater detail later, in the section "Rendering to a File."

If you select the More Options button, you initiate a dialog box that enables you to set several more options. Figure 30.8 shows the AutoCAD Render Options dialog box. The various options for this dialog are as follows.

Figure 30.8

The AutoCAD Render Options dialog box.

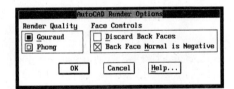

◆ **The Render Quality section.** This section determines the type of shading algorithm which will be used to render the drawing objects. Phong is the more sophisticated shading method and generates more realistic highlights, but takes longer. Gouraud is the default option.

◆ **The Face Controls section.** This section instructs RENDER how to handle back faces. *Back faces* are faces that face away from the viewer. Turning this on instructs RENDER to not bother to render the back faces and can reduce the time it takes to complete a rendering. How RENDER determines whether a face is a back face is determined by the Back Face Normal Is Negative option, which is on by default. When on, this option instructs RENDER to treat all faces that have a positive normal vector as faces that face the viewer. To have the back face option work correctly, you must define faces with points drawn in a counter-

clockwise direction. You need not worry about this when AutoCAD creates the surfaces for you, such as the surfaces created by REVSURF or TABSURF. If you use 3DFACE or PFACE to create faces, picking the points that define the surface, be sure to pick the points in a counterclockwise direction.

You also can instruct RENDER to discard back faces (default is off).

Gathering Statistics

You can use the STATS command to gather some information about your model and the last rendering.

> **STATS.** The STATS command enables you to display rendering statistics.
> Pull-down: *Choose* Tools, Render, Statistics
> Screen: *Choose* TOOLS, RENDER, Stats

You get a little flavor of the complexity of the model by the number of faces and triangles in your model. Naturally, the more complex the model, the longer the rendering takes. You can save the information to an ASCII file. As you create new renderings, AutoCAD appends the new statistics to the ASCII file you specify.

Setting Up Your Lights

Lighting is very important in the rendering process. Think of the way lights are used in the real world. You have lights for general lighting, lights to highlight particular features or areas, and even lights to color a scene. The LIGHT command enables you to define lights to perform all these tasks.

> **LIGHT.** The LIGHT command enables you to define and modify lights for rendering.
> Pull-down: *Choose* Tools, Render, Lights
> Screen: *Choose* TOOLS, RENDER, Lights

When you issue the LIGHT command, the Lights dialog box appears (see fig. 30.9).

You can choose between four basic sources of lights, each of which have different characteristics:

◆ **Ambient light.** *Ambient light* is the light that is all around and seems to come from everywhere and has uniform intensity. Ambient light also is known as *background light*.

30

◆ **Distant light.** A *distant light* is a light that is so far away that by the time the light rays reach the target, they all are parallel to each other and seem to come from one direction at a uniform intensity. Figure 30.10 shows how light rays emanate from a distant light source. A distant light is the equivalent of a sun and its intensity does not lessen with the distance from the source of the light.

Figure 30.9

The Lights dialog box.

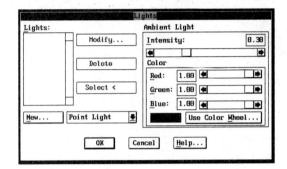

Figure 30.10

Light from a distant light source.

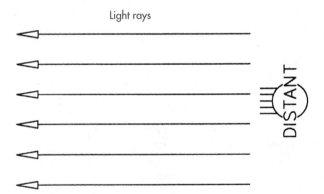

◆ **Point light.** A *point light* is a point source from which light rays emanate; a light bulb, for example, is a point light. Figure 30.11 shows how light rays emanate from a point light.

◆ **Spotlight.** A *spotlight* is a directed light source from which the light rays radiate in a concentrated cone. Within the overall cone of light is a brighter concentration of light rays, referred to as the *hot spot*. Figure 30.12 shows how light rays emanate from a spotlight.

The intensity of the light source is a function of the distance from the light source (the further away you are, the weaker the light). *Attenuation* is a term that describes the decrease in light intensity as a function of distance from the point light source; also referred to as *falloff*.

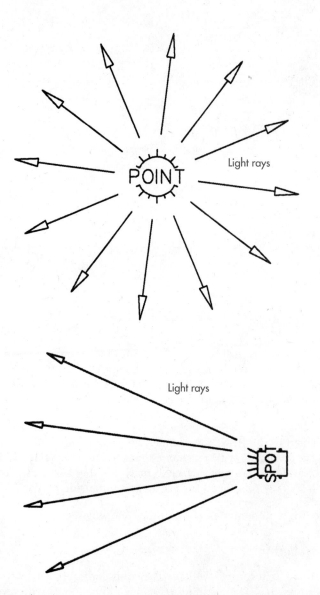

Figure 30.11

Light rays from a point light.

Light rays

Figure 30.12

Light rays from a spotlight.

Light rays

You can define the rate of attenuation as an inverse linear or an inverse square function. An *inverse linear attenuation* means that the intensity of the light is the direct inverse of the distance from the light source. *Inverse square* means that the intensity of the point is the direct inverse of the square of the distance from the light source. Using an inverse square relationship instead of an inverse linear relationship results in less light reaching an object (see fig. 30.13).

30

Figure 30.13

Attenuation and inverse square attenuation.

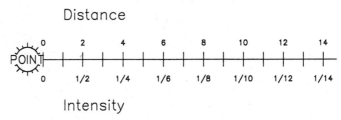

Inverse linear attenuation

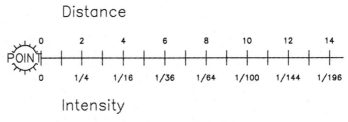

Inverse square attenuation

Rendering occurs because different surfaces reflect light in different amounts, giving you shades of a color. The amount of reflected light depends on the type of light (ambient, distant, point, or spotlight) and the angle of the surface to that light. A surface reflects the most light from a light source when it is at a 90 degree angle to the light rays.

The rendering performed by the RENDER command does not take shadows into account because the rendering algorithms assume that surfaces do not block light; that is, that light can travel through one surface to reach another surface. If you want to get renderings with shadows, you need to have an additional add-on package.

Defining light sources for a model is described in the following sections.

Assigning Colors to Lights

You can assign color to all light sources, which is the equivalent of placing a tinted lens in front of the light source. The default is the color white. You can, however, assign any color to a light. You can use several methods to assign colors. In several of the dialog boxes connected to the setting of lights, you see a button labeled Use Color Wheel. If you choose this button, the Color dialog box appears (see fig. 30.14).

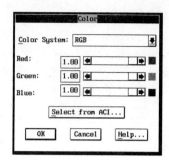

Figure 30.14

The Color dialog box.

The Color dialog box contains the following items:

◆ **RGB.** RGB is the default method for defining a color. You use the set of three slide controls to set the percentages of red, green, and blue to comprise the color. Equal percentages of each results in the color white. Zero percentages of each results in the color black.

◆ **HLS.** You can use the Color System edit box to change the system used to define colors from RGB to HLS. For HLS, the set of three slide controls change to represent the Hue, Lightness, and Saturation of a color. Hue determines the basic color. Lightness controls the amount of white in the basic color. Saturation controls purity (gray) of the color.

◆ **ACI.** If you choose the Select From ACI button, the Select Color dialog box appears, showing the first 255 color assignments (see fig. 30.15).

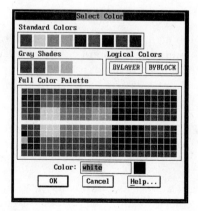

Figure 30.15

The Select Color dialog box.

30

Tip When you first start modeling, avoid assigning colors (other than the default white) to lights, especially if the model itself contains colors other than white. Colors can be confusing, and remember, lights of different colors mix to produce an intermediate color. If you use a green light on a red sphere, for example, you get a mix of the green and red.

The Light Icons

Every light source you define (except ambient light) results in a block that represents the light source being inserted into the drawing. These blocks are referred to as icons and you can edit them just like any other object in the drawing. If you want to move a light source, just use the MOVE command to move its symbol. The symbols are defined to be 1-by-1 unit symbols (see fig. 30.16). AutoCAD inserts the blocks with the default insertion scale factor of 1. You can use the Rendering Preferences dialog box to adjust this insertion scale factor.

Figure 30.16

Symbols for the lights.

Setting the Ambient Light

You use the Lights dialog box to set the ambient light. The intensity of the ambient light can be any value from 0 to 1.

If you set the ambient light level too high, your model can lack adequate contrast. Use ambient light to simulate the overall background light. For a dark room, for example, set it low; for a model in an open field, set it higher.

Creating a Distant Light

To create distant lights, open the Lights dialog box, set the <u>N</u>ew edit box to Distant Light, and then choose the <u>N</u>ew button, which opens the New Distant Light dialog box (see fig. 30.17).

When you create a new distant light source, you must name it, assign it an intensity (ranging from 0 to 1), assign it a color (default is white), and assign its direction relative to the model. An intensity of 0 turns off the light.

The light's direction is defined by two angles, an azimuth angle and an altitude angle. The *azimuth angle* is the direction in the XY plane, where north is 0 degrees. Positive angles are measured clockwise and negative angles are measured counterclockwise.

New Riders Publishing
INSIDE
SERIES

The *altitude angle* is the light's angle relative to the XY plane, ranging from 0 to 90 degrees, where 0 means the light comes from the side of the model and 90 means the light comes from directly above the model.

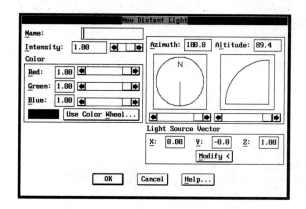

Figure 30.17

The New Distant Light dialog box.

You also can define the light's direction by defining the light source's unit vector. The *unit vector* is simply a set of three numbers that represent the X, Y, and Z displacements that define the line of sight for a unit length. To set these values, you can use the Modify button, which enables you to pick the target point at which to aim the light and the source point from which to aim the light. AutoCAD always treats distant lights as if they are located outside of the model, so it uses the two points only to define the direction from which the light rays come, not the actual location of the light.

Tip   To avoid confusion, always locate distant light outside of the model extents.

In the next exercise, you create two distant light sources.

Creating Some Lights

Continue to use the drawing CHAP30. Restore the view OVERALL.

Command: *Choose* Tools, Render Preferences	Issues the RPREF command and opens the Rendering Preferences dialog box
Change the icon scale to 100 *and choose* OK	Sets the insertion scale of the light icons
Command: *Choose* Tools, Render, Lights	Issues the LIGHT command and opens the Lights dialog box

30

continues

continued

Set the type of light in the drop-down list next to the <u>N</u>ew button to Distant Light. Choose the <u>N</u>ew button. Type the name **RISING**.

Choose the <u>M</u>odify button in the portion labeled Light Source Vector, which enables you to set the location and direction of the light.

`Enter light direction TO <current>:`	Sets the target point for the light
Using END object snap, pick ①	
(see fig. 30.18)	
`Enter light direction FROM <current>:`	Sets the source point for the light
Using END object snap, pick ②	

Use the slider bar to change the altitude to 45. You have now set the location of the distant light source and the direction of the light rays from the source. Choose OK to finish creating the distant light.

Choose the <u>N</u>ew button again to create a second distant light. Enter the name **SETTING**.

Choose the <u>M</u>odify button in the portion labeled Light Source Vector.

`Enter light direction TO <current>:`	Sets the target point for the light
Using END object snap, pick ①	
(see fig. 30.18)	
`Enter light direction FROM <current>:`	Sets the source point for the light
Using END object snap, pick ③	

Use the slider bar to change the altitude to 45. Choose OK. You now have two distant lights defined in the model. Choose OK again to exit the Lights dialog box.

Command: *Choose* Tools, Render, Render	Issues the RENDER command
Choose the Render Scene *button*	
Command: **REGEN** (Enter)	Issues the REGEN command and restores the wireframe

Save your work.

Creating New Point Lights

You create point lights by choosing the <u>N</u>ew button in the Lights dialog box after you set the type of light (in the drop-down list located next to the <u>N</u>ew button) to Point

Light. Choosing the <u>N</u>ew button in this instance initiates the New Point Light dialog box, as shown in figure 30.19.

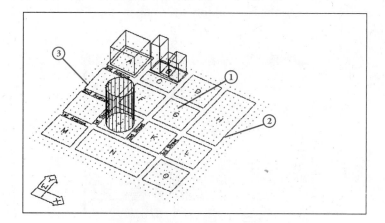

Figure 30.18

Creating new distant lights.

Figure 30.19

The New Point Light dialog box.

As with distant lights, when you create a new point light you assign it a name, intensity, color, and location. Additionally, you determine the light's rate of attenuation: inverse linear, inverse square, or none.

Because the light from a point light radiates in all directions, you need only specify a point light's location, not its direction. The intensity of the light can be any real number from 0 on up. An intensity of 0 turns off the light. The default intensity is 1 if you do not select an attenuation. If you use inverse linear attenuation, the default intensity is set to one-half the drawing extents. If you use inverse square attenuation, the default intensity is set to one-half the square of the drawing extents.

30

Creating New Spotlights

To create spotlights, open the Lights dialog box, choose the Spotlight light type from the <u>N</u>ew edit box, and then choose the <u>N</u>ew button, which opens the New Spotlight dialog box (see fig. 30.20).

Figure 30.20

The New Spotlight dialog box.

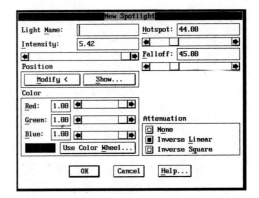

As with a point light, you assign a name, intensity, color, location, and attenuation type to a new spotlight. Additionally, you set two angles: the angle of the hot spot and falloff for the new light.

When you set the location of the spotlight, you pick a target point and the light's location. This is a directional source of light, and unlike a distant light (for which you also determine a direction of light), a spotlight casts light in only one direction and its location is not assumed to be outside the model.

The maximum value for the intensity varies according to the type of attenuation. If no attenuation is used, the maximum intensity value is 1. If an inverse linear attenuation is used, the maximum intensity is set to one-half the extents. If inverse square attenuation is used, the maximum intensity is set to one-half the square of the extents. The extents of the model is defined as the distance from the lower left coordinate to the upper right coordinate of the area occupied by the model.

The light from a spotlight is emitted in a cone of light. The included angle of the cone is referred to as the *falloff cone angle,* which you must define. The default value of the falloff cone angle is 45 degrees. Within the overall cone of light, there is a cone of concentrated light referred to as the *hot spot cone.* The included angle of the cone is referred to as the *hot spot cone angle* and its default value is 44 degrees. Figure 30.21 shows typical falloff and hot spot cones.

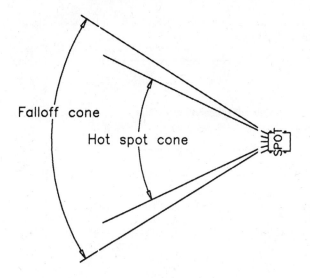

Figure 30.21

Spotlight definitions.

Modifying Existing Light Sources

To modify a light source, just highlight the light's name in the Lights dialog box and choose the <u>M</u>odify button. Alternatively, you can choose the <u>S</u>elect button to select the light's symbol in the drawing, then choose the <u>M</u>odify button.

You also can use standard AutoCAD editing commands, such as MOVE and ROTATE (or grip editing methods), to move the lighting icons around or to rotate their directions.

Deleting Existing Light Sources

To delete a light source, highlight the light's name in the Lights dialog box and choose the <u>D</u>elete button. Alternatively, you can choose the <u>S</u>elect button to select the light's symbol in the drawing and then choose the <u>M</u>odify button.

You also can erase the light's symbol in the drawing.

Tip   If you want to turn a light off temporarily, rather than delete it, you can set its intensity to zero. Alternatively, if you define scenes, you can use the SCENE command to delete the light from the scene (see the following section).

Creating Your Scenes

You know how to use DDVPOINT or DVIEW to achieve a viewpoint. You just learned how to create and position lights. Now, you can create scenes. A *scene* is nothing more

30

than a view that has a particular combination of lights. By default, the current scene is the current view with all lights being used.

> **SCENE.** The SCENE command enables you to define scenes to use with the RENDER command.
> Pull-down: *Choose* Tools, Render, Scenes
> Screen: *Choose* TOOLS, RENDER, Scenes

The SCENE command initiates the Scenes dialog box (see fig. 30.22).

Figure 30.22

The Scenes dialog box.

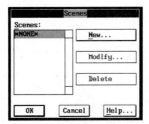

Scenes enable you to quickly switch back and forth between different views which use different lights. The list on the left shows all the currently defined scenes. The buttons on the right enable you to create new scenes, modify existing scenes, or delete a defined scene. To render a particular scene, select the scene from the list of defined scenes in the Render dialog box.

Creating New Scenes

When you choose the New button in the Scenes dialog box, the New Scene dialog box appears (see fig. 30.23).

Figure 30.23

The New Scene dialog box.

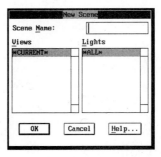

New Riders Publishing
INSIDE
SERIES

To create a new scene, you must first name the scene. The name can consist of as many as eight characters. After you enter a scene name, select a particular view from the list of saved views (left side of dialog box). These are views that you previously have used the DDVIEW command to save. If you just want to use the current view to define the scene, select the default view, *CURRENT*.

After you select a view, select one or more lights to associate with the view you selected. The default is to use all defined lights. The scene is now defined and you can choose OK.

In the next exercise, you create two scenes and render them.

Creating Scenes To Render

Continue to use the drawing CHAP30.

Command: *Choose* Tools, Render, Scenes	Issues the SCENE command and opens the Scenes dialog box
Choose the Ne̲w *button*	Specifies the New option

Enter the scene name **SUNRISE**. Select the view PERS1. Select the light RISING. Choose OK to finish creating the scene. The scene is now defined.

Choose the Ne̲w *button*	Specifies the New option

Enter the scene name **SUNSET**. Select the view OVERALL. Select the light SETTING. Choose OK to finish creating the scene. The scene is now defined. Choose OK again to exit the Scenes dialog box.

Command: *Choose* Tools, Render, Render	Issues the RENDER command and opens the Render dialog box
Select the scene SUNRISE *and choose the* Render Scene *button*	Renders the scene SUNRISE, which consists of the view PERS1 and the light RISING
Command: (Enter)	Repeats the RENDER command
Select the scene SUNSET *and choose the* Render Scene *button*	Renders the scene SUNSET, which consists the view OVERALL and the light SETTING
Command: **REGEN** (Enter)	Restores wireframe display

Save your work.

30

Modifying Existing Scenes

The Modify button in the Scenes dialog box enables you to modify a selected scene. The Modify Scene dialog box is very similar to the New Scenes dialog box. You can modify the view or lights associated with the scene.

Deleting Existing Scenes

The Delete button in the Scenes dialog box enables you to delete a selected scene. Deleting a scene does not delete the view or lights associated with the scene. To delete a view, use the VIEW command. To delete a light, use the LIGHT command.

Adding Materials to the Rendering

To add more realism to your model, AutoCAD provides you with the RMAT command, which enables you to define and apply materials to your model.

RMAT. The RMAT command enables you to define and assign materials to your model.
Pull-down: *Choose* Tools, Render, Materials
Screen: *Choose* TOOLS, RENDER, Mater'l

When you issue the RMAT command, you open the Materials dialog box, shown in figure 30.24.

Figure 30.24
The Materials dialog box.

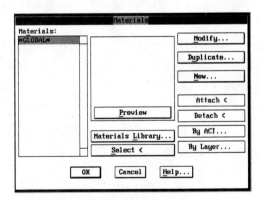

A material defines how a surface reflects light, and even the color of the reflected light, but does not let you assign textures to surfaces.

Importing Predefined Materials

AutoCAD comes with a library of predefined materials that you can apply to your model. You use the MATLIB command to manage the library of materials.

MATLIB. The MATLIB command enables you to manage material definition files.
Pull-down: Tools, Render, Materials Library
Screen: *Choose* TOOLS, RENDER, MatLib

Issuing the MATLIB command opens the Materials Library dialog box (see fig. 30.25).

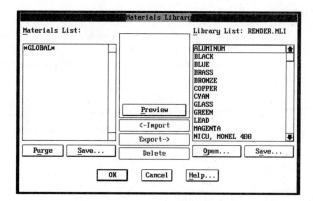

Figure 30.25

The Materials Library dialog box.

You also can use the Materials Library button in the Materials dialog box (opened by issuing the RMAT command) to invoke the MATLIB command.

Before you can assign materials to a model, you must define them or use the MATLIB command to import predefined materials into the drawing. The materials list on the left side of the dialog box is the list of materials currently defined in the drawing. The library list on the right side is a list of all materials in the current materials library file. A *materials library file* is a file in which you keep material definitions. By default, the current materials library file is RENDER.MLI.

To import a material from the library list, highlight it and choose the Import button. You can select multiple materials to import. You can preview the selected material before importing it by using the Preview button. If you have more than one material selected, the Preview button is disabled.

In the next exercise, you import several materials to use in the model.

30

Importing Materials

Continue to use the drawing CHAP30.

Command: *Choose* Tools, Render, Materials Library	Issues the MATLIB command and opens the Materials Library dialog box
Select Copper *from the list of materials and choose* Preview	Displays a sample of the selected material material
Select Glass and Steel *from the list of materials and choose* Import	Imports the selected materials into the drawing

You can select multiple materials, but you cannot preview more than one at a time; the Preview button is not active when you select more than one item at a time.

Choose the Import *button*	Imports the selected materials
Choose OK	Closes the Materials Library dialog box

In the next exercise, you assign the imported materials to your model.

Save your work.

Assigning the Imported Materials

After you import the materials, you can assign them to the model. You can use the Attach button in the Materials dialog box to assign materials to a particular object, the By Layer button to assign materials by layer, or the By ACI button to assign materials by color. You might run into a situation in which an object has been assigned a material for use during rendering. In addition, the object might reside on a layer to which a material is assigned and might be a color that renders as a certain material. In such complex situations, RENDER always gives priority to materials explicitly attached to objects, then to materials assigned by color, then to materials assigned by layer. If you want to preview the material before you assign it, select it from the materials list and then choose the Preview button.

At times you might want to find out what material has been assigned to a particular object. You can use the Select button to select the object and the object's material is highlighted for you.

In the next exercise, you assign the imported materials to the buildings and render the model.

Assigning Materials

Continue to use the drawing CHAP30. Restore the view Overall.

`Command:` *Choose* Tools, Render, Materials	Issues the RMAT command and opens the Materials dialog box
Select Copper *from the list of materials*	Sets the current material
Choose Attach	Specifies that you want to assign the current material to selected objects
`Select objects to attach "COPPER" to:` *Pick* ① *(see fig. 30.26)*	Attaches the material copper to the selected object
`Select objects:` (Enter)	Ends selection
Select Glass *from the list of materials*	
Choose Attach	
`Select objects to attach "GLASS" to:` *Pick* ②	Attaches the material glass to the selected object
`Select objects:` (Enter)	Ends selection
Select Steel *from the list of materials*	
Choose Attach	
`Select objects to attach "STEEL" to:` *Pick* ③	Attaches the material steel to the selected object
`Select objects:` (Enter)	Ends selection
Choose OK	Exit Materials dialog box
Choose Tools, Render, Render	Issues the RENDER command and opens the Render dialog box
Select the scene SUNRISE *and choose the* Render Scene *button*	

The colors of the buildings have changed. The colors come from the assigned materials.

continues

30

continued

Command: *Choose* Tools, Render, Render

Select the scene SUNSET *and choose*
the Render Scene button

Figure 30.26

Attaching
materials to
objects.

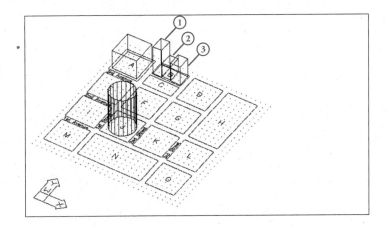

Modifying an Existing Material Definition

If you want to modify an existing material definition, use the RMAT command. Select
a material from the materials list and choose the **M**odify button, which opens the
Modify Standard Material dialog box (see fig. 30.27).

Figure 30.27

The Modify
Standard
Material dialog
box.

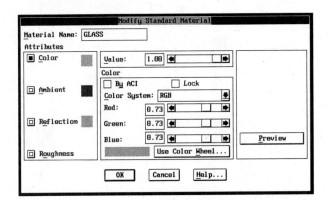

There are four components (or attributes) to a material definition, as follows:

New Riders Publishing
INSIDE
SERIES

◆ **Color.** This is the material's primary, or base, color, also referred to as *diffuse reflection*. You pick a color value for this attribute. Typically, you want the value of color and the value for reflection to add to 1. For a duller finish, keep the color value high relative to the reflection value. For a shinier finish, keep the reflection value high relative to the color value.

◆ **Ambient.** This determines the color of the material due to ambient light. You pick a color and value for this attribute. Keep the value for this attribute at 1.

◆ **Reflection.** This determines the color given off by shiny spots on the object. You pick a color and value for this attribute.

◆ **Roughness.** This determines the roughness of the material, which in turn determines the size of any shiny spots (reflective highlights) on an object. If the surface is very rough, no shiny highlights can exist; with smoother surfaces, the highlights exist. With lower values, highlights can exist and the lower the value, the more concentrated become the highlights. This attribute has an effect only when the value of reflection is other than 0.

You actually can assign a different color for the ambient and reflection attributes. If you want the highlight to appear intense, for example, you might want to assign the color white to the reflection attribute. Alternatively, you can use the Lock option to link the color of the ambient and reflection attributes to the base color. You can use the Preview button to preview the settings.

Creating Your Own Definitions

To create your own material, choose the New button from the Materials dialog box, which opens the New Standard Material dialog box—identical to the dialog box used to modify an existing material. The name you assign to your new material cannot exceed 16 characters.

Saving Modified and New Material Definitions

After you modify an existing material definition, you might want to save it to a materials library file so that you can use it in another drawing. To save a material definition, choose the Materials Library button in the Materials dialog box (or issue the MATLIB command), and choose the Save button under the materials list. This saves the materials list in the drawing to a file that you select. Using the Save button under the library list saves the library list to a file.

Tip   Before you begin to experiment with your definitions, be sure to make a backup copy of the file RENDER.MLI in case you need to restore the original definitions.

30

Setting Your Preferences

RENDER is controlled by a variety of settings. The Render Preferences dialog enables you to determine the destination for your rendering, the type of screen palette to use, and the types of procedures and options to be used to properly generate a rendered image of the current scene.

> **RPREF.** The RPREF command enables you to set the settings for the RENDER command.
> Pull-down: *Choose* Tools, Render, Preferences
> Screen: *Choose* TOOLS, RENDER, Prefer

You can set some rendering settings simply by using the RENDER command. Others, however, you can set only by using the Rendering Preferences dialog box (see fig. 30.28).

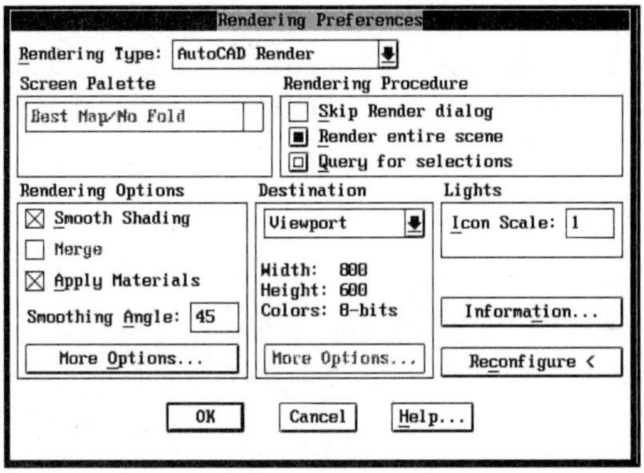

Figure 30.28

The Rendering Preferences dialog box.

In the Rendering Procedure section, you can choose Skip to skip the Render dialog box. If you enable this option, no dialog box appears when you issue the RENDER command. If you enable the Query for selections option, AutoCAD prompts you to select the objects to render.

In the Lights section, you can set the insertion scale of the light icons. The default value is 1. The icons were originally drawn to fit in a 1-by-1 area when plotted at a 1-to-1 scale. When you insert them into a large model, the icons might be too small. Setting the scale to the plot scale makes the icons visible. For example, if you plan to plot the model at 1/8"=1' scale, set the scale value to 96. If you change the scale, AutoCAD immediately resizes all existing light icons when you exit the RPREF command.

The Reconfigure button enables you to reconfigure the Rendering driver. For Windows, the configuration automatically is set to the current Windows graphics and printer drivers, which means that you have no real choice.

Saving and Retrieving Your Current Image

If you render to the current viewport, you can save the current image to a file. The image saved can be a rendered image, a shaded image, an image with hidden lines removed, or just the wireframe image.

Saving the Image

Use the SAVEIMG command to save the current image.

SAVEIMG. The SAVEIMG command enables you to save the image in the current viewport to a file.
Pull-down: *Choose* Tools, Image, Save
Screen: *Choose* TOOLS, Saveimg

When you issue SAVEIMG, the Save Image dialog box appears (see fig. 30.29).

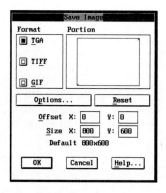

Figure 30.29

The Save Image dialog box.

In the Portion section, you determine what portion of the current image is saved. The choices are as follows:

In addition to specifying the portion to be saved, you can specify the size of the portion to be saved. By default, the entire portion is saved, but you can choose just a subarea by specifying an offset and/or size. You specify the offset and size in pixels. If you want to reset the offset and size values back to their default values, choose the Reset button.

30

You also have a choice of the format in which to save the image, as follows:

- ◆ **TGA.** The default format is Truevision V 2.0 format.
- ◆ **TIFF.** This is Tagged Image File Format.
- ◆ **GIF.** CompuServe Image Format.

Under Options, you then can choose whether to compress the file. The default is to not compress the file.

Replaying Saved Images

To redisplay an image file, use the REPLAY command.

REPLAY. The REPLAY command enables you to display a TIFF, GIF, or TGA image in the current viewport.
Pull-down: *Choose* Tools, Image, View
Screen: *Choose* TOOLS, Replay

The REPLAY command displays a standard file dialog box. Select the file to redisplay and AutoCAD restores the stored image. The image temporarily replaces the current contents of the viewport. You can restore the current viewport by executing the REDRAW command.

Merging Renderings

When AutoCAD renders an image, it utilizes an area of memory referred to as the *frame buffer*. Normally, before each rendering, this frame buffer is erased so that each rendering begins with a blank page. If you turn on the Merge option by using the RENDER or RPREF command, this buffer is not cleared before the new rendering is performed. The new rendering then merges with the existing rendering. You can use this option to place your rendering onto a background image by storing the background image in the frame buffer by using the REPLAY command and then rendering your model.

Rendering to a File

You can bypass the screen by rendering directly to a file. Rendering directly to a file is different from saving the current rendering to a file (SAVEIMG) because you have more choices for file formats and resolutions.

New Riders Publishing
INSIDE
SERIES

To choose to render to a file, select File output from the destination area. Then choose the More Options button under the destination edit box to display the File Output Configurations dialog box (see fig. 30.30).

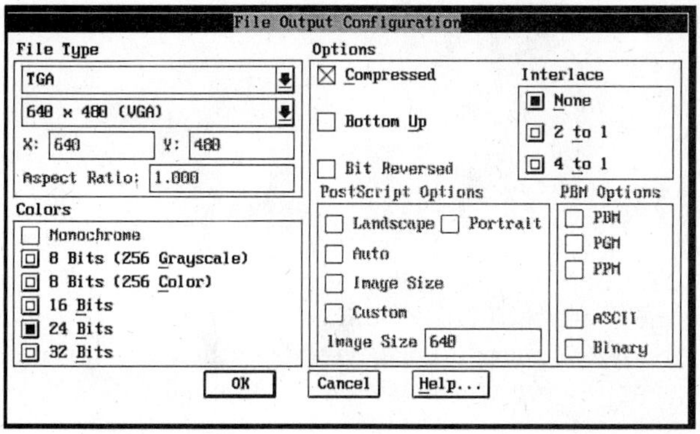

Figure 30.30

The File Output Configuration dialog box.

You can use this dialog box to set the format in which to save the image, the resolution, the number of colors, and other options related to the individual formats. In the File Type section, you can choose to use a GIF, X11, PBM, TGA, BMP, PCX, SUN, FITS, PostScript, TIFF, FAX G III, or IFF file format.

You can choose a variety of resolutions and colors. The key to selecting the appropriate settings for these two parameters is the device on which the file will be displayed or printed. If you generate files to be displayed on your own system, you want to set the resolution and colors to match your station's graphics card. If you send the files to someone else, the resolution and color settings should match that person's computer. The resolution and color scheme you use for the file is independent of the resolution and color scheme of the station on which it is produced.

In the Colors section, note that the first three choices, Monochrome, 8 Bits (256 Grayscale), and 8 Bits (256 Color), are pretty clear as to the number of colors those settings represent. But how about the choices labeled 16 Bits, 24 Bits, and 32 Bits? The number of colors they represent are 65,536, 16.7 million, and 4.3 billion, respectively. Not all color options are available for all file formats.

You also can use a compression scheme or set an interlace value to reduce the file size. These options are available only for certain file formats.

The other parameters shown in the dialog box are specific to Portable Bitmap and PostScript file types.

30

Tip The higher the resolution and color settings, the larger the resultant file, and the longer it takes to finish a rendering. Because the finer resolution and color scheme are effective only if the files are displayed on the appropriate equipment, setting these parameters to values greater than what is supported by the equipment used to view the files is pointless.

Putting Together a Slide Show

For complex models, the actual process of hiding or rendering a view can take some time. If you want to save the results of a HIDE or SHADE and replay them at a later date, you can use the MSLIDE command to make a slide of the current view. You then can use VSLIDE to view files you create using MSLIDE.

You even can put together a simple routine that displays your slides in an organized manner by using what is called a script file. A *script file* is nothing more than a text file that you put together. You include in the file the commands and responses you would normally type in from the keyboard. When you play the script file, the contents are executed just as if you are typing them.

Script files do have limitations. A script file cannot access commands from any of the menus. A script file cannot be interactive; you must supply in the script file all the commands and all the responses necessary for the commands. You can include any valid AutoCAD command in a script file. Script files can also include commands which were designed specifically for use in scripts. These commands, which control the script playback, are described in the following sections.

> **DELAY.** The DELAY command enables you to delay the execution of the next command in a script file for a specified period of time.

The format of the DELAY command is as follows:

DELAY *nnn*

nnn is the delay time in milliseconds.

> **RSCRIPT.** The RSCRIPT command causes the script file to repeat itself.

New Riders Publishing
INSIDE
SERIES

You place the RSCRIPT command at the end of the script file to cause the script file to be repeated.

> **'GRAPHSCR.** The GRAPHSCR command causes the drawing window to be brought forward.

GRAPHSCR and TEXTSCR are the command equivalent of the F1 function key.

> **'TEXTSCR.** The TEXTSCR command causes the text window to be brought forward.

A script file should have a file-name extension of SCR. A script file is a text file, so you can create one by using the MS-DOS EDIT or EDLIN commands, or the Windows Notepad or Write programs. You even can use your favorite word processor—just be sure to save it as a text file.

After you put together a script file, you execute it by issuing the SCRIPT command from within AutoCAD—just supply the name of the script file and watch the show.

> **SCRIPT.** The SCRIPT command executes a script file.
> Pull-down: *Choose* Tools, Run Script
> Screen: *Choose* TOOLS, Script

You can interrupt the script file execution by pressing the backspace or Esc key. You can resume an interrupted script by using the RESUME command.

> **'RESUME.** The RESUME command enables you to resume the execution of a script file after you interrupt its execution using backspace or Esc.

Unfortunately, you cannot use script files to present files that you use the RENDER command to produce, because the REPLAY command cannot accept a file name from the command line.

Tip   AutoCAD is very literal when it executes script files. Spaces are crucial because when you type in a space at the Command: prompt, it means something. So to avoid typing too many spaces, type one entry per line; do not try to string a command and the responses needed for the command on one line.

30

Considering Output Options

Images on a monitor are one thing, but you are bound to experience times when you wish you had that image on a slide or print or piece of paper. Several options have already been covered for images produced using SHADE and RENDER, but you can take advantage of other alternatives.

Using the Old Camera

You can get surprisingly good pictures or slides of your images by simply taking your camera and taking a picture of the image on your monitor. This is a low-cost and easy-to-implement procedure. You might need to experiment with lighting and positioning of the camera, but film is relatively cheap. When photographing the monitor screen, use a tripod and exposures of 1/30th seconds or longer to get good images onto film. In addition, consider using a telephoto lens to correct any curvature induced in the image by the curved monitor screen.

Screen Capturing Equipment

You also can purchase equipment that captures the images electronically and routes them to a slide generator. Typically, this type of solution requires a board that you install in your computer, which then intercepts the signal sent to your monitor and redirects it to the slide generator. The advantage of this equipment over just using a camera to produce the slides is that you do not have glare problems and the resolution of the slides generally is better.

Using Services

Some companies can take your AutoCAD drawing files, slide files, or other file formats (file formats supported by the RENDER command) and produce prints, slides, and even color hard copies of them. These services can be an economical alternative to purchasing your own equipment.

Graphics Printers

Plotters are designed to get your line work onto a piece of paper. To get rendered images onto paper, you must deal with a class of printers geared toward the output (usually color) of images. The equipment can range in cost from several hundred dollars to several thousand dollars. The determining factors are resolution and range of colors that the printer can produce. Now, you are not going to go out and buy an expensive graphics printer when you first begin to experiment with images, but you might want to investigate two especially attractive types of printers.

PostScript printers are designed to handle images and generally are used in conjunction with desktop publishing or word processing software. They are excellent at handling grayscale images. So check to see if anybody in your administrative staff already has a PostScript printer. If not, check to see if any available printers can accept add-ons to make them into PostScript-capable printers. For example, you can equip several models of HP laser printers to handle PostScript files.

Another low-cost printer capable of handling color images are inkjet printers available from several manufacturers, foremost of which is Hewlett-Packard. The printers do not give you photorealistic output, nor are they particularly fast, but for the price (several hundred dollars), the results are quite acceptable.

Using Optional Presentation Tools

You can use the HIDE, SHADE, and RENDER commands to generate images of your 3D models, but the quality of the images these commands produce is limited. The following are three major areas in which you might want more power:

- The capability to realistically account for shadows in a 3D model

- The capability to assign texture to the materials

- The capability to animate the images

If you want any of the preceding capabilities, you need to explore additional software. The software that is available can be divided into two categories:

- **Add-ons.** These packages work inside AutoCAD. Their main advantages are that they share AutoCAD's interface and they appear to the user to be just an extension of AutoCAD.

- **Stand-alone.** These packages work independently of AutoCAD but accept AutoCAD drawings. Generally speaking, the stand-alone packages are more powerful than the add-ons, but also are more expensive.

Exchanging Information with 3D Studio

3D Studio is a stand-alone package from Autodesk with features such as the following:

- Powerful drawing and editing tools that enable you to create your model inside 3D Studio

- Capability to import models from AutoCAD

◆ Photorealistic renderings with shadows, anti-aliasing, and textures

◆ Capability to produce animation

◆ CD full of prebuilt objects, textures, and backgrounds

3D Studio offers many more features than is reasonable to list here. It is, however, a separate program from AutoCAD and it requires a longer learning curve than a program that you integrate into AutoCAD. The commands that enable you to import from 3D Studio are 3DSIN and 3DSOUT.

3DSIN. The 3DSIN command enables you to import 3D Studio files into AutoCAD.
Pull-down: *Choose* File, Import, 3D Studio
Screen: *Choose* FILE, IMPORT, 3DSin

To export to 3D Studio, you use the 3DSOUT command.

3DSOUT. The 3DSOUT command enables you to export AutoCAD files to 3D Studio.
Pull-down: *Choose* File, Export, 3D Studio
Screen: *Choose* FILE, IMPORT, 3DSout

Add-On Packages

Two popular add-on rendering packages for AutoCAD are AutoVision (Autodesk) and AccuRender (Robert McNeel and Associates). Unlike 3D Studio, these packages are capable of creating photorealistic renderings and simple animations with shadows and textures, all within AutoCAD. For more information on these products, contact your local AutoCAD dealer.

When you decide on an additional package, keep the following things in mind:

◆ Have a firm idea of what you want the package to accomplish, be it animation or texture mapping.

◆ Be sure of the hardware requirements of the package. Know whether you will need to invest in additional hardware to get the most out of the software before you buy it.

◆ Make sure you can get support and training for the package.

◆ Be ready to test the packages with a set series of tests to help you compare speed, ease of use, and capabilities.

◆ If the files are being produced for clients, you need to know whether the files are compatible with the client's equipment or needs.

This chapter covered some of the basics of rendering and viewing 3D models. For complete coverage of rendering and modeling in AutoCAD, see New Riders Publishing's *AutoCAD in 3D*. New Riders Publishing's *Inside 3D Studio* contains complete coverage of modeling, rendering, and animation in 3D Studio. In the next chapter, you will be introduced to the new solid modeling features of AutoCAD.

30

Solid Modeling

In previous chapters you learned how to create 3D wire and surface models that look solid, but in fact are not. For example, you learned how to create a surface model that looks like a solid box, but in reality is more like a hollow box that has six sides. In terms of 3D modeling, there is a world of difference between a true solid box and a model that looks like a solid. Solids modeling formerly was an optional add-on package for AutoCAD, but is now incorporated into the basic R13 package. In this chapter, you learn how to do the following:

◆ Create basic solid shapes

◆ Create solids by extrusion and revolution

◆ Create complicated models by combining solids

◆ Edit solid models

◆ Create profile, section and cutaway views of a solid model

In the following Quick 5¢ Tour exercise, you create several solids and combine them to form a more complicated model. The model is a variation of the isometric model you created in Chapter 27, "Isometric Drawings."

Quick 5¢ Tour

Begin a new drawing named CHAP31 and use the default prototype drawing ACAD. Make a new layer named PART and set it current.

Command: *Choose* Draw, Solids, Box, Corner	Issues the BOX command
Center/<Corner of box> <0,0,0>: (Enter)	Sets the corner of the box at the default point
Cube/Length/<other corner>: @5,3,1 (Enter)	Sets the opposite corner, determining the X, Y, and Z dimensions and draws the box
Command: *Choose* View, 3D Viewpoint Presets, SE Isometric View	Issues the VPOINT command and displays a SE viewpoint
Command: *Choose* Draw, Solids, Cylinder, Center	Issues the CYLINDER command
Elliptical/<center point> <0,0,0>: *Using FROM and the ENDP object snap, pick* ① *(see fig. 31.1)*	Sets a base point for relative coordinates
<Offset>: @1.5,1.5 (Enter)	Sets the center of the cylinder
Diameter/<Radius>: 1 (Enter)	Sets the radius of the cylinder
Center of other end/<Height>: 2 (Enter)	Sets height and draws the cylinder
Command: (Enter)	Repeats the CYLINDER command
Elliptical/<center point> <0,0,0>: *Using FROM and the ENDP object snap, pick* ① *(see fig. 31.1)*	Sets a base point for relative coordinates
<Offset>: @1.5,1.5,0.5 (Enter)	Sets the center point of the cylinder
Diameter/<Radius>: 0.75 (Enter)	Sets the radius of the cylinder
Center of other end/<Height>: 2 (Enter)	Sets the height and draws the cylinder
Command: *Choose* View, Zoom, Out	Issues the ZOOM command with .5x
Command: *Choose* Construct, Subtract	Issues the SUBTRACT command

Select solids and regions
to subtract from...

`Select objects:` *Select the objects at* ① *and* ② *and press Enter*	Specifies the source objects
`Select solids and regions` `to subtract...`	
`Select objects:` *Select the cylinder at* ③ *and press Enter*	Subtracts the cylinder from the source objects
`Command:` *Choose* Construct, Fillet	Issues the FILLET command
`Polyline/Radius/Trim/<Select` `first object>:` *Pick* ④	Selects first edge
`Chain/Radius/<Select edge>:` `Enter radius:` **1** `Enter`	Sets fillet radius
`Chain/Radius/<Select edge>:` *Pick* ⑤	Selects second edge
`Chain/Radius/<Select edge>:` **R** `Enter`	Specifies the Radius option
`Enter radius <1.0000>:` **.25** `Enter`	Sets new fillet radius
`Chain/Radius/<Select edge>:` *Pick* ⑥	Selects third edge
`Chain/Radius/<Select edge>:` `Enter`	Ends selection and fillets the edges
`3 edges selected for fillet.`	
`Command:` *Choose* Tools, Hide	Issues the HIDE command

Save your drawing.

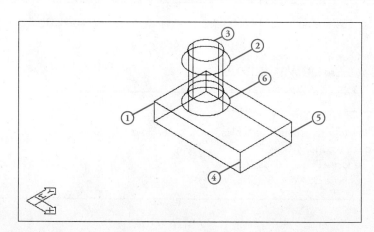

Figure 31.1

Creating the basic parts.

Creating the Basic Solid Shapes

In solid modeling, you use the Solids submenu of the Draw pull-down menu to create basic 3D shapes, such as boxes, cylinders, wedges, and so on. This menu issues solid modeling commands you can use to create solid shapes, boxes, spheres, wedges, cones, cylinders, and toruses.

Boxes and Wedges

AutoCAD has two commands you can use to create rectangular 3D solids: BOX and WEDGE. A *wedge* is simply a box cut in half diagonally. Figures 31.2 and 31.3 show examples of a box and a wedge, respectively.

Figure 31.2

Definition of terms for a box.

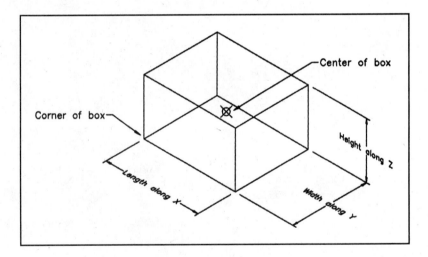

BOX. The BOX command enables you to generate a solid in the shape of a 3D rectangular box.
Pull-down: *Choose* Draw, Solids, Box
Screen: *Choose* DRAW2, SOLIDS, Box

WEDGE. The WEDGE command enables you to generate a solid in the shape of a right rectangular wedge.
Pull-down: *Choose* Draw, Solids, Wedge
Screen: *Choose* DRAW2, SOLIDS, Wedge

New Riders Publishing
INSIDE
SERIES

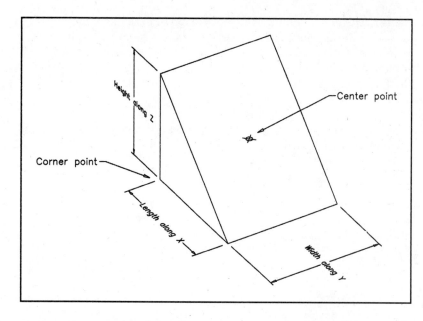

Figure 31.3

Definition of terms for a wedge.

31

The BOX and WEDGE commands have identical prompts. After you issue the BOX or WEDGE command, AutoCAD prompts you as follows:

`Center/<Corner of box> <0,0,0>:`

- ◆ **Corner of box.** The default is to specify a point to position the lower left corner of the box or wedge.

- ◆ **Center.** The other option you have for positioning the box or wedge is to locate the center point of the box.

After you pick a corner point or center point, the following prompt appears:

`Cube/Length/<other corner>:`

- ◆ **Cube.** If the solid you want to create is a cube, select this option and AutoCAD prompts you for the length of the cube. If you are working with a wedge, AutoCAD cuts the cube diagonally.

- ◆ **Length.** This option enables you to specify the length of the box or wedge. The length of the box or wedge is its dimension along the X axis. AutoCAD then prompts you to supply the width and height of the box or wedge. The width is the dimension measured along the Y axis, and the height is the dimension measured along the Z axis. The height can be a positive or negative number. If the height is positive, the object is extruded in the positive Z direction. If the height is negative, the object is extruded in the negative Z direction.

◆ **Other corner.** The default option is to specify a point to set the opposing, diagonal corner point. If you specify a point that has the same Z coordinate as the first point, AutoCAD also asks you for the height of the box. If you pick a point that has a different Z coordinate from the first point, AutoCAD calculates the height of the box based on the difference in the Z coordinates of the two points and does not ask you for a height.

AutoCAD always generates a box or wedge so that its edges are parallel to the X, Y, and Z axes of the current User Coordinate System (UCS), and always draws the top and bottom faces of the box or wedge parallel to the current XY plane.

 Tip

You can use relative coordinates for the second corner point to specify the length, width, and height of a box or wedge. For example, type **@3,2,4** for the second point to obtain a box or wedge that has a length of 3, a width of 2, and a height of 4.

Cones and Cylinders

Cones and cylinders have two basic shapes: elliptical and circular. Figures 31.4 and 31.5 show examples of elliptical and circular cones and cylinders, respectively. You use the CONE command to create cones and the CYLINDER command to create cylinders.

Figure 31.4

Definitions of elliptical and circular cones.

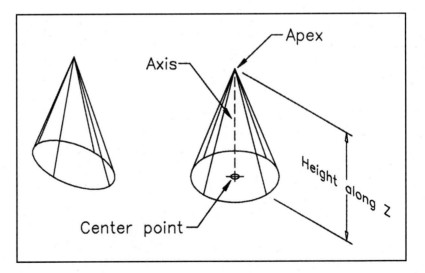

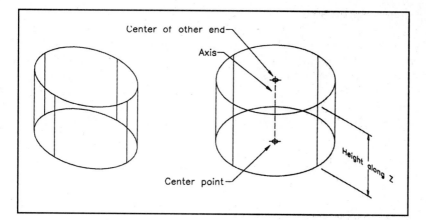

Figure 31.5

Definitions of elliptical and circular cylinders.

CONE. The CONE command enables you to generate a solid in the shape of a 3D right circular or elliptical cone.

Pull-down: *Choose* Draw, Solids, Cone

Screen: *Choose* DRAW2, SOLIDS, Cone

CYLINDER. The CYLINDER command enables you to generate a solid in the shape of a right circular or elliptical cylinder.

Pull-down: *Choose* Draw, Solids, Cylinder

Screen: *Choose* DRAW2, SOLIDS, Cylindr

You define cones and cylinders by drawing a circular or elliptical base and then specifying a height. You can define the height of a cone by placing an apex point. You can define the height of a cylinder by placing a center point for the opposite end of the cylinder.

The CONE and CYLINDER commands have the following options:

```
Elliptical/<center point> <0,0,0>:
```

- ◆ **Center point.** The default is to specify the center point of the circular base of a circular cone or cylinder.

- ◆ **Elliptical.** The Elliptical option enables you to define an elliptical base for an elliptical cone or cylinder. After you specify this option, the following prompt appears:

```
Center/<Axis endpoint>:
```

You can define the elliptical base by picking the endpoints of the axes (the default option) or by picking the center point and the endpoints of the axes (the Center option). See Chapter 7, "Drawing Basic Objects," for more information on creating ellipses.

After you define the base of the cone or cylinder, one of the following prompts appears:

```
Apex/<Height>: (cone)
```

```
Center of other end/<Height>: (cylinder)
```

♦ **Height.** The default enables you to specify a height that results in a right circular or right elliptical cone or cylinder. The height can be a positive or negative number. If you specify a positive height, AutoCAD extrudes the object in the positive Z direction; and if negative, in the negative Z direction.

♦ **Apex.** The Apex option enables you to define the orientation of the axis of the cone by picking the location of the apex of the cone. The difference in the Z coordinates of the apex point and the base of the cone determines the height of the cone. This option enables you to generate a cone that has a base that is not coplanar with the current UCS.

♦ **Center of other end.** The Center option is similar to the Apex option of the CONE command. It enables you to define the orientation of the axis of the cylinder by picking the location of the center of the other face. This option enables you to generate a cylinder that has a base that is not coplanar with the current UCS.

Spheres

You can use the SPHERE command to generate a solid in the form of a sphere (see fig. 31.6).

SPHERE. The SPHERE command enables you to generate a solid in the shape of a sphere.
Pull-down: *Choose* Draw, Solids, Sphere
Screen: *Choose* DRAW2, SOLIDS, Sphere

To generate a sphere, you must specify the center point of the sphere and the radius or the diameter of the sphere.

New Riders Publishing
INSIDE
SERIES

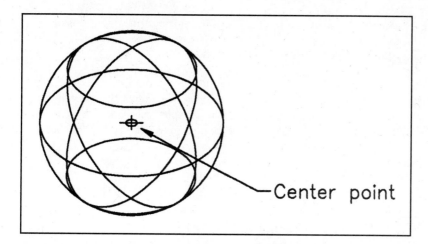

Figure 31.6

The sphere.

Toruses

You use the TORUS command to generate a circular tube (see fig. 31.7).

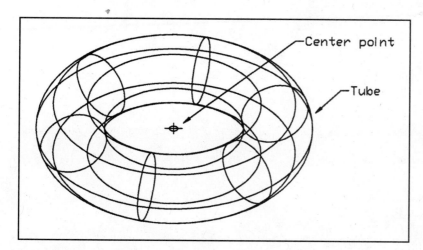

Figure 31.7

The torus.

TORUS. The TORUS command enables you to generate a solid in the shape of an O-ring (or donut).

Pull-down: *Choose* Draw, Solids, Torus
Screen: *Choose* DRAW2, SOLIDS, Torus

To generate a torus, you must specify the center point of the torus, the radius or diameter of the torus (as measured from the center point to the centerline of the tube), and the radius or diameter of the tube.

Tip You can generate some interesting shapes with the TORUS command. Specifying a tube radius larger than the torus radius results in a spherical shape with dimples at the top and bottom. Specifying a negative torus radius results in a football shape.

In the next exercise, you create the solids that you eventually combine to create the base of a bracket.

Creating the Building Blocks

Begin a new drawing named CHAP31A, using the default prototype drawing ACAD. Create a new layer named PART and set it current. Set the ISOLINES system variable to 6.

`Command:` *Choose* Draw, Solids, Box Corner	Issues the BOX command
`Center/<Corner of box> <0,0,0>:` (Enter)	Sets corner of box at default
`Cube/Length/<other corner>:` **5,5,1** (Enter)	Sets X,Y,Z dimensions of box
`Command:` *Choose* View, 3D Viewpoint Presets, SE Isometric View	Issues the VPOINT command and displays an SE viewpoint.
`Command:` *Choose* View, Zoom, Out	Issues the ZOOM command with a *.5x* scale
`Command:` *Choose* Draw, Solids, Cylinder, Center	Issues the CYLINDER command
`Elliptical/<center point>` `<0,0,0>:` **2.5,2.5,2** (Enter)	Sets center of cylinder base 1 unit above the box
`Diameter/<Radius>:` **.5** (Enter)	Sets radius
`Center of other end/<Height>:` **-4** (Enter)	Sets height of cylinder so that the cylinder goes right through the box
`Command:` (Enter)	Repeats the CYLINDER command
`Elliptical/<center point>` `<0,0,0>:` **2.5,2.5,3** (Enter)	Sets cylinder base 2 units above the box
`Diameter/<Radius>:` **.75** (Enter)	Sets radius of cylinder

New Riders Publishing
INSIDE
SERIES

```
Center of other end/<Height>:        Sets height of cylinder so that it
-2.25 (Enter)                        extends 0.25 units into the box
```

Your model should look like figure 31.8.

```
Command: HIDE (Enter)
```

Save your work. To restore the wireframe display, issue the REGEN command.

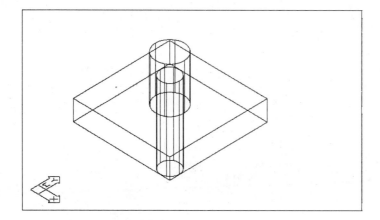

Figure 31.8

Drawing the solids for the base.

Controlling the Display of Solids

When a solid has a curved surface such as a sphere or cylinder, the curved surface is represented with lines when displayed in wireframe mode. These lines are referred to as *tessellation lines* (refer to fig. 31.8).

You use the system variable ISOLINES to determine the number of tessellation lines AutoCAD uses to represent a curved surface. The default value of ISOLINES is 4, which results in four tessellation lines for each curved surface. A value of 0 results in no tessellation lines. Increasing the number of tessellation lines might make it easier to visualize your 3D model. The drawback of increasing ISOLINES is that AutoCAD then takes longer to display curved 3D solids. Just how much longer depends on the complexity of the model and the speed of your system.

An alternative to ISOLINES is to instruct AutoCAD to display the silhouette edges of the curved surfaces by turning the system variable DISPSILH on (1). Displaying silhouette lines, together with fewer or no tessellation lines, can be more effective than increasing the number of tessellation lines in the wireframe display.

When you issue HIDE, SHADE, or RENDER, AutoCAD automatically replaces each face of the solid with a faceted surface that consists of numerous triangular-shaped pieces. The more pieces you use to represent the curved surface, the smoother the curved surface looks. Conversely, the more facets, the longer AutoCAD takes to perform a HIDE, SHADE, or RENDER.

You use the FACETRES system variable to control the number of facets AutoCAD uses to represent a curved surface. The value of FACETRES can range from 0.01 to 10, with a default value of 0.5. A high FACETRES setting results in more facets and a smoother surface. A lower setting results in fewer facets and a flatter surface.

When DISPSILH is on, AutoCAD suppresses display of faceted surfaces when you issue the HIDE or SHADE command.

Tip
Increase the FACETRES setting for smoother-looking curves when you generate the final renderings to give the solid smoother-looking curves. During the preliminary stages of checking the view, colors, and materials, however, you should keep the FACETRES setting low for faster processing.

To restore the wireframe display of a model or to see the effects of changing DISPSILH or ISOLINES, issue the REGEN command. In the next exercise, you modify the settings of DISPSILH and ISOLINES.

Modifying the Wireframe Display

Continue to use the drawing CHAP31A.

Command: **DISPSILH** (Enter)	Accesses the DISPSILH system variable
New value for DISPSILH <0>: **1** (Enter)	Enables the display of silhouette lines
Command: **REGEN** (Enter)	Regenerates the drawing to see the effect of changing DISPSILH
Command: **ISOLINES** (Enter)	Accesses the ISOLINES system variable
New value for ISOLINES <4>: **6** (Enter)	Increases the number of tessellation lines to be generated
Command: **REGEN** (Enter)	Regenerates the drawing to see the effect of changing ISOLINES

Save your work.

New Riders Publishing
INSIDE
SERIES

Building Complex Solids from Other Solids

You can build a solid by combining other solids. The building process requires that you do one of the following:

◆ Create a new solid to represent the union of several solids

◆ Subtract one or more solids from another solid

◆ Create a new solid to represent the intersection of several solids

◆ Create a new solid to represent the interference of several solids

The four commands you use to carry out the aforementioned processes are UNION, SUBTRACT, INTERSECT, and INTERFERE. You learned to use UNION, SUB-TRACT, and INTERSECT with regions in Chapter 12, "Drawing with Complex Objects." INTERFERE is introduced in this chapter. You can find union, subtract, and intersection items in the Construct menu, and you can find interference on the Solids submenu of the Draw menu.

The UNION command enables you to build a new solid by combining several solids. Figure 31.9 shows a union of a box and a cylinder.

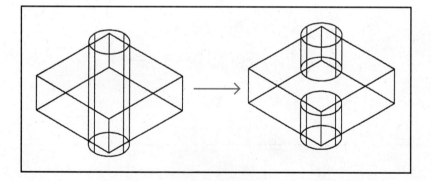

Figure 31.9

Union of a box and cylinder.

To use UNION, you simply select the solids you want to combine and AutoCAD generates a new solid. You can combine solids that do not even intersect; the result-ing solid looks like several distinct solids but handles as one object. More commonly, you merge several solids that actually intersect or touch.

The SUBTRACT command enables you to build a new solid by subtracting one or more solids from one or more source solids. Figure 31.10 shows an example of subtracting a cylinder from a box. First, you select the solids from which you want to subtract, then you select the objects you want to subtract.

Figure 31.10

Subtracting a cylinder from a box.

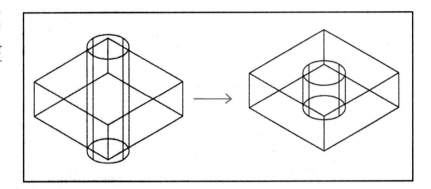

The INTERSECT command enables you to build a new solid from the common space occupied by two or more solids. Figure 31.11 shows the intersection of a cylinder and box.

Figure 31.11

The intersection of the cylinder and box.

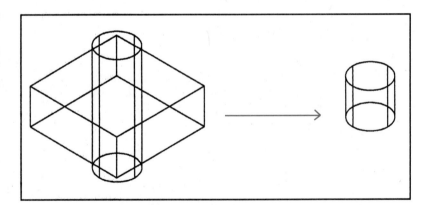

 Tip   Issuing UNION, SUBTRACT, or INTERSECT replaces the original solid objects with a new composite solid. The only way to recover the original solids after you use UNION, SUBTRACT, or INTERSECT is to issue the UNDO command. One way around this limitation is to copy the original solids to a separate layer before you create the composite solid. This way you easily can re-create the composite from the original solids.

New Riders Publishing
INSIDE
SERIES

The INTERFERE command is similar to INTERSECT. INTERFERE leaves the original solids intact, whereas the solid that INTERSECT creates replaces the original solids. Figure 31.12 shows the results of using the INTERFERE command.

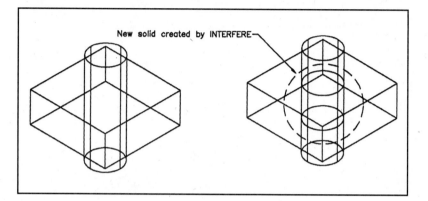

New solid created by INTERFERE

Figure 31.12

Interference of the box and cylinder.

31

INTERFERE. The INTERFERE command enables you to build a new solid from the intersection of two sets of solids.

Pull-down: *Choose* Draw, Solids, Interfere
Screen: *Choose* DRAW2, SOLIDS, Intrfr

Tip   Sometimes the solid you create when you use INTERFERE is obscured by the solids from which it was created. An easy way to move the new solid is to use the MOVE command and select the last object. Another thing you can do is to create the new solid on a separate layer from the original solids; INTERFERE creates the new solid on the current layer.

In the following exercise, you combine the solids you created earlier to form the base of the bracket.

Combining the Building Blocks

Continue from the preceding exercise.

Command: *Choose* Construct, Subtract   Issues the SUBTRACT command

Select solids and regions
to subtract from...

continues

continued

`Select objects:` *Select the box at* ① *and press Enter (see fig. 31.13)*	Selects the source object
`Select solids and regions to subtract...`	
`Select objects:` *Select the cylinders at* ② *and* ③ *and press Enter*	Selects the objects to be subtracted from the source object
`Command:` **HIDE** (Enter)	Displays a hidden line view of the model

`Regenerating drawing.`

The box now has a 0.5-unit radius hole and a 0.75-unit radius counterbore hole.

`Command:` **REGEN** (Enter)	Regenerates the wireframe

Save your work.

Figure 31.13

Subtracting the cylinders from the box.

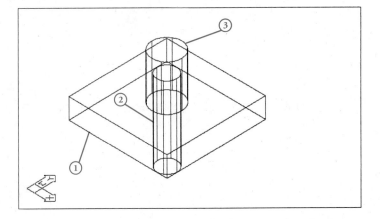

Extruding Solids

The EXTRUDE command is to solids what TABSURF is to surface models—a means of creating a 3D model from 2D objects.

New Riders Publishing
INSIDE SERIES

31

> **EXTRUDE.** The EXTRUDE command enables you to generate a solid by extruding 2D objects along the Z axis or along a path.
> Pull-down: *Choose* Draw, Solids, Extrude
> Screen: *Choose* DRAW2, SOLIDS, Extrude

You can extrude any closed 2D polylines, circles, ellipses, closed splines, and regions. A polyline object cannot have more than 500 vertices nor less than 3 vertices. An object to be extruded also is referred to as the *profile*. After you select the objects to be extruded, you see the following prompt:

```
Path/<Height of Extrusion>:
```

♦ **Height of Extrusion.** The default is to specify the height to extrude the selected objects along the Z axis. If the height is a positive number, the profile is extruded in the positive Z direction. If the height is a negative number, the objects are extruded in the negative Z direction. After you supply a height, AutoCAD prompts you for an extrusion taper angle.

```
Extrusion taper angle <0>:
```

The default angle is 0, which results in the sides of the solid being extruded perpendicular to the XY plane (no tapering) (see fig. 31.14). Positive angular values result in the sides being forced inwards (an inward taper), and negative angular values result in the sides being forced outwards (an outward taper). The absolute value of the taper angle must be less than 90 degrees.

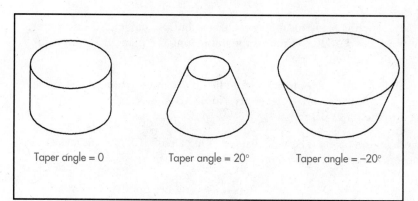

Taper angle = 0   Taper angle = 20°   Taper angle = −20°

Figure 31.14

The effects of a taper angle.

Stop It is possible to define a combination of an extrusion height and taper angle that would cause the solid to taper to a point before reaching its full height. Consider a rectangle with a size of 1" x 1". If you set the extrusion height to 1", and the taper angle to 45°, the solid would come to a point at a height of 0.7", which is below the 1" extrusion height. In this type of situation, EXTRUDE will fail.

◆ **Path.** The Path option enables you to extrude the selected objects along a path defined by a line, circle, arc, ellipse, elliptical arc, polyline (2D or 3D), or spline. The path should not be coplanar with the objects to be extruded. If the path includes curves, the curves should be gentle, not sharp. Sharp curves can force the extrusion to intersect with itself, which is impossible and causes EXTRUDE to fail.

The path can be an open path, such as a line, or a closed path, such as a circle. If the path is an open path, the beginning point of the path should be coplanar with the profile; otherwise, EXTRUDE moves the path to the center of and in the plane of the object to be extruded.

If the path is a spline, one of the endpoints of the spline should be perpendicular to the plane of the object to extrude; otherwise, the spline is moved to the center point of the profile and the profile is rotated to be perpendicular to the spline at the spline's start point.

Note AutoCAD cannot extrude along a closed 3D spline or a 3D polyline that has been spline fitted.

If the path contains segments that are adjacent but not tangent to each other, then at the joints, EXTRUDE miters the joint along the plane that bisects the angle that the segments form.

If the path is closed, the footprint should lie on the miter plane so that the start and end sections match up. If necessary, AutoCAD moves and rotates the footprint to the miter plane.

If more than one object is being extruded along a path, EXTRUDE makes sure that the extrusions end at the same plane.

EXTRUDE is similar to TABSURF, but differs on several key points, as follows:

◆ EXTRUDE creates a solid with closed ends, whereas TABSURF creates a surface with open ends.

◆ You can taper the extrusion if you use EXTRUDE but not if you use TABSURF.

◆ If you use EXTRUDE, you can extrude along a complex curved path defined in 3D space, whereas TABSURF enables you to extrude objects only along a straight line.

◆ EXTRUDE incorporates the object being extruded into the solid, whereas TABSURF leaves the profile intact and separate from the 3D mesh object.

In the following exercise, you use EXTRUDE to create one of the arms of the bracket.

Extruding the Arm

Continue to use the drawing CHAP31A. First create a UCS parallel to the face of the arms.

Command: *Choose* View, Preset UCS	Issues the DDUCSP command and opens the UCS Orientation dialog box
Select the FRONT *icon, turn on the* Absolute to WCS *option, and choose* OK	Creates a new UCS parallel to the front face of the bracket
Command: *Choose* Draw, Polyline	Issues the PLINE command
From point: *Using END object snap,* pick ① *(see fig. 31.15)*	Sets the start point of the polyline
Arc/Close/Halfwidth/Length/Undo/Width/ <Endpoint of line>: **@1.5,6** ⏎(Enter)	Draws the first segment of the polyline
Arc/Close/Halfwidth/Length/Undo/Width/ <Endpoint of line>: **@2,0** ⏎(Enter)	Draws the next segment
Arc/Close/Halfwidth/Length/Undo/ Width/<Endpoint of line>: *Using END object snap, pick* ②	Draws the next segment
Arc/Close/Halfwidth/Length/Undo/ Width/<Endpoint of line>: **C** ⏎(Enter)	Closes the polyline

Next, you will round the top of the arm with the FILLET command. You might need to pan the drawing down to see the top of the arm.

Command: *Choose* Construct, Fillet	Issues the FILLET command
Polyline/Radius/Trim/<Select first object>: **R** ⏎(Enter)	Specifies the Radius option

continues

continued

`Enter fillet radius <0.0000>:` **1** `Enter`	Sets the fillet radius
`Command:` `Enter`	Repeats the FILLET command
`Polyline/Radius/Trim/<Select first` `object>:` *Pick* ③	
`Select second object:` *Pick* ④	Fillets both polyline segments
`Command:` *Choose* Draw, Circle, *then* Center, Radius	Issues the CIRCLE command
`3P/2P/TTR/<Center point>:` *Using CEN* *object snap, pick* ⑤	Sets the center of the circle
`Diameter/<Radius>:` **.5** `Enter`	Sets the circle radius and draws the circle

Next, you convert the circle and polyline into two solids using the EXTRUDE command.

`Command:` *Choose* Draw, Solids, Extrude	Issues the EXTRUDE command
`Select objects:` *Select the polyline* *and the circle at* ⑤ *and* ⑥ *and* *press Enter*	Selects the objects to be extruded
`Path/<Height of Extrusion>:` **-.5** `Enter`	Sets the height of the extrusion
`Extrusion taper angle <0>:` `Enter`	Accepts the default taper angle and creates the solids

Finally, you subtract the hole from the arm.

`Command:` *Choose* Construct, Subtract	Issues the SUBTRACT command
`Select solids and regions to` `subtract from...`	
`Select objects:` *Select the arm at* ① *and press Enter (see fig. 31.16)*	Selects the source solid
`Select solids and regions to` `subtract...`	
`Select objects:` *Select the hole at* ② *and press Enter*	Selects the solid to be subtracted and subtracts it from the source

Save your work. Your drawing should now look like figure 31.16.

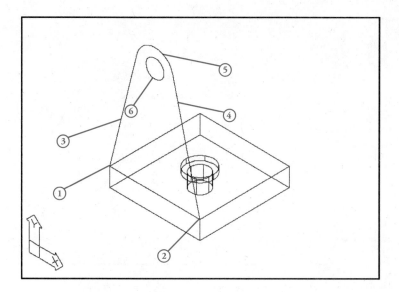

Figure 31.15
Creating the bracket arm.

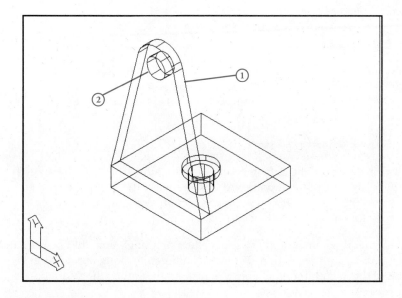

Figure 31.16
Subtracting the hole from the arm.

Revolving Solids

The REVOLVE command is similar to the REVSURF command. REVOLVE creates a solid of revolution as shown in figure 31.17.

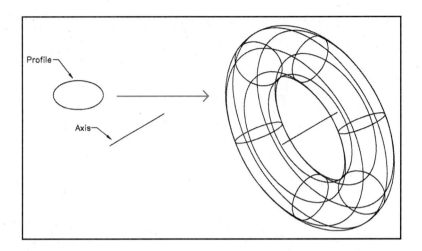

Figure 31.17

Revolving a circle to form a ring.

Profile

Axis

REVOLVE. The REVOLVE command enables you to generate a solid by revolving a 2D object about an axis.

Pull-down: *Choose* Draw, Solids, Revolve
Screen: *Choose* DRAW2, SOLIDS, Revolve

You can revolve any closed 2D polylines, circles, ellipses, closed splines, and regions. You cannot revolve a polyline that has segments that cross or intersect. After you select the objects you want to revolve, AutoCAD prompts you to define the axis of revolution, as follows:

```
Axis of revolution - Object/X/Y/<Start point of axis>:
```

◆ **Start point of axis.** The default enables you to define the axis of revolution by specifying its start and end points. After you specify the start point, you are prompted for the end point. The positive direction along the axis is in the direction of the start point to the end point.

◆ **Object.** This option enables you to select a line or a single straight-line polyline segment as the axis of revolution. The positive direction along the axis is in the direction of the axis endpoint nearest the pick point, to the other axis endpoint.

◆ **X.** This option enables you to define the X axis as the axis of revolution.

◆ **Y.** This option enables you to define the Y axis as the axis of revolution.

New Riders Publishing
INSIDE
SERIES

After you use one of the aforementioned options to define the axis of revolution, AutoCAD prompts you for the angle of revolution, as follows:

```
Angle of revolution <full circle>:
```

The *angle of revolution* is the angular distance the profile is revolved. The default angle is a full circle, or 360 degrees. If you specify an angle less than 360 degrees, you also must determine the positive direction of rotation using the right-hand rule. The angle you enter can be a positive or negative number.

Editing Solids

Of course, after you generate a solid, you want to be able to edit it. Just as you edit "normal" entities, you can use commands such as EXPLODE, FILLET, and CHAMFER to edit solids. You also can use grip editing methods to modify solids entities.

Exploding Solids

You can use the EXPLODE command on a solid object. The solid is then disassembled into a set of regions and bodies. You learned about regions in Chapter 12. You might not, however, be familiar with bodies; a *body* is a form of a NURBS surface (nonuniform rational b-spline, a method of creating complex curved surfaces). As a general rule, EXPLODE converts flat surfaces into regions and curved surfaces into bodies. In turn, you can explode regions and bodies into their constituent parts. You cannot use EXPLODE to disassemble a solid created from other solids back into its original components.

Filleting Solids

You can use FILLET to round the edges of a solid. If you use the same fillet radius to fillet several edges that meet at a common point, then FILLET produces at the common endpoint a rounded surface that is a portion of a sphere. In determining the direction of the curve, FILLET always generates a curved surface that produces a smooth, rounded transition between two adjacent surfaces, as shown in figure 31.18.

The prompt sequence for the FILLET command is a little different when you use it with a solid than when you fillet 2D objects. The initial FILLET prompt is as follows:

```
Polyline/Radius/Trim/<Select first object>:
```

Figure 31.18

Filleting an inside and an outside edge.

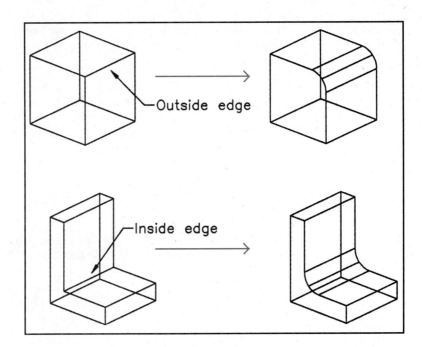

Here, you select the first edge of the solid to be filleted. AutoCAD then prompts you for the fillet radius, as follows:

```
Enter radius <0.2500>:
```

You do not have to use the Radius option to set the radius because AutoCAD prompts you for the radius whenever you select a solid. After you set the fillet radius, you see the following prompt:

```
Chain/Radius/<Select edge>:
```

◆ **Select edge.** The default enables you to select multiple single edges.

◆ **Chain.** The Chain option enables you to select one of the edges in a chain of edges you want to select. A *chain of edges* is a set of edges that are tangent to each other, such as the edges of the top surface of a box.

Stop In early versions of AutoCAD Release 13, the Chain option does not work. If you have one of the initial versions, check with your AutoCAD dealer to see if an upgrade is available. To find out what version you have, choose Help, About AutoCAD.

◆ **Radius.** The Radius option enables you to reset the fillet radius for the subsequent edges you select. You can use this option to apply different radii for different edges without having to stop and restart the command.

When you fillet solids, AutoCAD ignores the setting for the system variable TRIMMODE (the Trim option).

Chamfering Solids

You can use the CHAMFER command on any edge on a solid to generate a flat, transition surface between two adjacent surfaces (see fig. 31.19).

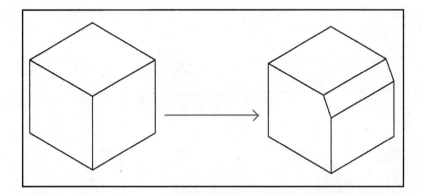

Figure 31.19

Applying CHAMFER to a box.

The prompt sequence for the CHAMFER command is a little different when you select a solid than when you select 2D objects. The initial CHAMFER prompt is as follows:

```
Polyline/Distance/Angle/Trim/Method/<Select first line>:
```

Here, you select the edge you want to chamfer. You then see the following prompt:

```
Select base surface:
Next/<OK>:
```

At any one edge, two surfaces meet. You must designate one of the two surfaces as the base surface. The *base surface* is the surface for which you want to chamfer the edges. One of the two surfaces that form the edge you selected are highlighted. At this point, you select the Next option to highlight the next surface or choose OK (the default option) to accept the highlighted surface as the base surface. You then see the following prompts:

```
Enter base surface distance <0.2500>:
Enter other surface distance <0.1000>:
```

Enter the distances by which you want each edge to be trimmed when AutoCAD draws the transition surface. The base surface distance is the distance by which the base surface you designated earlier will be trimmed. The other surface distance is the distance by which the other surface will be trimmed. AutoCAD then prompts you to select an edge to chamfer or to select a loop, as follows:

```
Loop/<Select edge>:
```

◆ **Select edge.** The default prompts you to select an edge to chamfer.

◆ **Loop.** The Loop option enables you to designate a continuous series of connecting edges (a loop) that you want to chamfer.

Whichever method you use to select edges, after you finish selecting edges or loops, press Enter to apply the chamfers.

In the next exercise, you finish assembling the bracket and create some fillets and chamfers.

Finishing the Bracket

Continue to use the drawing CHAP31A. First, you use CHAMFER to create a countersink for the hole in the arm.

Command: *Choose* Construct, Chamfer	Issues the CHAMFER command
(TRIM mode) Current chamfer Dist1 = 0.0000, Dist2 = 0.0000	
Polyline/Distance/Angle/Trim/Method/ <Select first line>: *Pick* ① *(see fig. 31.20)*	Selects base surface
Select base surface:	
Next/<OK>: Enter	Selects face of arm as base surface

The two surfaces that share the reflected edge are the face of the arm and the inside surface of the hole.

Enter base surface distance: **0.25** Enter	Sets first chamfer distance

New Riders Publishing
INSIDE
SERIES

```
Enter other surface distance
<0.2500>: 0.1 (Enter)
```
Sets second chamfer distance

```
Loop/<Select edge>: Pick ①
```
again and press Enter
Selects edge to be chamfered and completes the command

Next, you mirror the arm.

```
Command: Choose View, Set UCS,
World
```
Restores the World UCS

```
Command: Choose Construct, Mirror
```
Issues the MIRROR command

```
Select objects: Pick ① (see fig.
```
31.21) and press Enter
Selects the arm

```
First point of mirror line: Using MID
```
object snap, pick ②
Sets MIRROR base line

```
Second point: Using MID object snap,
```
pick ③
Sets MIRROR line

```
Delete old objects? <N> (Enter)
```
Completes the MIRROR command

Next, you merge the three solids into one.

```
Command: Choose Construct, Union
```
Issues the UNION command

```
Select objects: ALL (Enter)
```
Selects all the solids

```
Select objects: (Enter)
```
Combines three solids into one solid

Next, you fillet the four vertical corners of the base of the bracket.

```
Command: Choose Construct, Fillet
```
Issues the FILLET command

```
(TRIM mode) Current fillet
radius = 1.0000
```

```
Polyline/Radius/Trim/
<Select first object>: Pick ④
```
Picks first edge

```
Chain/Radius/<Select edge>:
Enter radius <1.0000>: 0.25 (Enter)
```
Sets radius of fillet

```
Chain/Radius/<Select edge>: Select the
```
*edges at ⑤, ⑥, and ⑦ and
press Enter*
Selects the remaining edges and completes the fillet

The bracket is now complete. Save your work.

Figure 31.20

Chamfering the edge of the hole.

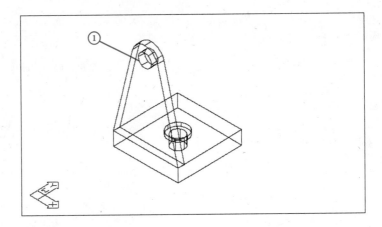

Figure 31.21

Mirroring the arm and filleting the edges.

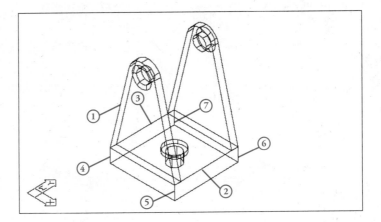

> **Note** Can you extend or trim solids? In a word, no. You cannot use the EXTEND, TRIM, LENGTHEN, or STRETCH commands to change the size of a solid.

Using Grip Editing with Solids

Grip editing works with solids, except for the Stretch option. Because you cannot stretch solids, the stretch grip mode works like the move grip mode. The grip points displayed vary with the type of object, as indicated in the following table.

New Riders Publishing
INSIDE SERIES

Object	Grip Point Location
Box	At each corner
Cone	At the center of the base of the cone and at the apex
Cylinder	At the center of the top and bottom surfaces
Sphere	At the center of the sphere
Torus	At the center of the torus
Wedge	At the corners

Using Object Snaps

You can use object snaps on 3D solids just as you do with 2D objects. Curved surfaces have CENter and QUAdrant object snaps just like arcs and circles. Straight edges have ENDPoint and MIDpoint object snaps. The TANgent and PERPendicular object snaps work, but the results are sometimes difficult to predict from a 3D viewpoint.

Stop   In early versions of Release 13, the INTersection object snap does not work on 3D solid objects. Try using the ENDPoint object snap or creating some 2D construction objects and snapping to them.

Measuring Mass Properties

As with regions, you can use MASSPROP to measure the mass properties of a solid. MASSPROP uses a density of 1 when it performs its calculations. You cannot change this density. With a density of 1, the value of mass and volume are identical. For solids, MASSPROP calculates the mass, volume, bounding box, centroid, moments of inertia, products of inertia, radii of gyration and principle moments, and XYZ directions about the centroid. The bounding box values describe the dimensions of an imaginary 3D box that encompasses the solid. The remaining properties are useful for various engineering calculations and are based on the solid's position relative to the current UCS. Therefore, you should set the location and orientation of the UCS before you calculate these properties.

Note   Unlike AME, the results of the MASSPROP command do not depend on any variable settings. It is, in fact, much more accurate than the MASSPROP command in the AME package.

In the next exercise, you calculate the mass properties of the bracket you just finished.

Getting Mass Properties

Continue to use the drawing CHAP31A.

Command: *Choose* Assist, Inquiry,   Issues the MASSPROP command
Mass Properties

Select objects: *Select the bracket*   Selects object to be queried

Select objects: (Enter)

```
--------------- SOLIDS ---------------~
Mass:          45.3530
Volume:        45.3530
Bounding box:    X: 0.0000 -- 5.0000
          Y: 0.0000 -- 5.0000
          Z: 0.0000 -- 7.8769
Centroid:      X: 2.5000
          Y: 2.5000
          Z: 1.9975
Moments of inertia:  X: 809.3703
          Y: 726.0549
          Z: 804.6635
Products of inertia: XY: 283.4563
          YZ: 226.4827
          ZX: 226.4827
Radii of gyration:  X: 4.2245
          Y: 4.0011
          Z: 4.2122
```

Press RETURN for more: (Enter)   Continues display of data

```
Principal moments and X-Y-Z directions about centroid:
          I: 344.9534 along [1.0000 0.0000 0.0000]
          J: 261.6381 along [0.0000 1.0000 0.0000]
          K: 237.7508 along [0.0000 0.0000 1.0000]
```

Write to a file ? <N>: (Enter)   Ends the MASSPROP command

Save your work.

Creating Section, Profile, and Cutaway Views

Section and cutaway views can be very useful to show the details of complicated 3D objects.

Section Views

You use the SECTION command to generate a region representing a cross section of a solid.

> **SECTION.** The SECTION command enables you to generate a cross-section view of one or more solids along a section (or cutting) plane.
> Pull-down: *Choose* Draw, Solids, Section
> Screen: *Choose* DRAW2, SOLIDS, Section

SECTION generates the cross section on the current layer as a region object lying in the cutting plane, which you specify by using one the following options:

```
Section plane by Object/Zaxis/View/XY/YZ/ZX/<3points>:
```

- ◆ **3points.** The default enables you to specify the section plane by picking three points on the plane.

- ◆ **Object.** Enables you to define the section plane by selecting a 2D object lying in the cutting plane. The 2D object can be a circle, ellipse, arc (circular or elliptical), 2D spline, or 2D polyline.

- ◆ **Zaxis.** Enables you to define the section plane by picking two points to define the origin and positive direction of the Z axis of the desired cutting plane. The first point you pick is the origin, and the second point establishes the positive direction of the Z axis. The section plane is the plane perpendicular to the Z axis you establish.

- ◆ **View.** Enables you to define the section plane parallel to the current viewport's viewing plane and intersecting a point you pick.

- ◆ **XY.** Enables you to define the section plane parallel to the XY plane of the current UCS and intersecting a point you pick.

◆ **YZ.** Enables you to define the section plane parallel to the YZ plane of the current UCS and intersecting a point you pick.

◆ **ZX.** Enables you to define the section plane parallel to the ZX plane of the current UCS and intersecting a point you pick.

The solids that you select to cut a section view through are not affected by the SECTION command; the solids are left intact by SECTION.

 Tip
After you produce the section (a region object), you easily can move it away from the solid(s) by using the Last option of the MOVE command (because the region is the last object drawn).

In the following exercise, you cut a section through the middle of the bracket you finished in the preceding exercise.

Cutting a Section

Continue to use the drawing CHAP31A.

`Command:` *Choose* Draw, Solids, Section	Issues the SECTION command
`Select objects:` *Select the bracket and press Enter*	Selects the bracket
`Section plane by Object/Zaxis/View/` `XY/YZ/ZX/<3points>:` *Using CEN object snap, pick* ① *(see fig. 31.22)*	Sets the first of three points needed to define the section plane
`2nd point on plane:` *Using MID object snap, pick* ②	Sets the second point
`3rd point on plane:` *Using MID object snap, pick* ③	Sets the third point and creates a region

A region is created that represents the cross section of the solid along the plane defined by the three points.

`Command:` *Choose* Modify, Move	Issues the MOVE command
`Select objects:` **L** `Enter`	Selects region created by SECTION
`Select objects:` `Enter`	

 New Riders Publishing
INSIDE
SERIES

```
Base point or displacement:
```
Using END object snap, pick ③

```
Second point of displacement: Pick a
```
point outside of the bracket

Moves the region away from the solid model

You now can do what you want with the section. You can transfer the section to another drawing file (using WBLOCK) or rotate it to lie in the XY plane so that you can annotate it.

Save your work.

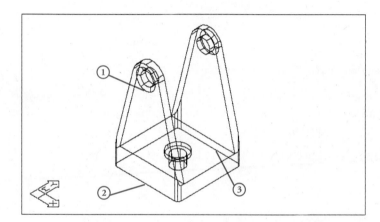

Figure 31.22
Cutting a section.

Cutaway Views

You also can use the **SLICE** command to slice a 3D solid into two parts (see fig. 31.23).

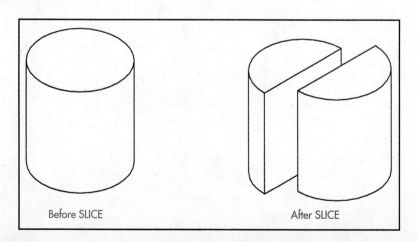

Figure 31.23
Slicing a solid.

Before SLICE   After SLICE

> **SLICE.** The SLICE command enables you to slice one or more solids into two parts along a slicing (or cutting) plane.
> Pull-down: *Choose* Draw, Solids, Slice
> Screen: *Choose* DRAW2, SOLIDS, Slice

You can use one of the following options to define the location of the cutting plane:

```
Slicing plane by Object/Zaxis/View/XY/YZ/ZX/<3points>:
```

These options are identical to the ones offered by the SECTION command.

After you locate the cutting plane, you see the following prompt:

```
Both sides/<Point on desired side of the plane>:
```

◆ **Point on desired side of the plane.** The default enables you to choose which portion of the sliced model you want to keep by picking a point on the desired side of the cutting plane.

◆ **Both sides.** This option enables you to retain both portions of the sliced model.

Tip Unlike the SECTION command, the SLICE command changes the selected solids. It is a good idea to make a copy of the objects before you slice the models, in case you ever need the original solids at a later date.

In the following exercise, you slice the model into two parts.

Slicing the Bracket

Continue to use the drawing CHAP31A.

Command: *Choose* Draw, Solids, Slice	Issues the SLICE command
Select objects: *Select the bracket*	Selects solid to be sliced
Select objects: (Enter)	
Slicing plane by Object/Zaxis/View/ XY/YZ/ZX/<3points>: **YZ** (Enter)	Sets the YZ plane as the cutting plane
Point on YZ plane <0,0,0>: *Using MID* *object snap, pick* ① *(see fig. 31.24)*	Sets a point on the YZ plane

New Riders Publishing
INSIDE
SERIES

```
Both sides/<Point on desired side          Retains both halves of the bracket
of the plane>: B (Enter)
```

Use the MOVE command to move one of the halves away from the other. You now have two solids rather than one. You can quit the drawing now because you do not use it again.

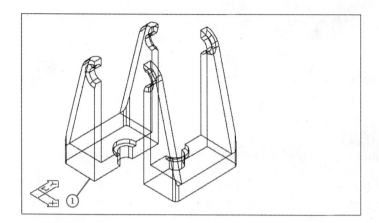

Figure 31.24

Slicing the bracket.

Profile Views

Unlike sections and cutaways, no command generates a 2D profile view of your model. You can, however, use several techniques to generate profile views. Each method has drawbacks.

DXB Views

One method of generating a 2D profile is to plot your drawing to a file, and then import the plot file back into AutoCAD. This involves configuring AutoCAD to plot to a DXB file, setting up the view you want to plot, plotting to the DXB file, and then using AutoCAD's DXBIN command to import the file. The DXB file acts as a virtual plotter that, in effect, captures the pen strokes of a normal plotter.

The major drawback to using a DXB file is that the 2D profile view that is generated consists of only straight lines with no colors or line weights and with everything on a single layer. All the drawing data (lines, arcs, circles, text, and so on) is converted to short line segments. This makes editing a DXB drawing very difficult.

Tip   If plotting to a DXB file, set the plot optimization to the highest level to prevent the drawing of overlapping lines.

PROJECT.LSP

Another way to generate 2D profiles is to use the IA Disk utility PROJECT.LSP. This lisp routine was included with AutoCAD R12 and provides a means of projecting 2D profiles from a 3D model. The routine, however, does not work with R13 solids. One way around this limitation is to use the SAVEASR12 command to convert your R13 solid model into a R12 wireframe model. Once converted to a wireframe, you then can run PROJECT.LSP on the 3D wireframe to create a 2D profile. See Appendix H, "The IA Disk," for information on loading and using PROJECT.LSP.

One of the disadvantages of PROJECT.LSP is that the resulting 2D profile needs significant editing. Overlapping and duplicated objects are common with PROJECT.LSP.

Paper Space

Another alternative is to use floating viewports in paper space. After you get the desired view in a floating viewport, you can use MVIEW's Hideplot option to remove the hidden lines from your plot. The foremost advantage of this method is that the profile view is really just another view of your model, so when you make changes to the model, AutoCAD automatically updates the profile views.

A major drawback to all of these techniques is that there is no automatic hidden line generation. The drafter must figure out which edges are hidden in the 2D view, and delete or change the linetype of those objects. For floating viewports in paper space, the hidden lines must be manually drawn and updated each time the model changes. For complex models, this process can be difficult and time-consuming. Currently, there is no way to automatically generate hidden lines when creating a 2D profile.

Exporting Solids

You might find on occasion that you have to import and export your solid model to the older AME solids modeling package (also made by Autodesk) or to other ACIS solids modeling software. You might, for example, need to perform stress analysis of a mechanical part you design using solids, or maybe check for fluid flow past a new propeller you might be designing. This type of analysis is not included with AutoCAD, so you will need to export your model to the software which would perform these types of analysis.

Exporting to AME

There is no direct means by which to export a R13 solid model to AME. Release 13 solids use a technology called ACIS to create solid objects. AME used a technology called PADL to create solid models in R12 (and R11). There is no way to convert ACIS solids to PADL models.

You can, however, use the SAVEASR12 command to convert the R13 solid model to a R12-compatible wireframe model. You then can use the wireframe objects in R12 to re-create the model as an AME solid model. For complex models, this involves significant work and should be avoided if possible.

Importing AME Models

Although exporting solid models to the AME package is impractical, importing AME models and converting them into solid models is possible, though not problem-free. The command you use is AMECONVERT.

AMECONVERT. The AMECONVERT command enables you to convert Version 2 or 2.1 AME solid models to AutoCAD solid objects.
Pull-down: *Choose* Draw, Solids, AME Convert
Screen: *Choose* DRAW2, SOLIDS, AMEconv

The procedure for transferring AME solids to R13 solids is as follows:

1. Open the R12 drawing file in R13. Release 13 automatically converts the file to R13 format. At this point, the AME solids still are identified as anonymous blocks.

2. Use the AMECONVERT command to convert the AME solids to the new AutoCAD solid objects.

3. Save the changes.

ACIS is a more accurate modeler than the AME CSG modeler ever was. As such, AMECONVERT can result in a less than perfect conversion. You might see some of the solid's surfaces shift in position relative to other surfaces; a fillet, for example, might shift so that it no longer provides a smooth transition from one surface to another. Always check the results of the AMECONVERT for such anomalies.

Linking to Other ACIS Modelers

If you ever need to import models from other ACIS-based modelers or export to them, you can use ACISIN and ACISOUT.

ACISIN. The ACISIN command enables you to import models from other ACIS solid modelers using the SAT file format.

Pull-down:　*Choose* File, Import, SAT
Screen:　　　*Choose* FILE, IMPORT, SATin

ACISOUT. The ACISOUT command enables you to export solid models to other ACIS solid modelers using the SAT file format.

Pull-down:　*Choose* File, Export
Screen:　　　*Choose* FILE, EXPORT, ACISOUT

> **Note**　The IMPORT and EXPORT commands have options for importing and exporting SAT files. Choosing an SAT file in IMPORT or EXPORT has the same result as using ACISIN or ACISOUT.

Your introduction to 3D modeling in AutoCAD is now complete. You have seen how to simulate 3D drawing through isometric drawing techniques, explored the use of User Coordinate Systems, and applied 3D viewing techniques to 3D models. You have examined AutoCAD's 3D objects and used AutoCAD's mesh creation tool to generate complex 3D surfaces. In this chapter, you were introduced to the new ACIS solid objects and saw how to use them to create complex 3D solid models. This is not, however, the end of AutoCAD's 3D capabilities. Powerful add-ons such as Designer, AutoSURF, and AutoVision all add to the 3D modeling and rendering capabilities of AutoCAD. For more on 3D modeling and rendering, see *AutoCAD in 3D,* by New Riders Publishing.

Part VIII

Appendixes

New Riders Publishing
INSIDE
SERIES

A P P E N D I X
A

Installation and Configuration

AutoCAD for DOS has significant advantages over its Windows sibling because it can address 386 or greater microprocessors in their native 32-bit mode. The DOS version also has less stringent memory, disk storage, and swap file requirements than does the Release 13 Windows version.

This appendix explains the requirements for the installation of AutoCAD Release 13 for DOS. It is essential to configure DOS properly if you want to attain optimum performance from AutoCAD. This appendix examines the following areas in depth:

◆ DOS configuration

◆ Memory management

◆ Installing AutoCAD Release 13

◆ Configuring AutoCAD's tablet menu

Discussing all possible configurations and variables in detail is not practical for this appendix. The purpose of this appendix is to acquaint you with the most important setup and configuration issues.

Additional information is available in the AutoCAD Release 13 *Installation Guide for DOS* and the README.TXT file available on the installation disks.

Tip   The user's guide that ships with DOS provides much useful information on configuration and memory management. Additional valuable information can be found in the Microsoft Knowledge Base. The Knowledge Base is available on the Internet (ftp.microsoft.com) and on many on-line services, such as CompuServe and Genie.

Installation Requirements

AutoCAD for DOS requires the following minimum hardware and software configuration:

◆ **An 80386 (minimum requirement), 80486, or Pentium-based computer.** Autodesk recommends a 386 system at least. 386SX and 486SX systems require a math coprocessor. In 386 and 486DX systems, the math coprocessor is designed into the CPU chip.

◆ **8 MB of RAM minimum.** The more RAM installed in your computer, the faster AutoCAD will run. Some 386 computers do not support addressing for more than 16 MB RAM. You can bypass this limitation by using a third-party memory manager, such as QEMM386 from Quarterdeck Office Systems, or by obtaining a BIOS update.

◆ **A hard disk that has enough free space for 26 MB of AutoCAD files and a 20 MB (minimum) swap file.** Additional disk space will be required for the storage of drawing (DWG) files.

◆ **A Video display adapter.**

◆ **Floppy disk drives.** At least one 1.44 MB or 1.2 MB floppy disk drive is required. Drives for 3.5-inch floppies with 1.44 MB storage remain the most popular floppy drives in PC systems today. The 5.25-inch drive with 1.2 MB storage is fast becoming obsolete.

◆ **IBM-compatible parallel port.** A parallel port is required for the network and international versions of AutoCAD.

◆ **Hardware lock.** A hardware lock is required for use on networks and for international single-user installations. It attaches to the workstation's parallel port. The hardware lock ships with all versions of AutoCAD that require it.

◆ **MS-DOS Version 5.0 or later.** MS-DOS Version 6.0 or 6.22 is strongly recommended.

Tip

Update your DOS operating system to version 6.0 or 6.22. DOS version 6.x offers valuable features for optimizing DOS performance.

Use SCANDISK regularly to check the condition of the directories and files on your hard drive. Use DEFRAG regularly to defragment files and optimize the performance of your hard drive. Use MEM to determine how your computer utilizes its memory, and use MEMMAKER to optimize memory usage.

Optional hardware includes the following:

◆ **A pointing device.** This device can be a mouse or a digitizing tablet with a stylus or puck.

◆ **Printer/plotter.** You need one or both of these to be able to produce hard-copy output of your drawings.

◆ **Digitizing tablet.** You need a digitizing tablet for tracing hard-copy or tablet menus.

◆ **Serial port.** You need a serial port to use with digitizers and some plotters.

◆ **CD-ROM drive.** Software installation from CD-ROM is easier, quicker, and far less painful than installation from floppy disks. Also, large data files and software libraries often are distributed on CD-ROM.

Configuring Your DOS Startup Files

When you boot your system, DOS reads two initialization files that configure your hardware, reserve space in memory, set device characteristics, customize the information that DOS displays, and launch memory-resident programs (TSRs) and other applications. These two files are CONFIG.SYS and AUTOEXEC.BAT.

You can use any ASCII text editor to view and edit these files. In fact, you can use any word processor to edit these files, as long as you save them as ASCII text files after you edit them.

The following text shows a typical CONFIG.SYS file:

```
device=C:\windows\himem.sys /v
device=C:\windows\emm386.exe noems x=C800-CFFF
DOS=UMB
device=C:\turbocom.sys
DOS=HIGH
shell=C:\command.com C:\ /e:512 /p
devicehigh /L:1,3280 =C:\ASPI.SYS
devicehigh /L:1,4704 =C:\DAFCDA.SYS
devicehigh /L:1,37520 =C:\PROIIS\SPEED_UP.SYS
buffers=1
files=50
```

CONFIG.SYS

This section discusses the settings and device drivers typically found in a CONFIG.SYS file. Be aware that the contents of CONFIG.SYS files on different systems vary according to the hardware and software used on the given system.

HIMEM.SYS and EMM386.EXE are discussed later in this appendix, in the section "Memory Management."

Buffers reserve memory to hold hard disk data during read and write operations. Each buffer uses approximately 532 bytes of memory. Your system setup determines the number of buffers that should be allocated. If your system uses SMARTDrive and disk compression (for example, DoubleSpace or DriveSpace) and DOS is loaded high, you should set BUFFERS=10. If you use SMARTDrive or other disk-caching software without disk compression, you should set BUFFERS=1. Use BUFFERS=20 or higher if you do not use SMARTDrive or some other form of disk caching.

FILES specifies the number of files that DOS can access at any one time. Autodesk recommends that you use FILES=50 or greater when you run AutoCAD. FILES does not use much memory; a large value helps when you use AutoCAD.

DOS=HIGH,UMB loads part of DOS into upper memory and provides support for loading device drivers and TSRs into the upper memory area to free conventional memory. The DEVICEHIGH command in CONFIG.SYS and the LOADHI command in AUTOEXEC.BAT load various device drivers into high memory.

SHELL defines the command interpreter that DOS is to use. By default, the system command interpreter is COMMAND.COM. The SHELL setting in CONFIG.SYS enables you to specify the amount of RAM available to use to store environment variable settings and other information. Use /E:256 or more for DOS 5.0 or later. If you

New Riders Publishing
INSIDE
SERIES

receive the error message `Out of environment space`, you might need to try a higher number. Increase the number, reboot, and try the operation that caused the error again. You might need to repeat the process several times before you successfully eliminate the error message.

DOS uses `STACKS` to handle hardware interrupts. The first number in `STACKS=9,256` is the quantity of stacks; the second number is the size of each stack in bytes. The number of stacks can be specified as 0 or a number in the range of 8 through 64. Stack size can be specified as 0 or a number of bytes in the range of 32 through 512. How much stack space you need on your system depends on the programs you run and if each program leaves enough stack space to handle hardware interrupts. If your computer becomes unstable or if you receive a `Stack Overflow` or `Exception Error 12` message, increase the number or size of stacks in your CONFIG.SYS file.

AUTOEXEC.BAT

The following is a sample of an AUTOEXEC.BAT file.

```
C:\windows\net start
LH /L:1,2320 c:\dce376dr.exe
@ECHO OFF
path C:\;c:\dos;c:\windows;c:\mouse;c:\batch;c:\xtgold
****************** Mouse Setup ************************
C:\windows\mouse
*********************************************************
LH /L:1,36640 C:\windows\MSCDEX.EXE /S /v /m:10 /d:mscd001
SET temp=c:\temp
```

`PROMPT` changes the appearance of the command prompt in DOS. The `$p` adds the current drive and path to the command prompt. `$g` adds > (the greater-than sign) to the command prompt. Other possibilities include `$t` for adding the time, `$d` for adding the date, and `$v` for adding the DOS version number to the display of the command prompt. This book assumes that you use `$p$g`.

DOS 6 has made the > sign and the display of the current drive and path the initial command prompt setting. There is no need to have the `PROMPT` command in your AUTOEXEC.BAT file if you are running DOS 6 and that is the appearance you want for your command prompt.

Entering **PROMPT** without any text following will clear the initial setting, and the command prompt will display as C> without any indication of path. If you enter **PROMPT $g**, the command prompt will display as >. If you enter **PROMPT $p**, the prompt will display only the drive and path, like `C:\`.

Tip   DOS versions 5.0 and 6.x now have extensive online help systems. To get information about a DOS command at the DOS command prompt, enter **HELP**, followed by the name of the command: **HELP COMMAND**. You can also enter most commands followed by **/?** to get help, like **COMMAND /?**.

The PATH command enables you to specify the directories DOS should search for executable files. MS-DOS recognizes up to 127 characters in the PATH command, including drive letters, colons, and backslashes. During initial installation, many programs add their directory to the PATH statement in the AUTOEXEC.BAT file. Because the PATH command uses conventional memory according to its length, you might want to examine your AUTOEXEC.BAT and remove unnecessary entries from your PATH statement.

Tip   Keep your AUTOEXEC.BAT and CONFIG.SYS files as uncluttered as possible. Keep your PATH down to the absolute minimum to save conventional memory and avoid possible conflicts.

The SET statement enables you to display, set, or remove DOS environment variables. SET commonly is included in the AUTOEXEC.BAT file to set a directory for the storage of temporary files. A program creates temporary files to hold data while a program runs. The program itself should delete temporary files after you close it. When an application or system crashes, the temporary files often remain in the directory established by the SET TEMP statement.

When you use DOS 5.0 or later, while the computer is booting and after Starting MS-DOS... appears on-screen, you can press F5 to bypass the CONFIG.SYS and AUTOEXEC.BAT files. Or, you can press F8 to step through your AUTOEXEC.BAT and CONFIG.SYS files one command at a time. By using F8, you can choose whether to run each line in both the AUTOEXEC and CONFIG files.

Tip   Using F8 to step through your CONFIG.SYS and AUTOEXEC.BAT files is an excellent troubleshooting tool for identifying entries that might be causing system problems.

SMARTDRV.SYS is a disk-caching utility that speeds up hard disk access. You can install another disk-caching utility instead, such as PC-CACHE from Central Point Software.

Stop   While disk caching is an important tool for speeding up access to program and data files, write caching can be dangerous. If your computer crashes or freezes while data is in the cache, not only do you lose that data, but it can corrupt the associated files. If you use DOS SMARTDRV, use the /X switch to disable write caching.

If you edit your CONFIG.SYS and AUTOEXEC.BAT files, your changes do not take effect until after you reboot your computer. To perform a warm reboot, press Ctrl+Alt+Del after you exit Windows.

Memory Management

Conventional memory is the 640 KB of memory located in the 0000 to A000 address range. Applications programs and DOS typically use this memory. A low resources or out of resources message often indicates that a system has limited conventional memory available.

The memory between 640 KB and 1 MB is the *upper memory area (UMA)*. You load device drivers and buffers (required by a variety of hardware, such as video display boards and network interface cards) and the ROM BIOS into the UMA. Most systems that use expanded memory load the expanded memory page frame into UMA.

Extended memory (XMS) is memory beyond 1 MB. You must have an extended memory manager, such as HIMEM.SYS, before you can access extended memory. AutoCAD for DOS requires extended memory and the use of an extended memory manager.

The first 64 KB of extended memory is called the *high memory area (HMA)*. The setup for MS-DOS 6.*x* automatically installs a portion of DOS to run in the HMA.

The extended memory area can be used only to store data, not to store executable code.

Expanded memory (EMS) is used to page 16 KB or 64 KB portions of memory into the expanded memory page frame, located in the UMA.

HIMEM.SYS and EMM386.EXE

MS-DOS provides two memory managers—HIMEM.SYS and EMM386.EXE—to manage extended and expanded memory.

HIMEM.SYS manages extended memory according to the XMS specification so that no two programs use the same area of extended memory. It also provides access to the first 64 KB of the extended memory area (the HMA).

EMM386.EXE performs two functions. It provides access to the upper memory area, and can make extended memory emulate expanded memory.

Many programs originally designed to run under DOS require expanded memory. To provide expanded memory for those programs, EMM386 can take a defined amount of extended memory and use it as expanded memory. The amount of extended memory used as expanded memory is determined by the switches used with EMM386 in the CONFIG.SYS file. Following are examples of different ways to set up extended memory usage:

```
DEVICE=C:\DOS\EMM386.EXE NOEMS
```

The NOEMS switch tells EMM386 not to allocate any extended memory as expanded memory.

```
DEVICE=C:\DOS\EMM386.EXE NOEMS X=C800-CFFF
```

The X=C800-CFFF switch instructs EMM386 to exclude a region of the upper memory area from use. Sometimes you must reserve a region of upper memory for a device, such as a network interface card or a graphics adapter.

```
DEVICE=C:\DOS\EMM386.EXE RAM=2048
```

The RAM=2048 switch instructs EMM386 to allocate 2 MB of extended memory as expanded memory. The quantity could be 512, 1024 (1 MB), or some other quantity.

```
DEVICE=C:\DOS\EMM386.EXE MIN=0
```

With the MIN=0 switch, no extended memory is reserved as expanded memory, but EMM386 dynamically allocates expanded memory as applications require it.

 Note Third-party software providers, such as Quarterdeck Systems, offer software that has the same functionality as HIMEM.SYS and EMM386.EXE. Some users believe Quarterdeck's QEMM as a memory manager is superior to the memory managers included with MS-DOS.

AutoCAD's DOS Extender

AutoCAD is a memory-intensive program that requires the use of extended memory. Included with—and an intrinsic part of—AutoCAD is an extension of the Phar Lap TNT 386IDOS-Extender 6.1 memory manager. This *Virtual Memory Manager* (VMM), in conjunction with DOS extended memory managers, uses two swapping systems for paging data between RAM and hard disk.

Virtual memory is the sum total of a system's physical RAM and hard disk storage available for swapping. When AutoCAD runs out of physical RAM during an AutoCAD session, the VMM pages the least recently used data to the hard disk in the form of a swap file. When the data is needed again, it is paged back to RAM and other data is paged to disk.

386IVMM and The AutoCAD Pager

One of AutoCAD's virtual memory systems is called 386IVMM, and it handles AutoCAD, AutoLISP, ADS, and protected-mode ADI drivers. 386IVMM creates a 400 KB swap file and a reserve swap file with an SWR extension every time you run AutoCAD.

The other virtual memory system is the AutoCAD pager. This system pages drawing files between disk and RAM as required. The AutoCAD pager uses as much memory as is specified in the ACADMAXMEM environment variable.

The STATUS Command

From the command line, enter **STATUS** for current information about your system's memory and storage. The STATUS command gives you the following information (see fig. A.1):

- ◆ Free disk space

- ◆ Virtual memory allocated

- ◆ Ratio between physical memory and virtual program size

- ◆ Total conventional memory

- ◆ Total extended memory

- ◆ Swap file size

Figure A.1

Result of issuing STATUS command.

```
Send F1 Text Screen                                              Go Text
Model space limits are X:    0.0000  Y:    0.0000  (Off)
                       X:   12.0000  Y:    9.0000
Model space uses       *Nothing*
Display shows          X:    0.0000  Y:    0.0000
                       X:   15.8496  Y:   11.5309
Insertion base is      X:    0.0000  Y:    0.0000  Z:    0.0000
Snap resolution is     X:    1.0000  Y:    1.0000
Grid spacing is        X:    0.0000  Y:    0.0000

Current space:         Model space
Current layer:         0
Current color:         BYLAYER -- 7 (white)
Current linetype:      BYLAYER -- CONTINUOUS
Current elevation:     0.0000  thickness:    0.0000
Fill on  Grid off  Ortho off  Qtext off  Snap off  Tablet off
Object snap modes:     None
Free disk: 22224896 bytes
Virtual memory allocated to program: 11048 KB
Amount of program in physical memory/Total (virtual) program size: 49%
Total conventional memory: 504 KB      Total extended memory: 14972 KB
-- Press RETURN for more --
Swap file size: 476 KB
Page faults: 399    Swap writes: 0    Swap reclaims: 18

Command: _
```

Tip Add as much RAM as possible to your system. Additional RAM is, without question, the single most effective way to improve AutoCAD performance.

Installing AutoCAD

For proper installation of AutoCAD Release 13 for DOS, make sure that your system meets the minimum requirements itemized at the beginning of this appendix. If you install from floppy disks, back up your disks before you begin. If you install from CD-ROM, you should back up the single floppy disk, known as the *installation disk,* that starts the installation process.

Installation Options

Insert the AutoCAD installation disk in the floppy drive and run the install program. AutoCAD prompts you to enter your name, your company's name, your dealer's name, and your dealer's telephone number. Enter the information as appropriate. Next, AutoCAD offers you the option of different types of installations and tells you how much disk space is required in bytes:

All files	40,618,500
Minimum installation	21,100,000
Typical installation	34,631,200

You can also customize your installation further by choosing whether to install:

New Riders Publishing
INSIDE SERIES

True Type fonts	1,693,200
Postscript fonts	603,350
Spelling dictionary	237,620
External database access	10,617,900
Example and sample files	4,102,900
Application development	1,631,100
Learning tools	799,300

Choose the installation that is appropriate for your system. Following the selection of components, AutoCAD prompts you for the letter assigned to your hard drive and for the directories in which to install Release 13. AutoCAD suggests two directories:

ACADR13\DOS

ACADR13\COMMON

AutoCAD explains that files in the \COMMON subdirectory can be used by either the DOS or Windows versions of AutoCAD Release 13.

Note   AutoCAD Release 13 for DOS can be installed from Windows. If installing AutoCAD from Windows, you are given the choice of installing the Windows version, the DOS version, or both versions. To install from Windows, use File Manager or Program Manager, and run SETUP.EXE from the AutoCAD installation disk.

A typical installation of both DOS and Windows versions of Release 13 requires 72 MB of hard drive space for AutoCAD files.

After choosing installation directories, if you use the CD-ROM installation disk, AutoCAD prompts ( ) for the letter of your CD-ROM drive and asks you to choose Metric or English Measurement Units. To complete the installation, select continue and insert disks as instructed.

If you are installing from CD-ROM, AutoCAD will immediately begin installation. The CD-ROM installation takes approximately seven minutes according to the speed of the PC, the hard drive, and the CD-ROM drive.

Upon completing the installation, AutoCAD asks if you want it to create an ACADR13.BAT batch file. AutoCAD displays the batch file that sets environment variables before running ACAD.EXE. It is recommended that you accept and utilize the ACADR13.BAT batch file. This batch file can always be edited, ignored, or deleted later if you find it does not suit your purposes. Environment variables are discussed in detail in Appendix C, "Optimizing AutoCAD."

A typical ACADR13.BAT file looks like the following:

```
SET
ACAD=C:\ACADR13\COMMON\SUPPORT;C:\ACADR13\DOS;C:\ACADR13\DOS\SUPPORT;C:\ACADR13\COMMON\FONTS
SET ACADCFG=C:\ACADR13\DOS
SET ACADDRV=C:\ACADR13\DOS\DRV
C:\ACADR13\DOS\ACAD %1 %2
```

Tip By using different batch files with different environment variable settings, you can run AutoCAD with varying configurations. The IA.BAT file created in Chapter 1 and used in this book is an example of a batch file for a special configuration. See Appendix C for an explanation of the IA.BAT file.

Configuring AutoCAD

The first time you run AutoCAD, you must configure AutoCAD for your system's hardware, network, and other configuration parameters. You need to know the type of graphics controller, plotter, and pointing device you have.

Video Display Driver

The first configuration item is the video display. AutoCAD searches the ACADDRV path (which is specified in the ACADR13.BAT batch file) for ADI drivers and lists available drivers for your selection.

If you are using a VGA display, Autodesk recommends selecting the Accelerated Display Driver by Vibrant Graphics. This accelerated display driver, created for AutoCAD and shipped with Release 13, adds a variety of features. These features include an Aerial View of the entire drawing in a window, a text window displayed on the graphics screen, and faster redraw, zoom, and pan.

Tip Remove any memory-resident (TSR for Terminate and Stay Resident) ADI display drivers before installing the Vibrant Graphics Accelerated Display Driver. This step will prevent memory conflicts from causing problems with configuration.

If you select the Vibrant Graphics Accelerated Display Driver, AutoCAD asks a series of questions concerning the setup of the display driver. These include:

```
Change Video Selections?

    Choices for video cards include: Generic VGA, ATI, Orchid, Diamond and
more.
```

New Riders Publishing
INSIDE SERIES

```
    Choice of Resolution and Colors—examples are 800×600×16, 800×600×256,
640×480×256, 1024×768×16, and so on.
    Single/Dual Screen? (Y/N)

Enter Custom Configuration Menu

    Display List Options
    Dual Screen Options
    Flip Options
    Font Selection
    Menu Color Scheme
    Palette Selection
    Screen Layout
    Bootup Features
    Load Config Presets
    Restore Previous Settings

Height, Width (to adjust aspect ratio)? <N>
Do you want a status line? <Y>
Do you want a command prompt area? <Y>
Do you want a screen menu? <Y>
```

Choose the selections best suited for your setup. Other display drivers offer similar customization options.

Digitizer

AutoCAD next requests that you choose an available digitizer. Drivers that ship with AutoCAD include:

```
CalComp 3300 Series ADI 4.2
Hitachi HICOMSCAN HD series ADI 4.2
Kurta XLP, ADI 4.2
Microsoft Mouse Driver ADI 4.2
Summagraphics MicroGrid v1.1 (Series II or later) ADI 4.2
Summagraphics MM Series V2.0 ADI 4.2
```

These ADI drivers are from Autodesk. If you have a driver from a specific manufacturer, follow that manufacturer's instructions for installing and configuring the driver. Make sure the driver is installed in your device driver subdirectory and that the ACADDRV environment variable is set to include that directory. The default directory suggested by AutoCAD during installation is ACADR13\DOS\DRV.

ADI Drivers

The *Autodesk Device Interface* (ADI) is a standard interface developed by Autodesk that gives all hardware developers specifications for writing device drivers that work with AutoCAD.

Stop Release 12 ADI 4.2 drivers will not work with Release 13. Release 12 ADI 4.2 device drivers are designed to run on 16-bit platforms. Release 13 requires Release 13 ADI 4.2 ADI drivers designed for 32-bit platforms.

Plotter

The next item on the configuration agenda is the Plotter. Plotter device drivers that ship with AutoCAD include:

```
CalComp plotters
Canon Bubble Jet and Laser printers
Epson printers
Hewlett-Packard plotters
Hewlett-Packard DeskJet and LaserJet printers
Houston Instrument plotters
IBM Proprinter
Postscript device
Raster file export
```

These, too, are ADI 4.2 device drivers from Autodesk. As with the digitizer drivers, if you have a driver from a specific manufacturer, follow that manufacturer's instructions for installing and configuring the driver.

Raster File Format

AutoCAD supplies ADI 4.2 drivers that plot drawings to a raster-format file. With a raster-format file, AutoCAD drawings can be used in illustrations, publishing, and multimedia presentations. The raster-format driver emulates a plotter and represents width and height in pixels. Among the raster formats supported by the AutoCAD ADI driver are GIF, TIFF, PCX, BMP, TGA, and Group 3 Fax.

File Locking

During the configuration process, AutoCAD asks if you want to enable file locking. File locking controls access to open files in network environments and prevents multiple users from altering active drawings.

With file locking enabled, AutoCAD places a write lock on any open file. The only user who can modify the file is the one who opened the file.

It is possible to open a file and place a read lock on a file. A read lock tells others on the network that someone has opened a file for viewing.

AutoCAD creates a lock file that uses the original file name with an extension related to the original file. When you are working in a drawing file or externally referencing a drawing, the lock file has a DWK extension. When you are saving, exiting, or inserting a block in an externally referenced drawing, the lock file has a DWL extension. See table A.1 for examples of a few different lock file extensions.

TABLE A.1
Examples of Extensions for Locked Files

File Type	File Extension	Locked File Extension
Drawing	DWG	DWK
Drawing	DWG	DWL
DXF	DXF	DFK
Shape	SHX	SXK
Plot	PLT	PLK
Menu	MNS	MSK
Menu	MNX	MXK

A lock file can contain one write lock but many read locks. AutoCAD does not create a lock file for an unnamed drawing. Upon closing a locked file, AutoCAD unlocks the original file and deletes the associated lock file. If AutoCAD is terminated abnormally, such as by a crash or by turning off the system with AutoCAD open, lock files will not be deleted. See Appendix B for instructions on cleaning up leftover lock files.

 Tip   If you install AutoCAD for a single user, do not enable file-locking. File-locking is necessary in a network environment, but does not serve a useful purpose in a single-user environment.

If you need to reconfigure AutoCAD for a different hardware device, the AutoCAD configuration menu enables you to identify and change parameters for the graphics display, digitizer, and plotter that make up your workstation configuration.

Reconfiguring AutoCAD

After you install and configure AutoCAD for DOS, you can examine or change your configuration setup.

The following exercise starts the configuration menu to make changes in your AutoCAD configuration.

Reconfiguring AutoCAD for DOS

Command: *Choose* Options, Configure   Issues the CONFIGURE command and displays
                                              current information in the AutoCAD Text Window

```
Current AutoCAD configuration

Video display:

 Your current display

Digitizer:

 Your current input device

Plotter (#):

 Your current plotters

Speller dialect:

 Language chosen
 (American English is an option)
```

Press RETURN to continue: Displays the configuration menu

```
Configuration menu
 0. Exit to Main Menu
 1. Show current configuration
 2. Allow detailed configuration
 3. Configure video display
 4. Configure digitizer
 5. Configure plotter
 6. Configure system console
 7. Configure operating parameters
```

To configure or change a device driver, enter the number of the item you want to change from the configuration menu. AutoCAD asks you questions about your hardware setup, and you respond with answers or a number from a list of choices.

Configuration depends on your specific hardware. AutoCAD prompts you to supply values for each device. If you need more information, consult your AutoCAD *Installation Guide for DOS* or the device driver manufacturer's documentation.

Tip If you need to reconfigure a device or restore its default settings, select that device type from the configuration menu, answer Yes at the Do you want to select a different one <N> prompt, then select the same device from the available device list.

Setting Up a Digitizing Tablet and Menu

A digitizing tablet can be used in two ways: as a digitizing device or as a screen pointing device. The following sections explain how to calibrate a tablet for digitizing purposes and how to configure a tablet to function as a pointing device.

After you calibrate your tablet, choose Options, Tablet, On to put the tablet into digitizing mode; choose Options, Tablet, Off to put the tablet into screen pointing mode.

Calibrating a Digitizing Tablet

A digitizing tablet can be used for tracing and digitizing drawings into AutoCAD. The tablet first must be calibrated to digitize points on a drawing and then map those points to the drawing coordinate system.

The tablet can be calibrated in either model space or paper space; the tablet will be calibrated in whichever space you are in at the time of calibration. If you switch from one space to another, tablet mode will be turned off.

If you turn tablet mode on, after switching from one space to the other, AutoCAD will tell you that you need to calibrate the tablet. If you switch back to your original space without having calibrated the tablet in the second space, the calibration settings you made in the original space are retained. Should you calibrate the tablet in the second space, however, the calibration for the first space will not be retained.

There is no way to store tablet calibration settings for later recall.

To calibrate, attach the paper you want to trace to the digitizing tablet. The paper must be flat and attached securely to the tablet; it can be placed at any angle.

Enter **TABLET** followed by **CAL** at the command line to calibrate the tablet. The menu will prompt you to enter digitizing points and coordinates for each point.

The accuracy of the drawing is directly related to the amount of points entered. After you enter the points, the calibration process performs a transformation, which maps points from the tablet to the drawing coordinate system. Transformation maps points on the drawing to their real coordinates and ignores the actual tablet points. You have a choice of three transformations:

◆ **Orthogonal.** Use orthogonal for dimensionally accurate drawings and for drawings with most points along single lines. Translation, Uniform Scaling, and rotation are specified with two translation points. Use two horizontally or vertically aligned points.

◆ **Affine.** Use Affine when horizontal dimensions are stretched in relation to vertical dimensions. This is usually the case with copies of drawings. Translation, independent X and Y scaling, and skewing are specified with three calibration points.

◆ **Projective.** This is similar to perspective projection of one plane onto another plane. With projective transformation, straight lines map into straight lines but parallel lines do not always stay parallel. Parallel lines that appear to converge are corrected with projective transformation. This can be used to digitize photographs.

With only two points entered, AutoCAD automatically performs an orthogonal transformation. With three or more points entered, AutoCAD determines which of the three transformations best suits the calibration. See figure A.2 for an example of the results of the computation for the three types of transformation. The table provides you with the information you need for selecting the best transformation for your application.

The following list explains the results reported in the table:

◆ **Outcome of fit.** The outcome may involve the following possibilities:

   ◆ **Exact.** Correct number of points for a transformation

   ◆ **Success.** More than enough points for a transformation

   ◆ **Impossible.** Not enough points for a transformation

   ◆ **Failure.** Sufficient points but transformation failed. This is typically due to colinear or coincident points.

   ◆ **Canceled.** The computational process was canceled. This only happens with projective transformation. Projective will show canceled when three points are entered. You can still choose projective transformation, however. AutoCAD will use the results computed for the transformation.

◆ **RMS Error.** RMS stands for root-mean-square; it measures how close the transformation is to a perfect fit. The smaller the number the better.

◆ **Standard Deviation.** This indicates the consistency of error over all the points.

◆ **Largest residual.** The largest error between where the point was mapped by the transformation and where the point would be mapped if the fit was perfect.

◆ **At point.** The point with the largest error.

◆ **Second largest residual.** The size of the error of the second least accurate point

◆ **At point.** The point with the second largest error.

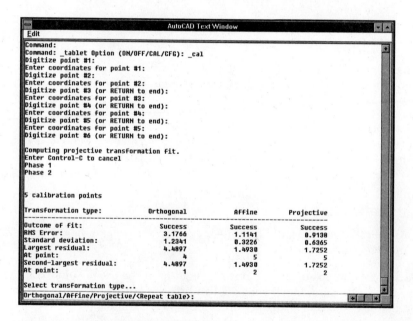

Figure A.2

The transformation table from the Tablet calibration procedure.

The figure shows an AutoCAD Text Window containing:

```
Command:
Command: _tablet Option (ON/OFF/CAL/CFG): _cal
Digitize point #1:
Enter coordinates for point #1:
Digitize point #2:
Enter coordinates for point #2:
Digitize point #3 (or RETURN to end):
Enter coordinates for point #3:
Digitize point #4 (or RETURN to end):
Enter coordinates for point #4:
Digitize point #5 (or RETURN to end):
Enter coordinates for point #5:
Digitize point #6 (or RETURN to end):

Computing projective transformation fit.
Enter Control-C to cancel
Phase 1
Phase 2


5 calibration points
```

Transformation type:	Orthogonal	Affine	Projective
Outcome of fit:	Success	Success	Success
RMS Error:	3.1766	1.1141	0.9138
Standard deviation:	1.2341	0.3226	0.6365
Largest residual:	4.4897	1.4930	1.7252
At point:	4	5	5
Second-largest residual:	4.4897	1.4930	1.7252
At point:	1	2	2

```
Select transformation type...
Orthogonal/Affine/Projective/<Repeat table>:
```

Using AutoCAD's Standard Tablet Menu

AutoCAD provides a standard tablet menu and includes a plastic template for an 11-by-11-inch digitizer tablet. To use the standard AutoCAD tablet menu, affix the AutoCAD standard plastic template to the digitizing tablet and use the AutoCAD TABLET command to configure the tablet (see fig. A.3).

Figure A.3

The standard AutoCAD tablet menu.

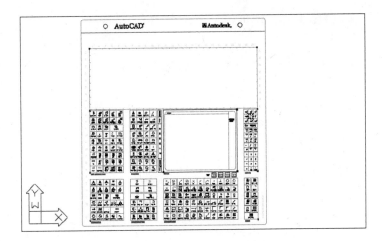

The TABLET.DWG Drawing

AutoCAD also comes with a drawing file, TABLET.DWG, which reproduces the plastic template menu. You can use this drawing to create a custom template drawing for your digitizer.

If you know how to edit drawings and customize the tablet menu, you can make your own tablet drawing, supporting the menu with your own tablet menu programs. If you customize your tablet menu, make a backup copy of TABLET.DWG, call it MYTABLET.DWG, and make your changes to the copy, not to the original.

Tablet Menu Configuration

This section assumes that you use an 11-by-11-inch or larger digitizer configured according to the *Installation Guide* (see fig. A.4).

If you use the AutoCAD template, place it on your digitizer. If you use the plotted TABLET drawing, trim the drawing, leaving about a 1/2-inch border, and tape it to your digitizer. Because tablets vary, and because every user trims and tapes differently, you must configure the tablet so that AutoCAD can know exactly where the tablet commands are located on the surface of the tablet.

Use the TABLET command from inside the drawing editor to configure the tablet. A series of donuts—tablet pick points on the drawing (or template)—are used as guides when defining each of the four menu areas on the standard AutoCAD tablet.

The standard menu is divided into four menu areas by columns and rows. In figure A.4, for example, the columns are numbered 1 to 25 across the top and the rows are lettered A to Y on the left. Menu area 1 is the top rectangular area. The first donut

New Riders Publishing
INSIDE SERIES

pick point is near A and 1 in the upper left corner. Menu area 1 has 25 columns and 9 rows of menu boxes.

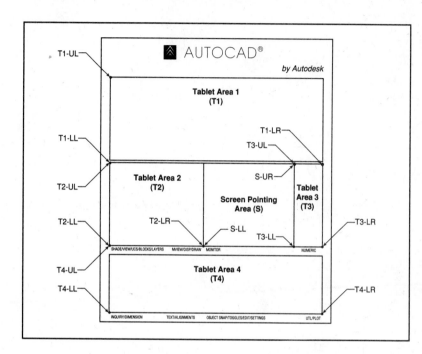

Figure A.4

Configuring the AutoCAD standard tablet menu.

When you configure the tablet, AutoCAD prompts you to pick three points for each menu area and to enter the number of columns and rows. For AutoCAD's standard tablet, use the default selections for columns and rows.

Autodesk recommends using a small area of the tablet that maps to the entire monitor display for the screen pointing area.

The following exercise takes you through the configuration of the AutoCAD tablet menu. If you have not used a tablet menu, it is wise to use the supplied AutoCAD menu and template before customizing your own tablet menu.

Configuring the AutoCAD Tablet Menu

Command: *Choose* Options, Tablet, Configure	Issues the TABLET command
Enter the number of tablet menus desired (0-4) <0>: **4** (Enter)	Specifies four menu areas on your tablet menu template

continues

continued

`Digitize upper left corner of` `menu area 1:` *Pick point* Menu 1 - UL	Selects appropriate donut (refer to fig. A.4)
`Digitize lower left corner of` `menu area 1:` *Pick point* Menu 1 - LL	Selects appropriate donut
`Digitize lower right corner of` `menu area 1:` *Pick point* Menu 1 - LR	Selects appropriate donut
`Enter the number of columns for` `menu area 1: (1-5015) <25>` **Enter**	Accepts the default
`Enter the number of rows for` `menu area 1: (1-1795) <9>` **Enter**	Accepts the default
`Digitize upper left corner of` `menu area 2:` *Pick point* Menu 2 - UL	Selects the appropriate donut
`Digitize lower left corner of` `menu area 2:` *Pick point* Menu 2 - LL	Selects the appropriate donut
`Digitize lower right corner of` `menu area 2:` *Pick point* Menu 2 - LR	Selects the appropriate donut
`Enter the number of columns for` `menu area 2: (1-2208) <11>` **Enter**	Accepts the default
`Enter the number of rows for` `menu area 2: (1-1814) <9>` **Enter**	Accepts the default
`Digitize upper left corner of` `menu area 3:` *Pick point* Menu 3 - UL	Selects the appropriate donut
`Digitize lower left corner of` `menu area 3:` *Pick point* Menu 3 - LL	Selects the appropriate donut
`Digitize lower right corner of` `menu area 3:` *Pick point* Menu 3 - LR	Selects the appropriate donut
`Enter the number of columns for` `menu area 3: (1-608) <9>` **Enter**	Accepts the default
`Enter the number of rows for` `menu area 3: (1-1812) <13>` **Enter**	Accepts the default
`Digitize upper left corner of` `menu area 4:` *Pick point* Menu 4 - UL	Selects the appropriate donut

A

Digitize lower left corner of menu area 4: *Pick point* Menu 4 - LL	Selects the appropriate donut
Digitize lower right corner of menu area 4: *Pick point* Menu 4 - LR	Selects the appropriate donut
Enter the number of columns for menu area 4: (1-1505) <25> (Enter)	Accepts the default
Enter the number of rows for menu area 4: (1-1392) <7> (Enter)	Accepts the default
Do you want to respecify the Fixed Screen Pointing area (N) Y (Enter)	
Digitize lower left corner of screen pointing area: *Pick point* Screen Menu - LL	Selects the appropriate donut
Digitize upper right corner of screen pointing area: *Pick point* Screen Menu - UR	Selects the appropriate donut

After configuration is complete, choose a few commands from the tablet and draw in the screen pointing area to test the configuration. The standard AutoCAD tablet menu is configured for your digitizer, and the configuration parameters are stored on your disk in a file.

Realizing the full power of AutoCAD for DOS, while using it problem-free, requires paying close attention to the configuration of your computer and the configuration of AutoCAD itself. It is necessary to optimize memory usage to the fullest extent possible with an understanding of swap files and disk utilities.

APPENDIX

B

Troubleshooting

 This appendix contains tips, hints, and solutions to the most common problems found when using AutoCAD for DOS.

Solving General Problems

When it comes to solving problems in AutoCAD, you might have to become something of a detective. There are good ways and bad ways to approach problem solving; the following list presents some general guidelines to solving problems:

1. Isolate the problem. If you can make the problem show up repetitively, it is easier to troubleshoot. Write down exactly what you were doing when the problem occurred. It might just be operator error; it might not.

2. Determine which part of the system is being affected by the problem (such as memory, disk, and so forth). Most error messages give a clue as to which part of the system the problem is with.

3. Analyze the problem to determine the best course of action. Take, for example, a problem that you have determined to be a memory problem. Is the problem a result of a TSR (terminate-and-stay-resident program) acting upon a DOS memory management problem. Once you have determined whether the problem is a TSR or memory management problem, you have eliminated quite a few possible causes of the problem.

4. Remove as many unknowns from the equation as possible. For example, an out of environment error is a memory management problem; therefore, do not look at TSR issues to solve this problem. (This becomes easier with experience.)

5. Come up with a solution and try it. Then start with step 1 again.

6. Repeat until the problem is solved.

 Tip Most problems can be solved in an hour or two at the most. If you have not solved the problem by that time, ask someone else. Utilize resources such as your AutoCAD dealer or CompuServe. Many answers to common problems can be found through these two resources.

Many of the errors or problems that occur in AutoCAD can be attributed to the setup of the machine. This includes, but is not limited to, the DOS environment and the AutoCAD environment. Each of these environments must be set up correctly for AutoCAD to run.

 Stop Also, none of the environments can be changed—either by the user or another program—while AutoCAD is running. This will result in a variety of errors. The rest of this appendix discusses a few common errors and their solutions.

Common Problems in the DOS Environment

The two most common problems in the DOS environment are an insufficient number of files, and conflicts with TSRs.

Insufficient Files

AutoCAD cannot open a file or issue a command when a FILES error occurs. This error is a result of the DOS environment. If you are working in AutoCAD and try to run a LISP routine or load an ADS file and you receive an error message telling you AutoCAD cannot load the file or cannot find the file, it may be caused by the FILES environment variable in DOS. The DOS CONFIG.SYS file has a statement called FILES=. For a standard AutoCAD installation, FILES should be set to 50. This setting enables AutoCAD and Windows to have as many as 50 files open at the same time, though running other programs concurrently with AutoCAD might require a higher number. Fifty is usually more than enough for a standard AutoCAD session. Use any text editor that creates pure ASCII text files and perform the following steps:

1. Modify the FILES= line of the CONFIG.SYS file to equal 50.

2. Save the file.

3. Reboot your machine to put the changes into effect.

Environment Space

The DOS environment space can also pose a problem. DOS reserves a certain amount of memory for SET variables (more commonly known as environment variables). When you start AutoCAD with the provided batch file, several variables are set. These variables tell AutoCAD where the key locations for needed files are. If your environment space is not large enough to accommodate all the variables, various parts of AutoCAD may not function correctly. If you load AutoCAD and receive a dialogue box that tells you AutoCAD cannot load the BASE.DCL file, there are two possible reasons: The environment variable is not set to the correct directory or the file does not exist. If you have run out of environment space, the first error is likely. There is not enough memory to hold the location of the BASE.DCL file. Fortunately, this is very simple to fix. Use your favorite text editor and modify your CONFIG.SYS file as follows:

1. Find the line that refers to your shell. It should look something like: SHELL=COMMAND.COM.... If this line does not exist, add it to the end of the CONFIG.SYS file.

2. Change the SHELL command to the following:

```
SHELL=C:\DOS\COMMAND.COM /e:1024 /p
```

The /e: statement sets the size of the environment space in terms of bytes. The /p switch makes this execution of the COMMAND.COM file permanent.

3. Save the file and reboot your system. This should solve the problem.

Do not waste memory by setting environment space larger than needed. You can determine the needed space as follows:

1. Make sure that all needed settings (except AutoCAD's) are made, then enter **SET>ENV.$** at the C:\> DOS prompt. This copies the environment settings to a file.

2. Use the DOS DIR command to list the directory listings of the ENV.$ file and of your AutoCAD startup batch file (such as IA.BAT or ACADR13.BAT).

3. Add the file sizes shown for the ENV.$ file and the batch file and use the result for the /e: value. Because the batch file contains a little more than just environment settings, the resulting value gives you an adequate factor of safety.

4. Delete the ENV.$ file.

TSR Conflicts

DOS TSRs also can be a problem. A TSR (terminate-and-stay-resident program) loads itself into memory and waits for a key event to occur before the TSR carries out its function. A key event may be something simple like the passage of time. A screen saver TSR waits for a predetermined amount of time of inactivity before trying to take more memory to run its program. This key is highly dependent upon the nature of the TSR. Most TSRs are well behaved and use only the memory they occupied when they were loaded. If a TSR takes over other memory when it is activated, memory corruption can occur if AutoCAD is running. The question is, how can you tell if it is a misbehaved TSR? A badly behaved TSR can cause AutoCAD to lock up when it appears nothing is wrong. If this happens repeatedly, go through your AUTOEXEC.BAT and CONFIG.SYS files and remove any unnecessary programs or drivers. (Refer to your DOS and Windows documentation, as well as Appendix A, "Installation and Configuration," of this book to find the minimum configuration needed to run AutoCAD). If the problem still occurs, then it is not caused by a TSR and you need to look elsewhere to solve the problem.

If the problem does not still occur, then one of the items you removed caused it. Add the items back one at a time, and test AutoCAD with each addition to determine the culprit.

Understanding AutoCAD Error Messages

AutoCAD keeps an error log of all errors that occur on the system in a file called ACAD.ERR. This file usually is located in the \ACADR13\DOS directory, but may end up in your current drawing directory. When AutoCAD detects an error, it displays the message on-screen and records it to this file. Sometimes errors are bad enough that AutoCAD cannot display the error problem on the screen. If this is the case, check the ACAD.ERR file to see if the error was recorded there. The following is an example error from an ACAD.ERR file:

```
FATAL ERROR:  Can't start display driver.

1/28/1995 at 12:13:06.690  Drawing: C:\
-----------
```

Each successive error is appended to this file. Some common errors that AutoCAD will notify you of are display driver errors, entity read errors, entity regen errors, and internal errors.

EREAD: Entity Read Error

Entity read errors occur when AutoCAD is reading a file from disk or from memory and it finds a corrupted entity or a sequence of bytes that makes no sense. File corruption can be caused by hardware errors (fairly rare), power surges, and abnormal program termination (crash) of an AutoCAD session. A file that displays this error might be recovered through AutoCAD's AUDIT and drawing RECOVER commands. Audit and drawing recovery both search the AutoCAD database for any errors and try to fix any errors that are found. If an error cannot be fixed, AutoCAD skips that section of the file and moves on to the next. This way, you might not recover all of the file, but you will recover at least some of it. Audit works from within files that are already open. To issue an Audit, complete the following steps:

1. Load the drawing into AutoCAD (if it is not already loaded).

2. Issue the AUDIT command.

3. When prompted by AutoCAD to fix any errors detected, enter **YES**. Now AutoCAD will fix any errors as it detects them.

4. Watch the text screen because AutoCAD will display errors as it finds them.

Drawing recovery is used when AutoCAD cannot completely load a drawing without an error. This process runs an AUDIT as AutoCAD loads the file. If the file cannot be recovered by this method, it might not be recoverable. Another method of cleaning up a drawing is to issue the WBLOCK command to remove unnecessary information from the drawing file. (Note that the WBLOCK command removes all unnecessary information). See Chapter 16 for more information on the WBLOCK command.

Tip   Frequently back up your files and use AutoCAD's autosave feature to avoid losing your valuable work.

EREGEN: Entity Regen

This error is similar to the EREAD error, but occurs when AutoCAD is trying to regenerate an object on the screen and finds an error in the translation process. AutoCAD crashes if this error occurs. As with EREAD errors, use the AUDIT or RECOVER commands to retrieve the file.

Internal Error

Internal errors are accompanied by a description of the error. The description looks rather cryptic and probably contains a minute section of the program code. If you get an internal error, AutoCAD will ask you if you want to save the file. If the error has the word write anywhere in it, it is probable that AutoCAD was performing a write operation to disk. This message probably is indicative of the fact that AutoCAD is running out of disk space. A write error problem may be solved by freeing up disk space, or by purchasing a larger hard drive.

SCANDR

This error message occurs when AutoCAD cannot update its temporary files due to an error of its own. Because AutoCAD crashes, you must go through the drawing recovery process described previously and hope to get the files back. Otherwise, revert to your backup files, which AutoCAD saves with BAK extensions. You can also revert to your auto save files. These files are created by setting the SAVETIME variable in AutoCAD. The auto save files generally have an extension of .SV$.

Exploring Other Problems in AutoCAD

Problems other than DOS and AutoCAD-specific problems can occur on your machine. These include the following:

◆ file locking

New Riders Publishing
INSIDE
SERIES

- cleaning up a crashed system

- 80386 and Pentium problems

- plotting ACIS solids

- memory manager problems.

File Locking

If you try to load a locked file into AutoCAD, your system should respond by telling you that the file was locked by *name* user on *mm/dd/yy* date. If you are on a single-user system, make sure file locking is turned off (see Appendix A, "Installation and Configuration"). If the file is locked, perform the following steps while in AutoCAD:

1. Choose File, Management, Utilities to display the File Utilities dialog box. Then click on <u>U</u>nlock File to open the Files(s) to Unlock dialog box.

2. Select the file(s) from the File(s) to Unlock dialog box and choose OK, then choose <u>Y</u>es when AutoCAD asks if you want to unlock the file.

This error usually occurs when the system crashes. When AutoCAD opens a file and file locking is turned on, a locked file with a DWK extension is created. If the system crashes, this file is not erased and the file still appears to be locked. The other way to solve this problem is to delete the lock file from DOS.

Cleaning Up a Crashed System

If AutoCAD crashes, a clean-up process is inevitable. Basically, two or three things need to be done. A *crash* is defined as a system shutdown without proper exit from AutoCAD (that is, a power outage, pressing your system's reset button, pressing Ctrl+Alt+Del, or system lockup with reboot). If this occurs, several files will be left in your current drawing directory. These files are the temporary files AutoCAD was using when it crashed. Some of these files might also be hidden. Before executing any of the following steps, make sure AutoCAD is not running (that is, shelled out). Perform the following steps to recover from a crashed system:

1. Run CHKDSK /F or, if you have DOS 6.0 or later, run SCANDISK. Both programs scan the hard drive for lost chains and clusters.

2. If the programs find lost chains, do not convert the chains into files; they are useless. SCANDISK might ask if you want to save the files; reply no. If it offers to salvage a directory, let it. It will convert it to a directory name such as DIR00001 in the root directory. When SCANDISK is finished, you can examine the directory's contents and see if it contains good files and/or subdirectories.

3. Delete all files with an AC$ extension in all of the directories that AutoCAD uses. These are crashed AutoCAD temporary files.

4. There might also be some other leftover temporary files. These files might have a filename similar to BBCDACFD. Delete these as well.

5. If file locking was turned on, you might have locked files to deal with. If that is the case, refer to the previous section.

Text and Support Path Problems

AutoCAD stores references to other files, such as xref and text font files, in the drawing file. When you use a file dialog box to specify a file, the full path is stored in the file name. If the drawing is later loaded on a system with a different drive letter or directory structure, this can cause problems. In some cases, AutoCAD then cannot find the referenced file, even if it is on the default support file search path. If AutoCAD can't find a text font file, and an alternate font substitution is set, the alternate font file will be substituted for display and plotting without warning. (The text styles will still reference the original font file even if it can't be found.) This can cause strange text appearance and alignment in the drawing. The font substitution is specified by the FONTALT system variable, which is set to the TXT font by default. We highly recommend that you set it to no substitution. That will cause AutoCAD to prompt you when it can't find a font file. To set FONTALT to no substitution, enter **FONTALT** at the AutoCAD Command: prompt, then enter a period at the New value for FONTALT , or. for none <"txt".: prompt. To prevent path problems do not use file dialog boxes to specify xref or files which are on the search path. Instead, choose the Type It button in the dialog box, then enter the file name without path at the prompt that appears, and AutoCAD will find the file and store its name without the path.

80386 and Pentium Problems

Some early 80386 chips are not compatible with AutoCAD. These chips (sometimes referred to as *B-Step chips*) will lock into an infinite loop when executing certain math coprocessor instructions. The error is in the 80386 chip itself and not AutoCAD or the math coprocessor. These errors are known as the Intel 80386 Erratum #17 and Erratum #21. The chips with the following markings exhibit these problems:

16 MHz chips	20 MHz chips	25 MHz chips
A80386-16	A80386-20	A80386-25
S40343	S40362	SX050
A80386-16		
S40344		

Errata #17 and #21 also can be detected by using the CHKBSTEP.COM program that ships with the DOS version of AutoCAD. This program is located in the ACADR13\DOS directory. You run the program by typing the command CHKBSTEP at the command prompt. The program will detect whether or not you have a B-step chip. If you do, first try to determine if it is an erratum #17 chip by changing the DOS memory extender. Use the command cfig386 -errata17 acad.exe to accomplish this. Next, try to run AutoCAD again. If the problem occurs again, you have an erratum #21 error and you must replace the 80386 chipset. (Contact your manufacturer to get a bug-free chipset).

Most early Pentium chips from Intel exhibit an FDIV error. This error occurs in double-precision floating-point divide operations. The Pentium chip truncates all numbers past the fourth decimal place; this error occurs once every 2 or 3 billion operations.

Because the error occurs rather infrequently, it does not pose a problem for most users. However, scientific, mechanical, or any precise type of drawing might show errors due to these chips. See Appendix H for a program that will test your Pentium chip for the error. If you decide you need to replace the chip, contact your manufacturer at Intel directly. They will replace the chip at no cost.

Plotting ACIS Solids

Plotting solids can sometimes be difficult because of the way AutoCAD interprets the geometry. When AutoCAD plots or hides complex solids, the geometry is converted to triangles and will be rendered with a faceted look instead of a smooth surface. Change the system variable DISPSILH to 1 to remove the triangles. This problem also occurs when using the HIDE command.

AutoCAD Patches

Because AutoCAD is such a large program, bugs are bound to pop up in the software. Many of these bugs are corrected by Autodesk as soon as possible. Even so, every once in a while, Autodesk releases patches for AutoCAD, in the form of patch files. The patches generally are available from CompuServe, in Autodesk's FTP site: ftp.autodesk.com (for those with Internet access), or directly from your dealer.

Some problems that you might not be able to solve are indeed the result of bugs, and the solution lies in applying the appropriate patches to AutoCAD. When the patches are applied, the AutoCAD version number changes; for example, Release 13 is the first release, whereas 13a is the first patched version. If the patch is considered a substantial upgrade, it will be given a revision number such as c1 or c2.

Note   As of this writing, Autodesk has released the Release 13c1 Maintenance Patch to both CompuServe and the FTP site.

The patches come with instructions for application—follow them explicitly. Before making any modifications, make sure you back up the ACAD.EXE file; this way, if the patches don't work correctly on your system. Also, write down your current AutoCAD configuration, because some patches make enough changes to require you to reconfigure after they run.

Looking at Memory Manager Problems

Both DOS and Windows include memory managers. (See Appendix A for a description). If you use a third party memory manager such as QEMM386 or 386MAX, be aware that some of the features may cause problems wen running AutoCAD. These programs load many TSRs and drivers above the DOS 640 KB barrier. (See DOS documentation about the 640 KB limitation.)

QEMM386 has a feature called Stealth that rearranges the memory between 640 KB and 1 MB on systems; this enables QEMM to load a large amount of drivers above 640 KB. Unfortunately, many programs are not compatible with the Stealth feature. Because this directly affects the mapping of parts of the video memory, high resolution applications such as Windows or AutoCAD might not run correctly. To be safe, do not use QEMM386's Stealth feature.

Also, be aware of which memory regions QEMM or any other memory manager is including or excluding for use in its optimizing process. You may or may not want certain regions of memory optimized, especially if you are using a network card in your system.

DOS Display Driver Problems

In DOS, you have to rely upon either AutoCAD, your Video Card manufacturer, or a 3rd party company, to provide the correct video display drivers for your card for AutoCAD. Usually, finding these drivers is not a problem. Occasionally, you may configure AutoCAD for a driver you are not sure will work with your video card. If you try this and it is not the correct driver, when you load AutoCAD, AutoCAD will crash because of an inconsistent video driver. If this happens, how do you change the AutoCAD configuration when you cannot get back into AutoCAD. Simple, just start AutoCAD with the -R parameter and this will immediately take you to the AutoCAD configuration screen where you can change video drivers and try another.

New Riders Publishing
INSIDE SERIES

APPENDIX

C

Advanced Configuration

DOS has environment variables and AutoCAD has system variables that configure your working environment. By understanding these variables and using them to your advantage you can optimize that working environment. This should result in a more satisfying and more productive experience as you work in DOS and AutoCAD.

Understanding DOS Environment Variables

You need to set DOS environment variables to optimize your use of AutoCAD. By using DOS environment variables, you can specify where AutoCAD finds its configuration and support files. You can also specify how much memory is used for temporary storage.

The DOS Environment Revealed

The DOS environment is a memory buffer that stores certain important variables. By using these environment variables, you can customize a variety of DOS settings. Examples include the function of the DIR command, the actions of the PATH command, and the display of the DOS prompt.

 Note The default size of the DOS environment is 256 bytes. The minimum size is 160 bytes, and the maximum size is 32,768 bytes. The DOS environment size can be changed in 16-byte increments; DOS rounds off the environment size to the nearest 16-byte boundary.

Use the /E switch with the SHELL command in your CONFIG.SYS files to change your environment size. The following line sets the DOS environment to 512 bytes:

```
SHELL=COMMAND.COM /E:512 /P
```

The /P switch establishes the default DOS command interpreter COMMAND.COM as the primary command interpreter.

An "out of environment space" error message means that your environment size is not large enough to store all of your environment variables. If you have removed any needless environment variables and you still get the "out of environment space" error message, increase the setting of the /E switch.

 Tip The DOS environment uses valuable conventional memory. Avoid using up too much conventional memory by needlessly setting too many environment variables or setting the environment size higher than needed.

When you reboot your system, all environment variables are reset. The only environment variables that will be restored are those set by the AUTOEXEC.BAT file. Setting other environment variables requires setting them in a batch file or from the DOS prompt.

New Riders Publishing
INSIDE SERIES

Entering **SET** at the DOS prompt displays your current environment. The DOS environment varies according to the setup of each computer. Listed below is a typical DOS environment:

```
PROMPT=$P$G
COMSPEC=C:\DOS\COMMAND.COM
PATH=C:\;C:\DOS;C:\WINDOWS;C:\MOUSE;C:\BATCH;C:\XTGOLD
TEMP=C:\TEMP
```

◆ **Prompt.** The PROMPT variable sets the appearance of the DOS prompt. PG is the default setting of the DOS 6.x prompt. PG tells the DOS prompt to display the active drive, the active directory, and the > sign.

◆ **COMSPEC.** The COMSPEC variable tells DOS the disk location of the command interpreter COMMAND.COM. If COMSPEC is set for a floppy disk drive, DOS prompts you to insert a floppy disk when it is looking for COMMAND.COM.

◆ **PATH.** The PATH variable specifies directories for DOS to search when you enter a command at the DOS prompt.

◆ **TEMP.** The TEMP variable specifies the directory for the storage of temporary files created by various applications.

Tip

If your system crashes while an application is active, check the directory specified by the SET TEMP environment variable. Files that the application would have deleted if there had not been a crash are typically found in this directory. Generally, you can delete these files because they are needlessly occupying valuable disk space. At times these temp files may contain data you may have thought you lost when the application or system crashed. You may be able to recover some of this data, particularly if the data is text or a database entry.

Other environment variables include:

◆ **COPYCMD.** The COPYCMD variable enables you to specify whether you want the COPY, MOVE, and XCOPY commands to prompt for confirmation before overwriting a file. The default setting calls for all of those commands to prompt for confirmation. The /-Y switch turns off prompt for confirmation, and the /+Y switch turns on prompt for confirmation.

◆ **DIRCMD.** The DIRCMD variable enables you to preset switches and parameters to the DIR command. Entering **SET DIRCMD=*.exe /P**, for example, makes the DIR command function as if you typed **DIR *.exe /P** at the command line. To reset the DIR command, enter **SET DIRCMD=** at the DOS prompt.

AutoCAD also adds environment variables, but before examining them, take a look at the SET command.

The DOS SET Command

The SET command sets, displays, or removes environment variables. The syntax for the SET command is:

```
SET variable=string
```

Real-life examples of SET command syntax follow:

```
SET PATH=c:\ACADR13
SET DIRCMD=dir *.exe /p
```

To restore an environment to its default state, enter:

```
SET variable=
```

Environment variable names such as DIRCMD and PATH are uppercase. If you enter them in lowercase, DOS automatically converts them to uppercase.

 Stop Do not leave space before or after the = sign when using the SET command. A space after the = sign will result in the use of the default environment value. A space before the = includes the space as part of the variable. For example, examine the following command, with an underscore (_) representing a space:

```
SET ACAD_=c:\ACADR13
```

This command defines a variable with the name of ACAD_ when you probably want to name the variable ACAD. A space is a lot harder to see than an underscore, and you may not pick up the error.

AutoCAD's Use of the DOS Environment

You can use a batch file to call the SET command. The IA.BAT batch file created in Chapter 1 uses SET to establish the AutoCAD environment:

```
SET
ACAD=C:\IA;C:\ACADR13\COMMON\SUPPORT;C:\ACADR13\DOS;C:\ACADR13\DOS\SUPPORT;C:\ACADR13\COMMON\FONTS
SET ACADCFG=C:\IA
SET ACADDRV=C:\ACADR13\DOS\DRV
C:
```

 New Riders Publishing
INSIDE SERIES

```
CD \IA\DWGS
C:\ACADR13\DOS\ACAD %1 %2
SET ACAD=
SET ACADCFG=
SET ACADDRV=
```

The ACAD environment variable specifies the search path for AutoCAD program and support files. After starting AutoCAD, the following directories are searched:

1. The current directory

2. The directory containing the current drawing

3. Directories specified by the ACAD environment variable

4. The directory that contains the AutoCAD program file (ACAD.EXE)

The ACADCFG environment variable specifies the directory for AutoCAD's configuration file, ACAD.CFG.

The ACADDRV environment variable specifies the directory that is home to the ADI driver files used by video displays, digitizers, and plotters.

The next three lines in the IA.BAT file are as follows:

```
C:
CD \IA\DWGS
C:\ACADR13\DOS\ACAD %1 %2
```

These three lines change to drive C, set the \IA\DWGS directory current, and then start AutoCAD from that directory. The %1 and %2 designations are parameters for the launching of drawing and script files. To run AutoCAD, for example, with a drawing named VIDEO.DWG and a script file named DEFAULTS.SCR, you enter the following at the DOS prompt:

```
IA video defaults
```

Simply enter IA at the DOS prompt to run AutoCAD without launching any drawing or script files.

The last three lines of the IA.BAT file are as follows:

```
SET ACAD=
SET ACADCFG=
SET ACADDRV=
```

These three lines reset the ACAD environment variables. These last lines of the batch file run only after you exit AutoCAD. Their purpose is to return conventional memory to DOS, a useful practice that can pay off when you run other DOS applications after exiting AutoCAD. These lines also avoid conflicts with other AutoCAD configurations.

Other AutoCAD Environment Variables

ACADALTMENU establishes the name of an alternative tablet menu. With this environment variable and with your tablet menus set up properly, you can swap between tablet menus. To load a tablet menu other than the one that ships with AutoCAD, add a line similar to the following to your AutoCAD batch file.

```
SET ACADALTMENU=c:\acadr13\dos\support\altmenu.mnu
```

ACADPLCMD provides an interface between AutoCAD and a plot spooler. A plot spooler acts as a buffer between your PC and your plotter and enables you to continue work on a drawing while plotting takes place in the background.

Writing plots to a file is required for plot spooling. You must answer yes to the configuration question Plot to file? if you want to always spool your plots, or you can specify *Plot to file* when you issue the PLOT command.

AutoCAD Pager Environment Variables

The AutoCAD pager manages the paging of data between physical RAM and the swap file. Use the following environment variables to customize the AutoCAD pager.

- ◆ **ACADMAXMEM.** The ACADMAXMEM variable specifies the maximum amount of RAM in bytes available to the pager. The default setting is the total amount of RAM available in the system minus a small amount of memory used for overhead. There is no reason to limit the amount of RAM unless you need to do so for compatibility with another program. Reducing the amount of memory available for the AutoCAD pager causes AutoCAD's performance to slow because swapping between RAM and the swap file will increase.

- ◆ **ACADPAGEDIR.** The ACADPAGEDIR variable designates the directory for the storage of the first page file. With this environment variable, you can specify the pager to use a directory on a drive that has plenty of available storage. The default directory is the current drawing directory. You might use ACADPAGEDIR if your hard drive is partitioned into multiple drives and the drive with the AutoCAD files is low on free disk space.

- ◆ **ACADMAXPAGE.** The ACADMAXPAGE variable specifies the maximum number of bytes that can be written to the first page file. If this variable is not set, AutoCAD will write to the first page file until the disk drive is full. If it is set,

AutoCAD will create a second page file once the first page file is full. The second page file is written to the directory specified in Option 5 of Config's Operating Parameters menu. The default entry is DRAWING; this places any temporary files in the same directory as the drawing that is being edited.

Understanding AutoCAD System Variables

AutoCAD uses its own system variables for setting a large variety of modes, sizes, and limits. You can access system variables by entering **SETVAR** at the Command: prompt or by choosing Options, System Variables from the pull-down menu. You can use the SETVAR command to examine but not change certain read-only system variables, such as ACADPREFIX.

Most AutoCAD system variables can be changed by the user. Many system variables can only be set on or off, where 1 represents on and 0 off. Dimension variables, for example, can only be set on or off. Other variables have several discrete settings, represented by integer values (like EXPERT). Some have multiple settings which may be combined (such as OSMODE), where each option has binary value (1 = ENDPoint, 8 = NODe), and the setting is represented by their sum. Still others hold real numbers, integers, or text strings that represent actual values of current settings in a drawing, or are used as defaults in commands (like FILLETRAD, GRIPSIZE, or HPNAME).

Settings for some system variables are stored with individual drawings, other system variables are stored in AutoCAD configuration files (ACAD.CFG or ACAD.XMX), and some system variables are not stored at all. See Appendixes F and G of this book for a complete list of system variables and dimension variables respectively.

A number of system variables, such as MENUECHO and RASTERPREVIEW, have multiple settings. For example, the values 0, 1, 2, or 3 establish different settings for the RASTERPREVIEW system variable, as described in the next section.

 Tip You can change a system variable transparently, but the change may not take effect until the interrupted command completes its action.

The AutoCAD programming interfaces: AutoLISP, ADS (AutoCAD Development System), and ARX (AutoCAD Runtime Extension System) can access system variables. System variables defined by AutoLISP, ADS, and ARX applications are called externally defined system variables. These programming interfaces with their ability to define and modify system variables are powerful tools for customizing AutoCAD.

To get a full list of system variables, you can choose Options, System Variables, List from the pull-down menu. Or, you can enter **SETVAR** at the Command: prompt, then enter **?**, and then press Enter.

The RASTERPREVIEW System Variable

New to Release 13 is the ability to preview a drawing in the File Open dialog box. The system variable RASTERPREVIEW controls the storage of drawing preview images and sets the format for storage. The default setting is 0; if you do not want to preview images, set RASTERPREVIEW to 3. Table C.1 shows the settings available for RASTERPREVIEW.

TABLE C.1
RASTERPREVIEW System Variable Settings

Setting	File Extension	Description
0	BMP extension	Saves the image in bitmap format
1	BMP and WMF extensions	Saves the image in both bitmap format and Windows Metafile format
2	WMF extension	Saves the image in WMF format
3	No preview image	

Tip Saving the preview image consumes time and disk space. If this causes you problems, you may want to disable the preview image function by setting the RASTERPREVIEW system variable to 3.

Setting Preferences

The Preferences dialog box enables you to specify units of measurement and to specify a prototype drawing.

To access the dialog box, enter **PREFERENCES** at the AutoCAD Command: prompt, or choose Options, Preferences from the pull-down menu. See figure C.1 for the Preferences dialog box.

The Measurement drop-down list gives you the option of selecting English or metric units.

New Riders Publishing
INSIDE
SERIES

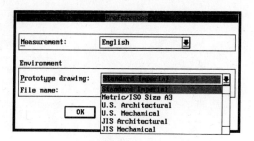

Figure C.1
The Preferences dialog box.

With the <u>P</u>rototype drawing drop-down list, you have the option of selecting a variety of different setup drawings. as shown in table C.2 below.

TABLE **C.2**
Prototype Drawings Shipped with Release 13

Type of drawing	Drawing Name
Standard Imperial	ACAD.DWG
Metric/ISO Size A3	ACADISO.DWG
U.S. Architectural	US_ARCH.DWG
U.S. Mechanical	US_MECH.DWG
JIS Architectural	JIS_MECH.DWG
JIS Mechanical	JIS_MECH.DWG

Tips for Managing AutoCAD

This appendix provides some helpful hints and tips for managing AutoCAD in a work environment. The following list includes some topics for discussion in this appendix:

- ◆ General management techniques

- ◆ Good drawing Practices

- ◆ Backing up critical system files

- ◆ System backups

- ◆ Hard disk management

- ◆ Managing multiple configurations

- ◆ Network management

- ◆ AutoCAD's built-in autosave feature

- ◆ File conversion between AutoCAD releases

These tips and hints are provided to help you with the everyday problems of maintaining an AutoCAD installation. Some of these problems include, but are not limited to: quick return to production in the event of a system failure, regular maintenance to help prevent problems and keep your computers running well, and compatibility issues with other platforms.

General Management Techniques

You can do several different things to help with the everyday general management and usage of AutoCAD. The simplest is keeping your directories organized. Organize your block libraries into distinct categories and keep all your blocks in directories related to the categories. An example of such an organization might occur in an Architect's office. Block libraries can be organized by the CSI Specifications categories. This breaks all the blocks an architect would use into about 15 categories and simplifies searching for these files. The same simple organization can apply to production drawings as well.

You can also implement drawing standards for your office. Many professional organizations already provide guidelines for CAD usage in the office. Drawing standards include, but are not limited to, a standard layer-naming system, standard dimension styles, standard text styles and fonts, standard borders, and standard colors used in the drawing. Of course, there can be many other standards besides these. It is sometimes a good idea to produce a manual outlining all the standards you want to have in your office. The implementation of these standards can be simplified by using prototype drawings. Many of the standards can be implemented in a set of prototype drawings. Multiple prototype drawings can be developed for interdisciplinary office, or for different projects that come through the office.

You should decide on a set of standards and implement them in your office. These standards should also include file locations and directory organization standards.

Good Drawing Practices

You can implement several simple drawing practices to increase production. The following practices are covered in this section: Purging files, Using Xref's, and setting system variables.

Get into the habit of purging your drawing every once in a while. Purging removes any layers, block definitions, and so forth that are not currently in use in the drawing. By removing these extra items, you reduce the file size of the drawing and the memory requirements needed by the system. On large drawings, this translates into an improvement in the overall editing time necessary for the drawing.

Use Xrefs when possible. *Xrefs* (or eXternal REFerence files) are similar to blocks, but do not take up near as much space in a drawing. Xrefs are also a good method of drawing management when several drawings are combined to form one larger drawing. Because an Xref is automatically updated every time it is loaded into a drawing, they are a good way to ensure accuracy when correcting or changing drawings that use another drawing as their base. An example of this is an electrical plan of a building where the floor plan is an Xref. Whenever the architect changes the floor plan, it is automatically updated in the electrical plan the next time the Xref is loaded into that drawing.

Change your system variables to help increase productivity. The EXPERT system variable controls how much AutoCAD prompts you for things such as regenerations. By changing the EXPERT system variable, you can enable or disable many of these prompts or warnings. Several different variables directly affect how fast AutoCAD can display the graphics. VIEWRES can be used to determine how many segments of a circle AutoCAD will draw on the screen. (This only affects screen redraws, not plotting.) The higher the number VIEWRES is set to, the longer it will take to draw arcs and circles. The lower the number, the rougher the arcs and circles will look, but they will redraw much quicker. Usually, a number around 100 is sufficient for the VIEWRES command. QTEXT can be used to disable the drawing of text on the screen. AutoCAD will draw a single line in place of the text when QTEXT is on. This can significantly reduce the redraw time of a drawing with a lot of text. FILL can also be turned off to prevent AutoCAD from filling in large areas of solid color on the screen, such as a wide polyline. This, again, will reduce the amount of time needed to redraw the screen.

By utilizing some of the techniques, you can significantly reduce the amount of time it takes AutoCAD to redraw a screen and reduce the chances of error in your drawings.

Backing Up Critical Files

After installing and configuring AutoCAD, you should make backups of several of the critical files on the system. You should back up these files in case any of the system files get corrupted during a system crash, an incompatible configuration locks up the system, or you want to restore the default settings quickly and easily. These files should be placed in a backup directory on the hard drive as well as on disks. The following files (with a brief description of each) should be backed up:

◆ **ACAD.INI.** (Location: \ACADR13\DOS) This file contains the configuration data about the AutoCAD working environment. If a user personalizes the AutoCAD environment, the customized ACAD.INI file should be backed up as well.

◆ **ACAD.CFG.** (Location:\ACADR13\DOS) This file is the most important AutoCAD file because it contains the encrypted authorization password and the system configuration, including the configurations for all plotters and display devices. Any time the AutoCAD configuration is changed, this file should be backed up.

◆ **ACAD.MNU.** (Location:\ACADR13\DOS\SUPPORT) This is the AutoCAD menu file. It is very easy, and often preferable, to customize the AutoCAD menus to suit the user. If you do so, you should back up the original default menus (even though they can be restored easily) and any menu files that have been customized.

All these files should be backed up because they can become corrupted at any time by viruses, hard disk errors, system crashes, and so on. Instead of having to reinstall or reconfigure AutoCAD, it is easier to copy the appropriate files from the backups.

Restoring system files can be automated by adding a few lines to the AUTOEXEC.BAT file in DOS. Set up the system so that every time the computer is booted, the backup files are copied into the appropriate working directories. It is not a good idea to modify the AUTOEXEC.BAT file to automatically back up the system files. If you make a backup of the important system files every time you boot the machine, and if the system crashes during bootup, the files could become corrupted. You don't want to back up the corrupted files!

Backing Up the System

At the end of every day, you should back up all changed files to disk for safety. You should always have at least two copies of a file in case one of the files gets corrupted. Also, scheduling regular backups of your entire system can help prevent major problems when the hard drive fails or part of the system board fails. Keeping an up-to-date backup of the drive makes for easy recovery of the files on the hard drive.

A tape drive or some type of removable optical media should be used for backing up the system. Floppy disks are not recommended because of the large number of disks generally required. (AutoCAD itself is 37 disks). A tape (both DAT and QIC) has a shelf life of 5–10 years, compared with a magneto optical disk's shelf life of 20 years. As expected, the MO is rather expensive when compared to a tape backup. If longevity is key in your backups, the MO drive is the best choice. If longevity is not very important, then a tape drive will suffice.

Most drives come with their own backup software to help ease the process of backing up the system. Many software programs will perform the backups unattended if you desire. Just make sure all the information will fit on the tape or disk.

A rotation schedule should be developed for backing up the complete hard drive. This rotation schedule ensures multiple versions of the system backups. Having multiple copies of system backups prevents the following problems:

◆ System backup tape loss, destruction, or corruption

◆ Corrupted system files being backed up on one set but not others

◆ Multiple copies of all files

A hard drive should be backed up once a week. A rotation of at least four tapes should be used. At the end of each month, a separate backup should be made and the original four tapes go back into the rotation. This provides a backup of the last four weeks of operation, as well as the monthly backups. The monthly backups should be stored off-site to provide the safest form of backup. Even if your office or workplace burns down, you always have a backup of the system and your files.

Note Unless you are running a network, disable AutoCAD's file locking. File locking can cause problems when the system crashes. Under a network environment, however, file locking must be enabled to avoid conflicts.

Managing Your Hard Disk

Keeping your hard disk up and running and in good condition can be difficult when using AutoCAD, especially if you are swapping to the disk constantly. When AutoCAD runs out of physical memory, it then uses hard disk space as "virtual memory." This constant reading and writing to the hard disk can cause hard drive fragmentation, and a system crash can leave unusable space on the hard drive. Several preventive steps can be taken to help care for your hard disk and improve the performance at the same time. A good utility suite such as Norton Utilities or PC Tools is highly recommended. At the very least, pick up a copy of DOS 6.2 or later. DOS 6.2 is a good investment because it contains a subset of portions of the Norton Utilities and PCTools. DOS 6.2 also has some of its own tools to help keep your hard disk in good working order.

Using one of these utilities, check the hard disk for errors when the system boots up. If you have Norton Utilities, run Norton Disk Doctor at bootup. If you have DOS 6.2, run SCANDISK at bootup. You can accomplish this by adding one line to the AUTOEXEC.BAT file. (Refer to the utilities' documentation for installing and running programs). Both of these programs will check the hard disk for errors, including lost chains, cross-linked and corrupted files, and corrupted directory structures. Running these utilities at boot time prevents many hard disk problems before they can start.

Your hard disk also should be defragmented at least once a week, especially under heavy usage. Two recommended utilities are the Norton Utilities' Speedisk or DOS 6.2's DEFRAG utility. (See your documentation on how to run these programs). As DOS works, it places files wherever it can on the hard drive, which can result in a file that is scattered around the hard drive. *Defragmenting* takes files and puts them back together in a contiguous space on the hard drive. Running these programs once a week will decrease the access time for files and increase the performance of your hard drive.

Managing Files

Managing large numbers of drawing files can become very difficult. There are numerous drawing management, scheduling, redlining, and revision control utilities available for AutoCAD. Autodesk's new Workcenter is well worth exploring, especially in the Windows environment. It combines drawing management, revision control, redlining, and other features in one easy-to-use package.

Managing AutoCAD on a Network

Managing AutoCAD in a network environment can present some of the following challenges:

◆ Setting up and maintaining shared COMMON directories

◆ File locking

◆ Maintaining multiple configurations across the network

◆ Performing appropriate backups

◆ Licensing control

All of these issues are the responsibility of the system administrator, the person who maintains the network and all machines attached to the network. This person has access to all machines, including the server, and should be the only one allowed to do backups. Many companies have one person devoted to this task, while other companies split the tasks up among several people.

There are two basic setups for AutoCAD on a network: single license versions of AutoCAD on each machine, and a network (or floating license) version of AutoCAD on the server. The network or floating license can be used to save money on the total

number of licenses purchased by a company. If all of the machines on the network are not using AutoCAD at the same time, buying a copy of AutoCAD for each and every machine makes no sense. A floating license, which allows a set number of people on the network to access AutoCAD, regardless of the machine they are on, would be a much better investment. You can then add or subtract licenses depending upon how many times you run out of licenses or reach your limit.

There are two network setups: client/server and peer-to-peer. In a client/server network, all programs and files that are to be shared across the network are placed on the network server. Because users will have some sort of access to the server, file locking is essential. Even if AutoCAD is installed as single license versions, make sure file locking is enabled in any network environment. File locking is necessary on the network to keep track of who is using which files. When file locking is enabled and a file is opened, a lock file is created. As long as the lock file is there, no one else on the network can modify the file. As a result, when a system crashes under this circumstance, you can end up with locked files.

A peer-to-peer network is one in which all machines can act as clients or servers, or both. In this type of network, it is very easy to designate one machine as the server by placing all of the COMMON files from AutoCAD on this machine and sharing those files with all other machines on the network. Employing a server reduces the amount of disk space required on the other machines. AutoCAD now uses a COMMON directory for files that are common across the various versions of AutoCAD. You can create the COMMON directory on any machine and enable all the others machines to use that directory as their common directory. This COMMON directory also is a good place to store any files or blocks that are to be shared with the rest of the office. This way all shared files are in a common location that is easily accessed by anyone on the network. Again, file locking is essential.

Managing Multiple Configurations

AutoCAD provides several methods for handling multiple configuration issues. The following list includes some of these issues:

◆ Creating batch files for various AutoCAD configurations, such as different plotters, display drivers, and so forth

◆ Setting up for discipline-specific work

◆ Multiple project setups

To create multiple configurations of AutoCAD on the same system, you need to be able to utilize different ACAD.CFG files. The process is discussed in Appendix C and summarized here:

1. Create a different directory for each unique configuration.

2. Create a startup batch file for each unique configuration (see your DOS documentation or the AutoCAD installation guide on how to do this).

3. When starting AutoCAD with a batch file, use the following environment variable: SET ACADCFG = *directory*, where directory is the location of the new ACAD.CFG file.

You must run each unique session of AutoCAD and configure each session as you like. Then, promptly make backups of each ACAD.CFG file.

A similar process can be used in DOS to set AutoCAD to project-specific directories. This way, when you start AutoCAD, it automatically defaults to the correct project directory that you specified. Follow the same procedure outlined above, but change step 3 to the following:

◆ Use the DOS Change Directory command to switch to the correct directory and then start AutoCAD from there. Alternatively, create different batch files that automatically switch to the correct directory before starting AutoCAD.

Setting up for discipline-specific work (architecture, engineering, and so forth) is a similar process, but you must enter AutoCAD to accomplish this. Implement the following procedure:

1. Create a batch file for each discipline.

2. Take each batch file, one at a time, and start an AutoCAD session.

3. When in AutoCAD, choose Options, Preferences to display the Preferences dialog box.

4. Under the Drawing Prototype drop-down list, choose the discipline drawing type you want to use. You may also choose Metric or English units at this point.

5. Choose OK to close the dialog box.

6. Exit the AutoCAD session.

This configuration information is saved to the ACAD.CFG file for each session. Make sure you have a backup of the file after you have completed your configuration changes.

Using the Autosave Feature

AutoCAD's autosave feature saves the current drawing file after a set time interval. This feature helps reduce the amount of time lost during power outages, system crashes, and other such catastrophes. To configure AutoCAD's autosave feature, you can either type **SAVETIME** at the Command: prompt and set the desired interval, or choose Options, Auto Save Time and set the time interval. The SAVETIME variable can also be configured through the CONFIG utility. Type CONFIG at the Command: prompt and choose item 7: Change Operating Parameters from the CONFIG menu. On the following menu, Item 7: Automatic-Save Feature is where you change the SAVETIME variable. The SAVETIME variable is stored in ACAD.CFG.

After the autosave feature is enabled, drawings are saved at the specified interval to the filename AUTO.SV*n*, where *n* may be blank or an incremental number.

Converting Release 13 Files to Earlier Releases

AutoCAD Release 13 files are not compatible with earlier versions of AutoCAD. To open a Release 13 file in Release 12, you must save the file in Release 12 format by using the SAVEASR12 command.

Some information might be lost in the translation process. All new Release 13 object types are converted to similar Release 12 objects. This conversion process may or may not create satisfactory results. An example of this is mtext objects in Release 13. When they are converted to Release 12, all styles using MTEXT will be converted to the STANDARD style using the TXT.SHX font. This is because mtext objects are not supported in Release 12.

To take a drawing from Release 13 to Release 10 or earlier, you must save the file as Release 12, create a DXF file using DXFOUT, and run the DXFIX.EXE utility that ships with Release 12. This will remove all the Release 12 information that Release 10 cannot understand. Again, more information may be lost.

 Stop When you open an old drawing file in Release 13, the only indication that it is an old version is an easily-missed Converting old drawing: message. When you save the drawing later, the drawing is saved as Release 13 unless you remember to use the SAVEASR12 command. Be sure to do so if others may need to reopen the file in Release 11 or 12.

D

Managing an AutoCAD system is not difficult, just time-consuming. Be sure to keep up with the general maintenance on a machine and the backups. Drawing and file maintenance can be developed through third-party software or your own in-house methodology. Just remember, keep the management as simple as possible to reduce the amount of headaches you might have during a crisis.

Command, Dialog Box, Alias, and Menu Equivalency Table

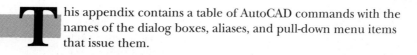

This appendix contains a table of AutoCAD commands with the names of the dialog boxes, aliases, and pull-down menu items that issue them.

Tip   You will also find useful annotated maps of pull-down menus in the back of this book.

In the Command Name and Options column, names and options shown in bold are new in Release 13. Many menu items issue specific options along with commands. For example, the View, Zoom, All menu item issues the ZOOM command with the All option. These options are indicated in the Command Name and Options column for those menu items, indented under the command name. In many cases, multiple options are issued; these are shown separated by commas. Often, menu items issue a command, pause for input, then issue specific options; this pause for input is indicated with a backslash—for example, \,Center for the Arc Start Center End menu item under the ARC command indicates that menu item issues the ARC command, pauses for the user to input a start point, and then issues the Center option.

In the Dialog Box column, the names shown are those that appear in the dialog box title bar.

Aliases are abbreviations that can be entered at the Command: prompt to issue commands. In the Alias column, the alias names shown in bold are in the standard ACAD.PGP file in the ACADR13\COMMON\SUPPORT directory and are normally available, whereas alias names shown nonbolded are defined in the optional ACAD.PGP file supplied on the IAW Disk (see Appendix H for more on this optional ACAD.PGP file). Aliases for dimensioning commands are prefaced with D, and commands beginning with DD that open dialog boxes are prefaced with DD.

In the Pull-Down Menu, Item column, items are shown in the form *Menuname, childmenuname, menuitemname*. View, Zoom, All translates to "Choose View to open the View pull-down menu, then choose Zoom to open the Zoom child menu, then choose All to issue the ZOOM command with the All option."

The — in any column indicates that an entry for the column is not applicable in that row of the table.

Note   The Dim: prompt is obsolete in Release 13. All of the R13 dimensioning commands can now be entered at the Command: prompt. Although the Dim: prompt is still present for compatibility purposes, the following commands, which were available at the Dim: prompt in earlier releases of AutoCAD, are obsolete and have been intentionally omitted from this table:

HOMETEXT, HORIZONTAL, NEWTEXT, OBLIQUE, ROTATED, SAVE, STATUS, TROTATE, UPDATE, VARIABLES, VERTICAL

New Riders Publishing
INSIDE
SERIES

continues

TABLE E.1
Command, Dialog Box, Alias, and Menu Equivalents

Command Name and Option	Dialog Box	Alias	Pull-Down Menu, Item
.X	—	—	Assist, Point Filters, .X
.XY	—	—	Assist, Point Filters, .XY
.XZ	—	—	Assist, Point Filters, .XZ
.Y	—	—	Assist, Point Filters, .Y
.YZ	—	—	Assist, Point Filters, .YZ
.Z	—	—	Assist, Point Filters, .Z
3D	—	—	—
3DARRAY	—	3AR	Construct, 3D Array
R,\\	—	—	Construct, 3D Array, Rectangle
P,\\	—	—	Construct, 3D Array, Polar
3DFACE	—	3DF	Draw, Surfaces, 3D Face
3DMESH	—	3DM	Draw, Surfaces, 3D Mesh
3DPOLY	—	3PL	Draw, 3D Polyline
3DSIN	3D Studio Import File	—	File, Import, 3D Studio
3DSOUT	3D Studio Output File	—	File, Export, 3D Studio
ABOUT	AUTOCAD(R)	—	Help, About Autocad
ACISIN	Select Acis File	—	File, Import, SAT
ACISOUT	Create Acis File	—	File, Export, SAT
AI_BOX	—	ABOX	—

E

TABLE E.1, CONTINUED
Command, Dialog Box, Alias, and Menu Equivalents

Command Name and Option	Dialog Box	Alias	Pull-Down Menu, Item
AI_DISH	—	ADSH	—
AI_DOME	—	ADOM	—
AI_MESH	—	AMSH	—
(AI_PROPCHK)	Modify	—	—
AI_PYRAMID	—	APYR	—
AI_SPHERE	—	ASPH	—
AI_TORUS	—	ATOR	—
AI_WEDGE	—	AWED	—
ALIGN	—	—	—
AMECONVERT	—	AC	Draw, Solids, AME Convert
APPLOAD	Load AutoLISP, ADS, ARX	—	Tools, Applications
APERTURE	—	—	—
ARC	—	A	—
\,C,\	—	—	Draw, Arc, Start, Center, End
\,C,A	—	—	Draw, Arc, Start, Center, Angle
\,E,A	—	—	Draw, Arc, Start, End, Angle
,E,D	—	—	Draw, Arc, Start, End, Direction
\,E,R	—	—	Draw, Arc, Start, End, Radius
\,C,\\	—	—	Draw, Arc, Center, Start, End

New Riders Publishing
INSIDE SERIES

Command Name and Option	Dialog Box	Alias	Pull-Down Menu, Item
C,\A	—	—	Draw, Arc, Center, Start, Angle
C,\L	—	—	Draw, Arc, Center, Start, Length
\	—	—	Draw, Arc, Continue
AREA	—	—	Assist, Inquiry, Area
ARRAY	—	ARR	—
R,\\	—	—	Construct, Array, Rectangular
P,\\	—	—	Construct, Array, Polar
ASEADMIN	—	ASA	Tools, External Database, Administration
ASEEXPORT	—	ASX	Tools, External Database, Export Links
ASELINKS	—	ASL	Tools, External Database, Links
ASEROWS	—	ASR	Tools, External Database, Rows
ASERUNREP	—	—	—
ASESELECT	—	ASS	Tools, External Database, Select Objects
ASESQLED	—	ASQ	Tools, External Database, SQL Editor
ATTEDIT	—	ATE	—
ATTEXT	Select Template File	—	—
ATTREDEF	—	ATR	Modify, Attribute, Redefine
BHATCH	Boundary Hatch	H	Draw, Hatch, Hatch

continues

TABLE E.1, CONTINUED
Command, Dialog Box, Alias, and Menu Equivalents

Command Name and Option	Dialog Box	Alias	Pull-Down Menu, Item
BLIPMODE	—	—	—
BLOCK	—	BL	Construct, Block
BMPOUT	Create BMP FIle	—	—
BOUNDARY	Boundary	BO	Construct, Boundary
BOX	—	—	Draw, Solids, Box, Corner
CE,\	—	—	Draw, Solids, Box, Center
BREAK	—	BR	Modify, Break, 1 point
\,F,@	—	—	Modify, Break, 1 Point Select
\,\	—	—	Modify, Break, 2 Points
\,F,@	—	—	Modify, Break, 2 Points Select
CAL	—	—	Tools, Calculator
CHAMFER	—	CH	Construct, Chamfer
CHANGE	—	—	—
CHPROP	—	—	—
CIRCLE	—	C	Draw, Circle
\,r	—	—	Draw, Circle, Center, Radius
\,D	—	—	Draw, Circle, Center, Diameter
2P,\	—	—	Draw, Circle, 2 Points
3P,\	—	—	Draw, Circle, 3 Points

New Riders Publishing
INSIDE SERIES

Command Name and Option	Dialog Box	Alias	Pull-Down Menu, Item
TTR,\	—	—	Draw, Circle, Tan, Tan, Radius
TTT,\	—	—	Draw, Circle, Tan, Tan, Tan
COLOR	—	—	—
COMPILE	Select Shape, Font File	—	Tools, Compile
CONE	—	CO	Draw, Solids, Cone, Center
E,\	—	—	Draw, Solids, Cone, Elliptical
CONFIG	—	CFG	Options, Configure
COPY	—	**CP**	Construct, Copy
CYLINDER	—	CY	Draw, Solids, Cylinder, Center
E,\	—	—	Draw, Solids, Cylinder, Elliptical
DBLIST	—	—	—
DDATTDEF	Attribute Definition	DDA	Construct, Attribute
DDATTE	Attribute Edit	DAT	Modify, Attribute Edit
DDATTEXT	Attribute Extraction	—	File, Export, Attributes
DDCHPROP	Change Properties	—	Modify, Properties
DDCOLOR	Select Color	DDC	Data, Color
DDEDIT	Edit Text	DDT	Modify, Edit Text
DDEMODES	Object Creation Modes	DDE	Data, Object Creation
DDGRIPS	Grips	DDG	Options, Grips
DDIM	Dimension Styles	DDI	Data, Dimension Styles
DDINSERT	Insert		Draw, Insert, Block

continues

E

TABLE E.1, CONTINUED
Command, Dialog Box, Alias, and Menu Equivalents

Command Name and Option	Dialog Box	Alias	Pull-Down Menu, Item
DDLMODES	Layer Control	DDL	Data, Layers
DDLTYPE	Select Linetype	DDLT	Data, Linetype
DDMODIFY	Modify (Varies)	DDM	Modify, Properties
DDOSNAP	Running Object Snap	DDO	Options, Running Object Snap
DDPSTYLE	Point Style	—	Option, Display, Point Style
DDRENAME	Rename	DDRE	Data, Rename
DDRMODES	Drawing Aids	DDR	Options, Drawing Aids
DDSELECT Settings	Object Selection	DDS	Options, Selection
DDSTYLE	—	—	—
DDUCS	UCS Control	DDUC	View, Named UCS
DDUCSP	UCS Orientation	DDUP	View, Preset UCS
DDUNITS	Units Control	DDU	Data, Units
DDVIEW	View Control	DDV	View, Named Views
DDVPOINT	Viewpoint Presets	—	View, 3D Viewpoint, Rotate
DELAY	—	—	—
DIM	—	—	—
DIMALIGNED	—	DALI	Draw, Dimensioning, Aligned
DIMANGULAR	—	DANG	Draw, Dimensioning, Angular

New Riders Publishing
INSIDE SERIES

Command Name and Option	Dialog Box	Alias	Pull-Down Menu, Item
DIMBASELINE	—	DBAS	Draw, Dimensioning, Baseline
DIMCENTER	—	DCEN	Draw, Dimensioning, Center Mark
DIMCONTINUE	—	DCON	Draw, Dimensioning, Continue
DIMDIAMETER	—	DDIA	Draw, Dimensioning, Radial, Diameter
DIMEDIT	—	**DIMED**	—
O,\	—	—	Draw, Dimensioning, Oblique
DIMLINEAR	—	DLIN	Draw, Dimensioning, Linear
DIMORDINATE	—	DORD	Draw, Dimensioning, Ordinate, Automatic
\,X	—	—	Draw, Dimensioning, Ordinate, X Datum
\,Y	—	—	Draw, Dimensioning, Ordinate, Y Datum
DIMRADIUS	—	DRAD	Draw, Dimensioning, Radial, Radius
DIMTEDIT	—	**DTED**	—
\,H	—	—	Draw, Dimensioning, Align Text, Home
\,A	—	—	Draw, Dimensioning, Align Text, Rotate
\,L	—	—	Draw, Dimensioning, Align Text, Left

continues

E

TABLE E.1, CONTINUED
Command, Dialog Box, Alias, and Menu Equivalents

Command Name and Option	Dialog Box	Alias	Pull-Down Menu, Item
\,C	—	—	Draw, Dimensioning, Align Text, Center
\,R	—	—	Draw, Dimensioning, Align Text, Right
DIMSTYLE	—	—	—
DIST	—	—	Assist, Inquiry, Distance
DIVIDE	—	DI	Draw, Point, Divide
DONUT	—	—	—
DRAGMODE	—	—	—
DTEXT	—	DT	Draw, Text, Dynamic Text
DVIEW	—	**DV**	View, 3D Dynamic View
DXBIN	Select DXB File	—	File, Import, DXB
DXFIN	Select DXF File	—	File, Import, DXF
DXFOUT	Create DXF File	—	File, Export, DXF
EDGE	—	ED	Draw, Surfaces, Edge
EDGESURF	—	ES	Draw, Surfaces, Edge Surface
ELEV	—	—	—
ELLIPSE	—	EL	Draw, Ellipse, Center
\,\	—	—	Draw, Ellipse, Axis, End
A,\\	—	—	Draw, Ellipse, Arc
END	—	—	—

New Riders Publishing
INSIDE SERIES

Command Name and Option	Dialog Box	Alias	Pull-Down Menu, Item
ERASE	—	E	Modify, Erase
EXPLODE	—	EXP	Modify, Explode
EXPORT	Export Data	—	File, Export
EXTEND	—	EX	Modify, Extend
EXTRUDE	—	EXT	Draw, Solids, Extrude
FILES	File Utilities	—	File, Management, Utilities
FILL	—	—	Options, Display, Solid Fill
FILLET	—	FI	Construct, Fillet
FILTER	Object Selection Filter	—	Assist, Selection Filters
GIFIN	—	—	File, Import, Raster, Gif
GRAPHSCR	—	—	—
GRID	—	—	—
GROUP	Object Grouping	GR	Assist, Group Objects
HATCH	—	—	—
HATCHEDIT	Hatchedit	HE	Modify, Edit Hatch
HELP	—	—	Help, Help
HIDE	—	HI	Tools, Hide
ID	—	—	Assist, Inquiry, Locate Point
IMPORT	Import File	—	File, Import
INSERT	—	—	—

continues

TABLE E.1, CONTINUED
Command, Dialog Box, Alias, and Menu Equivalents

Command Name and Option	Dialog Box	Alias	Pull-Down Menu, Item
INTERFERE	—	INTF	Draw, Solids, Interference
INTERSECT	—	INTS	—
ISOPLANE	—	—	—
LAYER	—	**LA**	—
LEADER	—	**LEAD**	Draw, Dimensioning, Leader
LENGTHEN	—	—	Modify, Lengthen
LIGHT	Lights	LI	Tools, Render, Lights
LIMITS	—	—	Data, Drawing Limits
LINE	—	**L**	Draw, Line
LINETYPE	—	**LT**	—
LTSCALE	—	—	—
LIST	—	LIS	Assist, Inquiry, List
LOAD	Select Shape File	—	Data, Shape File
LOGFILEON	—	—	Options, Log Files, Session Log
LOGFILEOFF	—	—	Options, Log Files, Session Log
MASSPROP	—	—	Assist, Inquiry, Mass Properties
MATLIB	Materials Library	MAL	Tools, Render, Materials Library
MEASURE	—	ME	Draw, Point, Measure
MENU	Select Menu File	—	Tools, Menu
MINSERT	—	MIN	Draw, Insert Multiple Blocks

Command Name and Option	Dialog Box	Alias	Pull-Down Menu, Item
MIRROR	—	—	Construct, Mirror
MIRROR3D	—	—	Construct, 3D Mirror
MLEDIT	—	MLE	Modify, Edit Multiline
MLINE	—	ML	Draw, Multiline
MLSTYLE	Multiline Styles	MST	Data, Multiline Style
MOVE	—	**M**	—
MSLIDE	Create Slide File	MSL	Tools, Slide, Save
MSPACE	—	**MS**	View, Floating Model Space
MTEXT	—	**T**	Draw, Text, Text
MULTIPLE	—	—	—
MVIEW	—	MV	View, Floating Model Space
MVSETUP	—	—	—
NEW	Create New Drawing	—	File, New
OFFSET	—	OF	Construct, Offset
OOPS	—	OO	Modify, OOPS!
OPEN	Open Drawing	—	File, Open
OSNAP	—	OS	—
FROM	—	—	Assist, Object Snap, From
ENDP	—	—	Assist, Object Snap, Endpoint
MIDP	—	—	Assist, Object Snap, Midpoint
INT	—	—	Assist, Object Snap, Intersection

continues

TABLE E.1, CONTINUED
Command, Dialog Box, Alias, and Menu Equivalents

Command Name and Option	Dialog Box	Alias	Pull-Down Menu, Item
APPINT	—	—	Assist, Object Snap, Apparent Intersection
CEN	—	—	Assist, Object Snap, Center
QUAD	—	—	Assist, Object Snap, Quadrant
PER	—	—	Assist, Object Snap, Perpendicular
TAN	—	—	Assist, Object Snap, Tangent
NODE	—	—	Assist, Object Snap, Node
INS	—	—	Assist, Object Snap, Insertion
NEA	—	—	Assist, Object Snap, Nearest
QUICK	—	—	Assist, Object Snap, Quick
NONE	—	—	Assist, Object Snap, None
PAN	—	**P**	View, Pan, Point
'	—	—	View, Pan, Left
'	—	—	View, Pan, Right
'	—	—	View, Pan, Up
'	—	—	View, Pan, Down
'	—	—	View, Pan, Up Left
'	—	—	View, Pan, Up Right
'	—	—	View, Pan, Down Left
'	—	—	View, Pan, Down Right

New Riders Publishing
INSIDE SERIES

Command Name and Option	Dialog Box	Alias	Pull-Down Menu, Item
PCXIN	—	—	File, Import, Raster, PCX
PEDIT	—	PE	Modify, Edit Polyline
PFACE	—	—	—
PLAN	—	—	—
PLINE	—	**PL**	Draw, Polyline
PLOT	Plot	—	File, Print
POINT	—	PO	Draw, Point, Point
POLYGON	—	POL	Draw, Polygon, Polygon
PREFERENCES	Preferences	PRE	Options, Preferences
PSDRAG	—	—	—
PSFILL	—	PSF	Draw, Hatch, Postscript Fill
PSIN	—	—	File, Import, Postscript
PSLTSCALE	—	—	—
PSOUT	—	—	File, Export, Postscript
PSPACE	—	**PS**	View, Paper Space
PURGE	—	PU	Data, Purge
QSAVE	—	—	File, Save
QTEXT	—	—	—
QUIT	—	—	File, Exit
RAY	—	—	Draw, Ray
RCONFIG	—	—	Options, Render Configure

continues

E

TABLE E.1, CONTINUED
Command, Dialog Box, Alias, and Menu Equivalents

Command Name and Option	Dialog Box	Alias	Pull-Down Menu, Item
RECOVER	—	—	File, Management, Recover
RECTANG	—	REC	Draw, Polygon, Rectangle
REDEFINE	—	—	—
REDO	—	—	Assist, Redo
REDRAW	—	**R**	View, Redraw View
REDRAWALL	—	RA	View, Redraw All
REGEN	—	—	—
REGENALL	—	—	—
REGENAUTO	—	—	—
REGION	—	REG	Construct, Region
REINIT	Re-Initialization	—	Tools, Reinitialize
RENAME	—	—	—
RENDER	Render	REN	Tools, Render, Render
RENDSCR	—	—	—
REPLAY	Replay	—	Tools, Image, View
RESUME	—	—	—
REVOLVE	—	REV	Draw, Solids, Revolve
REVSURF	—	RS	Draw, Surfaces, Revolved Surface
RMAT	Materials	MA	Tools, Render, Materials
ROTATE	—	RO	Modify, Rotate

New Riders Publishing
INSIDE SERIES

Command Name and Option	Dialog Box	Alias	Pull-Down Menu, Item
ROTATE3D	—	—	Construct, 3D Rotate
RPREF	Rendering Preferences	RP	Tools, Render, Preferences
RSCRIPT	—	—	—
RULESURF	—	RLS	Draw, Surfaces, Ruled Surface
SAVE	—	—	File, Save
SAVEAS	Save Drawing As	—	File, Save As
SAVEASR12	Save Release 12 Drawing As	—	File, Export, Release 12 DWG
SAVEIMG	Save Image	—	Tools, Image, Save
SCALE	—	SC	Modify, Scale
SCENE	Scenes	—	Tools, Render, Scenes
SCRIPT	Select Script File	—	Tools, Run Script
SECTION	—	SEC	Draw, Solids, Section
SELECT	—	—	—
W	—	—	Assist, Select, Window
C	—	—	Assist, Select, Crossing
G	—	—	Assist, Select, Group
P	—	—	Assist, Select, Previous
L	—	—	Assist, Select, Last
ALL	—	—	Assist, Select, All
WP	—	—	Assist, Select, Window Polygon

continues

E

TABLE E.1, CONTINUED
Command, Dialog Box, Alias, and Menu Equivalents

Command Name and Option	Dialog Box	Alias	Pull-Down Menu, Item
CP	—	—	Assist, Select, Crossing Polygon
F	—	—	Assist, Select, Fence
A	—	—	Assist, Select, Add
R	—	—	Assist, Select, Remove
SETVAR	—	—	—
SHADE	—	SH	Tools, Shade
SHAPE	—	SHA	—
SHELL	—	—	—
SKETCH	—	SK	Draw, Sketch
SLICE	—	SL	Draw, Solids, Slice
SNAP	—	—	—
SOLID	—	SOL	Draw, Polygon, 2d Solid
SPELL	Check Spelling	SP	Tools, Spelling
SPHERE	—	SPH	Draw, Solids, Sphere
SPLINE	—	SPL	Draw, Spline
SPLINEDIT	—	SPE	Modify, Edit Spline
STATS	Statistics	STA	Tools, Render, Statistics
STATUS	—	—	Data, Status
STLOUT	Create STL File	—	Files, Export, Stereolithography
STRETCH	—	ST	Modify, Stretch

New Riders Publishing
INSIDE SERIES

Command Name and Option	Dialog Box	Alias	Pull-Down Menu, Item
STYLE	—	—	Data, Text Style
SUBTRACT	—	SUB	Construct, Subtract
TABLET	—	—	Options, Tablet
TABSURF	—	TS	Draw, Surfaces, Extruded Surface
TEXT	—	—	—
TEXTSCR	AutoCAD Text Window	—	—
TIFFIN	—	—	File, Import, Raster, TIFF
TILEMODE	—	TI	View, Tiled Model Space (System variable)
0	—	—	View, Paper Space
TIME	—	—	Data, Time
TOLERANCE	Symbol	TOL	Draw, Dimensioning, Tolerance
TORUS	—	TOR	Draw, Solids, Torus
TRACE	—	—	—
TREESTAT	—	—	—
TRIM	—	TR	Modify, Trim
UCS	—	UC	—
W	—	—	View, Set UCS, World
O	—	—	View, Set UCS, Origin
ZA	—	—	View, Set UCS, ZAxis Vector
3	—	—	View, Set UCS, 3 Point

continues

TABLE E.1, CONTINUED

Command, Dialog Box, Alias, and Menu Equivalents

Command Name and Option	Dialog Box	Alias	Pull-Down Menu, Item
OB	—	—	View, Set UCS, Object
V	—	—	View, Set UCS, View
X	—	—	View, Set UCS, Xaxis Rotate
Y	—	—	View, Set UCS, Yaxis Rotate
Z	—	—	View, Set UCS, Zaxis Rotate
P	—	—	View, Set UCS, Previous
R	—	—	View, Set UCS, Restore
S	—	—	View, Set UCS, Save
UCSICON	—	—	—
UNDEFINE	—	—	—
UNDO	—	—	Assist, Undo
UNION	—	UN	Construct, Union
UNLOCK	—	—	—
VIEWRES	—	—	—
VLCONV	Visual Link Data Converter	—	—
VPLAYER	—	—	—
UNITS	—	—	—
VPOINT	—	VP	View, 3D Viewpoint, Tripod
NON,0,0,1	—	—	View, 3D Viewpoint Presets, Top
NON,0,0,-1	—	—	View, 3D Viewpoint Presets, Bottom

New Riders Publishing
INSIDE SERIES

Command Name and Option	Dialog Box	Alias	Pull-Down Menu, Item
NON,-1,0,0	—	—	View, 3D Viewpoint Presets, Left
NON,1,0,0	—	—	View, 3D Viewpoint Presets, Right
NON,0,-1,0	—	—	View, 3D Viewpoint Presets, Front
NON,0,1,0	—	—	View, 3D Viewpoint Presets, Back
NON,-1,-1,1	—	—	View, 3D Viewpoint Presets, SW Isometric
NON,1,-1,1	—	—	View, 3D Viewpoint Presets, SE Isometric
NON,1,1,1	—	—	View, 3D Viewpoint Presets, NE Isometric
NON,-1,1,1	—	—	View, 3D Viewpoint Presets, NW Isometric
VPORTS	—	—	—
VSLIDE	Select Slide File	VSL	Tools, Slide, View
WBLOCK	—	—	File, Export, Block
WEDGE	—	WE	Draw, Solids, Wedge, Corner
CE,\	—	—	Draw, Solids, Wedge, Center
XBIND	—	XB	—
B,\	—	—	File, Bind, Block
LA,\	—	—	File, Bind, Layer
LT,\	—	—	File, Bind, Linetype

continues

E

TABLE E.1, CONTINUED
Command, Dialog Box, Alias, and Menu Equivalents

Command Name and Option	Dialog Box	Alias	Pull-Down Menu, Item
S,\	—	—	File, Bind, Style
D,\	—	—	File, Bind, Dimension Style
XLINE	—	XL	Draw, Construction Line
XPLODE	—	—	—
XREF	—	XR	—
A,\	—	—	File, External Reference, Attach
O,	—	—	File, External Reference, Overlay
R,\	—	—	File, External Reference, Reload
D,\	—	—	File, External Reference, Detach
P,\	—	—	File, External Reference, Path
?,\	—	—	File, External Reference, List
B,\	—	—	File, External Reference, All
XREFCLIP	—	XRC	File, External Reference, Clip
ZOOM	—	**z**	—
2X	—	—	View, Zoom, In
.5X	—	—	View, Zoom, Out
W	—	—	View, Zoom, Window
All	—	—	View, Zoom, All
P	—	—	View, Zoom, Previous
X	—	—	View, Zoom, Scale

New Riders Publishing
INSIDE
SERIES

Command Name and Option	Dialog Box	Alias	Pull-Down Menu, Item
D	—	—	View, Zoom, Dynamic
C	—	—	View, Zoom, Center
Left	—	—	View, Zoom, Left
Limits	—	—	View, Zoom, Limits
E	—	—	View, Zoom, Extents
Vmax	—	—	View, Zoom, Vmax

E

APPENDIX F

System Variables Table

This appendix contains a table of AutoCAD system variables. You can use this table to find AutoCAD's environment settings and their values. Table F.1 represents all the variables available through AutoCAD, AutoLISP, and the AutoCAD Development System. Dimension variables are shown in Appendix G. The system variable name and the default AutoCAD prototype drawing (ACAD.DWG) settings are shown. A brief description is given for each variable, and the meaning is given for each code. Most variables are set by various dialog boxes or commands. These variables also can be set or checked by the SETVAR command, and most can be entered directly at the `Command:` prompt. However, those names shown italicized can only be directly accessed by the SETVAR command because AutoCAD has a command with the same name as the variable. All values are saved with the drawing unless noted with (CFG) for ConFiGuration file or (NS) for Not Saved. The Command Name column lists the commands that set the system variables. Variables marked (RO) are read-only, which means that you cannot change them.

 Note Variable names and features shown in bold are new in Release 13.

TABLE F.1
System Variables Table

Variable Name	Default Setting	Command Name	Variable Description
ACADPREFIX	"C:\ACADR13\COMMON\ SUPPORT;C:\ACADR13..."	—	(NS) (RO) Directory search path set by the DOS ACAD environment variable.
ACADVER	"13"	—	(NS) (RO) Release number of your copy of AutoCAD.
AFLAGS	0	DDATTDEF, ATTDEF	(NS) Current state of ATTDEF modes. The value is the sum of the following: 0 = No attribute mode selected 1 = Invisible 2 = Constant 4 = Verify 8 = Preset
ANGBASE	0.0000	DDUNITS, UNITS	The direction of angle 0 in the current UCS.
ANGDIR	0	DDUNITS, UNITS	The direction of angle measure from 0: 0 = Counterclockwise 1 = Clockwise
APERTURE	10	DDOSNAP, APERTURE	(CFG) OSNAP target size in pixels.
AREA	0.0000	AREA, LIST, DBLIST	(NS) (RO) Stores the last computed area.

New Riders Publishing
INSIDE SERIES

Variable Name	Default Setting	Command Name	Variable Description
ATTDIA	0	INSERT	Controls the attribute-entry method: 0 = Attribute prompts 1 = DDATTE dialogue box
ATTMODE	1	ATTDISP	Controls attribute display: 0 = OFF 1 = Normal 2 = ON
ATTREQ	1	INSERT	Attribute values used by insert: 0 = Uses default 1 = Prompts for values
AUDITCTL	0	—	(CFG) Controls whether AutoCAD creates an ADT file (Audit Report): 0 = No File 1 = ADT File
AUNITS	0	DDUNITS, UNITS	Sets Angular Units mode: 0 = Decimal Degrees 1 = Degrees/minutes/seconds 2 = Gradians 3 = Radians 4 = Surveyor's Units
AUPREC	0	DDUNITS, UNITS	Sets number of decimal places for angular units.
BACKZ	0.0000	DVIEW	(RO) The DVIEW back clipping plane offset in drawing units. (See VIEWMODE.)

continues

F

TABLE F.1, CONTINUED
System Variables Table

Variable Name	Default Setting	Command Name	Variable Description
BLIPMODE	1	—	Controls display of marker blips: 1 = Blips 0 = No Blips
CDATE	19941211.22041537	TIME	(RO) (NS) Current date and time in YYMMDD.HHMMSS format.
CECOLOR	"BYLAYER"	DDEMODES, COLOR	The color for new objects.
CELTSCALE	1.0000	LTSCALE, PSLTSCALE	Sets global linetype scale for new objects.
CELTYPE	"BYLAYER"	DDEMODES, LINETYPE	Sets the linetype for new objects.
CHAMFERA	0.0000	CHAMFER	The first chamfer distance.
CHAMFERB	0.0000	CHAMFER	The second chamfer distance.
CHAMFERC	0.0000	CHAMFER	The chamfer length.
CHAMFERD	0.0000	CHAMFER	The chamfer angle.
CHAMMODE	0	CHAMFER	(NS) Determines method AutoCAD uses to create chamfers: 0 = Requires two chamfer distances 1 = Requires chamfer length and angle
CIRCLERAD	0.0000	CIRCLE	(NS) Default radius value for new circles: 0 = None
CLAYER	"0"	DDLMODES, LAYER	The current layer.

Variable Name	Default Setting	Command Name	Variable Description
CMDACTIVE	0	CMDACTIVE	(NS) (RO) (Used primarily by ADS) Indicates that an AutoCAD command is active: 0 = None 1 = Ordinary command 2 = Ordinary and transparent 4 = Script 8 = Dialog box
CMDDIA	1	—	(CFG) Controls whether the PLOT command uses a dialog box or command prompts: 0 = prompts 1 = Dialog box
CMDECHO	1	—	(NS) Controls the echoing of prompts and input during AutoLISP functions: 0 = Disables echoing 1 = Enables echoing
CMDNAMES	""	—	(NS) (RO) Names of any active commands.
CMLJUST	0	DTEXT, TEXT	(CFG) Sets Multi-Line text justification: 0 = Top 1 = Middle 2 = Bottom

continues

TABLE F.1, CONTINUED
System Variables Table

Variable Name	Default Setting	Command Name	Variable Description
CMLSCALE	1.0000	DTEXT, TEXT	(CFG) Sets overall width of Multi-Line text: Scale factor 2 = Twice width of style def. Scale Factor 0 = Collapses multiline into single line Negative Scale Factor = Flips order of offset lines
CMLSTYLE	"STANDARD"	**MTEXT, DTEXT, TEXT**	(CFG) Sets the style for Multi-Lines.
COORDS	1	[^D] [F6]	Controls updating of coordinate display: 0 = Updated on pick points only 1 = Absolute continuously updated 2 = Relative only during prompts
CVPORT	2	VPORTS	The current viewport's number.
DATE	2449698.91977246	TIME	(NS) (RO) The current date and time in Julian format.
DBMOD	0	Most	(NS) (RO) Drawing modification status. Sum of the following: 0 = None 1 = Object database modified 2 = Symbol table modified 4 = Database variable modified

New Riders Publishing
INSIDE SERIES

Variable Name	Default Setting	Command Name	Variable Description
			8 = Window modified
			16 = View modified
DCTCUST	""	**SPELL**	(CFG)
			Current custom spelling dictionary and path.
DCTMAIN	"enu"	**SPELL**	(CFG)
			Current main spelling dictionary file:
			enu = American English
			ena = Australian English
			ens = British English (ise)
			enz = British English (ize)
			ca = Catalan
			cs = Czech
			da = Danish
			nl = Dutch (Primary)
			nls = Dutch (Secondary)
			fi = Finnish
			fr = French (unaccented capitals)
			fra = French (accented capitals)
			de = German (Scharfes s)
			ded = German (Dopple s)
			it = Italian
			no = Norwegian (Bokmal)
			non = Norwegian (Nynorsk)
			pt = Portuguese (Iberian)
			ptb = Portuguese (Brazilian)
			ru = Russian (infrequent io)
			ru I = Russian (frequent io)

continues

F

TABLE F.1, CONTINUED
System Variables Table

Variable Name	Default Setting	Command Name	Variable Description
			es = Spanish (unaccented capitals) esa = Spanish (accented capitals) sv = Swedish
DELOBJ	1	—	Controls whether objects used to create other objects are deleted from the database: 0 = Objects are deleted 1 = Objects are retained
DIASTAT	1	—	(NS) (RO) Last dialog box exit code: 0 = Cancel 1 = OK
DISPSILH	0	—	Controls display of silhouette curves of body objects in wireframe mode: 0 = Off 1 = On
DISTANCE	0.0000	DIST	(NS) (RO) Stores the distance computed by the DIST command.
DONUTID	0.5000	DONUT	(NS) Sets the default inner diameter for new donut objects.
DONUTOD	1.0000	DONUT	(NS) Sets the default outer diameter for new donut objects.

Variable Name	Default Setting	Command Name	Variable Description
DRAGMODE	2	DRAGMODE	Controls object dragging during editing commands: 0 = No dragging 1 = On (if requested) 2 = Auto
DRAGP1	10	—	(CFG) Sets regen-drag input sampling rate.
DRAGP2	25	—	(CFG) Sets fast-drag input sampling rate.
DWGCODEPAGE	"ansi_1252"	—	(RO) The code page used for the drawing.
DWGNAME	"UNNAMED"	—	(RO) The drawing name as entered by the user.
DWGPREFIX	"C:\ACADR13\DOS\"	—	(NS) (RO) The current drawing's drive and directory path.
DWGTITLED	0	NEW	(NS) (RO) Indicates whether the current drawing has been named or not: 0 = No 1 = Yes
DWGWRITE	1	OPEN	(NS) Indicates whether the current drawing is opened as read only: 0 = Read-only 1 = Read/write

continues

F

Table F.1, Continued
System Variables Table

Variable Name	Default Setting	Command Name	Variable Description
EDGEMODE	0	TRIM, EXTEND	Controls determination of cutting and boundary edges: 0 = Use selected edge without extension 1 = Extends selected edge to imaginary extension of cutting or boundary object
ELEVATION	0.0000	ELEV	The current elevation in the current UCS for the current space.
ERRNO	0	—	(NS) An error number generated by AutoLISP and ADS Applications. (See the *AutoLISP Release 13 Programmer's Reference* or the *AutoCAD Development System Programmer's Reference Manual.*) Not listed by SETVAR.
EXPERT	0	—	(NS) Suppresses successive level of Are you sure? warnings: 0 = None 1 = REGEN/LAYER 2 = BLOCK/WBLOCK/SAVE 3 = LINETYPE 4 = UCS/VPORT 5 = DIM

New Riders Publishing
INSIDE
SERIES

Variable Name	Default Setting	Command Name	Variable Description
EXPLMODE	1	EXPLODE	Controls whether the EXPLODE command support nonuniformly scaled (NUS) blocks: 0 = Does not explode NUS blocks 1 = Explodes NUS blocks
EXTMAX	-1.0000E+20,-1.0000E+20, -1.0000E+20	(RO)	The X,Y coordinates of the drawing's upper right extents in the WCS.
EXTMIN	1.0000E+20,1.0000E+20, 1.0000E+20	(RO)	The X,Y coordinates of the drawing's lower left extents in the WCS.
FACETRES	0.5000	HIDE, SHADE, RENDER	Adjusts smoothness of shaded and hidden-line removed objects. Valid from 0.01 to 10.0.
FFLIMIT	0	—	(CFG) Limits number of PostScript and TrueType fonts in memory. From 0 to 100. 0 is no limit.
FILEDIA	1	—	(CFG) Controls display of file dialog boxes: 0 = Only when a tilde (~) is entered 1 = On
FILLETRAD	0.0000	FILLET	Stores the current fillet radius.

continues

F

TABLE F.1, CONTINUED
System Variables Table

Variable Name	Default Setting	Command Name	Variable Description
FILLMODE	1	SOLID, FILL	Turns on the display of fill traces, solids, and wide polylines: 0 = Off 1 = On
FONTALT	"txt"	—	(CFG) Specifies alternative font when AutoCAD cannot locate requested font.
FONTMAP	""	—	(CFG) Specifies a mapped font file to use when AutoCAD cannot locate the font file.
FRONTZ	0.0000	DVIEW	(RO) The DVIEW front clipping plane's offset in drawing units. (See VIEWMODE.)
GRIDMODE	0	DDRMODES, GRID	Controls display of the grid in the current viewport: 0 = Off 1 = On
GRIDUNIT	0.0000,0.0000	DDRMODES, GRID	The X,Y grid spacing for the current viewport.
GRIPBLOCK	0	DDGRIPS	(CFG) Controls the display of grips for objects in blocks:

New Riders Publishing
INSIDE SERIES

Variable Name	Default Setting	Command Name	Variable Description
			0 = Off 1 = On
GRIPCOLOR	5	DDGRIPS	(CFG) The current color of unselected grips. Can be any AutoCAD color from 1 to 255.
GRIPHOT	1	DDGRIPS	(CFG) The current color of selected grips. Can be any AutoCAD color from 1 to 255.
GRIPS	1	DDSELECT	(CFG) Controls the display of entity grips and grip editing: 0 = Off 1 = On
GRIPSIZE	3	DDGRIPS	(CFG) The size of grip box in pixels; 0 = PICKBOX.
HANDLES	1	HANDLES	Controls the creation of entity handles for the current drawing: 1 = On
HIGHLIGHT	1	DDRMODES	(NS) Controls object selection highlighting: 0 = Off 1 = On

continues

F

TABLE F.1, CONTINUED
System Variables Table

Variable Name	Default Setting	Command Name	Variable Description
HPANG	0	BHATCH, HATCH	(NS) The current hatch angle.
HPBOUND	1	BHATCH, BOUNDARY	Type of object created by the BHATCH and BOUNDARY commands: 0 = Polyline 1 = Region
HPDOUBLE	0	BHATCH, HATCH	(NS) Controls user-defined hatch pattern doubling: 0 = Off 1 = On
HPNAME	"ANSI31"	BHATCH, HATCH	(NS) The default hatch pattern for new hatches.
HPSCALE	1.0000	BHATCH, HATCH	(NS) The default hatch pattern scale. Must be nonzero.
HPSPACE	1.0000	BHATCH, HATCH	(NS) The default spacing for user-defined hatch patterns.
INSBASE	0.0000,0.0000,0.0000	BASE	Insertion base point X,Y,Z coordinate of current drawing in current space and current UCS.

New Riders Publishing
INSIDE SERIES

Variable Name	Default Setting	Command Name	Variable Description
INSNAME	""	DDINSERT,INSERT	(NS) Default block name for INSERT or DDINSERT.
ISOLINES	4	—	Controls number of isolines per surface on objects.
LASTANGLE	0.0000	ARC	(NS) (RO) The angle of the last arc entered in the current UCS for the current space.
LASTPOINT	0.0000,0.0000,0.0000	—	The last point entered in the current UCS and current space.
LENSLENGTH	50.0000	DVIEW	(RO) The lens length of the current viewport perspective.
LIMCHECK	0	LIMITS	Controls object creation outside the drawing limits: 0 = Enables object creation 1 = Disables object creation
LIMMAX	12.0000,9.0000	LIMITS	The upper right limit of the WCS in current space.
LIMMIN	0.0000,0.0000	LIMITS	The lower left limit of the WCS in current space.
LOCALE	"en"	—	(RO) (NS) The ISO language code of the AutoCAD version being used.

continues

F

TABLE F.1, CONTINUED
System Variables Table

Variable Name	Default Setting	Command Name	Variable Description
LOGINNAME	""	CONFIG	(CFG) (RO) User name created by the CONFIG command or input when AutoCAD is loaded.
LTSCALE	1.0000	LTSCALE	Global linetype scale factor.
LUNITS	2	DDUNITS, UNITS	The Linear units mode: 1 = Scientific 2 = Decimal 3 = Engineering 4 = Architectural 5 = Fractional
LUPREC	4	DDUNITS, UNITS	Precision of decimal or fractional units.
MACROTRACE	0	—	(NS) Controls the Diesel, macro-debugging display. Not listed by SETVAR. 0 = On 1 = Off
MAXACTVP	16	—	(NS) Maximum number of viewports to regenerate at one time.
MAXSORT	200	—	(CFG) The maximum number of symbols and file names to be sorted in lists.

Variable Name	Default Setting	Command Name	Variable Description
MENUCTL	1	—	(CFG) Controls page switching of the screen menu: 0 = Does not switch with keyboard command entry 1 = Does switch with keyboard command entry
MENUECHO	0	—	(NS) Controls the display of menu actions on the command line; the value is the sum of the following: 1 = Suppresses menu input 2 = Suppresses system prompts 4 = Disables ^P toggle of menu echoing 8 = Displays DIESEL input/output strings
MENUNAME	"C:\ACADR13\DOS\ SUPPORT\ACAD.mnc"	MENU	(NS) (RO) Name and path of currently loaded menu.
MIRRTEXT	1	MIRROR	Controls how MIRROR reflects text: 0 = Retains text direction 1 = Mirrors text
MODEMACRO	""	—	(NS) A DIESEL language expression to control status-line display.

continues

F

TABLE F.1, CONTINUED
System Variables Table

Variable Name	Default Setting	Command Name	Variable Description
MTEXTED	"Internal"	DDEDIT	(CFG) Name of program to use for editing mtext objects.
OFFSETDIST	-1.0000	OFFSET	(NS) Default distance for the OFFSET command. Negative value enables the THROUGH option.
ORTHOMODE	0	[^O] [F8]	Sets the current Ortho mode: 0 = Off 1 = On
OSMODE	0	DDOSNAP, OSNAP	Sets the current object snap mode; value is the sum of the following: 0 = NONe 1 = ENDpoint 2 = MIDpoint 4 = CENter 8 = NODe 16 = QUAdrant 32 = INTersection 64 = INSertion 128 = PERpendicular 256 = TANgent 512 = NEArest 1024 = QUIck 2048 = APPint
PDMODE	0	POINT	Controls the graphic display of POINT objects.

New Riders Publishing
INSIDE SERIES

Variable Name	Default Setting	Command Name	Variable Description
PDSIZE	0.0000	POINT	Controls the size of POINT objects: Negative = Percentage of viewport size Positive = Absolute size 0 = 5% of graphics area height
PELLIPSE	0	ELLIPSE	The ellipse type created with ELLIPSE command: 0 = True ellipse 1 = Polyline representation of an ellipse
PERIMETER	0.0000	AREA, LIST, DBLIST	(NS) (RO) Last perimeter value calculated by AREA, LIST, DBLIST.
PFACEVMAX	4		(NS) (RO) Maximum number of vertices per face.
PICKADD	1	DDSELECT	(CFG) Controls whether selected objects are added to, or are replaced (added with Shift + select), the current selection set: 0 = Replace (Shift to add only) 1 = Added (Shift to remove only)
PICKAUTO	1	DDSELECT	(CFG) Controls the implied (AUTO) windowing for object selection: 0 = Off 1 = On

continues

TABLE F.1, CONTINUED
System Variables Table

Variable Name	Default Setting	Command Name	Variable Description
PICKBOX	3	DDSELECT	(CFG) Object selection pick box size, in pixels.
PICKDRAG	0	DDSELECT	(CFG) Determines whether the pick button must be depressed during window corner picking in set selections: 0 = Off 1 = On
PICKFIRST	1	DDSELECT	(CFG) Enables entity selection before command selection (noun/verb paradigm): 0 = Off 1 = On
PICKSTYLE	1	—	(CFG) Controls group selection and associative hatch selection: 0 = No group or associative hatch selection 1 = Group selection 2 = Associative hatch selection 3 = Group and associative hatch selection
PLATFORM	"386 DOS Extender"	—	(NS) (RO) Indicates the operating system in use. String value.

New Riders Publishing
INSIDE SERIES

continues

Variable Name	Default Setting	Command Name	Variable Description
PLINEGEN	0	—	Sets the linetype pattern generation around the vertices of a 2D polyline. Does not apply to polylines with tapered segments. 0 = Polylines are generated to start and end with a dash at each vertex 1 = Generates the linetype in a continuous pattern around the vertices of the polyline
PLINEWID	0.0000	PLINE	Default width for new polyline objects.
PLOTID	""	—	(CFG) Current plotter configuration description.
PLOTROTMODE	1	PLOT	Controls plot orientation: 0 = Rotation icon aligns at lower left for 0, top left for 90, top right for 180, lower right for 270 1 = Aligns lower left corner of plotting area with lower left corner of paper
PLOTTER	0	PLOT	(CFG) Current plotter configuration number.
POLYSIDES	4	POLYGON	(NS) Default number of sides for POLYGON objects (3-1024).

F

TABLE F.1, CONTINUED
System Variables Table

Variable Name	Default Setting	Command Name	Variable Description
POPUPS	1	—	(NS) (RO) Status of the currently configured display driver: 0 = Does not support dialog boxes, menu bar, pull-down menus, and icon menus 1 = Supports these features
PROJMODE	1	TRIM, EXTEND	(CGF) Current projection mode for TRIM or EXTEND operations: 0 = True 3d (no projection) 1 = Project to the XY plane of the current UCS 2 = Project to the current view plane
PSLTSCALE	1	—	Paper space scaling of model space linetypes: 0 = Off 1 = On
PSPROLOG	""	—	(CFG) The name of the PostScript post-processing section of the ACAD.PSF to be appended to the PSOUT command's output.
PSQUALITY	75	PSQUALITY	(CFG) The default quality setting for rendering of images by the PSIN command.

New Riders Publishing
INSIDE SERIES

Variable Name	Default Setting	Command Name	Variable Description
QTEXTMODE	0	QTEXT	Sets the current state of quick text mode: 0 = Off 1 = On
RASTERPREVIEW	0	SAVE, SAVEAS	Controls whether a preview image is saved and in which format the image is saved: 0 = BMP only 1 = BMP and WMF 2 = WMF only 3 = No preview image created
REGENMODE	1	REGENAUTO	Indicates the current state of REGENAUTO: 0 = Off 1 = On
RIASPECT	0.0000	GIFIN, TIFFIN	(NS) Controls the aspect ratio of imported raster images.
RIBACK	0	GIFIN, TIFFIN, PCXIN	(NS) The background color of imported raster images. Based on AutoCAD colors.
RIEDGE	0	GIFIN, TIFFIN, PCXIN	(NS) Controls the edge detection feature: 0 = Disables edge detection 1-255 = Threshold for edge detection

continues

F

TABLE F.1, CONTINUED
System Variables Table

Variable Name	Default Setting	Command Name	Variable Description
RIGAMUT	256	GIFIN, TIFFIN, PCXIN	(NS) Number of colors used when color images are imported.
RIGREY	0	GIFIN, TIFFIN. PCXIN	(NS) Imports images as grayscale: 0 = Disables grayscale image importing >0 = Converts each pixel to grayscale.
RITHRESH	0	GIFIN, TIFFIN, PCXIN	(NS) Controls brightness of imported images: 0 = Disables brightness control >0 = Only pixels brighter than value are imported
RE-INIT	0	REINIT	(NS) A code that specifies the type(s) of reinitializations to perform. The sum of: 1 = Digitizer port 2 = Plotter port 4 = Digitizer device 8 = Display device 16 = Reload ACAD.PGP
SAVEFILE	"AUTO.SV$"	CONFIG, PREFERENCES	(CFG) (RO) The default directory and file name for automatic file saves.

Variable Name	Default Setting	Command Name	Variable Description
SAVENAME	""	SAVEAS	(RO) (NS) Stores the file name you save the drawing to.
SAVETIME	120	CONFIG	(CFG) The default interval between automatic file saves, in minutes: 0 = Disable automatic saves
SCREENBOXES	0	CONFIG	(CFG) (RO) The number of available screen menu boxes in the current graphics screen area.
SCREENMODE	3	[F1]	(CFG) (RO) Indicates the active AutoCAD screen mode or window: 0 = Text 1 = Graphics 2 = Dual Screen
SCREENSIZE	1008.0000,578.0000		(RO) Size of the current viewport in pixels.
SHADEDGE	3	SHADE	Controls the display of edges and faces by the SHADE command: 0 = Faces shaded, edges not highlighted 1 = Faces shaded, edges in background color 2 = Faces not filled, edges in object color

continues

F

TABLE F.1, CONTINUED
System Variables Table

Variable Name	Default Setting	Command Name	Variable Description
			3 = Faces in object color, edges in background color
SHADEDIF	70	SHADE	Sets the ratio of diffuse reflective light to ambient light, expressed as a percentage of diffuse reflective light.
SHPNAME	""	SHAPE	(NS) The default shape name.
SKETCHINC	0.1000	SKETCH	The recording increment for SKETCH segments.
SKPOLY	0	SKETCH	Determines whether sketch uses lines or polylines: 0 = Generate lines 1 = Generate polylines
SNAPANG	0	DDRMODES, SNAP	The angle of SNAP/GRID rotation in the current viewport and UCS.
SNAPBASE	0.0000,0.0000	DDRMODES, SNAP	SNAP/GRID base point in the current viewport and UCS.
SNAPISOPAIR	0	DDRMODES, SNAP [^E], [F5]	The current isoplane for the current viewport: 0 = Left 1 = Top 2 = Right
SNAPMODE	0	DDRMODES, SNAP [^B], [F9]	Indicates the state of SNAP for the current viewport: 0 = Off 1 = On

Variable Name	Default Setting	Command Name	Variable Description
SNAPSTYL	0	DDRMODES, SNAP	The snap style for the current viewport: 0 = Standard 1 = Isometric
SNAPUNIT	1.0000,1.0000	DDRMODES, SNAP	The snap X,Y increment for the current viewport.
SORTENTS	96	DDSELECT	(CFG) Controls the display of object sort order: 0 = Disable SORTENTS 1 = Sorts for object selection 2 = Sorts for object snap 4 = Sorts for redraws 8 = Sorts for MSLIDE creation 16 = Sorts for REGENs 32 = Sorts for plotting 64 = Sorts for PostScript output Sum numbers to select more than one
SPLFRAME	0	—	Controls display of control polygons for spline-fit polylines, defining meshes of surface-fit polygons, and invisible 3D face edges: 0 = Off 1 = On
SPLINESEGS	8	—	The number of line segments in each spline curve.

continues

F

TABLE F.1, CONTINUED
System Variables Table

Variable Name	Default Setting	Command Name	Variable Description
SPLINETYPE	6	—	Controls the type of curve generated by PEDIT spline: 5 = Quadratic B-spline 6 = Cubic B-spline
SURFTAB1	6	—	Sets the density of a mesh in the M direction.
SURFTAB2	6	—	Sets the density of a mesh in the N direction.
SURFTYPE	6	—	Controls the type of surface generated by PEDIT Smooth: 5 = Quadratic B-spline surface 6 = Cubic B-spline surface 8 = Bezier surface
SURFU	6	—	Surface density in the M direction of 3D polygonal meshes.
SURFV	6	—	Surface density in the N direction of 3D polygonal meshes.
SYSCODEPAGE	ASCII	—	(RO) Code page used by the system.
TABMODE	0	TABLET	(NS) Controls the use of Tablet mode: 0 = Disables tablet mode 1 = Enables tablet mode
TARGET	0.0000,0.0000,0.0000	DVIEW	(RO) The UCS coordinates of the target point in the current viewport.

New Riders Publishing
INSIDE SERIES

Variable Name	Default Setting	Command Name	Variable Description
TDCREATE	2449698.91946285	TIME	(RO) Time of the creation of the current drawing in Julian format.
TDINDWG	0.00048947	TIME	(RO) Total amount of editing time elapsed on the current drawing in Julian format.
TDUPDATE	2449698.91946285	TIME	(RO) The date and time when the drawing was last saved, in Julian format.
TDUSRTIMER	0.00049144	TIME	(RO) User-controlled elapsed time in Julian format.
TEMPPREFIX	""	CONFIG	(NS) (RO) The directory for placement of AutoCAD's temporary files. Defaults to current drawing directory.
TEXTEVAL	0	—	(NS) Controls the checking of text input (except by DTEXT) for AutoLISP expressions: 0 = No 1 = Yes
TEXTFILL	0	TEXT	Controls the filling of Bitstream, TrueType, and Adobe Type 1 fonts: 0 = Display as outlines 1 = Display as filled images

continues

F

TABLE F.1, CONTINUED
System Variables Table

Variable Name	Default Setting	Command Name	Variable Description
TEXTQLTY	50	TEXT	Controls the resolution of Bitstream, TrueType, and Adobe Type 1 fonts: 0–100 (higher is better resolution).
TEXTSIZE	0.2000	TEXT	Default height for new text objects.
TEXTSTYLE	"STANDARD"	TEXT, STYLE	Default text style for new text objects.
THICKNESS	0.0000	ELEV	Current 3D thickness.
TILEMODE	1	TILEMODE	Enables and disables paper space and viewport objects: 0 = Off 1 = On
TRACEWID	0.0500	TRACE	The current width of traces.
TREEDEPTH	3020	—	A code number (4 digits) representing the maximum number of division for spatial database index for model space (first two digits) and paper space (last two digits). (CFG)
TREEMAX	10000000	—	The maximum number of nodes for spatial database organization for the current memory configuration. (NS)
TRIMMODE	1	FILLET, CHAMFER	Controls whether AutoCAD trims selected edges for fillets and chamfers:

New Riders Publishing
INSIDE SERIES

Variable Name	Default Setting	Command Name	Variable Description
UCSFOLLOW	0		0 = Leave edges intact 1 = Trim edges back Controls automatic display of the plan view in the current viewport when switching to a new UCS: 0 = Off 1 = On
UCSICON	1	UCSICON	Controls the UCS icon's display. Value is the sum of the following: 0 = Off 1 = On 2 = At origin
UCSNAME	""	DDUCS, UCS	(RO) The name of the current UCS for the current space: "" = unnamed
UCSORG	0.0000,0.0000,0.0000	DDUCS, UCS	(RO) The WCS origin of the current UCS for the current space.
UCSXDIR	1.0000,0.0000,0.0000	DDUCS, UCS	(RO) The X direction of the current UCS.
UCSYDIR	0.0000,1.0000,0.0000	DDUCS, UCS	(RO) The Y direction of the current UCS.

continues

F

TABLE F.1, CONTINUED
System Variables Table

Variable Name	Default Setting	Command Name	Variable Description
UNDOCTL	5	UNDO	(NS) (RO) The current state of UNDO. Value is the sum of the following: 1 = Enabled 2 = Single command 4 = Auto mode 8 = Group active
UNDOMARKS	0	UNDO	(NS) (RO) The current number of marks in the UNDO command's history.
UNITMODE	0	—	Controls the display of user input of fractions, feet and inches, and surveyor's angles: 0 = per LUNITS 1 = As input
USERI1-5	0	—	User integer variables. USERI1 to USERI5. Not listed by SETVAR.
USERR1-5	0.0000	—	User real-number variables USERR1 to USERR5. Not listed by SETVAR.
USERS1-5	""	—	User string variables (up to 460 characters long) USERS1 to USERS5. Not listed by SETVAR.
VIEWCTR	7.9248,4.5408,0.0000	ZOOM, PAN, VIEW	(RO) The X,Y center point coordinate of the current viewport in the current view.

New Riders Publishing
INSIDE SERIES

Variable Name	Default Setting	Command Name	Variable Description
VIEWDIR	0.0000,0.0000,1.0000	DVIEW	(RO) The camera point offset from the target in the WCS.
VIEWMODE	0	DVIEW, UCS	(RO) The current viewport's viewing mode. Value is sum of following: 0 = Disabled 1 = Perspective 2 = Front clipping on 4 = Back clipping on 8 = UCSFOLLOW On 16 = FRONTZ offset in use
VIEWSIZE	9.0816	ZOOM, VIEW	(RO) The current view's height in drawing units.
VIEWTWIST	0	DVIEW	(RO) The current viewport's view-twist angle.
VISRETAIN	0	VISRETAIN	Controls retention of Xref file layer setting in the current drawing. 0 = Off 1 = On
VSMAX	47.5487,27.2449,0.0000	ZOOM, PAN, VIEW	(RO) The upper right X,Y coordinate of the current viewport's virtual screen for the current UCS.

continues

F

TABLE F.1, CONTINUED
System Variables Table

Variable Name	Default Setting	Command Name	Variable Description
VSMIN	-31.6991,-18.1632,0.00	ZOOM, PAN, VIEW	(RO) The lower left X,Y coordinate of the current viewport's virtual screen for the current UCS.
WORLDUCS	1	UCS	(NS) (RO) Indicates if the current UCS = WCS: 0 = False 1 = True
WORLDVIEW	1	DVIEW, UCS	Controls the automatic changing of a UCS to the WCS during the DVIEW and VPOINT commands: 0 = Off 1 = On
XREFCTL	0	—	(CFG) Controls the creation of an XLG log file that contains XREF results: 0 = No file 1 = XLG file

Dimension Variables Table

This appendix contains a table of AutoCAD dimension variables. These variables generally are set by AutoCAD's Dimension Styles dialog box (DDIM command). They also can be set or checked by entering their names at the Command: or Dim: prompts. Use this table to find AutoCAD's dimension settings and their values. Table G.1 represents all the variables available for dimensioning through AutoCAD, AutoLISP, and the AutoCAD Development System. The dimension variable name and the default AutoCAD prototype drawing (ACAD.DWG) settings are shown. A brief description is given for each variable, and the meaning is given for each code. All values are saved with the drawing unless noted with (CFG) for ConFiGuration file, or (NS) for Not Saved. Variables marked (RO) are read-only, which means you cannot change them.

Note   Variable names and features shown in bold are new in Release 13.

TABLE G.1
Dimension Variables Table

Variable Name	Default Setting	Variable Description
DIMALT	Off	Enables alternate units dimensioning: 0 = Off 1 = On
DIMALTD	2	The decimal precision of the alternate units when used.
DIMALTF	25.4000	The scale factor of the alternate units when used.
DIMALTTD	2	The number of decimal places for tolerance values in alternate units.
DIMALTTZ	0	Toggles suppression of zeros for alternate unit dimension values: 0 = Off 1 = On
DIMALTU	2	Unit format for alternate units of all dimension families except angular: 1 = Scientific 2 = Decimal 3 = Engineering 4 = Architectural 5 = Fractional
DIMALTZ	0	Toggles suppression of zeroes for alternate unit dimension values: 0 = Off 1 = On
DIMAPOST	" "	The user-defined prefix and/or suffix for alternative dimension text.
DIMASO	On	Enables associative dimensioning: 0 = Off 1 = On
DIMASZ	0.1800	Controls the size of dimension arrows and affects the fit of dimension text inside dimension lines when DIMTSZ is set to 0.
DIMAUNIT	0	Angle format for Angular dimensions:

New Riders Publishing
INSIDE
SERIES

Variable Name	Default Setting	Variable Description
		0 = Decimal degrees 1 = Degrees/minutes/seconds 2 = Gradians 3 = Radians 4 = Surveyor's units
DIMBLK	""	Name of block to draw rather than an arrow or a tick.
DIMBLK1	""	Name of the block for the first end of dimension lines. (See DIMSAH.)
DIMBLK2	""	Name of the block for the second end of dimension lines. (See DIMSAH.)
DIMCEN	0.0900	Controls center marks or center lines drawn by DIM commands with radii: 0 = No center marks or lines <0 = Center lines are drawn >0 = Center marks are drawn
DIMCLRD	0	The dimension line, arrow, and leader color number; any valid color number; or the following: 0 = BYBLOCK 256 = BYLAYER
DIMCLRE	0	The dimension extension line's color. (See DIMCLRD.)
DIMCLRT	0	The dimension text's color. (See DIMCLRD.)
DIMDEC	4	The number of decimal places for the tolerance values of a dimension.
DIMDLE	0.0000	The dimension line's extension distance beyond ticks when ticks are drawn (when DIMTSZ is nonzero).
DIMDLI	0.3800	The offset distance between successive baseline dimensions.
DIMEXE	0.1800	The length of extension lines beyond the dimension line.
DIMEXO	0.0625	The distance by which extension line origin is offset from dimensioned entity.

continues

G

TABLE G.1, CONTINUED
Dimension Variables Table

Variable Name	Default Setting	Variable Description
DIMFIT	3	Controls the placement of text relative to the dimension: 0 = Text and arrow between extension lines if enough space; otherwise, outside 1 = Text and arrows between extension lines when text fits, arrows outside; otherwise, both outside 2 = Combination of 1 and 2 3 = Places whatever will fit between extension lines 4 = Creates leader lines when there is not enough space for text between extension lines
DIMGAP	0.0900	The space between the text and the dimension line; determines when text is placed outside a dimension.
DIMJUST	0	Controls the horizontal dimension text position: 0 = Center-justifies the text 1 = Positions text next to left extension line 2 = Positions text next to second extension line 3 = Positions text above and aligned with first extension line 4 = Positions text above and aligned with second extension line
DIMLFAC	1.0000	The overall linear dimensioning scale factor; if negative, acts as the absolute value applied to paper space viewports.
DIMLIM	Off	Presents dimension limits as default text: 0 = Off 1 = On (See DIMTP and DIMTM.)
DIMPOST	" "	The user-defined prefix and/or suffix for dimension text, such as "mm".

New Riders Publishing
INSIDE
SERIES

continues

G

Variable Name	Default Setting	Variable Description
DIMRND	0.0000	The rounding interval for linear dimension text.
DIMSAH	Off	Enables the use of DIMBLK1 and DIMBLK2 instead of DIMBLK or a default terminator: 0 = Off 1 = On
DIMSCALE	1.0000	The overall scale factor applied to other dimension variables except tolerances, angles, measured lengths, or coordinates: 0 = Paper space scale
DIMSD1	Off	Suppresses drawing of first dimension line 0 = Off 1 = On
DIMSD2	Off	Suppresses drawing of second dimension line: 0 = Off 1 = On
DIMSE1	Off	Suppresses drawing of first extension line: 0 = Off 1 = On
DIMSE2	Off	Suppresses drawing of second extension line: 0 = Off 1 = On
DIMSHO	On	Determines whether associative dimension text is updated during dragging: 0 = Off 1 = On
DIMSOXD	Off	Suppresses the placement of dimension lines outside the extension lines: 0 = Off 1 = On

TABLE G.1, CONTINUED
Dimension Variables Table

Variable Name	Default Setting	Variable Description
DIMSTYLE	"STANDARD"	(RO) Holds the name of the current dimension style.
DIMTAD	0	Controls vertical position of dimension text in relation to dimension line: 0 = Centers text between extension lines 1 = Places the text above dimension line except when dimension line is not horizontal and text inside lines is forced horizontal (DIMTIH = 1); the current DIMGAP value sets the distance from dimension line to baseline of lowest line of text 2 = Places the text on opposite side of dimension line from the extension line origins 3 = Places the text for a JIS representation
DIMTDEC	4	The number of decimal places for tolerance values for a primary units dimension.
DIMTFAC	1.0000	Scale factor for dimension tolerance's text height.
DIMTIH	On	Forces dimension text inside the extension lines to be positioned horizontally rather than aligned: 0 = Off 1 = On
DIMTIX	Off	Forces dimension text inside extension lines: 0 = Off 1 = On
DIMTM	0.0000	The negative tolerance values used when DIMTOL or DIMLIM is on.

New Riders Publishing
INSIDE
SERIES

continues

G

Variable Name	Default Setting	Variable Description
DIMTOFL	Off	Draws dimension lines between extension lines even if text is placed outside the extension lines: 0 = Off 1 = On
DIMTOH	On	Forces dimension text to be positioned horizontally rather than aligned when it falls outside the extension lines: 0 = Off 1 = On
DIMTOL	Off	Appends tolerance values (DIMTP and DIMTM) to the default dimension text: 0 = Off 1 = On
DIMTOLJ	1	Sets vertical justification for tolerance values relative to nominal dimension text: 0 = Bottom 1 = Middle 2 = Top
DIMTP	0.0000	When DIMTOL or DIMLIM is on, sets the maximum tolerance limit for dimension text.
DIMTSZ	0.0000	When assigned a nonzero value, forces tick marks (rather than arrows) to be drawn at the size specified by the value; affects the placement of the dimension line and text between extension lines.
DIMTVP	0.0000	Percentage of text height to offset dimension vertically.
DIMTXSTY	"STANDARD"	The text style of the dimension.
DIMTXT	0.1800	Height of the dimension text, unless current text style has a fixed height.

TABLE G.1, CONTINUED
Dimension Variables Table

Variable Name	Default Setting	Variable Description
DIMTZIN	0	Switches suppression of zeros for tolerance values: 0 = Off 1 = On
DIMUNIT	2	Sets units for all dimension style family members except angular: 1 = Scientific 2 = Decimal 3 = Engineering 4 = Architectural 5 = Fractional
DIMUPT	Off	Controls cursor functionality for user positioned text: 0 = Cursor controls only dimension line location 1 = Cursor controls text position as well as dimension line location
DIMZIN	0	Suppresses the display of zero inches or zero feet in dimension text, and leading and/or trailing zeros in decimal dimension text: 0 = Feet and inches 1 = Neither 2 = Inches only 3 = Feet only 4 = Leading zeros 8 = Trailing zeros 12 = Both leading and trailing zeros.

New Riders Publishing
INSIDE
SERIES

APPENDIX H

The IA Disk

A 3.5-inch floppy disk called the IA Disk is included with *Inside AutoCAD 13 for* DOS The book and disk are designed for use on your existing AutoCAD Release 13 system. The disk provides starting drawings and other files for many of the book's exercises, saving you time by avoiding routine drawing setup.

The disk also includes several useful AutoCAD utilities. The drawing files and other files required for the exercises are installed during the installation described in Chapter 1, along with the following free AutoCAD utilities (except for one named TEMPLATE! Free).

◆ **ARCHS.SHX.** A freeware AutoCAD text font that creates handlettering-style architectural text.

◆ **NRP_ACAD.PGP.** A file of aliases you can add to the ACAD.PGP file to define abbreviations for most commonly used AutoCAD commands. If you like using the keyboard instead of menus, this enables you to access commands with short abbreviations. For example, enter **DCON** to issue the DIMCONTINUE command instead of entering **DIMCONTINUE**.

◆ **P5TEST.LSP.** A little program that tests your Pentium processor for a floating-point division bug.

◆ **PSLWGS.** A set of PostScript code files that enable control over minimum line width and output color or gray level, on a color-by-color basis, for PostScript output using the AutoCAD PSOUT command.

◆ **PROJECT.LSP.** Defines commands that produce 2D drawings as "flat" projections of wireframe 3D models. This is useful for generating working drawings from a 3D model and for constructing other 3D wireframe and surface models. This appendix also describes how to convert Release 13 3D solid models to a format acceptable to PROJECT.LSP.

◆ **FROM.LSP.** Defines (nrp_from), an alternative to Autodesk's Release 13 FROM modifier. The FROM modifier is disabled when dragging during commands that feature dragging, such as INSERT and most editing commands. Dragging is disabled during NRP_FROM, while Autodesk disables FROM during dragging. NRP_FROM is available during editing commands, such as MOVE, to place something relative to another object.

◆ **PROPLINE.LSP.** A file that defines the NRP_DIMPL dimensioning command, which creates surveyor's bearing and distance dimensions such as N03°01'82"E 122.82' with a single pick.

◆ **TEMPLATE! Free.** A block cataloging and retrieval tool that works within AutoCAD. It works like the WBLOCK command, but automatically creates an icon menu from which the files can be selected and inserted into any drawing. Installation is described later in this appendix.

The installation and use of TEMPLATE! Free, and the setup and use of the rest of these utilities, are described later in this appendix.

 Note See the UPDATE.TXT file for license, copyright, and warranty disclaimer information. You can use the MS DOS Editor (the DOS EDIT command) or any word processor or ASCII text editor to read or print the UPDATE.TXT file.

All instructions in this appendix assume the following:

◆ That you are using the DOS operating system, version 5.0 or later. We recommend version 6.2 or later.

◆ That AutoCAD Release 13 for DOS is installed in the C:\ACADR13\DOS directory, and that AutoCAD runs and is configured properly.

◆ That you have performed all installation and setup steps in Chapter 1, and that the IA Disk files are installed in the C:\IA and C:\IA\DWGS directories.

New Riders Publishing
INSIDE
SERIES

Note Your floppy disk drive and hard drive letters or directory names might differ from those shown in this appendix. If they do, substitute your drive letter and directory names wherever you encounter drive letters (such as the A in A: or C in C:) or directory names (such as \ACADR13 or \IA).

The setup in Chapter 1 ensures that this book does not interfere with any other AutoCAD setup or projects on which you or your co-workers might be working.

Stop Perform all installation and setup steps in Chapter 1 before continuing in the book, or the book's exercises and the utilities described in this appendix will not work properly.

The following sections describe each of the IA Disk utilities.

Creating Handlettering Architectural Text with ARCHS.SHX

ARCHS.SHX is an architectural proportional single-stroke hand lettering font. For examples of the use of this font, see Chapter 23, "Techniques for Architectural and Civil Dimensioning." The font includes all the standard AutoCAD font characters, fractions down to 1/16", and special architectural characters for Angle, Center Line, Floor Line, Plate Line, Square, Greater Than, Less Than, and Copyright.

This font is part of a larger set of lettering fonts called the ArchFont Letter Sets V1.0, which includes ArchS, plus double and triple stroke equivalents, as well as a TXT-style replacement font.

ARCHS.SHX is Copyright 1994 by Chris Bryant, all rights reserved, and is *not* public domain. If you use the ArchS font and find it of value, a donation to Chris Bryant of any amount ($5 suggested) would be appreciated. Donors of amounts of $25 or more will receive a floppy disk with the entire ArchFont package plus the original SHP font definition files. The SHP files enable you to add additional characters of your own to the fonts. See the ARCHS.DOC file in the IA directory for more information and for copyright, license, and warranty statements.

The IA Disk installation in Chapter 1 placed the ARCHS.SHX and ARCHS.DOC files in the IA directory. To load ARCHS with the IA AutoCAD configuration, use the STYLE command, choose Type It in the Select Font File dialog box, and enter the name at the prompt that appears:

```
Font file <ARCHITECT>: ARCHS Enter
```

AutoCAD will then find the font in the IA directory and load it. See Chapter 13, "Annotation with Text," for more on loading and styling fonts.

Tip   Using the **T**ype It button and entering the font file name at the prompt that appears prevents AutoCAD from storing the path with the file name, avoiding file portability path problems.

To use this font with other AutoCAD configurations, copy the ARCHS.SHX and ARCHS.DOC files to the AutoCAD fonts directory (typically \ACADR13\COMMON\FONTS).

Note   The license for this font allows you to give it to others, but all copies must be accompanied by the ARCHS.DOC file.

Adding Command Aliases with NRP_ACAD.PGP

The NRP_ACAD.PGP file defines aliases (abbreviations) for most commonly used AutoCAD commands. The standard ACAD.PGP file defines about 18 aliases, such as L for the LINE command. If you prefer the keyboard to menus and tools, this NRP_ACAD.PGP enables you to access many more commands with short abbreviations. The aliases defined in NRP_ACAD.PGP are listed in Appendix E. The aliases in bold are those in the default ACAD.PGP file, and the rest of the aliases listed are the NRP_ACAD.PGP additions.

The IA Disk installation in Chapter 1 placed the NRP_ACAD.PGP file in the IA directory. To access the aliases in NRP_ACAD.PGP, you must add its contents to the ACAD.PGP file. To do so at the DOS command line, creating an ACAD.PGP file in the IA directory, perform the following steps:

1. Locate the ACAD.PGP file; it should be \ACADR13\COMMON\SUPPORT. Make a backup copy of the file, named ACAD_R13.PGP. You can use this to restore the original file if you ever want to do so.

2. Change to the C:\IA directory

3. At the C:\IA> prompt, enter the following:

```
COPY \ACADR13\COMMON\SUPPORT\ACAD.PGP + NRP_ACAD.PGP ACAD.PGP
```

New Riders Publishing
INSIDE
SERIES

When you restart AutoCAD, the new aliases will be available for use at the AutoCAD `Command:` prompt. You can also edit these aliases or add your own.

Testing Pentium Processors for a Division Bug

Millions of Intel Pentium processors have a flaw that occasionally causes them to make errors in floating point division. Intel states that these errors are so rare that they should not concern users of most applications. Some CAD industry experts say that these errors should not affect most CAD applications. However, if you have a flawed processor and request a replacement, Intel will provide one at no cost to you.

P5TEST.LSP, a tiny program that tests your Pentium processor for a floating point division bug, was placed in the IA directory during the IA Disk installation in Chapter 1. To test your processor, try the following exercise.

Testing Your Pentium Processor

Command: **(load "p5test")** (Enter)   Runs the test program and displays one of the two following messages:

```
Your Pentium chip appears to have a floating-point division bug.
If you are concerned, call Intel at 1-800-628-8686 for replacement.

You do not have a flawed Pentium processor chip.
```

Adding PostScript Width, Color, and Gray Level to PSOUT Output

The PSLWGS files enable you to control minimum line width, and output color or gray level, on a color-by-color basis in PostScript output produced by the AutoCAD PSOUT command. The IA Disk installation in Chapter 1 placed the PSLWGS.DOC, PSLWGRAY.PSF, PSLWRGB.PSF, and PSLWCMYK.PSF files in the IA directory.

All three PSF files define a minimum line width in inches for each AutoCAD color. Each file defines a "printed" color for each AutoCAD color, as follows:

◆ **PSLWGRAY.** Produces monochrome output, either as black or white or as shades of gray.

◆ **PSLWRGB.** Produces color output, specifying colors as combinations of the primaries RGB (Red-Green-Blue).

◆ **PSLWCMYK.** Produces color output, specifying colors as combinations of the primaries CMYK (**C**yan-**M**agenta-**Y**ellow-blac**K**). The CMYK color model is a PostScript level 2 feature, and is not be supported by all PostScript level 1 devices.

See the PSLWGS.DOC file in the IA directory for instructions on how to apply PSLWGS to PostScript output. You can use the MS DOS Editor (the DOS EDIT command) or any word processor or ASCII text editor to read or print the PSLWGS.DOC file.

PSLWGS is the work of Jon Fleming, who can be reached on CompuServe at 70334,2443. If you redistribute these files, be sure to include the PSLWGS.DOC file

Creating 2D Drawings from 3D Solids with PROJECT.LSP

PROJECT.LSP produces 2D drawings, as "flat" projections of wireframe 3D models onto the current UCS, for generating working drawings from a 3D model and as a tool for the construction of other 3D wireframe and surface models. Release 13 3D solid models can also be converted to a format acceptable to PROJECT.LSP. The IA Disk installation in Chapter 1 placed the PROJECT.LSP and PROJECT.DOC files in the IA directory.

PROJECT.LSP is copyrighted by Autodesk, Inc. and is included on the IA Disk with their permission. See the PROJECT.DOC file for copyright and warranty disclaimer, as well as further information on its use.

PROJECT.LSP works only in AutoCAD Release 10, 11, and 12 drawings. However, you can convert Release 13 3D models, including 3D solids, to Release 12 files and use them with PROJECT.LSP by following the process described later in this section.

PROJECT.LSP defines the following commands:

◆ **PROJECT.** Opens a menu with a choice of projections.

New Riders Publishing
INSIDE
SERIES

◆ **PROJECT1.** Produces a "flat" projection of wireframe 3D models (lines, arcs, circles, polylines, solids, points) onto the current UCS. This could be a useful aid for generating working drawings from a 3D model.

◆ **PROJECT2.** Projects an object normal from the current UCS onto a designated oblique construction plane. This can be useful in the construction of 3D wireframe and surface models.

To use PROJECT.LSP with *Inside AutoCAD13 for DOS*, do the following:

1. Strip your model of any objects new to R13 (such as ACIS solids, splines, ellipses, and so on) by using the SAVEASR12 command. Be sure to save the drawing to a new name to avoid overwriting the original file. ACIS solid models are converted into wireframe models. Surface models are retained, but any splines or ellipses are converted to polylines.

2. Open the new drawing (or insert it into your existing drawing, using the Explode button in the Insert dialog box or *filename in the INSERT command to insert it as individual objects).

3. Set your current UCS parallel to the view to which you want to project.

4. Load and execute PROJECT.LSP by entering **PROJECT** at the Command: prompt.

5. Select the objects you want to project.

6. After its initial load, you can enter **PROJECT**, **PROJECT1**, or **PROJECT2** at the Command: prompt.

After the projection is complete, you are offered the option of creating a block or a new drawing file out of the projection.

Managing Blocks with the TEMPLATE! Free Icon Menus

TEMPLATE! Free is a block cataloging and retrieval system that works within AutoCAD. It works like the WBLOCK command, creating drawing files for insertion into other drawings, but also catalogs images into an icon menu. The files can then be selected from the icon menu and inserted into any drawing using the normal AutoCAD insertion options.

TEMPLATE! Free is a useful program for anyone who saves only small numbers of symbols, or who uses symbols infrequently. TEMPLATE! Free is a freeware version of the commercial product TEMPLATE!. Many features contained in TEMPLATE! are available in TEMPLATE! Free with one big exception—TEMPLATE! Free will only save, insert, or catalog symbols that are stored in the subdirectory where TEMPLATE! Free is installed. TEMPLATE! enables users to store an unlimited number of symbols in an unlimited number of subdirectories that can be located anywhere, including network drives.

To copy the TMPLFREE.EXE archive file to the IA directory, put the IA Disk in disk drive A and enter the following at the DOS command prompt.

```
C:\> COPY A:TMPLFREE.EXE \IA\*.* Enter
```

Now, to complete the TEMPLATE! Free installation, perform the following steps. Remember to substitute your drive letter and directory names wherever you encounter drive letters (such as the A in A: or C in C:) or directory names (such as \ACADR13 or \IA) if yours differ from those shown.

1. Locate and note the path of the ACAD.PGP file. It should be \ACADR13\COMMON\SUPPORT, or if you installed the NRP_ACAD.PGP file, it should be \IA.

2. Place a formatted floppy disk in drive A (720K or larger).

3. Change to drive A:. The DOS prompt should now be A:\>.

4. At the A:\> prompt, type **C:\IA\TMPLFREE** and press Enter. This extracts the TEMPLATE! Free files from the compressed TMPLFREE.EXE archive file and copies them to the floppy disk.

5. Delete the TMPLFREE.EXE file from the IA directory.

6. At the A:\> prompt, type **INSTALL** and press Enter. This starts the installation program, asks you to specify the hard drive and path of the ACAD.PGP file, copies the files to a new C:\CADTECH directory, and modifies the ACAD.PGP file.

7. Add **C:\CADTECH;** to the ACAD= line of the IA.BAT file which you created in Chapter 1 (see Chapter 1 for an example exercise that similarly adds the C:\IA path).

Now that TEMPLATE! Free is installed, the following steps load it and run it:

1. Start AutoCAD.

2. At the AutoCAD Command: prompt, enter **(load "template")**. This loads the program.

New Riders Publishing
INSIDE
SERIES

3. At the AutoCAD `Command:` prompt, enter **TEMPLATE**. This opens the TEM-PLATE! Free dialog box and runs the program.

You can automate the loading of TEMPLATE! Free by adding the **(load "template")** line to the ACAD.LSP file in the IA directory.

See the TUTORIAL.TXT file for information on obtaining a short tutorial by fax. See the TEMPLATE.HLP file. It is the help file for TEMPLATE! and is available in the TEMPLATE! Free dialog box. CADDTECH Consulting provides free technical support to owners of the full version of TEMPLATE! See the README.DOC file for information on ordering the full version of TEMPLATE!, and for copyright, trade-mark, and licensing restrictions and disclaimers, and other information about TEMPLATE! Free. You can use the MS DOS Editor (the DOS EDIT command) or any word processor or ASCII text editor to read or print these files.

H

Specifying Relative Points with NRP_FROM

The AutoCAD Release 13 FROM modifier is disabled when dragging during com-mands that feature dragging, such as INSERT and most editing commands. This restricts the usefulness of the FROM modifier. New Riders provides an alternative called NRP_FROM. Dragging is disabled during NRP_FROM, while Autodesk disables FROM during dragging. NRP_FROM is available during editing commands, such as MOVE, to place something relative to another object.

The only advantage Autodesk's FROM modifier has over NRP_FROM is that NRP_FROM cannot be used with other AutoLISP- or ADS-defined commands, such as third-party programs or the ALIGN command.

The IA Disk installation in Chapter 1 placed the FROM.LSP file in the IA directory; the ACAD.LSP file in the IA directory loads it. You can use NRP_FROM by entering **(nrp_from)** at any point prompt. The following exercise gives an example of using NRP_FROM versus Autodesk's FROM.

Using the NRP_FROM Modifier

Command: *Draw several objects, select one of them, and choose* Modify, Move	Issues the MOVE command with the object selected

continues

continued

`_move 1 found` `Base point or displacement:` *Use an object snap to pick a point on the object*	Specifies the base point of the move displacement
`Second point of displacement:` *Choose Assist, Object Snap, From*	Issues Autodesk's FROM modifier
`_from` `** FROM command is not available while dragging. **`	Demonstrates limitation of Autodesk's FROM modifier, and reprompts
`Second point of displacement:` `(nrp_from)` (Enter)	Issues NRP_FROM and disables dragging
`From base point:` *Use an object snap to pick a point on another object*	Specifies a point relative to which the following offset is applied
`Offset: @1,1` (Enter)	Specifies offset (@ is required to match the syntax of Autodesk's From modifier) and moves the selected object

 Note Despite Autodesk's variously referring to their FROM modifier as a "command" and an "object snap," it is neither. It is an input point modifier that requires the use of object snaps for any practical use.

The FROM.LSP file, which defines NRP_FROM, is loaded by the ACAD.LSP file in the IA directory. To make its use as convenient as that of Autodesk's FROM modifier, you can add NRP_FROM to the AutoCAD menu. To add NRP_FROM to the pop-up menu and to the Object Snap submenu of the Assist pull-down menu, perform the following steps:

1. In DOS, copy the ACAD.MNU file from the \ACADR13\DOS\SUPPORT directory to the \IA directory.

2. Use the MS DOS Editor (the DOS EDIT command) or any word processor or ASCII text editor to open the ACAD.MNU file in the \IA directory and locate the following sections of the file, then add the lines shown in bold:

```
    ***POP0
[Osnap]
[From]_from
[NRP From](nrp_from)
[ — ]
[Endpoint]_endp
```

New Riders Publishing
INSIDE SERIES

```
[Midpoint]_mid
[Intersection]_int

    ***POP2
[Assist]
[Undo]^C^C_u
[Redo]^C^C_redo
[—]
[->Object Snap]
  [From]$M=$(if,$(getvar,cmdactive),,_osnap;)_from
  [NRP From](nrp_from)
  [—]
  [Endpoint]$M=$(if,$(getvar,cmdactive),,_osnap;)_endp
  [Midpoint]$M=$(if,$(getvar,cmdactive),,_osnap;)_mid
  [Intersection]$M=$(if,$(getvar,cmdactive),,_osnap;)_int
```

3. Save the file and exit the text editor.

4. In AutoCAD, use the MENU command to load the ACAD.MNU file from the \IA directory. The NRP From menu items you added will be available.

To use NRP_FROM in other AutoCAD configurations:

1. Copy FROM.LSP from the IA directory to ACADR13\COMMON\SUPPORT.

2. Make a backup copy of the ACAD.MNU file in the ACADR13\DOS\SUPPORT directory (name it ACADR13.MNU), then edit the original ACAD.MNU file in the ACADR13\DOS\SUPPORT directory, as described in the previous steps.

3. Use the MS DOS Editor (the DOS EDIT command) or any word processor or ASCII text editor to add (load "from") to the end of the ACAD.MNL file in the ACADR13\COMMON\SUPPORT directory.

4. Open a new or existing drawing to cause the ACAD.MNL file to be reloaded.

Creating Surveyor's Dimensions with NRP_DIMPL

Chapter 23 includes a series of exercises that create a dimension style suitable for surveyor's bearing and distance dimensions, like N03°01'82"E   122.82', but to create such a dimension requires listing an object's angle, copying the angle data into the Edit Mtext dialog box, and editing it. This procedure is cumbersome for frequent use. A quick and easy alternative is the NRP_DIMPL (for DIM Prop Line) command, defined in the PROPLINE.LSP file. It creates surveyor's bearing and distance dimensions with a single pick.

The NRP_DIMPL command requires a linear dimension style like the PROPLINE style, created in Chapter 23, for correct formatting and placement of the dimension. Although it does not require Surveyor's angle units to be set, doing so makes it easier to verify the results. The IA Disk installation in Chapter 1 placed the PROPLINE.LSP file in the IA directory; the ACAD.LSP file in the IA directory loads it.

In a drawing that contains the PROPLINE style, try using NRP_DIMPL in the following exercise. See Chapter 23 for creation of the style and information on how to make it available to any drawing. Of course, your distances and angles will vary from those shown in this exercise.

Creating Single-Pick Surveyor's Dimensions

Perform the following steps in a drawing file that contains the PROPLINE dimension style and several lines or polyline segments drawn at various angles, including a horizontal one drawn with ortho on.

Command: **NRP_DIMPL** (Enter)   Starts the NRP_DIMPL command

Pick object for PropLine dimension: Selects the object, and the point above
Pick a line or polyline   which the dimension will be placed

The NRP_DIMPL command places a linear dimension without further input, then asks you to choose between a North or South bearing:

N3d25'55"W or S3d25'55"E (N/S): **N**   Specifies a North bearing and places a
(Enter)   dimension like N03°25'55"W   120.75'

Try it again on other lines. When you try the horizontal line, you see the following prompt:

E or W (E/W): **E** (Enter)   Specifies East and places a dimension like E
220.17'

Note   The PROPLINE.LSP file, which defines NRP_DIMPL, is loaded by the ACAD.LSP file in the IA directory. If you will never use it, you can remove the following line from the ACAD.LSP file:

```
(defun C:NRP_DIMPL () (load "propline") (C:NRP_DIMPL))
```

Remember to check the UPDATE.TXT file for last-minute changes or corrections to the book or disk. You can read or print the UPDATE.TXT file by using the MS DOS Editor (the DOS EDIT command) or any word processor or ASCII text editor.

Index

M

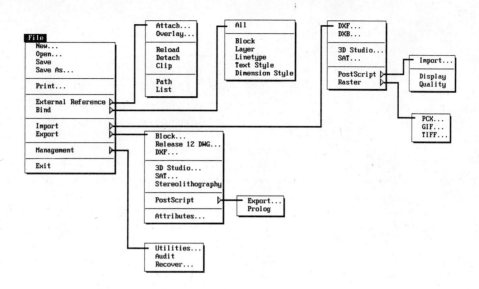

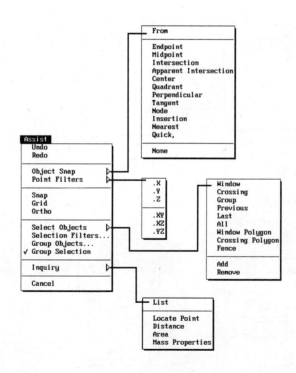

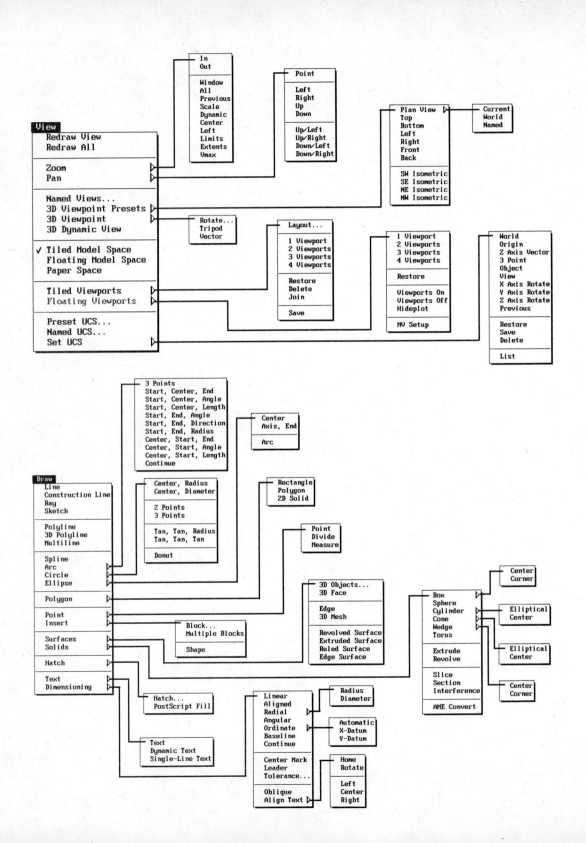

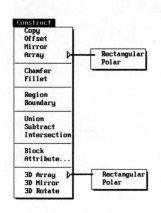

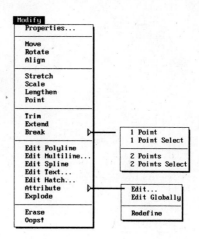

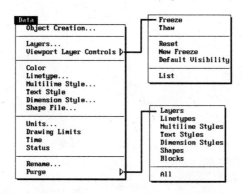

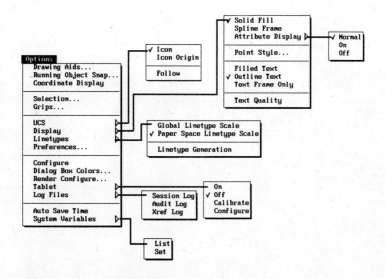

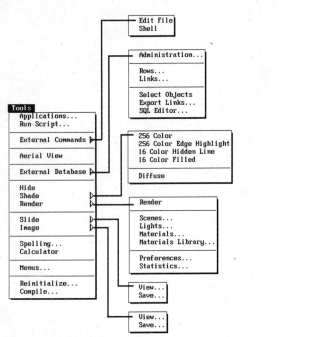

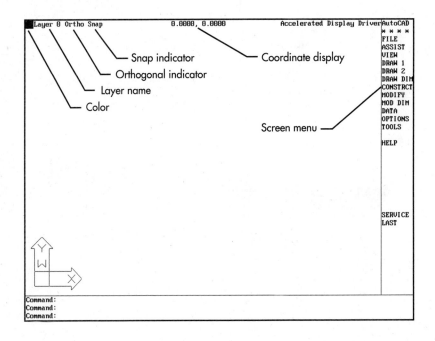

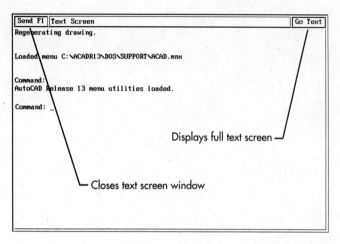

Text screen window